W9-BDZ-271

34 Beacon St
Boston 02106

*Career Guidance
and Counseling
Through the Life Span*

Second Edition

Career Guidance and Counseling Through the Life Span

Systematic Approaches

Edwin L. Herr
THE PENNSYLVANIA STATE UNIVERSITY

Stanley H. Cramer
STATE UNIVERSITY OF NEW YORK AT BUFFALO

Little, Brown & Company
Boston   Toronto

Library of Congress Cataloging in Publication Data

Herr, Edwin L.
  Career guidance and counseling through the life span.

  Rev. ed. of: Career guidance through the life span.
©1979.
  Bibliography: p.
  Includes index.
  1. Vocational guidance—United States. I. Cramer,
Stanley H. II. Herr, Edwin L. Career guidance through
the life span. III. Title.
HF5382.5.U5H39 1984   331.7'02'0973   83-25563
ISBN 0-316-35868-1

Library of Congress Catalog Card No. 83–25563

ISBN 0-316-35868-1

9 8 7 6 5 4 3 2 1

HAL

Published simultaneously in Canada
by Little, Brown & Company (Canada) Limited

Printed in the United States of America

DEDICATION

Samuel L. Herr (August 23, 1903—September 7, 1968),
  weaver, laborer, mechanic, school custodian,
  whose respect for the dignity of work was exceeded
  only by his respect for the dignity of people.

Louis Cramer (March 24, 1903—   ),
  yankee peddler, retail merchant, jobber,
  who stopped to smell the flowers.

Acknowledgments

The authors would like to thank the publishers and
authors for granting permission to use the following
material:

TEXT
Page 13: From Prediger, Roth and Noeth, *Nationwide
Study of Student Career Development: Summary of
Results* (Iowa City, IA: The American College Testing
Program, 1973), pp. 9–30. Copyright 1973 by the
American College Testing Program. Reprinted with
permission. *Page 16:* From *Career Guidance: Role and
Functions of Counseling and Guidance Practitioners in
Career Education: A Position Paper.* (American Per-
sonnel and Guidance Association, 1974), pp. 3–5. Copy-
right 1974, American Association for Counseling and
Development. Reprinted with permission. *Page 17:*
From *Position Paper on Counselor Preparation for
Career Development/Career Education* (Association for

Preface

Career guidance and counseling in the United States, and in much of the rest of the world, is in a dynamic state. Maturing theoretical perspectives, dramatic shifts in occupational structures, high unemployment rates among youths and adults, concerns about the quality of work life and worker productivity, and changes in the composition of the labor force have combined to change the content, processes, and consumers of career counseling. These factors have increased the national and international significance of career guidance and made more comprehensive its application across the life span.

In this book we chronicle the evolution of career guidance and counseling from the late 1800s to the present. In addition to tracing the roots of our field in vocational guidance and vocational psychology, we examine the concepts and language systems on which current approaches to career guidance rest. We also discuss the applications of systematic approaches to career guidance and counseling for children, youth, and adults in various settings: schools, colleges and universities, business and industry, and community agencies.

Several major themes are stressed in this edition. First is a recognition of the impact of career guidance as an instrument of human development and mental health. To understand this impact, it is necessary to probe the history of career guidance, contemporary shifts in social values and in the meaning of work, changes in the occupational structures, the theoretical approaches that have shaped current views of career guidance, and the career development of special populations. These topics are examined in Chapters 1–5.

The second primary theme emphasizes our belief that career guidance and counseling requires a developmental rather than a solely remedial approach. This belief mandates that it be conceived of as a systematic program designed to effect certain pre-planned or practitioner-client agreed upon behavioral outcomes. To aid the tailoring of career guidance programs to the special characteristics and needs of children, youth, and adults, we consider in Chapter 6 the stages and techniques of systematic planning for career guidance appropriate to different settings: work places, schools and universities, rehabilitation settings. In Chapters 7–11 we examine the developmental characteristics of and career guidance techniques particularly important to elementary, middle school, and high school students, and to adults in higher education, in the work place, and in other community settings. One salient feature of this second edition is the expanded treatment of career guidance and counseling in the work place. Chapters 12–13 give particular attention to special adult career problems of major concern in business and industrial settings.

The third major theme of the book is the identification of particular techniques, assessment devices, materials, and resources that can help career guidance specialists implement theories, planning strategies, and program models with individuals and groups. Although much pertinent information is interspersed throughout the book, Chapters 14–17 focus directly on these applications.

The fourth theme accents the research and social issues that must be resolved as career guidance moves to advanced levels of professional maturity. In Chapter 18 we address such issues.

To enhance the usefulness of this text, we have included Learning Activities and Objectives at the end of each chapter as well as appendices and a complete bibliography at the end of the text.

This text reflects not only ideas and knowledge we have gathered over years but also suggestions made by colleagues. First, we thank our reviewers who read the revised manuscript and offered their criticisms and recommendations: Reece Chaney, Indiana State University; W. Larry Osborne, the University of North Carolina at Greensboro; Edward E. Panther, University of South Florida; Nancy M. Pinson-Millburn, University of Maryland; and Robert L. Smith, East Texas State University. We wish to express our debt to the many persons cited in this book and to those, in particular, who gave us permission to quote extensively from their work. Just as concepts of career guidance have evolved over time, our own understandings of career guidance have been shaped by our many friends, colleagues, and associates who have shared their insights with us in person and in the professional literature. We are grateful to the long line of bright and talented people who have influenced our professional lives.

In particular, we wish to express our personal debts to Donald E. Super, Professor Emeritus, and to the late Charles Newton Morris, both of Teachers College, Columbia University. Each man in his unique way has served each of us as intellectual guides, friends, and mentors. We wish Chuck were here so we could tell him so; we are pleased to be able to acknowledge our gratitude to Don. Much of both men lives in this book.

Edwin L. Herr
Stanley H. Cramer

Brief Contents

Detailed Contents

1 / *Perspectives on Career Guidance and Counseling: Traditions and Emerging Challenges*

Career guidance is both an old and new term. It is old in the sense that it rests on the heritage yielded by three-quarters of a century of vocational guidance in America. It is new because its emphases, conceptual models, and consumer populations tend to go beyond those typically associated with earlier models of vocational guidance.

Emerging theoretical perspectives, rapid changes in occupational content, economic realities, legislative mandates, problems of youth and adult unemployment, concerns about the quality of work life and worker productivity, questions about the school-to-work transition, shifting labor force demographics (such as greater participation by women and minorities) have subtly but inexorably redefined the content, the time spectrum, the technologies, and the consumers of career guidance. Such pressures and forces have increased the comprehensive nature of career guidance and made it a process of international importance (Herr, 1982b).

The use of the term career guidance has been tentative for nearly twenty years, bursting into increasingly common usage only since the early 1970s. Career guidance, in its present form, has been stimulated by many phenomena: rapid and diverse social and occupational change, a maturing of theoretical perspectives about career behavior, and rising demand in many settings, populated by both youths and adults, for assistance in career planning, job search, and job adjustment skills. Career education, a major educational movement spawned in the 1970s, also was instrumental in reasserting the priority that career guidance needs to have in the schools, colleges and universities,

and workplaces. In this chapter we will examine the evolution from vocational guidance to career guidance during the twentieth century, describe some of the language, issues, and trends associated with this evolution, and place the support for career guidance into international perspectives.

In Chapter 2 we will examine contemporary meanings of work and ways to view the characteristics of the work place and work competencies. In Chapter 3 we discuss the occupational structure, its changing nature, and its classification, and in Chapter 4 we will consider the variety of current theoretical and research models essential to understanding career behavior in both macro and micro terms. In this case macro views attempt to explain the unfolding of career identity, choice, and adjustment across the life span; micro views attempt to explain specific processes of career development, e.g., decision-making. In Chapter 5 we will explore the career problems of specific population groups (e.g., women, handicapped, minorities, etc.).

In oversimplifying the issue, it is probably useful to suggest that Chapters 2–5 describe much of the *content* of career guidance: differences in occupational and life alternatives; the influences that shape work values, career identity, and choice-making strategies; the special circumstances relating to access and adjustment to work associated with gender, social circumstances, disability, and other factors. The remaining chapters of the book tend to describe the multiple *interventions* subsumed by the term career guidance. Thus, the descriptions of how work behavior is formed, the influences upon it, and how it is

1

individually manifested tend to be the objects or targets to which career guidance interventions are directed.

VOCATIONAL GUIDANCE: A TERM IN EVOLUTION

While it is possible to trace both philosophies and practices of vocational guidance far into antiquity (Williamson, 1965), our concern here is confined to the rise of vocational guidance in the United States, beginning in the late 1800s.

As the United States was rapidly emerging as a major industrial nation from the 1870s to the early 1900s, being fed by immigration to both coasts, and experiencing a large movement of persons from the farms to the cities, considerable attention began to be given to the effects of these events on the American people. Adequate education for children and effective placement of adults into a rapidly growing industrial complex were seen by many prominent spokespersons as social imperatives. Additional concerns of the times were: how to effectively distribute immigrants across the spectrum of occupations available; the need to bridge school with the realities of the adult world; the importance of reducing unnecessary job shifts caused by the large number of workers who moved from job to job because they were not aware of their capabilities or the opportunities available to them; and, general job dissatisfaction among workers.

These practical considerations were reinforced by the powerful influence of the reform movements of that time. The social reformers, the settlement house workers, and other groups concerned with human rights were making strong efforts to have workers viewed not as chattels of industry but rather as dignified persons with a right to determine their own destinies. Such a philosophy was evident in a document published by the U.S. Bureau of Education (predecessor of the U.S. Office of Education) in 1918, reflecting upon the conditions from which vocational guidance was rising:

> Education in a democracy, both within and without the school, should develop in each individual the knowledge, interests, ideals, habits and powers whereby he will find his place and use that place to shape both himself

and society toward ever nobler ends (Rosengarten, 1936, p. xix).

Influences leading to a rudimentary form of vocational guidance appeared at the turn of this century. Each of the following persons made a significant contribution to the creation of a climate susceptible to the assumptions and procedures upon which vocational guidance could be based: William Rainey Harper, on "The Scientific Study of the Student"; G. Stanley Hall on child study; Hugo Munsterberg on occupational choice and worker performances; John Dewey on restructuring of education, and Jesse B. Davis and Eli W. Weaver on educational and career problems of students.

At the beginning of the twentieth century, there was no scientific basis for vocational guidance as we know it today. Alfred Binet had not yet brought his intelligence scales from France. There was no *Dictionary of Occupational Titles* or *Occupational Outlook Handbook.* There were no comprehensive classification systems to describe the American occupational structure. Only an elementary understanding of individual differences and the crudest beginnings of aptitude or performance testing existed. Instead, palmistry, phrenology, and physiognomy were the methods widely used to obtain insights into one's future (Rosengarten, 1922).

Although there were some examples of vocational guidance in the schools in the late 1800s, the more likely sources for these services were philanthropic organizations, settlement houses, the Young Men's Christian Association and a number of private "vocation bureaus."

Enter Frank Parsons

In 1909 Frank Parsons, a man who is credited with being the primary architect of vocational guidance in the United States, came on the scene. An engineer by training, Parsons had spent much of his life dealing with various reform movements. During the 1880s and 1890s, he had been highly involved with settlement house activities along the northeastern coast, especially in Boston. Under the general credo that "It is better to choose a vocation than merely to hunt a job," Parsons established the Vocations Bureau in Boston. Parsons worked to provide a scientific base for assisting immigrants and others in effectively choosing work. He also became an outspoken critic of the Boston public school system.

Parsons contended that in the early education of youth, "We must train our students to full powers of action . . . in the various lines of useful work so far as possible according to their aptitudes as brought out by scientific tests and varied experience" (Stephens, 1970, p. 40). Parsons' posthumously published book, *Choosing a Vocation* (1909), elaborated various techniques which he found useful in helping adolescents to identify or diagnose their capabilities and to choose jobs with reasonable success expectations. To accomplish these goals, Parsons advocated a wide variety of means including reading biographies, observing workers in their settings, and examining existing occupational descriptions.

Parsons' most enduring contribution was his outline of the process of vocational guidance or, as he called the procedure, "true reasoning." In his view, vocational guidance consisted of three steps:

> First, a clear understanding of yourself, aptitudes, abilities, interests, resources, limitations, and other qualities. Second, a knowledge of the requirements and conditions of success, advantages and disadvantages, compensation, opportunities, and prospects in different lines of work. Third, true reasoning on the relations of these two groups of facts (Parsons, 1909, p. 5).

This schema defined the elements of what is now known as an actuarial or trait-and-factor approach to counseling. Such a position assumes that the individual can be described as possessing certain traits (interests, skills, aptitudes, and so on), that different occupations or educational alternatives can be described as requiring differing amounts and configurations of such traits, and that by matching individual traits and occupational requirements through a procedure such as "True Reasoning" a choice would occur. More importantly, Parsons' approach outlined the three-step procedure that required better and fuller information about individual differences and methods of assessment (first step), occupations (second step), and the decision-making process itself (third step). Although many other approaches to vocational guidance and counseling have been presented in the ensuing seventy years, much of the history of

vocational guidance in this century can be perceived in terms of which of Parsons' three steps was most dominant in the theoretical positions and practices of a particular decade (Herr, 1977).

From 1909 until the present, the first two steps, in particular, of Parsons' formulation have spurred research and developmental efforts. The first step has stimulated psychometric efforts to identify and measure individual differences and determine their relationship to occupational satisfaction or success. The second step has stimulated attention for the acquisition and use of occupational information. Together, the use of tests and information with clients has had a continuing effect on vocational guidance practices up to the present time. More recently, the third step, true reasoning, has been given considerable research and theoretical attention in the field under the general rubric of decision-making.

It is important to note that what is usually described in the professional literature as guidance and counseling began, in fact, as vocational guidance. The original intent of Parsons and his contemporaries was to provide direct assistance to persons needing to make occupational choices and was not oriented to the range of personal-social adjustments incorporated later into the province of guidance and counseling practitioners. Indeed, vocational guidance and vocational education were seen as complementary parts of a comprehensive reform movement, focusing on rational distribution of persons within a growing reservoir of occupational opportunity.

The Relationship of Vocational Education to Vocational Guidance[1]

Vocational education, while responding to the same kind of reformist flavor that gave impetus to vocational guidance, really antedated the latter. As the industrialization of the United States escalated during the late 1800s, criticism of public education as being too bookish, too elitist, and unrelated to the actualities of life became stronger

[1] Portions of this section have been adapted from Edwin L. Herr, *Guidance and Counseling, Vocational Education, Research and Development,* a paper prepared for the National Research Council's Committee on Vocational Education Research and Development. Washington, D.C., March 1975.

and more frequent. In 1862, the Morrill Act was passed, setting aside public lands to support agricultural education. (At that time, agricultural education was still the dominant form of vocational education outside urban areas in most of the nation.) The Morrill Act also gave impetus to experimental farms and to professional agricultural education. In 1871, U.S. Commissioner of Education John Eaton advocated the introduction of commercial subjects into the public schools. In 1876, Justin Smith Morrill, among others, recommended the support of practical, manual, and industrial education in order to distribute migrant workers among the occupations and industries that needed their services. Through the latter part of the nineteenth century, the American Federation of Labor (AFL) and other labor groups as well as the National Educational Association joined together in advocating the extension of comprehensive vocational education programs throughout the nation. The Smith-Hughes Act of 1917 (Herr, 1972) gave significant impetus to this change.

While others spoke of the economic and practical values of vocational education, Dewey (1900) advocated that such education also served exploratory goals by providing an opportunity for workers to learn about the social and cultural background of their vocations as well as the skills involved. That idea of exploration was echoed and extended by others, who were concerned not only about vocational training per se but also about the need to attend to the civic and the vocational intelligence of young workers.

Stephens has contended that:

> To many leaders of the vocational reform movement . . . it was apparent that vocational education was but the first part of a package of needed educational reforms. They argued that a school curriculum and educational goals that mirrored the occupational structure created merely a platform and impetus for launching youth into the world of work. What was clearly needed to consummate the launch were guidance mechanisms that would insure their safe and efficient arrival on the job. Without guidance experts it was argued, other efforts at reform would be aborted . . . Therefore, in the name of social and economic

efficiency, the argument continued, the youth who had been carefully trained would also have to be carefully counseled into a suitable occupational niche (Stephens, 1970, p. XIV).

Thus, for the first few decades of the twentieth century, guidance and counseling (really vocational guidance) was joined with vocational (industrial) education in response to the social and manpower problems of the day.

During this same period, vocational guidance tended to emphasize a "tryout-through-training" approach with much emphasis placed on occupational information. The information available was highly objective, only minimally related to the psychological appraisal of the individual, and delivered through counseling which was essentially directive and advice-giving in substance (Miller, 1973). According to E. G. Williamson, vocational educators predominated as vocational guidance practitioners in the early decades of the 1900s. Their confidence in the work description as being an adequate basis for vocational choice and their lack of training in psychology tended to restrict vocational guidance to providing information. Unfortunately, this information was largely untested in validity and did not give commensurate attention to the analysis of the individual (Williamson, 1965). In essence, step one of Parsons' formulation was abandoned in favor of step two. Paterson (1938) in speaking about the "genesis of modern guidance" indicated that the vocational guidance movement had become fixed at the level of vocational information. Williamson has argued that this situation existed until at least 1950, when the National Vocational Guidance Association broadened its objectives from the acquisition and proffering of occupational information to a more emphatic concern for the psychological good of the individual.

Thus, from 1900 to 1930, three trends prevailed: vocational guidance emphasized the study of occupations rather than the study of individuals; vocational educators predominated as vocational guidance practitioners; and vocational guidance and vocational education were largely seen as complementary components of a total effort to distribute students and others across the proliferating occupational structure.

Following World War I, however, vocational

guidance and vocational education lost this initial partnership. The demise of this relationship is due, at least partially, to the unwillingness of the National Education Association (NEA) to view vocational education and vocational guidance as parts of one unit. Indeed, in 1918, the NEA emphasized craft rather than technical training in vocational education and guidance for school education rather than for job education (Stephens, 1970).

From the 1920s to not more than a decade ago, vocational guidance and vocational education continued to withdraw from each other in practice and in principle, although counseling, in fact, was recognized and supported with "vocational education" funds by the George-Dean Act of 1938. More recently, but not categorically, counseling was further recognized and supported by the Vocational Education Act of 1963 and its amendments in 1968. In the Education Amendments of 1976 (PL 94–482), vocational guidance acquired a title of its own and categorical funding (see Title II, Section 134). Since 1976, amendments and proposed amendments to the vocational education act have continued to accent the importance of vocational guidance and to propose specific categorical funding or a setaside from total appropriations to employ and provide for the professional development of such specialists. The most recent example of such legislation is the Vocational Guidance Act of 1981 introduced in the Second Session of the 97th Congress and reintroduced in the 98th Congress. The explicit intent to support vocational guidance and the substantial setting-aside of monies in legislation for such purposes may tend to bring vocational guidance and vocational education back into the complementary relationship that had existed before World War I, although the importance of the availability of vocational/career guidance goes far beyond any special relationship it may have to vocational education.

Through the 1930s, 1940s, and 1950s, vocational guidance became the province primarily of school counselors (guidance counselors) whose functions tended to broaden and change as various educational movements came into prominence, for example, progressive education and life adjustment education. Vocational guidance was part of the professional repertoire of school counselors but by no means the central focus of their activity. At the same time, vocational educators continued to provide vocational guidance only to a restricted clientele, principally composed of students taking vocational education courses. This group constituted a relatively small portion of the total student population.

Two independent approaches to vocational guidance tended to arise in the 1920s and the 1930s: one provided by school counselors (guidance and counseling) and the other provided by vocational educators and specialists employed by the U.S. Department of Labor or by rehabilitation agencies. Except for a few major centers for vocational assistance during the depression, efforts to rehabilitate the physically handicapped, and the incorporation of vocational guidance procedures into military classification during World War II, vocational guidance, when it existed, was aimed at adolescents and young workers seeking initial employment.

During the 1920s, 1930s and 1940s, vocational guidance, as practiced by the relatively few school counselors then in existence, became increasingly responsive to several forces. One force was the growing knowledge of individual differences, the awareness of personality dynamics in vocational choice and work adjustment, and the general influence of a psychological approach to vocational guidance. A second force, also psychological, was a growing developmental view of the individual. Reinforced by perspectives such as those of Dewey, Stratemeyer, and the so-called progressives, American education took on "the rhetoric of child-centered pedagogy" (Cremin, 1961). During this period, progressives applied Freudian concepts to child study. Their efforts in the schools focused principally on mental health rather than on skill preparation except for the occupational education sponsored by and largely confined to definitions promulgated by the Smith-Hughes Act. Even more of a developmentalist notion was espoused by the advocates of a life adjustment approach to education. This approach advocated that the student learn facts across fields of knowledge relating to specific problems that recur in life, that the artificial barriers between school life and the life of the world beyond the school be minimized, and that the elements of each life situation have a cumulative effect in subsequent life stages and educational experiences. While using leisure time wisely and earning a living were among the persistent life situations with which students had to cope, life adjustment education related these situations to the affective life of the child and to longitudinal processes rather than to the more narrow definition of acquiring task skills in specific occupations.

A third force that affected perspectives on vocational guidance and counseling challenged information-giving as the primary technique, and instead advocated therapeutic treatment or psychotherapy as alternatives.

While the direct effects of the three forces just cited on guidance and counseling practitioners, mainly school counselors, are not easy to document, it is fair to suggest that collectively these forces tended to tie guidance and counseling to an educational mission, to a diagnostic-clinical rather than vocational and information-giving approach to students, and to the psychological or affective rather than performance aspects of individuals. As a consequence, vocational guidance became less than a top priority concern of school counselors.

On the other hand, the type of vocational guidance practiced primarily by vocational educators and manpower specialists was receiving a somewhat different form of stimulus. The Great Depression of the 1930s had reaffirmed the importance of job training in the various federal programs (CCC, and others) instituted during that time for the occupationally displaced. Vocational educators were active in developing such programs. More importantly, perhaps, the U.S. Department of Labor published the *Dictionary of Occupational Titles* and instituted the *Occupational Outlook Service,* giving a level of comprehensiveness and credibility to occupational information unavailable prior to that time. The Minnesota Stabilization Research Institute, as well as other similar agencies, undertook studies of vocational choice and adjustment in efforts to identify and demonstrate methods of educational and industrial rehabilitation of workers uprooted by industrial changes. One outcome of this activity was the development of new tests of vocational capabilities (Crites, 1969). Upon United States entry into World War II, the application of psychometrics to the selection and classification of personnel assumed massive proportions and the expertise of vocational educators was instrumen-

tal in the development of training programs for an increasingly technical military establishment.

These experiences caused vocational educators to change their perspectives on vocational guidance; they became strongly imbued with a market demand philosophy. Vocational educators viewed vocational guidance as a mechanism for matching individual and job or individual and education curriculum. Such an approach emphasized the importance of individual competency or aptitude for job training or available jobs. This was the criterion that vocational guidance addressed itself to rather than to individual preferences, interests, or values, criteria seen as primary in more psychologically based viewpoints.

The Precursors of Career Guidance and Counseling

For most of its first fifty years, whether responding to a market demand philosophy or a more psychologically oriented one, vocational guidance concerned itself with predicting occupational choice or occupational success from an individual's test scores prior to entry into the labor market. The primary emphasis has been on matching the aptitude for performance from the results of test profiles of those seeking employment to the requirements of available options, always attempting to maximize the compatibility between the two. Vocational guidance has been largely confined to one point in the life of the individual, that is, either entry into the labor market or readjustment with an immediate alternative after occupational dislocation. Further, its major reference point has been the requirements of the occupational structure rather than individual preferences or values.

Since 1950, this traditional view of vocational guidance has been significantly challenged. In that year, Robert Hoppock, president of the National Vocational Guidance Association, announced that the traditional view of vocational guidance was "crumbling" (Hoppock, 1950). In 1951, Donald Super recommended revision of the official National Vocational Guidance Association definition of vocational guidance, one which had stood since 1937: "the process of assisting the individual to choose an occupation, prepare for it, enter upon it, and progress in it" (Super, 1951). The 1951 revision recommended by Super amended this perspective by defining vocational guidance as "the process of helping a person to develop and accept an integrated and adequate picture of himself and of his role in the world of work, to test this concept against reality, and to convert it into a reality, with satisfaction to himself and to society."

This definition did not emphasize the provision of occupational information at a particular time, nor did it emphasize a simple matching of individual to job. Rather, it emphasized the psychological nature of vocational choice. Indeed, Super's definition effectively blended the personal and vocational dimensions of guidance, which previously had been arbitrarily separated, into a unified whole. The resulting base for conceptions of vocational guidance was self-concept oriented. It focused primarily on self-understanding and self-acceptance, to which occupational and educational alternatives available to the individual can be related. It suggested that the earlier rationale for vocational guidance was too limited, its emphasis on occupation alone outmoded, and its techniques applied too mechanically. As Crites has suggested, "More than any other career psychologist, Super has been instrumental in freeing career counseling from the static, single-choice-at-a-point-in-time concept of decision-making drawing attention to the potential contributions of sociology and economics to the field, and placing the study of career behavior in the context of human development" (Crites, 1981, p. 7).

TREATMENT OR STIMULUS?

Perhaps the most important point that Super's definition of vocational guidance makes is that vocational guidance can be construed in two different ways: (1) as a treatment condition or (2) as a stimulus variable (Crites, 1969, p. 22). These two conceptions are not mutually exclusive, but they do represent different perceptions of the needs of clients and of the time frame within which vocational guidance operates.

Treatment

If vocational guidance is seen as a treatment condition, then it will be seen as problem oriented or, at least, as appropriate primarily at decision points, thus restricted in time. In this sense vocational guidance and counseling will be viewed,

either directly or indirectly, as responding to taxonomies of vocational problems or to difficulties in choice by applying certain techniques or knowledge to resolve them. In such a perspective, the vocational guidance practitioner is likely to define the difficulties experienced by persons with whom he or she works in ways similar to those proposed by Williamson, Bordin, Byrne, and, more recently, Robinson.

Williamson (1939) has suggested that vocational problems can be described as:

1. No choice — Individuals cannot discriminate sufficiently among occupations to select one and commit themselves to it.
2. Uncertain choice — A choice has been made but the person is uncertain about it.
3. Unwise choice — There is a disagreement between the individual's abilities or interests and the occupation which he selects.
4. Discrepancy between interests and aptitudes — There is disagreement in the type or amount of these two traits as they interact or should interact in defining choice (p. 428).

Edward S. Bordin (1946, p. 174), commenting on Williamson's problem categories, suggested that "the assignment of the individual's difficulties to one of this set of classes of difficulties does not provide a basis for predictions of the relative success of different treatments." This observation led him to develop five other problem categories more psychologically oriented than those of Williamson:

1. Dependence
2. Lack of information
3. Self-conflict
4. Choice anxiety, and
5. No problem

Byrne (1958, p. 187) expressed displeasure at the generalization to high school students from the college samples used by Williamson and Bordin. He suggested that the problems could more adequately be described as:

1. Immaturity in situation
2. Lack of problem-solving skill
3. Lack of insight
4. Lack of information
5. Lack of assurance
6. Domination by authority (p. 187)

Robinson (1963) suggested another modification of these diagnostic constructs into the following categories:

1. Personal maladjustment
2. Conflict with significant others
3. Discussing plans [instead of Bordin's no-problem category]
4. Lack of information about environment
5. Immaturity
6. Skill deficiency (p. 332)

In each of these four sets of problem criteria — set forth by Williamson, Bordin, Byrne, and Robinson — symptoms and causes, or some interaction of the two, are confounded. The important point, however, is that they all imply a deficit of some type in the behavioral repertoire of the individual on the basis of which the strategies for vocational guidance treatment will be selected. Further, the assumption of all these criteria is that the problem in any one of the categories will surface at a decision point. Thus, vocational guidance will be effective as a post hoc response to a problem that is already present and which impedes the individual from progressing to some new phase of life, that is, entry into the labor force, selection of a specific occupation, advancement in an occupation, and so forth.

Stimulus

Conceiving of vocational guidance as a stimulus variable rests on a different set of assumptions from viewing it as treatment. As a stimulus variable, vocational guidance can be more effectively viewed longitudinally and developmentally. The time frame in which it will operate depends partly on the setting of the program and partly on the characteristics of the students or adults progressing through the setting.

As a stimulus variable, vocational guidance not only responds to existing problems, but it also aids one in acquiring knowledge, attitudes, and skills through which one can develop the behaviors necessary to cope with decision points, to acquire an occupational identity, or to develop career maturity. In the diagnostic categories previously identified, vocational guidance processes were triggered by presenting the problem of the person to be assisted. However, vocational guidance as stimulus is more future oriented and developmental, providing one with behaviors that anticipate choices and build career maturity, rather than situations in which one waits for crises to trigger action.

It seems obvious that vocational guidance conceived as a stimulus process fits well within any framework concerned with primary prevention. Indeed, the basic focus of vocational guidance as stimulus is educative, incorporating the philosophy and content of career models. The raison d'être of such an approach is the facilitation, indeed the maximizing, of growth rather than the repair of deficits.

Career Models Emerge

Since Super's redefinition of vocational guidance in 1951, there has been a subtle but important shift from occupational to career models in the vocational guidance literature. The occupational model described several paragraphs ago was the primary emphasis before 1951. Obviously, its influence has been continually significant, but it has competed increasingly with a series of broader perspectives on choice spawned by the career model.

By definition, career embraces a longer time frame than does occupational choice. Indeed, the concept of career embraces prevocational activity such as the effects on students of educational programs and options, as well as the post-vocational activity manifested by the retiree or the pensioner working part-time. Prime considerations in a career model are not the differences among occupations but, rather, the continuity or discontinuity in the individual's career development, the interactions of educational and occupational choices across time, and the sequence of occupations, jobs, and positions held.

Career models introduce several aspects into the concept of vocational guidance that are not apparent in the occupational model. One of these aspects concerns developmental career guidance. In such an emphasis, the vocational guidance practitioner is not only concerned with immediate choice of training or job; rather, he or she is concerned with intermediate and long-range goals and how immediate choices relate to those goals. Thus, personal values, the clarity of the self-concept, personal planfulness, and exploratory behavior vis-à-vis choice options become important variables to be considered in career guidance. In addition, personal behaviors, attitudes, and different kinds of skills are seen as appropriately developed by vocational guidance practitioners if they are not present in the student's or adult's behavioral repertoire.

Such conceptions of vocational guidance are not only concerned with an individual's potential performance on some set of occupational tasks but also focus on the attitudes and knowledge that facilitate or impede the choosing, learning, and using of such technical skills. More important, perhaps, such a model reinforces a view of vocational guidance as more than a set of services available at some specific decision point or available for persons who, for some reason or other, are experiencing choice conflicts or work adjustment problems. To summarize, career models emphasize the role of career guidance in systematically educating students or adults to the knowledge, attitudes, and skills that will be required of them at future choice points, in planning their educational programs, in selecting and preparing them for work, and in helping them anticipate and prepare for career paths available to them within a workplace. This approach is in contrast to intervention only after it has been clearly established that particular persons have not acquired the necessary skills and behaviors and are now experiencing problems because of these deficits in their behavioral repertoire. (This is what has previously been described as a treatment approach.)

The use of career models in vocational guidance slowly began to elevate the concern for self-understanding to the same level of importance as occupational understanding or task mastery. In this view, the primary objectives of vocational guidance are seen as developing the individual's skills to make a free and informed choice of career and appropriately preparing for that career, rather than for the needs of the labor market.

Wrenn (1964) summarized such a perspective well in this observation:

The planning for which the vocational counselor can be held responsible is planning for work satisfactions from both employed and nonemployed activity . . . One way to suggest the new emphasis is to say the counselor helps the student to define goals, not merely to inventory capacities. And it is clear that these must be life goals, not occupational goals only. There must be a dove-tailing of work in employed and non-employed settings if life is to be meaningful to the majority of people. . . . It is imperative that vocational counselors accept responsibility for helping students see their work life whole (p. 41).

In the late 1950s and early 1960s, such perspectives were part of a significant period of growth in school counseling, spurred on by the National Defense Education Act, Titles VA and VB, and the constant need to reassess what goals and directions such services should include. This also touched on the latter part of the dramatic period of change in counseling, spurred on by Carl Rogers' challenges to conventional clinical approaches, resulting in shifts to client-centered, nondirective techniques which deemphasized testing, prediction, and the use of information. Finally, this was the middle stage of the rise of career development theory and its major concern for the role of the person's self-concept as the stimulus for decision-making and commitment to various occupational and life goals. While each of these influences can be examined in great depth, suffice it to say that the interaction of these events and development continued to be incorporated into the concepts of vocational guidance. With them came a continuing assimilation into perspectives on vocational guidance of those emphases previously seen as the concern only of educational or personal counseling.

Of major concern to the shape of vocational guidance and counseling during the 1960s were discussion of its relationship to the process of decision-making and to the therapy process. Tyler (1961) suggested that such counseling concentrates on the individual's willingness to make choices and commitments in accord with a clear sense of ego identity. Moore (1961) argued that counseling, especially at the secondary school level, is concerned primarily with the counselee making choices. Samler (1968) advocated that vocational counseling should be a learning experience in decision-making. Brammer and Shostrom (1960) contended that vocational counseling allows counselees to discover facts about themselves and the working world "in a process whereby occupational choice limits are broadened and effective vocational planning really becomes a part of life-planning." Boy and Pine (1963) summarized many of the significant issues of the time as follows:

> The proponents of "vocational guidance" state quite emphatically that the school counselor's first job is vocational counseling and that therapeutic counseling is purely secondary. Yet in the light of the Super, Roe, and Ginzberg theories of vocational development, with their stress on the significant role of the self-concept in the process of vocational development, how can vocational counseling be divorced from therapeutic counseling? If, as Super indicates, the process of vocational development is essentially that of developing and implementing a self-concept, can effective vocational counseling take place just through dispensing and discussing occupational information without considering the psychodynamics of the self-concept? If vocational counseling is a primary task, should not school counselors provide the student with the opportunity to reach new insights, to explore and see his self-concept, to develop and to implement it? (p. 225)

COMPREHENSIVE CAREER GUIDANCE

By the late 1960s and early 1970s, the term career guidance was appearing in the professional literature almost as frequently as the term vocational guidance. Such shifts in terminology were not simply semantic but connoted shifting implications for the role and the purpose of the counselor. Career guidance, as a broadened interpretation of vocational guidance, began to communicate forcefully the importance of emphasizing the following as major organizing themes for career guidance:

1. Efforts to Develop Decision-Making — Career guidance is concerned with helping students and adults develop decision-making skills as well as defining, getting, and using information appropriate to different choices.

2. Concern for the Self-Concept — Decisions and plans express the self-concept of the chooser. It is necessary that career guidance help the student or adult achieve self-understanding before or as a part of occupational awareness. Thus, information about occupations needs to go beyond the facts of salaries or work content to include how these might relate to aspirations and values or how they would provide satisfaction for psychosocial needs.

3. Concern for Life Styles, Values, Leisure — Education, leisure, occupation, or career all interact to create or influence a life style. The way the student or adult comes to deal with such an issue is related to the clarity and characteristics of personal values. Career guidance, then, cannot attend to occupational choice without examining the educational or personal/social implications which it holds — its relation to personal values — in both the present and the future.

4. Free Choice — Career guidance is directed not to specific subsets of choices (vocational education) alone within a larger category (educational curricula) but to the range of choices available, the personal characteristics and aspirations to which these choices need to relate, and the likely outcomes of specific choices. Vocational education, general education, or college preparation, should certainly be seen as choice options to be considered, but their validity as choices lies in the comparative advantages each has over other possible choices in relation to specific personal criteria. Indeed, the safeguarding of individual integrity argues against any form of prescriptive guidance that coerces the person into pursuing specific careers or other life patterns.

5. Individual Differences — Fundamental to a free society is an acknowledgement of differences in individual talents, opportunities by which the range of these talents can be identified and nurtured, and the freedom of each individual to develop and express these talents in a unique way.

6. Flexibility and Coping with Change — Career guidance must help persons consider contingency planning, multiple routes to goals, flexibility in goals, and other notions of tentativeness as methods of coping with rapid change in social and occupational conditions.

By the 1980s, these concepts had become almost commonplace attributions to the purposes of career guidance. As suggested previously, career guidance was in a dynamic state, adding new concepts, new populations, new techniques. It was becoming increasingly *comprehensive.*

Comprehensive career guidance has come to mean many different things in the professional literature. Comprehensive has sometimes been used to mean programmed, preplanned, or systematic. At other times, it has meant longitudinal — articulated over an extended period of time, whether from kindergarten to grade twelve in the public schools, during the four years of college or university, over the six months spent in a halfway house or rehabilitation facility, or across the period of one's tenure within a particular firm, business, or government agency. At still other times, comprehensive has referred to a developmental content designed to equip consumers of career guidance with the attitudes, knowledge, and skills by which they can anticipate, plan, and act on a variety of career-related tasks. Finally, comprehensive has been used to connote the many ways intervention in career development can occur without confining counselors to a one-to-one framework (Herr, 1982b).

In the collective sense, it might be argued that rather than rejecting or being different from vocational guidance in its traditional forms, career guidance has absorbed vocational guidance techniques and expanded them in order to offer a more discriminating repertoire of interventions to a larger number of populations and settings. Within such a perspective, traditional approaches to vocational guidance (for example, matching person and job) still have a significant place within the broader perspectives of career guidance, depending on the needs of particular individuals.

Needs for Career Guidance and Counseling

A major implication of comprehensive career guidance is its applicability to many kinds of adult populations. As the evolution of vocational guidance to career guidance suggested, the traditional forms of vocational guidance have frequently been focused on adolescents and often delivered within the school. Increasingly, career guidance programs are being addressed to the total spectrum of adult populations, including retirees. These programs are occurring in community centers, in institutions for postsecondary education, in government agencies, and in business and industry.

Under the impetus of expanding knowledge of adult development, it has become obvious that in addition to the need to accommodate the special needs of women, racial and ethnic minorities, and handicapped populations, the special requirements of adults *qua* adults also must be responded to within the career guidance delivery system. This perspective does not disparage the significant assistance provided by rehabilitation agencies, employment services, or college career development and placement centers. Rather it suggests that however good these agencies are, they frequently deal only with very visible or very severe problems of occupational choice or adjustment. In many cases their interactions with clients are frequently very short lived and limited to points of crisis rather than to career planning and to helping an individual come to terms with the future. Such agencies often cannot deal with the person who is experiencing job alienation or dissatisfaction in subtle and quietly agonizing ways or the college student who views college as an end in itself rather than as an intermediate vocational decision. Neither can such agencies deal in depth with the woman who has been out of the labor force while her children were preschool, and now doesn't know where to seek information about starting a career. There are many such persons, but they are often invisible.

As one ages, one reassesses choices and plots one's possibilities of still attaining certain idealized goals, sometimes with anxiety and despair. As opportunities for advancement decrease, persons in their forties and fifties frequently take stock of how their achievements measure up to the self-concepts around which they had organized their self-esteem. If what they believe they have achieved falls significantly below what they expected from life, they may seek to change career patterns if time and circumstances still permit. In other instances, such opportunities may no longer be available to them, and they will have to accept the notion that it is too late for them to accomplish those visions on which their view of personal success rested. In either situation, career guidance is needed. In addition to these persons, many other persons will be at a stage of career deceleration as a way of anticipating retirement. Until fairly recently, little attention has been given to the career guidance needs of such persons, for assistance in considering volunteer work, managing of free time, part-time work, continuing education, and self-adjustments in which full-time work is no longer a central focus of identity.

Some observers report that a great many members of the work force are dissatisfied with the work they perform, but they do not know how to extricate themselves from these circumstances (O'Toole, 1973; 1975). Such persons need emotional support while they consider acting on their midcareer crises, and they need help to sort out the costs and benefits of executing the changes they are considering. Often such persons have been out of the educational mainstream long enough to have virtually no knowledge of training or career options currently available.

The studies of Northcutt (Knowles, 1977) and of others indicate that approximately 40 percent of the American adult population is coping inadequately with typical life problems (for example, getting work and holding a job, buying things, managing one's economic life, and parenting). Available evidence suggests that such persons need to experience skill-building approaches that are organized around the life crisis they are facing.

Some of the adults who need to be served by career guidance will have multiple problems of substance abuse, marital discord, child abuse, lack of transportation, or inadequate financial or nutrition management skills, which will need to be treated in multidimensional or "comprehensive" ways. To deal only with such persons' vocational needs and to assume that all of the other consequences of uneven unemployment will take care of themselves is unrealistic and inappropriate. Therefore, career guidance programs for such persons will need to interface more effectively with other agency programs in collaborative efforts so that the problems of work and social adaptation will receive simultaneous attention.

Most contemporary adults had little opportunity as adolescents to assess their own characteristics or to plan ways to which their values and goals could be achieved in various alternatives available to them. In line with the rationale of early perspectives on vocational guidance, it was assumed that choosing an occupation or, indeed, a college to enter was the end of the need for assistance by a counselor. As a result many adults continue throughout life unaware of their potentialities or preferences, often experiencing a vague but gnawing disaffection about what they are now doing or what the future will hold. In many instances, the career choices they made were random and often shallow commitments to those occupations or educational experiences which were available or visible at a time when they had to choose. Having never experienced the use of available exploratory resources, many such persons now experience an information deficit. They simply do not know what options are available, how to access them, or how to identify them.

These observations and those of Northcutt are supported by findings available from the National Assessment of Educational Progress (Westbrook, 1978) and from other reviews which indicate that a large percentage of adults are weak in basic skills and in occupational information, that they have had little opportunity to explore their personal characteristics with a counselor, and that they are unclear about their educational or career needs.

The presence of career education programs and comprehensive career guidance programs today may alleviate some of these problems among tomorrow's adult populations. But, because of the lack of universal availability of such programs, differences in their quality, and the population's mobility, they cannot totally eliminate such needs. Career guidance specialists in the future will need to provide a shifting blend of preplanned and spontaneous on-demand responses to the varying consumer groups with whom they will deal. Some, perhaps much, of the activity of these specialists will involve reducing stereotypes and regulatory barriers to opportunity now experienced by the elderly, ex-offenders, minorities, persons of different sexual preferences, women, and the handicapped.

The need for career guidance is certainly not confined to adults. Public school students and students in colleges and universities also continue to evidence demands for such assistance. In a major study of student career development conducted by Prediger, Roth, and Noeth (1973) involving 28,298 students in the eighth, ninth, and eleventh grades in 197 schools, selected findings included the following:

- More than three-fourths of the eleventh graders in the sample would like help with career planning. The proportion of eighth graders desiring such help is almost as high.
- Making career plans is by far the major area of need indicated by eleventh graders from a list of needs such as improving study, reading, or math skills, choosing courses, discussing personal concerns, or obtaining money to continue education after high school.
- Only 13 percent of the eleventh graders feel that they have received "a lot of help" with career planning from their school. Another 37 percent feel they have received "some help." However, half of the eleventh graders and slightly more eighth graders state that they have received little or no help with career planning.
- An overwhelming 84 percent of the eleventh graders indicate that they can usually or almost always see a counselor when they want to, which suggests, in view of the earlier findings cited, that the counselors in the sample are simply not providing help with career planning either individually or on a group basis. Certainly, time conflicts or the school's philosophy may constrain the counselors in this fashion, but as noted elsewhere in this report, it appears that retraining is critical in improving the counselor's performance.
- Over half of the eleventh grade girls chose occupations falling in only three of the 25 job families used to assess their preferences. The three were clerical and secretarial work, education and social services, nursing and human care. Seven percent of the boys prefer such occupations. Nearly half of the boys' choices fall in the technologies and trades cluster of job families in contrast to only 7 percent of the girls' choices. Thus, we have a fairly dramatic example of the pervasive influence of work role stereotype related to sex which unnecessarily restricts the career options considered by both males and females.
- With respect to job preparation, approximately 40 percent of the eleventh graders are uncer-

tain as to whether their educational plans are in line with the occupations they are considering, and approximately one-fourth are not sure if they will be able to complete the steps necessary for entering these occupations (Prediger, Roth & Noeth, 1973).

With respect to the need for career guidance in postsecondary education, one study of graduate and undergraduate students indicated that the most prevalent problem perceived by students involved vocational choice and career planning; 48 percent of the males and 61 percent of females indicated that they were having problems in this realm (Kramer, Berger, & Miller, 1974). Other research (Snyder, Hill, & Derksen, 1974; Williams et al., 1973) supports the fact that approximately one-half of America's college-going population feels a need for some assistance with career planning and/or career choice.

One of the most enduring education statistics is the fact that roughly 50 percent of those who enter college graduate in four years from the same institution they originally entered. There is no magic attached to graduating from the same institution in four years or in remaining in the same institution. However, this tendency by so many college students to change courses of study and institutions or drop out entirely is at least partially caused by a lack of considered goals in the first place. Many persons think no further than gaining access to college. They have no real purpose to which to commit their energies after matriculation, and they are not clear about the ultimate career goals to which a considered choice of curriculum could be related. These persons, like many of the adults previously described, experience identity crises, choice dilemmas, and information deficits, many of which could be reduced with adequate career guidance.

In sum, comprehensive career guidance programs have come to serve all elements of the population – children, youth, and adults – in formal educational settings and in a wide range of community agencies as well as in business and industry. As both the needs for and the responses to career guidance have become more comprehensive, the need for clarity about the meanings of key concepts in career guidance has also grown. In the next section we will provide definitions of many of the major concepts used throughout the book.

A Vocabulary for Career Guidance

Every occupation and profession has its own language system, its own way of using symbols to identify boundaries of domain, time, and space within which its work activities and prerogatives occur. So it is with career guidance. Key definitions allow the philosophical themes that give career guidance a sense of coherence and common cause to be translated to a more operational level.

Some of these key definitions follow:

Career–Various conceptions of career exist, and observers tend to emphasize different aspects of the term. For example, McDaniel (1978) has contended that career means more than one's job or occupation. It is a "life style" concept that also involves a sequence of work or leisure activities in which one engages throughout a lifetime. Hansen and Keierleber (1978) have argued for an expanded concept of career that includes helping individuals make choices related to work, education, and family as interrelated phenomena affecting role integration. Gysbers and Moore (1981) have proposed that the term life career development be substituted for the term career in order to reflect self-development over the life span through the integration of the roles, settings, and events in a person's life. Raynor and Entin (1982) maintain that,

A career is both a phenomenological concept and a behavioral concept. It is the link between what a person does and how that person sees himself or herself. A career consists of time-linked senses of self that are defined by action and its outcomes. A career defines how one sees oneself in the context of one's social environment – in terms of one's future plans, one's past accomplishments or failures, and one's present competences and attributes (p. 262).

In perhaps the most frequently used concept of career, Super (1976) has defined it as:

The course of events which constitutes a

life; the sequence of occupations and other life roles which combine to express one's commitment to work in his or her total pattern of self-development; the series of remunerated and nonremunerated positions occupied by a person from adolescence through retirement, of which occupation is only one; includes work-related roles such as those of student, employee, and pensioner together with complementary avocational, familial, and civic roles. Careers exist only as people pursue them; they are person-centered. It is this last notion of careers, "they exist only as people pursue them," which summarizes much of the rationale for career guidance (p. 4).

Careers are unique to each person and created by what one chooses or doesn't choose. They are dynamic and unfolding throughout life. They include not only occupations but prevocational and postvocational concerns as well as how persons integrate their work life with their other life roles: family, community, leisure.

Career Development–The total constellation of psychological, sociological, educational, physical, economic, and chance factors that combine to shape the career of any given individual; those aspects of an individual's experience which are relevant to personal choice, entry, and progress in educational, vocational, and avocational pursuits; the process by which one develops and refines such characteristics as self- and career identity, planfulness, and career maturity. The lifelong behavioral processes and the influences on them that lead to one's work values, choice of occupation(s), creation of a career pattern, decision-making style, role integration, self- and career identity, educational literacy and related phenomena. Career development proceeds — smoothly, jaggedly, positively, negatively — whether or not career guidance or career education exist. As such, career development is not an intervention, but the object of an intervention.

Career Maturity–The repertoire of behaviors pertinent to identifying, choosing, planning, and executing career goals available to a specific individual as compared with those possessed by an appropriate peer group; being at an average level in career development for one's age (after Super, 1957).

Career Management—The personal state of actively and consciously participating in shaping one's career and accepting responsibility for the activities and choices made toward those ends (Hansen & Tennyson, 1975).

Career Education—The totality of experiences by which persons acquire knowledge and attitudes about self and work and the skills by which to identify, choose, plan, and prepare for work and other life options potentially comprising career; an effort aimed at refocusing American education and the actions of the broader community in ways that will help individuals acquire and utilize the knowledge, skills, and attitudes necessary for each to make work a meaningful, productive, and satisfying part of his or her way of life (Hoyt, 1978).

Career Guidance—A systematic program of counselor-coordinated information and experiences designed to facilitate individual career development and, more specifically, career management; a major component of career education integrating family, community, and school to facilitate self-direction; a set of multiple processes, techniques, or services designed to assist an individual to understand and to act on self-knowledge, and knowledge of opportunities in work, education, and leisure and to develop the decision-making skills by which to create and manage his or her own career development. May include the development of job search, job interview, job adjustment skills and placement into a chosen occupation. McDaniel (1978) has summarized many of these concepts in his definition of career guidance as an organized program to assist an individual to assimilate and integrate knowledge, experience and appreciation related to: (1) self-understanding; (2) understanding the work society and those factors which affect its constant change, including worker attitude and discipline; (3) awareness of the part leisure may play in a person's life; (4) understanding of the necessity for the many factors to be considered in career planning; and (5) understanding the information and skills necessary to achieve self-fulfillment in work and leisure (p. 17).

Career Path—A term typically used in business and industry to describe a series of positions available in some occupational or specialized work area ordinarily connoting possibilities for advancement.

Career Ladder—A term typically used in business and industry to describe opportunities for upward mobility in an occupational area or across occupational areas within a firm. Usually portrays increasing levels of experience and skill. "A succession of jobs available to an individual worker with each job successively offering increased responsibility and wages and more desirable working conditions" (Evans & Herr, 1978, p. 32).

Career Lattice—A term typically used in business and industry to portray all of the opportunities in a firm or a subdivision of a firm including those available for upward and for horizontal mobility (such as lateral transfer). As such it portrays the opportunities to shift from one career ladder to another (Evans & Herr, 1978, p. 34).

Occupation—A group of similar jobs found in different industries or organizations.

Job—A group of similar, paid positions requiring some similar attributes in a single organization (Super, 1976).

Position—A group of tasks to be performed by one person; in industry performed for pay. Positions exist whether vacant or occupied; they are task and outcome defined, not person centered (Super, 1976).

Leisure—Time free from required effort or for the free use of abilities and pursuit of interests (Super, 1976).

Avocation—An activity pursued systematically and consecutively for its own sake with an objective other than monetary gain, although it may incidentally result in gain (Super, 1976).

Career Awareness—The inventory of knowledge, values, preferences, and self-concepts that an individual draws on in the course of making career-related choices (Wise, Charner, & Randour, 1978).

Perspectives on Counselor Role in Career Guidance

The historical evolution of approaches and definitions pertinent to career guidance has led to considerable speculation about counselor role. These perspectives have been captured in various role statements and in a number of articles. Several of the more prominent statements are examined in the following paragraphs.

Among the first statements dealing with the role of guidance specialists in career guidance was that made in a joint position paper of the American Vocational Association–National Vocational Guidance Association Commission on Career Guidance and Vocational Education. This paper was officially adopted by NVGA in May 1973 and by AVA in July 1973, recommending that the responsibilities of the guidance team (such as counselors and related specialists) include:

Program Leadership and Coordination
1. Coordinate the career guidance program.
2. Provide staff with the understanding necessary to assist each student to obtain a full-competency-based learning experience.
3. Coordinate the acquisition and use of appropriate occupational, educational, and labor market information.
4. Help staff understand the process of human growth and development and assess needs of individuals.
5. Help staff plan for sequential student learning experiences in career development.
6. Coordinate the development and use of a comprehensive, cumulative pupil data system that can be readily used by all students.
7. Identify and coordinate the use of school and community resources needed to facilitate career guidance.
8. Coordinate the evaluation of student learning experiences and use the resulting data in counseling with students, in consulting with the instructional staff and parents, and in modifying the curriculum.
9. Coordinate a job placement program for the school and provide for job adjustment counseling.
10. Provide individual and group counseling and guidance so that students will be stimulated to continually and systematically interrelate and expand their experiences, knowledge, understanding, skills, and appreciations as they grow and develop throughout life (pp. 13–14).

In December 1974, the Board of Directors of the American Personnel and Guidance Association

adopted a statement describing the role and functions of counseling and personnel practitioners in career education. This statement recommended that counselors provide leadership in:

1. Identifying individual career development tasks and implementing programs to accomplish them;
2. identifying and classifying educational and occupational information;
3. assimilating and applying career decision-making methods and materials;
4. eliminating the restrictions that racism and sexism place on opportunity;
5. expanding the variety and appropriateness of assessment devices and procedures necessary for sound personal, educational, and occupational decision-making;
6. emphasizing the importance of career counseling and of achieving its goals (pp. 3–4).

These six functions are considered to be inseparable leadership duties for counselors in career education. The APGA statement also considers it essential for counselors to participate actively in the career education process in seven additional ways:

1. By serving as liaison between educational and community resource groups.
2. By conducting assessment surveys of career guidance needs among students.
3. By organizing and operating part-time and full-time educational, occupational, and placement programs.
4. By conducting job adjustment activities.
5. By contributing to revisions of the curriculum.
6. By helping involve the family in career education.
7. By participating in efforts to monitor and assess activities and communicating the results of those activities to other practitioners and clientele (p. 5).

In 1976, the Association of Counselor Education and Supervision adopted a position paper on Counselor Preparation for career development/career education (Association for Counselor Education and Supervision, 1976). This position paper contends that counselors engaged in career guidance, regardless of their employment setting, should have knowledge and competencies in the following fifteen areas:

1. Career and human development theory and research, and the skills necessary to translate this knowledge into developmental career guidance and career education programs.
2. Career information resources, and the necessary skills to assist teachers, administrators, community agency personnel, paraprofessionals, and peers to integrate this type of information into the teaching-counseling process.
3. Career assessment strategies, and the skills necessary to assist individuals to use these data in the decision-making process.
4. Individual and group counseling practices, and the skills necessary to assist individuals in career planning using both approaches.
5. Career decision-making processes, and the skills necessary to implement programs designed to facilitate career decision-making for clientele in educational and community agency settings.
6. Job placement services, and the skills necessary to assist their clientele to seek, acquire, and maintain employment.
7. The unique career development needs of special clientele groups (women, minorities, handicapped, disadvantaged, adults, etc.), and the skills necessary to assist them in their development.
8. Sexism and racism, and the necessary skills to reduce institutional discrimination in order to broaden the career opportunities available for all persons.
9. The roles that life style and leisure play in career development, and the skills necessary to assist clientele to select and prepare for occupations that coincide with various preferences.
10. Consultation strategies and the skills necessary to assist others (teachers, parents, peers, etc.) to deliver indirect career guidance services.
11. Synthesizing strategies, and the skills necessary to assist individuals to understand the interrelatedness of their career decisions and life roles.
12. Program development and curricular infusion strategies, and the skills necessary to design and implement career awareness, self-development, career exploration, and job placement programs within educational and community agency settings.
13. Organizational development and change processes, and the skills necessary to facilitate change in educators' attitudes toward career education.
14. Program evaluation techniques, and the skills necessary to acquire evidence of the effectiveness of career guidance and career education programming.
15. Educational trends and state and federal legislation which may influence the development and implementation of career guidance programs (pp. 10–11).

These three position papers, although written for somewhat different purposes, share a generally common view about the roles for which the counselor or career guidance practitioner should be responsible. They each view the counselor as an activist involved in both group and individual activities designed to promote knowledge, attitudes, and skills which individuals need for self-definition and career planning. Rather than being confined to a one-to-one mode of interaction in an office situation, the counselor is seen as a collaborator, a resource person, and a consultant to parents, teachers, and community representatives, to emphasize and facilitate the contributions these persons can make to the career development of youth or adults. In general, each paper advocates that the counselor play a developmental role, providing experiences by which persons can acquire mastery behaviors appropriate to effective career development, rather than a treatment or remedial role for youth or adults who have faced choice dilemmas and found their skills wanting.

In each of these position papers, counselors are expected to understand career development, to be able to assist educators to realize career development implications for curriculum modifications, and to create learning opportunities relevant to the broad range of human talent. It is also expected that counselors will work with others in effecting placement of students and adults in educational and occupational opportunities in the community through which their career development can be enhanced.

A developmental approach to career guidance is not likely to mean that counselors will have no further responsibility for crisis counseling, for remediation in the traditional sense, or for assisting students or adults at particular decision points. In all likelihood, such needs will always be prevalent, although it is assumed that the incidence of crises can be reduced if counselors use developmental techniques to equip individuals with self-understanding, career awareness, and decision-making skills. It is also assumed that emphasizing developmental approaches to career guidance allows the counselor to have a positive effect on the lives of more persons than can a counselor who relies exclusively on one-to-one, crisis-oriented approaches. It is not assumed that the eclectic use by counselors of developmental career guidance approaches will eliminate the need for individual counseling. Rather, it is expected that such requirements will continue to help students and adults personalize and test the insights they obtain from career guidance emphases in curriculum, work experience, simulations, and other approaches. A major assumption is that the counselor functions related to career guidance can be viewed in terms of the competencies taught and brought together into a program, and that they can ultimately be related to the outcomes sought by students or adults.

Mitchell (1975) has suggested that the competencies emerging from career development emphases can be classified into seven broad categories:

Career Counseling Competencies–Skills in using new assessment instruments and other techniques designed to stimulate client exploration of self and of possible options and to relate specific occupational and educational decisions to life roles and total life style.

Program Planning Competencies–Skills by which the counselor can "team with other staff members to plan developmental, comprehensive career guidance programs that are integrated into the curriculum and are designed to include every student in the school or every client in the agency."

Implementation Competencies–Skills, for example, to stimulate career development exploration, techniques for helping groups who have

special needs, ability to deal with effects of cultural socialization on the career development of men and women.

Consultation Competencies–Skills necessary in effective cooperation with other staff members and with representatives of community agencies.

Linkage Competencies–Skills necessary to advocating client needs and mechanisms to meet them with various community agencies.

Staff Development Competencies–Skills necessary to conducting workshops and minicourses for staff members, parents, and other persons in areas appropriate to facilitating career development (for example, planning, evaluation, information dissemination).

Evaluation Competencies–Skills related to the design, carrying through, and reporting of evaluation of career guidance programs in relation to accountability (pp. 701–702).

The position paper on the counselor's role in career education promulgated in 1974 was subsequently refined and elaborated under the press of experience. In 1980, as a function of a national study of the role of the school counselor in career education, there emerged a matrix of career guidance competency requirements related to different functions and purposes in which the counselor might be expected to engage. Figure 1.1 presents this matrix.

Finally, the competencies identified by Mitchell and the 1980 APGA Study of the School Counselor in Career Education are extended by the comprehensive set of competencies approved by the Board of Directors of the National Vocational Guidance Association in 1981 as essential to vocational/career counseling. The latter advocates that the counselor should demonstrate minimum competencies in six areas. Selected examples include:

General Counseling–Examples: knowledge of general counseling theories and techniques; ability to use counseling techniques in effectively assisting individuals with career choice and life/career development concerns; skills in building a productive relationship with the client; ability to assist the client identify internal personal factors as well as contextual factors related to life/career decision-making.

Information–Examples: knowledge of education,

Figure 1.1
Competency (Role) Areas and Statements (APGA Study of School Counselor in Career Education)

Career Guidance Program Components

	Counselor Knowledge/ Expertise Component	Leadership Component	Management Component	Direct Services Component	Indirect Services Component
PLANNING/ DESIGN	Understand program management concepts Understand concepts of career education, guidance, and career development Understand staff development and in-service education techniques and procedures Understand community and labor market composition and trends Understand concepts of collaboration in the delivery of educational programs	Involve educational staff and community resource persons in planning and designing activities Institute communication networks among appropriate populations	Assess student career development needs Apply program management concepts Assess the effectiveness of the existing career guidance program Establish program goals and objectives Design specific career guidance services and activities Coordinate career guidance program with career education and total educational thrust at the institution Prepare budgets Develop calendars and time lines depicting sequence of program activities	Plan and design activities and services to facilitate career development needs of students	Participate in the design of school and non-school activities which extend the goals and objectives of the career guidance program
IMPLEMEN-TATION	Understand career development theories Understand counseling theory and techniques Understand decision-making theory Understand group dynamics Understand needs of specific groups within institutions and the community (women, handicapped, ethnic minorities, etc.) Understand the role and function of information in education and counseling Understand curriculum design and content Understand measurement and appraisal techniques	Coordinate school and community resources Develop program support from administration, board of education, instructional staff, community and students Develop and implement a public relations system Provide input to curriculum revision	Manage the career guidance program Conduct staff development sessions	Counsel individuals and small groups Conduct student assessment (ability achievement, interest, personality, etc.) Disseminate occupational and educational information Conduct career awareness, explorations and experience programs Operate student service activities (e.g., career center, job placement program, etc.)	Consult with teachers, parents, and administrators regarding students Conduct information programs for parents and community representatives Provide direct input and technical assistance to persons implementing career education activities Conduct staff development training
EVALU-ATION	Understand essential, integral, and continuous nature of evaluation Understand range and variety of data collection and assessment methodologies Understand program standards and guidelines from government agencies and accredited and professional associations Recognize exemplary career guidance practices, methods, and techniques	Demonstrate exemplary career guidance program aspects	Conduct comprehensive evaluation of the career guidance program Monitor activities conducted by self and others Utilize broad-based input to the evaluation system (students, teachers, parents, etc.) Prepare and disseminate interpretive communication evaluation results Communicate findings to career guidance program decision-makers Improve and modify the career guidance program decision-makers Improve and modify the career guidance program process Identify exemplary practices, methods, and techniques Conduct evaluation of the effectiveness of staff development training	Evaluate the effectiveness and value of specific career guidance activities and services	Disseminate findings from career guidance and career education programs to appropriate populations

training, employment trends, labor market and career resources; basic concepts related to vocational/career counseling including career development, career pathing, and career patterns; career development and decision-making theories; resources and techniques designed for use with special groups; strategies to store, retrieve, and disseminate vocational/career information.

Individual/Group Assessment-Examples: knowledge of appraisal techniques and measures of aptitude, achievement, interest, values, and personality; strategies used in the evaluation of job performance, individual effectiveness, and program effectiveness; ability to interpret appraisal data to clients and other appropriate individuals or groups of people.

Management/Administration-Examples: knowledge of program designs, needs assessment techniques and practices and performance objectives used in organizing and setting goals for career development programs; knowledge of management concepts and leadership styles used in relation to career development programs; ability to prepare budgets and time lines and to design, compile, and report on evaluation of career development activities and programs.

Implementation-Examples: knowledge of program adoption and planned change strategies and of personal and environmental barriers affecting the implementation of career development programs; ability to implement individual and group programs in career development for specified populations; ability to implement a public relations effort on behalf of career development activities and services; ability to devise and implement a comprehensive career resource center and to implement pilot programs in a variety of career development areas.

Consultation-Examples: knowledge of consultation strategies and models; ability to provide effective career consultation to influential individuals, the general public, business and professional groups; ability to convey program goals and achievements to key personnel in positions of authority; ability to provide data on the cost effectiveness of career counseling and career development activities.

Although there are other excellent analyses of competencies for career guidance personnel (for example, Phillips-Jones, Jones, & Drier, 1981), the statements examined here generally represent the perspectives of professional associations and are therefore both representative of thinking among practitioners and influential in shaping such thinking.

Trends in Counselor Role in Career Guidance

Professional association position papers, proposed or actual legislation, and articles such as that of Mitchell provide the conceptual fuel that triggers trends in counselor role. Some of these trends are extensions of those which have been in process for much of the past decade; others are now emerging. In general, the authors of this book believe such trends as the following will be prominent aspects of or issues in career guidance for the next decade.

Application of Systematic Approaches to Career Guidance. In the first version of this book (Herr, & Cramer, 1972), we advocated that vocational guidance be seen as a total system of interacting techniques and personnel that could facilitate the individual acquisition of knowledge, attitudes, and skills leading to effective career behavior. Much of that has been incorporated into current models of career education and guidance. Although we continue to believe that counselors must apply systems thinking to the programming of career guidance, the term systems connotes to some a task so formidable that they reject it as a real solution to advancing the effectiveness of career guidance.

As a compromise, then, in the first edition and now in this one, we have proposed that, if speaking of a systems approach to career guidance suggests too threatening or too overwhelming a task to be realistic, the term systematic approach might be better. Regardless of which term one uses, however, the trend for the counselor seems apparent. In the future, the goals of career guidance and the methods by which these goals will be met must be identified in each setting — educational institution, agency, work place — for both accountability and programming effectiveness.

If any criticism of guidance and counseling is enduring, it is that it is difficult to assess its outcomes or to know in any specific sense what it contributes to broad social or educational goals.

Shaw (1968) was among the first to note that most descriptions of guidance services have been confined to what is done (such as individual counseling, testing, maintenance of records, information-giving), rather than to why these things are done. Such questions as: How will students or adults be different as a function of guidance and counseling? or, What specific client outcomes are sought from different guidance and counseling processes? have not typically been addressed. In short, descriptions of guidance programs have largely dealt with the processes to be expected rather than the products. However, in an era of accountability, legislators, administrators, and consumers are frequently heard to say, "We want to know what you intend. What are your goals? How do you distinguish your contributions from those of other educational or social processes?"

Systems thinking or a systematic approach endeavors to specify clearly the ends sought and the specific methods by which such ends will be realized. In the process, a systematic approach to career guidance would recognize that objectives must be stated explicitly, that the relationship of the counselor's contributions to these objectives must be stated clearly in relation to the contributions of other persons, and that ways of assessing whether or not career guidance objectives are being met must be identified and carried through. The basic question for career guidance programming is: Which resources or combination of resources (people, places, media) are appropriate for fostering what type of development in what type of learner under what conditions (time, place, size of group, and so on) to achieve what purposes (Phillips, 1966)? This requires a statement of program goals, behavioral objectives for students or clients, linkage of career guidance processes and resources to behavioral objectives, and an evaluative procedure. (Chapter 6 will deal with such planning in considerable depth.)

The Counselor as Applied Behavioral Scientist. In order to plan systematically for career guidance and to respond to individual differences, the counselor will likely become more eclectic in the future. Rather than being theory-bound or a practitioner of one process (such as individual counseling), the counselor will need to use a range of techniques and processes both with groups and with individuals. The application of these techniques will need to be tailored to specific problems presented by individuals or to developmental purposes. In general, the applications of these techniques will cause the counselor to have a broad acquaintance with a range of theories, concepts, and ideas bearing on human development and the empirical evidence of the effectiveness of these ideas. There seems to be no question that among the techniques to be employed by future career guidance practitioners, there will be heavy reliance on structured group experiences to build skills required by particular clients (for example, assertiveness, planning, decision-making, job search and interview).

The Counselor as Change Agent. In providing a comprehensive program of career guidance, the counselor will likely depart from the one-to-one mode of interaction with clients as a principal strategy. Increasingly, counselors will be involved in collaborative efforts with teachers, parents, administrators, community agency personnel, and employers to modify the environments that shape their clients' lives. Creating positive climates for learning; modifying curriculum content; working with employers to provide work-study experiences, exploratory opportunities, realistic employment requirements, and more mentally healthful work environments; and actively seeking job placement for clients, are examples of the activities in which counselors are likely to become engaged. There seems to be little question that counselors will need to persist in giving their skills away to educators, parents, and management or supervisory personnel in industry in efforts to sensitize these individuals to the needs of all persons for self-esteem, achievement, and opportunities to share in decision-making and governance. In such circumstances, the counselor will likely serve as a consultant or a resource person to these "significant others" who influence the lives of various groups of persons in different educational or work places.

Shifting Theoretical Models. Career guidance will stimulate increased attention by counselors to developmental psychology as well as to economics, anthropology, sociology, and organizational behavior as the conceptual frames of reference on which their practice is based. A counselor with psychology as the only discipline is likely to assume that client problems are due to personel deficits or ego structures. When the other behavioral sciences are addressed, individual transactions with the environment come more readily into view. As such, the effects of the belief systems, the types of information, and the characteristics of the social or work environments become equally likely and important subjects for the counselor's attention.

In particular, the career guidance practitioner must have thorough grounding in career development theory. Broadly conceived and multidisciplinary in orientation, most of these perspectives indicate that how we view ourselves and our choices is learned, either negatively or positively, beginning in early childhood and continuing throughout our lives. Such views see decision-making as the mechanism by which the person translates personal views of self and orientations to the past, present, and future into what one believes one can do, what one chooses to do, and what one does. Career development behavior is, in large measure, the prime conceptual set for career guidance practice.

In addition to serving as a conceptual foundation for career guidance, career development theory also serves as the source of concepts that can be used to plan group developmental experiences for students or adults and for modifying curriculum. This body of theory and research provides answers, even if incomplete, to the counselor's quest for information about what behaviors are necessary to develop an information processing strategy; what knowledge, attitudes, values, or skills comprise effective decision-making; or what developmental tasks persons in different age ranges ought to be able to master. This set of understandings permits the counselor to serve intelligently as a resource person or a collaborator in creating experiences to facilitate career development in clients.

Beyond the conventional views of career behavior that have been so important in influencing contemporary career guidance practice (for example, Super, 1957; Holland, 1973; Ginzberg, 1972; Tiedeman, 1961), other perspectives will be required in the future to fully comprehend career development. For example, Free and Tiedeman (1980) have argued convincingly that the study of economics has much to contribute to effective career guidance practice. They contend that both econometric and psychometric models need to be included in the foundational study of individual behavior and counseling. Besides economics per se, several other models of behavior, motivation, or decision-making are useful to career guidance; they rest on concepts in organizational and industrial psychology. Among them are the work on achievement (McClelland, 1965); equity theory (Goodman & Friedman, 1971); expectancy/valence theory (Vroom, 1964; Lawler, 1973), human capital theory (Osterman, 1980); and opportunity theory (Roberts, 1968). Several of these theories are discussed in some detail in Chapter 4.

Other concepts that must be incorporated more fully into career guidance are those related to employment and unemployment. Such terms are frequently treated as though they were unidimensional rather than being composed of various types of conditions affecting certain groups of people more than others. Career guidance specialists with a simplistic view of the factors causing unemployment tend to think that their profession will reduce unemployment. Although career guidance is likely to facilitate "employability" in persons, however, it cannot create jobs for them. Employment has to do with fiscal and monetary policy, changing product demands, international tensions, energy resources, shifting population demographics, and other factors that influence what types of jobs will exist, how many, and where. Thus, naive overpromise about what career guidance can do must be restrained through increased recognition of economic realities if career guidance is to be viewed as a credible and mature intervention system. In addition, uninformed understandings of the factors causing and maintaining unemployment cause some counselors, like some lay citizens, to assume that after receiving career guidance or training, if one is still unemployed, one must want to be. One might legitimately make that assumption if this nation were providing full employment. It is not. Therefore, we sometimes inadvertently blame the victims of unemployment for being victims (Herr & Watts, 1981).

Another area that affects the integrity of comprehensive career guidance programs is the characteristics of labor markets. Doeringer and Piore (1971) have described a dual labor market in the United States that has different ports of entry for workers depending on the industry involved, and different levels of security, benefits, training, and possibilities for internal mobility. Obviously, the primary and the secondary labor markets require different job search strategies, skills, and personal characteristics. Without being aware of such distinctions both the consumers and the career guidance practitioner are likely to waste energies in efforts which are insufficiently targeted or unresponsive to actual hiring dynamics. It is also useful to recognize that federally funded programs (such as the Job Training and Partnership Act) also represent a labor market beyond the dual labor market presented by Doeringer and Piore. And, there are informal labor markets that tend to be outside the corporate or organizational structures and represent different forms of self-employment (Gershuny & Pahl, 1979–1980).

In the future, conceptual models dealing with both career behavior and career intervention will demand more attention to the broad areas of role integration, sex-role shifts, and dual-career couples. Super (1981) has portrayed nine major life-career roles – child, student, leisurite, citizen, worker, spouse, homemaker, parent – which different persons play for different amounts of time with different stability and intensity. More needs to be known about these roles and their effects on the conception and delivery of comprehensive career guidance programs. Similarly, issues of role integration, sex-role shifts, and dual career planning must be incorporated into the future models of and the delivery of comprehensive career guidance (Hansen & Keierleber, 1978; Keith, 1981).

Beyond role integration, sex roles, or dual career roles is the area of special populations. Future trends in comprehensive career guidance theory and practice will include more refined attention to such populations. Among those which will undoubtedly receive increased effort are undecided or indecisive individuals, emotionally disabled or mentally retarded youth and adults (Karayani, 1981), and the physically handicapped.

Finally, as comprehensive programs of career guidance become more sophisticated, it seems crucial that increased attention be given to the comparative effects of career guidance interventions. Journals are now filled with advertisements and exhortations about the value of different types of approaches or resources. On balance, however, these approaches and resources are not being criticized with regard to problems, population types, or settings. It seems crucial to the future effectiveness and credibility of comprehensive career guidance programs and systems that systematic attention be given to such intervention effects.

Career Guidance and Leisure

Comprehensive career guidance programs of the future will need to concern themselves with the range of roles affected by whether or not work is seen as a central commitment of individuals. As suggested at several places in this book, one of those roles is leisurite (Super, 1981). In some types of work, it may not be possible to find personal fulfillment or satisfying human relationships or a sense of achievement. In such instances, persons will need to look elsewhere for outlets for such needs. The leisure world of volunteer activity, hobbies, and nontechnical learning may serve such needs for self-fulfillment. Some persons may be forced into extended periods of leisure because of work dislocation, reduced work time, or early retirement. Some may seek leisure opportunities because they are not committed to work as a central concept in their lives. Regardless of which of these reasons motivate persons to engage in leisure activity, how they choose and conceptualize the use of leisure in their lives will be a legitimate and growing emphasis in career guidance.

Bloland and Edwards (1981) have argued for a career counseling conceptualization that blends work and leisure. They recognize work and leisure as playing complementary roles in the lives of people but also hold that leisure can play two roles when it seeks to make up for dissatisfaction felt in work. They build their theoretical structure on the work of Kando and Summers (1971), who suggested that leisure can respond in two ways to dissatisfaction at work: (1) supplemental compensation (positive feelings through leisure are also adequately experienced through work); (2) reactive compensation (avocational activities are used to recover from unpleasant work experiences).

Rimmer and Kahnweiler (1981) have studied the potency, evaluation, and activity associated with the terms work, leisure, education, the future, and self among college students and found them to be perceived as interrelated components of their lives. Whether such relationships would also be true for other subpopulations is not known, but some evidence suggests that leisure time is a mixed blessing for many people (Herr & Watts, 1981). Obviously, the availability of leisure time varies among people, and their ability to use it without additional stress or conflict also varies widely. Clearly such ambivalence and ambiguity about how leisure fits into life priorities, how decisions about effective uses of leisure can be made, and how leisure can fulfill needs unmet by work are together important elements of future models of career education and career guidance.

Career Guidance as Content or Curriculum

One of the major outcomes of developmental career guidance as it has emerged during the past fifteen years or so has been the rise of career guidance workshops, group approaches, self-directed modules, and other programs. Some of these are designed to facilitate individual decision-making by "educating persons to choose." Others are built around specific clusters of career development tasks found to be most significant at different chronological life periods or at particular transition points. They may include attempts to influence the development or acquisition of a positive self-concept, interpersonal skills, control over one's life, the discipline of work, presenting oneself objectively, knowledge of resources, preferred life styles, and other career management tasks (Tennyson, Kansen, Klaurens, & Antholz, 1980). Some researchers are advocating the need to train youth and adults in affective work competencies (Kazanas, 1978). Nelson (1979) has described the methods and materials for teaching occupational survival skills. Hopson and Scully (1981) have presented a British version of life skills teaching that includes much career-related content. The Employment and Training Admin-

istration of the U.S. Department of Labor (1980) published a program entitled *Self-Directed Job Search: An Introduction* to help former CETA participants to acquire skills for obtaining and being effective in work.

There are many other examples of career guidance content available. Those identified here suggest that such content must be tailored to the special needs of different youth or adult subpopulations, that such content approaches can be expanded to focus on whatever types of self-development, skill acquisition, or exploratory behavior is necessitated in different work environments or educational settings, and that such content has become an integral part of comprehensive career guidance programs.

Herr (1982a) has suggested that depending on the population and the purpose to be served, career guidance content in group programs tends to deal with three categories of skills: work context skills, career maturity or guidance skills, and decision-making skills.

Work context skills are related to the psychological aspects of the situation in which work activity is carried on but can be viewed separately from the technical skills of work performance.

In some nations observers would suggest that these are the elements of industrial discipline; in others they would be called affective work competencies. In any case they include knowledge and skills associated with employer-employee relations and supervisor-worker relations, interpersonal skills in relation to co-workers, willingness to follow rules, adaptability, punctuality and regularity in attendance, pride in work, self-discipline, and efficiency. Such work context skills tend to be those which research studies and surveys of employer preference have shown repeatedly to be at the heart of work adjustment, job satisfaction, and work satisfactoriness. Their lack is at the core of reasons for workers being discharged; with some modification in language, the lack of these skills probably also contributes to school vandalism, mediocre achievement, tardiness, and other behavioral problems. Although more subtle and psychological than work performance skills or numeracy and literacy they can nevertheless be analyzed and taught.

Guidance Learnings. In many ways, however, the teaching of work context skills is incomplete without attention to a second category of individual learning described as guidance or as related to career maturity. Indeed, it is conceivable that many of the problems now associated with the work context (such as worker alienation and mid-career crisis) are really problems of self-learning or deficits in other guidance-related skills. Such learnings, like work context skills, are more psychological than technical, and they can be taught. Guidance skills are typically those now described under the rubric of career development. They concentrate on assisting persons to become aware of their self-characteristics (such as aptitude, values, interests), their career opportunities (such as occupational alternatives, educational options, the relationship between subject matter and jobs), and the bringing together of self- and career opportunities into a plan for action. In essence, guidance learnings are designed to help persons become more purposeful, goal directed, and capable of self-management. They include attention to decision-making skills, job search and interview strategies, and general planfulness. They also include concern for such emphases as the ability to use exploratory resources to reality-test choices, constructive use of leisure, personal economics skills, and other pertinent areas of behavior by which one is helped to get and keep a job. In general, they argue that forging a career requires two types of knowledge: self-knowledge and job knowledge.

With respect to self-knowledge, persons need to be assisted to come to terms with who they are; what kinds of commitments they are willing to make; what their aptitudes, interests, values, and goals are; and how competent or confident they feel. In essence, self-information is a base for anything else; that is, knowing one's strengths and weaknesses, preferences, and goals defines an evaluative foundation to which any option or action can be referred to determine its relevance. This base of information also helps one determine what information one has, what one needs, and what should be secured.

Job knowledge includes the range of work options available and how these might be accessed. This requires having knowledge about and considering the personal relevance of such matters as the characteristics of curricular majors available, their prerequisites and content; the relationship between subject matter and occupations in which that subject matter is required; the outcomes of pursuing various curricula (What is the placement record? Into what kinds of jobs are people placed?); the matching of personal characteristics with those required in preferred curricula or occupations; and so forth.

In addition, considerations of occupational and other opportunities will likely require information about methods of access. Are the preferred occupations available locally? If not, where are they available? How are potential employers identified? What is the best procedure for contacting an employer? What information or procedures are pertinent to the completion of letters of inquiry, resumes, applications? What types of questions or other conditions are likely to prevail in an interview situation? How does one follow up a contact with an employer?

A third area of emphasis beyond that of work context skills or guidance learnings is that dealing with the *decision-making* process itself. One could argue that such a distinction is overly pedantic; that this learning is typically incorporated into the learnings previously described. That may be true, but decision-making skills are, nevertheless, a type of content that has integrity in its own right as a systematic method that can be applied repeatedly to process information, weigh alternatives, and project action consequences. Perhaps most important, decision-making is the way people can establish relations between actions in the present and the future expectations about the consequences of those decisions. Thus, decision-making becomes an important way of manifesting an internal locus of control.

The Use of Technology. Many counselors have been trained to believe that the primary, if not total, explanation for behavioral change in their clients is counselor personality (for example, the provision of empathy, unconditional positive regard, and so on). Assuming that such a premise is too limited a concept of the counselor's role with diverse client needs, career guidance has incorporated into the counselor's professional repertoire several forms of technology that extend the counselor's potential to effect behavioral change. Games, work samples, films, problem-solving kits, self-assessments, and computer interactive systems are but a few of the means developed recently to provide learning and simulated experience designed to increase client exploration and planning. Technology applied to career guidance is likely to expand rather than recede and, thus, the career guidance person of the future will need, in addition to other expertise already cited, to be comfortable with and competent in the use of such resources.

Special Needs Populations

Although the specific group characteristics may change, there will continue to be groups of persons who have special needs for career guidance. Ordinarily, these are groups that have been denied equity in their access to educational and occupational opportunities because of racial and sexual bias or discrimination because of age or disability. Bias or discrimination of any kind is a waste of human resources and it is a matter that career guidance persons can help reduce or eliminate. Counselors have many possibilities for action both at the client level and at the institutional level. In the first place, it is a matter of helping youth and adults free themselves of the psychological limits on choice that they experience because they have incorporated other people's beliefs that females or persons of particular racial, age, or physical disability characteristics should not consider certain educational or job options. Frequently they have also internalized the implied reasons for restricting such choices; for example, they believe that if one has some set of group characteristics (such as race or sex) one is *ipso facto* inferior or less able then others. In the second place, it is a matter of helping employers, parents, teachers and other gate keepers of opportunity not to restrict free access to jobs and education on the basis of such stereotypes. Elsewhere in this book, techniques useful in dealing with specific career problems of different special needs populations are discussed. We will say here only that the reduction of bias will include the whole repertoire of counselor and career guidance strategies including those of cognitive restructuring and support groups as well as resource, collaborative, and consultative roles. The requirements

for such emphases need to be considered basic to any rationale for a planning model in career guidance for the foreseeable future.

INTERNATIONAL APPROACHES IN CAREER GUIDANCE

Career guidance, career education, and more traditional forms of vocational guidance have become international phenomena. They are not exclusive inventions or provisions of the United States. Many nations have implemented or refined mechanisms designed to facilitate individual decision-making, ease the transition from school to work, or assist with problems of unemployment, underemployment, and job adjustment.

Just as in America, other nations have developed approaches to infuse subject matter with career development concepts, created decision-making courses and experiences, established career resource centers in communities and in educational institutions, expanded contacts between schools and the larger community, developed computerized employment services and occupational training programs. Many of these countries have developed work-study, shadowing, apprenticeship, and retraining schemes that are more comprehensive than our own. Other nations have devoted major attention to the problems of the disabled or of women.

Obviously, the approaches taken by other nations are colored by their own political belief systems, economic conditions, cultural traditions, and conceptions of free and informed choice of educational and occupational opportunity. As a result, such approaches are not necessarily interchangeable across national boundaries. This is not the point. The point is that as nations experience particular levels of industrialization, occupational specialization and diversity, and as available information about the possibility structure existing in that nation expands, needs for career guidance grow and change.

Societies throughout the world are in transition. In some, the changes are revolutionary; in others, evolutionary. It is a rare nation, if it exists, that is not influenced by turmoil surrounding its economic climate, achievement images, value structure, employment or unemployment rates, educational structure, male/female relationships, quality of life, and other matters that bear on the kind of work available, who does it, and how they get access to it and advance within it. Obviously, career development in each nation is a function of the prevailing political, economic, educational, and industrial systems of that nation and of the resources devoted to career guidance or career education and the forms they take.

Societies vary on at least two dimensions in their approaches to helping youth and adults with career development (Watts & Herr, 1976). The two dimensions can be distinguished by (1) whether the primary locus is the needs of society or on the needs of the individual, and (2) whether the approach basically accepts the status quo or is concerned with changing it in prescribed directions. Figure 1.2 graphically illustrates the point. Each of the four cells in that figure carry different implications for the nature and content of career guidance. Basically each asks, Is the purpose of career guidance human development, facilitating individual free choice and purposeful action, or developing human capital and deciding how it will be used for the good of the state? Career guidance can be and is developed in various nations from each of the answers possible.

Within this broad context of national differences, Super (1974) has suggested that in examining career guidance practices among the developed nations, four conflicting trends are apparent. They are:

1. *Manpower utilization versus human development.* In the former situation, career guidance can be viewed as an instrument of national policy by which persons can be directed and trained in educational and occupational areas reflecting economic and social needs. Or, in the latter instance, career guidance can be seen as reflecting a national policy that emphasizes self-fulfillment, social welfare, and personal happiness. These are not necessarily mutually exclusive views but it is likely that in most nations one of the two possibilities predominates as the basis for career guidance.

2. *Occupational choice versus vocational development.* The basic conflict here has to do with whether one views career guidance as leading to an immediate occupational choice or as a process of helping individuals clarify and act on intermediate and future goals. In the latter perspective, even when immediate choice is under consideration, is it considered in relation to such matters as the place of work in the preferred life style, preferences for leisure, life goals broadly conceived, or the relationship of this job or position to those one hopes to achieve in the future?

3. *Information dissemination versus counseling.* The fundamental issue in this conflict is whether the provision of accurate information about educational and occupational information is adequate in itself or whether persons need the assistance of specially trained persons to sort out the implications of such information in relation to personal interests, values, needs, and abilities.

4. *Professional guidance versus lay guidance.* This conflict has to do primarily with the form and intensity of the training persons need in order to do effective "career guidance" and whether a nation can afford to commit the resources and the training necessary to professionalize its career guidance practitioners.

Figure 1.2
International Approaches to Helping Youth and and Adults with Career Development

	Needs of Society	Needs of the Individual
Change	Social Change Approach	Individual Change Approach
Status Quo	Social Control Approach	Non-Directive Approach

Although each of these four conflicts is couched in international terms, it is possible to argue that there are advocates for each of the positions reflected in different sectors of this nation. Nevertheless, the prevailing professional rhetoric, if not always the practice, of career guidance favors those elements of the four conflicts that emphasize human development, vocational development, counseling, and professional guidance. Saying this, however, does not preclude the fact that in the United States, as in other nations, career guidance is a sociopolitical process significantly affected by the characteristics of the society in which it is found. Theories, techniques, and programs of career guidance are never value free. Under any model of implementation, career guidance represents some form of environmental modification that in turn carries a set of assumptions with political overtones. In any transactional view of individual-environment interaction, it is societal factors — political, religious, economic, historical — which largely determine the types of problems that are appropriate for counselors or career guidance practitioners to deal with. This perspective is played out in the legislative entitlements or definitions of service that can be provided, in the policy focus as well as the resources committed to career guidance as counseling.

To pursue further the notion of societal effects on career guidance, it is possible to argue that the types of questions which youth and adults bring to career guidance specialists or counselors are related to how they view the current societal belief systems about such matters as personal choice, achievement, social interaction, self-initiative, marriage, prestige, occupational or educational status, and many other aspects of life. The resulting anxieties, deficits, or indecisiveness that these persons experience as they compare themselves with what society in the form of parents, teachers, peers, spouses, employers, self-improvement books, or the mass media say they should believe or do represent a large part of the content with which career guidance specialists or counselors deal (Herr, 1982b).

Flowing from such a point of view is the notion that the questions different societies "permit" or encourage their citizens to ask about themselves and their future and the resources placed at the disposal of the individual to sort out answers to these questions vary cross-culturally in fairly dramatic ways. Herr (1974, 1978) has attempted to analyze the types of work-related questions populations are likely to ask whose nations differ on an industrial development continuum. In particular he distinguishes among the types of work, information systems, work-related questions, and guidance processes likely to exist in the least developed societies, developing nations, and developed or postindustrial nations.

As one moves across these three categories of industrial development, the roles of familes change as information disseminators and reinforcers of certain socially stratified occupational or educational choices; "have nots" change from a majority to a minority position in the society; occupational diversity and service roles increase; work becomes less visible and increasingly "walled off" from those who must choose it; information about opportunities becomes more sophisticated and more abundant; personal questions shift from those primarily addressed to physical survival and increasingly become more existential ("Who am I?" "What do I want to be?"); career guidance and counseling tend to become more conceptually based and seen as specialized occupations (professions) in their own right. While such perspectives are overly simplified and, indeed, caricatures of reality, they do cast into bold relief that career guidance mechanisms do not exist in a political, social, or economic vacuum. They are interactive, if not symbolic, with the characteristics of the societies in which they exist.

The likelihood that the availability of career guidance will expand across the nations of the world is difficult to predict. If, however, the relationships previously suggested between industrialism and the diversity of roles available, education and work, the need to provide information about work and encouragement of achievement in systematic rather than random ways are valid, then career guidance in some form seems inevitable in virtually every nation. Perhaps the more salient point is that in an increasingly technological world, both international organizations and governments have become more aware that the major questions regarding technology are not technical, but human questions (Drucker, 1970). Among these questions are not only those of how to develop workers able to discharge the occupational task specific skills required to design, operate, and maintain the various forms of technology, but, more importantly, how to help persons come to terms with such matters as their work values, work commitments, work productivity, and the personal discipline associated with these matters.

Summary

In this chapter we have examined briefly the historical evolution of the concepts and content of what is now being called career guidance. We have introduced the notion of *comprehensive* career guidance to reflect its importance to all segments of the population — children, youth, and adults — as well as its growing availability in community agencies, business and industry, and educational settings. We have suggested that it is necessary to think in terms of a career guidance program that is systematically planned, has clear statements of counselor competencies, and reflects a series of national trends that show its future directions. We have also identified a partial vocabulary of terms pertinent to career guidance as well as some issues that are yet to be resolved. Finally, we have considered some perspectives on career guidance as an international phenomenon.

In Chapter 2 we will examine contemporary meanings of work and ways to view the characteristics of the work place and work competencies. In Chapter 3 we will discuss the occupational structure, its changing nature, and its classification. In Chapter 4 we will consider the variety of current theoretical and research models essential to understanding career behavior in both macro and micro terms. In this case macro views attempt to explain the unfolding of career identity, choice, adjustment across the life span; micro views attempt to explain specific processes of career development, e.g., decision-making. In Chapter 5 we will explore the career problems of specific population groups (women, handicapped, minorities, and so forth).

Chapters 2, 3, 4, and 5 describe much of the *content* of career guidance: differences in occupational and life alternatives; influences on work values, career identity, choice-making strategies; the special circumstances relating to access and adjustment to work associated with gender, social circumstances, disability, and other factors.

The remaining chapters of the book tend to describe the multiple *interventions* subsumed by the term career guidance. Thus, the descriptions of how work behavior is formed, the influences on it, and how it is individually manifested tend to be the objects or targets to which career guidance interventions are directed; the content with which such interventions are concerned.

LEARNING ACTIVITIES

1. Discuss with a colleague, "Why are there apparent discrepancies between most educational or guidance programs and the needs that persons indicate are important to them?"
2. Write a brief essay contrasting the meanings of the terms *career* and *occupation*.
3. On a flow chart, trace the major changes that have occurred in career development practices since 1907.
4. Construct an inventory of needs that the various research studies suggest career guidance should serve.
5. Summarize the various position statements on counselor role in career education and career guidance and place into categories the major counselor competencies recommended. Analyze those competencies you now possess and those you need to acquire. Develop a plan by which you might acquire the skills you need.
6. Contact your State Department of Education and secure any position statements they have available regarding the philosophy and content of career guidance and career education.
7. Develop a glossary of terms contained in this chapter (such as career guidance, career development, career education, and so on), and define them in your own words.

8. Consider what types of skill development might be served by career guidance content delivered through group approaches.
9. Inventory five major issues that relate to international approaches to career guidance. Describe for yourself how program planning and resource utilization might resolve each of the issues.
10. Make a list of the trends in career guidance identified in this chapter. Can you think of others? If so, add them to your list and consider how you would present these to a meeting of policymakers concerned with the future directions of career guidance.

OBJECTIVES

After reading this chapter, engaging in the learning activities, and reading the references suggested, you should have met the objectives that follow. If you have not, it would probably be useful for you to review the material in Chapter 1 before proceeding further. You should now be able to:

1. List at least three of the major historical trends that stimulated vocational guidance in this country before 1950.
2. Name three ways in which the term career implies a difference from the term occupation.
3. Describe how using career models rather than occupational models changes the counselor's role.
4. Identify at least three organizing themes for career guidance that arose during the 1960s and early 1970s.
5. Describe at least five counselor competencies that major position papers of professional organizations would recommend.
6. Discuss four or more trends affecting counselor role that are stimulated by career education, career development theory, and the change from vocational to career guidance.
7. List at least three issues affecting career guidance that must be dealt with in the future.
8. Summarize research findings describing the needs for career guidance by students and other persons.
9. Distinguish between the definitions of career guidance, career development, and career education.

2 / *Work: Some Contemporary Perspectives*

Counseling has sometimes been called a verbal profession. How a counselor responds to clients' problems and concerns depends on the labels and the definitions by which these questions, problems, or concerns are classified.

So it is with career guidance. The first chapter identified some of the terms of major significance to the understanding and practice of career guidance. It was suggested there that the career guidance practitioner will function differently if the client's immediate concern is choosing a specific job, considering a choice of occupation, or deliberating about how such matters might fit with life style, family roles, availability and use of leisure, and aspirations as these combine to shape a career. The point is that job, occupation, and career are not interchangeable. They represent different choices for the client and for the career guidance practitioner.

The word we want to focus on in this chapter is *work*. A central organizing goal of career guidance is the facilitation of the choice and implementation of work in one's life. When one chooses a job one chooses a whole series of things in addition to the work content or tasks to be performed. One also chooses the persons with whom one will work, the role expectations of others, the social status ascribed to the job, the likely types of leisure in which one will engage and with whom one will likely experience leisure, how much and when vacation will occur, the types of continuing education or training required, the style of supervision, whether one's use of time is rigidly prescribed or discretionary, and the "work culture" in which the job tasks will be performed. Given such diverse and interactive outcomes from a

choice of work, it is paradoxical that work itself is rarely discussed in career guidance. Indeed, work is frequently treated as a monolithic abstraction, almost as though all work is the same or as if the word work has a single meaning.

DEFINITIONS OF WORK

Although work can be defined in a variety of ways, some definitions summarize several major concepts. For example Super (1976) defines work as:

> The systematic pursuit of an objective valued by oneself (even if only for survival) and desired by others; directed and consecutive, it requires the expenditure of effort. It may be compensated (paid work) or uncompensated (volunteer work or an avocation). The objective may be intrinsic enjoyment of the work itself, the structure given to life by the work role, the economic support which work makes possible, or the type of leisure which it facilitates (p. 20).

This definition does not equate work and occupation as is often the case. Rather, it allows for work to be nonpaid, to be outside the formal job structure identified as occupation, to include homemakers, members of alternative communities, and those self-employed in the invisible and illegal economy as workers (Miller, 1980).

Super also proposes definitions for other words appropriate to a language of work. They include:

Labor–Productive work for survival or support, requiring physical or mental effort.

31

Employment–Time spent in paid work or in indirectly paid work such as homemaking.

Leisure–Time free of required paid or unpaid work, in rest, play or avocations.

Play–Activity that is primarily recreational and relaxing; engaged in for its own sake; it may be systematic or unsystematic, without objective or with a temporary and personal objective; it may involve the expenditure of effort, but that effort is voluntary and easily avoided by the player (p. 22).

Super's definitions of work and related terms are basically psychological; they tend to place the perceptions, definitions, and motivations relative to work within the individual's actions. Another way to define work is from a sociological perspective. In this connection, Braude (1975) contends that:

The sociologist argues that the human being is not an economic animal and that only, nor is he a psychological mechanism and that only, nor is he wholly political or exclusively cultural. If man is human at all, the sociologist says, this humanity stems from the necessary inclusion in groups and in the web of groups that make up society (p. 4).

Flowing from this perspective, Braude goes on to argue that,

Narrowly conceived, work is simply the way in which a person earns a living. From a broad perspective, a person works in order to maintain or enhance any of the statuses that are his by virtue of his membership in a multiplicity of groups. . . . As long as the person defines, or has defined for him, the activities in which he is engaged as in some manner related to his survival, either physical or social, then we can say that person is working. . . . The work that any individual performs is articulated with that of others who work and with the containing social structure by its location within the division of labor (pp. 12–13).

These definitions of work and related terms suggest that such concepts are complex. They deal with both individual perceptions and actions as well as the social interactions and roles through which individual behavior is played out. Indeed, Braude (1975) maintains that work needs to be understood within a context of people, position, and purpose.

In spite of the conceptual complexity associated with work, frequently in career guidance we talk of choices, options, decisions without using the word work. We act as though everyone understood that work is implied and as though the meaning of work were similarly understood by everyone using it. In doing so, however, we corrupt the richness and diversity of what the word work stands for. For example, if we confine our use of work only to task performance or work content, we are likely to emphasize a counselee's aptitudes, achievement, and work performance potential. In doing so, we may overlook the fact that in either choice of or adjustment to work the issue for a particular client may not be task performance but rather how one understands the work place and its expectations, one's ability to get along with co-workers or to share values and interests with them, or one's preferences for the intensity and style of supervision. As one focuses on each of these emphases possible assessments, questions, and reality testing experiences emerge that are different from those appropriate to thinking only about whether one can learn or do work tasks per se.

In this chapter we will consider the meaning of different perspectives on work for career guidance. In particular, we will consider: work values and the meaning of work to different groups of people; job satisfaction; work and mental health; employment and unemployment; the transition to work; work and leisure; affective work components; and occupational survival skills. We will briefly deal with such notions as the division of labor, specialization, work tasks, work roles, good and bad work. In short, in this chapter, we hope to increase the reader's sensitivity to the language of work and its meaning for the practice of career guidance. Since other chapters speak directly to dealing with specific career problems, we will concentrate here on linking various categories and concepts of career guidance to differences in the meanings and concepts of work.

The Concept of Work

From the earliest days of recorded history, work has been the subject of controversy. It has been seen as punishment or as the way to eternal salvation. It has been viewed as fit only for slaves to do so that their masters would have unfettered leisure or as the context in which humankind can achieve its most creative and influential purposes. Anthropologists and historians have argued that work has been instrumental in creating civilizations by its need to cause people to engage in mutual effort to survive and to advance their quality of life. The division of labor that differentiates persons into classes of functional activity has been seen by some sociologists as the basis for social stratification, classes, castes and other types of social systems.

The current issues surrounding work are so pervasive and so central to human existence that Pope John Paul II devoted a papal encyclical to the subject in 1981: "Laborem Exercens" (On Human Work). This was the first such statement the Roman Catholic Church had delivered on work in nearly ninety years. Selected statements from the encyclical strike directly at the meaning of work and its dynamics:

> Because fresh questions and problems are always arising, there are always fresh hopes, but also fresh fears and threats connected with the basic dimension of human existence: man's life is built up every day from work, from work it derives its specific dignity, but at the same time work contains the unceasing measure of human toil and suffering and also of the harm and injustice which penetrate deeply into social life within individual nations and on the international level.

Secretary of Education Bell (Riegle, 1982) has conveyed a sense of the meaning of work somewhat differently than Pope John Paul II, but no less dramatically:

> Work in America is the means whereby a person is tested as well as identified. It is the way a youngster becomes an adult. Work shapes the thoughts and life of the worker. A change in atmosphere and life-style can be effected by an individual by simply changing the way he or she makes a living. For most of us in adult life, being without work is not living (p. 1114).

Whether viewed through a secular or spiritual lens, such a powerful medium obviously carries diverse meanings for individuals choosing or engaging in work. Although virtually all paid work has the potential to meet the economic needs of human beings, all work, paid and non-paid, has the additional potential to meet broad social and psychological needs: effective interaction with others, personal dignity, a sense of competency or mastery, identification with some purpose or mission larger than oneself, and human relationships.

Table 2.1 suggests the range of needs or purposes that work can provide. Work undoubtedly serves more purposes or needs than suggested there, however. In any case, such purposes or needs are not necessarily mutually exclusive. The same person may attempt to achieve several different types of economic, social, and psychological purposes from work simultaneously, even though one category may be emphasized in shaping work motivation.

Some types of work do not gratify many of the needs in Table 2.1, whereas other types potentially gratify all. In part, this distinction occurs when work tasks are routine and repetitive, seen only partially by their participants as contributing to a final product, when the individual is made servant to the machine and deskilled in the process, or when they offer only limited possibility for personal achievement. Such notions raise in the minds of some observers a dichotomy of "good work versus bad work" (Schumacker, 1981). Bad work is an unpleasant necessity; good work is a process that ennobles the product as it ennobles the producer. Meaningless work is seen as an abomination, as bad; good work is seen as giving purpose to life, speaking not just to one's physical engagement but to how the work engages the soul and the spirit.

However metaphysically uplifting such thoughts are, they tend to cast the organization and content of work into a simple dichotomy that does not exist, for the most part, in absolute terms. Rather, individuals tend to define work as good or bad depending on how it meets their particular needs.

As O'Toole (1981) has argued, "When it is said that work should be 'meaningful' what is meant is that it should contribute to self-esteem, to the sense of fulfillment through the mastering of one's self and one's environment, and to the sense that one is valued by society" (p. 15). These are psychological processes that individuals perceive and

Table 2.1
Different Purposes Work Can Serve

Economic	Social	Psychological
Gratification of wants or needs	A place to meet people	Self-esteem
Acquisition of physical assets	Potential friendships	Identity
Security against future contingencies	Human relationships	A sense of order
Liquid assets to be used for investment or deferred gratifications	Social status for the worker and his/her family	Dependability, Reliability
Purchase of goods and services	A feeling of being valued by others for what one can produce	A feeling of mastery or competence
Evidence of success	A sense of being needed by others to get the job done or to achieve mutual goals	Self-efficacy
Assets to purchase leisure or free time	Responsibility	Commitment Personal evaluation

attribute to work differently. Indeed, as O'Toole has suggested in another context, what almost all authors find when studying workers in different types of "bad" work — work that could be better done by machines or animals — is that such people attempt to interject some meaning into the hours in which they labor; they cope with unrewarding work by creating a sense of community. "If the task itself is meaningless, meaning can at least be attached to the social interaction with fellow workers" (p. 8).

In this connection, Fretz and Leong (1982) after a comprehensive review of pertinent research studies concluded:

One finding that occurred with striking frequency in studies in the life span and worker adjustment sections was the moderating impact of the interpersonal context. When workers desire and have satisfying affiliative relationships on the job, the descriptive effects of limited job scope, job dissatisfaction, person-environment misfit, and the like were often minimized. If more direct investigation of affiliative context support these scattered findings, there are obvious intervention implications — facilitating more satisfactory affiliative conditions may often be easier and less expensive than employee relocation, job enrichment, and the like. Some jobs are simply not pleasant; maximizing the value of the

interpersonal context may be the most direct route to maximizing employee stability and performance (p. 152).

Given the propensity for workers to master, or cope, or to interject meaning into work that by some external criterion would be seen as bad or repetitive, it is not difficult to understand that even when workers report boredom and monotony (see Morse & Weiss, 1962, p. 30), they also report that work is a prime source of personal definition or identity, and they would continue to do it even if they became wealthy enough to stop working (Vecchio, 1980). Although that attitude may be true in general, Super (1982) has noted differences in the salience of work to people in different nations and regions of nations. Yankelovich (Calhoun, 1980; Yankelovich, 1981; Yankelovich & Lefkowitz, 1982) among other observers, reports that in the United States work values are changing. His surveys suggest,

Under the impact of [women's liberation] the rigid division of labor in the family is beginning to break down. People are growing balky on the job; they seem less willing than in the past to endure hardships for the sake of making a living. Some unions are now stressing non-economic issues at the bargaining table. Many people are seeking jobs that may pay less well but offer a more agreeable life style. And even the high value we place on economic growth as the main goal of our society is cast in doubt (p. 33).

Changes in the Meaning of Work

Yankelovich goes on to contend that we are now in the throes of a transformation of work values and the work ethic. In his view the work ethic is so central to American culture that if its meaning shifts, the character of our society will shift along with it. In the next chapter we will examine the shifts from goods-producing to service-and knowledge-producing as the major outcomes of work. We will talk about the nature of the knowledge explosion and the effects on work of such technological advances as silicon chips and microprocessers. But it is important to realize that those changes have to do with content of work. What Yankelovich and others in this chapter are concerned about is how people view the "meaning" of work to themselves, how central it is to their self-definitions. In Yankelovich's view such meanings are changing. He compares his studies of American life themes in the 1960s with those current today. Such themes link work with people's life values and are the ingredients of the term *work ethic*. Table 2.2 compares the themes identified by Yankelovich in the mid-1960s with those from his research reports in 1981.

Ginzberg and his associates in the Conservation of Human Resources Project and several earlier projects at Columbia University have been studying work in America since 1939. They avoided proposing a general theory of work throughout these years because of the complexity of the forces affecting work shifts in America and throughout the world. Ginzberg, however, reported a series of propositions in 1975 that describe the views he and his colleagues hold about the fundamental shifts occurring in the role of work in the lives of individuals in contemporary America. Many of them complement the findings of Yankelovich, or are precursors of them. Among the major observations are the following (Ginzberg, 1975):

- It is erroneous to postulate a marked decline in the work ethic in America and especially to attribute it to youth alone. We believe that

changes have been underway for some time in the ways in which large numbers of Americans of all ages relate to work.

- Similarly, we believe it is an error to single out any particular occupational group, such as blue-collar or service workers, and argue that they have lost pride in workmanship and are no longer willing to give a day's work for a day's pay. Our counterpoint is that if such trends can be validated, they can be found in all occupational groups, although not necessarily to the same degree. . . .

- The American work ethic may be altered as small-scale independent enterprise gives way still further to large organizational structures characterized by hired management, salaried professionals, and bureaucratical staffs. . . . Nevertheless, we can expect that as a society moves away from a subsistence standard of living, and if we are more successful in establishing and maintaining a high level of employment, people's attitudes toward their work and their careers will be significantly altered. . . .

- Allowance must also be made for the successful efforts of ever larger groups of workers — professional and managerial, other white-collar, blue-collar, and (recently) service workers — to develop structures through which they are able to influence the conditions under which they work, output norms, rewards, promotion ladders, and job security. . . .

- Today, more and more young people do not get regular jobs until they are in their early or mid-twenties. There is little doubt that this markedly elongated preparatory process affects their expectations and responses as members of the labor force.

- An interesting clue to what may well be a deep malaise is seen in the small but growing number of people who have had successful careers but who decide in midstream to make a break and seek a new occupation. Although the reasons for these attempts at breakaway are many and diverse, they seem to be rooted in varying degrees of dissatisfaction with the work these individuals have been doing.

- It is often difficult to assess the specific contribution of the individual in our society, because work is increasingly performed in groups and because the key to group cohesion and perfor-

Table 2.2
Trends in the Work Ethic in the 1960s and the 1980s

1960s	1980s
The Good Provider Theme The breadwinner — the man who provides for his family — is the real man *The Independence Theme* To make a living by working is to "stand on one's own two feet and avoid dependence on others." *The Success Theme* Hard work always pays off *The Self-Respect Theme* Hard work of any type has dignity whether it be menial or exalted. A man's inherent worth is reflected in the act of working.	*Reduced Fear of Economic Insecurity* For most people economic security continues to dominate their lives. But today people take some economic security for granted. A substantial minority say that they are now prepared to take certain risks with their own economic security for the sake of enhancing the quality of life. *Economic Division of Labor Between the Sexes* The economic discipline that maintained the rigidity of sex roles in the past has weakened. The idea of women working for purposes of self-fulfillment rather than economic motives gains wider acceptance all the time. *The Psychology of Entitlement* A broad new agenda of social rights is growing and a psychological process is developing whereby a person's wants and desires become converted into a set of presumed rights. *The Adversary Culture Challenges the Cult of Efficiency* The average American has begun to wonder whether too great a concern with efficiency and rationalization is not robbing life of the excitement and pleasure desired. *The Changing Meaning of Success* An increasing number of people are coming to feel that there is such a thing as enough money. A "big earner" who has settled for an unpleasant life style is no longer considered more successful than someone with less money who has created an agreeable life style. People are no longer as ready to make sacrifices for economic success as they were in the past.

mance lies in "political arrangements" among the members and the leadership. Thus, personal acceptability is often confused with technical competence....

• Another important concomitant of how large organizations operate and one that has an impact on how people work is the restricted room at the top — a limitation that quickly becomes clear to most employees. Once they recognize it, many recalculate the probabilities of attaining one of the key prizes and the costs that attach to the effort....

• About 40 percent of all working persons are women; we know little about what different groups of women want from work, except that many of them have begun to fight against the discrimination to which they have been subjected. Moreover, most working women are married, and changes in their career aspirations will inevitably lead to changes in the lives of their husbands and children.

- Finally, we must recognize that the close links that formerly existed between work and income have been loosened with consequences that are just beginning to surface (pp. 63–65).

To argue that the meaning of work is changing is not to say that all persons in the work force accept such changes or act in accordance with them. Yankelovich attributes what he calls the nontraditional values, those now emerging, primarily to persons under thirty-five and particularly to the college-educated. In his view, although the percentage is shrinking, the majority of workers still hold traditional values in which work motivation derives from money, status, and security.

With respect to the effects of college education on the expectations or meanings attributed to work, it is important not to overgeneralize to distinctions between white-collar and blue-collar work. One might project, on the assumption that educational levels are different between blue-collar and white-collar work, that the meanings of work are also different. That may well be true, but the relationship is not a simple one. For example, Wright and Hamilton (1979), consistent with previous research, did not find in national survey data that education and job satisfaction were significantly related among blue-collar workers, nor did they find substantial dissatisfaction with work. For example, in a 1976 study Hamilton and Wright found that the proportions of white male manual workers who were "very satisfied" with their work varied from 42.9 percent of those with less than a high school degree to 42.4 percent among high school graduates and 37.7 percent for those with some college or more. Adding the proportions "very" and "moderately" satisfied together, the figures were 84.1 percent, 81.4 percent, and 78.1 percent respectively. They go on to state, "While the assertion that rising education among blue collar workers leads to enhanced work discontent can be found nearly everywhere, evidence that would support it appears to be in relatively short supply. In fact,

there appears to be emerging evidence against it" (p. 64). In their 1979 study, Hamilton and Wright undertook to provide additional details on the job outlooks of the college-educated working class. They point out that the college-educated working class as defined here are almost exclusively a college dropout population; no more than 15 percent of the group has completed four years of higher education. Nevertheless, the researchers found that the college-educated manual workers are about as eager and involved as other members of the working class. Indeed, no disproportionate dissatisfaction with work could be found among the college-educated manual workers. In addition, they found that the people who actually perform manual labor are much more positive about what they do than are the intellectuals who write about how "miserable" and "degrading" manual labor in the industrial society is. Beyond this, the alternative jobs available to them in lower clerical and sales categories pay substantially less than many manual jobs, do not necessarily offer more diversity and challenge, and do not offer better opportunities for mobility.

The meanings attached to work differ not only across groups but also across time. As suggested previously, work has been seen differently through history. Toffler (1980) has described such shifts in terms of three waves of change across the world: agricultural, industrial, advanced technological. Each of these brings with it different forms of work and meaning. Maccoby and Terzi (1981) suggest that there have been four major work ethics throughout American history and that elements or residuals of each of these coexist today: the Protestant ethic, the craft ethic, the entrepreneurial ethic, and the career ethic. In addition, they contend that a fifth ethic, that of self-fulfillment, is rapidly emerging as a major motivation to work. The point of such observations is that "each work ethic implies a different social character, different satisfaction and dissatisfactions at work, and a different critique of society" (p. 165).

According to Maccoby and Terzi, the Protestant ethic stimulated a character driven to work for the glory of God and for personal salvation and one that could not tolerate unethical and undisciplined behavior. The craft ethic is represented by persons oriented to "savings and self-sufficiency, to independence and self-control, and to rewards on earth. The craftsman is most satisfied by work which he controls, with standards he sets" (p. 165). The entrepreneurial character suggests risk-taking, boldness, the exploitation of opportunities and people, and a dislike of the bureaucracy, red tape, and regulation that stifle free enterprise and personal initiative. The career ethic represents other-directedness, a striving to get ahead, to become more attractive and valuable in the marketplace, survival of the fittest rather than seniority and loyalty as the prime requisite of promotion and reward. The emerging ethic of self-fulfillment represents those who seek challenge, growth, and work that is not so consuming that it denies a place for family, community, leisure, and other aspects of life. The presence of such a profusion of work ethics affirms that both those who are in the process of work choice and those who are engaged in work represent a pluralism of purpose and motivation.

Such multiplicity of work values or meanings complicates the task of career guidance significantly. Similarly, it complicates the seeking of answers to such questions as, Has the motivation to work declined? The probable answer to such a question is more questions: What kind of work are you talking about? Which group of workers holding what type of work ethic are you considering? Beyond such questions, however, it appears that despite certain popular rhetoric to the contrary, Americans' motivation to work is still quite high, although certain jobs and styles of supervision are not looked on with much favor.

As Maccoby and Terzi (1981) among others have reported, when they asked people if they would continue to work even if they could live comfortably for the rest of their lives without working, most people choose to work. Indeed, as the rise in the proportion of women and minorities in the labor force indicate, more and more people are trying to gain access to work, and the demand for paid employment of all types continues to grow. As we will discuss in the following section, reporting that most people want to work or are seeking work is not the same as saying that people are satisfied with the work available to them or with their personal fit with the job they have.

JOB SATISFACTION

From the meanings of work just discussed, it is obvious that in most of the work in which people engage we find a confrontation of the individual with the organization. The ingredients of this confrontation yield satisfaction or dissatisfaction, feelings of incompetence or inferiority, and motivation to be productive or work alienation.

Among the more controversial issues facing the American business/industrial labor complex and, indeed, government policy is that of job satisfaction or job alienation. Sometimes the professional literature, the popular press, and certain research findings leave one with the impression that only during the exploration or anticipation phases of youth are processes of self-understanding, finding meaning in achievement, or choice important. Therefore, efforts to assist persons to deal successfully with such needs are most frequently available in schools and colleges, places primarily occupied by youths, rather than in settings primarily occupied by adults.

Such a perspective belies the reality that adults must continue to cope with trying to implement a self-concept in their life styles, in their work, in their choices, and in their planning. Efforts to grapple with skills in interpersonal relationships and in learning or relearning continue for most people as long as they live. As Gross (1975) has observed, "Socialization is far from complete in childhood; it goes on throughout persons' lives, involving adjustment to and becoming members of schools, universities, occupations and becoming socialized to appropriate roles in old age." Caplow (1954) has suggested that organizational socialization involves individual accommodations in terms of "skills, self-image, involvements, and values."

In general, studies of job satisfaction indicate that it is proportionate to the satisfaction of needs about which the person feels most strongly (Katzell, 1964). Some data indicate that employees whose morale or attitude toward work is poor and who are dissatisfied, tend to be absent more frequently, have high accident rates, or quit work more regularly. Other data suggest that the dissatisfied worker uses low productivity as a form of aggression or reprisal. This literature views work adjustment as essentially a psychological process by which the individual interacts and comes to terms with one's work environment.

The widely quoted report, *Work in America* (O'Toole, 1973), sponsored by the U.S. Department of Education to study the institution of work and its implications for health, education, and welfare took a rather pessimistic view of job satisfaction in America. The report concluded that large numbers of American workers at all levels are not satisfied either overtly or covertly with the quality of their working lives. The sources of this discontent are seen to be diminished opportunities for work autonomy, impersonal corporate and government bureaucracies, specialization, and shifting values toward work itself. In particular, it is assumed that with low-level economic and security needs met, more and more workers seek satisfaction in work from its self-actualizing possibilities, its opportunities to gratify interests, and the need for satisfying human relations. Many popular books and mazazines, often taking their cues from this report, have echoed wide dissatisfaction and a feeling of boredom among the American labor force.

Some research does show that assembly-line workers are more alienated or dissatisfied than workers in craft-based work or work involving high technology. Such relationships have also been found in comparisons of these types of jobs internationally (Shepard, Kim, & Hougland, 1979). But as other research has shown (Hamilton & Wright, 1976) that is a relative matter. Most manual workers are satisfied with their work.

Other observers contend that although there is clearly a percentage of people (typically assessed at about 10 percent of the work force) who are dissatisfied with their work for many reasons, job satisfaction in general is growing. They further argue that it is erroneous to believe that all workers seek self-actualization in work, that it occupies a central place in their life commitments, or that satisfaction in work cannot be acquired from rising economic or fringe benefits.

The U.S. Department of Labor has indicated that there is no objective evidence of any widespread, dramatic decline in job satisfaction over the last ten or twenty years. On the other hand, the younger, the less educated, and the less skilled sectors of the labor force do register less satis-

faction than do professional-technical workers, managers, officials, and proprietors. What does seem clear is that the majority of American workers require something more than adequate remuneration from their jobs in order to feel satisfied (such as working conditions, challenge, and so on). In general, they seem to be getting these added satisfactions. In 1973 a poll conducted by the Survey Research Center of the University of Michigan found that 90 percent of American workers were satisfied with their jobs (U.S. Department of Labor, 1974). In that same year, another poll conducted by the Gallup organization put the satisfaction figure at 88 percent (U.S. Department of Labor, 1974). Recent studies continue to suggest that most workers like and value their work (Rabinowitz, Falkenbach, Travers, Valentine, & Weener, 1983).

Although we will show in subsequent sections of this chapter that many young workers have trouble adjusting to first jobs because of personality traits, poor attitudes toward supervision, or other attitudinal factors, this does not necessarily mean that the desire to work in the majority of youth has eroded. Indeed, in a recent study of the Bureau of Labor Statistics, cited by the Joint Economic Committee of the Congress (1980), it was noted that the commitment to the work force by young adults (ages 20–24) is far stronger than in the past. Indeed, it is now equal to that of the 25–44 age group where labor force participation is highest. In addition, evidence points to the fact that these workers are eager to make a contribution to the world. Nevertheless, existing literature seems to suggest that subgroups within the youth culture reject the traditional work ethic, materialism, and conventional social norms as they understand them.

Person-Job Fit

A study conducted by the University of Michigan's Survey Research Center concluded,

> It does not appear that young workers have a lower commitment to work than their elders. The problem lies in interaction between work itself and the changing social character of today's generation, and in the failure of decision makers in business, labor, and government to

recognize the fact. . . . The young worker is in revolt not against work but against the authoritarian system developed by industrial engineers in business and industry who felt that "the worker was stupid, overly emotional, insecure and afraid of responsibility" (Special Task Force to the Secretary of Health, Education and Welfare, 1973).

This report and many others during the 1970s generated public debate about the quality of work life. Embedded in such debate are experimentation with new approaches to designing work organizations, employee health and well-being, workplace participation and democratic management, productivity and the quality of work life, the relationship of satisfaction to performance, and work-related stress and dissatisfaction (Lawler, 1982). The core of such concerns is the fundamental fit between person and job.

Hackman and Oldham (1981) have picked up this theme in their research. Unlike many other theorists about job satisfaction and productivity, they link it directly to the fit of person to job. They state,

> One of the major influences on organizational productivity is the quality of the relationship between people who do the work and the jobs they perform. If there is a good "fit" between people and their jobs, such that productive work is a personally satisfying experience, then there may be little for management to do to foster high motivation and satisfaction — other than support the healthy person-job relationship that exists. But if that fit is faulty, such that hard and productive work leads mainly to personal discomfort and distress, then there may be little that management can do to engender high productivity and satisfying work experience (p. 173).

They further maintain,

> Even as work organizations have continued to get bigger, more mechanical, more controlling of individual behavior, and more task specialized, the people who work in these organizations have become more highly educated, more desirous of "intrinsic" work satisfaction, and perhaps less willing to accept routine and monotonous work as their legitimate lot in

life. . . . Ways of structuring jobs and managing organizations that worked early in this century, it is argued, cannot work now because the people who populate contemporary organizations simply will not put up with them (p. 175).

Another way of saying this is that the descriptions of workers as passive, confused, irrational, and nonresistant to manipulation by management, which were promulgated by the Hawthorne studies is now being viewed as more mythology than fact (Bramel & Friend, 1981).

Such perspectives argue that an extremely important role for career guidance in business and industry is that of worker classification and assessment as well as job redesign based on models of management that allow for greater worker participation in decisions about work processes, flexitime, quality circles, worker ownership of product quality, and so forth. The current infatuation of American management with Japanese management styles, for example, contrasting theories X and Y with Z (Ouchi, 1981), relate directly to such issues.

Against this background of person-job fit, there continues to be a concern about the effects of underemployment or overeducation of many Americans. O'Toole (1975) has, for example, written about the "Reserve Army of the Underemployed." He means that there are far fewer challenging jobs than there are persons with educational credentials that qualify them for such jobs. Although the educational level of the population has continued to go up, and in particular the number of college-educated persons has risen significantly as a proportion of the total labor force since World War II, the economic system has not kept up with the "job content inflation" associated with the rise in educational credentials or with the employment expectations of younger workers.

O'Toole foresees potentially grave social, political, and economic problems flowing from the overeducated, underutilized work force that is constantly growing in this country. In particular, he has noted the possibilities of class conflict, job dissatisfaction, credentialism, decreasing economic productivity, and dwindling public support of education and its institutions.

Even where Americans do not now profess job dissatisfaction, a substantial proportion feel that they are overeducated. One survey (Quinn et al., 1971) indicated that 30 percent of American workers had more education than they thought was needed to do their jobs.

The other side of the problem is undereducation. In one sense, it is more difficult to underestimate undereducation than it is overeducation. Nevertheless, the trend in America continues to be that the less education one has, the more likely it is that he or she will be unemployed. Unemployment is typically low in the professional and skilled occupations and is generally high for the less skilled segments of the labor force. By 1980 several federally assisted programs (for example, CETA) were expected dramatically to decrease the number of Americans in the labor force with eight years or less of schooling from about 12.5 million (19 percent) in 1970 to about 9.1 million (11.8 percent) by 1980 (Bjorkquist, 1970). Although, in general the educational attainment of American workers is rising (by 1970 the average worker had 12.3 years of education), a substantial percentage of the population remains undertrained for specific skilled jobs and undereducated for general adult competency. Both overeducation and undereducation are further discussed in Chapter 3.

Theories of Job Satisfaction

Theories about job satisfaction continue to have a central place in the literature of career development. In many of them issues of person-job fit, over- or undereducation of workers, and job redesign are at least implicit. Many of the theoretical approaches to be reviewed in Chapter 4 deal directly with job satisfaction and how it is psychologically motivated. In particular, the reader is encouraged to read the work of Vroom (1964), Lawler (1973), and Raynor and Entin (1982), on expectancy theory; Bandura (1977) on self-efficacy theory; Tiedeman and O'Hara (1963) on anticipation and implementation; Holland (1966) on person-situation congruency; Roe's (1956) use of Maslow's Prepotent needs theory; or Super's (1980) perspectives on self-concept and career maturity as each of these relates in some way to job satisfaction or dissatisfaction. Indeed, virtually all of the work in Chapter 4 which deals with either the choice of or the adjust-

ment to work has implications for the understanding of job satisfaction.

In addition to the perspectives considered in Chapter 4, several not discussed there are useful to consider in this section. For example, the task force that considered the status of work in America (O'Toole, 1973, pp. 36–96) attempted to summarize what was then known about worker satisfaction. They noted that the level of satisfaction with one's work is directly related to the level of:

1. prestige of the job
2. autonomy, control over the conditions of work
3. cohesiveness of the work group, which facilitates interaction
4. challenge and variety of the task
5. employer concern and involvement of employees in decision-making
6. wages with respect to both amount and "relative deprivation" felt by the worker; his or her perception of adequacy of wages when compared with those of others performing similar tasks
7. mobility potential of the job: workers want to feel that there exists in a job a potential for movement upward through the skill hierarchy, the occupational hierarchy, the organizational structure in which the work is performed, or any combination of the three
8. satisfactory working conditions
9. job security

These nine perspectives describe the types of areas in which career guidance programs in business and industry can provide information, support, encouragement, or skill building approaches that can facilitate job satisfaction. In an elaboration of some of these elements, Hall and Schneider (1973) have proposed a model of organizational career development based on psychological success and failure. In it they suggest that need for competence leads the individual to seek situations where self-esteem will be enhanced and avoid situations where self-esteem is likely to be reduced. They base their model on three propositions.

1. Increases in career self-image, career commitment, and self-esteem will result from success in attaining a career relevant goal that satisfies the following criteria:

   — The goal was set by the person.

- The path to the goal was defined by the person.
- The goal was perceived as challenging or difficult but attainable.
- The goal was central to the person's self-image.
- The goal was attained.

2. The extent to which a person's initial job assignment provides the conditions for psychological success (challenge and autonomy) will continue to be positively related to career commitment, performance, and success in subsequent years. An initial job experience of psychological failure may conversely be related to decreased commitment, performance and success in later years.

3. The transition from one organizational status to another is often accomplished by significant changes in the person's self-image, satisfaction, and attitudes toward work (pp. 3–8).

In the model proposed by Hall and Schneider good performance leads to satisfaction. In this respect it is congruent with the various interpretations of expectancy theory cited in Chapter 4. The opposite way to view the relation between motivation, performance, and satisfaction (Steers & Porter, 1975) is that performance follows from satisfaction rather than leads to it. In this regard two classic examples of approaches to job satisfaction will be cited: the theory of work adjustment by Lofquist and Dawis (1969) and the two-factor theory of Herzberg (1968). Basically, in such models the fit between individual needs, skills and abilities, and technical organizational requirements is the seedbed for satisfaction and if such satisfaction is attained high performance will ensue.

Both the Lofquist and Dawis and the Herzberg models emphasize that work is more than the accomplishment of some set of tasks. It is also a place of human interaction and psychological reinforcement. The latter may be far more significant in creating job satisfaction than the former.

Lofquist and Dawis (1969) contend that job satisfaction and work adjustment result from correspondence between individual and environment. The major assumptions that underlie this theory include the following:

- Each individual seeks to achieve and maintain correspondence with his or her environment.
- Work represents a major environment to which most individuals must relate.
- In the case of work, then, correspondence can be described in terms of the individual fulfilling the requirements of the work environment, and the work environment fulfilling the requirements of the individual.
- The continuous and dynamic process by which one seeks to achieve and maintain correspondence with one's work environment is called work adjustment.
- This stability of the correspondence between the individual and the work environment is manifested as tenure in the job.
- Satisfactoriness and satisfaction indicate the correspondence between the individual and the work environment. Satisfactoriness is an external indicator of correspondence derived from sources other than the worker's own self appraisal. Satisfaction is an internal indicator of correspondence; it represents the individual worker's appraisal of the extent to which the work environment fulfills his or her requirements.
- The levels of satisfactoriness and satisfaction observed for a group of individuals with substantial tenure in a specific work environment establish the limits of satisfactoriness and satisfaction from which tenure can be predicted for other individuals.
- The work personalities of individuals who fall within the limits of satisfactoriness and satisfaction for which substantial tenure can be predicted may be inferred to be correspondent with the specific work environment.

An important aspect of this theory and the program of related research is the correspondence between the individual's needs and the reinforcer system that characterizes the work setting. Such a view is similar to the early work of Henry A. Murray (1938) and the recent work of Holland (1973) in assessing the importance and the degrees of tolerance associated with person-situation congruence. Lofquist, Dawis, and their various colleagues have distinguished work settings and occupations on the basis of their profile of reinforcers of individual behavior: twenty-one different reinforcers are seen as potentially comprising a work setting (see Table 2.3); different persons will have needs profiles that accord with or are incompatible with the reinforcer profile of any given occupation or setting. Their job *satisfaction* and tenure in that setting will vary accordingly.

To assess an individual's job *satisfactoriness* one can compare the individual's scores on ability tests, such as the General Aptitude Test Battery, with Occupational Aptitude Patterns (U.S. Department of Labor, 1962) for different occupations. Together these two assessments — of individual satisfaction, correspondence of needs and occupational reinforcers, and satisfactoriness, correspondence of individual abilities with occupational requirements — were integrated into the Minnesota Occupational Classification System in 1975 and coordinated with the Dictionary of Occupational Titles and the Holland Codes cited elsewhere in this book. Such views are complemented by those of Herzberg.

Herzberg's perspectives have been called two-factor, dual-factor, or motivation hygiene theory. Herzberg's theory of work behavior (for example, Herzberg, 1968; Herzberg, Mausner & Snyderman, 1959) has stimulated considerable discussion, debate, and research on motivation, satisfaction, and performance in work. It has also been used as the basis for job enrichment and redesign programs in industry. Put simply, Herzberg's theory includes two sets of factors. The first has to do with job environment; these are the hygiene factors. The second has to do with the job content; these are the motivation factors. The first set deals with the drive to avoid pain and to gratify the range of acquired wants that have been socialized around such a drive. These "hygiene" factors, which are extrinsic to the job, include company policy and administration, supervision, interpersonal relationships, working conditions, salary, status, and security. The absence of these makes for job dissatisfaction; their presence reduces or eliminates job dissatisfaction but does not elicit satisfaction or high performance. In order to achieve the latter, the second set of factors, called motivators, is necessary. The motivators induce growth, satisfaction, higher performance. Included are achievement, recognition for achievement, the work itself, responsibility, and growth or advancement. Without motivators, one can achieve a work environment in which workers are free of dissatisfaction and conflict with management but they may also lack productive effort or high performance. To obtain the latter, one may need different types of job loadings or redesign, which include removing some controls while retaining accountability; increasing the accountability of individuals for their own work; giving a person a complete unit of work rather than a fractionated, repetitive piece in which they cannot see a whole product; granting additional authority to an employee about how he or she does his or her job; making periodic reports of performance productivity directly available to the worker rather than to the worker's supervisor.

Table 2.3
Occupational Reinforcers

Ability utilization	Recognition
Achievement	Responsibility
Activity	Security
Advancement	Social service
Authority	Social status
Company policies & practices	Supervision-human relations
Compensation	Supervision-technical
Co-workers	Variety
Creativity	Work conditions
Independence	Autonomy
Moral values	

Career Guidance and Job Satisfaction

The models of job satisfaction, motivation, and work performance discussed here and in Chapter 4 provide both conceptual stimuli and a potential blueprint for the variety of activities in which counselors and career guidance persons can engage effectively in business and industry. These will be detailed more fully in Chapters 11 and 13. Suffice it to say here that what is known about job satisfaction supports such counselor activity as:

- educating first-line supervisors and managers to current perspectives on job satisfaction, work motivation, and work performance
- providing information to workers about career paths, career ladders, the avenues and requirements for mobility within the organization
- classifying workers by technical skills and psychological needs to maximize person-job fit with regard to content, supervisory style, and related factors
- conducting workshops and seminars to increase workers' understanding of their educational opportunities, their employability skills, and their understanding of the organizational characteristics with which they interact
- consulting with managers about job redesign and work enrichment schemes
- providing support groups for workers in various types of transitions (such as new jobs, geographical relocations, overseas transfers, shifting family structures)
- providing individual counseling about work behavior and career development

WORK AND MENTAL HEALTH

There are strong links between work and mental health. In a major study of mental health in America and the contrasts in patterns of help-seeking from 1957 to 1976, Veroff, Kulka, and Douvan (1981) report that about 10 percent of their respondents in 1957 and in 1976 either used help or could have used help with job problems or vocational choice (p. 190). Undoubtedly, this number is understated since several other problem areas reported probably also included job-related problems (such as situational problems involving other people, non-psychological situational problems, "nothing specific — a lot of little things," marriage). The researchers also found that younger workers are more distressed in their work, more aware of their own shortcomings, and more sensitive to difficulties, and that they seek greater gratification from their work life. Older people are more often locked into a job to which they are already adapted and hence tend to make the best of what they have.

Veroff, Kulka, and Douran found profound differences between the college educated and the less educated in their reactions to work. The college educated expect work to fulfill their desires for interesting and exciting experiences; they are more ego involved in work satisfaction or dissatisfaction because they have been socialized to expect highly personal expression in work. Sex differences in reactions to work and adaptation to work settings were also found. Surprisingly it was found that men are less ego involved in work than women.

In essence, such findings suggest that some groups are more likely to risk psychological distress associated with work than others. However, the findings of Veroff, Kulka, and Douvan suggest that distress about work is only minimally related to readiness for self-referral.

> Evidently adaptation to work is a psychological process which if unsuccessful is as likely to stimulate thoughts of self-help as of seeking help from professionals. Indeed one might surmise that people often diagnose their own psychological problems at work as being ones which require that they "get themselves together" or find other work or another job. This option of leaving a job as a solution to a work problem may possibly reduce the association between work distress and readiness for self-referral (p. 89).

Unemployment and Mental and Emotional Distress

Whether it leads to readiness for self-referral or not, distress about work and unemployment itself are associated with a range of personal and social problems. For example, Levine (1979) has reported on both the reactions to unemployment and the emotional consequences of unemployment. He reports that reactions to unemployment tend to unfold in three stages: (1) optimism, (2) ambiguity, and (3) despair. Although there are individual differences in coping with these stages, the virtually predictable emotional and cognitive consequences, according to Levine, include: boredom, identity diffusion, lower self-esteem, guilt and shame, anxiety and fear, anger, and depression. These are not benign emotional reactions.

Liem and Rayman (1982) have reviewed studies of the social and private costs of unemployment. They indicate, "Prolonged unemployment is commonly a serious threat to health and the broad quality of life. These costs, furthermore, are borne not only by individual workers, but also by their families and communities" (p. 1116). They go on to indicate, "There is good evidence that losing one's job can increase health risks, exacerbate chronic and latent disorders, alter usual patterns of health-seeking behavior, and exact numerous other social and interpersonal costs" (p. 1116).

Among the specific problems found in the research literature to be associated with unemployment and economic decline are first admissions to psychiatric hospitals, rises in rates of infant mortality, increased deaths from cardiovascular and alcohol-related diseases, and sharp increase in suicide rates, greater demand for mental health services due to increased psychological impairment of the population (Brenner, 1973, 1979); threats to the structural interdependence between the family and the workplace (Kantor, 1977); stress in the children of unemployed parents — such as moodiness at home, new problems in school, strained relationship with peers (Liem & Rayman, 1982), digestive problems, irritability, and retarded physical and mental development (Riegle, 1982); child and spouse abuse, and juvenile delinquency (Riegle, 1982). The "ripple effect" of unemployment touches not only the individual who is unemployed but all parts of the system of which he or she is a part. For each of the persons involved it is common to have manifested a wide range of physical, emotional, and social stresses and strains. In Chapter 13, unemployment and its effects are explained in detail.

Work Pathology

Beyond the general relationships between work and mental health just cited, there are also more serious matters. For example, there are problem employees whose work pathology and psychopathology often merge. These are persons for whom corporations have long provided units dedicated to occupational mental health (McLean, 1973). Staffed by psychiatrists or clinical psychologists, such units are frequently augmented by the referral of problem employees to outside consultants through employee assistance plans or through various health care or insurance plans. As counseling psychologists and other career guidance specialists are increasingly employed by corporations and government agencies, treatment of such problems in the work site may become more common.

In considering serious problems of mental illness in the work place, it is sometimes difficult to know whether work induces mental illness or persons bring mental illness to work. Huffine and Clausen (1979) have engaged in one of the few long-term studies of the effects of mental illness on careers. They intensively studied thirty-six married, white men after they had entered a Washington, D.C., area mental hospital between 1952 and 1958 as first-admission patients with diagnoses of functional psychosis, affective disorder, severe psychoneurosis, or character disorder. Their data revealed that, in and of itself, being labeled mentally ill does not determine the course of a man's career even though he may be confined for months in a public mental hospital. They found that men whose symptoms subsided — either at the end of the initial episode or within a few years thereafter — did not suffer gross occupational setbacks. Indeed, it was found that the career of a man who was able to establish his competence before the initial onset of mental illness stands a good chance of surviving prolonged, even severe, symptoms.

However, about one-third experienced lower occupational status and more repeated failure than before admission. Success in spite of mental illness tends to depend on success of previous socialization into a work role and competence developed before becoming mentally ill. Where these two conditions exist, the result seems to be a resilient work role, making it unnecessary to sacrifice a career to mental illness. Although this study did not pursue them, factors in the character and structure of the work place may also facilitate or impede reestablishment of a career after an episode of mental illness. This is an area yet to be fully probed, but it is likely to have important implications for the supportive role that can be played by the career guidance specialist or counseling psychologist in industry. At a minimum it is likely that such professionals will need to assist managerial and supervisory personnel as well as the afflicted person's co-workers to understand what behaviors might be expected in different forms of mental illness and, indeed, that it is likely that no symptoms will be observable at all because of the control exerted by medication and other treatment.

Some forms of work pathology may require specific types of differential treatment in the work place. Neff (1977) has suggested several broad patterns of what might be considered work psychopathology. The underlying theme of such problems may be difficulty with authority figures, with interpersonal relations, with the meanings of work, or related conflicts. In particular, he reports five patterns of behavior that lead to failure at work. The patterns, in paraphrased form, include the following:

Type 1. These are people who appear to have major lacks in work motivation; a negative conception of the role of worker. Such people have not been socialized to value work for themselves or they attribute negative stereotypes to the work role (such as "work is for squares"). They may view work as societal pressure for them to conform to a regimentation they prefer to avoid or resist. They pursue impulse gratification now, rather then deferred gratification and planning for the future. Persons so characterized, particularly in the extreme cases, may be made to work under powerful social coercion but will likely meet only minimum standards of productivity and will require continuous, close supervision. From a counseling view such persons need to be assisted to develop an internal locus of control and to be placed in work settings that provide graduated incentives for productivity.

Type 2. These are individuals who experience fear and anxiety as the predominant responses to demands to be productive. A fairly common type, such persons may be fearful of inability to perform effectively or have little positive self-regard. Their previous life is likely to have been a series of failures. They may interpret constructive criticism as personal threat; be acutely uncomfortable, perhaps immobilized by anxiety in a competitive situation; treat opportunities for cooperative work with others as situations likely to expose personal vulnerability. Such persons are likely to respond favorably to conditions arranged to offer them success experiences. These individuals probably require supervisory support and encouragement while discovering that there are work roles that can be performed without constant personal deprecation. They may sometimes require a constantly sheltered work role that does not demand new and rapid challenges or expectations. Therapeutically, such persons could likely profit from cognitive restructuring or rational-emotive approaches that focus on their self-labeling and its behavioral consequences (Ellis, 1962; Meichenbaum, 1977).

Type 3. This type includes people whose basic behavioral style is open hostility and aggression. They perceive supervision and criticism as attacks to which to respond with anger or violence. In such people the work expectations of society are internalized as restrictive and hostile demands on them. Such persons are frequently energetic and able if placed in work they can do independently of others. They frequently do not have difficulty in finding employment but in maintaining it. The typical reason for dismissal or quitting is inability to get along with others because of, in the extreme circumstances, manifestations of paranoid psychosis or in other situations intense irritability, physical aggression to others, or constant anger. This type of behavioral problem is very difficult to deal with in a work setting, although it may respond to long-term therapy or newer approaches to anger management and reduction (Schlichter & Horan, 1981; Novaco, 1976).

Type 4. Included here are persons whose behavior is characterized by marked dependency. Because of socialization problems in early childhood, the individual internalizes precepts that personal welfare depends on pleasing authority figures; that independent behavior by the worker can threaten such a relationship; that childlike compliance is the chief defensive strategy to be used in any circumstance (home, school, work) where others are perceived as all-powerful authority figures. Such persons may work effectively to please a supervisor as long as close and continuous management is present. They typically require constant emotional support from the supervisor, whose patience is likely to be sorely tried in attempting to respond to the constant personal irresponsibility and emotional immaturity displayed by the worker.

Such persons are likely to require selective placement in situations where they receive considerable personal approval and support. Therapeutically, they need assistance in examining their view of authority relationships and the types of trade-offs they are consciously or unconsciously engaging in through their dependency behaviors.

Type 5. These persons display a marked degree of social naivete. Such individuals simply lack knowledge about themselves as workers, about work content, and about the realities and demands of the work environment. In such cases, the focus of the counselor is not on the individual's rejection of work or resistance to components of the work place but on ignorance. The procedure is to provide the worker with social learning or a specific educational experience in which information about the organization and expectations of work is primary.

The five types of inadequate work patterns suggested by Neff are hypothetical but represent some of the potential interactions to be observed between work and the mental health of some workers. Without some type of intervention, persons characterized by such work behaviors will likely fail, quit, or be dismissed. Career guidance practitioners, counseling psychologists, or other human resource development specialists will need to provide differential treatment to cope with the variety of problems.

Persons who are having mental health problems in their work place may not display psychiatric symptoms – paranoia, character disorders, severe psychoneurosis – although they may be depressed, preoccupied with family problems, experiencing alcohol abuse, or otherwise behaving ineffectively. In short, they may have become problem employees.

Peace (1973) suggests that problem employees can be seen first as simply employees with problems. If sufficient help is not received they may become problems to themselves. If self-understanding and other forms of assistance do not occur at this point, the employee may then become a problem for management. In this view, employees never become a problem for management until they have first become problems to themselves. The problem employee is a person who has an emotional problem which he or she has neither solved nor escaped. Becoming a problem employee is not a voluntary process but one that evolves as the worker acts in ways that make sense in the tangled emotions being experienced but that alienate or anger co-workers, supervisors, and others.

From a somewhat different perspective, Nolan (1973) defines a problem employee as "one who does not conform to the social vocational role expected of him at his place of employment" (p. xi). From this standpoint, physical disability, psychological maladjustment, neurosis, and so forth are not in themselves characteristics of problem employees. Nor is a person in good physical and psychological health necessarily a nonproblem employee. The actual definition of a problem employee depends on the standards set by the work organization. Many factors affect such definitions and thus preclude a simple listing of personality traits or deficits as in themselves problematic. The possibilities across a spectrum of worker types have been identified by Nolan (1973) as follows:

1. Some job applicants have psychological problems at the time of hiring; they may get worse, improve, or stay the same upon employment.
2. Some employees who may or may not have been maladjusted at the time of employment develop problems at a later date. These problems may or may not be influenced by the job setting.
3. Some employees show average or superior job performance in spite of – or because of – their problem.
4. Some employees who are not technically regarded as psychologically handicapped still cannot function effectively under certain work conditions or leadership types (p. xiii).

Obviously, career guidance practitioners in industry will have many opportunities to engage in career counseling, skill-building, classification, consultation, education, and referral as the relationships between work and mental health take on renewed attention in the future.

WORK AND LEISURE

The values ascribed to work and leisure and the interaction between the two terms have been matters of significant discussion for many centuries. The debate has escalated in the past two decades as the onset of automation, robotics, and other machine-machine systems have altered the character of many forms of work. Supposedly, technological advances have freed people to engage in more leisure activities. For some, leisure seems synonymous with idleness or fewer hours of work. To other observers, the effective use of leisure is in itself a serious matter since idleness and the inadequate use of leisure can bring with them anxiety, frustration, crime, and other social problems.

In the most obvious counterpoint, the type of work one engages in affects how much time is available for leisure pursuits, what these pursuits are likely to be, and with whom and when they will occur. But leisure and how it is used also have to do with quality of life. McPhearson and Guppy (1979), for example, describe retirement and aging as representing for many a transition from a work to a leisure role. Others suggest that persons must balance work and leisure as sources of need satisfaction (Leclair, 1982). The questions in such cases are: Can leisure also provide the self-esteem potentially available from work? Can leisure be growth-producing just as work can potentially be? Does leisure deserve the same sort of attention and resources as does planning for work or other aspects of career?

The answers to such questions are debatable. In recent decades, leisure has rarely been seen as having merit in itself either as a life style or in excessive portions as a complement to work. As the meanings of work and work ethics in this society are changing toward greater emphasis on holistic approaches to well-being and self-actualization, the part that leisure plays in such circumstances is being rethought by many observers.

Concepts of Leisure

One of the concepts useful to thinking about leisure is that time is a commodity to be rationally used (Wilson, 1981). Therefore, the planning of a career involves considering how one will use the time available. It has sometimes been suggested that the only thing all humankind shares is twenty-four hours a day. How we use these hours is what differentiates us. Obviously, the partitioning of time available into work, leisure, family and community roles, idleness, and learning is a matter of values as well as of resources and information.

The use of time interacts with the use of language. As has been said both here and in the first chapter, language shapes how we view people and problems and what we do about them. Language sets limits on perception; we can see only that which we have been linguistically trained to see. As Wilson (1981) has so effectively articulated,

> Our language is beautifully adapted to the world of organized work, but ill-adapted to the world of unorganized leisure. We have many words and many perceptual frames to describe the product of goods or the rules of bureaucratic behavior. But one's tongue twists or falls silent when we try to tell of contemplation or love, of writing a poem, or pondering a philosophy (p. 283).

Within this context, Wilson reminds us, "One of our great hazards in considering leisure is that it is so commonly thought of as a residue, an empty category of experience that is 'left over' when other life sustaining activities have been accomplished" (p. 284). Instead, in his view, leisure requires alertness, involvement, immersion. It is an active rather than passive process, in which one is not compelled to engage but which is frequently the condition in which "peak experience," growth, and self-actualization can occur. Kelly (1981) goes beyond this position in his wedding of leisure sociology and existential theory to contend that the essential variety of leisure offers "an especially apt environment for trying out identities not fully established and the non-serious consequences of play affording opportunity for risk in self-presentation" (p. 312).

A Leisure Typology

Gunter and Gunter (1980), using concepts of freedom of choice, time, and involvement, have identified several modes or styles of leisure that can be useful as reference points for career counselors.

Pure Leisure. Pure leisure represents an ideal state in the blending of individual choice and involvement. In reality, it is a type of sporadic experience rather than an ongoing life style: the fantasy of child's play, the separation and timeliness that often accompanies the reading of a good book or the hearing of a beautiful symphony, the spontaneity of a comfortable evening with friends, the simple escape from work and other distractions that sometimes occurs in travel or games. Usually experiences of pure leisure are temporary rather than continuous leisure-styles. In fact, there is increasing evidence that much leisure of great importance for maintaining psychological equilibrium may be "interstitial" and found in minutes and moments interspersed through any day (Czikszentmihalyi, 1975).

Anomic Leisure. How to use the increased leisure options society bestows on us, particularly in the absence of institutional roles and involvements, is a problem. Although some persons would consider such a situation the essential element of the good life, the lack of structural constraints and obligations may cause leisure to be viewed with dislike, antipathy, confusion, and a sense of powerlessness. At various points in life (unemployment, retirement, shortened work weeks, enforced vacations or holidays) individuals may have an abundance of free time and for a variety of reasons be unable to cope with it. A variation on this classification has been described as a polarity, compensation, or oppositional view of leisure in which the distinctions between work and leisure are sharply defined. Leisure is seen as filling the void left by work.

Institutional Leisure. One's work involvement or involvement with other institutions, such as family, community, politics, or religion, may be so intense as to minimize one's freedom of choice outside of the penetration of these institutions throughout our life style. The most negative form of institutional leisure occurs for the workaholic. A more positive form occurs for the individual who is so wrapped up in the work role being played that the choice of leisure tends to blend institutional involvements with free time. This may happen through continuing education, travel, conducting business on the golf course, reading, or meetings, which are work related but seen by the individual as interesting, rewarding, growth producing. It is the quality rather than the form of the activity that makes it leisure. Allen (1980) has described this type of leisure as a fusion, spillover, or extension model in which no clear distinction exists between what is one's leisure and what is one's work.

Alienated Leisure. Although the institutional pervasiveness of leisure may be similar to that in the previous category, in this form of leisure there is little personal satisfaction or positive psychological identification with it. Here the institutional structure may consume the person's leisure time out of necessity, not choice. Family responsibilities — such as many children or aged parents — may require constant attention and time; work roles may require constant community involvement in meetings, dinners, and other tasks to preserve image and public relations. Persons in this category pursue leisure activities from duty or habit but really do not derive satisfaction or choice from them.

Leisure Counseling

Although such a typology does not exhaust personal approaches to leisure, it nevertheless sets a crude map of the different roles counselors might play in helping clients come to grips with leisure issues. In some cases, the question is one of identifying the leisure opportunities that exist. In others, the question is one of values clarification toward work and leisure. In still other cases, the individual needs to be helped to consider in depth the lack of leisure they are experiencing and their unhappiness about such a situation. Counselors need to help some persons find leisure "moments" during their daily activity or consider leisure to try on personal roles that may not yet be fully formed. It seems obvious that the constructive choice and control of leisure in one's life are extremely important to self-esteem, holistic health, and other positive characteristics. A lack of such conditions is conducive to stress, "burn-out," possibly antisocial acts of vandalism, crime, and so on.

McDowell (1976) has defined leisure counseling as "a helping process which facilitates interpretive, affective, and/or behavioral changes in others toward the attainment of their leisure well-being" (p. 9). Edwards (1980) maintains, "Leisure counseling is a process that occurs when a trained leisure counselor helps one person or a group of persons, of any age, to determine their present leisure interests, attitudes, and needs — then assists them in choosing and following leisure pursuits that are practical, satisfying, available, and unharmful" (p. 1). LeClair (1982) suggests that leisure counseling is "a process using contemporary counseling techniques to facilitate the awareness of client's thoughts, feelings, and values toward leisure as well as to develop the client's decision-making skills involved in leisure participation" (p. 294). Just as in other areas of controversy and possible stereotyping, counselors must consider their own values about leisure and the different models of leisure in which clients might engage so that they can provide resources and effective planning assistance.

THE TRANSITION TO WORK

The transition to work among youth, displaced homemakers, and other groups who have not had previous experience in the labor force has become a major international problem. In particular, the school-to-work transition has become the object of concern and research throughout the world.

As Herr and Watts (1981) have suggested, from a parochial perspective it is easy to believe that the large number of unemployed youth in the United States is a phenomenon confined to this nation and a signal of deeply ingrained economic difficulties. Whether or not the latter is true, the former is not: problems of youth employment are not confined to the United States but range throughout the industrialized and the nonindustrialized nations of the world.

The International Labor Office (ILO) reported in 1977 that:

In the nine Common Market countries those under the age of 25 looking for jobs have more than doubled since 1975 and now account for one out of every three of the five million unemployed. . . . Teenagers are hardest hit, especially those looking for their first job. Even in countries with relatively low levels of joblessness, such as Sweden and Norway, teenage unemployment is twice or thrice higher than that of other workers (International Labor Office, 1977a).

In another ILO study (1977b) in an Asian country it was found that 79 percent of the unemployed were under 25 years of age and nearly half of them had not yet reached the age of 18. The magnitude of the total problem is dramatized by ILO statistics that indicate that young people under 20 make up one-third of the population of the industrialized countries and one-half of the population in the developing countries.

The official U.S. Department of Labor statistics comparing youth unemployment rates for selected countries in 1978 showed the United States leading with 19 percent; Italy, 16.8; France, 16.1; Canada, 15.6; Australia, 13.1; Germany, 7.2; Great Britain, 7.0; Sweden, 5.5; and Japan, 4.1 (U.S. Department of Labor, 1979). The teenage-to-adult ratios also vary significantly from nation to nation. Italy, for example, has experienced a ratio of teenage unemployment seven times higher than the adult rate. In the United States the recent ratios of youth-to-adult unemployment have tended to be three or four times as high. Canada, Britain, and Japan tend to have the lowest ratios of teenage-to-adult unemployment, with differentials of about two to one.

The reasons for differences in youth unemployment and for differentials between youth and adult unemployment relate to the labor market policies of each country, the availability of transition services (such as job orientation, guidance, counseling, and placement), female participation in the work force, the characteristics of the industrial base of the nation, the number of legal and illegal immigrants in the country available for temporary work in agriculture, construction, and other activities in the secondary labor market, and other pertinent factors.

Research shows that as a group, young workers in the United States enter the labor force gradually rather than abruptly on the completion of school (Stevenson, 1978). A trial-and-error period typically precedes complete assimilation into the labor force. Large numbers of teenagers and young adults combine school and work before completing the transition. This process is made possible largely through opportunities for part-time employment in the secondary labor market (including fast food restaurants, service stations, agriculture, odd jobs, retail stores). However, a growing body of research indicates that beyond a predictable period of experimentation, joblessness among out-of-school teenage youth carries with it a "hangover effect." Adams and Mangum (1978) show,

> Those who have unfavorable early labor market experiences are less likely than others to have favorable experiences later, education and other background characteristics held constant. Thus, early labor market experiences are related to subsequent measures of labor market success. They cannot be treated as benign phenomena which "age out" nor as simple individual problems which have no implications for social policy or governmental intervention (Garraty, 1978).

Frequent unemployment and other poor labor-market experiences during the early years have a deleterious effect later, in part because periods of unemployment represent loss of work experience, information, and skills that may put the person at a competitive disadvantage in the eyes of an employer and may also have an injurious effect on attitudes toward work.

The demoralizing effects of prolonged unemployment have been documented in many reports in the United States and in Great Britain, among other nations (for example, Adams, Mangum & Lenniger, 1978; Harrison, 1976; Marsden, 1975). Such studies have shown that unemployment is destructive enough for adults, who have already achieved a work identity, and who because of their life experience and knowledge may find it

possible to see unemployment as a social rather than a personal problem. Young persons or women entering the labor force for the first time have no such identity or experience to sustain them, and their resulting sense of rejection and worthlessness may well reinforce negative self-images that have already been established at school or in the family.

The most serious problem in this regard is found among those youths who are both out of school prematurely and out of work. In addition, major transition problems are frequently experienced by certain groups of disadvantaged youth, particularly but not exclusively black males and females, Hispanic youth, Native Americans, and inner-city and rural poor. Thus, the youth population is composed of subpopulations who vary in their ability to master the movement from school to work. Obviously, the reasons for such circumstances are diverse — racial discrimination, economic circumstances, geographic differences in part-time opportunities, and inadequate occupational skills have each been cited as contributing to the transitional problems of youth.

Whether or not the unemployed young are also the unemployed middle aged is not now clear, but that is certainly true in many instances. What is clear is that career guidance approaches in the future will need to acknowledge more fully than has been traditional the different types of unemployment, how they come about, and who is affected by them.

Classes of Unemployment

Unemployment is composed of different categories and causes (Kroll, 1976). In conventional labor market terms, it is possible to divide unemployment into four categories: structural, frictional, seasonal, and cyclical. Although these types of unemployment are not totally independent they are sufficiently distinctive to be worthy of mention.

Seasonal Unemployment. Some unemployment is a function of climate or predictable shifts in weather sufficient to affect such industries as tourism, recreation, agriculture, or construction. Although seasonal unemployment is on the average less lengthy than other forms of unemployment, there is relatively little that career guidance, education, or government schemes can do to change the timing or characteristics of such unemployment. Career guidance can be helpful in informing people that it occurs, identifying the industries most likely to be affected by seasonal unemployment, and helping persons considering entrance into such industries to develop attitudes of flexibility toward the type of work they do.

Cyclical Unemployment. Fiscal and monetary policies can repress consumer demand and general business activity, therefore causing unemployment. Manipulation of the tax structure, shifts in the demographic characteristics of the population, changes in the proportions of discretionary income and savings, international events, natural disasters, and governmental attempts to control inflation, each contribute to cyclical unemployment. This type of unemployment is relatively unaffected by the availability of career guidance or, indeed, by the nature of the training of the work force. Career guidance can assist workers who have been dislocated by cyclical unemployment to pursue other types of work and to recognize that the unemployment they are experiencing is not a function of their personal inadequacy but rather of external forces affecting realignments in job configurations and availability.

Frictional Unemployment. When workers are initially entering the labor force after schooling is completed or when they are being reabsorbed into the labor force as they are moving from one project to another or between occupations, frictional unemployment occurs. Ordinarily of short duration, this form of unemployment occurs as workers locate and move into available jobs. Although some time loss is inescapable between leaving school or one job and identifying and moving to another, the amount of time spent in such movement is likely to be reduced if potential workers are provided with job search skills and accurate knowledge of job opportunities. Career guidance can be a significant influence in reducing the *length* but not the presence of frictional unemployment.

Structural Unemployment. A mismatch between the skills of those seeking jobs and the job requirements themselves creates structural unemployment. Such circumstances are likely to occur when new technologies or geographic relocations of particular industries create major shifts in the organization and content of work. These changing skill requirements give undereducated, inappropriately educated, geographically immobile, inexperienced, and physically and emotionally handicapped groups a significant disadvantage and make them likely to be unemployed for a long time. The responses of career guidance to such a form of unemployment include referral to skill training programs, assistance in developing job entry and job search skills, interpretation of labor market information, clarification of unemployment benefits and resources, emotional support during retraining and job search, brokering and advocacy with employers, and job development in which tailored work stations are solicited in behalf of individual clients. The overarching problem in such a condition is that career guidance practitioners cannot create or recreate jobs that political, technological, and economic conditions have caused to disappear or to be in limited supply.

Such perspectives on the different causes and characteristics of unemployment accent the need for career guidance programs and practitioners to tailor their responses to the presenting problems of groups or individuals.

Employment Transition Problems

Whether or not unemployment is at issue, persons entering the labor force without a substantial base of experience are likely to experience a variety of transition problems to which career guidance programs must be prepared to respond. The sophistication and the organization of contemporary work frequently walls off young people from what jobs they might choose and how information about available work might be obtained. Many counselors and teachers suffer from the same lack of knowledge. In some cases, students find that what they studied in school is unrelated to available jobs or to new processes, materials, or technological developments (Burdetsky, 1976). Furthermore, as a nation, energy crises and international complications have directly affected the content and organization of work. Our nation has come to realize the incredible complexity and intense interaction of the technological and human problems facing us in the foreseeable future. It has become evident that many of the problems experienced by our work force are not simply technical, but psychological and sociological.

As much as many persons need to acquire occupational task skills, they also need assistance to clarify or strengthen their self-attitudes and to change their personal habits, emotional responses to life situations, attitudes toward work, planning skills, and methods of adjusting to new jobs.

Several studies appearing during the 1960s indicated that many persons experiencing difficulties in obtaining and keeping jobs did so because they lacked skills in job seeking and on-the-job behavior, which were separate from the ability to do the required work. For example, Eggeman, Campbell, and Garbin (1969) queried a national sample of 763 Youth Opportunity Center counselors from forty-eight states about the major problems faced by youth in the transition from school to work. Eighty-six percent of the counselors indicated that the major problem was inadequate job preparation. In this study, inadequate job preparation was broadly defined to include inadequate training, inadequate job skills, lack of information about work and training opportunities, lack of knowledge of the real demands of work and of employer expectations, lack of educational requirements, and lack of prior work experience. Slightly more than 71 percent of the counselors indicated vocational behavior as a third-ranked category of poor worker adjustment. Included under vocational behavior were poor work habits (absenteeism, tardiness, and so on), inability to fill out forms and handle interviews, inability to accept supervision, inability to get along with fellow workers or to cope with real demands of work, poor attitudes toward work, and so forth.

Garbin, Salomone, Jackson, and Ballweg (1970) analyzed worker adjustment problems of youth and concluded that youthful employees often fail on their jobs, not because they lack technical competencies, but because they lack skills relating to the nontechnical complex, what we describe elsewhere as affective work competencies or

work context skills. In a somewhat different view, Reubens (1974) has reported that basic literacy and good work attitudes may be more important for employment than occupational skills. She contends that an increasing number of employers already look for these qualities first, rather than for traditional vocational skills.

In the study of Eggeman, Campbell, and Garbin (1969) previously cited, 78.2 percent of the Youth Opportunity Center counselors surveyed reported that personality problems hamper youth's adjustment to the world of work. More specifically, 72 percent mentioned job-seeking or on-the-job behavior as a major problem. After reviewing the research of Fleishman (1968) and Ley (1966) among others, as well as their own research, Garbin et al. (1970) contended, "The basic difficulty of many youth is not that of finding a job, but in keeping one" (p. 4). As a function of their research on the adjustment of 642 young workers in Columbus, New Orleans, and Omaha, they found that the most difficult kinds of things that workers had to learn in job performance were: technological (46.7 percent); interpersonal (19.2 percent); personal (14.8 percent); and organizational (4.3 percent). They indicated that a preparation for work involves more than inculcating prospective workers with technological skills.

Similar to, but a bit more comprehensive than, the 1960s studies we have cited was the extensive survey of the work entry problems of youth conducted by Haccoun and Campbell (1972). The results of their survey were used by Crites (1976) in his discussion of "thwarting conditions" that new workers may experience as they attempt to become established in a job. According to Haccoun and Campbell and to Crites, there are two classes of thwarting conditions: (1) those dealing with job performance problems; and (2) those dealing with job entry, career planning, and management problems. Each of these classes of "thwarting conditions" contains a number of pertinent problems, as shown in Table 2.4.

Recent research adds increasing insight into the "thwarting conditions" related to the transition to work and work adjustment. Ashley et al. (1980) studied in depth the adaptation to work of thirty-eight males and thirty females, from 17 to 30 years of age. The results of the study indicate that for those who adapt to work successfully,

Table 2.4
Work Entry Problems of Youth

I. On the job performance problems
　　Responsibility, maturity, attitudes, and values
　　Work habits
　　Peer and supervisory adjustment
　　Communication
　　New roles
　　Automation and changing technology
　　Self-image
　　Alienation

II. Job entry, career planning, and management problems
　　Job-seeking
　　Interview and test-taking
　　Geographic mobility
　　Family and personal situational adjustment
　　Job layoffs and rejections
　　Educational preparation and job placement
　　Career planning and management
　　Occupational aspirations and job expectations
　　Youth image
　　Military
　　Prejudice and discrimination
　　Prior work experience
　　Trade unions

a sequence of adjustments in five areas may be involved.

Performance Aspects. In the initial phase of adjustment, on job entry, the performance aspects of adaptation occupied the center of employees' concern. Some of the performance-related adjustment problems they encountered included learning what was expected and how to do the new job tasks, doing unusual job tasks (often not in the job description) or learning new ways to do old ones, coping with idle time or sporadic work schedules on the job, and dealing with a great volume or variety of work tasks or unexpectedly complex job tasks, physical or mental fatigue or inefficiency, and production quotas and standards.

Organizational Aspects. Informal (unofficial) rules, procedures, and hierarchies presented a major challenge to most workers coming into a new job. They frequently found a distinct difference between the official and the unofficial rules of the job. Workers seemed to feel that

satisfactory adjustment had a lot to do with a good initial orientation. Most workers recognized a need to know about the company, its functions and activities, and how workers fit into the total organization of the company.

Interpersonal Aspects. Overlapping in time with performance aspects was the need to begin to adapt to co-workers because their assistance was needed in order to achieve adequate adaptation in performance. Subjects who could not relate to co-workers were unhappy in the work situation. Many of the subjects reported feeling that they had adjusted to the new job when they "felt accepted" by their co-workers. Several workers reported difficulties in adjusting to supervisory styles that conflicted with their own attitudes, values, or work styles. For some of the young workers, especially those in a full-time work environment for the first time, interpersonal aspects of the jobs (such as teamwork, dealing with disagreeable co-workers, adjusting to supervisors, getting assistance from others) represented the most difficult part of adjusting in the work environment.

Responsibility Aspects. As adaptation proceeds and performance and interpersonal aspects of the job come under control, adjustment problems related to responsibility tend to emerge. These include proving oneself, making use of training opportunities, getting ahead, getting raises, and related tasks.

Affective Aspects. In essence throughout the adaptation process, adjustment to work is affected by the worker's attitudes and feelings. Subjects indicated the importance of maintaining a good work attitude and a willingness to work hard, regardless of how good or bad the particular job was seen to be. They also reported that self-awareness and good feelings about oneself and one's job performance were important aspects of adaptation to the job.

In another study of functional competencies for adapting to the world of work, Selz, Jones, and Ashley (1980) asked four national respondent groups (general adult population, high school seniors, public school teachers, and employers) to establish the priority of competencies important to occupational adaptability. Fifty percent or more of all samples thought one would have a great deal of difficulty at work if one did not have the following abilities:

- use reading, writing, and math skills the job calls for
- use tools and equipment the job calls for
- get along with others
- deal with pressures to get the job done
- follow rules and policies
- have a good work attitude

Affective Work Competencies

What seems to be repeated in the studies reported here of either transition to work or work adjustment is that although job skills and "task teachability" are important so, too, is what some nations call "industrial discipline" and Kazanas (1978) has described as "affective work competencies." Many of us have long contended that people typically do not lose their jobs because they cannot perform them but rather because of

"personality." We have used that term in a vague, almost glib, way to represent some complex of behaviors that do not fit the expectations of the work setting, and so we have dismissed the person. Kazanas' research confirms that what has so often been characterized as personality factors in unemployment can really be defined in terms of the characteristics, habits, values, or attitudes comprising affective work competencies. He contends that within management theory and behavioral research in industry, there has been a shift in emphasis from cognitive and psychomotor behavior to the social and psychological components of affective behavior.

A review of the research on why employers discharge or fail to promote employees identified fifteen behaviors, the first seven of which were common across studies (Kazanas, 1978, p. 32):

1. carelessness
2. laziness
3. absence/tardiness
4. disloyalty
5. distraction
6. too little or too much ambition
7. lack of initiative
8. dishonesty
9. noncooperativeness
10. lack of courtesy
11. unwillingness to follow rules
12. troublemaking
13. irresponsibility
14. lack of adaptability
15. misrepresentation

The opposite of the reasons for being dismissed are the affective work competencies identified by employers as important to work adjustment (Kazanas, 1978, p. 34):

1. punctuality
2. honesty
3. reliability
4. dependability
5. initiative
6. helpfulness
7. cooperation
   a. willingness to cooperate
   b. ability to get along with others
   c. character skills — performance as a co-worker

8. willingness to learn
9. sense of humor

Affective work competencies, like other work context skills, can be taught and must be seen as part of the content of career guidance programs. Such skills reflect a worker's understanding of the sociology and of the psychology of the "work culture." With such an understanding of the organizational structure and expectations that mediate the performance of work, career guidance personnel can encourage the development of affective work competencies not simply as arbitrary or capricious value sets but as "occupational survival skills" (Nelson, 1979).

Although worker deficits in employability skills reported here have been studied primarily in young workers as they enter the labor force, a growing research base has shown similar deficits in information, planning, or job-seeking skills among older workers experiencing occupational dislocation. The studies of Northcutt (Knowles, 1977), for example, suggest that only 40 percent of the American adult population is coping adequately with typical life problems (such as getting work and holding a job, buying things, managing one's economic life, and parenting). Evidence suggests that such persons need to experience skill-building approaches that are organized around the type of life crises they are facing. These observations are supported by findings from the National Assessment of Educational Progress (Westbrook, 1979), which indicates that a large percentage of adults are weak in basic skills and in occupational information; they have had little opportunity, tested or otherwise, to examine their personal characteristics with a counselor; and they are unclear about their educational or career needs.

Multidimensional Barriers to Work

For disadvantaged adults particularly but not exclusively, transition to work and work adjustment are multidimensional problems. Often when people are provided job training or occupational information or encouragement or career counseling and they still do not get work and adjust to it, we assume that they do not really want to work, they prefer welfare, or they are lazy. It is more likely that we have provided help in only one of the dimensions of life that is affecting their transition to and effective induction into work. Miller and Oetting (1977) identified some thirty-seven specific barriers to work in eleven categories, which were reported by 409 economically and vocationally disadvantaged persons in the Denver area. These barriers included child care, health, transportation, social and interpersonal conflicts, financial problems, legal problems, emotional-personal problems, drug and alcohol abuse problems, job qualifications, discrimination, and language and communication problems. In such perspectives we again see the need for career guidance approaches to take a multidimensional view of individual problems with work and a differential treatment approach to the resolution of the various problems experienced by any given individual.

Finally, it is useful to reaffirm that the transition to work and the adjustment to work are not single events but dynamic ones likely to recur throughout the life of adults. In 1978, the College Entrance Examination Board conducted a major study probing career changes for adults (Arbeiter, Aslanian, Schmerbeck, & Brickell, 1978). They concluded that some 40 million adults in the United States anticipated making a career change and were engaged in various life transitions — entering, progressing in, and exiting not only specific jobs, but also career fields. As part of this study, it was found that the spur to much career change lies in requirements for learning or, on the other side of that issue, life transitions tend to trigger learning, either voluntary or mandatory. These findings have been further explored in another national study that has examined life changes as reasons for adult learning (Aslanian & Brickell, 1980). Clearly, the nature of work in America is interwoven with the need to learn as one moves into a new job, adapts to a changing job, and advances in a career. Therefore, as work in the American society increasingly replaces experience with knowledge as a major criterion of admission and success, career guidance programs and practitioners must also respond to such conditions. We will need to provide clients with assistance in sorting out alternative and often nontraditional forms of learning and their implications for personal time commitments, travel, residency, and occupational preparation. Such assistance must be provided with an awareness of the fact that adults deciding to return to school also have many personal responsibilities and emotional demands on their time and energy. Also at issue may be adult problems with learning such as lack of self-confidence in one's ability to learn, unrealistic expectations of progress, theoretical or irrelevant learning tasks, seeking help too late or from the wrong sources, lack of efficient reading and study habits, press of time, and related matters (Porter, 1970).

Papalia and Kaminski (1981) have discussed various counseling skills required in an industrial environment. They indicate that career counselors should advise and counsel on programs offered by local and regional institutions of higher education. They should help employees prepare and process material related to tuition reimbursement, matriculation, admission, or assessment of prior learning. Of particular importance is the career counselor's role in negotiating for an industry the offering of special credit and noncredit courses, either in-house or at a campus location, locating special resource personnel needed to offer special programs and renting space and equipment from area educational facilities so that industry can conduct its own programs in these locations.

Adult Career Problems

Campbell and Cellini (1981) have developed a diagnostic taxonomy of adult career problems. In doing so, they have indicated that across the stages of adult career behavior, four common tasks tend to recur. They are: (1) decision making; (2) implementing plans; (3) achieving organizational/institutional performance at an acceptable level; and (4) accomplishing organizational/institutional adaptation so that the individual can effectively take part in the work environment. They then develop a diagnostic taxonomy of problems in each of these areas that can be used to classify client problems. The taxonomy is reproduced in Table 2.5.

In broad terms this taxonomy represents an array of adult career problems to which differential treatments can be related. It also provides a structure from which groups of persons needing similar assistance could be inferred and relevant skill building efforts constructed.

In using such a classification scheme, other research reminds us that it is a mistake to lump together all midlife or, indeed, other career changes that occur throughout adulthood. Thomas (1980), for example, found four distinct groups of changes among seventy-three men who had left professional and managerial careers between the ages of 34 and 54. The four groups — labeled the drift-outs, opt-outs, force-outs, and bow-outs — differed on several variables including amount of education completed, additional education undertaken to change careers, time taken to make the change, radicalness of change, and the importance of personal values in deciding to leave their former careers. Undoubtedly, other differentiations could be made among blue-collar changers and other subpopulations. However, the needs for content and process in career guidance will likely differ from group to group of changes.

CONCLUSIONS

The rationale for career guidance and for continuing research into career development implies that work is fundamental to how one feels about oneself (Sarason, Sarason, & Cowden, 1975). In addition, virtually any analysis of human development indicates that access to work is crucial to the ability to move effectively from adolescence to adulthood. Such a concern has particular vitality in those nations with highly developed technology and great affluence, such as the United States and other industrialized nations.

Tyler, Sundberg, Rohila, and Greene (1968) found in an extensive cross-cultural study of vocational choice patterns of adolescents that the more complex and affluent a society becomes, the freer one is from choice constraints, and thus the more the choice process becomes internalized. At the current level of American societal development, it is likely that the direction of one's life is determined more by one's own choices than by external social conditions. Finally, the premise on which this book rests is that career behavior and development, as well as access to work, are based on knowledge, skills, and attitudes that can be fostered rather than left to chance.

To take the above positions is not to be unaware of utopian forecasts that the United States is be-

Table 2.5
Diagnostic Taxonomy Outline: Problem Categories and Subcategories

1.0. Problems in career decision-making
  1.1. Getting started
     A. Lack of awareness of the need for a decision
     B. Lack of knowledge of the decision-making process
     C. Awareness of the need to make a decision, but avoidance of assuming personal responsibility for decision-making
  1.2. Information gathering
     A. Inadequate, contradictory, and/or insufficient information
     B. Information overload, i.e., excessive information which confuses the decision maker
     C. Lack of knowledge as to how to gather information, i.e., where to obtain information, how to organize, and to evaluate it
     D. Unwillingness to accept the validity of the information because it does not agree with the person's self-concept
  1.3. Generating, evaluating, and selecting alternatives
     A. Difficulty deciding due to multiple career options, i.e., too many equally attractive career choices
     B. Failure to generate sufficient career options due to personal limitations such as health, resources, ability, and education
     C. The inability to decide due to the thwarting effects of anxiety such as fear of failure in in attempting to fulfill the choice, fear of social disapproval, and/or fear of commitment to a course of action
     D. Unrealistic choice, i.e., aspiring either too low or too high, based upon criteria such as aptitudes, interests, values, resources, and personal circumstances
     E. Interfering personal constraints which impede a choice such as interpersonal influences and conflicts, situational circumstances, resources, and health
     F. The inability to evaluate alternatives due to lack of knowledge of the evaluation criteria — the criteria could include values, interests, aptitudes, skills, resources, health, age, and personal circumstances
  1.4. Formulating plans to implementing decisions
     A. Lack of knowledge of the necessary steps to formulate a plan
     B. Inability to utilize a future time perspective in planning
     C. Unwillingness and/or inability to acquire the necessary information to formulate a plan
2.0. Problems in implementing career plans
  2.1. Characteristics of the individual
     A. Failure of the individual to undertake the steps necessary to implement his/her plan
     B. Failure or inability to successfully complete the steps necessary for goal attainment
     C. Adverse changes in the individual's physical or emotional condition
  2.2. Characteristics external to the individual
     A. Unfavorable economic, social, and cultural conditions
     B. Unfavorable conditions in the organization or institution central to the implementation of one's plans
     C. Adverse conditions of or changes in the individual's family situation
3.0. Problems in organization/institutional performance
  3.1. Deficiencies in skills, abilities, and knowledge
     A. Insufficient skills, abilities, and/or knowledge upon position entry, i.e., underqualified to perform satisfactorily
     B. The deterioration of skills, abilities, and/or knowledge over time in the position due to temporary assignment to another position, leave, and/or lack of continual practice of the skill
     C. The failure to modify or update skills, abilities, and/or knowledge to stay abreast of job changes, i.e., job obsolescence due to new technology, tools, and knowledge

3.2. Personal factors
    A. Personality characteristics discrepant with the job, e.g., values, interests, and work habits
    B. Debilitating physical and/or emotional disorders
    C. Adverse off-the-job personal circumstances and/or stressors, e.g., family pressures, financial problems, and personal conflicts
    D. The occurrence of interpersonal conflicts on the job which are specific to performance requirements, e.g., getting along with the boss, co-workers, customers, and clients.

3.3. Conditions of the organization/institutional environment
    A. Ambiguous or inappropriate job requirements, e.g., lack of clarity of assignments, work overload, and conflicting assignments
    B. Deficiencies in the operational structure of the organization/institution
    C. Inadequate support facilities, supplies, and resources, e.g., insufficient lighting, ventilation, tools, support personnel, and materials
    D. Insufficient reward system, e.g., compensation, fringe benefits, status, recognition, and opportunities for advancement

4.0. Problems in organizational/institutional adaptation

4.1. Initial entry
    A. Lack of knowledge of organizational rules and procedures
    B. Failure to accept or adhere to organizational rules and procedures
    C. Inability to assimilate large quantities of new information, i.e., information overload
    D. Discomfort in a new geographic location
    E. Discrepancies between the individual's expectations and the realities of the institutional/organizational environment

4.2. Changes over time
    A. Changes over the life span in one's attitudes, values, life style, career plans, or commitment to the organization which lead to incongruence between the individual and the environment
    B. Changes in the organizational/institutional environment which lead to incongruence between the individual and the environment, e.g., physical and administrative structure, policies, and procedures

4.3. Interpersonal relationships
    A. Interpersonal conflicts arising from differences of opinion, style, values, mannerisms, etc.
    B. The occurrence of verbal or physical abuse or sexual harrassment

---

coming a leisure society — that work will be replaced by free time in which individual tastes and cultural pursuits will abound unimpeded by the need, the desire, or perhaps even the opportunity to pursue a livelihood as historically defined. Those who predict such a social condition assume that present definitions of work will become obsolescent and that work will need to be redefined as machines become capable of performing most of the tasks in producing goods.

Since 1945 our society has largely replaced the words "stability" and "scarcity" as characteristics of our economy with the words "change" and "abundance" even though all groups in the population do not share such conditions equally. This reversal has occurred largely because of science and technology's fantastic abilities to harness energy and to translate this energy into person-machine systems. No occupational group is unaffected by the explosion of knowledge, changing social values, movement to corporate hierarchies, occupational and geographic mobility, new housing patterns, and similar phenomena that attend the fundamental realignment of our occupational structure and our economic base.

To assume, however, that work is disappearing, or that a society with leisure as its principal characteristic has emerged is still premature (McMahon, 1970; Levitan, 1973). It appears more accurate to suggest that many new types of work are appearing and that much of the work to be done requires new levels of personal commitment and capability. To emphasize this latter point, one can compare the help-wanted ads of any metropolitan newspaper with similar ads of twenty or twenty-five years ago. The job titles alone reflect significant changes in the type of work being done now and the number of job choices possible.

In the future, work may become less attractive as an economic necessity because of growing welfare benefits or the possibilities of guaranteed income; it may occupy fewer hours each week, even though it is more central in one's life due to the continuing education necessary to perform it; or it may occupy a longer period in one's total life because of longer life expectancy. But there is no evidence that work will cease to be a central force in defining individual life styles in the foreseeable future. Therefore, a broad understanding of work and its potential meaning to different clients is crucial to the effective practice of career guidance.

Summary

We have talked in this chapter about the terms that are associated with work and its meaning to different groups as well as its relationship to leisure, job satisfaction, mental health, and related concepts. These topics are discussed in terms of their implications for the practice of career guidance.

LEARNING ACTIVITIES

1. Review newspaper editorials in a major city newspaper and identify discussions that pertain to the quality of work life, individual productivity, or the meaning of work in contemporary society.
2. Observe advertisements in various media and consider how they stimulate personal questions of psychological identity in relation to work.
3. Keep a record for one month of decisions and dilemmas confronting you. Analyze the skills or knowledge they demand of you and compare them with the occupational and employability skills discussed in this chapter.
4. Discuss with a group of young workers their experiences with adjusting to work. Are they congruent with the induction problems discussed here?
5. Interview personnel officers in an industrial organization and union officials about their view of job satisfaction. Is it eroding or improving? What factors do they think stimulate job dissatisfaction? Do the two groups differ in their perceptions? If so, why do you think that occurs?
6. Review your personal preferences for leisure. To what degree are these preferences affected by your preferences for work? Is there a relationship between them? Do your friends see work and leisure differently?
7. Inventory your stereotypes about the meaning of work to different types of workers. Does the research reported here support your stereotypes? Would your perceptions of how people view different types of work interfere with your ability to counsel them? In what ways do you think your stereotypes about work need to be changed?
8. Construct a workshop plan by which you would help young workers anticipate the "thwarting conditions" with which they might be faced on entering work. Identify the strategies they might use to counteract these conditions.
9. Prepare a presentation for a group of persons contemplating midcareer change. Identify the psychological and economic problems they might face and what they might do about these situations.
10. Disucss with some local psychologists or personnel people in industry their perceptions of work and mental health. How important do they think work is to effective human development? What resources are available in the community to assist persons having severe emotional and mental health problems in the work place? List such sources and the services they provide.

OBJECTIVES

After reading this chapter, engaging in the learning activities, and reading the references suggested, you should have met the objectives that follow. If you have not, it would probably be useful to review the material in Chapter 2 before proceeding further. You should now be able to:

1. Define work and leisure in your own words.
2. Compare psychological and sociological definitions of work and identify their differences.
3. List at least three purposes work can serve in each of the following areas: economic, social, and psychological.
4. Describe the major trends in the American work ethic in the past twenty years. Compare those prevalent in the 1960s with the trends prevailing currently.
5. Be able to discuss current perspectives on job satisfaction. Does job satisfaction lead to improved performance or does improved performance lead to job satisfaction?
6. Identify three ways career guidance in business and industry can help improve job satisfaction among workers.
7. Contrast the theories of job satisfaction proposed by Hall and Schneider, Herzberg, and Lofquist and Dawis.
8. Summarize three major mental health problems with which a career guidance specialist might be confronted in business and industry.
9. Define leisure counseling and identify three ways it interacts with career guidance.
10. Construct a graph differentiating the four major types of unemployment, indicating who is likely to be affected by each, what factors cause it, and how career guidance can affect it.
11. Develop an outline of the thwarting conditions and the work entry problems of youth and tell how each might be prevented and treated as it occurs.
12. Define "affective work competencies" and list five of these. Discuss their meaning for career guidance.

3 / The American Occupational Structure

It is important for counselors to understand the characteristics of the occupational structure because individuals must know what is possible — what opportunities exist now and will exist in the future — if they are to engage in effective decision-making. In one sense, career decision-making is the process of relating relevant characteristics of self to appropriate aspects of the worlds of work, education, and training. An intimate knowledge of that external world is necessary if counselors are to help counselees reduce that huge universe to manageable proportions. When career counseling is directed toward immediate placement, all that is required is an understanding of the current occupational structure. When, however, career counseling has its more common emphasis, on some future point of choice and entry, counselors and counselees must operate on the basis of informed speculations about the changing occupational structure.

THE CHANGING SCENE

Futurism is popular today, and a great many futurists are attempting to predict what the United States will be like ten, twenty, fifty, or a hundred years from now (Toffler, 1980; Naisbitt, 1982). All agree on only one point: the future will bring change. Beyond this simplistic conclusion, however, futurists agree on very little. Whether predictions emanate from historical and qualitative analyses or from more empirical and quantitative bases, conclusions suggest that the occupational structure of the United States is one of those societal elements that will undergo

the greatest upheaval. What precise form this flux will take, however, is arguable. We may view this problem in terms of the difficulty of making occupational projections and in terms of scenarios for the future.

Occupational Projections

The relative accuracy of occupational forecasts is moot. Virtually everyone, both labor forecasters and their critics, agree that forecasts are not completely accurate, nor can they ever be. Where the two sides differ is in their appraisal of how useful a less than accurate prediction is. For example, the Bureau of Labor Statistics has conducted several studies that illustrate that the projection record is imperfect, "but . . . the projections have been reasonably accurate in the majority of cases" (Pilot, 1980, p. 6). "Reasonably accurate" means an underestimate or overestimate for major occupational groups ranging from 6.7 to 9.1 percent. For specific occupations, absolute percentage errors will average about 20.8 percent. Is this error rate great enough to discourage the use of labor market projections in career planning? Probably not, especially when we consider that in translating most Bureau of Labor statistics, writers change numbers to descriptive statements. Such is the case, for instance, with the *Occupational Outlook Handbook*, which extrapolates BLS numbers to employment growth phrases such as "Much faster than the average for all occupations," or "More slowly than the average for all occupations." Evaluating the 1975 projections of occupational employment, Carey (1980) and Christy and Horowitz (1979) concluded that

62

such factors as recession, inaccurate estimates of technological change, and obsolescent data on projections of employment by industry, among other factors, caused most error in prediction. Further complications in projecting labor supply and demand are sex related. In looking at projections made between 1959 and 1976, Ryscavage (1979) concluded that the predictions were too low for women and too high for men. To respond to these factors, forecasters now collect data on employment by industry every three years.

To improve occupational projections, the Bureau of Labor Statistics provides forecasts based on alternative assumptions about the future in terms of economic growth (Carey, 1981b). In addition, they have created an industry-occupation matrix, which describes industry employment by occupation. These changes in forecasting help to gainsay the arguments of critics such as O'Toole (1982) who maintain that the two major errors of past prognosticators have been in assuming that the future is a simple extrapolation of the present and in basing forecasts on a singular view of coming events rather than on the interactive effects of several simultaneous forces.

Hence, many factors combine to make occupational forecasting a less than exact science. If we could control important variables, we could increase our forecasting efficiency. It is unlikely, however, that we shall ever be able to account totally for such influences as: changes in demand for products or services, the rate and type of technological innovation, the composition of the population, work attitudes in flux, changes in training opportunities (such as CETA), and alterations in retirement patterns (such as nonmandatory, mandatory, early). Forecasts are based on very large numbers over extended periods of time. As such, they are likely always to have some degree of error; therefore, caution is advised in the use of such data.

We may conclude that although this propensity for error will persist, and although our forecasts are likely never to be very elegant, the data on labor forecasting are accurate enough to be useful to counselors and to individuals in career planning. Indeed, we have no choice. We must use future-oriented data. The lag between preparation for an occupation and entry into that occupation is frequently protracted over years. One needs

some idea, however imperfect, of what the occupational demand is likely to be at time of entry as well as at time of choice.

Future Scenarios

Futurists present their visions as *scenarios*, potential slices of future history. As we read various futurists, we are struck with the great number who are akin to the biblical Jeremiah. The future, they maintain, will be terrible unless we repent our ways. Unfortunately, even "downside" futurists do not seem to agree on what it is that we have to repent. Contrasted to this jeremiad outlook are those (few) futurists who are Pollyannas. Everything will be all right; we have survived and flourished until now; we shall prevail in the future. Sandwiched between the doom-and-gloom crowd and the head-in-the-sand bunch are the realists. Many of these realistic futurists offer fascinating predictions that have implications for career guidance and counseling.

To read Peter F. Drucker twenty years ago, for example, is to see today. Drucker (1968) long ago predicted the massive shift to "knowledge work" and the consequent creation of a knowledge society. He accurately foresaw that knowledge workers would require more from work than the tangible reward of pay. What Drucker has described is what is called the "information economy" (Hamrin, 1981). The American labor force is now largely occupied with information handling. In fact, more people are engaged in manipulating information than in mining, agriculture, manufacturing, and personal services combined. This change is largely the result of advances in microelectronic technology, wherein data can be handled in a few picoseconds (one second contains as many picoseconds as there are seconds in 31,700 years). The shift has moved America from an agricultural society to an industrial society, and now to a service-based, information-oriented society. The term "compunications" is sometimes given to this phenomenon of the marriage of microelectronics and information processing. Dickson (1977) points out that by whatever name — postindustrial society, technotronic era, or postwelfare society — we are talking about a society that is service rather than goods oriented and that is dominated by a professional/technical class (rather than the businessmen who dominated the industrial society).

The increase in technology brings new occupations and different work modes. The incipient field of robotics is one consequence. Robotics takes us one step further along the automation-cybernetics continuum. We are witnessing ever more complex machines under the control of people. This, in turn, will lead to greater needs for training, as individuals do more intellectual, higher-level work. We are also witnessing machine-machine systems, which monitor, control, initiate, and terminate work with only a little supervision, done by a few skilled technicians. Eli Ginzberg (1982) points out the profound influences of our mechanized society and the increasing effects of mechanization in the future — mechanization of agriculture, mining, design and manufacturing, commerce, and office work. He observes that in 1820, approximately 70 percent of the American population was engaged in agriculture; now about 3 percent are in agriculture and approximately 70 percent are in service. Goods are produced with fewer operatives as our machines get bigger and better. Even in a very large goods-producing company such as General Electric, only 40 percent of employees are directly involved in production. The obvious consequences of the new technologies and machines is job displacement. Hahn (1980) suggests, "Among the various responses to technological side effects have been demands for the social management of technology, a rising antitechnology mood, and technology assessment (TA) — the review of possible and probable impacts, prior to the introduction of a new technology" (p. 35).

It is clear that the advance of our scientific technology has not been accompanied by similar progress in our social technology. Gordon (1979), for example, sees little progress in the development of social policies to encourage the career development of women while protecting the welfare of the family. Issues such as maternity benefits, child care, and part-time or flex-time work are still not resolved. Currently, child care is available to only 10 percent of working mothers (Burr, 1980). Occupational stress and the quality of work life also await the development of effective social technologies. Many, for example, are predicting a more participatory work force. Ras-

kin (1980) predicts, "Autonomous work teams, the opportunities of rotated leadership, two-way communication on everything important to the worker in his job, plus a widening list of joint policy decisions at the shop level are inevitable" (p. 97). Although this view may be overly optimistic, it is clear that we shall have to spend more energy in improving the quality of work. Social technologies will have to find solutions to management dilemmas, improve decision-making, address participatory problems and humanization, attack special problems of population subcategories, and deal with individual-group relations, to cite just a few areas in need of development (Cellarius & Platt, 1972). Many of these problems are sensibly addressed by Hays (1982).

The next decade or two will be crucial in at least four areas that will affect the nature of work and the composition of the labor force. One area is *energy*. We have gone through periodic energy crises, and these have spurred research into alternative energy sources: coal, solar, tar sands, shale, fission, fusion, wind, and so forth. Continuing energy problems, real or manufactured, will mean decreased mobility and a more conserving society. These two factors can appreciably affect the kind, quantity, and quality of work in the future. A second area is the *biosciences*. We appear to be on the threshold of both exciting and frightening developments. Genetic modification can lead to the creation of new antiviral agents, new substances, new life forms (Amara, 1978). These advances are also likely to affect the life span of workers and provide for a longer career life. A potentially huge industry is waiting to be developed. A third area is *materials*. We are likely to see the creation of new materials, to find substitutes for old ones, to recycle, and to use renewable resources in different ways (such as liquid fuel by hydrogination). Finally, we have already alluded to the *information sciences*, which will surely continue to have a profound effect on both home and office. Because of new information processing machines, for example, fewer secretaries may be required.

Current occupations will, of course, serve as the foundation of these new occupations of the future. Whether stemming from technological progress or from social concerns, new occupations are invariably related to old. A gene splicer is still likely to be a biologist. A fiber optics technician probably will be a physicist. Environmental engineers can be air pollution control engineers, radiological health engineers, solid waste engineers, industrial hygiene engineers, sanitary engineers, water pollution control engineers, environmental compliance engineers, but they are still engineers. New occupations tend to spring from existing ones. They do, however, tend to merge disciplines (biochemists, geophysicists, bionicists).

One of the major problems generated by a movement toward a knowledge society is over-education. Several commentators have warned about a potential oversupply of college graduates. The U.S. Department of Labor suggests that only approximately one-quarter of all job openings will require four or more years of college (U.S. Department of Labor, 1974). Given current rates of college attendance and economic growth, that figure translates into an annual surplus of approximately 140,000 graduates. This situation is seen as one of inflated credentialism and has led some observers to maintain that problems of job satisfaction, underemployment, and unfulfilled ambitions will be exacerbated (Berg, 1975; Harrison, 1973; O'Toole, 1975; U.S. Department of Health, Education, and Welfare, 1973). In fact, in the very near future, there will be no profession for which supply does not exceed demand (unless, of course, "demand" is redefined). Various solutions to this potentially dangerous situation have been proffered: educational upgrading (Berg, 1975); equalizing access to higher education, ending credentialism, and equalizing income distribution (Jencks, 1972); job redesign (USOE, 1973); profit sharing; total employment; reducing college enrollments (Bird, 1975); upgrading job requirements (Gordon, 1974); a national personpower policy (Fleming, 1974); and career education (Hoyt, 1975), among others. There is obviously no easy solution. For years we have known that too little education was a career handicap; now we must cope with what was once unthinkable — that too much education may be equally constricting.

This relatively new development in no way should obscure the fact that undereducated and unskilled workers are still the major problem area in the labor force. The less one is educated, the more likely it is that one will be unemployed. Labor force entrants — particularly those entering the labor force for the first time — account for three-quarters of unemployed teenagers (U.S. Department of Labor, 1974). At the other end of the spectrum, men aged 55 to 64 without a high school diploma leave the labor force in significantly greater proportion than high school and college graduates of comparable ages. The undereducated are also the unskilled and the poor. Of this group, many have latent ability, and, if motivated and trained, could contribute meaningfully to the labor force. Unemployment is typically low in the professional and skilled occupations and is generally high for the less skilled segments of the labor force. Although the general educational attainment of the American worker is rising, a substantial proportion of the population remains undertrained for specific skilled jobs and undereducated for general adult competency. As we have observed, people do not need just more education. There is ample evidence to suggest that individuals can be retrained and gain entrance to an occupational level previously unavailable to them (Bjorkquist, 1970). Hence *undereducation* may not be as much of a problem as is *inappropriate* education.

Later in this chapter, we shall investigate further some likely changes in the American occupational structure. For now, it is sufficient to remind ourselves that just a few short years ago there was no aerospace industry, no computer industry, no airport security guards, no television industry, and no Pac Man.

THE PAST, PRESENT, AND FUTURE OF THE LABOR FORCE

The Past

Several striking changes have occurred in the American occupational structure during the last forty years.

- Employees in goods-producing industries have remained relatively constant, while employees in industries providing services have increased dramatically. Consequently, more than twice the number of workers are now involved in the provision of services as are employed in the production of goods.

- Employees in blue-collar occupations have increased relatively little, while employees in the white-collar occupations have increased markedly. Currently, approximately 60 percent of workers are classified as white collar.
- The average educational attainment of the labor force has risen appreciably. More than 87 percent of workers now have at least a high school education. About 36 percent of all workers age 18 and over have completed at least one year of college (Young, 1980).
- The proportion of women workers in the labor force has increased significantly. About one-quarter of all managers are now women. Over 50 percent of American women now work outside the home.
- The number of blacks in the professions has increased. About 12 percent of blacks are now in professions (Erickson, 1980). Blau and Duncan (1967) investigated the problem of occupational mobility in America and included that there was no "rigidification" despite the

fact that many people feared that the occupational structure presented no opportunity for mobility. The sole exception to their findings were blacks. Since 1967 considerable progress has been made, and it is now doubtful that mobility is closed for any group in America.

- Part-time work has increased considerably. Over one in every five workers is a part-time employee.
- Job turnover has increased; that is, the average number of jobs held over a work lifetime has gone up (for males).
- Self-employed workers decreased strongly until the 1970s. They have, however, increased steadily since 1972 (Fain, 1980).

The Present

The current labor force (all persons working and looking for work) in America is probably most accurately portrayed by the results of the 1980 Census of Population (U.S. Bureau of the Census, 1982). Data pertinent to 1980 include the following:

Total persons 16 and over	171,182,857	
Labor force	106,065,807	62 percent
Civilian labor force	104,531,047	
Females 16 and over	89,435,850	
In labor force	44,740,543	50 percent
Civilian labor force	44,600,005	
Females with child under 6	13,554,175	
In labor force	6,211,979	46 percent
With child 6–17	16,960,095	
In labor force	10,713,045	63 percent
Classification by sector		
Employed 16 and over	97,631,061	
Private wage and salary workers	73,781,491	76 percent
Federal government	3,784,035	4 percent
State government	4,552,762	5 percent
Local governments	8,389,001	9 percent
Self-employed	6,617,700	7 percent
Unpaid family workers	506,072	1 percent
Total		102 percent^a
Classification by occupation		
Employed 16 and over	97,631,061	
Managerial and professional specialty occupations	22,320,685	23 percent
Executive, administrative, and managerial	10,196,035	
Professional specialty occupations	12,124,650	
Technical, sales, and administrative support	29,464,636	30 percent
Technicians and related support occupations	3,013,725	

Sales occupations	9,727,163	
Administrative support, including clerical	16,723,748	
Service occupations	12,680,131	13 percent
Private household occupations	563,644	
Protective service occupations	1,473,088	
Service occupations, except protective & house	10,643,399	
Farming, forestry, and fishing occupations	2,758,089	3 percent
Precision production, craft, & repair occupations	12,515,360	13 percent
Operators, fabricators, and laborers	17,892,160	18 percent
Machine operators, assemblers, & inspectors	9,120,394	
Transportation & material moving occupations	4,359,494	
Handlers, equipment cleaners, helpers, & laboratory workers	4,412,272	
Classification by industry		
Employed 16 and over	97,631,061	
Agriculture, forestry, fisheries, & mining	3,927,232	4 percent
Construction	5,765,627	6 percent
Manufacturing	21,798,171	22 percent
Transportation	4,230,987	4 percent
Communications and other public utilities	2,826,010	3 percent
Wholesale trade	4,250,145	4 percent
Retail trade	15,795,183	16 percent
Finance, insurance, and real estate	5,821,955	6 percent
Business and repair services	4,073,316	4 percent
Personal, entertainment, & recreation services	4,092,479	4 percent
Professional and related services	19,782,125	20 percent
Public administration	5,267,831	5 percent
Classification by family		
Families	58,975,810	
No workers	7,549,060	
One worker	19,484,635	
Two or more workers	31,942,115	

^{a}Rounding error

The accuracy of these data in describing the current labor force will vary. At the time of this writing, for example, the national unemployment rate was 6.6 percent. That rate changes; consequently, it affects the proportion of workers in various categories.

The Future

Now let us look at the more difficult task. Given the flaws in forecasting discussed earlier in this chapter, what will the occupational structure be in ten or fifteen years? We can present Bureau of Labor Statistics and the "best guess" estimates of knowledgeable people.

The most profound influence on the occupational structure will be the changing age composition of the population. We are all aware of the "baby boom" generation that will be at prime

working age from 1985 to 1995. The changing age proportion in the population can be seen graphically in Figure 3.1 if one compares actual 1965 percentages to projected 1990 percentages (keep in mind that there will be approximately 50 million more Americans in 1990 than there were in 1965). Data here are adapted from Dearman and Plisko (1981), p. 10.

The median age in America is expected to rise from 28.1 in 1965 to 32.8 in 1990. Geographically, the Northeast and north central states are projected to continue to lose population, while the South gains and the West gains somewhat less (Rones, 1980).

The changing age of the labor force has a potentially deep effect. Jackson et al. (1981) suggest that:

As the baby-boom cohorts entered the labor market, there were large numbers of appli-

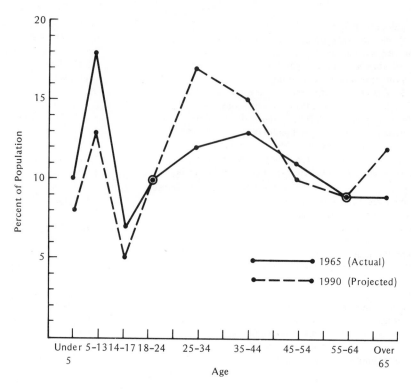

Figure 3.1
Percentage Change in Population 1965 to 1990

cants for most jobs, and as a result, companies could afford to ignore human-resource development. As the smaller cohorts born in the late 1960s replace the babyboom cohorts . . . this will change. Companies will have to compete for entry-level workers, and the resources they devote to this competition will increasingly reduce those available to reward continuing employees. But continuing employees will demand rewards. Their numbers will make the typical nonpecuniary reward, promotion, possible for a decreasing percentage of cohorts, and with neither money nor promotion, employees' dissatisfaction will increase (p. 130).

Drucker (1982) echoes this feeling, indicating that, in fact, jobs for the young will have to be restructured. No longer will fast promotions prevail, for even capable individuals will have to spend many years not far removed from the entrance level. Consequently, he makes an eloquent plea for career assistance in the workplace:

But, above all, there is need to counsel the young. There is need to make sure they have someone to whom they can talk in the organization, if only to unburden themselves. There is need of someone who is concerned with the problem of the young getting to the place in the organization – or outside the organization, for that matter – where their strengths are most likely to be productive and recognized (pp. 170–171).

In Chapter 11, we will detail some of the possibilities for this type of career counseling within organizations.

This relative shortage of youth and the great increase in prime-age workers – those with expectations of promotion – will inevitably lead to increased competition for desirable jobs. Therefore, the labor force will probably have to be more mobile in seeking employment and advancement. From the late 1960s through the 1970s the labor force increased by over 2 percent annually. Beyond 1985 it is expected to increase less than one percent per year — barring a new baby "boomlet" or female participation increasing at a greater rate than predicted (Fullerton, 1980). Even though the growth rate of the work force will decrease, minorities will be represented at a higher rate: 25 percent of new entrants. Such increase will be attributable to higher immigration rates, the increasing number of illegal aliens entering the labor force, and the generally higher birthrate of minorities (Amara, 1978).

As indicated earlier in this chapter, the government is becoming more cautious in its occupational projections. It now provides three alternate projections based on differing estimates of economic and social development. On that basis, Table 3.1 displays the projections of the Bureau of Labor Statistics for occupational employment through 1990.

Examination of Table 3.1 reveals that white-collar occupations are expected to expand faster than blue-collar, service, or farm occupations. Of the white-collar group, technical and professional workers are projected to grow less quickly than they have in the last twenty years. About two-thirds of the professional and technical jobs are accounted for by teachers, medical professionals, health technologists and technicians, engineers, and engineering and science technicians. Because of the retardation in the growth of teaching jobs, a predicted slowdown is not surprising, even though medical and health fields are predicted to grow appreciably. Managers and administrators (one in five of whom are self-employed) are not expected to increase very much. Salesworkers may be expected to experience greater than average growth in both retail and nonretail trade. Finally, in the white-collar category, clerical workers (who account for more jobs than any other occupational group) are also expected to grow faster than the average rate of employment growth.

Within the blue-collar groups, craft and kindred workers (of whom about half are mechanics and construction trade workers) are expected not to grow dramatically and are very sensitive to the three alternative conditions. Operatives (over 80 percent of whom work at manufacturing jobs) are projected to grow slowly.

Among the service workers, dramatic increases are expected, especially in food service and health service occupations. It is anticipated that private household workers will decrease. Finally, farm workers are expected to continue the decline that has persisted for decades as a result of technological innovation.

Some of the specific occupations projected to grow fastest are:

- Accountants and auditors
- Aero-astronautic engineers
- Architects
- Automotive mechanics
- Blue-collar worker supervisors
- Bookkeepers, hand
- Cashiers
- Child-care attendants
- Computer operators
- Computer programmers
- Computer systems analysts
- Correction officials and jailers
- Data processing machine mechanics
- Dental assistants
- Dental hygienists
- Elementary school teachers
- Employment interviewers
- Food preparation and service workers, fast food
- General clerks, office
- Guards and doorkeepers
- Helpers, trades
- Janitors and sextons
- Kitchen helpers
- Licensed practical nurses
- Nurses aides and orderlies
- Office machine and cash register servicers
- Paralegal personnel
- Peripheral EDP equipment operators
- Professional nurses
- Physical therapists
- Sales clerks
- Secretaries
- Tax preparers
- Travel agents and accommodation appraisers
- Truckdrivers
- Typists
- Veterinarians
- Waiters/waitresses

The point that all these changes emphasize is that trends in occupational and industrial growth necessitate continual adjustments in career deci-

Table 3.1

Employment By Major Occupational Group, Actual 1978, and Alternative Projections for 1990

[Numbers in thousands]

Occupational group	1978		1990							Percentage change in employment, 1978–90			
			Low-trend		High-trend I		High-trend II				Low-trend	High-trend I	High-trend II
	Number	Percent	Number	Percent	Number	Percent	Number	Percent					
Total	97,610	100.0	119,590	100.0	127,907	100.0	121,447	100.0			22.5	31.0	24.4
White-collar workers	48,608	49.8	60,730	50.9	64,712	50.6	61,570	50.7			24.9	33.1	26.7
Professional and technical workers .	15,568	15.9	20,038	16.8	21,119	16.5	20,295	16.7			28.7	35.7	30.4
Managers and administrators . .	8,802	9.0	10,484	8.8	11,257	8.8	10,677	8.8			19.1	27.9	21.3
Salesworkers	6,420	6.6	7,989	6.7	8,632	6.8	8,079	6.7			24.4	34.5	25.8
Clerical workers	17,818	18.3	22,219	18.6	23,705	18.5	22,519	18.5			24.7	33.0	26.4
Blue-collar workers	31,812	32.6	37,720	31.5	40,694	31.8	38,330	31.6			18.6	27.9	20.5
Craft and kindred workers . . .	11,705	12.0	14,366	12.0	15,555	12.2	14,668	12.1			22.7	32.9	25.3
Operatives	14,205	14.6	16,399	13.7	17,697	13.8	16,584	13.7			15.4	24.6	16.8
Nonfarm laborers	5,902	6.0	6,955	5.8	7,441	5.8	7,078	5.8			17.8	26.1	19.9
Service workers	14,414	14.8	18,946	15.8	20,074	15.7	19,220	15.8			31.4	39.3	33.3
Private household workers . . .	1,160	1.2	982	0.8	993	0.8	988	0.8			−15.4	−14.4	−14.9
Other service workers	13,254	13.6	17,965	15.0	19,081	14.9	18,232	15.0			35.5	44.0	37.6
Farmworkers	2,775	2.8	2,193	1.8	2,426	1.9	2,327	1.9			−21.0	−12.6	−16.3

NOTE: Due to rounding, sums of individual items may not equal totals.

70

sions. Using the best information now available, counselors and counselees can plan for the future insofar as supply and demand factors affect career decisions. For example, we have already witnessed the fact that reduced openings for teachers caused many college students to major in other fields and caused those who majored in education to enter other occupations. In the past, two out of every three women college graduates entered teaching. Obviously, even with predictions for upturns in the employment of teachers at the elementary school level and existing shortages in several secondary school subject areas, women have been forced to broaden their outlook on career opportunities.

There are many predictions about changes in the *nature* of work as well as, as we have just seen, in the *type* of work. It is difficult to know which, if any, of the incipient efforts to change the nature of work are likely to become popular. A simple cataloging of some of these predictions should illustrate the potential effect on career counseling.

- *job redesign* to utilize the particular talents of individual workers and accommodate higher levels of education
- *job sharing* in which two or more individuals share a full-time position on a less than full-time, full-pay basis
- *flexible scheduling*, or flex-time, whereby individuals put in an eight-hour day but are able to choose (within prescribed parameters) when these daily eight hours are worked
- *quality control circles* whereby workers negotiate and are responsible for quality standards of both work and materials
- *more part-time jobs* to allow homemakers and retirees to earn supplementary income
- *sabbaticals*, much as in academia, for personal and organizational development
- *job rotation* to relieve monotony and to increase breadth of worker understanding
- *flexibility of rewards* wherein workers may choose the combination of pay and benefits that best fits their needs
- *power sharing*, or democratization, leading to greater cooperative group governance.
- *flexible retirement*, including time of retirement (early, later than usual) and type of re-

tirement (phase out, as in a four- , three-, or two-day week, or all at once)
- *nontraditional rewards*, such as time off for high-quality work, bonuses for safe work
- *improved career ladders* so that individuals may perceive an escape from plateauing at a terminal level
- *home-based work* whereby individuals produce goods or perform services in their own homes
- *educational benefits*, both through the formal educational system and at the work site, paid for by the organization (including opportunities for retraining and retooling)

The contours of the future with regard to the quantity and quality of work in America are not sharply focused. However, counselors and counselees who are willing to try to form some sense of what those contours will be are likely to be rewarded.

RELATION OF THE OCCUPATIONAL STRUCTURE TO CAREER GUIDANCE AND COUNSELING

Several parts of this text have and will identify the antecedents and the processes of career decision-making. Weaving throughout this discussion are the factors that produce individual differences shaping personal styles of approach to choice and implementation of choice. In this chapter, perhaps the important point to be made is that such considerations are valid only if a diversity of choices exists, and if any given individual has the political and social freedom to choose among opportunities. The fact that these two conditions do exist in the United States has historically impelled the provision of career guidance to foster not only freedom of choice but informed choice as well.

Individuals must choose something; in terms of this book, they must choose an occupation and, indeed, a career pattern from among the thousands of the existing possibilities. For example, the *Dictionary of Occupational Titles* (DOT) lists over 20,000 jobs. New jobs are created each day; obsolescent jobs are phased out of existence daily.

If, however, as we have contended several times

in this book, personal identity is acquired through such characteristics. as commitment, planning, seeing oneself and what one does in the present as affecting the future, then career guidance should aid the choice of an occupation within the broad context of "career." This context connotes not simply a choice at a point in time, but also a series of immediate and intermediate choices made to achieve one's goals at a future time.

In order for individuals to relate themselves to the educational and occupational alternatives available to them, they need some "handles" to help them see how these alternatives differ. Later in this text, in Chapter 16, we will detail many types of occupational information, both regionally based and national and directed both toward current vacancies and likely future developments.

To bring some order into what can well be a chaotic situation, various schema have been devised to classify, in logical ways, the thousands of individual jobs and the variety of educational and training programs. Each scheme emphasizes at least one characteristic for differentiating occupations. As will be indicated in Chapter 6 (career guidance objectives), in Chapters 7–12 (the application of career guidance practices at different developmental levels), and in Chapter 14 (information systems), these occupational differences can be used to give substance to efforts at assisting career development and choice; to reality-test one's characteristics against job requirements; and to create filing systems or person-machine interaction systems to provide better access to information.

One of the prime differences between occupational alternatives relates to levels and kinds of education or training (Herr & Cramer, 1968). A system of classifying differences in educational and training opportunities by overt and covert criteria will not be elaborated on here — except as it is included in the variables for classifying occupational characteristics in the DOT. However, it is important, when considering the range of opportunities in the American occupational structure, to recognize the relationship between level and kind of education and level and kind of work.

Occupational Classification Systems

From ancient times, there have been attempts to classify occupations. Hopke (1979) points out that primitive societies classified workers into two categories: physical laborers and nonlaborers (such as priests, chiefs, and medicine men). Others talked of a three-class system: peasants, nomads, and the priestly or educated classes. As society became more complex, so did work and its classifications. Some of the classifications were indeed fanciful and curious. For example, there have been classifications by physical characteristics, such as brain weight and head size (Sorokin, 1927). The brains of physicians and university teachers averaged 1500 grams; the brain weight of unskilled laborers averaged only 1410 grams. The head size of full professors was 35.79 centimeters; of associate and assistant professors, 35.72; of instructors, 35.64; of students, 34.58.

As we have become more sophisticated, classifications of occupations have been formulated for various purposes on both *a priori* and *post hoc* bases and with their roots in economics, psychology, and sociology. Some are careful attempts at empirical derivation; others are slightly better than incense burning. Among the major classification systems are the following (after Hatt, 1962):

- By *industry* as in the Census Classification below.
- By *socioeconomic group*, for example, bourgeoisie, proletariat; blue collar, white collar; lower, middle, upper.
- By *ability and/or aptitudes*. Ghiselli (1966) has demonstrated, as indicated in Chapter 4, that "in terms of their requirements, jobs are not organized into clear cut and separate groups. Rather there is a continuous variation among jobs, and they form clusters which do not have distinct boundaries. Second, jobs which superficially appear to be similar in terms of nature of work may have quite different ability requirements, and jobs which appear to be quite different may have very similar requirements" (p. 111). This finding that, despite mean occupational differences on ability dimensions, the heterogeneity of ability within occupational groups is substantial has been verified over the

decades (Fryer, 1922; Stewart, 1947; Thorndike and Hagen, 1959).

- By *occupation*. An obviously cumbersome method if one uses single occupations, since there are over 20,000 titles listed in the *Dictionary of Occupational Titles*. By groupings of occupations, according to the Census Classification, or the DOT, the system is sensible.
- By *interests*. Most interest inventories classify occupations by interest patterns of those in the occupations. Jackson and Williams (1975) contend that they have isolated twenty-three distinct occupational clusters on the basis of interest. The United States Employment Service (USES) operationalizes the worker trait by occupational group concept in terms of eleven basic occupational interest factors (Droege and Padgett, 1979), which are now used in the U.S. Department of Labor's *Guide to Occupational Exploration* and for which an interest inventory is available. Thus one can combine the General Aptitude Test Battery (GATB) and the Interest Inventory for a broader assessment than was previously possible with USES materials. The USES Occupational Interest areas are: artistic, scientific, plants and animals, protective, mechanical, industrial, business detail, selling, accommodating, humanitarian, leading-influencing, and physical performing. Holland's classification, although based on personality types, may also be considered an attempt at classification by interests. Holland himself, however, has indicated that different occupations include a variety of types and subtypes (Holland and Holland, 1977).
- By *field and level*. Anne Roe's two-dimensional classification by eight fields of interest and six levels of occupations, described in detail later in this chapter, has proven to be a useful taxonomy. Meir (1978) has demonstrated that the field-level matrix is indeed orthogonal; that is, fields and levels are mutually independent.
- By *field, level, and enterprise*. Super (1957) suggested adding a third dimension to Roe's schema to indicate the enterprise or the general setting where work is performed. A representation of this idea will be presented later in this chapter.
- By *income*. The range of income within occupational groups is so wide as to make classification on this basis almost meaningless. As with ability classification, there are mean differences among occupations, but the within-occupation variability is substantial.
- By *type of work*. This type of classification can take many forms, ranging from dichotomies such as physical-nonphysical to the more sophisticated descriptions of people-data-things activities outlined later in this chapter and contained in the discussion of the DOT. The Minnesota Occupational Classification System attempts to classify occupations by a combination of ability requirements, work reinforcers (need satisfiers), and environmental style dimensions (Dawis et al., 1979).
- By *educational or occupational prerequisites*. Again, the DOT system of classifying occupations according to educational level is a good example of this type of taxonomy. Classifications such as these are easily implemented in practice by means of occupational materials such as the Bureau of Labor Statistics' "Jobs for Which You Can Qualify If You're a High School Graduate," or "Jobs for Which You Can Train through Apprenticeship," or "Jobs for Which You Will Probably Need a College Education."
- By *occupational duties performed*. Part of the DOT presents occupational descriptors, the tasks performed by persons in the occupation. Although such information is basic to anyone considering an occupation, it is so narrow that classification solely on this basis is rather unwieldy.
- By *life span*. It is possible to classify occupations according to such dimensions as early entry–early leaving, early entry–late leaving, late entry–late leaving. A professional athlete, for example, would have an early entry–early leaving occupation, whereas a physician would have a late entry–late leaving occupation.
- By *rewards*. Rewards may be financial, honorific, working conditions, or a combination of these factors. In one sense, the status classifications of occupations described later are examples of this type of taxonomy.
- By *age*. Kaufman and Spilerman (1982) have demonstrated that the majority of detailed

census occupations conform to one of five basic age profiles: (1) occupations in which young workers are overrepresented (such as entry-level occupations); (2) occupations in which middle-aged workers are concentrated (such as supervisors, foremen, managers); (3) occupations in which the elderly are overrepresented (such as contracting occupations); (4) occupations with a uniform age distribution (such as crafts); and (5) occupations with a U-shaped age distribution (such as undesirable jobs).

The USOE Clusters

The career education movement stimulated the development of a new occupational cluster system by the USOE. Because of the prestige of that office and because of the funds for career education that emanated from that source, the fifteen-cluster taxonomy quickly became a highly utilized classification system. Commercial materials, especially, were rushed to market, packaged with the USOE cluster framework. Similar to many other clustering models, the USOE clusters begin with the assumption that all work can be classified, involving either the production of goods or the provision of services. These two activities are then organized into fifteen occupational clusters. Within each cluster there is a hierarchy of occupations ranging from professional to the unskilled.

1. *Business and Office* (e.g., data processor, bookkeeper, accountant, file clerk)
2. *Marketing and Distribution* (e.g., salesperson, marketing researcher, economist, systems analyst)
3. *Communications and Media* (e.g., reporter, photoengraver, script writer, electronic technician)
4. *Construction* (e.g., architect, paperhanger, bricklayer, roofer, plasterer)
5. *Manufacturing* (e.g., machine operator, chemist, welder, tool and die maker)
6. *Transportation* (e.g., pilot, truck driver, auto mechanic, aerospace engineer)
7. *Agri-Business and Natural Resources* (e.g., farmer, miner, farm agent, wildlife manager)
8. *Marine Science* (e.g., seaperson, diver, fisherperson, marine biologist)

9. *Environment* (e.g., forest ranger, meteorologist, geologist, tree surgeon)
10. *Public Services* (e.g., counselor, fireperson, policeperson, probation officer)
11. *Health* (e.g., psychologist, veterinarian, dentist, speech pathologist, chiropractor)
12. *Recreation and Hospitality* (e.g., waitress, chef, golf pro, cashier)
13. *Personal Services* (e.g., beautician, priest, mortician, TV repairperson)
14. *Fine Arts and Humanities* (e.g., dancer, author, jeweler, piano tuner)
15. *Consumer and Homemaking Education* (e.g., interior decorator, seamstress, home economist, model)

These clusters are undergoing continual revision and expansion. For example, the California State Department of Education has further subdivided each cluster into major occupational groups. These major occupational groups are then partitioned into major job families which, in turn, can lead to the identification of specific occupations (Weagraff, 1972).

Despite its current widespread use, the USOE cluster classification system is not without its critics. Some of the criticisms revolve around issues of cost and other practical considerations of implementation. Some center on challenging the theoretical assumptions underlying the categories. The most obvious perceived disadvantage of the USOE clusters, however, is the problem of overlap. For example, Weagraff (1974) points out that jobs in the "parks" field could be a part of at least three separate clusters: public service, natural resources, or recreation and hospitality. Similar obfuscations could occur with a large number of jobs. Although this criticism is not unique to the USOE clusters (it applies equally to several other clusters), it does speak to potential weaknesses in the system that must be overcome if it is to be more effective than other systems. There are several attempts currently underway to construct an empirically based cluster taxonomy of occupations. Perhaps the most noteworthy of these attempts is that being researched at North Carolina State University (Boese & Cunningham, 1976).

Census Classifications

Since 1790 the U.S. Bureau of the Census has conducted a decennial accounting of the demographics of this country. Recent legislation increases the frequency of that nationwide census of population. In order to provide a framework within which to classify the work world, the Bureau of the Census has devised two distinct classification systems: one that is descriptive of the industries in which people work, and another that is related to occupational categories. Each of these is briefly discussed below.

Industrial Classification. A commonly employed classification model is the federal government's Standard Industrial Classification System (SICS). It offers a comprehensive listing of types of industry within eleven major categories (note similarities to USOE clusters):

1. agriculture, forestry, and fishing and mining
2. construction
3. manufacturing
4. transportation
5. communications and other public utilities
6. wholesale trade
7. retail trade
8. finance, insurance, and real estate
9. business and repair services
10. personal, entertainment and recreation services
11. public administration

These categories, in turn, are divided into eighty-four less broad industrial classifications. For example, Retail Trade is composed of eight subcategories:

- building materials, hardware, garden supply, and mobile home dealers
- general merchandise stores
- food stores
- automotive dealers and gasoline service stations
- apparel and accessory stores
- furniture, home furnishings, and equipment stores
- eating and drinking places
- miscellaneous retail.

Finally, these eighty-four categories are further

delineated by specific industries within them. Basically, the SICS describes *where* people work; it gives little or no indication of what people do. It is a classification system that is useful in gathering statistics and sometimes in filing occupational information. Otherwise, it has little utility for direct career guidance and counseling.

Occupational Group Classification. The 1980 Census of Population Occupational Classification is as follows:

Managerial and professional specialty occupations
Executive, administrative, and managerial occupations
Professional specialty occupations

Technical, sales, and administrative support occupations
Technicians and related support occupations
Sales occupations
Administrative support occupations, including clerical

Service occupations
Private household occupations
Protective service occupations
Service occupations, except protective and household

Farming, forestry, and fishing occupations

Precision production, craft, and repair occupations

Operators, fabricators, and laborers
Machine operators, assemblers, and inspectors
Transportation and material moving occupations
Handlers, equipment cleaners, helpers, and laborers.

These census classifications are valuable, because they periodically update the distribution of workers into occupational categories and by industry. Thus, they provide data to a variety of consumers in terms of an accepted classification system.

Status Classifications

Another classification system is based on the status of occupations. Status level is usually determined by the perceived prestige of an occupation, which, in turn, is based on such factors as the amount of money earned, power, the type of work involved, the degree of responsibility for social welfare, the amount of education necessary, and other prerequisite factors. Some people mistakenly believe that earning power is the primary criterion of status. That this is not so is evident by examining the various prestige scales. For example, one scale ranked 100 occupations according to prestige (Smith, 1943); ranked highest was U.S. Supreme Court Justice, and ranked lowest was the occupation of professional prostitute. Available data suggest that a "successful" prostitute makes considerably more money annually than does a jurist sitting on the highest court.

The classic prestige scale is the one established by the National Opinion Research Center of the University of Chicago. It is generally referred to as the NORC Scale of Occupational Prestige and presents the following prestige hierarchy of occupations (National Opinion Research Center, 1947):

- Government officials
- Professional and semiprofessional workers
- Proprietors, managers, and officials (except farm)
- Clerical, sales, and kindred workers
- Craftsmen, foremen, and kindred workers
- Farmers and farm managers
- Protective service workers
- Operatives and kindred workers
- Farm laborers
- Service workers (except domestic and protective)
- Laborers (except farm).

The NORC Scale closely parallels another prestige ranking system, Duncan's Sociometric Status Index of 1950. The average status score for all occupations is 30. In relation to that average, the following occupational group scores prevail:

- Professional, technical and kindred workers 75
- Managers, officials, and proprietors (except farm) 57
- Sales workers 49
- Clerical and kindred workers 45
- Craftsmen, foremen, and kindred workers 31
- Operatives and kindred workers 18

- Service workers (except private household) 17
- Farmers and farm managers 14
- Farm laborers and foremen 9
- Private household workers 8
- Laborers (except farm and mine) 7

These occupational status rankings as well as others have remained relatively stable for the past half-century (Hodge, Siegel, & Rossi, 1964; Counts, 1925; Deeg & Paterson, 1947; Hakel, Hollman & Dunette, 1968; Braun & Bayer, 1973; Medvene & Collins, 1974; Kanzaki, 1976). The results may be somewhat suspect, because perceptions of the status of newer occupations cannot be compared with earlier perceptions since the occupations did not exist. Also, most respondents utilized to establish prestige hierarchies are college students. This fact could prejudice the results, since Spaeth (1968) has demonstrated that academic performance and intellectual ability largely determine what a person regards as occupational prestige. Hence, it may be dangerous to generalize the results of occupational status studies.

As an example of the typical sort of response of college students in the prestige ranking of occupations, Table 3.2 presents a ranking of 94 careers requiring a college degree. Most are sensible, but some are nonsensical. The results of the study indicated that: (1) the phenomenon of occupational egocentrism was operating, in that students gave higher status rankings to the occupations they were training for than the average rating for the same occupation by all other students; and (2) more than 5 percent of the students indicated that they were not familiar with about 40 percent of the occupations, suggesting a relatively widespread lack of occupational awareness.

It is important to realize that as early as the ninth grade, students are acutely aware of occupational prestige values (Slocum, 1966). Yet, although high school students are aware of occupational prestige values, the value of a specific occupation is not a good predictor of their occupational likes and dislikes (Slocum & Bowles, 1968). Contrary to popular belief, high school students find a wide range of occupations attractive, independent of occupational prestige.

The relative constancy of occupational prestige over time is not to say that the occupational

Table 3.2
Ninety-four Careers by Rank Order in Descending Mean Rating Scores
(n = 318)

Occupation	Rank	Mean Rating	Occupation	Rank	Mean Rating
Physician	1	89.5	Marketing research worker	49	53.9
Lawyer	2	86.4	Soil scientist	50	53.2
Dentist	3	83.5	Interior designer and decorator	51	53.1
Veterinarian	4	80.2	Urban planner	52	52.8
Biochemist	5	79.3	Political scientist	53	52.7
Engineer	6	77.8	Programmer	54	52.4
Chemist	7	77.2	Technical writer	55	51.1
Optometrist	8	76.4	Dietitian	56	50.9
Physicist	9	76.1	Sociologist	57	50.6
Engineering and science technician	10	74.4	Commercial artist	58	50.4
Architect	11	73.7	Rehabilitation counselor	59	50.3
Osteopathic physician	12	73.5	Secondary school teacher	60	50.0
Geophysicist	13	70.4	Forester	61	49.7
Pharmacist	14	67.9	Musician/music teacher	62	49.4
Psychologist	15	67.3	Geographer	63	49.3
College and university teacher	16	67.0	Public relations worker	64	49.0
Systems analyst	17	65.3	Historian	65	48.4
Flight engineer	18	65.2	School counselor	66	48.0
Pilot and copilot	19	64.9	Advertising worker	67	47.8
Accountant	20	64.8	Career planning and placement counselor	68	47.6
Life scientist	21	64.4	Kindergarten and elementary school teacher	69	46.9
Oceanographer	22	64.2	Airline dispatcher	70	46.7
Podiatrist	23	62.8	Actuary	71	45.4
Physical therapist	24	62.8	Social worker	72	44.9
Registered nurse	25	62.5	Home economist	73	44.3
FBI special agent	26	62.1	Cooperative extension service worker	74	44.3
Mathematician	27	61.6	Singer/singing teacher	75	43.5
Geologist	28	61.4	Range manager	76	43.5
Landscape architect	29	60.2	Insurance agent/broker	77	43.5
Statistician	30	60.2	Employment counselor	78	43.2
Industrial designer	31	60.1	Personnel worker	79	43.2
Hospital administrator	32	59.5	Industrial traffic manager	80	42.7
Food scientist	33	59.5	Purchasing agent	81	42.6
Meteorologist	34	59.3	Medical record librarian	82	42.5
Speech pathologist and audiologist	35	59.1	Hotel manager and assistant	83	42.5
Bank officer	36	58.7	Newspaper reporter	84	42.3
Anthropologist	37	58.4	Licensed merchant marine officer	85	42.2
Clergy	38	57.3	Insurance underwriter	86	42.0
Dental hygienist	39	57.2	Securities salesperson	87	40.2
Astronomer	40	56.9	Recreation worker	88	39.7
Economist	41	55.8	Insurance claim examiner	89	39.1
Actor/actress	42	55.5	Manufacturer's salesperson	90	38.2
City manager	43	55.3	Insurance claim adjuster	91	37.5
Medical laboratory worker	44	54.8	Librarian	92	33.9
Occupational therapist	45	54.4	Dancer	93	31.3
Chiropractor	46	54.4	Sanitarian	94	27.1
Soil conservationist	47	54.3			
Draftsman	48	53.9			

structure is unresponsive to generational changes. A classic example was the great upsurge of scientific and engineering careers stimulated by Sputnik and the resulting reactions all the way through the space program. Then, because of federal deemphasis of the space program and subsequent massive technical and scientific unemployment, the United States found itself with a surplus of scientists and engineers. Thus, fewer students opted for training in these areas. Now, however, scientists and engineers are again in demand. Also in the late 1960s and early 1970s, we witnessed a reluctance of college graduates to enter large, corporate business and industrial structures, either because of the perceived depersonalization of such organizations, because of a movement away from material goals on the part of many students of that generation, or because of some other factor. Now, one of the "hot tickets" in colleges and universities is the business major, and corporate recruiters on campus are inundated with interviewees. For years, the agribusiness industry was a relatively unpopular major; now students are in strong competition to secure majors in that area.

The point is that to some extent the way in which occupations are perceived and consequent interest in entering them are contingent on supply and demand. Supply and demand, in turn, are shaped by priorities in the society and by the prevailing work ethic of each generation. To an equal extent, some occupational areas seem to endure, as is the case with the health sciences.

In any case, occupational status classification systems are useful, in that they permit individuals in the process of career development and choice to project into the future in order to discern probable changes in occupational status levels. If young people are to appreciate the dignity which they can bring to all work, they must understand the bases on which some occupations are perceived as prestigious and on which others are not. If occupational prestige is a consideration in career decision-making, it is important that individuals understand the factors that determine prestige.

Psychological Classification Systems

Holland's Classification System. Many classification schemes are based on the psychological characteristics of workers. One example is the

system developed by John Holland and his associates at the Johns Hopkins University (Holland, 1973). In Chapter 4, Holland's theory of career development is described; you will note that it is based on a theory of personality types. Evolving out of this theory are six classes of occupations: realistic, investigative, artistic, social, enterprising, and conventional. Each of these has five to sixteen subclasses; within each subclass, occupations are arranged by the years of general education required. In all, 456 common occupations — comprising about 95 percent of the labor force in the United States — are included. All occupations are arranged in a system that uses the six Holland code letters:

- Realistic Occupations (R) include skilled trades, many technical and some service occupations
- Investigative Occupations (I) include scientific and some technical occupations
- Artistic Occupations (A) include artistic, musical, and literary occupations
- Social Occupations (S) include educational and social welfare occupations
- Enterprising Occupations (E) include managerial and sales occupations
- Conventional Occupations (C) include office and clerical occupations.

The two or three classes that persons in a specific occupation most resemble are designated in order by the code letter for those classes. Thus counselors, for example, are designated SEA, meaning that they most of all resemble people in social occupations, that they next most resemble people in enterprising occupations, and that they still less resemble people in artistic occupations. If one takes the six categories and looks to possible combinations, over 100 possible combinations emerge. One of the difficulties with the Holland system is that for some combinations, no occupations have as yet been identified.

To relate his classification scheme to a more familiar system and one which provides occupational information, Holland further identifies occupations by their fourth edition DOT code numbers. These numbers provide a description of the occupation and estimates of interests and aptitudes associated with it. Thus, the occupation of counselor is described by its DOT designation, 045.107–010, and by the three occupational classes or types that counselors most resemble, SEA.

Finally, a 1–6 designation describes the level of educational development demanded by an occupation. Levels 5 and 6 refer to college training; levels 3 and 4 mean high school and some college, technical, or business training; levels 1 and 2 mean only elementary school or no special training. We now have the complete Holland classification for the occupation of counselor.

4th Edition	DOT	ED	CODE
Counselor	045.107–010	5	SEA

The Holland classification system has now been applied to interest measurement and to a variety of other aids in career planning. Many of these will be described in later chapters. There has been a great deal of research that attempts to validate Holland's occupational groupings and to establish their effectiveness in career research, career guidance, vocational education, and social science. Thus far, the Holland taxonomy has generally withstood the rigors of close empirical scrutiny and stands as an excellent example of an attempt to classify occupations psychologically. As shall be seen in Chapter 14, the Holland system has been converted into a career guidance delivery system, through the *Self-Directed Search*, and it provides one of the reporting frameworks for the Strong-Campbell Interest Inventory. There remain some very real questions regarding aspects of the translation of Holland's theoretical model to an operational model (such as the validity of self-estimates of aptitudes), but the system has value in that it does what any good occupational classification scheme should do – it breaks down the complex and confusing occupational world into manageable categories to which individuals can then relate important self-characteristics.

Field, Level, and Enterprise

Most occupational classification systems are unidimensional – that is, they classify occupations on the basis of a single factor or variable. As has been previously noted, it is possible (and desirable) to classify occupations by combining two or more variables into a multidimensional scheme. One of the first attempts of this sort was made by Roe (1954) and later modified by Moser, Dubin, and Shelsky (1956). Her classifi-

cation system combines eight fields and six levels. The eight fields, which are based on the work of interest measurement researchers, are: outdoor-physical, social-personal, business contact, administration-control, math-physical sciences, biological sciences, humanistic, and arts. Her levels are based on the responsibility, education, and prestige involved in an occupation. These levels are: professional and managerial (higher), professional and managerial (regular), semiprofessional and low managerial, skilled support and maintenance, semiskilled support and maintenance, and unskilled support and maintenance.

It soon became apparent that still another dimension was needed to describe an occupation fully. The concept of enterprise, roughly related to industrial classification, was added by Super (1957), who drew a tridimensional model of occupational classification in terms of field, level, and enterprise (see Figure 3.2). The tridimensional classification scheme clearly depicts the fact that occupations differ in at least three dimensions: in terms of the field of activity or interest; in terms of level of ability, education or training, autonomy, authority, prestige, and rewards; and in terms of the enterprise in which work is performed.

The field level-enterprise classification system is another attempt to bring order into the potential chaos of our awareness of the thousands of existing jobs. The assumption is that no single dimension is adequate to do this job; therefore, several dimensions must be combined. If counselors understand such a multidimensional structure and also understand their counselees, then they can help individuals relate their self-characteristics to the occupational structure.

Standard Occupational Classification

Development of a Standard Occupational Classification (SOC) started in 1966 and is basically an attempt to bridge the Census Classification and the DOT. It includes the best features of the International Standard Classification of Occupations (ISCO), the Canadian Classification and Dictionary of Occupations, and the British Classification of Occupations and Directory of Occupational Titles. The classification covers all occupations in which work is performed for pay

Figure 3.2

A Scheme for Classifying Occupations by Level, Field, and Enterprise

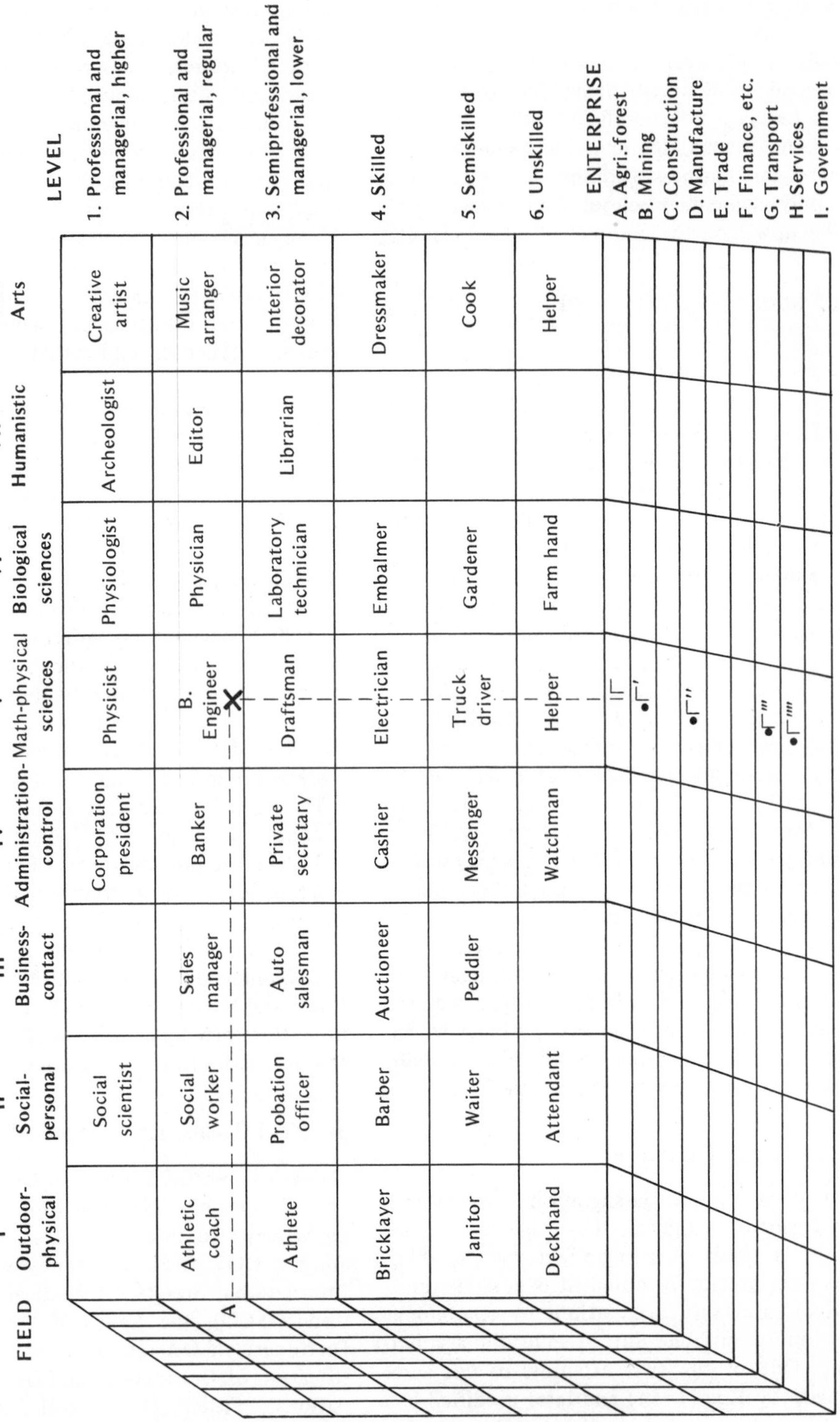

LEVEL

1. Professional and managerial, higher
2. Professional and managerial, regular
3. Semiprofessional and managerial, lower
4. Skilled
5. Semiskilled
6. Unskilled

ENTERPRISE

A. Agri.-forest
B. Mining
C. Construction
D. Manufacture
E. Trade
F. Finance, etc.
G. Transport
H. Services
I. Government

FIELD	I Outdoor-physical	II Social-personal	III Business-contact	IV Administration-control	V Math-physical sciences	VI Biological sciences	VII Humanistic	VIII Arts
1		Social scientist		Corporation president	Physicist	Physiologist	Archeologist	Creative artist
2	Athletic coach	Social worker	Sales manager	Banker	B. Engineer	Physician	Editor	Music arranger
3	Athlete	Probation officer	Auto salesman	Private secretary	Draftsman	Laboratory technician	Librarian	Interior decorator
4	Bricklayer	Barber	Auctioneer	Cashier	Electrician	Embalmer		Dressmaker
5	Janitor	Waiter	Peddler	Messenger	Truck driver	Gardener		Cook
6	Deckhand	Attendant		Watchman	Helper	Farm hand		Helper

or profit but does not include volunteer work. The SOC tries to reflect the current United States occupational structure on the basis of work performed and place of work. It is structured on a four-level system: division, major group, minor group, and unit group. It runs from gross description to finer detail as one goes from division to unit; and it includes DOT numbers and census occupation codes.

There are twenty-two divisions. Each division has major groups (designated by a two-digit number), minor groups (designated by a three-digit number), and unit groups (designated by a four-digit number). The divisions are:

Executive, administrative, and managerial occupations
Engineers, surveyors, and architects
Natural scientists and mathematicians
Social scientists, social workers, religious workers, and lawyers
Teachers, librarians, and counselors
Health diagnosing and treating practitioners
Registered nurses, pharmacists, dieticians, therapists, and physician's assistants
Writers, artists, entertainers, and athletes
Health technologists and technicians
Technologists and technicians, except health
Marketing and sales occupations
Administrative support occupations, including clerical
Service occupations
Agricultural, forestry, and fishing occupations
Mechanics and repairers
Construction and extractive occupations
Precision production occupations
Production working occupations
Transportation and material moving occupations
Handlers, equipment cleaners, helpers and laborers
Military occupations
Miscellaneous occupations

To illustrate the progressively finer distinction, let us consider the division of Mathematicians and Natural Scientists.

17 Computer, mathematical, and operations research occupations (major)
  171 Computer scientists (minor)
    1712 Computer systems analysts (unit)

    1719 Computer scientists, not elsewhere classified
  172 Operations and systems researchers and analysts
    1721 Operations researchers and analysts
    1722 Systems researchers and analysts, except computer
  173 Mathematical scientists
    1732 Actuaries
    1733 Statisticians
    1739 Mathematical scientists, not elsewhere classified
18 Natural scientists
  184 Physical scientists
    1842 Astronomers
    1843 Physicists
    1845 Chemists, except biochemists
    1846 Atmospheric and space scientists
    1847 Geologists
    1849 Physical scientists, not elsewhere classified
  185 Life scientists
    1852 Forestry and conservation scientists
    1853 Agricultural and food scientists
    1854 Biological scientists
    1855 Medical scientists

This system is obviously useful for research and classification purposes. It remains to be seen how utilitarian it will be for the development of career-related materials and for other practical applications.

The Dictionary of Occupational Titles (DOT)

Perhaps the most widely used occupational classification system is that employed in the *Dictionary of Occupational Titles*. The DOT was first issued in 1939 to meet the needs of the public employment service system to standardize occupational information in order to facilitate job placement, employment counseling, career guidance, labor market projections, and person-power accounting. Subsequent editions of the DOT appeared in 1949 and 1965. The fourth edition was published in 1978. Unfortunately, at the time of this writing, there is some doubt because of budget restrictions whether this valuable resource will be continued.

The fourth edition of the DOT contains information relating to approximately 20,000 jobs. This figure represents about 1400 fewer jobs than in the third edition and is a consequence of the deletion of some 3500 jobs and the addition of approximately 2100 new occupational definitions.

All jobs in the fourth edition of the DOT are designated by a nine-digit number. Previously, a six-digit number had been used; however, three additional digits have been added to provide each occupation with its own code in order to expedite computerized analyses. The first of the nine digits refers to an occupational category, of which there are nine:

0/1. Professional, technical, and managerial occupations
2. Clerical and sales occupations
3. Service occupations
4. Agricultural, fishery, forestry, and related occupations
5. Processing occupations
6. Machine trades occupations
7. Benchwork occupations
8. Structural work occupations
9. Miscellaneous occupations.

These nine occupational categories are divided into 82 two-digit occupational divisions, which are then subdivided into 549 three-digit occupational groups. For purposes of illustration, the two-digit occupational divisions and the three-digit occupation groups relating to the 0/1 occupational category and the 00/01 division are presented below.

Example of Two-Digit Division
0/1 Professional, Technical, and
Managerial Occupations

00/01 Occupations in architecture, engineering, and surveying
02 Occupations in mathematics and physical sciences
04 Occupations in life sciences
05 Occupations in social sciences
07 Occupations in medicine and health
09 Occupations in education
10 Occupations in museum, library, and archival sciences
11 Occupations in law and jurisprudence

12 Occupations in religion and theology
13 Occupations in writing
14 Occupations in art
15 Occupations in entertainment and recreation
16 Occupations in administrative specializations
18 Managers and officials, n.e.c.
19 Miscellaneous professional, technical, and managerial occupations

Example of Three-Digit Group
00/01 Occupations in Architecture,
Engineering, and Surveying

001 Architectural occupations
002 Aeronautical engineering occupations
003 Electrical/electronics engineering occupations
005 Civil engineering occupations
006 Ceramic engineering occupations
007 Mechanical engineering occupations
008 Chemical engineering occupations
010 Mining and petroleum engineering occupations
011 Metallurgy and metallurgical engineering occupations
012 Industrial engineering occupations
013 Agricultural engineering occupations
014 Marine engineering occupations
015 Nuclear engineering occupations
017 Drafters, n.e.c.
018 Surveying/cartographic occupations
019 Occupations in architecture, engineering, and surveying, n.e.c.

The middle three digits of the nine-digit code number refer to worker traits. Jobs require that people function in relation to data, people, and things. Each of these three items has a hierarchy of relationship levels, and the code digit refers to the highest level within the hierarchy at which a worker is required to function. Following are the hierarchies for each digit.

DATA (4th Digit)
0 Synthesizing
1 Coordinating
2 Analyzing
3 Compiling
4 Computing

5 Copying
6 Comparing
   PEOPLE (5th Digit)
0 Mentoring
1 Negotiating
2 Instructing
3 Supervising
4 Diverting
5 Persuading
6 Speaking-Signalling
7 Serving
8 Taking Instructions – Helping
   THINGS (6th Digit)
0 Setting Up
1 Precision Working
2 Operating – Controlling
3 Driving – Operating
4 Manipulating
5 Tending
6 Feeding – Offbearing
7 Handling

Hence, the more a worker functions with complex responsibility and judgment, the lower the number on each list; the less complicated the function in relation to data, people, and things, the higher the number. Compiling data is a more complex task than copying data; instructing people is more complicated than serving them; and precision work with things is more intricate than manipulating them.

The final three digits of the nine-digit code indicate the alphabetical order of titles within the six-digit code groups. Many occupations may have the same first six digits. Therefore, the last three digits serve to differentiate a particular occupation from all others. If a six-digit code is applicable to only one occupational title, the last three digits will be 010.

To illustrate, let us "read" the nine-digit codes for a sample occupation: marine architect.

Marine Architect (001.061-014)
0 = A professional, technical, and managerial occupation
0 = An occupation in architecture, engineering and surveying
1 = An architectural occupation
0 = Synthesizes data
6 = Speaks to people
1 = Precision work with things

014 = Alphabetically distinguishes from other 001.061 occupations (for example, landscape architect).

Each entry in the DOT contains the following information: (1) The Occupational Code Number; (2) The Occupational Title; (3) The Industry Designation; (4) Alternate Titles (if any); (5) The Head Statement (summary of occupation); (6) Task Element Statements (specific tasks worker performs); (7) "May" Items (duties performed by worker in some establishments but not in others); (8) Undefined Related Titles (if applicable). To illustrate, the entry for marine architect is listed below.

001.061-014 ARCHITECT, MARINE
           (profess. & kin.) architect, naval;
           naval designer.
Designs and oversees construction and repair of marine and craft and floating structures, such as ships, barges, tugs, dredges, submarines, torpedoes, floats, and buoys: Studies design proposals and specifications to establish basic characteristics of craft, such as size, weight, speed, propulsion, armament, cargo, displacement, draft, crew and passenger complements, and fresh or salt water service. Oversees construction and testing of prototype in model basin and develops sectional and waterline curves of hull to establish center of gravity, ideal hull form, and buoyancy and stability data. Designs complete hull and superstructure according to specifications and test data, in conformity with standards of safety, efficiency, and economy. Designs layout of craft interior including cargo space, passenger compartments, ladder wells, and elevators. Confers with MARINE ENGINEERS (profess. & kin.) to establish arrangement of boiler room equipment and propulsion machinery, heating and ventilating systems, refrigeration equipment, piping, and other functional equipment. Evaluates performance of craft during dock and sea trials to determine design changes and conformance with national and international standards.

The fourth edition of the DOT is a single volume of 1371 pages and provides essentially the same data that were packaged in two volumes of the third edition. The DOT user will find it separated into nine sections: an introduction and summary listings, master titles and definitions, term titles and definitions, occupational group arrangement, glossary, alphabetical index of titles, occupational titles arranged by industry designation, industry index, and an appendix which explains the data, people, and things system.

There are three basic arrangements of occupational titles. *The Occupational Group Arrangement* is appropriate if the user has sufficient information about the job tasks, wants to know about other closely related occupations, and/or wants to be sure he or she has chosen the most appropriate classification using the other arrange-

ments. *Occupational Titles Arranged by Industry Designation* is appropriate if the user knows only the industry in which the job is located, wants to know about other jobs in an industry, and/or wants to know about work in a specific industry. *The Alphabetical Index of Occupational Titles* is appropriate if the user knows only the occupational title and cannot obtain better information.

In summary, the fourth edition of the DOT should present few problems of usage for the counselor. Besides its direct value as a comprehensive reservoir of information on approximately 20,000 separate jobs, the DOT provides a framework for use in a variety of other career-related resources (such as Holland's SDS, CIS, and so on).

Summary

Occupational classification schemes provide ways of examining the American occupational structure, an understanding of which is essential to career guidance and counseling. Such classification systems are valuable in that they provide a framework for the delivery of career guidance services. The occupational system helps us to understand the total social system of our society, since it is a society's primary structuring element. We have described several unidimensional and multidimensional systems. Each, in its own way, provides a means of bringing manageable form and order into the potential chaos of occupational investigation.

LEARNING ACTIVITIES

1. Use the list of twenty-five occupations in the Kanzaki article in the chapter references. Ask various groups to rank the occupations according to social status. If you have a large enough N, perform several crossbreaks (such as male vs. female, college-educated vs. non-college-educated, and so on). How do your results compare to the Counts, Deeg and

Paterson, Hakel, Hollman, and Dunnette, and Kanzaki studies? If you wish, you may use the ninety-four occupations of the Clark and Seals study in this chapter and perform the same analyses.

2. Read any of the following books (or any other similar volume) in which scholars attempt to define the future of work. Write an essay in which you indicate your agreement or disagreement with the author.

   Dickson, Paul. *The future of the workplace: The coming revolution in jobs.* New York: Weybright and Talley, 1976.

   Kahn, H., Brown, W., & Markel, L. *The next 200 years: A scenario for America and the world.* New York: William Morrow, 1976.

   Kerr, C., & Rosow, J. M. (eds.) *Work in America: The decade ahead.* New York: Van Nostrand, 1979.

   Sheppard, C. S., & Carroll, D. C. (eds.) *Working in the twenty-first century.* New York: John Wiley & Sons, 1980.

   Theobald, R. *An alternative future for America's third century.* New York: Swallow, 1976.

   Toffler, Alvin. *Future shock.* New York: Bantam Books, 1970.

3. Check with your state employment office to see if they have any regional projections regarding supply of and demand for workers. Discuss with the forecaster or other representatives how these projections were evolved.
4. Discuss with a classmate the advantages and disadvantages for practice of several different classification schemes.
5. Locate someone whom you feel is underemployed (that is, who is in an occupation not commensurate with his or her education or training). Discuss with that person the reasons for underemployment, his or her feelings regarding the situation, and so forth.
6. The problem of obsolescence in education or training is staggering. Locate and interview a person in a profession or trade regarding the ways in which he or she keeps "current."
7. Using the DOT, define two of the following occupations according to code number:
   a. back washer
   b. frog shaker
   c. banana spotter
   d. car whacker
   e. bank boss
   f. kiss setter
   g. tie puller
   h. hand shaker
8. Discuss with a classmate the implications of several statements in this chapter regarding likely future changes in the occupational structure.

OBJECTIVES

After reading this chapter, engaging in the learning activities, and reading the suggested references, you should have met the objectives that follow. If you have not, it would probably be useful for you to review the material on the American Occupational Structure before proceeding further.

1. List at least four reasons that cause occupational forecasting to be a less-than-exact science.
2. Describe the effects of both undereducation and overeducation.
3. List at least three changes in the American occupational structure over the past twenty-five years.
4. List at least five projected changes in the occupational structure over the next twenty-five years.
5. Name at least ten of the USOE clusters.
6. Define the two major categories involved in census classification.
7. Describe, in general terms, the hierarchy of status classification.
8. Name the six categories of Holland's classification system.
9. List Roe's eight fields and her six levels.
10. Describe the four-tier organization of the SOC.
11. Describe the code number system of the DOT.

4 / *Career Development and Choice: Theory and Applications*

In this chapter we will consider the conceptual frames of reference designed to explain how individual career development unfolds across the lifespan as well as how particular personal attributes and characteristics of the social structure influence career development. Such perspectives represent the conceptual foundations for career guidance, career education, and related interventions in individual career development. In Chapter 5 we will deal more specifically with how the models described in this chapter fit the needs and characteristics of women, minorities, and other special groups.

In a collective sense, the conceptual perspectives reviewed in this chapter deal with several interacting emphases: (1) the flow of understandings, experiences, commitments, values, and skills by which one forges the many facets of personal identity — self, educational, occupational, and career; (2) the process of decision-making as the way one expresses personal identity in a choice; and (3) the functional relationships between time, social structures, and personal attributes. This does not imply that we review all the conceptual perspectives here. That is not possible within the limited space available in this chapter. Rather the intent here is to highlight major conceptual approaches which attempt to explain the acquisition of work related behavior, the anticipation of career options, and adjustments to the settings in which that behavior will be implemented.

As studies pertinent to career development have ensued, the concepts involved have tended to broaden. Some research is more pertinent to occupational choice at a specific point in time or to adjustment within a work setting than to career development across time. Some research is concerned with the structure of choice, work behavior, or "career maturity" within a particular life stage whereas other research is concerned with how such structures change over time, and with the continuities and discontinuities in career patterns throughout life. Increasingly research and speculation in career development have shifted from almost a total concentration on adolescence and young adulthood to greater attention to career behavior in middle and late adulthood. As a result, it can be argued that career development theory and life-span developmental psychology are growing more congruent in their perspectives and methodology, if not deliberately then certainly inadvertently. Life-span developmental psychology is an empirical, multidisciplinary science that is concerned with the description and explication of ontogenetic (age-related), normative history-graded (evolutional) influences, and nonnormative life events as they influence behavioral change from birth to death (Goulet & Baltes, 1970) as well as with the relationship between intervention and life-span development (Fuchs, 1978; Danish, 1981). See Chapter 17 for perspectives from life-span psychology on needed research in career development. In their idealized sense, both life-span psychology and career development, as a special instance of life-span psychology, are more than the additive result of different age-related studies with different groups of subjects in different educational or work settings. The intent in both cases is more holistic and longitudinal in understanding the influences on and the life histories of persons as they engage in the various roles available to them across time. In fact, the available career development theory and research do not meet the idealized criteria just suggested but derive for the most part from less systematic and more disparate sources. Warnath (1975) among others has criticized the state of theory in career development. Nevertheless, these sources combine to provide an impressive set of insights into the career-related or work-related behaviors that are the targets for the interventions that career guidance represents.

Even though career development theory is, as yet, fragmented and incomplete (particularly when addressed to women and to the disadvantaged segments of society), what is presently known provides a basis for programmatic efforts to spur the development of effective career behavior. If one views the confluence of approaches, theory, and research with objectivity and boldness, one finds tentative sets of constructs and propositions to explain differential career behavior and decision-making, as well as to provide guidelines for aiding such processes.

CAREER DEVELOPMENT AND VOCATIONALIZATION

Katz (1973, p. 89) has stated that "the content of vocational guidance is defined as the opportunities for choice that society permits among educational and occupational options." Placing that idea in a broader view suggests that the content of career guidance includes not only choices among educational and occupational options but also those of life style — the degree to which work will be a central way of fulfillment for a particular individual and the ways the person will cope with the possibility of free and informed choice in pursuing personal direction and planning.

An overriding goal in career guidance is the facilitation of free and informed choice in the individual. The assumption is that choice cannot be free unless it is informed. A further assumption is that the types of information available to an individual depend on how free the person is to consider different options or life styles. The latter, of course, can be diminished or strengthened by political conditions, historical events, family circumstances, and many other phenomena. Given that reality, however, in order for one to choose

freely, one needs knowledge, not only about what is available from which to choose but also about the personal characteristics that might be emphasized in evaluating and acting on available choices. This latter goal requires, in addition to knowledge, clarification of personal values, interests, and attitudes as these relate to self-characteristics; environmental alternatives (occupational, educational, personal, social options); and the decision-making process itself.

Career development, as the term will be used in this chapter, refers to the body of speculation and research that focuses on understanding the factors underlying free and informed choice, the evolution of personal identity in regard to work, and the transition, induction, and adjustment to work. Borow (1961) has summarized the matter well in his statement that theories and research, which examine career development, are in reality "a search for the psychological meaning of vocationally relevant acts (including the exploratory vocational behavior of youth) and of work itself in the human experience." More recently, Super (1980, p. 283) has stated that, "careers have been viewed variously as a sequence of positions occupied by a person during the course of a lifetime (Super, 1957), as a decision tree portraying the decision points encountered by a person going through school and into the world of work (Flanagan & Cooley, 1966), and as a series of life stages in which differing constellations of developmental tasks are encountered and dealt with" (Buehler, 1933; Super, 1957). Thus, the universe of perspectives of which career development theory and research are comprised is wide indeed.

Most theories of career development view vocational behavior as a continuing, fluid process of growth and learning, and they attach considerable importance to individual self-concepts, developmental experiences, personal history, and the psychosocial environment of the individual as major determinants of the process. Thus, career development can be said to be dealing with one aspect of socialization, that which might be called vocationalization (Crites, 1969, p. 88).

The socialization process, if it is successful, "insures that the maturing child will accept and internalize the system of beliefs and norms governing relationships among people. These beliefs and norms become the basic frame of reference within which the adult experiences his world" (Bradburn, 1963, p. 334). "The socialization process, then, speaks to the articulation of the motivational system of the personality with the structure of the social system" (Parsons, 1951, p. 32). As Gross has observed (1975), "although traditional studies of socialization have focused on infancy and childhood, recent research has turned to adult socialization. Such research suggests that socialization is far from complete in childhood; it goes on throughout persons' lives." The importance of Gross' observations has been amplified in the virtual explosion of perspectives on adult career development that have become available in the recent past (for example, Levenson, 1978; Lowenthal, 1977; Gould, 1978).

The process of vocationalization, or career development as it is described throughout this book, speaks to the various factors — psychological, sociological, cultural, economic — which, across time, result in self-career identity, decision-making ability, and career maturity. Vocationalization, as we see it, has to do with those processes and factors which aid or impede one's acquisition of the values, knowledge, and skills leading to effective career behavior.

Most importantly, however, our contention is that the individual processes of vocationalization, as described by career development concepts, can be understood, anticipated, and influenced by systematic programs of career guidance or career education. Career development concepts, then, are not descriptions of the inevitable; rather, they are descriptive of the possible and sometimes the probable behavioral results, if no intervention occurs to help the individual cope consciously with such possible or probable outcomes as they relate to his or her goals.

APPROACHES TO CAREER DEVELOPMENT AND CHOICE

Career development is concerned with broader phenomena than those represented by the term occupations; it is synonymous with the earlier term vocational development. The emphasis in the psychological or sociological study of careers (career development in this context) is on the continuities and discontinuities in the lives of groups (Super, 1954). The psychology and sociology of occupations, on the other hand, stress characteristics of single or categorized occupations (Super, 1969b).

The occupational model is primarily concerned with prediction from one point in time to another. "It takes prediction data at an early stage of the career and uses regression methods to predict success to one occupation, or uses discriminant analyses as a means of assessing the likelihood of being found, later, in each of several possible occupations." On the other hand, the career model "is one in which the individual is conceived of as moving along one of a number of possible pathways through the educational system and on into and through the work system" (Super, 1969a, p. 3). Both of these models are important for different reasons. To make an arbitrary distinction, the occupational model, which stresses matching or actuarial relationships of person and job, is central in career guidance applied to an immediate job or occupational choice; the career model undergirds career guidance as a stimulus to intermediate and long-range career planning. Put another way, the major unit of concern in an occupational model is the differences in work content across occupations and their relationship to individual aptitudes and interests. The major unit of concern in a career model is the clarity and accuracy of the self-concept as the evaluative base by which to judge available options.

In addition to its other foci, career development is intimately related to the factors that motivate or impede decisions. But as Tiedeman (1961, p. 18) has pointed out, "Vocational development not only occurs within the context of a single decision; vocational development ordinarily occurs within the context of several decisions. . . . Each decision is also to be considered in relation with a wider context of past and future decisions leading to the presentation of career." Further, Hershenson and Roth (1966, p. 368) contend, "Vocational development may be conceived of as a decision-making process which creates two trends: (a) narrowing the range of possibilities, and (b) strengthening the possibilities which remain. Through the successive refinement of these trends, events are experienced, construed and acted upon until a career choice is arrived at."

Types of Approaches

The approaches describing career development or some aspect of it have been classified several ways. Hilton (1962) has labeled them as models of attribute matching, need reduction, economic man, social man, and complex information processing. Osipow (1968, pp. 10–11) has classified such approaches as trait-factor approaches, sociology and career choice, self-concept theory, and vocational choice and personality theories. Crites (1969) discusses them as nonpsychological theories (such as accident, economic, cultural, and sociological) and the psychological theories (such as trait-and-factor, psychodynamic, developmental and decision). Pitz and Harren (1980) have described those theories dealing specifically with career decision making as normative (or prescriptive) and behavioral (or descriptive). In the former case, the theorist focuses on procedures for making optimal decisions, decisions that best meet some criterion. In the latter, the theorist is concerned with describing the decision-making process itself. Holland and Gottfredson (1976) have described the two main traditions for understanding careers as the developmental view and the differential view. Miller (1974), Pietrofesa and Splete (1975), and other observers classify career development perspectives with somewhat different systems. Super (1981) has recently contended, "The approaches and theories of the past 75 years fall into three main categories: those that match people and occupations, those that describe de-velopment leading to matching, and those that focus on decision making" (p. 8). As shown in Table 4.1, several types of approaches are included under each of the three main categories.

These attempts at classification highlight the factors, emphases, or disciplinary bases that distinguish one theory or research effort from another. In general, the categories depicted are not mutually exclusive or independent but they attempt to explain differential career behavior and choice from somewhat varied vantage points. Jepsen and Dilley's (1974) comparisons among many of the models of career development reported here have shown, "They are similar to each other but certainly not to the point where parts of one can be interchanged for parts of another" (p. 345).

The elements comprising our current understanding of career development emerge from inquiry carried on in different disciplines, primarily sociology, economics, and psychology (developmental, differential, vocational, and personality). For our purposes in this chapter, career development approaches and their proponents will be considered in the following sequence: trait and factor, actuarial or matching; decision; situational or sociological; psychological; and developmental. Where possible, the disciplinary antecedents or roots of each approach will be identified.

Trait-and-Factor, Actuarial, or Matching Approaches. Trait-and-factor or matching approaches, coupled with actuarial methods, consti-

Table 4.1
Types of Approaches to Occupational Choice and Career Development

Matching	Developmental	Decision-Making
Differential Aptitudes Personality	Life-stage and identification	Process
Situational Structure Context Socialization	Life-span, life-space and personal constructs	Style
Phenomenological Self-concept Congruence	Stage and determinants Path models Regression models	Process-style-situation

tute a venerable theme in career guidance. Rooted in the psychology of individual differences, applied psychology, and differential psychology, these approaches conceive of the person as an organization of capacities and other properties that can be measured and related to the requirements of training programs or occupations. Based on empirically derived information on differences among people occupying various occupations or correlates of choice or satisfaction, trait-and-factor approaches are more descriptive of influences on choice than they are explanatory of career development.

In the trait-and-factor approach, the individual is regarded within a pattern of traits — such as interests, aptitudes, achievements, personality characteristics — which can be identified through objective means, usually psychological tests or inventories, and then profiled to represent the individual's potential. Trait-and-factor approaches consider occupations similarly, that is, as susceptible for profile according to the "amounts" of individual traits they require. When one profile is overlaid on the other, the probable degree of fit between person and job can be identified.

Such an approach represents the essence of the occupational model previously identified in this chapter and in Chapter 1. As Super (1969b) has noted, vocational psychology, from its beginnings until shortly after 1950, was essentially a psychology of occupations. The occupation was the subject, and the persons in it were the sources of data on the occupation. Thus, from an actuarial standpoint, predictions can be made using individual traits as predictors and the degree to which these traits are possessed by successful persons in different occupations as the criteria. Further, the techniques and results of the numerous studies combining different traits and different occupational requirements also provide a means of appraising an individual's possibilities.

Miller (1974) has suggested that the assumptions underlying the trait-and-factor approach include:

1. Vocational development is largely a cognitive process; decisions are to be reached by reasoning.
2. Occupational choice is a single event. In the spirit of Parsons, choice is stressed greatly and development very little.

3. There is a single "right" goal for everyone in the choice of vocation. There is little or no recognition that a worker might fit well into a number of occupations.
4. A single type of person works in each job. This is the other side of the coin of the third assumption. Taken together, these two notions amount to a one-person, one-job relationship — a concept congenial to the trait-factor approach.
5. There is an occupational choice available to each individual (p. 238).

Historically, trait-and-factor studies have provided the technical foundation for elaborating the three-step process of vocational guidance as laid down by Parsons (1909). As psychological instruments have been developed to assess individual traits, and as knowledge has been accumulated about differences in occupational and educational requirements including aptitudes, interests, and personality factors, vocational guidance processes have become an increasing scientific aid to choice. This approach stands in contrast to pre-Parsonian assumptions, that subjective descriptions of occupational or training requirements are a sufficient basis for choice.

The assumptions on which trait-and-factor approaches rest, while contributing significantly to the current character of career guidance, can lead to a narrow perspective on career development. Trait-and-factor approaches have been primarily oriented to specific occupations or tasks as the criteria toward which predictor variables such as aptitudes, mental ability, socio-economic characteristics, interests, values, personality manifestations, and other variables are directed. However, career development is not concerned solely with the choice of an occupation; it is also concerned with the process by which such choices can be purposefully integrated within a patterning of decisions, thereby maximizing freedom of choice and implementing the personal meaning of the way one conceives his or her traits.

Yet, there is reason to believe that the classical trait-and-factor approaches will continue. O'Hara (1969, p. 29), for one, has asserted that all vocational counseling must be set in the context of career development, but that "persons at any stage are chiefly concerned with the immediate decision to be made, and only remotely concerned with prediction of career development." Thus, trait-and-factor approaches and career development models are complementary, yet useful singly for different purposes. Indeed, the acceleration of multivariate designs and computer availability will undoubtedly add increased insight to this approach.

As Cooley (1964) has indicated, the trait-and-factor problem today is not simply the task of relating a predictor, such as a test score, to some final occupation but the consideration of patterns of attributes and their relationship to the sequence of decisions young persons must make in establishing themselves in the world of work. If such a procedure becomes available, it will diminish a major weakness of trait-and-factor approaches — the view of individual traits and environmental requirements as relatively static rather than dynamic. Such an approach can underestimate one's potential to learn and to grow or the propensity of educational and occupational requirements to change fairly dramatically in a period of a few years.

Used correctly, the trait-and-factor approach has significant utility for career guidance and career education. For example, Cunningham (1969) has identified 103 human attributes (traits) in the cognitive, psychomotor and affective domains and is relating these to 622 work elements (factors required in 814 occupations). When completed, this information will permit persons to determine how closely a range of relevant self-dimensions specifically match the requirements of various occupational clusters. Currently, the information provided by the Worker Trait Groups, found in the *Dictionary of Occupational Titles*, can provide similar exploratory insights although not as detailed as those developed by Cunningham will likely be.

Clearly, if used with insight into the predictive limitations of trait-and-factor procedures, such information can be valuable in providing a person with a sense of the "odds" one faces in pursuing specific choices or the incremental differences that exist between where one is now and where one hopes to be in terms of various educational or occupational options.

A persistent finding limiting the overall usefulness of trait-and-factor, or actuarial, approaches has been that the typical measures used predict training success more effectively than job success

(Super & Crites, 1962). For example, on the basis of various traits, one can reasonably predict with accuracy whether an individual will successfully complete a carpenter's apprenticeship or some type of formal education (such as medical school). Those trait patterns are less likely to predict whether the person will be a successful carpenter or physician after completion of training. Roe (1956) reported that many studies have examined trainability but few deal with job proficiency following the training period. After analyzing 127 studies, Brown and Ghiselli (1952) concluded that there is no certainty that a test that predicts a worker's ability to learn to perform a task also predicts how well one will perform following training. Thorndike (1963) observed that prediction of performance in school- and work-training programs may be the most one can expect of our current test batteries.

Thus, despite all that the trait-and-factor approach has to commend it — statistical sophistication, testing refinement, and technological application — the resulting predictions of individuals' success in specific occupations have been discouragingly imprecise. For example, Tiedeman (1958, p. 9), in a review of trait-and-factor studies on predictions of vocational success, concluded: "In every study, the choice and successful pursuit of a goal has proven to be a function of one's aptitudes, but in every instance the most striking feature of the distributions of aptitudes for the people making the various choices was their overlap." And, as a result of a massive actuarial study examining the traits of 10,000 men and the careers in which they were found a decade or so later, Thorndike and Hagen (1959, p. 350) wrote: "We should view the long-range prediction of occupational success by aptitude tests with a good deal of skepticism and take a very restrained view as to how much can be accomplished." The point seems to be that aptitudes and other predictors of occupational success are important, but so are other manifestations of personality such as values, energy levels, perseverance, and so on.

If one were to subscribe to the trait-and-factor approach as the sole description of vocational development and decision-making, one would have to assume that people have a much greater degree of self-insight than most seem to have — self-insight not simply of the measurable aspects of the self but of the self as a wholly functioning organism, and the relationships between self and the personally important components of the options among which one can choose (Hilton, 1962). In addition, if one considers the counselor as the major source of information about self-characteristics and occupational factors, one must face the possibility that the counselee is accepting such information on the basis of faith in an authority figure. Consequently, choices made are not affirmations of identity developed from insights into self-characteristics and a personal view of the world. Rather, they are made because it is expedient to assume that the person will find success in an occupation on the basis of statistical findings that he or she fits into certain occupational populations.

As indicated previously, trait-and-factor approaches maintain that choice is primarily conscious and cognitive. Such a premise seems more hopeful than valid as succeeding approaches to career development in this chapter will demonstrate. Choice occurs not only as a function of relating an individual's traits to the characteristics of alternatives but also as a function of complex interaction between the person's developmental history and environment. In fact, the richness or impoverishment of the reservoir of experience, the accuracy and relevance of the information possessed, the distortion in appraisal of self-characteristics or possibilities of reaching aspirations, the scope and nature of the self-concept system, as well as many other combinations of factors, also enter into choice, frequently making it more psychological than logical.

Before leaving trait-and-factor approaches, we will review selected research that discusses the interrelationships or the interaction between specific traits and different criteria usually associated with occupational and educational choice. The studies cited are by no means exhaustive, but they do suggest the types of predictors, criteria, and relationships used in trait-and-factor approaches.

Abilities. Briefly, it is obvious that a person's intelligence or other aptitudes play a significant part in the occupational level he or she is likely to attain, the training the person is likely to be admitted to or succeed in, and the work he or she is able to perform. Intelligence and aptitude do not relate in the same fashion to each of these pos-

sibilities. As noted earlier, intelligence and/or specific aptitudes typically correlate more highly with success in training than with success in work performance — principally because the latter is based on a wider range of expectations and criteria than is the former. There are differences between learning to do something and applying one's knowledge in a work setting in which one's work skills must be integrated with those of others, performed under rigid deadlines, or conditioned by other dimensions eliciting personality traits. The evidence continues to support the conclusion of Super and Crites (1962, p. 99): "Given intelligence above the minimum required for learning the occupation, be it executive work, teaching, packing or light assembly work, additional increments of intelligence appear to have no special effect on an individual's success in that occupation."

As proposed by several theorists considered in subsequent sections of this chapter — such as Roe and Holland — there is a relationship between ability and the levels attained within career fields. For example, Elton (1967) has reported findings regarding field (engineering) and the career role within that field (researcher, teacher, administrator, salesman, or practitioner). His data suggest that personality plays a part in the vocational choice of engineering, but ability influences the career role within a specific field. Other researchers (such as Winer, Cesari, Haase, & Bodden, 1979) have found positive relationships between cognitive complexity, an ability factor, and career maturity. It is important to acknowledge that variations in abilities occur not only between groups but also within groups. This is also true of the other traits that follow. A major point represented by the between- and within-group variation is that no one trait is the dominant influence in the forms of choice made.

Needs and Interests. Other traits relevant here are needs and vocational interests, which have been found to be closely related (Thorndike, Weiss, & Dawis, 1968). Suziedelis and Steimel (1963) also found a number of significant relationships between specific predominant needs and particular interest patterns. Correspondence between needs, vocational interests, and curricula areas was found in a study which showed that personality identifications of students (following Holland's model) were related to their initial vocational choices (Osipow, Ashby, & Wall, 1966).

This relationship between needs, occupational interests, and personality identifications has also been demonstrated when typologies other than those of Holland are used. Riesman's characterization of inner-directed and outer-directed personalities was employed by Kassarjian and Kassarjian (1965) to examine the potential relationships between these two personality types, occupational interests, and social values. It was found that inner-directed and outer-directed personalities did differ in their occupational interests, and that inner-directed persons scored higher on the theoretical and aesthetic value scales and lower on the economic, social, and political scales than their outer-directed contemporaries. Bohn (1966) has reported similar findings. Mossholder, Dewhirst, and Arvey (1981) studied differences in vocational interest and personality characteristics among 241 development and research engineers and scientists. They found that development personnel exhibited greater interest in supervisory related areas, but researchers showed a tendency toward high specialization and academic interests. Development personnel described themselves as more dominant, defensive, and achieving, yet less critical than research personnel.

It is not just typological characteristics in general that relate to occupational interests, values or achievement but specific individual characteristics within such typologies. For example, it has been found that undecided college students are more dependent than more decided students but are equal in achievement to them (Ashby, Wall, & Osipow, 1966). And, Hummel and Sprinthall (1965) found that when mental ability and social status variables are held constant, underachievers are less adaptive in ego functioning than achievers. It also seems apparent that racial, ethnic, and cultural background affects choice. For example, one study comparing the vocational interests of black and white ninth-grade students in North Carolina (Chansky, 1965) found that blacks were more interested in occupations requiring interpersonal relations whereas whites prefer thing-oriented work.

Educational and vocational interests are also related. In one study, Miller and Thomas (1966) found that an educational interest tends to be related subsequently to several vocational interests, some of which do not directly correspond to the academic area being examined. They explain that preference for being a functioning member of an occupational group does not necessarily indicate that the student will prefer the training or the courses involved for reaching that occupation. The fact that there is a close relationship between some school subjects and some occupations is obvious. Indeed, one of the major goals of career education is to assist students to clarify and act on such relationships. What has yet to be achieved is an understanding of the instrumental relationships between those subjects and specific occupations that are not directly related, particularly in terms of attitudes and other elements constituting psychological readiness.

The relative importance of interests to vocational decisions has been studied by Bordin, Nachmann, and Segal (1963). Certain occupations evidently satisfy specific needs, and these needs are related to interests (Kohlan, 1968). On these relationships, there has recently been a significant merger between the work of Strong and that of Holland, perhaps most clearly in the format and scoring of the Strong-Campbell Interest Inventory. Although the rationale and empirical base of each differs, they do identify differences in occupations similarly in regard to the interests held by people who occupy them (Campbell & Holland, 1972). With respect to career maturity, Wigington (1982) has demonstrated that high scores on the Kuder Occupational Interest Scales are significantly correlated with scores on the Career Maturity Inventory.

Melamed and Meir (1981) have also demonstrated relationships between interests, job congruity, and selection of avocational activity. Using employed persons from 21 to 65 years of age in Australia and in Israel they found (1) people tend to select leisure activities congruent with their personality patterns; (2) people in congruent occupations (as measured by personality pattern and occupational code) were vocationally satisfied and conceived their preferred activities as an extension of the type of activities they do at work; and (3) people in incongruent occupations are vocationally dissatisfied and compensate for this by selecting compensatory leisure activities, and they tend to show higher salience (importance) for their avocational activities than for their work activities.

A continuing dilemma exists concerning the part that interests play in comparison with the part that abilities play in the making of a vocational decision. For example, Holland and Nichols (1964) report that of National Merit Finalists, 50 percent changed college majors because of lack of interest, whereas only 25 percent indicated lack of aptitude as a reason. Sharf (1970) states that male students report interest as more significant than ability in vocational decision-making, although the difference is not as great as the 2:1 ratio reported by Holland and Nichols. Hughes (1972), in studying 400 men employed full-time, found that they worked at occupational levels predictable from the summation of intelligence and self-evaluation rather than from vocational interests consistent with the Holland approach. Reeves and Booth (1979) found in a study of 2429 Navy enlisted personnel assigned to training as hospital corpsman that when interest measures were added to an aptitude measure, predictive validity was increased significantly.

Stereotypes and Expectations. Expectations and stereotypes also appear to influence vocational decision-making. Information that people have regarding occupations is often indirect and stereotypic. Such stereotypes have been found to develop by the beginning of elementary school or earlier (Rosenthal & Chapman, 1980; White & Brinkerhoff, 1981) and are frequently sex-linked (Garland & Smith, 1981). As they go about making a vocational choice, they may search for environments that they perceive will meet their needs and expectations (Holland, 1963), and it seems likely that stereotypes of occupations are held by such searchers and that these are part of a foundation for vocational choice (Hollander & Parker, 1969, 1972).

It is also likely that vocational decisions are affected by the prestige or status people assign to various occupations. Typically, high school students express preference for high-status or prestige occupations, even though they cannot realistically expect to enter these occupations (Clack, 1968). Students eventually realize that abilities, interest, and skills directly affect access to and success in occupational and educational options and must be considered in choice-making.

Ott (1978) found in a sample of sixteen institutions that female engineering students differ in important respects from male engineering students. Among these differences were role expectations: men tend to be more concerned with income and financial security; women with aiding society. Also, even though the women students tended to be very high achievers and hard workers who participated in a wide variety of high school activities, they tended to have lower expectations for performance in college than men.

Significant Others. If educational interests and vocational interests are related, one can assume that adults, parents, and others have an influence on youth and young adults through identification, support, and encouragement of occupational preferences. Day (1966) found that:

1. Some students do choose teachers as vocational models.
2. Teachers also exert influence on the vocational plans of many students whether or not they are vocational models.
3. Boys are significantly more influenced by teachers than are girls.
4. Teacher influence is generally proportional to the amount of formal training required for an occupation.

That the influence of teachers and counselors on students' vocational plans, interests, values, preferences, and choices is not more persuasive may be partially explained by Watley's findings (1966), that these adults are selective in the students they advise, encourage, or otherwise influence toward certain occupations and, one can speculate, toward any occupation.

Values. There is considerable evidence that what an individual values both in work itself and in the rewards that work is perceived as offering affects vocational decisions and is internalized fairly easily in development (Super, 1962; Thompson, 1966; Hales & Fenner, 1972; Perrone, 1973; Drummond, McIntire, & Skaggs, 1978). Values, however, cannot be viewed in isolation. The values a person holds are the products of upbringing, environment, education, and a host of other variables (Hershenson, 1967). For example, although there are distinctive differences in the occupational value structure of parents and their offspring, there is greater similarity between values of daughter and mother than between those of father and son (Wagman, 1968).

Another complicating factor with regard to values and vocational choice is cause-effect. Do values determine career choice, or does career choice determine values? Underhill's research (1966) suggests that careers vary substantially in this relationship. For example, in the humanities, in education, and in law, values appear stronger; whereas in medicine, engineering, physical sciences, and business, the career choice predominates. Whatever the cause-effect or lack of it, it is clear that occupational groups can be differentiated by discriminant analysis in terms of the values and personalities of their membership (Irvin, 1968). Some research also suggests that the patterning of work values is positively related to the vocational maturity of persons and to academic success (Knapp & Michael, 1980). Thus, vocational maturation for both males and females involves the development of differentiated work values (Miller, 1974). Jurgensen (1978), over a thirty-year period, ranked the importance of ten factors that make a job good or bad as perceived by some 57,000 applicants for jobs in a public utility. He found the order for men to be security, advancement, type of work, company, pay, co-workers, supervisors, benefits, hours, and working conditions. Women considered type of work more important than any other factor, followed by company, security, co-workers, advancement, supervisor, pay, working conditions, hours and benefits. The interesting finding was that changes in these rankings over thirty years were almost inconsequential. Other research suggests that work values are independent of job knowledge. Therefore, it cannot be assumed that being clear about one's work values also means having enough job knowledge to make realistic choices. It would seem then that work values and job knowledge need to be addressed separately in the career counseling process (Sampson & Loesch, 1981).

Residence. Evidently, the size of the community from which an individual comes is related to the

type of vocational choice made. For instance, in one study involving almost 10,000 high school seniors, the proportion choosing high-status occupations increased as the size of the community increased. When sex, intelligence, and socioeconomic status were controlled, differences in occupational choice by community were eliminated for girls but maintained for boys (Sewell & Orenstein, 1965). In general, then, youth reared on farms, in rural, nonfarm areas, or in small cities aspired to lower-prestige and lower-paid occupations than did youth raised in larger communities. "As the population density of an area increases, aspiration levels and occupational attainment tend to rise" (p. 555).

Family. Family influences, including childrearing patterns and socioeconomic level, also appear to have an effect on occupational choice and on career maturity. Indeed, Levine (1976) has suggested that the influence of social and economic origins on later life is so well documented that it could almost be considered axiomatic. Some representative studies of such phenomena follow. Basow and Howe (1979) examined the influences of various models on the careers of 300 randomly chosen college seniors. They found that parents were the most influential models, and nonparent, nonteacher adults were the least influential. They also found that females were significantly more affected by female models than were males.

Using almost 80,000 college freshmen, Werts (1968) compared fathers' occupations with sons' career choices. His results suggest that certain groups of occupations, such as physical sciences, social sciences, and medicine, are inherited. Although we can only guess why there is an association between a father's occupation and his son's career choice, this relationship apparently does exist. In some cases, the obverse may hold true — that is, fear of parental competition, generally irrational and unconscious, may affect occupational choice (Malnig, 1967). Hollander's (1972) studies of male high school and college students found that maternal influences on vocational interests are stronger in high school and paternal influences stronger in college years. Oliver's research (1975) indicated that a girl's father is more important than her mother in determining the degree of her career commitment as a collegiate undergraduate.

Oliver concluded that antecedent family variables influence the development of motivational patterns that are associated with career and home-making orientation in college women. Smith's findings (1980) showed that whether the mother worked was a major influence on high school girls' orientation toward the role of housewife versus paid employee. Anderson (1980) found that high school seniors used the educational achievement of their same-sexed parent as a primary factor in setting their educational goals. In general such a process served to lower the educational goals of the females in the sample.

Roe's theory of vocational choice, described later in this chapter, rests on the hypothesis that child-rearing processes determine subsequent vocational choices. Medvene (1973) found that the long-term developmental effects of parental avoidance, concentration, and acceptance are important to both emotional-social and educational-vocational clients who come to college counseling centers. An individual's nurture may thus be more important than nature in ultimate occupational choice.

Family factors may also influence whether an individual has or has not made an occupational choice. In the Career Pattern Study, apparently those individuals followed up at age 25 who had made a choice were more accepting of a father or a father substitute than those who had not made a choice (Marr, 1965), although the choice was not found to be related to parents' occupational level. In a study of sixth graders, Creason and Schilson (1970) found that children generally express occupational preferences higher than their fathers' occupational levels.

Finally, family socioeconomic status is related to career choice. In one study, middle-class white boys and lower-class black girls expressed greater preference for white-collar and professional occupations than did lower-class black boys or middle-class white girls (Clark, 1967). However, in this instance, the race variable tends to complicate class differences. Another study (Omvig & Thomas 1974) comparing higher and lower socioeconomic males and females indicates that established norms are of little value in interpreting vocational interest results to inner-city disadvantaged students, especially males. Socioeconomic differences are associated with differences in information about

work, work experience, and occupational stereotypes, which, in turn, affect vocational interests. Dillard's study (1976) of black youth concludes that socialization or vocationalization processes, significantly influenced by the family, rather than ability differences in reading achievement accounts for career maturity differences in this sample. MacKay and Miller (1982) found that elementary school children from middle and upper socioeconomic backgrounds choose white-collar and professional occupations as goals more often than children from lower socioeconomic backgrounds; that these attitudes are firmly established by the time a child is in grade 3; and that there is a positive relationship between socioeconomic level and complexity of data manipulation in occupational choices.

Adjustment. General psychological adjustment also affects vocational choice. The career development pattern of emotionally disturbed students is not so smooth as that of well-adjusted students (Osipow & Gold, 1967), and usually such students tend to have artistic, musical, and literary interests (Sternberg, 1956; Drasgow & Carkhuff, 1964). Schaffer (1976) studied the work histories of male psychiatric patients. The results indicate that the more severe the maladjustment, the less likely the men were to have been employed above the semiskilled level, and that there was a direct relationship between severity of disorder and unemployment time. In addition, job satisfaction and success were found to vary as a function of the personality characteristics of the different diagnostic groups.

In one study, Crites and Semler (1967) followed up 483 fifth graders when they were in the twelfth grade. The results indicate that fifth grade adjustment is related not only to later adjustment and educational achievement but also to vocational maturity. Thus, general adjustment does appear to be related to vocational adjustment. Heath's research (1976) has shown that psychological maturity, whether measured in adolescence or adulthood, very consistently predicted vocational adaptation.

Perhaps it is best not to force vocational exploration and decision-making for maladjusted individuals but to wait for the appropriate time. Berdie (1968) suggests that considerable change occurs in the personality of typical students from grades nine through twelve and that a college freshman is somewhat better adjusted personally than he or she was as a high school freshman. There is also evidence (Hollender, 1967) that vocational choices become more realistic with advancing age. Hence, especially in the case of the maladjusted individual, delay in vocational decision-making may be desirable.

Risk-Taking. Another personality variable that seems to be related to vocational choice is risk-taking. Early work by Ziller (1957) found that there was a significant relationship between vocational choice and a propensity for risk-taking. Subsequent studies (Burnstein, 1963; Mahone, 1960; and Morris, 1966) also found evidence that risk-taking plays a part in vocational decision-making. However, a large-scale study by Slakter and Cramer (1969) has demonstrated that although there is some evidence that risk-taking is related to vocational choice, the current measures of risk-taking are too crude to capitalize on this relationship. Witmer and Stewart (1972) have reported findings that show preference for taking risks reflects a general life style. Thus, the high-risk person's openness to new experiences and that person's rejection of tradition may indicate self-confidence in dealing adequately with life contingencies.

All that can be said at this time is that a relationship between risk-taking and vocational choice does seem to exist, but we do not know as yet the extent or understand the dynamics involved.

Aspirations. Level of aspiration appears to contribute to vocational choice. At least in males, level of aspiration seems relatively constant during secondary schooling (Flores & Olsen, 1967). Level of aspiration is also frequently related to level of self-esteem, with persons of higher aspiration also persons of higher self-esteem (Prager & Freeman, 1979). Level of aspiration usually affects curriculum choice and hence vocational choice. It would appear that typical eighth- or ninth-grade boys are, therefore, ready to make such choices. These findings about aspiration have been extended in a national sample of young men and women between the ages of 14 and 24, showing that the category of a person's earlier job (using

Holland's classification) forecasts the category of later jobs, and that there is significant agreement between a person's current occupation and vocational aspiration (Nafziger, Holland, Helms, & McPartland, 1974). It also has been found that aspirations, expectations, and vocational maturity are related in graduate students and rehabilitation clients. Thus, whether one's expectations are similar to one's aspirations appears to depend on past success-failure experiences, education, and consequent vocational maturity (Walls & Gulkus, 1974). When vocational aspirations and job opportunities as determinants of later jobs held are studied, it is found that men more often achieve congruence between their aspiration and their field of employment by changing aspirations to match the job field rather than the other way around and that early jobs are more predictive of later field of work than are early aspirations (Gottfredson & Becker, 1981).

Summary of Traits and Factors

Although the above analysis is not exhaustive, it is clear that a great many variables enter into career decision-making: work values, occupational stereotypes and expectations, residence, family socioeconomic status and child-rearing practices, general adjustment, personality factors including needs and propensity for risk-taking, educational achievement, level of aspiration, and gender. Each of these is influenced by and overlaps with the others. They are in dynamic interrelationship. The preponderance of one or more variables in vocational decision-making depends heavily on the individual making the choice. Some individuals are more influenced by certain factors than others (Healy, 1968). A major characteristic of trait-and-factor approaches is that they describe relationships between variables and choices, but they do not explain how such variables develop. We must turn elsewhere for such insights.

DECISION THEORY

Increasingly apparent in the professional literature are attempts to theorize about educational and occupational choice through the use of decision models. The major factor that differentiates these models from others reviewed in this chapter is their primary emphasis on the *process of decision-making*. For purposes of this section, a variety of approaches with diverse conceptual roots are reviewed, such as cognitive, economic, mathematical, social learning.

In historical terms, decision-making models are economic in origin. A fundamental assumption in many of these approaches, based on Keynesian economic theory, is that one chooses a career goal or an occupation that will maximize gain and minimize loss. The gain or loss is, of course, not necessarily money but anything of value to the individual. A given occupation or career pathway might be considered as a means of achieving certain possibilities — for example, greater prestige, security, social mobility, or a spouse — when compared to another course of action. Implicit in such an approach is the expectation that the individual can be assisted to predict the outcomes of each alternative and the probability of such outcomes. The person will then choose the one that promises the most reward for his or her investment (such as time, tuition, union dues, delayed gratification) with the least probability of failure.

More specifically, a major notion in decision theory is that an individual has several alternatives or courses of action. In each of them, certain events can occur. Each event has a value for the individual, a value that can be estimated through some method of psychological scaling. Also, for each event a probability of its occurrence can be estimated through actuarial prediction. If, for each course of action, the value of each event is multiplied by its probability and these products are summed, the sound choice from this point of view would be the alternative in which the sum of the expected "values" is the greatest (Hills, 1964). Such a perspective has led to the use of decision trees, flow charts, and game trees to describe the decision-making process. The different paradigms explaining decision theory provide counselors with models, graphs, and concepts that help them to discuss the process of decision-making directly with their clients. As such, the paradigms provide cognitive maps of the decision-making process itself as well as how different variables or behaviors affect the process.

Expectancy Theory

In one major conceptual form, decision theory is frequently expressed in mathematical terms as an expectancy x value theory of motivation (Raynor & Entin, 1982) or as expectancy/valence theory (Vroom, 1964; Lawler, 1973). For more than fifty years, many investigators have used the concepts embedded in these approaches to understand relationships among variables in a dynamic state as they affect individual behavior or as they have attempted to understand the relationship among inputs to choice or work motivation more generally. As a cognitive theory of motivation, individuals are viewed as rational persons who have beliefs and anticipations about future events in their lives. Steers and Porter (1975) summarize the theory in the following way: "It argues that motivational force to perform — or effort — is a multiplicative function of the expectancies, or beliefs, that individuals have concerning future outcomes times the value they place on those outcomes." Vroom (1964) uses the term valence to refer to affective orientations, positive or negative, toward outcomes, but distinguishes these preferences (valences) from the actual satisfaction they offer (their value). In general, it is assumed that means acquire valence as a consequence of their expected relationship to ends. But, in this view, positive valence, particularly in the face of uncertain outcomes, is not sufficient to motivate choice or action. It must be combined with expectancy, the degree to which the individual believes that preferred outcomes can be attained (are probable). Finally, it is assumed that people choose from among alternative acts the one that has the strongest positive or weakest negative force (value) and the most likelihood of occurring.

Lawler (1973), in a very similar approach to that of Vroom, also uses the terms valence and expectancy to explain individual action. He suggests that all of the theorists using such a framework maintain that the tendency to act in a certain way depends on the expectancy that the act will be followed by a given consequence (or outcome) and on the value or attractiveness of that consequence (or outcome) to the actor. Lawler (1973) continues this line of thinking by distinguishing two types of expectancies about which people are concerned $(E \to P)$ and $(P \to O)$. The first, effort $\to$ performance, has to do with the person's estimate of the probability that he or she can accomplish the intended performance (such as perform the tasks required, meet a deadline) in the particular situation. The second, performance $\to$ outcomes, has to do with subjective probability estimates that if a particular performance is achieved it will lead to certain outcomes (a pay raise, promotion, some other reward). In extending Vroom's position, Lawlor argues that motivation or choice is a function of both the attractiveness of outcomes, the valence, and the two expectancies cited: that one can do what needs to be done and if one is able to do so, the probability that a desired outcome will result. An additionally useful characteristic of Lawlor's view is his analysis of how people achieve perceptions of $E \to P$, their ability to perform. Among others he cites communications from other people, learning, personality factors, self-esteem, and past experiences in similar situations as influencing one's perceptions about the ability to perform as required in a particular situation.

The most recent extension of expectancy x valence notions has been used by Raynor and Entin (1982) as the basis for a general theory of personality, motivation, and action. The basic hypothesis of the theory is:

> When doing well *now* is seen by the person as a necessary prerequisite for earning the opportunity to try for later success (termed a contingent path), individual differences in achievement-related motives (the motives to achieve success and to avoid failure, M_S and M_{AF}, respectively) are accentuated and become apparent in action, so that success-oriented individuals $(M_S > M_{AF})$ are more motivated to do well but failure-threatened individuals $(M_{AF} > M_S)$ are more inhibited by the prospect of failure, as compared to when immediate activity has no such future implications (termed a noncontingent path) (p. 3).

Raynor and Entin integrate these concepts and others with theory concerning self-identity, self-image, self-evaluation, and self-esteem. In oversimplified form, they found that earning the opportunity to continue along a contingent path

was important for self-evaluation because attainment of the future goal that was contingent on immediate success is anticipated to provide feelings of self-worth.

Wheeler and Mahoney (1981) in applying an expectancy model to occupational preference and occupational choice reinforce the fact that economic and psychological models have not tended to distinguish between occupational preference, occupations to which people are attracted, and occupational choice, the occupations persons actually choose to enter. The former is a function of valence as it was discussed in the previous section; the latter is a function of the attraction to an occupation, the expectancy of entering an occupation, and the costs of preparing for an occupation. Applying such a model to the preferences and the choices of ninety-eight business and thirty psychology students, they found strong support for the distinction between the two concepts. Occupational preference was a function of pure attraction. Choice involved a compromise among attraction, expectancy of attaining an occupation, and expected costs. They also found that this process is likely to differ for various groups since different groups are more strongly influenced by economic cost-benefit analysis and other groups are primarily influenced by the attractiveness of the occupation regardless of how much it costs to attain that occupation.

Self-Efficacy Theory

Although a social learning theory of career development as proposed by Krumboltz et al. (1975, 1979) will be discussed later in this chapter, it has an application that parallels what has just been described as expectancy theory. Bandura (1977) has proposed a view of behavior change that he has called self-efficacy. Bandura contends that behavior changes and therefore decisions made are mediated by expectations of self-efficacy: expectations or beliefs that one can perform a given behavior. The theory states that the level and strength of self-efficacy will determine (1) whether or not a coping behavior will be initiated, (2) how much effort will result, and (3) how long the effort will be sustained in the face of obstacles. This model proposes four principal sources from which expectations of self-efficacy are derived: performance accomplishments, vicarious experience, verbal persuasion, and emotional arousal. As does Lawlor, previously cited in expectancy theory, Bandura also distinguishes between an outcome expectancy and an efficacy expectancy. An outcome expectancy refers to the person's estimate that a given behavior will lead to particular outcomes. An efficacy expectation is an estimate that one can successfully execute the behavior required to produce the outcomes sought. Efficacy expectations vary on such dimensions as magnitude, generality, and strength.

According to Bandura (1977) self-efficacy appears to be able to be increased and strengthened as a result of various types of treatments, but several general concepts are important to the understanding of the theory. First, people cognitively process information differently. Depending on how they judge the many factors bearing on their performance, they will vary in their perceptions of self-efficacy. Second, people have many different types and amounts of efficacy-relevant experiences. Providing one new source of efficacy information will not necessarily affect the overall level of self-efficacy. However, preliminary research data (Bandura, 1977; Bandura, Adams, & Meyer, 1977) suggest that with understanding of the concept of self-efficacy, the sources from which it is derived, and its potential effect on vocational behavior, intervention procedures can be devised to increase individual levels of self-efficacy.

In direct and indirect ways the concepts and the language of both expectancy theory and self-efficacy theory permeate many of the career guidance interventions designed to facilitate the decision-making process. The observant reader will note such relationships in many of the approaches that follow.

Decision-Making Paradigms

Many paradigms describing the decision-making process have evolved from earlier conceptions of problem-solving or scientific analysis. Pitz and Harren (1980), for example, have indicated that any decision problem can be described in terms of four elements:

1. the set of *objectives* that the decision-maker seeks to achieve

2. the set of *choices*, or alternative courses of action, among which the decision-maker must choose
3. a set of possible *outcomes* that is associated with each choice
4. the ways each outcome might be assessed with respect to how well it meets the decision-maker's objectives, the *attributes* of each outcome (pp. 321–322).

In turn, a typical view of the sequence of events in decision-making might include the following steps:

- defining the problem
- generating alternatives
- gathering information
- processing information
- making plans and selecting goals
- implementing and evaluating plans (Bergland, 1974)

Clarke, Gelatt, and Levine (1965) would suggest a somewhat different labeling of the decision-making paradigm which has implications for the information required by the person doing the choosing. In paraphrased form, the stages are as follows:

Information about alternative actions – Before deciding what to do, a person needs to know what alternative courses of action are possible.

Information about possible outcomes – The person needs to know to what results the alternative actions available are likely to lead.

Information about probabilities linking actions to outcomes – How likely are alternative actions to lead to different outcomes? What are the probabilities – high, medium, low – of certain results occurring from different actions?

Information about preferences for the various outcomes – The person needs to consider the values he or she wishes to apply to different outcomes.

Together these emphases in decision-making suggest that the individual needs both a prediction system and a value system to make decisions among preferences and expectancies for action within a climate of uncertainty. Gelatt (1962), as a result of synthesizing Bross's model of statistical decisions (1953) as well as the analysis of decision sequences reported by Cronbach and Glaser (1957), proposed a decision-making framework in which information is the "fuel" of the decision-maker and actions taken may be terminal (final) or investigatory (that is, instrumental in both acquiring and requiring more information). Within this framework, Gelatt contended that there are essentially three elements of the decision-making process, each of which requires different information. Figure 4.1 summarizes this point.

The Gelatt perspective emphasizes the need for accurate and complete information in each of the systems necessary to a choice of and values about a particular situation, and it implies that risks vary among outcomes of possible actions. In one sense, the better the information a decision-maker has, the clearer are the risks that the person takes in implementing different actions. The risks are not necessarily reduced, but it is assumed that knowing them provides the chooser a more rational basis for deciding what magnitude of risk is worth taking or whether the probabilities of a pay-off occurring for the risk involved are too low. Obviously, the degree of risk one is willing to take varies among persons and leads to different choice-making styles — some people are highly aggressive, others quite cautious, still others are in between these bipolar reference points. Jepsen (1974) has reported research showing that individual differences in decision-making can be classified in terms of strategy types in adolescents. He clustered groups of adolescent decision-makers into twelve types based on how they organized data about themselves and career options. These clusters reflect differences in planning activity.

Examples of three of the twelve types will illustrate Jepsen's view of individual differences in this area:

Strategy-type 3. Sought little career information and viewed current actions as relevant to planning. Considered only a few occupational alternatives and few reasons for considering either occupations or post-high school actions. Few outcomes were anticipated for preferred post-high school activity.

Strategy-type 6. Named many alternative occupations and post-high school activities and reasons for each. Many possible outcomes were anticipated, many intrinsic and self-appraised reasons were given. Planning activity was very high.

Strategy-type 9. Very few actions were taken on plans and little information was sought. Vaguely stated and low-level occupational alternatives were reported, and a single class of reasons was given for considering them.

A similar point can be made relative to the valuing of outcomes likely from different actions. Each person clearly or vaguely applies a scale of values important to him or her to each available alternative in a decision. The strength of the values in relation to the probability of the outcome actually occurring is seen by some observers as the crux of the decision process (Katz, 1963, 1966, 1969). Katz (1966) has suggested, in a model of guidance for career decision-making, that an index of "investment" be developed to represent the substance of what an individual risks

Figure 4.1

A Graphic Conception of the Gelatt Model

	Information Necessary
Predictive System	Alternative actions
	Possible outcomes of actions
	Probabilities of outcomes of actions
Value System	Relative preferences among probable outcomes
Decision System	Evaluation of priorities or rules

or loses in preparing for or electing any career option. This assumes that the person can be helped to determine the "odds," the chances of success in entering or attaining some alternative. More importantly, however, it means that knowing the odds is sufficient for decision-making. As Katz has indicated, persons must also assess the importance of success to themselves in each option or the seriousness of failure. To make such assessments immediately places one's decisions in a value domain. Thus, decision-making includes the identifying and the defining of one's values: what they are and what they are not, where they appear and where they do not appear.

Another way of conceiving the application of decision theory to choice is seen in the approach of Kalder and Zytowski (1969). In this model, the elements consist of inputs (such as personal resources, intellectual and physical characteristics, time, capital), alternatives (possible actions at a choice point), and outputs (the probable consequences of various actions). Again one undergoes a process of scaling what one has to give up to get various outcomes and how probable such occurrences are. The chosen alternative is assumed to be the one that offers the highest net value — the best value available when input costs and output costs are balanced. Implicit in such a model is the assumption that the decision-maker has sufficient information about personal characteristics and the alternatives available to rank the values, utilities, and sacrifices associated with each possible action.

Other theorists and researchers have considered some of the specific aspects of the decision models as proposed by Gelatt, Katz, Kalder and Zytowski. For example, within the valuation of alternatives, Tillinghast (1964) contends that planning and deciding by the counselor and the counselee inevitably include some combination of choices concerned with (1) the probable, (2) the possible, and 3) the desirable. Concern with *the probable* focuses on alternatives stressing security, stability, and safety — for example, jobs likely to remain relatively unaffected by the changing times, colleges with admission requirements safely within the demonstrated scholastic ability of the counselee, and emotional and social expressions of the counselee that are safely within the boundary of "socially sanctioned utterances."

A choice orientation toward *the possible* holds that the rewards of success are more important than the consequences of failure; thus danger, erratic and vague influences, excitement, and unpredictable events are not things to be avoided in trying to maximize security. In this context, the counselor is concerned with what the individual might be, rather than what that individual easily can be or is and emphasizes widening the counselee's perceptual field with respect to choices and plans.

Alternatives emphasizing *the desirable* are not what could be or even what might be, but rather what must be or should be. This choice orientation gives little attention to statistical reality as it now exists in situations or as it might be reasonably projected. Tillinghast suggests that counselees of this orientation are likely to be described as dedicated, single-minded, or even unrealistic, but he maintains on their behalf that to consider only those courses of action in which the odds for success are 90 out of 100 (the probable), is to deny a large portion of life's potential.

Some decision theorists (Davidson, Suppes, and Siegel, 1957) describe the process of making a decision between uncertain outcomes as requiring reconciliation of several general factors: the relative valuing of the outcomes, the cost of attaining the outcomes, and the probability that each outcome may occur. This approach, similar to what Hilton (1962) has labeled "probable gain," and essentially what Kalder and Zytowski describe as sacrifices associated with various inputs, includes the dimension of investment. It suggests that within any choice or decision, the individual must assess personal resources and how much of them, tangible or psychological, he or she wants to commit to a particular alternative in such a manner as to maximize gain and minimize loss. Garbin (1967, p. 17) has stated in this regard, "A vital facet of the decision-making process involves a consideration of the requirements, rewards, and duties inherent in the several available alternatives at the point of choice as balanced with considerations of personal capacities, interests, and values."

Brayfield (Brayfield & Crites, 1964) has stressed the importance of considering choice as occurring under conditions of uncertainty or risk. According to him, the individual assigns a reward value (utility) to alternative choices and appraises the chances of being able to realize each of them (subjective probability). As a result, the person will attempt to maximize the expected value in making a decision. Thoreson and Mehrens (1967, p. 167) have also addressed this point. They state, "Objective probabilities are not directly involved in the decision-making process, but are only involved insofar as they are related to subjective probabilities. The question that arises is the extent to which certain information (objective probability data) actually influences what the person thinks are his chances (subjective probability) of an outcome occurring."

Similarly, Blau, Gustad, Jessor, Parnes, and Wilcock (1956, p. 533) contend, "A choice between various possible courses of action can be conceptualized as motivated by two interrelated sets of factors: the individual's valuation of different alternatives and his appraisal of his chances of being able to realize each of the alternatives."

Although formal decision theory conceives of decision-making as (1) a process, (2) having an essentially rational base, and (3) involving the selection of a single alternative at a particular point in time (Costello & Zalkind, 1963), the influence of individual subjectivity in interpreting information about oneself and about various options gives substantial credence to Hansen's (1964–1965) position, that decisions are frequently more psychological than logical. Every counselor must keep the possibility of personally introduced bias in information constantly in mind, as clients are assisted to determine what sorts of information they need and what the acquired information means. Rather than assuming that the client will process information rationally and comprehend its full implications instead of filtering it through a personal set of incomplete or stereotyped images, the counselor must be directly involved in ensuring that the client considers pertinent information with as much objectivity as is possible.

Another approach to occupational decision-making is based on principles of learning theory. Miller (1968, p. 18) has proposed that a vocational decision is "any behavior that consistently and significantly relates to eventual participation in an occupation." He argues that there are four categories of decision behavior: overt physical activities, overt verbal statements, covert emotional or physiological changes, and covert verbal

responses or thoughts. According to him, any learning theory of vocational decision-making should involve accurate prediction, explanation, and control of vocational decision behaviors. In order to achieve this — prediction, explanation, and control — the learning theorists must first identify those behaviors which constitute the decision. Once this task is accomplished, the environmental stimuli pertaining to the decision would have to be isolated. These stimuli might include positive and negative reinforcers, general learning principles of classical and instrumental conditioning, stimulus-response sequences, convergences and divergences, and other principles of learning. The primary requirement for a learning theory model of vocational decision-making is a relatively complete set of information about an individual's past history. In summary, Miller (1968) states:

> In order to predict decision behaviors the learning theorist would want to know for an individual the discriminative stimuli that control his overt and covert responses, the relative strengths of his learned and unlearned motives along with effective reinforcers, and the strengths, composition, and relations among S-R mechanisms. Given such information the learning theorist would expect to be able to predict all kinds and combinations of decision behaviors with an extremely high degree of accuracy (p. 22).

An application of learning theory principles to vocational decision-making is offered by Krumboltz and his colleagues (Krumboltz & Thoresen, 1964; Krumboltz & Schroeder, 1965). In this series of studies, students were encouraged to seek occupational information by means of behavioral counseling methods, which, of course, are based on social learning principles. If information-seeking behavior can be considered an aspect of decision-making, then the Krumboltz et al. experiments indicate clearly that vocational decision-making, by means of the applications of principles of learning theory, can be broadened to include a wide range of behavior.

More recently, Krumboltz, Mitchell, and Gelatt (1975, pp. 4–8) and Krumboltz, Mitchell, and Jones (1979) have proposed a social learning theory of career selection. They indicate that although "real life is always more complicated than our theories," it is possible to call attention to the events most influential in determining career selections. In particular, they point to the following four categories of influencers:

1. Genetic endowment and special abilities (such as race, sex, physical appearance and characteristics, intelligence, musical ability, artistic ability, muscular coordination).

2. Environmental conditions and events (such as number and nature of job and training opportunities, social policies and procedures for selecting trainees and workers, neighborhood and community influences, rate of return for various occupations, technological developments, labor laws and union rules, changes in social organizations, physical events (earthquakes, floods), family characteristics, community and neighborhood emphases).

3. Learning experiences such as *Instrumental Learning Experiences* (ILEs), in which antecedents, covert and overt behavioral responses, and consequences are present. Skills necessary for career planning and other occupational and educational performances are learned through successive instrumental learning experiences. *Associative Learning Experiences* (ALEs) in which the learner pairs a previously neutral situation with some emotionally positive or negative reaction, observational learning and classical conditioning are examples).

4. Task approach skills (such as problem-solving skills, work habits, mental set, emotional responses, cognitive processes that both influence outcomes and are outcomes themselves).

These four types of influences and their interactions lead to several types of outcomes:

1. Self-observation generalizations (SOGs) — overt or covert statements evaluating one's own actual or vicarious performance in relation to learned standards.

2. Task approach skills (TASs) — cognitive and performance abilities and emotional predispositions for coping with the environment, interpreting it in relation to self-observation generalizations, and making covert or overt predictions about future events. With relation to career decision-making specifically, might include such skills as value-clarifying, goal-setting, alternative-generating, information-seeking, estimating, planning.

3. Actions — entry behaviors that indicate overt steps in career progression (such as applying for a specific job or training opportunity, changing a college major).

The Krumboltz, Mitchell, and Gelatt model accents the instrumentality of learning experiences in producing preferences for activities as well as task approach skills. Krumboltz, Mitchell, and Gelatt (1976) state, "It is the sequential cumulative effects of numerous learning experiences affected by various environmental circumstances and the individual's cognitive and emotional reactions to these learning experiences and circumstances that cause a person to make decisions to enroll in a certain educational program or become employed in a particular occupation" (p. 75). Within a decision theory frame of reference, then, this model suggests that becoming a particular kind of worker or student is not a simple function of preference or choice but "is influenced by complex environmental (e.g., economic) factors, many of which are beyond the control of any single individual." These factors can be learned by the individual, and career decision-making skills can be systematically acquired. Both the studies of Ware (1980) of the effects of social learning on the acquisition of career-related preferences among college students and Weiss (1978) on the social learning of work values in organizations show preliminary support for a social learning theory of career development.

A final approach still within the general domain of decision theory — with particular relevance to the outcomes of premature choosing and the resulting restrictions on full career development — is what has been called complex information processing (Hilton, 1962). The advocates of this approach contend, "The reduction of dissonance among a person's beliefs about himself and his environments is the major motivation of career decision-making." Although James (1963) has recommended that Hilton substitute "conflict" for "dissonance," the roots of this approach are Festinger's (1957) early theory of cognitive dissonance. That theory, here grossly oversimplified for purposes of space, indicates that the magnitude of information and the number of factors to be considered in decision-making are so great that the individual chooses prematurely, without fully considering the implications of the choice, in order to reduce the besieging pressures as the torrents of information relevant to the choice are sorted out. The person then reinforces the choice by rationalization: selective attention to those data making the choice appear satisfying to self and to external observers. Although the chooser "knows" there are other options and better ones, particularly over the longer range, it is comforting to make a selection and suppress the costs of its unrealism by a variety of self-deceptive devices. Such a process is not unlike what happens when one is "bitten by the new car bug." Suddenly, the tires on the old car seem balder, there exist previously unheard noises in the engine, the newspaper seems to be full of warnings that in another year new car prices will escalate dramatically, and so on. Such selective perceptions help to reduce the dissonance in the choice. Career choices are also rationalized through a similar process.

SITUATIONAL OR SOCIOLOGICAL EMPHASES

Both rigid adherence to a particular set of educational or occupational goals and floundering in decision-making, vocationalization, or career development, stem from situational circumstances, the social structure of which one is a part. This is due both to limited avenues through which one can implement choice and from limited knowledge of available opportunities. Beyond such matters, however, the social structure represents the context in which each person negotiates his or her identity, belief systems and life course.

Watts et al. (1981), in comparing the evolution of career development theory in Britain with that of the United States, has suggested:

It is intriguing that theories of career development in the USA have been so heavily dominated by psychologists whereas in Britain the contributions of sociologists have been much more prominent. The dominant focus in the USA has been on the actions of individuals, while in Britain indigenous theoretical work has been more preoccupied with the constraints of social structures. . . . The failure of the American social-structural evidence to have much influence on career development theory seems to be due basically to cultural and his-

torical factors. From the beginning of its independent existence, the USA has been formally committed to the proposition that all men are created equal. . . . As a result, there is belief that the individual controls his own destiny; that if he has appropriate abilities, and if these can be appropriately developed, his fate lies in his own hands (p. 3).

The observations of Watts are very helpful in capturing the essence of situational or sociological perspectives on career development. Such approaches remind us that decision-making, the development of self-identity, and life chances do not occur in a vacuum. They occur within political, economic, and social conditions that influence the achievement images and belief systems on which individuals base their actions. They occur as person-environment interactions (Super, 1957).

Person-Environment Interactions

Hollingshead (1949), Warner, Melker, and Eells (1949), and Hoggart (1957) among others have reported on the effects of social class on occupations chosen and on other aspects of work identity and career. In the first section of this chapter, family effects were identified as important predictors of occupational choice and of work adjustment. Although not the only important mediator of social class or social status in children, family characteristics represent the seedbed for differences in the socialization, or vocationalization, of the young across social classes.

Many propositions have been advanced to explain situational effects on career development. For example, Caplow (1954), Miller and Form (1951), and most recently Bandura (1982) have discussed the accident theory of vocational choice or development, which stresses chance as a determinant of personal opportunities for choice.

Chance Encounters: In the most recent exposition of such a view, Bandura's, the central thesis is that chance encounters play a prominent role in shaping the course of human lives. For his purposes, "A chance encounter is defined as an unintended meeting of persons unfamiliar to each other. . . . Human encounters involve degrees of fortuitiveness. People often intentionally seek certain types of experiences, but the persons who thereby enter their lives are determined by a large element of chance" (1982, p. 748). Bandura also describes how fortuitous symbolic encounters mediated through another's actions profoundly affect life paths. Symbolic encounters might include hearing a particular lecture, reading a particular book, unexpectedly witnessing a particular event on television or in reality, which has such an effect on an individual that it stimulates the pursuit of a new life path. According to Bandura, some chance encounters "touch people only lightly, others leave more lasting effects, and still others branch people into new trajectories of life" (1982, p. 749). He suggests that psychology is not able to predict fortuitous occurrences, nor does it have much to say about their occurrence except that personal bents and social structures and affiliations make some types of encounters more probable than others. Here we find the particular importance of social class, family background, geographic residence, and similar contexts increasing the likelihood of some encounters and decreasing the likelihood of others.

Bandura further suggests that if psychology cannot predict the likelihood of chance encounters, it can provide the basis for predicting the nature, scope, and strength of the effect they are likely to have on human lives. He suggests that "neither personal proclivities nor situational imperatives" operate as independent shapers of the course of lives. Chance encounters affect life paths through the reciprocal influence of personal and social factors. He then outlines the personal and social factors that are likely to determine the effect of chance encounters. Table 4.2 shows these factors in paraphrased chart form from his narrative of the process.

Bandura's work to date rests primarily on observation and biographical data. It is an attempt to develop into an effective conceptual framework the psychological processes that are subsumed or activated by what is more popularly called chance or accident. In this sense, he makes the following point: "Fortuitous influences may be unforeseen, but having occurred, they enter as evident factors in causal chains in the same way as prearranged ones do" (p. 749). Bandura has not attempted to speculate about the number of people whose career development is a function of chance en-

counters or how such a view applies across occupational groups. There are other findings, however, that bear on such matters.

Preparation and Planning. Hart, Rayner, and Christensen (1971) studied the degree of preparation, planning, and chance in occupational entry among sixty men representing professional, skilled, and semiskilled occupational levels. They found that most men at the professional level entered their occupation primarily through planning and preparation. At the skilled level, some men entered their occupations through planning, whereas many others were primarily influenced by chance events. Those who entered occupations at the semiskilled level were primarily influenced by chance events. Partially based on the earlier work of Hart et al., Salomone and Slaney (1981) studied the perceived influence of chance and contingency factors on the career choices of 447 female and 470 male nonprofessional workers. In some contrast to the findings of Hart et al., Salomone and Slaney found that chance factors were much less important than were personal qualities in influencing vocational decisions. The authors conclude,

> Perhaps the "chance theory" was seen as a reasonable alternative by sociologists writing in the 1940s and 1950s but clearly, the workers of the 1970s — including nonprofessional skilled and unskilled workers — appear to assess their personal inclinations (interests and needs), their skills and abilities, and their personal and family responsibilities before making vocational choices. . . . In large measure, they perceive themselves as using rational processes to arrive at their occupational decisions (p. 34).

Culture and Social Class Boundaries. But the factors bearing on choice or development are not restricted to chance or intervening variables. The breadth of the individual's culture or social class boundaries has much to do with the choices that can be considered, made, and implemented. No more vivid an example exists than that of people raised in poverty. As Moynihan (1964) has pointed out, the circumstances in which poverty flourishes produce a distinctive milieu that conditions the social responses, educational attainment, voca-

Table 4.2
A Synthesis of Bandura's Perspectives on Factors Influencing Chance Encounters

Personal Determinants of the Effect of Chance Encounters	Social Determinants of the Effect of Chance Encounters
Entry Skills Interest, skills, personal knowledge likely to gain acceptance or sustain contact with another	*Milieu Rewards* The types of rewards and sanctions an individual or group provides if a chance encounter alters a life path
Emotional Ties Interpersonal attractiveness tending to sustain chance encounters so that certain social determinants might operate	*Symbolic Environment and Information* Images of reality provided by other than direct experience; different individuals or groups furnish different symbolic environments
Values and Personal Standards Unintended influences more likely to be important if persons involved share similar standards and value systems	*Milieu Reach and Closedness* Chance encounters with a relatively closed milieu — e.g., cults, communal groups — have the greatest potential for abrupting reordering life paths
	Psychological Closedness Belief systems provide structure, directions, and purpose in life. Once persons, through chance encounter, get caught up in the belief system of a particular group, it can exert selective influence on the course of development and erect a psychological closedness to outside influence. Beliefs channel social interactions in ways that create their own validating realities.

[handwritten annotation: BLACK PEOPLE ARE NOT WHITE PEOPLE WITH DARK (BROWN) SKIN.]

tional ambition, and general intellectual level of the overwhelming majority of those raised within it. Poor people are not just rich people without money. Their life space, possibility structures, level and types of reinforcement, models, and social resources all differ as a function of their social status. However, it is important to avoid speaking glibly about social class differences. Leacock (1968, p. 845) reminds us, "Unfortunately, lower class culture is fast becoming a new stereotype behind which the individual is not revealed more fully, but instead is lost." Nevertheless, an important factor in the career development of an individual is the effect of the culture and society on the goals one is conditioned to value. Within this context are found such elements as family income levels, social expectations, levels of social mobility, and psychological support for patterns of educational and occupational motivation.

Lipsett (1962) has argued that counselors must understand the implications of the following social factors for a particular individual as they interact with career development:

1. Social class membership — for example, occupation and income of parents, education of parents, place and type of residence, ethnic background.
2. Home influences — for example, parental goals for the individual, influence of siblings, family values and counselee's acceptance of them.
3. School — for example, scholastic achievement, relationships with peers and faculty, values of the school.
4. Community — the "thing to do in the community," group goals and values, special opportunities or influences.
5. Pressure groups — the degree to which an indi-

vidual or his or her parents have come under any particular influence that leads him or her to value one occupation over another.

6. Role perception — the individual's perception of self as a leader, follower, isolate, and so forth; the degree to which one's perception of self is in accord with the way others perceive one.

The important concern here is that the factors identified by Lipsett operate directly or indirectly in every individual's life. The degree to which they operate as determinants or constraints in development and choice, however, can be assessed only in the individual case.

Counselors must be alert to how much clients have accepted the attitudes and values held by the various aspects of their environments, have personally tested such perspectives, and whether those perspectives facilitate or restrain choice-making. The ways social class background shapes career development can be seen in the research of Gottlieb (1967). In this study, which used 1327 male adolescents (Caucasian and black) enrolled in the Job Corps as a sample, no support was found for the proposition that the lower-class culture has a built-in set of values that discourage social mobility. Rather, it appears that lower-class parents, though wanting their children to succeed, lack the abilities to help them move into more advantageous social positions and "there are few other adults in their lives who have the ability to help the youngster in both the business of goal clarification and goal attainment" (Gottlieb, 1967, p. 120).

Zito and Bardon (1968) examined a similar phenomenon in terms of achievement imagery. In particular, they attempted to determine how black adolescents in an urban area perceived the probabilities of success and failure in both school and work. They found that achievement imagery, or the need to achieve, is equally strong in black adolescents from the same urban environment, regardless of intelligence and type of program. However, they also found that school-related material tends to threaten black adolescents with failure, even though work-related material arouses fantasies of successful achievement of goals. Ogbu (1974) argues that black and Mexican-American students reduce their efforts in school tasks to the level of rewards they expect as future adults.

Stevic and Uhlig (1967) examined the concepts that youths with an Appalachian background have about their probable life's work. When comparing a group of students remaining in Appalachia with a group of students who had migrated to an Ohio city, they found that:

1. Appalachian youth who stay in the geographic area have a significantly lower aspirational level than do students who have migrated from it.
2. Youth who remain native to Appalachia have different personal role models and characteristics for success than those students who have migrated from it.
3. A major problem in raising the occupational aspirations of Appalachian students appears to be lack of information and opportunity rather than lack of ability (p. 438).

LoCascio (1967) studied continuity-discontinuity in vocational development within many different populations. He described developmental units as continuous, delayed, and impaired, according to differences in behavioral repertoires, learning, and the incorporation of learning. It appears that the career development of those labeled as disadvantaged is more likely to be delayed or impaired than that of their more fortunate contemporaries. Research by Ansell and Hansen (1971) suggests that disadvantaged high school students are slower by about two years than their middle-class counterparts in developing the ability to select a vocation. Studies by Schmeiding and Jensen (1968) of American Indian students and by Asbury (1968) of rural disadvantaged boys, similar to those previously cited studies of blacks and Appalachian youth, support LoCascio's as well as Ansell's and Hansen's conclusions.

A major study of youth unemployment has clearly shown that social class and racial differences exist in the amount of unemployment experienced by various subpopulations of youth (Adams & Mangum, 1978). Indeed, such social class differences are also apparent in the use of resources and other types of mechanisms to aid in the transition from school to work. Similar findings have been reported in another major work on the youth labor market (Osterman, 1980).

Social class factors limit career development not only among the poor and the lower classes. The expectations or demands on middle and upper-middle class youth can also be socioeconomically restrictive. Krippner (1965), in a study of the educational plans and preferences of upper-middle class junior high pupils, found that most of them were expected to attend college, and that neither pupil dislike of school nor poor achievement deterred these students from agreeing with their parents that higher education should be given high priority. He stated, "It seems incredible that nine out of ten parents, whose children are the poorest students in their class, should give their sons and daughters the impression that they are to attend college. Many of these boys and girls are working two grades below their present school placement, yet this fact is apparently ignored" (p. 259).

Gribbons and Lohnes (1966, p. 69), in their studies of students in the Boston area, found a similar factor operating: "We may tentatively conclude that students in the lowest aptitude levels expect more education and think that their parents want them to have more education than is realistically possible or even beneficial." In terms of the college mystique that currently operates in our society, it is frequently observed that middle- and upper-middle-class students are in college because they have not had an opportunity to consider any other avenue for meeting their personal goals. It is probably accurate to suggest, however, that if such a choice proves to be wrong, the middle- or upper-middle-class youths have a greater range of alternatives available to them than have their less advantaged contemporaries.

Perhaps the most important point gleaned from sociological studies of career development and choice is that although the preferences of individuals across various social or economic classes are essentially the same, lower-class expectancies of being able to achieve their preferences are less. In other words, what they would prefer to do is not what they expect to be able to do (Kurolesky, Wright & Juarez, 1971). Such inconsistency may stem from a recognition of their inability to do what they prefer because of lack of intellect or aptitude (Osipow & Gold, 1967; Clack, 1968). But the more pertinent reason seems to be their recognition of cultural constraints that will prohibit them from access to their preferred choices. Thus, it is likely that occupational preferences will reflect the family's occupational level and,

therefore, the child's socioeconomic milieu. As Super (1969a, p. 3) has asserted, the individual's "starting point is his father's socioeconomic status; he climbs up the educational ladder at a speed fixed both by his psychological and social characteristics and by the resources provided by his family environment."

Although the personal aspirations of an individual raised in an environment unsupportive of planfulness or commitments to long-range goals may be the same as for those reared in more favored circumstances, if the person does not have the knowledge or the techniques to cope with the environment, that individual is at a considerable disadvantage in achieving the prerequisites for reaching personal goals.

Some sociologists even argue that developmental notions of career guidance based on individual choice are unrealistic. Roberts (1977), a British sociologist, is one of the foremost proponents of such a view. In essence he does not believe that most people choose, in any precise sense of that term. Instead, they are chosen or act as opportunities arise rather than in some longitudinal pre-planned way. He summarizes the point as follows: "The notion that young people possess freedom of choice and that they can select careers for themselves upon the basis of their own preferences is pure myth. It is not choice but opportunity that governs the manner in which many young people make their entry into employment" (p. 145). As factors affecting such a circumstance, he identifies the mechanisms of educational selection, the patterns of recruitment into different types of employment, home background, and other social structure factors.

Whether one is as adamant about social structure factors in career development as is Roberts, situational approaches to career development suggest that the socioeconomic structure of a society operates as a percolator and a filter of information. In essence, one's position among the social strata making up a nation has much to do with the kind of information one gets, the alternative actions one can take, and the kind of encouragement one receives. Persons are often selectively rewarded or reinforced in certain kinds of behavior depending on the group to which they belong. Women's Liberation, Black and Brown Pride Movements, Gay Liberation, and the Grey Panthers are examples of reactions against the constraints in opportunity imposed because of stereotyped images held by various segments of our society.

In a pluralistic culture such as America today, persons of different ethnic or racial backgrounds are likely to differ in the types of role models available to them. Perhaps more important, different cultures allocate values differently and these values have consequences for behavior. Unfortunately, these value differences are rarely responded to by school or by helping professionals (Harrington, 1975).

Although the mass media, and television in particular, may convey general achievement images that all of us are encouraged to emulate, information about how such images are accomplished or planned and prepared for is not as accessible. Thus, career guidance has a major responsibility to reduce the correlations between membership in certain groups and success. Individual competence and desire, not group membership, must become the criterion by which relevant information and encouragement are provided to people regardless of their sex, race, or other situational determinants. Having a pluralistic population does not mean having a caste system in which some persons remain at low status levels, because they are denied information or opportunity to seek other levels in the society.

Finally, in considering many of the situational effects on choice in graphic form, it is useful to consider the Blau, Gustad, Jessor, Parnes, and Wilcock paradigm (1956). Their schematic of the choice process is a classic synthesis of the factors occurring together within the individual and the environment as the person moves toward occupational entry. Essentially, this same paradigm accents the effects of the social structure on choice. As they observe:

The social structure — the more or less institutionalized patterns of activities, interactions, and ideas among various groups — has a duel significance for occupational choice. On the one hand, it influences the personality development of the choosers; on the other, it defines the socioeconomic conditions in which selection takes place. These two efforts, however, do not occur simultaneously. At any choice point in their careers, the interests and skills in

terms of which individuals make their decisions have been affected by the past social structure, whereas occupational opportunities and requirements for entry are determined by the present structure (p. 539).

This twofold effect of the social structure is schematically presented in Figure 4.2. The left side of the figure suggests that the molding of biological potentialities by the differentiated social structure (Box 3) results in diverse characteristics and individuals (Box 2), some of which directly determine occupational choice (Box 1). At the same time, as indicated on the right side, the social structure changes (Box III), resulting in a socioeconomic organization at any point in time (Box II), some aspects of which directly determine occupational selection (Box I). These two developments, separated only for analytical purposes, must be joined to explain entry into occupations.

The Blau et al. paradigm suggests that geography, the historical moment in time, occupational characteristics, political factors, and the occupational possibility structure and its requirements affect anyone's career development. Stopping there, however, understates situational effects on choice, because while interacting with such external circumstances, the individual has also incorporated and will act on the belief system held by family, peers, neighborhood, ethnic, and religious groups that also define his or her "situation."

Psychological Approaches

Psychological approaches to career development stress intrinsic individual motivation more than the other approaches discussed thus far do. Tying the psychoanalytic, need, and self-emphases into a single body of psychological approaches, Crites (1969, p. 91) observes: "Each of them proposes that the most significant factor in the making of a vocational choice is a motivational or process variable. For this reason, they contrast sharply with the trait-and-factor theories, which emphasize the observable characteristics of the individual and not the inferred states or conditions which prompt him to behave as he does."

The major assumption of the psychological approaches is that because of differences in personality structure, individuals develop certain needs

Figure 4.2

The Blau, Gustad, Jessor, Parnes, and Wilcock Paradigm

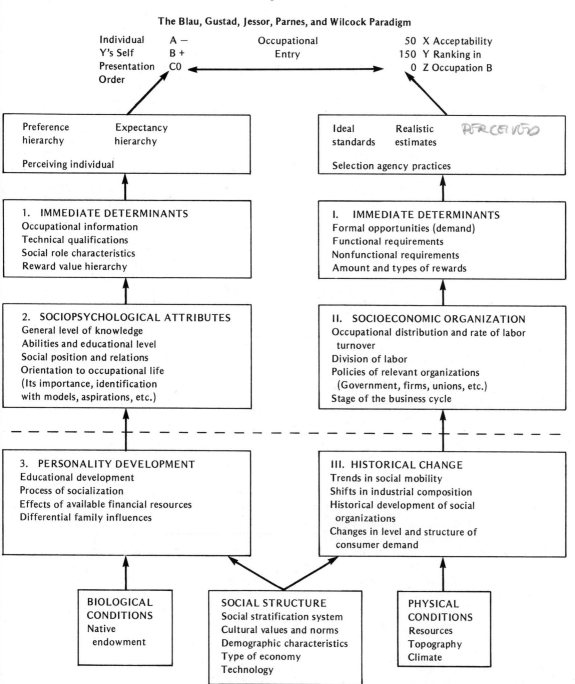

Individual   A −   Occupational   50 X Acceptability
Y's Self   B +   Entry   150 Y Ranking in
Presentation C0   0 Z Occupation B
Order

Preference hierarchy — Expectancy hierarchy
Perceiving individual

Ideal standards — Realistic estimates *PERCEIVED*
Selection agency practices

1. IMMEDIATE DETERMINANTS
Occupational information
Technical qualifications
Social role characteristics
Reward value hierarchy

I. IMMEDIATE DETERMINANTS
Formal opportunities (demand)
Functional requirements
Nonfunctional requirements
Amount and types of rewards

2. SOCIOPSYCHOLOGICAL ATTRIBUTES
General level of knowledge
Abilities and educational level
Social position and relations
Orientation to occupational life
(Its importance, identification
with models, aspirations, etc.)

II. SOCIOECONOMIC ORGANIZATION
Occupational distribution and rate of labor
  turnover
Division of labor
Policies of relevant organizations
  (Government, firms, unions, etc.)
Stage of the business cycle

3. PERSONALITY DEVELOPMENT
Educational development
Process of socialization
Effects of available financial resources
Differential family influences

III. HISTORICAL CHANGE
Trends in social mobility
Shifts in industrial composition
Historical development of social
  organizations
Changes in level and structure of
  consumer demand

BIOLOGICAL CONDITIONS
Native
endowment

SOCIAL STRUCTURE
Social stratification system
Cultural values and norms
Demographic characteristics
Type of economy
Technology

PHYSICAL CONDITIONS
Resources
Topography
Climate

Source: Reprinted with permission, from Peter M. Blau, et al., "Occupational Choice: A Conceptual Framework," *Industrial & Labor Relations Review*, Vol. 9, No. 4 (July 1956), p. 534. © 1956 by Cornell University. All rights reserved.

or drives and seek satisfaction of these needs or drives through occupational choices. Thus, it is contended that different occupational or, indeed, curricular areas are populated by persons of different need types or personality types. These approaches rather consistently develop a classification of personality or need, and then relate it to gratifications available in different environments — occupational or educational. In one sense, the distinguishing characteristics of these approaches are the disciplinary lenses through which career-related phenomena are viewed and the emphasis on the antecedents of vocational behavior as a function of some form of self-classification, conscious or unconscious.

Freud's Psychodynamic View

At the core of any psychodynamic view of work or other aspects of life is the "depth psychology" of Sigmund Freud. As is well known, Freud devoted much of his life to creating a theory of personality encompassing both its conscious and unconscious aspects and the notions of how childhood personality development profoundly influences adult life, including one's work life. However, the most comprehensive application of classic psychoanalytic concepts to occupational choice or career development has been made by Bordin, Nachmann, and Segal (1963), called the Michigan Group. Although preceded by Brill's (1948) psychoanalytic concepts of guilt and exhibitionism and of the pleasure and reality principles to explain the choice attraction of various vocations, Bordin, Nachmann, and Segal have extended the emphasis on the gratification that various types of work offer to meet certain individual impulses. Much like Brill, they consider "work as sublimation — but in the broad sense of all activity other than direct gratification, rather than in the narrower sense of pregenital impulses turned into artistic activities" (p. 110). For the more commonly described traits such as interests and abilities, they substitute individual modes of impulse gratification, the status of one's psychosexual development, and levels of anxiety. More specifically, they maintain that connections exist between the early development of coping mechanisms and the later development of more complex behaviors. They assert that adult occupations

are sought for their instinctual gratifications, as need for these is developed in early childhood, and that in terms of personality formation and the needs inherent in the individual structure, the first six years of life are crucial.

From analyses of such roles as accountants, creative writers, lawyers, dentists, social workers, clinical psychologists, plumbers, physicists, and engineers, Bordin and his colleagues have conceived an elaborate matrix of the basic need-gratifying activities found in different occupations. They have divided psychic and body-part classifications into those activities important to psychoanalytic thinking. They then related these to the potential gratification, the objects from which gratification is available, and the sexual mode of gratification that exists in each of the occupations indicated above. According to Bordin et al., the psychic dimensions by which occupations can be described include the ability of the occupation to satisfy anal, exhibiting, exploratory, flowing-quenching, genital, manipulative, nurturing, oral, aggressive, rhythmic, and sensual needs. The means by which occupations potentially respond to these needs are their instrumental modes — such as tools, techniques, or behaviors used — and the objects dealt with — such as needs of clients, pipes and plumbing fixtures, and money.

To illustrate the Bordin, Nachmann, and Segal position, it might be useful to consider the antecedents relating to a person whose occupation is a lathe operator. The hypothesis would be that such a person's primary instinctual gratifications during the first six years of life came from oral aggressive activities — biting, chewing, and devouring. The theory would hold that these activities are converted from teeth to the fingers to knives, saws, and drills and, possibly, to biting and cutting words and ideas. In the case of the lathe operator, the assumption would be that the gratification found in oral aggressiveness tends to become fixation, manifested in personality, and now finds its adult counterparts in such activities as the use of tools for cutting, grinding, and drilling.

Adler's View

Although Freud's work has been acknowledged repeatedly as the dominant conception of psychology, namely personality theory, future historical writings may give a larger share of that prominence to Alfred Adler. Many current emphases in holistic psychology, the importance of the self-concept as a stimulus to behavior, the individual's ability to hold goals consciously and to plan in accordance with them, the transactional nature of individual personality as a product of social forces, and many concepts of normality have their roots in Adlerian perspectives.

In strong opposition to Freud's major premise that human behavior is essentially determined by inborn instincts, Adler believed that such behavior was motivated by social urges. He fashioned a humanistic theory of personality that was the antithesis of Freud's view (Hall & Lindzey 1957).

Adler stressed a subjective, creative system of behavior through which persons search for experiences that aid in fulfilling their unique style of life. The self, then, is an important cause of behavior and, indeed, the focus of individual uniqueness. The individual is conscious of inferiorities and of goals held. According to Adler (1927), the major goal of individuals is to overcome inferiority and to obtain superiority within some notions of social interest. There are innumerable ways to strive for superiority, and how this is accomplished fits into a unique style of life. In a sense, persons perceive, learn, and retain what fits the style of life and ignore everything else. In doing so, however, Adler believes that humankind possesses a creative self by which personality is built out of the combined material of heredity and experience. The creative self gives meaning to life, and formulates both goals and the means to goals (Adler, 1935).

Although Adler did not make work a central concern of his theory, there is no question that his concepts of personality describe work motivation and the work setting as a place to implement social interest, unique life styles, and superiority. Many of Adler's concepts will appear in different guises in more recent theories described in this chapter.

Maccoby's Research

Maccoby (1980) recently examined Fromm's extension of Freud's concepts as related to how work influences the potential for pathological versus healthy development. Fromm contended that individual development occurs through stages, from helplessness and dependency to the increasing capacity for independence, reason, mutuality, and creative expression. This process depends on biological maturation and social training, which derives from family influences and those of other agents of society, including work. Maccoby points out that within Fromm's model, psychopathology can be understood as a person's regressive attempt to recreate an infant's sense of total protectiveness, by controlling the world and by seeking a feeling of omnipotence. The result is to become more unconsciously driven, more helpless, and ultimately more despairing. Within this context, work can be viewed as playing a major role in determining an individual's developmental level. Work can stimulate life-affirming attitudes and growth and development, or through frustration and oppression stimulate regressive attitudes. As Maccoby points out, for those on the borderline between normalcy and psychopathology, stressful work or an unhealthy work environment can trigger regressive solutions and behaviors, unproductive attitudes, and similar negative behavior. Presumably decisions made in such a psychic frame of reference would reflect the individual's view of work as repressive or as challenging and growth producing.

Maccoby (1976) has also applied psychoanalytic and socioeconomic concepts to the understanding of upward mobility in high-technology corporations. He described this process of social selection as a function of the corporate "psychostructure," which selects and molds certain kinds of behavior in order to achieve congruence between the work requirements and the character of those who do the work. Maccoby found that in these corporations individuals who move upward on the career path must be highly motivated to do what the organization requires them to do and to restrain personal traits that do not fit the requirements of the work place and the images afforded by the psychostructure. Again, on the negative side, depending on the psychostructure operating, such requirements can attract certain types of emotional disturbance, or stimulate dependency, compliance, and other regressive behavior leading in turn to substance abuse, underdeveloped feelings of compassion and affection, and other related phenomena.

The psychoanalytic view of occupational choice

or career development has less research to validate its assumptions than most of the other emphases discussed in this chapter. In addition, criticisms have been leveled at the theory's inadequacy to consider the effects of external forces on choice such as economic, cultural, or geographic limitations, although such criticisms are not often focused on such persons as Adler or Fromm. Finally, the psychoanalytic position of Freud, in particular, suggests that career guidance or career education could do very little after early childhood to alter individual career development. The role of the counselor would be limited to helping persons identify the pertinent mode of gratification they seek and the occupations that might satisfy those needs.

Roe's Approach

The theoretical and research efforts of Roe (1956) also apply personality theory to career development. Indeed, as Osipow (1968, p. 17) has pointed out, Roe marries two major personality theories: (1) the earlier work of Gardner Murphy (1947) — in particular, Murphy's canalization of psychic energy and emphasis on the relationship between early childhood experiences and later vocational choices; and (2) Maslow's (1954) theory of prepotent needs to vocational behavior. Roe also accents genetic factors as these interact with need hierarchies to determine vocational behavior and choice. "In other words, given 'equal' endowments genetically, differences in occupational achievement between two individuals may be inferred to be the result of motivational differences which theoretically are likely to be the outcomes of different childhood experiences" (Osipow, 1968, p. 18).

Roe, from her studies of different types of scientists (1953), concluded that some personality differences evolve from childrearing practices (such as rejecting, overprotecting, democratic) and that these differences are related to the kinds of interaction that such persons ultimately establish with other people — toward them or not toward them — and with things. Affected strongly by the psychoanalytic notion that the first few years of life encompass the primary experiences shaping adult behavior, she identified the substance of three primary childrearing practices.

She describes the first as *emotional concentra-*

tion on the child, which includes the opposite extremes of overprotective and overdemanding behavior. Children who have been intensely conditioned to receive need gratification from their parents if certain contingencies were met might choose occupations that would give them a high level of feedback and reward — such as the performing arts. The second childrearing pattern is that of *avoidance of the child*. The continuum of parental responses in this pattern might include emotional rejection of the child as well as physical neglect. The hypothesis here would be that the child would look to nonpersons and things, and would have limited contacts with others as bases for gratification. In such instances, scientific and mechanical interests are likely to develop as ways of finding gratification without reliance on others. The third childrearing practice is *acceptance of the child*, which might involve either casual acceptance or loving acceptance, incorporating the child into the family unit as one among equals in a democratic process. In this third childrearing practice, it is assumed that a child's independence is encouraged, and that he or she may seek occupations that balance personal and nonpersonal interests without the need for isolation from others or intense approval from them.

Roe suggests then that there are relationships between the psychic energy, genetic propensities, and childhood experiences that shape individual styles of behavior, and that the impulse to acquire opportunities to express these individual styles is inherent in the choices made and the ensuing career behavior. Thus, the strength of a particular need, the delay between the arousal of the need and its satisfaction, and the value that the satisfaction has in the individual's environment are the conditions — shaped by early childhood experiences — that influence career development. These inputs to Roe's thinking can be summarized into two perspectives on the origin of vocational interests, that (1) career directions are first determined by "the patterning of early satisfactions and frustrations," and that (2) the modes and degrees of need satisfaction will determine which needs will become the strongest motivations" (Roe & Siegelman, 1964, p. 5).

As Roe's work was taking shape after World War II, so was that of Maslow, whose theory has probably been the most influential yet developed in shaping the concepts of needs. To elaborate her need constructs, Roe has applied Maslow's theory of prepotent needs to career behavior. Maslow (1954) arranged human needs in a hierarchy in which he conceived the emergence of higher-order needs as contingent on the relative satisfaction of lower-order, more primitive needs. The needs in ascending order are:

1. Physiological needs
2. Safety needs
3. Needs for belongingness and love
4. Needs for importance, self-esteem, respect, independence
5. Need for information
6. Need for understanding
7. Need for beauty
8. Need for self-actualization

Perhaps one or two simple illustrations of the meaning of Maslow's hierarchy will be useful here. For example, one might cite the instance of a child doing poorly in school who comes from a home where food is scarce and the parents are considering divorce. A teacher might chastise the child for not doing his or her homework and not caring about school. The more accurate view is that the child is preoccupied with satisfying physiological and safety needs. Until these can be relatively taken for granted, the child is unlikely to be motivated by needs for information or understanding. A similar translation can be made in seeking certain kinds of work. The person who has lived through a depression where work is limited and large numbers of people have no money or little food is likely to view the security aspects of work more positively than the person who has not been exposed to such poverty and is freer to seek high-order needs in work.

Roe's concerns with specific childrearing practices, the manner in which the parents interact with the child, the resulting need structure, and the ensuing orientation toward or away from persons have been translated into a useful field and level classification of occupations, including the following (Roe, 1956, pp. 143–152):

Fields	*Levels*
I. Service	1. Professional and Managerial (1)
II. Business Contact	
III. Organizations	2. Professional and Managerial (2)
IV. Technology	

V. Outdoor	3. Semiprofessional, Small Business
VI. Science	
VII. General Culture	4. Skilled
VIII. Arts and Entertainment	5. Semiskilled
	6. Unskilled

To understand the concept of fields and levels, an example might be useful. Persons entering service occupations (Group 1), it is assumed, are primarily oriented toward persons and probably come from a home which generated a loving, overprotective environment. Within a service occupation, the level attained — the level being based on work complexity or responsibility — is dependent on genetic factors manifested in intelligence as well as the style of environmental manipulation.

More than any of Roe's other contributions, this field and level classification, which also has been described as a circular array (Roe, 1956) of occupational groups contiguous in their emphasis on people (Groups I, II, III, VII, VIII) or on things (Groups IV, V, VI), has been supported by Perrone (1964). He found that high school boys with similar scores on cognitive measures tend to prefer similar occupational groups as defined by Roe's eight groups. Indeed, when job changes are examined they are found to be nonrandom. That is, people typically move from one job in one group to another in the same group as defined by Roe's classification scheme. They do not typically move to a group in which the orientation or activity is in direct opposition to the initial group (Hutchinson & Roe, 1968). A fuller description of Roe's occupational classification scheme was provided in Chapter 3.

Attempts to test other aspects of Roe's theory, particularly the effects of the family on later vocational behavior, have seen far less positive results or at least very ambiguous results (Crites, 1962; Brunkan & Crites, 1964; Brunkan, 1965). However, one study with rather interesting findings is that of Green and Parker (1965). They administered to a seventh-grade sample of boys and girls living with their parents, the Roe and Siegelman's (1964) Parent-Child Relations Questionnaires. The responses provided data about the current home atmosphere of the children. These data were then examined to see whether the occupational preferences of these children indicated person or nonperson orientation. It was found that for boys the perception of either parent as warm and supporting results in person-oriented occupational choices and that for girls cold parental relationships result in nonperson career choices.

Both the personality approach of Bordin, Nachmann, and Segal and that of Roe imply that occupational choices are made as aspects of self-classification, whether the central focus is impulse gratification or need satisfaction. Thus, occupational choices and career patterns are affirmations of personal behavioral styles.

Holland's Theory

Holland's (1966, 1973) approach gives explicit attention to behavioral style or personality type as the major influence in career choice and development. In this sense, Holland's work is part of a long tradition of conceptualizations of individual differences in personality type encompassing the work of such persons as Spranger (1928) and Murray (1938). Spranger described six basic types of individuality: theoretic, economic, aesthetic, social, political, and religious. Murray proposed a series of needs and press (environmental characteristics, reinforcers, rewards), which he combined into a need-press paradigm designed to explain differential behavior in organizations.

Indeed, Holland's contributions are equally prominent in the area of environmental assessment and in understanding person-situation interactions as they are in understanding individual behavior. Much of his effort has been devoted to developing structures for understanding and predicting the behavior of persons in different types of environments. Holland and his associates have also made extremely important contributions to the understanding of vocational interests in relation to personality characteristics; to the importance of both academic and nonacademic accomplishments to life; and to the development of instruments useful both in testing his theoretical propositions and in translating his theory into career guidance tools. The most notable of the latter are the Vocational Preference Inventory and the Self-Directed-Search. Finally, Holland's theory has generated hundreds of studies in the past decade that have tested, refined, and extended his propositions with diverse populations, in different settings, and in many nations of the world. We will identify a few studies to suggest some of the lines of ongoing inquiry after we identify the primary assumptions of the theory.

Holland assumes that the individual is a product of heredity and environment. As a result of early and continuing influences of genetic potentialities and the interaction of the individual with his or her environment, there develops a hierarchy of habitual or preferred methods for dealing with social and environmental tasks. The most typical way in which an individual responds to the environment is described as modal personal orientation.

Four assumptions constitute the heart of Holland's theory:

1. In our culture, most persons can be categorized as one of six types: realistic, investigative, artistic, social, enterprising or conventional.
2. There are six kinds of environments: realistic, investigative, artistic, social, enterprising and conventional.
3. People search for environments that will let them exercise their skills and abilities, express their attitudes and values, and take on agreeable problems and roles.
4. A person's behavior is determined by an interaction between his personality and the characteristics of his environment (Holland, 1973, pp. 2-4).

To emphasize the person-situation correspondence, Holland has classified work environments into six categories analogous to the six personal orientations. In other words, he describes the person and the working environment in the same terms. Accordingly, Holland makes explicit, more than do most of his contemporaries, that occupations are ways of life, environments which manifest the characteristics of those inhabiting them as opposed to being simply sets of isolated work functions or skills. In addition, Holland has extended his examination of types of occupational environments to educational environments, particularly collegiate.

In condensed and paraphrased form, the major emphases of the six personality types and their relationship to pertinent occupations are:

1. The *Realistic* (R) type has a preference for activities that require the explicit, ordered, or

systematic manipulation of objects, tools, machines, animals; and an aversion to educational or therapeutic activities. Examples of occupations which meet the needs of Realistic types are surveyor and mechanic.

2. The *Investigative (I)* type has a preference for activities that entail the observational, symbolic, systematic, and creative investigation of physical, biological, and cultural phenomena in order to understand and control such phenomena; and an aversion to persuasive, social, and repetitive activities. Examples of occupations which meet the needs of Investigative types are chemist and physicist.

3. The *Artistic (A)* type prefers ambiguous, free, unsystematized activities that entail the manipulation of physical, verbal, or human materials to create art forms or products; and has an aversion to explicit, systematic, and ordered activities. Examples of occupations which meet the needs of Artistic types are artist and writer.

4. The *Social (S)* type prefers activities that entail the manipulation of others to inform, train, develop, cure, or enlighten; and has an aversion to explicit, ordered, systematic activities involving materials, tools, or machines. Examples of occupations which meet the needs of Social types are social science teacher and vocational counselor.

5. The *Enterprising (E)* type prefers activities that require the manipulation of others to attain organizational goals or economic gain; and an aversion to observational, symbolic, and systematic activities. Examples of occupations which meet the needs of Enterprising types are political scientist, salesman, and executive.

6. The *Conventional (C)* type prefers activities that entail the explicit, ordered, systematic manipulation of data, such as keeping records, filing materials, reproducing materials, organizing written and numerical data according to a prescribed plan, operating business machines and data processing machines to attain organizational or economic goals; and has an aversion to ambiguous, free, exploratory or unsystematized activities. Examples of occupations which meet the needs of Conventional types are accountant and clerk (Holland, 1973, pp. 14–18).

Obviously, it is unlikely that persons fall solely into one of the major personality types described. Therefore, a coding system has been devised to indicate the person's primary and secondary types (Holland, Vierstein, Kuo, Karweit, & Blum, 1970). These codes are reflected in three-letter combinations – each letter corresponding to the first letter of one of the six types. For instance, a code of RIA would indicate that the person is most like the Realistic type, next most like Investigative, and third most like Artistic. Holland and his colleagues have also classified 456 occupations according to the same three-letter code system. For example, for the code RIA, two occupations are listed – architectural draftsman and dental technician. It is assumed that a person obtaining the code RIA should begin to explore these two occupations and then break into related areas through the use of the *Dictionary of Occupational Titles* and other pertinent references.

Holland, like Roe, addresses himself to level hierarchies within occupational environments. The level hierarchy, or the particular responsibility or skill level within an occupational field which one gravitates to, is dependent on the person's intelligence and self-knowledge. Self-knowledge refers to the amount of accuracy of self-information as contrasted with self-evaluation, which refers to the worth the person attributes to him or herself. A complementary description of Holland's scheme was offered in the previous chapter.

In summary, Holland's theory (1973, pp. 2–10) contends that individual behavior is a function of the interaction between one's personality and environment, and that choice behavior is an expression of personality. Thus, people seek those educational and occupational settings which permit expression of their personality styles. Since persons inhabiting particular environments, occupational or educational, have similar personality characteristics, their responses to problems and interpersonal situations are likely to be similar. For these reasons, interest inventories are personality inventories, and vocational stereotypes held by individuals have important psychological and sociological implications. Put another way, it is possible to suggest that as persons explore occupational possibilities, they use stereotypes of themselves and stereotypes of occupations to guide their search. If their preferences are clear and their information about self or occupations accurate, they will likely make effective choices. If their understanding of their personality type or appropriate occupations is unclear, they are likely to be indecisive and vacillate among possible choices. In Holland's view, the adequacy of information about the self and various occupational possibilities is crucial.

Finally, Holland hypothesizes that congruent interactions of people and environments belonging to the same type or model, in contrast to incongruent interactions, are conducive to more stable vocational choice, higher vocational achievement, higher academic achievement, better maintenance of personal stability, and greater satisfaction.

In 1976, Holland and Gottfredson extended and clarified some of the earlier theoretical propositions. They did so by exploring four major questions:

1. How do personal development, initial vocational choice, work involvement and satisfaction come about?

> People grow up to resemble one type or another because parents, schools, and neighborhoods serve as environments which reinforce some behaviors more than others and provide different models of suitable behavior. The reinforcement consists of the encouragement of selected activities, interests, self-estimates, and competencies. . . . Different cultural influences as well as other aspects of the interpersonal milieu, such as sex-role socialization, race, religion, and class promote the development of some types more than others by differential encouragement of the experiences (activities, interests, competencies, etc.) that lead to different types (p. 21).

2. Why do most people have orderly careers when the individual jobs in their work histories are categorized using an occupational classification scheme?

> The majority of people manage to find work that is congruent with their type. More explicitly, the average person searches for or gravitates toward work environments in which his/her typological predilections and talents (activities, competencies, perceptions

of self and world, values, traits) are allowed expression and rewarded. . . . By definition, well defined types know what activities and competencies bring them satisfaction and congruency. . . . Orderly careers are also encouraged by the stereotyped ways in which employers perceive a person's credentials (p. 21).

3. Why do people change jobs? What influences their search for new jobs?

> People change jobs because they are dissatisfied, because they are incompetent, because other workers wish them to leave, and for other personal and environmental reasons: better climate, physical disability, dissatisfied relatives, more money, and other influences. In theoretical terms, people leave because of excessive person-environment incongruency, or because of an opportunity to increase their congruency (p. 21).

4. Why do some people make vocational choices that are congruent with assessment data, others do not, and still others are undecided?

> People with consistent and well-defined personality patterns are expected to be "good" decision-makers because of the implications of differentiation and consistency: integration of preferred activities, competencies, occupational preferences and self-estimates; and compatibility of primary dispositions. . . . [Some personality] types may be better decision-makers than others. . . . The making of decisions at appropriate times (end of high school, end of sophomore year, when to change jobs, when to marry, etc.) may reflect only different rates of development and different environmental contingencies (p. 22).

As indicated at the beginning of this section, Holland himself and his associates have been extremely productive in both generating and testing his theoretical propositions. As one might expect with a theory that is both comprehensive in the questions it stimulates and dynamic, the findings reported are somewhat mixed, although they typically support the theoretical propositions. Some selected findings follow.

Laudeman and Griffith (1978) studied the relationship among personality typology, environmental orientation, and values of six different groups of male seniors at a midwestern university. Each group represented one of Holland's primary personality types through the following majors: mechanical engineering, electrical engineering, elementary education, accounting, marketing, and art or music education. Holland's Vocational Preference Inventory (VPI) was used to assess personality types and the Allport-Vernon-Lindsey Study of Values was used to measure six basic values or motives in personality. Although there were some inconsistencies among engineering and education major with regard to their highest mean scores on the VPI personality scales, the researchers concluded that male college seniors in this sample did generally reflect personality types and value dimensions that correspond with their major field of study in accordance with what would be predicted by Holland's theory. Scanlan (1980) has applied Holland's occupational classification system to self-employed men and found it useful in differentiating what he described as craft entrepreneurs and opportunistic entrepreneurs. He also found that in accordance with the theory, the educational interests of the respondents, the types of occupations they held before self-employment, and the types of work on which craft and opportunistic entrepreneurs spend their time in the course of operating their

businesses all reflect the three-letter Holland codes by which they were differentiated.

Holland's notion of consistency has also been tested in different ways. This concept, advanced in 1973, is related to his six major personality types, which are arranged in a model that corresponds to their intercorrelations (see Figure 4.3).

In looking at the hexagons for men and women, one can see that those personality types with the highest positive correlations are arranged together on the outside of the hexagon, whereas those types with the smallest correlation are the farthest apart on the diagram. The intermediate distances have correlations of intermediate size.

Consistency, according to Holland, is the degree to which the dominant and subdominant interest types (the first two expressed vocational choices) of a person or an environment are similar to each other as demonstrated by their adjacent position or closeness on the hexagonal model. The assumption is that persons whose dominant personality (interest) types are essentially consistent would be more integrated in their characteristics (traits, values, perceptions) than persons whose interest types are much more disparate. Such consistent persons would be more vocationally mature. Further, consistent persons would likely be more predictable and higher achievers than inconsistent persons. Erwin (1982) examined changes in college majors, course withdrawals, and other indices of academic performance in relation to Holland's

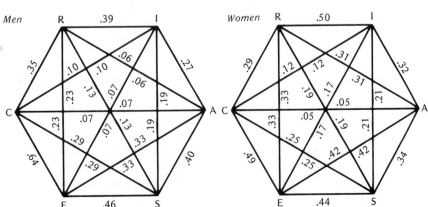

Figure 4.3
Holland's Hexagon for Men and Women

construct of consistency but found only weak support for the construct as it was measured in this study. However, Wiley and Magoon (1982) studied the construct of consistency in social personality types (211 college freshmen) in relation to persistence in college and academic achievement. They found significant results in favor of the construct. For example, high- and medium-consistency subjects persisted in college at a higher rate than low-consistency subjects and the relationship between consistency and college grade point averages was also significant.

Related to the studies of Erwin and Wiley and Magoon of the usefulness of Holland's typology for predicting persistence and performance in college, Bruch and Krieshok (1981) studied Holland's notion of congruence, person-situation compatibility, among theoretically oriented engineering majors. The researchers hypothesized that high congruence (an investigative student in an investigative major) compared to moderately high congruence (a realistic student in an investigative major) would result in greater persistence and better academic performance. The hypotheses were confirmed in that high student-curriculum congruence (I-type student in I-type major) demonstrated greater academic achievement and persistence in the initial engineering major over a two-year period than did student-curriculum congruence, which was moderate. Spokane (1979) followed up 232 women and 386 men in their senior year who had taken the Strong Campbell Interest Inventory in their freshman year. He found that congruent students were more satisfied and differentiated than incongruent students and that they perceived themselves to be more congruent. Barak and Rabbi (1982) in a study of 293 undergraduate students randomly stratified across majors representing different Holland categories, found that consistent students tend to persist in college, do not change majors, and achieve more than inconsistent students. Consistency in this study related to people who possess a consistent personality pattern and an integration of similar interests, competencies, values, traits, and perceptions, and was reflected here in the degree to which students at registration made the first two choices of major in the same or adjacent Holland category (investigative-investigative, investigative-realistic, and so on).

Another line of research dealing with Holland's theory has to do with its validity for men and women and across racial groups. Doty and Betz (1979) studied the concurrent validity of Holland's theory for men and women employed in an enterprising occupation. In general, the findings suggested that, at least within an employed sample, Holland's theory is valid for both men and women as defined by equally high scores on the E-theme in the Strong Campbell Interest Inventory and the Self Directed Search and by relationships between enterprising scale scores and job satisfaction. Walsh, Bingham, Horton, and Spokane (1979) studied the differences between 155 college-degreed black and white women employed in three traditional male occupations (engineering, medicine, and law). They found that white and black women in the same occupation tended to obtain similar mean scores on the VPI and the SDS. Ward and Walsh (1981) also studied the concurrent validity of Holland's theory for employed non–college degreed black women. The subjects were 102 black women working in occupations representing each of the six vocational environments described by Holland. Four scales of the VPI and four scales of the SDS successfully differentiated the work environments of the women consistently with Holland's theoretical propositions.

A further line of inquiry concerning Holland's work has to do with its relationship to other classification systems. Jones (1980), for example, has shown how the Holland typology can be useful with the *Guide for Occupational Exploration* published by the U.S. Department of Labor in 1979. Rounds, Davison, and Dawis (1979) used a multidimensional scaling procedure to examine the fit of Holland's hexagonal model to the General Occupational Theme scales of the Strong Campbell Interest Inventory, which are based on the Holland model. The fit for males was good. For females, the relationship was less good, suggesting caution in the use and interpretation of the SCII occupational themes for females.

Gottfredson (1980) compared six schemes for describing occupations in order to examine the construct validity of Holland's typology of work environments and to estimate the amount of information shared by these commonly used classification systems. The five occupational classification systems studied, in addition to the Holland system, included occupational prestige, activities and requirements presented in the DOT, self-direction, the twelve major census categories, and the occupational reinforcer patterns formulated in the Minnesota Theory of Work Adjustment (Lofquist & Dawis, 1969). Acknowledging limitations in both the data available for the occupations examined and the differing or uncertain validity of the classification schemes used, Gottfredson's evidence does support the construct validity of Holland's occupational scheme. She finds that it is superior to the census classification scheme in its potential flexibility and interpretation. She does recommend, however, that the Holland work typology be supplemented by a measure of occupational prestige so that the resulting information would include a paradigm of work type by level.

Rounds, Shubsachs, Dawis, and Lofquist (1978) classified 181 occupations, for which reinforcer rating data were available, into the six Holland environmental models. The Minnesota Job Description Questionnaire provides ratings of twenty-one reinforcers (such as ability utilization, achievement, activity, advancement, authority) in different occupations (see Chapter 2). The authors concluded that the results provided only modest support for Holland's environmental formulations, particularly that of consistency. They also reported finding a different order of intercorrelations among the Holland Scale than has been used to construct the hexagon (RCSIAE or REAISC rather than RIASEC as proposed by Holland). Finally, they suggest that descriptions of occupational environments based on vocational interests and vocational preferences, as is Holland's, differ from those based on environmental characteristics (occupational reinforcers and behavioral requirements) such as the Minnesota Theory of Work Adjustment. Gottfredson (1980) has suggested that the data of Rounds et al. be reevaluated to account for the effects of prestige level. Super (1981), however, would likely be somewhat more supportive of the findings of Rounds et al. since he contends that the one fundamental methodological flaw in most of Holland's work "is the fact that both Holland's predictors and his criteria have been preferences. . . . The predictor has usually been either the score on an interest inventory

consisting of occupational titles or expressed vocational preferences classified according to Holland's hexagon. The criterion has been the vocational preference (another occupational title) expressed at some later date" (p. 20).

Holland's theory continues to stimulate other lines of inquiry, raise new questions, and find new applications. Although much research remains to be done on the hypotheses generated by the theory, it continues to be an important conceptual structure for considering choice, persistence, and performance in educational and occupational settings.

Hoppock's View

To complete this section on personality approaches to career development, it is worth noting Hoppock's Composite View (1976). Summarizing several extant theories, Hoppock proposes a series of straightforward speculations about occupational choice that give prominence to need satisfaction:

1. Occupations are chosen to meet needs.
2. The occupation that we choose is the one that we believe will best meet the needs that most concern us.
3. Needs may be intellectually perceived, or they may be only vaguely felt as attractions which draw us in certain directions. In either case, they may influence choices.
4. Occupational choice begins when we first become aware that an occupation can help to meet our needs.
5. Occupational choice improves as we become better able to anticipate how well a prospective occupation will meet our needs. Our capacity thus to anticipate depends on our knowledge of ourselves, our knowledge of occupations, and our ability to think clearly.
6. Information about ourselves affects occupational choice by helping us to discover the occupations that may meet our needs and by helping us to anticipate how well satisfied we may hope to be in one occupation as compared with another.
7. Information about occupations affects occupational choice by helping us to discover the occupations that may meet our needs and by

helping us to anticipate how well satisfied we may hope to be in one occupation as compared with another.

8. Job satisfaction depends upon the extent to which the job that we hold meets the needs that we feel it should meet. The degree of satisfaction is determined by the ratio between what we have and what we want.

9. Satisfaction can result from a job which meets our needs today, or from a job which promises to meet them in the future.

10. Occupational choice is always subject to change when we believe that a change will better meet our needs (Hoppock, 1976, pp. 111–112).

Developmental Emphases

Developmental emphases on career behavior and decision-making differ from the approaches previously discussed, not because they reject the latter but rather because they are typically more inclusive, more concerned with longitudinal expressions of career behavior, and more inclined to highlight the importance of the self-concept.

Ginzberg, Ginsburg, Axelrad, and Herma (1951) – a team composed of an economist, a psychiatrist, a sociologist, and a psychologist respectively – were early leaders in speculating about career development as a process that culminates in an occupational choice in one's early twenties. In particular, they asserted: "Occupational choice is a developmental process: it is not a single decision, but a series of decisions made over a period of years. Each step in the process has a meaningful relation to those which precede and follow it" (p. 185). Ginzberg and his colleagues identified four sets of factors, the interplay of which influences the ultimate vocational choice: individual values, emotional factors, the amount and kind of education, and the effect of reality through environmental pressures. These factors undergird the formation of attitudes, which converge to shape occupational choice. More particularly, Ginzberg et al. saw choice as a process delimited by life stages, in which certain tasks are faced by preadolescents and adolescents. Within the interaction that occurs as these tasks are confronted, compromises between wishes and possibilities

contribute to an irreversibility as the process unfolds.

Ginzberg and his associates have labeled the gross phases of the vocational choice process – the period of development – as fantasy (from birth to age 11), tentative (11 to 17), and realistic (age 17 to early twenties). Except for fantasy, each of these periods has subaspects. Thus, the tentative period is divided into stages of interest, capacity, value, and transition. Following this period, there emerges the realistic period, which is broken into exploration and crystallization.

Ginzberg et al. have given credence to the notion that vocational behavior finds its roots in the early life of the child and develops over time. They have indicated that vocational behavior and career choice become increasingly reality-oriented and specific as one moves toward the choice itself.

In the reformulation of his theory twenty years after the first statement, Ginzberg (1972) suggested some modifications. First, he now believes that the process of occupational choice-making does not end at young adulthood. Rather, it is likely to occur throughout the individual's working life with changes in goals or work situations requiring decision-making and remaking. Second, Ginzberg has dampened his emphasis on the irreversibility of occupational choice. Finally, he has substituted the term *optimization* for the earlier term *compromise*. The point here is that individuals constantly try to improve the occupational fit between their changing selves and circumstances. Thus, as shifts continue to occur in work and other aspects of life, the person must deal with new decisions designed to balance possible gains against economic and psychological costs. Ginzberg's reformulated theory now includes the following elements (paraphrased):

1. Occupational choice is a process that remains open as long as one makes and expects to make decisions about work and career. Often occupational choice and working life are coterminous.

2. The decisions made during the preparatory period (principally schooling through adolescence) will help shape later career, but changes occurring in work and life will also influence career.

3. Decisions about jobs and careers are individual attempts to optimize the fit between personal priority needs and desires and the work opportunities and constraints that occur.

Super's Developmental Approach. Probably the developmental approach that has received the most continuous attention, stimulated the most research, influenced most pervasively the field of vocational psychology, and is the most comprehensive is that promulgated by Super and his many colleagues in the Career Pattern Study (Super et al., 1957; Super et al., 1963; Super, 1969a, 1969b; Jordaan & Heyde, 1979). This approach is an integrative one, stressing the interaction of personal and environmental variables in career development.

Super's proposal came shortly after Ginzberg's original propositions. Super had provided early input into the Ginzberg statement but believed that it was deficient in several respects (Super, 1953). According to his view, the Ginzberg position did not take into account previous pertinent research (such as the nature of interests in vocational choice); it failed to describe "choice" in an operationally acceptable way; it made a sharp distinction between choice and "adjustment" when, in fact, the two were blended in adolescence and virtually indistinguishable in adulthood; and it failed to delineate the process of compromise.

In response to these conditions, Super formulated his own theory comprised of ten major propositions, each of which was testable and, indeed, could provide the framework for a longitudinal research study. His original propositions follow:

1. People differ in their abilities, interests, and personalities.
2. They are qualified, by virtue of these characteristics, each for a number of occupations.
3. Each of these occupations requires a characteristic pattern of abilities, interests, and personality traits, with tolerances wide enough, however, to allow both some variety of occupations for each individual and some variety of individuals in each occupation.
4. Vocational preferences and competencies, the situations in which people live and work, and hence their self-concepts, change with time and experience (although self-concepts are generally fairly stable from late adolescence until late maturity), making choice and adjustment a continuous process.
5. This process may be summed up in a series of life stages characterized as those of growth, exploration, establishment, maintenance, and decline, and these stages may in turn be subdivided into (a) the fantasy, tentative, and realistic phases of the exploratory stage, and (b) the trial and stable phases of the establishment stage.
6. The nature of the career pattern (that is, the occupational level attained and the sequence, frequency, and duration of trial and stable jobs) is determined by the individual's socioeconomic level, mental ability, and personality characteristics, and by the opportunities to which he is exposed.
7. Development through the life stages can be guided, partly by facilitating the process of maturation of abilities and interests and partly by aiding in reality testing and in the development of the self-concept.
8. The process of vocational development is essentially that of developing and implementing a self-concept: it is a compromise process in which the self-concept is a product of the interaction of inherited aptitudes, neural and endocrine make-up, opportunity to play various roles and evaluations of the extent to which the results of role-playing meet with the approval of superiors and fellows.
9. The process of compromise between individual social factors, between self-concept and reality, is one of role-playing, whether the role is played in fantasy, in the counseling interview, or in real life activities such as school classes, clubs, part-time work, and entry jobs.
10. Work satisfactions and life satisfactions depend upon the extent to which the individual finds adequate outlets for his abilities, interests, personality traits and values; they depend upon his establishment in a type of work, a role which growth and exploratory experiences have led him to consider congenial and appropriate (Super, 1953, pp. 189–190).

In a major sense, Super has made explicit the

intimacy of career development and personal development. He has synthesized much of the early work of Buehler (1933), Hoppock (1935), and of Ginzberg, Ginsburg, Axelrad, and Herma (1951) in his longitudinal attempt to focus developmental principles on the staging and the determination of career patterns. He has characterized the career development process as ongoing, continuous, and generally irreversible; as a process of compromise and synthesis within which his primary construct — the development and implementation of the self-concept — operates. The basic theme is that the individual chooses occupations that will allow him to function in a role consistent with his self-concept and that the latter conception is a function of his developmental history. (The male pronoun is used precisely here, because Super's research and theory have dealt with men, not women.) Further, because of the range of individual capabilities and the latitude within occupations for different combinations of traits, he has indicated that most people have multipotentiality.

Although Super's approach has been labeled typically as a developmental self-concept theory (Osipow, 1968, p. 117), Super himself has labeled it differential-developmental-social-phenomenological psychology (Super, 1969b). Such a label indicates the confluence of knowledge bases to explain career development that this approach has attempted to synthesize and order.

Super gives prominence to individuals' mastery of increasingly complex tasks at different stages of career development. Here he has attempted to synthesize the work of Miller and Form (1951) and of Havighurst (1953) by integrating these two perceptions of life-stage phenomena into a more elaborate set of constructs. Miller and Form, after extensive analysis of the work histories of a sample of men, conceived the following work periods as descriptive of a total life perspective: initial (while in school), trial (early, short-lived, full-time work), stable (normally mature adult), and retirement (after giving up employment). These work periods in concert with those of Buehler (1933) — growth (childhood), exploration (adolescence), establishment (young adulthood), maintenance (maturity), and decline (old age) — provided the outline of Super's thesis, although he focused on the exploratory and establishment stages.

These two stages are divided into substages. The exploratory stage breaks down into the tentative,

transition, and trial (with little commitment) substages; the establishment stage, into the trial (with more commitment), stabilization, and advancement substages (Super, 1969b). He has further formulated gross developmental tasks — crystallization, specification, implementation, stabilization, and consolidation — which rest on substages and metadimensions contributing to increasing vocational maturity (Super et al., 1963). Within these stages are factors internal as well as external to the individual that influence the choices made. These factors continue to narrow the array of options the individual considers. There is an emphasis, then, on vocational convergence and greater specificity in behavior.

For nearly a quarter of a century, Super, his colleagues, and a great number of doctoral students have carried on the Career Pattern Study to attempt to validate and refine this theory. This longitudinal effort has studied the lives of more than 100 men from the time they were in ninth grade until they were well into adulthood, 35 years of age and beyond, as they have gone about occupational choice, preparation, and participation in work.

Many research studies and publications have been developed in conjunction with the Career Pattern Study. Some of these will be dealt with specifically in Chapter 6. Implications for career guidance and career education have also been developed.

In the course of the Career Pattern Study, insights into life stages and the developmental tasks which comprise them have become refined. The following table (Table 4.3) synthesizes from several writings by Super and Jordaan a current view of Super's perspectives on the life stages and their composition.

Each of the career development tasks identified can be further subdivided into the specific behaviors required to complete the task. For example, Table 4.4 reports a factor analytic model of vocational maturity in ninth grade which provides an outline of elements to which either instruction or guidance processes might be related. This level of specificity has provided much of the content for career educational models as well as systematic planning for career guidance and counseling. In Chapter 6, we shall deal with these matters more fully.

In a recent analysis of vocational maturity in

Table 4.3
A Synthesis of Super's Conception of Life Stages and Developmental Tasks

Growth	Exploration	Establishment	Maintenance
Birth Self-concept develops through identification with key figures in family and school needs and fantasy are dominant early in this stage; interest and capacity become more important with increasing social participation and reality testing; learn behaviors associated with self-help, social interaction, self-direction, industrialness, goal setting, persistence. Substages: *Fantasy* (4–10 years) Needs are dominant; role-playing in fantasy is important. *Interest* (11–12 years) Likes are the major determinant of aspirations and activities. *Capacity* (13–14 years) Abilities are given more weight and job requirements (including training) are considered. Tasks: Developing a picture of the kind of person one is. Developing an orientation to the world of work and an understanding of the meaning of work.	*14 years* Self-examination, role try-outs and occupational exploration take place in school, leisure activities, and part-time work. Substages: *Tentative* (15–17) Needs, interests, capacities, values, and opportunities are all considered, tentative choices are made and tried out in fantasy, discussion, courses, work, etc. Possible appropriate fields and levels of work are identified. Task — Crystallizing a Vocational Preference *Transition* (18–21) Reality considerations are given more weight as the person enters the labor market or professional training and attempts to implement a self-concept. Generalized choice is converted to specific choice. Task — Specifying a Vocational Preference *Trial-Little Commitment* (22–24) A seemingly appropriate occupation having been found, a first job is located and is tried out as a potential life work. Commitment is still provisional and if the job is not appropriate, the person may reinstitute the process of crystallizing, specifying, and implementing a preference. Task — Implementing a Vocational Preference	*24 years* Having found an appropriate field, an effort is made to establish a permanent place in it. Thereafter changes which occur are changes of position, job, or employer, not of occupation. Substages: *Trial-Commitment and Stabilization* (25–30) Settling down. Securing a permanent place in the chosen occupation. May prove unsatisfactory resulting in one or two changes before the life work is found or before it becomes clear that the life work will be a succession of unrelated jobs. *Advancement* (31–44) Effort is put forth to stabilize, to make a secure place in the world of work. For most persons these are the creative years. Seniority is acquired; clientele are developed; superior performance is demonstrated; qualifications are improved. Tasks: Consolidation and Advancement	*44 years* Having made a place in the world of work, the concern is how to hold on to it. Little new ground is broken, continuation of established pattern. Concerned about maintaining present status while being forced by competition from younger workers in the advancement stage. Tasks: Preservation of achieved status and gains. **Decline** *64 years* As physical and mental powers decline, work activity changes and in due course ceases. New roles must be developed: first, selective participant and then observer. Individual must find other sources of satisfaction to replace those lost through retirement. Substages: *Deceleration* (65–70) The pace of work slackens, duties are shifted, or the nature of work is changed to suit declining capacities. Many men find part-time jobs to replace their full-time occupations. *Retirement* (71 on) Variation on complete cessation of work or shift to part-time, volunteer, or leisure activities. Tasks: Deceleration, Disengagement, Retirement

Table 4.4
A Factor Analytic Model of Vocational Maturity in Ninth Grade

Factor I Planning Orientation
    A. Acceptance of Responsibility
    B. Specificity of Information (more immediate types)
    C. Specificity of Planning
    D. Steps Taken to Obtain Information
    E. Awareness of the Need for Choices

Factor II The Long View Ahead
    A. Awareness of the Need for Ultimate Choices
    B. Specificity of Information (remoter types)
    C. Entry Planning
    D. Awareness of Factors in Choice
    E. Awareness of Contingency Factors
    F. Acceptance of Responsibility

Factor III The Short View Ahead
    A. Specificity of Planning
    B. Awareness of the Need for Immediate Choices
    C. Acceptance of Responsibility for Choice
    D. Steps Taken to Obtain Information for High School

Factor IV The Intermediate View
    A. Awareness of Factors in Choice
    B. Awareness of Need for Intermediate Choices
    C. Specificity of Post-High School Plans
    D. Awareness of Contingency Factors

adulthood, Super (1977) postulates that the same five factors are important in midcareer as are important in adolescence: planfulness or time perspective, exploration, information, decision-making, and reality orientation. However, he contends that the tasks, the topics to be explored, and the kinds of information needed by 40-year-old adults are different from those important to adolescents. He further contends, "Although the content of decisions differs, decision-making principles are the same at any age and in dealing with any life stage."

From 1976 to 1979, Super lived and worked in England and began to test his theoretical propositions in that nation. While doing so, he also elaborated aspects of his conceptual models.

One aspect of his recent formulations is a Life-Career Rainbow (1980; 1981) to depict how various roles emerge and interact across the life span. He suggests that most people play nine major roles in their life, which emerge in approximate chronological order as follows: (1) child (including son or daughter), (2) student, (3) leisurite,

(4) citizen, (5) worker (including unemployed worker and nonworker as ways of playing the role), (6) spouse, (7) homemaker, (8) parent, and (9) pensioner. The constellation of interacting, varying roles constitutes the career (1980, p. 284). The principal theaters in which these roles are played include: (1) the home, (2) the community, (3) the school (including college and university), and (4) the workplace. Although there are other roles and other theaters, the ones identified tend to be the most common.

Each role tends to be played primarily in one theater, although some roles, such as worker, may spill over; that is, from the workplace to the home, and cause conflict and confusion. It is in role shaping, redefining the expectations of others and of the role itself with one's conception of it, as well as in the choice of positions and roles, that the individual synthesizes personal and situational role determinants.

With respect to the relationship between earlier performance and later positions and roles, Super maintains, "The nonoccupational positions occupied before the adult career begins influence both the adult positions which may be occupied and the way in which their role expectations are met. Thus the amount and type of schooling is one determinant of occupation entered, and the first occupational position, both its type and job performance, is one determinant of later occupational positions open to the individual" (1980, p. 286). Similarly, relationships occur between earlier and later performance throughout life and, indeed, between preretirement and satisfaction with one's life in retirement.

Super goes on to suggest that the fact that people play several roles simultaneously in several theaters means that occupation, family, community, and leisure roles affect each other. "Success in one facilitates success in others, and difficulties in one role are likely to lead to difficulties in another" (1980, p. 287).

Super indicates, "The simultaneous combination of life roles constitutes the *life style*; their sequential combination structures the *life space* and constitutes the *life cycle*. The total structure is the *career pattern*" (1980, p. 288). Accordingly, roles increase and decrease in importance with the life stage and according to the developmental tasks that are encountered with advancing age.

Decision points occur before and at the time of taking on a new role, of giving up an old role, and of making significant changes in the nature of an existing role (1980, p. 291). Super has identified a graphic model of career decision-making that involves cycling and recycling and is rational, prescriptive, developmental, and emergent. It is shown in Figure 4.4. What this model does not portray is that the time intervals at any one step may vary greatly. Depending on the circumstances that surround the career decision point, the total model may emerge over years, days, or weeks.

Finally, Super (1980) contends:

The decision points of a life career reflect encounters with a variety of personal and situational determinants. The former consist of the genetic constitution of the individual modified by his or her experiences (the environment and its situational determinants) in the womb, the home, and the community. The latter are the geographic, historic, social, and economic conditions in which the individual functions from infancy through adulthood and old age (p. 294).

These determinants affect *preferences, choices, entry* into the labor force and assumption of the worker role and role *changes*. Figure 4.5 portrays these two categories of determinants lifting up or pressing down on the individual.

Tiedeman's Paradigm. The work of Tiedeman and his associates, particularly O'Hara, added perspective to some elements of Super's propositions. In regard to Tiedeman particularly, Super (1969a) has stated:

Some men continue to change occupations throughout life, while others have stable periods followed by new periods of trial, which in turn lead to stabilization for a second or third time. Thus, there are stable (direct entry into the lifework), conventional (trial leading to stability), unstable, and multiple-trial careers. The life stage processes continue more or less throughout life, repeating themselves in the sequence: INITIAL – TRIAL – STABLE – DECLINE. Tiedeman's (1958) use of this concept in theorizing about position choice, each decision concerning the occupancy of a position involving exploration, establishment, and maintenance, is a useful refinement (p. 4).

Tiedeman alone, and with O'Hara, views career development as part of a continuing process of differentiating ego identity. In these terms, how a person's identity evolves is dependent on early childhood experiences within the family unit, the psychological crises — as defined in terms of Erikson's constructs (1963) — encountered at various developmental stages and the agreement between society's meaning system and the individual's meaning system as well as the emotional constants of each.

In essence, Tiedeman has emphasized an occupational decision-making paradigm within the staging phenomena (à la Erikson) making up career development. Tiedeman has maintained that Super's developmental perspective is probably an accurate way of viewing the process of career choice, but he further believes that an explicit statement about the characteristics of individual decisions needs to be made. To this end, Tiedeman has offered the following model of decision-making (Tiedeman, 1961):

Figure 4.4
A Developmental Model of Emergent Career Decision Making

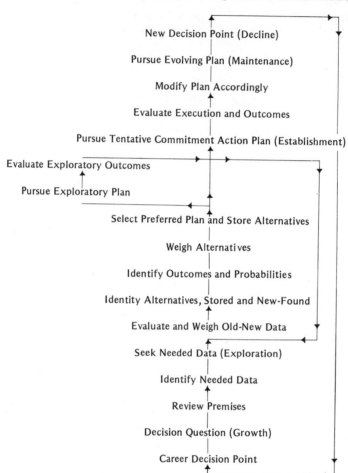

New Decision Point (Decline)

Pursue Evolving Plan (Maintenance)

Modify Plan Accordingly

Evaluate Execution and Outcomes

Pursue Tentative Commitment Action Plan (Establishment)

Evaluate Exploratory Outcomes

Pursue Exploratory Plan

Select Preferred Plan and Store Alternatives

Weigh Alternatives

Identify Outcomes and Probabilities

Identity Alternatives, Stored and New-Found

Evaluate and Weigh Old-New Data

Seek Needed Data (Exploration)

Identify Needed Data

Review Premises

Decision Question (Growth)

Career Decision Point

I. The Period of Anticipation
   A. Exploration (random and acquisitive activity)
   B. Crystallization (emerging of patterns in the form of alternatives and their consequences leading to clarification and comment)
   C. Choice (organizing in preparation for implementations)
   D. Specification (clarification)
II. The Period of Implementation and Adjustment
   A. Induction (person largely responsive)
   B. Reformation (person largely assertive)
   C. Integration (satisfaction)

Each of these stages is intended to represent a change in the dominant condition of the decision process. Indeed, each decision-making stage is represented by a qualitatively different psychological state.

Tiedeman's model is not limited to the formulation of a choice (anticipation) but also considers what happens when one attempts to implement that choice (induction). Basically, this process indicates that there is constant reciprocity between the person's self-concept and the environmental expectations as decisions are made and implemented. If the individual's ability to take on role expectations as defined by the environment is not

Figure 4.5
Personal and Situational Determinants of the Worker Role

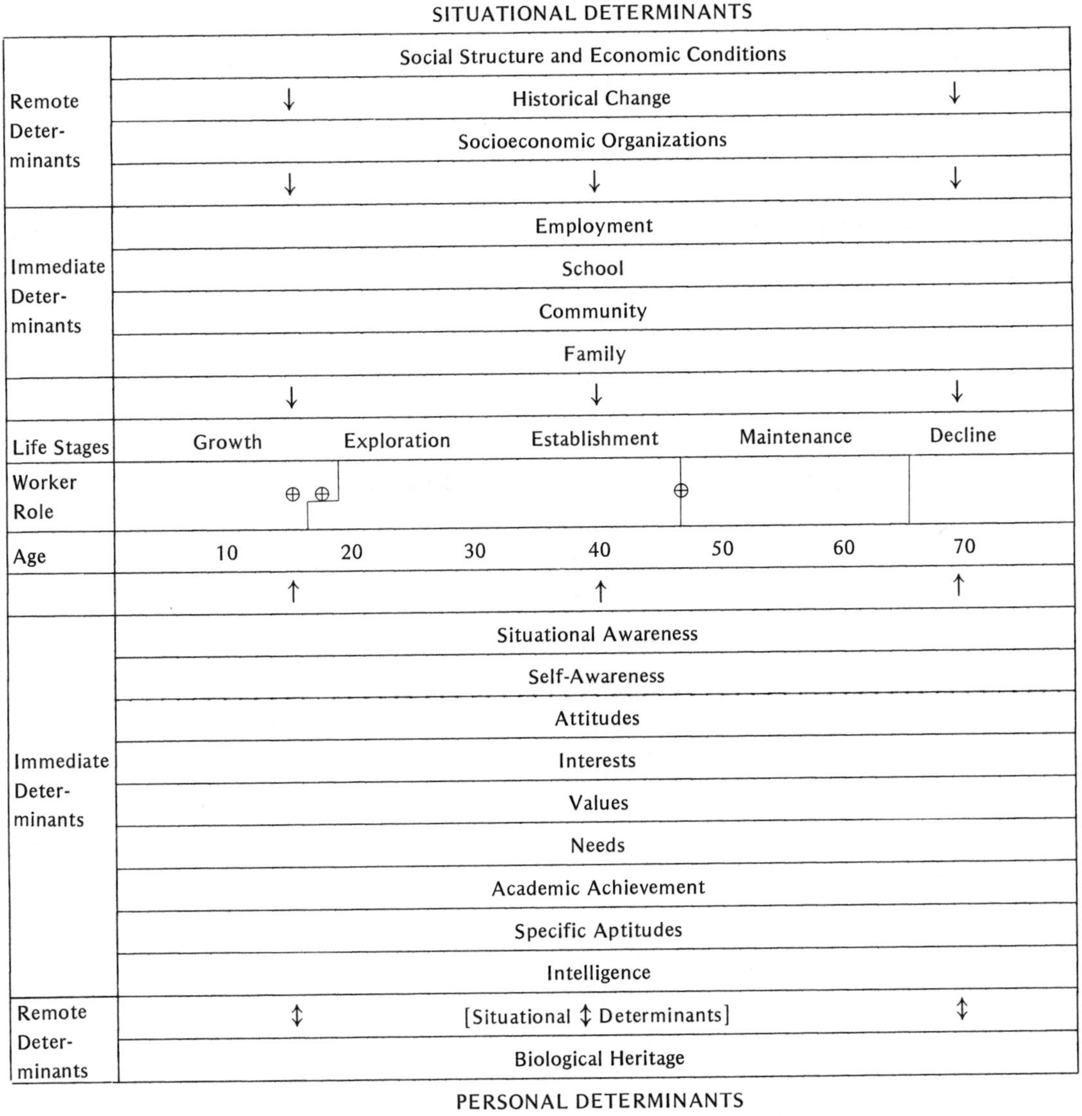

SITUATIONAL DETERMINANTS

Remote Deter-minants	Social Structure and Economic Conditions				
	↓		Historical Change		↓
	Socioeconomic Organizations				
	↓		↓		↓
Immediate Deter-minants	Employment				
	School				
	Community				
	Family				
	↓		↓		↓
Life Stages	Growth	Exploration	Establishment	Maintenance	Decline
Worker Role	⊕ ⊕		⊕		
Age	10	20　　30	40　　50	60	70
	↑		↑		↑
Immediate Deter-minants	Situational Awareness				
	Self-Awareness				
	Attitudes				
	Interests				
	Values				
	Needs				
	Academic Achievement				
	Specific Aptitudes				
	Intelligence				
Remote Deter-minants	↕		[Situational ↕ Determinants]		↕
	Biological Heritage				

PERSONAL DETERMINANTS

stretched beyond tolerance, the person will stay in the position and integrate these expectations into the ego concept. However, if this does not happen, the person will likely reinstitute the process of anticipation.

Tiedeman and O'Hara also suggest that individual personality is shaped by perceptions of career choices and also somewhat by the individual's conformance to the norms and values of those persons already established within the occupational setting. They stress the intimacy of self-concept and career concept as a person gradually matures through many small decisions.

Tiedeman's later work has become increasingly

independent and critical of Super's developmental perspectives. For example, in 1977, Dudley and Tiedeman observed, "In brief, Super did not provide any conceptualization of the personality as an active force with complex inner organization; he did not provide an adequate notion of the person as an agent in formation of a career pattern" (p. 6).

In his recent collaboration with others (Dudley & Tiedeman, 1977; Peatling & Tiedeman, 1977; Tiedeman & Miller-Tiedeman, 1977) Tiedeman has been increasingly instrumental in emphasizing the power of the individual to create a career and in advancing notions of autonomy, competence, and agency as major ingredients to such processes. He and his colleagues are pursuing ways to facilitate conceptions of the human career as a holistic concept, in which career and the process of career development are one.

Tiedeman and his colleagues have viewed career development as a "within to without" phenomenon rather than the reverse, which is more typical in conceptions of career development. In this view, anticipation of choice, the first major category of behavior in the original Tiedeman paradigm (1961) is seen as a creative process of hierarchial restructuring in which the individual continues to transform self and environmental subsystems as movement toward accommodation or implementation occur. The conceptualizations have been aided by the evolution from a cubistic model to a pyramidal one. The cubistic model (Miller & Tiedeman, 1972) suggests that three dimensions are involved in leading a decision-guided life that is proactive (from within to without) rather than reactive (from without to within). Each of the basic conditions is comprised of three steps along the way to greater maturity, sophistication, or consciousness in action: 1. *problem condition* — steps: problem forming (vicarious), problem solving (acting out), solution using (autonomous use). 2. *psychological states* — steps: exploration, clarification, accommodation. 3. *self-comprehension* — steps: learning about, doing, doing with awareness (Miller & Tiedeman, 1972). This schematic provides a language system by which one can help the individual with self-comprehension and movement toward greater control of personal decision-making and the recycling of it. Miller-Tiedeman (1977) subsequently simpli-

fied the cubistic model into a pyramid containing many of the same concepts and others particularly important to her efforts to facilitate decision-making with adolescents. The pyramidal model of decision-making comprehension includes four levels — learning about, problem-solving, solution-using, solution-reviewing — which are each elaborated and coupled with a hierarchy of decision strategies.

In sum, Tiedeman and, in particular, Miller-Tiedeman are evolving a conceptual, linguistic, and process structure designed to accept the power of the person to create and to be in human career. Although other approaches to career development do not oppose such notions of individual power to create a career, Tiedeman and Miller-Tiedeman seem dedicated to self-empowerment as the central proposition in such a process.

Knefelkamp and Slepitza. An interesting model of career development that actually blends a developmental and cognitive approach has been advanced by Knefelkamp and Slepitza (1976). Although research continues on this model, it will likely play a prominent role in emphasizing a comprehensive view of career development, at least among college students.

Extending the earlier work of Perry (1968), which focused on the ethical and intellectual development of college students, Knefelkamp and Slepitza postulate that college students move from a simplistic categorical view of career through four stages culminating in a complex, pluralistic view of career. The movement of college students through these stages can be predicted and described through the unfolding of nine variables, each of which represents a substage. Figure 4.6 portrays these relations.

The stages, in paraphrased form, are as follows:

1. Dualism — This stage is dominated by simplistic, dichotomous thinking about career planning that largely is controlled by information obtained from external sources.

2. Multiplicity — In this stage, student decision-making becomes more cognitively complex and more oriented to the possibility of making right and wrong choices. More factors are considered in the process and cause-and-effect relations are worked into the decision-making process.

Figure 4.6

Variables of Qualitative Change
Knefelkamp/Slepitza Model of Career Development

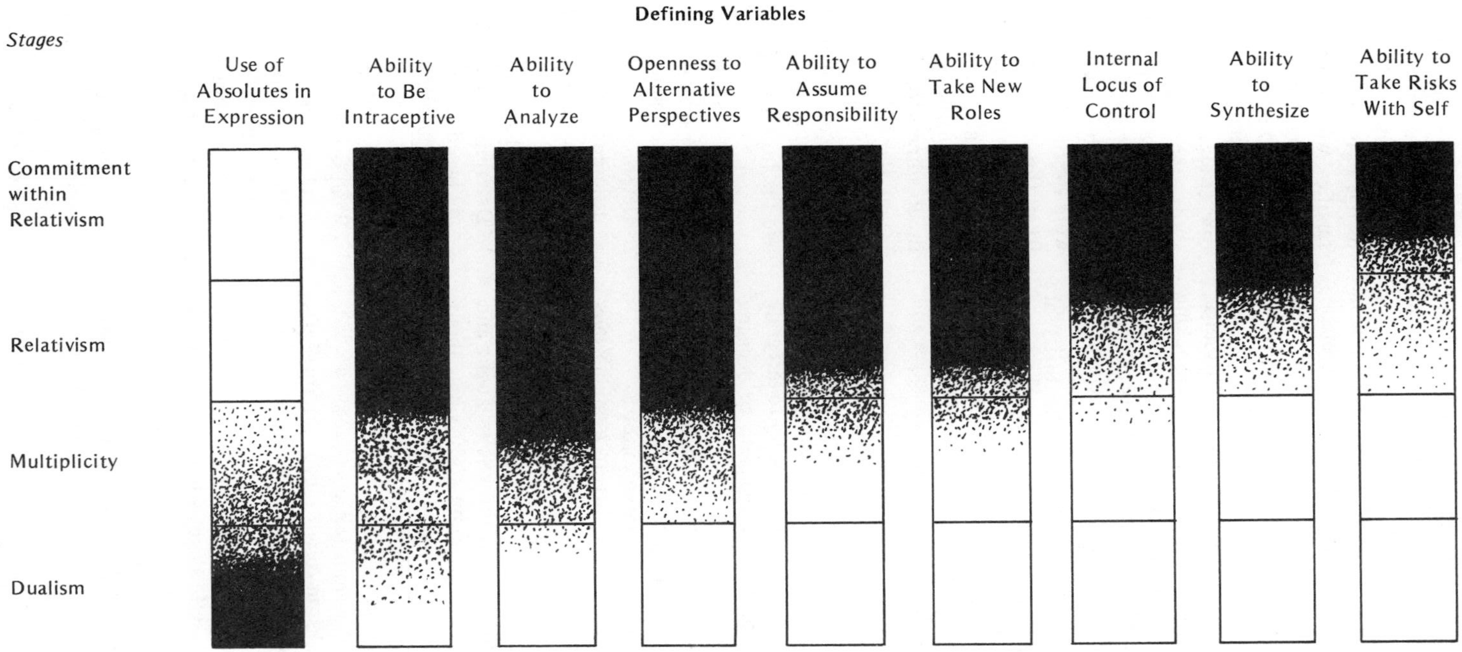

Defining Variables

Columns (Defining Variables): Use of Absolutes in Expression, Ability to Be Intraceptive, Ability to Analyze, Openness to Alternative Perspectives, Ability to Assume Responsibility, Ability to Take New Roles, Internal Locus of Control, Ability to Synthesize, Ability to Take Risks With Self

Stages: Commitment within Relativism, Relativism, Multiplicity, Dualism

Degree of density corresponds with presence of variable

131

3. Relativism – In this stage, the student's point tends to shift from a predominantly external to a predominantly internal one. Students are more analytical in their decision-making, tend to assume responsibility for decisions made, and they create a decision-making process which is tailored to their own characteristics and perceptions.
4. Commitment within Relativism – In this stage, increased responsibility for the decision-making process is taken, choice of a career is seen as a personal commitment, career identity and self-identity become more closely intertwined.

The nine variables that affect the maturity of career planning among college students, as the stages just cited evolve, include:

1. Locus of Control – the external-internal sources students use to define themselves and their environments.
2. Analysis – the individual's ability to break down a decision into its diverse elements and to consider cause and effect relationships.
3. Synthesis – the individual's ability to integrate the diverse aspects of a problem or decision into a whole.
4. Semantic Structure – the continuum of absolute-open verbs and qualifiers students use in their written and spoken expressions.
5. Self-Processing – the ability to examine oneself and take into account one's defining factors.
6. Openness of Alternative Perspectives – the degree to which a student knows about and considers alternative points of view about options.
7. Ability to Assume Responsibility – the student's willingness to accept the consequences of actions or decisions taken.
8. Ability to Take on New Roles – the student's ability to accommodate the characteristics of new roles or activities.
9. Ability to Take Risks with Self – the student's ability to risk self-esteem when new learnings and experiences so demand.

Gribbons and Lohnes' Career Development Study.
Gribbons and Lohnes (1968; 1982) have been engaged in a longitudinal study of career development, entitled the Career Development Study

(CDS), for more than twenty years. The 111 subjects of the study (57 boys and 54 girls) began to be studied when they were eighth graders in 1958 in five eastern Massachusetts communities. These families were scattered in socioeconomic status and fathers' occupations. The students had in common exposure to an eighth-grade group guidance treatment based on *You: Today and Tomorrow* (Katz, 1958). Throughout the years of the study, the subjects were interviewed intensively and were contacted by questionnaire, correspondence, and by telephone. Early in 1980 a final data collection was completed when the subjects were 34 or 35 years old. Contact was made with 91 of the 108 living subjects.

Much of the data were collected by first using the Readiness for Vocational Planning Scale, which was subsequently abbreviated and retitled the Readiness for Career Planning Scale. To a large extent the CDS has attempted to validate many of the concepts first proposed in the research framework for Super's Career Pattern Study.

Specifically, the Career Development Study has had the following specific objectives:

1. Test the theory of occupational choice that proposes a process running through a sequence of developmental stages.
2. Determine whether there are significant sex differences in career sequences.
3. Describe in detail 110 real careers over 11 years of development, and seek unifying mathematical and psychological models for them.
4. Determine the extent to which career decisions are based upon selected self-concept and other factors, answering such questions as:
   What is the role of intelligence in choosing, entering, and remaining in an occupation?
   What is the role of values in making choices?
   What is the impact of value shifts as they occur with maturation?
   What effects do familial and societal pressures have in shaping occupational aspiration?
5. Accomplish a successful multidimensional scaling of early vocational maturing from an interview protocol, naming the resulting scales, as a set, Readiness for Vocational Planning (RVP).
6. Explore the statistical dependence of numerous criteria of career development on the RVP scales, collecting the criteria in followup inter-

views every two years for a total of 11 years. (Gribbons & Lohnes, 1982, p. 25)

In their first major report in 1968, Gribbons and Lohnes examined the concept of Readiness for Vocational Planning as a measure of vocational maturity during adolescence. Their research identified eight variables, which in combination correlated highly with readiness for vocational planning at the eighth-grade and postsecondary school levels. They are (pp. 15–16):

Variable I. Factors in Curriculum Choice – Awareness of relevant factors, including one's abilities, interests and values and their relation to curriculum choice; curricula choice to occupational choice.

Variable II. Factors in Occupational Choice – Awareness of relevant factors, including abilities, interests, values; educational requirements for choice; accuracy of description of occupation.

Variable III. Verbalized Strengths and Weaknesses – Ability to verbalize appropriately the relation of personal strengths and weaknesses to educational and vocational choices.

Variable IV. Accuracy of Self-appraisal – Comparison of subject's estimates of his general scholastic ability, verbal ability, and quantitative ability with his actual attainments on scholastic aptitude tests, English grades, and mathematics grades.

Variable V. Evidence of Self-rating – Quality of evidence cited by subject in defense of his appraisal of his own abilities.

Variable VI. Interests – Awareness of interests and their relation to occupational choices.

Variable VII. Values – Awareness of values and their relation to occupational choices.

Variable VIII. Independence of Choice – Extent of subject's willingness to take personal responsibility for his choices.

Gribbons and Lohnes found that vocational maturity – as measured by the eight Readiness for Vocational Planning scales cited – increased from grades eight to ten. They also indicated that an overlapping of scores in these two grades showed that some eighth-graders had already achieved considerable vocational maturity while some tenth-graders evidenced a considerable lack of it.

More important as a rationale for vocational development is their findings that levels of eighth-grade vocational maturity are predictive of educational and occupational planning, educational aspirations, and level of occupational aspirations in the twelfth grade; of field and level of actual occupation two years after high school; and of two-year, post–high school career adjustment. The RVP scales failed to discriminate among those students manifesting Differential Career Processes – constant maturity, emerging maturity, degeneration, and constant immaturity – but they did demonstrate a trend from idealism in the eighth grade to realism in the twelfth grade, with brighter students (above IQ 105) appearing to choose more consistently with their measured intelligence than less bright students.

Following the portion of their study reported in 1968, Gribbons and Lohnes revised the Readiness for Vocational Planning because it had proven to be too time consuming and cumbersome. Its place was taken by the Readiness for Career Planning, a shorter scale (twenty-two items rather than forty-five) that was simpler to score.

When the authors compared their 1980 data with the variety of data they had examined at different decision points throughout the preceding twenty-two years, they made a number of conclusions. These are selectively summarized and paraphrased as follows:

1. By 1980 very few of the subjects were in the occupations to which they had aspired as eighth graders in 1958. Only six men and six women were in the same or closely related occupations. As a result, Gribbons and Lohnes contend that career guidance in secondary education should not focus on counseling about specific occupational titles, but only as these illuminate principles that apply to discriminations among broad career fields and levels (p. 115).

2. By 1980, eight women and six men remained in the same socioeconomic class that their families had occupied in 1958, whereas twenty-four women and twenty-three men moved one or more levels higher and fifteen men and fifteen women moved lower in socioeconomic level from that occupied by their families in 1958.

3. By 1980 only twenty of the fifty-two persons who aspired to college as eighth graders had

actually achieved the goal (54 percent males, 15 percent females).

4. A general result of the longitudinal study is that it has been shown that career patterns can be conceptualized, operationally defined, measured, and predicted. Career transitions are in part predictable from probability laws fitted to career process variables and in part predictable from antecedent trait profiles of subjects (p. 126).

5. The Career Development Tree from Project TALENT research appears to be the most useful mapping of career patterns over adolescence and into young adulthood. A curriculum that would produce understanding of this mapping would produce a considerable sophistication in world view and a frame of reference for exploring personal multipotentiality (p. 126).

6. Inputs to the computation of career predictions need to include:

Current career plans

Sex

Socioeconomic status

Ability factors (verbal knowledge, mathematics, English, visual reasoning)

Vocational maturity factors

Scholasticism

Interest factors (science, cultural, business, outdoors and shop) (pp. 126–127)

7. The majority of adolescents are poorly oriented with respect to career development tasks and fully one-third to one-half of young adults at age twenty-five appear to be in career development troubles (p. 127).

8. Educational variables prefigure career variables. "We think it is in their failure to sponsor understanding of the career values of education that educators miss their main opportunity to promote best career development possible in students" (p. 128).

9. "Career guidance in our schools should begin in the elementary years with curriculum units designed to teach understanding and the value of careers and education as they intertwine in our civilization. In the junior high years, students should begin to interact with a computer measurement system that will help them to assess their personality and project their multipotentiality.... Ways must be found to communicate the scientific knowledge we now have about career development to young people in our schools, in modes

that encourage better relations of self to society, better self direction and greater acceptance of responsibility for personal history. The knowledge is technical, involving probability laws and trait-statistical maps. It requires computer communications. We must have a computerized career information system as an integral part of a career guidance curriculum in our schools" (pp. 128–129).

10. Finally, in comparing the men and women subjects over the twenty years of the study, women, as a group, were able to aspire to less and to achieve less than men. Sex-role stereotypes appear to have been the primary source of the special difficulties for women.

The most mature stage of career development in this process model suggests that career maturity can also be conceived in terms of self-actualization as used in other places in this book.

Adult Development. Among the major emphases in career development in the past ten years is adult career development. As suggested in several other places in this chapter, much of the early work in career development theory and research was focused on adolescent exploration, anticipation, and the formulation of preferences, although the major theorists have speculated about adult development as well as adolescent development. It is now clear that exploration and change do not end with adolescence but continue throughout life.

Summarizing the work of major theorists in adult development, Schlossberg (1978) has advanced five propositions about adult development that reflect some of the change that occurs. These propositions follow in paraphrased form:

1. *Behavior in adulthood is determined by social rather than by biological clocks.* In childhood and adolescence, biological development or deterioration is a greater factor than in adulthood. Beyond the changes occasioned by menopause or the possible rapid physical change of late, late adulthood, most of the effects on behavior in adulthood are social, not biological. Social norms about when and how certain behavior should occur — when one should marry, settle down in a job, or retire — tend to affect perceptions of and stimulate action regarding major life events. To

be out of synchronization with such events may cause feelings of uncertainty, anxiety, or inadequacy. Although these age-related norms may be changing under the influence of the increasing numbers of adults returning to school, changing careers in midlife, entering new careers after retirement, and trying out new marital and life styles, socially defined age-appropriate behavior remains a very powerful influence on life-career behavior.

2. *Behavior is at times a function of life stage, at others of age.* As will be shown in Chapter 6 (Table 6.2), many theorists have identified distinct chronological periods in which specific tasks, problems, structures, and states of mind are likely to occur. Levinson et al. (1978) to be discussed in the next section advocates such a view. Other theorists (such as Lowenthal, Thurnher, & Chiriboga, 1976) attribute less importance to age per se and much more importance to what types of events or the tasks the person is actually dealing with. This is a "stage approach."

3. *Sex differences are greater than either age or stage differences.* In the various adult life stages, men and women differ dramatically, partly because of early socialization and partly because their identities tend to be defined differently. The identities of men tend to be defined primarily in terms of direct achievement. Women, on the other hand, define their identities more in terms of vicarious achievement, not through their own activities and accomplishments but through those of the dominant people in their lives (usually men) (Lipman-Blumen & Leavitt, 1977).

4. *Adults continually experience transitions requiring adaptations and reassessment of the self.* In opposition to notions that adulthood is one of stability and certainty, the concept of transitions suggests that adults are constantly experiencing change either deliberately, because it is chosen, or inadvertently, because of forces external to the self. Such changes can engender growth, new concepts of self, or crisis and deterioration. In either case stress accompanies the transition and requires adaptation.

5. *The recurrent themes of adulthood are identity, intimacy, and generativity.* Identity, intimacy, and generativity, as defined by Erickson (1950), recur throughout the individual's life. Identity may become an issue whenever the indi-

vidual faces a transition. This in turn raises questions of generativity: What meaning does my life have? What have I contributed to the world? What have I created? Intimacy refers to free, open, spontaneous, affectionate, trusting responses with all of those with whom we have close human ties. These relationships tend to sustain energy and motivation to develop identity and to cope with matters of generativity. They are apparently crucial to successful adaptation to transitions.

Although the work of Ginzberg et al. and Super et al. are quite pertinent to understanding career behavior in adulthood, it is useful to accent here the efforts of several other theorists as well.

The Importance of Adult Transitions. As the propositions of adult development provided by Schlossberg suggest, transitions are the central focus of much current theoretical attention. Indeed, Perry (1982) has contended that "special needs populations" can be conceived of in two ways: (1) as those who are experiencing equity difficulty in gaining access to education and work because of bias, discrimination, quotas, prejudice, and other forms of social gate-keeping; and (2) those who are at risk because of transitions — changing families, mid-career job dislocation, retirement. In much of the literature transitions are portrayed as frightening or traumatic. Indeed, as Schlossberg (1981) has asserted, the current definitions of transition have actually grown out of crisis theory. However, some theorists (such as Parkes, 1971) prefer the term psychosocial transition to play down the notion of crisis. It is in this perspective that Levinson et al. (1978) talk of *developmental transition* to represent "a turning point or boundary between two periods of greater stability" (p. 57).

It is probably fair to argue that Levinson, Darrow, Klein, Levinson, and McKee (1978) have extended the models of Havighurst, Ginzberg et al. and Super et al. by adding the notion of transition to each of the life stages portrayed in those models. In other words, one does not abruptly change life stages (exploration to establishment, establishment to maintenance), but instead engages in a period of activity over time that represents a transition to the next life stage. Levinson et al. use the term *era*, much as other theorists use the term stage or phase (p. 18). According to Levinson et al. there are four such eras in life: childhood and adolescence, ages 0–22; early adulthood, 17–45; middle adulthood, 40–65; and late adulthood, 60 on. The transition between eras consistently takes four or five years — not less than three and rarely more than six. Transitions are developmental periods that link the eras and provide some continuity between them, a boundary zone. "The nature of each era is reflected in the evolution of a man's careers in work, family, and other settings, his involvement in solitary and social enterprises, and his broader life plans and goals" (p. 30). The pronoun 'his' is used precisely here because Levinson's work like that of Super was based on research with men. He and his colleagues studied forty men in considerable depth over several years, as the empirical base for his theoretical perspective. They split the subjects into four groups of ten men each from one of four occupational subgroups: hourly workers in industry, business executives, university biologists, and novelists.

In addition to eras and transitions, Levinson et al. use several other terms to describe career development as they see it. Primary among these is *individual life structure*. The life structure refers to the patterning of one's life at a given time and to the engagement of the individual in society. Levinson (1977) contends that a life structure has three aspects:

1. The nature of the man's *sociocultural world*, including class, religion, ethnicity, race, family, political systems, occupational structure, and particular conditions and events, such as economic depression or prosperity, war, and liberation movements of all kinds.
2. His *participation in this world* — his evolving relationships and roles as citizen, worker, boss, lover, friend, husband, father, member of diverse groups and organizations.
3. The *aspects of his self* that are expressed and lived out in the various components of his life; and the aspects of the self that must be inhibited or neglected within the life structure (1977, p. 100). In Levinson et al. (1978) this aspect is expanded to reflect the idea that a man selectively uses and is used by his world, through his evolving relationships and roles as

citizen, lover, worker, boss, friend, husband, father, member of diverse groups and enterprises. Participation involves transactions between self and world (p. 42).

In this view (Levinson, 1977; Levinson et al., 1978) adult development is the evolution of a life structure through alternating stable periods and transitional periods. The primary developmental task of a stable period "is to make certain crucial choices; build a life structure around them and seek to attain particular goals and values within this structure" (p. 100). Each stable period has its distinctive tasks that reflect the requirements of that time in the life cycle. The primary developmental task of a *transitional period* is "to terminate the existing structure and to work toward the initiation of a new structure" (1977, p. 100). In this process a man reappraises the existing life structure, explores possibilities for change in the world and in the self, and moves toward the crucial choices that will form the basis for a new life structure in the next stable period. Each transitional period also has its own distinctive tasks reflecting its place in the life cycle.

Levinson et al. (1978) describe choices as the primary components of the life structure. To describe and analyze the life structure is to consider the choices a person makes and how he deals with the consequences. "Every choice is saturated by both self and world. To choose something means to have a relationship with it. The relationship becomes a vehicle for living out certain aspects of the self and for engaging in certain modes of participation in the world" (p. 44).

Other Major Approaches to Adult Development. Several other approaches to adult development are useful in extending our views of career development. Unfortunately, space here does not permit a fair treatment of them. Suffice it to say they can be divided into those which emphasize "phasic" or "stage" approaches (Lasker, Moore, & Simpson, 1980). Phasic approaches are those in which certain types of development are seen to occur during relatively fixed periods of life: they are age-related. Levinson et al. (1978), Super (1957), Ginzberg et al. (1951), Erikson (1950), and Gould (1978) would be examples. The stage approach involves identification of levels of maturity that are essentially independent of age but vary with the psychological capabilities and development of different individuals. Loevinger (1976), Perry (1968), Knefelkamp and Slepitza (1976) are representative of such approaches. Together, these theorical approaches reinforce the importance of change for notions of career development, of differences in individual interpretations of events and in their capabilities to act on them, and of the interactive nature of self and society. Chapter 6 gives a summary of the life stage emphases or tasks proposed by many of the theorists described in this section (Table 6.2).

IMPLICATIONS FOR CAREER GUIDANCE AND COUNSELING AND CAREER EDUCATION

In the several approaches covered in this chapter, career development is described as a process shaped by an interplay of self-references; self-knowledge; knowledge about training; educational and occupational opportunities; genetic and early childhood influences; evolving personality styles; and patterns of traits that individuals express cognitively and psychologically in their choice behavior and career identity. The collective finding of these descriptions of career development is that like all human behavior, it is complex and is part of the total fabric of personality development.

Career development is characterized by progressive growth and learning operating from infancy through adulthood within a network of impinging forces internal and external to the individual. Within this context, choice behavior involves a series of interdependent decisions that are to some extent irreversible and are intimately tied to the individual's personal history, to personal perceptions of the future, and to both antecedent experiences and future alternatives.

Most of the existing approaches to career development are based on limited samples of rather privileged persons; most often these samples are of men rather than women. They are, in general, addressed to those in the middle range of socioeconomic characteristics rather than to those who veer from this classification in either direction. Consequently, these approaches tend to empha-

size the continuous, uninterrupted, and progressive aspects of career development that seem possible primarily in those whose choice barriers are minimal, for whom both psychological and economic resources are available to aid purposeful development, and in whom a high correspondence between self-concept and vocational concept is most probable. Such criteria do not fit all the persons about whom career guidance practitioners or educators must be concerned.

Another characteristic of these current approaches to career development is that although they predict that individuals with particular need hierarchies or self-concepts will reject occupations and career patterns that do not seem compatible with their personal characteristics, little attention is given to the possibility that work itself is not central to the life styles or aspirations of some persons, or that it has connotations that repel rather than attract. As Zytowski (1965, p. 746) has stated, "They assume that all men want to work, that the idea of a vocation has a positive valence as a goal, or that the effect attached to career behavior is positive." For many persons, however, choices are based not on what they want to do but on what they do not want to do. For these people, choice seems to be more nearly a matter of moving away from the undesirable rather than moving toward an ideal (Gross, 1967). For other persons, work is not the central commitment for investment of identification or energy that many theories assume.

Another point of concern in present descriptions of career development is the age or level of maturity required to make choices. "Most would feel that a certain maturing process must take place before youth (ages 14 to 18) can sensibly make choices — especially vocational ones" (McDaniels, 1968). McDaniels rebuts this assumption by stating that youth "are not too young to choose, only too poorly prepared to make choices." Thus, in much of the thinking about career development, there is insufficient attention to the heterogeneity in every group within the population whether classified by age, sex, race, social class, or any other basis.

Perhaps the most important point of all in analyzing current approaches to career development is that the theories largely describe what happens if nothing is done to influence the process. Although several longitudinal approaches have emerged — for example, Super's Career Pattern Study (1957), Crites' Vocational Development Project (1969), Gribbons and Lohnes' Readiness for Vocational Development (1968) — their purpose has not been systematically to influence career development but only to describe it at different stages of life. Taking due cognizance of the caveats expressed, the following career development implications would seem to provide a conceptual base for planning career guidance or career education activities.

1. The concept that people are only economic animals and that work is chosen only for the livelihood it offers is too simplistic. Work also provides a means for meeting needs of social interaction, dignity, self-esteem, self-identification, and other forms of psychological gratification.
2. Individual differences in performance and in preference exist among people, and these can be related to differences among people occupying various occupational and educational roles.
3. Personal, educational, occupational, or career maturation is comprised of complex learning processes that begin in early childhood and continue throughout life.
4. Choice occurs not as a point in time but in relation to antecedent experiences and future alternatives.
5. Decision-making is continuous, tentative, and often more psychological than logical.
6. Because of the importance to adult behavior of early childhood experiences in the family, the school, the community, intervention to facilitate positive career development needs to begin during the first decade of life. This is the nursery of human nature, when attitudes are formed that are ultimately reflected in career commitment or rejection.
7. Career development is comprised of tasks with which persons must cope in each life stage. Many of these tasks are culturally defined; some are age related; some are stimulated by transitions.
8. Value systems, both individual and cultural, are important in shaping career development.
9. Career information must include not only ob-

jective factors such as earning possibilities, training requirements, and numbers of positions available but also the social and psychological aspects of careers as well.

10. To be effective, career information should be provided in contests, actual or simulated — for example, gaming, field trips, career-sensitive curricula, work study, role playing, computer-mediated information retrieval — by which individuals can project themselves into possible career roles, act them out, and test their meaning.
11. Since occupational and career choices are methods of implementing an individual's self-concept or expressing their personality style or type, information about self-characteristics — attitudes, aptitudes, values — is as necessary as career or occupational information. Unless the person knows what personal resources he or she has to commit to choice and the outcomes sought, the person has no guidelines by which to evaluate whether anything is of value to him or her.
12. Career development concepts provide the substance for program goals for career guidance and career education that can be translated into behavioral expectations for students or adults and pertinent experiences created to facilitate such behaviors for persons in different life stages.
13. Career development theory indicates that decision-making involves action. Therefore, ways need to be found to help persons take responsibility for their own learning and for their own direction. Persons need to be helped to develop planning skills and the courage to execute their plans.
14. Persons need to be helped to develop an awareness that they do have choices, to determine at any given time what kind of decision is involved and the factors inherent in the decision that make a personal difference.
15. An individual's career development is not isolated from development in physical, emotional, and mental areas.
16. Choice opportunities for most persons are so complex that career guidance in the family or neighborhood is likely to be inadequate for today's realities.
17. Occupational choices and career patterns are

basic to one's life style and reflect developmental experiences, personality, goals, and so forth.

18. Career choice can be an essentially rational process if the person knows how to select and obtain appropriate information and then is able to apply the decision-making process to it.

19. Career choice is frequently a compromise between the attractiveness of an alternative, the likelihood of attaining it, and the costs of attaining it.

Summary

In this chapter, the concept of career development has been defined and applied to the term vocationalization, and the possibility of influencing such development rather than leaving it to random events has been suggested. Finally, five major approaches to describing career development —trait-and-factor, decision, situational, psychological, and developmental emphases — have been discussed and some of their implications identified.

Whatever the process of occupational or career decision-making, it is clear that choice involves a series of minidecisions made over a relatively long period of time. If systematic assistance in making these decisions can be provided, there is an increasing likelihood that the decisions will be "good" — appropriate for the chooser. The factors that enter into a vocational decision and the process by which that decision is made are highly complex. Content and process are intricately related. What a systematic approach to career guidance accomplishes is to bring some order into what is typically a chaotic, haphazard choice.

Finally, it is important to reassert that the present perspectives of career development are incomplete in describing the behavioral development at issue. They have not been formulated as a result of or in conjunction with repeated or longitudinal studies as much as one would hope. Neither do they use enough samples from female or disadvantaged populations that one can feel confident of the similarities or dissimilarities across subcultures that are implied in some of these theories. The particular career problems and the ways theoretical approaches fit various special populations will be discussed in Chapter 5.

LEARNING ACTIVITIES

1. Outline the life stages and developmental tasks of Super's approach to career development, and identify how they might be used in organizing career guidance.
2. Write a brief essay defining the term self-concept.
3. Describe how a teacher or counselor might use Festinger's Theory of Cognitive Dissonance to help persons weigh alternative behaviors related to some problem situation.
4. Select the approach to career development in which you are most interested. Describe why you are so inclined and what implications this approach has for career guidance practice.
5. Analyze each of the approaches to career development and tell what it says about careers as a developmental process versus careers as a specific choice.
6. Identify each of Holland's six personality types and write a brief description of the personality characteristics of each type.
7. Compare expectancy theory and self-efficacy theory. List three similarities and two differences of each.
8. Define the term transition and consider why it has become so important in thinking about adult development.
9. Define an exploratory stage in career development and list its implications for career guidance practice.
10. Develop a rationale for the systematic teach-

ing of a decision-making skill to persons at different developmental stages.

11. Compare the five major approaches to career development by listing the unique aspects of each and any similarities that exist.

12. Construct a matching exercise, identifying in one column the theoretical approaches, in a second column the names of persons associated with each approach, and in a third column, the major concepts of each approach.

OBJECTIVES

After reading this chapter, engaging in the learning activities, and reading the references suggested, you should have met the objectives that follow. If you have not, it would probably be useful for

you to review the material in Chapter 4 before proceeding further. You should now be able to:

1. Describe the relationships between socialization, vocationalization, and career development.

2. Distinguish the characteristics of a career model from those of an occupational model.

3. Identify at least three major concepts each of a trait-and-factor approach, a decision theory approach, situational emphases, psychological emphases, and developmental emphases.

4. Name at least two theorists associated with each of the five major approaches that describe career development and choice.

5. List at least seven implications for career guidance and career education, which flow from the different approaches, to explain career development and choice.

5 / Career Development and Counseling of Special Populations

Chapter 4 presented a summary of what we know about so-called majority groups. Several other populations are thought to be sufficiently distinct from these groups on whom career development normalization data have been gathered that they should be treated differently. We agree that these other populations have some unique concerns; we also believe that much of what we have learned about career development can, in fact, be applied to these populations. Differences in career development between these populations and the "norm" may, in fact, be more a matter of degree than of kind.

There are a great many possible special populations. For example, workers on late shifts represent one of every six full-time employees (Hedges & Sekscenski, 1979). It is assumed that these workers have unique problems that cause them to suffer from sleep disturbances, digestive and nervous disorders, and disruptions of family life, all of which negatively affect marriages. Hence, we might well treat this population separately. Because of space limitations, however, we must limit the populations we will discuss. The populations we have chosen are: women, the culturally different, immigrants, and the disabled.

In each case, we will present an overview of research relating to the population and offer suggestions for counseling. In some of these areas, the research is conflicting. We have tried to make as much sense as possible out of these inconsistencies and to be temperate in our conclusions. With each group, we would suggest, the counselor can draw on a great deal of conventional career development theory. This chapter should provide information to supplement that knowledge.

WOMEN

Throughout this volume, we will look specifically at the unique career development needs of females. We emphasize women because of their recent large-scale entry into the labor market and because we are learning more about their career development each day. That knowledge guides practice and instructs us how to apply differential interventions to enhance female career development.

No less an authority than Freud (1930) pointed out, "No other technique for the conduct of life attaches the individual so firmly to reality as laying emphasis on work; for his work at least gives him a secure place in a portion of reality, in the human community" (p. 80). If he were living now, he would have to delete the masculine pronouns, for the work imperative holds as much for women as it does for men. There is no differentiation in the capacity of work to meet the psychological, social, and economic needs of both men and women.

During the 1970s the number and percentage of women in the labor force rose continually. Waldman et al. (1979) sum up the progress of women workers during the decade.

More than a million women per year, on average, joined the labor force; the greatest percentage increase in women's labor force rates occurred for those with children under age 6. The dual-worker family became a more solid part of American life, and the number of women maintaining their own families, very frequently with young children at home, rose to the highest level ever recorded in the country. (p. 40)

In a more detailed summary of the current status of women workers, the Women's Bureau of the United States Department of Labor has promulgated *20 Facts on Women Workers* (Women's Bureau, 1982). In somewhat edited form, these facts follow.

1. The majority of women work because of economic need. Two-thirds (66 percent) of all women in the labor force in March 1982 were single (25 percent), widowed (5 percent), divorced (11 percent), or separated (4 percent), or had husbands whose earnings in 1981 were less than $15,000 (21 percent).
2. About 47 million women were in the labor force in 1981. This compares with 32 million in 1971.
3. The average woman worker is 34 years old. At that age she can expect to work about eighteen more years.
4. Sixty-two percent of all women 18 to 64 years of age were workers in 1981, compared to 91 percent of men. Fifty-two percent of all women 16 years and over were workers. Labor force participation was highest among women 20 to 24 (70 percent).
5. Women accounted for 43 percent of all workers in 1981. Black women made up nearly half (49 percent) of the black labor force; white women represented 42 percent of all white workers; and Hispanic women were 39 percent of all Hispanic workers.
6. The influx of women into the work force during the 1970s has resulted in nearly equal labor force participation rates for women, by race or ethnic origin.
7. Women accounted for three-fifths (60 percent) of the increase in the civilian labor force in the last decade — more than 13 million women compared with nearly 9 million men.
8. More than one-fourth (28 percent) of all women workers held part-time jobs in 1981; a great majority of them (78 percent) were employed on a voluntary part-time basis. About 66 percent of all part-time workers were women.
9. In 1977 the average woman 16 years of age

could expect to spend 27.7 years of her life in the work force, compared with 38.5 for men.
10. The more education a woman has, the greater the likelihood that she will seek employment. Among women with four or more years of college, about three out of five (58 percent) were in the labor force in 1981.
11. The average woman worker is as well educated as the average man worker. In March 1981 both had completed a median of 12.7 years of schooling.
12. Women workers with four or more years of college education had about the same income as men who had only one to three years of high school. When employed full-time year round, women high school graduates (with no college) had about the same income on the average as fully employed men who had not completed elementary school.
13. Women are still concentrated in low-paying dead-end jobs. As a result, among full-time year-round workers the average woman earns only about three-fifths (59 percent) of the average man's earnings. The median wage or salary income of year-round full-time workers in 1981 was lowest for black women and highest for white men.
14. Women continue to constitute large proportions of workers in traditional occupations. They were 80 percent of all clerical workers in 1981 but only 6 percent of all craft workers; 62 percent of service workers but only 45 percent of professional and technical workers; and 63 percent of retail sales workers but only 28 percent of nonfarm managers and administrators.
15. The unemployment rate was lowest for adult white men (20 and over) and highest for young black women (16 to 19) in 1981.
16. The number of working mothers has increased more than tenfold since the period immediately preceding World War II (1940), and the numbers of working women more than tripled. Fifty-nine percent of all mothers with children under 18 years of age were in the labor force in March 1982; 50 percent of mothers with preschool children were working.
17. About 55 percent of all children under 18 had working mothers in March 1982; 46 per-

cent of all children under age 6 had mothers in the labor force.

18. Women are maintaining an increasing proportion of all families; about 1 out of 6 families was maintained by a woman in March 1982 compared with 1 out of 8 in 1972.

19. Women represented 63 percent of all persons below the poverty level who were 16 years of age and over in 1981.

20. The proportion of poor families maintained by women increased substantially between 1971 (40 percent) and 1981 (47 percent). By 1981 some 70 percent of poor black families with 3.1 related children under 18 were maintained by women. Similarly, 50 percent of poor Spanish-origin families with 909,000 related children and 39 percent of poor white families with 3.1 million related children were maintained by women.

These data clearly indicate the effect of women in the work force. However, they do not emphasize the point that the sex composition within many professional and managerial occupations is indeed changing in the direction of greater female participation. Although it is true that women in America are concentrated in few occupations and that one-third of all women in the labor force are working in just seven occupations — secretary, retail sales clerk, household worker, elementary school teacher, bookkeeper, waitress, and nurse (Bem and Bem, 1973) — it is also true that substantial progress has been made. For example, women now make up 10 to 20 percent of all engineering students (Seltz-Petrash, 1980), they now exceed 24 percent of all full-time students in graduate science programs in comparison to only 13 percent in 1973; they constitute about one-quarter of freshman medical school enrollments (as opposed to 9 percent in 1973); and they now earn better than 15 percent of the law degrees awarded (versus less than 6 percent in 1970). By any standard, these figures represent progress. In addition, women are now receiving about one-fifth of the graduate degrees in architecture and veterinary medicine, and two-fifths of the masters degrees in communications and mathematics (Stevens & Marquette, 1979).

Two factors have combined to cause this significant change in the composition of the work force.

Antidiscrimination laws and executive orders have been enacted or enforced more rigorously. Simultaneously, the consciousness-raising of women, related to careers, has been a target of women's rights groups and of professional helpers (counselors and other human relations workers). Both of these endeavors have attempted to alter the composition of the labor force. In large measure they have succeeded. The still obvious imbalance in the labor force has resulted from discriminatory practices in employment and in entry to advanced training for certain occupations and from a low level of aspiration among women. The career "undershooting" of women, in turn, has been ascribed to occupational stereotyping, early childhood conditioning, fear of failure, fear of success, and a variety of other child-rearing and socialization practices. Hence, attempts at changing the sex composition of the labor force have centered on legally removing discrimination barriers on the one hand, and on changing the career aspirations of women on the other.

It is clear from the preceding data that the strategy has been successful (although still too slow in the opinions of many). In the last edition of this volume we predicted that more progress would be made in the decade ahead than in the whole previous history of work in America. We are on the way to being correct in that prediction. In addition to the legislative and aspiration raising efforts described above, however, another factor is causing changes in the work force. Traditional women's occupations are now precisely those which are most in oversupply — teacher, librarian, social worker, and so on. Women in higher education are forced by the labor market to select nontraditional careers or to be unemployed.

In the following sections, we will summarize the research on various aspects of the career development of women. After these summaries, we will present implications for the counseling of women. Specifically, we will investigate stereotypes, temporal differences, traditional versus pioneer versus homemaker career studies, theory lacks, role models, and male-female differences.

Stereotypes

As we shall see in Chapter 7, sexual stereotyping of occupations begins at a very young age. For many individuals, this stereotyping remains endemic to careers throughout life. For example, using a sample of third- and fifth-grade students, MacKay and Miller (1982) discovered that boys had more complex interaction with things in their occupational choices (environments) than did girls. As Krefting and Berger (1979) indicated in their research, interacting with things is perceived as masculine, interacting with people is perceived as feminine, and interacting with data is seen as both masculine and feminine.

Knell and Winer (1979) demonstrated with a sample of youngsters aged 3 to 5.7 years that boys' perceptions are more stereotyped than girls, but that girls' perceptions can conform more to stereotypical thinking by reinforcement from stories that present stereotypical models. The opposite, however, was not apparent; that is, well-established stereotypes evidently are not easily counteracted by reading material. The implication here is that reading content would have the greatest effect on the young child and would decrease as career-related sex stereotypes become stronger. The idea that young boys' perceptions are even more stereotyped than those of girls is given further support in the work of Tremaine and Schau (1979) and by Teglasi (1981), who found that boys' selections of both toys and occupations in grades K–6 were more sex-typed than were the selections of girls. Hence, the need for early elimination of sexual stereotyping in careers is as important for males as it is for females.

The stereotyping continues through middle school where boys give higher ratings (in terms of perceived respect for an occupation and its importance in the community) to male jobs, whereas girls give higher ratings to female jobs (O'Bryant, Durrett & Pennebaker, 1978). In one interesting study, Frost and Diamond (1979) found that children in fourth-, fifth-, and sixth-grades who stereotyped children's jobs (babysitting, lawn mowing, car washing) also sex stereotyped adult occupations, thus suggesting the etiology of later stereotyping behavior. By high school, sex stereotyping of interests and mathematical ability has become well ingrained (E. Lunneborg, 1982) and may be fostered even further by brief self-assessment instruments (they make males appear less interested in service and females appear less interested in technical jobs than do more standard

measures of these characteristics). Women in adolescence and young adulthood also demonstrate that they select from only a few occupational possibilities and too often on a sex-typed basis (Brito & Jusenius, 1978). Results of research with adolescents consistently shows that females have lower occupational expectations than males, largely as a consequence of traditional sex-role socialization (Rosen & Aneshensel, 1978). For adolescent females, there is reason to believe that domestic and work role expectations are related to both generalized sex-role attitudes and specific plans for adult domestic roles (Aneshensel & Rosen, 1980). In short, too many females see the sexes in stereotypical ways and feel that women and men should enact different domestic and occupational roles. Even at the college level, students' interest in an occupation can be altered by suggestions of male or female domination in the occupation. When, for instance, male college students are told that in ten to fifteen years, women will constitute 50 to 60 percent of all attorneys, their interest in law as an occupation is significantly less (Collins, Reardon & Waters, 1980).

One promising approach to understanding the dynamics of sex-role stereotyping in careers is suggested by Hackett and Betz (1981). They propose self-efficacy theory as an explanation. This theory suggests that because of differential socialization, women lack strong expectations of personal efficacy for a variety of career-related behaviors. Hence, they fail to realize their capabilities and talents in work. Self-efficacy expectations, it is assumed, are lower among women than men. If one performs a task successfully, expectations of efficacy for that task are increased. It is hypothesized that women have fewer opportunities to demonstrate successful task accomplishments. They may also have fewer chances to watch other people succeed, to experience success vicariously. It is thus thought that they may lack same-sex models. Anxiety frequently prevents the development of facilitative efficacy expectations, and females are considered more likely to have anxiety responses. Finally, information about personal efficacy comes from the verbal encouragement and persuasion of others. It is thought that females receive less encouragement from counselors and others. So expectations of personal efficacy tend to be weakened for women.

All in all, sex stereotyping of occupations still restricts the career development of females (and males). The primary point of attack is, logically, at the earliest age possible; intervention becomes increasingly difficult as stereotypes become more ingrained.

Time Parameters

There is a need for continual evaluation and upgrading of career needs, aspirations, and life plans of women. Research quickly becomes obsolescent, and the findings of the very recent past are not necessarily applicable to the present or the future.

Two studies, conducted independently and using different instrumentation, compared female college students' attitudes toward education, family, and work in 1969 and 1973 (Parelius, 1975; Voss & Skinner, 1975). Both reported differences in female sex-role perceptions between the 1969 and 1973 groups (for example, an increase in the percentage planning a "double-track" career-homemaking pattern, a reduction in the percentage planning to interrupt their careers for child-rearing, stronger commitment to sexual equality, and, in general, a greater extrafamilial orientation). Voss (1980) later compared groups from 1966, 1973, and 1976 on their perceptions of the female sex-role. She discovered that men are indeed expressing a more liberal female stereotype, but that they may not behave as they talk. She also discovered subgroup differences in their perceptions of female sex-roles (such as college major differences).

Another example of the need for updating is provided by Zuckerman (1979) who investigated college students' educational and career goals, preferred and expected career commitment, and sex-role attitudes. One of her findings is that "variables that predicted nontraditional goals or attitudes in previous studies may not be significant predictors for today's college students. This appears to be especially likely for women, since roles that were considered nontraditional in earlier studies have become very popular" (p. 253). One final example: Spitze and Huber (1980) looked at data on sex-role status from 1938 and 1978 and concluded that there were strong historical effects; that is, that trends in attitudes over time may be explained more by the general climate

during a given period than by changes in specific individual experiences and attributes.

The inference is clear: counselors must remain in touch with the literature and developments of the times. We are all aware of counselors who appear to be caught in a time warp, assuming that everything is as it was. When dealing with the changing status and needs of women, especially, such ingenuousness can be harmful.

Traditional versus Pioneer versus Homemaker

Studies relating to what distinguishes career-oriented women from non-career oriented women or women in traditional occupations from women in "pioneer" occupations offer few guidelines for practice. They are frequently conflicting in results and simplistic in conclusions. Among the more instructive studies, however, are those which hint at factors distinguishing one group of women from another in terms of career orientation. These studies make the following suggestions: A female exposed to a maternal model of work competence tends to be more career oriented (Baruch, 1972). Those who are career oriented or who are planning nontraditional careers achieve higher grades, make a career choice later, come from more advantaged homes, and experience more personal identity and acceptance conflicts (Moore & Veres, 1976; Standley & Soule, 1974; Faunce, 1971; Astin & Myint, 1971; Navin, 1972; Richardson, 1974). They have fathers with higher educational levels and are more likely themselves to be childless (Greenfeld, Greiner, & Wood, 1980). They tend to receive more encouragement from teachers, counselors, friends, and significant others (Stake & Levitz, 1979). They exhibit higher esteem needs (Betz, 1982). They manifest stronger career-centeredness and career salience (Marshall & Wijting, 1980; Illfelder, 1980; Yanico, 1981). None of these studies, however, provides truly definitive answers.

We have not progressed a great deal in our knowledge of these differences (traditional versus pioneer versus homemaker). For example, Lemkau's (1979) review of studies from 1932–1976 turned up no constellation of personality and background factors that were characteristic of the woman who pursues a male-dominated occupation. She does conclude with a description of what might be a typical or modal woman in a male-dominated occupation.

She is the oldest child of a stable marriage. Her mother is probably as well-educated as her father and was employed during her childhood. Her father is better educated than most and employed in a professional or managerial position. In keeping with the educational and employment status of her parents, her family tended to be upwardly mobile. If her atypical role is one requiring high education, the probability that she, or one, or both parents was foreign born is higher than expected in the general population.

This prototypic woman reports having been close to both parents. She recalls that her parents emphasized achievement, hard work, and education, conveying by work and example that competence was as appropriate for girls as for boys. She reports that they were supportive of each other in diverse endeavors, and that they encouraged her to experiment with "masculine" as well as "feminine" activities and behaviors.

As an adult, she shares with her male counterpart those characteristics related to competence on the job, having even more than he of such "right" traits as assertiveness, intelligence, and imagination. Except for a tendency to be more oriented toward ideas and things and less to the social environment, she does not differ from the more typical woman on positive aspects of the feminine stereotype. She does not fit the stereotype of the "castrating" career woman whose competence is developed at the expense of sensitivity or expressiveness. While she is experiencing some stress in her role, she is generally emotionally healthy with unusual resources for coping with difficulties she encounters (pp. 236–237).

In terms of career-oriented women versus housewives, Betz (1982) has demonstrated that there is at least one characteristic held in common: the highest need for both groups of women appears to be self-actualization, simply pursued in different ways. There are also obvious differences. For instance, as one might suspect, employed women are more feminist (liberal in sex-role attitudes) than are full-time housewives (Ferree, 1980). Ul-

timately, whether a woman works outside the home or not seems to depend on the interaction between career and family task demands and her own values (Faver, 1982).

Comparing traditional women to pioneers to housewives is, in the final analysis, highly complex. It has been repeatedly demonstrated that female career patterns are much more complex than those of males (Stockton et al., 1980). Add this finding to the fact that there is extreme overlap among these three groups of women on almost all possible variables – within-group variation is almost as large as between-group variation – and it is easy to understand why no clear and consistent findings have emerged.

A few studies have sought to link Holland's theory of careers and female occupational choice differences. One study (Wolfe & Betz, 1981) substantiated a strong association between congruence and traditionality of choice; that is, women whose choices are in nontraditional career fields are significantly more likely to be making choices congruent with their personality type than are women choosing traditional career fields. Another study (Swatko, 1981) showed that nontraditional women score higher than traditional women on Holland's investigative and enterprising scales, both of which represent predominantly masculine environments.

One fascinating study followed up 352 of Terman's gifted women who were part of his original sample (Holahan, 1981). The mean age of these women was 66 at the time of follow-up. This population of very bright individuals was categorized into three groups: homemaker ($N = 139$), job ($N = 57$), or career work history ($N = 136$). In general, the homemakers were not dissatisfied with their lives (although they said that they would have chosen careers had they to do it all again). Career women were generally satisfied; job holders were not (a job holder is one who has done work for income but who would not call it a career). The group with lowest life satisfaction was composed of those who worked for income alone and who had lost a spouse through death or divorce. However, in a backward look from the vantage of young old age, the majority of Terman's women, careerists and homemakers, expressed high life satisfaction.

Finally, sex-role self-concept (masculine, feminine, androgenous) does not appear to be related to curriculum choice in college (Lyson & Brown, 1982) or to persistence in either traditional or nontraditional majors (Yanico & Hardin, 1981). It does, however, seem related to career ambitions in both traditional and nontraditional occupations.

All in all, then, there is little that we can say with certainty about differences among women who choose pioneer careers compared to those who select traditional careers and compared to those who elect to be full-time housewives. Although we can speak of some modal characteristics, there is great variance in each of these three groups. Zuckerman's (1979) conclusion may be accurate: "Parental role models and other variables that were significant predictors of college women's goals in the 1950's and 1960's are much less important now that 'non-traditional' goals are more widely accepted" (p. 318).

Role Models

Earlier literature suggested that career models, especially female models, appeared to exert a strong influence on the career aspirations of women (Almquist, 1974; Angrist, 1972; Elliott, 1973). Whether the model is a working mother, an occupational model — who is also enacting simultaneous roles of wife, mother, and worker — or a professor, she has been reported by career-oriented women as influential in the formulation of their career goals.

The popular media have played up the idea of "mentor" in the work progress of successful career women. The notion here is that of an established powerful figure in an occupational field (usually male) who takes a female under his aegis and guides and, in a sense, manipulates her rise in that field. Subsequently, the idea of a mentor (also termed, occasionally, "patron" or "rabbi") in the career development of women has proven to be useful. We know that mentors beget mentors in that those who had a mentor become mentors for others; we know that mentor relationships are most often established in the first five years of one's career; we know that more women are becoming mentors as their numbers increase in top management positions; and we know that most women are now advised that the route to upper-level jobs is through a mentor (Roche, 1979;

Thompson, 1976; Shapiro et al., 1978; Baron, 1977).

More recent studies have also confirmed the importance of role models in the career development of women. P. W. Lunneborg's (1982) research has demonstrated that both male and female role models influence the careers of women who hold a nontraditional work orientation. These models (in high school, college, and graduate school) were positive influencers and included parents, siblings, teachers, friends, and other adults. In terms of parents, the encouragement and support of *both* a mother and a father is most important in fostering nontraditional careers (Auster & Auster, 1981). In a somewhat more detailed study, Weishaar, Green, and Craighead (1981) attempted to determine how college major choice is influenced by role models who serve as reinforcers, for males as well as for females. Their major finding was that *no one* was reported most frequently as an influencer of college major. When an adult was mentioned, it was most often a same-sex parent, although clearly fathers and other adult males gave their daughters reinforcement, especially those selecting nontraditional careers. On the basis of their findings, the authors recommend the use of vocational role models to influence women to pursue nontraditional careers. One attempt at doing so with children at a very early age is noteworthy because it ended in failure (Weeks, Thornburg, & Little, 1977). Kindergarteners were exposed for two weeks to nontraditional role models and curriculum materials, but there was no significant change in their vocational preferences. The investigators suggest that the lack of positive results may be due to the fact that the children received too little too soon. The two weeks may not be enough time, and more protracted exposure may be required. Also, children at that age may not be developmentally ready to handle a sophisticated concept.

In a more detailed look at the family as role models influencing the career salience of women, Bielby (1978) used eight-year longitudinal data on women who graduated from college in 1961 and were periodically surveyed through 1968. She confirmed the frequently found negative relationship between socioeconomic class and career salience of women (career-oriented women come from less economically privileged homes), but she failed to find any other factor (such as maternal employment or sex-role ideology) that would account for much variance in career salience.

Such conflicting findings may be artifacts of methodological shortcomings more than anything else. The suggestion is very strong that for both males and females the developmental support and encouragement of important adult figures is an essential variable in career development.

Aspects of Sex Differences

There is presently no clear theory relating to the career development and choice of women. Rose and Elton (1973) and Zytowski (1969), among others, have argued for a separate theory of career choice for males and females. Barnett (1971) has offered some interesting thoughts that might lead to such a theory, but her effort illustrates the confounding of sex with other personal variables in decision-making. For example, she states:

> For a college woman, her decision to pursue a career is intimately related to her femininity, her need for independence, her self-concept, and her plans for marriage. It is influenced also by the expectations of her social group, family, and college peers and her responses to these groups. For each woman, the planning process and the feelings accompanying it reflect her position with respect to these four factors (p. 311).

This statement seems sensible. But it would appear equally sensible if, in the above statement, one substituted male adjectives and pronouns. Perhaps male-female distinctions in career development and career choice are not so much a matter of kind as a matter of degree. Notions of masculinity and femininity are certainly important in career choice. Are they more important for women? Probably. Plans for marriage are important in the general life planning of both men and women. Are they more important for women? Probably. Perhaps what is needed is a theory of career development and career choice that is applicable to both sexes, but that might weight various factors according to gender, and

weight other factors according to such variables as age, race, socioeconomic class, and so on.

There are studies on a variety of sex differences in career development, career choice, and career behaviors. Siegfried et al. (1981) found support for the idea of sex differences in job preferences; that is, preferences for various job characteristics classified as either motivators (such as challenging work, voice in decision, contribution to society) or hygienes (such as salary, fringe benefits, job security). They concluded that both males and females in college ranked the motivators high in importance, but females also gave nearly the same importance to hygiene factors. Sex differences were so real that, using multivariate analysis, the investigators were able to predict a subject's sex simply by looking at the rank of motivators and hygiene factors. Another study of sex differences, using Project Talent data (Card, Steel, & Abeles, 1980), determined that although women had higher grades and higher test scores than men in high school, eleven years after high school the men had acquired more education and were earning more money. The authors attributed these sex differences primarily to greater conflict for women between the roles of spouse/parent and the roles of student/worker. Variables that measured the onset, duration, and extent of family-related commitments were more strongly related to female than to male realization of potential.

These types of very real male-female aggregate differences in earnings are much discussed issues in the popular media. There have been several refinements in the way in which these data are examined that help to explain the differences somewhat. Rytina (1981) has demonstrated that when women constitute only a small proportion of the workers in an occupation, their earnings are much lower than those of their male counterparts. In the female-dominated and low-paying occupations, the earnings of women are closer to those of men. Hence, occupational sex segregation negatively affects female earnings and perpetuates male-female earnings differences, although these differences are not translated into lesser job satisfaction for females (Lee, Mueller, & Miller, 1981). Further refinement comes in a study by McLaughtin (1978), who looked into the matter of occupations of equal prestige for which male-female earnings were decidedly unequal. He discovered,

The earning potential of prestige-equivalent occupations differs such that males tend to be clustered in occupations with greater income potential even within categories of prestige. This is consistent with the notion that many men and women who attain equally prestigious occupations do not attain equal occupational earning potential (p. 920).

Karpicke (1980) provides one final example of sex differences that substantiates the degree-versus-kind argument made earlier in this chapter. For college students she studied sex differences in success avoidance, home-career conflict, and attitudes of significant members of the opposite sex as influences on career planning. Further, she was interested in determining sex differences in and the accuracy of counselors' perceptions regarding these variables. Her results suggest that undergraduate females have significantly more success avoidance and home-career conflict than male students, but that this fact may not be so important in career planning as originally was thought. She concludes,

> The results of this study suggest that the theoretical career development literature for women is not accurate in its emphasis on the integration of the female sex role into a woman's career plans. Although two of the variables measured (success avoidance and home-career conflict) were more important to women than to men, they do not appear to be focal concerns for the career planning process of either sex. Continuing efforts need to be made to determine factors that influence the career planning processes of both sexes and to provide counselors with empirical data on which to base career counseling intervention strategies (p. 245).

Discontinuities in Female Career Development

Although more and more women are displaying continuous, uninterrupted career patterns, discontinuities obviously abound. The major source, formerly, of male discontinuity was the Selective Service System's propensity for drafting into military service. This discontinuity has not been a problem for several years. For women, the primary source of discontinuity is children.

Walker, Tansky, and Oliver (1982) examined 1973 interview data gleaned from the Quality of Employment Survey conducted by the University of Michigan Survey Research Center. The 1455 workers surveyed included 470 regularly employed women, 179 of whom were sole wage earners. The researchers analyzed the data in terms of male-female differences in work values. They concluded that only one value – convenience – was consistently different for men and women. Women assigned it a higher priority. The presence of children in the home (preschool or school age) was negatively related to most work values for women. In other words, working mothers experience reduced work involvement, perhaps because the presence of children causes working women to reassess the importance they give to work. Although the data on which these conclusions are based are over a decade old, there is little reason to doubt their current applicability.

Another study investigating women's careers (Rosenfeld, 1979) used data on 5083 women who were surveyed from 1967 to 1977. The conclusion was that men are likely to remain continuously employed whereas women tend to have intermittent employment. Once again, the discontinuities were generally related to changes in the extent of home responsibilities. The discontinuity of career development in women is seen as a paramount barrier to occupational upward mobility status.

Some see a chicken-egg argument in relation to women's fertility and employment. Which causes which? Does child-bearing constrain labor force participation or can we use labor force activity to predict a woman's expected fertility? Cramer's (1980) research suggests that the dominant effects are from fertility to employment in the short run and from employment to fertility in the long run. Variables such as race and sex-role attitudes, however, may affect this conclusion. Scanzoni's (1979) work also illustrates that work consistency of women and the fertility control patterns that enhance that consistency vary in time (the period in which one lives) and across time (short- and long-run consequences). Although sex-role attitudes may be significant in continuous or discontinuous female employment, that has not yet been demonstrated. In fact, the research of Spitze and Waite (1980) failed to predict a fertility-employment link on the basis of sex-role attitudes.

In any case, career interventions with women should include assurance that females understand the nature of continuous and discontinuous career patterns and the effect of fertility on those phenomena. In Chapter 12, we will further discuss these consequences for women who seek to return to the labor force or who seek to enter it for the first time after a protracted period of child-bearing and child-rearing. Such women have rarely considered the consequences of discontinuity before the fact and frequently, therefore, experience trauma after the fact.

Career Counseling of Women

Given differences in the career development of women, what are the implications for career counseling of females in contemporary society? One must assume that at all levels, but especially at the higher occupational levels or in nontraditional careers, women will exhibit more conflict than men, will experience differences in job-seeking patterns, and will have to overcome more obstacles to career advancement (Leviton & Whitely, 1981). Lang (1978) offers several suggestions to assist nontraditional women:

1. Expect challenges — testing of boundaries, prejudices, loneliness, and so on.
2. Embrace your uniqueness — accept unique career aspects of self.
3. Be creative — make creative responses and decisions; be assertive; keep a sense of humor.
4. Play the power game — understand the rules and how things happen.
5. Analyze and build significant male relationships — both at work and at home.
6. Seek role models — observe and learn from a successful female role model in your field.
7. Be human — be aware of and attend to self-needs and desires.

Although these suggestions apply equally to men and women, the intensity with which they must be pursued differs for women. Some of these suggestions can be implemented through such techniques as networking, peer counseling, and professional support. Networking is "a process of identifying existing social networks, enhancing connecting networks along new lines, and chan-

neling information through these created guidance networks" (Voight, Lawler, and Falkerson, 1980, p. 106). These networks are made up of contact persons for educational and employment advice and placement. It is ironic, in contemporary society, that while "old boy" networks are being vilified and legislated against as a job-finding technique, networking can be valuable for women in job-finding and promotion. Peer counseling can range from simple support groups to more action-oriented endeavors. Professional support and counseling can assume a variety of forms.

The application of professional counseling to the career adjustment of "young-old" women is a case in point (Bartlett & Oldham, 1978). These are women between the ages of 45 and 64. Bartlett and Oldham recommend for this population midlife, occupational change, preretirement, and life-style counseling. In midlife counseling, counselors may provide "personal" counseling for those experiencing unanticipated *internal* changes (illness, divorce, death), while for those who undergo unanticipated *external* changes (unemployment), career counseling is thought to be appropriate. In occupational change counseling, the counselor assists the person to assess motivation for change and the dynamics of the presenting problem. In preretirement counseling, preventive attention and follow-up are suggested to smooth the transition. Finally, in life-style counseling, counselors help older women to become aware of their personal qualifications, instill in them an attitude of planfulness, and promote adaptability. In all cases, reassurance of personal worth may be necessary. Again, all of the preceding suggestions are sensible for men as well as for women.

Counseling adult women college students is another example of professional interventions to aid women. Smallwood (1980) surveyed a sample of this population and concluded that their four major needs are: (1) adequate child care facilities; (2) accommodating job schedule realities (help with securing off-campus employment coordinated with class schedules, flexibility of class scheduling, and so on); (3) academic reentry (such as special academic counseling and encouragement); and (4) financial and personal counseling needs (such as divorce or major life change). One example of career/life planning for women is offered by Kitabachi, Murrell, & Crawford (1979) who recommend a three-stage sequence: self-awareness, self-appraisal, and taking action. Not surprisingly, with the possible exception of Small-wood's need (1), these needs apply in kind to adult male college students.

Early counseling interventions with females are thought to be important as influencers of career decision-making. One study (Sauter, Seidl, & Karbon, 1980) demonstrated that women who elected traditional or nontraditional career paths experienced different high school counseling and held different attitudes toward women's roles. Traditional women were more conservative and sex dichotomized in their attitudes. Further, high school counseling was reported as an influence only by women who selected traditional female careers, suggesting that counselors encourage sex stereotyping. Thus, early counseling interventions in themselves are apparently not so important as the type of intervention. What is called for, according to the authors, is nonstereotyped counseling that addresses career opportunities for women and helps them to appraise their abilities and ambitions. Another high school counseling intervention was designed and implemented by Brenner and Gazda-Grace (1979), who put three groups of male and female students through a nine-session decision-making course that emphasized recognition and personal values, knowledge of relevant information and the ability to use it, and knowledge of an effective decision-making strategy. One group was composed of all women; two other groups were composed of equal numbers of men and women. The results showed that women in the all-female group were better able to make career decisions than were those in the sexually mixed group. It may be that segregating women for treatment is an appropriate strategy in teaching career decision-making, or it may be that a different type of group leadership is necessary depending on the sex composition of the career group.

The idea of counselor stereotyping and sex bias is, of course, not new. Male counselors seem to ascribe different motivations (such as success avoidance) to male and female undergraduates, and even female counselors do not accurately perceive sex differences in motivating factors

(Karpicke, 1980). Mercado and Atkinson (1982) offer evidence that male counselors encourage male and female high school students to explore occupations along sex-stereotypic lines. Further, a physical-attractiveness bias may enter vocational counseling. Indeed, given what we know about the psychology of attractiveness – that attractive individuals are ascribed all sorts of positive characteristics and non-attractive people are not – it would be surprising to discover that it did not. Such biases are difficult to counteract. One attempt to do so is reported by Rudnick and Wallach (1980). They organized a conference for counselors and math and science teachers to explore nontraditional female choices. This type of preservice and inservice education apparently is necessary on an ongoing basis. Another successful workshop for women, entitled "Choices and Changes," is reported by Sandmeyer (1980). She organized groups to explore four themes: Expanding Horizons, Narrowing the Focus, Translating Self to the Employment Context, and Looking Ahead. Initial evaluations were positive. One final example of a program recommended for women is that advocated by Newman (1978) who suggests a structured counseling experience organized around the focus of helping women to deal with three facets of life: individual needs, relationship needs, and life-work needs and satisfactions. She recommends a life-planning program to "foster responsible self-realization and growth in a group setting by providing frameworks for developing information about yourself, your skills, abilities, and needs (first phase) and for organizing these data to achieve the goals you identify as significant (second phase)" (p. 260). Individual counseling, role models, seminars, workshops, group discussions, and resource centers are all used to achieve these ends.

THE CULTURALLY DIFFERENT

There are many minorities on which we might possibly focus. We will limit our attention to only two: blacks and Latinos. Significant minority populations of Native Americans, Asian Americans, and other culturally different segments of the population will also be referenced in other chapters.

Blacks

Although there has been a recent increase in research on career development and behavior of precollege blacks, there has been relatively little on higher education and adulthood. Most post-secondary research has concentrated on access: Do black students in compensatory programs achieve as well as regularly admitted students? Are admissions tests as predictive for blacks as for whites? Much less research has been devoted to process and exit-related concerns: What effect does the collegiate experience have on the values and attitudes of blacks? Why do blacks tend to gravitate toward certain occupational fields? What are unique black career-related problems?

Nevertheless, there are some useful findings. First of all, the black student is as likely as any other to come to higher education with ambition, an appreciation for work, and high career expectations (MacMichael, 1974), although sex-role influences may inhibit the career and educational aspirations of black women as they do white women (Gurin & Gaylord, 1976). At the same time, the career development of black students is more likely to be delayed or impaired than that of the more advantaged populations (LoCascio, 1967). This lag can manifest itself at the college level in such problems as a discrepancy between a desire for a college education and a career choice that does not require that level of education, a general lack of knowledge of alternatives, possible skills deficits, and an unclear picture of oneself in relation to the world of work. These problems are hardly unique to blacks, but they may be more characteristic of black students as a group than of whites.

Smith (1975) reviewed the research on the career development and behavior of blacks and drew the following profile:

The profile of the Black individual as portrayed in the research cited is a portrait of a vocationally handicapped person. According to the studies examined, the average Black, if one can speak of average individuals of any racial group, is one who may lack positive work role models; does not manifest a lifetime commitment to a career as a way of life; is work-alienated; and places a greater priority on job security rather than self-fulfillment in an occupation. More-

over, he tends to have a negative self-image which fosters identity foreclosure and a rigid closing out of self and directions. His aspirations are high, but his expectations of achieving his desired occupational goals are low. He has limitations placed upon his occupational mobility because of his racial membership; evidences interests that are more person than thing-oriented; (and) is vocationally immature (p. 55).

One researcher who has produced a body of solid information on the career development of blacks is Dillard (1980). He cites several factors that impede the career development of blacks, ranging from restricted opportunities to background factors. These impediments, according to Dillard, make inappropriate for blacks theories based on white, middle-class vocational development. He argues, for example, that lower-class blacks have few positive work-related experiences, limited educational experiences, poor environmental resources, negative orientations to work, and restricted access to career and employment information. Further, he observes that few opportunities are available for lower socioeconomic young blacks to view and accept work habits from a role model, especially a paternal model. In terms of black women, he maintains that compared to white women, they are forced to consider to a greater extent family and racial and sexual discrimination in work decisions. With lower-class blacks, Dillard suggests that because of situational factors, primary work values are likely to be extrinsic rather than intrinsic: self-expression is less a concern than is bread on the table. Finally, in terms of aspirations, Dillard proposes that rather than studying black-white differences, we ought to be investigating within-group black differences: male versus female, urban versus rural versus suburban, lower-class versus middle-class, and so on. Dillard's ideas are sensible and worthy of implementation. He recognizes the ever-present confounding variable of socioeconomic class. Until we can control clearly for socioeconomic class in racial comparisons, research on between-group and within-group differences in career development will be less helpful than it might otherwise be. For example, Dillard and Campbell's (1981) study of parental influences on the aspirations of Puerto Rican, black, and anglo children demonstrated no clearly direct linear influence. The aspirations that some parents hold for their children are influences in adolescent vocational development. For others, however, regardless of ethnicity or race, there seems to be no influence. Why, we do not know.

There is no doubt that in the aggregate blacks are disadvantaged, not only compared to the white majority but also compared to other minorities. In 1977, for example, the unemployment rate for black workers was 13.1 percent, while for whites it was 6.2 percent, and for Hispanics it was 10.1 percent. In that same year, the median family income for all American families was $16,009; for Puerto Ricans, $7,972; for Mexicans, about $12,000; for Cubans, over $14,000; and for blacks, $9,563. Thus, only Puerto Rican families are more destitute (Newman, 1978). To be sure, strides have been made. Since World War II, the earnings of black men have increased faster than those of white men. Since 1975, however, these gains have stabilized. Up to 1975, the gains were usually attributed to the declining proportion of blacks in the South, increased education, and a period of relatively full employment. In general, additional increments of education translate into additional earnings for blacks at about the same rate as for whites. On-the-job training, however, seems to pay off more for whites than for blacks (Taylor, 1981).

At one time in America there were considerable differences among blacks in the North and in the South in terms of occupational earnings and status. In some respects these differences persist (Hogan & Pazul, 1982). For example, northern-born black men pursue different career patterns from blacks who migrate from the South. Blacks who are native to Milwaukee, Wisconsin, emphasize the intrinsic rewards associated with jobs, whereas southern-born migrants to Milwaukee emphasize the extrinsic rewards. "As a result, the northern natives tend to value a high status job, even if it is low-paying, while the migrants prefer job with higher pay even if it is relatively low status" (Hogan & Pazul, 1981, p. 1127). This situation is changing, however. Regional differences in black occupational attainment and status are declining as a result of decreased emigration from the South and some selective return of migrants to the South (LaGory & Magnani, 1979).

With so many blacks unemployed, it is natural that many would see discrimination as a major cause (along with skills deficits and lack of work readiness). Indeed, how a worker perceives the possibility of employment discrimination affects several attitudes, including locus of control. Becker and Krzystojiak (1982) studied labor market discrimination and concluded that among blacks, beyond racial identity, their perceptions of employment discrimination influenced their tendency to blame external forces for their plight (blacks who feel they are discriminated against experience twice as much externality as blacks who report no awareness of discrimination). Clearly, those blacks who perceive discrimination in employment are affected in terms of their subsequent work attitudes, values, and behaviors.

What is bias and what is not bias in employment? Research has not yet provided us with definitive answers. Several studies have investigated aptitude measurement, for example, as a source of bias. Work sample examinations, especially, have been carefully examined for ethnic differences that might lead to a conclusion of bias. Backman, Lynch, and Loeding (1979) concluded that the TOWER System of Vocational Evaluation produced higher mean scores for whites than for blacks in all aptitude areas except motor skills. These differences were not attributable to amount of education. Further, the work samples were designed to represent job tasks rather than academic achievement. These findings suggest that the use of a separate set of norms for ethnic, sex, and disability groups may be appropriate. These norms are provided. Although the differences are apparently real, for whatever reason, it is also possible to exaggerate black-white differences. Brugnoli, Campion, and Basen (1979), for instance, used work sample ratings for mechanics to show that when observers are asked to make global evaluations after viewing an applicant's performance on a task representing an irrelevant job behavior, race-linked bias tended to be present. When observations were of relevant behaviors and were required to be specific rather than global, however, the work bias was not present. This finding suggests that careful training of evaluators can result in reported differences in aptitudes being less vulnerable to change through racial bias.

Another factor that has impeded the full realization of black career progress has been constriction of the curricula in which black students enroll in higher education. There has been little change since 1972, when Bayer reported that blacks tended to choose majors predominantly in the social sciences, education, and health fields. Few chose the physical sciences, engineering, biological sciences, or agriculture. These findings are consistent with other research (Kimball, Sedlacek, & Brooks, 1973; Hager & Elton, 1971). Smith (1980) proposes that counselors encourage black and other minority students to explore nontraditional careers. Minority students, it is argued, must be exposed sequentially and continuously to science and mathematics courses from a very early age; they must be encouraged to take science and mathematics courses; and both industry and the schools must provide them with up-to-date career information. If minorities acquire the necessary skills, increase their career awareness, and receive increased parental and school career planning, Smith believes that they will choose from a broader array of alternatives.

Gottfredson (1978) has pointed out that blacks are considerably under-represented in enterprising occupations (see Table 5.1). Enterprising occupations (such as sales and management) usually provide high income with less education than do other job families. Black youth, it is thought, should be exposed to more information about and experience in enterprising occupations. Why blacks are not more highly represented in enterprising occupations is difficult to know. Past discrimination may have been directed more to managers, administrators, and salespersons than to educators, health personnel, ministers, and other social service workers. Whatever the reason, blacks should become more involved in types of work that offer higher income differentials. Entreprenurial business activities represent one such occupational category.

The restricted choices of minority students is also noted by Turner, Johnson, & Patterson (1981) who view the problem as basically one of an expectation-readiness gap. Hence, they advocate training in career decision-making as an appropriate focus for minorities in higher education. They describe a program for minority undergraduates at Western Michigan University that begins with summer orientation. The goals of the program are:

- to promote and facilitate students' involvement in continuous evaluation
- to provide the necessary resource materials and guidance to enhance effective career exploration
- to assist students in reality testing of their tentative career choices
- to facilitate reality-based career decision
- to encourage and assist in the development of a life plan to support and strengthen career decisions
- to encourage minority students' use of counseling, testing, and placement services

It is hoped that this emphasis on self-assessment and initial career exploration, reality testing, and implementation will lead to a more comprehensive distribution of career choices among blacks and other minorities.

Latinos

Latinos or Hispanics are a heterogeneous minority within the general population. Their heritage may be Mexican, Cuban, Puerto Rican, Central American, South American, or from Spain itself. The largest Hispanic ethnic group are the Mexicans, with over 7 million legal workers in America; there are about 2 million Puerto Ricans; there are approximately a million Cubans; and there are about 2.5 million persons of other Hispanic origin or descent (Newman, 1978). Some (such as Cubans) originally came to this country for political reasons, whereas others immigrated for economic reasons. Each of these major Hispanic groups has different unemployment rates and sex differences in work force participation, although all groups are basically less well off than the general population. Among the Puerto Ricans, there is a great deal of movement between the mainland and America (in 1977, half of all working-age mainland Puerto Ricans lived in New York City). Cubans, on the other hand, have little or no movement back to Cuba. Cubans and Mexicans tend to be unemployed for shorter durations than do Puerto Ricans. These figures emphasize the heterogeneous character of "Hispanics."

Hispanic workers are concentrated more in the lower-paid, lesser-skilled occupations than the

Table 5.1
Percentage of Men Aged 36–65 in Each Type of Work: By Race
and Educational Level

Type of Work	Years of Education					
	≤ 8	9–11	12	13–15	16+	Total
	Whites					
Real	82.0	70.5	55.2	31.8	10.2	53.8
Inv	3.4	3.7	5.1	8.1	20.8	7.4
Art	0.2	0.6	1.4	2.8	4.0	1.6
Soc	1.9	2.7	3.7	5.1	19.2	5.8
Ent	10.6	18.4	27.6	41.8	38.6	25.6
Conv	2.0	4.0	7.0	10.4	7.2	5.8
(N)	(4,040)	(3,892)	(5,951)	(2,239)	(3,164)	(19,286)
	Blacks					
Real	92.0	89.2	72.9	50.0	15.6	81.0
Inv	0.8	0.6	3.8	6.4	12.2	2.3
Art	—	—	0.8	2.1	4.4	0.5
Soc	2.2	2.6	6.1	13.8	46.7	6.3
Ent	3.7	3.7	8.0	10.6	12.2	5.4
Conv	1.2	4.0	8.4	17.0	8.9	4.5
(N)	(727)	(351)	(262)	(94)	(90)	(1,524)

total work force. More than half of the employed Hispanic women are either clerical workers or nontransport operatives (dress makers, assemblers, machine operators, and so on), both low-paid occupations. Hispanic men are disproportionately employed as operatives, service workers, and craft workers. Although a great percentage of Hispanics are *not* employed in agriculture, contrary to popular stereotype, about 7 percent work in that area compared to 1 percent of the white population. Although these data present a picture of Hispanic ethnic groups as generally underrepresented in the more remunerative occupations of society, some progress is being made. The children of first- and second-generation immigrants expect higher-status and better-paying jobs in the economy. The major task facing these groups is to acquire the education and occupational skills necessary to effect these aspirations.

Ayres (1979) offers some suggestions for working with the over 12 million Hispanics (5.6 percent of the United States population). She points out that as a socioeconomically disadvantaged minority, young Hispanics may have limited ex-

posure to and experience with occupations and, consequently, choose from among few alternatives. They may not have basic job-seeking skills (such as filling out applications), and they may need encouragement, motivation, and reinforcement to pursue occupations and opportunities not traditionally considered reachable by Hispanics.

Of course, the major difference between Hispanics and other major American minorities is language. According to Herrera (1978), the United States is the fifth largest Spanish-speaking country in the Western Hemisphere (after Mexico, Argentina, Columbia, and Peru). Those whose native language is not English tend to complete fewer years of schooling. Since over half of the American Hispanic population are children or adolescents, this lack of language facility translates into very high dropout rates. From this dilemma springs the controversy of bilingual education. Some want Spanish to be the first language of instruction and bilingualism the goal. Add to this strong family ties and cultural traditions (for example, Hispanics tend to have a deeply engrained sense of fatalism and destiny), and the career counselor has more than the "normal" problems with which to contend. There is not only heterogeneity among ethnic groups of Hispanics; there are also clear individual differences. Treating people as individuals while recognizing the cultural context from which they come is a fine-line activity.

Several organizations are dedicated to providing services especially for Hispanics. These organizations provide college financial assistance (for example, National Hispanic Scholarship Fund), special career and academic counseling (Aspira), and vocational training and job placement (the Puerto Rican Forum). In addition, Hispanics are a targeted and preferred group for various federal programs, because of their lower levels of educational attainment, occupational and employment status, and income when compared to the general population.

As with blacks, Hispanics have been the focus of a number of studies which seek to determine occupationally relevant differences between them and the white majority. These studies have not always provided useful data. It may be that, as Dillard advocates for blacks, we are better off studying within-group differences for Hispanics. One study (Gould, 1982) investigated the career progress of 111 Mexican-American college graduates and concluded that differences in their career progress were largely attributable to individual differences rather than ethnicity. Further, he found that,

> In spite of the number of cultural differences enumerated for Mexican-Americans, the personal factors related to career progression were not unlike those which one would expect as being salient for a group of Anglo Americans. Hence, based on the results of this study, there is no reason to believe that the correlates of upward progression which have been identified in the literature are inappropriate for identifying Mexican-American candidates who have the greatest potential for career progression (pp. 107–108).

These correlates include such factors as grades, tolerance for ambiguity, work ethic, psychological success, and need for achievement. In terms of the last variable, Gould (1982) had previously determined that those Mexican-Americans with a

moderate need for achievement were found to have higher upward mobility than those with high or low need achievement, suggesting that employing organizations resent either too high or too low a level.

In a similar vein, Scott and Anadon (1980) investigated the ACT Interest Inventory profiles of Native Americans and Caucasian college-bound students and found the profiles of both groups to be very similar. In general, whenever white and nonwhite racial groups are compared in terms of responding to interest inventories, they are found to respond in basically like fashion.

Counseling the Culturally Different

There are not many quality books and articles on counseling the culturally different. Guidelines are little different from these for counseling people in general. Perhaps, as we maintain is the case with women, differences are more in degree than in kind. The counselor should know the cultural milieu of culturally different clientele, just as he or she should understand the cultural context of any client. Professional helpers should possess certain characteristics for working in a culturally skilled manner with various ethnic groups (or a representative of any cultural context, for that matter). These characteristics include beliefs/attitudes, knowledges, and skills (Division 17 Education and Training Committee, 1982).

Beliefs/Attitudes

1. The culturally skilled counseling psychologist is one who has moved from being culturally unaware to being aware and sensitive to his/her own cultural heritage and to valuing and respecting differences.
2. A culturally skilled counseling psychologist is aware of his/her own values and biases and how they may affect minority clients.
3. A culturally skilled counseling psychologist is one who is comfortable with differences that exist between the counselor and the client in terms of race and beliefs.
4. The culturally skilled counseling psychologist is sensitive to circumstances (personal biases, stage of ethnic identity, sociopolitical influences, etc.) which may dictate referral of the

minority client to a member of his/her own race/culture.

Knowledges

1. The culturally skilled counseling psychologist will have a good understanding of the sociopolitical system's operation in the United States with respect to its treatment of minorities.
2. The culturally skilled counseling psychologist must possess specific knowledge and information about the particular group he/she is working with.
3. The culturally skilled counseling psychologist must have a clear and explicit knowledge and understanding of the generic characteristics of counseling and therapy.
4. The culturally skilled counseling psychologist is aware of institutional barriers which prevent minorities from using mental health services.

Skills

1. At the skills level, the culturally skilled counseling psychologist must be able to generate a wide variety of verbal and nonverbal responses.
2. The culturally skilled counseling psychologist must be able to send and receive both verbal and nonverbal messages accurately and "appropriately."
3. The culturally skilled counseling psychologist is able to exercise institutional intervention skills on behalf of his/her client when appropriate.

These suggestions for desirable characteristics are certainly beyond contention, but they also apply to *any* clientele, not simply the culturally different. There certainly is no doubt about the counselor's need to understand the characteristics of the ethnic or racial group of which the counseled individual is a part and to have all of the attending and responding skills characteristic of a good counseling relationship.

These guidelines are interesting, however, in that they suggest that culturally different counselors may sometimes need to refer clients to others who may be more skilled in assisting people of a given ethnic or racial group with problems that center on membership in that group. This strategy is quite different from that recommended by some who would have only members of a given

ethnic or racial or sexual group counsel individuals in that group. Ruiz and Padilla (1977), for example, argue that with Latinos,

> To be effective, the counselors must "speak the language" of the client, both literally and figuratively. The number of Latino professionals already available is infinitesimally small, and the disproportionately small number of Latinos enrolled in baccalaureate or doctoral programs indicates underrepresentation of Latinos in the professions is going to continue in the foreseeable future. The short-run solution to this problem is two-fold; teach Spanish and Latino culture to non-Latino counselors, and teach counseling skills to Latinos at the paraprofessional level (p. 407).

We reject the implications that in the long run only like-ethnics should counsel ethnics; by extension, only substance abusers should counsel substance abusers, only gays counsel gays, only divorced counsel divorced, only unemployed counsel unemployed, only schizophrenics counsel schizophrenics, and so on, *ad absurdum*.

A thoughtful model of Minority Identity Development (MID) has been offered by Atkinson, Morten, and Sue (1983). Although this model has not been tested to any appreciable extent, it does offer a framework for intervention with minorities at various developmental stages. In summary form, the model appears in Table 5.2.

This model suggests that in stage 1, minority individuals prefer the cultural values of the majority culture over their own. In stage 2, dissonance sets in and results in confusion and conflict. The dominant culture is no longer clearly superior to the minority member's own culture. In stage 3, there is a rejection of the dominant culture, a sort of reaction formation, and the person totally endorses the minority views. In stage 4, the person begins to think less in terms of minority-group dogma and more in terms of forming individual reactions. Finally, in stage 5, conflicts are resolved and individuals become comfortable with themselves and with their heritage. The recurrent theme throughout each of these stages is oppression, first as an individual experiences it and later as he or she strives to eliminate it both in one's own life and in society. We have previously referred to the great heterogeneity on all variables

Table 5.2
Summary of Minority Identity Development Model

Stages of Minority Development Model	Attitude toward self	Attitude toward others of the same minority	Attitude toward others of different minority	Attitude toward dominant group
Stage 1 — Conformity	self-depreciating	group-depreciating	discriminatory	group-appreciating
Stage 2 — Dissonance	conflict between self-depreciating and appreciating	conflict between group-depreciating and group-appreciating	conflict between dominant held views of minority hierarchy and feelings of shared experience	conflict between group-appreciating and group-depreciating
Stage 3 — Resistance and Immersion	self-appreciating	group-appreciating	conflict between feelings of empathy for other minority experiences and feelings of culturo-centrism	group-depreciating
Stage 4 — Introspection	concern with basis of self-appreciation	concern with nature of unequivocal appreciation	concern with ethnocentric basis for judging others	concern with the basis of group depreciation
Stage 5 — Synergetic Articulation and Awareness	self-appreciating	group-appreciating	group-appreciating	selective appreciation

that exists within any minority group. The MID model is another example. Within any given culturally different ethnic or racial group, identity issues may be resolved to a greater or lesser degree by individual members. The task of counselors is to determine at which stage an individual is functioning and to determine how facilitating or how self-defeating that stage might be in terms of career development.

Another sensible model has been developed by Gurin and Pruitt (1978) especially for black women, although there is no reason why it should not apply to all minorities. It stems from the Student Development Model for Tomorrow's Higher Education (THE Model), developed by the American College Personnel Association. In summary, the model is as follows:

1. *Goal-Setting* — For what do you strive? What are your short-range, intermediate, and long-range goals and tasks? What behaviors need to be de-

veloped or eliminated? What information do you require? What discrimination must be overcome? What are the psychological and social costs of achieving your goal? In general, what planning must occur to reach your goal?

2. *Individual Assessment* — What baseline development data are available to help one formulate specific personal objectives and behavioral change strategies? How can we be sure that standardized test data on abilities, interests, and so on are not misused for minority individuals? What alternative assessment techniques are appropriate?

3. *Instruction* — How can counselors help individuals to acquire knowledge and skills that are essential to their development? What information must minorities possess to ensure good decision-making? How can career education contribute in the schools? How can realistic expectancies be engendered and nourished by means of gradual skills acquisition? How can we ensure success experiences? How can role models be utilized? How

can values best be inculcated or clarified? How can we teach minorities to achieve what they want to achieve? What are the roles of assertive skills training, job socialization skills, and so on?

4. *Consultation* — How can counselors best work with minority clients, their families, employers, and other groups and individuals that affect their lives? How can counselors help to get the schools to intervene effectively in minority lives? How can minority parents be motivated and given the knowledge and skills to help their children? How can counselors acquire counseling skills?

5. *Milieu Management* — How can the school and the workplace be shaped to enhance minority career development? Can "social engineering" increase the opportunity structure? What, for example, is the effect of specific college climates on minority student development? How can employers provide an organizational atmosphere that fosters minority progress? How can we increase access to and progress in educational and employment institutions?

All of these research findings and suggestions for practice distill to the following guidelines for career counseling of the culturally different:

1. Counselors should, above all, possess all of the generic counseling knowledge, skills, understandings, abilities, and behaviors thought to be appropriate in any helping relationship.

2. Counselors should recognize their own attitudes and values as these impinge on counseling specific ethnic and racial groups; they must work to ensure that these internal frames of reference do not form roadblocks to successful counseling. Obviously, white, majority counselors should uncover any possible biases toward blacks, Latinos, or other groups; but professionals who are themselves culturally different should undergo similar self-scrutiny regarding the majority.

3. Counselors should be aware of the cultural context from which individuals come, but they should not assume that individuals are bounded by that culture. They are first and foremost *individuals* and only secondarily representatives of a specific racial or ethnic group.

4. Counselors should understand what aspects of career helping may need special attention with specific culturally different groups. All groups,

minority or majority, will need the same career skills, attitudes, knowledges, and so forth; some groups may need emphasis on one aspect of career development.

5. Counselors must help minorities to understand and internalize that they *do* have a choice in career development; that given certain decisions and behaviors, certain consequences are likely to occur.

6. Counselors should help culturally different individuals understand that although they may encounter discrimination, they cannot be discouraged by it or consider themselves perpetual victims of it. They can be taught to deal with it and to use the vehicles available to surmount it.

7. Counselors must be sure that they understand which deficits and discontinuities in the career development of the culturally different are consequences of socioeconomic class and which are the result of membership in some specific racial or ethnic group. Slaney (1980), for example, has suggested that many black-white differences in career variables may be a reflection of socioeconomic differences as much as racial differences.

IMMIGRANTS

America, of course, is a land of immigrants as are, most notably, Canada and Australia. Massive occupational assimilation has challenged American social service agencies for over a century. There are both legal and illegal immigrants to America.

Legal and Illegal Immigrants

The legal immigrants in recent years have emigrated primarily from Southeast Asia (most notably the Indochinese, Laotians, Cambodians, Taiwanese, and Philippinos); Cuba, Haiti, and other West Indian islands; Colombia, Honduras and other Central American countries; and Russia (specifically, Russian Jews). In addition, immigration quotas have been maintained for other countries that have traditionally supplied the United States with new citizens. Huge influxes of refugees are both a threat and a promise to America. The promise is one of enhanced human resources and the richness of cultural pluralism. The threat is to indigenous minorities. For instance, putting together data supplied by Bach and Bach (1980) with U.S. Census data, we conclude that there are as many Southeast Asian refugees in America who have come since 1975 as there are Native Americans.

The basic challenge for these refugees is to find adequate employment to ensure economic self-sufficiency. This task is not so easy, considering that refugees, especially those whose emigration was largely unanticipated, frequently are not fluent in English. Others who are admitted for humane reasons come with severe health problems. They have adjustment difficulties, but after a while, the labor-force participation of most immigrant groups tends to match that of the general population. Those who leave a country under considerable stress, however, do tend to work a longer work-week, to represent a smaller proportion of white-collar workers, and to have a greater proportion of service workers.

Refugees are likely to settle in geographical enclaves, probably since the majority are prone to have friends or relatives already there. It is well known that Southeast Asians have gravitated to California and Texas in large numbers, both initially and through secondary migration (movement from one state to another, once in America). Louisiana and Virginia are also states with large Southeast Asian populations. Cubans and West Indians have settled heavily in Florida; Russian Jews and Colombians in New York City.

Some come to this country in hard economic times, and the assistance available to them is, therefore, minimal. Add that fact to the language problem, exploitation by employers, and the normal anxiety of being a stranger in a strange land, and it is easy to comprehend some of the difficulties faced by immigrants.

The experience of the Cuban refugees is instructive (Bach, 1980). They came in two waves: early, beginning in 1959 and late, in 1980, when Castro loosened restrictions on emigration. In some respects, these immigrants were more fortunate than most Third World immigrants who settle in American cities, for most had some urban industrial work experience. Most Cuban immigrants, like most immigrants of whatever country of origin, soon became members of an ethnic work-

ing class — in this case, the Cuban-American working class. The jobs they got were likely to be as crafts-workers, machine operatives, or unskilled laborers. Few (especially in the latest wave) were professionals or managers. Many earlier immigrants had to take positions at a lower status level than they held in Cuba. All in all, occupational adjustment, especially in hard times, is not easy for immigrants, but they eventually assimilate. Obviously, the more help they get, the easier the task.

Illegal immigrants, on the other hand, have an even more difficult task, since they are in constant danger of deportation and thus subject to exploitation. Sehgal and Vialet (1980) point out that over 1 million illegal aliens are apprehended in America each year (mostly Mexican because of concentration on the border) — more than double the total, on average, admitted legally each year. These are only the ones who get caught. Estimates of total numbers of illegal immigrants range from 2.9 to 5.7 million. Some slip illegally into the country; others enter legally and later violate the terms of their visas. The illegals and visiting labor force participants, it is assumed, are a source of cheap labor to exploiters who also do not have to pay much attention to working conditions. It is argued that they thus displace native workers. Unfortunately, the problem is such that counselors are not typically involved.

Once immigrant groups are in the country for a time, both generational changes and occupational advancement tend to lead to greater exogamy (marrying outside of the immigrant group) and thus greater assimilation into American culture (Schoen & Cohen, 1980). Assimilation usually takes place by starting at the bottom and gradually moving up. Some people, however, remain in an enclave economy, working within immigrant-owned firms.

Legal immigrants, especially those whose emigration has been sudden, unanticipated, externally induced, and stressful, face many adjustments. Occupational adjustment may be the greatest of these.

There is a difference also in the adjustment of white versus black immigrants. De Freitas (1981), for example, discovered through his research that:

Black immigrants in New York City experience

significant occupational mobility during their first few years after arrival. Downward mobility is especially severe among those with high level occupational backgrounds in the country of origin. These results are consistent with hypotheses derived from previous research on the adjustment difficulties experienced by white immigrants. However, unlike most white immigrants who are able to subsequently recover much of their lost occupational status through upward mobility, foreign-born black professionals, managers, and craftsmen appear less likely to regain their former occupational levels. Despite certain employment advantages when compared with indigenous blacks, foreign-born blacks are substantially underrepresented in high-pay, high-status occupations relative to white males (p. 45).

Counseling Immigrants

How can immigrants best be counseled about career concerns? To answer this question intelligently, we really need to know more about the vocational development of immigrants than we do now. In most cases, immigration represents a discontinuity in career development for an individual. The nature and effect of that discontinuity has not been studied in very much depth.

One exception is the excellent work underway in Israel by Krau (1981, 1982). Although the findings from the Israeli experience are not completely applicable to the American scene, they have enough face validity to be worth further exploration and testing here. For example, Krau investigated how individuals cope with basically unanticipated emigration and whether cognitive dissonance might be a motivator explaining immigrants' behavioral strategy. Using eighty-nine new, educated immigrants to Israel (mainly from Russia and Romania), who were provided an accountancy training program by the Ministry of Absorption, Krau discovered that any preparation for a career change took place basically *after* arrival in the new country. To cope successfully after the fact of immigration, some people reduce their self-image to become congruent with the lower status of their new career. For example, they tend to become less self-assertive. Some people, however,

deny that their status has been lowered. Such denial results in less expressed satisfaction. In short, one can accept a lowered status and adopt a self-image that is congruent with that lowered status and, eventually, over time, work back to a higher level. Or, one can deny the reality of lowered status and risk a poorer adjustment. Counseling such individuals thus involves helping them to minimize denial efforts.

Krau has built a model of career development of immigrants. The stages of the model include crystallization, vocational retraining, job entry and trial, establishment, and maintenance. Although immigrants experience discontinuity because of emigration, Krau's model suggests that once they reach a new country, the process of career reconstruction is one of continuity. In his model, he matches coping behaviors with specific career developmental tasks of immigrants. His paradigm is partially presented in Table 5.3.

Preliminary research on the validity of the model is encouraging. From these early findings, it does appear that the model of career stages accurately represents what most immigrants go through as they become integrated into the work world and culture of their new nation. Further, "skills critically defining the adjustment to one career stage are success predictors for the acquisition of behaviors of greater complexity needed to adjust to the requirements of the following period" (Krau, 1982, p. 328). Some highly educated, skilled, language-fluent immigrants may pass directly from the crystallization stage to job entry and trial, skipping the retraining stage. If the model holds, the counselor must determine where the individual is likely to experience the greatest difficulty in coping behavior and must work preventively to ensure a smoother transition.

Finally, a caveat: simply because immigrants are grouped for census purposes does not mean that they are alike. Southeast Asians are a good example. Not only are the cultures different among the countries, but within nations immigrants will represent divergent cultures. Long-standing regional and national antipathies may make emigrants from one country loathe to be in a group with others from another nation or even their own. Great care should be exercised in setting up any career intervention to be certain that the

Table 5.3
A Career Development Model of Immigrants

Career stage	Problem-creating condition	Coping behavior
Crystallization	Language difficulties	Learning
	Lack of information on labor market and on job requirements	Help-seeking behavior
	Cognitive dissonance over status incongruence	Reducing cognitive dissonance
Vocational retraining	Cognitive dissonance over status incongruence	Reducing cognitive dissonance
	Need to accept also unfamiliar occupation	Emotional acceptance of new occupation
	Lack of skill in new occupation	Acquisition of occupational knowledge and skills
Job entry and trial	Competition on the labor market	Competitive behavior
	Short employment interviews and tests	Efficiency in test situations and display of vocational knowledge and skills
Establishment	Job requirements	Conforming to requirements
	New work community	Openness to social contacts and new values
	Need for enculturation	
	Need for economic security	Effort to achieve a permanent income
Maintenance	Job requirements	Conforming to job requirements
	Need to heighten living standard and position in community	Effort to catch up economic community standards
		Effort to assert oneself in the community

group is not so heterogeneous that it is unworkable.

THE DISABLED

In Chapter 11, we will look at career counseling in institutions devoted to vocational rehabilitation. In Chapter 9, we will discuss the implications of PL 94-142, the law governing the education of handicapped students. This section is intended to complement those parts of the book and to consider career-relevant aspects of a final special population, the disabled.

Career Development of the Disabled

There is considerable confusion in the field regarding the difference between *disability* and *handicap*. We prefer the distinction drawn by

Dunham and Dunham (1978). They consider the disabled person to be one who is structurally, physiologically, and psychologically different from a normal person because of accident, disease, or developmental problems. A person who is handicapped, they maintain, feels less adequate than others, either in general or in a specific situation. A disability, then, need not be a handicap.

Hence, by the disabled, we mean a population that has a disability or several disabilities that may or may not be a vocational handicap. The disability may be *physical* (such as amputations, birth defects, cancer, heart problems, burns, deafness, blindness, multiple sclerosis, muscular dystrophy, orthopedic, spinal injury), *intellectual* (mental retardation, learning disability, brain damage, speech and language disorders), *emotional* (mental illness, substance abuse, alcoholism, obesity and other eating disorders), or *sociocultural* (as discussed earlier in this chapter). In any case, best estimates are that in the United States over 10 percent of the population have chronic physical, mental, or emotional conditions that limit their activity sufficiently to make a substantial career difference.

It may be reasonably expected that severe disability, either congenital or adventitious, will have a profound influence on an individual's career development. To a great extent this is true, but the effect is largely unpredictable by type of disability. Classic studies by Wright (1960) and Shontz (1975) have demonstrated that for persons with disabilities, the within-group variability in terms of personality patterns and general adjustment is as great as the variability between them and the rest of the population. To be sure, those with disabilities may have certain functional limitations that restrict their freedom in choosing from among the vast array of occupations, and if the disability is not congenital, there is bound to be some discontinuity in career development. Hershenson (1974) agrees that adjustment is not predictable or specifically affected by the disability, but he does point out the functional limitations of chronic conditions. For example, if work competence is affected (as by manual dexterity problems), there may be an effect on work personality or work choice.

These exceptional individuals are presumed also to be the victims of considerable prejudice by potential employers and possible bias by counselors (Ioracchini & Aboud, 1981; Pederson, Holwill, & Shapiro, 1978; Florian, 1978; Hosie, 1979). It is no doubt true that attitudes rooted in the concept of stigma affect behavior toward the disabled, just as sexism, ageism, and racism exist; but some research suggests that attitudes toward the disabled vary by type of disability. In the past, for example, employers appeared to be more willing to hire the physically disabled than to hire the functionally disabled (such as the psychiatrically disabled). Some more recent evidence, however, hints that these attitudes may be softening (Stone & Sawatzki, 1980). As is the case with many stereotyped attitudes, they can frequently be altered by providing experiences permitting the development of greater empathy with the subject of the stereotype. With the disabled, for instance, Ibrahim and Herr (1983) used a role-playing situation in which individuals assumed a disability, and the experience had a significant effect in building positive attitudes toward those actually having that disability.

It is obviously impossible to deal with every disability within the confines of this volume. Each disability is, in fact, the focus of a large body of literature related specifically to career development within that disability. Further, the reason for being of rehabilitation counselors is to assist in the vocational rehabilitation of those with disabilities. All we are attempting to do in this chapter is to make the "generalist" career counselor aware of the possible functional limitations and the possible delayed, discontinuous, or impaired career development of those with disabilities.

Career Counseling of the Disabled

In a classic 1963 article, McDaniel argued that in cases of traumatic disability, the individual was required to regress to the tentative and realistic phases of the exploratory stage. In these substages, the task of the disabled is to define and accept a modified self-concept with certain new limitations, to test these formulations in reality, and to find new ways to satisfy aspirations. Ultimately, according to McDaniel, the process of vocational redevelopment will be affected by pretrauma experiences in career, personal, and social circumstances; the types of concepts and decisions requiring modification; the specific type of disabling factors; and the availability of assistance and information. In the two decades since McDaniel's original theoretical conceptualization of vocational redevelopment for the disabled, little has changed. We have more sophisticated tools, but the basic idea of career redevelopment and what it entails has not appreciably changed, even though different theoreticians may offer different contexts for redevelopment. Two examples are presented here, both of which deal with needs: one is based on Maslow's need hierarchy and a second is based on a trait-and-factor orientation applied to the Theory of Work Adjustment.

Maslow's need theory has been operationalized by Lassiter (1981) to apply to the disabled and their vocational redevelopment. Within this context, he describes needs and their applications to work and work adjustment in competitive work settings.

1. Physiological Needs
   a. Need to learn to work in a wheelchair (for example, using the bathroom, traveling from home to job, taking a coffee break, meeting with fellow workers, dealing with different job performance tasks).
   b. Need to learn new ways of being productive (for example, coping with a work schedule different from others; using specially structured pieces, instruments, or machines to enable the client to meet job demands; receiving an individualized instructional program in mobility).
   c. Need for the client to accept responsibility for personal hygiene (for example, attend to toilet and other personal needs, learn to care well for his or her body and avoid medical complications and illnesses in order to avoid absenteeism, loss of productive activity, and more severe disablement).
2. Safety Needs
   a. Strong desire of the client to remain in work similar to previous job and a preference for association with people on the job who are familiar.
   b. Need for a job that appears to offer tenure and stability with decent health and retirement plans, and so on.
   c. Need for a smoothly functioning, orderly position.
3. Belongingness and Love Needs
   a. Need for finding new ways of developing feelings of belongingness.
   b. Need for analyzing the potential for caring and being cared for that might be provided in the job setting if certain job modifications or support groups were developed.
4. Esteem Needs
   a. Need to experience new feelings of competence and self-confidence that come from a person's exposure to new interpersonal skills and new tasks.
5. Needs for Self-Actualization
   a. Need for self-awareness and self-actualization.
   b. Need to develop one's inner space (thoughts and feelings).
   c. Acceptance and optimization of a life of severe disability.

A different needs perspective is provided by those who advocate the use of the Theory of Work Adjustment with the disabled (Dawis & Lofquist, 1978; Lynch & Maki, 1981). The Theory of Work Adjustment is discussed at several points throughout this volume. Although at least one study (Vandergoot & Engelkes, 1977) found the theory to have no more usefulness than traditional counseling as a structure, many are enthusiastic about its application to the disabled. The theory suggests, in part, that individuals have work needs; occupations provide work reinforcers; if reinforcers equal or exceed needs, people will be satisfied at work. In other words, individuals adjust to work through the interaction between work personality and work environment. Melding this theory with a trait-and-factor approach, Lynch and Maki suggest that the counselor working with a disabled client use the traditional trait-and-factor steps: (1) *analysis* — getting information about the client; (2) *synthesis* — interpreting information about the client; (3) *diagnosis* — using interpretation of the data, combined with consideration of the functional limitations of the client, to identify assets of the individual; (4) *prognosis* — determining future options and developing a plan of action; (5) *counseling* — helping clients to know themselves and to use available resources to achieve their potential; and (6) *follow-up* — monitoring adjustment in the placement situation.

Part of counseling with the disabled (just as with the nondisabled) will involve assessment of a client's aptitudes, interests, work values and needs, and so forth. Sinick (1979) has urged counselors to give individual rather than group tests to the disabled, to use timed tests carefully and cautiously, to provide rest periods and several testing sessions, and to utilize work samples. He further advocates the use of an interview to discuss interests, values, and needs rather than the use of an interest inventory, since the disabled may be deprived of many life experiences that form the content of common interest measures. Depending on the type of disabling condition, work samples may be useful assessment tools. Gannaway, Sink, and Becket (1980), for example, used the Singer Vocational Evaluation System (VES) and reported good predictive efficiency in a county social service vocational rehabilitation project. Stodden, Casale, and Schwartz (1977), on the other hand, found little practical use for work sample measures when applied to the mentally retarded.

Another area of importance in counseling the disabled is job readiness. Job readiness involves providing disabled clients with training in such job-relevant aspects as increasing their motivation and willingness to work, getting them medically stabilized, ensuring their ability to function well interpersonally and emotionally and to follow orders, having specific work skills, and demonstrating good work habits. One study (Tesolowski & Halpin, 1979) compared the work personality characteristics of physically handicapped sheltered-workshop employees participating in a job-readiness program and concluded that they had significantly better work personality characteristics than a comparable group that had not had job-readiness training. Similarly, there are other reports in the literature of job-readiness programs for specific disabilities. Fay et al. (1979), for example, describe a successful job readiness program, based on modeling and role playing, and centered on the development of social skills for alcoholics.

Another major consideration in the career counseling of the disabled is placement, which receives much more emphasis in the rehabilitation literature than in the more general career literature. Flannagan (1974), Echols (1972), Murphy (1977), and Minton (1977) have all stressed the counselor's role in placement in the rehabilitation process. Studies of the effectiveness of placement in vocational rehabilitation have consistently demonstrated that the time spent in this activity has a high "payoff." For instance, Zadney and James (1977) showed that as a counselor spent more time on activities having a direct bearing on placement, total rehabilitation increased and cases that were closed as "not rehabilitated" decreased.

Career education and similar experiences also are frequently used in the vocational development or redevelopment of the disabled. Marinoble (1980), for instance, advocates the use of community jobs, just as with nondisabled students, to provide a direct, independent career education experience for disabled students. In such a situation, students can reinforce social skills, and put

to use work behaviors learned in the classroom. In colleges PL 93-112 requires career offices to provide services to the disabled without discrimination. Many career centers have adapted their services to assist the disabled. The visually impaired, for example, are provided specially designed materials in braille and specific programs directed toward meeting their unique needs (White, Reardon, Barker, & Carlson, 1979). Career materials abound that are tailored for every type of disabling condition. Special career and educational information can be found for the hearing impaired (Happ & Altmaier, 1982; Lombana, 1979), epileptics (Hood & Brown, 1979), and virtually every other category of disability.

Finally, in terms of career education for the disabled, Brolin and Gysbers (1979) suggest that the focus of the counselor should be on helping individuals to develop crucial life skills for successful living and working. In three areas — daily living, personal-social, and occupational — the authors offer twenty-two competencies that the disabled need to acquire for successful career development. Career-related competencies would include, for example, the daily living skill of utilizing recreation and leisure, the personal-social skill of problem-solving, and the occupational skills of knowing and exploring occupational possibilities, selecting and planning occupational choices, exhibiting appropriate work habits and behaviors, exhibiting sufficient physical-manual skills, obtaining a specific occupational skill, and seeking, securing, and maintaining employment. To help the disabled achieve these goals, Brolin and Gysbers urge that counselors exercise the following career functions (p. 261):

1. Conduct career assessment for the handicapped as an integral part of an overall assessment program.
2. Develop and use community resources.
3. Become an advocate for handicapped individuals in the context of an overall program of advocacy.
4. Develop and monitor individual learning programs in cooperation with other educators and with parents.
5. Consult with parents concerning the career development of their children.

6. Consult with other educators concerning the development of self-awareness and decision-making skills in handicapped individuals.
7. Work with handicapped individuals in the selection of job possibilities.
8. Carry out individual and group counseling with the handicapped on an ongoing basis.

In summary, Herr (1982) has collated a list of the knowledges and skills necessary for counselors who work frequently with the disabled (pp. 21–22).

Knowledge

Federal and state legislation, guidelines and policies dealing with exceptional persons.

Rights of exceptional persons

Types of classification, diagnostic tools or processes and their limitations vis à vis work potential or skill

Informal assessment procedures for assessing interests, values, goals

Characteristics of different types of exceptionality, their etiology, and their likely effects upon work behavior

Opportunities available in the local labor market for persons with different types of skills and different types of difficulties

The meaning of functional limitation and its use in counseling

Models of career development applicable to the congenitally or adventitiously disabled

The effects of social stigma, labeling, stereotype upon the self-concept of exceptional persons

Characteristics of the handicapped related to employment skills, training programs, and potential occupational and educational opportunities

Ways of working with other specialists to facilitate a comprehensive approach to career exploration, career preparation, and career placement of exceptional persons

Examples of job redesign by which employers can accommodate the capabilities and/or functional limitations of various types of exceptionality

Methods of developing individual educational programs (IEPs) or individual employment plans

Fears, concerns, and needs of parents or spouses of exceptional persons and ways to work with total family unit

Models of developing daily living, mobility, job search, and work skills

Reference materials and directories pertinent to different categories of exceptionality: *Vocational Preparation of Retarded Citizens* (Borlin, 1976); *Workers Worth Their Hire* (American Mutual

Insurance Alliance, 1970); *Work and Human Behavior* (Neff, 1977); *Career Exploration and Preparation for Special Needs Learners* (Phelps & Lutz, 1977); *Guidance, Counseling and Support Services for High School Students with Physical Disabilities* (Technical Education Research Centers, 1977).

Skills

Ability to interpret and advise about legislation, policy, guidelines and rights which affect exceptional persons and their family members

Ability to use diagnostic and informal assessment procedures with exceptional persons

Ability to assess functional limitations and to use them in helping clients engage in occupational exploration and career planning

Ability to apply knowledge of career development theory to assist in the analysis of self concept portrayal or developmental task deficits of individual clients

Ability to effectively provide individual and group counseling of persons of different types of exceptionality and their families

Ability to work with other specialists in team approaches to clients for educational or employment planning and placement

Ability to work with employers in developing job restructuring for different types of exceptional persons

Ability to plan and implement different types of skill building workshops or experiences necessary for employability and work adjustment

Summary

In this chapter we have considered four sarily mutually exclusive special populations: women, the culturally different, immigrants, and the disabled. For each, we have pointed out unique aspects of career development or redevelopment that require counselor interventions. These interventions emphasize techniques somewhat different from those used with the general population or call for different emphases in the use of common techniques. Also, we suggested that unconscious stereotyping, leading to bias, may be present in counselors or employers; and we offered information to gainsay such stereotyping. Finally, we are persuaded that when we learn more about the career development of these special populations, we shall ultimately conclude that the career differences between each of these groups and the majority are differences more of degree than of kind.

LEARNING ACTIVITIES

1. Set up a systematic model that describes a course, workshop, or seminar addressed to some unique career need of one of the four special populations described in this chapter. Include behavioral objectives, activities, materials, and evaluation.
2. If you live near a large city, make an appointment to visit the local office of the Immigration and Naturalization Service and talk with a representative. Gather data on numbers of immigrants in your geographical area, common vocational and other adjustment difficulties, sources of assistance, and so forth.
3. Inventory all of the resources for career counseling provided for women in your community. Include continuing education, higher education, YWCAs, church groups, local, state, county, and federal agencies, women's rights organizations, private agencies, and so on. Are these efforts coordinated? Redundant? What recommendations, if any, would you make to improve service delivery?
4. Arrange a visit to the nearest office of the Division of Vocational Rehabilitation, Goodwill, or any other organization devoted to helping the disabled achieve vocational rehabilitation. What major problems exist? How are they being addressed?
5. Investigate any source of educational or occupational information directed specifically at members of any of the four special populations, for example: E. Gollag & A. Bennett. *The college guide for students with disabilities* (Cambridge, Mass.: Abt, 1976); J. S. Mitchell. *I can be anything: Careers and colleges for young women* (New York: College Board, 1978). How do these sources differ from the standard materials?
6. Talk with a counselor who works in a program for college youngsters who are educationally and economically disadvantaged. What are the major career problems the counselor confronts? What special techniques or materials are required in working with this population?
7. Talk with a representative of your state Employment Service. Ask for data on any of the four special populations described in this chapter. What special problems are encountered?
8. In his book, *America now: The anthropology of a changing culture* (1981), Marvin Harris states:

> From the holistic point of view of this book, the most important point bearing on crime and unemployment among black males is that during and after World War II blacks migrated in unprecedented numbers from farms to cities in search of union-wage factory jobs. This was scarcely a voluntary movement since it coincided with the end of the epoch of small farms and with the final stages of the industrialization of agriculture. But it was precisely during this same period that the great shift from goods production to service-and-information production was taking place. This resulted in a massive pile-up of unemployed black workers inside the run-down cores of the nation's largest cities (p. 136).

If Harris is accurate, what are the implications? What are possible solutions? What are roadblocks to implementing the solutions?

OBJECTIVES

After reading this chapter, engaging in the learning activities, and reading the suggested references, you should have met the objectives that follow. If you have not, it would probably be useful for you to review the material on special populations before proceeding further.

1. Identify at least three career needs especially pertinent to women, to the culturally different, to immigrants, to the disabled.
2. Describe at least five characteristics of the population of working women.
3. Define "stereotype" and explain how it affects the career development of women.
4. Distinguish among a few parameters that separate traditional women workers from pioneer women workers from homemakers; the career development of men from the career development of women.
5. Summarize the literature relating to the influence of role models in the career development of women.
6. Give at least two reasons for discontinuity of career development in females.
7. List at least three useful principles in the career counseling of women.
8. Name at least three unique characteristics of the career development of blacks, of Latinos.
9. Provide at least three tenets relating to the career counseling of the culturally different.
10. Identify at least two unique constraints in the career development of immigrants.
11. Describe the likely career development stages of immigrants.
12. Define the difference between handicap and disability.
13. List at least four career competencies required by counselors who deal with the disabled.

6 | *Systematic Planning for Career Guidance*

According to Katz (1974), managers at all levels need three distinct types of skills: (1) the ability to produce the organization's goals or services, *technical* skill; (2) the ability to work in groups as a leader or member, *human* skill; (3) the ability to see how organizational units and functions are integrated, *conceptual* skill. Each of these could easily describe the professional in career guidance, regardless of the setting: business and industry, education, community agency. The purpose of this chapter, however, is to consider conceptual skills as they are reflected in systematic planning for career guidance.

If career guidance is to be more than a series of random events or activities, and limited encounters between counselors and counselees, it must be built on systematic planning or a systems approach. Such planning requires the completion, in a logical order, of a set of steps that seek to answer several general questions: (1) Why have a career guidance program? (2) What will be the goals of the career guidance program? (3) How will the goals of the career guidance program be achieved? and (4) How will it be determined if the career guidance goals have been achieved?

THE PROCESS OF SYSTEMATIC PLANNING

A systematic approach to program planning rests on the concept of systems analysis, which in turn is concerned with the examination of the interrelationships among the parts of a system in order to formulate goals and objectives. Science, the defense establishment, and industry have used systems analysis and related methodology for several decades to make complex, interactive units manageable and more amenable to monitoring and evaluation. Depending on its relationship to other components within an institution, career guidance may be seen as a system in its own right or as a subsystem of a larger whole (see, for example, Byham, 1982).

Program planning, whether for career guidance or other purposes, is required to ensure that the goals are clearly understood, that the techniques or processes comprising the program are related to the goals, and that the criteria on which the program will be judged are explicit. These elements underlie the program's accountability and are the steps leading to its evaluation.

In essence, a systematic approach to career guidance suggests that if you wish to end with a particular type of employee, student, or client behavior (for example, career maturity, self-understanding, decision-making skills), you build toward that goal by comprehensively taking into consideration the functional relations between the elements and people who effect such a goal. In conceiving such a system in relation to career guidance, the counselor or career administrator needs to take into account the interdependent effects of such variables as:

1. learner or client characteristics
2. resource characteristics available in a school, employment or community setting (such as budget, materials available, referral sources, exploratory sites, personnel who can be involved)
3. counselor characteristics

169

4. effectiveness of counselor techniques
5. administrative characteristics or management requirements
6. community or institutional expectations

Within this context, the basic question underlying the planning for career guidance is: Which resources or combination of resources (people, places, media) are appropriate for fostering what type of development in what type of learner or client under what conditions (time, place, size of group, and so on) to achieve what purposes (Phillips, 1966)? In systematic planning, then, one must begin with a statement of what is to be achieved in career guidance and counseling, what goals are to be accomplished, and what student, employee, or client development is to be facilitated. A basic premise of this book is that an understanding of the various approaches to career development provides the *content* for these considerations. (Chapter 4 was devoted to identifying the major emphases in career development theory and research, and much of this chapter extends the analysis of career development approaches more specifically. These aspects of career development should be reviewed as appropriate here.) This emphasis on beginning with goals for the program is in contrast to beginning with counselor techniques that can be performed. In too many instances, counselors do what they know how to do without questioning why they are doing these things or what goals they are attempting to achieve. In the process, they lose sight of answers to such questions as, Why Career Guidance? or How will students, employees, or clients be different as a result of exposure to career guidance? Without answers to such questions, however, career guidance programs lack direction and are likely to be pressured into areas for which counselors are not prepared or in which their skills are ineffective.

Ryan's Functions

Ryan (1974) has identified six functions necessary to a systems approach to career education. In modified form, they include:

1. *Establishing a conceptual framework* — Determine the rationale, define the basic concepts, specify the basic assumptions on which the program will be based.
2. *Possessing information* — Gather, evaluate, and store data about the community, available resources, facilities, the population to be served. Determine what other information is necessary.
3. *Assessing needs* — Compare the ideal program as built from the rationale, assumptions, and concepts of step 1 with the existing situation in the setting where this program is to be installed. Determine the discrepancies between what the program should be and what it now is. Assess the perceptions of parents, employers, managers, employees, teachers, students, or other consumers, administrators, and community representatives about what priorities the program should meet; these could be described as the assessed needs to which the program will be directed. Which of these groups you query depends on whether you are implementing a career guidance program in business and industry, a community agency, or an educational setting.
4. *Formulating the management plan* — Specify program goals and performance objectives for students, employees, or clients. Identify the processes that will be related to the program goals. Specify the resources and constraints that need to be considered in putting the plan together.
5. *Implementing the program* — Put the program plan into action. Provide in-service to staff involved, order materials or resources necessary, offer the experience or processes related to program goals.
6. *Evaluating the system* — Monitor ongoing operations as well as the changes in knowledge, skills, and attitudes of the participants. Determine whether the program is meeting its goals and whether individual elements are effective.

Rimmer's Components

More recently, Rimmer (1981) has proposed that the program planning and evaluation model should consist of seven major components. They include:

1. Inform and involve key groups.
2. Define the problem/goals.
3. Conduct needs assessment.
4. Formulate objectives.
5. Design program components.
6. Implement the program.
7. Evaluate the program.

The six steps described by Ryan or the seven steps proposed by Rimmer have been described by others with variations applied to particular problems or emphases (see Mannebach & Stillwell, 1974; AIR, 1975; Chiko, Tolsma, Kahn, & Marks, 1980). In fact, there is no one right way for such planning, but however it proceeds, it should be logical and comprehensive. Reduced to its essence, the three phases of designing a program are:

1. Determine and describe what is to be achieved.
2. Do what is necessary to achieve the desired result.
3. Check to see that you have succeeded in doing what you set out to do (Gammuto, 1980, p. 84).

A FIVE-STAGE MODEL

The broad aspects of the various stages of planning for a career guidance program are described in Table 6.1. Each of the stages of planning portrayed in Table 6.1 has its own unique requirements and characteristics. The rest of this chapter will be devoted to discussing the stages. Before we do so, however, we should remember that regardless of which planning paradigm one accepts, a systems approach is fundamentally a decision-making process. Indeed, a planning system really involves the generation of a system of hypotheses. In stage 1, program goals are really hypotheses that imply that if such program goals are met, the conditions existing before the program will be eliminated or improved. Similarly, behavioral objectives are hypotheses that if persons obtain the behaviors specified, the program goals will be achieved. In stage 3, the selection of alternative program processes can be conceived of as a series of hypotheses that one process is more likely than another to result in the desired behavior for which it is accountable. The evaluation, summa-

tive or formative, designed to monitor the program is really a series of tests of the hypotheses implicit in stages 1–3. Indeed, the evaluation scheme that evolves can be conceptualized almost as a pre/post test with the program elements considered to be treatments; the original conditions considered as baseline data; and, the output or behavioral outcomes which result from the program as posttest data. Obviously, most career guidance programs cannot or will not be evaluated using pure experimental designs but it can be helpful to think of much of program planning as being analogous to such conceptualizations.

Stage 1 – Developing a Program Rationale and Philosophy

Stage 1 includes all the thinking and data collection that relates to developing a program philosophy and rationale. It includes securing information about the characteristics of the setting in which the career guidance program is to operate and the resources to be committed to that effort. Such planning also includes developing needs surveys (questionnaires or structured interviews) to determine what consumers (students, employees, or other adults) and others believe the focus of the career guidance program should be. Together, these data will help determine what the current status of career guidance in the particular setting is and what different groups believe it should be. At the conclusion of stage 1, counselors should have formulated a statement that clearly answers the question, Why Career Guidance?

Another aspect of stage 1 is to review current research and theory on what the program's directions might be, what behaviors might be affected by the program, what basic concepts and assumptions should be considered. In Chapters 1–4, contributions have been made to such an analysis and should be reviewed. Chapter 4, in particular, speaks to the conceptual elements that give career guidance its general rationale. Many of these insights could be translated into program philosophy for a particular setting.

Basically, programs in career guidance will have one of three emphases or a combination of these three. (1) In a *stimulus approach* consumers are

Table 6.1

Stages in Planning for and Implementing a Career Guidance Program

Stage 1	Stage 2	Stage 3	Stage 4	Stage 5
1. Develop a program philosophy	1. Specify program goals	1. Select alternative program processes	1. Describe evaluation procedures	1. Identify milestones (crucial events) that must occur for program implementation
1.1 Review research and theory pertinent to career guidance and career development	2. Specify individual behavioral objectives to be achieved	2. Relate program processes to program goals or specific behavioral objectives	1.1 Summative evaluation to assess whether total program goals are being met	1.1 When staff in-service will occur
1.2 Specify program rationale		3. Identify resources necessary to implement various program processes	1.2 Formative evaluation to assess whether program elements are contributing effectively to program goals	1.2 When information about the program must be prepared and sent to consumers
1.3 Describe theoretical and philosophical basis for program		4. Identify personnel (teachers, counselors, human relations specialists, administrators, community representatives, first-line supervisors, parents) who have contributions to make to various program processes	1.3 Identify evaluative data to be secured, from whom, and by whom	1.3 When materials and resources for the program must be ordered
1.4 State assumptions			1.4 Build or secure data-collection instruments	1.4 When base-line data on participants will be collected
1.5 Define concepts			1.5 Decide on the form of data analysis and who will be responsible	1.5 When program will be introduced
2. Collect comprehensive data on what consumers (students, adults) and others (parents, employers, teachers, administrators, community representatives) believe should be program priorities			1.6 Identify persons or groups to whom evaluative data will be provided and in what form	
3. Collect data on the current program — goals, resources, etc.				
4. Identify where the target population — students, workers, other adults — currently stand on their career development				
5. Determine discrepancies between what current program is and what it should be				

172

assisted to anticipate and explore opportunities and how these relate to their personal abilities, preferences and circumstances. In essence, the intent is to facilitate career development. (2) In *induction and adjustment* to a setting, the intent of the career guidance program is to assist persons to translate their preferences or choices into action, consolidate these choices, and advance within the settings in which they are implemented. (3) In a *treatment approach* individuals may anticipate and explore but also must undergo remediation or reconstruction of their attitudes, knowledge, and skills.

However a program emphasis is conceived, planning for it needs to include insights into the behaviors that the program intends to affect. These insights need to be translated into a program philosophy and rationale. For example, if the career guidance program is to emphasize stimulus, then career maturity and the elements comprising it may be helpful input to conceptualizing program philosophy and rationale. Although insights into the behavioral structure of career maturity are useful not only to a stimulus approach to career guidance, the other two career guidance program emphases have other bodies of insight that are useful in conceptualizing and planning their particular intent.

Concepts of Career Maturity as Input for a Stimulus Approach. Before one can properly specify program goals or performance objectives for the career development, vocationalization, or stimulus of students or adults, one must identify the overall goal. That goal which appears most frequently in the literature and which seems to have the most face validity is *career maturity*. Although useful as an ultimate goal, however, it is too global to be useful for intermediate purposes unless it can be dissected into its elements. Thus, it is necessary to convert the elements of career maturity into unifying themes and behavioral descriptions and place these along a developmental line leading to career maturity at some point in life, such as high school graduation, tenth grade, sophomore year in college, release from a rehabilitation facility, or at specific career transition points, such as when an employee is ready to be promoted to a new role.

When attempting such a task, however, one must realize that, just as in other developmental processes, individuals will differ in their readiness for various elements or aspects of career development and in the ways by which they develop this readiness. Not everyone will reach the same point at the same time, nor will all proceed through the elements of career development at the same pace. As previously indicated, the speed of such movement and the readiness for it will depend on the individual's personal history and many extrinsic and intrinsic factors.

The objectives of career development, then, rest on statements of expectations for specific target groups, which necessitate judgments of what individuals ought to be able to achieve and behavioral descriptions of these activities. But one must also realize that for optimum effect, career development should be personalized. Although the literal realization of such a goal may be too much to expect, any attempt systematically to aid career development requires an emphasis both on diagnosis and on the provision of diverse learning experiences. It is simply not enough to say to a person, "Be career mature." Each one needs to understand what being career mature means, what the consequences of career maturity are, how one acquires career maturity, and what opportunities are available to aid such an effort.

In essence, a systems approach to career maturity at its best would represent a planned continuum of experiences for individual students, employees, or clients. The individual should be exposed to the program on the basis of assessed readiness and move progressively toward the goal of career maturity.

Fostering career maturity seems to require both individualizing and personalizing (Shane, 1970). As will be shown later in this chapter, there are certain elements of effective behavior that all persons need to acquire individually. But there are also times when, as individual goals become clearer, the person needs the opportunity and the assistance to "create him or herself"; that is, to develop ways of creating goals and a life style independent of others.

Before directing further attention to the goals of vocationalization, it is important to consider career maturity itself more specifically. Although Carter (1940) and Strong (1943) each examined the relationship between interest patterning and levels of maturity in adolescents and adults, the meaning of career maturity has taken on a greater comprehensiveness since approximately 1950. For example, Ginzberg, Ginsburg, Axelrad, and Herma (1951) reported, "To some degree, the way in which a young person deals with his occupational choice is indicative of his general maturity and, conversely, in assessing the latter, consideration must be given to the way in which he is handling his occupational choice problem" (p. 60). Extending this definition, Super (1957, p. 186) indicated that in a gross sense career maturity can be described as "the place reached on the continuum of vocational development from exploration to decline." Later still, Crites (1961, p. 259) described it as "the maturity of an individual's vocational behavior as indicated by the similarity between his behavior and that of the oldest individuals in his vocational life stage."

A clarification of these definitions of career maturity is provided by Super (1957), who differentiated Vocational Maturity I (VMI) from Vocational Maturity II (VMII). He defines VMI as "the life stage in which the individual actually is, as evidenced by the developmental tasks with which he is dealing in relation to the life stage in which he is expected to be, in terms of his age" (p. 132). VMII is defined as "maturity of behavior in the actual life stage (regardless of whether it is the expected life stage), as evidenced by the behavior shown in dealing with developmental tasks of the actual life stage compared with the behavior of other individuals who are dealing with the same developmental tasks" (pp. 57, 132).

These definitions of Vocational Maturity I and II raise several other points. One is that career maturity differs when defined as the vocational behavior expected of persons at different points in life. What is career maturity at age 10 will not be at age 16 or 25 or 35. Second, although in VMI there is an expectation that gross characteristics of career development describe broad chronological periods in life, VMII attends to how a particular individual is coping with career development in a personal sense. In other words, it asks, Where is this person now, and what knowledge, attitudes, or skills does he or she need to progress to higher levels of career development? Similarly, it would

be possible for corporations and other settings to define the types of career maturity necessary at different transition points within the career paths available. Third, VMI and VMII introduce the concept of developmental tasks as means by which career development progresses.

Most of the examples of ingredients important to career maturity, reported on later in this chapter, have evolved from the work of Super and his colleagues in the Career Pattern Study. Some readers may consider this an imbalance. However, as Norton (1970) has noted, whether one examines the concurrent, related work of Vriend (1968), Crites (1965), Gribbons and Lohnes (1968), Nelson (1956), or Westbrook (Westbrook & Cunningham, 1970), the essential criteria of career maturity remain fairly constant. What does change, however, across these approaches to career maturity are the methods of measuring the presence of specific elements of career maturity. In Chapter 14 we will discuss these measurement strategies and their availability for counselor use.

It is important to realize that if career maturity is to be used as the goal of career development, and if a systems approach to achieving it is to be mounted, measures of career maturity are needed in order (1) to assess personal readiness to make educational-vocational decisions or to participate in particular types of career development experiences; (2) to serve as diagnostic instruments for determining treatment; and (3) to evaluate the effectiveness of strategies for aiding vocationalization (Westbrook & Cunningham, 1970). Many such assessment devices are described in Chapter 16.

The Mastery of Developmental Tasks as a Function of Career Guidance. Several theorists, including Havighurst (1953), Erikson (1963), Super (1957), Super, Starishevsky, Matlin, and Jordaan (1963), Tiedeman and O'Hara (1963), and Gribbons and Lohnes (1968), have either directly or indirectly wedded particular developmental tasks with stages of increasingly mature vocational behavior. Thus, we can assume that the developmental task concept is useful, both as a description of the changing demands on individuals as they move through life and as a means of organizing those demands — whether knowledge, attitudes, or skills — into a systems approach to career development.

In terms of the first use of developmental tasks just cited, Havighurst (1953, p. 2) has provided the following definition: "A task which arises at or about a certain period in the life of the individual, successful achievement of which leads to happiness and success with later tasks, while failure leads to unhappiness in the individual, disapproval by society, and difficulty with later tasks." This definition has come to be accepted almost universally. As Zaccaria (1965) has reported, those who formulate developmental tasks generally agree on the following statements:

1. Individual growth and development is continuous.
2. Individual growth can be divided into periods or life stages for descriptive purposes.
3. Individuals in each life stage can be characterized by certain general characteristics that they have in common.
4. Most individuals in a given culture pass through similar developmental stages.
5. The society makes certain demands upon individuals.
6. These demands are relatively uniform for all members of the society.
7. The demands differ from stage to stage as the individual goes through the developmental process.
8. Developmental crises occur when the individual perceives the demand to alter his present behavior and master new learnings.
9. In meeting and mastering developmental crises, the individual moves from one developmental stage of maturity to another developmental stage of maturity.
10. The task appears in its purest form at one stage.
11. Preparation for meeting the developmental crises or developmental tasks occurs in the life stage prior to the stage in which it must be mastered.
12. The developmental task or crisis may arise again during a later phase in somewhat different form.
13. The crisis or task must be mastered before the individual can successfully move on to a subsequent developmental stage.
14. Meeting the crisis successfully by learning the required task leads to societal approval, happiness, and success with later crises and their correlative tasks.
15. Failing in meeting a task or crisis leads to disapproval by society (p. 373).

The developmental task concept can be used to describe an average set of demands with which the individual must cope, as well as a way of looking at how a given individual is attaining such an expectation, at what points he or she is having difficulty, what specific experiences or competencies the person needs to acquire, and what resources might aid his or her development. Such a concept makes it possible to provide sequential developmental experiences that will prepare the individual to meet emerging developmental tasks and to prescribe (on an individual basis) alternative methods of coping with developmental task difficulties. In short, facilitation of developmental tasks offers a rationale for career guidance as well as a potential organizing theme for program planning.

Further, individual variation in accomplishing developmental tasks can be considered in the following ways: "A given task has a unique meaning to each individual. . . . Secondly, individuals vary with respect to their general approach to developmental tasks. . . . The third idiographic dimension of developmental tasks is the patterning of developmental tasks" (Zaccaria, 1965, p. 374). As previously pointed out, Lo Cascio (1967) has identified three basic patterns for mastering developmental tasks: continuous developmental pattern, delayed developmental pattern, and impaired developmental pattern. The individual differences that produce such differential patterns are values, attitudes, need systems, age, sex, and temperament, as well as cultural factors, such as socioeconomic status.

If one accepts developmental tasks as an organizing structure for conceptualizing career development or facilitating career maturity, one must then determine what the developmental tasks are that move one along a continuum to career maturity. There are several conceptualizations from which to draw. Table 6.2 presents major emphases in these various approaches. It is obvious that the emphases are not parallel in

Table 6.2
Examples of Theoretical Conceptions of the Development of Vocationally Related Behavior

	Tiedeman (1961)	Gesell, Ilg, & Ames (1956, pp. 376–382)	Ginzberg et al. (1951)	Buehler (1933)	Havighurst (1964, p. 216; 1972)
Birth to Age Ten			FANTASY Interests	GROWTH	Birth 5–10 I. Identification with a worker – father, mother, other significant persons. The concept of working becomes an essential part of the ego-ideal. Principal developmental tasks of middle childhood 1. Developing fundamental skills in reading, writing and calculating 2. Learning physical skills necessary for ordinary games 3. Learning to get along with age mates 4. Learning an appropriate masculine or feminine social role 5. Developing concepts for everyday life 6. Development conscience, morality, and a scale of values 7. Achieving personal identity
Age Ten to Fifteen	Anticipation or Preoccupation Exploration Crystallization Choice Clarification	10. Plans for careers: indefinite; careers chosen are varied, often unrelated 11. Very few have no idea of what they want to do. More than tens make single choice, choices become more realistic; occupations chosen become smaller. 12. Trend toward a single, definite choice continues. Fewer make several choices or express indecision. Boys are more likely than girls to be definite and express only one choice. 13. Marks peak for single definite choices about future work. Tends to assert choice without indecision.	TENTATIVE Capacities	EXPLORATION	10–15 II. Acquiring the basic habits of of industry: Learning to organize time and energy to get a piece of work done (school, work, chores). Learning to put work ahead of play in appropriate situations

Table 6.2 (continued)

Erikson (1965, 2nd Ed.)	Super (1969)	Gould (1978)	Levinson (1978)	Hall (1978, pp. 81–84)
Basic trust (basic mistrust) Autonomy (shame and doubt) Initiative (guilt) Industry (inferiority) Fundamentals of technology First sense of division of labor and of differential opportunity Outer and inner hindrance				
Identity (role confusion): Ego identity and the tangible promise of career Occupational identity Sexual identity	Substages: Tentative Transition Trial (with little commitment) Developmental tasks crystallizing a vocational preference; specifying it			

Table 6.2 (continued)

Tiedeman (1961)	Gesell, Ilg, & Ames (1956, pp. 376–382)	Ginzberg et al. (1951)	Buehler (1933)	Havighurst (1964, p. 216; 1972)
	14. Show less certainty in career choice. More individuals make multiple choices and a greater variety of choices than at ages 13 or 15; now recognize the difficulty of a single choice. 15. Many quite indefinite about their choice of future career. Group as a whole names many fewer careers than earlier, but finds it difficult to decide on a single choice.			
Implementation or Adjustment Induction Reformation Integration	16. More decisiveness appears. A considerable variety of choices is mentioned. Sex-typed choices predominate for boys and girls.	R E A L Values I S T I C		III. Acquiring identity as a worker in the occupational structure; choosing and preparing for an occupation. Getting work experience as a basis for occupational choice and for assurance of economic independence. Principal developmental tasks of adolescence. 1. Achieving new and more mature relations with agemates of both sexes 2. Achieving masculine or feminine social role 3. Achieving emotional independence of parents and other adults 4. Achieving assurance of economic independence 5. Selecting and preparing for an occupation 6. Acquiring a set of values and an ethical system as a guide to behavior 7. Preparing for marriage and selecting a mate 8. Starting a family 9. Getting started in an occupation

Age Fifteen to Twenty-five

Table 6.2 (continued)

Erikson (1965, 2nd Ed.)	Super (1969)	Gould (1978)	Levinson (1978)	Hall (1978, pp. 81–84)
Intimacy (isolation): The capacity to commit oneself to concrete affiliations and partnerships and to develop the ethical strength to abide by such commitments Ethical sense True genitality		Major Theme 1. Leaving our parents' world	Early Adult Transition (17–22) 1. Terminate pre-adulthood — start moving out of the pre-adult world — question the nature of the world and one's place in it — modify or terminate existing relationships with important persons, groups, and institutions — Reappraise and modify the self that formed it 2. Begin early adulthood — Explore its possibilities — Imagine oneself a participant in it — Consolidate an initial adult identity — Make and test some preliminary choices for adult living Four major tasks from 17 to approximately 30 1. Forming a dream and giving it a place in the life structure	

Table 6.2 (continued)

Tiedeman (1961)	Gesell, Ilg, & Ames (1956, pp. 376–382)	Ginzberg et al. (1951)	Buehler (1933)	Havighurst (1964, p. 216; 1972)
Age Twenty-five to Forty-five			E S T A B L I S H M E N T M A I N T E N A N C E D E C L I N E	IV. Becoming a productive person; mastering the skills of an occupation; moving up the ladder within the occupation V. Maintaining a productive society. — Achieving adult civic and social responsibility — Assisting teenage children to become responsible and happy adults — Developing adult leisure-time activities — Relating oneself to one's spouse as a person — Adjusting to aging parents — Accepting and adjusting to the physiological changes of middle age — reaching and maintaining satisfactory performance in one's occupational career. VI. Contemplating a productive life. — Adjusting to decreasing strength and health — Adjusting to retirement and reduced income — Adjusting to death of spouse. — Establishing an explicit affiliation with members of one's age group — Establishing satisfactory physical living arrangements — Adapting to social roles in a flexible way

Age Forty-five to Sixty

Table 6.2 (continued)

Erikson (1965, 2nd Ed.)	Super (1969)	Gould (1978)	Levinson (1978)	Hall (1978, pp. 81-84)
	Substages: Trial (with more commitment) Stabilization Advancement Developmental tasks		2. Forming mentor relationships 3. Forming an occupation 4. Forming love relationships and family.	
	Stabilizing in the chosen vocation consolidating one's chosen status advancing in the occupation	Major Themes 1. I'm nobody's baby now 2. Opening up to what's inside	Levinson (1978) Age 25-45 Entering the Adult World (22-28) Fashion a provisional structure that provides a workable link between the valued self and the adult society. 1. Explore possibilities for adult living; keep options open; avoid strong commitments; maximize the alternatives 2. Create a stable life structure — Become more responsible and make something of my life	
Generativity (stagnation) productivity creativity Ego integrity (despair)	The concern is how to hold the place achieved in the world of work. Preserving or being nagged by a self-concept. Little new ground is broken, but continuation along established lines.			
Integrity vs. Despair (Disgust)	Pace of work slackens, duties are shifted. Part-time jobs may replace full-time jobs. Cessation of occupational activities occurs. Adjustment to a new self-involvement in leisure-time activities occurs.	The End of an Era: Beyond Mid-Life 1. The life of inner-directedness finally prevails; I own myself	The Age Thirty Transition (28 to 33) — Make important new choices or reaffirm old ones Settling Down (33-40) 1. Tries to establish a niche in society — anchor life more firmly — develop competence in a chosen craft — become a valued member of a valued world	Start at 45-60 — awareness of advancing age — awareness of body changes relating to aging — knowing how many career goals have been or will be attained — search for new life goals — marked change in family relationships — change in work relationships — sense of work obsolescence

Table 6.2 (continued)

Tiedeman (1961)	Gesell, Ilg, & Ames (1956, pp. 376–382)	Ginzberg et al. (1951)	Buehler (1933)	Havighurst (1964, p. 216; 1972)

Age Sixty to Death

the sense that each discusses developmental tasks as Havighurst defined them. Nor do they agree on the exact time span in which particular development ensues. They do, however, agree that career development occurs in crucial steps with each systematically related to those preceding and succeeding it. These steps also relate to turning points in each developmental stage, where individuals either progress or fall back as a function of their success in grappling with the central issues of the stage.

In a sense, each of these discussions of development also supports the concept of the movement of the individual, first in coming to terms with the self as differentiated from the environment and, then, with the expansion of the personal social radius, in coming to terms with such rela-

tionships as self and institution, self and environment, and self in process (Herr, 1969). Tennyson has talked about this phenomenon as becoming some *one* before becoming some *thing* (Tennyson, 1967). Hershenson (1968) has stated it as a series of unfolding vocational questions from birth through adult life such as, Am I? Who am I? What can I do? What will I do? What meaning does what I do have for me?

Although the illustrations in Table 6.2 are too gross to be directly translated into goals for career guidance, other pertinent points are discernible. For example, what does Havighurst's first stage (identification with a worker) suggest for a student who comes from a home and a culture in which there are no productive workers? If the achievement of later tasks depends on such iden-

Table 6.2 (continued)

Erikson (1965, 2nd Ed.)	Super (1969)	Gould (1978)	Levinson (1978)	Hall (1978, pp. 81–84)
			(*Age 25 to 45*) — define a personal enterprise, a direction in which to strive 2. Work at advancement — strive to advance, to progress on a timetable 3. Becoming one's own person — accomplish the goals of the settling down enterprise — become a senior member in one's world — speak more strongly with one's voice — have a greater measure of authority The Mid-Life Transition (40 to 45) 1. A period of questioning of the life structure	— feeling of decreased job mobility and increased concerns for job security

tification, then education or some other social intervention (such as career guidance) must respond to that lack. In accordance with the general rationale of developmental tasks that missed stages leave a deficit in dealing with later tasks, the question becomes: What resources, what role models, what experiences can the school, the corporation, or agency provide to help this particular person acquire a concept of work as a part of his or her orientation for the future? Or, suppose we are talking about a male who has, in Super's terms, never been able to advance in an occupation. Do we simply consider this person a "loser" and try to dismiss him from the workplace or instead allow him to drift along at a mediocre level of productivity assuming he can do no better? Or, do we attempt to determine what prevents him

from advancing? Is it his fear of responsibility? His preoccupation with family problems? His lack of clarity about the requirements of particular career paths in the work setting? Each of these hypotheses and others is reasonable and can be pursued in a career conference with the worker. Once the problem is defined, a career guidance approach can be instituted to help the person become more purposeful and productive. But such outcomes are matters of philosophy, knowledge of behavior, and program planning.

Another example of the longitudinal shaping of tasks relevant to ultimate vocational behavior is provided by Stratemeyer, Forkner, McKim, and Passow (1957, pp. 208–214). In Table 6.3, the concept, Using Effective Methods of Work, is broken into a constituent element, planning, which is in turn subdivided: for example, deciding on and clarifying purpose, budgeting time and energy. Each aspect is then extended across chronological age periods, which move from gross to more specific manifestations of the behavior. Such a procedure permits the elaboration of a conceptual scheme that begins with the earliest point at which education may intervene and successfully builds experiences basic to enhancing career maturity. This scheme also permits a gross profile to be described of the experiential background that an individual is expected to have but that may not be present in his or her history. Thus, the scheme can be used to show present and future behavioral expectations, as well as to determine what experiences need to be acquired now and what successes an individual needs to move from one particular developmental plateau to a more effective behavior.

Both Tables 6.2 and 6.3 provide a frame of reference for formulating specific program goals and individual objectives. In each the themes presented are more global than objectives should be. They do not provide behavioral descriptions that permit evaluation of an individual's accomplishment of the goals set for him or for her. Before turning to the development of program goals or the matter of behavioral descriptions, let us consider some current research findings on career maturity.

Current Research Pertinent to Career Development and Career Maturity. Research of particular relevance to career maturity has been accomplished in the Career Pattern Study (Super, 1969a, b; Super, Starishevsky, Matlin, and Jordaan, 1963; Jordaan and Heyde, 1979; and Crites, 1974); in the Career Development Study (Gribbons & Lohnes, 1968); and in Project Talent (Flanagan, Shaycoft, Richards, & Claudy, 1971). Each of these research studies has identified the elements of career maturity, particularly as they have implications for preadolescents and adolescents, but the findings are also useful in considering the needs of adults.

The Career Pattern Study has focused principally on the exploratory and establishment steps of career development. It has been assumed that these are the stages crucial to education and, in particular, to curriculum development and guidance. As Table 6.2 illustrates, the developmental tasks that span these two life stages (from approximately age 14 to 25 plus) are as follows (you might wish to review the appropriate sections discussed in Chapter 4):

Table 6.3
Using Effective Methods of Work

	Childhood	Later Childhood	Youth
Planning, deciding on, and clarifying	Identifying immediate purposes in general terms	Determining major issues involved in achieving purposes	Extending ability to identify aspects and long-time implication affecting purposes
Determining sequence of steps to achieve purpose	Planning immediate next steps	Making longer-range plans	Extending range and details of planning
Budgeting time and energy	Planning time allotments with the help of others	Developing the ability to make independent decisions as to use of time	Budgeting time in terms of more activities and a larger time span
Evaluating steps taken	Deciding on the success of immediate steps	Considering the effectiveness of progress toward longer-range plans	Taking increased responsibility for evaluating progress toward goals

- crystallizing a vocational preference
- specifying it
- implementing it
- stabilizing in the chosen vocation
- consolidating one's status
- advancing in the occupation

Crystallizing a vocational preference has to do with the individual's "formulating ideas as to fields and levels of work which are appropriate for him, self and occupational concepts which will enable him, if necessary, to make tentative choices, that is, to commit himself to a type of education or training which will lead him toward some partially specified occupation" (Super, Starishevsky, Matlin, & Jordaan, 1963, p. 82). Specifying a vocational preference is the "singling out of a specific occupation and the attitude (not the act) of commitment to it" (ibid.). Implementing the preference is converting it into a reality. Thus, these separate stages are divided between all the factors in formulating a preference, on the one hand, and those in formulating an actual choice on the other. In this context, choice can be represented by entering a postsecondary educational program designed to prepare one for a preferred goal or in entering employment and receiving on-the-job training in a particular area of work performance.

The implications of this line of reasoning are that the major emphasis in career development to the twelfth-grade level is on enabling the individual to crystallize and specify preferences or to anticipate the act of choice. However, it is also obvious that many adolescents or high school graduates have not attained such maturity. Thus, college student personnel programs, industrial relations efforts, and rehabilitation programs or other community-based programs will need to provide opportunities for clients and workers to develop these same insights and skills in an abbreviated, accelerated time frame. Indeed, as other parts of this book indicate, many adults served by community agencies or by career services in business and industry are as ignorant about themselves and their opportunities as are children and youth. Therefore, the same type of planning content will be useful in developing programs focused on a stimulus approach.

What, then, are the behaviors or attitudes that foster the crystallization or specification of a vocational preference? What subelements could be set forth in a chart similar to Table 6.3? One such list is as follows, paraphrased from the work of Super, Starishevsky, Matlin, and Jordaan (1963):

1. *Awareness of the need to crystallize* — Fundamentally, this attitude acts as precursor of those which follow. It has to do with developing an attitude of readiness to involve oneself in the succeeding elements. This is perhaps more adequately described by Jordaan (1963) as becoming oriented to the need to explore.

2. *Use of resources* — This element is principally a set of instrumental behaviors by which one copes with exploration, whether it is focused on self-understanding or occupational description; it is present in relation to many persons or objects: parents, counselors, teachers, materials, part-time jobs, employers.

3. *Awareness of factors to consider in formulating a vocational preference* — This involves knowledge of the possible bases for preferences — whether intellectual requirements, relationship between interests and appropriate outlets, need for alternatives, or availability of outlets for different self-characteristics, that is, security, prestige.

4. *Awareness of contingencies that may affect vocational goals* — The existing evidence (Super & Overstreet, 1960, p. 51) suggests that this element and items 2 and 3 collectively contribute to narrowing preferences and adding stability to those preferences which remain. Fundamentally, this element concerns the factors that may impede implementation of a particular preference, and the alternatives that can be actualized if necessary.

5. *Differentiation of interests and values* — This element is the ability of the individual to differentiate the personally important from the unimportant and to concentrate attention on certain objectives and activities rather than others as a basis for decision-making and for action.

6. *Awareness of present-future relationships* — This factor is concerned with coming to terms

with the interrelationship between present activities and intermediate or ultimate vocational activities: for example, understanding educational avenues and their requirements as these provide access to different fields or levels of occupational activity.

7. *Formulation of a generalized preference* — All the factors described to this point should culminate in the formulation of a generalized preference, or crystallization. This level of preference is less a specific occupation than a general one out of which further specification will ensue. In such cases, the preference represented by a particular occupational title is likely to symbolize related activities that are liked rather than a specific occupation.

8. *Consistency of preference* — Consistency may be primarily verbal, or it may be manifested instrumentally in course selection and in such areas as extracurricular or part-time occupational activities.

9. *Possession of information on the preferred occupation* — This element represents possession of more specific information about the generalized preference. It is characterized by greater variety and accuracy of information and by better understanding than is represented by the formulation of a generalized preference.

10. *Planning for the preferred occupation* — The focus here is on deciding what to do and when and how to do it. As Super and Overstreet demonstrated in their work in 1960, specificity both of planning and of information are measurable characteristics of vocational maturity in early adolescence.

11. *Wisdom of the vocational preference* — This is in large measure a criterion of the previous elements. Although certain external criteria can be applied, it is generally assumed that wisdom is really more a function of the process by which a preference is developed than the preference itself.

12. *Specification* — This level of vocationalization represents elaboration of the preference, that is, more specific information and planning, a greater commitment to the preference, and a refinement of the steps already described, with a sharper focus on the particular

preference and the steps preceding implementation (pp. 84–87).

Analyses (Super, 1969a, 1974; Jordaan & Heyde, 1979) of the studies within the Career Pattern Study concerned with the elements just identified affirmed the importance of planfulness and time perspective at the ninth grade. Also, although ninth-grade boys did not understand themselves or the world of work enough to make sound vocational or prevocational decisions, these manifestations of career maturity were related to ability, to opportunity for the arousal of interest and the use of abilities, and to taking advantage of such opportunities.

Further, these studies found that career maturity factors common at both the ninth and twelfth grades included occupational information (educational, psychological, and economic) as well as planning, independence, crystallization of interests, and specification and implementation of preferences (Super, 1969a). Super further reported that the available data suggest that the "realism of the late teens is more the reality of the self, of its abilities and interests, than that of opportunities beyond the realm of personal experience." More important, however, is this finding:

Vocational maturity in the ninth grade, judged by occupational information, planning and interest maturity, was significantly related to vocational success in young adulthood. . . . In the twelfth grade vocational maturity, judged by the same measures as in grade 9, proved even more valid. Information about training and education required for the preferred occupation yielded a significant number of anticipated relationships. Those with educational and occupational level attained by age 25 were moderately high, and those with career development and stabilizing-floundering were fair . . . measures of awareness of choices to be made and of information and planning bearing on the choices, which seemed to have some construct validity in ninth grade and twelfth grade have predictive validity for vocational development in young adulthood (pp. 5–6).

These studies have somewhat tempered earlier findings (Super & Overstreet, 1960) that ninth-grade boys cannot yet make sound decisions about fields or even levels of work. In other words, these later studies show that aspects of career maturity at the ninth grade more accurately predict career maturity at the twelfth grade and at age 25 than had been found earlier. Further, since these studies demonstrate that some students reach a career maturity at ninth grade that predicts career maturity at age 25, they support the theory that career guidance or education can stimulate career development for a great many other students.

Additional support for direct attention to career development as a dimension of general education is implicit in findings reported in another article by Super (1969b, p. 18), in which he states, "Boys who are given opportunities in school and out-of-school and who use these opportunities during their school years tend also to make good use of their later career opportunities." Thus, it has been found that measures of career maturity in high school predict career success better than do the conventional predictions based on test scores or grades, and better than occupational success; in other words, how boys deal with developmental tasks at one stage tells something about their maturity later in life. It further stresses that in the early growth years, the foundations of later careers are laid.

In comparing career maturity in adolescence and in middle adulthood, Super (1977, p. 296) contends that although the decision-making principles remain the same, the content differs in particular in the "universality of awarenesses and information needed in adolescence, compared to the particularity required in adulthood." These aspects of particularity can be seen in the dimensions with the model of career development he has proposed for the midcareer.

As indicated in Chapter 4, throughout the history of the Career Pattern Study, the self-concept in career development has been the synthesizing agent. Super (1951, 1953) has proposed that:

In expressing a vocational preference, a person puts into occupational terminology his ideas of the kind of person he is, in entering an occupation, he seeks to implement his self-concept,

and in stabilizing in an occupation he attempts to achieve self-actualization. In a chronological sense, three phases of self-concept evolution occur: formation, translation and implementation. Through growth and learning as well as the constant interaction of the individual with external influences the self-concept system is modified and adjusted until a synthesis is finally evolved (p. 185).

Each of the crucial phases of the evolving self-concept has certain emphases and processes integral to it (Super, 1969b):

1. The formation process includes exploration of the self and of the environment, the differentiation of the self from others, identification with others who can serve as models, and the playing of these selected roles with more or less conscious evaluation of the result (reality testing).
2. The translation of self-concepts into occupational terms may take place through identification with an adult role model ("I am like him" or "I want to be like him"), experience in a role in which one has been cast, or learning that some of one's attributes should make one fit well into a certain occupation.
3. The implementation process involves action as in obtaining the specialized education or training needed for the preferred occupation or finding employment in it (p. 19).

In sum, theory and research support the self-concept as a dynamic factor in shaping individual behavior. As Herr has noted (1970):

Motivation, perseverance, choice, and generalized behavior each relate to the labels persons apply to the different aspects of the self and to the elements which comprise the contexts or situations with which they do or expect to interact. Self-labels, or self-concepts, represent the pieces making up the composite self-picture, the self-concept system, one uses to trigger or restrain particular modes of behavior under specific contingencies. One's self-concept may be an accurate representation of the self, it may be distorted, or it may be obscure either in general or under specific conditions (p. 67).

Two other items of potential input in formulating career guidance goals and objectives will be considered before a synthesis of the research findings is reported. The first is a sociological perspective on preparation for work life (Gross, 1967). Gross has contended that such preparation involves four emphases:

1. Preparation for life in an organization, involving authority, security quests, impersonality, routine, conflict, mobility, and demotion.
2. Preparation for a set of role relationships.
3. Preparation for a level of consumption involving a certain style of life.
4. Preparation for an occupational career, involving changes in the nature of jobs, and different types of jobs depending on the position in the life cycle (p. 417).

Each of these represents potential themes for organizing career development activities.

The second perspective is on the ingredients of human effectiveness (Blocher, 1966). Blocher contends that basic to an individual's human effectiveness is a knowledge of the social roles one is likely to play and the implications of others' structured expectations about appropriate behavior in these roles. In terms of career development, the analysis of social roles should extend to the opportunities available for the expression of individual characteristics such as leadership, creative or original contributions, helping relationships, and unusual levels of accomplishment. Tied to such analysis of social roles is the second emphasis — coping behaviors. Blocher suggests that possession of a range of coping behaviors and knowledge of the consequences of these in relation to social roles enhance personal effectiveness. Finally, he contends that developmental tasks and the discontinuities between social situations and available coping behaviors are additional themes worthy of vocationalization efforts. Some observers prefer the notion of mastery behavior to that of coping behavior. They view the latter as at a middle range rather than at the highest level of human effectiveness (Smith, 1977).

Suggested Input to Program Goals of Stimulus or Exploration. The theory and research emanating from Super's Career Pattern Study, the related

work of Gribbons and Lohnes, and the sociological and psychological perspectives of Gross and Blocher have been treated as examples of appropriate input in formulating career guidance program rationale, program goals, and indeed, performance objectives that are concerned with facilitating exploration, choice, and anticipation. However, before turning to the specific matter of formulating program goals and objectives per se, some synthesis of the aforementioned data is necessary.

In order to attain different aspects of career maturity, students, employees, or other adult clients need a comprehensive body of information that links what they are doing educationally at particular times to future options in both education and work. They need to know what curricula or training opportunities will be available to them, what factors distinguish one curriculum or training opportunity from another, what components make up separate curricular pathways, what personal factors are relevant to success in different curricula, and how the various curricula are linked to different field and level responsibilities in the occupational world.

Students and adult clients also need self-knowledge. They need to be able to differentiate personal values and personal interests as these relate to personal strengths and weaknesses in abilities — verbal, quantitative, scholastic. They need to be able to assess these elements of the self, to incorporate their meaning into the self-concept, and to relate this self-information to the choices with which they will be confronted.

Students and adults also need to understand the characteristics of the organizations in which they work or are likely to work as these determine role relationships, social relations, flexibility of coping behavior, level and kind of consumption, and changes probable throughout their occupational history.

Transcending this necessary base of knowledge is the motivation to use it in purposeful ways, or, as Clarke, Gelatt, and Levine (1965, p. 41) observe, to develop "an effective strategy for analyzing, organizing, and synthesizing information in order to make a choice." In the making of decisions, there are skills that can be learned. Once a person has made a plan for some segment of life with which he or she is content to live, that person can make the next plan more intelligently and with less hesitation or conflict. But it must be remembered that one cannot make occupational or career decisions without educational implications and vice versa. Nor can effective planning and choice-making occur without one's recognizing and assessing the psychological and emotional implications of various decisions.

The studies of Super and his colleagues emphasize attitudes of planfulness, recognition of possible alternative actions, and ways to assess the desirability of outcomes on the basis of personal preferences and values. Students and adults can be helped to evaluate the sequence of outcomes of immediate choice — proximate, intermediate, ultimate — as well as the factors that are personally relevant at experiential branch points, the probabilities associated with these factors, and the personal desirability of the three outcomes in the sequence. The fostering of planfulness and of career development involves providing the person not only with knowledge, but also with opportunities to apply the knowledge to his or her personal characteristics. Vocationalization efforts must, among other things, help individuals commit to work a sense of value, ego-involvement, personal endeavor, and achievement motivation.

Table 6.4 synthesizes, in gross terms, some of the emphases within the time spans most appropriate to vocationalization, through young adulthood, thus providing an organizing framework for developing goals and objectives for career guidance programs emphasizing exploration and choice. Although these tasks normally occur in adolescence and young adulthood, career guidance programs for older adults that focus on exploration and choice will likely need to include such content.

Input for Programs of Induction or Orientation.
Before leaving stage 1 it is important to note that conceptualizations of input to the ingredients of career maturity are basic to planning for career guidance programs that have stimulus, career exploration, or the facilitation of anticipation or choice as their major goals. To date, most planning concepts have been devoted to such purposes rather than to induction or orientation. The lack of conceptualization appropriate to these areas

is fertile soil for both the application of theory and research. Nevertheless, there are career guidance programs in which the major goals are induction or orientation. Such programs have various settings. They are particularly prevalent in colleges and universities and in business and industry. They are concerned with the behaviors of persons as they attempt to implement their preferences in the realities of a curriculum or a work setting and as they advance beyond exploration and anticipation to actual implementation of their preferences, induction into the realities of the work environment, and advancement in the occupation or the corporation they have chosen for themselves.

If Super's work in specifying the ingredients of career maturity is the major input to planning career guidance programs concerned with exploration and anticipation, Tiedeman's (1961) concepts are helpful in considering induction or orientation. As discussed in Chapter 4, Tiedeman has described the period of implementation and adjustment, which follows the period of anticipation, as comprised of three emphases: induction, reformation, integration. This process suggests that in the early stages of *implementation*, the individual is largely responsive to environmental expectations, work norms, role definitions, personal possibilities available in the setting, and so on. If the individual's ability to take on these role expectations is not stretched beyond limits of tolerance and can be accommodated in the self-concept system, the individual is likely to remain in the position and move to the second stage, *reformation*. In that stage the individual is likely to become more assertive, take more control of the setting or job, begin to impose certain personal demands on it, and begin to shape it to fit personal preferences and characteristics. In the third stage, *integration*, both the individual and the work setting are likely to have undergone some reciprocal shaping and change. Many of the role expectations of the setting have become part of the individual's work identity and self-concept resulting in the individual's job satisfaction. And the environment has been rearranged to accommodate the personal idiosyncrasies of the worker as he or she plays out the role expectations. As the environment reinforces the individual worker's satisfactoriness and the

Table 6.4

Synthesis of Inputs to Vocationalization and Career Maturity Through Young Adulthood

Approximate Ages					
Pre-school	5–9	10–14	15	18	19–25

Formation of self-concept → Translation of self-concept into vocational terms → Implementation of self-concept

Developing preference or anticipation →   choice → induction → reformation → integration

Fantasy →   Tentative   Realistic

                                               Trial (with little commitment)   Trial (more commitment) → stabilization → advancement

Awareness of the need to crystallize (orienting) → Use of resources (exploring) →

Formulating interests →   Relating interests and capacities   Relating interests and capacities to values

Developing a vocabulary of self →   Awareness of factors to consider in formulating a vocational preference

Developing a vocabulary of work →   Awareness of contingencies which affect vocational goals

Rudiments of basic trust in self and others → Differentiation of interests and values

Rudiments of initiative →   Awareness of present-future relationships

Rudiments of industry →   Accepting oneself as in process

Knowledge of fundamentals of technology →   Relating changes in the self to changes in the world

Differentiating self from environment →   Acquiring basic habits of industry

Identification with a worker →   Learning to organize one's time and energy to get work done

Developing sex social role →   Learning to defer gratification, to set priorities

Learning rudiments of social rules →   Achieving personal identity

Learning fundamental intellectual,
physical and motor skills →

                                               Acquiring knowledge of life in organizations

                                               Preparation for role relationships

                                               Preparation for level and kind of consumption

                                               Preparation for an occupational career

                                               Formulation of generalized preference

                                               Possession of information concerning the preferred occupation

                                               Planning for the preferred occupation

Preparing for marriage
selecting a mate
Developing capability
for intimacy
starting a family
Becoming a productive
person
Mastering the skills
of an occupation
Moving up the ladder
within the
occupation

                                               Choosing and preparing for occupation

                                               Achieving more mature relations with peers of both sexes

                                               Achieving emotional independence of parents and other adults

Developing planfulness

Developing decision-making strategies   Independence of choice

Role-playing
Identification } → Role-playing, curricula exposure → reality testing → work-study

attitudes of others → identification → self-appraisal

190

worker gains satisfaction, integration leads to consolidation and advancement.

Schein (1971) has described induction into an organizational career in a conception of stages and transitions that also provides input to the planning of a career guidance program. This is portrayed in Table 6.5.

Schein's work connects the stages of one's career in an organization with the processes that might be put in place in a career guidance program to facilitate that stage. The latter reflects what will be discussed in stage 3 of this chapter.

Input to Treatment Program Goals. In the third emphasis in planning a career guidance program, one must often anticipate the need for treatment by some group of consumers. These are persons whose career development has been arrested or impaired or who have undergone trauma or disease sufficient to make their ability to choose or to experience work adjustment problematic. Many paradigms exist to explain such phenomena. A classic one is that of Leona Tyler (1969) who has differentiated counseling into choice and change. The assumption is that persons who need to accomplish personality change, independence from others, and similar psychological maturity cannot deal with choice dilemmas until they resolve the more fundamental personality issues with which they are currently preoccupied. Another useful paradigm is that of Goodstein (1972) who portrays indecision and indecisive behavior in relation to anxiety as an antecedent or a consequent of behavior. D'Alonzo and Fleming (1973) have suggested that the main psychiatric factors among employees and therefore the problems encountered in mental health programs in industry (as well as career guidance programs in business and industry) are:

1. Improper discipline during childhood and youth ("Momism," at home, or on the job)
2. Job adjustment and responsibility; the need of all people to face reality with its attendant successes and failures; learning to accept criticism and to compensate for defects
3. Family problems
4. Health worries
5. Miscellaneous fears, phobias, anxieties, etc (p. 164).

Together these types of behavior are manifested in absenteeism, excessive turnover, alcoholism, industrial accidents, lowered productivity, and labor strikes.

As discussed in Chapter 2, Neff (1977) has identified several types of problem employees and the characteristics of their work psychopathology.

Type I includes people who appear to have major lacks in work motivation; they have a negative conception of the role.

Type II includes individuals whose predominating response to the demand to be productive is manifest fear and anxiety.

Type III includes people who are predominantly characterized by open hostility and aggression.

Type IV includes people who are characterized by marked dependency.

Type V includes people who display a marked degree of social naivete (pp. 238–243).

Each of these types of persons requires differential treatment typically of a significant intensity as well as differences in level of supervision, information, and personality change.

On balance, career guidance programs do not emphasize treatment of severe psychological problems however they are defined. But persons with severe problems of motivation or adjustment do come to career guidance programs for many reasons, including denial of the severity of their problems, because the career guidance program is the only mental health provision available, or because these persons believe philosophies and activities of career guidance will be helpful to them. Therefore, even though the career guidance program itself does not deal with treatment, it frequently must include in its program planning, procedures by which such persons will be referred or therapists will be placed on a consultative retainer to deal with such cases as they arise.

A Program Rationale for Planning. In summarizing stage 1 (developing a program rationale and philosophy), a particular school or college, corporation, or agency may synthesize from the foregoing steps a program rationale that includes the following assumptions:

1. Individuals can be equipped with accurate and relevant information translated into terms of

Table 6.5
Interaction of Worker and Organization in Career

Basic Stages and Transitions	Statuses or Positions	Psychological and Organizational Processes; Transactions between Individual and Organization
1. Preentry	Aspirant, applicant, rushee	Preparation, education, anticipatory socialization.
Entry (trans.)	Entrant, postulant, recruit	Recruitment, rushing, testing, screening, selection, acceptance ("hiding"); passage through external inclusion boundary; rites of entry; induction and orientation.
2. Basic training novitiate	Trainee, novice, pledge	Training, indoctrination, socialization, testing of the man by the organization, tentative acceptance into group.
Initiation, first vows (trans.)	Initiate, graduate	Passage through first inner inclusion boundary, acceptance as member and conferring of organizational status, rite of passage and acceptance.
3. First regular assignment	New member	First testing by the person of his own capacity to function; granting of real responsibility (playing for keeps); passage through functional boundary with assignment to specific job or department.
Substages 3a. Learning the job 3b. Maximum performance 3c. Becoming obsolete 3d. Learning new skills, etc.		Indoctrination and testing of person by immediate work group leading to acceptance or rejection; if accepted further education and socialization (learning the ropes); preparation for higher status through coaching, seeking visibility, finding sponsors, etc.
Promotion or leveling off (trans.)		Preparation, testing, passage through hierarchical boundary, rite of passage; may involve passage through functional boundary as well (rotation).
4. Second assignment Substages	Legitimate member (fully accepted)	Processes under no. 3 repeat.
5. Granting of tenure	Permanent member	Passage through another inclusion boundary.
Termination and exit (trans.)	Old-timer, senior citizen	Preparation for exit, cooling the mark out, rites of exit (testimonial dinners, etc.).
6. Post-exit	Alumnus emeritus retired	Granting of peripheral status.

personal development level and state of readiness.

2. Individuals can be assisted to formulate hypotheses about themselves, the choice points that will be in their future, and the options available to them.

3. Individuals can be helped to develop appro-

priate ways of testing these hypotheses against old and new experiences.

4. Individuals can be helped to come to terms with the educational and occupational relevance of what they already know or will learn about themselves and their futures.

5. Individuals can be helped to see themselves in

process and to acquire the knowledge and skills that will allow them to exploit this process in positive, constructive ways.

6. Individuals acquire feelings of personal competence or power from self-understanding and the ability to choose effectively.

In addition, analysis of community, administrative, and consumer groups will have offered support or rejection of these assumptions and their priority in a career guidance program. Information will be acquired about whether or not the students or adults to be served by the program already possess such knowledge, skills, and behaviors or whether such outcomes need to be facilitated. As these judgments are made, they need to be translated into actual program goals and behavioral specifications for the students or adults who will be involved with the program.

Preceding the statement of program goals and behavioral objectives, most programs would typically have an introductory statement dealing in broad terms with several topics explaining, Why career guidance? These topics might include:

- current social and occupational conditions faced by youth and adults
- needs for career planning and other career guidance elements as perceived by students (adults) and community groups
- the present career guidance program
- assumptions which guide new program thrusts
- basic concepts of program directions

The particular content of such preliminary statements will vary from one setting to another. What is important in one setting with one type of population may not be important in another. The resources available (personnel, materials, money) to support the program as well as the amount of time the program will be in contact with the student or adult population to be served (12 years, 3 years, 4 years, 6 months, 3 sessions) will need to be considered as the actual program goals to be adopted are decided on.

Stage 2 – Stating Program Goals and Behavioral Objectives

Following the formulation of a rationale and philosophy for the career guidance program that answers, "Why career guidance?" it is necessary

to decide on what will actually comprise the program. A review of career development theory will suggest many behaviors, types of knowledge, or skills that a career guidance program might facilitate. However, conducting needs assessments, analyzing resources available, and deliberating on the characteristics of the target groups to be served in a particular setting will likely reduce the many possibilities to those which constitute the most important goals for a particular program.

In stage 2 of systematic planning, the primary purpose is to translate the needs for career guidance in a particular setting, as identified in stage 1, into program goals and behavioral expectations for the consumers to be served. Program goals and behavioral expectations are actually hypotheses that say that, if these goals are accomplished, the needs to which career guidance responds in this setting will be met or reduced consistent with individual differences manifested by persons served by the program.

Program Goals. Program goals and behavioral expectations for students or clients differ in their specificity and in their purpose. Program goals are general statements of program purposes or outcomes. Program goals should not deal with the processes by which they will be accomplished but concentrate instead on the outcomes to be achieved. Program goals should reflect the philosophy, theory, and assumptions underlying a program as defined in stage 1 of systematic planning.

Examples of program goals in a particular setting might be as follows. As a result of the career guidance program all clients will:

1. develop vocabulary for distinguishing self-characteristics such as interests, aptitudes, values, roles, and self-concept
2. Understand their unique pattern of personal characteristics (such as abilities, interests, values, attitudes, and so on)
3. attain a positive self-concept (that is, a sense of self-respect, personal worth, and respect for one's own uniqueness)
4. understand the variety and complexity of occupations and career opportunities available locally and within the state
5. understand the relationships between edu-

cational opportunities and occupational or career requirements

6. determine the basic characteristics and qualifications related to preparation for and performance of various occupational roles

7. understand the concept "life style" and its relationship to career development

8. learn how to effectively use a range of exploratory resources

9. develop effective decision-making strategies and the skills necessary in carrying them out

These goals are client- or student-centered. In general terms, they make explicit the career guidance program's purposes, and they imply criteria by which their accomplishment might be judged. These are the global statements of outcomes around which the program will be structured. Decisions about behavioral expectations, processes, resource needs, evaluative strategies will each flow from the statement of program goals.

Behavioral Objectives. Behavioral objectives, as compared to program goals, are more specific expressions of behavior. The specifying of statements of behavioral expectations for students or clients that underlie program goals is one of the most difficult aspects of systematic planning. It necessitates making value judgments of what people ought to be able to achieve, and it requires describing these in behavioral terms. Further, it frequently requires a range of behavioral expectations underlying each program goal so that individual differences in readiness or experience can be recognized.

As compared with program goals, behavioral statements for clients or students should describe observable performance or behaviors — outcomes that describe what individuals will be able to do, not what will be done to them. Program goals are usually stated so broadly that it is difficult to know when an employee or student has reached them, but behavioral objectives are measurable. Writing objectives requires you to think of the performances that indicate that the program goal has been reached. In addition to writing objectives that are likely to be important to all consumers of the career guidance program, it is always important to remain flexible enough

to accommodate individual objectives of a crisis nature or those which do not fit directly within the planned program emphases.

Approaches to Writing Objectives. The current emphases in objective development stress the importance of defining the outcomes of career guidance in terms of observable human performance, citing the conditions under which it should be demonstrated, and determining the standard or criterion of success. Within this context, however, there are several suggested ways of stating objectives based on different purposes.

Tyler (1950, p. 30) asserts: "The most useful form for stating objectives is to express them in terms which identify both the kind of behavior to be developed in the student and the content or area of life in which this behavior is to operate." An objective of vocational guidance stated in Tyler's terms would be as follows: "To write clear and well organized reports of requirements in preferred occupations." Such an objective does not discuss the procedures for accomplishing the goal, but it does specify the skill — to write clear and well-organized reports — and the domain of concern — requirements in preferred occupations — which are important components of the goal.

Goals stated in the terms advocated by Tyler resemble what McAshan (1970) has termed minimum-level behavioral objectives. Goals stated at this level can be used to denote program goals without specifying precise expectations for individuals or the criteria on which evaluation is based.

Probably the best-known approach to writing objectives is that advanced by Mager (1962). According to this approach, a statement of objectives is a collection of words or symbols that describe an educational intent. Such a statement should include: (1) what the individual will be doing (terminal behavior) when demonstrating his or her achievement, (2) the important conditions under which the terminal behavior is to occur, and (3) a criterion of acceptable performance or standard that indicates when the learner has successfully demonstrated his or her achievement. An objective relevant to career guidance developed in line with these criteria is as follows: Given ten occupations, the student must be able to correctly identify, by labeling, the minimum educational requirements of at least nine of them.

The latter format for writing objectives provides, to a greater degree than others, behavioral descriptions which when analyzed with other data permit evaluation of whether an individual has accomplished the established goals. However, such a format represents the potential dangers of becoming too restrictive either in criterion of success used, the evaluation activities, or the requirement that all persons accomplish goals in the same way.

Obviously, each career guidance program will need to develop independently a set of operationally stated objectives to guide its program effort in fostering career development in the students or clients for whom it is responsible. The particular objectives developed will reflect the clients' characteristics as well as the available resources. Measures of individual performance of these objectives will also be necessary. In schools, agencies, business or industrial settings, or other career guidance settings, where there is great variability in the personal histories of the students or the clients, it will also be necessary to assess the degree to which individuals or groups can already perform the behavior. Finally, as such a system is implemented, it will be necessary to evaluate continuously whether the career guidance activities designed to accomplish the objectives are actually bringing about changes in the behavior of the persons exposed to them.

Table 6.6 presents some sample objectives that might be used at different educational levels to facilitate particular emphases on career development. They are not exhaustive, nor are they necessarily the right objectives for a given situation. Indeed, they only make sense as they relate to different program goals, and as they describe behaviors that seem to relate to such goals. They do blend, however, some of the research inputs contributing to career maturity previously discussed in this chapter with strategies for developing objectives. As the key illustrates, separate objectives roughly approximate different levels of the cognitive and affective domains identified by Bloom et al. (1956) and by Krathwohl,

Bloom, and Masia (1964). For example, an objective followed by a (C, K) indicates that the objective is from the cognitive domain and assesses knowledge; an (A, Re) means that the objective is the affective domain and assesses *receiving*. The reader is also encouraged to study the work of Simpson (1972), if the development of psychomotor objectives is called for.

Fundamentally, Table 6.6 indicates that the development of behavioral objectives, using a Mager approach, should include either quantitative or qualitative criteria for assessing the behavior. If used for a career guidance program which will extend over a long period of time, these behavioral objectives should be consistent with student or client capability at different developmental levels. Essentially this same format can be used in developing career guidance objectives for college student personnel programs, or for adults in business and industry, although the time available for such programs will probably be less than in the public schools and the clientele more diverse.

Gronlund (1970), in reviewing the format proposed by Mager for developing objectives, suggests that such an approach is most useful when the desired outcome is to have all students or clients perform alike at a specified minimum level. In particular, such a format could be used at lower levels of cognitive activity, such as the acquisition of vocabulary, knowledge, or facts for labeling occupational distinctions, educational characteristics, or self-traits like interests and aptitudes. Levels of knowledge such as these are basic to higher-order activities like analyzing, applying, synthesizing, and evaluating, and in Gronlund's perception they are minimum essentials (1970, p. 33). Gronlund maintains that in addition to stating objectives in terms of minimum essentials, it is necessary to state more complex objectives in such form that they encourage each person to progress as far as possible toward predetermined goals. Thus, the objective to be attained is stated in a general form and is followed by specific samples of representative behaviors at different levels of complexity. Being able to accomplish any one of the behaviors is sufficient to satisfy the goal. However, not every person must accomplish the same behavioral objective and, therefore, individualization is possible. An example of this

Table 6.6
Sample Objectives to Facilitate Career Development
at Different Educational Levels

Elementary School	Junior High School	Senior High School
In an oral exercise, the student can identify at least six types of workers who contributed to building his school (C,K)	The student lists correctly the different educational areas that are available both in the immediate and distant future, the nature and purpose of each, the possible outcomes of each in terms of levels of occupational activity (C,C)	The student reality-tests broad occupational preference by systematically relating it to personal achievement in different courses, part-time work, extracurricular activities (A,O)
In a flannel-board presentation, the student can label, according to their tools or clothing, ten different types of workers found in the community (C,K)	The student verbally differentiates self-characteristics (e.g., interests, values, abilities, personality traits) and expresses tentative occupational choices that might provide outlets for each (C,C)	The student analyzes his or her present competency in skills necessary to broad occupational preference and develops a plan by which these can be enhanced where necessary (C,An)
In an oral exercise, the student can state how different workers contribute to his or her well-being and the welfare of the community (C,K)	The student can accurately appraise on a written profile his or her measured ability, achievement level, and current interests (C,An)	Given a part-time job in school or out of school, the student is able to list the advantages and disadvantages it might offer in terms of personal interests or values (C,C)
After viewing a movie, the student can identify most occupations in the community and describe how they support each other (C,K)	The student can place on a skilled/unskilled continuum twenty occupations about which he or she has read (C,K)	From a series of case studies about working conditions as they affect individuals with different characteristics, the student can identify patterns of coping behavior and discuss their personal implications under similar circumstances (C,E)
The student can check vocabulary items correctly as being names of interests, aptitudes, abilities (C,K)	From a dramatization portraying five different ways of valuing different methods of handling daily events, the student can consistently identify and describe the value set with which he or she feels most comfortable (A,V)	
From a list of fifty occupations, the student can identify those which occur primarily indoors or outdoors (C,C)		The student executes plans to qualify for an entry-level position by choosing appropriate courses at the high school level (A,V)
The student can select from a list of ten alternatives the five best reasons for planning his or her time (A,Re)	The student can weigh alternative outcomes from different kinds of work in relation to the public welfare and rank order these outcomes in terms of personal preference (A,O)	The student produces a plan of alternative ways of accomplishing educational (occupational) goals if the first choice is not successfully implemented (C,Sy)
The student can correctly list major breakdowns of the occupational structure: e.g., communications, manufacturing, distribution, transportation, or professional/skilled/semiskilled/unskilled (C,C)	The student observes five films and then lists the major differences in the technological processes observed (A,Re)	Given ten choices, the student decides on a broad occupational area to study in depth. In a written proposal, the student outlines the resources needed to develop this study, the plans necessary to gain access to these resources, and the particular outcomes he or she desires to obtain (C,E)
The student can prepare a graph showing the different educational alternatives available: junior high school, high school, community college, area vocational technical school, college, apprenticeships, armed forces (C,Ap)	Using the *Dictionary of Occupational Titles*, the student can identify ten occupations that are ranked highest in dealing with people, things, or data (C,Ap)	
The student can arrange in appropriate rank order the number of years of schooling associated with different	After a field trip to a factory, the student can tell in his or her own words the differences in work conditions or procedures observed	The student can differentiate between the major occupations that make up a broad occupational area

Table 6.6 (continued)

Elementary School	Junior High School	Senior High School
educational alternatives (C,C) The student can classify the titles of courses available in the junior high school and senior high school and the types of content with which they are concerned (C,C) The student can choose from a list of twenty occupations those offering salaries within particular ranges (C,K) The student voluntarily discusses the importance of work and how education helps one to work effectively (A,Rs) The student can select from a table models of tools or instruments used in ten different occupations (C,An) The student can role play three occupations which are of most personal interest (C,Sy) The student can demonstrate how certain knowledge and skills acquired in different school subjects are applied in different work roles (C,Ap) The student can identify the skills in which he or she feels most confident and role plays workers who might need these skills (C,E) The student can role play interpretations of the values workers might hold in four different occupations (C,E) The student is willing to share with others the planning and presenting of a play about work and being a worker (A,V) The student discusses the importance of teamwork in different work settings, cooperates with others in order to reach a common goal, and can express the importance of his or her contributions and that of others in reaching a common goal (A,O)	in different parts of the plant (C,An) The student is able to assess in rank order the personal value of each of ten occupational clusters (C,An) The student can describe in essay form how knowledge and skills acquired in different subject matter areas relate to performing different work roles (C,Ap) The student can identify and define ten forms of continuing education following high school including apprenticeships, on-the-job training, correspondence courses, armed forces service schools, evening schools, reading (C,C) The student completes an assigned job analysis according to instructions and on time (A,Rs) The student can compare correctly the social roles which describe a supervisor and a follower (C,Sy) The student can tell a story in his or her own words about how an individual suffering a particular limitation can overcome weakness and maximize strength in education or in work (C,Sy) The student can identify, locate, and describe the use of five directories listing post-secondary educational opportunities at college, junior college, and technical levels (C,Ap) The student can identify in a gaming situation future decisions to be made in order to reach different goals (C,Sy) The student can identify, assess, and defend an analysis of possible steps that might be taken to minimize personal limitations and maximize assets (C,E) The student continuously explores and synthesizes the relationships	or a job cluster in terms of (1) the amount and type of education needed for entrance, (2) the content, tools, setting, products, or services of these occupations, (3) their values to society, (4) their probability of providing the type of life style desired, and (5) their relationship to personal interests and values (C,E) The student considers five different categories of post-secondary education, chooses one, and defines the reason for choosing it (C,C) The student develops a plan of access to the next step after high school, either educational or occupational, listing possible alternatives, whom to contact, application dates, capital investment necessary, the self-characteristics to be included on a resumé (C,Ap) Given an identified social problem—e.g., air pollution, rehabilitation of drug users, the development of new uses for materials, creating by-products of fishery harvesting—the student can create a lattice of occupations at different levels which might contribute to resolving the problem. (The student may use as a reference the *Dictionary of Occupational Titles* or the *Occupational Outlook Handbook*) (C,E) The student makes adjustments in planning, use of resources, and exploratory experiences necessary to maintain progress toward achievement of goals (A,O) The student verbalizes feelings of competence and adequacy in those tasks which have relationships to personal vocational preference (A,CCV) The student is able to define the congruence between personal

Table 6.6 (continued)

Elementary School	Junior High School	Senior High School
During school activities, the student expresses or demonstrates a positive attitude toward self, others, education, and different types of work roles (A,CCV)	between tentative choices and demonstrated abilities (A,V)	aspirations, values, and preferred life style (C,E)
	The student is able to select two persons from history and discuss why he or she would like to emulate them (A,V)	The student is able to use his or her ratings by teachers and peers to confirm self-perceptions of competence or preference (C,Ap)
	The student can produce a list of resources or approaches available for learning about and assessing the world of work (C,E)	The student takes specific steps to implement a post-secondary educational plan (A,CCV)
	In a role-playing situation, the student can project or portray the personal and social significance that work might have in the lives of individuals at different levels within the occupational structure (C,E)	The student takes specific steps to implement a post-secondary vocational preference (A,CCV)
	The student can describe possible personal and environmental contingencies that could impinge on future decisions (C,E)	The student demonstrates ability to judge personal choices in terms of situations, issues, purposes, and consequences rather than in terms of rigidity or wishful thinking (A,CCV)
	The student can differentiate between the several broad occupational areas in terms of (1) a potential satisfaction each might offer, (2) the nature of the work tasks performed, (3) the future impact technology could have on particular occupational areas, (4) the future demand for workers in broad occupational areas (C,E)	
	The student can demonstrate judgments about how different types of work can be better made to meet individual needs (A,O)	

KEY: (C,K) = Cognitive-Knowledge; (C,C) = Cognitive-Comprehension; (C,Ap) = Cognitive-Application; (C,An) = Cognitive-Analysis; (C,Sy) = Cognitive-Synthesis; (C,E) = Cognitive-Evaluation; (A,Re) = Affective-Receiving; (A,Re) = Affective-Responding; (A,V) = Affective-Valuing; (A,O) = Affective-Organization; (A,CC) = Affective-Characterization by a value or a value complex.

kind of objective appropriate to career guidance is as follows:

Objective: Understands the interdependence of the occupational structure.
1. States the principle of interdependence in his or her own words.
2. Gives an example of the principle.
3. Identifies work orientations — such as, data,

people, things — which contribute to interdependence.
4. Distinguishes between field and level lattices in job families as representative of interdependence.

None of the methods of writing objectives is more correct or desirable than any other. The format to use depends on the purposes to be served, the general style of the planning system being developed, or the previous format for goal and behavior setting being used in the particular setting. Indeed, many existing models of systematic planning blend the Tyler, McAshan, Mager, or Gronlund models of writing objectives into a system that is locally relevant.

With the rise of career education since 1971, many efforts have been undertaken to formulate models of tasks that persons need to acquire in order to master the many elements comprising career maturity. One such model is the specification of career management tasks by Tennyson, Hansen, Klaurens, and Antholz (1975). Their paradigm reflects a developmental view of career development, including the specification of tasks appropriate to different life stages. These career management tasks and the stages associated with them are shown in Table 6.7.

Each of these tasks could be considered a program goal around which career guidance efforts would be implemented. This model also identifies career management tasks appropriate to persons beyond high school, or, indeed, into adulthood. These tasks include:

I. developing interpersonal skills essential to work
II. developing information processing skills about self and the world of work
III. reintegration of the self

Table 6.7
The CDC Career Management Tasks

Attending Stages — Grades K–3
1. Awareness of self
2. Acquiring a sense of control over one's life
3. Identification with workers
4. Acquiring knowledge about workers
5. Acquiring interpersonal skills
6. Ability to present oneself objectively
7. Acquiring respect for other people and the work they do

Responding Stage — Grades 4–6
1. Developing a positive self-concept
2. Acquiring the discipline of work
3. Identification with the concept of work as a valued institution
4. Increasing knowledge about workers
5. Increasing interpersonal skills
6. Increasing ability to present oneself objectively
7. Valuing human dignity

Asserting Stage — Grades 7–9
1. Clarification of a self-concept
2. Assumption of responsibility for career planning
3. Formulation of tentative career goals
4. Acquiring knowledge of occupations, work settings, and life styles
5. Acquiring knowledge of educational and vocational resources
6. Awareness of the decision-making process
7. Acquiring a sense of independence

Organizing Stage — Grades 10–12
1. Reality testing of a self-concept
2. Awareness of preferred life style
3. Reformulation of tentative career goals
4. Increasing knowledge of and experience in occupations and work settings
5. Acquiring knowledge of educational and vocational paths
6. Clarification of the decision-making process as related to self
7. Commitment with tentativeness within a changing world

IV. acquiring a sense of community
V. commitment to a concept of career
VI. acquiring the determination to participate in change
VII. creative application of management skills to life roles

In relation to each of these tasks are behavioral indicators that research suggests underlie the task identified. Each of the career management tasks is broken down into performance objectives and enabling objectives. For example, at the senior high school level the first management task is "reality testing of a self-concept." The performance objective and enabling objectives associated with this task are:

PO #1 Describes his own abilities, aptitudes, and other personal resources in relation to the requirements for preferred occupations.
    EO #1 Identifies both actual and potential personal objectives.
    EO #2 Describes the physical, mental, social, economic, and educational requirements of his preferred occupation.

The Minnesota model (Table 6.7) just described is illustrative of a number of models that have evolved from a comprehensive theoretical base and systematic planning. Another is the National School-Based Comprehensive Career Education Model I developed in 1971. The planning in this model included the identification of elements, themes, goal statements, and performance objectives. Each element is composed of several themes and these, in turn, are further reduced to more explicit statements of expected behaviors. An example might be the element, self-awareness, as it applies to grade 9. The appropriate theme under that element would be: "The student will come to recognize the relationship of his interests, aptitudes, and achievements to realization of his career aspirations." This element and theme are in turn translated into goal statements and performance objectives as shown in Table 6.8.

Another approach that graphically identifies the various levels of planning is that formulated in the Career Guidance, Counseling and Placement Project at the University of Missouri —

Columbia (1973). In this project, four domains facilitating a "career conscious individual" have been identified as pertinent to career guidance. They include: self-knowledge and interpersonal skills, knowledge of work and leisure worlds, life-career planning knowledge and skills, and basic studies and occupational preparation. Within each of these domains there are several steps: the identification of concepts pertinent to the domain, the specification of goals related to the concepts identified, the identification of developmental goals tied directly to an educational level, the translation of developmental goals into performance objectives indicating specific behavior an individual will be able to demonstrate as a result of a particular learning experience, and the identification of activities which will facilitate such learning. Table 6.9 portrays the presentation of only one such concept within the domain of life-career planning knowledge and skills.

Business and industry as well as various government agencies have begun to introduce career development systems that use the types of program goal statements and behavioral objectives cited in the previous examples. Specificity of the goals and behavioral statements is frequently less elaborate but the general models are similar. For example, Leibowitz and Schlossberg (1981) have identified a framework from which career planning skills can be identified, defined, and operationalized. These skills are arranged in stages of importance to both employees and managers. As such they can serve as the planning framework for training workshops or for the development of career guidance programs in which managers have a major role. For each of the cells of this model, specific behavioral objectives can be defined and specific strategies identified to accomplish such goals. Table 6.10 presents the planning model proposed by Leibowitz and Schlossberg for industry.

Many other models of systematic planning could be identified here. Virtually all states and many industries and government agencies have now developed such approaches to career education and career guidance. These many examples offer a pool of goals and objectives from which one might select those appropriate to a given setting and, most importantly, to the conceptual frame-

Table 6.8
Goal Statements and Performance Objectives for one Aspect of
Self-Awareness at Grade 9

Goal Statement	Performance Objective
A1.0 Students will utilize their aptitudes as measured by The General Aptitude Test Battery to access and explore related occupational information (WTG's).	A1.1 Students will be able to identify occupations (WTG's) which are related to their aptitudes.
B1.0 Students will develop a definitive notion (in their own words) of their aptitude strengths and weaknesses.	B1.1 Students will be able to rank their aptitudes (9 aptitudes of the GATB) according to their strengths.
	B1.2 Students will be able to list aptitude clusters representing their overall strengths and weaknesses (e.g., strengths in perceptual areas, strengths in performance areas, strengths in intellectual and academic areas).
C1.0 Students will utilize their aptitude strengths and weaknesses, likes and dislikes, personal achievements, etc. to project themselves into possible satisfying occupational situations (WTG).	C1.1 Students will be able to name and describe in essay form at least three occupations which they feel would be satisfying to them and explain why they feel the occupation would be satisfying.
D1.0 The student will apply or utilize understanding about his interests, personal achievements, aptitudes to develop educational and career goals.	D1.1 The student will compile a list of occupational and educational goals and explain his reasons for formulating his goals and objectives.
	D1.2 Given all the curriculum alternatives for the local school district, the student will be able to plan a course of studies consistent with his educational and occupational goals.

work for career guidance which one develops in stage 1 of one's planning.

Sources of goals and objectives that deserve special mention are:

- *Career Development: A California Model for Career Guidance Curriculum, K–Adult* (1972). Edited by Joe Cunha, Darryl Larramore, Bruce Lowrey, Anita Mitchell, Thomas Smith, Dale Woolley. California Personnel and Guidance Association, 654 East Commonwealth Avenue, Fullerton, California 92631.
- *Curriculum Design and Instructional Objectives Catalog.* Publication Office, American Institutes for Research, P.O. Box 1113, Palo Alto, California 94302.
- *Objectives for Career and Occupational Development.* National Assessment of Educational Progress, 300 Lincoln Tower, 1860 Lincoln Street, Denver, Colorado 80203.

- *Measures of Self Concept.* Instructional Objectives Exchange, Box 24095, Los Angeles, California 90024.
- *Pupil Personnel Services, A Handbook for Program Development and Evaluation.* Frank Wellman and Earl J. Moore. Missouri Evaluation Projects, University of Missouri, Columbia, Missouri, August 1975.

In summary of stage 2 in systematic planning, a few points need reinforcement.

1. The specification of program goals and behavioral objectives for students or clients should not occur in a vacuum. These program directions should flow from a conceptual framework and a needs assessment pertinent to the local agency setting.
2. Behavioral objectives provide an inventory of possible emphases that can help a counselor

Table 6.9
Approach to Planning for Career Guidance, Counselor Placement for State
Departments of Education Developed by University of Missouri–Columbia

Domain:
Career Planning

Concept:
One's future is influenced by present planning.

Goal 3.2:
For the individual to understand the relationship
between present planning and future outcomes.

Dev. Goal 3.2: K–3	Dev. Goal 3.2: 4–6	Dev. Goal 3.2: 7–9	Dev. Goal 3.2: 10–12
For the individual to understand the consequences of his decision-making.	For the individual to understand that previous decisions will affect present and future decisions.	For the individual to understand the need to re-examine decisions regarding future long-range career responsibilities.	For the individual to understand the need to reconsider goals and formulate new plans when necessary.
Objective 3.22: The individual will describe situations in which his decisions affect others.	Objective 3.21: The individual will identify situations in which one decision has led to a series of other decisions.	Objective 3.21: The individual will identify skills or knowledge utilized in a preferred occupation which may transfer to another.	Objective 3.23: The individual will describe situations in which new information might cause him to reconsider his goals and formulate new ones.
Activity: Glasser Classroom Meetings	Activity: Decision Logs	Activity: Interviewing	Activity: Career Exploration Groups

Table 6.10
Career Planning Process Model

	Stage 1	Stage 2	Stage 3
Employee Responsibility	Explore	Understand	Take Action
Manager Responsibility	Listen and Support	Identify Clarify	Select Strategy
Manager Roles Required	Communicator Counselor	Communicator Appraiser	Communicator Counselor Appraiser Coach Mentor Advisor Broker Referral Agent Advocate

and counselee define what problems or skill deficits should be worked on.
3. Depending on the form in which behavioral objectives are written, both the career guidance activities to facilitate them and the criteria on which they might be evaluated can be specified.

Stage 3 – Selecting Alternative Program Processes

The major problems in systematic planning for career guidance occur in stages 1 and 2 – deciding what needs exist, developing a conceptual framework for the program and translating such insights into program and performance goals. Once the directions for the program are specified, it is then necessary to identify those processes which can facilitate the identified goals. The Missouri model referred to a few paragraphs earlier indicated one form of tying activities or career guidance processes to performance objectives.

A major question in selecting program processes in relation to either program goals or performance objectives is what behavior is intended. The second question is what processes might facilitate these behaviors: individual counseling? group career development? work-study? behavior modification? values clarification? role-playing? It is conceivable that any one of these processes or many other acceptable techniques might be useful. However, it is necessary to decide which available technique or process is likely to be the best. Viewed in this context, any career guidance technique or process must be considered a means to an end. It must also be evaluated in terms of the time available, resources required, competencies of personnel available, costs involved, and such other criteria as are appropriate in a particular setting. Table 6.11 suggests examples of the broad range of techniques or processes that could be used to facilitate career development and from which decisions can be made in relation to different program goals or behavioral objectives.

Figure 6.11 indicates how many such techniques are combined in one corporation's career development system. A leader in this kind of programming, Connecticut General Insurance Company, the employer of over 14,000 people, has had a continuing commitment to employee career

mobility. A brief portrayal of the techniques used in this process includes various combinations of counseling, special services, education/training, referral and placement activities.

Extending such points further, Table 6.12 indicates how input from a needs assessment conducted on a particular target population, in this case female undergraduate students living in a dormitory of apartment suites, can be related to processes (programs) tailored to meet such needs. This depiction also includes in the right column examples of criterion variables by which to evaluate the effectiveness of the various processes of concern.

Hypothetical examples of how program goals, performance objectives, and activities/techniques can be presented for planning purposes follow. (See Table 6.13.) A longitudinal program would include goals, behavioral objectives, activities, and evaluation methods arranged at different educational levels or within sequences appropriate to a particular agency or corporate constituency. Obviously, a total program would include more goals than identified here but the essence of their formulation is reflected in the examples given. Again, it should be noted that any format may be used in a systematic approach to programming, as long as it is structurally sound and contains objectives consistent with the experiences required by those serviced by the program.

Stage 4 – Developing an Evaluation Design

Although stages 1 and 2 of systematic planning require the most deliberation and compromise among the different directions a career guidance program might take, stage 4, the evaluation stage, seems to be the most threatening to many counselors. Apparently, some counselors equate evaluation with some highly sophisticated and esoteric skills beyond their ability to comprehend. Such a perspective is incorrect but widely held.

Evaluation has been defined by Trantow (1970) as "essentially an effort to determine what changes occur as the result of a planning program by comparing actual changes (results) with desired changes (stated goals) and by identifying the degree to which the activity (planned program) is responsible for the changes" (p. 3). The key word here is "planned." Evaluation cannot occur

Table 6.11
Examples of Techniques to Facilitate Career Development

— films	— defining terms
— discussions	— committees
— developing bulletin boards	— role play
— making occupational role books	— job analyses
— creating listings of characteristics of self in relation to educational and occupational alternatives	— debate
— analyzing expectations of work	— interview: workers, employers, Employment Service Counselors, college admissions people, post-secondary AVTS personnel
— collecting newspaper articles or magazine stories	— gaming
— writing short themes	— test interpretations
— developing games about interests	— making posters
— self-ratings	— contrast or compare characteristics of work or education
— field trips	— library research
— resource people	— keep personal records for purposes of analysis
— examination of want ads	— publishing newspaper about career development concerns
— work samples	— doing follow-up study
— work study	— shadowing workers
— part-time work	— apprenticeships
— panels of recent graduates in different work or educational settings	— internships
— profile census data	— computer-assisted programs
— individual counseling	— career guidance curriculum
— testing	— work simulations
— group career counseling	— relaxation tapes
— social modeling	— behavioral rehearsal
— desensitization	— career resource center
— seminars on career paths/career ladders	— individual counseling
— peer discussion groups for women and minorities	— skills inventory — job matching system
— career path publications	— on-the-job training
— in-house career counselors	— job rotation

unless it is effectively planned. Nor can it occur if we are not clear about the goals we wish to accomplish or the ways these will be measured. If we have completed the stages of the systematic planning process outlined earlier in this chapter, the goals and the behavioral objectives the program seeks to accomplish should be clear. The question we need to raise now is: What evidence will we accept that the goals or objectives have been met? Some possibilities might include:

• Ratings of student, employee, or client performance by teachers, parents, counselors, or employers.
• Judgments by experts of whether program goals have been met.
• Follow-up studies of how students, employees,

or clients plan, apply decision-making skills, make accurate self-estimates after exposure to career guidance.
• Scales of student or client attitude about themselves or career exploration or work.
• Staff reaction sheets about changes in student or client behavior during a career guidance program.
• Student or client opinion of how their behavior has been changed or improved as a result of career guidance.
• Observations of student or client understandings and skills in role playing or actual situations.
• Changes in school attendance, work punctuality, or other quantitative indices related to career guidance goals.

• Scores on published standardized instruments such as the
> Assessment of Career Development
> Career Maturity Inventory
> Career Development Inventory
> Cognitive Vocational Maturity List
> ETS Guidance Inquiry
> Readiness for Vocational Planning
> Adult Career Concerns Survey

These instruments measure different aspects of personal knowledge of career development be-

haviors with regard to: (1) what the person knows about personal attributes, occupational information, job selection, course and curriculum selection, school and career problem solving; (2) what the person *has done* in regard to: involvement in career planning activities, involvement in wide range of worker activities, involvement in activities related to preferred occupation(s); and (3) one's attitudes, preferences, and perceptions with regard to self, work, and information resources. For a comprehensive analysis of the specific content of each of these

Figure 6.1
Connecticut General's Overall Career Development System

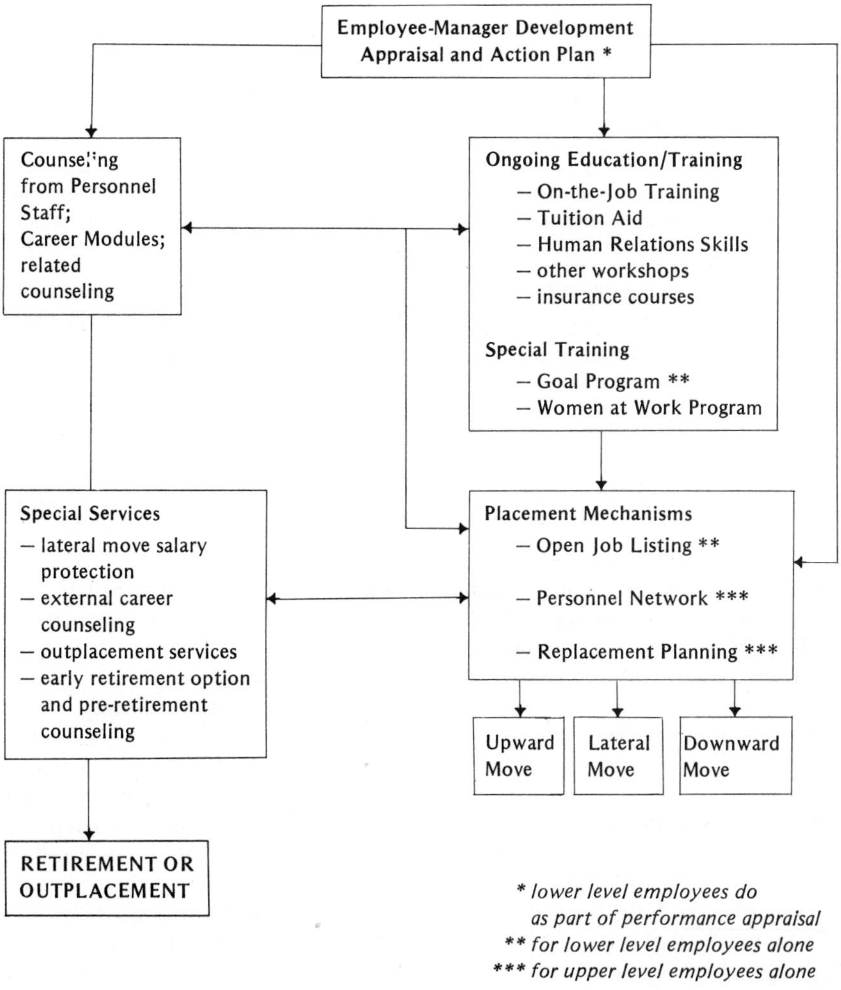

Employee-Manager Development Appraisal and Action Plan *

Counseling from Personnel Staff; Career Modules; related counseling

Ongoing Education/Training
— On-the-Job Training
— Tuition Aid
— Human Relations Skills
— other workshops
— insurance courses

Special Training
— Goal Program **
— Women at Work Program

Special Services
— lateral move salary protection
— external career counseling
— outplacement services
— early retirement option and pre-retirement counseling

Placement Mechanisms
— Open Job Listing **
— Personnel Network ***
— Replacement Planning ***

Upward Move | Lateral Move | Downward Move

RETIREMENT OR OUTPLACEMENT

* lower level employees do as part of performance appraisal
** for lower level employees alone
*** for upper level employees alone

Table 6.12
Counseling Service Planning Chart

Sample Population Sub-group Description	Goal Area of Strongest Need and Goal Statements Within That Area	Examples of Programs to Serve Needs	Examples of Criteria for Goal Achievement
Female undergraduate students living in dormitory of apartment suites	Work-Study Skill Development:		
	Know how to manage finances	Discussion seminar; Speakers	Answer correctly 90% of items on written test
	Outline and take notes effectively	Study skills group	Take notes during classroom lecture that cover 90% of main points
	Write in manner that is coherent and interesting	Writing improvement lab	Write paper that includes all basic elements of good writing
	Speak so easily understood	Speech course: group counseling	Satisfactory rating by all members of the group
	Increase reading rate and comprehension	Speed reading course	Rate increase of 25% and comprehension increase 20%
	Concentrate for longer time on studies	Individual counseling; group counseling; peer support network	25% increase in time spent reading textbooks
	Complete assignments on time	Group counseling; peer support network	Meet all assignment deadlines
	Prepare effectively for tests and exams	Study skills group	Receive satisfactory score on at least two tests
	Know how to use library	Study skills group; library workshop	Can describe to satisfaction of group how to find library resources

instruments, with regard to the emphases cited above, see Westbrook (1974), Super (1974), Kapes & Mastie (1982), and Cook, Hepworth, Wall, & Warr (1981). There are also other published instruments dealing with work values, interests, and planning which are pertinent to evaluation and which will be discussed in Chapter 14.

The basic point to be made here is that the type of evaluation and the resulting data will differ in accordance with the setting and the type of behavior being assessed. It depends on what the program goals are, what types of energy and personnel time can be committed to evalua-

tion, what fiscal support is available for evaluation, and what evaluative competencies exist in the career guidance staff or can be obtained from outside experts.

A system of evaluation is concerned with: whether the total program is meeting its goals, typically referred to as summative or product evaluation; and whether the individual processes or activities designed to accomplish particular goals or behavioral objectives are doing so effectively or more effectively than other possible processes or activities, typically referred to as formative or process evaluation.

Put in a very simplistic way, summative or

product evaluation requires that you have data about student or client performances in areas related to program goals before the career guidance program or procedure was implemented and similar data about the students or clients after the career guidance effort. This is necessary so that you can judge what changes took place, whether they were sufficient to justify the program, and what they mean for future program efforts. Summative or product evaluation is essentially concerned with the aggregate effects of the program in terms of its goals, rather than how well specific techniques or activities contributed to such outcomes.

Process evaluation is usually concerned with more experimentally oriented questions than is product evaluation. It seeks answers to whether individual behavioral objectives are met effectively by the techniques related to them, whether particular activities are more effective with some subgroups rather than others, and which program techniques or activities are most effective for what purposes with what groups.

Regardless of whether the intent is to evaluate the products or the processes of career guidance, there is a logical sequence of steps which should be undertaken (Herr, 1976).

1. *Identifying goals and stating objectives*
   This step has been covered sufficiently in this chapter so it will not be discussed further here.
2. *Choosing criterion measurements*
   This is a very crucial step. After evaluation criteria have been identified — goals for the program and objectives for the processes — ways of measuring them must be identified or devised. Criteria differ in the precision with which they can be measured. Commercially published instruments are available which can be used to evaluate some career guidance goals; for other goals, locally devised rating scales, self reports, observations, questionnaires will have to suffice. The point of overriding importance is ensuring that whatever information is gathered is clearly relevant to what the program goals and objectives are, not something else.
3. *Establishing levels of performance or standards*
   It is necessary to decide at an individual or a group level what is acceptable. From an in-

dividual standpoint, this may mean deciding for each program goal, how many behaviors (1, 3, 5) must be successfully demonstrated or how many examples (1, 5, 10) must be listed, labeled, or otherwise shown within a particular behavior. From a group standpoint, it may be necessary to decide that some percentage of persons meet some portions of objectives (at least 70 percent of the group will complete 75 percent of the required objectives) in order for the project to be considered successful. There is no magical formula here. The judgment will likely be a judgment of what might be a reasonable improvement over baseline data.

4. *Specifying program elements*
   In summative evaluation, the boundaries of the career guidance program need to be identified. What specific elements in an agency, a school, a corporation, or a college are considered to comprise the career guidance effort. By considering this question carefully, we can reassess the validity of the career guidance program goals and reinforce their distinctiveness from those being carried on by other parts of the agency or institution in which the career guidance program is located.

   In process evaluation, the critical issue is identifying the behavioral objectives or goals for which a particular activity or technique is being done. How do these differ for different program processes? Do all the techniques or activities implemented have clear purposes in client or student behavior or are they being done for their own sake?
5. *Designing the evaluation*
   This step is analogous to planning the preparations for a trip. It involves laying out the data collection format and identifying the persons who will participate. The specific questions to be considered include:
   a. Who will be involved? — Will the career guidance staff conduct the evaluation alone? Will outside experts, state agency personnel, or some other group be involved in collecting or analyzing information? What amount of staff time is available for evaluative efforts and how will other responsibilities be covered?
   b. Sampling — From whom and about whom

Table 6.13
Examples of Presenting Program Goals, Performance Objectives, and Activities/Techniques

Ninth-Grade Program in Self- and Career Awareness

Program Goal	Subgoal	Performance Objectives	Career Guidance Techniques
1. To increase individual self-awareness.	1.A. Reinforce awareness of one's strengths.	1.A.1. The student will be able to show, in front of the group, a 5–10 minute oral description of him or herself as if his or her best friend were describing him or her for membership in a club.	1.A.1. The counselor will introduce a group discussion on the various components of a person (e.g., physical, emotional) and how these form a self-concept.
		1.A.2. The student is able to write a two-page report for the counselor describing how his or her three greatest strengths have helped in situations with people within the previous two weeks.	1.A.2. The counselor will explain the concept of a personal journal and its place during the entire course. The students will begin theirs with a one-page feeling reaction write-up of their responses.

Vocational Rehabilitation in a Regional Correctional Facility

Program Goal	Behavioral Objectives	Career Guidance Techniques
1.To help the client use available educational and occupational information for formulation of tentative vocational goals.	1.A.1. The client can verbalize a basic understanding of the personal and situational factors and decisions which shaped his work history.	1.A.1.1. Group sessions with a counselor.
	1.A.2. From the "help wanted" columns in regional newspapers the client can identify jobs which (1) he is prepared for now, (2) he could probably do with some remedial education and/or vocational training, and (3) are probably out of his reach.	1.A.2.1. Test and interest inventory results interpreted and discussed in individual counseling sessions. 1.A.2.2. Use of career information kits and occupational briefs adopted to client's reading level. 1.A.2.3. Use of tape recording of job descriptions, films, and displays to reach those clients with low reading levels.
	1.A.3. In a gaming situation, the client can identify future decisions which must be made to reach the tentative goals he has set.	1.A.3. Department-made adult game adapted from the life-career game.

A College Program for Returning Women Students

Program Goal	Behavioral Objectives	Career Guidance Activities
1. To help students develop decision-making skills.	1.A.1. The student will identify and assess specific reasons for selecting a particular course of study or career choice.	1.A.1.1. Role play the decision-making paradigm in regard to an interview with a department head about reasons for choosing a course of study. 1.A.1.2. Discussion groups to provide support for decisions being made and carried out. Groups will challenge, suggest, foster, and support decisions. 1.A.1.3. Taped interviews with representatives of various curricula will be considered in terms of placement record, role expectations, content in various courses of study.

Business and Industry

Program Goal	Behavioral Objectives	Career Guidance Activities
1. To help employees achieve desired job or career change.	1.A. The employee will be able to identify the career change resources available in the Counseling/Career Planning, Education/Training and Job Opportunities units of the corporation.	1.A.1. Provide the employee with a copy of organizational chart of major career change mechanisms available in the company. Discuss the functions of each component and what services are available in each unit. 1.A.2. Have the employee identify intermediate career goals and identify the company provisions for job information and job transfer, programs of education and training provided, and career planning workshops available on topics of personal interest.
2. To increase employees' awareness of career paths and placement information	2.A. The employee will understand the use of career paths for personnel classification steps, placement, and mobility within the company.	2.A.1. Lunchtime discussions will be held with all employees to acquaint them with the use of career paths charts in their department as well as open job listings, personnel networks, and replacement planning. Representatives of the training section will identify the various training opportunities available to support different career path moves.

should information be obtained? What size groups will be involved? How can we ensure that the data we collect are representative of the persons about whose behavior we are most concerned?

   c. Timing — When will information about the products or processes of career guidance be collected? Continuously? Immediately when a student or client completes an encounter with a career guidance activity? Six months after a person finishes his career guidance experience? At random times? Such decisions obviously affect the amount of effort which the evaluation process will require, what kinds of questions can be raised, how comprehensive the design will be.

6. *Collecting data*

How will the information desired be obtained? Questionnaires? Interviews? Observations? Commercial Instruments? Are you going to purchase them or develop them locally? How much lead-time will be required to get these things accomplished before evaluation can begin? Can the information be machine scored and/or coded to protect confidentiality? Does the content of the data collection instruments clearly relate to the goals and objectives (criteria) to be evaluated?

7. *Analyzing data*

How you analyze the information you collect depends upon the kind of information you collect. Are the data ranked or on an interval scale? Do you have baseline data about students or clients for comparison purposes with post-career guidance information about these persons? Do you need between group or within group comparisons? The form of the information collected, the purpose of the evaluation, the research skill of the evaluator, the time and money devoted to the evaluation will each affect the kind of information analysis which needs to be undertaken. Some people equate evaluation and statistics. Different statistical methods do help you summarize numerical information and, to be used appropriately, these methods each require the information to be of particular types. But they have no magic nor is any one statistical procedure better than another. For many pur-

poses, simple comparisons by frequency count, percentages, or graphic representation (pie chart, bar graph) will be adequate to answer the evaluation questions. In other situations, correlation, analysis of variance or covariance, or path analysis may be more appropriate.

8. *Interpreting data*

While statistical treatment of data can provide findings about many kinds of questions, the meaning of these answers becomes a matter of value judgment by someone or some group. The findings may be that 70 percent of the program goals were met for 60 percent of the persons involved. That's a statistical fact but is it an acceptable indicator of program quality? Does it point to areas of needed program improvement? How does it compare with the characteristics of persons before the program began? The meanings of these questions are not matters of statistics but matters of counselor or administrative judgment — the ultimate substance of evaluation. As a part of systematic planning, it is important to know who will make such judgments and for what purposes.

9. *Reporting and using data*

Evaluating a career guidance program or procedure always implies that the results may signal the need for change or a clearer indication of the status of the counselor's or the program's accountability. In either case, it is likely that administrators, boards of education, corporate boards of directors, trustees, legislators will need to be apprised of the outcomes of the evaluation process. Although these persons may be influential in deciding on personnel, facilities, resources, or program directions, they may have little understanding of either career guidance or of research. Therefore, the information collected and its analyses, no matter how complex, must be put into terms that these decision-makers can understand. Pictures, graphs, slides and a clearly presented verbal report are typically preferred over statistics to convey essential information about career guidance to those who need to know. If handled effectively such approaches represent major methods of communication, public relations as well as accountability to the counselor's various publics. The major focus of evaluation here is on assessing a program's impact in such a way that decision-makers can consider the support to provide it in the future and what changes need to be. Nevertheless, it is important to note that the basic data on which evaluative judgments are based also are important as feedback to the individual so that insights pertinent to career maturation can be gained (p. 2).

The evaluation stage constitutes a feedback loop in systematic planning of career guidance programs. It both provides insight into whether the program is meeting its goals and also provides the base for action to improve the program.

Stage 5 – Milestones

The last stage of systematic planning is really an adjunct to the other four stages. It is the specifying of critical times when major events must take place if the career guidance program is to become functional, or different or evaluated at some specified time. In simple terms, milestones can be considered the time frame for the implementation of the planned program.

Let us assume that a school district, college, or corporation has totally reconstructed its career guidance priorities and developed a planned program which is due to begin in September. It is now the previous December and the four stages of systematic planning have been accomplished. We are now beginning stage 5, the specification of the things which must happen if the career guidance program is going to become operational in September. What schedule of events should we consider? Some examples would include:

Milestones

February 15 – Develop an inventory of all equipment and resources that need to be ordered for the career guidance program.

March 1 – Complete all purchase orders for resource and equipment needs. Begin assembling an in-service package to be presented to all staff involved in the career guidance program.

March 15 – Schedule presentations on program progress for administrative group and board of directors in May.

March 20 – Identify evaluation instruments that need to be purchased and order them.

April 15 – Complete in-service package. Schedule in-service presentations in early June.

May 15 – Present orientation to program progress for administrators and directors.

June 15 – Complete in-service of career guidance staff, community representatives, and instructional staff or first-line managers to goals, objectives, processes, and evaluative design for the Career Guidance Program.

July 1 – Check on the status of resources and equipment purchases. Follow-up on missing items.

July 15 – Check on the availability of evaluative instruments. Meet with consultant personnel to finalize rating scale satisfaction inventory, or other such services.

August 1 – Assemble a public information package for news media and institutional publication. Describe the needs for the program, its goals and objectives, and when it will be implemented.

September 1–10 – Collect baseline data on how students, clients, employees currently stand on behavioral expectations (knowledge, attitudes, skills) underlying program goals.

September 15 – Implement program.

These are possible milestones that need to be met before a program is implemented. In many instances, these milestones would be more detailed or there would be more milestones to accomplish. On implementation, another set of milestones pertaining to data collection, analysis, and interpretation would need to be followed for the first year of operation. Both the milestones and the events described are changeable. Never-

theless, planning systematically is aided by utilizing milestones. In the last analysis, that is the central point of this chapter – the need for systematic planning and the incorporation of the techniques which will facilitate it.

Summary

In this chapter, we have proposed that the systematic planning of a Career Guidance Program occurs in five stages. These include developing a program philosophy, specifying program goals and behavioral objectives, selecting alternative program processes, describing evaluation procedures, and identifying milestones. In each of these stages, a number of questions and decisions must be dealt with. We have discussed here examples of each of these stages and the types of content appropriate to them.

LEARNING ACTIVITIES

1. Demonstrate your understanding of the planning concepts in this chapter by:
   a. selecting a particular age and sex group,
   b. investigating the developmental characteristics of that group,
   c. stating appropriate assumptions about the career guidance needs of this group,
   d. formulating two or three program goals and examples of their behavioral objectives,
   e. suggesting several activities to accomplish the objectives, and
   f. identifying criterion measures for evaluating the achievement of program goals.
2. State the assumptions of the Mager and the Gronlund approaches to writing behavioral objectives, and give two examples of each method.
3. Construct a flow chart of the stages of systematic planning and compare its steps to those of a traditional problem-solving approach. How are they similar? How are they different?
4. Discuss the differences between individual and programmatic assessment.
5. Write a brief statement of the effects on

assessment of converting program goals into behavioral objectives.
6. Make a list of career guidance functions you know how to implement or hope to learn to implement. After each one, indicate what student or client behavior it would likely affect or change.
7. Formulate a brief needs assessment instrument of your own and circulate it among several of your colleagues or friends. Ask them to identify needs to which career guidance should be directed.

OBJECTIVES

After reading this chapter, engaging in the learning activities, and reading the references suggested, you should have met the objectives that follow. If you have not, it would probably be useful for you to review the material in Chapter 6 before proceeding further. You should now be able to:

1. List at least three reasons for systematic planning of career guidance.
2. Name the functions associated with taking a systems approach to career guidance.
3. Identify the five major stages of planning for career guidance used in this chapter.
4. Describe at least three ways to formulate input for a career guidance program philosophy and rationale.
5. Discuss the concept of career maturity and name four or more characteristics associated with it.
6. Differentiate between program goals and behavioral objectives and give at least two examples of each.
7. Identify at least two approaches to writing

behavioral objectives and briefly discuss the merits of each.

8. Discuss why it is important to identify program goals and objectives before selecting the activities or content of a career guidance program.

9. List at least five methods of evaluating career guidance programs.

10. Write a brief explanation for including "milestones" in the planning of career guidance programs.

7 / *Career Guidance in the Elementary School*

The provision of career guidance in the elementary school is not a new add-on to or a dramatic reversal of typical elementary school emphases. Self-knowledge, knowledge of future educational and occupational alternatives, and development of the rudiments of decision-making by students generally have been considered important in both elementary school philosophy and practice. Current models of career guidance reinforce the need for systematic activities and information to occur throughout the elementary school curricula and to involve teachers and counselors in many forms of cooperative effort.

Career guidance in the elementary school is not intended to force children to make premature choices. Rather, it focuses on awareness of choices that will be available, ways to anticipate and plan for them, and their relation to personal characteristics. Many students need to know that they will have opportunities to choose and the competence to do so. These students also need to become aware of themselves, how they are changing, and how they can use school experiences to explore and prepare for the future.

Among the assumptions that give career guidance credibility in the elementary school are:

1. awareness that styles of choice behavior in adolescence and adulthood are affected by the types of developmental experiences that occur in childhood

2. evidence that many of the materials and texts used in elementary schools portray the world of work or of future education inaccurately and foster unnecessary sex-typing of occupations or restricted views of available educational or occupational possibilities

3. acknowledgment that feelings of personal competence to cope with the future grow with knowledge of one's strengths, ways to modify weaknesses, skills in planning and using available exploratory resources, understanding of relationships between schooling and its application in work and other community roles.

A consideration of the characteristics of elementary school children will help to place some of these assumptions into perspective.

THE ELEMENTARY SCHOOL CHILD

Children of elementary school age are fundamentally generalists, in the sense that they are typically open to and interact with a broad range of stimuli and modes of behavior. In their unbridled enthusiasm and curiosity, they have not yet been constrained by many of the social realities and stereotypes that plague and distort the perceptions of their older brothers and sisters and many adults with whom they identify. Yet they are vulnerable in the sense that attitudes and perceptions about life and their place in it are formative and are readily influenced by the environmental circumstances surrounding them, including inaccurate information and sex stereotyping.

Environmental Influences

Environmental circumstances take many forms and have varied relationships to the growth and development of elementary school children. For

214

example, Rich (1979) has demonstrated that children are most knowledgable about occupations located in their own community. Therefore, if they come from a predominantly rural community, for example, with few occupations and these mostly of low status, it is these to which they will likely aspire. She argues that such circumstances put rural students at a comparative disadvantage to their urban counterparts. She further contends that acquiring knowledge "about nonlocal occupations or more specifically about middle- and high-status occupations, could provide rural students with an equal opportunity to make more varied and more optimal occupational choices" (p. 325).

Environmental circumstances go beyond geography. A particularly powerful one is socioeconomic status. Holland (1981) found, in a study of 300 randomly selected sixth-grade students enrolled in twenty-two public schools in Georgia, that socioeconomic status was more useful in predicting the maturity of career attitudes than self-concept, race, sex, place of residence, and age. The data indicated that the higher the student's socioeconomic status the higher the score obtained on the Attitude Scale of the Career Maturity Inventory (CMI).

A further major environmental circumstance affecting the career attitudes of children are their relationships with their parents and the attitudes of the latter toward work. Miller (1978) has examined the childhood antecedents to career maturity attitudes in young adulthood and found some support for the hypothesis that parental attitudes and behavior reported as having occurred during childhood are positively associated with career maturity attitudes among community college students. Parental attitudes and behavior that impede general development and well-being were found to be associated with attitudes indicative of career immaturity. As discussed in Chapter 2, prolonged unemployment tends to also be associated with increases in child abuse, substance abuse, marital discord, intense anxiety, and insecurity. Such circumstances are likely to influence the views of work held by children in families significantly affected by unemployment.

Berry (1979) has reported that research indicates that many problems of older children, youth, and adults are a result of unresolved com-

munication problems stemming from childhood (p. 515). She argues the importance of this matter for communication theory, which she contends "explains human growth and development itself because it is the social matrix from which the self-concept emerges and takes shape and it is the self-concept that gives direction to human life. . . . It is communication that (1) puts the individuals in touch with their own thoughts and feelings and (2) ties person to person and every person to a group" (p. 516). In this view, social interference with communication development takes place when the pattern of communication between the parent and child is unsatisfactory, at least from the child's point of view. Obviously, such disturbed communication patterns will affect not only the child's view of self but interactions with others in the school and, subsequently, in the work place.

As a function of such environmental circumstances and others, levels of aspiration, achievement motivation, and self-perceptions have their genesis in the early years of the family and of schooling. Here are the roots of the behavior that will manifest itself many years later under the labels of career identity and commitment, or conversely, juvenile delinquency, early school leaving, and underemployability. If Luchins' primacy effect (1960) is a valid premise – that the information obtained first carries the most weight in ultimate decisions – then in the case of elementary school age children, education and career guidance must focus considerable attention on attitude development, decision processing, and self-awareness, as well as on knowledge of the broad characteristics and expectations of work. These are the ingredients of career development that underlie growing career maturity.

Children's Values Toward Work

Many persons believe that the elementary years are too early for career guidance goals. They believe that concerns about self-understanding and planning for the future are better left to the junior high school and beyond. Although adults might feel more comfortable if they did not need to plan career guidance responses to children's developmental needs in the elementary school, children do have such needs.

As elementary school children move through the elements of fantasy so characteristic of growth and learning at that life period, work is an important concern to them. By the time they have completed the first six grades of school, many of them have made tentative commitments to fields of work and to self-perceptions. The point here is not that the choices are irreversible or that this phenomenon is good or bad, but, rather, that it occurs. Parker (1970), for example, found that fewer than 10 percent of 29,000 students in the seventh grade in Oklahoma described themselves as not having vocational goals. Simmons (1962) discovered that the elementary school children in his study were very much aware of occupational prestige. Creason and Schilson (1970) found that of a sample of 121 sixth graders who were asked about their vocational plans, none indicated that they had no vocational plans, none indicated that they had no vocational preferences, and only eight indicated that they did not know why they chose their particular preference. In a related study, Davis, Hagan, and Strouf (1962) found that out of a sample of 116 twelve-year-olds, 60 percent had already made tentative choices. Nelson (1963) has demonstrated that as early as the third grade, children have well-developed attitudes regarding occupations and levels of education and that as early as ages 8 and 9, children tend to reject some occupations as holding no interest for them.

Hales and Fenner (1972, 1973) have reported research findings indicating that values related to work begin to form in childhood and that these values enter into preadolescent vocational behavior. In particular, their research has shown that "although sixth-grade pupils differ in the work values which they hold, the work values of different groups (male-female, social classes) are more alike than they are dissimilar" (1973, p. 31). They further contend that an exploration of work values by elementary pupils may be useful in initiating analysis of the world of work from a perspective that is less dominated by sex and social class roles than is true of interests and aspirations. Borow (1970), too, has proposed that career development in the elementary school can be better understood if it is presented within the context of values and the valuing process. Cooker's research findings (1973) are similar to those of Hales and Fenner (1973), although he suggests somewhat sharper sex differences in values with boys who value such things as money and control more than girls, and girls who place more importance on altruism and helping others than boys. This latter finding suggests that the valuing process does begin in the preschool period. In other words, whether or not education and career guidance respond to this fact, the evidence shows that elementary school students have already begun to assimilate perceptions and preferences that may be wholesome and meaningful or distorted and ultimately harmful to aspirations and achievement.

Additional Perspectives

Some additional perspectives on the ability of elementary school children to conceive of themselves in occupational terms, the sex differences in such behavior, and the knowledge of elementary children about occupations and related phenomena can be obtained from the findings of the National Assessment of Educational Progress's Career and Occupational Development Project. The national study included some 28,000 nine-year-olds (Miller, 1977). Selected findings from this assessment include:

1. Nine-year-olds can describe things they do well and things they cannot do well, although for the most part they are too young to relate these directly to occupational activities. It is harder for them to state their limitations than their strengths. More whites and children from homes where parents possess education beyond high school than blacks or children whose parents have not completed high school are able to list both strengths and weaknesses.

2. Nine-year-olds have limited methods of evaluating their own abilities or are unable to do this. Females more often judge by what others say or by tests and grades, whereas males more often judge by personal comparison or comparison with a piece of data.

3. Most nine-year-olds are able to state strong and weak interest activities but fewer are able to state weak than strong interests.

4. Nine-year-olds generally have high knowledge of the duties and requirements of visible occupations, although there is evidence of sex differences in the knowledge of specific occupations.

5. When given a list of twenty-six household skills and maintenance-building skills that are work-related and done without assistance, most nine-year-olds indicated that they had done many of the activities (for example, babysat, repaired a toy, shopped at the store, planted vegetables or flowers, painted an object).

6. About 60 percent of nine-year-olds have participated in out-of-school learning experiences such as special training and lessons. Males, blacks, and children whose parents have less than a high school education have had fewer such experiences than other groups.

7. Most nine-year-olds can give acceptable responses to exercises that measure their skills in working effectively with peers, co-workers, and others.

8. Most nine-year-olds do not perceive themselves as being responsible for their own behavior.

9. Most nine-year-olds show resourcefulness in completing a task assigned to them when the instructions are clear. However, fewer nine-year-olds are able or willing to take the initiative to seek assistance in completing a task that is unclear to them.

10. About 60 percent of nine-year-olds see the responsibility for selecting what work they will do for a living as belonging to someone other than themselves. Blacks and those whose parents are less than high school graduates are less apt to see their future work as their own decision than whites or those whose parents have more than a high school education.

Importance of the School Years

The first ten years of life have been called, correctly, the "nursery of human nature." This is the period of life when a child's goals, achievement motivation, and perceptions of self as worthy or inferior begin to be formulated. The concepts children acquire during this life stage directly influence later school success, career identity, adult interests, and general perspectives on life.

Elementary school children, in their play and school groups, are concerned with individual differences, work, adult life patterns, and personal feelings of competence, which they translate into self-perspectives and preferences for some work or educational activities to the exclusion of others. Whether based on accurate information or not, such perspectives direct the child's behavior unless subsequent experiences change such directions.

One can speculate that not all the information and influences from which these preferences and perceptions are derived are appropriate or accurate. Frequently, unrealistic career plans are made at this level because of the emphasis in parent and community attitudes, as well as in textbooks, on prestige fields, frequently defined as those requiring college preparation. Such an emphasis obscures consideration of other occupations that employ large proportions of workers, offer equally potent gratifications, and are growing in demand. During the past twenty years, various studies have shown that only a small fraction of the many existing types of work are presented to children in elementary school texts and in basal readers. Frequently, the occupations presented reinforce sex-typing (male chef, female waitress; male physician, female nurse) or other unfortunate distortions (Herr, 1977).

This phenomenon is but one evidence of the increasingly rigid walls between the preadolescent (and the adolescent) and the occupational niches and educational options to which they must relate. Far too often, large segments of the student population — those from the culture of poverty and those from homes in which the children are economically favored but psychologically disadvantaged — have no systematic models of effective behavior or of enthusiasm to which to relate and no environmental support for developing personally and socially fulfilling behavior. Although all children probably have some adult models, they probably do not all have models who display a range of adequate behavior and also a consistent vocational identity that provides a stable base for the child's self and occupational explorations. For many elementary school children, stultifying conditions and lack of vocational stimulation occur when attitudes and acquisition of the tools of the culture are in their seed stages.

The effects of a stagnated or unresponsive home or school life can be inferred from Hunt (1961). He points out that, according to Piaget,

> The rate of development is in substantial part, but certainly not wholly, a function of environmental circumstances. . . . The greater the variety of situations to which the child must accommodate his behavioral structures, the more differentiated and mobile they become. Thus, the more new things a child has seen and the more he has heard, the more things he is interested in seeing and hearing. Moreover, the more variation in reality with which he has coped, the greater is his capacity for coping (pp. 258–259).

There is, then, the danger that when the educational process does not create flexibility of behavior and awareness of ways to obtain goals, the seeds of an anomic situation are inadvertently planted. If we hold a carrot up to children, a culturally valued goal, whether a prestige occupation or a certain level of educational attainment, without expending equal energy in developing command of the means whereby children can obtain these goals, we have negated our concepts of individual differences and education as a process of development. Further, we are operating from a narrow view of ability and reinforcing a restrictive definition of individual talent.

Research indicates that many youngsters who drop out of school physically at age 16 have already, in fact, dropped out of school psychologically as early as grade 3. Frequently, this occurs because they fail to sense relationships between what they study in school and life as they experience it outside of school. Some generalize school failures or feelings of incompetence to all academic experiences. They acquire a psychological set that generates resistance to schooling and to the possibility of working toward a self-fulfilling future. Probably such children are not the majority of elementary school children. Many children do develop awareness of their personal uniqueness, possible life options, method of planning, and ways of becoming responsible for one's future.

Unless opportunities for the latter to occur are systematically planned and the elementary school curriculum is augmented with career guidance activities, many other children may learn inadequate behaviors or incorrect information about themselves or their opportunities.

Many of the career guidance goals, or career education emphases, identified in this chapter or earlier ones have long been a part of the elementary school's philosophy. Dewey (1931), for example, believed that the child's knowledge began by doing and that industrially oriented themes, problems, and activities provided the potential to satisfy native tendencies to explore, to manipulate tools and materials, and to construct and create. Indeed, Dewey saw that industrial themes or problems could serve as a correlating medium for other subjects (1931), and as opportunities to acquire knowledge of the industrial world, the fundamental processes of economic life (1900), and the sociocultural backgrounds of vocations (1931). However, restricted or incomplete information and a lack of systematic planning have reduced the power of many schools to achieve these goals. By implementing the stages of planning identified in Chapter 6 and incorporating many of the activities identified later in this chapter into a school's offering, however, one should be able to make contemporary manifestation of such goals accessible to more students.

COUNSELORS AND CAREER GUIDANCE

The elementary school counselor has many responsibilities and techniques for discharging this professional role. Historically, the processes used by elementary school counselors have been defined as the three Cs: counseling, coordinating, consulting. How much each of these is used depends on the needs and resources which characterize a local setting. The American School Counselors Association (1977) has stated, "Consistent with the philosophy of education, elementary school counseling concerns itself with children in the developmental process of maximizing their potential. The elementary counselor works within the educational framework and the child's total environment to enable each child to arrive at an identity and learn to make choices and decisions that lead to effective functioning as a worthwhile being" (p. 1).

It is within such a context that planning for career guidance becomes important for an elementary school counselor. There are many ways to conceive the planning process; several examples follow.

Halverson (1970) has proposed several principles of career development based on characteristics of elementary school children that are useful to planning.

1. The need for goals and objectives that are defined in terms of educational needs and interests of students at this stage of development.
2. The consideration of career development within the larger concept of all the goals of the elementary school. It should not be a new, fragmented, or separate piece of the curriculum but instead an integral part of goals already validated for elementary education.
3. Curriculum planning as it is influenced by career development should not be dominated by college-preparatory emphases.
4. Readiness for learning in terms of career development must take into account what has already been learned or experienced by the student, the projected goals that relate to the student's expressed or identified needs, and the general level of his or her intellectual, social, and emotional maturity.
5. Concrete experiences and learning must precede learning of the abstract. Younger children function more successfully in the concrete realm than in the abstract, with the readiness for abstractions increasing with age.
6. If goals for career development are adopted, experiences and activities must be sequenced in such a way as to maximize the likelihood that students will achieve these goals.
7. There are many subject areas and activities in the elementary school which can be vocationalized. Thus, career development can be integrated with other instructional goals.

Gysbers (1969), quoting the developmental work of Frank Wellman, has labeled the learning phases that relate to career development and span the elementary and early junior high school years as perceptualization, conceptualization, and generalization. Perceptualization focuses on the processes necessary for an individual to become aware of self and environment and to differentiate between them. In the conceptualization phase, essentially grades 4 to 6, concept formation is mediated by past experiences and is given direction by value systems, which are shaped by stereotypes, community and family input, and the student's knowledge about work. In the generalization phase the student uses the already formed concepts about differences among people and occupations to generalize within these domains.

As the individual moves through increasingly complex phases of awareness about self-characteristics and the local world, he or she also moves from being a nonspecialized consumer of input to a more action-oriented investigator of selective types of input, and finally in the junior high school/senior high school years becomes a candidate for future educational experiences or for a particularized work role. This general overview of career development roughly parallels the paradigms of Ginzberg, Super, Tiedeman and O'Hara, as discussed in Chapter 4. It also reflects the notions of Piaget (1929) about the stages of cognitive development, of Kohlberg (1968) about moral reasoning, or of Dewey (1931) about behavior appropriate learning. Collectively these views suggest that the content of guidance or education — in this case career development concepts — will be most effective when they are attuned to the patterns of thought that are natural to a child of the age concerned. For elementary school children such content is learned better when approached at a concrete rather than abstract level.

Goals for Career Guidance in the Elementary School

On balance, the goals of career guidance in the elementary grades are to provide experiences by which students can do the following (Herr, 1976):

1. Realize that understanding one's strengths, values, and preferences is the foundation for education and occupational choices.
2. Understand that it is possible to achieve future goals by planning and preparation in the present.

3. Achieve a sense of personal competence to choose and to meet the requirements of educational and occupational alternatives.
4. Consider the implications of change in one's self, in one's options, and in relation to the need for continuing education throughout life.
5. Understand the similarities between problem-solving and personal decision-making skills.
6. Develop an unbiased, nonstereotyped base of information from which to plan later educational and occupational decisions.
7. Understand that schooling is made up of many opportunities to explore and to prepare for life.
8. Recognize the relationships between academic skills — reading, writing, computation — and other subject matter and how these are used in future educational and work options.
9. Identify occupations in which people work with others, with ideas, or with things.
10. Consider the relationships between occupation, career, and life style.
11. Describe the purposes that work serves for different people.
12. Consider the importance of effective use of leisure time (pp. 1–2).

Depending on the setting and the characteristics of the children being served, many other goals might be developed for a local program of career guidance. Others have been suggested in Chapter 6, and a careful reading of this text will suggest still others. Indeed, it may be more important for "significant others" to understand the developmental needs of children than for the children themselves. Such goals for career guidance in the elementary school can be useful in classes in parenting or in efforts to stimulate community volunteers or PTAs to help give children work-relevant exploratory experience. Regardless of which goals are finally chosen, however, several thoughts need to be borne in mind.

The goals and the characteristics of elementary school children discussed earlier in this chapter should make one point very clear. If career guidance in the elementary schools is to make a difference, simply providing periodic occupational units in which students are told about work is not sufficient. As a result of a study

of the types of occupational information used in vocational decision-making by 294 boys in grades 4, 6, 8, 10, and 12, Biggers (1971) concluded, "Less effort might be devoted to novel ways of disseminating information and more effort given to helping students learn to use the information." He further maintains, "Guidance programs beginning in the elementary grades must recognize the need and plan appropriate experiences to increase the student's ability to use information in vocational decision-making, which is the reason for disseminating vocational information in the first place" (p. 175).

Biggers' observations are well worth noting. To be useful in the elementary school, information must be available in a wide range of reading levels and other sensory modes. In addition, activities will have to meet the diverse needs of students in their initial forays into career development. Parents need to be involved, and when this is not possible, some children need to be provided with adult occupational models. Counselors will have to be activists, initiating and coordinating experiences for different children both within the educational process and outside it. Educational materials and the attitudes of teachers will need to be influenced to contribute to vocationalization. Speaking specifically to the role of elementary school counselors in facilitating such processes, the American School Counselors Association (ASCA) states: "As children reach the upper elementary grades, effort is directed through the curriculum toward increasing student awareness of the relationship between school and work, especially the impact of educational choices on one's life style and career development" (ASCA, 1981, p. 9).

Parental Influence. The involvement of parents in this process is not limited to their role as the prime source of influence on their child's occupational perceptions at the time he or she begins school. Rather, at the elementary school level in particular, counselors should develop strategies to help parents answer these questions: Why career guidance? When does career development begin? Is home environment related to career development? When should my child begin to explore occupations? What are schools and employment agencies doing in this field? How much education will my child need to succeed in different careers? Should a parent ever choose an occupation for his or her child? Should a parent encourage a child to work part-time while in high school? Do young people give sufficient thought to the choice of an occupation? (Knapp & Bedford, 1967). By using such a strategy, counselors are making parents collaborators rather than isolates in the guidance process and in the education of their children.

Since parents have direct control over the environment in which their children are raised, they have the unique opportunity to expose them to experiences designed to enhance their self-fulfillment. As their children enter education, parents share but do not give up the responsibility for their development. Unfortunately, the complexity and dynamic quality of the current occupational structure make it very difficult for most parents to serve as the chief career guidance agents for their children. Indeed, parents are frequently worried about their own occupational future, unsure of how their work contributes to a final product or fits into a total institutional pattern, or confused about the multitude of jobs they see around them. In short, parents are often unclear about how they can be an effective part of their children's development. Often they need reassurance from counselors that they can make such a contribution and understanding of what form it might take. Although not confined to the elementary school, specific ways that parents can contribute to the career guidance program include these:

1. Encourage and assist their children to analyze their interests, capabilities, and limitations.
2. In those work areas with which they are most familiar, help their children relate worker traits, conditions of work, life styles of workers, and potential opportunities for work.
3. Discuss work values that parents have experienced in themselves and others and relate some of the consequences.
4. Discuss the economic condition of the family and help the youth to plan what education and training will help them break out of the constraints of these conditions.
5. Provide encouragement and information as

to how their child can use the knowledge, experience, and services of relatives, friends, fellow workers, and community or state agencies in exploring, planning, and preparing for their work role.
6. Provide the necessary example and counsel to their children during crucial developmental periods to help them establish and maintain a positive self-concept.
7. Display the attitude that *all* persons have dignity and worth no matter what occupational position they hold.
8. Provide situations so that their children can experience decision-making and carry responsibility for the consequences of their decisions.
9. Provide open communication between home and school so that the experiences and the consultation possibilities in both environments can be used to meet the needs of the children involved.
10. Encourage their children to explore a wide spectrum of alternatives, both educationally and occupationally, without stereotyping or labeling any alternatives to discourage the child's consideration of them.
11. Be sensitive to and accept the ambivalence or tentativeness that children frequently exhibit about self-images or images of future career alternatives.
12. Without defensiveness about their lack of specific information, help their children contact specialists or find information relevant to their concerns.
13. Learn about the relationships between specific educational patterns and occupations in order to assist their children to plan their educational experiences effectively.
14. Provide opportunities for work within the home and the community with the opportunity to accept responsibility.

The Relationship of Goals to Program Functions

As indicated in Chapter 6, program goals and behavioral statements of career guidance objectives should precede functions. The former should be cast as behavioral descriptions so that the counselor or teacher can evaluate whether the student has met the objectives specified for a grade or other educational level. Assuming for the moment that one has selected from Chapter 6 — or has developed locally — objectives pertinent to one's school setting and students, what functional options are available to accomplish the objectives? Several suggestions have already been offered in this chapter. The strategies should be concrete rather than abstract, at least in grades 1–3; they should involve action rather than simply verbalization; they should use multi-media approaches as much as possible. As suggested previously, children are doers. Children need to explore and try on different work roles.

Concrete Strategies for Implementing Goals. O'Hara (1968) adds several other observations that can be used to guide the selection and use of functions for fostering vocationalization or career development. First, the characteristics of career development discussed in this book are largely "acquired needs" pertinent to students in the United States and other developed nations of the world but are not necessarily part of the developmental needs of children in other cultures. Therefore, one must establish a readiness for career guidance or career education. One way to do this is to reinforce, through social approval from teachers, counselors, and parents, those behaviors of children which are oriented to consideration of choices, information seeking, and participation in exploratory activities. If some teachers provide these experiences and encourage children to participate in or exhibit career development, but other teachers convey by attitude or behavior that these things are unimportant, many students are not likely to persist in the behavior. For example, if an elementary school child is trying to raise questions about work or choice-making but is constantly patted on the head and told not to worry about those things now, the child is not likely to continue to consider them important. If they were, this teacher, who is a significant influence in the child's life, would deal with them.

Second, since many of the problems to which early efforts at career development are directed are remote, real or simulated experiences must be provided in which children can make decisions and experience the consequences of those decisions. This may be done by permitting children

to plan a particular project and then by analyzing the results, or by working through illustrative case materials or games, identify decision factors and alternative outcomes. From such immediate experiences, bridges are built from the academic world to the world of work. Further, ways must be found to convert daily intellectual problems into occupational problems, thus allowing children to learn a variety of responses to problem-solving circumstances.

The child must also be helped to develop cues by which personally important concepts and ideas can be distinguished from unimportant ones. The child also needs to have translated into his or her terms such concepts as relative importance, compromise, irreversibility, synthesis, and developmental process.

In order to differentiate or integrate self-characteristics and characteristics of the occupational world, the child must be assisted to develop a broad repertoire of pertinent words — the language of occupations. Without them, students lack the tools for manipulating and symbolizing the world as it pertains to them.

Hunt (1970) has stressed the importance of symbolization to the student's ability to deal with the physical world, the social world, and the inner world as they relate to career development. She sees each of these three abilities as competencies that children must acquire as foundations for career development. In extending this line of reasoning, she recommends that children study workers primarily as problem-solvers. Regardless of whether the medium used to help students develop an understanding of different occupations is a field trip, demonstration, film, or reading, students should be encouraged to ask:

1. What is the nature of the problem of living that this person routinely solves?
2. What is the nature of this person's competencies?
3. What special tools does this person use for solving problems?
4. What special facilities does this person need?
5. Could I do what this person is doing?

In addition, Hunt has argued that from kindergarten through the third grade, the emphasis should be more on manipulative direct experience than on vicarious experience. In line with Gysbers' conception of the perceptualization phase, the emphasis at these grade levels is on, Who am I? rather than, What do others do for me or tell me about? This also means that the tools or the media that are made available in these experiences must be physically manageable. Besides gaining an understanding about work, children must gain perceptions of themselves as successful with these tools or media. At the fourth- to sixth-grade levels, Hunt suggests that although concrete, direct experiences are still vital, the array of tools and media needs to be expanded to provide more and more problem-solving challenges requiring exploration of information and acquisition of basic skills.

What is implicit in the positions of O'Hara and Hunt is made explicit in Arbuckle's position (1963–1964), that people and work are irrevocably related. Thus, occupational information is valuable to the degree that it can diminish an outside-the-person focus and stimulate the child's learning and exploration as a part of seeing himself or herself in process, as having and exhibiting freedom of choice. This emphasis on people as workers and as problem-solvers also reinforces for the elementary school child the importance of "me" and "my characteristics" as primary influences on "my future."

Sequencing Career Guidance Experiences

Halverson's observations (page 219) indicate the importance of sequencing career development experiences from concrete to abstract. First-grade activities should differ from sixth-grade ones, even though the themes or the attitudes to be developed remain constant. In considering sequencing, one must also consider sexual differences as these affect knowledge about or realistic attitudes toward career development.

Norris (1963) has suggested a career guidance sequence in the elementary schools, particularly in terms of occupational information:

Kindergarten. The child learns about the work activities of his mother, his father, and other members of his household.

Grade 1. The child learns about work in his immediate environment — his home, school, and neighborhood.

Grade 2. The child learns about community helpers who serve him as well as about familiar stores and businesses in the neighborhood.

Grade 3. The child studies the expanding community. Emphasis is placed upon transportation, communication, and other major industries.

Grade 4. The child learns about the world of work at the state level including main industries of the state.

Grade 5. The child's studies broaden to cover the industrial life of the nation. Major industries of the various sections of the United States are selected.

Grade 6. The child's program is expanded to include the entire western hemisphere. Life in Canada and in South and Central America is contrasted with life in the United States (p. 56).

Bank (1969, p. 285) has provided a derivation of Norris' grade-level theme by focusing on occupational role models exemplifying particular emphases. Examples of his approach include:

Kindergarten	School role – models	Principal Teacher School secretary University professor
First Grade	Community role – models who help feed us	Grocer Milkman Waitress
Second Grade	Community role – models who protect our health	Dentist Nurse's aide Doctor
Third Grade	Models who protect our health – personal hygiene	Barber Beauty operator
	Models who provide shelter	Plumber Building cleaner
	Models who protect us	Lawyer Fireman Policeman
Fourth Grade	Models who provide transportation	Gas station manager Bus driver Airline stewardess
Fifth Grade	Models who provide communication	Postman Printer Photo-journalist
Sixth Grade	Models who provide for business	Banker Office secretary Salesclerk

Beyond the examples of using occupational role models to sequence career guidance experiences for elementary school children, many career education projects have identified specific concepts appropriate to each grade or educational level by which to organize activities or experiences for children. These approaches are very much like those suggested in Chapter 6. Although there are many examples available, two will illustrate the point here.

The Concepts of Awareness and Accommodation. Bailey and Stadt (1973, pp. 351–359) have suggested that grades K–6 can be divided into two stages: Awareness (K–3) and Accommodation (4–6). These in turn can be broken into subgoals as follows:

Awareness (K–3)
1. awareness of self
2. awareness of different types of occupational roles
3. awareness of individual responsibility for own actions
4. development of the rudiments of classification and decision-making skills
5. learning cooperative social behavior
6. development of respect for others and the work that they do

Accommodation (4–6)
1. development of concepts related to self
2. development of concepts related to the world of work
3. assuming increased responsibility for planning one's time
4. application of decision-making and classification skills
5. development of desirable social relationships
6. development of work attitudes and values

Each of these concepts provides an impetus to the development of career guidance experiences that will facilitate the behaviors, attitudes, or knowledge involved. Somewhat similar is the sequence of concepts that guides the career development exemplary project in the District of Columbia Schools (1976). There are many subconcepts distributed across K–6, but the subconcepts and career development activities at each grade level are derived from five:

1. There is dignity in all work.
2. The life of a culture depends on its workers who produce goods and services.
3. There are many different kinds of work.
4. Mankind uses tools for work.
5. Work has rewards.

In addition to such concepts, children would likely be helped to realize that school is a child's work and that its rules, expectations, and content are organized in many ways parallel to the adult world of work.

Examples of Program Content

These approaches to sequencing show awareness of the developing radius of the interests of elementary school students and their increasing capacity for abstractions. They do not, however, directly suggest what content to include or what emphases would lead to knowledge of industrial characteristics, or of the factors that distinguish industries. Kaback (1960) more than two decades ago reported examples of ways to accomplish the latter. In general, these are still valid. In a first-grade project, a teacher used a broken chair leg to stimulate consideration of work and tools. After some discussion, the children decided that a broken chair leg required a carpenter. Then they decided on the tools, processes, and materials needed to repair the chair leg: "(1) Remove the broken piece of wood, (2) cut a new piece of wood, (3) nail the new piece of wood onto the chair." The children then went to the woodworking ship and accomplished this task. Following the repair job, they discussed the qualities needed to perform a good job. They then discussed other work activities of a carpenter. From this point they moved into discussions of the work done by their parents. Finally, they analyzed the work activities of these different occupations in terms of knowledge of the alphabet (filing), physical capacities (bending, sweeping), mental expectations (knowing what to do next). Such activities, with a little ingenuity, can be expanded in many different ways to provide impetus to career development.

A somewhat different way of sequencing content has been advocated by Ridener (1973). Based on twenty-three concepts that are to provide the

K–6 curricula, this approach emphasizes "careers of the month," in which instructional guides tie occupations and careers to specific subject matter at each grade level. Thus, each month careers associated with different subjects are highlighted, but no one curriculum reinforces the career concepts throughout the year. The suggested sequence is to introduce career concepts in a variety of ways throughout the school in September. In October, language arts careers are highlighted; November, math careers; December, science careers; January, social science careers; February, fine arts careers; March, vocational education careers; and April, health and physical education careers. Finally, in May, activities occur by which the concepts focused on throughout the year can be reviewed and reinforced.

Schmidt (1976) working with a team of elementary teachers and counselors in the Colorado Springs School District designed a career guidance program built around two components. The first was concerned with increasing self-concepts of elementary children and the second built on the first to help students explore careers. The self-concept component was divided into four basic areas: strength-building in which students were taught how to identify strength in others; values identification by which students could be helped to clarify their own value systems; goal-setting in which students established minigoals important to larger aspirations and monitored their progress in achieving these; and life management in which they discussed obstacles to their self-made goals and developed strategies for overcoming them. Component 2, career awareness, involved the use of several types of commercial resources. One, *Career Kits for Kids*, was used in grades K–2 and allowed students to role-play different types of workers and wear hats and uniforms that fit each particular role. Real workers in the selected areas were invited in to provide actual work process examples for the children and show them the tools used in the occupations. In addition, puppet shows and songs were made up by the children about different forms of work. The second commercial resource used in this component was a series of six filmstrip units (*Career Discoveries* – Guidance Associates) that dealt with broad career areas such as "people who influence others" or "people who make things." The emphases here

were on the types of persons in different jobs, their life styles, and the strengths or values, and goals they brought to their job. Again, guest speakers were used and students compared their personal profiles developed in the self-concept component to those appropriate to different work options.

Related to the types of content and method suggested by Schmidt, it was implied by Sander, Westerberg, and Hedstrom (1978) that the world of children's literature offers a wide variety of ways to explore decision-making or other career guidance objectives. They summarize ten stories from children's literature that could be useful. Included are stories dealing with decision-making and the consequences of making unwise choices, self-awareness and economic awareness, and other topics.

Somewhat similarly, Nelson (1980) has described the CREST program, which through three storybooks for children and related materials and activities, translates the concepts of choice awareness in a way that is intended to be understandable and engrossing for children. It helps them see the many ways in which they are in charge of themselves and the many alternatives they have as they choose their ways. Research on the project indicated that children in the experimental condition were able to produce more choices, and those choices were judged to be more positive, than were those of children in the control condition. Teacher responses were also found to be quite positive about the value of the CREST program.

An interesting approach is the T4C program, which operates from kindergarten through grade 6 in many New Jersey schools (New Jersey State Department of Education, 1973). This approach integrates world-of-work concepts within traditional subject areas and emphasizes hands-on experiences by which students can become acquainted with various technological processes. Each T4C classroom has a complete set of hand (and sometimes power) tools and teachers have guides for forty-seven learning episodes that can be tied into various subjects at different grade levels. Episodes include "Discovering Machines" and "Merchandising" in kindergarten, "Writing Poems for Silk Screen Cards" in first-grade language arts classes, "Exploring Electricity," in third-grade natural sciences, and "Weather Station" in sixth-grade science. In each episode, simple problems using appropriate technologies are completed by the children, written about, and demonstrated in other ways.

Wircenski, Fales, and Wircenski (1978) reported on a project for a combined second- and third-grade class in the Lafayette, Indiana, schools. The specific objectives were to help the children learn the following concepts:

1. that the world of work is composed of many interrelated jobs in order to plan, design, advertise, manufacture, distribute, and service goods
2. that all jobs are important
3. that cooperation among all workers is very important

These objectives were met by engaging the class in constructing a small wooden wagon and by carrying out activities related to the manufacture of the wagon in various subject areas. Students were assigned to various manufacturing tasks after job specialization required to assemble the wagon was studied. Examples of the uses of related subject areas were: music, a promotional song was written and sung by the students; art, a company logo was designed and advertising materials produced; English, various writing assignments dealing with the history of work, the importance of manufacturing, and career opportunities available were produced; math, material and supply needs were calculated and related production times and likely salaries were computed; social studies and science, the principles of manufacturing were studied. As part of the project each student was interviewed, hired, and trained for his or her job. In engaging in the project, students were also exposed to the importance of work ethics, leadership, cooperation, and respect for others.

Fifield and Petersen (1978) have described the use of job simulation to enhance vocational exploration in the elementary schools. At the time of the report, more than thirty units based on the fifteen USOE career clusters, discussed in Chapter 3 and in other places in this book, were being rotated through classrooms in Logan, Utah. The units were either located in classrooms or in mobile units moved among elementary schools.

According to the authors, the following steps were taken to develop each simulation unit:

1. A mock-up site was prepared (for example, for the auto brake repair unit, a car fender appropriately mounted with backing plate and brake parts was provided; for the plumbing unit, the section of a wall in which a wash basin and pipe fixtures were installed was provided). In most cases, the mock-up used a workbench or work area where materials and tools were organized. . . .
2. Appropriate materials and tools were assembled and made available for each unit. . . . The student was required to perform only the essential tasks in completing each simulated unit. Real tools associated with the respective jobs were used and the mock-up for the job was designed as realistically as possible.
3. Instructions and directions were narrated on a cassette tape that was accompanied by a set of written directions and appropriate pictures. . . .
4. Supportive career materials, such as videotapes, catalogues, career brochures, and other literature pertaining to the occupations were used as the principal source of illustrative materials (p. 329).

Each unit was designed to be completely self-contained so that the teacher could strictly serve as a monitor.

In addition to using the USOE clusters as organizing themes and content for career development in the elementary schools, McGee and Silliman (1982) use interest measurement as a basis for career awareness activities. In particular, they describe the five sections of *What I Like To Do* (Meyers, 1975) — play, academics, the arts, occupations and reading — as the basis for developing small-group guidance activities. They then suggest sample activities that can be used in working through the individual sections of the inventory. Included would be use of slides and newspaper or magazine pictures showing different people working, student journals in which written assignments related to "What I want to be" are maintained, interest trading corners, library research, writing brief job descriptions, bulletin board projects, interviews with workers.

In two socioeconomically different elementary

schools, Goff (1967) showed that measurable increments in vocational knowledge, in occupational aspiration, and in realism of occupational choice can be attained through a planned vocational guidance program. Stress was placed on developing a respect for all levels of human endeavor, gaining an understanding of personal strengths and limitations, and acquiring satisfaction in learning tasks themselves. Children were asked to work through the making of occupational choices for the purposes of testing and discussion as well as for reinforcement of the idea that early and specific choices were not expected at the elementary school levels.

In an attempt to determine whether primary-grade children could gain occupational awareness important to vocational attitude and value formation, Wellington and Olechowski (1966) found that eight-year-old youngsters could: develop a respect for other people, the work they do, and the contributions they make in providing production and services for everyone; understand that occupations have advantages and disadvantages for the worker; and understand some of the interdependent relationships of workers. The group of students with whom Wellington and Olechowski worked was first exposed to a unit of study entitled "Shelter." The building industry and the variety of workers in it were explored. Initial indications were that at the conclusion of this unit youngsters did not yet understand the workers' roles and functions. Follow-up discussions then focused on methods of increasing the children's understanding. The students were assigned to interview a variety of workers. With the assistance of the teacher and the counselor, they developed questions to ask in the interviews. The interviews and the class discussions that followed were taped. After the children listened to the tapes and completed their discussions on the building industry and its workers, there was a significant increase in their understanding and awareness of working people and their work. The important point is that the initial lack of increased student awareness was a result of faulty techniques, not of student ability to grasp the concept.

Handel (1973) has suggested three techniques found to be useful as career guidance activities: career corner, seminar special, brainstorming. Found to be useful with fifth and sixth graders,

career corner is comprised of a large pegboard with manila packets containing information about various careers placed in an activity area. Pertinent film loops, filmstrips, and tapes can also be placed in the activity area and keyed to the information on the pegboard. Students can develop their own synopses of information in which they are interested and place them into a personal job bank folder for future use. The seminar special consists of devoting periodic morning meetings to visits from persons in the community who bring objects they use in their work for the children to handle. These objects provide a focal point to discuss the career area each adult visitor represents. With some cross-class scheduling, several adults can be involved in adjacent rooms each morning and students can move between them. Brainstorming, in this situation, was confined primarily to counselor-teacher discussions of the range of possibilities by which teachers could reinforce career development concepts in their subject matter. Although ultimately providing career guidance input to classrooms, this technique was found to increase rapport between the counselor and teachers and promote a team effort in career guidance.

In Detroit, Michigan, an elementary school employment service has been developed to give children the opportunity to learn about the rules of work and to have work experiences in and after school (Leonard, 1972). Additional goals are for children to learn how to fill out job applications, develop positive attitudes toward work and a sense of responsibility toward a job, and understand the relationship between their school life and the world of work. Procedures are developed by which students can apply for, consider the requirements of, interview for, and be hired for such jobs as safety patrol member, service squad member, future teacher, lunchroom helper, room helper, audio-visual aide, office helper, custodian's helper, and library staff member. Hedstrom (1978) has described a similar project in the Kentwood, Michigan, schools.

All the projects reviewed here, although derived from somewhat different sets of objectives, give evidence of being responsive to the guidelines in this chapter. Their activities are also congruent with Kaback's (1966) observation, "The younger the child the greater the interest in the actual job performance itself. Most children are natural born actors; they want to act out in order to understand what it feels like to be a carpenter or a ballplayer" (p. 167).

There are several important implications in Kaback's statement. First, in terms of the media of career development, dramatizations, role-playing, and simulation have potential for children figuratively to project themselves into the characteristics of roles important to differences in occupations. An example of this is Cook's (1968) twenty-five-minute operetta, *When I Grow Up*. It is used from kindergarten to third grade to help children establish an awareness of different work roles and to help in self-concept development. Second, it is possible to help students identify with attainable occupations represented in their immediate neighborhoods or community. Finally, if children base their occupational preferences on job performance itself, this is a prime time to introduce them to the relationships between interests and occupational areas.

Laramore and Thompson (1970) have suggested encouraging students to dream about what they would like to do as adults and then pantomime those jobs, letting other students guess who they are and what they are doing. Other suggestions they provide include:

1. Have students discuss their hobbies and attempt to relate them to occupations.
2. Have upper-grade, elementary school children discuss any part-time jobs which they hold around the home or in the community with regard to what they like, the satisfactions they get, or how they spend the money obtained.
3. Have students write a résumé of their own skills (weeding, cutting grass, baby-sitting, ironing) and have them discuss how they might sell these skills to prospective employers in their neighborhood (pp. 263–264).

Some elementary schools actually provide employment opportunities and personnel offices to serve different career guidance expectations. For example, the Schulte School in Sturtevant, Wisconsin, takes the position that children should assume responsibilities and make a meaningful contribution to the operation of the school.

They also believe that students should understand the relationship between their activities in school and the real world outside the classroom (Elleson & Onnink, 1976). To these ends, they have created an employment office, Jobs Inc., operated by the school counselor, which helps school staff members find needed workers and to help elementary school students find school jobs that they prefer.

Other interesting examples of providing students "hands-on" experiences to take responsibility and to learn work procedure in the elementary schools are available. For example, Leonard (1972) has described an effective way to build career guidance experiences into a self-contained classroom situation and curriculum. He advocated the creation of a Popcorn Factory in which students play the roles of various workers in the factory and the teacher can use such content to make spelling, reading, writing, and arithmetic more meaningful while expanding each student's perspective on work and on himself or herself.

CAREER GUIDANCE TECHNIQUES IN THE ELEMENTARY SCHOOL

Throughout this chapter we have suggested many career guidance techniques appropriately used in the elementary school. However, many others can be used to achieve particular program goals and behavioral objectives. Even the extensive list of techniques that follows is not exhaustive, since creative elementary school counselors and teachers will find additional ways to achieve selected career guidance goals. These may be used with individual students or groups of students, by the counselor or by a teacher. Many can also be used by the counselor in serving as a resource to teachers.

Curriculum Infusion – Career Units

Provide reading reference books or biographies that portray personal decision-making.

Show guidance films on selected topics.

Read poems such as Robert Frost's *The Road Not Taken* and have students compare to decision-making in their own lives.

Have students create and then discuss "I wish" poems.

Analyze short stories based on characters portraying different interests or values.

Select a career cluster requiring competence in particular subject matter (such as math, science, language) and identify occupations related to it.

Have students research some aspect of change — such as a means of transportation — compile pictures depicting changes and occupations affected, arrange a bulletin board display related to the project.

Do oral reports on different occupations with the student pretending to be the worker in the report.

Have students write a paper on, "The kind of person I am," "The kind of person I want to be," or "How I have changed in the past year."

Make a movie with students serving as plot writers, camerapersons, graphic artists to illustrate communication careers.

Have students prepare an autobiography and address at least three ways in which their life is influenced by family, school, and peers.

Display words in a prominent place that refer to leisure-time occupations such as lapidary, numismatist, spelunker, philatelist, bibliophile. Have students look up the meaning of these words and consider how they relate to the use of leisure time.

Build interest centers around different career clusters or ways to assess self characteristics.

Provide listening centers that include individual earphones, recording devices, record players, tapes and cassettes dealing with worker interviews, study skills, and topics related to self-understanding.

Group Activities

Play "Let's Pretend" or "What's My Line" using occupations or careers as the content.

Role play photo problems for children in grades 1–3. Mount photographs depicting various problems or situations pertinent to self-understanding or occupational differences on display board, and have children role play their interpretation of the photos.

Have students discuss unfinished stories available in the *NEA Journal* and in other sources that cause them to consider alternative solutions to various problems.

Have students design posters depicting the steps or conditions important to responsible decision-making.

Have students probe a problem-solving situation by making up the behavior of puppets.

Have students design table games in order to play different approaches to decision-making, career options, or other life situations.

Divide class into "green" and "purple" groups, for example. Have students simulate discrimination of one color, analyze the behaviors involved, and relate to interpersonal skills or work adjustment.

Write a skit using terms from the world of work.

Develop crossword puzzles using terms from the world of work.

Use the help-wanted section of a newspaper to identify words from the world of work.

Have students compose questions and take part in a class "quiz show" based on occupations and educational alternatives.

Have students compose a help-wanted advertisement for a particular job.

Bring in a tool or material, uniform or a picture of one, and use these as the basis for a creative writing lesson about the objects or workers who use them.

Have students write about a fantasy or daydream about doing a certain job, draw pictures of themselves doing it, and identify the tools necessary. Discuss in class.

Using local job-related events, have students develop career pyramids to illustrate the interdependence of jobs required to accomplish the goal (such as build a new apartment house, airport, supermarket).

Have students produce a short cartoon strip about some aspect of the world of work that went wrong.

Have students collect pictures of workers whose occupations are clearly a means of self-expression, such as writer, musician, artist, and generate class discussion on the way in which other occupations are a means of self-expression; pictures may be used for bulletin board.

Have students participate in everyday decisions such as what to do in free time, which homework assignment to do first, where to eat lunch.

Have students plan a class party or field trip, identify the compromises that must be made, and list the risks or consequences.

Have students design creative drama skits that deal with self-concept, values, making choices, and other pertinent topics.

Have students compare lists of interests, abilities, and achievements with occupations in which these are important.

Have students identify feelings from pictures (sad, happy, and so on) and relate them to past situations in which they experienced these feelings.

Have students identify different roles they play, list them on the board, and have discussions on how these roles are learned or why they are important.

Have students maintain a diary in which they note things that make them feel unique, worthwhile, and deserving of respect.

Have students construct a career pyramid that illustrates the different types of jobs in a career area at different levels of education and responsibility. For example, in health careers, discuss the range of opportunities from the ambulance driver or sanitary inspector to the most sophisticated specialist.

Have students compose a brief job profile for a worker in each of the career clusters.

Given a series of pictures illustrating various community workers (police officer, truck driver, salesperson, teacher, construction worker), have the students give a job title for each, discuss the work activities involved and the problems they solve.

Have students describe ten different workers who built, maintain, or operate the school.

Have students list major problems facing society and then identify an occupation or career cluster that they think will have greatest effect on solving the problems.

Using a list of twenty to fifty occupations, have students give an example of a need or function of the community which is met by each occupation.

Using a list of ten to fifteen common occupations, have students describe those which are (1) mostly outside work, (2) mostly inside work, (3) both inside and outside work.

Using pictures of people at work, have students distinguish between those involving the production of goods or services.

Have students match pictures of tools and what they are used for (for example, rake–leaves, hammer–nails, saw–boards, screwdriver–screws). Discuss the use of tools for different purposes in school and in work.

Have students identify two commonly used tools in each career cluster.

Have dress-up clothes available for children to try on and pretend to be the workers. Discuss how they feel when they act out a particular worker's role and what would they like to know about such a worker.

Students will select an occupation of their choice and through a variety of media (resource books, filmstrips, interviews), develop an accurate description of a typical life style for the worker in a chosen occupation.

Using a supply of magazines, have students locate one picture that breaks down the traditional male-female occupational role-typing (male nurse, female physician, male secretary, female truck driver). Discuss.

Students may keep a log of all the examples of occupational stereotyping that they discovered while watching TV.

Using a list of leisure-time activities (baseball, art, photography, rock collecting) have each student identify at least one occupation that could result from an interest in each activity.

Have students pantomime a leisure activity in which they engage. Other students try and guess the activity. Play "Twenty Questions" based on leisure-time activities of the students.

Have students plan and carry out a Hobby Fair in which each student is invited to bring an example of his or her hobby, and demonstrate or describe the hobby to the class.

Have students make a class display of various famous people engaging in their leisure field career.

In a role-playing situation, have students break into pairs and role-play an employer who is interviewing an applicant for a job. The interviewer wants to know why the person wants the job — besides the money.

Have children engage in comparison shopping while visiting a shopping center. Have children compare the costs of a box of eight crayons. Discuss.

Community Involvement

Community career surveys.

Take field trips to sites that allow students to see how subject matter is applied to solve work problems or is necessary to facilitating work activity.

Invite resource persons to discuss how personal characteristics contribute to daily functioning or ask them to discuss their vocational history in relation to what they now do.

Have students "shadow" selected workers on the job to view the work activity in which they engage and the other types of workers with whom they interact.

Invite the director of the local adult education class to visit the school, discuss the program with students, and explain why adults take courses.

Develop and organize list of resource speakers and field trips to observe the workers' roles in various occupations.

Visit a local factory and observe the entire production process. Assign small groups to study one aspect of the process thoroughly, make a display of it, and present it to the total class.

After an opportunity to interview a worker, have the student orally describe the career exploration of the worker, and the way in which the worker applied career exploration to the process of deciding to enter the career in which he or she is presently employed.

After talking with two adults in very different occupational roles, have students list four ways in which their occupation influences the life style of each (amount of "spare" time available, money to buy various items, travel versus staying in one location, hobbies, friends).

Interview a parent or relative to discover the personal satisfactions obtained from working and leisure activities.

Have students visit a local sports equipment store and discuss with the manager the growing demand for sporting equipment for leisure time.

Have the class visit a local craftsperson or invite the person to visit the class. Have that person discuss his or her work in terms of speed, efficiency, economy, and quality. If possible, have the students compare the handcrafted product with its mass-produced counterpart. Stress that society needs both types of products.

The career guidance techniques identified here are of little use unless they are planned for and integrated into a systematic effort. For example, a field trip is often merely a reward for students or teachers and has little intrinsic value. Its value can be significantly enhanced if students are prepared to look for certain things while at the field site, and if they have an opportunity to discuss their observations on return from the site. The same is true of most of the other items mentioned in the foregoing list. In isolation, these techniques are of very little value. When tied to specific program goals and behavioral expectations for children, introduced in a planned and meaningful way, and opportunities made available to reinforce the learning they represent, such techniques have a powerful cumulative effect in moving elementary students toward progressive career maturity.

To achieve such goals in career guidance, the elementary school counselor, in cooperation with teachers, needs to consider:

1. how to individualize those career guidance techniques which will be used
2. how to increase teacher, parent, and student knowledge of career development and the ways career guidance techniques facilitate it
3. how to coordinate career guidance activities
4. how to develop or acquire special materials
5. how to implement cooperation, planning, and evaluation, as suggested in Chapter 6

Obviously, some students will not achieve the behaviors identified throughout this chapter as necessary to career development by means of curricular or other group modes. Problems involving personal relationships, decision-making and problem solving, adjustment to one's failures and successes, and meeting the demands of everyday living (Gibson, 1972) are best handled in an individually tailored counseling mode. The stimulus modes identified in most of the chapter examples lay an information base from which self-understanding, career awareness, and related

coping or mastery tasks can arise. Individual and group tasks supplement each other depending on individual readiness and the tasks to be achieved.

Summary

In this chapter, we have described an array of themes and practices that can be used in elementary school career guidance efforts to stimulate career development in children. Attention has been given to the characteristics of development manifested by elementary age children, and these characteristics have been set forth as the criteria to which career guidance efforts must be attuned. The major themes discussed were the importance of the elementary school as a shaper of attitudes toward the self and toward different aspects of the environment, and the need of individual students to develop a vocabulary for distinguishing environmental characteristics and important aspects of their evolving selves. Relationship of goals to program function and the sequencing of career guidance program content and techniques have been discussed.

LEARNING ACTIVITIES

1. Observe an elementary school classroom for a day and formulate an impressionistic profile of elementary school boys and girls as you have seen them behave.
2. Write a brief essay discussing the perspective of elementary school children on workers, the formulation of interests, and the research on tentative goal-setting by elementary school children.
3. Compile an inventory of behaviors of elementary school children that career guidance activities might affect, using Chapters 4 and 6 as reference sources.
4. Create a skeletal outline of the components of an elementary school career guidance program, and write a brief introductory rationale that explains why the program is important.
5. Review elementary school textbooks, and

identify both accurate and inaccurate perspectives on work they contain.
6. Examine career guidance materials for the elementary school and list occupational or sex stereotypes you believe are inappropriate.
7. View "Sesame Street," "The Electric Company," and "Mr. Rogers Neighborhood" television programs. Identify components of career guidance content included in each and contrast the styles of presentation of each program.
8. Secure from your State Department of Education position statements about career guidance in the elementary school and any lists of exemplary programs they have available.
9. Discuss with an elementary school counselor and elementary school teacher their views of needs for career development among elementary school children. Compare their views.
10. Describe at least three roles an elementary school counselor might play to initiate, support, or implement career guidance in grades K–6.

OBJECTIVES

After reading this chapter, engaging in the learning activities, and reading the references suggested, you should have met the objectives that follow. If you have not, it would probably be useful for you to review the material in Chapter 7 before proceeding further. You should be able to:

1. Name three or more reasons for providing career guidance in the elementary school.
2. List at least five characteristics of elementary school children that are pertinent to career guidance efforts.
3. Identify at least three planning considerations relative to career guidance in the elementary school.

4. Summarize in your own words six to eight goals for career guidance programs in the elementary school.
5. State two or more examples of sequential programs of career guidance in the elementary schools.
6. Discuss at least ten career guidance techniques you wish to acquire skill in performing.

8 | *Career Guidance in the Junior High/Middle School*

When examining the guidance needs and characteristics of students at separate educational levels — elementary school, junior high school/middle school, and senior high school — it is tempting to declare that one of these is more important than another. Yet the essence of career development is that each of these life stages demands mastery of different emphases within an evolving consciousness of self-characteristics and of the life options to which these characteristics relate. In other words, career development as mediated through the educational process must be responsive to the developmental tasks that surface as children grow, as well as to the characteristics of the institutions that influence their mastery of these developmental tasks. If either career guidance or career education is going to be a developmental process, the program must be continuous and cumulative. The outcomes obtained by students at one educational level must serve as the foundation for the subsequent segments of the program at the next educational level. Developmental tasks were discussed in Chapters 4 and 6; you may wish to review them here.

In most career education models, programs for grades 7–9 emphasize exploration and planning. This does not imply that the elementary school emphases of self- and career awareness have been completed, but rather that as children grow, they face new demands. Thus, they must develop increasingly complex behaviors. Indeed, it is likely that for most students self- and career awareness will continue to be refined as self- and career exploration and planning proceed in the junior high or middle school and beyond.

The need for pre- and early adolescents to acquire knowledge and skills important to exploration and planning comes from their opportunities to engage in activities farther from home and independent from the family as well as the nature of the school itself. The eighth and ninth grades are the first instances in the typical student's life of formal choice-points; times when the individual is faced with external pressures to make a public decision and a potentially long-range commitment among competing alternatives. Such decisions are reflected in expectations of choice among specific courses, high school curricula, a particular high school or area vocational technical school to attend, or, in some instances, whether to remain in school at all.

The junior high/middle school is a transition period, between childhood and adolescence as well as between general and specialized education. As such, its processes and goals reflect either solutions or further exacerbations of what Coleman (1974) perceives as the gap between "youth and adulthood" or what Marland (1974) sees as the gap between "education and work." Thus, factors such as present-future relationships, values, delayed gratification, personal responsibility, and choice consequences have real implications for individual students. How and to what degree the attitudes, knowledge, and skills making up these factors are acquired has implications beyond immediate adjustment at the junior high or middle school level. Such development is also predictive of success and satisfaction in the senior high school years and beyond.

Before turning to specific aspects of career guidance in the junior high school/middle school, it is useful to think about the developmental characteristics of students of this age. Unless these matters are taken into consideration, much career guidance activity is likely to be irrelevant. For ease of writing, "junior high school" will be used in this chapter to include both middle school and junior high school students.

CHARACTERISTICS OF JUNIOR HIGH SCHOOL YOUTH

Junior high school students are not the same creatures who inhabited the elementary schools a year or two earlier. As a result of experience and growth, their horizons have widened. With pubertal changes near, either in themselves or their peers, their perceptions of life have changed. Junior high students are more able than elementary age children to comprehend relationships and to use abstract terms and symbols. They are preoccupied with belonging and conformity, being highly influenced by their like-sexed peers and less so by their opposites; they are also taking tentative steps toward independence from their families. They are making more definitive strides in sorting themselves from the mass of students with whom they interact as they try on the multiple social roles that accompany school and community experience.

Junior high school students are immersed in the continued development, refinement, and strengthening of basic skills begun in the elementary school, and they are beginning to converge on the more specialized experience of the senior high school. Their time focus is shifting, however subtly, from the immediate present to the future. Because choices of curricula and of the specific high school or vocational school they will attend a year or two hence are rapidly approaching, their sensitivity to work and its relevance to them as persons in the process of becoming is accentuated.

These problems of selecting a high school to attend and choosing courses in high school are matters of significant proportions in the junior high school. Frequently, this is true because junior high school students or their parents are unaware that when one chooses an educational course of action, he or she reduces or at best alters the alternatives available in the future. Jordaan and Heyde (1979) observe,

Although they may not realize it, these curricular choices are also for many students prevocational choices. The commercial curriculum is in effect prebusiness; the industrial arts curriculum, preparation for a skilled trade; the college curriculum, preprofessional; and the general curriculum, a sort of no man's land with no clear-cut prevocational implications. . . . In pursuing a given curriculum they are, whether they know it or not, increasing the probability of being admitted to or excluded from certain fields of work and training programs (p. 2).

These perspectives are particularly true in the election of those courses which permit the student maximum freedom to qualify for educational opportunities beyond the secondary school while the student is reality-testing whether or not such further education is necessary for goal achievement. Since, at the junior high school level in particular, school *is* work, the opportunity to use personal encounters with the different content and context of courses in order to explore present and future alternatives is important; it is also manageable.

Although the alternatives from which a junior high school student can choose are limited, they represent, nevertheless, the opportunity to practice collecting and analyzing information about alternatives, to anticipate outcomes, and to develop decision plans. Since such dimensions are crucial to successful career development, curricular decisions made in the junior high school provide the opportunity to help students consider how to maximize freedom of choice and assume responsibility for choices made while there is still time for reversing a choice and charting new educational routes if necessary.

The years of junior high school are by design transition years. Intensive, almost frenzied, exploration can be expected whether the school aids it or simply allows it to proceed (Stamm & Nissman, 1973). It is a period when such career development concepts as compromise and the congruence or incongruence between aspirations and expectations become operational as realities, and when idealistic fervor or naivete get their initial temperings in the reality-testing of curricular, athletic, and part-time work experiences. It is also a time when values emerge with enough continuity to be measurable (Perrone, 1973). Indeed, research shows that the development of work values is well underway by the fifth grade and that eighth graders display value profiles like those of fifth graders (Hales & Fenner, 1972). Unless the educational experiences provided students at this level are timely and immediate to the questions that students are asking themselves, it is unlikely that they will have a significant influence on student behavior or choice-making. This is a time, then, when change in the self and the world can be used as a focal point for planning, and when student responsibilities through participation in planning can be related to the consequences of decisions. The research of Campbell and Parsons (1972) has shown that the majority of junior high students exhibit a readiness for vocational planning. The question is, Are schools and counselors prepared to help in this process?

Sex Differences

Junior high school years are also a time when sex differences exert important influences in curriculum choice, and when choice considerations become different in kind for males and females (Cass & Tiedeman, 1960). Brough (1969) has reported that sexual differences are related to the voluntary seeking of counseling in the junior high school, with girls exceeding boys in mean number of interviews as well as in educational-vocational planning and personal-social development. He interprets these findings as:

First, the sex-role values of the middle-class culture permit females a great degree of dependency on adults and a longer period of child-teacher closeness. By the junior high years boys are already expected to reflect independence and "manliness" [authors' note — and this apparently precludes, in comparison with girls, their seeking help with problems]. Secondly, while most all students reach the age of puberty during grades seven through nine, the average age of puberty for boys is two years later than that of girls, or ages 15 and 13 respectively. Since this developmental stage involves considerable emotional crisis in our culture, it is not unusual for junior high school girls to feel

the adolescent press with a greater frequency and intensity than boys (p. 70).

In the previous chapter, little emphasis was placed on differences in career development strategies based on sex. The intent was not to gainsay the influence of sex-typing on occupational stereotypes or on appropriate choices to be considered. Rather, the assumption was that boys and girls both need a language of vocations, an orientation to preference, the rudiments of how to differentiate interests and aptitudes and relate them to future educational options and the occupational clusters available. These experiences should be gained within a context that is not sex-biased. In the junior high school, sex effects become far more pronounced and perhaps make different guidance emphases necessary. As indicated in the summary of Chapter 4, career development theories give only cursory attention to differences between males and females, but it is obvious — if for no other reason than the advanced biological maturity of girls — that differences will occur in the ways young men and young women approach occupational and career choices. Zytowski (1969), as well as Fitzgerald and Crites (1980), among others, have presented preliminary theories of career development for women.

Fortner (1970) reported that in one sample of 400 junior and senior high school girls, when compared with a similar sample of 170 boys, the girls tended to show preference for professional, managerial, and skilled positions more than did the boys and for semiprofessional, small business, semiskilled, and unskilled less than did the boys. It was found that measured intelligence or scholastic aptitude was significantly correlated with these levels of preference.

Entwisle and Greenberger (1972) explored the effects of adolescent-sex, race, IQ, social class, and residential locus on their attitudes toward women's work role. The sample consisted of 270 male and 305 female ninth graders attending six Maryland schools described as black inner-city, white inner-city, black blue-collar, white blue-collar, white rural, and white middle-class. The findings showed a marked difference between boys and girls concerning the women's role, with boys consistently holding more conservative opinions. Both sexes disapproved of women holding "men's" jobs. Black students were less opposed to women working than were white students, but they were just as negative toward their doing the same work as men. Both black and white inner-city students were generally willing for women to work. Blue-collar girls were more conservative than inner-city girls on women's roles. The greatest differences between girls' and boys' views were found among the middle-class white sample. High IQ girls were generally found to hold more liberal views than average and low IQ girls, and high IQ girls from blue-collar homes were found to be the most liberal about women's roles.

A further related issue is that of sex differences in work values. Wijting, Arnold, and Conrad (1977) studied the variance in work values of 1402 boys and girls in grades 6, 9, 10, and 12. They reported that the most salient pattern of work values in this sample was an intrinsic work orientation, with high values being placed on activity, involvement, and on pride in one's work, and a devaluing of extrinsic rewards (such as money and social status). With minor variations, they found this pattern to be true of girls, not boys. They found that boys generally devalued the intrinsic rewards of work and positively valued money and social status. These researchers also found that these work values tend to increase in their crystallization from grade 9 to grade 12. With respect to vocational maturity attitude, Herr and Enderlein (1976) found, in a study of 1553 students from ninth to twelfth grades in three school systems and across sex and curricular classifications, that females displayed a higher mean Vocational Development Inventory — Attitude Scale score at all grade levels than did males. Crites (1978) reports,

> Recent longitudinal research . . . indicates . . . that sex differences do emerge during the high school years. . . . At each succeeding grade level (above the seventh grade) females had statistically reliable higher mean scores on the attitude scale than males. In other words, their attitudes toward the process of career choice matured at a faster rate than that of males (p. 5).

Pedro, Wolleat, and Fennema (1980) indicate that, for whatever reason, there is growing evidence that women's educational and occupational options are limited by the preparation in mathematics they receive while in high school. In this study they compared plans to study mathematics in high school among 400 female and 322 male ninth- and tenth-grade students from nine high schools in midwestern communities. Even though this sample was skewed toward higher-than-average enrollment in mathematics, they found the female students planned to study less mathematics than their male classmates, both during and after high school, even though they were achieving as well as their male counterparts. In addition, when career plans were studied, they found that the ninth- and tenth-grade females in this sample tended to select the stereotypical female career areas that generally require little mathematics. As the authors note, with only the minimal preparation in mathematics, the female students will not be able to choose from the full range of options should they change their occupational plans later. This is particularly true in a society where the emerging occupations are those of high technology.

In related research, Neely (1980) has reported the results of a comparison of the scores on the Career Maturity Inventory of seventy-two male and fifty-two female ninth-grade students in a midwestern town of 25,000 residents. The girls' mean scores on the Attitude Scale fall significantly higher than the boys' mean scores. The girls' scores on the competency subtests were also found to be significantly higher than the boys' on self-appraisal, goal selection, and problem-solving.

The work patterns and the proportions of women in the labor force have changed significantly during the past several decades. It is expected that for the foreseeable future, women will enter the labor force in greater percentages than will men. Thus, as cultural constraints about what is acceptable work or schooling for women continue to fall away, it is expected that women will continue to seek more schooling and more employment than ever before.

By 1990 it is expected that 55 percent of all women 16 years of age and older will be employed (Smith, 1979a). Specific projections are as follows:

> Nearly all of the projected additions to the female labor force will be within the age group

twenty-five to fifty-four, most will be married, and the majority will have minor children. Much more rapid growth of the female labor force should be anticipated if the gap between women's and men's wages begins to narrow, or if attitudes about the appropriate activities for men and women in our society continue to change as much as they have over the past decade (Smith, 1979b, p. 14).

Yet, although this process is accelerating, the pathways and the continuity with which these pathways can be pursued are still different for boys than for girls. Homemaking is still a major vocation for women and bearing at least one child continues to be pervasive among married women. These two factors alone cause either temporary or long-term discontinuities in the career development of women, even though they less rarely negate the important presence of women in the labor force for much of their lives. As day-care centers, financial subsidies for home care of children, and other supports to working mothers are expanded, women will become more significant in their leadership and in their distribution throughout the occupational structure. These possibilities need to be considered in multiple role planning.

The other reality factor remains. Even though social reinforcement for working women is increasing and legislation bars overt obstacles, psychological barriers still tend to cause girls to have fewer job choices than do boys. Reasons for this phenomenon can be found in curriculum content selected by girls as well as in factors in the larger society.

Nieva and Gutek (1981) suggest that the continuing tendencies to consider jobs as male or female encourages the development of two labor markets — a male labor market and a female labor market (p. 5). As Hawley (1980) has indicated, although occupational segregation is slowly diminishing as women in greater numbers begin to enter male-dominated fields, "over one-half of the female workers in the United States are now concentrated into clerical, operative, or service positions while professional women are concentrated in the areas of teaching and nursing" (p. 1).

Similar to the discrimination that prohibits access to some occupations because of racial criteria, sex-typing can be expected to restrict women's access to some occupations in the foreseeable future even though women jockeys, coal miners, baseball umpires, commercial airline pilots, and long-haul truckers are no longer without precedent. Counselors continue to have a major job in helping to reduce high correlations between sex and occupation.

Girls tend to be "set" in a career earlier than boys (by about age 15), even though they may enter a career pattern with less thought than boys because of the residual effects of stereotyping of choices they are encouraged to pursue. According to Hollender's research (1971), significantly more females than males report a definite vocational choice during this period. For these reasons, Havighurst (1965) among others has advocated that counseling for girls should be different from that for boys. Whether counseling should be different in fact or should emphasize different things earlier is debatable, but it is not debatable that since the male's identity is more typically cloaked in a career fabric than is the female's, girls have a different problem of identity achievement from that of boys. Cultural influences have historically assigned to boys in this country a primary role as the breadwinner and, thus, have reinforced in many ways that career development of males is the more important — not necessarily because of the benefits to the male himself but because of the importance of the choices he makes to the well-being of his future family. Although this notion is changing, many of the historical effects remain in the attitudes of various persons.

Research also indicates that the occupational preferences of males and females at the junior high level and beyond are not the same, and this is true for both whites and blacks (Omvig & Thomas, 1974; Nafziger, Holland, Helms, & McPartland, 1974; Powell & Bloom, 1963; Woal, 1974). Although it is not clear why these differences occur — perhaps the incorporation of early sex stereotyping, maybe a lack of information across occupations — counselors need to help the student be clear that such differences are consciously held and not simply a result of information or experiential deficits. Thus, if career guidance strategies are to respond to the needs of females and to help them come to terms with career development — career maturity and identity — these strategies must be mounted no later than the junior high school period. To wait diminishes the likelihood that career development can be influenced for females in optimum ways.

Approaches to Gender Differences in the Junior High School

A very basic strategy by which counselors can attempt to facilitate realistic exploration of career motivations in junior high school girls is by exposing them to nontraditional role models (Katz, 1973). Similarly, Cramer, Wise, and Colburn (1977) examined the use of "stereotype debunking" as a method of combating sex stereotyping. It was found by Piost (1974) that showing a female computer programmer in a career film significantly increased the career motivation of eighth-grade girls for that career compared to their considerably lessened preference for the career when a male model was used in the same film.

Wilson and Daniel (1981) used a role clarification and decision-making workshop to help seventh- and eighth-grade students overcome sexrole stereotypes. Using a variety of activities — such as considering the lives of famous women, songs illustrating social norms and social change in men's and women's roles, discussion of characteristics required for different occupations, interest inventories, analysis of nontraditional jobs — they found in comparing an experimental with a control group that a relatively brief workshop (five sessions) is effective in influencing traditional sex-role attitudes.

Vincenzi (1977) has examined a related approach to minimizing occupational stereotypes that, although it used sixth graders as subjects, could be adapted to the junior high school. In this instance, eighty girls and ninety-seven boys from nine sixth-grade classes were chosen randomly and assigned to experimental and control groups. The experimental group students were exposed to two 30-minute sessions a week for ten weeks. During these sessions, the experimental group:

1. reviewed and discussed magazine articles concerning women working at jobs traditionally sex-typed as masculine and men at jobs traditionally sex-typed as feminine

2. examined and discussed the definitions of a stereotype and identified stereotypes other than occupations
3. met seven women who work in traditionally masculine occupations. Each woman spoke for thirty minutes, gave a short demonstration, and explained her job and why she chose it. Occupations discussed were doctor, lawyer, chemist, television reporter, architect, telephone linesperson, and auto mechanic

The research findings of this approach indicated that the number of occupations viewed as sextyped by the experimental group was significantly reduced and that the experimental group improved significantly over the control group in the incidence of occupational stereotyping.

Another method of dealing with such concerns is to use women in nontraditional careers as guest speakers or as persons for students to shadow on the job. Such persons can also demonstrate the efficacy of multiple role planning. Beyond these types of recognition of sex differences at the junior high school level, counselors also need to help teachers and parents recognize sex stereotyped activities and reinforcement in teaching materials, in educational policies about course options segregated by sex (such as home economics and shop), and in reading materials of various kinds. Title IX of the Education Amendments of 1972 as amended in 1974, 1976, 1980 has made quite clear that segregation of the sexes in courses, athletics, or other school-related activities can be illegal at worst and inappropriate at the best. Counselors obviously have responsibilities to advance the gender-fair notions implicit in this legislation. Put more positively, counselors can help teachers and parents to enthusiastically support career exploration that is unfettered by traditional sex biases. Such efforts once begun must continue in the senior high school, in higher education, and among adult populations.

Differences in Maturity

Of the entire educational span, the junior high school years have the widest range of maturity levels in the student population. The effects of pubertal changes, differences in the rates of male and female growth, and the general unevenness of physical, emotional, and intellectual development within and between the population of girls and boys contribute to this spectrum of maturational differences. Differences in readiness, questions of general academic progress, preoccupations with bodily change, peer conflicts, boy-girl relationships, and rebellion against family restrictions — each co-exists with and often confounds the continuing process of career development. Sherman (1967) states:

> The timing of prevocational orientation may be crucial. Once students get involved in the junior high school milieu their own social and physical maturation and the existing organizational structures (both formal and informal) and the rewards offered from these environments in which they live all influence them. They turn their attention to diverse pursuits, such as popularity, prestige, athletic achievement, and appear to develop different life styles, each with a different set of values. If students are helped to focus on career development prior to becoming a part of this milieu, it could help them to build a kind of core attitude toward their personal futures which might provide a slightly different perspective on the many other concerns of this age which are so much a part of growing up (p. 5).

Differences in maturity among junior high school students, particularly with regard to career development, is also apparent in data provided by the National Assessment of Educational Progress's Project on Career and Occupational Development (Aubrey, 1977). Selective findings about a national sample of some 38,000 thirteen-year-olds follows:

1. Most thirteen-year-olds can state things they can do well and things they cannot do well. Females are slightly better able to do both than males and whites are somewhat better than blacks at these types of self appraisal.
2. While almost all thirteen-year-olds can identify something they would like to do better, only about three-fourths have actually tried to find out how to do it better. Blacks and students whose parents have not completed high school are somewhat less able to state

how to find out how to improve their abilities and limitations, although both of these groups indicate an extremely strong interest in school and academic areas and a desire to improve in these areas.

3. Males more often judge how well they do a preferred activity by a personal comparison while doing an activity while females tend to more often judge by what others say.
4. Overall, males and females are equally knowledgeable about highly visible occupations. However, there is some evidence that there are sex differences in the understanding of specific occupations.
5. Approximately 70 percent of thirteen-year-olds are interested in a current hobby, sport, game, or activity that they feel would be of use for obtaining a job. Group and individual sports are the major categories selected as most useful in obtaining a job. School and academics rank near the bottom.
6. The vast majority of thirteen-year-olds state that at least one school subject has taught them something of use in a job. Of eleven academic areas, mathematics receives a larger percentage of responses linking this discipline to work and jobs than the combined total of the remaining ten.
7. When asked to list ten things to be considered in choosing a job or career, most thirteen-year-olds can list two things and less than half of them can list more than five. While they have difficulty in stating specific factors to consider in choosing a job or career, most do think about a future job.
8. The first choices of thirteen-year-olds for future jobs tend to be occupations generally requiring college degrees or lengthy training periods beyond high school rather than jobs now held by the majority of the work force.
9. Practically all are able to state types of work they do at home. The work done by thirteen-year-olds at home could provide career development programs with a starting point for an exploration of future careers and occupations.
10. There is a difference among sub-groups of thirteen-year-olds with regard to how many have visited places of interest in the com-

munity and acquired related learning experience.

11. Nearly 80 percent of thirteen-year-olds have participated in out-of-school learning experiences such as special training and lessons. Blacks and children whose parents have not graduated from high school have had fewer such experiences.

12. In general, thirteen-year-olds have been exposed to a host of out-of-school experiences without assistance. By connecting their present skills and interests with future career choices, they could begin the process of initial planning on a positive note with individual student direct involvement.

13. Over half (59 percent) have attempted to find a part-time or summer job.

14. A high percentage of thirteen-year-olds are able to list three or more ways people their age could earn money, but minority group students and those whose parents have not completed high school have less information in this regard.

15. Thirteen-year-olds seem to have sensitive and aware attitudes toward work.

16. Three-fourths of thirteen-year-olds feel they ultimately should make the decision as to what job they would take to make a living.

A Time for Early School-Leaving

The junior high school years are a period when many students will permanently absent themselves from formal education. Some of these students will have begun to drop out of school psychologically in the elementary grades. Others will do so in grades 7, 8, or 9. Still others who have found no meaning in school will not only terminate their psychological interaction with the education process, but they will also remove themselves physically. In several other places in this book, what the future holds for those without a high school diploma or marketable skills is discussed. Suffice it to say here that career guidance and the broader educational process must respond to potential dropouts not merely by encouraging these students to remain in school or by lecturing them about the monetary value of a high school diploma, but by altering the educational structure to make it more meaningful.

The realities are that many students who drop out are not getting anything in school that helps them get a better job, and they know it! In many instances ways have not been found to move concrete, task-oriented instruction into the junior high school, where these students can get "hands on" experiences that relate to real work as they see it. Nor is there opportunity to combine general education and work-study opportunities at the junior high school level.

The point is that for some youngsters at this level, purely academic content holds no appeal at all unless it has immediate relevance to salable skills and this relevance is made obvious. These students in the junior high school need access to a skill-centered curriculum like that contained in vocational education at the comparable level. If they do not receive this opportunity, the chances are that they will leave the school as unemployable. Some of these young people do not have the tolerance or the ego-strength to wade through a morass of personally meaningless experiences until the ninth, tenth, or eleventh grades, when they can get more meaningful educational experiences. However, these students should still be provided with experiences other than occupational task-specific skills to foster career development. Indeed, within the context of skill development, not only can they be helped to see where they might go, but prescriptions of the specific ways of implementing their goals can be developed. For those for whom skill-centered training is most relevant and is the prime source of success experiences, training in decision-making and planning that transcends job layouts can facilitate self-understanding and recognition of alternative ways of using evolving skills. Within this context, the concept of continuing education as a way of refining one's skills and becoming a more effective problem-solver at work can be wedded to a knowledge of available apprenticeships, on-the-job training, postsecondary vocational technical schools, military service schools, and other pertinent experiences. It is clear that such task-centered, skill-oriented, and concrete experiences would be helpful to all students if used to relate self-characteristics to the alternatives available, but it is even clearer that such experiences are critical to preventing dropouts.

PLANNING CONSIDERATIONS

While there are commonalities between the role of the middle/junior high school counselor and the roles of elementary and senior high school counselors, there are also differences. For example, the American School Counselors Association (1977) contends that: "Orientation to junior and senior high schools, educational placement, career development, and group activities to promote greater self-direction, particularly in value formulation and decision-making, are all areas with special implications for the middle/junior high school counselor" (p. 3). Obviously, such experiences must be planned and coordinated.

In addition to the general planning considerations for career guidance discussed in Chapter 6, the introductory sections of this chapter suggest several specific characteristics of junior high school students that must be considered.

1. Since the junior high school is a transitional experience from the structured and general education of the elementary school to the less structured but more specialized education of the secondary school, students must be provided broad opportunity to explore their personal characteristics as well as those of the educational options from which they must choose. Opportunities to relate curricular options to the possible and subsequent educational and occupational outcomes seem highly desirable.
2. Since wide ranges in career maturity, interests, values, and abilities characterize junior high school students, a wide variety of methods are needed to accommodate the range of individual differences. Minority students and students whose parents have not completed high school frequently have not had the developmental experience or occupational knowledge enjoyed by whites or students from homes in which parents are well educated. These students may need special programs to facilitate their understanding of opportunities available to them, their requirements, and how to access them.
3. Since females are more likely than males to have made definitive vocational choices, career guidance programs must ensure that such choices were made deliberately and on the basis of accurate, pertinent information.

4. Although students in the junior high school are capable of verbal and abstract behavior, exploration will be enhanced if they are given concrete, hands-on, direct experiences as well.
5. Fundamental to the rapid changes that students experience in the junior high school is a search for personal identity. Therefore, career guidance programs must encourage students to explore their feelings, needs, and uncertainties as a base for evaluating educational and occupational options. Values clarification and other similar processes are helpful in this regard.

Goals for Career Guidance in the Junior High School

There are many statements of career guidance goals for junior high school youth. One example is that of the National Conference on Guidance, Counseling, and Placement in Career Development and Educational Occupational Decision Making. The objectives recommended there were (Gysbers & Pritchard, 1970):

1. The student further differentiates his self-characteristics (interests, values, abilities, and personality characteristics) from those of others, and can identify broad occupational areas and levels which may be more appropriate for him.
2. The student differentiates between the several broad occupational areas in terms of (a) a potential satisfaction each might offer him, (b) the nature of work tasks performed, (c) the future impact technology might have on particular occupational areas, (d) the contribution and importance of particular occupational areas to our society, and (e) the future demand for workers in broad occupational areas.
3. The student identifies different educational areas that are available both in the immediate and more distant future, the nature and purpose of each, the avenues toward which each can lead, and tentatively assesses what each offers him in terms of his possible vocational choices. He demonstrates how knowledge and skills acquired in different subject matter areas relate to performing different work roles. He recognizes the personal and social significance that work has in the lives of individuals at

varying levels within the occupational structure.

4. The student identifies future decisions he must make in order to reach different goals. He identifies those personal and environmental efforts that impinge upon his future decisions. He assesses possible steps he might take in minimizing negative factors and maximizing positive ones and considers the possible consequences each has for him.

5. The student makes a choice of a broad occupational area to study in greater depth.

6. The student can differentiate between the major occupations that make up a broad occupational area and can make some differentiation of these occupations in terms of (a) the amount and type of education needed for entrance, (b) the content, tools, setting, products or services of these occupations, (c) their value to society, (d) their ability to provide him with the life style he desires, (e) to what extent they can satisfy his interests and values, (f) in what ways they do and do not seem appropriate for him.

7. The student selects education or training in the light of his tentative broad career purposes (pp. 73–74).

Another example of career guidance objectives in the junior high school suggests that students should learn to (Herr, 1976):

1. attain realistic understanding of themselves
2. develop skill in using various sources of self-, educational, and occupational information
3. understand different educational options available in high school and beyond, the nature and purpose of these, and the types of postsecondary education or career options to which they lead
4. distinguish between career clusters in terms of the major occupations which make them up and in terms of such matters as (1) the amount and type of education needed for entrance, (2) the content, tools, settings, products, or services with which these occupations are associated, (3) the potential of such occupations to satisfy personal interests and values, (4) the potential of such occupations to provide the type of life style desired

5. consider life in an organization and the various roles played
6. identify ways of effectively managing work and leisure time
7. consider the behavioral implications of taking personal responsibility for what one wants to become
8. identify broad career areas and levels of educational aspiration which are personally appropriate
9. plan their high school program based on accurate information, tentative career goals, and accurate self-appraisal
10. formulate plans for implementing the decisions made (pp. 1–2).

You may also wish to review the CDC management tasks in Table 6.7.

Examples of Program Content

Career guidance programs or activities designed to incorporate many of the goals we have cited are now available in many middle and junior high schools. Both the substance and the format of these career guidance approaches vary widely. Some examples follow.

The concept of change — change in characteristics of the self and in environmental options — has been mentioned elsewhere in this book as a possible unifying thread in career development and decision-making. At the junior high school, such a theme can be related to the accelerating application of new technological discoveries to the occupational structure; it can reinforce the validity of preparing oneself to be versatile and yet firmly grounded in the fundamental processes that undergird all occupations. The concept can be related to work habits, mechanical principles, electrical principles, structural design and architectural evolution, chemical and biological principles, numerical operations and measurements, or verbal communication as this relates to different role relationships. Therefore, students can be increasingly encouraged to ask of occupational and educational areas, Do I like it? What does it take? Do I have what it takes? Such questions can be tested in various courses, as well as in the simulated or work experiences that will be discussed later in this chapter. Students can be encouraged to ask, Why am I taking chemistry or algebra or

English? and How can I use it? Teachers must be encouraged to respond to these questions as meaningful, with fairly specific answers. This is the sort of climate that supports career development and connects what students are being exposed to educationally with the occupational world. It can expand students' awareness of possibilities.

When teachers are asked to consider how the subject they teach is related to occupations or careers at different levels of education or in different interest categories, a basic difficulty often is that their formal backgrounds have not prepared them to respond to such questions. One important resource to offset this condition has been prepared by the Minnesota Department of Education. The Bureau of Pupil Personnel Services of this agency has developed a series of charts describing the relationship between subject-matter courses and selected careers. An example of these is available in Table 8.1, presenting information on careers related to social studies.

Obviously, this table does not exhaust all the possibilities, but it does represent a method of connecting what one studies with how it might be used. At any point in the educational process, discussions, role-playing, field trips, or other activities could be conducted to point up how social studies might be used in that particular occupation. One could relate social studies to a people-data-things conception of the occupational structure or to other emphases, always trying to extend student perceptions or possibilities and the ways of access to them.

In order to offset the limited experience of some teachers to get involved with work-related material in their subject matter, various school districts have taken different approaches to this circumstance. Some districts pay groups of teachers to work during the summer developing short units in the major subject areas on specific career topics. In this fashion, regular curriculum can continue but with a change in emphasis that accommodates more career-oriented content. For example, in a Utah school district, as a result of such a summer workshop, sample units were developed by teacher teams and then distributed to all teachers in that subject area within the school district for testing and refining in the school curriculum. One such unit was newspaper report-

ing as a career in ninth-grade English classes. Many other school districts have developed learning activity packages that can be integrated into various educational levels and subject matter. Coordinators of Career Education in State Departments of Education are prime resources to identify examples of these in each state.

Career Clusters. One method of helping students relate their characteristics to occupational alternatives through exploration as well as develop increasingly sophisticated skills important to a family of occupations is career clustering. Career clustering has been integrated into many school-based career education models or projects.

In junior high school, the objective of career clustering has been to expose students to the full range of occupational choices that will be available later and to the notion of the relationships among occupations comprising a particular career family, to knowledge of the relative advantages and the requirements of each, as well as to provision of entry skills appropriate to a broad family of related occupations (such as construction or health care).

Career education has strongly emphasized career awareness and career exploration prior to career preparation. It has further advocated that career preparation makes the student occupationally flexible. In this context, then, occupational or career clusters can be used to organize curriculum directed toward the preparation of students with skills, knowledge, and attitudes required for job entry into a family or cluster of occupations. This means that instructional teams can be developed to integrate mathematics, science, communications, and social studies around typical problems found in career clusters. Techniques such as flexible or modular scheduling, team teaching, independent study, and individualized instruction can be used to address differences in content or learning styles. Career clusters are also career guidance devices in that they provide students with awareness and exploratory opportunities across several clusters of occupations. As indicated in Chapter 3, there are fifteen career clusters developed by the USOE and used in most national career education models.

Each of the clusters has been divided into subclusters, which are further divided into discrete

Table 8.1
Selected Careers Related to Social Studies

Level	Service	Business, Clerical, and Sales	Science and Technology	General Cultural	Arts and Entertainment
B.A. or above	Social worker Psychologist FBI agent Counselor YMCA Secretary Clergy	Government official Industrial executive Market analyst Economist Buyer Arbitrator	Archaeologist Paleontologist Anthropologist	Judge Lawyer Philologist Editor News commentator Reporter Librarian	Museum curator Historian (Dramatic arts)
High School plus technical	Police sergeant Detective Sheriff Employment interviewer	Union official Bank teller Salesperson Wholesaler Retailer		Justice of the peace Radio announcer Law clerk	Tour conductor Travel bureau director Cartoonist
High School graduate	Police officer Religious worker Bus drivers	Floor walker Interviewer (poll) House canvassers and agents		Library assistant	Museum guide
Less than High School graduate	Train porter Taxi driver Bellhop Elevator operator Usher	Peddler Newspaper carrier		Library page Copy person	

occupational functions at increasing levels of specificity requiring varying types of education from unskilled levels to graduate or professional education. Some states have developed modifications on these fifteen clusters. Some cities have developed curriculum guides that can be used in exploratory or group guidance programs at grades 7 and 8. Many commercial materials and audio-visual products have also been developed to deal with one or more of the 15 clusters to stimulate student exploration and career awareness.

Winter and Schmidt (1974) reported on how they used a cluster approach to integrate career education into the eighth-grade language arts curriculum at Scott Carpenter Junior High School in Westminster, Colorado. In particular, they developed seven modules including: introduction to careers, self-awareness, decision-making, occupational clusters, economic awareness, investigating an occupational cluster, and planning for the future.

The first module caused students to define the word career, to identify typical career patterns for men and women, and to identify reasons for working. The filmstrip, "Why Work at All?" was shown to stimulate student discussion on reasons for working.

In the self-awareness module, students were expected to identify their strengths and weaknesses as related to their abilities and interests and to match these with at least two potential careers. The relationships between school subjects and possible jobs were also examined. Workbooks, personal checklists, interpretations of results of the Ohio Vocational Interest Survey, and the writing of personal character sketches were activities used to support this module.

The major content of the decision-making module was the curriculum on decision-making, entitled *Deciding*, developed by the College Entrance Examination Board in 1972.

The occupational clusters module was presented through the "Popeye" comic books published by King Features Syndicate, which use cartoon characters to present information about jobs in each cluster. Students also constructed people pyramids showing how people from different clusters work together to produce different products.

The economic awareness module focused on how economics affects each student's life. Such concepts as economic systems, supply and demand, inflation, depression, and elements of production were discussed.

A variety of approaches was used in the module on investigating an occupational cluster. The Widening Occupational Roles Kit (WORK), *Job Family* booklets, and *Job Experience* Kits (all from Science Research Associates) were used as major resources for students in identifying a specific preferred cluster or area within a cluster to study. In addition, students wrote to at least one firm that offered jobs in the preferred cluster asking for information about the job and the firm. Students also took field trips to pertinent sites and had resource speakers from different occupations come to class to discuss their jobs.

In the planning module, students compiled lists of skills they would need to meet the requirements of jobs in the occupational cluster most related to their interests and aptitudes. Students also planned a tentative high school program of studies that would provide the necessary skills. During this module, the relevance of flexibility and tentativeness in planning as well as employment trends and the rapidity of change were considered.

The model reported by Winter and Schmidt is an excellent application of clustering and related concerns now developed in the junior high school. The possibilities for expanding or modifying such modular approaches to serve career guidance objectives in a local school are restricted only by the initiative and ingenuity of the local staff.

Using Community Resources in Career Guidance. One approach to facilitating career development among junior high school students is to systematically involve the use of community resources. Pinson (1980) has made the helpful observation, "Community in the abstract can be simplified if one views it through a student's eyes as three sets of establishment adults: school staffs, parents, and employers (less clear to the students is a fourth set of adults . . .: organized labor)." Throughout Chapters 7, 8, 9, and 13 a variety of suggestions have been made about how school staff can facilitate the career development of students within subject matter areas. In Chapter 7, the role of parents in facilitating the career development of their children was discussed. Those observations about parents like those about the characteristics of school staff are relevant here as well.

In talking about using community resources in career guidance in this section, we will emphasize the resources of business and industry and organized labor as resources for junior high school students. In this respect, Pinson (1980) has extrapolated from various documents and statements recommendations from business and industry about how they can be useful in career guidance. Selected recommendations and priorities include:

1. Using the business and industry community to validate civic and social outcome measures as well as the work competency indices developed by schools as exit requirements.
2. Utilizing community work stations as frequently for observation and exploration by elementary and middle-school youth as for actual work experience at the secondary school level.
3. Involving business and industry in ways that further curriculum objectives in all subject areas: i.e., assisting students to conduct a job search in the yellow pages could indirectly increase their reading achievement levels (p. 138).

With respect to the contributions of organized labor to career guidance, Pinson recommends such ideas as:

1. Ongoing career development programs should more closely reflect the interests and needs of today's adult workers, as opposed to "the child as an adult."
2. Reconsider and revise the framework of work experience to take into account labor's views of economic realities: for example, more non-paid work experience during school tenure.
3. Encourage the infusion of labor studies as part of a comprehensive thrust at all school levels. Involve union representation at the curriculum design level.

Although many of these perspectives are equally valid for the senior high school, there are some specific programs oriented to the use of community resources in junior high school career guidance programs that are worthy of note. One of these follows.

In Concord, Massachusetts, students work with a team of teachers and counselors in a community

program (Ryan, 1972). The first part of the program is designed to alert students to the world of work. As part of that phase, students are asked to choose one of four concurrent courses that have been jointly developed by Rotary Club members from the community and the counselor/teacher team. Each course is given on a Friday morning for five weeks at an appropriate community site. Supervision at the site is provided by a teacher, a Rotary Club community course reader, and parent volunteers. The four courses offered are Health/Medicine, Manufacturing, Food and Its Processing, and Community Retailing. Throughout these courses, students maintain journals describing perceptions of adults observed in the occupation studied. In the sixth week of the program, students in the separate courses are brought together for the sharing of impressions, knowledge, and recommendations. During the next five weeks, students may choose from four additional courses: Knowing Your Town, Construction and Home Building, Food and Its Retailing, and Service Industries. Finally, for several Friday mornings, students are placed with adult workers who are in occupations preferred by individual students.

This approach has many virtues. One of them is its systematic integration of learning and observation. Another is its purposeful use of the community as a learning laboratory. Third, such a program brings adults into contact with the concerns and interests of young persons and provides a natural method for the two groups to interact. Fourth, perhaps less directly, the program helps students develop reasons for a sense of pride and accomplishment in their schoolwork, beyond that of academic achievement.

When considering community involvement in career guidance at the junior high school level, parents are frequently a neglected resource. Fletcher (1976) has suggested several possible ways parents can become integral parts of the career guidance program. They can volunteer to take students to work with them and they can have students work with them as interns if they own a business. They can drive students to field trips, serve as career center aides, or serve as resource speakers in classes on career guidance seminars. Retired grandparents can come into career guidance classes and show students how hobbies can be related to careers. Fletcher suggests further that it is useful to develop a resource file of parents' careers for various uses in career guidance. Such a file could classify these occupations by the U.S. Office of Education career clusters described in Chapter 3 and earlier in this chapter. Finally, Fletcher indicates that parents often feel left out of career planning, because they do not understand the relationship of classwork to future careers. Helping them through PTAs or other methods to understand these relationships is likely to stimulate their positive involvement in the career development of their own children and to provide a powerful resource bank to supplement the career guidance efforts of the counselor or teacher.

Career Guidance Strategies for Decision-Making and Problem-Solving

The examples just cited respond to elements of career development at a rather gross level and are basically similar to those activities recommended for the elementary school. To meet more specific goals, some differences in strategy or context are useful. Paolitto (1977) has maintained that the junior high school is a natural setting for group counseling as a major vehicle of personal learning for early adolescents. More specifically, Kinnick (1968) has compared the use of group discussions and group counseling to increase student ability in problem-solving and decision-making.

Kinnick has described group discussion as "the cooperative and constructive deliberation on a common problem by a group attempting to reach agreement on a solution to that problem" (p. 350). Typically, group discussion involves a group of eight to fifteen members, engaged in exchanging information, knowledge, and ideas for the following purposes: (1) to provide a means of helping students learn problem-solving skills, (2) to help particular students improve their ability to solve their particular problems, and (3) to help students learn to work with others toward a common goal. Group discussion could be stimulated by the use of case materials presenting different types of problems with which junior high school students can identify (such as choosing curricula, decision-making, choosing a college, how to study, job analyses); or by the use of film strips or films dealing with similar content, field trips, or resource

persons. Variations on the discussion method could be initiated through the use of role-playing, sociodrama, or plays focusing on particular content or problem areas.

Group counseling that focuses on problem-solving, according to Kinnick, does not depart markedly from group discussion. The emphasis of the latter is on problems, whereas the stress in group counseling is on the person's approach to problems, and thus involves more personal references, identity issues, and emotionality. One may assume, then, that more personal problems would be examined in group counseling than in most group discussions. In either of these groups, however, problem-solving as a creative process of evaluation, information collection and analysis, synthesis and planning, can be aided by means of (1) lifelike, group settings for making decisions and choices, (2) the influence of peers through group interaction and group norms, (3) the opportunity for free expression of opinions and emotions with less personal reference, and (4) the opportunity to give and receive support as a group member (Wright, 1959, p. 554).

Regehr and Herman (1981) undertook to teach the skills of career decision-making and self-assessment to ninth-grade students. Two of four classes were selected from ten ninth-grade classes in a large junior high school in Calgary, Canada, to serve as experimental and control groups for the study. The experimental program was conducted over three months in eleven 50-minute periods. Sessions 1–7 were directed at teaching self-assessment skills to the students. These skills were continually viewed in a "work" or career context. Sessions 8–11 dealt with teaching the skills of decision-making and examining them within a career framework. Following each session, students were instructed to keep a log of their reactions, thinking, and feeling about each of the sessions. Prepost testing was done exclusive of the sessions and included the Attitude and Competence Scales of the Career Maturity Inventory (CMI), the Internal-External Locus of Control Scale (I-E) and a questionnaire specifically designed for this program.

Surprisingly, a multivariate analysis found no significant difference in overall career maturity between the experimental and control groups. It appeared that since the control group was in a group guidance class that included a career unit, they may have been taught essentially the same skills as those taught more directly in the experimental program. Beyond this possibility, the researchers indicated that other explanations were differences in student readiness to explore career related information and the lack of familiarity they had with discussing personal values and beliefs about themselves, and that isolated programs intended to foster career development may not be able to compensate for what Wise, Charner, and Randour (1976) have described as the influences of career development. These influences include family, school, mass media, and community groups, which represent interactive components of comprehensive and systematic approaches as described elsewhere in this book.

Motsch (1980) studied the efficacy of peer social modeling in assisting girls with career exploration. She assigned 180 ninth-grade girls to one of four treatment conditions or to a control group. She assigned an additional thirty-six girls randomly selected from another high school to a second control group. A videotape of a female counselor and a female high school student discussing different career information-seeking behaviors presented the modeled behaviors. The four treatment conditions included: (1) videotape only, (2) videotape plus reinforcement, (3) videotape plus reinforcement plus stimulus materials, and (4) stimulus materials plus reinforcement, (5) Control Group I, and (6) Control Group II. The findings were,

> Peer social modeling is related to increasing both the variety and frequency of information-seeking behaviors; more specifically, that a counseling group using modeling, positive reinforcement, and overt practice of the modeled behaviors with stimulus materials is more likely than the other treatment conditions investigated to provide an increase in the variety and frequency of information seeking behaviors among ninth grade girls (pp. 238–239).

Even more directly focused on the fostering of decision-making skills is the work of Krumboltz and his students. Ryan and Krumboltz (1964) found that systematically reinforcing decision and deliberation statements of students in counseling did increase the rate of deliberation and decision statements significantly and that this reinforced behavior generalized to noncounseling settings.

Yabroff (1969) has demonstrated the importance of specific information if the counselor wishes to increase the realism of choices of ninth-grade students. He used experience tables (probability tables based on what has happened to students having different levels of achievement, and so on, when such students entered colleges, employment, or high school courses) to reinforce the importance of obtaining (1) specific facts about the choice, (2) a knowledge of alternatives, and (3) some estimate of the possible consequences. Yabroff found that his sample of ninth-grade students selected high school courses and made post high school plans more commensurate with their abilities than did students who did not receive such information.

Much of the work in social modeling and imitative learning as stimuli to information-seeking or decision-making has been designed for use with senior high school students. Many of these techniques will be described in Chapter 9. Chapter 14 will contain a more complete analysis of decision-making and the career guidance intervention strategies designed to influence it.

Simulation as a Career Guidance Strategy. In discussing simulation, This (1970) has stated:

> Desirable as it may be, it is not always possible to bring reality into the classroom or into the training situation. When this is not possible, we try to replicate in the learning experience the nearest thing we can to the phenomenon of the real world. It does not matter whether we are talking about a piece of equipment or an emotional experience. We call this simulation (p. 20).

The following elements are generally considered to be necessary for an effective simulation program:

1. a supportive climate
2. exposure of the individual's normal behavior
3. feedback
4. experimentation
5. a cognitive map
6. practice
7. planning application

In a sense, most of the work reported in the previous section has used some form of simulation of reality to stimulate exploratory behavior in students. In each instance, some form of technology, such as films, modeling, audiotapes, has been used. Until recently, educational technology has been more concerned with how to communicate than what to communicate. It has, however, clear and powerful potential for simulating real-life experiences as an aid to career development, decision-making processes, contingencies, and outcomes. It can also serve as a medium for information retrieval accessed on the basis of student characteristics.

Johnson and Myrick (1972) have described the use of a simulation technique for middle school students called MOLD (Making Of Life Decisions). In this simulation each student follows six basic steps:

1. Completes a personal profile sheet describing abilities and interests.
2. Becomes involved with small group procedures that assist him or her in self-appraisal.
3. Explores career fields and makes a tentative career choice based on his or her abilities and interests.
4. Plans on paper the next year of his or her life, making decisions about his or her education, job, home life, and leisure activities. The student chooses from alternatives actually available in the community, not fictional or hypothetical possibilities.
5. Receives feedback on his or her decisions, such as grades earned in each course and whether or not he or she got a job applied for. This feedback is derived from probability tables which take into account such variables as ability, study time, and chance.
6. Uses the results and plans the following year. In this way, contingency plans and consequences of immediate decisions can be accounted for.

This simulation was used with a filmstrip on career and educational planning, a review of materials in the guidance center, and small-group discussion of reasons for personal choices, where personal strengths were identified and reinforced.

Information Retrieval

In recent years, several projects have attempted to tie together exploration, simulation, and information retrieval with computer technology. Such computer-based systems will be discussed in Chapter 16. Here we will look at three approaches in the middle/junior high school. In a larger sense, the examples cited throughout the chapters on the elementary school, the junior high school, and the senior high school are ways of delivering information, of responding to the characteristics of the consumers, and of giving students a context in which they can project themselves into the information and reality-test its personal meaning.

Harris and Wallin (1978) studied whether occupational information does influence the career choices of seventh-grade students. The sample for the study included 133 (63 girls, 70 boys) seventh-grade students who were randomly assigned to three groups varying in the amount of information about occupations provided to the students. The results of the study supported the "idea that the career horizons of [seventh grade] boys and girls can be expanded by helping them to become more aware of occupational requirements, duties, conditions of work, and opportunities" (p. 53). Group C, the group that received the most comprehensive information about job descriptions, training needed, and potential earnings, was found to consider a wider range of career alternatives than did the other two groups.

Betz, Engle, and Mallison (1969) took a random sample of 350 non-college bound high school graduates from four north central states and studied their perceptions of the education and guidance they had experienced. A significant conclusion was that the youth interviewed could not articulate a meaningful concept of self. These youth, contrary to some other data, did not perceive parents as being especially helpful in resolving personal, educational, or vocational problems and concerns, and there were no other significant adults to help them because counselors were perceived as not available, too busy, too involved with college-bound students, or simply unknown to this group. Finally, these ex-students agreed that a dichotomy in information available, encouragement, and help with vocational-identity questions favoring the college-bound over the non–college bound exists in the schools from which they came.

These findings and others (Otte & Sharpe, 1979) affirm that the ingredients of career development discussed throughout this book are important to all students, not just a certain stratum of them. They also reemphasize that although information availability and help with sorting out one's self-implications are not the whole of vocationalization or career development, they are an important component of it. Finally, by implication, it is clear that the provision of information cannot be delayed until students are at the point of leaving school but useful, meaningful data must be continuously accessible throughout the course of education.

CAREER GUIDANCE STRATEGIES AND WORK

For many students, work is the best try-out experience. For some, organized work-study programs are ways of shortening the period of economic and psychological dependence under which so many youth chafe. If such work experience is also to facilitate career development, it should be more than casual, unsystematic ventures into whatever chance opportunity presents itself. The behavioral goals cited in Chapter 6 are pertinent here also. They represent motivational as well as diagnostic possibilities to which work can be related. However, if such goals are to be realized, education and the business-industry complex must come together in mutually creative exchanges in order to provide such opportunities systematically. One requirement would be that schools accept responsibility for helping youngsters find part-time or summer jobs in which they can use what they have learned. Equally important, guidance and counseling activities must be directed to helping students examine the work they are doing as they are doing it, if it is to help the vocationalization of these students.

One attempt in the junior high school to use work as a way of accomplishing some of the goals cited here is the Forsyth Program conducted in Forsyth County, Georgia. This is an effort to re-

construct, at grades 7–9, the total educational environment so as to make it meaningful to socio-economically disadvantaged students who are indifferent to existing curricula or to work. The concrete elements of a particular vocational program such as industrial arts, home economics, or agriculture are used as the core of the basic academic curriculum (math, science, and communication skills). Students are placed in work stations within the school or outside the school, and their experiences are used as the basis for group counseling sessions. The group counseling sessions are conducted by an educational and work-experience coordinator (a person with both counseling and vocational education background). This person also places and supervises students in their work stations and coordinates the activities of those teachers assigned to work with students in the project (Bottoms & Matheny, 1969; Royston, 1970).

It is obvious that paid work has limited possibilities for fostering behavioral modification or career development in the junior high school in many parts of the nation because of federal, state, or local restrictions on age, the amount of time a student can commit to work, and the type of work he or she can do. There are, however, junior high school students to whom none of these restrictions apply. There are others for whom opportunities could be made available if job needs were communicated to educators or counselors by such community agents as the Chamber of Commerce, industrial personnel people, representatives of the National Alliance of Business, or the United States Employment Service.

OTHER CAREER GUIDANCE ACTIVITIES AND TECHNIQUES IN THE JUNIOR HIGH SCHOOL

As is obvious, career guidance in the junior high school can be accomplished in many ways and related to many objectives. Teachers can achieve some career guidance objectives by making their subject matter more career oriented. Teachers and counselors can collaborate in some program efforts. Counselors can achieve many career guidance objectives alone. Activities that take students into the community for exploratory purposes can be helpful. In addition to the approaches to career guidance that have already been described here, the following list of other possible activities or techniques that have been tried in career education or career guidance settings across the nation might suggest ways to meet needs:

Curriculum Infusion

- Using census data, have students compare and contrast the composition of the United States labor market in 1940 and currently. Have them consider the percentages of workers employed in such areas as blue-collar versus white-collar families, or goods-producing versus service-producing industries. Discuss why shifts have occurred in these percentages.
- Divide class into small groups and have them compete in naming the most occupations in goods- or service-producing occupations.
- Given a unit in consumer economics or similar topic, have students define in a two-page paper what job rewards mean to them. Consider such areas as fringe benefits, salary, vacations, shift work, life style, supervision, independent action.
- Given a list of activities (hobbies, sports, pets, clubs, and so on), have the student differentiate between those which require interpersonal skills and those which do not.
- After reading a biography of a famous person, have students identify risks the person took in implementing a career goal. Discuss.
- Have students write a theme describing a decision they made in the past that involved compromise.
- Teach students good study habits and relate these to good work habits.
- Develop "student days" in which students follow school and community officials in their daily job tasks. Have students report back to the class on what they learned about the various occupations and their responsibilities.
- Present students with a description of a hypothetical individual whose job was done away with through technological change. Have students work in groups to decide what that person might do to capitalize on existing skills and knowledge.
- Following group discussion on the effects of technology on the world of work have students

identify at least six occupations that existed twenty years ago and have now been combined with other occupations or have ceased to exist.
- Develop bulletin board displays illustrating the variety of tools and materials used by various occupations relating to subject areas taught in school.
- Plan a film series illustrating various career clusters. This could be available for viewing during lunch periods, study halls, and so on.
- Given a situation of poor interpersonal relations between a subordinate and a supervisor, have the students role-play three ways to improve those relations.
- Following a class discussion on the effects of technology on our society, have students name two areas (such as marine science, space exploration, ecology) that are most likely to create new occupations within the next ten years.
- Display posters in each subject matter area illustrating the contributions of workers in related occupations.
- Have students prepare bulletin board displays depicting marketable skills relating to subject area.
- Have students look through job ads in local newspapers to identify as many marketable skills as possible. Have them relate identified skills to specific subject areas taught in school.
- Given a preferred occupation, have the student demonstrate in a role-playing situation examples of communication skills necessary for successful performance of the occupation.
- Examine current events in the news media with regard to present career, economic, social, political climate and changes that will confront students when they plan for and enter the work world.
- Set up career cluster explorations in industrial arts classes which give pertinent hands-on experience in each cluster.
- Organize extracurricular career interest groups.
- Develop bulletin board displays illustrating the educational pathways to various careers (that is, four-year college, graduate, and professional schools, two-year college, trade school, on-the-job training, apprenticeship programs, and so on).
- Select a consumer product and trace it back to its original raw material, showing the interde-

pendency of various occupations necessary to produce the product.

Decision-Making and Acquisition of Career Information

- Tape record a simulated interview between a counselor and a student engaged in the decision-making process or some aspect of it. Have students listen to the tape and discuss their view of what went on.
- Use a variety of simulated decision-making games and compare the steps they portray (such as Life Career Game, Consumer, Economic System).
- Given a decision of curriculum that students will confront in the future, have them list the alternatives, advantages, and disadvantages of each, make a tentative decision. Consider the consequences likely to occur in terms of future educational and occupational possibilities.
- Have students list major decisions regarding their future which they must make:

  1. within two years (such as high school course selection)
  2. within five years (such as trade school, college, occupation)
  3. within ten years (such as where to live, work, marriage)

Have them consider at least three alternatives in each decision that will be available and discuss the implications of each.

- For a hypothetical situation in which an individual clearly made an inappropriate occupational selection, have students identify reasons why the occupation was inappropriate for the person in question.
- Using a tentative identification of a preferred occupation, have the student list chronologically the steps that need to be taken to prepare to enter the occupation.
- For the 15 USOE career clusters, have students give at least two reasons why they would or would not consider occupations within each cluster.
- For a preferred career cluster, have students select four occupations within that cluster and gather information about them. Have them state the criteria by which they chose the four and on which they might rank them.

- Through individual or group counseling, have students develop a set of personal criteria for use in exploring occupations.
- Using a list of ten qualities desired by individuals in fellow workers, have the students discuss at least one way in which each quality could improve individual chances for advancement in a selected career.
- Using a list of twenty common occupations, have students classify each in terms of its relationship to data, people, and things using the categories "highly related, related, not related."
- Have the students list examples of talents or other contributions he or she might make to a hypothetical talent show.
- Create a series of posters or displays illustrating women doing a variety of occupations previously thought of as masculine roles and men in such occupations as nursing, secretarial work, and so on.
- Use a "Problem Bucket" to which students anonymously contribute problems facing them. Discuss problems in small groups and explore possible solutions.
- Conduct job clinics relating to those jobs open to junior high school students, such as babysitting, lawn work, newspaper delivery, and so on.
- Play "match-up" games in which students are expected to choose the correct types of educational requirement for various occupations.
- Have the student develop a tentative outline of the course of study he or she plans to pursue in high school including program choice, required courses, and electives.
- Have students list ten occupations in which socialization skills and interpersonal relationships are crucial (such as salesperson, teacher) and ten occupations in which these skills are less important (such as research scientist, chemist, veterinarian).
- Invite business personnel into the school to conduct mock job interviews with students and discuss the results with them.
- Using a list of six occupations commonly stereotyped as to sex roles, have the student look up each occupation in available resource materials and be able to give specific reasons why such stereotyping is wrong.
- Have students role-play a decision situation involving the need for compromise.

- Make posters illustrating various phases of the decision-making process.
- Have students solve a scrambled letters puzzle based on decision-making terminology.
- Have students identify the entry-level skills for five occupations within an occupational cluster of their choice. (Make use of career information, field trips, talks with workers in the field, and so on.) Have the student identify those skills he or she feels could now be performed and those in which additional training needs to be acquired.

Community Involvement

- After listening to resource speaker on a career of his or her choice, have students list at least four new ideas concerning that career area which each had not previously considered.
- Have students tape record an interview with a worker whose job has come into existence in the past ten years as a result of scientific technology. Discuss the implications for planning that the interviews suggest.
- After a field trip to a setting representative of a particular occupational cluster, have the student list tools or materials he or she observed workers using.
- After having interviewed a person who works in the student's general field of interest (career or career cluster), have the student describe in a

group discussion how this person's occupation is an integral part of his or her total life style.
- Develop a directory of entry-level jobs in the community including job descriptions, requirements, contact persons, and procedure for applying.
- Have students engage in volunteer community service work in hospitals, nursing homes, orphanages, and so on. Discuss their experiences in helping others in class and explore the potential occupations related to them.
- Invite local employment service counselors to talk with students about jobs available in the community.
- Develop a Youth Employment Service to bring students seeking part-time work together with employers having short-term or odd jobs.
- Develop performance contacts with students relative to community projects that would help them acquire career awareness.
- Given an opportunity to observe an experienced individual and a trainee in a specific career cluster, have the student compare at least five different levels of capability between the two individuals as they perform their work roles.
- Design a Human Resource Book that lists members of the community who are willing to share their knowledge and expertise with students. Identify these persons by address, phone number, occupational title and area of expertise.

Summary

In this chapter we have examined the implication for career guidance of youth occupied primarily by exploration, planning, and identity formation. We have noted the effects on the development of career guidance programs that are associated with gender, differences in maturity, and early school leaving. Themes and practices recommended in Chapter 7 for use at the elementary school level have been longitudinally extended and reshaped to make them appropriate for the middle/junior high school. Examples of program content, activities, and techniques appropriate to youth are described and, where possible, relevant research findings are presented.

LEARNING ACTIVITIES

1. Discuss with vocational education teachers, Bureau of Employment Security personnel, or union officers the opportunities for either full- or part-time work available to junior high school students (ages 13, 14, 15, 16) and what regulations govern such activity.
2. Compose a behavioral profile of a typical junior high school boy and girl as you have experienced them. Compare your composition with the description in this chapter.

3. Construct a graph in which you depict each of the steps of the decision-making process and describe what counselor activities might facilitate such steps.
4. Discuss with a close colleague your feelings about whether girls should have different or earlier career guidance than boys. Consider the basis for your feelings about this matter.
5. Compile a taxonomy of objectives for career guidance in the junior high school following the stages suggested in Chapter 6.
6. Secure from your state's Department of Education information about the content of each of the career clusters being used by each agency.
7. Explain the meaning of career exploration. Define what elements or tasks compose it. Refer to Chapters 4 and 5 for examples of content appropriate to junior high school students.
8. Develop a written rationale for the systematic teaching of decision-making skills to junior high school students.
9. Identify at least ten career guidance techniques you wish to learn or already are competent to use. State for each one the behavioral objectives for students it might facilitate.
10. Construct an outline of self- or career-related questions junior high school students might wish to have answered and list suggested alternative sources of information related to these questions.

OBJECTIVES

After reading this chapter, engaging in the learning activities, and reading the references suggested, you should have met the objectives that follow. If you have not, it would probably be useful for you to review the material on career guidance and the junior high school before proceeding further.

1. Describe at least five typical behavioral characteristics of junior high school students.
2. Discuss three reasons for providing planned career guidance activities in the junior high school.
3. Identify at least four factors that should be taken into account in planning career guidance efforts in the junior high school.
4. List in your own words five or more appropriate goals for career guidance efforts in the junior high school.
5. Name three or more counselor actions that would facilitate decision-making in junior high school students.
6. Describe at least one example of a career guidance program that has been infused into curriculum in a junior high school.
7. Identify two ways of getting teachers involved in career guidance activties in the junior high school.
8. Name at least ten career guidance techniques that could be implemented in the junior high school, either by the counselor alone or with the help of teachers.

9 | Career Guidance in the Senior High School

The major factor with which senior high school students must deal is the imminence of reality as defined by the rapidly approaching separation from senior high school and their passage into the independence of young adulthood. Like other factors in decision-making and intermediate choices, reality — defined as how the alternatives of postsecondary school life are considered by the individual — will have different implications for each individual.

Postsecondary school reality for different students might be cast in any one of the following forms:

1. Choosing a postsecondary vocational or technical school to pursue some skilled specialty.
2. Gaining access to a college and selecting a major field of study with its myriad implications for later vocational endeavors.
3. Converting part-time work experience while in school into a full-time position in the labor market.
4. Entering the labor market for the first time.
5. Deliberating about military service, marriage, combining work and continuing education.
6. Acquiring an apprenticeship opportunity.

However, there will also be many students for whom none of these possibilities seems viable or appealing; for them, the future and its reality represent threat or trauma. Some of these students see the future beyond high school as a confrontation with their indecisiveness about life and their place in it. Others will find the burden of decision-making untenable and will try to escape or postpone facing such an awareness directly (Hayes, 1981).

CAREER MATURITY AMONG SENIOR HIGH SCHOOL STUDENTS

Although little is known specifically about when adolescents state their occupational choices or the numbers of them who are essentially decided about such commitments, some rough estimates are available. Crites (1969) reviewed several pertinent studies and concluded that about 30 percent of students are undecided during the high school and college years. This is somewhat more than Fottler and Bain's recent finding (1980a) of 18 percent undecided among a sample of high school seniors in Alabama and less than Marr's longitudinal study (1956), which reported that 50 percent of the subjects did not make a choice until about age 21. Hollender's research (1974) has shown that decisiveness among senior high school students varies with the intellectual characteristics of students. Among male students, there are significant increases in decidedness from the lowest intellectual quartile to the highest. Females showed a similar trend, although the percentage decided dropped in the top intellectual quartile perhaps because of the conflicts bright girls continue to experience between nurturant roles and further educational achievement. Whichever of the numbers or trends regarding decisiveness in the senior high school population one accepts, it is clear that career development needs among senior high school students are wide-ranging.

Differences in Career Aspirations

Such data tend to confirm that within the subpopulations comprising senior high school students there are substantial differences in career development and maturity needs for career guidance. Many factors produce these differences (for example, levels of parental support, gender and racial background, self-concept, health and physical development). Dillard and Campbell (1981) compared the influence of 304 Puerto Rican (154), black (154), and Anglo (99) parents on the career behavior of their 194 adolescent children in grades 9 to 12. Represented were both intact and nonintact families with middle and lower socioeconomic characteristics. They found that these parents differentially affected their children's career development. For example, it was found that parental career *values* did not have much influence on their children's career aspirations in any of the three groups. However, the parental career *aspirations* for their children were significantly related to the child's career aspirations in both black and Puerto Rican families but not in the Anglo families. Mothers in the black group seemed to contribute more strongly to their children's career development than did fathers of the same ethnic membership. In general, Anglo parents' career values or aspirations are much weaker predictors of children's career development than are those of black or Puerto Rican parents.

Plata (1981) compared the occupational aspirations of forty normal and forty emotionally disturbed male adolescents randomly selected from a midwestern public school (twenty from a general studies program and twenty from vocational education) and from a special education program administered in a state institution for the mentally ill in which the students were residents (20) or part of an outpatient population (20). He found, using the Occupational Aspiration Scale, that the level of occupational aspiration for regular normals (students in general secondary school studies) was significantly higher than for either of the emotionally disturbed groups. The latter scores reflected that emotionally disabled adolescents do maintain their aspirations "at a low level or that their level of occupational aspiration vacillates" (p. 134). This finding is in keeping with a series of earlier research studies. However, in addition, it was found that the level of occupational aspirations of normal, vocational students did not differ significantly from either of the emotionally disturbed groups but was significantly lower than the normal students enrolled in general, academic secondary school studies. Thus, we find again that there are subgroups of secondary school students who differ on their occupational aspirations. Although emotional disturbance apparently depresses such aspirations it does not explain the fact that the normal, vocational students in the sample also had low occupational aspirations.

Pound (1978) studied the self-concept of some 500 male and 500 female students randomly sampled from six high schools in western New York in attempting to predict career maturity for race and sex subgroups. Using the attitude scale of the Vocational Development Inventory (now CMI) and the Tennessee Self-Concept Scale(s) as predictors he found that the self-concept does appear to have a different effect on career maturity depending on the race and sex of the participants. He further indicated,

> When male students evaluate self concept, they are heavily influenced by external sources.... For white females, the findings suggest that internal resources play a major role in developing an evaluative statement of self-concept. Finally, the results would indicate that for Black females, statements related to positive or negative feelings toward self are developed from multidimensional sources favoring neither internal nor external frames of reference (p. 67).

He further contends that when predicting career maturity, different predictors are important for different racial and gender groups and, similarly, different influences affect "the frame of references chosen by students in evaluating their self concept."

In a study somewhat related to that of Pound, Karayanni (1981) compared the career maturity of emotionally maladjusted and emotionally well adjusted high school students in two medium-sized schools in north central Florida. Eighty-nine students were classified as emotionally maladjusted from their scores on the Minnesota Counseling Inventory (MCI) and 92 were classified as well-adjusted using the same procedure. Using the Attitude Scale of the Career Maturity Inventory as the dependent variable, Karayanni found significant differences in career attitude maturity between well-adjusted and maladjusted students. The well-adjusted students had a significantly higher score on the CMI-Attitude Scale than did the emotionally maladjusted students. He interpreted this to mean that any disturbance in personality will affect an individual's vocational development. Although he did not find sex differences in career attitude maturity scores, when they were pooled without regard to level of adjustment he did find significantly higher scores for white students than for black students.

Perrone, Male, and Karshner (1979) have studied the career development concerns of talented students. Their findings include the following:

1. The talented are often told, "You can be anything you want," which somewhat negates and denies what and who they already are, placing them on a treadmill of continually becoming something beyond their immediate selves. This anything-is-possible attitude often makes it difficult for talented students to acknowledge their weaknesses and any evidence of personal limitation is ignored or rejected.
2. Talented persons may receive a great deal of reinforcement from others for their endeavors, making it difficult to sort out what they value from what others value for them. In attempting to set priorities they often adopt the value systems of powerful or influential models, which may make it hard to measure up.
3. Talented persons sometimes have a tendency to commit themselves to career choices prematurely, based on subject-matter fields in which they achieve considerable recognition and success (p. 18).

Fottler and Bain (1980b) studied the occupational aspirations of 2112 seniors from fourteen high schools in Alabama. The sample was described as 54.3 percent females, 26.4 percent nonwhites, 50.8 percent enrolled in a college preparatory program, average age 17.4 years. A comparison of the career aspirations of males and females indicated that approximately twice as many males (5.6 percent) as females (2.8 per-

cent) aspired to a managerial position. Beyond this finding, however, the data do not suggest that females' aspirations are lower than males'. Indeed, females tended to aspire to professional and technical occupations slightly more than the males, while aspiring to managerial occupations less. At lower levels of occupational aspirations, traditional patterns emerged: females aspire to clerical and service positions, and males aspire to be craftsmen, operatives, or laborers. Professional and sales were the only two occupational groupings for which there were not statistically significant differences in the proportion of male and female aspirations. At least two concepts are evident in these data. First, compared to earlier studies the "motivation to manage" among students of all ages is low and declining. Second, there apparently are deep-rooted attitudes that continue to direct both sexes toward traditional occupational roles.

Garrison (1979) also studied gender differences in career aspirations of high school seniors. He compared three statewide surveys of twelfth-grade students (1970, 1973, and 1976) in public high schools in Virginia. The number of students in each survey was 57,195, 58,558, and 62,181 in 1970, 1973, and 1976 respectively. He found that the career choices of high school males and females are becoming more similar, particularly in regard to high status professional occupations. His data suggest that male aspirations for these jobs are declining while female aspirations are rising dramatically, lessening gender differences in choice. He also found a declining percentage of females choosing clerical-sales jobs and middle-states professions. In sum, he sees the potential for a reduction in sex segregation growing as men's and women's orientations to the labor force become more similar.

Dunne, Elliott, and Carlsen (1981) found somewhat similar results to those of Fottler and Bain. They studied the occupational aspirations of 1900 tenth, eleventh and twelfth graders in twenty-six rural high schools in five regions of the United States. They found that the females had both higher educational and occupational aspirations (when measured by the Duncan SEI Scale) than did males. In addition, they found that although the young rural women tended to aspire to female-stereotyped jobs, they did not restrict themselves to as narrow a range of choice as has been found in many other studies. However, beyond the female-stereotyped occupations, females tended to consider neutrally perceived occupations (such as artist, draftsperson), not jobs stereotyped for the opposite sex (such as logger, plumber, construction worker). Females in this sample did not seem to consider home-making to be a career to which they aspired.

Aspirations by high school students toward particular types of occupations has been studied by Heilman (1979). She found that projections of more balanced sex ratios (30 to 50 percent) encouraged greater occupational interest among women, but a totally balanced sex ratio (50/50) tended to reduce their occupational interest. Heilman suggests that, for males, changes in sex composition appear to alter the perception of social rewards to be derived from a career, whereas for females they alter the perceived likelihood of success. In addition, the data suggested that gradual increments in the number of women in nontraditional occupations, for example up to 30 percent, did not cause major changes in men's interests or images of the field while increasing women's likelihood of viewing these occupations as realistic possibilities. Macke and Morgan (1978) studied the work orientation of some 1067 high school senior girls, both black and white, in Louisville, Kentucky. It was found that such work orientations were related to mothers' work *behavior* rather than to work values or proscriptions against maternal employment. It was also found that with equal commitment to families, black girls were 20 percent more likely to expect to work after having children than were white because of economic circumstances.

Differences in Career Development

Another view of the differences in career development among senior high school students comes from the National Assessment of Educational Progress Project on Career and Occupational Development referred to in the previous two chapters. About 37,500 seventeen-year-old boys and girls from across the nation were included in the sample. Selected findings follow (Mitchell, 1977).

- Most seventeen-year-olds have talked seriously to someone about their future plans. Their plans are discussed with parents twice as often as with counselors, advisors, or peers. Only about two-thirds felt that the person(s) they talked to was aware of their abilities.
- Males tend to have more confidence in their ability to do things well than females.
- When asked to match occupations with required physical characteristics or learned skills, most seventeen-year-olds are able to match at least five of nine correctly but less than 10 percent could match all correctly. Blacks and persons from low socioeconomic backgrounds in cities were significantly lower than other groups in their ability to make such occupational matches.
- Prestige and status are cited more than twice as often as challenge and responsibility, personal satisfaction, opportunity and advancement as reasons for accepting a promotion to a supervisory job.
- Only 2.2 percent of the respondents saw school or academic areas as activities that might be useful for a job. Students are not able to draw linkages between formal or informal academic learning and performance on a job.
- The principal resource named for finding out the requirements of a job is observation of the job field. Reading about it and contacting a personnel office are also frequent responses. Only about one-quarter of the respondents see the counselor among their top five sources of job requirement information. The responses to the questionnaire item indicate that students are not sufficiently aware of sources of job information or how to access these sources.
- Nearly all seventeen-year-olds have thought about the kind of job they would like to have in the future. More than two-thirds have considered professional jobs, with more males than females aspiring to be professionals.
- Females see themselves as clerical workers in service occupations, and as homemakers and housewives. Males see themselves as craftspersons, farmers and farm managers, laborers, managers or administrators, proprietors and owners, in the military and in protective services. Thus, the data indicate that seventeen-year-old males and females choose sex-stereotyped jobs.

- Most have worked at a part-time or summer job; economic independence is the main reason for doing so. Females more than males name part-time clerical, sales, and service jobs, whereas more males name craftsperson, farm laborer, laborer, and operative.

As career guidance activities are implemented, students in the senior high school are likely to be found more rigid in their educational and occupational values and preferences than are their younger contemporaries. Thompson (1966) has reported that ninth- and tenth-graders' views of their vocational choices may be well established when they enter high school and may not change readily. Astin (1967), too, has shown that on the basis of Project Talent data derived from a sample of 650 male high school seniors, the students' measured interests and expressed career choices at the ninth-grade level were the best predictors of career outcomes at the twelfth-grade level.

Work Values

Of particular importance in understanding senior high school students is the status of their work values. Perrone's seven-year longitudinal study (1973) of 170 students in a suburban Wisconsin village found that students beginning in the junior high school and continuing into grades 11 and 12 expressed rather constant value levels of three types: security, affiliation, and independence. More specifically, boys valued a good income more than girls did. Girls valued helping others, working with people, and having time for one's family more than did boys. Senior boys valuing independence had higher IQ scores than did those valuing security and affiliation. Senior girls valuing independence and affiliation had higher IQ scores than did those valuing security. Boys and girls valuing security had lower grade point averages than did those valuing independence and affiliation. As seniors, boys had higher occupational aspirations than did girls — the first time this difference occurred in this sample from the junior high school forward.

In a study of work values of 116 fifth-, eighth-, and eleventh-grade students in a small Appalachian school system, Hales and Fenner (1972) found that the development of work values was well underway for most children by grade 5 and continued with remarkable similarity through grade 11. As compared with the fifth and eighth graders in this sample, eleventh graders valued altruistic jobs and work that permits self-realization more highly than did the fifth or eighth graders. This finding did not suggest a value shift as much as an apparent response by eleventh graders to the immediacy of choice and an apparent determination to embark on such choice from a position of one's own strengths. Reflecting the farming, small retail, and semiskilled trades characteristic of this geographic region, students generally gave priority to work that is steady and dependable, pays well, permits the use of personal skills and interests, and benefits other people. However, the deviation of scores on the scales measuring such values suggests that there were many variations in the student values profiles, even though this group of students was quite homogeneous in socioeconomic characteristics and other characteristics.

With respect to the consistency or inconsistency of work values among students from the junior high school through the senior high school, other research indicates that they are affected by several factors that have implications for working with any student. For example, sex differences in work values have been reported in the studies cited here and in others (see Olive, 1973; Wijting, Arnold, & Conrad, 1977). The social positions of parents and racial differences are also related to students' work values (Ermalinski & Ruscelli, 1971; Thomas, 1974).

Relationships Among Curricula, Work Values, and Career Maturity

The longitudinal study of Kapes and Strickler (1975) suggests somewhat less consistency in work values from ninth to twelfth grades than do the other two studies reported. However, particularly significant is their finding that different high school curricula appear to cause different changes in work values. For example, home economics students tend not to change their work values from ninth to twelfth grade, whereas college preparatory students change their work values much more during the same period. Thus, some curricula tend to reinforce a set of work values whereas others tend to challenge such values. This research further clarifies the status of work values in the senior high school. Rather than having totally different shifts in work values, students are more likely to have work values changing in intensity, with strong values growing stronger and weak values growing weaker.

Herr and Enderlein (1976) found a similar relationship between high school curricula and career maturity, as did Kapes and Strickler (1975) with work values. Their research indicated that students in the academic program were more career mature in ninth grade than students in vocational education, general, or business education. Although academic students were still the most career mature at twelfth grade, students in business education had almost equaled them. Students in the other two curricula remained significantly less career mature than either the academic or business education students. Apparently, curricular content interacts with student characteristics differently in stimulating both work values and career maturity.

In a subsequent longitudinal study of 1007 of Herr and Enderlein's students, Herr, Weitz, Good, and McCloskey (1981) examined the relationship of high school curriculum and personal characteristics while in high school to postsecondary educational and occupational patterns when these persons were 24 to 27. Young adults from an academic curriculum background were found to be significantly more career mature in their career-related exploratory behavior at ages 24–27, using the adult form of the Career Development Inventory as the criterion measure, than persons from vocational curricula. Apparently postsecondary school educational or occupational experiences do not equalize the gap in career maturity observed between academic and vocational students during the secondary school. Indeed, these data continue to suggest that persons who have completed a vocational education curriculum in high school enter career establishment with significantly fewer and less complete developmental exploratory experiences than do persons from academic curricula. These findings are undoubtedly confounded somewhat by differences in ability and socioeconomic background found among persons who enter the academic or the vocational curriculums in secondary schools.

Nevertheless, career development knowledge and experiences for students in the secondary school apparently differ in major ways, and the resulting differences in career maturity persist into young adulthood.

What this longitudinal study did not find, as compared with the earlier study of Herr and Enderlein (1976) were sex differences in career maturity. They earlier found that female students were significantly more career mature regardless of curriculum in high school than boys. However, as measured by their concern about and completion of career development tasks, Herr, Weitz, Good, and McCloskey (1981) found no sex differences in career maturity by ages 24–27. Thus, it appears that following high school, women do not capitalize on the advantage in career attitude maturity either because of experiences of homemaking and child-rearing or institutional discrimination. An alternate hypothesis (Pedro, 1982) developed in a study of high school females in a nonurban high school in the Midwest is that one needs to understand whether females plan to achieve directly or vicariously in career and job areas in order to understand the extent of involvement for planning in these areas. Thus, gender-specific and general career maturity variables need to be considered in understanding the career development of female high school students and their subsequent career behavior.

In attempting to identify specific predictors of postsecondary educational and occupational behavior, Herr et al. (1981) found that in addition to sex and curriculum, the best predictors of postsecondary educational level completed were high school GPA and father's occupation. Of present occupational status, in addition to sex and curriculum completed, the top three predictors were satisfaction with current occupational plans and progress toward them, high school GPA, and career maturity in high school as measured by the Attitude Scale of the Vocational Development Inventory (now the CMI). Of current salary, the top three predictors, in addition to sex and curriculum, were satisfaction with current occupational plans and progress toward them, career maturity or high school as measured by the Attitude Scale score of the Vocational Development Inventory, and certainty of occupational plans.

Jordaan and Heyde (1979) have completed a somewhat more comprehensive longitudinal analysis of the vocational maturity of high school boys. This study traces the vocational development of a group of boys from approximately age 15–18, or grades 9–12. Some of their findings (pp. 184–186) follow. Few twelfth graders and still fewer ninth graders had decided on an occupation or a specialty within an occupation. Vocational preferences from the ninth to the twelfth grade tended to be "unstable, uncertain and unrealistic," with twelfth-grade preferences having little similarity to those expressed in the ninth grade. Some two-thirds of the twelfth graders and even more ninth graders had no confidence in their goals. In twelfth grade nearly half of the boys were considering goals that were not consistent with their socioeconomic background or their measured interests and abilities. Most boys in the twelfth grade, as in the ninth grade, knew little about the occupation they thought they might enter; their use of appropriate resources of information, their knowledge of the world of work, and their plans for achieving their goals were often seriously deficient. Only about half of the twelfth-grade boys knew what they would or should do to qualify for their prospective occupations, and few had done any contingency planning.

As compared with the ninth grade, even with the deficits in knowledge and planning, twelfth-grade boys are considering fewer occupational possibilities and fields of work. There is, as theory would suggest, a movement toward greater crystallization and specificity in choice from the ninth to the twelfth grade. In speaking of the typical twelfth grader, as compared to the typical ninth grader, Jordaan and Heyde suggest:

His interests are more adult, and he has somewhat more confidence in them. He is more aware of the significant characteristics of occupations and has more information about occupations that interest him. He has more specific plans for obtaining the required training, education, and on-the-job experience. He shows greater readiness to assume personal responsibility for securing a beginning job or the required education and training. However, his vocational preferences are no more realistic

or appropriate, judging by intellectual requirements, interests involved, or socioeconomic accessibility, than they were when he was in the 9th grade (p. 186).

In theoretical terms, Jordaan and Heyde (1979) contend that the data they examined support the conclusion "that awareness of concern with present and future decisions, awareness of factors to consider in making decisions, occupational information, and planning are important aspects of vocational maturity in adolescence" (p. 195). As suggested elsewhere, particularly in Chapters 4 and 6, such behaviors are also related to career behavior at age 25 in other studies by Super and his colleagues. As such they represent important organizing themes around which program goals and career guidance activities in the senior high school can be planned.

IMPLICATIONS FOR CAREER GUIDANCE IN THE SENIOR HIGH SCHOOL

Since students in the senior high school will have arrived at these differing degrees of career maturity by differing routes of continuity or discontinuity, career guidance activities must have three emphases: *stimulating career development, providing treatment*, and *aiding placement* (the latter refers to student movement to the next educational level or to the immediate life of worker, consumer, and citizen). Conceptually, it is important to recognize that in terms of career development, some senior high school students will be no more mature than are elementary school students. Therefore, they will need to acquire, in a shorter time, the vocabulary, self- and career awareness, and exploratory experience that might have been expected to occur earlier. Treatment will need to occur when, even after being provided information and other exploratory experiences, students are still unable to make a choice or a commitment to some plan of action (Crites, 1981).

Which of the three career guidance emphases is implemented must depend on where the individual student is in career development and what he or she needs most at a given time: reassurance, information, reality-testing, emotional release, attitude clarification, or work exposure. Obviously, career guidance activities at the senior high school level, as at other educational levels, must be predicated on individual needs, readiness, and motivations.

The principal emphases in career guidance activities for different individuals must be on the intensity of planning, readiness to participate in life as an independent person, and goal-directedness of the individuals to be served. In support of such premises, the National Conference on Guidance, Counseling, and Placement in Career Development and Education-Occupational Decision-Making (Gysbers & Pritchard, 1969) recommended the following objectives for career guidance activities in the secondary school:

1. The student develops awareness of need for more specific implementation of career purposes.
2. The student develops more specific plans for implementing career purposes.
3. The student executes plans to qualify for entry-level jobs by taking appropriate courses at the high school level, by on-the-job training, or by pursuing further training in college or postsecondary vocational education leading toward qualifications for some specific occupation (p. 74).

These objectives must be elaborated and cast in behavioral terms as recommended in the preceding chapters, particularly Chapter 6. But the significant point here is that career guidance activities in the senior high school must take each student from where he or she is in coping with developmental tasks integral to career development, and lead that person to the creation and the achievement of a set of specific preferences and plans to implement them. For many students, the senior high school years are the crucible in which they test their vague aspirations by developing specific strategies for converting these aspirations into reality. Career guidance, in its repertoire of emphases, represents the last opportunity for many students to rehearse in a protected context different coping behaviors and alternative actions and plans, and to assess these against a backdrop of self-characteristics and value sets before their induction into the adult society.

PLANNING CONSIDERATIONS IN THE SENIOR HIGH SCHOOL

Within the systematic stages of planning for career guidance outlined in Chapter 6, there are several concerns of particular importance in relating career guidance to senior high school students.

1. Because many students will complete their formal education with the senior high school and thereby terminate their opportunities for the systematic analysis and facilitation of their career development, efforts need to be undertaken to reach all students with career guidance opportunities.
2. The major career guidance emphasis in the senior high school needs to be on the specific and comprehensive planning of immediate, intermediate, and future educational and occupational choices after high school. However, for many reasons, not all senior high school students will be ready for such planning. Many students will need intensive self- or career awareness and exploration opportunities, either because they did not have such experiences in the junior high school or because they were not ready to profit from them at that time.
3. Due to the nature of senior high school students and the diversity of their goals, career guidance in the senior high school should include counseling and developmental guidance experiences dealing with study habits, human relations at work, career and educational planning, job search techniques, and job interview skills.
4. Decisions must be made about how career guidance and placement will correspond or differ in the senior high school. Will placement be seen as a process spanning the total senior high school period or an event primarily dealt with in the twelfth grade? Will counselors take sole responsibility for educational and occupational placement or will they share these elements with other persons (such as vocational teachers, employment service counselors) in the school and the community?
5. The senior high school student is confronted with internal and external pressures to make

decisions and to pursue specific types of outcomes. Career guidance can help students deal effectively with these pressures.

6. The verbal and conceptual skills of high school students are more developed than those of junior high students, permitting career guidance to proceed along multiple and complex dimensions.
7. Since the major combinations of possibilities following high school are reasonably clear — college, other postsecondary education, work, nonwork, military, or governmental service (such as VISTA, Action) — career guidance should help senior high school students to consider the advantages and disadvantages of each.

Goals for Career Guidance in the Senior High School

Unlike goals for elementary and junior high school populations, those for senior high emphasize specific planning and awareness of life roles as a consumer and as one engaged in leisure time pursuits. Examples of program goals that might be adapted to a particular senior high school (Herr, 1976) include helping students learn to:

1. show relationships between their achievements, values, preferences, educational aspirations, and career preferences
2. analyze current personal competency in skills necessary to career preferences and develop plans to strengthen these skills where necessary
3. assume responsibility for career planning and its consequences
4. prepare to qualify for entry-level jobs by taking appropriate courses, by cooperative education, or by on-the-job training
5. prepare to qualify for post-secondary education by taking courses required by the type of program and institution desired (community college, college, trade, or business school)
6. develop knowledge and skills pertinent to life as a consumer
7. develop skills pertinent to effective use of leisure time
8. systematically reality test career preferences

by relating them to achievement in courses, part-time work, or extracurricular activities
9. identify alternative ways of accomplishing desired educational or occupational goals if preferred choices are not available
10. describe the major forms of continuing education following high school (for example, apprenticeships, on-the-job training, correspondence courses, military service schools, evening schools, reading, college), and list those most related to career preferences
11. identify the steps required to gain admission after high school including whom to contact, application dates and procedures, and the capital investment necessary
12. make accurate estimates of personal traits and achievements and present these effectively on a resume and in an occupational or educational interview
13. develop specific plans to implement career goals
14. execute career plans (pp. 1–2).

Consistent with the setting and the program design, the facilitation of some of these goals might be best achieved by teachers, others by the counselor, and still others in cooperative activity among various specialists or community persons.

Sequencing Career Guidance Experiences in the Senior High School

A persistent theme in the chapters on career guidance in the elementary and junior high schools has been the need for many of the objectives of career development to be met within the goals of particular curricula. Implied has been the need for students continuously to connect what they are doing educationally with consequences in terms of occupational and educational alternatives, the life styles they represent, and their general requirements. Mention has also been made of the importance of teacher attitudes in encouraging planfulness among students, an appreciation of the spectrum of occupational alternatives in which knowledge of various subject matter is useful and in some cases necessary, and other elements of career maturity.

Exploring Educational and Career Opportunities.
At the root of these recommendations is the fact

that students need to come to terms with a variety of personal questions and with clarifying a self-concept. Hoffman (1973), in discussing self-understanding for productive living, has observed, "The questions teachers should be encouraging students to ask are 'Who am I?' 'What influences me?' and 'How can I control the influences upon me?' Once these answers are found, or at least sought, the most neglected area of education will take its proper place as the most important" (p. 79). Livingston (1970) has viewed the matter in the following perspective:

> One reason university graduates have had so much difficulty making the transition from academic life to the world of work is that they have failed to develop in school the self-identities needed to enable them to make firm career commitments. Their formal education has not nurtured the traits of individuality, self-assurance, and responsibility or developed the attributes that would permit them to become active agents in their own career success (p. 40).

Bruner (1973) has offered this opinion: "Neuroses of the young are far more likely to revolve around work than around sex. The delay of vocational or job decisions fostered by our school system has provided difficulty for students to identify themselves in adult roles." He suggests that the "first order of business in the transformation of our mode of education is to revolutionize and revivify this idea of vocation or occupation" (p. 22).

The school counselor has a role in directly encouraging the development of such experiences as well as in collaborating with teachers to assist them in the career development of students. The school counselor needs to exert leadership in helping administrative and curriculum groups respond to the architect's dictum that form should follow function as plans are made to incorporate more flexibility, interdisciplinary integration, variable time blocks, individualized programming, multimedia approaches, and self-teaching devices than now exist in many educational systems.

Some Examples of Programs. There are fewer examples of comprehensive sequential career guidance or career education activity at the senior

high school level than at the elementary or junior high school. Presumably, this is true because the organizational structures of these three educational levels differ. In particular, the typical senior high school structure is built around the need for students to acquire the knowledge and skills inherent in a subject rather than adapting subject matter to specific students' needs.

In essence, career education and career guidance both rest on the need to infuse general education subject matter with a greater career orientation. At a fundamental level, this requires incorporating and adopting many of the themes and activities emphasized in Chapter 8 and supplementing them with simulation, group processes, or work-study opportunities. For example, a continuing career development theme in courses designed to prepare students for college will diminish the persistent assumption that college is an end in itself. College, too, is an intermediate occupational choice for the vast majority of students who enter. With such an emphasis, students can be helped to see college less as a way of deferring career thinking and more as one way to achieve particular career goals. As will be indicated later, many of the students for whom college immediately follows high school can also profit from direct work experience or from access to vocational education experiences in the school itself, in order to heighten the purpose with which they approach college.

Not all the students to whom career development strategies have relevance in general education and career guidance will have college as their major intent or work after high school as their immediate goal. Hoyt mounted a major research project some years ago concerned with those whom he has described as "the specialty oriented" (Hoyt, 1965). He contrasted the specialty-oriented with the liberal arts–oriented student, who also has postsecondary education aspirations but is inclined to trade, technical, or business school training rather than college. He speaks of the specialty-oriented as those whose prime educational motivation is to acquire an occupational skill or set of skills that could be used to enter the labor market.

Hoyt indicates that for the specialty-oriented student, guidance practices should include increased use of information in the counseling process and counseling for specific decision-making. He asserts, "I think far too many students leave the secondary school today with, at best, some general notions of what they may do but without the slightest idea of when or how they will be able to convert these general notions into realistic actions" (p. 235).

One of the most comprehensive approaches to career development and career guidance in the senior high school is that found in Mesa, Arizona. One of the original six field-test sites for the national school-based career education model, Mesa went through an extensive process of system-wide evaluation and project developments using a variety of consultants from around the nation. Using essentially a systems approach, guidance personnel built into the guidance program an accountability component that could be based on student needs. The steps on which the Mesa guidance personnel designed their efforts included:

1. A detailed needs assessment which included assessing the demographic characteristics of the students to be served and the outcomes from guidance which students desired in four areas: intrapersonal, interpersonal, academic learning, educational-vocational.

At the senior high school, the top priority outcomes were:

Academic Learning

I need to improve my memory
I need to improve my understanding of what I need
I need to improve my ability to concentrate
I need to know how to study better
I need to become more comfortable when giving information or speaking in class

Educational-Vocational

I need to understand my abilities, interests, and other characteristics
I need to consider more than one alternative for what I should do after high school
I need to know how and where I can find occupational and educational information and guidance
I need actual on-the-job experience to know

what it's like to be employed and to learn more about jobs
I need to know what jobs are available to me

Interpersonal

I need to better solve problems I have with my parents
I need to be a better listener and more responsive to the feelings and needs of others
I need to accept criticism better
I need to have more confidence so I can be at ease with other people

Intrapersonal

I need to be more satisfied with my life, my achievements, and myself
I need someone to talk to when personal problems arise
I need to set goals so I can stop drifting along with no particular purpose in life
I need to be more skillful in making decisions and solving problems

2. An objective status assessment of on-going programs in terms of how counselors were using their time and toward what ends.

3. A reconciliation of the "What is" with "What ought to be."

4. Built a guidance model based on the outcomes of steps 1 and 3.

5. Designed a program based essentially on student needs.

6. Programmed an implementation schedule for delivery of the program to the target population.

7. Designed evaluation strategies to determine if, in fact, the program delivered its objectives.

8. Built in a systematic evaluation and feed-back system to insure that all parts of the program remained sensitive to changing student needs.

9. Began a task analysis to determine competencies required by practitioners to deliver the program.

10. Did a beginning competency analysis to determine present competency level of practitioners.

11. Began the design of in-service programs to bring practitioners to appropriate competency levels.

12. Began the development of transportable practitioner training packages (Mesa Public Schools, 1974).

What has emerged from this analytic process are a series of guidance "units" administered in various subjects through a teacher/counselor team relationship and a reconceptualized counselor role in career guidance. A major emphasis of the guidance program is the delivery of various guidance learnings as an integral part of the existing curriculum and classroom activities. The format for the guidance learnings sought in the curriculum were teacher-counselor booklets or resource guides for each unit. In each of these guides the following topics were included:

1. goal statements and performance objectives of the unit
2. length of unit and each lesson within it
3. materials necessary to deliver the unit
4. enrichment activities
5. new vocabulary
6. teacher preparation tasks
7. a brief descriptive statement of each lesson
8. answer keys to end-of-unit tests, where appropriate
9. points to cover in individual or group discussions with students

In originally implementing these units, the counselors did the teaching. Subsequently, teachers took responsibility for the teaching but, as necessary, counselors continued to monitor units, lead group discussions, counsel individual students, and assist in other ways. In such circumstances, both the teachers and counselors became resource people. They checked on student progress; led small-group discussions on important points; conferred with individual students when the need dictated; suggested supplementary activities to both fast and slow learners; helped students with end-of-unit evaluation procedures; and facilitated student learning by making certain that appropriate materials, resources, and people were available as the students needed them.

Another comprehensive sequential approach to career guidance is that developed through indepth planning in the Corning-Painted Post Area Schools (N.Y.). Table 9.1 presents the program outcomes for which the guidance program became accountable. As can be seen, the guidance program is responsible for five goal areas, each with specific

themes around which guidance programming takes place in each grade.

Table 9.2 presents the activities of the guidance program in each of the goal areas by grade. Referring back to the planning concepts of Chapter 6 will help reinforce your understanding of these commitments to activities as hypothesis testing. The assumption is that each of the activities cited by grade and by goal will be instrumental in achieving the outcomes in each of these cells. The overall matrix provides administrators and the public information about what the guidance program includes, how it changes over time, and what broad goals it is accountable for. What is not included here because of space limitations is the specific behavioral outcomes for students, which the processes are intended to facilitate as the broad goal areas are translated into student knowledge, attitudes, and skills at each grade level.

A further example is what Brown (1980) has described as a Life-Planning Workshop (LPW) for high school students. The LPW is conducted in structured small groups that cover seven components in six to eight one-hour meetings. The components are:

1. Why People Behave as They Do — Emphasizes that behavior is goal-directed and explores the concept of accepting responsibility for one's own behavior.
2. Winners and Losers — Emphasizes how losers can become winners by accepting responsibility, making good decisions, and planning ahead.
3. Your Fantasy Life — Explores the relationship between fantasy and planning.
4. Your Real Life — Outlines what students consider to be a set of realistic life expectations regarding education, career, close relationships, leisure and community involvement. Compares fantasy and realistic expectations and uses a lifeline exercise (Knickerbocker and Chesney, 1975) to help students note where they are now and key decisions are made throughout life.
5. Setting Life Goals — Deals with the decision-making process and planning using a force-field analysis approach that requires students

Table 9.1
Corning-Painted Post Area Schools Core Guidance Program by Outcomes

Goal	Grade						
	6	7	8	9	10	11	12
Knowledge of Self	Values	Interests	Aptitudes	Aptitudes	Work values	Interests	Values Aptitudes Interests Achievements
Knowledge of Work and Education	Sex-role stereotyping		Local opportunity	Occupational and educational resources Occupational structure	Attitudes toward and rewards of work	Job seeking survival skills Leisure Education/ work link	Education/ work link
Decision-Making		Decisions and values	Course selection Curriculum selection	Course selection	Course selection Decision-making skills	Course selection Post-high school planning	Post-high school planning
Remedial and Consultation	Behavior change →						
Placement	Academic adjustment	Academic adjustment	Academic adjustment Course selection Curriculum selection	Academic adjustment Course selection	Academic adjustment Course selection	Academic adjustment Course selection	Academic adjustment Post-high school plans

to list forces that contribute to or retard goal attainment.

6. Short-Term Life Planning, High School Graduation — Helps students identify all requirements for high school graduates and the positive and negative forces relating to the attainment of that goal.

7. Long-Term Life Planning — Takes students through both short-term and long-term planning in education, career, close relationships, leisure, and community development. Shows students that each of these areas is related to all others and is potentially a source of personal fulfillment.

Because the field testing of such an approach has shown initially positive results, it could be used within curriculums or as the substance of group counseling or special career guidance units.

Another career development class was implemented and evaluated by Mackin and Hansen (1981). The population for the class was eleventh- and twelfth-grade students at an inner-city high school in Minneapolis. Students were administered the Attitude Scale and three of the Competency Subscales of the Career Maturity Inventory (CMI) as part of a pre/post design. The Career Development Curriculum designed by the senior author served as the independent or treatment condition provided over eleven weeks. The Career Development program was based on development tasks for high school students drawn from the Career Development Curriculum developed by Tennyson, Hansen, Klaurens, and Antholz (1975) which has been described at several places in this book. The goals of the curriculum are: (1) to increase self-awareness; (2) to increase career awareness; and (3) to increase decision-making and planning skills. Self-Awareness consists of four units — self-concept, interests, abilities, and values and needs. Activities include student completion of a self-esteem measure, an adjective list, an occupational family tree, the Strong Campbell Interest Inventory, Holland's Self-Directed Search, standard achievement and aptitude assessments, selected readings, values auctions, and a paper dealing with self and society.

Career Awareness included two units: Career Development and The Future. Activities included constructed personal lifelines, life-career rainbows, guest speakers, field trips, and occupational fantasy trips. Guest speakers included persons who would provide role models counteracting prevailing stereotypes of sex-types or racially typed roles.

Decision-Making and Planning was devoted primarily to "teaching decision-making skills and helping students identify goals and plans for the attainment of these goals. Emphasis is on learning a process of decision-making. Activities used include selected exercises from *Decisions and Outcomes* (Gelatt, Varenhorst, Carey, & Miller, 1973), analysis of decision-making styles, a force-field analysis of student plans, and a career plans paper.

Although the sample size was small ($N = 15$) and there was no control group, the results were quite positive. Students were found to have significantly increased their scores on the attitude scale, self-appraisal scale, and goal-selection of the CMI. On class-evaluation scales, the students indicated that the class was helpful in the eight areas of intended effect: interests, values, skills, needs, occupational and school information, setting goals, making decisions, and making plans.

Variations on this approach that are specifically addressed to the reduction of sex-role stereotyping have been stimulated by Project BORN FREE. Training materials and approaches as well as the conceptual bases for this program are described in several important articles (such as Hansen & Keierleber, 1978).

A final example of a sequential approach has been designed to create a team effort to support career planning for academically disadvantaged students in East Lyme High School, Connecticut (Matthay & Linder, 1982). The team included two special educators, two counselors, and two cooperative work experience coordinators. Fifty-one tenth-grade students comprised the population of students who were included because of lack of decision-making skills, lack of motivation toward finishing high school, and low academic test scores (significantly below grade level and below state and local norms in standardized reading and math tests).

Participants in the program's career awareness classes met for forty-five minutes every day for one semester, participated in weekly individual counseling with the school counselors, and received tutoring from the special educators as

Table 9.2

Corning-Painted Post Area Schools Core Guidance Program by Activities

Goal	Grade						
	6	7	8	9	10	11	12
Knowledge of Self	"Bread and Butterflies" "Deciding" Discussion	SRA, "What I Like to Do" "Picture Inventory Exploration Survey" (P.I.E.S.) Discussion	Differential Aptitude Test (DAT) Discussion	Guidance Information Systems Continued Interpretation of DAT and SAT	"Work Values Inventory" Value Clarification Exercises (e.g., values auction) Guidance Information System "Harrington-O'Shea" Systems Continued Interpretation of DAT and SAT	"Strong-Campbell Interest Inventory" or "Career Assessment Inventory" Guidance Information System "Armed Services Vocational Aptitude Battery" Continued Interpretation of DAT and SAT	Senior Interviews "CEEB" and "ACT" "ASVAB"
Knowledge of Work and Education	"Jobs and Gender" "Job Prejudice" Discussion		Speakers Field Trips Career Days Interviews Shadowing Lecture and discussion Want Ads	Media Center "Hands-on" Lecture and discussion Career Days Guidance Information System Audio-visual Presentations Reading Assignments	Media Center "Hands-on" Lecture and discussion Career Days Guidance Information System Audio-visual Presentations Reading Assignments	Media Center "Hands-on" Lecture and discussion Career Days Guidance Information System Audio-visual Presentations Reading Assignments	Media Center "Hands-on" Lecture and discussion Career Days Guidance Information System Audio-visual Presentations Reading Assignments
Decision-Making		"Deciding" Discussion	Course Selection Curriculum Selection	Course Selection	Course Selection "Harrington-O'Shea System" Guidance Information System	Course Selection Post-high School Planning "Career Motivation Process"	Post-high School Planning "Career Motivation Process" "Short Job Search"

Remedial

Identification
Counseling
Referral
Consultation (team conferences, individual conferences, in-service training, departmental meetings, articulation meetings, curriculum review, special needs, faculty meetings, staff development days, case conferences, parent conferences, parent-counselor advisory groups, parent group meetings, home visits, newsletters, industry visitations, career days, industry internships, periodic meetings with industry, agency consultations, media communications, college days, agency board participation, health and welfare association.

Placement

School Visitations	Student Handbooks	Student Handbooks	Course Selection
Principal-Counselor Presentations	Open Houses	Open Houses	Group and Individual Conferences
Student Handbooks	Newsletters	Newsletters	Individualized Test Interpretation and
Open Houses	Team-Parent Conferences	Team-Parent Conferences	Achievement Review
Newsletters	Individual Conferences	Individual Conferences	
Team-Parent Conferences		High School Visit	Post-high School Plans
Individual Conferences			Post-high School Plans

271

needed. The classes consisted of action activities, individual assessments of interests, aptitudes, and exercises, values clarifications discussions, activities, maintenance of journals, career decision-making exercises, audio-visual presentations, speakers, field trips, interviews with workers, assigned readings, and individual and group counseling. The content of the program included self-awareness, career awareness, and specific career discovery.

Based on pre/post testing, open-ended feedback from students, and the observations of students by teachers and counselors, the results of the program were found to be as follows:

1. Students became more familiar with regional career opportunities and trends and increased their job-search and decision-making skills.
2. Thirty-nine of the fifty-one students were found to have improved academic performance, improved class and school attendance, more positive self-images, more dedication to their school work, greater drive toward choosing career goals, and increased initiative to make meaningful choices about future goals.
3. Thirty-eight of the participating students planned to enter the cooperative work experience program in either their junior or senior year. Eight others felt the program was helpful in assisting them to consider entering vocational education programs.
4. Twenty-four of the students indicated that the program provided them an impetus to complete their high school education.
5. Students reported improved understanding of the relationship of school courses to specific careers and an understanding of the background knowledge and skills essential for successful job performance.

Space does not permit the examination of such other excellent examples of sequential career guidance approaches as Careers in Literature and Life (Bienstock, 1981) or Operation Guidance, which is a comprehensive and systematic approach to career guidance developed by the Center for Vocational Education at The Ohio State University (Campbell, Suzuki, & Gabria, 1972). Suffice it to say that the latter system involves carefully designed modules to assist schools to perform context validation, state behavioral objectives,

methods selection, and testing. Although other examples of sequential career guidance activities in senior high schools might be cited, those given suggest examples of the content and organization that are frequently found.

Career Guidance Strategies to Foster Decision-Making

In most of the sequential approaches to career development in the senior high school, helping students acquire decision-making skills is a major objective. In some cases, this goal is made explicit and in other cases it is assumed to be a by-product of the other career guidance activities implemented. Regardless of whether these are seen as part of a sequential program, many guidance techniques have been used to promote decision-making behavior among senior high school students.

Many appropriate techniques are discussed in other parts of this text. Those discussed here relate directly to senior high school students. In one study, Jones and Krumboltz (1970) examined the matter of stimulating occupational exploration through film-mediated problems. The experiment was replicated in two high schools; one a predominantly white middle-class school and the other a school in which 46 percent of the students were Mexican-American and Puerto Rican, 7 percent were black, 1 percent were Oriental, and the remainder were white. In both of these high schools, three versions of an experimental film were shown; the film presented five jobs that represented a cross-section of employment opportunities available for men and women in banking. A representative problem situation in each job was enacted on film for five or six minutes to the point where a decision had to be made.

The three versions of the film differed in the type of response each requested from the students in the experimental group: active-overt participation (students recorded their solutions in workbooks), active-covert participation (students were asked to think about their solutions but did not write them down), passive participation (no questions were asked of the students). One control group of students viewed regular banking career films; another read printed banking career information, and questions for them to consider were suggested; a third control group read printed general career information. The conclusions were (1) that the experimental film versions were more effective than were materials selected for comparison, and (2) that the participative versions of the experimental film were more effective than the passive version.

In another study, Krumboltz and Schroeder (1965) randomly assigned fifty-four eleventh-grade volunteers for educational and vocational counseling to three treatments: (1) reinforcement counseling (information-seeking responses reinforced), (2) model-reinforcement counseling (tape-recording of a male counselee played to each student prior to reinforcement counseling), and (3) a control group. The findings were (1) that the experimental groups engaged in more information-seeking outside the interview than did control group members; (2) that reinforcement counseling produced significantly more information-seeking outside the interview (such as reading resources, talking about opportunities) for females but not males as compared to control-group behaviors; (3) that model-reinforcement counseling produced significantly more information-seeking outside the interview for males than for females as compared to controls; and (4) that the ratio of information-seeking to other responses in the interview was positively correlated with external information-seeking.

In a related study, Krumboltz and Thoresen (1964) randomly assigned 192 eleventh-grade pupils to individual and group counseling settings in which the following four procedures were used by counselors: (1) reinforcement of verbal information-seeking behavior, (2) presentations of a tape-recorded model interview followed by reinforcement counseling, (3) presentation of film or filmstrip plus discussion as a control procedure, and (4) inactive control. The findings were (1) the model-reinforcement and reinforcement counseling produced more external information-seeking than control procedures; (2) that with a male model, model-reinforcement counseling surpassed reinforcement counseling for males but not females; (3) that group and individual settings were about equally effective on the average, but interactions were found to be affected by counselor variables, schools, set of subjects, and treatments.

Meyer, Strowig, and Hosford (1970), in a similar study, assigned 144 female and male eleventh-grade students in three rural high schools to four behavioral-reinforcement counseling treatments and controls in individual and small-group settings. Baseline data on the information-seeking behaviors of the students were collected before initiating the treatments. Local high school counselors were trained and used as the experimental counselors. The treatments used were: (1) reinforcement of verbal information-seeking behavior, (2) tape-recorded model interview plus reinforcement, (3) sound film plus reinforcement, and (4) no-treatment control. The findings were (1) that all behavioral-reinforcement treatments produced significantly more information-seeking behaviors than no-treatment control procedures; (2) that on the average, reinforcement counseling was as effective as model reinforcement and film reinforcement for promoting the criterion behaviors; (3) that insignificant differences occurred between small-group and individual counseling settings; and (4) that for most treatments, females showed a greater amount and variety of information-seeking behavior than males.

Young (1979) compared the effectiveness of a value confrontation procedure and a procedure based on verbal operant conditioning in enhancing career development attitudes and increasing the frequency of information-seeking in ninety rural adolescent males. The subjects were identified as internally or externally controlled, according to their locus of control scores, and then randomly assigned to one of the two experimental treatment groups or a control group. The specific purpose of the value confrontation was to create an awareness of dissatisfaction about one's career planning and to relate this to inconsistencies in one's belief system. For these students, the dissatisfaction about their career planning had already been reported on the Career Development Inventory-Secondary School Form. It was brought to their attention by the counselor. The counselor then related how "good" career planners and "poor" career planners ranked the focus values "logical" and "responsible" and the priority of the values "ambitious," "logical," and "responsible" over other values (p. 16). At four times during the procedure students had the opportunity to examine their own hierarchy of values.

The reinforcement counseling treatment was to make the subjects aware of the relative strength of their career planning orientation, resources for exploration, and information and decision-making. Subsequent to the interpretation of the CDI, the counselors verbally and nonverbally reinforced those statements of the subject which were evidence of vocationally mature responses. These were expressions of behavior or of intentions. Seven weeks after the treatments it was found that the value confrontation procedure resulted in significantly greater frequency of information-seeking for internally controlled subjects when compared to the reinforcement counseling and control procedures. No statistically significant differences on the career planning orientation criterion between the cognitive and behavioral treatment groups were evident.

Collectively, the studies reported here, although not exhaustive, provide insight into the potential of reinforcement-behavioral counseling, modeling, imitative learning, and filmed and audiotaped presentations of specific stimulus materials to influence different components of decision-making and information-seeking behavior among high school students. Perhaps more important, they demonstrate that sex and other individual characteristics are related to the effects of these approaches. In other words, they emphasize the necessity of matching technique with individual characteristics and needs.

Finally, it is apparent that although these approaches have validity for facilitating career development objectives, they also hold promise for the treatment of specific behavioral deficits. In terms of the latter, Woody (1968) has discussed the use of behavioral techniques in career counseling. In particular, he has described the following behavioral techniques as having validity in career guidance and counseling: social recognition and object rewards, social modeling, verbal reinforcement, systematic desensitization, assertive practice, and clinical suggestion.

Although highly effective in facilitating aspects of decision-making among high school students, behavioral-learning-reinforcement approaches are not the only useful techniques. Flake, Roach, and Stenning (1975) have reported significant changes on Career Maturity Inventory scores for tenth-grade students exposed to short-term counseling involving discussion of general career plans, testing with and interpretation of the Gordon Occupational Checklist and the General Aptitude Test Battery and analysis with the student of his or her personal responses to the Career Maturity Inventory.

Amatea and Cross (1980) described a career guidance program designed for ninth- through twelfth-grade students and their parents, entitled *Going Places*. The program includes six components that are presented through discussion, small-group activities, reading materials, skill rehearsal, and at-home tryout and specialization. The program consists of six 2-hour sessions, one per week. Through the use of a behavioral contract, participants commit themselves to homework that applies skills learned in the group sessions. The unique aspect of the program is the combination of parents and their children in the same group systematically learning about personal and occupational data and other specific career-planning skills. The goals of this program are

(a) to develop a supportive family environment to encourage career planning and decision-making; (b) to provide an overview of the important elements involved in career planning and decision-making; (c) to encourage the development of self-management skills in goal setting and decision-making as useful tools in career planning; (d) to develop self-exploration skills and compile a base of self-information; (e) to encourage the development of organizing principles for viewing the work world as a method for expanding job options and comparing self and occupational data; (f) to develop systematic information-getting skills useful in exploring occupational and training paths; and (g) to provide information on various occupational and training paths (pp. 277–278).

Evaluated by anecdotal data from twenty-four students and twenty-four parents who participated in three different programs, reactions to the content and the format of the program were found to be very favorable. However, the authors did suggest several caveats. For example, since the program is designed primarily for literate, motivated parents and students, its content and format will not suit all types of students, parents, and family groups. In addition, the program is not designed to deal with deep-seated conflicts between parents and children in which career is a central issue; thus, families need to be screened before inclusion in the group. Finally, in order to accommodate the needs of parents, such a program typically needs to be offered in the evening.

Laramore (1979) too, has outlined a process of group career counseling for families that requires 8 to 10 three-hour sessions, one per week. The first session is devoted to providing an information base for the parents and children, rapport-building activities, and an effort to dispel some common myths about career choices. In sessions 2–6 activities that reveal skills, attitudes, interests, and values are introduced and shared. During this time group members maintain a data sheet about each other group member and they clip want ads and other information that they think will be useful to each of the other members. These are filed in individual envelopes and given directly to the member in the seventh session. At this "career options" session, members share why they chose which information for each other. Then decision-making steps are discussed and related to the possible career options for each individual. For the eighth session, members must have written a letter of application, a resume or qualification brief for one of the jobs. General information on effective job-seeking skills is then given. In sessions 8–10 group members role-play job interviews, and these are videotaped as possible and critiqued so that individual performance can be improved. In the last hour group members share their plans of action and discuss implications and possibilities.

Neely and Kosier (1977) report using the eighteen sequenced tasks of the Vocational Exploration Group (Daane, 1971) with both handicapped and nonhandicapped high school boys and girls. Using self-ratings and observations about work potential as criteria, the findings tended to support the utility of short-term group approaches in the career development of high school students, including the handicapped. Myers, Lindeman, Thompson, and Patrick (1975) have reported that the Educational and Career Exploration System (ECES), a computer-based system, significantly affected experimental students' planning orientation and uses of resources for occupational exploration but did not significantly increase their possession of occupational information or their

decision-making skills as compared with students exposed only to a regular guidance program. Thus, it was suggested that this system might supplement a local guidance program in those areas where the latter was less effective than ECES. At the end of this chapter, other methods of facilitating decision-making in senior high school students are listed. General helping strategies are also provided in Chapter 14.

Career Information Systems

Although in Chapter 16 we will discuss in depth the use of career information, it is useful here to consider the findings of a national survey of career information systems in secondary school conducted by Educational Testing Service and funded by the National Institute of Education (Chapman & Katz, 1981). This study included stratified samples from the 17,856 secondary schools in the United States that have grades 10–12 and are not devoted exclusively to special populations. School questionnaires were sent to 3412 schools, and student questionnaires were sent to 4883 students in 155 schools stratified from the total school sample.

The findings of the questionnaires indicated that a wide variety of offerings are available to students. These include six categories of publications, computer systems, guidance activities, and contact with educational professionals. Obviously, no school has all of the resources identified, and some schools have very little. About a quarter of the schools in the sample have a computer system of any sort; only 18 percent use simulations. The top ten resources and the nationwide percentage of schools that use them are as follows (p. 248):

Resource	Percentage of Schools Using
Occupational Outlook Handbook	92
Conference with counselors	83
Dictionary of Occupational Titles	83
Career days, speakers, etc.	75
Occupational handbooks for the military	75
Vocational school directories	74

Externally produced AV materials	71
College directories arranged by occupation	70
Occupational information units in subject matter course	62
Job site tours	59

Management of these guidance resources is typically in the hands of professionals – the director of guidance and staff or the coordinator of career education and staff. Over 60 percent of the schools reported that they have a staff member who serves as a director or head of career guidance, and fewer than 6 percent of the schools nationwide said that they did not employ a full-time equivalent guidance counselor. Although counselors report spending less than a quarter of their time with students discussing occupational choice and career planning, roughly two-thirds of the counselors indicate that "a great deal" of this time is spent in directing students to occupational information or in answering students' questions about occupational information. More than half of the counselors said that they spent "a great deal" of this time interpreting occupational information and assisting students with career decisions.

On the negative side, the findings do indicate that although 92 percent of the schools have the *Occupational Outlook Handbook* some 8 percent or 1400 schools do not. Some 6 percent of schools do not have a full-time equivalent guidance counselor. That figure translates into over 1000 schools. Thirty-five percent of schools (6000 or more) have no one serving as director of guidance. In at least 30 percent of the schools it is likely that much of the career resource material is obsolete.

When one turns to the information in the student questionnaires, there is considerable evidence that the resources students use most, although not exclusively, are *not* those provided by the school. Students seem to use informal resources more than formal ones. Parents or relatives, friends, and employed workers ranked 1, 2, and 3 as persons students had talked with about occupations. Counselors and teachers lagged far behind. Parents or relatives and someone in the proposed line of work were named as frequently

as formal publications, and considerably more frequently than counselors and teachers, as the source of information about the education and training requirements for entry into an occupation the student was considering, and about its earnings, job security, the opportunity it provided to help others, and the activities the work entailed.

Additional information about the use of reference materials is also reported on the student questionnaire. Although reference books have been used at least once by almost 80 percent of the students, less than 50 percent of the students have used them more than once. Magazines are used a little less frequently than reference books, and pamphlets and briefs less than that. Half of the students who are aware that their school has a computer terminal have ever used it and the same applies to microfiche (such as VIEW). Although over 60 percent of the students have been exposed to a film or other audio-visual medium for career information, fewer than 50 percent of them have ever participated in any of the other eight experiential activities about which they were asked: simulation, special course in career planning, career day, work-study, job shadowing, tour of a business, meeting with former students, meeting with employed workers. These student reports exist in the face of the finding that over 75 percent of the schools offer career days and over 40 percent offer special courses in career planning.

The survey found a relationship between the type of student and the resource used. For example, low-ability females in nonacademic programs tended to use teachers as their career resource more than the average of other students; tenth and eleventh graders used counselors more than the average; nonwhite high-reading-ability females used books, magazines, and pamphlets more than did the average. Similar relations of resource and student type were found for other groups. The researchers were appropriately cautious in interpreting these findings but they do give credence to the importance of offering experiences and resources that differ on the basis of the ability, experience, development, learning style, and interests of the users.

A final point to be made is that this survey suggested that students do not lack career resources but rather a usable context in which to place the information. In essence, as Katz suggested more than two decades ago, students "often don't know what information they need, don't have what information they want, or can't use what information they have" (Katz, 1963, p. 25). The problem, then, for any career guidance system is to help students determine what questions to ask, what information will answer their questions, and where to find the information they need; help them structure the information and interpret it; and help them arrive at a strategy for making decisions based on information (Chapman and Katz, 1981, p. 252). However mundane it sounds, students need to be educated to a paradigm of decision-making in which information plays a role and is seen as naturally integrated into the awareness, exploration, and action elements of such a paradigm.

Also at issue in such a survey is counselors' intention and preparation to serve as a career resource themselves. Sobol (1978) studied the characteristics and activities of sixty-nine counselors in high schools in the Dallas, Texas, area. It was found that 87 percent of the counselors help students choose college, 75 percent help students choose between college and vocational education, 70 percent help students get jobs, and 51 percent set up job interviews for students. In addition, it was found that most of these counselors try diligently to keep abreast of their field. Seventy-two percent reported that they study job opportunities by various means: for example, 58 percent use labor market forecasts, 43 percent bring in guest speakers, 62 percent talk to business representatives. The other side of the matter is that the school counselors tend to emphasize the current job market rather than the projected job market of five or ten years in the future. About 42 percent of the counselors do not use labor market forecasts at all and about 16 percent are not aware that such forecasts are available to them. Obviously, for those counselors who do not know about or use labor market forecasts their use as a career resource to students is limited, as is the likelihood that students will develop a context for their information-seeking behavior that includes consideration of intermediate and future goals as well as immediate choices.

An interesting technique for disseminating information on the relationship of curricula to specific job titles, to conceptualize jobs held by graduates of different programs, or to help students identify specific career opportunities in local industry has been described by Lipsett (1980).

Figure 9.1 illustrates how different emphases within a business administration curriculum are related to clusters of jobs. Figure 9.2 illustrates how jobs held by graduates of a particular curriculum could be portrayed. Figure 9.3 depicts career paths in local industry. As Lipsett has suggested, although such career charts are not panaceas, they can be integrated into career counseling, a career information course, or other career exploration activity. Obviously, such visual display of important information can be an important adjunct to any of the career information systems we have identified.

CAREER GUIDANCE AND VOCATIONAL EDUCATION

One of the most fruitful efforts of the school counselor will be direct collaboration with vocational educators to reshape both the image and the substance of their disciplines. Vocational education has been called "the bridge between man and his work" (Advisory Council on Vocational Education, 1968) and that part of education which makes an individual more employable in one group of occupations than another (Evans & Herr, 1978). We contend that such labels must come to describe more of the total educational process. If any part of education (or all of it) is to deserve this label by bringing into the lives of individual students the complex of experiences necessary to bridge education and work, more than specific occupation task-training is involved. This very specificity of trade or job training is what has led to cries of obsolescence in vocational education and of unresponsiveness to the dynamics of the occupational structure.

From a career guidance standpoint, the important thing to remember about vocational education is that it has been seen for too long as useful to only a highly restricted sample of the total student population rather than to all or most students. Its image has been that of a second-class alternative for those with low verbal skills or for

Figure 9.1
Business Administration

Typical Job Titles Related to Principal Curricular Areas

Economics	Accounting	Marketing	Personnel	Finance
Economist	Public Accountant	Sales Representative	Employment Interviewer	Bank Loan Officer
Labor Market Analyst	Tax Accountant	Sales Manager	Recruiter	Bank Branch Manager
Long Range Planner	Cost Accountant	Branch Sales Ofc. Mgr.	Employee Benefits Specialist	Bank Operations Manager
Utility Rate Specialist	Auditor	Market Researcher	Job Evaluator	Bank Examiner
Municipal Research Specialist	Bank Examiner	Advertising Copy Writer	Training Specialist	Broker (stocks & bonds)
Business Forecaster	Estimator	Advertising Manager	Job Analyst	Treasurer
	Budget Director	Account Executive	Employee Counselor	Investment Counselor
	Credit Manager	Buyer (store)	Labor Relations Specialist	Controller
	Controller	Merchandise Manager	Personnel Director	
	Office Manager	Store Manager	Industrial Relations Director	
		Publicity Director	Compensation Administrator	
		Market Forecaster		
		Circulation Manager		
		International Trade Specialist		

Typical Job Titles in Functional Subspecialties

Factory Operations	Information Management	Real Estate	Insurance
Production Control Mgr.	Computer Programmer	Appraiser	Underwriter
Production Planner	Systems Analyst	Broker	Actuary
Cost Accountant	Manager of Information Systems	Sales Representative	Claims Examiner
Foreman		Property Manager	Sales Representative
General Foreman		Mortgage Officer	
Manufacturing Manager			

Traffic	Purchasing	Banking
Traffic Manager	Purchasing Agent	Operations Manager
Shipping Clerk	Buyer (industrial)	Branch Manager
Operations Manager	Inventory Control Manager	Loan Officer
	Warehouse Manager	Cashier
		Investment Officer
		Investment Counselor

Figure 9.2
Jobs Held by Retailing Graduates

Entry Jobs	First Level Management	Second Level Management	Higher Management
Assistant Buyer	Buyer	Division Manager	Store Manager
Salesperson	Department Manager	Merchandise Manager	Area Manager
Assistant Interior Designer			V.P. Merchandising

Specialized Professional Jobs	Related Jobs Outside of Retailing
Sales Forecaster	Account Executive
Manager, Visual Design	Sales Manager
Credit Manager	Sales Representative
Personnel Manager	Manufacturer's Representative
Interior Designer	Advertising Manager
Fashion Coordinator	Chamber of Commerce Executive
Market Researcher	
Training Specialist	
Training Supervisor	

those with interests in working with their hands rather than their minds. In the process, many students in such programs and many vocational educators have become defensive about their alleged inferior status, have moved further into an isolationist stance divorcing themselves from so-called academic education, and have tied themselves to training experiences rigidly defined by time and content. This latter condition has occurred not necessarily because vocational educators want it that way but because factors such as legislative funding and union or apprenticeship regulations have, in some instances, forced such restrictions.

Regardless of the reasons for the situation, many students who desperately need what vocational education can offer have been blocked from this access. Such a condition has added fuel to the arbitrary separation of students into supposedly homogeneous categories of college-bound and non–college bound, with the educational experiences offered each group seen essentially as mutually exclusive.

The means of releasing more of the potential contribution of vocational education to career development and, indeed, to career guidance lies not in assigning or recruiting more students for a vocational education track but in making vocational education an equal partner with all other aspects of the educational process. All the relationships between "general education" and career development that have been suggested throughout this book apply to vocational education with equal force. They must be incorporated into a reshaping of the many thrusts of vocational education in such a way that the lines, or at least the images, that presently separate vocational education and general education are made to blur or vanish.

These comments about vocational education are not intended to preclude the continuation of specific job training for some students, but rather to convey the urgent need to broaden the present interrelationships and pathways within vocational education and between it and other educational experiences. Indeed, it is important that even more specific vocational education programs be developed that truly respond to both the low and the high ends of the intellectual continuum — whether the preparation is for becoming a helper, a waiter, a lawnmower repairperson, an industrial landscape gardener, a heavy construction equipment operator, or a computer programmer. The need is to create more tactics not only for fitting youth to programs but also for fitting programs to youth. The existing lock-step in many states of certain training durations and specified training experiences as the only route to vocational

Figure 9.3
Company's Career Opportunities With a Bachelor's Degree in Business or Equivalent

	Labor Grades			
Grade 07	Grade 08	Grade 09	Grade 10	Grade 11

FINANCE DIVISION

Grade 07	Grade 08	Grade 09	Grade 10	Grade 11
Accountant		General Accountant	Supv. Gen. Accounting	
			Supv. Cost Accounting	
Applications Programmer I		Sr. Applications Programmer	Mgr. Applications Programming	
Systems Analyst			Senior Systems Analyst	Mgr. Systems Analysis
				Mgr. Credit & Collections

MARKETING DIVISION

		Sec. Supv. Administrative Services		
				Advertising Manager

MANUFACTURING DIVISION

		Asst. Traffic Manager		
		Production Control Mgr.		Mgr. Order Analysis
				Mrg. Customer Service

education must be broken to exploit the enlarging opportunities in the occupational structure for individuals with a wide range of capability.

If career guidance is to be fully effective, vocational education courses must not only teach skills for specific occupations or skills across families of jobs; they must also develop within students the elements of career development that will free them to discern the alternative ways to use these skills and to attain the personal competence to capitalize on these skills. Further, more avenues must be created for all students to move freely between general and vocational education, with the criteria for such movement being individual need, readiness, interest, motivation, and the blend of academic and vocational experiences to meet these criteria.

Integrating the Work Experience with Schooling. Obviously, neither traditional concepts of vocational education or the newer forms such as the cluster concept, nor a greater freedom of movement between general and vocational education is the only way to provide career guidance and career development. At the senior high level, the integration of work experience with schooling can be a reality. The age and sex of the student are no longer the contingencies they were at the junior high school level. Blocks of time can be developed when students will actually report to jobs instead of school for two or three weeks or a term at a time.

Although the economic appeal is obvious, the training and exploratory value of work experience must be fitted to individual needs. Hence, if a

Figure 9.3 (continued)

Labor Grades				
Grade 12	Grade 13	Grade 14	Grade 15	Grade 16
Chief Accountant				Mgr. Accounting Operations
Sec. Mgr. Cost Accounting	Mgr. Cost Accounting		Chief Factory Accountant	
	Mgr. Systems Analysis & Applications Programming			Mgr. Data & Office Services
Asst. Mgr. Purchasing		Manager Purchasing		
		Mgr. Order Processing		
Traffic Manager				
Mgr. of Prodn. Ordering				
				Mgr. of Services

particular student is interested in electronics, a program can be made available by which he or she can complete required high school work and simultaneously secure on-the-job training through part-time employment. With creative business-industry-education cooperation, programs can be mounted that provide training at work stations in the community in the late afternoon or morning hours, with the rest of the day devoted to general education in the school. For some students, this can be pretechnical training, for others, a permanent job, and for still others, precollege exploration. The integration of such experiences is inherent in the school-based and experience-based models of career education described in Chapter 13.

Probably the most common name for programs

of work-study is cooperative education. A specific definition of this term is found in Section 195 of Title II of the Education Amendments of 1976, where the Vocational Education Act of 1963 is amended.

The term "cooperative education" means a program of vocational education for persons who through written cooperative arrangements between the school and employers, receive instruction, including required academic courses and related vocational instruction by alteration of study in school with a job in any occupational field, but these two experiences must be planned and supervised by the school and employers so that each contributes to the student's education and to his or her employability.

Work periods and school attendance may be on alternate half days, full days, weeks or other periods of time in fulfilling the cooperative program.

Cooperative education or work experience programs are essentially a process of behavioral change for students through experience. At one level, experience comes from immediately determining how what one learns in the classroom is applied at work. At another level, it comes from being adult-oriented at the work station rather than adolescent-oriented. In this sense, students have the opportunity to experience work norms as lived by adults rather than speculate about such things with one's adolescent peers. Finally, cooperative education programs assist students to see themselves and the work done as a whole. Frequently, classroom study fragments employability traits, work habits, human relations, and communications into small increments for purposes of learning. But in the real world all of these elements are part of a complete and constantly unfolding fabric that requires individual judgment and discrimination if career maturity is to result.

Work experience programs also allow the student to test which career development tasks have already been incorporated into his or her behavioral repertoire and which still need honing. In this way, work experience programs provide goal direction to learning and to student planning. A work experience in these terms is not just experience for its own sake but is related to employability. As such, it represents a prime medium for career education, and for developing affective work behaviors and other behaviors that help students acquire a positive career identity and execute it in effective action. In sum, cooperative education can be seen as a powerful tool in career guidance on the secondary school level.

The Relationship of Career Guidance to Vocational Education.[1] Hohenshil (1980) has aptly reported the prevailing view of vocational education of guidance and counseling:

[1] Parts of this section are adapted from Herr, E. L. Career Development and Vocational Guidance. Chapter 6 in *Education and Work*. Edited by Harry F. Silberman. Chicago, Illinois: The University of Chicago Press, 1982.

Vocational education has long been a strong supporter as well as critic of guidance and counseling. On the one hand, there is no other area of education that has financially supported guidance as much for so long. . . . On the other hand, [vocational educators] have also believed that many counselors are neither well prepared nor have the interest in making career development a priority in their guidance programs. There is a generalized feeling that school counselors place too much emphasis on "college and therapy" at the expense of the development and implementation of well planned career guidance (p. 668).

In general, as partial validation of Hohenshil's observations, the literature on career guidance, vocational guidance, or vocational counseling *in* vocational education is not large. Rather, the literature speaks primarily, and more broadly, to vocational guidance or career guidance in secondary schools, sometimes differentiating the needs and treatment of vocational education students and sometimes not. There are, however, studies which suggest that vocational students receive less vocational or career guidance than other students. Examples of some of these studies follow.

In 1966 Campbell and his colleagues undertook a national study of the status of guidance and counseling in secondary schools by comparing the viewpoints of school administrators, counselors, teachers, and students on guidance issues. Some 353 high schools and 7000 respondents were included in the study. Among other findings it was reported that in most schools no one assumed the primary responsibility for assisting students to decide on and enter into vocational programs (Campbell, 1968).

Kauffman and his colleagues (1967) in two major studies of vocational education found that over half the vocational students, but less than one-third of those who followed an academic or general program, reported that they had never discussed their course choices with a counselor; of those students who reported that they had had some formal guidance, three-quarters had a favorable estimate, but vocational students were less likely than students in other curricula options to report favorably.

Palmo and DeVantier (1976) studied the counseling needs of vocational students over an academic year in one vocational-technical school. A similarity of concerns and problems existed among the students. The majority expressed difficulties with teachers, failure in school, peer relationships, home problems, and vocational/career plans. In particular, although vocational students have tentatively chosen a vocational path by enrolling in a vocational curriculum, approximately 30 percent of the students in this study were dissatisfied or confused by their choices and were not really aware of the alternatives available to them. The vocational students expressed a need "for more vocational counseling and additional materials that might help them with impending decisions" (p. 174).

Stern (1977) has summarized other studies of vocational students or graduates that reflect, however indirectly, their needs for career guidance. Such findings are that vocational students are no more knowledgeable about the world of work than nonvocational students, as likely to drop out as other students, no more satisfied with their jobs than graduates of the general track, and somewhat less satisfied than commercial and college preparatory graduates.

Career Guidance in Vocational Education. Career or vocational guidance *in* vocational education is typically seen as a *support* to the latter. Although there is a historical rhetoric as well as more recent legislative support for vocational guidance and vocational education as a partnership, that view does not always predominate in practice.

Support services can be defined in many ways. By tradition aspects of education tend to be included that facilitate the central role of instruction but are not themselves primarily instructional. Guidance and counseling generally meet these criteria and can play important support roles before and after vocational education instruction. For example, career or vocational guidance has a significant role in attracting, recruiting, or selecting students for vocational education options. Because of the many educational choices for youth, attracting appropriately motivated and talented students becomes a major concern to vocational educators in any setting. Vocational guidance can convey the image and possibilities of vocational education to potential enrollees, parents, sending schools, and other sources of input to vocational education programs.

A second role for career or vocational guidance in vocational education is that of *assisting* in the selection of students for admission to various vocational education programs. Such a role involves individual assessment of aptitudes and preferences that, in turn, must be considered in relation to probabilities of success and satisfaction as these derive from *research* about differences in vocational education curricula and the characteristics of those who are successful in them. When individual desires and the realities of course availability or probabilities of success come into conflict, school counselors can help potential enrollees consider the alternatives in as nonarbitrary manner as possible. Whether or not such conflict exists, school counselors have a major role in ensuring that students are properly motivated and equipped to take advantage of the vocational education instruction chosen. Where such a condition does not occur, career guidance personnel need to assist students in choosing a different option in vocational education or to exit from it into another option that promises to meet their current needs.

A third role of career or vocational guidance in vocational education is directly related to instruction itself. As will be discussed in the following section on placement, vocational education students need access to instruction in work-context skills and guidance or career-development skills as well as in specific technical and occupational skills. Since these skills are composed of attitudes, emotions, psychological factors, and cognitive and informational aspects, school counselors often become involved with their provision. Counselors may work with vocational teachers as collaborators or consultants as such learnings are infused into curricula. Or, in some instances, school counselors may take direct responsibility for providing such instruction. Through separate group courses, seminars, interactive computer-assisted instruction, gaming, role-playing, and other techniques students can gain work-context and personal guidance learnings. As this occurs, career guidance as a support service tends to blur into career guidance as subject matter.

A fourth support service contribution to vocational education is the role of career guidance in the placement of students. Conceived in traditional terms, placement of vocational education graduates into suitable employment or post-secondary education has been seen as an event, not a process. The assumption has been that, in the case of work for instance, when a student is about to complete the vocational education program, he or she would be brought into direct contact with an employer(s) seeking a person with such training. The rationale for such an assumption is that the student is employable – possesses the appropriate attitudes, marketable skills, job search and interview behaviors – and only needs assistance to obtain a suitable employer. The role of career or vocational guidance was conceived as that of matchmaker at the point when the student exited the vocational education system.

Increasingly, placement is being conceived as a process, not an event. As such it is seen as a stream of career development and guidance learnings that are acquired concurrently with occupation-specific task learnings throughout the students' vocational education experience, not just when the student is about to enter work full-time. In this sense, assisting vocational education students to focus on their learning and performance capabilities; gain decision-making capacity; formulate an awareness of their options, how to prepare for them and gain access to them; and acquire job search and job interview behavior are seen as not only preparing these persons for the school-to-work transition but for placement as a natural extension of all vocational education. Career guidance, then, is seen as a central component of this process, not something abrupt and different from it.

PERSPECTIVES IN VOCATIONAL PLACEMENT

Historically, career guidance, counseling, and placement have been considered mutually exclusive functions. Our contention is that although they are not synonymous, neither are they mutually exclusive or discrete functions.

There are obviously many ways to think about

the vocational placement of students in the work place or other educational settings after they finish their secondary schooling. As suggested in the previous section, many people treat placement as an event; an independent activity that can be seen differently than other dimensions of a career guidance program. Such a view can create problems where none need to exist, because it assumes that placement is different or unable to be accommodated within guidance programs or by their personnel.

In some contexts, the term placement is used vaguely. As a result, it is hard to determine if placement means locating jobs, or creating awareness of job needs and then matching students with the available jobs, or building capabilities within students to handle job search and job adjustment. It would seem that both aspects of placement – job development and student development – should be combined if the program is to be effective. Such a view would see placement as integral to career or vocational guidance.

If there is a difference between career guidance and placement, it largely lies in the fact that the first concept is heavily involved with facilitating self- and career-awareness, exploration, formulating and choosing preferences. Placement, though not excluding these concerns, is more oriented to creating processes by which choices can be converted into action through gaining entry into available jobs or educational opportunities consistent with such preferences. Thus, career guidance is concerned with anticipating and sorting among alternatives; placement is concerned with implementing choices and adjusting to them. These differences in emphasis, however, do not preclude both objectives or processes being included in a career/vocational guidance program.

Part of the way to handle such disparities is to think about placement as a process, not an event. In a systems approach, career guidance as a stimulus to career development is a process that leads to placement. In a very real sense, effective placement of students into the labor market is the end result of their readiness for vocational planning, crystallizing a vocational preference, acquiring job search and employability skills and other attitudes, knowledge, and skills pertinent to the career guidance process.

Viewing placement as a process does not preclude the fact that individuals come to placement in different conditions of readiness for decision-making and for assuming the responsibility for implementing a choice. The assumption is that these conditions will depend on the students' exposure to elements of career development, career education, or career guidance in concert with reinforcement, encouragement, and modeling in their family background and general or vocational educational experiences from elementary school through the senior high school. If such development has not occurred in the personal history of the student to be placed, the counselor alone or in cooperation with others needs to assist the student, within an abbreviated time frame, with the prerequisites to placement the individual lacks. This obviously may include some type of assessment to find out where the student stands with regard to the *process of choice* — independence, planfulness, possession of occupational information, knowledge of the decision-making process, his or her attitude toward choice — and to help him or her think about the *content of choice* — which includes the placement alternatives available, their characteristics, and their likely consequences.

If placement is viewed as a transition process for the student as well as a point in time, then as part of the career guidance program, the school counselor can, among other things, help the student prepare psychologically for placement. This may require role-playing interview situations, assistance in completing or recognizing the importance of employment applications, or making compromises because of the restricted provision of jobs available in the local setting. It will also involve support and follow-up while the individual is moving through the placement process. In some cases, the counselor must lend strength to individual students who encounter initial rebuffs in the job-seeking process until the student's self-confidence and self-esteem are reinforced.

To be effective in the placement process, it is obvious that the school counselor needs to have the time and the ability to communicate with persons outside the school who are active in placement — personnel or training people in business and industry, employment service counselors, rehabilitation counselors, and others. Such communication requires that the counselor be

able to talk knowledgeably about the competence, goals, and characteristics of persons to be placed, as well as to secure information about openings that is relevant, accurate, and localized. In this regard, knowledge of regional labor trends as well as knowledge of available local jobs is important to the counselor, as is knowledge of training opportunities, career paths, and career ladders in local industry.

Since not all students to be placed will be high school graduates, school counselors concerned with placement will need to know of jobs available for the school dropout as well. At the point of placing dropouts, the counselor needs to reject the temptation to admonish them about how much monetary difference exists between them and high school graduates or why this choice condemns them to a lifelong position of unskilled or semiskilled work. In some instances such an admonition would be in error. For instance, as Redfering and Cook (1980) have shown in their study of high school dropouts ($N = 100$) and high school graduates ($N = 100$) in which half of each group had received vocational training and the other half had not, the existence or absence of vocational training was a more potent influence on income level and job complexity than was completion of high school. Therefore, rather than moralizing about the decision of the student, the appropriate course of action is to provide the dropout with help in obtaining employment, information about ways to continue the student's education, and the reassurance that opportunities exist for resuming a high school program.

A further question that needs attention is, What will we include in the placement domain? Do we mean by placement, facilitating student entry into jobs or postsecondary educational opportunities? Or, do we mean, in addition, student placement into cooperative education, part-time employment, volunteer placement, summer employment, and a range of exploratory opportunities? Crawford (1976) has indicated that at the secondary school level one must consider at least five goals: (1) placing graduates in full-time or part-time jobs; (2) placing dropouts; (3) placing students in part-time jobs; (4) coordinating preplacement training; and, (5) advising students of occupational opportunities available through continuing education. Whether or not one accepts

Crawford's goals, the answers to the preceding questions will have very significant implications for who should be responsible for placement, how much time should be committed to placement, what resources are needed, and what the content of placement should be.

The fact is that placement for students entering the labor market has seldom been seen as a major responsibility of the school. It is true that vocational educators in different curricula, business teachers, and some school counselors have engaged in placing students. But it is less true that these activities have been performed with purpose under the rubric of career guidance or have been seen as a natural extension of this process.

And yet job placement, like other educational outcomes, cannot occur effectively unless it is seen as important and planned effectively. A recent study conducted at the National Center for Research in Vocational Education (1982) examined the factors relating to the job placement of former secondary vocational education students. They found that a strong commitment to job placement is one of the most important factors affecting job placement. National Center researchers found that higher job placement seems to exist in those schools where administrators, counselors, and teachers possessed both a clear understanding of the importance of job placement and a consistent belief that the major purpose of vocational education is the placement of students in jobs related to their training. They further found that enthusiasm for the goal of job placement is also an important part of this process. McKinney, the project director, stated, "There has to be a philosophical position on the part of the school system that job related training and effective job placement programs are two very important and two very interrelated processes" (p. 1).

Ways to Facilitate Job Placement

The study suggested that several activities seem to facilitate higher job placement rates in all labor markets. These include:

- maintaining regular contact with employers regarding the job placement of students
- providing coordination for job placement activ-

ities through a centralized job placement service and including teachers in job placement activities
- helping students acquire the basic education skills needed to obtain a job and to perform on the job, and
- orienting the vocational education curriculum to the needs of employers in the community.

We reemphasize that placement is more than an isolated event; it is a process that brings students and employers together. If the school already participates in work-study or cooperative education programs, part of this task has already been accomplished. If it does not, strategies to enlist school-industry-business cooperation must be devised. Cooperative linkage with employment service counselors is one step in this direction; vocational resource conferences, community advisory groups, utilization of chambers of commerce, and the National Alliance of Business are others.

In our experience, developing a part-time job brokering system within a career resource center or trying to set up summer employment for juniors, seniors, or students of legal age has been very helpful to the students and it has raised the consciousness of employers that the school exists, that there are students seeking work, and that the counselors are interested in learning about employer needs and the characteristics of work in their firms. This is particularly helpful in the urban area, where the students of several local high schools are competing for placement. Goeke and Salamone (1979) have described several useful related projects such as developing a rent-a-kid program to foster part-time work, job-finding clubs for seniors, or informal work-study apprenticeship programs in conjunction with employers in the private sector.

Buckingham and Lee (1973) have recommended that placement programs include job clinics. Essentially, job clinics are workshops on broad topical areas that help students acquire job search and acquisition skills related to such areas as:

- effectively completing job applications
- personal appearance
- employer tests — civil service testing, scholastic testing
- job interview behavior

- telephone tips for talking with potential employers
- transportation to work
- job referral cards to employers
- tips in applying for jobs

Gysbers et al. (1973) have outlined the responsibilities of a specialized staff member or counselor who can act as coordinator of placement services. This outline implies some aspects of program content but also suggests the outreach dimension of the program as well as the need for collaboration between career guidance personnel, other educators, and community representatives. The responsibilities of such a person might include:

1. Conduct staff development sessions for the counselors for such purposes as understanding the economics of local industry, child labor regulations, union regulations, services of the State Employment Service and follow-up activities.
2. Solicit and maintain support of administration and instructional staff.
3. Inform local employers of the placement services, cooperative and vocational education programs, and provide names and telephone numbers of counselors and others involved in placement.
4. Plan and conduct a well-organized public information program to keep parents, employers, and community members informed of placement services.
5. Seek cooperation from community and civic organizations to encourage such events as career days, work-exploration contracts, parent days, and job preparation and entry clinics.
6. Organize and initiate follow-up activity with guidance staff: plan a method to maintain continuous contact with graduates and former students.
7. Assist counselors in developing a system of job order forms, referral cards, reply cards, and evaluation forms for employers (pp. 75–78).

Also of concern in placement is the identification of a person or persons responsible for placement and, possibly, the location of a placement center. Although placement is clearly a part of career guidance, a pertinent question is, Should counselors take the total responsibility for placement, or should they serve to coordinate a variety of placement activities? There is no one correct answer to this question. It depends on school resource commitments and structures. Whether or not counselors should assume total responsibility for placement, they must consider it a significant part of their responsibilities. The existence of a placement center is again dependent on school structures and resources. In many instances, placement centers have been included as part of *career resource centers*. In this sense, placement information and procedure can be integrated with computer terminals, manpower information, career guidance references, student follow-up data, group processes, resource persons, and other aspects of the career guidance program.

Regardless of who does the job placement, Brown and Feit (1978) contend that five categories of skill are required.

- determining students who need placement
- survey of job opportunities
- prereferral assessment and training
- referral
- placement follow-up

Each of these skills has been part of the repertoire of most counselors, although frequently they have not been brought into the direct service of job placement. That such application needs to become a more integral aspect of career guidance programs seems no longer to be debatable.

CAREER GUIDANCE TECHNIQUES FOR THE SENIOR HIGH SCHOOL

Throughout this chapter, examples of career guidance techniques have been discussed for use with different student populations and for different purposes. The following inventory of career guidance techniques used in various programs throughout the nation may provide additional ideas for adaptation in the local setting. Many of these activities could be directly integrated into various subject matter areas as part of a career education infusion strategy or equally well used as part of group or individual career guidance strategies.

Curriculum Infusion

After reading a vocational biography, have students describe how a career decision made by the subject influenced areas of his or her life such as choice of friends, family life, location of residence, and so on.

Have students complete a sample job and/or college application, write a job resume, and successfully role-play a job or college interview.

Have students engage in appropriate research and prepare a term paper discussing the concept of supply and demand as it related to a changing labor market.

Develop a short unit in each subject matter area on how technology has affected the occupations related to that subject area (for example, implications of technology for office clerical workers as part of business education program, and so on).

Have students demonstrate in a written assignment the ways in which technology has multiplied the number of jobs, and have them associate this fact with the necessity for interdependence among workers in a particular industrial setting (that is, steel plants, space industry, and such).

Have students define in writing the specific steps they must go through to obtain some future educational or vocational goal. The steps should be listed in chronological order.

In art class have students design and prepare a brochure describing student skills, desires for part-time work, and related matters to be sent to the community.

Have students prepare a resume listing the various skills they possess.

After reading a biography in which the "career pattern" of a famous individual is described, have students identify the decision points in that person's life, the occupational roles played, and the stages of preparation leading to each role. Have students use this information to prepare a written assignment describing the "career pattern" of the subject in question.

After studying "industrialism," the student might write a short essay on the factors leading up to and resulting from mass production techniques as they developed in the United States during World War II.

At the beginning of any course, the teacher might help each student write a brief assignment as to the relationship of the course to some educational or occupational goal of the student. Students could also formulate a list of individual goals pertaining to the course, that is, skills, knowledges, or attitudes they hope to develop.

Group Guidance Processes

Have students construct an occupational family tree in which they research the occupations held by each of their grandparents, parents, and siblings. Have them examine gender-specific reasons for choices as appropriate. Apply specific questions to the tree: Which family member am I most like? Why? What do my family members want me to choose? Why?

Develop life planning workshops in which life roles and the coping skills required in them are analyzed and shared.

Given a career-related problem (such as selection of a college, trade or technical school; comparison of two or more occupations; need for financial assistance), have students locate appropriate informational resources.

Given ninth-grade educational plans, have senior high school students modify the plan to correspond with changing concepts of the self.

For a series of case studies illustrating examples of people making career decisions, have the students identify those examples which represent poor planning, and indicate what steps could have been taken that were not.

Have the students write a long-range career plan identifying the specific steps each must take to reach preferred future goals.

Have students develop a tentative long-range occupational plan on entering high school. This should be in writing and kept on file. It should include short-term as well as long-term goals and steps to reach such goals. The plan should be periodically reviewed and evaluated in individual counseling sessions.

Have each student develop in writing a plan of access to his or her next step after high school, either educational or occupational, listing possible alternatives, whom to contact, application dates, capital investment necessary, and self-characteristics to be included on applications or resumes.

Have students differentiate between the major

occupations that make up the occupational cluster of their choice in terms of (1) the amount and type of education needed for entrance and advancement, (2) the content, tools, settings, products, or services of these occupations, (3) their value to society, (4) their probability of providing the type of life style desired, and (5) their relationship to personal interests, abilities, and values. Discuss in group sessions.

Have students list at least six factors they are seeking in a career (such as opportunity to travel, meeting new people, responsibility, opportunity for advancement, and so on). Discuss in group sessions.

Given information concerning labor force trends from 1970 to 1980 or beyond, have the students discuss ways these trends might affect their own career selections.

Use the Decisions and Outcomes curriculum prepared for the College Entrance Examination Board as the basis for a group guidance unit on decision-making.

Discuss the kinds of decisions people of varying age groups must make: 5-, 10-, 18-, 21-, 35-, 50-, 65-year-old persons. Relate these to long-term planning concerns.

Present students with a series of hypothetical situations describing an individual with a decision-making dilemma (an individual who wants to be a professional athlete but has not displayed sufficient ability). Have students discuss and consider what compromises exist.

Devote a section of the school newspaper to profiling the skills and abilities of selected graduating seniors, to posting job openings, and to providing various job tips.

Create a job-finding club for seniors to facilitate the learning of job-search and related procedures.

Draw on past experiences in decision-making, and have students discuss how a decision that was made was influenced by some external factor (family, friends, geography).

Have students list the relative advantages and disadvantages of each of the career alternatives they are considering in terms of their relationship to expressed life-style goals.

Have students take specific steps to implement a career-based decision before leaving high school (such as apply to a job or post-high school training program, engage in job or college interview).

Using appropriate resources, have each student develop a list of entry-level skills needed for an occupational area of his or her choosing.

Have students engage in mock job interviews.

Have each student list at least six courses or school experiences in which he or she has been successful and relate these successes to the attainment of marketable skills currently possessed.

For an identified social problem, such as air pollution, rehabilitation of drug users, the development of new uses for materials, or creating by-products of fishery harvesting, have students create a lattice of occupations at different levels (professional to unskilled) that might contribute to resolving the problem.

Have students read books that depict work as a means of self-expression and discuss what this means for choice.

Have students identify important skills or competencies related to some educational or occupational goal. Have them compare their progress in attaining these with that of the previous year in terms of: (1) little or no progress, (2) fair progress, (3) great progress.

Have students list ten means of furthering their education beyond high school (such as college, trade school, apprenticeship, on-the-job training, military, peace corps, reading, and so on), and discuss the advantages and disadvantages of each.

Have students differentiate between the major occupations that make up a preferred career cluster in terms of the amount and type of education needed for entrance.

For an occupational area of his or her choice, have the student list in order the educational experiences (courses and training) needed to enter and advance in that occupation.

Have students contrast and compare a recent interest inventory with one taken in junior high school.

Community Involvement

Invite outside resource persons to review their own career patterns and emphasize the planning in which they engaged, the information they used, and information they would like to have had but did not.

Establish a placement service to provide (part-time, summer, or simulated) job experiences for students to try out job skills.

Have resource persons from the local Bureau of Employment Security discuss such matters as local employment trends, unemployment rates, and related factors.

Take field trips to local industries followed by a discussion of how new technologies or automation has affected each one.

Cooperate with the local Bureau of Employment Security to establish a program designed to inform students of local job opportunities.

Establish a rent-a-kid activity program to facilitate the development and information about part-time jobs in the community.

Interview employers regarding personal qualities they look for in employees. After an opportunity they interview employers in management or supervisory positions regarding qualities necessary for career success, have students write a short paper relating job attitudes to job success.

After an opportunity to observe and interview workers in job settings relating to an occupational cluster of his or her choosing, have the student list the materials, tools, and processes associated with the observed occupations.

Have students do a "job analysis" of an occupation of their choosing.

Have students participate in part-time work experiences in a job related to an occupational cluster of their choosing.

Using a list of community agencies, businesses, and so on and a description of their functions, have students select one and work there for a week, demonstrating punctuality, regular attendance, and the ability to perform tasks under the direction of a supervisor. Success will be judged by the job supervisor.

Send follow-up questionnaires to working graduates, requesting their assistance as contact persons for students wanting occupational information about the kind of work in which they are now employed or as job-lead resources for current students.

Summary

In this chapter we have discussed career development in the senior high school as it is conditioned by the imminence of various forms of reality with which students must cope. Continuing themes regarding a systematic approach to career development which were begun in elementary school finally converge at the senior high school level. Implications for intensity of planning and the fostering of goal-directedness in different individuals are considered as correlates of different forms of behavior following high school. The mutual contributions of vocational education and general education to career education are examined as recommendations are developed for greater meshing of these two elements of the educational process. In addition, career guidance and placement processes have been discussed. Finally, career guidance techniques appropriate to the senior high school have been identified.

LEARNING ACTIVITIES

1. Organize a local advisory committee consisting of students, faculty, administrators, business and industry representatives, parents, government agency personnel, college instructors, and vocational educators to discuss the needs for career guidance and placement in the senior high school and identify how each group might contribute.

2. Set up a meeting with vocational educators in your school or community (home economics, trade and industrial educations, industrial arts, business education, cooperative education) and discuss the responsibility for placement of their students and the procedures followed.

3. Meet with a manager of your local Employment Security Office and discuss what role

this agency plays in placement, what services they offer school students, what types of information about employment they can provide for use by students, and what policies they follow in cooperating with schools.

4. Talk with a group of senior high school students about their perspectives and their confidence regarding what they want to do after high school. Explore with them the quality of help in career guidance they have received from the school and what they would like to have.

5. Formulate a rationale for planning career guidance efforts in the senior high school with which you are familiar or in which you hope to work.

6. Visit any demonstration or operational career education programs in your state. Examine the assumptions on which the program is based and the sequential format of its activities.

7. Describe in your own words the rationale for decision-making activities, the techniques you would use in facilitating such skills, and the preparation you would need to make to lead such efforts.

8. Tour a vocational education center. Talk with the counselor about how the existing curricula differ, how students are selected for each, what happens to the graduates of the different curricula, how vocational education and general education come together in these programs, and which curricula are primarily for college-bound students.

9. Explain why placement responsibilities need to be assumed by the senior high school, and identify three major issues related to the implementation of a placement program.

10. List at least ten career guidance techniques you wish to learn or are now competent to

use. For each one, state the behavioral objectives or program goals it might facilitate.

OBJECTIVES

After reading this chapter, engaging in the learning activities, and reading the references suggested, you should have met the objectives that follow. If you have not, it would be useful for you to review this chapter before proceeding further.

1. Describe at least five typical characteristics of a senior high school population.

2. Identify at least three reasons for providing career guidance in the senior high school.

3. Discuss at least four factors pertinent to planning for career guidance in the senior high school.

4. Describe in your own words at least five goals appropriate to the provision of career guidance in the senior high school.

5. Name at least two examples of sequential career guidance projects in the senior high school.

6. List four or more methods of facilitating decision-making in the senior high school, and summarize in your own words the research findings supporting their use.

7. Identify at least three ways by which vocational education can help meet the goals of career guidance.

8. Distinguish two ways in which career guidance and placement are similar or the same and two ways in which they differ.

9. List at least ten career guidance techniques that could be implemented in the senior high school by the counselor alone.

10. Name at least ten career guidance techniques that teachers could integrate into their subject matter.

10 | Career Guidance and Counseling in Higher Education

An extraordinary proportion of Americans are enrolled in either two-year or four-year postsecondary and higher educational institutions. In 1979 over 11.5 million students were enrolled for either degree or nondegree credit (National Center for Educational Statistics, 1981).

In terms of high school graduates pursuing first-time degree credit, approximately six of every ten secondary school diploma recipients are entering college (National Center for Educational Statistics, 1980), a ratio unmatched in any other country of the world. Hence, despite some very real problems besetting higher education in America (largely related to the population curve), it is clear that substantial numbers of Americans are choosing continued formal schooling through pursuit of higher education.

It is equally clear that a significant portion of these students are experiencing difficulties in relating their educational pursuits to the world of work. In one study of graduate and undergraduate students at Cornell University, Kramer, Berger, & Miller (1974) reported that the most prevalent problem perceived by students involved vocational choice and career planning; 48 percent of the males and 61 percent of the females indicated that they were having problems in this realm. Other research (Snyder, Hill, & Derksen, 1974; Williams et al., 1973; Carney & Barak, 1976) substantiates the fact that approximately half of America's college-going population feels a need for some assistance with career planning or career choice.

A more recent study assessed the academic, career, and personal needs of 1625 students at the University of Georgia (Weissberg et al., 1982). Career development needs were expressed by a greater percentage of students than experienced either academic or personal needs. For example, over 80 percent of the students wanted to explore job opportunities related to their majors and to obtain work experience in a career area; 77 percent desired to develop effective job-seeking skills; and 72 percent wanted to learn how to prepare for their careers. Over half said they would very much like to explore their career interests, values, and abilities, to obtain information, to talk to a counselor about career plans, and to learn how occupations can affect their future way of life. In contrast, only four personal needs (time management, relief of speech anxiety, budgeting, and self-confidence) and only five academic needs (study skills, writing skills, test anxiety reduction, ease in class participation, and effective library use) were cited by more than 50 percent of undergraduates, and none of these needs was expressed by more than two-thirds of the students. Clearly, in this study career needs were perceived as paramount when compared to personal and academic needs.

Affirmation of this trend comes in a needs analysis conducted by Walters and Saddlemire (1979). They surveyed freshmen at Bowling Green State University and concluded that 85 percent of students indicated need in six areas of career information stated as:

1. information on the occupations that my chosen major will prepare me for
2. knowledge of places and people on campus that can help in my career planning
3. more direct experiences such as part-time work or job visits in occupations that I am considering

292

4. better understanding of myself to choose an occupation that closely fits my values, goals, and life-style preferences
5. knowledge of the job market
6. help to plan college courses that will give more flexibility in choosing among different occupations (pp. 227–228)

All of these studies taken together make clear the need for career guidance and counseling services in our postsecondary institutions — technical, two-year, and four-year.

CHARACTERISTICS OF THE POPULATION

Certain selected characteristics of the college-going population have a bearing on the provision of career guidance services. Among these are: reasons for choosing higher education, student cultures, age distribution of the clientele, outcomes of advanced schooling, and socioeconomic backgrounds of students.

Reasons for Going to College

Higher education in America is not a part of the compulsory educational system; consequently, going to college involves a deliberate choice. The reasons for that decision are many and varied. There is a large body of research that pertains to student motivations for attending college. Basically, these studies suggest several categories of college-goers:

The Self-Fulfillers. These students are primarily concerned with a search for personal identity and self-fulfillment. They expect the collegiate experience to offer a flexible and supportive environment in which self-expansion can occur. Although vocational ends may be present, they are neither immediate nor primary. For many others, college is seen as a setting in which to pursue assortative mating.

The Careerists. These students view themselves as attending college primarily for vocational reasons; that is, to receive the specific preparation or credentials necessary to enter into a specific profession or occupation or to prepare for ad-

vanced training and education. The collegiate experience is seen as a means to an end rather than as an end in itself. Other motivations may be present, but they are peripheral to the major goal of occupational preparation.

The Avoiders. For these students the college decision is more a matter of avoidance than it is of positive, conscious, and deliberate striving for a goal, either career or self-fulfillment oriented. In the 1950s and 1960s, these were the students who pursued higher education in order to avoid the draft. They are individuals who seek to put off choosing other alternatives, either because of lack of readiness to make these choices, because of a perceived repulsion in the alternatives available, or because of an inability to make a choice. In effect, they are buying time.

These three categories, which, of course, are not mutually exclusive, describe most reasons for the college choice, albeit in simplified form. The point is that many students in each category — the self-fulfillers, the careerists, and the avoiders — will ultimately have a need for career guidance. The self-fulfiller, at some point, realizes that although personal development and enhancement of mind and spirit are indeed laudable goals, most people in our society are expected and required to work. The careerist not infrequently discovers that an original career choice is inappropriate and searches for occupational alternatives. The avoider eventually becomes cognizant that one cannot procrastinate career choice forever.

Student Cultures

Related to the notion of student motivations for higher education attendance is the idea of student cultures. There have been many classifications offered with the purpose of delineating the clientele of higher education according to the diverse systems of values and activities to which they subscribe. Perhaps the most widely cited of these taxonomies is that devised by Clark and Trow (1966). They perceive four dominant student cultures: collegiate, vocational, academic, and nonconformist.

The *collegiate* culture is one with a high school orientation, involving "expensive play." Students in this category are engaged primarily in the pursuit of fun. The *vocational* culture is composed of those students who view college as a kind of off-the-job training, an organization of courses and credits leading to a diploma and a better job than they might otherwise expect. Their pursuit is for skills and a diploma. The *academic* culture is made up of those students who have an identification with the intellectual concerns of the serious faculty members. They are pursuing knowledge. Lastly, the *nonconformist* culture is seeking an identity. They are students who are involved with ideas, and who use off-campus groups as points of reference. They maintain a critical detachment from college and evidence a generalized hostility toward the college administration.

As with initial motivations for college attendance, student cultures are not mutually exclusive. Further, students can slide from one to the other with relative ease. Changes in student cultural identification usually entail alterations in career thinking to which career specialists must respond.

Age Distribution

The prevalent feeling is that the college-going population is overwhelmingly 18–21 years of age. The facts, however, gainsay this myth. Approximately one-third of undergraduate college students are outside the "normal" age range. Hence, the college population represents diverse levels of maturity, life experience, occupational exploration, work experience, and a host of other variables. Concomitantly, the types of need for career guidance also vary.

Sex Composition

A nineteenth-century male bastion, higher education in the twentieth century has experienced a rapid and continued growth of female students. From 1972 to 1978, the number of women 25 years old and older attending college more than doubled (The National Center for Education Statistics, 1981). The latest data show that females are in the majority in higher education. As we have indicated frequently, females at various developmental stages present a different and, in many ways, a more complicated set of career guidance concerns than do males. The clientele of higher education is no exception.

Socioeconomic Class

There are some linear relationships between family income and college attendance. As family income increases, the probability of a youngster going to a four-year college also increases. Obversely, as family income increases, the probability of vocational school attendance decreases. Two-year college attendance (transfer and terminal) is mixed when related to family income. These same family socioeconomic factors that influence college-going may also influence student expectations of college. Traditionally, higher education has been viewed as a means to upward mobility. As our society has become increasingly educated and affluent, it may be that a substantial proportion of the American middle class now views higher education as a means simply to hold on to what they have.

Outcomes of Advanced Schooling

Most people choose higher education because they feel it will lead to worthwhile personal or monetary returns. However, it is very difficult to assess the outcome of advanced schooling. Despite some recent contrary reports in the mass media, it is reasonably clear that as a group, college graduates will earn significantly more than high school graduates. Yet it is not easy to partial out the influence on earnings of a college education considered separate from ability and other personal factors.

In summary, students in higher education are a heterogeneous group in terms of age and socioeconomic status, motivation for college attendance, and sophistication of career planning. Women and minorities are attending college in increasing numbers and present career concerns that require special attention. Diverse student cultures offer a framework within which to view and to understand the college population. Finally, the outcome of higher education suggests a "payoff" in terms of careers, although many of the reasons for that advantage may have relatively little to do with the collegiate experience itself.

PLANNING CONSIDERATIONS

Eli Ginzberg (1971) has suggested that higher education has been remiss in carrying out responsibility for career guidance. He states:

> We have seen that the college setting is not a sympathetic environment for the provision of educational and career guidance. The presumption is that when students encounter problems in these areas the faculty is available to counsel them. But most faculty members know little about the world beyond academe. They are generally able to assist prospective graduate students, but often cannot help undergraduates who plan to enter the world of work. Colleges still have to recognize and respond to the need of many students for career guidance as a contribution both to increasing the value of the educational experience as well as to facilitating later work adjustment.

> We have spoken earlier of the special problems of the community college. Thus it should suffice here to note that they, too, frequently neglect vocational guidance despite the fact that occupational training is probably the most important function they perform. Unfortunately, the prestige associated with an academic rather than a technically oriented program of studies has led many administrators and faculty to downgrade students in the latter track and to neglect their guidance needs (p. 135).

Ginzberg is probably correct. As one searches the professional literature, one can discover few statements, until recently, relating to the provision in higher education of a comprehensive career guidance and counseling service. Placement, in the narrow brokerage sense of bringing employers and prospective employees together, has traditionally existed on most campuses. So, too, has the opportunity for contacts, whereby a professionally trained counselor assists a student to consider various career alternatives. These two activities — placement and limited individual career counseling — have historically existed as discrete pursuits on college campuses. Only recently has there been a movement toward combining the career planning and placement functions; only lately has the concept of programmatic, integrated, and systematic delivery of career guidance services in higher education become a visible phenomenon.

Institutional Commitment. The first planning consideration relating to the provision of career

guidance and counseling in higher education involves *institutional commitment.* Two- and four-year colleges and universities must recognize the legitimacy of the career helping function as a bona fide part of the total higher educational enterprise. Further, these institutions must provide the trained person-power and facilities necessary to effect the career guidance function.

There is evidence that institutions of higher education have made this commitment. Koehn's (1978) survey of the status of career-planning programs in California colleges indicates a great broadening from the simple broker role. Skills identification, values clarification, and speakers on the content of particular fields and job search skills were activities common at every institution. Credit-bearing career planning courses were offered at over 40 percent of the schools. About two-thirds offered sequential experiences at a somewhat less than course level. Still, problems existed including unpredictable attendance, staffing difficulties, space, lack of academic credit for courses, and general faculty ennui or, in some cases, antipathy. Further evidence comes from Reardon, Zunker, and Dyal (1979). Their survey of 302 institutions demonstrated the frequency of career planning programs and services shown in Table 10.1. In general, the larger the institution, the more varied the career services and the higher the career counselors' satisfaction with them.

Table 10.1
Frequency of Career Planning Programs and Services and Chi-Square Differences for Institutional Size

Activity	% Yes
1. Occupational Information	88
2. Resume Preparation	81
3. Interview Preparation	81
4. Educational Information	78
5. Individual Assessment Information	76^a
6. Referral (Campus)	74
7. Referral (Community)	72^b
8. Self Help Materials	71
9. Group Career Counseling	68
10. Faculty Consultation	61^b
11. Testing	58
12. Resource Speakers	56
13. Advising Undeclared Majors	52
14. Decision-Making Training	51
15. Multimedia Materials	36^a
16. Academic Advising	36
17. Orientation	35

18. Mini-Career Courses	33
19. Study Skills	30
20. Special Women's Programs	30^a
21. Staff In-Service Training	30^b
22. Assertiveness Training	39
23. Career Planning Course (Credit)	39
24. Career Planning Course (Noncredit)	29^a
25. Card Catalogue (Cross Referenced)	28
26. Job Simulation	26
27. Employability Skills Training	26
28. Curriculum Infusion of Career Materials	19
29. High School Visitation	17
30. Faculty In-Service Training	16
31. Computer Assisted Guidance	11

$^a p < .05.$

$^b p < .01.$

Some go even further in expanding the old brokerage role beyond career planning and career counseling and advocate a complete amalgamation of counseling and placement on the college campus (Robb, 1979). As phrased by Chervenik, Nord, and Aldridge (1982):

> Career planning and placement are a wedded pair, interlocked and interrelated. The emphasis that may be given to one or the other depends on the operation's constituency, location, and direct assistance from employer representatives. In short, the objective of career services is to help students to understand the career planning and placement process, so that throughout life they will be prepared to cope with the inevitable changing situation: a future with jobs and circumstances unknown at this time (p. 51).

Commitment of faculty, even with institutional commitment, remains a troublesome problem. There is still a sort of antivocationalism in many faculty who represent arts and sciences disciplines. No cure for this vexing condition has yet been discovered, but there is some evidence to suggest that faculty who are involved in in-service training for career guidance in higher education are more likely to infuse career concepts into their classrooms than are faculty who receive no special training (Ryan & Drummond, 1981).

A second planning consideration in higher education relates to the *immediacy* of students' career guidance needs. Procrastination, dilatory behaviors, and other delaying tactics in decision-making become less attractive alternatives as the imminence of the "real world" intrudes into students' lives. The Scarlett O'Hara syndrome — "I'll think about it tomorrow" — produces an increasing sense of uneasiness; one's tomorrows become fewer as one approaches a choice of major field or a career. As the graduation rite of passage comes closer, most students receive intensified pressure from parents, relatives, friends, and others to specify career goals. A few short years ago, the student was being asked what he or she wanted to be "when you grow up." Now, grown up, the student can no longer have the luxury of responding with some vaguely conceived career goal. The problem is in the "here and now," not in the long-range future.

This principle of immediacy affects delivery of services in times of tight budgets. Blocher and Rogers (1977) report that when limited funds caused a shortage of career helping personnel at George Mason University, a decision was made to concentrate priorities on services to seniors rather than on underclass students, since the needs of seniors were more immediate.

Third, in planning comprehensive career guidance programs in higher education, institutions should offer a *complete range of services*. Hale (1974) has proposed some useful distinctions among the types of career guidance services that should exist on a campus. *Career advising* is viewed as academic advisement by a faculty member, who translates career choices into educational goals and programs and relates academic curricula to career opportunities. *Career counseling* is perceived as psychological procedures used to assist students with self-evaluation and recognition of capabilities and interests. *Career planning* is seen as a process of relating the outcome of self-evaluation to information currently available about the world of work. These services should lead to an integrated, coordinated system which is composed of five elements: (1) a structured and comprehensive university-wide program of career education; (2) a central agency offering career information, career counseling, and career planning and placement in a one-stop service for students and academic advisors; (3) a cadre of specially qualified and prepared academic advisors selected from among faculty of the many subject disciplines; (4) a central administrator in academic affairs who can devote full-time to the supervision and coordination of the career education, counseling, and academic advisement system; and (5) a Commission on Academic Advisement and Counseling (for advisory and coordinating functions).

In summary, the primary planning considerations relating to the provision of career guidance and counseling in higher education include institutional commitment, responsiveness to immediate needs, and comprehensive, articulated delivery of services.

Goals for Career Guidance

Goals for career guidance in higher education should be such that all types of career concerns and needs are addressed. It is, therefore, unlikely that many students will require each of the outcomes that follow; however, almost all students in higher educational institutions could probably benefit from one or more. In a truly comprehensive career guidance program, provision will be made to achieve the following goals:

Assistance in the Selection of a Major Field of Study. A majority of freshmen will change their major field at least once during their collegiate experience. Indeed, this phenomenon is to be expected, for the first two years of study at most colleges and universities are so structured as to allow students to explore academic experiences. Each change of academic discipline entails a commensurate alteration in career planning to which career guidance should respond.

At South Dakota State University, for example, undeclared majors take a one-credit course in career planning and development and meet with an advisor at least twice each semester (Menning, 1981). The course allows them to explore various alternatives before declaring a major. For many college students, choice of major is tantamount to choosing a future vocation. Goodson (1978) has conducted research at Brigham Young University which suggests that in the chicken-egg type of relationship between choice of major and choice of occupation, the more career-oriented students choose an occupation first, whereas the less career-oriented students choose a major first. There is some evidence that the faculty adviser system produces few effective results in terms of student career decision-making (Moore, 1976;

Russel and Sullivan, 1979). Something more substantial is required.

Assistance in Self-assessment and Self-analysis. As we have repeatedly stated in this book, career planning presumes self-knowledge of several types. Reasonable career choices cannot be made by individuals who do not have a fairly clear notion of who they are, their strengths and weaknesses, what they value, their motivations, their psychological characteristics, and their interests. In short, students must be aided to discover both a personal and a vocational identity which can subsequently be related to the world of work.

Assistance in Understanding the World of Work. At the collegiate level, it is likely that most students will have a broad and basic understanding of the occupational structure. However, many students may need help in exploring specific segments of that structure in personally relevant terms (for example, What work is related to a given major? What is the employment outlook in a specific occupational field? What are the diverse opportunities available within a single chosen field?).

Assistance in Decision-making. Information, whether pertaining to the self or to some area external to the self (that is, career options), is of little use if it is not effectively processed. Such information must be translated into short-range and long-range career goals and then reality-tested. A personal plan must be evolved that, ideally, is consistent with the information that one has gathered.

Assistance with Access to the World of Work. Placement, in a broad sense, is more than an attempt to dovetail students seeking employment with available jobs. It consists of an array of services designed to help students with access to the world of work. It ranges from the scheduling of students for on-campus recruitment interviews to the dissemination of placement folders to prospective employers; but, it also entails assistance in developing student skills in "selling" oneself: resume preparation, interviewing behaviors, job searching procedures, and so forth. In fact, in one survey of the needs of graduating students, four of the top five expressed needs related to these types of activities. They were: writing a resume, finding graduate school and scholarship information, getting to graduate school, and conducting a job search (Gallagher & Scheuring, 1979).

Assistance in Meeting the Unique Needs of Various Subpopulations. Some identifiable segments of the college population present special concerns for the career counselor. Among these subpopulations are visible minorities (such as blacks, chicanos, Puerto Ricans, native Americans, certain Asians, older men and women, and so on) and less visible minorities (such as gay students). Campuses with relatively large proportions of distinct minorities may well wish to mount programs directed toward meeting the career guidance needs of such groups, in so far as these needs extend beyond "normal" boundaries (that is, coping personally and legally with discriminatory practices, locating specialized sources of assistance, and such). Another group that may require additional career aid is women. Chapter 5 in this volume deals with the unique career concerns of various minorities and women. We here point out some examples of other types of collegiate groups that may need special attention.

Foreigners constitute almost a quarter-million students in American colleges and universities. Several observers (Walter-Samli & Samli, 1979; MacArthur, 1980) have pointed out that these students present specific career concerns. For instance, they study so long in America that they frequently are not aware of current career opportunities in their own home countries. Counselors need to be sensitized to their culturally engendered modes of coping with complex decision-making. They need periodic reviews of progress and evaluations of the training to be sure that there are links to opportunities in their home countries. Preparation for reverse culture shock is another problem. Life style, equipment, and role expectations will all be different from what they experienced in America. Some will expect the college or university to offer assistance in job placement at home. Foreign graduate students seem to have realistic career plans, but foreign undergraduate students frequently do not (Salimi & Hsi, 1977). These undergraduate students, there-

fore, present an even more intense need for career assistance.

Another college subpopulation with unique career concerns is the adult student. Returning or first-time entrants to the college classroom are increasing, and there are those who argue that new and different career services are necessary for adults (Hitchcock, 1980). Others, however, maintain that modification of existing services is sufficient (Heppner & Olson, 1982). For example, the University of Missouri at Columbia responded by hiring older peer counselors, offering expanded hours for counseling, and providing in-service training in thirteen areas, including such topics as: the process a person goes through in returning to school, the process a person goes through in changing jobs or whole career fields, time and money management, issues faced by special groups, and the appropriateness or inappropriateness of various assessment tools for adults. College students over 28 years of age are more likely than younger students to be high achievers. Married women are more likely to achieve than unmarried women (Von der Embse & Childs, 1979). It is argued that adults' problem-solving orientation to learning and a desire to apply new knowledge immediately contribute to this higher academic achievement. Life experience and motivational factors seem to make adults more ready for learning and more open to career counseling. Some colleges offer a separate reentry course for these adults, especially women (Lance, Lourie, & Mayo, 1979) and provide them with a designated counselor and other specific resources to meet their common needs.

A third subpopulation requiring a special type of career attention is the liberal arts student. Especially in an age of vocationalism, liberal arts majors may require different services from their more career-oriented counterparts. Several of the specific techniques for career interventions with these students are described later in this chapter. Because their needs are unique, specific sources of jobs for liberal arts students have been compiled (Zehring, 1979), and studies have concluded that liberal arts graduates do not face so terrible an employment prospect as many fear. Cappeto (1977), for example, traced the immediate and long-term employment prospects of undergraduate business majors versus liberal arts majors. He discovered that business graduates had a large advantage in terms of initial employment (for example, on graduation day, 75 percent of the business graduates had job offers as compared with 44 percent of social science graduates, 41 percent of humanities graduates, and 26 percent of science graduates). Within five months after graduation, however, employment differences were much less sharp: 2.17 percent of business graduates were unemployed compared with 4.19 percent of science graduates, 4.9 percent of social science graduates, and 9.52 percent of humanities graduates. Still, the problem of helping students to translate liberal arts education into employable skills is formidable and requires special effort.

These are but three examples of specific collegiate subgroups that may require intensive effort by career counselors. The list of such groups could be expanded. Some colleges, for instance, pay special attention to the career needs of student athletes (Wittmer et al., 1981). Others provide special career services for veterans, especially Viet Nam veterans.

Sequencing Career Guidance Experiences

The primary thrust of this book is that career guidance experiences at every life stage should proceed in an orderly, systematic, sequenced, integrated, and articulated fashion in accordance with the common and unique needs of the particular clientele. Career guidance in higher education is no exception.

Parker (1974) has highlighted the fact that career practices in higher education can evolve in two distinct ways. On the one hand, an institution can subscribe to or invent a theory of student career development and then devise a program consistent with that theory. On the other hand, an institution can proceed on an obverse course: a college can be almost forced into a program on the basis of available resources and then fit that program into a theory on a post hoc basis. Frequently, this latter procedure is the case. Parker states:

Although it is much neater if an institution can take time to develop a rationale or a theoretical structure from which programs and organizations can emerge, it is not always possible. Frequently, decisions are made on an expedient

basis; too often they are left that way, and we have to "just make the best of it." It is, however, possible to do more than that: If one is operating from a solid base of theory, he can always bring programs and organizational structures into a reasonable "best fit" (p. 253).

Thus, the first requisite in sequencing career guidance experiences in higher education is that activities either logically emanate from or fit into a theory of student development. For example, a systems approach, TRIPOD, has been instituted at Moravian College, Bethlehem, Pa., and is based on Holland's theory of career development (Kirts & Fischer, 1973). This approach provides sequenced phases of career assistance, beginning with self-assessment, progressing through an educational and occupational exposure phase, and culminating in training for job hunting techniques, evaluation of job opportunities, and interview-taking. The advantages of TRIPOD are precisely those to be gained from any systematic, developmental program:

1. It provides a sequential developmental process which facilitates the natural occurrence of vocational maturing.
2. It promotes increased self-awareness on the part of the student and helps him relate that awareness to the world of work.
3. It is designed to be operated in a way that produces minimal conflict with academic philosophies and functions, yet seeks to use the academic community as a vital and integral resource to aid the program.
4. It promotes a team approach involving both counseling and placement personnel, each with its own thrust and emphasis, yet bound together by common overall objectives.
5. It provides maximum flexibility in that students may take advantage of as many or as few activities as they deem necessary and as their time allows. Entering freshmen have the opportunity to fully utilize the entire program, but even seniors may participate to the extent that they can make an intelligent search into the job market.
6. It allows for academic planning on the part of students in a way that assists them in selecting courses of study that will better prepare them to meet their objectives (p. 49).

A variation of the comprehensive program model may be found in the notion of modular service delivery. Abbott, McLean, & Davidshofer (1978) and Hageseth (1982) describe a two-session workshop format (fifty minutes or less per session) in which activities are carefully structured and the subject matter is restricted to a single theme. At Virginia Commonwealth University, these modules are conducted by graduate students. Modules include workshops on life planning, vocational exploration, decision-making, and choice implementation. Some institutions, such as Henderson State College, Arkansas, have expressed the sequential nature of their career programs in diagrammatic form (Luther & Smith, 1974); see Figure 10.1.

The point with all of these systematic programs is that each stage builds on a previous stage to ensure comprehensive interventions. Simultaneously, a student may enter at any stage of self-perceived or counselor-perceived need. Finally, all segments of the career-helping community have clearly delineated responsibilities in order to minimize the possibility of fragmented services.

EXAMPLES OF PROGRAM CONTENT

Basically, colleges and universities have used four major approaches to deliver career guidance: (1) courses, workshops, and seminars that offer structured group experiences in career planning; (2) group counseling activities that are generally less structured and emphasize broader, more affective aspects of human and career development; (3) individual counseling opportunities that accentuate diverse theoretical orientations to career concerns; and (4) placement programs that culminate the career planning and decision-making process.

Figure 10.1
A Sequential Model for a Career Program

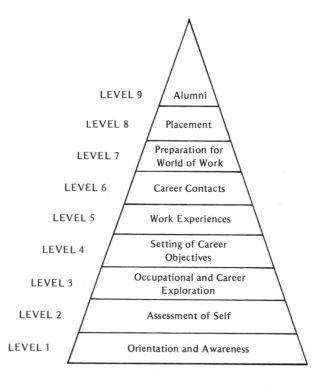

Courses, Workshops, and Seminars

An increasingly popular career guidance delivery mode is the structured group experience in the form of a course, workshop, or seminar. At Dickinson College, Carlisle, Pa., the PATH Program has been devised to assist liberal arts students to relate their studies to career alternatives, to recognize the marketable skills they possess, and to provide a framework for future job-hunting (Figler, 1973). Presumably, liberal arts students have developed communication skills and a breadth of viewpoint in problem-solving; but these skills must be related to the job market. The PATH Program attempts to assist liberal arts students to dovetail their skills and the world of work by exposing them to four group sessions of approximately ninety minutes each. These sessions are conducted with certain "ground rules."

1. Imagine that your vocational future is completely open. Make no prior assumptions about your vocational goals or inclinations.
2. Try not to censor your responses to the exercises. You will not be forced to disclose anything that you would prefer to keep to yourself.
3. Job labels are to be treated as just symbols, within which you can move around and create your own type of work experience.
4. The objective is to create your own vocation, weaving it together like a patchwork quilt, from the many different things you like to do.
5. The expectation of this program is *not* that you will have a clear, final idea of what you want to do when the program is completed.
6. This program can be used and reused at any of several times in your life (p. 48).

In Session I, students are exposed to structured exercises that focus on the Present Self. These include a discussion of childhood fantasies, a listing of things one likes to do, and a description of both achievements and failures with emphasis on the personal qualities or traits which contributed to each successful or unsuccessful outcome. Session II emphasizes the Future Self. Students respond to the question, Who will you be? in as many as ten different ways, both vocational and nonvocational. They discuss an ideal vocation and summarize antivocations; in other words, they consider both points of personal attraction and repulsion in future work. Session III is devoted to Self-Assessment. The stress is on the relationship of major field of study to career possibilities, along with a self-inventory of abilities, personal traits, and satisfactions. Finally, participants are asked to review occupational literature and to choose tentatively four occupational titles that seem most attractive. Session IV emphasizes an Evaluation of Occupations. Occupations are considered one at a time in relation to abilities, personal traits, and satisfactions rated on a 1–10 point scale. Each student compares his or her ideal occupation developed in Session II with the occupations evolved in the later sessions.

At Cornell University, female students took a course entitled Career Environment and Individual Development (Babcock & Kaufman, 1976). This course met seven weeks, once a week, for two hours, and was credit-bearing. The primary focus was the relationship between careers and individual behavior. To accomplish this end, value clarification exercises were employed, and students were taught decision-making methods, theories of occupational choice, job satisfaction factors, sources of occupational information, work-power projections, and techniques of career planning. Large- and small-group discussions were frequent, and videotapes were used. Assignments included reading, an interview with a worker in a chosen occupation, "shadowing" a person at work, keeping a decision-making diary, and writing a final paper on personal career plans. Students who took the course were matched with comparable samples who had received individual counseling and with a no-counseling control group. The course was more effective than individual counseling and no-counseling in facilitating the career development of women as measured by Super's Career Development Inventory and by Graff and MacLean's Counseling Assessment Form. Specifically:

1. Students in the class showed a significantly greater gain on self-knowledge and the relation of that knowledge to occupations than did students in the other groups.
2. Students in the class reported having engaged

in a greater number of planning activities to become informed about careers than did the students in the other groups.

3. Students in both the class and the walk-in (counseling) groups reported greater gains in changes in expressed occupational choice than did the students in the control group.

4. Students in the walk-in group reported much assistance in interviewing techniques and writing resumes and cover letters; students in the class reported no assistance in these areas.

5. Students in class reported much assistance in making a comprehensive self-appraisal but the walk-in group reported little or no assistance in that area (p. 265).

The authors concluded that "a systematic learning experience structured around values clarification strategies, decision-making exercises, and readings and discussions on job satisfaction and workpower projections can be employed effectively in a college setting as a model for facilitating students' vocational development" (p. 265).

In another study comparing the effectiveness of various career guidance delivery modes, Smith and Evans (1973) confirmed the superiority of a structured career guidance program over individual counseling and no-counseling in increasing the career development of students. Meeting once a week for five consecutive weeks, students convened in large and small groups to focus on decision-making, values, interests, behavioral traits, and social influences. The individual counseling consisted of two to four sessions and included test interpretations and discussions of values and decision-making. A control group received no treatment. The authors concluded that a systematic learning experience structured around a strategy for decision-making can be effectively employed in a college setting to facilitate career development.

Several career courses for undecided two-year college students are reported by Wollman, Johnson, and Bottoms (1975). In the General College at the University of Minnesota, a Career Planning Seminar met for one hour each week for eleven weeks, and students were awarded two credits. The seminar was built around the use of the "Programmed Guide to Career Decision-Making," a package of fifteen career exploration units

(Magoon, 1969). Fundamentally, this program involves five steps: (1) Identifying the Problem (How do I go about the process of learning more about myself and the world of work so that I can make sound occupational and educational plans?); (2) Gathering Appropriate Information (including self-clarification and understanding of the world of work); (3) Exploring Alternatives and Selecting a Tentative Choice (synthesizing information and selecting two tentative occupations); (4) Implementing a Choice (developing an action plan); and (5) Evaluating the Decision Periodically. Evaluating the course with pre-/post-tests, the authors concluded that:

1. students' knowledge about sources of career counseling, internships, occupational information and educational programs substantially increased

2. each student reported an increase in the ability to gather and analyze information about occupations

3. each student felt more competent in analyzing his or her compatibility with occupations

4. about two-thirds of the students reported that as a result of the seminar they had increased the number of occupations they would consider as occupational possibilities (p. 678)

Other career-planning curriculum interventions were effected at Metropolitan Community College in Minneapolis, Minnesota. Three elective courses were offered for credit: Career and Personal Adjustment, Women in the '70's, and Occupational Skills Development. Career and Personal Adjustment teaches a process of self-examination, information-gathering and analysis, and personal planning. Women in the '70's looks at women and work from a feminist point of view. Occupational Skills Development is a "Self-selling" course involving resume preparation, interviewing techniques, letters of application, labor market trends, and sources of placement assistance.

Working with students at Everett (Washington) Community College, Adams (1974) implemented a program designed to be preventative in nature in the sense of decreasing student failure rate. He formed four groups of entering freshmen, all of which had the same high school grade point average. Group I was a control group. Group II completed the ACT Guidance Profile, had opportunity to review an extended list of possible majors at the time of major choice, and were advised by counselors rather than by clerical personnel in admissions. Group III came to the college for an on-campus interview with a counselor in addition to completing the Guidance Profile. The counselor assisted the student in planning the first quarter's work and remained both the academic advisor and counselor of the student. Students in Group IV received the same treatment as students in Group III, except that Group IV students were enrolled in a course called Career Planning as part of the first or second quarter's work.

The course attempted to provide a relaxed atmosphere in which students could integrate their value structures, abilities, and motivations into a realistic educational/vocational pattern. Students took the Kuder DD and the GATB, became familiar with the use of occupational information, had assigned readings, wrote an autobiography, viewed various filmstrips, were exposed to guest workers from diverse fields, role-played job interviews, discussed values, interviewed a worker, wrote an intensive research paper on an occupational field, and completed a resume. In addition, each student had at least one synthesizing interview with the counselor who taught the course. At the end of one full academic year, the course group achieved a substantially and significantly higher GPA than the control group and reported more positive attitudes toward college. Students in groups II and III also experienced positive gains in relation to the control group but not nearly so large or significant as for students in the course. Adams' study represents one of the most persuasive pieces of evidence of the effectiveness of a structured group experience on career planning and college achievement.

These courses, seminars, and workshops are illustrative of those prolific in higher education. Each, in its own way, seeks to bring a systematic order to the often chaotic process of career planning. For further information on such structured group experiences see Comas and Day (1976), Hollis and Hollis (1976), Cohn (1972), Gillingham & Lounsbury (1979), Schrank (1982), Krolik & Nelson (1980), Cochran, Hetherington, & Strand (1980), Tillar & Hutchins (1979), Bartsch & Hackett (1979), and Heppner & Krause (1979).

Group Counseling

The distinction between group counseling and more structured group guidance activities is frequently subtle, and the boundaries between the two are often obfuscated. Traditionally, group counseling has involved less formal structure, more affect, and greater utilization of the resources of group members. However, attempts at group counseling with a career focus in higher education often combine both structure and relative nonstructure, as the following examples of group counseling efforts illustrate.

An effort at structured group counseling for undecided students at Louisiana State University focused on self-examination and decision-making (Kuehn, 1974). Groups met for three two-hour sessions with nine students in each group. Participants engaged in a variety of simulation and gaming activities (such as the Desert Island Game), participated in values clarification exercises, took the Strong Vocational Interest Blank, were introduced to occupational information resources, and explored personality type identifications related to careers, among other activities. Initial, highly informal evaluations were positive. It may be difficult for some to discern any difference between what Kuehn describes as group counseling and the courses, workshops, and seminars previously described. Indeed, there seems to be no difference except that the number of students accommodated in the group was fewer than typical of the latter type groups.

At the University of Miami, one-shot, coeducational, ninety-minute discussion groups are held in the dormitories. The groups are termed "Span of Life Discussions" (Kantor & Bartlett, 1974), and they are geared to helping students achieve heightened cognizance of the decisions they make in college and the effect of these decisions on the total span of their lives. Each session develops according to the composition and size of the group and according to the major concerns of the group members. These concerns typically include evaluation of the students' education to date and vocational and professional goals, male-female relationships, present life concerns, and concern for the future (quality of life). Student evaluative comments were both positive and negative. Positive student self-reports relating to the experience included the following:

1. increased awareness of value differences and conflicts among individuals and groups and acceptance of this fact
2. increased consciousness of one's individual values
3. re-examination and possible modification or strengthening of one's values
4. increased ability to make decisions and take actions that indicate and reinforce one's values
5. increased awareness of the necessity of taking responsibility for one's choices and decisions (p. 147)

A case-centered group counseling approach had students at California State College, Hayward, California, present themselves as cases (Sprague & Strong, 1970). The other group members then attempted to help the individual with questions and suggestions. Seven group members met for one hour a week for nine weeks. Each student sat for a battery of tests (SVIB, Kuder, Form DD, EPPS, and Allport-Vernon-Lindzey Study of Values). Results were combined with ACT scores, and each member was furnished a separate profile of results. The general goals for the group experience were:

1. Each member of the group was to become an expert in the problem-solving method as applied to the process of vocational choice. The sessions attempted to improve the skills of each member as a "vocational counselor."
2. Each member was to develop a comprehensive picture about himself, his interests, abilities, and needs as applied to his choice of productive goals and work.
3. Each member would benefit from the group interaction in obtaining support from his peers, having an opportunity for informational exchange, and would develop better organization in thinking and problem-solving (p. 36).

After two orientation sessions, the remaining seven weeks were devoted to focusing on a different student each week. Evaluations of these groups have been rather loose, but the results are generally positive.

Other group counseling of a career nature has emphasized one theoretical orientation or another. For example, Kurtz (1974) describes the use of a Transactional Analysis format in vocational group counseling. By applying structural analysis (analysis of the influence of childhood experiences and of parental messages on the attitudes and beliefs of the adult), the counselor assists students in increasing self-knowledge; by applying script analysis (investigating specific life dramas that persons compulsively play out), the counselor helps students to make more rational career choices. A third transactional analysis concept, the use of contracts, is viewed as a method of increasing students' information-seeking behaviors. In these groups, between six and nine students meet for five 90-minute sessions and go through a six-part program of structured exercises and discussion. Part I involves a series of exercises designed to achieve group development, to clarify group goals, and to introduce basic transactional analysis concepts. Part II exercises are intended to focus participants' attention on understanding the influence of parental values, attitudes and commands on their decision-making and on separating self-values from present values if the two are incongruent. In Part III, child-structured exercises are used to help members separate childhood fantasies from present realities. The fourth part utilizes structured exercises aimed at getting students to reality-test their plans, gather self-information, and estimate success probabilities of various alternatives. Part V focuses on the future, and the counselor tries to help participants to break down rigid or fixed "scripts" for their lives. Finally, Part VI entails discussion with a goal of integrating all previous information. Very little formal evaluation has been effected that assesses the effectiveness of this orientation as applied to career counseling.

Aiken and Johnston (1973) used positive verbal and nonverbal reinforcement with groups of undecided male freshmen and sophomores at the University of Missouri in an effort to get students to seek information and to act independently relative to their own educational or career plans. In two or three, one and one-half hour group sessions, students significantly increased their information-seeking responses when compared to a control group, although the differences tended to diminish over time. In any case, this study, as well as others presented in this chapter, demonstrates that career exploration behaviors can be taught.

The professional literature is replete with other examples of program content for career group counseling. Some have investigated the use of subprofessional counselors in career group counseling (Pate, Simpson, & Burks, 1969–1970); others have attempted to integrate a behavioral approach to career group counseling within the structure of an academic course (Parker, Bunch, & Hagberg, 1974); still others have concentrated on liberal arts students (Hazel, 1976) or some other subpopulation within higher education.

There have been some further comparisons regarding the relative career helping effectiveness of structured group experiences versus more counseling-oriented groups. A study by Perovich & Mierzwa (1980) is typical of the design and results of this type of research. They compared Vocational Information Groups (VIG) to Self-Growth Groups (SGG) to Control Groups (CG). VIGs in eight work sessions considered eight specific content areas for which vocational information was provided in a group context that allowed group member interaction (such as career development, strategies for employment, decision-making skills, sex role stereotypes). The SGGs were aimed at self-growth through greater self-understanding by means of encounter with other group members. FIRO-B techniques were used as a starting point; T group techniques were employed for the remainder of the eight work sessions. The control group received no treatment. With the VIG, college students achieved desirable gains in vocational maturity, planning awareness, and self esteem, and there were no sex differences. With the SGG, vocational maturity increased but not self-esteem or planning awareness. Both types of groups achieved results significantly better than the control group. The conclusion is that a structured group experience is preferrable in meeting the vocational needs of college students.

Individual Counseling

It is probably fair to say that most individual counseling of a career nature in higher education (at least in the past) has been of the "test 'em and tell 'em" variety. Although continuing to recognize the importance of human assessment as a requisite to career planning and decision-making, most modern counselors are placing increased emphasis on the importance of value clarification and the recognition of total life patterns in the counseling process. The trait-and-factor orientation that so long has dominated individual career counseling is still prevalent, but it has been supplemented by a consideration of the total life goals, commitments, and values of the individual.

At Harvard University, for example, one-to-one career counseling with undecided students concentrates on helping individuals to view themselves as unique and valuable persons (Ginn, 1973–1974). Once that goal is accomplished, direct personal counseling proceeds in accordance with removing the particular impediment that is keeping the undecided student from making a decision. Basically, one or more of three problems is operative: "(1) insufficient data about the kinds of work alternatives and what these would entail; (2) unwillingness to choose among the variety of alternatives for fear of limiting their options . . .; and (3) basic disagreements with, or distaste for, the options with which they are confronted, arising from the belief that commitment to social change is violated by most of these options" (p. 44).

The number of individual career counseling sessions and the sophistication of the counselor appear to have little effect on a student's gaining an increased certainty of career choice. Ullrich (1973) has demonstrated that students report an increased certainty of career choice whether seen for only two interviews or more frequently and whether the counselor is experienced or inexperienced. Satisfaction with that career choice, however, was not increased as a result of counseling. It appears that most students who seek individual career counseling are experiencing some discomfort with their situation. Wade and Shertzer (1970) studied students who came for career counseling at the University of Evansville, Indiana, and found them to have a higher anxiety level than those students who did not seek counseling. After testing and counseling sessions, however, anxiety levels diminished to the point where there were no differences between counseling seekers and nonseekers.

Samaan and Parker (1973) compared advice-giving with behavioral reinforcement counseling and reported that the latter technique produced superior results in achieving information-seeking behavior and activity, a finding consonant with several other studies in the professional literature.

Allied to the counseling strategy for the delivery of career guidance in higher education is consultation. Conyne and Cochran (1973) have noted the influence of faculty members on the career development of students and have suggested an outreach consultation strategy for influencing the academic press of an institution in the service of career development. To accomplish this goal, the career development specialist both acquires information from faculty and disseminates information to them.

In career counseling, it is useful to have a diagnostic taxonomy which helps the counselor to understand the nature of the student's career problems and thus to suggest intervention strategies. One such paradigm has been devised by Bordin and Kopplin (1973). They identify five basic motivational conflicts that students frequently bring to career counseling: (1) Synthetic Difficulties (such as diverse interests, restricted experience, realistic obstacles); (2) Identity Problems (such as inappropriate sex model, unrealistic identity, lack of identity); (3) Gratification Conflicts (student looking for maximum gratification from an occupation and minimum conflict); (4) Change Orientation (student dissatisfied with self and attempts to change self by means of career choice); and (5) Overt Pathology (pathology so severe that career choice is difficult).

Morrill and Forrest (1970) have suggested that there are several types of career counseling that fall along a continuum.

Type 1. Counseling that aids the client with a specific decision by providing information and clarification of issues.

Type 2. Counseling that aids the client with a specific decision by focusing on decision-making skills rather than only on the decision at hand. This has application for the specific situation as well as later choice points.

Type 3. Counseling that views career as a process rather than an end-point toward which all decisions lead. Thus, the focus changes from the objective of making the correct ultimate choice and once-and-for-all pronouncement of identity

to the process of making a continual series of choices.

Type 4. Career process counseling that focuses on creating in the individual the ability to utilize his personal attributes to achieve self-determined objectives and to *influence* the nature of future choices rather than merely adapt to external pressures (p. 301).

They propose that career counseling should be consonant with the developmental process: The focus should be narrow when only a specific decision in the developmental process is being considered and broad when the concern is the individual in relation to his or her career process.

Peer Counseling

One development that is apparently gaining in popularity on the college campus is the use of peer counselors. Ash & Mandelbaum (1982), Knierian & Stiffler (1979), and Zehring (1976) have advocated the effective use of peers in career counseling in order to supplement understaffed programs. Such paraprofessionals, it is argued, have a natural rapport with their peers and can be trained to perform the more rudimentary tasks attendant to counseling. One interesting side effect is that professional staff evidently are stimulated by the enthusiasm of the peer counselors.

These brief examples have been presented to illustrate that individual career counseling should take into account the "whole person" and an individual's given needs at a specific developmental time. Further, the concepts of cognitive flexibility, which will be described in Chapter 14, are urged. There is little evidence that any theoretical counseling orientation is superior to any other in the totality of career counseling. Techniques from a given "school" of counseling may be appropriate for certain types of career counseling (such as behavioral for increasing information-seeking behaviors) and techniques from another orientation for other types of career counseling (such as "insight" counseling for self-awareness and understanding). Individual career counseling appears to be effective in achieving a variety of desirable outcomes (for example, anxiety reduction, increasing certainty of career choice, decision-making, and so on); however, as noted previously in this chapter, group methods have been demonstrated to be at least as effective in achieving certain types of career-related outcomes.

Placement

In the early days of higher education in America, the placement function was largely carried out through the "old boy" network. Mentors helped their students to get jobs. Over the years, a formal placement structure evolved. Almost two decades ago, Thomas (1966) surveyed eighty-two placement offices at colleges and universities throughout the country in order to determine the purposes to which these offices directed themselves. On the average, the following seven goals emerged in rank order.

1. to assist students in the investigation of career opportunities
2. to assist in the fulfillment of the purposes of the university
3. to maintain liaison between the university and employers of its products
4. to assist alumni in matters pertaining to employment opportunities
5. to provide part-time, temporary, and/or summer student placement services
6. to act in a public relations capacity
7. to perform research in areas related to placement activity (p. 87)

These purposes still exist; however, increased attention is being afforded the career planning function. What used to be almost purely employment counseling is now expanded to career counseling in many college and university placement settings. To be sure, placement offices are still repositories of both occupational information and employer information, are a vehicle for bringing together industrial, business, and educational recruiters with student and alumni job-seekers, and are dispensers of student and alumni career dossiers to potential employers. But many placement offices are offering a broader array of career guidance and counseling services. In addition to increased career planning with individual students, placement offices are keeping academic departments aware of changes in particular labor markets, offering orientation to the world of work programs, and enacting other structured group ex-

periences to produce better work world citizens. In short, the days are gone on most campuses of simply posting job openings and scheduling recruiters.

At the two-year college level, for example, Parker (1975) has neatly summarized a comprehensive placement function in a combination flow chart, organizational diagram, and job description (see Figure 10.2). This model is intended to achieve six placement goals:

1. provide assistance to present and previously enrolled students in locating part-time or full-time employment which is compatible with their educational background, employment experience, and career aspirations
2. act as a liaison between student applicants and prospective employers to ensure ethical hiring practices
3. develop, maintain, and strengthen contacts with business and industry to identify employer personnel needs and promote/interpret college programs
4. integrate the activities of career placement services with the instructional program to the extent of developing special materials and/or courses related to employment
5. act as a resource tool for students, faculty, and counselors in career planning and course development
6. maintain an efficient records system, including an adequate follow-up procedure with which to accurately evaluate student job performance, student attitudes toward placement services, and appropriateness of college programs as they relate to employment trends (p. 254)

Placement-type activities in colleges include the preparation of manuals to help students in the job-search process (O'Neil & Heck, 1980), alumni panels (Cherichello & Gillian, 1980; Sampson, 1980), assisting with the graduate school application process (Marshall, 1979), public relations activities (Dwight, 1979), informational interviewing of employers (Boll & Briggs, 1979), and interchanges with business and industry (Lamb, 1980). One interesting study in this latter realm was conducted by Ducat (1980) who investigated the effects of cooperative education placements on the career exploration and occupational self-concepts of community college students. She dis-

Figure 10.2
Model of a Comprehensive Placement Function

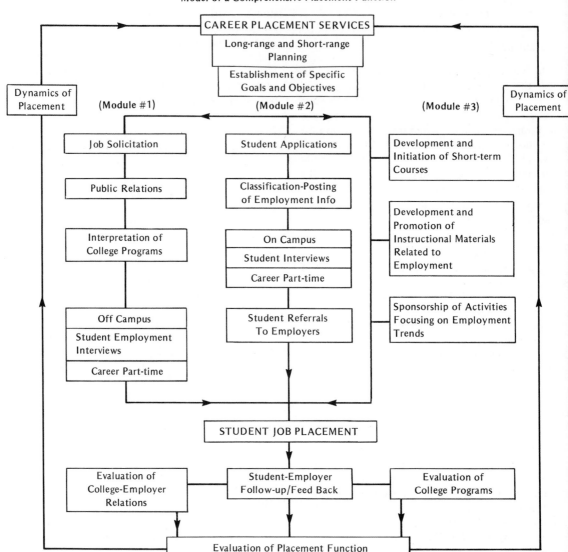

covered that the internship experience seems to activate uncertainty that stimulates vocational exploratory behavior and ultimately leads to a more favorable view of self. In short, cooperative internships may be better laboratories than the classroom for enhancing vocational exploratory behavior and self-perceptions.

Related to the placement function, Figler (1978) has delineated twenty generic life skills in five categories that individuals should use when they conduct a career search. Counselors can also use this skills inventory to diagnose client deficiencies. Thus, the skills inventory can serve as a needs assessment.

Self-Assessment Skills

1. identifying and clarifying one's *values*
2. sensitivity to one's *feelings*
3. identifying one's *skills*
4. *creativity* in imagining new career possibilities
5. recognizing extent of one's *risk-taking* proclivities
6. translating self-assessment into action by *goal-setting*

Detective Skills

7. building a *prospect list* of people, organizations, and so on
8. learning how to create contacts through a *personal referral network*
9. taking initiatives in the search process through *assertiveness*

Research Skills

10. using available *printed materials*
11. obtaining information from people in careers as an *inquiring reporter*
12. gathering data about a field or employer through *participant observation*

Communication Skills

13. gathering information by effective *listening*
14. encouraging people to talk by *questioning*
15. expressing oneself with *self-disclosure*
16. communicating through *writing*

Transition Skills

17. involving others as a *support group*
18. selling oneself through *self-marketing*
19. preparing to move to a target area through *long distance*
20. surviving financially through an *interim* job

This is a typical array of job-seeking skills, job-survival skills, job-advancement skills, and the like. Aspects of these important skill areas are addressed throughout this book. At this juncture, however, we would note that "how to" books on these skills represent an obvious growth industry and that writing them provides employment for many people.

These books have certain common elements. The writing is typically of the "selling" genre and leans heavily on metaphor and alliteration. The message is intended to be inspirational and uplifting, almost a homily on the need for faith and endurance in the process. The advice is slanted toward assertive, aggressive selling of a product — oneself. Not infrequently, the book is addressed to some specific segment of the population (women, business types, redundant workers, and so forth).

At the present time, the best that can be said about these books is that they do not seem to do any harm. As far as we know, there has not been a published study that demonstrates the superiority of any of these methods over hit-and-miss efforts or over any other of these methods. We recommend none of them; we recommend all of them.

One of the problems to be overcome in the provision of career guidance and counseling in higher education is the potential destructiveness of "territorial imperative" thinking. As higher education has increasingly accepted its role in enhancing the career development of students, various campus bailiwicks of helpers have staked claim to the career assistance function — placement, counseling, and advisement offices; academic departments; and units directed at specific subpopulations in academe (such as minority programs). This compartmentalization has the potential of producing a fragmented, piecemeal, hit-or-miss, redundant provision of services or of resulting in a coordinated, comprehensive, integrated program. Care should clearly be taken to ensure the latter outcome.

CAREER GUIDANCE TECHNIQUES

In addition to the techniques previously described in this chapter, the following procedures and ideas are illustrative of the types of activities that can be used in the career guidance and counseling of college students.

- Arrange seminars involving recruiters and faculty in various allied fields.
- Set up internship programs to provide field experiences in subject matter disciplines.
- Role-play job interviews and videotape them for student feedback.
- Have students interview individuals currently working in their field of interest.

- Videotape recruiters and amass a library of such tapes for student viewing "on demand."
- Administer personality assessment instruments and provide group and/or individual interpretation (such as Eysenck Personality Inventory, Edwards Personal Preference Schedule, Omnibus Personality Inventory, and so on).
- Conduct a credit-bearing or credit-free course or seminar in general or specific aspects of career planning.
- Administer various interest inventories and provide group or individual interpretation (such as Strong-Campbell Vocational Interest Blank, Kuder Form DD, and so on).
- Develop shadowing programs to enable students to experience "real" day-to-day work situations.
- Have students study Roe's field and level occupational classification system.
- Administer various career planning forms and discuss the results (such as Self-Directed, Programmed Guide to Career Decision-Making, and so on).
- Teach the use of the *Dictionary of Occupational Titles* and the *Occupational Outlook Handbook*.
- Administer and interpret various career development or career maturity inventories (such as Super's Career Development Inventory, Crites Career Maturity Inventory, and so on).
- Arrange faculty-staff panels to talk about curriculum and careers in their fields.
- Conduct values clarification exercises as they relate to career planning and decision-making. See Sidney Simon, L. Howe, and H. Kirschenbaum, *Values Clarification: A Practical Handbook of Strategies for Teachers and Students* (New York: Hart, 1972); J. W. Pfeiffer and J. E. Jones, *A Handbook of Structured Experiences for Human Relations Training* (Iowa City, Iowa: University Associates Press, 1968–1978); Volume I–V; and others.
- Arrange student panels composed of various majors to talk about their students and aspects of making a decision about a major.
- Devise illustrative case study materials for use as a stimulus in career group guidance.
- Have individuals in a group present themselves as "cases" to the other group members.

- Use status rankings of occupations as a discussion vehicle.
- Use the residence halls, the student union, and other areas as outreach career guidance possibilities.
- Set up mobile career information units (such as vans) and circulate around the campus.
- Locate jukeboxes, tape machines, or other audio media in high traffic locations around the campus to disseminate curricular and career information.
- Establish career information libraries or resource centers in libraries, unions, residence halls, etc.
- Utilize the campus radio or TV stations for a regularly scheduled career program.
- Have a regularly appearing career planning column in the student newspaper.
- Organize cooperative work programs for students in various courses.
- Integrate a career planning unit within an existing academic course (such as Speech, any introductory course).
- Establish a computer-based academic advisement or career guidance system.
- Engage in in-service, up-dating workshops with faculty advisors.
- Have students write vocationally relevant autobiographies.
- Use films and filmstrips to stimulate discussions.
- Teach students to write a resume and have them write their own resume.
- Engage in decision-making simulation and gaming activities (such as those in *Women and Deciding*).
- Have students engage in individual study of an occupation or an occupational field.
- Have students take job satisfaction inventory and discuss the results.
- Directly teach theories of career development or theories of career decision-making.
- Show the film *Future Shock* and discuss the implications for career planning.
- Study the occupational structure according to one or more classifications (such as industrial, census, Holland, cluster).
- Use the "Looking Ahead to a Career" slides to acquaint students with current and future per-

sonpower needs (available from the National Audiovisual Center, Washington, D.C. 20409).
- Have students read Studs Terkel's *Working*, Charles Reich's *The Greening of America*, or

almost any book by Peter Drucker. Discuss the career implications.
- Have students conduct a career-related project as part of an academic course requirement.

Summary

In this chapter, we have considered characteristics of students in higher education as they relate to career planning and decision-making. Interventions designed to assist students with career concerns have been discussed. Guidelines were offered relating to the effective and efficient delivery of career guidance services. If students were exposed to the type of career-related interventions described in earlier chapters of this volume, the need for such intensive career assistance at the collegiate level would probably be lessened. Currently, however, the higher educational setting is replete with students who have career problems to which career helpers must respond.

LEARNING ACTIVITIES

1. Within this chapter are listed six goals of career guidance and counseling in higher education. Form these goals into a simple questionnaire. On the campus, approach every tenth undergraduate at random and ask the person to indicate his or her own perceived need in relation to the goals. Administer about twenty questionnaires and tally the results. What percentage of students indicated needs to achieve which goals? You might also ask them if they know if assistance is available on campus to achieve the goals — where and how. If there is a discrepancy between stated career needs of students and perceived availability of career helping assistance, how do you account for this gap? What might be done to remedy such a situation?

2. Interview workers in career planning and placement regarding the functions which they perform. What factors do they perceive as inhibiting more effective functioning? What

services do they feel are performed well? What kinds of activities would they engage in if they had additional person-power?

3. Conduct a survey of all career planning, counseling, and placement activities on a given campus. Include centralized efforts, special program services (for example, minority students, women, and others), departmental programs, advisement, and so on. Can you discover any overlap of services? If so, how would you redesign the career helping enterprise on campus?

4. Select any given undergraduate population and any given focus for career planning with that population (such as undecided students and choice of major, seniors and employability skills). Outline a course, workshop, or seminar which would be appropriate for the group which you selected.

5. For activity 4, set up a systematic model that describes a single session of the course, workshop, or seminar. Include behavioral objectives, activities, materials, and evaluation.

6. Discuss with a classmate your personal experiences with career-related needs and the help (or lack of it) which you received as an undergraduate.

7. Most colleges and universities maintain a "career reading room," "career resource center," or some similarly named repository for career-related materials. Visit the center on your campus and make some judgments regarding the comprehensiveness of materials, ease of use, help provided for students' effective use, and so on.

8. Develop a written statement to the vice-president for student affairs in which you present a rationale for increased budgetary resources for the career guidance, counseling, and placement functions.

OBJECTIVES

After reading this chapter, engaging in the learning activities, and reading the suggested references, you should have met the objectives that follow. If you have not, it would probably be useful for you to review the material on career guidance in higher education before proceeding further.

1. Describe at least four characteristics of the higher education population.
2. Name three planning considerations relevant to the provision of career guidance in higher education.
3. List at least five goals for career guidance in higher education.
4. Describe a systematic, sequential program for the delivery of career guidance services in higher education.
5. Describe the use of courses, seminars, and workshops, group counseling, individual counseling, and placement in career guidance in higher education.
6. Distinguish at least one difference among the delivery modes in objective 6.
7. Name at least ten career guidance techniques that could be used in higher education.

11 | *Career Counseling in the Work Place and in the Community*

This chapter concentrates on the types of career counseling and guidance activities that are taking place in various institutions within the community and in some of the diverse organizational structures that constitute the work place. In each of these two settings, the principles pertaining to both developmental and remedial activities described in the earlier chapters are put to use.

We will begin with a discussion of career counseling in the work place – the stores, the factories, the laboratories, the offices, the agencies in which people vocationally function. We will follow this discussion by giving brief attention to the provision of career guidance and counseling in several agencies within the community: rehabilitation agencies; the Veterans Administration; the United States Employment Service; correctional programs; Jewish Vocational Service; federal or state programs for the disadvantaged, dislocated, or women; and continuing education programs.

CAREER HELPING IN THE WORK PLACE

One of the fastest growing opportunities for career assisting is that pertaining to business and industry in its broadest sense. Fast growing, however, does not mean common. Two surveys of the extent of career development activities in corporations, for example, demonstrate that the movement is, at best, incipient. Griffith (1980) received responses from 118 of the Fortune 500 companies from which he solicited information. He concluded that less than 25 percent of workers in the 118 responding corpora-

tions were being reached by career development services. These services included the ones shown in Table 11.1.

In a more comprehensive study, Walker and Gutteridge (1979) report on career planning practices in 225 of the 1117 firms they surveyed. Their results (Table 11.2) indicate that career planning practices in industry are more informal than systematic.

Other surveys (Abdelnour & Hall, 1980; Career Development Bulletin, 1979; Griffith, 1981; Morgan, Hall, & Martier, 1979; Cohen, 1977; Gutteridge & Otte, 1983) report similar stirrings within organizations, both private and public. Many of these surveys are unsophisticated in construction and analysis, are based on inadequate samples, and are atheoretical. Nevertheless, they do demonstrate the notion that career development in the work place is receiving increased attention and thought. In some ways the current state of the literature pertaining to career planning in organizations is reminiscent of the writing and research related to the condition of school counseling in the late 1950s and early 1960s – role studies, suggestions, reports of tentative programs, recommendations for practice, rudimentary attempts to link theory with practice, and very little empirical or evaluative research.

The Rise in Interest

Why the increased attention? It would be pleasant to report that corporate America is motivated by humanistic concerns to let employees become all they are capable of being. Alas, that is probably not the case, although

Table 11.1
Rank of Career Development Services Offered by 118
Corporations to All Employees by Frequency

Rank	Service	Frequency n (%)	Median Years Offered
1	Support for external training	98 (83.1)	8
2	Alcohol/drug counseling	67 (56.8)	6
3	Retirement planning	66 (55.9)	5
4	Support groups for minorities/ women	56 (47.5)	4
5	Job separation counseling	51 (43.2)	6
6	Career exploration	35 (29.7)	3
7	Career ladders	25 (21.2)	3.5
8	Teaching of advancement strategies	17 (14.4)	2
9.5	Personal financial planning	12 (10.2)	3
9.5	Family/marital counseling	12 (10.2)	2

Table 11.2
Career Planning Practices[a]

Practice	Doing	Planning	Discontinued	Never Done
Informal counseling by personnel staff ($n = 222$)	197 (88.7%)	11 (5.0%)	1 (0.5%)	13 (5.9%)
Career counseling by supervisors ($n = 217$)	121 (55.8%)	38 (17.5%)	0	58 (26.7%)
Workshops on interpersonal relationships ($n = 213$)	104 (48.8%)	26 (12.2%)	5 (2.3%)	78 (36.6%)
Job performance and development planning workshops ($n = 210$)	89 (42.4%)	46 (21.9%)	0	75 (35.7%)
Outplacement counseling/ related services ($n = 212$)	79 (37.3%)	4 (1.9%)	4 (1.9%)	125 (59.0%)
Psychological testing and assessment ($n = 211$)	74 (35.1%)	17 (8.0%)	40 (19.0%)	80 (37.9%)
Workshops and communications on retirement preparation ($n = 212$)	71 (33.5%)	51 (24.1%)	0	90 (42.5%)
Testing and feedback regarding aptitudes, interests, etc. ($n = 208$)	68 (32.7%)	20 (9.6%)	28 (13.5%)	92 (44.2%)
Referrals to external counselors and resources ($n = 209$)	61 (29.2%)	8 (3.8%)	8 (3.8%)	132 (63.2%)
Training of supervisors in career counseling ($n = 212$)	53 (25.0%)	67 (31.6%)	2 (0.9%)	90 (42.5%)
Career counseling by specialized staff counselors ($n = 210$)	43 (20.5%)	16 (7.6%)	2 (1.0%)	149 (71.0%)
Individual self-analysis and planning ($n = 211$)	33 (15.6%)	39 (18.5%)	2 (0.9%)	137 (64.9%)
Assessment centers for career development purposes ($n = 213$)	31 (14.6%)	37 (17.4%)	8 (3.8%)	137 (64.3%)
Life and career planning workshops ($n = 210$)	24 (11.4%)	36 (17.1%)	2 (1.0%)	148 (70.5%)

[a]Bases of percentages vary with responses. Nonresponses are excluded from percentage calculations.

Figure 11.1
Relationship Between Career Effectiveness and Organizational Effectiveness

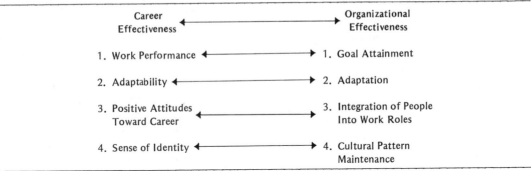

certainly every company gives the idea lip service. In fact, a variety of pressures external to the work place and a growing recognition that good career management is also "good business" have led to the enhanced emphasis on career planning and development. Equal employment opportunity enforcement, union pressures for career ladders, shortages of certain specialized personnel, and other pressures on organizations have combined to cause extant, narrowly defined programs to expand or to goad companies into establishing initial programs. Of course, the serendipitous by-product of inaugurating a program to foster organizational development is that the individual, too, benefits.

Hall (1976) schematically demonstrates the reciprocal benefits of organizational and individual attention to career development concerns (Figure 11.1).

Ritzer (1977) sees work life as basically an arena in which various types of conflict are likely to occur at all occupational levels. The solution to conflict in the work place is, in his judgment, best applied in the setting in which it occurs. Safety and health hazards, stress hazards, and hazards stemming from threatening interactions on the job (such as police work) should be addressed in the setting from which they arise. Factors such as work overload, work underload, working conditions, changing causes of stress throughout an individual's work life (Cooper & Marshall, 1980), supervision problems, role ambiguity and conflict, and other problems of work are addressed throughout this volume. In the most pessimistic sense possible, Williams (1980) points out the stressors presumably caused by

the work environment, and suggests that the organizations in which people work have a responsibility to eliminate or assuage the stressors.

The work environment in twentieth century society is also one of stress. People congest in large cities working for impersonal companies or governments. They hurry to and from work engaging in work that is often personally unsatisfying and under conditions that could be labeled inhumane. Natural bodily rhythms are subjected to clock time, and the noise of the factory often impedes communications. White collar co-workers are frequently competitors, while labor and management engage in posturing and confrontation (p. 23).

We may conclude that there is increasing excitement about the prospects of career development programs within organizations. At the same time, such programs are typically neither comprehensive nor common, and several issues and problems require resolution.

Career-related functions performed within organizations vary from setting to setting. They also change according to who is performing the role of career helper — career development specialist, supervisor, consultant. One of the most comprehensive listings of career functions in industry is provided by Leibowitz and Schlossberg (1981) and is reproduced in Table 11.3. Their perspective is that of how a manager or supervisor can perform a career-helping role. There is a potential problem, of course, when the person who evaluates work performance is also the person who serves as the "counselor." Although some people maintain that the task is not only possible but also desirable (Meckel, 1981), there is clear potential for role conflict and employee suspicion.

The difficulty in reconciling the apparently incongruous tasks of assessment of individuals by the organization and of career counseling by those who perform that function is made explicit by Burack and Mathys (1980) who list the essential differences between these two modes of operation (Table 11.4). In any case, Table 11.4 hints at the broad array of possible *supervisor* activities. On the level of the functions of a *career counselor* in industry (or the career development specialist as opposed to a supervisor or manager) the literature is less instructive. One article (Merman & McLaughlin, 1982) suggests eleven counselor activities to achieve a like number of desired outcomes. The work is presented here in adapted form:

	Role	*Employee or Organization Outcome*
1.	Advisor or Information Giver	Acquiring needed information to make informed choices.
2.	Teacher/ Facilitator	Developing of skills needed for present and/or future positions.
3.	Process Consultant	Improving of self-concept through awareness of goals, values, strengths, and weaknesses.
4.	Strategic Planner	Taking personal responsibility to manage one's own career and market self for internal or external career opportunities (for example, motivation, assertiveness, marketing, career management, and job search).
5.	Consultant to Organization	Making organization responsive to employee needs for career development.
6.	Creator and Enabler	Taking responsibility for complete control of own career (for example, providing situations for employees to learn in a nonthreatening atmosphere).

	Role	*Employee or Organization Outcome*
7.	Facilitator/ Teacher (see #2)	Becoming an active problem solver and understanding and developing process skills.
8.	Integrator	Developing trust that the organization understands his or her needs including the effect of career changes on personal life styles.
9.	Consultant/ Mediator	Coordinating personal needs and organizational mission.
10.	Facilitator/ Philosopher/ Futurist	Participating in helping the organization identify the effect of current issues, trends, and social values.
11.	Manager of a System/Conceptualizer	Organization develops an appropriate and evolving career management system using emerging technologies.

Pervading the literature, there is the recurring theme of a tension between individual needs, goals, and aspirations on the one hand and the organization's needs and requirements on the other. Usually, career helping is effected either by a disinterested third party or by a third party who is passionately committed to the individual as opposed to any institution. It is not surprising, then, that human resource management specialists are gingerly entering the career development field *in situ*. Organizations have some fears about possible negative consequences of increased career development activities in the work place. These roadblocks to progress include: the raising of false expectations in the minds of employees regarding promotional possibilities (Zenger, 1981); overplanning that tends to provide more regulation than is necessary (Cleveland, Orr, et al., 1975); management ignorance about the advantages of career counseling (Gambrill, 1979); lack of organizational self-insight (Schein, 1978); servicing large demand once programs are established (Morgan, Hall, & Martier, 1979); difficulty in evaluating the results of career development programs (Connelly, 1979); and perceptions of getting help as an indication of weakness (Knowdell, 1982). Although none of these concerns has been documented as occurring, they are significant possibilities that must be fully addressed if career planning in organizations is to be effective.

Organizational Career Patterns

Some preliminary work offers tentative paradigms of "normal" developmental career patterns in organizations. The types of career patterns that are possible for individuals in organizations seems to depend very much on the type of management espoused by the organization. For example, Ouchi and Jaeger (1978) and Ouchi (1981) have distinguished three types of management styles in organizations. Type A, American in orientation, is characterized by short-term tenure in employment, quick promotions, and specialized career paths. Type J, Japanese in origin, is marked by more long-range, secure employment, slow promotion, and nonspecialized career paths. It is argued that a third style, Type Z, would be appropriate for American organizations. Type Z would be distinguished by long-term, although not guaranteed employment, slow promotion, and moderately specialized career paths. All three management styles hold implications for individual career development patterns within organizations.

Assuming the typical extant American system, however, Dalton, Thompson, and Price (1977) suggest four progressive *professional* career stages in organizations: apprentice, colleague, mentor, and sponsor. Each stage involves different activities, relationships, and psychologically related developmental tasks. This categorization is very general and not based on any theoretical or research foundation.

Hall (1976) also presents a global notion of career stages within organizations and their concomitant tasks. He describes early career, middle career, and late career stages and offers examples of the type of tasks attendant to each stage.

Early Career–for example, develop action skills, a specialty, creativity, innovation; deal with feelings of rivalry and competition

Middle Career–for example, develop skills in training and coaching others and a broader view of work and organization, train to update and integrate own skills, reorganize thinking about self

Late Career–begin to establish self in activities outside the organization, gradual detachment from organization, shift from power role to one of consultation, guidance, wisdom

A somewhat more specific model is provided by London and Stumpf (1982). Using Buehler's original categories as adapted by Super (described earlier in this volume), they offer developmental requirements associated with mastery of each adult career stage.

Stage I: *Exploration and Trial* (e.g., taking a job offer, experiencing training and job challenges, setting goals, getting feedback)

Stage II: *Establishment and Advancement* (e.g., developing expertise, experiencing success or failure, reinforcing self-image, forming a career strategy, finding a mentor)

Stage III: *Mid-Career*

(a) *Growth* (e.g., evaluating goals, fearing stagnation, adjusting career direction, needing change, working through midlife crisis)

(b) *Maintenance* (e.g., realizing the value of job security, fearing the risk of change, expressing loyalty to the organization, having a feeling of pride in professional accomplishments, becoming a mentor, etc.)

(c) *Decline* (e.g., sensing failure, insecurity, and crisis, anticipating early retirement with few plans, disengaging from work and nonwork prematurely, developing physical and/or mental illness)

Stage IV: *Disengagement* (e.g., psychologically preparing for retirement, finding new interests and sources of self-improvement, learning to accept a reduced role)

Most of the descriptive material relating to career stages in organizations is based on very small samples or on observations of individuals within selective industries or occupational groups. For example, one classification evolved from a

Table 11.3
Roles and Associated Questionnaire Items

Communicator

- Holds formal and informal discussions with employees
- Listens to and understands an employee's real concern
- Clearly and effectively interacts with an employee
- Establishes environment for open interaction
- Structures uninterrupted time to meet with employees

Counselor

- Helps employee identify career-related skills, interests, values
- Helps an employee identify a variety of career options
- Helps employee evaluate appropriateness of various options
- Helps employee design/plan strategy to achieve an agreed-upon career goal

Appraiser

- Identifies critical job elements
- Negotiates with employee a set of goals and objectives to evaluate performance
- Assesses employee performance related to goals and objectives
- Communicates performance evaluation and assessment to employee
- Designs a development plan around future job goals and objectives
- Reinforces effective job performance
- Reviews an established development plan on an ongoing basis

Coach

- Teaches specific job-related or technical skills (OJT)
- Reinforces effective performance
- Suggests specific behaviors for improvement
- Clarifies and communicates goals and objectives of work group and organization

Mentor

- Arranges for an employee to participate in a high-visibility activity either inside or outside the organization
- Serves as a role model in an employee's career development by demonstrating successful career behaviors
- Supports employee by communicating to others in and out of organization employee's effectiveness

Advisor

- Communicates the informal and formal realities of progression in the organization
- Suggests appropriate training activities which could benefit employee
- Suggests appropriate strategies for career advancement

Broker

- Assists in bringing employees together who might mutually help each other in their careers
- Assists in linking employees with appropriate educational or employment opportunities
- Helps employee identify obstacles to changing present situation
- Helps employee identify resources enabling a career development change

Referral Agent

- Identifies employees with problems (e.g., career, personal, health)
- Identifies resources appropriate to an employee experiencing a problem
- Bridges and supports employee with referral agents
- Follows up on effectiveness of suggested referrals

Table 11.3 (continued)

Advocate
- Works with employee in designing a plan for redress of a specific issue for higher levels of management
- Works with employee in planning alternative strategies if a redress to management is not successful
- Represents employee's concern to higher-level management for redress on specific issues

study of approximately 200 scientists and engineers who may or may not be representative of other types of personnel in organizations. From the experience of these subjects, the investigators (Graves, Dalton, & Thompson, 1980) postulate four stages of careers that occur within organizations.

Stage 1 is characterized by work in collaboration with and under the guidance of a senior researcher or formal supervisor. Work is never completely one's own, for assignments are part of a larger project or activity. The scientist or engineer tends to do routine, detailed work. A task at this career stage is to balance the need to be dependent and the need to show initiative if one is to advance to a higher stage. Stage 1 is basically an apprenticeship.

Stage 2 finds the engineer or scientist having his own project or area of responsibility. The worker assumes responsibility for a specific portion of a project or for a process. He works with relative independence and is judged by the results that are produced. It is in this stage that the worker acquires a reputation for competent work

Table 11.4
Career Counseling Versus Appraisal Interviewing: Similarities and Differences

Element	Career Counseling	Appraisal Interviewing
Focus	• helps individual take charge of own career	• determines potential value of employee to organization
Time frame	• short-run to long-term	• immediate
Information	• individual gets more information than organization	• organization gets more information than individual
Direction	Individual ⇄ Organization	Individual ⇄ Organization
Type	• career paths, ladders • job requirements • organization politics	• judge past performance • assess potential • establish promotability • compare against performance standards
Climate	• supportive, nonthreatening	• neutral, threatening, and/or at times helpful (developmental)
Result	• helps person to establish goals, means, completeness, logic, and next step in own career • where specific targeted jobs are involved, will involve needs analysis to establish individual developmental requirements along his or her career path	Traditional approach: • hire or reject • recommendation to promote or transfer Developmental approach: • supply useful career-related information • work out means to achieve job objectives

and establishes his credibility. It is a stage characterized by independence and specialization.

In stage 3, the worker assumes responsibility for the guidance of others. He applies a greater breadth of technical skills and works for the benefit of others in the organization. His task is to develop and stimulate others through ideas and information. He becomes a mentor as he develops from a perspective of self to a perspective of others.

Finally, in Stage 4 the worker becomes a significant influence over the future direction of a major part of the organization. More than a mentor now, the scientist or engineer sponsors and develops many promising people. He has wide interactions both inside and outside of the organization. He becomes either an upper-level manager, an idea innovator, or an internal entrepreneur.

A still more specific delineation of the normal course of careers in organizations is provided by Schein (1978). He divides the career life cycle into four stages: entry, socialization, midcareer, and late career.

Entry Stage Tasks

1. Making a preliminary occupational choice that will determine the kind of education and training to pursue.
2. Developing a viable "dream" — an image of the occupation or organization that can serve as the outlet for one's talents, values, and ambitions.
3. Preparing oneself for the early career through "anticipatory socialization," in order to develop what one considers to be the attitudes and values necessary for succeeding in one's chosen occupation.
4. Facing the realities of finding a first job.

Socialization Stage Tasks

1. Accepting the reality of human organization (for example, dealing with people, communicating).
2. Dealing with resistance to change.
3. Learning how to work; coping with too much or too little organization and too much or too little job definition.
4. Dealing with the boss and deciphering the reward system — learning how to get ahead.

5. Locating one's place in the organization and developing an identity.

Mid-Career Stage Tasks

1. Finding career anchors (a "career anchor" is an occupational self-concept resulting from self-perceived talents and abilities, self-perceived motives and needs, and self-perceived attitudes and values — in short, the pattern of self-perceived talents, motives, and values to guide, constrain, stabilize, and integrate the person's career). Five career anchors have been identified; four others are hypothesized. (A tenth career anchor, *warrior*, has been identified among army personnel (Derr, 1980). Warriors have a basic psychological need for high adventure and action).
   a. technical/functional competence
   b. managerial competence
   c. security and stability
   d. autonomy
   e. creativity
   f. basic identity
   g. service to others
   h. power, influence, and control
   i. variety
2. Specializing versus generalizing

Late-Career Stage Tasks

1. Becoming a mentor.
2. Achieving a proper balance of involvement in work, family, and self-development.
3. Letting go and retiring.

Each of these attempts at defining the course of careers within organizations, as well as other attempts to describe the work life cycle (see, for example, Miller & Form, 1951), potentially provide a theoretical base for in-house career development programs.

The Career Counselor in the Organization

Several people have urged career counselors to intensify their role in organizations, especially in industry. Indeed, such a concept is not new; one can point to isolated instances of counseling by psychologists within industry as far back as the 1920s (Baker, 1944). Several contemporary writings about psychologists functioning as counselors within industry describe in a sort of "how I spent my summer vacation" way the activities of academics on sabbatical leave who tried to link "town and gown" more closely by working within industry in their geographical area. One such endeavor was undertaken by Lipsett (1980). During his sabbatical, he set up an office within a 1700-person plant and counseled employees. These employees had four basic categories of problems. The first group wanted help in changing from perceived routine occupations (such as secretary) to those perceived as less routinized and more satisfying (such as sales). The second group desired educational counseling, mainly in order to qualify for job advancement. The third group wanted to explore qualifying for management. The fourth group brought to the counselor problems of work adjustment (such as relations with supervisors). Lipsett concluded that disseminating information played an important part in his functioning and that test results, career path charts, and educational and occupational information resources were necessary in the industrial setting.

A college counselor used another leave to set up services at a 200-person Smith Corona laboratory (Papalia & Kaminski, 1981; Papalia & Moore, 1979). These services then continued on a part-time basis after the leave. The counselor typically spent his time focusing on personal adjustment, academic counseling, and career decision-making. In addition, the counselor helped to develop training programs which carried academic credit at his institution. He further acted as a group facilitator for human relations, problem solving, decision-making, organizational development, leadership training, and communication skills. Part of his role also included referrals to local agencies (e.g., Catholic charities) and outplacement counseling. Finally, he arranged for the offering of flextime courses dealing with such topics as "Transactional Analysis for Managers" and "The Psychology of Personal Adjustment."

A somewhat less provincial approach is taken by Leonards (1981) who speaks more universally about the possibilities of corporate psychology. He believes that counseling psychologists are most appropriate for corporate clientele because of their emphasis on working with healthy personalities. Foci would include counseling for resolution of mid-career issues, for pre-retirement planning, and for specific career development

concerns. Further contributions to the corporate body would come from the counselor's assisting in organizational development, program evaluation, and general psychological consultation.

Continuing with speculation regarding the role of a counseling psychologist in industry, both Toomer (1982) and Osipow (1982) offer ideas about how psychologists can transcend a career role in organizations and can contribute to many areas. Toomer's ideas of the roles and relationships of counseling psychologists in business and industry appear to speak to almost everything *but* career counseling. Figure 11.2 indicates a broad range of roles and functions he would propose.

Osipow's ideas about applications in organizations for counseling psychologists are more specific in their career-relatedness. He suggests, for example, 16 possibilities for useful contributions.

1. Helping employees and managers identify hazards in work
2. Training people to identify their work styles (especially those that might be deleterious to them) and teaching them to change them
3. The effects of repetitive work on people
4. The effects of transfers to new locations, especially if forced
5. Special stresses and strains in the two-career couple family
6. Special stresses experienced by people employed in boundary spanning roles (e.g., jobs which require employees to "split" allegiances)
7. The special stresses in people with high interpersonal demands in their jobs
8. Preparation for retirement
9. Dealing effectively with the process of job evaluation
10. Dealing with the special problems of entrepreneurs
11. Dealing with the problems of job loss
12. Dealing with the special problems of small business people
13. Dealing with the special problems of professionals
14. Health care issues
15. Self-help and self-care
16. Family counseling

Each of these articles is representative of the

Figure 11.2
Counseling Psychologist in Business and Industry: Roles and Relationships

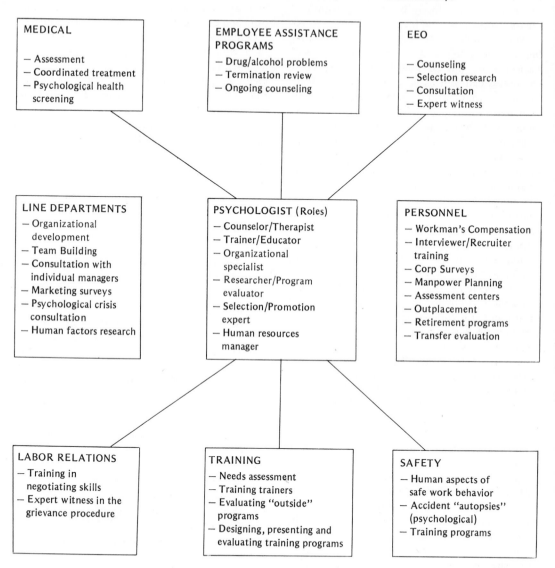

current state of the career counselor in industry. They offer tentative, exploratory proposals of how specialists can function to enhance career development in the organization. There are not, as yet, definitive answers to a number of questions. These questions are addressed later in this chapter.

Examples of Career Programs

As indicated by survey results, many organizations have formal, functioning career development programs. General Electric, AT&T, AirCal, Aetna, and Xerox, for example, all have formal materials and procedures to assist their employees with career development concerns. We here offer a brief description of several illustrative programs in order to give a flavor of the activity that is taking place.

Since 1975 a program at Livermore Laboratory in California has served the 7000-plus person workforce by means of three major components: a career assessment center, individual career counseling, and several career assessment workshops. The workshops are conducted during working hours for about seven weeks. They are limited to eighteen participants per session, and require approximately forty hours of participant time. Workshops progress from overviews of career planning to assessment of values and interests, to decision-making concerns, to an achievement motivation program. Evaluations based on participant self-reports have been generally positive (Knowdell, 1982).

Related to this program is the establishment of a Career Resource Center at Livermore (Moir, 1981). This is a typical example of such centers which are, of course, common outside of business and industry but are rarer within the work place. The center is run by a full-time office assistant who is supervised by a professional career resource specialist. It contains educational information, career planning information and resources, data on the world of work, books and cassettes related to personal growth, supervisory/management training materials, computerized career information, professional periodicals, self-study courses, and announcements of off-site training.

One common strategy related to career development in organizations is the assessment center (Moses & Byham, 1977). There is little doubt that the assessment center is used more for personnel selection than for individual development, more for identifying potential managers than for diagnosing employee strengths and weaknesses. The concept began in World War II with selection of spies for the OSS and now concerns itself largely with selection for higher management and for management trainees. In a few situations, the assessment center is also used to select sales and technical personnel and other nonmanagement workers. Techniques used in assessment centers include: in-basket exercises (an individual is provided with data relating to problems and must, within a specified time period, demonstrate ef-

fective decision-making); related management games and simulations; leaderless group discussions; analysis and presentation of complex situations; role playing exercises; essay writing; psychological aptitude and personality tests; and others. These techniques are designed to assess oral and written communication skills; leadership; ability to organize and plan; decision-making ability; tolerance for stress and behavioral flexibility; and energy, forcefulness, creativity, and risk taking among other traits (Bender, 1973). There is obvious potential for byzantine behaviors by assessors; consequently, those involved in assessment center activity have produced a guiding document, *Standards for Ethical Considerations for Assessment Center Operators.*

At the University of California, Santa Barbara campus, a career development program serves staff employees (largely women) in groups of twelve (Eng & Gottdanker, 1979). The program consists of a self-assessment (such as SDS or POI) and subsequent exercises focusing on skills analysis, personal work and environmental goals, self-imposed barriers, assertion and self-expression skills development, job interviews, and role-playing of interpersonal conflict situations. The aims of the program include increases in awareness of career options, understanding of how to achieve new goals, and self-confidence. Self-reports of participants suggested substantial changes in both attitudes and actual career shifts.

At the Internal Revenue Service, a program, Interpersonal Relations Training for Upward Mobility (IRT Program), focuses on giving women the assertiveness skills necessary for career advancement (Hultman & Cunningham, 1978). The program consists of twelve videotapes of problem situations, group discussion, and role-playing exercises. Evaluations indicated that most participants improved their ability to recognize ineffective work responses.

The Gulf Oil Corporation in Pittsburgh and Chatham College have combined resources to offer a program to help women assume an active personal role in future planning and to use information effectively in implementing plans (Fort & Cordisco, 1981). These ends are addressed by means of assessment activities (values, interests, temperament, and selected aptitudes), individual advising (by one person from Gulf and one from

Chatham and directed at educational information and career goals), and workshops (lectures, discussions, homework, and so on). Evaluations are loose but suggest positive growth on the parts of participants.

One advantage of providing career counseling services in the work place is that tailor-made assessment instruments can be used that have potentially greater face validity and predictive validity than more generic instruments. For example, the Social Security Administration, which employs 80,000 people, has developed its own Career Interest Profile (Barad, 1977). The CIP instrument was designed to assess interests in each of twelve focal occupations (such as public contact claims, disability examining, social insurance policy and procedures, supervisory). The potential for such made-to-order assessment devices is obvious.

Many organizations have excellent in-house educational and occupational information materials. One is the Aetna Life and Casualty Company. They publish several volumes for their employees in a *Develop Yourself* series. For example, *Develop Yourself: A Guide to Education and Training* is an almost 250-page catalog of all the education and training offered at Aetna. Each course is listed in terms of the purpose of the course, for whom it is designed, what its content is, how long it lasts, what the prerequisites are, how to get registered, and how much, if anything, the course will cost. This document puts to shame many college catalogs. A companion volume, *Develop Yourself: A Career Path Handbook*, is intended to provide Aetna's 36,000 employees with information about job possibilities within the company in fourteen job clusters and the career progression usually followed.

Published material, however, need not be voluminous to be effective. The Carborundum Corporation publishes for its employees a series of career ladders in each plant location relating to such occupational areas as engineers, factory operations, cost engineering and scheduling, construction, engineering technologists, chemists, procurement, and administration. The career ladder for cost engineering and scheduling is shown in Figure 11.3 as an example of how effective a graphic of a simple career ladder can be.

These examples of program content indicate that many of the techniques developed outside of organizations are being put to use within the work place. Also, however, specific techniques and materials are being developed to meet the unique needs of particular organizations.

There is, of course, disagreement about what are appropriate or inappropriate approaches to career programs in organizations. Kolb and Plovnik (1977) have described four limitations to existing career development programs. In paraphrased form, they are:

1. They are too work oriented (rather than dealing with total life interests). Therefore, the focus should be on life rather than on occupation. Participants should examine the relationships among work, family, leisure, spiritual/developmental needs, and so on.

2. They are too specialization centered; that is, they focus only on one's dominant interests or proven abilities. Rather, they should center on career as a here-and-now issue. Participants should be helped to reinterpret personal history and readjust goals in light of emerging life circumstance.

3. They are too planning oriented. Some people thrive on goals; others do not. Therefore, emphasis should be on immediate personal choices rather than on long-range planning. Individuals should be brought into closer contact with the choice-making process.

4. They are too outcome oriented; that is, they emphasize outcome at the expense of process. Thus, individuals do not learn a process to apply in the future. Emphasis, therefore, should be on the learning process itself as opposed to outcomes.

In our judgment, this either-or discussion sets up a mutually exclusive, dichotomous model when, in fact, the presumably antithetical elements are both necessary. Concentration on one at the expense of the other is a mistake. Programs are needed that focus on both if career in the sense that the term is used in this book is to be addressed adequately. There certainly are no extant "rules" for providing career assistance in the work place. Developers are relatively unfettered in their attempts to implement a concept. That same freedom, however, leads to several questions.

Figure 11.3
Cost Engineering and Scheduling Career Ladder for Exempts without Engineering Degrees
(Engineers: See Engineering Career Ladders)

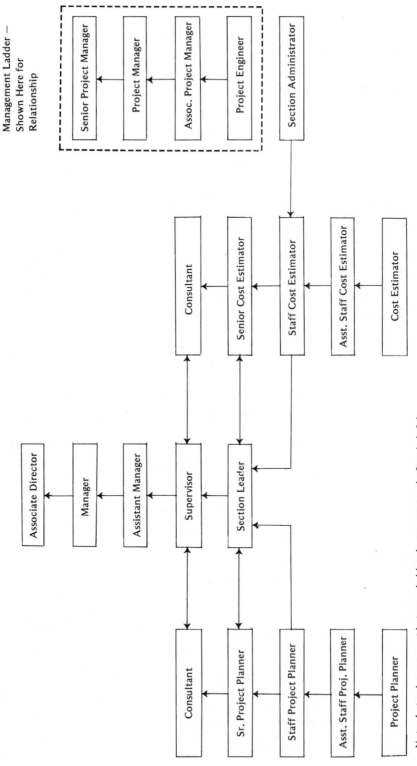

325

Issues and Needed Research

Throughout our discussion in this chapter, we have pointed to unresolved issues and to several questions that lend themselves to researchable answers. To conclude our exploration of career counseling in the work place, we summarize these concerns.

1. Can career counseling effectively occur within the work place when there appears to be a basic conflict between the necessity for performance evaluation and the desirability of threat-free career development activity? Can both organizational and individual needs be met within the corporate body?
2. Who should provide career development services within industry? Supervisors? Career counseling specialists? Generic training and development personnel? Some new hybrid of human resource development specialist and career counselor?
3. What are the appropriate functions necessary to achieve which career development outcomes in organizations?
4. What methods and materials are best for what types of adult clients and/or concerns?
5. What evidence can be gathered to prove, disprove, or alter current theoretical notions about adult career development?
6. How do career identities develop? How are they shaped by work experiences? (Super & Hall, 1978)
7. How can we define success in career development? What criteria are appropriate? Are money earned, satisfaction, career maturity, and other outcome measures appropriate?
8. How can we best evaluate to demonstrate the effectiveness of career development programs in organizations? Can we successfully reconcile equal employment concerns and organizational needs?
9. What can be done to secure pervasive organizational support for career development programs?
10. Is there a "critical mass" of personnel and materials necessary in order to provide minimally acceptable career development services? Is there a minimum number of employees required before a program should be established?
11. Is it possible to use generic career development systems to apply in various organizations, or must systems be tailored to the unique needs and populations of each institution in the work place?
12. What types of research are required to produce improved performance appraisal, a greater understanding of supervisor/supervisee relations, and so on?
13. What are the differential career development needs of diverse subpopulations within the organization (such as clerical, supervisory, managers, production, sales)?
14. How can many of the adult career concerns and special populations described in Chapters 5, 12, and 13 best be addressed within the structure of work place organizations?
15. Are career development concerns best handled at several locations or at a "home" office?

Proprietary Placement Agencies

A word about proprietary "career counseling" firms or placement agencies is in order. The general stance toward these organizations is *caveat emptor* (Lilley, 1978). There are obviously some perfectly legitimate private employment agencies and career counseling firms. In general, one can be reasonably confident about a placement firm when the employer pays the fee. In no case should a job seeker ever pay money "up front" to a placement agency. In terms of career counseling, we have had called to our attention firms that for a fee of $2,000–$3,000 will do no more and no less than "standard" career helping procedures: testing, exploration of self, exploration of the world of work, and decision-making assistance. Again, as a general rule, no group or individual career counseling should ever exceed a cost more than $300–$400. Even then, potential counselees should shop around a community for the "best deal" that balances quality service with moderate cost. Sometimes, additional "personal" counseling may be necessary before an individual can be said to be truly job ready, and additional counseling may add to the cost of basic career counseling. One should be wary, however, of such circumstances.

CAREER HELPING IN THE COMMUNITY

Within the community, adults or others who wish to receive career counseling have several possibilities for service. However, many of these organizations do not exist in some communities; if they do exist, they are often inadequately publicized. The rest of this chapter presents an overview of the more common of these types of organizations.

Two surveys have investigated the extent of adult counseling resources and the types of programs that are offered in the community. Obviously, many of the resources identified relate to career counseling. About a decade ago, Harrison and Entine (1977) conducted a survey for the American Institutes for Research. They gleaned useable responses from 367 adult programs. Of this sample, about one-third were sponsored by colleges and universities; one-fifth were under the aegis of community colleges; 18 percent were housed within private agencies (such as YWCA or B'nai B'rith); 16 percent were located within government agencies; and 12 percent were affiliated with a school district. Operating within this structure, these programs provided career classes, workshops, seminars, and small-group interactions, frequently on an outreach basis (shopping centers, libraries, and so on). Most of the career programs disseminate information (sometimes by telephone and mobile vans), provide testing and test interpretations, engage in job placement and job development, or do all three.

A second, more recent study (Whitson et al., 1979) examined CETA-sponsored adult counseling programs in three major American cities. Within these programs, the career services provided were typical of those reported by Harrison and Entine: intake, assessment, counseling, training, placement, and referral. Frequently emphasized were job search techniques, interviewing skills, and resume preparation training. Many of the programs for adults provide more than career counseling, of course, but we are here concerned simply with career assisting opportunities.

The U.S. Employment Services

The U.S. Employment Service is the national umbrella for fifty state services. In some states, these are called the Job Service, whereas in others they are called the Employment Service. For instance, the New York State Job Service has over 150 local offices that provide career assistance. There is no charge either to employers or to job seekers, since the Job Service is funded by Federal Unemployment Insurance Tax revenues. The Job Service provides help to both employers and to job seekers. In terms of service to employers, the Job Service typically offers:

Job Matching–Computer matching of qualified candidates and available jobs.

Applicant Selection and Job Openings Referral–interviewing and referral of applicants to jobs (with preference to certain target populations)

Interstate Clearance (nonagricultural)–recruitment of workers from other areas to meet needs in a given area

Job Bank–computerized listings of jobs for given metropolitan areas

Federal Bonding Program–fidelity bonding for qualified workers if inability to obtain bonding is a barrier to employment

Labor Market Information–current and projected labor statistics throughout any given state (for example, labor force, wages and salaries, hours and earnings of factory and production workers, collective bargaining settlements, employment of minorities and women, occupational projections)

Apprenticeship–registering of all apprentice training programs and developing training standards

Cooperation with Department of Commerce–Job Incentive Program (tax incentives to business to create jobs), Industrial Development Program (On the Job Training, WIN, Private Industry Council, and so forth)

Testing Program–gives, for employers, tests of general aptitudes, clerical skills, literacy, and interests

Occupational Analysis–in-depth technical services in selection, turnover, absenteeism, job assignments, training, direction, personnel practices, and procedures

GAMOT (Gate Applicant Master Order Technique)–provides large companies with an efficient means of screening large numbers of applicants

Tax Credits–informs companies of various tax breaks for employing certain target group individuals (at the time of this writing, for instance, SSI recipients, handicapped referred from Vocational Rehabilitation, youth from economically disadvantaged families, Vietnam veterans under 35)

On the Job Training–helps employer defray costs of hiring and training new workers

WIN/OJT–Work Incentive Program helps people who receive aid to dependent children go from welfare to economic independence. WIN sponsors on-the-job training (see above)

The U.S. Employment Service, through its state agencies and local offices, also provides direct service to individuals. Some offices are full service in that they handle all occupational codes in the *Dictionary of Occupational Titles*; others are special-service offices (for example, serving only industrial and service occupations). Offices may also have casual labor sections (day work), domestic sections (housekeeping, cleaning), a professional unit, a restaurant registry, a nurse registry, a substitute teacher registry, an expert for aliens and immigrants, among many other specialized programs.

Within the Job Service Office, there are three basic positions related to career counseling. *Placement interviewers* (or employment interviewers) initially see all applicants. On the basis of the data they gather in the interview, they refer applicants to appropriate job openings, to training programs, or to counseling. Their function is basically one of face-to-face information-gathering and primary placement. *Job development specialists* are primarily concerned with just that — finding employers who are willing to list available jobs with the Jobs Service. In many cases, this involves convincing employers that there are great benefits for working through the employment service. *Employment counselors* have applicants referred to them who require testing or counseling. Assessment, of course, is accomplished by using the General Aptitude Test Battery (GATB), the most fully developed test battery in the world. A newer interest inventory also appears to

be of the same high caliber. Issues for counseling might involve midcareer change, reentry into the work force, lack of clear vocational choice, skills assessment, and the like. This is a higher-level civil service position than either of the two previously described. Other specialists provide additional services in the Jobs Service. Some offices have a veterans employment aide or a veterans representative. There may be Job Corps Units, Home Relief Placement, or other specialty units.

All in all, the Jobs Service provides adults and some out-of-school youth with a valuable service. Because of time demands, the counseling is frequently not so intensive as either the employment service counselor or the client would prefer. Within these constraints, however, the Job Service gives people a fine opportunity to receive some career assistance.

Rehabilitation Agencies

For those people who are disabled in some way, various rehabilitation agencies in the community can provide invaluable career help. To qualify for the career services of an agency of this type, an individual must be handicapped in seeking or in keeping employment because of some mental or physical disability. Further, there must be some reasonable probability that the services will indeed bring employment benefit to the individual.

The generally accepted goal of vocational rehabilitation is to assist the disabled individual to be able to work and, thus, to be self-sufficient (Mund, 1978). The major community agencies for helping to achieve this goal are the local offices of the Division of Vocational Rehabilitation (DVR). Specialty agencies (for the blind, cerebral palsied, and so on) also provide career services to the disabled. Besides providing guidance and counseling, such agencies help clients by means of physical and mental restoration services, training, maintenance and transportation, family services, interpreters for the deaf, readers for the blind, and placement, to cite just a few types of assistance.

There is obviously employer discrimination and prejudice toward the disabled. These employer attitudes largely reflect those of the public in general. Hence, vocational rehabilitation counselors must not only work with clients to get them ready for employment, but also educate employers to get them to hire the disabled. Work readiness for clients may entail providing work at a rehabilitation center or in a sheltered workshop ("a work-oriented rehabilitation facility with a controlled working environment and individual vocational goals, which utilizes work experience and related services for assisting the handicapped person to progress toward normal living and a productive vocational status") [Association of Rehabilitation Facilities]. Such a workshop may be transitional or long-term. About one-half million individuals per year are in such workshops. It may further involve providing clients with job-seeking skills or using vocational exploration groups to allow information and feedback. In general, vocational rehabilitation consists of intake, work-tryout, work conditioning and training, job placement, and follow-up. Evaluation is usually by means of traditional psychometric instruments as well as by work samples. An extremely useful concept in working with the disabled is McDaniel's (1963) notion of vocational redevelopment rather than vocational development. (See Chapter 5.)

The idea of *disability* has been considerably expanded by some vocational rehabilitation practitioners. It may now include, for example, not only physical disability and mental retardation, but also alcoholism, substance abuse, mental illness, learning disabilities, speech and language disorders, and social and economic disadvantage. This illustrative list suggests, as Hershenson (1974) has observed, that the differences between the disabled and the nondisabled are smaller than the differences within each group.

For mental patients, there is ample documentation that work is a needed form of activity (Anthony & Buell, 1974; MacKota, 1980); that community-based settings lead to more successful vocational rehabilitation than do hospital-based settings (Beard, Melamud, & Rossman, 1978; Stein & Test, 1980; Davis, 1979); and that employer hiring bias toward the psychiatrically disabled continues to exist (Lytel, 1978). Ciardiello and Bingham (1982) have demonstrated that even the most chronically disturbed individuals are capable of work.

The process of career helping for such individuals is really no different from that for other populations (although some of the substance obviously changes). Namely, as Anthony (1980) describes the process, it is one of: (1) determining client needs; (2) developing a rehabilitation plan; (3) providing work adjustment training; and (4) engaging in placement.

There are several guidelines that pertain not only to the psychiatrically disabled but also to other disabled populations:

1. Past general history and prior work history are good predictors of future work adjustment for the disabled.
2. Continual support, at least for the short term, is necessary.
3. A step-by-step, systematic program is best for the career helping of the disabled (see, for example, Beley & Felker, 1981).
4. Vocational skill building (rather than a concern with diagnosis or symptomatology) is extremely important.
5. Tests of self-concept or ego strength are probably more useful predictors of work adjustment than are more traditional psychological tests.

Whether the service is provided in a rehabilitation center, a rehabilitation workshop, or a rehabilitation residence, the goal is still one of removing both internal and external barriers to a client's working. These barriers, as defined by Wright (1980), consist of an *occupational handicap* (the inability to perform at a satisfactory level all of the essential requirements of an occupation), an *employment handicap* (difficulty in getting a suitable job because of discrimination), a *placement handicap* (difficulty in placing a client on a job because of his or her occupation or employment handicap (or both)), or a *vocational handicap* (any difficulty in adjusting or readjusting to the world of work). The rehabilitation literature is replete with references to the concept of *vocational adjustment* or *work adjustment*. This concept is actually nothing more than the total of the confluence of the worker's job satisfaction and the employer's idea of job satisfactoriness.

Since the 1973 Rehabilitation Act, counselors are responsible for providing each client with an Individualized Written Rehabilitation Program (IWRP). This movement toward systematic delivery and accountability requires a written statement of counselor and client responsibilities in the rehabilitation process, services to be provided, intermediate and long-range vocational goals, criteria for evaluation, review process, and post-employment services.

Toward the end of removal of barriers to seeking and keeping employment, the rehabilitation career helper assesses, counsels, and engages in job development and placement. Job development usually involves securing job opportunities for those disabled clients who are not easily placed. As counselors actually place the clients, they must attend to such considerations as work tolerance (capacity for protracted effort), work readiness, job-seeking skills (including employment interviewing, job orientation, and possible job modification to accommodate a disability).

Sometimes generic career counseling and vocational rehabilitation coexist in the same agency. Brolin (1975) describes one such case at the Vocational Counseling and Rehabilitation Services in St. Louis, Missouri. Urban clients may be served in one of two ways:

1. career guidance for any adult having problems clarifying educational goals, work abilities, or other job possibilities
2. rehabilitation services, including comprehensive work evaluation, social security disability determinations, personal adjustment training, training for job seeking skills, and job placement (p. 687)

In total, rehabilitation agencies provide excellent career services for the physically, emotionally, intellectually, or sensorily disabled. Although they are relatively new organizations (largely since 1920), they have established a fine record of helping disabled individuals achieve usefulness as workers.

Veterans Administration

Over a decade ago, Super and Bohn (1970) observed that some of the most influential practice of counseling was that which took place within the Veterans Administration (VA) organizational structure. As they indicated, "The vocational counseling practices and standards of the Veterans Administration set many precedents, having a lasting effect on vocational counseling and on the psychological specialty of counseling psychology" (p. 176).

Within the Veterans Administration, vocational counseling occurs in two distinct settings (Russella & Brophy, 1982). One is the Department of Medicine and Surgery (DMS), which operates through hospitals and outpatient clinics. The other is the Department of Veterans Benefits (DVB), which functions through fifty-eight regional offices. The psychological services offered in DMS are both vocational and personal; those offered through DVB are primarily vocational counseling and vocational rehabilitation counseling (although there may be some personal adjustment counseling). The clientele is not restricted simply to veterans. Also eligible for services are spouses and survivors of veterans.

Counseling positions within this agency (or any federal agency) are governed by Civil Service regulations. According to the U.S. Civil Service Commission's *Position-Classification Standards* (1968), counseling psychologists perform most of the career services. The positions related to the title may range from psychological technician to rehabilitation counselor to counseling psychologist, with major differences in training and responsibility through the titles. The description for counseling psychology, for example, is as follows (pp. 6–7):

Counseling psychology includes the educational, vocational, and rehabilitation counseling of the physically or mentally handicapped or others in need of or seeking vocational guidance. Counseling psychologists in the Federal service are principally employed in connection with the educational counseling of veterans and nondisabled war orphans who are entitled to receive educational benefits from the Federal government, or with vocational counseling of physically and mentally disabled veterans or others who are entitled to vocational rehabilitation benefits.

Counseling psychologists help the client to (a) learn about his abilities, capacities, interests, goals, and personality needs, (b) identify and explore educational and vocational possibilities, and (c) select from among them the goals that are appropriate to his personal needs, characteristics, and circumstances. They also help the client develop realistic education, training, and career plans for achieving these goals. As necessary, counseling psychologists help clients modify attitudes, feelings, or behavior patterns that interfere with their making progress in educational, vocational or rehabilitation planning.

Psychologists assist the client in arriving at considered decisions and choices regarding the educational, vocational or rehabilitation problems he currently faces. They also help him learn the bases for making valid decisions when he is confronted later by other educational and vocational choice situations.

Counseling psychologists have, in addition to their basic education and training in psychology, specialized knowledge about occupations and occupational trends, and about educational facilities and programs. They are familiar with the physical, mental, educational, and experience requirements of various occupations and with interrelationships among occupations. They know specialized training resources and other community facilities for rehabilitating the handicapped.

At the highest Civil Service levels, counseling psychologists also

provide highly skilled counseling services to clients with difficult and complex problems of personal adjustment or vocational rehabilitation. They typically deal with such clients as:

1. multiple paraplegics or other homebound clients who have severe emotional or family relations problems resulting from their disability;
2. chronic mentally disturbed patients or alcoholics; or
3. mentally disturbed or other clients with a long history of unsatisfactory vocational adjustments (p. 27).

Some individuals regard this federal emphasis on vocational aspects on the part of counseling psychologists as too restrictive (Ivey, 1976). Others are in agreement with continuing the primary role of career in the functions of a counseling psychologist (Osipow, 1977). In any case, the role of a counseling psychologist in the Veterans Administration emphasizes career counsel-

ing — somewhat less for DMS than for DVB. Hence, the VA is a valuable resource for career counseling for veterans, for their spouses, and, in some cases, for certain other dependents.

Jewish Vocational Services

Many organized religions provide counseling services, either limited to their own constituencies or on a nonsectarian basis. Catholic Charities, for example, is one such organization. In terms of career counseling, however, by far the best developed services are those offered through Jewish-sponsored organizations.

A Jewish Occupational Council exists to link organizations that provide Jewish Vocational Services in about thirty larger cities in the United States and Canada. There is a long heritage in America of the B'nai B'rith Vocational Guidance Service, which has provided the profession at large with many useful educational and occupational materials. The clientele at the Jewish Vocational Services is nonsectarian, and fees are charged according to a sliding scale based on income and the ability to pay. Of those who come to the service, generally about 30 percent are between the ages of 15-21; about 60 percent are 22-45; and about 10 percent are over 45. Typically, clients are provided with a series of interviews and tests of interests, abilities, and aptitudes. Each service maintains a reasonably complete educational and occupational library. Both individual and group counseling are available.

These agencies, and many of the better community agencies that provide career counseling services, are usually members of the International Association of Counseling Services (IACS). This accrediting group enforces standards on its membership in terms of such criteria as: professional education, supervised practice, and experience of the director and staff; professional association membership; professional practices: and administrative aspects. Membership in IACS assures that an agency conforms to certain minimal standards.

Correctional Programs

It is difficult to imagine any group that has more career deficiences than ex-offenders. As a group, their education is minimal, their work history is limited, and their work skills are either rudimentary or completely lacking. Add to all of these deficits the stigma of being an ex-offender, and we are presented with a picture of internal and external barriers to career development that are formidable indeed. Smith and Warner (1977) point to a prison population that even prior to incarceration was unemployed, undereducated, and underskilled.

Within about 800 prisons in America are almost 400,000 inmates, overwhelmingly men and almost half black. These data are only for those in state or federal prisons and do not include those in local or county jails. Add to this population almost 200,000 parolees, about one-quarter of whom will eventually return to prison. This recidivism is caused, at least in part, by an individual's inability to find work (Hodanish, 1976–1977; Ellis, 1976; McGinnis et al., 1977).

Attention to the career aspects of individuals is always regarded as both a means of prevention and a source for remediation. Because the unemployment rate for ex-offenders is four to five times that of nonoffenders (Larkin, 1975), employment programs for ex-offenders are viewed as a necessary part of any rehabilitation. However, there are over 300 occupations in America that restrict the hiring of ex-offenders. Some restrictions are logical (for example, occupations that allow access to drugs or firearms), but some are absurd (beautician, photographer, tatoo artist, taxi driver).

Many states now have comprehensive programs geared to employment of ex-offenders. In fact, there are over 1000 separate programs, all of which emphasize vocational training. In addition, they are likely to include some form of assessment, individual and group counseling, career education (such as job-search skills), placement, work-release, and follow-up. Within correctional institutions, educational programs also have been historically stressed, probably stemming from the eighteenth-century notion of teaching inmates to read the Bible in order to set them on the right path. It is now possible for prisoners to extend their education to the point of earning college degrees.

Although geared to a very specialized clientele (and one that most of us would just as soon not

join), programs for ex-offenders offer help to a population that desperately needs it.

Federal and State Programs for Disadvantaged, Dislocated, and/or Women

Because of high unemployment rates, the increase in women and minorities in the labor force, changes in the economy that cause massive dislocation of workers, and other factors, the federal and state governments have sponsored various programs to provide career-assisting services to adults in the community. In the past decade, such legislation as the Vocational Education Act, the Comprehensive Employment and Training Act, the Career Education Act, the Older American Act, and the Women's Equity Act, to cite just a few examples, has provided funds and mandates for career guidance and counseling in various degrees. Because of all these diverse legislative programs and the number of other agencies and institutions providing career assistance, however, the services offered have frequently been isolated or have lacked depth. As Miller (1982) describes the problem:

> The major need in designing adult career development programs is to provide comprehensive and coordinated program models. Historically, programs for adults have been short term programs focusing on specific needs. This has resulted in the development of services that are less client-focused and that do not address comprehensive career development needs. (p. 364)

Brolin (1975) suggests that one solution to the problem is to designate an existing agency in each large community (such as the Employment Service) to serve as a referral source for career guidance services. There is no doubt that there is considerable duplicative effort taking place in most communities, especially in terms of programs for women and minorities.

With plant closings becoming more common and with more workers consequently becoming dislocated, there is a need for community-based response in the form of career services. We are here speaking of more than typical outplacement counseling that organizations provide to a small number of their workforce either by hiring an outside firm or by utilizing their own personnel. We are talking of trauma — abrupt dislocation of large numbers of workers (as with International Harvester, Bethlehem Steel, the auto industry, and so on). Some pioneer work by Taber, Walsh, and Cooke (1979) describes a program in Michigan that responded to a plant closing. Management, unions, a local university, and community representatives formed an alliance to respond to the upheaval. One of the first actions of this group was to establish an in-plant counseling program to help the workers define their problems and contact the appropriate helping agencies. It became clear that workers had several deficits that needed to be addressed. For example:

People did not have information about possible helping agencies.

Employees did not recognize their problems.

Employees did not seek assistance until it was too late.

Employees lost fringe benefits (such as health insurance) as well as wages.

Employees did not have job-seeking skills.

Employees had complexly interrelated problems.

The authors suggest that the employees lacked "bureaucratic competence" — the ability to deal successfully with bureaucratic agencies. However, what this project tried to provide was "community competence" — the capacity of a community to provide resources so that people can make informed decisions about their own problems. Getting all of the extant services in a community to form a comprehensive, coordinated, proactive system to respond to the emergency was no small task.

The counseling program consisted of getting two plant employees who were well-known and respected members of the union to provide counseling for hourly employees. The counselors were trained intensively for three days to familiarize them with resources and services available in the community. The purpose of the counseling was not psychological or directly career assisting. Rather, it was to diagnose problems, to put workers in contact with appropriate agencies, and to follow up. In short, the counselors served

as a proactive element usually lacking in a community.

Community programs for the disadvantaged, the dislocated, and/or women are available under a variety of names that change as often as administrations in Washington and in state capitals: Job Corps, Displaced Homemakers, CETA, and so on. Some attempts have been made to ensure consistency and good practice in the operation of such programs. For example, the "Legislative Provisions for the Improvement of Guidance Programs and Personnel Development" was a cooperative project of the National Center for Research in Vocational Education, the American Personnel and Guidance Association, the American Vocational Association, and the American Institutes for Research. This project produced voluminous written materials and provided training for practitioners related to the establishment of community-based career counseling programs. Some of these materials are very good; some are not.

In any case, there are federal- and state-funded programs available for the disadvantaged, the dislocated, and women. Their number and focus will vary with trends in public policy. There is a need to coordinate these career services within any large community.

Continuing Education Programs

The Harrison and Entine study (1977) cited earlier in this chapter indicated that almost one-third of the opportunities for career counseling in the community are sponsored through continuing education programs either by colleges, universities, and two-year colleges or by public school districts. Raines (1972) proposes that these educational institutions conduct parallel programs, one serving the institution and its clientele and the other serving the community.

Lewis and Lewis (1977) also see educational institutions providing communities with a variety of educational and vocational services. They believe people are more likely to seek career help from an educational institution than from a community agency. As they see the role of the educational institution in dealing with adults,

Counselors can help community members to examine the possible place of further education in their lives and make decisions based on their values, their strengths, and their concrete knowledge about the options that might be open to them. Programs like this have been particularly effective in opening new doors to women, to individuals seeking midcareer changes, to retirees searching for new vocations or avocations, and to low income individuals. ... Many colleges have been successful in reaching mature community members through centers designed for their needs and connected with the institution's division of continuing educa-

tion or community education. It might be possible to bring such programs even closer to the people by offering workshops, short courses, and counseling opportunities through civic or neighborhood organizations with ongoing memberships and multipurpose functions (p. 285).

One final word: if community agencies or other public delivery systems fail, there are those who suggest that the private sector is waiting in the wings to take over the necessary functions.

Summary

In this chapter we have discussed the provision of career helping to adults in the organizational settings in which people work and in the communities in which they live. In the former case we observed the incipient nature of the career services and the potential for conflict in their delivery. In the latter case we noted the array of alternatives available and highlighted the need for more coordinated effort. Opportunities certainly exist; however, getting people and available services together remains a problem.

LEARNING ACTIVITIES

1. Arrange to interview a training and development specialist, personnel director, or vice president for employee relations of a large company. Ascertain the extent of career assistance available within the particular organization. Ask about perceived roadblocks to future development.

2. Interview the director of any of the agencies described in this chapter that provide services for adults. What strengths and weaknesses can you discern?

3. Suggest a system to ensure minimum overlap and maximum usage of the adult career counseling opportunities within your community. What are the barriers to instituting such a system? How might these barriers be overcome?

4. Read any issue of the *Training and Manage-*

ment Journal. What similarities and differences do you note between this journal and such generic career-oriented journals as the *Journal of Vocational Behavior* or the *Vocational Guidance Quarterly*?

5. Address yourself to any of the fifteen issues or needed research items listed within this chapter. Suggest some possible resolution of issues or specific types of research that might prove useful.

6. Interview several workers at various levels who are employed by a large organization. Determine what career assistance they are now receiving and what assistance they wish but do not now have.

7. For a given local organization, outline the contents and functioning of an assessment center. Suggest a basic library and appropriate assessment devices (for what purposes). How would you evaluate the effectiveness of such a center?

8. Make an inventory of all opportunities for adult career counseling and guidance in your community. Are any significant community populations without potential resource? Are there any populations that seem to be overserved?

9. Ask a sample of adults whether they would use an adult career counseling service. If not, why not? Check the accuracy of their perceptions of such things as the cost of such services, the types of experiences provided, and the likely outcome.

10. Check out the private employment services and the private, proprietary career counseling services in your community. What conclusions do you draw?

OBJECTIVES

After reading this chapter, engaging in the learning activities, and reading the suggested references, you should have met the objectives that follow. If you have not, it would probably be useful for you to review the material on career counseling in the work place and in the community before proceeding further.

1. List at least six types of career assistance activities extant in organizations.
2. Describe three reasons for increased interest by organizations in career planning activities.
3. Differentiate between individual career planning and organizational career planning.
4. Define career, career planning, career management, and career development as these terms are used by organizations.

5. Enumerate at least five functions of a career counselor in organizations.
6. Define an organizational career pattern and list at least one task at each stage of a given pattern.
7. Describe an assessment center.
8. Specify at least five issues or needed research related to the provision of career counseling in the work place.
9. Describe the general career functions of the U.S. Employment Service.
10. Describe the career services offered by a typical rehabilitation agency.
11. Outline the general career services provided by the Veterans Administration.
12. Characterize the career assistance provided by Jewish Vocational Services.
13. Offer a depiction of what career help is available for offenders and ex-offenders.
14. Describe the career assistance offered in federal or state programs for the disadvantaged, dislocated, or women.
15. Depict the typical career helping services provided through continuing education programs.

12 | *Special Adult Career Concerns I*

Until fairly recently, anyone interested in career counseling might well have wondered if there is a career life after adolescence. Early work in career development and behavior focused on factors and processes leading to the initial choice of an occupation and rarely addressed adult career development. Further, researchers and theorists generally were grounded in the specialties of child and adolescent psychology and ignored that portion of the career life span subsequent to exploration and initial choice.

Awakening to adult career behavior began with an interest in gerontology (that branch of knowledge dealing with aging and the aged). Thus, the last of the career life cycles was probably the first to be studied intensively with adults. Concerns about preretirement and retirement spawned a good deal of research. In fact, most postadolescent research since World War II has been related to old age (Goulet & Baltes, 1970). The development of the middle-aged and older worker was still given little attention.

Developmental psychology, which is concerned with changes in behavior over periods of weeks, months, or years, has begun to investigate whether career changes with age extend beyond young adulthood. Specifically, developmental and vocational psychologists have been taking initial steps to determine if career behaviors and other psychological characteristics are ontogenetic (age-related). Increasing attention, both in the popular press and in professional journals, has been addressed to the notion of adult life stages. Scholars such as Roger Gould (1972), Daniel Levinson et al. (1978), Wortley & Amatea (1982), Raynor and Entin (1982), Farrell and Rosenberg (1981),

and George Vaillant (1977), and lay writers such as Gail Sheehy (1976, 1981) have turned the search for an explanation of the adult life cycle into a chic pursuit. This early research is tentative and is based on population samples that are both small and narrowly delimited. Yet it is a beginning. In relation to career behavior, this new and enthusiastic interest in adults is evidenced by the creation of various committees, commissions, and special interest groups within professional organizations, by a rapidly increasing number of articles relating to adult career behavior, and by new legislation.

Indeed, the language applied to the career development and behavior of adults reflects these popular concerns. Terms like career menopause or career climacteric are used with an assurance that is in direct contrast to what is actually known about the important changes that may occur in adult career behavior. In fact, we are only beginning to collect systematic data on adults, and there is some question about whether we possess any useful theory of general development in which to use these collected data. Of the human being's three score and ten years, relatively little attention has been focused on the last five decades of life. Using Piaget and Erickson (or other behavioral scientists), we can build a reasonable model of development from infancy through adolescence; however, beginning with the young adult and through senescence, we are merely in the incipient stages of acquiring knowledge.

To be sure, there are those who, in the past, have addressed themselves to adult behavior in general and adult career behavior in particular. Not the least of these has been Charlotte Buehler

(1933), to whom Donald Super and others have acknowledged a great debt in the development of their own work. Her attempts to evolve a comprehensive psychology of the entire course of life have provided a stimulus and a framework for many subsequent researchers. Among others, David Tiedeman and Robert O'Hara (1963) have also provided some valuable thoughts and data on adult career stages. And we are just now beginning to receive the benefit of data from longitudinal studies such as the Career Pattern Study (Super, 1977, 1980; Super & Kidd, 1979) and Project Talent (Flanagan, 1978; Abeles, Steel, & Wise, 1980), whose initial early adolescent subjects have now reached early adulthood or incipient middle age. One example will suffice to point out the kinds of data that are emerging from longitudinal studies. The twenty-one-year follow-up of the original 111 person sample in Gribbons and Lohnes' (1982) Career Development Study (CDS) compared the original stated 1958 career aspirations of the then eighth graders with the actual occupations for the 91 remaining subjects in 1980. Results reveal the substantial changes that occur between early adolescence and adulthood; few were in their original choice occupation. Since much previous career development research has been accomplished using expressed vocational choice of students rather than actual entry into an occupation, these differences represent significant implications for theory-building. In general, the CDS sample showed major shifts for males to business from the sciences and for females to housewifery from education, the humanities, and the arts.

Thus, we do know something about adult behaviors and needs — at least enough to make an informed start at comprehensive delivery of career facilitating services; but there is much more to learn before the "science" of career facilitation with adults replaces the current "art." This chapter summarizes some of the existing knowledge, describes some of the delivery systems in use, and generally provides an introduction to the career counseling of adults. Osipow (1983) has summarized our current condition:

Clearly, attention to mid-career transitions is burgeoning. Many interventions have been devised to try to help people deal with the associated stresses and strains. These interventions remain to be proven with respect to their effectiveness. What does appear to be clear is that the cultural determinants that have indicated career stages and development in younger people seem as they get older to operate to produce predictable stages in many people, at least in professional and managerial levels and very likely in other levels as well. Probably these events are subject to continual revision as a function of changes in society and the continuing reorganization of its work structure, as well as demands for different kinds of human resources. (p. 223)

FACTORS UNDERLYING COUNSELING ADULTS

Obviously, the adult population is completely heterogeneous. It is not a population contained within a single institution, such as the school. The targets of career counseling, therefore, potentially include each person in the labor force and each adult seeking to enter the labor force. However, for our purposes here, some delineation is necessary. In the following chapter, we will discuss several adult subpopulations: (1) unemployed, dislocated, and discouraged workers; (2) "burned out" workers; (3) working mothers; (4) dual-career couples; (5) job seekers; and (6) dissatisfied workers. In this chapter, we will concentrate on four adult subpopulations: (1) midcareer changers; (2) women entering or reentering the labor force after a period of child-rearing; (3) the older worker; and (4) preretirees and retirees.

Characteristics of the Population

Career counseling of adults should be viewed within the context of changes in society, many of which have been discussed in Chapter 3. In general we may point to the following characteristics that significantly affect the career counseling of adults.

1. *Changing marital patterns* — The marriage rate remains lower than in times past, women are getting married later in life, and the divorce rate is substantial (for example, one out of

every three married women 30 years old has been or will be divorced).

2. *Changing child-bearing and child-rearing patterns* — The birth rate has declined significantly from the past. Changes in the birth rate have caused increases and decreases in the number of workers in various age groups of the population, affecting both the opportunities open for workers and the types of goods and services in demand by society. Because of divorce, less than 70 percent of all children under 18 live with their two natural parents.

3. *Changing occupational patterns* — The alteration of the occupational structure causes unemployment, underemployment, and frustration as well as opportunities. The information economy or the service economy requires different workers from those needed in a goods producing, industrial economy. The nature of work itself is in flux.

All of these factors can have a profound effect on the kind and frequency of career counseling services required by the adult population.

Within this context of external changes, adults are also experiencing internal changes — mental, physical, and emotional — that are in symbiotic relationship with their work. The process of aging is indeed complex, stemming from endocrine changes; aspiration-achievement discrepancies; stagnation-versus-growth Ericksonian issues; the greater reality of death and dying; changes in relationships with spouse, children, and parents; role changes; and other factors. Each of these changes in life may affect attitudes toward and performance at work, just as the experience of work can affect attitudes toward and general behavior in one's nonwork life. The types of problems with which adults may need to cope in terms of career are numerous. One attempt at a taxonomy of these career problems is that devised by Campbell and Cellini (1981). They characterize adult problems into four categories: (1) problems in career decision-making; (2) problems in implementing career plans; (3) problems in organizational/institutional performance; and (4) problems in organizational/institutional adaptation. The full taxonomy is presented in Chapter 2.

Work by Phillips (1982a, 1982b) offers some further instructive data about adult career development and behavior. She investigated career decision-making behavior over time in ninety-five males who participated in the Career Pattern Study and discovered that exploratory behavior tends to decrease and that decisions are less exploratory and more terminal from age 21 to age 36. Career decisions, then, are made differently at different stages of development. Phillips also, strangely, discovered that increasing commitment with age (a condition thought to be highly desirable) did not necessarily lead to higher levels of career outcomes (such as career success, job satisfaction, systematic career progression). Whether this finding was an artifact of her sample or whether this result is indeed the case is important, since current career development theory is postulated on the desirability of increasing career commitment.

Studies that investigate the counseling needs of adult students offer additional data to guide career interventions. Goodman (1981, p. 468) lists nineteen appropriate potential adult client groups.

1. adults seeking general personal counseling in the areas of self, family, work, and social interaction
2. personal and family resources planning and management seekers
3. life planning, career planning, and career management clients
4. persons seeking job search, job campaign, and placement coaching
5. unemployed and underemployed college graduates (men and women) exploring career alternatives
6. middle-aged men and women (mostly empty-nest housewives) seeking to enter or reenter gainful employment
7. middle-aged men and women seeking to make a change in employment or career
8. the laid-off or fired middle-aged, middle-class, educated male
9. the female executive or professional under career or job stress
10. the black professional or executive dealing with career problems and stress that accompany transfer or promotion
11. people moving into and out of government and academic employment

12. the certified school teacher seeking career alternatives
13. the fledgling entrepreneur attempting to become self-employed by starting a small business
14. the second-, third- and fourth-career planner
15. adults in alternative work patterns such as share-a-job situations where two or more workers share one position and income
16. new careers for older workers: part-time and volunteer work
17. counseling in employee assistance programs: both public and private sector employer-provided employee assistance programs
18. counseling for avocational and leisure time activities
19. counseling institutionalized populations in prisons, rest homes, nursing homes, hospitals, and so on

Perrone, Wolleat, Lee, and Davis (1977) surveyed 1817 adults who ranged in age from under 21 to over 50 regarding their major concerns as adult students. Of the twenty-five items to which they reacted, the five highest contained two career concerns: needing more information about jobs and occupations, and needing to know more about one's vocational abilities.

Given all of this documentation of the career needs of adults, we turn now to discussions of planning considerations with adults and of career counseling techniques with adults.

Planning Considerations

The framework for service delivery with adults is more problematic than it is with younger clients. Compared to programs and theory effected in educational institutions and with younger counselees, the field lacks historical perspective, empirically verified techniques, validated materials, and pertinent theory. Nevertheless, the career counseling of adults will probably be made more efficient and effective if attention is given to the following suggestions regarding planning.

1. Goals and objectives should be based on some model of the needs of adults at various stages of adult life and with diverse presenting problems. Although the body of knowledge pertaining to the needs of subpopulations of adults

(as described in this volume) is in incipient form, it is growing daily; there does exist enough useful material to make a "first beginning." Particularly helpful to the counselor will be journals about which many counselors new to counseling adults may not be aware: *Industrial Gerontology, Journal of Gerontology, Monthly Labor Review, Industrial Sociology, Journal of Employment Counseling, Personnel Administration, The Gerontologist,* and *The Family Coordinator.*

2. The physical centrality of adult career counseling services, the hours of operation, and the publicizing of such services should be such that the populations to be served readily know what career counseling opportunities exist and that the facilities can be reached with minimum discomfort and maximum ease. Preretirement counseling located in places of employment; women's programs attached to continuing education programs of high schools, colleges, and universities; improved dissemination efforts by the U.S. Employment Service branches; and counseling with senior citizens within centers for the aged are all examples of attempts to expedite service delivery.

3. Middle-class adults who seek career counseling are typically highly motivated. Those people in earlier stages of career development frequently require that a readiness be established; the challenge for the counselor of adults is to capitalize on the readiness and motivation that the adult brings to career counseling.

4. Adults generally will have little tolerance for the abstract in career counseling. There is an immediacy, an urgency, and a concreteness to their concerns. They are, on the average, able to phrase their questions in self-referent terms that are concise and meaningful.

5. The bases on which adults ought to make decisions are probably little different from those required by decision-makers at an earlier stage of development. They should have a knowledge of self, a knowledge of the world of work, and decision-making skills. In some subpopulations of adults (such as midcareer shifters), these characteristics may be relatively well developed; in others (such as women seeking to enter the non-household labor force for the first time at a relatively advanced age), these requirements may be as undeveloped as in the average adolescent.

6. The delivery of services should be systematic,

although the progression may be accelerated because of the accrued experience of the clientele. In short, goals must be translated into activities, suitable materials for the conduct of these activities must be discovered or invented, and evaluation should occur to determine the extent to which goals have been achieved as a result of the activities provided.

7. Specificity is a keynote in planning. Throughout most of the school years, relatively broad and broadening goals such as career awareness exploration, conceptualization, perceptualization, and generalization are laudable ends in themselves. With some adults, it may be necessary to achieve these goals, but the counselor must go on from that point to help adults to narrow generated alternatives, to negotiate systems, to focus interests, to secure employment, or otherwise to deal in self-relevant specifics. Expansion is a primary goal for the young; specificity is an aim with the adult.

8. For many adults, career counseling will have to occur within the context of a strong awareness of family implications. Adult decision-making affects more people than simply that person, unlike most earlier decision-making. Often, career decisions of adults will involve simultaneous demands on spouses, children, and the extended family. The obverse may also pertain; that is, marital crises seem increasingly to stimulate a career change.

9. A great many adults will simply want information. Others may want "counseling" but also want information. Thus, information dissemination becomes a highly important service for adults.

Career Counseling Techniques

Almost any career counseling technique used with younger populations can, of course, be used with adults. Basically, the goals are the same; self-knowledge of various types, its relationship to the worlds of work and education or training, and effective decision-making skills, among others. Many of the techniques that the counselor will use in working with adults are implicit in the goal statements for each adult subpopulation and in the planning considerations just presented. Specifically, as counselors work with adults, they will want to remember the following unique consider-

ations that should be added to their repertoire of career helping strategies and behaviors.

1. Especially with unskilled adults from lower occupational levels, *motivation* is a primary focus of career assistance. Readiness and motivation for work are frequently lacking in some adults, despite the axiom that people want to work. Counselors must, then, seek to establish within some adults the desire to work.

2. Although much career counseling with adults can be developmental (in the sense of commonalities at given stages of life), a good deal of the focus of adult career counseling will be crisis-generated and crisis-centered. Frequently, therefore, what have come to be termed *crisis intervention* techniques will be utilized. Crisis intervention provides quick, short-term relief in an emergency situation. The counselor deals with the immediate problem rather than with the underlying causes of the problem in providing the temporary relief.

3. Many adults will be searching for what has loosely been defined as *self-actualization*. However, their expectations and perceptions that some future work will enable them to achieve self-actualization often prove to be unrealistic. Counselors should work with adults within a framework of *reality*. This is not to say that adults ought to be discouraged from having their heads in the clouds; rather, they should be simultaneously aided to keep their feet on the ground.

4. The *dissemination of information*, a cognitive activity anathema to some counselors, is an important strategy in the career counseling of adults. Adults want answers to specific questions; counselors should provide those answers. For example, a study by Kasschau (1974) reviewed the available evidence evaluating retirement preparation programs. She describes two types of programs: (1) counseling programs that focus primarily on the development of favorable attitudes toward retirement; and (2) planning programs that concentrate mainly on information dissemination and as a stimulant-to-planning device. On the basis of her review, Kasschau concludes that in terms of both client satisfaction and effectiveness of the programs, retirement preparation efforts should emphasize the planning function. In other words, they should raise appropriate questions and provide concrete, objective, relevant

information regarding such areas as finance, legal aspects, and health.

5. *Testing* and the use of test results with certain adult subpopulations should be approached with tentativeness. Several researchers have pointed out that norms for adult populations are frequently nonexistent, and that there is often not a demonstrated relationship between test score and job performance for a specified adult clientele.

6. Bocknek (1976) has cautioned that *counseling techniques* that have evolved from work with younger adults (such as reflection of feeling) may not be appropriate for older adults even though they have been successful with younger clients and, in fact, may ignore the developmental needs of this chronologically advanced population (such as historical perspective). He further notes that much counseling is practiced *by* younger adults who are often guilty of conscious or unconscious age bias. Troll and Nowak (1976) have described three types of age bias: (1) age restrictiveness (setting arbitrary or inappropriate age limits for any behavior); (2) age distortion (misperception of the behavior or characteristics of any age group); and (3) age-ism (negative attitudes towards any age group). Thus, counselors will want to test their current repertoires of counseling techniques in terms of their salience for adults and will need to engage in self-examination for possible age bias.

7. In a perceptive article, Schlossberg (1976) summarizes the various foci of adult counseling. She suggests:

To be effective, the counselor of adults must first have a knowledge of the decision-making process that can be used in diagnosing the problems of the individual client — and in particular determining whether the client is at the anticipatory or the implementation stage and in devising appropriate interventions. Occasionally, the counselor may have to go beyond the function of counseling the individual into program development and social activism. The second requisite is an awareness of adult development and an ability to penetrate beyond what the client says to what is left unsaid. Finally, the counselor must be aware of any tendency to define options and possibilities

solely in terms of the client's age. Only when counselors are able to free themselves from (or at least control) age bias can they help the client make free and informed choices. (p. 36)

With these planning considerations and techniques in mind, then, for the career counseling of adults, we will turn to a consideration of the four subpopulations previously identified in this chapter.

MIDCAREER CHANGES

It is difficult to discover exactly how many Americans change careers each year, partly because of differing definitions of *what* constitutes a career change (a shift from one Holland or Roe category to another? from one occupational title to another? from one job to another?). We believe that Kelleher's (1973) data are probably reasonably accurate, although they are ten years old. She estimates that about 8 percent of Americans change occupations each year, of whom about 40 percent are over 35 years of age.

Reasons for Change

The reasons that people voluntarily change jobs are many and varied. Sinick (1975) offers the following partial listing of motivations for or causes of career shifts.

initial career not person's own choice
career inappropriate from outset
original aspirations not met by career
purpose of first career accomplished
change of career required by changing goals
satisfaction sought for higher level needs
dead end reached in terms of advancement
inadequate outlet for creativity
insufficient challenge to abilities
data-people-things involvement inappropriate
incongruence with vocational interests
desire to implement avocational interests
disproportion between prescribed and discretionary duties
insufficient variety in work content
work pressures and deadlines too demanding
work becomes too physically demanding
work context source of dissatisfactions

- employer policies and practices dissatisfying
- purpose of employer enterprise incompatible
- co-workers divergent in values and lifestyles
- personality conflicts with supervisor or co-workers
- earnings outstripped by living expenses
- desire to "keep up with the Joneses"
- social status of occupation inadequate
- insufficient time for leisure activities
- greener grass in another field. (pp. 7–8)

Entine (1977) has suggested a broader taxonomy of reasons for midcareer change. He has proposed that causes can be either internal or external and unanticipated or anticipated, thus leading to a 2 x 2 classification model, as exhibited in Figure 12.1.

In a similar manner, Thomas (1980) used the experiences of seventy-three men who had left professional and managerial careers between the ages of 34 and 54 to devise a typology of career changers. His schematic representation is presented in Table 12.1.

Not too long ago there was a prevalent notion

that voluntary career shifters were "oddballs," individuals who because of some personality flaw or character disorder were deficient in adaptive skills, professional malcontents, or otherwise lacking in some way. In fact, most studies of career shifters versus career persisters indicate no differences in emotional adjustment; midcareer change does not necessarily constitute floundering or pathological behavior (Hiestand, 1971; Neopolitan, 1980; Clopton, 1973). Clopton, as a result of his doctoral research involving highly educated males, categorized career shifters into three types:

Type A – Shifts undertaken as a direct consequence of some major event that impels the shifter to reformulate the meaning of his life and personal goals.

Type B – Shifts that result primarily from the shifter's gradual disenchantment with his first career. The typical pattern is that the shifter first becomes aware of being more bored and/or disillusioned with his work; he begins casting about for a different profession which he feels would permit fuller utilization of his potential.

Figure 12.1
Causes of Midcareer Change

	Internal	External
Unanticipated	Examples: Serious Illness Divorce Death of Spouse or Children 1	Examples: Unemployment Work Dissatisfaction Job Obsolescence Rapid Inflation 2
Anticipated	Examples: Empty Nest Labor Force Reentry Voluntary Career Change 3	Examples: Planned Retirement Promotion and Advancement 4

Table 12.1
Typology of Career Changers

| | | Pressure from self to change | |
		Low	High
Pressure from environment to change	Low	"Drift-outs" 17 (Routine)*a*	"Opt-outs" 12 (Self-determined)
	High	"Force-outs" 25 (Situation-determined)	"Bow-outs" 19 (Accommodation)

*a*Titles in parentheses are those used by Murray et al. (1971) in their original formulation of this typology.

Type C–Shifts that occur after a shifter realizes that, although he still enjoys his first career, there is another profession which would give him at least as much, and possibly more, satisfaction. Typically, in such cases, the second career begins as an avocational interest and develops gradually to the point of becoming a full-time commitment. (p. 11)

Some researchers have found career shifters to be less mentally healthy that persisters. Vaitenas and Wiener (1977), for example, determined that in their sample of sixty-five changers in business-managerial occupations, these changers were characterized by emotional maladjustment and fear of failure and low differentiation and consistency of interest when compared to a control group of nonchangers. Sarason (1977) offers an explanation of why some studies find midcareer shifters to be less functional than nonshifters. He argues that unhappiness in work comes about because of a mismatch between one's personal characteristics and the particular work demands or work environment in which these characteristics are utilized. If the discrepancy is large enough, the person will become anxious and dysfunctional, evidence possibly psychopathological symptoms, and change careers. We prefer to believe that voluntary midcareer shifts are acts of a mentally healthy personality.

Brim (1976) hypothesizes as does Sarason that career shifts in middle age may be caused by an aspiration-achievement gap, but does not necessarily see this situation as producing a pathological reaction. He states:

The aspirations in life that men set for themselves are primarily expressed through the institution of work. Over the course of the working life, from entry to the mid-life period, it is likely that although aspirations may be adjusted downward on occasion, one usually believes there is enough time left for the desired level of achievement to be reached in future years. But during mid-life most American males must adjust their career aspirations of earlier years downward to fit current reality. A man may be told that he has risen as high as he can go in his place of work; that his present position must be accepted by him as the achievement level for his lifetime (p. 3).

Developmentalists see midcareer changes as simply an alternative available in a predictable stage of adult life. Levinson et al. (1978), in their taxonomy of adult male development, suggest that midcareer shifts are most likely to occur during what they have termed the Becoming One's Own Man (BOOM) stage (35-39). It is during this stage that men are evidently most prone to experience constraint and oppression in work and to seek resolution of these feelings. This study receives support in the research of Hill and Miller (1981). In their study of academics, Entrekin and Everett (1981) identified a similar stage that comes a bit later in life. The ages 30-44 are described as a "settling in" period; 45-49 are seen as a span of years in which the individual "reaches out" and becomes restless, exhibiting more change needs; 50-54 are viewed as a "settling down" time; and after 55, the individual academic is thought to be "finishing" his career. Others have described a similar phenomenon that can occur anywhere from the late thirties to the early fifties as "midolescence" (McMorrow, 1974; Sagal & DeBlassie, 1981).

Others see midcareer change as a case of incongruity based on Holland's categories. Wiener and Vaitenas (1977) report that their forty-five changers showed much more incongruity of modal type and environment than did their sixty-six stable controls. Congruency in terms of Holland's theory has also been found to be related to more stable careers in women and men (Rose & Elton, 1982; Gottfredson, 1976) and to more career-mature individuals (Guthrie & Herman, 1982). These findings are gainsaid by other studies, however. For example, Robbins, Thomas, Harvey, and Kandefer (1978) found no support for the notion of congruity as a motivator for career change. In their sample of managerial and professional men 33–54 who changed careers, about 42 percent changed to careers more congruent with their personality, 40 percent to careers less congruent, and 18 percent made no change in terms of a Holland category.

Still others see midcareer change as an attempt to more nearly meet values and needs. For instance, Snyder, Howard, and Hammer (1978) studied professors who remained teachers versus professors who became administrators and concluded that changers had significantly higher power needs, whereas those who remained professors had higher autonomy needs. Thomas (1979) used a sample of men who changed from higher-status careers between 34 and 54 years of age to determine that value change appeared to be the major motivation for a career shift. Isaacson (1981) believes that changing worker needs and interests are major reasons for career change.

It appears that midlife phenomena are present in both primitive societies (Gutmann, 1967) and modern societies other than American. Collin (1979), for example, indicates that midcareer change is apparently as observable in Great Britain as it is in America. Further, the midlife potential for crisis evidently pervades all races, ethnic groups, and subcultures. Miles (1981), for instance, describes unique midlife problems for blacks, who begin to question their worth in life from a perspective of lifelong handicap and disability because of a lack of education, discrimination, unemployment, and other factors.

In any case, whether midcareer changes are caused by frustration and anxiety, by growth, achievement, and expansion motives, by a recognition of one's individual differences, or by some other factor or a combination of factors, the midcareer shifter should be viewed, in general and barring evidence to the contrary, as a mentally healthy individual. Those in the process of midcareer change are usually at least in their late twenties and beyond. In a chronological sense, they are middle-aged, and with middle age come many changes. Several researchers have attempted to place these changes within a helpful structure. Peck (1975), for example, has expanded on Erikson's middle-age-related seventh stage, generativity versus stagnation. Peck suggests that this stage of life is further characterized in the healthy adult by: (1) a change from valuing physical powers to valuing wisdom; (2) a shift from sexualizing to socializing in human relationships; (3) a transformation from emotional impoverishment to emotional flexibility; and (4) a transition from mental rigidity to mental flexibility. Seen in the light of these desirable attributes, most midcareer shifts would be natural manifestations of a psychologically healthy organism.

Those Who Change

Who goes through midlife career change? Every occupation is represented, but some are more visible than others. Classic cases of midlife career change can be found in the ranks of those who put in twenty years or so in the military or in municipal activities, such as fire and police protection, and then retire at a relatively young age, free to pursue a second career. In the 1970s, thousands of engineers and scientists became unemployed because of substantial cuts in space and defense spending; these workers in declining industries were often forced to seek unrelated types of employment, or to take lesser paying jobs in the same occupation. More recently, the field of education has experienced cutbacks, causing teachers and other educational personnel to switch career paths. Whether voluntary or involuntary, it is clear that midlife career change is a visible phenomenon and that a significant proportion of workers will not fit the one life-one occupation mode.

Early research in career patterns gave little attention to the idea of *voluntary* career changes. Drawing on Miller and Form (1951), Super (1957) described four types of career patterns for men.

1. *The stable career pattern.* In this category are found most professional careers, many managers, some skilled workers and to a lesser extent semi-skilled and clerical workers. They are persons who have gone directly from school or college into a type of work which they have consistently followed: in other words, they have essentially skipped the trial work period.

2. *The conventional career pattern.* In this pattern the sequence of jobs follows the typical progression from initial to trial to stable employment. This pattern is most typical of managerial, skilled, and clerical workers, but characterizes some professionals and domestic workers.

3. *The unstable career pattern.* Here the sequence is trial-stable-trial: the worker does not succeed in establishing himself permanently in what might have been a lifetime job or occupation, but instead gives up his potential career in one field and goes off in a different direction in which he may or may not establish himself. This sequence is seen most often in semi-skilled, clerical, and domestic workers.

4. *The multiple-trial career pattern.* This is the pattern of frequent change of employment, with no one type sufficiently prolonged or dominant to justify calling the person established in a career. This type of sequence is observed most often in domestic, clerical, semi-skilled workers, who not infrequently shift from one type of work to another and accumulate the most disconnected of work histories (pp. 73–74).

Categories 3 and 4 above pertain to midlife career shifters, but there is little cognizance of the voluntary or involuntary shifts of well-established workers within an occupation. As we have seen, such shifts by those who have indeed established themselves in an occupation are not at all rare.

In summary, midlife career changes — second careers — are becoming increasingly common. Those in the midst of such voluntary or involuntary shifts require assistance in career planning.

There is currently no pervasive delivery system for providing this aid, although isolated programs directed toward this end do exist.

Counseling Midcareer Shifters

Unlike younger decision-makers, midlife career shifters typically have accrued experience and developed judgment that enable them to approach the career decision-making process with maturity and knowledge. Even so, the career counselor working with this population will want to discover certain common factors even within this group. Some of these factors are addressed in the following goals.

1. Assist the individual to explore, specify, and evaluate the clarity of the reasons for a career shift. Is the individual confused and anxious as a result of an involuntary career shift, secure and optimistic because of the prospects of a voluntary career shift, or some combination of both? Are stress factors with which an individual has difficulty coping in a current job likely to be present in an intended job? Does the individual appear distressed, depressed, or dysfunctional? How carefully has the individual planned? These and other questions relate to the goal of shift clarification.

2. Assist the individual to acquire all necessary information relevant to a career shift. Does the individual recognize the relationship between education or training and the proposed work shift? What steps are necessary to effect the change? Where and how does one get the necessary information? One comprehensive review of the literature (Pascal et al., 1975) concluded that redirection schemes usually emphasize aptitude diagnosis, provision of realistic job information, on-the-job instruction, and placement assistance.

3. Help the individual to envision the possible effects of a career shift. Will there be financial ramifications? Will family life be affected? Will life style change appreciably? Will geographical relocation be required? What will be the immediate, intermediate, and long-range consequences?

4. Aid the individual to develop appropriate job-seeking or education-seeking behaviors. Can the person write an effective resume? Does the individual have good skills as an interviewee? Has he or she narrowed down to manageable propor-

tions the education or training universe? Does the person have adequate information? These concerns will be treated in detail in the next chapter.

5. Assist the individual to clarify abilities, interests, and personal characteristics. Will the attributes of the person facilitate or impede the transition to a different career, occupation, or job? Are there characteristics germane to the person that would make his or her functioning unsatisfying in any job? Are there any physical, mental, or emotional problems to be considered?

6. Assist, if appropriate, to place the individual in a job. Certain settings wherein counselors work with midcareer shifters will have placement as a goal (such as the Employment Service or Outplacement Counseling). Other agencies that do not perform a brokerage role may well consider performing this function if no alternative is readily available.

One model for assisting midcareer counselees is offered by Finnegan, Westefeld, and Elmore (1981). Their model is not too different from one designed to work with any population. They present four goals: (1) for people to gain information about themselves in order to make constructive choices; (2) for the participants to gain information about their environment that might influence work choices; (3) for the participants to realize that midlife reassessment is not unusual, that others are faced with it, and that there are ways of coping with it; and (4) for members of the workshop to gain skills in decision-making for occupational midlife reassessment and change (p. 70). To accomplish these goals, they concentrate on five major themes: abilities, interests, values, confinements (barriers to moving to a new job), and environment (speculation about an ideal work setting).

It is important that changers utilize the services of counselors. Armstrong's (1981) study of middle-aged returnees to higher education sought to determine how they arrived at their decisions. Few of the sample used counseling services; rather, they relied on habitual decision response patterns that were based largely on choosing from among limited alternatives on the basis of little information. Brown (1981) discusses several models for assisting adults at midlife: self-help groups; informational models (career information hotlines, job

information seminars, occupational libraries, and so on); developmental models (concern with total life/career development); and structured group models (carefully structured activities based on a systematic model). These are not necessarily mutually exclusive models for assisting midlife clients. Examples of these types of programs can be found in the work of Marlowe (1981), Waters and Goodman (1977), and Gerstein (1982).

Finally, Golembiewski (1978) offers several suggestions on how organizations can assist midcareer transitions for workers. These include:

1. . . . a greater awareness of the organizationally-relevant features of the transition is required, as it applies to all employees.
2. . . . organizations should develop a more acute ethical and economic sense of the costs/benefits of aiding their members through a mid-life transition.
3. . . . great emphasis should be placed on continuous checks of career progress against individual needs.
4. . . . the several rhythms of the life cycle must be acknowledged and responded to, both in individual behavior as well as in organization policies and procedures.
5. . . . employing organizations and professional organizations should better tailor their various systems and policies to human cycles and needs.

Golembiewski suggests some further specifics that organizations might undertake to help employees through midlife transitions. These include facilitating by:

- recognizing mid-life transitional phenomena and by providing resources to help employees cope and understand, as via training programs held in-house or sponsored by professional associations
- subsidizing mid-career changes, the derivative benefits being most apparent in cases involving individuals at senior levels of responsibility whose departure requires a chain of promotions and reassignments
- negotiating contracts with "permanent part-timers" at all levels of organization who are seeking some better balance between "making it" and satisfying broader needs or interests

- helping employees cope with realities that can severely complicate mid-life transition, such as by subsidizing career changes for individuals who have been passed over for promotion
- establishing procedures and traditions by which mid-life transitionists can devote greater attention to integrative and supportive activities that facilitate the development of others, as by serving as a mentor, in contrast to the emphasis on the competitiveness and development of self characteristics of earlier life-stages
- establishing policies and transitions whereby full-time employees can accept lesser job responsibilities at reduced compensation, as opposed to such approaches as "up or out" systems.

Since organizational responses are generally slow (see Chapter 11), it is likely that in the foreseeable future, midcareer shifters will be helped to rearrange their internal structures rather than the organizations within society acting to facilitate changes. In any case, we are now starting to understand the dynamics of midcareer shifts and to devise helpful interventions.

WOMEN ENTERING OR REENTERING THE LABOR FORCE

In Chapter 5 we discussed some career considerations unique to females. A specific aspect of careers relating to adults is the case of women who enter or reenter the labor force after a period of child-bearing and child-rearing.

Career Patterns

Super (1957) has classified the career patterns of women as follows:

1. The *stable homemaking career pattern*. This category includes all women who marry while in or very shortly after leaving school or college, having expected to do so and having no significant work experience.

2. The *conventional career pattern*. In this pattern of working followed by homemaking the young woman leaving school or college goes to work for a period of several months or several years, in an occupation which is open to her with-

out training beyond that which she obtained in her general education, in brief professional education substituted for general education, or in some relatively brief post-high school or post-collegiate education. Clerical work, teaching, nursing, occupational therapy, or secretarial work illustrate these types of occupations. They are generally viewed as stop gaps, but may be thought of as life careers, with subsequent changes of aspirations. They are often valuable as an opportunity for developing independence and a sense of being a person in one's own right. Marrying after this relatively brief work experience, the young woman becomes a full-time homemaker.

3. *The stable working career pattern*. The sequence in this type of career pattern is one of entering the work force on leaving school, college, or professional school and embarking on a career which becomes the woman's life's work. She may perceive it as a life career from the start: a small percentage of young women do have strong career (as contrasted with homemaking) motivation and interest [*note:* this was in *1957*]. Or she may at first view her working career as a preliminary to marriage, or a working career to resume after a period of full-time homemaking.

4. *The double-track career pattern*. This is a pattern of the woman who goes to work after completing her education, marries, and continues with a double career of working and homemaking. She may take occasional time out for childbearing. The pattern is most common near the upper and lower ends of the occupational scale, among women physicians and scientists, and among women domestics, presumably because the challenge of the work, or the income it produces, is important to the woman in question. The double role is in neither case easy, for the married working woman usually has two jobs, one with and one without pay.

5. *The interrupted career pattern*. Here the sequence is one of working, homemaking, and working while or instead of homemaking. The young woman works for some time, then marries, and then, when her children are old enough for her to leave them, when financial needs — including those from being widowed or divorced — or interest in working become dominant, she returns to work. . . .

6. *The unstable career pattern*. In women, this

type of career pattern consists of working, homemaking, working again, returning to full-time homemaking, etc. It results most often from irregular economic pressures which make extra earnings necessary despite homemaking preferences or needs, or from poor health necessitating giving up employment, or from a combination of these. This pattern is observed most often at the lower socioeconomic levels.

7. *The multiple-trial career pattern.* This pattern is the same in women as the similarly named pattern in men: it consists of a succession of unrelated jobs, with stability in none, resulting in the individual having no genuine life work (pp. 77–78).

In this chapter, we are concerned with women in patterns 2, 4, 5, and 6. As we saw in Chapter 5, more women have entered and are entering the labor force; a significant proportion of those women are reentering the world of work and education after a substantial hiatus or are older women entering for the first time. These women feel considerable insecurity, stress, and a variety of emotions and uncertainties that beg for professional career interventions. Mogul (1979) has aptly described their condition from a psychiatric perspective.

Women resuming outside work after an interval . . . have to struggle simultaneously with the realities of the work world, friction at home, and their own inner conflicts. The more a woman's sense of herself was grounded in her identity as wife and mother, the greater the readjustment in her sense of self when she reenters the occupational world. The sense of femaleness, attractiveness, and lovability is often related to being dependent, and less competent than men, so that doubts about important parts of the self are stirred up as other parts are developed. To be aggressive and actively self-promoting — necessities in the school or work world — are characteristics to which (an older) generation of middle-aged women did not aspire in their youth. Since women primarily grew up to be those who nurture and give to others and are sensitive and vulnerable to real or imagined disapproval from people who are important to them, the sense of guilt and failure is almost unavoidable as they begin to do for themselves.

In order to change her lifestyle during her middle years without either too much guilt and inhibition or too much angry repudiation of her former life, a woman has the psychological task of testing and making room for new identities and new self-perceptions without entirely discarding old ones that had offered gratifications and grounds for previous self-regard. It is helpful to have social and family support for these changes and also to have derived solid gratifications from the previous role. (p. 1140)

Riley (1982) envisions more and more reentry or first-time entry women and labels the process "cohort norm formation." Women in their thirties and forties are responding to social changes by moving in new directions: going to school, pursuing careers, or structuring family lives in innovative ways. When they do, however, as Slaney, Stafford, and Russell (1981) have demonstrated, they experience considerably more career indecision than do high school or college women. This finding adds further evidence to support the need for career interventions for reentry women. In addition, Lenz and Shavitz (1977) have pointed out the social and psychological barriers facing reentry women: job discrimination, lack of marketable skills, guilt feelings, and a low opinion of their own abilities. Coupled with all of these factors is the problem of what Berman (1980) describes simply as being a woman in an era of changing values.

Reasons for Returning to a Career

Women return to careers for many reasons. The most obvious cause is financial. In an age of inflation, it is frequently necessary for both husband and wife to work in order to maintain a standard of living gained when only the husband worked, let alone to increase a standard of living. In times of high unemployment, a wife may be the only marriage partner able to find work. Divorce and widowhood also may cause financial strain that necessitates reentry. In any case, financial necessity, however idiosyncratically defined, is a major work motivator for reentry women. A second reason for work outside the home is fulfillment. Bernard (1970) has observed that declining birth rates mean fewer years of child-bearing and child-rearing and that housekeeping duties are much easier, thus leaving women technologically unemployed in the sense of traditional motherhood. In many cases, such a condition leads to ennui, frustration, feelings about a lack of personal worth and identity, and so on. There is some persuasive research to suggest that for women an acute crisis stage in many adult lives may come at the empty-nest period (Thurnher, 1974). With the termination of the family life cycle, when children have left the home and nurturant demands are no longer present, many women review their life, find themselves fighting feelings of impotence, helplessness, and despair, and search for outlets to fill the void resulting from the empty nest. Lowenthal and Weiss (1976) report that in a study of middle-aged individuals, including various socio-economic and age and sex classifications, the most poorly adapted subjects in the sample were women in the empty-nest stage. Paradoxically, they suggest that few of these women would voluntarily seek counseling.

The typical woman in America enters the labor force immediately after schooling and works for a few years before marriage and having a child. Few women permanently leave the labor force. Most return or never leave at all. Shortages of skilled workers in many professional, managerial, clerical, skilled craft, and service occupations offer women an excellent employment prospect. Nondiscrimination legislation helps to break down barriers to higher-level occupations and to traditionally male dominated fields. New opportunities in expanding occupations are available. When these opportunities are combined with the trend toward more education for women and toward smaller families (thus muting the effects of fertility on work), the likely result is a modest increase in the labor force participation of women.

Counseling Reentry Women

Much of the counseling for reentry women depends on how long the women have been absent from paid employment and how big a hiatus exists between termination of formal education or training and entry into the labor force. For most women in late entry or in reentry situations, the following goals would seem to be appropriate.

1. Reinforce positive feelings about self-worth and ability to make a contribution in the work force outside the home. Many women lack specific salable skills or possess obsolescent training; they irrationally translate these lacks into feelings of little personal worth. They should be aided to separate employability skills deficits from personal worth estimates. Many married women may have difficulty realizing an identity separate from their husbands after years of making their self-development subservient to family needs. Will they be able to assume a multiroled existence after a period of essentially restricted roles?

2. Provide any information that may be lacking about basic career decision-making: personal assets and limitations, values and attitudes, the world of work, resources, and so on. Despite social sophistication and a generally mature life orientation, women in this category may be vocationally illiterate and may require the most rudimentary types of career information.

3. Assist in exploring changes in life style that may be occasioned by first-time entry or reentry into the labor force. What are the possible consequences of paid employment on marital relationships, continued child-rearing, division of labor in the home, leisure activities, and so forth? Will paid labor result in actual economic benefit? In some cases, it will not.

4. Help clients to understand the implications of full-time versus part-time work. Only a minority of women work full-time the year round.

5. Prepare women to deal with possible discrimination, both overt and covert. What possible discriminatory attitudes may be encountered among management? What possibilities exist for subtle or blatant sexual harrassment by employers or by fellow workers? Do hiring, promotion, and retention practices present barriers because of sex? Do compensation differences exist that cannot otherwise be explained? What are intentional and unintentional sexist questions posed in an interview? How does one combat discrimination on a personal level?

6. Provide specialized experiences, if necessary, in such areas as consciousness-raising and assertiveness-training.

7. Explore entry-level jobs with extant education versus possible jobs with additional education or training. Will any job do because of immediate

economic necessity, or does she really want a vocation for the rest of her life, or is it some combination of both? Where and how does she obtain the additional education or training?

8. Provide a referral system for placement assistance; provide placement services if no alternative is available; and provide job-seeking and job-hunting skills.

9. Provide follow-up and continuing support. Once the individual has begun to work, there may be needs for assurance, enhancement of coping skills, and general support. Further, the counselor may be able to secure feedback about the types of assistance that might have been provided in the prework situation but were overlooked or not given sufficient attention.

Many excellent programs have been devised to deal with issues of sex in the career development of women, and reentry women in particular. These programs have produced some fine materials for use with the subpopulation. See, for example, EDC/WEEA Publishing Center, 55 Chapel Street, Newton, MA 02160.

As for most other special populations, there is a separate statement of principles for counseling and therapy of women (American Psychological Association, 1979). These principles begin where generic counseling competencies leave off and are largely directed toward eliminating sexism in counseling by urging the end of sexist language, banishing of preconceived notions about goals for women, forbidding sexual relationships between counselor and client, recognizing unique women's issues and concerns, and remaining professionally alert to the burgeoning literature on women. Worrell (1980) expands on the theme by defining many populations of adult women, one of which is reentry and adult women. Here she includes women "returning to work or school, displaced homemakers, or empty nest women, and aging and retiring women" (p. 479). She sees reentry counseling as generic counseling with special perspectives on sexual issues, identity crisis management, and aging.

There are many reports of successful programs designed for reentry women. Sandmeyer (1980) offered a three-day workshop, called "Choices and Changes," intended to aid women aged 26–35 in decision-making for either late entry into

the occupational world or career change. A second example concerns career/life planning aspects of counseling with divorced women. Kitabchi, Murrell, and Crawford (1979) offer suggestions for such counseling, and include the additional variable of *loss* (as in the death of a relationship). They advocate a three-stage group process, progressing from self-awareness through self-appraisal to taking action.

THE OLDER WORKER

Generally speaking, the older worker is considered to be over 45. Although age discrimination in employment hiring practices has been theoretically reduced by federal employment acts, there is little doubt that this category of worker faces considerable prejudice in terms of hiring or retention policies and that career problems are heightened for this age group. The Work in America Institute (1980) has pointed up this problem and has recommended actions for employers to make policies age-neutral and responsive to our aging work force. These include:

- review of nondiscriminatory hiring and separation practices to be certain that de facto systems are not operating despite apparent compliance with Equal Employment Opportunity
- review of age distribution of employees within an organization to be sure that older workers are not over- or underrepresented in any area
- examination of alternatives for older workers, such as part-time work, job sharing, work schedule variations, and flex time.

Roscow (1983) echoes some of these suggestions and places the issue of older workers in perspective. He states:

In fact, the raising of the mandatory retirement age to 70 is producing shifts in the labor force trends. By the end of the next decade, employers will be more motivated to attract older workers than ever before. This will necessitate a loosening of social security regulations, more flexible working arrangements for older people (hours, weeks, and months), phased/gradual or tapered retirements, job redesign to accommodate physical and psychological abilities and needs, and a general set of personnel policies that are more responsive to the older character of the work force. This also represents a great area for personnel management experiments and change, in anticipation of the coming age shift (pp. 16–17).

Attitudinal and Developmental Factors

When unemployment strikes the older worker, it is likely to be for longer periods of time, and the process of looking for work is frequently fraught with barriers that produce debasement, humiliation, and frustration. As age increases, occupational mobility decreases, thus cutting down the alternatives for the older worker. Jaffe (1978) investigated the labor force experience of older workers and concluded that among unemployed men aged 45 and over, about 42 percent were unemployed for fifteen weeks or longer; for younger men, only 28 percent were unemployed that long. For women, the corresponding percentages were 35 and 21. These workers experience considerable difficulty getting placed in a job. U.S. Employment Service data have consistently demonstrated over the years that older workers are a substantial proportion of their clientele (30 percent plus) but that these workers are placed on a less than proportional basis (usually less than 20 percent). Rudd and Coveney (1979) looked at the employment experience of a sample of these men and concluded that although they held positive attitudes toward work, they were cynical about the effectiveness of job-seeking efforts; consequently, their attempts to get work tended to be limited after a while; they became discouraged. They lost their jobs and they failed to find new ones because of changes within themselves or changes in occupational patterns in the economy. Because of their unique problems, the discipline of industrial gerontology has come into being to study the employment and retirement problems of middle-aged and older workers.

The labor force participation of workers over the age of 65 in America has actually declined in linear fashion since just before the turn of the century. In 1890 about 68 percent of all men over 65 were in the labor force; by 1930 that figure had dropped to 54 percent; and by 1970 only 25 percent of all men over 65 were still in

the labor force (Graney & Cottam, 1981). In fact, the industries that employ the most people in America have provided few opportunities for older people's participation. It will be interesting to see how much the raised mandatory retirement age will affect these data.

Many of these problems are caused by the natural physical consequences of aging. Marbach (1968) has summarized the characteristics of jobs that, in the opinion of some, are unsuitable for older workers:

> As concerns manual work, there are in the first place jobs which call for occasional bursts of considerable energy or a long period of sustained exertion without any break; jobs which oblige the worker to stand or to maintain an unnatural posture; jobs with excessive environmental stresses; those calling for a rapid, uninterrupted rate of work; finally, as far as perceptual and mental processes are concerned, jobs which make excessive sensory demands or necessitate accurate discrimination, a great deal of decision-making and choice, or the need to remember for very short periods (pp. 28–29).

The fact is that for most older workers, intellectual functioning is not impaired. Whenever health has been preserved, verbal scores have remained relatively stable. There is, however, a persistent and progressive decline in performance on most speeded tasks. Hence, older workers are likely to remain stable in their cognitive abilities and to deteriorate in their psychomotor performance. Of course, when extreme old age is considered, the general trend in cognitive functioning is downhill. These conditions are perhaps responsible for the fact that the lowest retirement rates are found in white-collar and service occupations, and the highest rates exist in blue-collar and agricultural occupations.

In a comprehensive review of age-related differences in work attitudes and behavior, Rhodes (1983) reached some general conclusions with which we agree. She found that age is related to overall job satisfaction, satisfaction with work itself, job involvement, internal work motivation, and organizational commitment. Age appears to be negatively related to turnover intention. There also seems to be an increase with age in needs for security and affiliation and preferences for extrinsic job characteristics and having friendly co-workers and supervisors. In terms of career development, she states,

> Recent studies based on life cycle and career stage models suggest that determinants of job satisfaction and job involvement change depending on one's career stage. Preliminary evidence suggests that task characteristics are more strongly related to job satisfaction and involvement in the trial or early career stage (after a learning period), personal characteristics achieve salience in the midcareer stage, and reward variables, although important throughout, become particularly important in the late career stage (p. 356).

The four out of each ten American workers who are older face some formidable factors that work against their quickly finding new employment when they are displaced from jobs. Among these factors are: (1) many employers' unfavorable attitudes toward older workers; (2) substitution of cheaper labor (such as illegal aliens, women) for older workers; and (3) changes in occupations, industry, and the geographical distribution of jobs that favor the hiring of younger workers who are more flexible and mobile.

This lack of flexibility of older workers is often referred to as the problem of obsolescence. Obsolescence is workers' lack of up-to-date knowledge and skills needed to perform effectively. In terms of employer bias, a study by Craft, Doctors, Shkop, and Benecki (1979) indicates that age does not seem to be a primary determiner of an employer's perception of personal work-related traits, but it does affect the hiring decision because of the potentially shortened work life. The same holds true for older women who face greater unemployment difficulties than their younger counterparts (Pursell & Torrence, 1980). Employer attitudes are also affected by fears that older workers have more accidents. Root's (1981) data indicate that this is not so: older workers are hurt less than younger workers, but they are hurt more seriously when they do have an accident. Rhodes (1983) corroborates this finding, explaining that perhaps the negative association between age and accidents is caused by the fact

that older workers who are less capable of meeting the physical aspects of jobs leave these more physically demanding and hazardous jobs.

Reducing the Negative Effect of Ageism

Several approaches have been advocated to reduce the negative effect of ageism in hiring, promotion, and retention. One suggestion has involved job redesign. Such a technique is frequently applied on an informal, personal basis in small enterprises, but it is now being advocated on a massive scale. Essentially, job redesign involves a determination of a job's physical demands and the minimum physical capacities necessary for its performance. Particularly noted are points of strain that might suggest job modification or reallocation to the benefit of the older worker. The attempt is to dovetail worker abilities and job requirements, taking into account both worker needs and production demands. Thus, employment opportunities for older workers can be extended by removing pressures in the work environment. Job reorganization might also entail allowing workers of greater experience to handle more complex tasks, while inexperienced workers tend to the simpler, more physical aspects of a job. One must be careful here, for there is some evidence that job enrichment may actually decrease job satisfaction among older workers (Phillips, Barrett, & Rush, 1978).

A related technique has involved the concept of functional age (McFarland, 1973). The theory is that it is unfair and wasteful to judge workers on the basis of chronological age; therefore, the idea is to rate a worker's functional ability on the job — to determine what the worker can do operationally. One such measurement system, GULHEMP, provides a seven-category scale to assess mental, physical, and personality variables related to work output, responsibility, communication with fellow workers, and potential for retraining or reallocation (Koyl, 1974).

A third approach to accommodating older workers is retraining them in order to establish eligibility for jobs with specific training requirements. Getting older workers to be motivated for and to engage in retraining is, however, frequently difficult to accomplish.

Perhaps some distinctions should be made between the younger older workers (45–54) and the older older workers (55–70). One study of laid-off space industry workers found that the 45–54 age group had no more difficulty in finding reemployment than did all other workers. The 55–70 group, however, experienced great difficulty; they held fewer jobs, were unemployed longer, and eventually earned lower pay when they did find employment (Turner & Whitaker, 1973).

Kieffer (1980) summarizes some of the suggestions made to assist older workers now on the job. He advocates:

- more effective performance evaluation programs
- identification of alternative jobs or work arrangements in the same or related organizations
- alternative job placements
- development and improvement of counseling services relative to further careers or retirement
- improvement or adaptation of selection systems for training, development, and promotion
- updating of advisory services on pensions and fringe benefits
- review of terminating procedures
- mental health counseling (p. 11)

Counseling the Older Worker

As we have indicated previously, older workers are likely to experience employment difficulties that make them particularly vulnerable to trauma in the career domain. Therefore, many of the goals of career counseling with these clients involve reassurance and immediate assistance.

1. Provide support in building and maintaining positive attitudes toward one's worth and dignity. Is the individual confusing temporary rejection as a worker with rejection as a human being? Does the individual have a work history of rejection? Does the person express feelings of hopelessness, worthlessness, obsolescence, despair? Is confidence shattered?

2. Explore possible retraining and other avenues for improving their employment opportunities.

3. Provide any and all geographic information. Does the individual know where the best markets for employment are? Is mobility a problem?

4. Assess the actual reasons for employment difficulties. For example, is the person coming for assistance because of layoff, resignation, sickness, retirement, or firing?

5. Assist individuals to gauge accurately their present state of motivation, the expectations they hold for future employment, and their perceptions of themselves as workers.

6. Especially with managerial, professional, and technical occupations, aid the individual to consider the relative importance of such factors as salary, use of abilities, status, amount of responsibility, security, opportunities for advancement, chance to make a contribution, and so on. Also important is the need to explore the possibilities and consequences of occupational downgrading and salary decrease.

7. Assist in developing job-seeking behaviors, if necessary.

8. Provide placement and follow-up services if no other opportunities exist in the area served; refer to appropriate agencies and institutions if placement services are available.

One example of a program for older workers should provide a flavor of the types of activities in use. Smith and Golden (1982) report on six-meeting, twelve-hour job readiness workshops, miniworkshops, and an employment information showcase. Fifteen to twenty-eight participants were placed in each of twelve groups. Designed for workers 55 and older, the program had three major goals:

1. to develop a mechanism to disseminate vocational guidance information materials, and training to unemployed or underemployed adults . . . , to assist in finding gainful employment or volunteer work to supplement retirement incomes or to enhance life styles

2. to develop and compile vocational guidance materials related to the concerns of older job seekers and those who work with this audience in finding gainful employment or meaningful volunteer work

3. to alert potential employers of the skills and abilities of older individuals as a means of both reversing age discrimination and informing older adults that they possess characteristics desired by employers. (p. 30)

PRERETIREMENT
AND RETIREMENT

We sometimes forget that retirement and the time immediately preceding it are a part of one's career life; these times are as fraught with potentially anxiety-producing events as are any others. Most of that anxiety for those who have had a work life revolves around the possibility that the loss of work will cause serious problems of adjustment. In Chapter 2 we devoted attention to the purposes that work serves in maintaining an individual's psychological and social well-being. Jahoda (1979, 1981) has investigated the functions that work performs in keeping people mentally healthy. She suggests that employment provides five beneficial consequences other than simply earning a living.

> First, employment imposes a time structure on the waking day; Second, employment implies regularly shared experiences and contacts with people outside the nuclear family; Third, employment links individuals to goals and purposes that transcend their own; Fourth, employment defines aspects of personal status and identity; and finally, employment enforces activity (1979, p. 312).

On the face of it, retirement removes these five sources of psychological well-being; if nothing is substituted, it is logical to assume that loss of work has the potential for inducing psychological malaise. For that reason, some people try to retire partially and ease into the stage, but this partial retirement is prevalent mainly among the self-employed (Quinn, 1981). Many would like to stay in the job market, but discrimination, a lack of job opportunities, and other factors combine to force them to retire completely (Rones, 1980; Gray & Morse, 1980; Stagner, 1979; Burkhauser & Tolley, 1978). Hence, despite the raising of the retirement age, early retirement among men has actually increased (Rosenfeld & Brown, 1979). Men, in general, plan to retire earlier than they actually do, however (Ekerdt, Bosse, & Mogery, 1980).

On the other hand, some see loss of work as merely an informal, nonceremonious rite of passage (Atchley, 1976; Roscow, 1974; Ward, 1979; Kaiser, Peters, & Babchuk, 1982), a transition between the world of work and retirement. Even so, retirement for some comes as a great surprise. Several national surveys have indicated that over 40 percent of individuals who state that they never expected to stop working are retired four years later (Goudy, 1981). Some studies (Butler, 1975) describe a "retirement syndrome," characterized by anxiety and depression; other studies (Bell, 1979) find that even people who were strongly committed to work do not demonstrate negative changes in retirement either immediately after the fact or eighteen months later.

Much of the conflict among findings may be an artifact of the samples used in the studies. We know that several individual differences seem related to successful retirement, and these dimensions may be more or less present in different samples. Among the dimensions that appear to be involved in a positive retirement transition are: adequate income (Morrison, 1975; Schmitt & McCune, 1981), voluntary rather than involuntary retirement (Meier, 1975), good health (Spreitzer, Synder, & Larson, 1980; Walker & Lazer, 1978), specificity of plans and staying active (Rockwell, Hood, & Lee, 1980; Graney & Zimmerman, 1981; McPherson & Guppy, 1979), and history of an orderly rather than a discontinuous career (Maddox, 1972; Glamser, 1981). To extend Super's career maturity idea, some people appear to be retirement mature whereas others seem to be retirement immature (Kingson, 1981; Johnson & Riker, 1981). The notion that stress occurs when individuals are forced into a life stage before they are ready seems reasonable (Walker, Kimmel, & Price, 1981). Because of these individual differences in adjustment to retirement, studies that seek to place retirement among the hierarchy of stressful life events usually show it to be in the middle range (Holmes & Rahe, 1967; Paykel, Prousoff, & Ulenhuth, 1971; Lundborg & Theorell, 1976; Ilfield, 1976).

Attitudes Toward the Aged

Our society's attitudes toward the aged have been less than benevolent. In many ways we have rejected the older population. Some people apparently view age itself as an anathema and shun those who are old. About one-fifth of our current aged population is foreign born, and xenophobia (fear of foreigners) may well cause negative attitudes. Our old tend to have much less formal education than does the general population, and in a society that values educational attainments, the old are likely to experience prejudice because of this. Finally, as is well known, the old are poor; a great many who do not work are living on an annual income below that established by the U.S. Department of Labor as representing poverty level. Thus, age itself, discrimination toward the foreign born, lack of education, and poverty combine to evoke negative attitudes toward the aged in America. In a few years, as the aged population becomes more indigenous and their level of education (as well as their numbers) increases, these attitudes may soften. At the present time, however, they are real and destructive and give credence to Jonathan Swift's assertion: "Every man desires to live long, but no man would be old."

Withers (1974) has catalogued many of the myths about the aged and work that affect retirement (although recently many of these myths have been destroyed by legislation). He lists the following fallacies:

- The right age for retirement is 65.
- Work capacity always declines with age.
- Older workers cannot be retrained.
- It does not pay to retrain older workers, because they retire so soon afterward.
- It is futile to retrain older workers, because no one will hire them.
- Older workers cannot be hired by companies with insurance programs, because it is impossible to fit them into these programs.
- It is undesirable to hire older workers as a group; they are poorly educated.
- In retirement, income can be greatly reduced because old people consume less per person and need less income than younger people.
- Older workers should be retired because in our advanced technological economy their labor is not needed. They should make room for younger workers (p. 24).

All of these statements cannot accurately be applied to all older workers. Older workers are as heterogeneous as the labor force in total, and broad generalizations such as these are simply inaccurate when applied indiscriminately to older workers.

Adjustment to Retirement

Ultimately, adjustment to retirement is very much an individual matter. Some will welcome retirement and will embrace leisure and the relative lack of structure with guiltlessness and joy. Others will fret and stew, experience trauma, and never adjust. It has been argued, for example, that "Leisure is not quite leisure when you do not have to work" (Hochschild, 1973, p. 19). In other words, free time becomes a constant excess with which one must cope rather than a welcome temporary release from a basically time-structured life. Generally, retirement causes people to think about leisure more in terms of *pleasure* than in terms of *freedom*. Hence, retirement can be either a period of enrichment and opportunity to pursue avocational and leisure interests or a source of depression connected with the loss of a culturally dominant social role.

Much of the literature on retirement conceives that stage as a period of disengagement, a reversal of expansion, a period characterized by less involvement in social participation. Disengagement, however, is perhaps an erroneous concept. Those who adjust well to retirement are more likely to reengage society in a different way than they are to disengage society. To be sure, some retirees disengage, but others simply reorient the direction and intensity of their engagement.

Several studies attempt to categorize retirees according to adjustment in retirement or by activity level. The American Health Care Corporation's study, *Aging in America: Trials and Triumphs* (1980), divided its sample of 514 randomly selected older persons into three groups:

Enjoyers — 27 percent — successfully cope with aging. Usually they are healthy, well-educated males who are financially secure.

Survivors — 53 percent of the sample — are reasonably successful copers with age. They are largely men and women of average health, less than a high school education, and basically adequate financial resources.

Casualties — 20 percent of the sample — are not very successful in coping. Usually they are female, without much education, in relatively poor health, and of low income.

Walker, Kimmel, and Price (1981) divide their sample of 1511 recent retirees from major corporations into four groups:

The Rocking Chair Group — 44 percent of the sample — voluntarily retired at about 62–65, are generally healthy, and are reasonably content with their retirement associates, finances, and activities.

The Reorganizer Group — 24 percent of the sample — retired voluntarily at 62–65, were generally better educated, more financially secure, and healthier. They looked forward to beginning a new pattern of activities and usually worked as volunteers.

The Holding On Group — about 19 percent — continued to work for pay. Some involuntarily retired and needed the income. Most had not thought about retiring or made plans for retirement. Availability of jobs for this group is absolutely necessary.

The Dissatisfied Group — 13 percent of the sample — were working neither voluntarily nor for pay and had a hard time keeping busy. Income and health were relatively poor. They had little retirement satisfaction.

In short, these two surveys indicate that people of various educational levels, incomes, and activity focus can retire successfully by adopting different styles. They also suggest that, as Dillard (1982) advocates, teaching specific retirement life styles may be a useful preretirement counseling activity.

Counseling for Preretirement and Retirement

Retirement is indeed a time of appraisal and reappraisal. It is simultaneously a look backward and a look ahead. The goals that appear appropriate in working with this group are as follows:

1. Assist in planning. Provide information relating to health, finances, housing, appropriate agencies for the elderly, and a variety of other concerns relating to daily living.
2. Clarify affective reactions to retirement. Individuals vary in their reactions to retirement. The counselor should not assume any universal reaction: trauma, joy, anticipation, disengage-

ment, reengagement, and such are equally likely responses. Forced versus voluntary retirement will probably evoke within the counselee two appreciably different sets of concerns.
3. Make appropriate referrals to community agencies designed to deal with particular aspects of the aged.

In terms of this latter suggestion, Blai (1982) has put together a compendium of resources for older persons who desire to work. State employment service offices, agencies on aging, YWCAs and YMCAs, and Forty-Plus Clubs are all possibilities. In addition, various volunteer agency programs exist: Foster Grandparents Program (FGP), Retired Senior Volunteer Program (RSVP), Volunteers in Service to America (VISTA), Peace Corps, Senior Companion Program, Service Corps of Retired Executives (SCORE). Also, the United States Department of Labor sponsors the Senior Community Service Employment Program (SCSEP), which employs economically disadvantaged older persons in part-time community service jobs.

Corporations have taken increasing action to provide their employees with preretirement programs, although the effect of these programs has not been carefully evaluated (Olson, 1981). Unfortunately, some of the careful evaluations we do have show few, if any, significant longitudinal differences between groups that have had a preretirement program and those that have not (Glamser, 1980), although in the short run, there may be significant differences in favor of treatment groups (Fitzpatrick 1979; Morrow, 1981). Nevertheless, their number is growing. A survey of Chief Executive Officers and Personnel Directors of the Fortune 1000 companies (Research & Forecasts, Inc., 1980) confirms progress, but also indicates that a majority of the companies still have no retirement preparation program, and 40 percent doubt that they have the "expertise" in-house to develop one. Of those which do have a program, Table 12.2 presents a breakdown of the topics covered in terms of three categories: *narrow* programs that concentrate on financial questions; *intermediate* programs that cover finances plus health, leisure, and legal questions; and *broad* programs that cover virtually everything. Hence, most

Table 12.2
Topics Covered by Retirement Preparation Program as Reported by Personnel Directors

□ = reported by more than 50%

	Narrow	Intermediate	Broad
Social Security and Medicare	77%	87%	98%
Financial benefits and options	73	85	97
Physical and mental health	14	81	100
Leisure	9	76	100
Legal aspects	23	68	98
Employment	0	28	92
Housing	0	40	90
Community resources	5	49	88
Options for employment after retirement	18	19	83
Interpersonal relations	9	25	68
Life planning	14	21	61
	*	*	*
	(22)	(53)	(59)

*Adds up to more than 100 percent because individuals give more than one answer.

programs are focusing on both higher-order and lower-order human needs.

Loesch (1980) suggests "life-flow leisure counseling" as an antidote to possible diminution of self-satisfaction and self-definition caused by loss of work in retirement. This system involves exploration of interests, values, satisfactions, and personal characteristics and subsequently integrating and synthesizing this information into leisure pursuits. Leisure counseling, in fact, is a part of virtually every prepackaged retirement planning program. For example, the National Council of Older Americans' eight-module program contains one on leisure and another on life style (Fitzpatrick, 1980).

Finally, in terms of issues related to this very young activity of counseling the old, Atchley (1979) reports on a conference designed to assess research needs. Among the more interesting research questions are the following:

Physical and Mental Ability for Employment

1. How does functional capacity interact with occupation to influence the decision to retire or the timing of retirement? How do subjective and objective health factors compare as predictors of functional capacity for employment?
2. To what extent do various diseases such as heart disease, diabetes, or arthritis influence functional capacity for employment? Do these factors influence the decision to retire or the timing of retirement directly or do they operate through their effects on functional capacity for employment?
3. How do mental health factors such as anxiety or depression influence the decision to retire or the timing of retirement?
4. How does physical aging compare with health factors in predicting functional capacity for employment?
5. How do the following compare as factors influencing functional capacity for employment?
   a. physical and mental aging
   b. disability due to disease or accident
   c. obsolete psychomotor skills
   d. obsolete knowledge
   Does the relative importance of these various factors differ by occupation and how?

*Economic and Noneconomic Rewards
by Employment*

1. To what extent does the fulfillment of individual occupational goals influence the decision to retire or the timing of retirement?
2. How are the meanings attached to the job related to the type of retirement, the decision to retire, or the timing of retirement?
3. Do people feel a need to replace job rewards (both economic and noneconomic) in retirement? If so, does this influence the decision to retire or the timing of the retirement?

Social-Psychological Characteristics

1. What are the determinants of attitude toward retirement?
2. What are the determinants of attitude toward the job?
3. How do attitudes toward the job influence attitudes toward retirement?
4. How do significant others influence attitude toward retirement?
5. How do attitudes toward retirement influence the decision to retire or the timing of retirement?
6. How does the perceived effect of retirement on prestige affect the decision to retire or the timing of retirement?

Personality Factors

1. How does a positive orientation toward planning (active manipulation of environment) influence the decision to retire or the timing of retirement?
2. All other things being equal, is the Type A person (i.e., hard-driving, competitive, pressed for time) more or less likely to retire or retire early compared to the Type B person?
3. Do inner-directed people retire more frequently or retire sooner compared to other-directed people?

Information

1. What effects do retirement planning programs have on the decision to retire or the timing of retirement?
2. To what extent is the decision to retire the result of a "rational" process?

System Pressures to Retire

1. What effects do varying employer retirement policies, employer pressures toward retirement, and organizational characteristics have on the decision to retire and the timing of retirement?
2. How do employer policies, unemployment, job retrogression, peer pressures, employer pressure, and family pressures compare as influences on the decision to retire and on the timing of retirement? (pp. 47–48)

Summary

In this chapter we have outlined factors that contribute to an increasing need for adult career counseling. We have presented characteristics of four adult subpopulations: midcareer shifters, women entering or reentering the labor force after child-rearing, older workers, and preretirees and retirees. We have suggested specific foci for the career counseling of these groups. We have further presented general guidelines for the career counseling of adults. In the following chapter we will discuss several additional adult subpopulations for which the counselor requires specialized career knowledge and skills.

LEARNING ACTIVITIES

1. Select a popular book directed toward self-help in the career process. Any large bookstore will have many from which to choose (for example, Bolles, *What Color Is Your Parachute?*; Campbell, *If You Don't Know Where You're Going You'll Probably End Up Somewhere Else*). Read the book and make an assessment of its content, face, or logical validity. Do the statements made and the advice offered seem appropriate in light of what we know about adult career development and

behavior? Is there anything potentially harmful about the book? Who might benefit from such a volume?

2. Several magazines relating to females in the work force have come into existence in the last several years. Among these are: *MS, New Woman, Women's Work*, and *Working Woman*. Choose one such periodical and evaluate it in terms of its potential helpfulness.

3. Interview an adult who is representative of one of the four subpopulations described in this chapter. What primary career-related concerns are expressed by the person? What are the psychological effects of these concerns? How could career counseling interventions help this person? What form should such interventions take? Are they currently available in the community?

4. Locate an individual whose primary responsibility is career counseling of adults. Interview the person in terms of his or her perception of what is done for clients and what impedes a more complete provision of services (personpower, materials, and such).

5. Monitor the mass media for articles and programs pertinent to the four subpopulations of this chapter.

6. Select a work of fiction wherein the protagonist is attempting to cope with one of the four adult problem areas. Describe the pertinent dynamics.

7. Select one of the magazines or periodicals directed to the retired population (such as *Dynamic Maturity, Retirement Living, Senior Power, Modern Maturity, Retirement Life*). Analyze the concerns dealt with in such publications and the face validity of the articles.

8. Below is a partial listing of films relating to various aspects of preretirement and retirement. View one or more and summarize the salient features.

> *The Rest of Your Life.* Albed Ed Council, Distribution Center, Galien, Michigan 49113
>
> *Retire to Life.* Administration on Aging. University of Oklahoma, Norman.

Planning the Quality Life. Harvest Years. Cascade, California.

New Wrinkles on Retirement. University of Georgia, Center for Continuing Education, Athens, Georgia 30602

Decisions, Decisions. Family Interaction Center/MRI, 555 Middlefield Road, Palo Alto, California 94301

Critical Decades. National Medical Audiovisual Center (Annex). Station K, Atlanta, Georgia 30324

9. Conduct a community survey to discover what assistance is available for preretirees and retirees in each of the following areas: financial planning, physical health, legal services, attitudes toward retirement, death and dying, sex and aging, life enrichment (such as volunteerism, second careers, use of leisure), housing and transportation, and consumerism.

OBJECTIVES

After reading this chapter, engaging in the learning activities, and reading suggested references, you should have met the objectives that follow. If you have not, it would probably be useful for you to review the chapter before proceeding further.

1. List four adult subpopulations for which career counseling is appropriate.

2. Enumerate at least three changes in American society that give rise to career-related problems.

3. Identify for each of the four adult subpopulations, two typical behavioral characteristics.

4. Describe at least five planning considerations entailed in the career counseling for adults.

5. List at least three goals for career counseling with each of the four subpopulations.

6. Specify at least two career counseling techniques or foci appropriate for each of the four subpopulations.

13 | *Special Adult Career Concerns II*

As we saw in Chapter 12, even with the most advantageous career development, a person may experience problems related to work. These difficulties, in turn, can frequently affect nonwork behaviors. Most people will need to make career adjustments as they negotiate the various career development stages. Some will need to make only minor changes; others will be forced to make profoundly troubling ones. Even after adjustments, problems will continue to arise from within the individual (for example, expectancy-reality discrepancies) or from outside the individual (for example, economic downturns causing unemployment). The potential frustrations of these in the labor force are many, and counselors can work in both a developmental mode and a remedial mode to help people to address these areas of concern.

In this chapter, we will discuss six more adult career concerns. For each we will present an overview of the particular problem; we will review representative research on the problem; and we will offer implications for counseling those who are experiencing it. We will begin with a look at the unemployed, dislocated, and discouraged worker. A discussion of so-called burnout will follow. Attention will then be directed to family effects of working mothers. The family theme will be continued with a consideration of dual-career couples. We will explicate three aspects of job-seeking behaviors (locating job sources, writing application letters and resumes, and interviewing). We will conclude with a reflection on aspects of job dissatisfaction. Much of the literature in these areas is contradictory; consequently, this chapter represents what might best be considered a state-of-the-art report.

UNEMPLOYED, DISLOCATED, AND DISCOURAGED WORKERS

Virtually every stress assessment instrument includes recent job loss. It is generally acknowledged that such an event is traumatic and produces considerable anxiety, stress, and disequilibrium. Indeed, the involuntary loss of a job or prolonged unemployment can be among life's more upsetting occurrences. For career counselors, dealing with those who have experienced involuntary job loss (whatever the reason) is especially challenging.

The Nature of Involuntary Job Loss

The number of people who are involuntarily unemployed will vary, of course, depending on economic conditions and other factors. Obviously, the worse the economic conditions, the greater the unemployment; the greater the unemployment, the larger the number of discouraged workers. Discouraged workers are people who desire jobs but who do not look for them because they believe a search will be in vain (Finegan, 1978). There are approximately one million such workers (more or less depending on conditions) in America. They want to work and, if jobs were more plentiful, they would be working. Discouraged workers, however, are *not* figured into unemployment statistics, since only those people who are looking for work are included in determining the unemployment rate.

Involuntary unemployment can take several forms, as we indicated in Chapter 2. *Frictional unemployment* is a term used by economists to designate a "temporary problem faced by indi-

360

viduals between jobs, those who have quit their jobs to search for better ones, and those who are looking for their first job" (Weinstein, 1979, p. 25). About one-half to two-thirds of the unemployed typically fall into this category. *Cyclical unemployment* refers to job losses caused by level of economic activity (such as recessions) and, unlike frictional unemployment, may see workers out of work for months or longer. This type of unemployment is most deeply felt in the manufacturing and construction industries, but clearly no industry is immune. Finally, *structural unemployment* is "long-term joblessness that results from changes in the kinds of workers needed by the economy" (Weinstein, 1979, p. 25). These are people replaced by new technology, by import competition, or by changes in the geographical location of industry, for example. Generally, such workers have to be retrained or relocated before they can find employment.

There do not appear to be significant racial differences among displaced workers, seniority held constant (DiPrete, 1981). There do, however, appear to be age, race, sex, and education differences in the willingness of the unemployed to relocate in search of work (Mueller, 1981). In general, the young, blacks, men, and persons with lower educational levels are more willing than others to relocate. Such people frequently rely on the support of friends or relatives in the new setting. All of this is not to say that the young, women, and minorities are not more susceptible to layoffs than other cohorts. They are, simply because of "last in, first out" retrenchment practices.

Several social and legislative buffers help to assuage the shock of involuntary job loss. The best-known program is *unemployment insurance*, the amount of which varies from state to state. In addition, some workers, through their unions, can qualify for *supplemental unemployment benefits* (SUBs) or some variation of SUB pay (such as Layoff Benefit Security or Savings Programs). Another program is *Worker Adjustment Assistance*, available to those who have lost their work because of import policies. *Public service employment* is also usually helpful in times of high unemployment, especially for the disadvantaged. We are all familiar with programs like the Job Corps and Summer Youth Programs. Other legis-

lation affects special groups of workers only, such as the railroad industry and the transit and airline industries. These programs will vary in number and intensity depending on the administration in power in Washington.

In addition to this legislated assistance, other programs are designed to aid displaced workers (Millan, 1979). Many of these palliative measures are the result of collective bargaining agreements. Work rules that specify standard crew sizes, for example, shelter some jobs — and at the same time, may be responsible for layoffs. Slack work provisions enable work-sharing or put restrictions on overtime to protect workers. Employee transfer among company facilities is another negotiated protection. So, too, are plans to absorb cutbacks by normal attrition, seniority provisions that give greatest job security to those with longest service, early retirement opportunities, and advanced notice of layoff (unfortunately, usually only a week or less). It is not easy to design a responsive system for involuntary job losers that will support them and, simultaneously, encourage them to seek new jobs. Dealing with the material needs of the dislocated, discouraged, and unemployed, however, is easier than dealing with the psychological effects of job loss.

The Psychological Effects of Job Loss

In Chapter 2 we discussed the relationship between work and mental health. Here we will provide more detail on that relationship.

The more an individual is motivated to work, the more likely he or she will be to experience depressive affect as a result of unemployment (Feather & Davenport, 1981). Such individuals are more likely to blame external economic conditions for their unemployment than they are to blame themselves. It is not surprising that depressive affect is a concommitant of the unemployed, motivated worker. Parkes (1971) poignantly describes the meaning of loss of work:

Loss of job deprives a man of a place to work, the company of workmates, and a source of income. It, therefore, produces several changes in his life space. What corresponding changes can be expected in the assumptive world? Clearly assumptions about the sources of money and security will change and the individual's faith in his own capacity to work effectively and to earn are also likely to change. His view of the world as a safe secure place will change, his expectations of his future and that of his family will change, and he is likely to have to replan his mode of life, sell possessions and maybe even move to a place where his prospects are better. Thus his altered assumptive world will cause him to introduce further changes in his life space, to set up a cycle of internal and external changes aimed at improving the "fit" between himself and his environment. (pp. 103–104)

There have been some attempts to link reaction to job loss with reactions to more permanent loss (such as death and dying stages or grief stages). Both imminent and actual loss, it is hypothesized, produce predictable stages of reaction. In England, for example, Harrison (1976) has suggested a transitional cycle that begins with shock, proceeds into optimism, evolves into pessimism, and ends with fatalism. Schlossberg and Leibowitz (1980) describe five stages progressing from job loss to adaptation: disbelief, sense of betrayal, confusion, anger, and resolution. In general, those who suffer traumatic job loss tend to become immobilized and depressed, ultimately accept reality and test themselves and the job market, and usually reacquire some self-esteem (although they may tend to have less than the employed). Of course, some never recover and remain in a depressed state, blaming themselves and falling into a state of inertia. For a few, the experience of downward mobility associated with unemployment can be so intensely traumatic that it may increase the likelihood of suicide (Breed, 1963). Hayes and Nutman (1981) have summarized the relationship between unemployment and mental health by pointing out the financial, social, and human costs of high levels of unemployment.

In financial and social terms it means that more hospital places are required. In human terms it means that the chances of resettlement, an essential element in the treatment of many disorders, is greatly reduced. Finally, if unemployment is a factor which increases the possibility of mental disorders, then in times of high unemployment not only is there a probability of an increase in the number of people suffering from some sort of mental illness, but the means by which these people may be treated are decreased. (pp. 80–81)

Brenner (1973) has conducted a series of meta-analyses over thirty years that point to the fact that high unemployment periods tend to correlate with an increase in admissions to mental health facilities and in suicides, homicides, imprisonment, and death rates. Disillusionment, disaffection, and boredom because of inactivity are frequent complaints. The unemployed may also report feelings of failure and uselessness; they may express feelings of isolation and rejection that they attribute to their unemployment. Although not clinically indicating any specific mental disorder or group pathology, such feelings clearly represent stress reactions that impede optimal functioning.

Others report that although the initial shock of job loss is indeed traumatic, the long-term effects may be less devastating than is typically thought (Kasl, Gore, and Cobb, 1975; Little, 1976). What is usually described here is a situation akin to a phoenix rising from the ashes, a rebuilding of a war-torn city, or a successful artificial hip implant. It is clear that it would be much better not to have a condition to which the individual must muster resources and react; however, since the situation exists, those who attack it and gain employment are thought to be the better for it. In short, one must stretch to find the brighter side of dislocation and unemployment.

Counseling Involuntary Job Losers

Needs analyses of unemployed persons — especially minority individuals — have demonstrated that they want career planning help, especially in career assessment (Atlas, 1978). The specific form of such assistance has not, as yet, been determined with any certainty. Schlossberg and Leibowitz (1980) have proposed a conceptual model based on experiences with "riffed" (reduction in force) workers at NASA's Goddard Space Flight Center in 1977. They base their model on job loss as a transition, a "life change or turning point requiring an alteration in everyday patterns of behavior and thinking and necessitating new coping strategies" (p. 205). Their model consists of three components: (1) the characteristics of the particular transition; (2) the characteristics of support systems, with special emphasis on institutional supports; and (3) the characteristics of the individual, particularly the resources brought to the transition. Schematically, the model appears in Table 13.1.

As a result of applying their model to the Goddard situation, Schlossberg and Leibowitz describe ways in which the trauma and pain of job loss can be mitigated by institutional efforts. They recommend a program that includes job-finding training and job-lead identification. Hiring a consultant firm of out-placement specialists is one response; using internal personnel officers is another. In either case, the atmosphere ought to allow participants to experience and express their feelings. The organization can time the staging of terminating events so that employees are gradually allowed to rehearse new roles. It can further have available all information-related events. It can provide support, also, for those who must do the actual firing.

Similar recommendations are made by Hayes and Nutman (1981), who suggest five ways in which the unemployed can be helped:

1. enhancing or maintaining the individual's self-esteem by helping him or her manage anxiety and develop more effective problem-solving skills
2. improving the fit between the individual and his or her life space

3. promoting job-seeking skills
4. developing new work-related skills
5. developing positive attitudes toward work and acceptable work habits (p. 112)

They suggest that effective work orientation programs for the unemployed have certain common characteristics. Among these are:

Job orientation — Preparation for a specific job appears to yield more successful results than preparation for work in general.

Training methods — Role play and self-directed discussion groups do not appear to be so successful as those methods which involve work experience, feedback on progress toward work related goals and immediate positive reinforcement.

Liaison and support — Counseling and liaison between the training and the work setting are frequently associated with success.

Identity and experience of training staff — Professional educators (especially those based in colleges and universities) appear to be less effective than resource persons who seem to have a more intimate knowledge and understanding of the immediate work environment.

Course content — More successful courses focus on work attitudes and work behavior rather than on the more general issues such as those associated with being disadvantaged and unemployed.

Indeed, Salipante and Goodman (1976) have convincingly demonstrated that when dealing with the long-term unemployed, successful programs tend to focus on the participant's work at-

Table 13.1
A Model for Studying Job Loss

Characteristics of the particular transition	Characteristics of pretransition and post-transition support systems	Characteristics of the individual
Onset: sudden vs. gradual	Intimate family relationships	Psychosocial competence
Source: internal or external	Network of friends	Coping orientation
Timing: on-time or off-time	Instuional support	Experience with similar transitions
Duration: permanent, temporary, uncertain	Workshop	Other stressful events during the year
Affect: positive or negative	Job finding assistance	
Degree of Stress	Severance pay	

titudes as well as developing job skills. Programs that deal with the development of job skills in isolation are less successful. Thus, the existence of counseling was found to increase retention rates. A contrasting finding, however, is reported by Fottler (1978), who investigated the variables associated with the success of 104 manpower program participants over time. He found that *frequency* of counseling did not affect success of participants. He suggests that perhaps some minimal level of counseling is necessary, but that additional counseling does not increase success rates. Most studies, however, seem to agree that skilled counseling, when combined with specific job training, can contribute to successful programs when dealing with the hard-core unemployed. Counseling is clearly a valuable component in programs directed toward assisting the dislocated, most especially those who have been dislocated from managerial or professional positions.

The dislocation from work is, at worst, cataclysmic and, at best, upsetting. The ensuing unemployment causes problems of lack of stimulation (even rats and monkeys are disturbed by lack of activity) and feelings of depression and reduced self-esteem. Long-term and chronically unemployed individuals frequently need to change work attitudes as well as to acquire specific job skills. Other persons may require an assessment of work assets and training in job-seeking skills. Underemployment is a frequent result of white-collar dislocation. In all cases, career counseling that is tailored to the unique needs of dislocated, unemployed, or discouraged workers can be a useful part of a total support system.

BURNOUT

Beginning in the early 1970s, a time of disillusionment, Herbert Freudenberger and his colleagues, who were working in free clinics in New York City, first applied the term *burnout* to career behavior (Freudenberger, 1974). Since then, the term has come into common usage both in career literature and in the popular media. It has been variously defined as a phenomenon, a syndrome, and a set of symptoms. Most writing on the issue is anecdotal, informally observational, and confined to consideration of only a few occupational groups (for example, mainly business, child care, mental health, education, health care, law enforcement, and social service). Frankly, at this time, we are uncertain whether burnout is a bona fide consequence of stress, a natural part of career development stage theory, simply another aspect of job satisfaction, or nothing at all.

Webster's Third New International Dictionary defines burnout partially as follows: "to cause to fail, wear out, or become exhausted by making excessive demands on energy, strength, or resources, . . . to cease to be in a condition to perform a normal function by reason of unusually prolonged exposure to fire or heat, . . . to fail, wear out, or become exhausted by reason of excessive demands on energy, strength, or resources." The difficulty in applying a commonly used term in a new way is that it can lose its meaning through careless use. For example, one article defines stages of burnout in teachers as "first degree burn (mild), second degree burn (moderate) and third degree burn (severe)" (*Instructor* Special Report, 1979, p. 57). Another terms it a "smoldering" problem (Daley, 1979). One could envision even more far-fetched analogies. How about burnover, which is an imperfectly burned brick that requires reburning? We could extend the term to refer to an ameliorative situation whereby burned out workers are refired with new energy. The point is that the term burnout is metaphorical and lends itself to facile and loose use of language. Counselors should be wary of unspecified or unproven statements relating to burnout.

What Is Burnout?

Freudenberger (1980) defines burnout symptomatically as a depletion of an individual's physical and mental resources, and he attributes the etiology of burnout to excessive strivings to attain some unrealistic goal imposed by oneself or by the values of society. Symptoms include just about everything: loss of "charisma," fatigue, headaches, sleeplessness, quickness to anger, suspicion, paranoia, and depression, among many others. Such symptoms, of course, can be caused by something other than burnout, so it is indeed difficult to isolate their cause. Freudenberger views the work situation as the precipitating factor of burnout, especially in the helping professions, in that devotion to helping and unrealistic expectations combine to lead to burnout.

Cherniss (1980a) is another who has considered burnout in the helping professions. He defines burnout as a "process in which a previously committed professional disengages from his/her work in response to stress and strain experienced on the job" (p. 18). In his conception, burnout is a three-stage process. In stage one, the worker feels *stress* because of an imbalance between resources and demands. In the second stage, the worker experiences *strain*, an immediate, short-term emotional response to anxiety, tension, and fatigue. In the third stage, the worker tries to *cope defensively* by altering attitudes and behavior (for example, treating clients mechanically). It is this third stage that is thought to be "true" burnout. Cherniss' stress-related conception has received some preliminary, rudimentary, and small-scale research validation (1980b).

A third major writer in the field of burnout is Maslach, who, with various associates, especially Pines, has described a variety of behaviors related to burnout (Maslach, 1976; Maslach, 1978; Maslach & Jackson, 1981; Pines & Maslach, 1978; Pines & Maslach, 1979). Most of her thoughts pertain to mental health workers. In that context, she views burnout as a "loss of concern for the people with whom one is working characterized by an emotional exhaustion in which the staff person no longer has positive feelings, respect, or empathy for clients" (Maslach, 1978, p. 113). The job induces stress; the worker cannot cope; burnout results and manifests itself in such observable behaviors as low morale, excessive absenteeism, psychosomatic symptoms, and an increase in family and marital conflict, to cite just a few presumed personal consequences. Maslach also contends that dealing with certain *types* of clients and *numbers* of clients make a worker especially vulnerable to burnout. For example, it is alleged that those who work with higher populations of schizophrenics are more likely to burn out and that those who work with too many clients are similarly more susceptible.

Several work-related stages have been described that might be confused with what is thought to be burnout. For instance, *rust-out* (Howard, 1975) is a term applied to individuals who are under-

employed, who are in occupations that do not make full use of their education and training, or who do not have enough pressure and challenge on the job. Their skills atrophy and, it is consequently argued, they may develop symptoms akin to those ascribed to burnout. Similarly, some writers attempt to distinguish between *tedium* and burnout (Pines & Maslach, 1980); the former is used to refer to a condition arising from "constant or repeated emotional pressure associated with an intense involvement with people" (p. 15), whereas the latter results from "any prolonged, chronic pressures" (p. 15). It is difficult to comprehend this type of mutual exclusivity. Some speak of *stagnation* in the context of burnout, but mean something different (Edelwich & Brodsky, 1980). Stagnation refers to becoming stalled after an initial burst of enthusiasm. One final illustration is that of *plateauing* (Ference, Stoner, & Warren, 1977). Plateauing refers to an individual's reaching a vertical position in an organization beyond which he or she will never progress. The thought of no further vertical (or even horizontal) movement, it is hypothesized, could cause symptomatic reactions similar to those of burnout.

Hence, the term *burnout* is not at all clear in meaning. Just as intelligence is sometimes cynically defined as that which intelligence tests measure, burnout may soon come to be regarded as that which burnout instruments assess. Unfortunately, we do not now have a burnout assessment instrument that has been sufficiently tested, although at least one looks promising. Instruments by Helliwell (1981), Freudenberger (1980), and Justice, Gold, and Klein (1981) are in the early development stages. The most advanced instrument is the Maslach Burnout Inventory (Maslach & Jackson, 1981), which consists of four subscales: Emotional Exhaustion ("I feel used up at the end of the workday"); Depersonalization ("I've become more callous toward people since I took this job"); Personal Accomplishment ("I feel I'm positively influencing other people's lives through my work"); and Personal Involvement ("I feel personally involved with my [students', clients'] problems").

The source of stress or burnout is thought by most observers to be the interaction between personal factors (such as personality) and the situational stress variables of the occupation (supervision, job tasks) as both of these variables are embedded in the culture (attitudes toward work). The stresses emanating from an occupation itself are neatly summarized by Yates (1979) who draws on the work of Cooper and Marshall (1976). His representation is shown in Figure 13.1.

The correlates of burnout are just beginning to be recognized (assuming that one accepts the definition of burnout used by various investigators). Forney, Wallace-Schutzman, and Wiggens (1982) surveyed twenty-four career development professionals who reported that burnout seemed to be associated with such environmental correlates as repetitive work tasks, lack of advancement opportunities, work overload, feedback and supervision issues, organizational politics, boredom, and time pressures. In another study, which utilized a larger sample than is usually found in burnout studies, Schwab (1981) studied 461 teachers and concluded that role conflict and ambiguity were significantly related to burnout. Sarata and Jeppesen (1977) interviewed human service professionals (nurses, psychologists, social workers, and so on) and used a measure of job satisfaction as an indication of burnout to determine that information, variety, and opportunities for learning appeared to impede burnout. If one regards stress and burnout as tantamount (a la Maslach), then another study by Farber and Heifetz (1981) indicates that burnout may be correlated with excessive workload and working with very disturbed people. This latter finding has been repeated by Emener and Rubin (1980).

Another group of studies has looked at the relationship between burnout and life events. Pines, Aronson, and Kafry (1981) report a significant negative correlation between tedium (as defined earlier) and positive life events (conversely, the more negative life events there are in a person's life, the higher the tedium scores). Sarason and Johnson (1979), again using a job satisfaction measure equated with burnout, found that negative life changes are associated with lower levels of job satisfaction. Several researchers have preliminarily determined that males and females tend sometimes to react differently to the same occupational stressors (Tung, 1980; Thompson, 1980). Other researchers suggest that reactions to occupational stress will differ by *level* of employment (Axelrod & Gavin, 1980; Parasuraman &

Alutto, 1981). Some research also points to the relationship of on-the-job and off-the-job stress, including that severe reactions come about only when *both* types of stress are present (Pardine et al., 1981).

To summarize thus far: most investigators of burnout regard it as a reaction to occupational stress (in addition to research previously cited, see, for instance, Cedoline, 1982; Daley, 1979; Gardner and Hall, 1981; Savicki and Cooley, 1982; Veninga and Spradley, 1981). Consonant with the stress literature, these reactions may be physical, mental, and/or emotional. Most authors agree that burnout is not the result of a single event; rather, it is a cumulative phenomenon, beginning with barely noticeable changes and proceeding through increasingly intense reactions until it becomes a crisis that, if left unresolved, can cause chronic depression, alcohol and substance abuse, even suicide. All of this does not explain why and how an individual's internal resources moderate external stressors. Why, for some individuals, is the same stressor likely to result, in Selye's (1975) terms, in *eustress* (positive) whereas for other individuals it results in *distress* (negative)? It is not our purpose to review in any systematic way the formidable collection of literature on stress and coping. We are convinced that stress is at least a contributor to burnout (and perhaps ultimately will be found to be synonymous with it).

There is much, however, that is still unexplained by viewing burnout in terms of stress theory, as a stage phenomenon, or in terms of general job satisfaction. One possible route to filling in missing knowledge may be that suggested by Warnath and Shelton (1976) who view counselor burnout as basically the result of an expectation-reality gap. Another possibility is proposed by Tiedeman (1979) who views burnout as an "existential dilemma" associated both with experiencing normal career development and coping with the normal tasks of midlife that all of us experience but that, for some, produce a crisis reaction (such as the so-called midlife career crisis). In all speculations, what remains constant is a situation-person effect. What differs is the extent to which situation or person produces the effect. We do not now have any clear notion of the relationships among stress, coping styles, worker characteristics, career development, job satisfaction, and burnout

Figure 13.1
Sources of Stress at Work and Their Consequences for the Individual

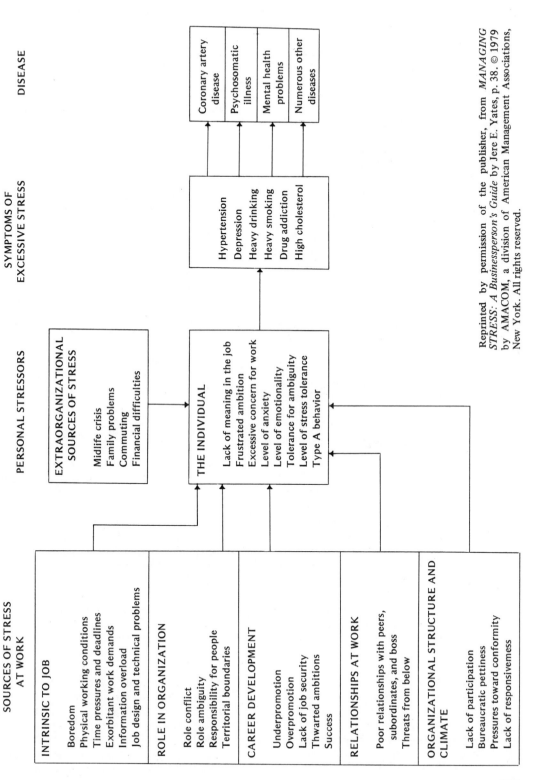

SOURCES OF STRESS AT WORK

PERSONAL STRESSORS

SYMPTOMS OF EXCESSIVE STRESS

DISEASE

INTRINSIC TO JOB

Boredom
Physical working conditions
Time pressures and deadlines
Exorbitant work demands
Information overload
Job design and technical problems

ROLE IN ORGANIZATION

Role conflict
Role ambiguity
Responsibility for people
Territorial boundaries

CAREER DEVELOPMENT

Underpromotion
Overpromotion
Lack of job security
Thwarted ambitions
Success

RELATIONSHIPS AT WORK

Poor relationships with peers, subordinates, and boss
Threats from below

ORGANIZATIONAL STRUCTURE AND CLIMATE

Lack of participation
Bureaucratic pettiness
Pressures toward conformity
Lack of responsiveness

EXTRAORGANIZATIONAL SOURCES OF STRESS

Midlife crisis
Family problems
Commuting
Financial difficulties

THE INDIVIDUAL

Lack of meaning in the job
Frustrated ambition
Excessive concern for work
Level of anxiety
Level of emotionality
Tolerance for ambiguity
Level of stress tolerance
Type A behavior

Hypertension
Depression
Heavy drinking
Heavy smoking
Drug addiction
High cholesterol

Coronary artery disease
Psychosomatic illness
Mental health problems
Numerous other diseases

Reprinted by permission of the publisher, from *MANAGING STRESS: A Businessperson's Guide* by Jere E. Yates, p. 38. © 1979 by AMACOM, a division of American Management Associations, New York. All rights reserved.

367

(however defined). Until we do, counselors should be a bit more tentative and less facile as they discuss burnout.

The Prevention and Treatment of Burnout

There are two ways in which a worker can cope with burnout (especially if one considers stress as tantamount to burnout). The first method is a sort of do-it-yourself response. There are an increasing number of popular self-help books that offer one system or another for coping with stress (Selye, 1975; Yates, 1979; Friedman, 1974; Veninga & Spradley, 1981; Freudenberg & Richelson, 1980; Potter, 1980). At a professional level, somewhere in the literature of most fields there are articles on coping with burnout.

A second way of coping with burnout or preventing it is for professional counselors to address the question. They can do so in two ways: alter the work environment or change the individual. We present several suggestions for effecting each of these approaches. Keep in mind, however, that many of these suggestions are made based on one or another idiosyncratic definition of burnout.

The Environment. Various organizational strategies have been proposed to deal with the problem of burnout. Among these are:

1. allowing "time-outs" in which workers are allowed time off from the job to recuperate psychologically and to recharge themselves
2. training supervisors to recognize and to deal with potential burnout-inducing situations and actual burnout
3. providing enhanced opportunities for vertical career development (such as career ladders, in-service training, conference attendance)
4. allowing worker participation in policy-making
5. allowing more worker autonomy in decision-making
6. providing more explicit organizational recognition of achievement
7. permitting reduction of workload and variety in type of client served
8. experimenting with such variables as flex-time, job rotation, job enrichment, and job sharing

9. providing for employee counseling within the organization
10. offering comprehensive employee orientation programs
11. sponsoring organizational workshops on stress management and support groups
12. clarifying organizational goals and policies
13. identifying chronic sources of stress and frustration
14. providing career planning assistance
15. reducing the intensity involved in a job
16. identifying and addressing sources of role ambiguity and role conflict
17. trying to use more employee abilities and skills
18. providing workers with adequate resources to perform the required work
19. reducing "busy work" (such as too many meetings)
20. using epidemiological techniques to try to reduce the contagion effect of burnout
21. reducing isolation of workers
22. allowing enough lead time for work
23. providing employees with as much security as possible

The Individual. Individual approaches to the amelioration or prevention of burnout will vary according to what theoretical concept is seen as the cause. If stress is viewed as the precipitating factor, for example, then it is viewed differently by theorists of the psychoanalytic, learning and behavioral, developmental, sociological, physiological, neurobiological, or environmental schools. Most of the suggestions to help individuals cope with or prevent burnout are really atheoretical or spring from a preliminary set of frequently random postulates about the nature and etiology of burnout. With this caveat in mind, we present several of these suggestions in order to give a sense of the current activity.

Several suggestions involve preservice preparation for helping workers to cope with the possibility of burnout (Lattanzi, 1981; Savicki & Cooley, 1982; Warnath & Shelton, 1976; Warnath, 1979; Partin & Gargiulo, 1980). Although there is some danger of a self-fulfilling prophecy here, preservice attention is sensible. It is assumed that such preparation will present a realistic picture of what a particular type of work will be and will thus reduce the potential expectation-reality gap. If the expectations of a new occupation are more in line with the actualities of the work setting, it is thought, stress will be less. If workers are not disillusioned by false ideals in their preparation, it is argued, they cannot be disappointed when they face reality.

In both preservice and in-service programs, the basic concerns are the same. These include training in the recognition of sources of work stress, techniques of dealing with the stress, and evaluation of that application. Writers vary in suggesting how one should specifically cope. Garte & Rosenblum (1978), for example, urge that the way to "light fires" in burned out counselors is by means of *leisure therapy*, which is defined as "the process of utilizing leisure activities for the purpose of increasing personal and professional effectiveness" (p. 159). They offer several suggestions, for instance, of how work and play might be integrated: using a hobby such as photography or writing in the service of the organization for which one works, taking "invigorating" coffee breaks, or playing a regular bridge game at lunch.

Others, who advocate holistic health education, would offer different suggestions (Argeropoulos, 1981). They would prescribe vigorous exercise, nutrition, relaxation techniques (such as meditation, self-hypnosis, deep breathing, progressive relaxation, yoga, autogenic training such as biofeedback), use of support groups to foster self-awareness and self-acceptance, organizational skills, specific coping skills training, and alteration of self-defeating belief systems.

Helliwell (1981) presents a long list of suggestions for helping individuals to deal effectively with burnout. These include: encouraging introspection, eliminating negative messages, reducing care and concern (psychological withdrawal), and increasing alternative activities to work (such as family, outside interests). Other ideas are of the "straighten up and fly right" variety: stop feeling sorry for yourself, simplify your life, and don't spend time with pessimistic people, to cite just a few. In a slightly different vein, Freudenberger (1980) recommends an Alcoholics Anonymous approach: learning to accept things that cannot be changed, and focusing on things that can be.

Forney, Wallace-Schutzman, and Wiggens (1982) suggest the use of Rational Emotive Therapy (RET) techniques in order to discover various "myths" that foster self-defeating attitudes. These myths include such statements as "my job is my life" and "I must always perform at a peak level and with a lot of energy and enthusiasm" (p. 437). The idea is to challenge such myths with rational thinking.

Cedoline (1982) encourages a balanced life between work/play, challenge/leisure, stress/relaxation, companionship/solitude, and discipline/self-indulgence. This balance would be brought about by a stress management program. In this program, the first step is to identify what kinds of stress one is experiencing, what job conditions are most stressful, and what one does or says to oneself under pressure. The second step is designed to help people read their own stress symptoms. For six weeks they keep a daily log of stressful events. Individuals are told to record what events preceded the feeling of stress, when in the day the stress occurred, what the feelings were like, and what response resulted. Each day is rated on a ten-point scale (1 = disaster; 10 = a cinch). The next step is selectively to apply coping techniques depending on whether the stress is caused by external locus of control problems, occupational feedback or communication deficits, work overload, role conflict or ambiguity, or training deficits. If specific behavioral objectives are devised for this program, it could hold much promise.

Support groups are frequently advocated as a response to or a prevention of burnout (Gardner & Hall, 1981; Spicuzza & De Voe, 1982). Spicuzza and De Voe have developed a Mutual Aid (MA) group system for burned-out individuals. They see these groups as places where people "can discover or reassess their sense of self, search for their own personal meaning in society, diminish their feelings of solitude within a group structure, and perhaps promote social change" (p. 96). These are lofty goals indeed. They see MA groups as consisting of eight to twelve members and as being either homogenous or heterogeneous. The groups are directed at a combination of socialization, instruction, discussion of business, and evaluation (of previous meetings). Emphasized are the needs for participants to take risks and to practice and experiment with new behaviors. Finally, Pines et al. (1981) offer a coping grid that can summarize burnout-coping strategies (Figure 13.2).

Figure 13.2
Stress Situations and Response Effectiveness

	CONTINUOUS	INTERMITTENT
MUTABLE	Direct-active (alter the source)	Direct-active still possible May wish to ignore depending on periodicity
IMMUTABLE	Indirect-active generate own relief or May need to escape situation: catharsis and self-change insufficient	Catharsis or diversion (temporary) Change self (permanent): adjusting to an intolerable situation

WORKING MOTHERS

The many roles we play in life are obviously inter-related. A worker may also be a daughter, a wife, and a mother, for example. The symbiotic effect of different roles is considerable. In our example, work can affect family; family can affect work behaviors. A mythology has arisen over the years, however, regarding precisely what the effects are. In this section we will consider some of the family factors related to work and attempt to draw some conclusions on the basis of available research.

Effects on Children

About half of all children under 18 have working mothers (Waldman et al., 1979). The traditional pattern has been for women to enter post-school work, to take a hiatus from work for an extended period of child-bearing and child-rearing, and often to return to work when the last child has reached school age. This traditional pattern is eroding in favor of more continuous work careers (Shapiro & Mott, 1979).

Although a great many studies address the effects of maternal employment on children, many suffer from methodological shortcomings. For example, some studies try to take into consideration substitute care for children while the mother is at work, but often the quality of that care is not assessed. Also, these studies frequently do not control for the mother's occupational and educational status, the age of the child when the mother started working, maternal job satisfaction, attitudes of other family members toward maternal work, the husband's sharing of the management of the home, parental personality characteristics and sex-role beliefs, the size of the family, and the career pattern of the mother. Add to these complications the facts that sample sizes are often small, that definitions of key terms frequently differ from study to study, that most data are gathered from self-reports, and that there is rarely a theoretical anchor for such studies. Although it would be easy to dismiss the findings of this body of research as unacceptably derived, such an indictment would be too harsh. There is much that is instructive.

Several reviews of the literature (Etaugh, 1974, 1980; Smith, 1981, Hoffman, 1979) provide us with some summary conclusions. Etaugh concludes, "Available data indicate that high-quality nonmaternal care does not appear to have adverse effects on the young child's maternal attachment, intellectual development, or social-emotional behavior" (1980, p. 309). Etaugh (1974) further emphasizes that strength of attachment between mother and child is related more to the quality and intensity of their interactions than to the frequency. Stable and stimulating caretaking appears to be related to the personal and cognitive development of the child, however that caretaking is defined. Further, adjusted mothers (whatever their role) tend to have adjusted children through adolescence (with the possible exception of lower-class boys and girls whose mothers work full-time). Maternal employment does not appear to affect children's school achievement, but it does seem positively to affect educational and occupational aspirations (especially in terms of daughters choosing less traditional careers).

Smith (1981), as a result of her review, is less confident about the lack of negative effects on both preschool and school-aged children, arguing, "For the vast majority of infant and preschool children . . . we simply do not know what the effects of maternal employment are" (p. 197). This conclusion appears to us to be overly cautious. We believe that the data are clear enough to provide some reasonable implications for practice, which will be discussed later in this section. At the same time, we certainly agree with the need for better conceived and executed research.

The two major variables affecting a woman's decision to work are the presence or absence of children and the family's financial condition. Child-bearing, in general, used to have a strong negative effect on outside employment. Now, both economic exigency and personal satisfaction appear to combine to make working mothers of even small children common (Hoffman, 1979). This situation is presumed by many to lead to interrole conflict between the roles of mother and employed worker which, in turn, is thought to lead to stress (Dunlop, 1981; Beutell & Greenhaus, 1982). Not the least source of stress is supposed to be the guilt engendered by a mother's working rather than tending primarily to child care. Ever since Bowlby (1958) introduced the notion of maternal deprivation to explain the cognitive, affective, and social deficits of children in institutions (based on research having severe methodological flaws), and ever since Harlow (1953) did his work with monkeys and maternal behavior, generalizations have been made to the maternal work situation. The leaps made have been huge and inappropriate.

Research on the effects of maternal employment on infants and preschoolers and adolescents offers several conclusions about which we can be reasonably certain:

1. When the child is enrolled in high-quality, center-based care, the intellectual effects are neither harmful nor helpful, except for children who grow up in high-risk environments. For these children, quality day care seems actually to help to maintain or to raise IQ scores.
2. Maternal employment does not seem to alter the emotional bond between mother and child.
3. Maternal job satisfaction appears to be positively related to development in preschoolers.
4. There is absolutely no convincing proof of the deleterious effects of maternal employment on preschoolers. At the very least, maternal employment seems to do no harm.
5. Maternal employment likely has a positive effect on a daughter's career involvement and commitment. When combined with factors such as the educational and occupational status of the mother, sex-role ideology, and encouragement of both parents, maternal work has an interaction effect that leads to a decrease in a daughter's sex-typing and to more assertive career planning (Jones & McBride, 1980; Smith, 1980; Bielby, 1978; Haber, 1980; Dellas, Gaier, & Emihovich, 1979).
6. Adolescent children of working mothers do not appear to experience any proven, consistently harmful effects (Hannson et al., 1981; Gold & Andres, 1978).
7. Female adolescents may react somewhat differently to maternal employment than do male adolescents (Burke & Weir, 1978).

In summary, there is, thus far, no evidence that maternal employment victimizes children. There are data to suggest, at least in some areas that have been researched, that maternal employment reduces children's sex role stereotyping and has a positive influence on a daughter's career development. It is important to emphasize that while the literature does not demonstrate any other great gains for children which can be attributed to maternal employment, it also shows conclusively that maternal employment, in general, does no harm to children.

Effects on Mothers

In the previous section we alluded to the possibility of interrole conflict and resulting stress as a result of maternal employment. The general conclusion reached in most of the research studies is that there is basically no difference in adjustment and satisfaction between working and nonworking mothers (Nye, 1963; Feld, 1963; Keith & Schafer, 1980; Radloff, 1975; Newberry, Weissman, & Myers, 1979; Parker, Parker, Wolz, & Harford, 1980; Wright, 1978; Townshend & Gurin, 1981; Beckman, 1978). A few studies have actually indicated measurably positive results as a consequence of maternal employment (Feree, 1976; Macke, Bohrnstadt, & Bernstein, 1979; Walker & Walker, 1980; Kessler & McRae, 1982; Holahan & Gilbert, 1979). There is no doubt that working mothers experience more stress than do nonemployed mothers; however, rewards appear to counterbalance the stress and, for most maternal workers, the stress stemming from interrole conflict does not become debilitating. At least one writer concludes the converse (Smith, 1981). However, we believe her argument for the negative effects of employment on a mother's identity development, life satisfaction, and stress is not warranted by the available data.

Beckman's study (1978) provides a good summary of the rewards and costs of maternal employment. She collected data by means of interviews and tests from both professional and nonprofessional married women. Her sample reported that the rewards of parenthood were the opportunity to watch the child grow and develop, the warm relationship with the child, the teaching role, and biological fulfillment, or fulfillment of the female role. Among the perceived costs of parenthood for these married workers were restricted freedom and lack of opportunity for career mobility and privacy. The rewards of work were thought to be opportunity for social interaction, achievement, challenge and creativity, self-definition, esteem and independence, and, of course, economic benefit. The costs of employment were reported as increased time pressure, interruption of routine, and interference with the needs of children. Given these rewards and costs, it is not surprising that maternal work does not appear to affect a mother's well-being in any substantially negative manner.

Effects on Families

If maternal employment does not seem to affect adversely either child-rearing or the mother's well-being, does it have an effect on the marriage or on the family?

Early research reported an inconsistent but generally weak negative relationship between maternal employment and marital satisfaction. Later research, more sophisticated in design and controlling for more variables, suggests that it is not maternal employment per se that determines marital satisfaction; rather, it is the extent to which that employment infringes on fulfillment of role expectations and thus causes conflict (Houseknecht & Macke, 1981). This finding of lack of effects has been most forcefully presented in a study by Locksley (1980), who provides strong evidence against the hypothesis that such negative outcomes in contemporary society as rising divorce rates, juvenile delinquency, and illegitimacy are attributable to a mother's participation in the wage economy. Booth (1977) demonstrated that husbands of employed women evidenced no more marital discord and stress than did spouses of housewives. In general, wife employment status and marital adjustment research produces trivial differences, if any, between dual-worker versus single-worker families (Staines, Pleck, Shepard & O'Connor, 1978). This finding may vary over the life cycle, however (Keith, Goudy & Powers, 1981).

Further evidence comes from surveys of work and family life conflicts (Pleck, Staines & Lang, 1980). These surveys indicate that about one-third of all workers (male and female) living in families report either moderate or severe work-family conflicts. This figure rises by about seven percentage points for those who are parents. This total is relatively small. What is more significant is that working women did not report any greater conflict than did working men.

The notion is frequently put forth that if the wife's occupation is less rewarding than the husband's in terms of pay or status, marital satisfaction is likely to be higher. If, however, the wife's occupation is higher than the husband's, it is assumed that marital satisfaction will be lower. A study by Richardson (1979) clearly refutes this idea. Richardson found that wives with higher occupational prestige and continuous labor force participation were happier with their marriages than were wives with equal occupational prestige yet discontinuous labor force participation. Hence, occupational inequality in marriage does not appear to be sufficient to cause marital discord. Pearlin's (1975) data also support this conclusion.

It is generally accepted that men are more satisfied with marriage than are women. It is also generally accepted that the pressure of young children is likely to be associated with lower life satisfaction and poorer marital adjustment. Maternal employment does not seem to be a factor in these findings. In general, marital adjustment for working wives is greatly enhanced, as might be expected, by a supportive husband (for example, one who approves of his wife's employment, shares in household duties, and advocates a similar belief system). In general, also, higher occupational and educational status is associated with better marital adjustment in dual-worker couples.

Implications for Career Counseling

The great majority of women will experience some interrole conflict. They must be assisted to anticipate it; those who are having difficulty with the experience should be helped to deal with it. Many young women still believe that worker and mother are mutually exclusive roles, and that if mothers work some horrendous harm will befall their children, their marriage, or themselves. Young women, before the fact, and mothers, after the fact, should be aided to see that these ideas have no basis in reality. The general rule should be that if a woman feels good about herself, if she has a mate who is supportive of her work and who is willing to help with housework and child-rearing, maternal employment will not only be unharmful, but it may be beneficial.

There are several strategies for assuaging potential and real home-career conflict. Several years ago, Hall and Lawler (1971) described three types of coping behaviors for maternal workers:

Type I: structural role redefinition – the process of redefining the expectations of others
Type II: personal role definition – the process of modifying your own expectations of your behavior
Type III: responsive role performance – no redefinition of expectations either of self or of others, but attempt to do everything expected of you ("superwoman")

It seems appropriate that women understand these three alternatives and the possibility that Type III behavior will add to stress and strain rather than ameliorate it.

Another strategy for lessening career-home conflict is for the couple to delay parenthood and to engage in associated behaviors, such as to drop out of the labor force during perceived "critical" periods of child-rearing or to remain childless by choice (Wilkie, 1981). At several points in this book we have stressed the necessity for all individuals, but for females especially, to adopt an attitude of planfulness. Choosing between traditional and nontraditional roles is one such decision. Zaslow & Pederson (1981) offer four suggestions, for example, in counseling couples regarding child-bearing.

1. Women assuming full-time caregiving roles may be more satisfied with the choice if they have carefully assessed the options for eventual return to employment as well as considered a means to maintain professional competence while unemployed. Women planning to combine career and family roles may need to assess the availability of substitute care and the possibility of flexible work hours, part-time employment, or employment that does not involve separation from the baby. The evaluation requires an examination of needs, feelings, and options.

2. Couples may be encouraged to seek out other parents who have made similar sex-role choices.

3. After the couple chooses how to delegate career-home responsibilities, the counselor must help the couple deal with the pressures inherent in that choice.

4. The support of the spouse is crucial in adjustment to maternal employment, and the counselor may help each spouse to understand the

implications of the other's choice for himself or herself.

Beutell & Greenhaus (1982) suggest a similar intervention strategy:

It may be useful for spouses to discuss the possible effect of similar/dissimilar career orientations on their work and family roles. Spouse workshops or seminars may be appropriate vehicles for initiating and reinforcing such discussions (p. 108).

Stake (1979) also presents some useful suggestions:

Given present sex role expectations, women's career involvement and women's role factors are related; therefore, women's role factors must be considered in any complete discussion of career involvement. Furthermore . . . women who have little confidence in their abilities will have more difficulty coming to grips with the conflicts of home and career. It seems that these women would benefit from an exploration of self-concept issues, particularly in regard to their feelings of competence and attitudes toward the traditional women's role. Through this process of personal counseling these women may be better able to consider available alternatives and to develop realistic plans that would take into account their needs, their motives, and their potential for growth (p. 40).

Laramore (1979) has suggested career counseling for families in which parents and children help each other to make "good" career decisions and clarify goals.

Although there is a great deal of talk about the "subtle revolution" in realigning family roles, and although there is a great deal of attention given by academics to the decline of the "good provider" stereotype (Bernard, 1981), women still assume the more sex-traditional share of burdens in household management. When all is said and done, males must be educated to factors of maternal employment as much as women are.

At the very least, the considerable body of literature on maternal employment indicates that such work will not harm children, the mother herself, or the marriage. Maternal employment may actually have beneficial effects in each of these areas. Since the prevailing folklore is different from the facts, a massive reeducation of American men and women may be necessary.

DUAL-CAREER FAMILIES

We have just addressed the problems of dual-*worker* families or dual-*earner* families. Now we will consider a growing phenomenon in Western cultures, the dual-*career* family. This term is usually reserved for couples where work represents a high commitment for both parties and the wife's work is continuous. If we define dual-career even more specifically — as requiring both spouses to be in professional, technical, or managerial jobs — then approximately 14 percent of the American labor force would fall into this category (*Monthly Labor Review*, 1981). This discussion, then, represents another look at family roles within the context of career development.

The Nature of Dual-Career Families

The idea of dual-career families began to be popularized about 1969 and stemmed from a study of graduates of British universities. Rapoport and Rapoport (1971, 1976) are generally given credit for calling attention to the phenomenon. They viewed dual-career couples as a new structural family type, one in which both heads of household pursue careers and simultaneously maintain a family life together, thus emphasizing the importance of work and family for both males and females.

Since the Rapoports' early work, there have been many studies relating to the dual-career family. These studies have suffered from several methodological limitations. Most of the samples have been small and restricted in their representativeness (for example, too many use academics as their sample). Also, very few concentrate on or even include the male perspective; they focus on the wife. The perspectives of both spouses would seem to be important. And, definitions of what constitutes a dual-career family vary from study to study. Finally, the data in these studies is most often collected by means of interviews or other forms of self-report. This technique is, of course, common for sociological studies, but it neglects more psychological aspects and other data-gathering possibilities.

The accumulated research that we do have, however, even with its methodological shortcomings, offers some instructive findings. One apparent conclusion is that dual-career families — which we presume represent one of our most sophisticated and nontraditional structures — are, in fact, usually asymmetrical in terms of domestic responsibilities (Paloma & Garland, 1971; St. John Parsons, 1978; Bryson et al., 1976; Epstein, 1971; Johnson & Johnson, 1977; Yogev, 1981; Sundby, 1980; Wallston, Foster, & Berger, 1978). Females apparently do considerably more than half of household management chores. This "tolerance for domestication" is manifested in nonegalitarian family functions. It may be that the wife is unwilling to change or is willing to assume the burden because of a fear of changing the family environment. Another possible explanation has been offered by Rapoport and Rapoport (1971), who describe an *identity tension line*, a point beyond which the violation of sex-role socialization becomes uncomfortable for the individual, either male or female. In any case, the tendency toward a traditional division of labor in performing domestic tasks means that wives retain the major responsibility for child-rearing and for household maintenance.

If asymmetry occurs in the majority of dual-career couples, then it is naturally hypothesized that this combination of family and work roles produces overload, identity and self-esteem dilemmas, multiple role cycling, discomfort, role conflict, violation of norms, and decreased leisure — all of which may result in stress. In fact, stress is prevalent in dual-career families (Rice, 1979; Skinner, 1980; Willis, 1979), but couples in such a structure generally believe that the stress would be greater if the wife were not pursuing a career. In short, some heightened stress by the woman is perceived as a relatively small cost.

The nonegalitarian burden for women in the home may be one reason that the wife's career is frequently subordinated to the husband's. In Holmstrom's (1972) sample of academics in Massachusetts, for example, the wives more often put their careers second to that of their husbands. In addition to conscious choice, however, discrimination apparently operates to make dual-career wives less successful, in general, than their husbands (Butler & Paisley, 1977; Pingree et al., 1978; Rosen, Jerdee, & Presturch, 1975). This discrimination runs from overt antinepotism regulations to more subtle forms of sexual prejudice. The dual job-hunting constraints generally favor the male's landing a better job. There is a sort of self-fulfilling prophecy operating here in that managerial skepticism about a woman's ability to handle adequately both work and family sets up a barrier to her entry into higher levels within occupations. Sometimes the only solution is the so-called commuting marriage (Gross, 1980), where husband and wife are geographically separated for extended periods of time.

If there are all of these difficulties in dual-career families, why bother? The answer is that, in general, those involved in dual-career marriages are happy, and the dual career itself is thought to be a primary contributor to that adjustment. Huser & Grant (1978), for example, found that dual-career wives were more self-actualizing than their non–dual career counterparts. Studies by both Sekaran (1982) and Hardesty & Betz (1980) suggest that if dual-career wives did not pursue their careers, they would be unhappy, for these women are more similar to working males than they are to nonworking females; that is, there is no difference in career salience between husbands and wives in dual-career families. Yogev (1981) indicates that academic wives strongly feel that their careers improve their marriage. Men and women in dual-career marriages tend each to rank family first and career second in priority. So long as the wife's job status does not have to be lowered to accommodate the dual-career couple, marital adjustment appears to be high (Hiller & Philliber, 1982). Men tend to report more spouse fulfillment and contentment, greater intellectual companionship, and increased income as decided advantages in dual-career marriages. This latter advantage, however, does not always hold. St. John Parsons (1978) points out that increased income is not always a benefit because of the increased cost of the dual-career life style (for example, child care and domestic help). Women typically report greater self-expression and realization of their potential and a greater sense of independence and competence for their children as a result of the dual-career nature of the family.

Dual-career marriages are characterized by greater self-reliance and self-sufficiency than non–dual career couples (Burke & Weir, 1976) and have more inner direction and self-acceptance (Huser & Grant, 1978).

Counseling for Dual-Career Couples

Any career-family counseling is essentially life style counseling. The symbiotic relationship between family and career requires both males and females to understand life roles. Most marriages have relationship issues, but these may be intensified in the dual-career family. Addressing changing spouse needs and identity, the shifting balance of power, competition, and continual revision of the initial marital contract are the sine qua non of any successful marriage.

There are some suggestions for employing institutions to effect changes in order to make life easier and fairer for dual-career couples. Hall and Hall (1978), for example, recommend many company policies, among which are these: (1) programs for dual-career couples to help them to learn the process of managing two careers; (2) support structures for transfers and relocation; (3) provision of flexible work environments; and (4) revision of development, transfer, and nepotism policies. Companies have not yet advanced to the point where such suggestions are widely implemented. Consequently, adjustment in dual-career marriages is usually effected by the individuals themselves working to deal with internal and external constraints.

The two characteristics that appear in almost every successful dual-career marriage are flexibility and the internal security of the individuals (Maples, 1981). Sundby (1980) enumerates eight other factors that seem to be prevalent in successful dual-career families. These are (1) knowing each other well before marriage; (2) awareness of self and sense of identity; (3) compatibility in decision style; (4) high energy level for the woman; (5) moderate to low social interchange needs; (6) stable help with child care and household management; (7) adequate or better combined financial earnings; and (8) job security or possibilities for career development. These factors might serve as the structure for discussions with

dual-career couples both before and during marriage.

In general, women may use either role definition or role expansion to cope in dual-career marriages (Gilbert, Holahan, & Manning, 1981). In the first, they alter the demands made on them either internally or in negotiations with others. In the second, much as with the "superwoman" working mother, they try to meet all of the role demands. Role definition obviously produces less stress than role expansion, and wives can be assisted to define their dual roles more effectively. In terms of enhancing definition, Parker, Peltier & Wolleat (1981) recommend nine adaptation techniques:

1. asking each other for assistance and support
2. talking to other couples who share a similar life style
3. limiting the number of obligations that are taken on at any one time
4. discussing expectations, goals, and needs with each other
5. scheduling time (especially time for being alone singly and together)
6. looking for help outside the family for domestic, maintenance, and child-care needs
7. seeking help from an employer or supervisor to make adjustments in the work setting
8. taking time to get away from the stress and relax
9. planning for emergencies – having back-up plans for situations that are not a part of the schedule (e.g., sickness, trip out of town) (p. 18).

Some of these types of ideas have been put into effect by Kahnweiler & Kahnweiler (1980) in a workshop aimed at college undergraduates. The object is to raise awareness in college men and women of issues in the dual-career family. This sort of preventive approach may prove useful, but more careful evaluation is necessary. In such a workshop, a list of eleven myths regarding dual-careers generated by Gingrich (1982) might be useful as stimulators of discussion.

1. A dual-career couple has extra money and is usually financially secure.
2. It's better to marry someone who is in your field.

3. After we get married, we'll see who gets a job first, and the other person will look in that area until they get one.
4. In an equal relationship, neither of us will need to compromise our careers.
5. We want children, but it will work out later after we get our careers established.
6. If our careers come in conflict, it will eventually work out because we love each other.
7. Living together before we get married will be better to see if our careers are compatible.
8. If we find a lot of conflict, the only answer is divorce, separation, or a dissolving of the relationship.
9. Business and most other employers are not aware of the career searching situations dual-career couples face.
10. There is never enough time to keep two careers, a home, friendships, individual activities, and a relationship going.
11. It is difficult to get a job and have others understand your unique situation because the traditional housewife and breadwinner standard is still in the majority (pp. 28–29).

It is, of course, important that counselors understand their own attitudes toward the dual-career family. Both Boswell (1981) and Gray (1980) suggest that it is mandatory for counselors to explore their own feelings toward sex roles and to overcome any biases that might be present.

Dual-career couples face potentially heightened stresses and strains when compared with those experienced by dual-worker or dual-earner couples. A knowledge of these possibly harmful issues and a sense of how to intervene to prevent or to remedy them are necessary for the counselor.

JOB-SEEKING BEHAVIORS: THREE ASPECTS

This chapter focuses on some potential problem areas related to work. These areas may be the result of dysfunctional behaviors, or they may be the cause of dysfunctional behaviors. For example, getting a job is the most fundamental of work skills. Failure to get a job – repeated rejection – can lead to what Zehring (1975) calls *rejection*

shock; that is, negative emotional and physical symptoms, depression, low self-esteem, alienation, lack of motivation, and so on. Ultimately, the repeatedly rejected applicant becomes a discouraged worker (as defined earlier in this chapter). We assume that if people in the labor force possess job-seeking skills, they will be more likely to become employed. Job-seeking, according to Stevens (1973) is, "a small segment of vocational behavior exhibited in the process of vocational development prior to work adjustment and contingent upon occupational choice" (p. 209). Three of these job-seeking skills have been researched: job sources, application letters and the resume, and interviews.

Job Sources

The job search is the initial phase of job-seeking behavior. How do people go about locating potential jobs? Which methods of job location appear to be most useful or effective? The answers to these questions are not formed as yet with any precision. There are so many conditions in the research that generalizations are few.

One way to address the question is to ask how employers go about filling the jobs that they have available. Angresano's (1980) study of employer hiring practices provides some information. Unfortunately, the focus of interest in this study was only on small and large firms likely to hire graduates of vocational/technical training institutions. Nevertheless, the findings are instructive. The primary methods used by these employers for recruiting workers to fill vacancies were: internal promotion, newspaper advertisements, and selection from a pool of walk-in candidates. The principal criteria used for selecting workers were experience with another employer at a similar job, on-the-job training, and a personal interview (as opposed to the completion of a formal training program). The implication is that, at least for voc/tech blue-collar jobs, workers should be advised to seek entry-level jobs and work their way vertically by means of demonstrated performance.

From the job-seekers' perspective, Allen and Kearny (1980) studied the relative effectiveness of alternative job sources for two-year college graduates. They categorized job sources as either *formal* (state employment services, private employment agencies, executive search firms, college placement offices, union hiring halls, advertisements in newspapers and professional journals) or *informal* (personal references from friends, relatives, and faculty members). Their conclusion was that for two-year graduates seeking initial entry into the labor market, formal job sources resulted in more favorable outcomes. For engineering technology majors, however, this advantage lessened over time; for business alumni, formal sources held up. These results are a little different from those of other studies, which seem to show slightly more favorable results for those who use informal sources (Reid, 1972; Granovetter, 1974). Factors such as the level of job desired, general economic conditions, and specific formal or informal sources used are apparently powerful moderator variables and thus make generalizations difficult.

The general rule would seem to be that job-seekers should use all available job sources, formal and informal, in their search. This area appears to be one where, if people have to err, they are better off using too many sources than too few. The common advice of using all available resources in the job search would indeed seem to be appropriate. In addition to establishing this set in counselees, counselors can work to be sure that job-seekers understand all of the formal and informal sources open to them.

Letters of Application and Resumes

As indicated in a previous chapter, most authorities view the job-seeking process as something akin to a battle campaign. The literature is replete with military terminology, and there is also a great deal of the old-time football coach at half-time exhorting his players to "get out there and fight." Some go so far as to say that the job hunt is no more nor less than selling a product – in this case, oneself. Consequently, general marketing guidelines should be applied to selling oneself (Pelletier, 1981). Some job seekers, of course, react strongly against the notion of marketing oneself like a new cereal or a detergent. Others argue that if the technique is good enough to elect a president of the United States, it is good enough to get a job. All the Madison Avenue hoopla

aside, all job-seeking involves presenting oneself in the best light possible. With the exception of face to face contact with an employer, the most popular method of picturing one's assets is an application letter and a resume. These offer both opportunities and potential dangers.

In terms of letters of application, Stephens, Watt, and Hobbs (1979) present the results of a survey of employer preferences regarding the form and substance of such communications.

It appears that the letter most likely to bring forth a positive response would be short, error-free, and grammatically correct. The format of the letter does not make much difference. The style of the letter is probably not as important as previously thought. An emphasis on employer benefit gets varied responses, although the "hardsell" approach is viewed negatively and should be avoided. The letter should not rehash the resume, but should merely introduce it. Attempts at sophistication through the use of metaphor, simile, and quotations are not well received by personnel officers. A succinct, straightforward letter to introduce the application or resume is the safest way to avoid detracting from the profile displayed in those documents. The potential for prejudicing the reader by a poorly constructed introductory letter appears to be a real possibility (p. 242).

Hence, it does not really matter, it would appear, what form – block or semiblock, for example – the letter takes. What is most important is that the letter be error free, a finding previously highlighted by Mansfield (1976), and that it be short and direct.

With regard to the resume itself, several guidelines, based on some research, should prove useful. For example, Olney (1982) replicated an earlier study to determine what changes might have occurred in employer preferences regarding what should be included on the resume. He discovered some substantial changes in the rankings, as indicated in Table 13.2.

Stephens, Watt and Hobbs (1979) effected the same sort of research on resumes as on the previously reported application letters. They viewed preferences for both content and format of the resume. Their conclusions are similar to those of earlier research by Field and Holley (1976):

Table 13.2
1981 Ranking and Comparison of 15 Resume Items

	1981 $(N = 174)$	1974a $(N = 165)$	Amount of Change
Related work experience record	1	2	+1
Salary requirements	2	7	+5
Listing of college courses	3	12	+9
College education record	4	3	−1
References	5	4	−1
Nonrelated work experience record	6	1	−5
College grade point average	7	11	+4
Military experience	8	5	−3
Civic, church, and social work	9	14	+5
Hobbies, outside interests	10	8	−2
High school record	11	13	+2
Draft status	12	9	−3
Personal data (age, etc.)	13	10	−3
Marital status	14	6	−8
Applicant's picture	15	15	0

a(Keyser, 1974)

It seems that the resume most likely to elicit a positive response should be neat and error-free. It should be specific, with high information content, but should also be succinct, and a single page if possible. The manner in which the information is positioned on the page and the way in which italics are used is unimportant. The color and quality of the paper are also unimportant. Even the use of shortcuts, such as abbreviations, is not as serious a liability as was previously thought. It is effective to marginally differentiate the resume by offering a unique or unusual format. Radical differences in format, however, will detract from the resume's appeal. The generally preferred order of presentation of content items is personal data, education, work experience, awards and achievements, affiliations, and references (p. 33).

In this same study, 60 percent of the respondents indicated that they formed some opinion of the applicant solely on the appearance of the resume and cover letter. Therefore, the importance of an error-free, succinct, clean resume and cover letter cannot be overemphasized.

There is a plethora of books and kits intended to assist individuals to write resumes. At the Uni-

versity of Colorado, Wilkinson and Rosenberg (1979) designed, implemented, and evaluated a resume preparation workshop for students. Although such workshops are common, one noteworthy result of the evaluation was that students who talk with a counselor or with friends about resumes produce a more effective product than those who get their information only through reading materials. This finding suggests that all of the books and kits available are best not used in isolation.

Several of the most valuable surveys relating to the variables considered either positive or negative in the job-seeking process are those of Endicott (1965, 1975) at Northwestern University. Citing negative features that personnel officers report as a result of reading resumes and interviewing applicants, Endicott presents the following list of the most common reasons for not offering a job to a graduate (rank ordered):

1. poor personal appearance
2. overbearing know-it-all
3. inability to express self clearly; poor voice, diction, grammar
4. lack of planning for career; no purpose or goals
5. lack of confidence and poise

6. lack of interest and enthusiasm
7. failure to participate in activities
8. overemphasis on money; interest only in best dollar offer
9. poor scholastic record – just got by
10. unwilling to start at the bottom – expects too much too soon
11. makes excuses, evasiveness, hedges on unfavorable factors in records
12. lack of tact
13. lack of maturity
14. lack of courtesy
15. condemnation of past employers
16. lack of social understandings
17. marked dislike for school work
18. lack of vitality
19. fails to look interviewer in the eye
20. limp, fishy handshake
21. indecision
22. loafs during vacations preferring lakeside pleasures
23. unhappy married life
24. friction with parents
25. sloppy application blank
26. merely shopping around
27. only wants a job for short time
28. little sense of humor
29. lack of knowledge of field of specialization
30. parents make decisions for him
31. no interest in company or industry
32. emphasis on who he knows
33. unwillingness to go where we send him
34. cynical
35. low moral standards
36. lazy
37. intolerant with strong prejudices
38. narrow interests
39. spends much time in movies
40. poor handling of personal finances
41. no interest in community activities
42. inability to take criticism
43. lack of appreciation of value of experience
44. radical ideas
45. late to interview without good reason
46. never heard of company
47. failure to express appreciation for interviewer's time
48. asks no questions about the job
49. high-pressure type
50. indefinite response to questions

One might well ask what some of these factors have to do with job performance, and one might well argue the placement of these factors on the hierarchy; nevertheless, what they tell us about business and industrial managers is useful in preparing individuals to write good resumes and give good interviews.

The Job Interview

A third aspect of the job-seeking process is the interview, either with a recruiter who grants interviews to all or with someone who sees the people who pass some initial screening. In either case, job seekers have an opportunity to present themselves in the best possible light. However, their chances for selection may become imperiled for a variety of reasons, many of which, as we have just seen, are unrelated to the requirements of the job.

One area of research has been interview biases and psychological sets. We are reasonably clear that certain personal characteristics establish a negative mindset in the majority of interviewers. Unfortunately, much of this research employs college student samples rather than actual interviewers. There is an obvious leap in application in such cases. Nevertheless, we may conclude that certain prejudices are more likely than not to be present in employment interviews. One of these interview biases is age. Craft et al. (1979) suggest on the basis of their research that although interviewers may not be affected in their perceptions of a person's work-related traits on the basis of age, they tend to make more negative decisions in hiring because of the potentially shortened work-life of the older worker. In addition to age, there is evidence that being overweight affects interviewers; fat applicants are viewed as significantly less desirable employees than are average-weight persons despite objectively identical performances (Larkin & Pines, 1979). Nonverbal behaviors (such as eye contact, smiling, head movements, body movements, tone of voice) also appear to affect interviewers (Barbee & Keil, 1973; Young, Beier & Beier, 1979; Young & Beier, 1977; McGovern & Tinsley, 1978). In fact, in one experiment (McGovern, Jones, & Morris, 1979), even student subjects were able to discriminate nonverbal behaviors as well as an experienced professional group of interviewers in making employment evaluations about potential applicants.

Vecchiotti and Korn (1980) studied the values of college students in the humanities and sciences and those of recruiters and found a number of differences. Recruiters, for example, seem to prefer the masculine Stereotypic Value Profile as measured by the Rokeach, regardless of the sex of the applicant, thus confirming the match between business values and masculine values. Tucker and Rowe (1979) used college students in another study to establish psychological sets on the basis of expectancy theory and to confirm the notion of self-fulfilling prophecy in the employment interview. For some subjects, an interviewer received a favorable letter of reference; for others, an unfavorable letter; and for still others, a neutral letter. Interviewers who got the unfavorable expectancy seemed to give the applicant less credit for past successes and to hold the applicant personally responsible for past failures. The final decision was closely related to these causal interpretations of past outcomes. One possible way to counteract these tendencies is to use several interviewers and a group-consensus approach (Rothstein & Jackson, 1980). This method, however, is obviously not very cost effective.

In another study of congruence between interviewer and interviewee values, Giles and Feild (1982) demonstrated that college recruiters consistently overemphasized the importance to applicants of intrinsic factors (such as chance to use one's abilities, interesting work, opportunity for recognition in one's profession) and underestimated the importance of extrinsic factors (fair and considerate supervision, good pay, desired geographical location of job). Hence, college recruiters indeed seem to have inaccurate stereotypes of what job factors, intrinsic or extrinsic, were important to applicants. Renwick and Tosi's (1978) study suggests that the less information interviewers have, the less likely they are to reach conclusions on the basis of stereotypes.

It is clear, then, that psychological sets, stereotypical reactions, and biases affect interviewers' judgments in the interview process. In addition, as we have noted in an earlier chapter, the time of day in which the interview is conducted seems to be a determining factor as well as the quality of the person who preceded one in the interview

room and whether or not the recruiter has a quota to meet. On the assumption that counselors cannot do a great deal to change interviewer behavior, they have turned to "coaching" the interviewee on methods to minimize interviewer bias and to maximize their self-presentation.

Galassi and Galassi (1978) synthesized a great deal of the research on interviews and suggested a four-phase intervention in preparing clients for the interview. They label Phase I "Developing Realistic Expectations." In this phase, clients are instructed about the format (structured or unstructured), content (client-centered), and length (short) of interviews, the roles of the interviewer and interviewee, the probabilities of positive decisions, and the way the interview is used in the decision process. In Phase II, "Developing Interviewing Skills," the focus is on effective self-presentation techniques (such as dressing appropriately, using standard speech, developing other communication skills, expressing work attitudes and traits, minimizing subjective impressions, handling problem questions). Phase III, "Using Effective Training Procedures," refers to counselors selecting the best methods and techniques available to promote achievement of the desired outcomes. In general, the recommendation is for the use of several techniques rather than a single one (such as modeling, role playing, video feedback, discussion, written materials, relation training, behavioral rehearsal, systematic desensitization, self-instructions, identification and disputation of counterproductive beliefs, etc.). Five or six hours of total instruction is considered minimally adequate. Finally, the fourth phase, "Preparing for Rejection Shock," involves helping clients to deal with some inevitable rejection through reinforcement, support groups, and keeping life changes to a minimum during the job search.

Zelenak (1978) compared three methods of preparing clients for job interviewing. She established a group marked by assertive training, another characterized by a didactic approach, and a third that received no treatment and acted as a control group. Each treatment group received fifteen to eighteen hours of instruction and practice. The three groups demonstrated no significant differences in interviewing skills, suggesting that the frequently recommended technique of assertiveness training is not a useful adjunct to interview preparation programs. More comprehensive employability programs also usually include training in interviewing skills as well as resume preparation and application letter writing (Rosove, 1982).

There are several compilations of the most frequently asked questions in job interviews (for example, Nealer & Papalia, 1982; Martin, 1979; Endicott, 1975). Combining these into a single list produces the following questions.

1. What are your long-range and short-range goals and objectives? When and why did you establish these goals?
2. What specific goals, other than those related to your occupation, have you established for yourself in the next ten years?
3. What do you see yourself doing five years from now?
4. What do you *really* want to do in life?
5. What are your long-range career objectives?
6. How do you plan to achieve your career goals?
7. What are the most important rewards you expect in your career?
8. What do you expect to be earning in five years?
9. Why did you choose the career for which you are preparing?
10. Which is more important to you, the money or the type of job?
11. What do you consider to be your greatest strengths and weaknesses?
12. How would you describe yourself?
13. How do you think a friend or professor who knows you well would describe you?
14. What motivates you to put forth your greatest effort?
15. How has your educational experience prepared you for a career?
16. Why should I hire you?
17. What qualifications do you have that make you think that you will be successful in a company like ours?
18. How do you determine or evaluate success?
19. What do you think it takes to be successful in a company like ours?
20. In what ways do you think you can make a contribution to our company?

21. What qualities should a successful _____ possess?
22. Describe the relationship that should exist between a supervisor and those reporting to him or her.
23. What two or three accomplishments have given you the most satisfaction? Why?
24. Describe your most rewarding educational experience.
25. If you were hiring someone for this position, what qualities would you look for?
26. Why did you select the school you did?
27. What led you to choose your major field of study?
28. What subjects did you like best? Why? What subjects did you like least? Why?
29. If you could do so, how would you plan your course of study differently? Why?
30. What changes would you make in your school? Why?
31. Do you have plans for continued study? An advanced degree?
32. Do you think that your grades are a good indication of your academic achievement?
33. What have you learned from participation in extracurricular activities?
34. In what kind of a work environment are you most comfortable?
35. How do you work under pressure?
36. In what part-time or summer jobs have you been most interested? Why?
37. How would you describe the ideal job for you?
38. Why did you decide to seek a position with this company?
39. What do you know about our company?
40. What two or three things are most important to you in your job?
41. Are you seeking employment in a company of a certain size? Why?
42. What criteria are you using to evaluate the company for which you hope to work?
43. Do you have a geographical preference? Why? Will you relocate? Does relocation bother you?
44. Are you willing to travel?
45. Are you willing to spend time as a trainee?
46. Why do you think you might like to live in the community in which our company is located?

47. What is a major problem you have encountered? How did you deal with it?
48. What have you learned from your mistakes?
49. Why did your business fail?
50. Why are you leaving your present job?
51. What can you do for us that someone else can't?
52. How good is your health?
53. Do you prefer line or staff work? Why?
54. What kind of salary do you expect?
55. What are your biggest accomplishments in your present or last job?
56. How long would it take you to make a contribution to our firm?
57. What new goals or objectives have you established recently?
58. Why haven't you obtained a job so far?
59. What is your feeling about alcoholism? Divorce? Homosexuality? Women in business? Religion? Abortion? (Such questions are inappropriate but are sometimes asked. Be careful.)
60. Would you describe a few situations in which your work was criticized?
61. What was the last book you read, movie you saw, or sporting event you attended?
62. How would you define success?
63. Are you creative? Give an example. Are you analytic? Give an example.
64. Have you fired or hired people before? What do you look for?
65. Tell us all about yourself.
66. How do you feel about working for a _____
67. Do you consider yourself a leader? Give an example.
68. Who thinks more of you, your subordinates or your superior?
69. What interests you the most and the least about the position we have?

JOB DISSATISFACTION

In Chapter 2 we presented an overview of job satisfaction in America; in Chapter 15 we will discuss some of the more common measures of job satisfaction. One of the purposes of this chapter is to explore job dissatisfaction and its implications for those adults who require career counsel-

ing. We conservatively estimate that there are 4000 articles, books, dissertations, and monographs on job satisfaction. It is clearly impossible to address more than a small proportion of these studies.

Summary of Job Satisfaction Studies

To recapitulate what was concluded in Chapter 2 and to expand those findings, we offer the following summary:

1. Most research in job satisfaction is atheoretical and correlational.

2. Results are often contradictory.

3. National surveys indicate that somewhere between eight or nine of every ten American workers report themselves to be basically satisfied with their jobs (Quinn, Staines & McCullough, 1974; Portigal, 1976; Katzell, 1979; Weaver, 1980).

4. The proportion of satisfied workers in America has not changed greatly over the last quarter-century.

5. Positive relationships have generally been found between job satisfaction and: higher occupational levels (Kalleberg & Griffin, 1978); higher educational levels (Quinn & Mandilovitch, 1980); higher pay — or at least a threshold of pay; enriched jobs; autonomy; considerate and democratic supervision (Srivastva et al., 1975; Valenzi & Dessler, 1978; Gilmore, Beehr, & Richter, 1979); positive views of top management (Ruch, 1979); participation in decisions affecting one's work and working conditions; interaction with influential and significant others; relatively small organizations and work groups; adequate resources (Katzell, 1979); Holland personal codes and occupational environments (Maynard, 1979); age, in the sense that satisfaction tends to increase with age in a nonlinear, U-shaped form (Glenn, Taylor, & Weaver, 1977; Cohn, 1979; Muchinsky, 1978; Near, Rice & Hunt, 1980); and better health (House, 1974).

6. Low job satisfaction seems to be related to certain other characteristics: unpleasant, hazardous work; role conflict, ambiguity, and overload (Abdel-Halim, 1981; Helwig, 1979; Wright & Gutkin, 1981); inability to use skills; repetitive tasks; inability to interact in a work group; pro-

union activity (Schriesheim, 1978; Bigoness, 1978); poor supervision, such as lack of feedback and recognition; discriminatory hiring practices; lack of mobility in the organization; promotional inequity; and low wages (Kasl, 1977).

7. There appear to be no definitive conclusions regarding the relationship between job satisfaction and a variety of other variables. In some cases, there are no measureable differences; in others, the results are equivocal. Among the variables that have been researched are: turnover and absentee rates (Taylor & Weiss, 1972; Muchinsky & Tuttle, 1979; Cheloa & Farr, 1980); sex (Sell, Brief, & Aldag, 1979; Voydanoff, 1980; Miller, 1980; Weaver, 1980; Enderlein, 1975; Lee, 1982; Lee, Mueller, & Miller, 1981); race (Wilson & Butler, 1978; Moch, 1980; Weaver, 1978); work performance (Porter & Lawler, 1968; Jacobs & Solomon, 1977); and life satisfaction (Bamundo & Kopelman, 1980; Rice, Near, & Hunt, 1980; Schmitt & Mellon, 1980; Orpen, 1978; Sarason & Johnson, 1979; Bell, 1978; Wiener, Vardi, & Muczyk, 1981).

A great deal of this lack of relationship or the inconsistent results is probably due to the fact that until fairly recently not much attention has been paid to the likely influence of moderator variables. Moderator variables are third variables that influence the relationship between job factors and job satisfaction. Some of the moderator variables that have been examined are: self-esteem (Greenhaus, 1971); higher-order need strength (Dreher, 1980); interests; ability; job characteristics (Brass, 1981; Helpingstine, Head, & Sorensen, 1981); job involvement (Lefkowitz & Brigando, 1980); career stages (Gould, 1979; Stumpf & Rabinowitz, 1981; Gould & Hawkins, 1978); worker alienation (Vecchio, 1980a; Lefkowitz & Brigando, 1980); and religious affiliation (Vecchio, 1980b). Each of these moderator variables has been found to affect the relationship between job factors and job satisfaction.

Age is another moderator variable that makes it very difficult to describe a simple relationship between job factors and job satisfaction. A study by Cohn (1979) is a good example of this situation. He investigated the importance of intrinsic (noneconomic) factors in work satisfaction as determinants of an individual's sense of well-being

as related to age. He discovered that, as with most such studies, intrinsic factors were lower for men during the later stages of labor-force participation. Why? These declines were not an artifact of lower levels of satisfaction. Rather it appears that older men derive their satisfactions from the *consequences* of work rather than the *experiences* of work. In other words, noneconomic factors of work assume less importance to individuals as they age — the *type* of satisfaction changes while overall satisfaction, as has been indicated earlier, tends to rise with age. A complicated relationship, indeed.

This diverse emphasis on intrinsic or extrinsic factors and on methodological problems in the measurement of job satisfaction — for example, single-question versus multifactor measures (McGehee & Tullar, 1979) — further complicate matters. In any case, we know something about job satisfaction and we continue to learn. What we know and learn can be applied to assist the dissatisfied worker.

Counseling the Dissatisfied

If job satisfaction has no consistently proven relationship to either work productivity or absenteeism and turnover rates (if job involvement is controlled for), then one might well ask why employers should be concerned. Basically, other than the human concern that workers are themselves better off happy than unhappy, there is no compelling utilitarian reason why employers should be involved in trying to ensure the satisfaction of their workers. There is considerable reason, however, why counselors should be well-versed in the job satisfaction literature and should be able to apply its findings in helping dissatisfied workers.

It is important for the individual to recognize the centrality of work in his or her life. This knowledge, in turn, can help individuals to understand their work place and non–work place behaviors (Maurer, Vredenburgh, & Smith, 1981). And when we consider, as House (1974) determined, that measures of work satisfaction are the strongest predictors of longevity (exceeding even general happiness and physical factors), then we realize how important it is to be satisfied at work.

Dissatisfied workers often express a global sort

of malaise — the career "blahs" — and are unable to articulate, without assistance, the specific facets of their job dissatisfaction. It is important that they know the specifics of their discontent, for that knowledge, in large measure, determines what can be done to remedy the situation. For this reason, we recommend either the formal or informal use of one of the better developed instruments designed to measure job satisfaction. For example, in Chapter 2 we discussed job satisfaction in the context of the Theory of Work Adjustment. The reader will recall that this theory suggests that jobs have differing work reinforcers, that individuals have differing vocational needs or preferences for work reinforcers, and that how closely these two elements dovetail determines an individual's satisfaction. If the theory is accurate, then people should be helped to know their own vocational needs and where or where not these needs are being reinforced by occupations and jobs. One can do this formally by administering and interpreting to clients the *Minnesota Importance Questionnaire* (Rounds, Healy, Dawis, & Lofquist, 1981) or informally by trying to assess verbally the same dimensions. The twenty relevant need dimensions are (Lofquist & Dawis, 1975):

Ability utilization – I could do something that makes use of my abilities.
Achievement – The job could give me a feeling of accomplishment.
Activity – I could be busy all the time.
Advancement – The job would provide an opportunity for advancement.
Authority – I could tell people what to do.
Company policies and practices – The company would administer its policies fairly.
Compensation – My pay would compare well with that of other workers.
Co-workers – My co-workers would be easy to make friends with.
Creativity – I could try out some of my own ideas.
Independence – I could work alone on the job.
Moral values – I could do the work without feeling it is morally wrong.
Recognition – I could get recognition for the work I do.
Responsibility – I could make decisions on my own.

Security – The job would provide for steady employment.
Social service – I could do things for other people.
Social status – I could be "somebody" in the community.
Supervision-human relations – My boss would back up the workers (with top management).
Supervision-technical – My boss would train the workers well.
Variety – I could do something different every day.
Working conditions – The job would have good working conditions.

If the instrument is administered, it can be interpreted in terms of the needs that are indicated as important, in terms of a hierarchy of needs, in terms of normative data that are available, in terms of likelihood of satisfaction with a particular occupation or clusters of occupations, and in terms of basic values. In a less formal way, a counselor might simply encourage an individual to talk about the specific characteristics of a job that appear to be producing dissatisfaction, using the categories as a sort of checklist. If the twenty needs seem too unwieldy, the counselor might want to use the six factors into which the twenty needs seem to cast themselves: *Safety* (Supervision-Human Relations, Supervision-Technical, Company Policies and Practices), *Autonomy* (Responsibility, Creativity), *Comfort* (Activity, Independence, Variety, Security, Working Conditions, Compensation), *Altruism* (Social Service, Moral Values, Co-Workers), *Achievement* (Ability Utilization, Achievement), and *Aggrandizement* (Social Status, Recognition, Authority, Advancement).

Once the satisfiers and dissatisfiers are identified, the client can be assisted to change those things that can be changed, either within the job or by moving to a new type of job or the same type of job in a different setting; and to accept those things which cannot be changed or otherwise to come to grips with elements of self or work.

Similar use can be made of another very popular job satisfaction instrument — the Job Descriptive Index (JDI) — either by actual administration and scoring or by utilizing the taxonomy devised for the instrument. The JDI emphasizes extrinsic rather than intrinsic rewards of work. It asks respondents to describe their work rather than their feelings about that work. There are five subscales and a total score possible. The five subscales are: *Work on Present Job* (fascinating, routine, satisfying, boring, and so on), *Present Pay* (adequate, insecure, underpaid), *Opportunities for Promotion* (infrequent promotions, fairly good chance for promotion), *Supervision on Present Job* (hard to please, quick-tempered, knows job well), *People on Your Present Job* (ambitious, stupid, no privacy). One can, in fact, use any instrument to devise a structured interview guide to assist clients in exploring their vague notions of dissatisfaction. The typical areas to be investigated are job involvement, amount of work and the stress and strain of that work, relations with one's co-workers and with one's supervisors, status, finances, opportunities for advancement, security or lack of it, working conditions (physical and nonphysical), opportunities to express a variety of needs, and progress toward career goals. Examining dissatisfactions with work in this sort of context will ultimately lead to a consideration of general life roles and the place of work in the total life context. Eventually, the counselor and client will need to consider the chicken-egg conundrum of the effect of work on life satisfaction and the effect of life satisfaction on work. Although the results of research are equivocal for groups, as we have indicated previously, they are less obfuscated for any given individual. If job dissatisfactions are affecting other aspects of one's life, it is important that this fact be faced squarely and that alternatives be examined. Likewise, if the converse pertains — if life unhappiness is affecting work — that too should be explored. Testing aspects of self and the work environment that are causing dissatisfaction is a first step in attaining job satisfaction.

For some workers, this quest for causes will focus on extrinsic factors of work; for others, the emphasis will be on intrinsic factors. Causes of stress and dissatisfaction will vary over an individual's career. Consequently, an understanding of where the individual is in terms of career stages will be of use to the counselor. In some careers, there will be little or no opportunity for upward mobility, a situation that inherently encourages dissatisfaction. Alternative sources of gratification, such as community work or a hobby, may be effective substitutes. For some individuals, investigating job dissatisfaction from a Marxian perspective might prove useful. Concepts of powerlessness, alienation, meaninglessness, isolation, and self-estrangement are other ways of expressing the type of dissatisfaction that is described more traditionally as lack of autonomy, relations with co-workers, and so on. It is interesting to note the paradox that Marxian ideology is most often prevalent in time of full employment. In hard times, there seems to be much less talk of powerlessness and alienation.

We have concentrated on what the counselor can do to help the individual deal with dissatisfactions of work. We have avoided discussing what can be done by organizations in terms of various types of job enrichment, better supervision, and so on. The motivation for such organizational changes will have to emanate from a belief that job satisfaction for its own sake is an appropriate end.

Job satisfaction is a complex phenomenon, the causes of which will vary according to stage of individual career development, and a variety of moderator variables. Counseling the dissatisfied involves determining the specific extrinsic and intrinsic factors giving rise to the dissatisfaction and applying methods of changing or of dealing with the issues.

Summary

In this chapter, we have considered six special adult career concerns. We have tried to indicate that even in the most continuous and mature of career development patterns, such problems may be present. Enough information has been offered about unemployed, dislocated, and/or discouraged workers, burnout, working mothers, dual-career couples, job-seeking behaviors, and job dissatisfaction to give the counselor a basic understanding of each of these areas and an idea of how to intervene either to prevent or to remedy the problem.

LEARNING ACTIVITIES

1. In a bookstore, locate any resume "kit" or any of the scores of books aimed at helping individuals who are in the process of job seeking. How does the advice offered match with the research findings presented in this chapter? What discrepancies exist?

2. Interview someone who has lost a long-time job because of a plant or business closing or because of some adventitious event. Try to get a sense of the psychological and the economic effects of the event. What useful buffers did the individual find to job loss? What needs were not being met by existing services?

3. Design a systematic intervention aimed at one of the following groups: dislocated workers, dual-career couples, or job seekers. Be sure to include behavioral objectives, activities to achieve the objectives, materials to use in the activities, and an evaluation.

4. Role-play a job interview and have a third party critique the interview. Or, you may wish to videotape the interview. This activity should give you a sense of your own interview behaviors and alert you to how you react to the interview behaviors of others.

5. If you are married and one-half of a dual-career couple, think of your own situation in relation to such concepts as "tolerance for domestication," "identity tension line," or similar ideas.

6. Talk with a helping relationship worker or any worker in the human services about burnout. Simply offer the term without redefining what you mean. Ask the individual to describe burnout in himself or herself or in colleagues. Determine if the individual is talking about stress, about normal behaviors of a career development stage, about job dissatisfaction, or about all three variables.

7. Prepare a short questionnaire to assess the feelings of working mothers about several issues raised in this chapter. What do they perceive the effects of their work to be on their children, themselves, and their marriage? Go to a day care center (or otherwise secure a population). Administer the instrument, tally the results, and interpret them.

8. Prepare your own resume and cover letter. Pair off with someone who has accomplished the same task. Critique each other's work in relation to the research findings reported in this chapter.

9. Locate an article from a newspaper or a magazine on any topic addressed in this chapter. Form some judgments on how much in the article is sensationalized or folklore and how much is consistent with what is actually known at this point.

10. Using the MIQ categories or the JDI categories, think about which aspects of job satisfaction would or do give you pleasure and which would be or are dissatisfiers.

OBJECTIVES

After reading this chapter, engaging in the learning activities, and reading the suggested references, you should have met the objectives that follow. If you have not, it would probably be useful for you to review the material on specific adult concerns before proceeding further.

1. Define three types of unemployment.

2. Describe three types of legislated assistance and three types of negotiated assistance available to the unemployed.

3. List five possible psychological effects of job loss.

4. Describe four possible foci in counseling job losers.

5. Offer one definition of burnout.

6. Recognize that burnout may simply be stress, normal career development stage behavior, or job dissatisfaction rather than a separate and definable "syndrome."

7. List five correlates of burnout (however it is defined).

8. Enumerate five possible organizational responses to burnout.

9. Suggest five possible individual responses to burnout.

10. Summarize the research on the effects of working mothers on children; on mothers themselves; on marriages.

11. List at least two behavioral objectives for counseling working mothers.

12. Define dual-career couple.
13. Describe three differences between dual-worker families and dual-career families.
14. Characterize appropriate counseling for dual-career couples.
15. Distinguish between formal and informal job sources.
16. Summarize the research on resumes and cover letters with regard to form and substance.
17. List ten common failings in the job interview.
18. Recognize the relationship between job satisfaction and work productivity, absenteeism, and turnover.
19. List five specific aspects of job satisfaction.

14 / Helping Strategies in Career Guidance and Counseling

Career guidance and counseling exist because of freedom of choice. Theoretically, individuals in our society (as opposed to some other countries) have an almost unlimited number of career and educational options from among which they can choose, free of political constraints. Because career choice is unique and relatively unfettered for individuals, they must be given assistance in decision-making. That assistance typically takes the form of helping individuals to discover those personal characteristics that make a career-related difference; aiding them to be aware of the array of educational and occupational alternatives from which they may choose; and assisting them to process the dimensions of these two worlds on both affective and cognitive levels.

There are several purposes of guidance and counseling, depending on the particular type of problem. Some counseling is directed at eliminating or at improving dysfunctional or maladaptive behaviors. Other counseling emphasizes developmental and preventative aspects of helping in order to, in Shakespeare's words, "Meet the first beginnings (and) nip the budding mischief before it has time to ripen to maturity." Still other counseling is aimed at assisting in decision-making. These latter two purposes, development and decision-making, are the goals of career guidance and counseling.

To accomplish these goals, two strategies are commonly employed: individual counseling and group methods. Each of these helping strategies will be discussed in terms of its relevancy for career development and decision-making.

INDIVIDUAL COUNSELING

Definition

There are hundreds of definitions of counseling, focusing on process, relationship variables, content, techniques, outcomes, counselor characteristics, and so on. We regard career counseling as (1) a largely verbal process in which (2) a counselor and counselee(s) are in dynamic interaction and in which (3) the counselor employs a repertoire of diverse behaviors (4) to help bring about self-understanding and action in the form of "good" decision-making in the counselee, who has responsibility for his or her own actions.

Counseling requires some as yet undetermined threshold of verbal ability on the part of the counselees. One can help a person who is not yet verbally fluent but not typically through counseling. For example, some stereotypical behaviors of severe retardates (rocking, self-punishment, and such) can be eliminated by behaviorally manipulating the environment. Counseling, however, entails sensible verbalizations.

Being in dynamic interaction refers to the fact that both the counselor and the counselee(s) are constantly changing as individuals and that the relationship between them is in a continual state of flux. There is movement in the successful career counseling experience toward the development or resolution of factors affecting the decision-making process.

There is mutual participation in the counseling relationship. If the counselor assumes all responsi-

389

bility for participation, then the interview is nothing more than advice-giving. If the counselee is given all responsibility for participation, then the interview becomes a soliloquy. Although some catharsis may result, little else of value emerges. These extreme examples of the structure-nonstructure or the directedness-nondirectedness continuum suggest that the counseling relationship is not a superordinate-subordinate one; the counselor and the counselee are equally responsible for participation. Because of individual differences in personality, types and levels of training, and experience, some counselors will tend to be more active than others. Likewise, some counselees will tend to be more verbally active in the relationship than others. But both counselor and counselee must interact in dynamic fashion if counseling is to affect the counselee's decision-making.

In terms of this relationship, some conditions are thought to be facilitative, others are judged to be impeding. Briefly, this notion suggests that a counselor's effectiveness transcends any theory of counseling or the use of specific techniques. The crucial variables in success are assumed to be attitudes and sensitivity that create a "therapeutic" atmosphere. For example, Carkhuff (1983) maintains that the primary dimensions are the counselor's empathic understanding of the counselee, the respect shown for the counselee, the counselor's genuineness within the counseling session, and the concreteness or specificity with which problems are confronted. Geis (1970) suggests that other conditions might be equally facilitative: communicated competence, authoritativeness, confidence, wisdom, noncondemnation of the counselee as a person, objectivity, flexibility, high intelligence, absence of serious emotional disburbance, absence of communicated disruptive personal values, and personal style. Still other researchers suggest additional counselor variables that effect a therapeutic relationship: amount of counselor self-disclosure (Jourard & Jaffe, 1970); ability to make accurate predictions (Watley & Vance, 1964); and so on. There is neither space nor intent to review exhaustively the counseling literature. The point is simply that there do seem to exist some conditions that facilitate career counseling. We may assume that their absence retards the progress or, at the very least, does not

help the process or assist the counselee toward counseling relationship goals.

The career counselor employs a repertoire of diverse behaviors. Each theory of counseling proposes its unique and sometimes not-so-unique set of procedures and techniques for dealing with the counselee. We are convinced that there are very few "truths" in counseling. Each counseling approach can lay claim to its share of successes — at least insofar as one can gauge successes from reports of clinical activity and can accept varied definitions of the term. Clients, however, vary; each comes with need systems, backgrounds, psychological sets, and states of readiness that militate against undifferentiated treatment. Some counselees want information; some want help in "thinking through" a problem; some wish assistance in exploring feelings; some desire aid in ridding themselves of unwanted anxieties. And so it goes. Each counselee stimulus presents the counselor with an opportunity to make a differentiated, tailored response. Counselors frequently speak of inappropriate responses made by a counselee; however, the obverse is equally possible. The counselee who seeks information and finds himself or herself confronted by a counselor who clarifies, explores, diagnoses, reinforces, extinguishes, or engages in all sorts of behaviors *except* giving information has reason to wonder about the appropriateness of the counselor's response. All of these behaviors are appropriate as responses to various stimuli; their indiscriminant use, however, is likely to be counterproductive. Counseling procedures or behaviors ought to vary according to the needs of the counselee.

Perhaps the most reasonable suggestion is that of Sprinthall, Whiteley, and Mosher (1966), who urge that the counselor remain "cognitively flexible." Cognitive flexibility refers to the counselor's remaining open-minded, adaptable, and resisting premature closure in perception and cognition. The opposite of flexibility is rigidity; a rigid counselor has no tolerance for ambiguity, has an excessive need for structure, and has great difficulty in adapting to the needs of the counselee. Flexibility, thus, implies an avoidance of either excessive structuring or complete ambiguity and the use of a repertoire of behaviors consonant with client needs.

In other words, certain types of counselor behaviors are appropriate in certain situations and are inappropriate in others. For example, if one goal of career counseling is to promote counselee information-seeking behavior, evidence suggests that the behavioral technique of reinforcement is effective. On the other hand, there are specific career counseling concerns (such as valuing) that might be better approached by other procedures or techniques. It may help at specific times to clarify or reflect feelings. It may be useful at other times to summarize, restate, or interpret. There are occasions when a counselee is ready for confrontation, and that technique will be effective. On a more cognitive level, the counselor may want to point out alternatives directly or to provide information. At still other points, in the manner of some behavioral, rational-emotive, or transactional analysis counselors, homework assignments may be given. At times, the counselor might even want to persuade the counselee. These examples of counselor behaviors are by no means exhaustive; however, they do exemplify the diversity of approaches in a career helping individual relationship, and their very diversity argues for their discriminative use.

Finally, career counseling should bring about self-understanding and action. Knowledge of self and its subsequent relationship to the worlds of work, education, or training are the aims of career counseling. Action suggests that the clearest criterion of counseling success is outcome, that is, decision-making behavior of an appropriate nature. The individual, not the counselor, selects from informed alternatives and acts on that choice. Career counseling is action-oriented in that it is ultimately concerned with affecting behaviors (decision-making). It is helpful, therefore, just as with any other segment of a comprehensive career helping service, to approach individual counseling on a systematic basis: specifying goals in behavioral terms, evolving procedures to accomplish those behaviors, utilizing whatever resources may be required, and evaluating to determine if behaviors have been achieved.

Some Systematic Individual Counseling Models

Stewart et al. (1978) have devised an approach called "systematic counseling," in which "the various aspects of the counseling process are clearly identified and organized into a sequence designed to resolve the client's concerns efficiently as well as effectively" (p. 2). Their paradigm could easily be used in career counseling. Drawing on learning theory, systems analysis, and educational technology, the model is designed so that an agreed-on objective is stated in behavioral terms, a wide variety of learning experiences is logically structured to achieve the objective, and constant monitoring and feedback occur. The model is described in terms of thirteen sequenced functions. Beginning with the fourth function and proceeding through the tenth, the sequence runs as follows:

Function 4.0 – During the first interview, the counselor explains the counseling relationship to the client. This involves explaining briefly the purpose of counseling, the respective responsibilities of the counselor and client, the kinds of things focused on in counseling, and the limits under which counseling is conducted.

Function 5.0 – The counselor then proceeds to construct a model of the client's concerns, i.e., he engages the client in conversation about the difficulty so as to understand the problem in all relevant aspects. He then verifies or checks his picture of the client's concerns with the client himself.

Function 6.0 – Next, counselor and client decide upon a mutually acceptable goal and specific learning objective for counseling.

Function 7.0 – The next major phase is to determine and implement a strategy for attaining the client's learning objective. Major strategies include information-seeking, decision-making, and behavior modification. . . . A plan of attack including intermediate objectives and specific steps to be taken by the client and counselor is decided upon, and these steps are then carried out.

Function 8.0 – In this phase, client performance is evaluated both in terms of improvement over the initial, presenting level of problem behavior and in terms of whether the learning objective has been attained. If the objective has not been attained, it is then necessary for counselor and client to "recycle" through (repeat) Function 7.0. . . . after which performance is again evaluated.

Function 9.0 – After the objective has been attained and there is no apparent need for further counseling, the counselor proceeds to terminate regular contact with the client. He begins by explaining the rationale and procedures for termination and resolves any client or counselor resistance to termination. Next, he conducts transfer of learning, emphasizing how the strategies and skills learned during the counseling process can be applied by the client to future problems. Finally, he establishes a plan for monitoring the client's performance for a reasonable time after the termination of counseling.

Function 10.0 – In this phase, the counselor follows up or monitors the client's performance. This procedure usually involves one or more of the following: (a) observing the client's behavior directly; (b) asking the client how he is progressing in brief checkup interviews; (c) requesting information from others in the client's environment who are familiar with his performance; and (d) examining records and other written data concerning the client's behavior. If the client encounters difficulty, provision is made for further counseling.

Another systematic counseling model which is more directly pertinent to career choice has been developed by Herr, Horan, and Baker (1973). In this model, counselor behaviors are specified, accompanying necessary conditions are detailed, and criteria for successful performance are suggested. The entire eighteen-step sequence is presented in Table 14.1.

Another endeavor to bring a logical, sequenced procedure to individual counseling has been described by Gunnings (1976). What is termed a "systemic approach" to counseling (the art of intervening into the lives of individuals through systems understanding and modification) entails seven progressive steps.

1.0 Identification of symptoms
2.0 Exploration of problem causation (self-concept in relation to environmental variables)
3.0 Discussion of problem-solving strategies and techniques (alternatives and consequences)
4.0 Selection of problem-solving strategies and techniques

5.0 Implementation of selected strategies (long- and short-term)
6.0 Evaluation of effectiveness of problem-solving process
7.0 Expansion of client's use of model (transfer to various situations)

There are other systematic individual counseling models in the literature (Brown & Brown, 1977). These systematic models extend from industrial applications (Marlowe, 1981), to "multimodal" career counseling (Smith & Southern, 1980; Lazarus, 1976; Gerler, 1980), to the briefest of interventions with ninth-grade girls (Prediger & Noeth, 1979), to attention to systematic decision-making by counselors rather than by counselees (Turner, 1979; Roberts, 1978), among many other applications. It is probably fair to state that currently, whatever the theoretical orientation of career counselors, the preferred mode of delivery is systematic, more or less as delineated in this volume. Each systematic approach has in common the notion that the goals of intervention should be specified in terms of the client's behavior; that a logical, differentiated series of techniques and strategies to achieve those goals should be effected; and that monitoring of progress and evaluation of results is important. No doubt the current push for accountability in mental health services will spawn a great many more models of this type.

A Broad View of Career Counseling

Career counseling should not be viewed in a narrowly defined sense. It cannot be separated from various orientations to counseling that, in general, take into account an individual's total personality, culture, and environment. Brammer and Shostrom (1960) point out that career counseling can be construed in several ways. First, career counseling can be regarded simply as a process of confirming a choice already made by a counselee. Second, career counseling can be considered largely as a process of clarifying career objectives. Finally, one can view career counseling as allowing counselees to discover facts about themselves and the working world and to process that information in decision-making. In this latter orientation, career counseling is a process whereby

Table 14.1
Sequential Counselor Behaviors in Systematic Vocational Counseling

Counselor Behavior	Necessary Conditions	Criteria for Successful Performance
1. Counselor defines the purpose of counseling, and the roles of the counselor and student.	At the outset of the initial interview (unless the student discusses his concerns immediately, then before the end of the initial interview).	Definitions should correspond to a predetermined standard.
2. Counselor helps the client define the problem via specific counseling skills (see Ivey). *If the problem is one of vocational choice then the following counselor behaviors ought to ensue. Other kinds of student problems may require different types of counselor activity.*	During the initial interview and in as many subsequent interviews as are required.	The problem is defined when the student so indicates (e.g., "Yes, that's it," or "You really do understand me!").
3. Counselor determines if vocational choice is the primary concern (e.g., "It seems that although you have a lot of things on your mind, you're mainly interested in coming to some sort of vocational decision").	After the student has expressed all he cares to concerning his problem or his reason for seeking counseling.	The student responds in an affirmative manner.
4. Counselor explains the decision-making paradigm (e.g., "Arriving at a good vocational decision means that we have to look at all the alternatives, then weigh them in the light of information about you and the advantages and disadvantages of each course of action. I can't make the decision for you, but together we can arrive at and implement one").	Immediately following Counselor Behavior No. 3.	The student indicates that he understands the process.
5. Counselor explains the preparatory behaviors needed to make a good decision (i.e., he provides an overview of the counselor behaviors depicted below).	Immediately following Counselor Behavior No. 4.	The student states that he understands the process.
6. Counselor determines if the student has sufficient motivation (e.g., "How do you feel about proceeding along these lines?").	Usually after Counselor Behavior No. 5. May be repeated after subsequent Counselor Behaviors.	The student indicates willingness to proceed. (If the student hesitates, or is unwilling to proceed, then recycle to Counselor Behavior No. 2 or terminate.)
7. Counselor asks the student to identify all possible alternatives which come to mind.	The alternatives may be identified in the interview and/or as a between-interviews assignment.	The student compiles a complete list of alternatives (oral or written).

Table 14.1 (continued)

Counselor Behavior	Necessary Conditions	Criteria for Successful Performance
8. Counselor identifies any additional alternatives which come to his mind and are ethically appropriate.	Counselor exhibits this behavior only if criterion for No. 7 is considered to be inadequate by either the counselor or the student.	A joint list of alternatives is compiled.
9. Counselor assembles all relevant information about the student (e.g., test scores, academic performance, vocational experience and interests) from records and/or from student inquiry.	This information may be gathered during the interview or, if not immediately available, between interviews.	All existing relevant information about the student is available for discussion.
10. Counselor assembles additional information about the student (e.g., schedules further testing).	Counselor exhibits this behavior only if the criterion for No. 9 is considered to be inadequate by the counselor.	All relevant information is compiled.
11. Counselor presents to the student any information about the student relevant to the potential vocational decision (e.g., predictive statements derived from expectancy tables).	Immediately following Counselor Behaviors No. 9 and/or 10.	The student indicates that he understands this information.
12. Counselor requests that the student identify the advantages and disadvantages of the alternatives which have been identified.	During the interview (in the context of counselor-student discussion) and/or as a between-interviews assignment.	The student provides a set of such statements.
13. Counselor identifies any additional advantages and disadvantages which come to his mind.	Counselor exhibits this behavior only if the criterion for No. 12 is considered to be inadequate by either the counselor or the student.	A joint list of such statements is compiled.
14. Counselor asks the student to evaluate the alternatives (e.g., "In terms of what we know about you and the various alternatives, which alternatives seem most promising?").	Immediately following Counselor Behaviors No. 12 and/or 13.	The student rank orders the alternatives from most to least preferred.
15. Counselor helps the student obtain additional information about the most promising alternative(s) (e.g., He verbally reinforces the student for reading about the prospective profession(s) and talking to members of the prospective profession(s). He may also schedule modeling or simulation experiences for the student),	The additional information is usually accumulated outside of the counseling interview.	The student gathers this information or participates in the scheduled experiences.

Table 14.1 (continued)

Counselor Behavior	Necessary Conditions	Criteria for Successful Performance
16. Counselor helps the student implement the most promising alternative.	Immediately following Counselor Behavior No. 15.	A tentative course of action is selected and tried out.
17. Counselor determines if the selected alternative is satisfactory.	Immediately following Counselor Behavior No. 16.	The student reports that he is happy with the decision. (If not, recycle to Counselor Behavior No. 16, "next most promising alternative.")
18. Counselor terminates the counseling relationship.	Immediately following Counselor Behavior No. 17.	The student has learned the decision-making paradigm and is able to engage in independent action.

occupational choice limits are broadened, and effective career planning really becomes a part of life planning.

This broader perspective on career counseling has been recognized by the Association for Counselor Education and Supervision (ACES) of the American Personnel and Guidance Association. An ACES position paper (1976) recommends "that all students and adults should be provided with career guidance opportunities to ensure that they":

1. Understand that career development is a lifelong process based on an interwoven and sequential series of educational, occupational, leisure, and family choices.
2. Examine their own interests, values, aptitudes, and aspirations in an effort to increase self-awareness and self-understanding.
3. Develop a personally satisfying set of work values that leads them to believe that work, in some form, can be desirable to them.
4. Recognize that the act of paid and unpaid work has dignity.
5. Understand the role of leisure in career development.
6. Understand the process of reasoned decision-making and the ownership of those decisions in terms of their consequences.
7. Recognize that educational and occupational decisions are interrelated with family, work, and leisure.
8. Gather the kinds of data necessary to make well-informed career decisions.
9. Become aware of and explore a wide variety of occupational alternatives.
10. Explore possible rewards, satisfactions, lifestyles, and negative aspects associated with various occupational options.
11. Consider the probability of success and failure for various occupations.
12. Understand the important role of interpersonal and basic employability skills in occupational success.
13. Identify and use a wide variety of resources in the school and community to maximize career development potential.
14. Know and understand the entrance, transition, and decision points in education and the problems of adjustment that might occur in relation to these points.
15. Obtain chosen vocational skills and use available placement services to gain satisfactory entrance into employment in relation to occupational aspirations and beginning competencies.
16. Know and understand the value of continuing education to upgrade or acquire additional occupational skills or leisure pursuits.

Historically, the genesis of school counseling is "pure" career counseling. In the 1930s, many counselors began to realize that pure career counseling is a goal as illusory as the Loch Ness monster; consequently, they began to assimilate into career counseling those variables usually subsumed under the rubrics of educational counseling and personal-social counseling. This development did

Table 14.2

Examples of Self and Environmental Factors Influencing Career Choices

Personal Attribute Factors	Value Structure Factors	Opportunity Factors	Cultural Forces Factors
Intellectual ability	General values	Rural-Urban	Social class expectancies
Differential aptitudes	Work values	Accessibility of occupational	Family aspirations and
Skills	Life goals	opportunities	experiences
Achievements	Career goals	Accessibility of educational	Peer influences
Experiential history	Perceived prestige of	opportunities	Community attitudes and
Achievement motivation	occupations and curricula	Scope of occupational	orientation toward education
Responsibility	Stereotyped attitudes toward	opportunities	or work
Perseverance	occupations and curricula	Scope of educational	Teacher influences
Punctuality	Psychological centrality of	opportunities	Counselor influences
Warmth	occupations or curriculum	Requirements of occupations	General role model influences
Risk-taking proclivities	in values	Requirements of curricula	Image of educational or
Openness	People-data-things orientation	Availability of compensatory	occupational options within a
Rigidity	Attitudes toward work	programs	culture
Ego strength	Work ethic	Exposure to interventions	High school climate and reward
Self-esteem	Leisure	Status of the economy	system
Decision-making ability	Change needs		College climate and reward
Vocational maturity	Order needs		system
Sex	Nurturance needs		Primary referent groups
Race	Succorance needs		influences
Age	Power needs		
Physical strength	Stability		
Health	Security		
	Altruism		

not strike a responsive chord in some ardent vocationalists, one of whom wrote an article advocating that the schools rid themselves of a "piece of educational rubbish" — that rubbish being all counseling in the schools *except* career counseling (Kitson, 1934). In some respects, this argument has persisted to the present. Some individuals still regard career counseling, defined in a narrow sense, as the only legitimate work of school counselors; any other emphasis is looked on as at best secondary and at worst harmful. Such a perspective is poppycock. One must look to the total life goals of individuals and to their subsequent life styles. One must look to a host of personal and educational variables crucial to continuous career decision-making. One must adopt a career counseling viewpoint that is integrative.

As indicated earlier in this volume, there are those who consider career counseling "a great swindle," arguing that career choices defy logic and predictable order (Baumgardner, 1977). The great majority of counselors take a more informed and balanced view. They acknowledge that clients have limiting aspects (see Table 14.2), that counselors have their blind spots and limitations, and that the economy is virtually unpredictable; nevertheless, they point out that a broad view of career counseling, applied with skill, can do a great deal to mitigate malevolent and random influences on career development and choice and to help individuals to adapt to and cope with the buffetings of life. Parkinson, Bradley, and Lawson (1979), for example, suggest that career counselors can attack these influences by means of such counseling activities as: encouraging adventurous job exploration, teaching coping skills, assisting clients to make emotional evaluation explicit, and teaching "luck." Herr (1977) and Osipow (1977) provide further cogent argument to rebut the fatalistic approach of Baumgardner.

The Counselor and the Counselee's Internal Frame of Reference

If career counseling is regarded in the broad sense of the term and if career development and choice are more than the results of haphazard external events, then much of career counseling will be focused on the counselee's internal frame of reference. At the outset, the objectives of counseling include assisting the counselee to cast in bold relief those factors which are an amalgama-

tion of personal attributes, values, opportunities, and cultural factors (see Table 14.2). Over three decades ago, Super (1951) proposed a definition of career guidance that emphasized not solely the provision of occupational information at a particular time or a simple matching of person and job, but rather a "process of helping a person to develop and accept an integrated picture of himself and his role in the world of work, to test this concept against reality, and to convert it into a reality, with satisfaction to himself and to society" (p. 89). This definition blends those dimensions of counselors sometimes arbitrarily separated into the personal and the vocational (as we have seen), into a totality with interlocking relationships. Further, this process is seen as oriented to the self-concept, primarily focusing on self-understanding and self-acceptance. To these can be related the relevance of external factors, which define the environmental options available to the individual.

This approach also stresses the importance of counseling's resting on a base of self-attitudes and value sets, which the individual understands and accepts and uses to maximize his or her own freedom to choose the opportunities that seem to meet needs, desires, and inner urgings. In addition, a counseling relationship so defined means that the counselee and the counselor come to understand which personal characteristics are individual and unchangeable and which are modifiable. The counselee can then proceed from self-understanding to the matter of engaging in appropriate career-related behaviors.

Appraisal Information. In order to deal effectively with the latter dimension of the counseling process, the counselor will need to be an appraiser as well as an interpreter of data about the counselee. Essentially, three broad classes of information are important (Goldman, 1971). The order in which they are dealt with is in large measure a result of the individual counseling orientation.

The first set of appraisal information is concerned with personal attribute data — predictor variables. Given counselors may determine that they should begin counseling a given individual by presenting what they have learned about the counselee through information from tests of aptitude, achievement, interest, and personality; school grades; hobbies; work history; family background; expressed attitudes. Frequently, counselors who start from this base treat each of these pieces of information as fixed and unmodifiable, as having immutable relationship to certain future outcomes that the individual should consider. Because of the overwhelming amount of information that can be collected about a given individual, much of it may be irrelevant to the counselee's questions. Or, the counselee may accept the interpretation of the predictor variables as having a sophistication or expertness that permits him or her little room in which to maneuver. More important, counselees may play passive and dependent roles, awaiting with little personal investment or acceptance, the expert's judgment about what they can and cannot do or what they should do or should not do. Recall that counseling is an activity of mutual participation. Such a counseling orientation, however, places the counselor in the role of expert and the client in a subordinate, dependent position, thereby making participation less than mutual.

A second set of appraisal data relates to certain pathways which counselees might follow. Should they take vocational education? Should they take a specific educational sequence? Should they attend a post–high school business or trade school? Should they return to school? Should they change jobs? Should they go into the armed forces? Should they enter college? Some counselors may choose immediately to compare the requirements for each of these avenues with the information available about predictor variables that describe the particular counselee. This approach, like starting immediately with predictor variables, is a trait-and-factor approach which, if treated superficially or mechanically, can be irrelevant to the real issues. For example, students who ask where they should go to college may really be asking whether they should go to college at all. Or asking, Why are my parents so insistent on my attending college? Are there some other things I might do which can get me where I want to be? A counselor who senses the underlying questions may choose, instead of immediately turning to college catalogues and the predictor variables that describe the student, to help the student sort out what he or she would expect to gain as a result of pursuing one pathway rather than another. What outcomes does the counselee consider personally important values?

A third piece of appraisal information with which the counselor might begin are the outcomes that are of consequence to the person at his or her present level of development. What kind of person are you? What do you see as your major strengths and limitations? As you think about the future, are you primarily interested in obtaining satisfaction from the work activity in which you are engaged or from the work situation? Do you feel the need for regularity and security, or do you desire variety and change? Do you like to work alone or with others? Are you principally concerned with income levels? Prestige? What possible choices have you already considered and why? What are your values? What influences are most important to you as you have shaped personal answers to these questions — parents, peers, generalized attitudes in the community, etc.?

A Counseling Cycle. From the beginning of the counseling relationship, this approach encourages the counselee to tune in to himself or herself and to organize those parts of self and self-concept which one thinks are of most significance. Super (1957) addresses this point in the following manner:

> Since vocational development consists of implementing a self-concept, and since self-concepts often need modification before they can be implemented, it is important that the student, client, or patient put his self-concept into words early in the counseling process. He needs to do this for himself, to clarify his actual role and his role aspirations; he needs to do it for the counselor, so that the counselor may understand the nature of the vocational problem confronting him.

This calls for the cyclical use of nondirective and directive methods. Schematically, vocational counseling can be described as involving the following cycle:

1. nondirective problem exploration and self-concept portrayal
2. directive topic setting, for further exploring
3. nondirective reflection and clarification of feeling for self-acceptance and insight
4. directive exploration of factual data from tests, occupational pamphlets, extracurricular experiences, grades, etc., for reality testing

5. nondirective exploration and working through of attitudes and feelings aroused by reality testing
6. nondirective consideration of possible actions, for help in decision-making (p. 308)

Such a frame of reference then gives the counselor and the counselee an opportunity to identify those predictor variables and those avenues which appear to be most relevant to the counselee. Furthur, having such a frame of reference from which to operate allows the counselor to help the counselee identify and clarify possible distortions between his or her self-perception and the behavior that the information suggests.

For example, people who overestimate their mechanical skills may not perform very effectively as machinists. In other words, such individuals ascribe to themselves characteristics they actually do not possess. Following our previous line of thought, these counselees' personal characteristics and values do not seem to be congruent. Such a situation raises several questions for the counselor and the counselee. Is the degree to which one possesses mechanical skills modifiable? Are the elements of mechanical skills perceived by the counselor to be present but actually lacking a matter of spatial visualization, intelligence, manual dexterity, or experience? If the former types of variables are operative, the chances of becoming an effective machinist are minimal. If experience is the deficit, are there pathways in education or the community through which one can heighten skill proficiency through experience? Another question is, of course, What prompts the person to want to be a machinist? Is it the work activity or the work situation? Is it because the person knows people who are machinists and is influenced by them, or is it because the person has been told that machinists are in great demand and thus gain good income and security? Is it because the person wants to remain in the community and the machining industry is a prominent one? If the person is concerned about something besides the work activity as a machinist, are there other skills or strengths on which to capitalize to gain the same outcomes that were perceived to result from becoming a machinist?

The second part of this concern is that choosing an occupation also includes choosing a life style. In western culture, one is largely labeled by one's occupational title. From an existential frame of reference, Simon (1966) has contended that occupational choice is ultimately a result of an array of decisions leading to self-objectification. These sequential decisions give people the option of standing out as fully responsible before their peers, of being objectified, or of conforming to certain stereotypes that permit them to escape the painful process of having others see them as they really are. Hence, it is the ego strength they build and commit to these decisions that ultimately determines whether or not they are going to spend the rest of their lives in dynamically realizing their potential or spend it in the frustration of fighting their own innate drives toward fulfillment. But it must be realized that this, too, is an important ingredient of choice — deciding how much of self one desires to express in occupational commitment. How ego-involved is the counselee in work, in a choice of education or training, in school, in family? How committed is the individual? How committed can the individual become?

A counselor and a counselee need to understand that a measured interest may indicate that one will direct effort to an area but does not say how much effort will be applied to get there. To cite an extreme analogy, a person may have an interest in going to Tahiti, and this interest may remain constant throughout life. But interest alone does not indicate that the individual will take the steps or raise the finances to get to Tahiti. So it is with tentative occupational aspirations. Individuals will have to be helped to examine whether they have the dedicated involvement required by specific choice options. This, too, is a matter of values and characteristics of the self that may or may not be present or possible to acquire.

But the capacity for deep involvement relates also to the meaning one attaches to a particular life style. How important is it to a particular counselee to be tagged a machinist? Is it important enough to delay certain personal gratifications through a lengthy apprenticeship? Is it important enough to labor over applied mathematics or physics? Is it important enough to accept the midnight shift rather than "normal" work hours? Is it important enough to gamble on attaining seniority as security against layoffs? Is it important enough to practice being punctual, reliable, dependable? Is it important enough to try to be a machinist even if the odds are high against success? These are not necessarily the right questions, but they are all types of questions counselors and counselees must work through as personal attribute and value factors, as the self and the self-concept, are described and clarified. The process of doing so is the process of decision-making.

In other chapters of this text, we have reported research comparing the effectiveness of individual counseling with other helping modes in enhancing the career development and behaviors of counselees. Sometimes individual counseling is found to be less effective in achieving desired career-related goals than are structured workshops, seminars, courses, and other intervention methods. Herr (1976) has implied that such findings may be specious, because the counseling treatments are rarely as carefully and specifically defined as are the comparative intervention methods. In other words, the counseling treatment is frequently generic, broad, and unstructured, whereas the comparative treatment is goal specific, narrowly delimited, and structured.

Three recent reviews of career counseling outcome would appear to support Herr's speculations. Holland, Magoon, and Spokane (1981) concluded:

> The experimental evaluations of counselors, courses, career programs, card sorts, interest inventories, workshops, and related treatments imply that the beneficial effects are due to the common elements in these divergent treatments: (a) exposure to occupational information; (b) cognitive rehearsal of vocational aspirations; (c) acquisition of some cognitive structure for organizing information about self, occupations, and their relations; and (d) social support of reinforcement from counselors or workshop members. In addition, the strong tendency to find some positive effects for both diffuse interventions . . . and specific interventions . . . occurs because the average client knows so little about career decision making and career problems that a small amount of new information and support makes a difference.

At the same time, the general failure to find different effects for different treatments demonstrates a large hole in our understanding of client-treatment interactions and indicates the need for more analytical and less shot-gun evaluation (pp. 285–286).

Fretz (1981) also concluded that most career interventions (individual counseling, group-oriented, or self-directed) appear to be beneficial and that there is no consistent body of data to suggest that any one mode of intervention is more effective than any other. Fretz attributed the lack of differential outcome to the failure of researchers to explicitly describe treatments, client characteristics, and outcomes; lack of nonrandom assignment of subjects to treatments; attempts to manipulate too many variables; use of a single outcome criterion rather than several; and nonreporting of intercorrelations among variables.

Finally, Spokane and Oliver (1983) reviewed career counseling outcome studies by calculating effect sizes (difference between the mean of a treated group and mean of a control group divided by the standard deviation of the control group on a given outcome measure). This procedure yields a finer delineation of differences between groups in a meta-analysis. On the basis of this more elegant statistical treatment of the data, the authors reached the following conclusions regarding differential effectiveness:

1. Clients receiving any vocational intervention are better off, on the average, than 81 percent of the untreated controls.
2. Clients receiving individual vocational interventions are better off, on the average, than 79 percent of untreated controls.
3. Clients receiving group/class vocational interventions are better off, on the average, than more than 89 percent of untreated controls.
4. Clients receiving a variety of alternative treatment (for example, computer-assisted, audio-taped, self-directing) are, on the average, better off than 59 percent of untreated controls.

All in all, the research on career counseling outcome is comforting and, taken as a whole, provides powerful documentation for the continued existence of legitimate career helping. It is, whatever the reasons, clearly more persuasive than outcome research in any other subset of human intervention activity.

Decision-Making

In Chapter 4, we presented a review of decision-making theories of career choice. Chapters relating to the provision of career guidance services from elementary school through adulthood each stress, in varying degrees, the importance of decision-making skills. Decision-making is a learned process crucial to career choice and behavior. Therefore, the nature of decision-making and its relationship to helping strategies is discussed below.

Classifications. For purposes of explication, decision-making can be classified in several ways. First, we may consider *institutional decisions* versus *individual decisions.* The former relate to judgments that affect organized groups of people; the latter pertain to choices that have largely personal consequence. The literature of management and administration is replete with discussions of institutional decision-making, and the findings are summarized herein as they relate to effecting systematic service delivery within such institutions as schools, colleges, agencies, and others. Second, we may regard decision-making methodology in terms of *mathematical model decisions* versus *nonmathematical model* decisions. Mathematical decisions rely mainly on the rigid logic of the calculus of probability, whereas nonmathematical decisions are the result of a less formal symbolic logic. Statisticians tend to be skeptical of any decision theory that cannot be realized mathematically and experimentally; they assume complete information and rationality. Since human beings are sometimes not rational, and since they frequently make choices on the basis of incomplete information, decision-making is often more psychological than logical, and less rigorous methods are employed. These nonmathematical models of decision-making are usually called *descriptive* models. Thirdly, we may speak of *group decision-making* versus *individual decision making.* Here we are concerned with the process of decision-making. The literature of social psychology and group dynamics suggests that under certain types of conditions and for specified types of problems, groups consistently outperform individuals in decision-making. Unfortunately, career choice is not one of those problems; it tends to be approached individually and, of course, it should be. Finally, we may regard *decisions under certainty* versus *decisions under risk.* In the former, an individual or institution will know with absolute certainty that a decision will be followed by a 100 percent probability of a given consequence. This state is often not so simple as it appears, for there may

be many consequences possible, each a virtual certainty, and choice must still be made. In the latter case the degree of risk may range from a knowledge of different probabilities of occurrence to complete uncertainty.

When we speak of an individual and career-related choices, then, we refer to individual decisions that are basically nonmathematical in a formal sense (although probability data may be available), which are individually effected, and which, typically, are made under conditions of risk.

In terms of conditions of risk, we may think of four possibilities. *Certainty* is that condition described above wherein choice A will surely lead to event B. *Objective probability* is a condition of risk wherein an individual becomes informed of the "odds" relating to the consequences emanating from the making of a given decision. Largely by the use of regression equations or less formal expectancy tables, individuals can be compared with others having similar characteristics and can be given relatively objective, actuarial probabilities of success or failure in some future event. *Subjective probability* is a risk condition in which individuals translate objective probabilities into personal or psychological terms. They may overestimate low probabilities or underestimate high ones, depending on their propensities for risk-taking and other factors. *Uncertainty* is a risk condition that exists when the consequences of a decision are not completely known or when the probabilities suggest that the outcome desired is not totally certain.

One of the aims of career counselors is to remove as much uncertainty as possible. The counselor accomplishes this condition by assisting the individual to grasp the objective probabilities (aptitudes, interests, work opportunities, education and training opportunities, and such) and to understand the manner how these objective data may be subjectively or psychologically processed (attitudes, values, aspirations, and others). To do so requires a strategy for decision-making.

In their review of the literature relating to career decision-making models, Jepsen and Dilley (1974, p. 335) concluded that these models:

- are similar in many ways to decision theory and to each other but certainly not to the point where parts of one can be interchanged for parts of another
- vary substantially on their assumptions about

the decision-maker and the conditions under which the decision is made

- are applicable to different types of decisions
- are more complementary than competitive

They consider both long-range and short-range changes in the individual and combine this "distance in time" dimension with an "amount of understanding" or informational dimension in the schematic diagram shown in Figure 14.1.[1]

Assumptions underlying intervention strategies. Hence, the decision-making model that the counselor chooses to utilize may well depend on the particular stage of career development of the individual in relation to the immediacy of the career-related decision and the amount of information the individual is assumed to possess. Whatever model one chooses, however, there are certain basic assumptions that undergird all intervention strategies in assisting individuals to make decisions.

1. Many factors in decision-making will be outside the control of the decider. These factors include such variables as the state of the economy and accessibility of education and training opportunities.

2. Individuals are rarely able to acquire and to process *all* relevant information in making some career-related decisions. They will tend to select out those data which they deem important or readily available, or someone else thinks are important. This condition leads to what Simon (1960) has termed "the principle of bounded

rationality," whereby individuals typically realize their inability to acquire the entirety of information and to define the complete range of possible outcomes, and so settle for a strategy of decision-making that will lead to "good enough" decisions. Subsequently, that "good enough" decision may lead to what Festinger (1957) has described as "cognitive dissonance," a rationalization process in which decisions made on the basis of bounded rationality are justified as the best decisions possible. Janis and Mann (1977) describe this process as "bolstering."

3. Decisions will generally be made under a condition of suboptimization (Miller & Starr, 1967). People usually have many objectives; to choose one is to lower the probability of attaining others. Choice optimizes the chances of a given outcome occurring and simultaneously suboptimizes the chances of conflicting outcomes. This condition suggests that short-range decisions that may seem good when they are made may be suboptimizing in the sense that they seriously affect the flexibility of a long-range plan.

4. The evaluation of a career-related decision is frequently more a matter of process than of outcome (Dilley, 1967). If outcome is employed as the criterion of a good career decision, then one must look to long-range favorable results. Counselors seldom have that luxury. As a result, process criteria are more frequently used. We tend to judge a career-related decision as "good," if it is logical and consistent when it is made or if it was the consequence of prescribed procedures and consonant with some specific model of decision-making. It is possible, then, for decisions that are judged "good" when they are made in terms of the process to be ultimately "bad" decisions in terms of outcome; conversely, it is possible, though unlikely, that "good" outcomes can result from "bad" process.

5. Individuals can be taught how to make career-related decisions. There are dozens of decision-making programs, each different yet each similar, that have reported at least short-range success. Some of these paradigms will be discussed later in this chapter. Further, there is evidence that, once taught, a decision-making strategy and skills in decision-making have transfer value (Evans & Cody, 1969).

6. Although we know that a great variety of factors influence individual career decision-making,

---

[1] Among the models used to evolve the diagram were the following: D. V. Tiedeman and R. P. O'Hara, *Career Development: Choice and Adjustment*, New York: College Entrance Examination Board, 1963; T. L. Hilton, "Career Decision-Making," *Journal of Counseling Psychology*, **19**, 1962, 291–298; V. H. Vroom, *Work and Motivation*, New York: Wiley, 1964; C. C. Hsu, "A Conceptual Model of Vocational Decision-Making," *Experimental Publication System*, **9**, 1970, Ms. #270–276; F. M. Fletcher, "Concepts, Curiosity, and Careers," *Journal of Counseling Psychology*, **13**, 1966, 131–138; M. R. Katz, "The Name and Nature of Vocational Guidance," in H. Borow (Ed.), *Career Guidance for a New Age*, Boston: Houghton Mifflin, 1973; H. B. Gelatt, "Decision-Making: A Conceptual Frame of Reference for Counseling," *Journal of Counseling Psychology*, **9**, 1962, 240–245; D. R. Kaldor and D. G. Zytowski, "A Maximizing Model of Occupational Decision-Making," *Personnel and Guidance Journal*, **47**, 1969, 781–788.

Figure 14.1

Theoretical Vocational Decision Types

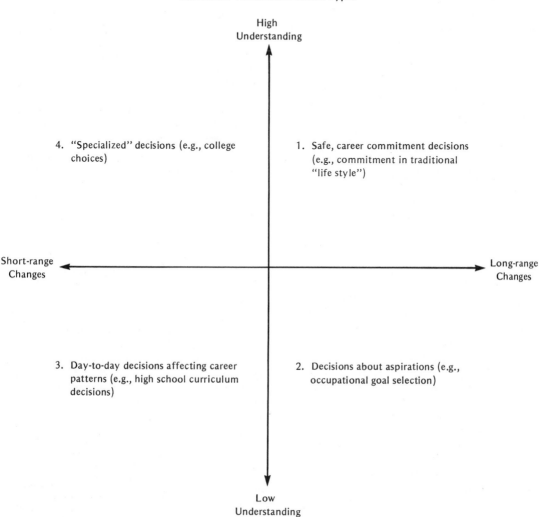

High
Understanding

4. "Specialized" decisions (e.g., college choices)

1. Safe, career commitment decisions (e.g., commitment in traditional "life style")

Short-range Changes

Long-range Changes

3. Day-to-day decisions affecting career patterns (e.g., high school curriculum decisions)

2. Decisions about aspirations (e.g., occupational goal selection)

Low
Understanding

we do not presently have any definitive indication of which factors predominate for which individual under what conditions and of how these differential weightings evolve. We know relatively little about the correlates of decision-making (O'Neill et al., 1980). There is some evidence to suggest that the following factors bear a relationship to decision-making abilities: values (Katz, 1966, 1980; Blaikie, 1971); propensity for risk (Slakter & Cramer, 1969; Davidshofer, 1976); achievement motivation (Wish & Hasazi, 1973; Tseng & Carter,

1970); and age (Okun, 1976; Guttmann, 1978). Among the factors that have been investigated and for which the relationship with decision-making is conflicting or unclear are: sex (Fox, 1973–1974; Milley & Bee, 1982; Harren, Kass, Tinsley, & Moreland, 1978; Lunneborg, 1978; Moreland, Harren, Krimsky-Montague, & Tinsley, 1979; Barrett & Tinsley, 1977; Neice & Bradley, 1979; Slaney, 1980; Foote, 1980; Sacks & Eisenstein, 1979; Brenner & Gazda-Grace, 1979); interests (Lowe, 1981; Lunneborg, 1975); vocational maturity (Holland & Holland, 1977; Phillips & Strohmer, 1982: Ware, 1980); anxiety (Hawkins, Bradley, White, 1977; Brown & Strange, 1981); and self-esteem (Gordon, 1981; Super & Hall, 1978; Barrett & Tinsley, 1977). In the final analysis, there may be several correlates (O'Neil et al., 1980).

7. We do not have a clear notion of why deciding individuals emphasize one or another of these factors or others and how that situation develops. It is possible to construct a taxonomy that delineates the kinds of influences that impinge on career decision-making. The interaction of these internal and external variables is paramount in the decision-making process. Personal attributes and characteristics, value structures, opportunity factors, and cultural forces, separately and in combination, are brought to bear in decisions (see Table 14.2). Their combination, weighting, and content vary from individual to individual.

This fact has led some researchers to propose a taxonomy of decision-making *styles*. Arroba (1977) proposed six styles of decision-making:

Logical – situation appraised coldly and objectively, choice made on the basis of what is best
No thought – no objective consideration
Hesitant – postponement of final commitment to an alternative, inability to make a decision
Emotional – decision based on what the person subjectively wants or likes
Compliant – decision made in accordance with the perceived expectations of the situation or of others, passivity
Intuitive – decision based only on a personal feeling of rightness or inevitability (p. 151)

Her proposals were later tested and basically confirmed by Hesketh (1982). Janis and Mann (1977), who have produced some of the most significant work in decision-making, have suggested four defective patterns of decision-making:

Unconflicted adherence – The individual simply denies any serious risks from current course of action.
Unconflicted change to new course of action – The individual simply denies any serious risks in making a decision or change.
Defense avoidance – The individual avoids any-

thing that might stimulate choice anxiety or painful feelings and gives up looking for a solution.
Hypervigilance – The individual becomes extremely emotionally excited as the time constraints of decision-making are made more pressing.

Harren (1979) offered three vocational decision-making styles in undergraduate students: (1) *rational*, involving objective deliberation and self-appraisal; (2) *intuitive*, involving emotional self-awareness and fantasy; and (3) *dependent*, involving denial of responsibility. This classification system has been the focus of corroborative research by Rubinton (1980), who suggests that rational decision-makers do best with rational interventions whereas intuitive decision-makers do best with intuitive interventions, and by Harren, Kass, Tinsley, and Moreland (1978), Lunneborg (1976), and Daniels (1982).

Finally, Jepsen (1974) has conducted some extremely interesting preliminary research which attempts to identify specific career decision-making styles or "strategy-types" in adolescents. Looking at the way adolescents organized data about themselves and career options, he clustered similar groups of decision-makers into twelve types of decision structures that reflect differences in planning activity and post–high school plans with a few differences in long-range plans. Of the twelve types, several are outlined below for illustration.

Strategy-Type 3. Sought little career information and viewed few current actions as relevant to planning. Considered only a few occupational alternatives and few reasons for considering either occupations or post–high school actions. Few outcomes were anticipated for preferred post–high school activity.
Strategy-Type 6. Named many alternative occupations and post–high school activities and reasons for each. Many possible outcomes were anticipated, many intrinsic and self-appraised reasons were given. Planning activity was very high.
Strategy-Type 9. Very few actions were taken on plans and little information was sought. Vaguely stated and low-level occupational alternatives were reported, and a single class of reasons was given for considering them.

These attempts at describing decision-making styles differ in terms of the population from which they were derived (secondary school students, college students, adults), the time involved (one point in time or a span of time), and the methodological design. Each, however, offers some potentially fruitful areas for further investigation.

8. Each model of career decision-making assumes motivation or tries to establish readiness on the part of the chooser to take responsibility for career decisions. Too frequently, career guidance is analogous to the Boy Scout who helped the "little old lady" across the street — when she did not want to go. The intentions are good, but the perceived needs of the person being assisted are ignored, or the individual is not helped to internalize the importance of the choices which must be made.

Some Approaches. These commonalities, then, cut across all programs for teaching decision-making. Some of the better known of the decision-making approaches were described in Chapter 4; others will be described below or are treated more fully in order to demonstrate how particular theoretical emphases get translated into practice.

Martin Katz of the Educational Testing Service has spent years developing a system with which to assist two-year college students in the career decision-making process (Katz, 1973, 1980). Katz works from the assumption that values are the major synthesizing force in decision-making. "The basic choice is essentially a choice between arrays of values, or value systems" (1973, p. 116). Consequently, he has constructed the System of Interactive Guidance and Information (SIGI), a computer-based process designed to help students to examine their values, to explore options, to retrieve information that is related to their values, and to get relevant interpretations of the data. In effect, students are learning a strategy for relating information to values and are thus increasing their competence in decision-making. Students may go through the system as often as they like, each time taking an active role in controlling inputs. It is, in fact, a humanistically conceived interactive system which attempts, by means of a detailed exposition of objectives, scope, and sequence, to assist individuals to:

- understand the sequential nature of choices
- gain a knowledge of options in the domain of human values
- recognize that value systems can change
- become aware of the full array of conditions of work and attitudes toward work
- grasp the rewards and satisfactions characteristic of each specific option at each choice point so the individual can detect the fit of these characteristics to his own values as he perceives them at that time
- become aware of the cost and consequences of each decision
- know and understand the probabilities of entry and success in each option considered at any choice point
- acquire information about ways and means of proceeding (1973, pp. 122–123)

Katz's computer-based system of value-oriented decision-making is given independent support by Blaikie (1971). An Australian sociologist, Blaikie has devised a theoretical model of occupational choice centered on values, for which he has gathered some empirical support in relation to career choices in higher education. His theoretical model contains eight propositions:

1. Individuals have goals and seek means to realize them; action is goal-oriented.
2. The values which an individual holds determine the relative importance given to these goals; individuals give highest priority to those goals which accord with the values they hold.
3. Values are internalized, initially, during primary socialization as a part of an individual's symbolic universe, and are subsequently either modified by processes of secondary socialization or largely replaced by re-socialization.
4. Individuals choose an occupation in which they perceive they can realize the occupational goals which they give the highest priority.
5. When individuals perceive restrictions related to their possible employment in occupations which are seen to accord best with their high priority occupational goals, they will choose an occupation which they perceive will be least likely to hinder the realization of their high priority occupational goals; they will minimize value deprivation.

6. Students enter university as inhabitants of diverse symbolic universes.
7. During their university course, secondary socialization, and perhaps re-socialization occurs, entailing a change in goal priorities.
8. Therefore, changes in occupational choice between entering and leaving university may be determined by:
   a. Changes in goal priorities;
   b. Changes in the perception of the possibility of realizing high priority goals in the occupation chosen initially;
   c. Changes in the perception of the probability of obtaining employment in an occupation (pp. 317–318).

Hence, the content of career decision-making might well place a high emphasis on values and valuing. Further, Katz has demonstrated that an interactive, computer-based system can be used as an aid in teaching a decision-making strategy.

Another career-related decision-making process is based on the idea of diverse types of information being equally important as content and on a problem-solving strategy of making choices (Hamilton & Jones, 1971). This problem-solving model contains six skill areas.

Skill Area #1: *Understanding the Problem* – Being willing to work toward setting and achieving educational and vocational goals.

Skill Area #2: *Searching for and Using Information* – (a) Personal information on abilities, interests, preferences, etc., and (b) information about related opportunities in the worlds of education and work.

Skill Area #3: *Getting Alternatives* – Thinking of several possible educational and vocational goals.

Skill Area #4: *Selecting Goals and Making Plans* – (a) Choosing the goals (first and second choice) that seem like the best bet for the individual, and (b) making plans for reaching them.

Skill Area #5: *Carrying Out Plans* – Carrying out plans, switching to a second best goal if necessary.

Skill Area #6: *Finding Out If It Works* – (a) Judging whether the first (or the second best) goal has been achieved, and (b) describing what helped and what hindered the individual's efforts along the way.

The College Entrance Examination Board has published a series of workbooks designed to help individuals learn a process with which to make decisions. Junior high school students can use *Deciding* (Gelatt, Varenhorst, & Carey, 1972); *Decisions and Outcomes* (Gelatt, Varenhorst, Carey, & Miller, 1973) is intended for older students and adults; and females can employ *How to Decide: A Guide for Women* (Scholz, Prince, & Miller, 1975).

Deciding and *Decisions and Outcomes* are practical implementations of the model of decision-making devised by Gelatt et al. and described in Chapter 4. They take students and adults through a systematic process for making decisions. *Deciding* is divided into three units: values, information, and strategy. Through various exercises, discussions, outside activities, role-playing, and simulations, the user is given practice in employing a learned decision-making process. Clear and concise behavioral goals are stated for each unit. The complete program can be implemented in as few as fifteen or as many as forty-five class periods.

The values component includes:

- the importance of values in the decision-making process
- the individual, personal nature of values
- a definition of values
- recognition of values in others
- clarification of own values
- identification of values of groups
- converting values into objectives for use in making decisions

The information component includes:

- possible alternative actions
- possible outcomes (consequences of various actions)
- probability of outcomes (relationship between actions and outcomes)
- desirability of outcomes (personal preferences)

The strategy phase of the program includes:

- conditions of risk and certainty
- common strategies (such as wish, safe, escape, combination, impulsive, fatalistic)

Figure 14.2 represents a typical exercise from *Deciding*.

Figure 14.2

Using Values in Making Decisions

Listed below are some typical values of both adults and teenagers. They are based on what a group of teenagers have said are typical values. There probably are others that you feel are more important.

Opinion of others	Family	Independence
Prestige and recognition	Honesty	Money
Helping others	Creativity	Education
Immediate pleasure		Responsibility

Read over the stories that follow. They are about people who have to make decisions. Choose what *you* think the person would decide under the circumstances. Write that decision in the proper space. Select from the list of values above the value you think that decision represents. If you do not find one there that you think fits, write in your idea of the value.

1. Mr. Slagel is production editor at Straightforth Publications, Inc. He is making $18,000 a year, enjoying the chance to write, use his creative ideas, and see some of them developed. His oldest son will be entering college next September, which will be a drain on the family finances. There are four other children in the family. He is called into the president's office and offered the job of assistant vice-president at a salary of $30,000 a year. He would be handling financial accounts, personnel problems, and sales. There would not be time for creative work and the parts of his job he enjoys.

   Mr. Slagel decides to_____

   He values_____

2. Susan is interested in music and has studied the violin for the past four years. She also enjoys children—babysitting with them, teaching them, playing with them. In May, she is invited to join the community chamber group for the summer. She would be paid $2 an hour. At the same time she is asked to be recreational leader working with handicapped children. She would be paid $2 an hour for the recreational job too. She is not able to accept both invitations.

   Susan decides to_____

   She values_____

3. John is great at working on cars and engines. Next year his high school is starting a new course in auto mechanics. He has one elective not committed to subjects he absolutely has to take. However, he wants to go to the state university, which requires that he take another year of foreign language. John's decision is what course to take for that elective.

   John decides to_____

   He values_____

4. While in his junior year, Joe was thrown out of high school because he got into a fight with his shop teacher. For several months afterwards he did odd jobs and hung out with a few of his friends on his street. Later he and one of his friends were arrested for disturbing the peace. Given a choice between going to jail, returning to school, or joining the army, he enlisted. Since returning from Vietnam, Joe has worked as a dishwasher, delivery boy, hospital attendant, and volunteer playground supervisor. None of these jobs lasted more than three months. Joe would like to do something with himself, perhaps continue with training like that he received in the Army as a medic. But his friends aren't very helpful, and Joe doesn't feel he has much of a chance to improve his present situation.

   Joe decides to_____

   He values_____

Decisions and Outcomes and *How to Decide: A Guide for Women* are expanded and more sophisticated workbooks that are structured in similar ways to *Deciding*. That is, they encourage the clarification of values, the use of relevant information, and the development of a decision-making strategy. Content in *How to Decide* is geared specifically for females. These very well conceived and executed workbooks exemplify systematic efforts to teach the art of decision-making in a logical, ordered manner. They are illustrative of many similar programs that are available and are listed in Chapter 16.

A cross-cultural decision-making program in workbook format is worthy of mention because it is a very well done attempt to operationalize a theoretical approach to decision-making. Bearing some resemblance to the College Board products, this program was devised for use in Great Britain and certain Commonwealth countries. Called *Decide for Yourself* (Law, 1973), it is divided into five stages: (1) influences and choices; (2) values and needs; (3) abilities, skills, and qualifications; (4) personal styles; and (5) focus. Students actively participate in self-assessment, determine values and influences, and are helped to relate these types of knowledge to the world of work.

Janis and Mann (1977) propose five distinct stages of decision-making: (1) appraising the challenge; (2) surveying alternatives; (3) weighing alternatives; (4) deliberating about commitment; and (5) adhering despite negative feedback. Within this system, a feedback loop permits reversions to earlier stages. The evaluation of a "good" decision is conducted in terms of seven specific criteria:

1. thoroughly canvasses a wide range of alternative courses of action
2. surveys the full range of objectives to be fulfilled and the values implicated by choice
3. carefully weighs whatever he knows about the costs and risks of negative consequences, as well as the positive consequences, that could flow from each alternative
4. intensively searches for new information relevant to further evaluation of the alternatives
5. correctly assimilates and takes account of any new information or expert judgment to which he is exposed, even when the information or judgment does not support the course of action he initially prefers
6. reexamines the positive and negative consequences of all known alternatives, including those originally regarded as unacceptable, before making a final choice
7. makes detailed provisions for implementing or executing the chosen course of action, with special attention to contingency plans that might be required if various known risks were to materialize (p. 11).

Harren (1966, 1979) offers a model of decision-making that includes stages of awareness, planning, commitment, and implementation. Within this context, self-esteem and identity are thought to be important. The tasks of decision-making are to achieve autonomy, interpersonal maturity, and a sense of purpose. Harren describes the model in terms of four conditions: (1) *interpersonal evaluation* (positive and negative feedback); (2) *psychological states* (level of anxiety); (3) *tasks conditions* (specific career relevant tasks, defined in terms of imminence, alternatives, and consequences); and (4) *context conditions* (interpersonal relationships defined in terms of mutuality, support, and probability. Pitz and Harren (1980) suggest that a "good" decision under these circumstances should be evaluated in terms of four behavioral criteria:

1. *Information-seeking.* What information has the person sought about alternatives being considered?
2. *Range of alternatives.* How many and what variety of choices has the person identified and considered?
3. *Knowledge of alternatives.* How much knowledge does the person have about the choices and how accurate is it?
4. *Rationality of choice.* How consistent is the person's behavior with the principles of expected utility theory?

Each of the preceding programs demands counselee involvement in the actual choice process. Other programs are more mechanistic, in the sense that the program has inherent in it the capacity to make the actual choice. Holland's *Self-Directed Search* (1970), for example, processes student input data in such a way that choices on the basis of the data provided by the users are fed back to them for further exploration. In a sense, the system processes the data and makes the choices for the user rather than the user processing the data and making the choice. Even in this type of system, however, the user must subsequently choose from among the alternatives suggested by the mechanical processing.

Common to virtually all of these career decision-making programs and to other not specifically described here are several foci: (1) a knowledge of self, variously defined, but usually including aptitudes, interests, achievements, personality characteristics, attitudes and values, with different emphases placed on each by different programs; (2) a knowledge of the world of work, variously described, but according to some generally accepted classification system (such as *DOT*, cluster, field and level, and others) and including work-related factors (such as rewards of work, requirements of work, and others); and (3) a decision-making strategy, variously conceived, but usually entailing a step-by-step, rational, logical, by-the-numbers procedure. Currently, no career decision-making system has been proven to be more effective than any other, although each lays claim to success. Comparative studies in this regard would prove interesting and useful.

On the other hand, these models of decision-making differ on a variety of parameters. First, they vary in nature: mathematical or descriptive. Second, they vary in terms of the decision-making variables that are considered most important (values, interests, self-concept, abilities, motivation). Third, they differ in terms of the emphasis placed on environmental variables (economics, cultural factors, social conditions, residence). Fourth, they diverge in their assessment of the amount and type of information necessary for good decision-making. Fifth, they place differing accent on the probability factor. Sixth, they differ in their perception of the stages that decision-makers experience. Finally, they differ in terms of evaluation (for example, outcome or process).

We have been addressing the concept of career decision-making programs that can be used with individuals but are, basically, designed to be uti-lized with groups. Of course, a decision-making model also can be effected in individual counseling. For example, Krumboltz (1966) has urged that if one of the goals of counseling is learning the decision-making process, then such counseling goals as the following should be explicit:

- generating a list of possible courses of action
- gathering information about each feasible alternative course of action
- estimating the probability of success in each alternative on the basis of the experience of others and projections of current trends
- considering the personal values that may be enhanced or diminished under each course of action
- deliberating and weighing the facts, probable outcomes, and values for each alternative
- eliminating from consideration the least favorable courses of action
- formulating a tentative plan of action subject to new developments and opportunities
- generalizing the decision-making process to future problems.

Bergland (1974), in a thoughtful review and synthesis of the career decision-making literature, has suggested that the basic strategy of decision-making is problem-solving. Consequently, he offers a series of stages that the decision-maker should be helped to negotiate:

1. defining the problem
2. generating alternatives
3. gathering information
4. developing information-seeking skills
5. providing useful sources of information
6. processing information
7. making plans and selecting goals
8. implementing and evaluating plan (p. 352).

Almost every decision-making approach in career counseling and guidance is directed toward narrowing down choices. However, there are exceptions. For example, Frederickson, Rowley and McKay (1975) argue that since individuals are "multipotential" (that is, they can respond adequately to a variety of appropriate environments), they can, in fact, rely on chance or accident. They will be capable of adapting and developing the necessary skills to perform well in almost any occupation. If this be so, the funneling type of decision-making is inappropriate. Rather, a five-stage process is used by the counselor in getting individuals to recognize their own flexibility and elasticity in anticipating and in dealing with change:

1. *Readiness:* the building of vocational maturity, wherein the individual gains a social, physical, and psychological acceptance of the responsibility for implementing a career decision
2. *Awareness:* of self and of the world of work
3. *Exploration:* a systematic and planned inquiry into the world of work with a wide view and examination of different occupations
4. *Reality testing:* balancing choices within a risk-taking structure
5. *Confirmation:* a particular time in which a career decision is confirmed (p. 37).

Although this five-stage process is intended to be a developmental experience throughout formal schooling, the implication is that it can be accelerated by intensive counseling.

Some models of career decision-making do not focus on the totality of choice. Instead, they emphasize decision-making in a particular segment of career choice. Such a model is described by Weissman and Krebs (1976) in their approach, which begins with self-exploration and ends with establishing alternatives. Remember that most career decision-making paradigms insist that individuals choose from among alternatives. Here, generating alternatives in problem-solving is emphasized rather than the more common procedure of selecting a few from among the many alternatives. In individual counseling, students are encouraged to imagine future-oriented, ideal career situations; then they are asked to select one idea and to translate it into goal language (what they specifically might do to implement the idea). Then they are assisted to imagine all of their strengths that would help reach the goal and all weaknesses that would prevent the reaching of the goal. The relative strengths of each positive and negative factor are then plotted in a sort of force-field analysis. The strongest weakness or block is selected for focus regarding ways to remove or to weaken the block. Finally, an action plan is evolved to answer pertinent questions: Where do I begin? How do I begin (letter, tele-

phone, meeting)? In short, students are assisted to engage in "introspective dialogue" to aid in problem resolution and to develop career alternatives.

Other individual counseling approaches for decision-making use various terminology descriptive of the process. Thomas (1972) refers to "feasible alternatives" counseling, a system based on a rational, active student-counselor partnership in which the emotional loading of alternative courses of action is assessed and transferability to noneducational or noncareer concerns is emphasized. The counselor and the counselee discuss in depth the feasible alternatives. Counselees keep a written record of the process for future use. Magoon (1969) suggests a decision-making counseling process called Effective Problem-Solving (EPS), a twelve-step, question-stimulated, workbook system. Mitchell (1973) speaks of "catalytic counseling" as a method for teaching students how to decide. This process is based on the application of computer systems, but the application is clinical and no hardware is used. Rather, the counselor programs facts to students and helps them personalize the data. The counselor acts as a catalyst to stimulate persons to think about any event in terms of the alternatives in their unique situations. A final illustration is Nelson's (1976) concept of "choice awareness," a decision-making paradigm for elementary school children. An outgrowth of Transactional Analysis principles, the model overarches all types of choices, only one of which is pertinent to career and educational decision-making. It addresses choices related to caring, ruling, enjoying, sorrowing, and thinking/working. It is the latter choice category that pertains largely to career behaviors. "Positive and negative options are examined, the consequences of each are explored, and the responsibility for choice-making is left squarely to the individual whose choice it is" (p. 463).

In summary, all of these decision-making models for use in individual counseling are action-oriented. By whatever terminology they are called, they address choice in a staged, systematic manner. They are intended to assist individuals in filtering objective data through subjective systems of risk-taking, emotionality, utility determination, and so on. Again, no single model has been determined to be superior to any other; yet each implies its unique success. They suggest to counselors that virtually any model of assisting an individual in career decision-making — extant or yet to be invented — can be successful if based on sound theoretical and research findings, and if operationalized in logical, consistent ways.

Indecision and Indecisiveness. Before leaving the topic of decision-making, it is necessary to point out the difference between undecidedness and indecisiveness and to describe several recent decision scales that are largely in the experimental stage. Crites (1969) has defined *indecision* as "the inability of the individual to select, or commit himself to a particular course of action which will eventuate in his preparing for and entering a specific occupation" (p. 305). He specifies three possibilities for indecision: (1) the multipotential individual who is unable to designate one goal from among many choices; (2) the undecided individual who cannot make a choice from among available alternatives; and (3) the uninterested individual who is uncertain about a choice because of lack of an appropriate interest pattern. In contrast, *indecisiveness* emanates from general personal problems rather than from doubts related to a specific career choice, perhaps because of the pain involved in decision-making. In indecision there may be lack of information or knowledge of how to sort through alternatives; in indecisiveness a generally dysfunctional personality orientation may cause such choice anxiety that an individual is rendered incapable of making a decision. Seldom are these distinctions made explicit when, for example, counselors speak of decided and undecided students.

Several decision scales are now being used, largely for experimental and research purposes. Osipow, Carney, Winer, Yanico, and Koschir (1976) are responsible for the Career Decision Scale (CDS), a sixteen-item instrument designed originally for college students. It yields scores for four types of indecision: (1) lack of structure (lack of confidence, choice anxiety, potential choice avoidance); (2) perceived external barriers (for example, financial or parental); (3) approach-approach (difficulty in deciding among alternatives; and (4) personal conflict (difficulty choosing between occupations that reflect differing personal values) (Osipow, 1980). A study by

Barak and Friedkes (1981) found that clients who basically lacked structure received most benefit from counseling; those in the personal conflict and perceived external barrier categories gained the least from counseling. Other studies (Hartman & Hartman, 1982; Hartman, Utz, & Farnum, 1979) apply the scale to both high school students and graduate students.

Another decision scale is the Vocational Decision-Making Difficulty Scale (VDMD) developed by John Holland (Holland, Gottfredson, & Nafziger, 1975). Slaney, Palko-Nonemaker, and Alexander (1981) identified four factors of indecision measured by this scale: (1) lack of information; (2) lack of clarity of an individual's place in the world of work; (3) choice anxiety; and (4) questions about ability. Slaney (1980) and Slaney, Palko-Nonemaker, and Alexander (1981) discovered significant differences between the VDMD and the CDS. Holland, Gottfredson, and Power (1980) categorized decision-making difficulties as: (1) problems of vocational identification, (2) lack of information or training, (3) environmental or personal barriers, and (4) no problems. In an earlier study (Holland & Holland, 1977) a large majority of an undecided group were identified as simply delaying decisions until reality demanded action. Their indecision was not a matter of lack of information or immaturity. They believe that some students suffer, however, from an "indecisive disposition" resulting from a failure to acquire the necessary cultural participation, self-confidence, tolerance for ambiguity, concept of identity, and environmental and self-knowledge necessary for decision-making. The point that indecision is not necessarily pathological is well taken and should temper the tendency of counselors to feel that decisions need to be made before they are necessary. After all, almost three out of every four college freshmen express some form of indecision, tentativeness, or uncertainty about selecting a major (Titley & Titley, 1980; Grites, 1981; Menning & Whittmayer, 1979).

A third scale, the Vocational Decision Scale (VDS), has been developed by Jones and Chenery (1980). Three indecision subtypes were identified: (1) general self-uncertainty (indecisiveness, lack of self-confidence regarding decision-making ability and occupational ability, lack of clarity about onself); (2) low choice/work salience (lack of relationship between interests or abilities and occupational field, low motivation); and (3) transitional self (scarcity of educational and/or occupational information, conflict with significant others).

Other scales are: Harren's (1979) Assessment of Career Decision-Making (ACDM), an instrument based on Tiedeman and O'Hara's stages of exploration, crystallization, choice, and clarification; Lunneborg's (1976) Career Decision-Making Questionnaire (CDMQ); and Appel, Haak, and Witzke's (1970) Career Decision Readiness Inventory (CDRI).

Finally, in addition to all those interventions previously mentioned that are designed to enhance career decision-making, there is evidence that decision-making can be improved through the use of behavioral interventions (Snodgrass & Healy, 1979), group experiences (Bartsch & Hackett, 1979; Evans & Rector, 1978), individual counseling (Kirlighan, Hagesth, Tipton, McGovern, 1981), self administered instruments (Krivasky & Magoon, 1976), and simulations (Katz, Norris, & Pears, 1978).

GROUP PROCESSES

The second major strategy for implementing career guidance and counseling programs is the use of groups of one type of another. Many chapters of this text are liberally laced with examples of the use of group processes in such activities as disseminating information, utilizing educational and career information, developing attitudes toward career planning and work, and learning decision-making. Therefore, in this section we present only a brief overview of the group strategy in career guidance.

Rationale

It should be evident that in any systematic approach a great many objectives of career guidance and counseling can be achieved through group methods. Traditionally, it has been maintained that group procedures provide *efficiency* and *effectiveness*. If, for example, the dissemination

of information is a goal of career guidance at a specific point along the career development continuum, it is clearly more efficient to present the information once to a group than to present it individually to each member of the group. Also, if the goals of career guidance entail problem-solving or if the immediate objective of career guidance is to treat dysfunctional behaviors that may be affecting career development, then group methods are appropriate, for groups have been found to perform consistently better in certain types of problem-solving tasks and under certain conditions than do individuals attacking the same problem. In terms of correcting dysfunctional behaviors, it is reasoned that since these behaviors are typically learned in group situations, they are best unlearned or relearned in the same milieux or substitute behaviors learned.

Currently, the majority of all employed persons work within the framework of corporate structures wherein the primary modus operandi is the group as a procedural vehicle. It would seem beneficial for individuals, especially youngsters, to become used to functioning in this manner as a part of their preoccupational experience. Some suggested themes by which such career-related learning might be facilitated in groups are presented in Chapters 6–10.

The use of group methods is further justified by the fact that various career guidance curricula and theories of career development suggest universal career needs. These are needs that are presumed to be required or felt by all individuals; therefore, common learnings of this sort may be facilitated in groups. The relevance of these learnings to an individual's unique situation may be recognized through both group and individual methods.

Characteristics of the Group

Counselors may work with collections of individuals or aggregates rather than with true groups. In a social psychology sense, a group is characterized by at least six criteria (Hansen & Cramer, 1971):

1. Members of the group are in *interaction* with one another; that is, there must be at least two-way communication.
2. Members of the group share a *common goal*.

This goal may be set by the group itself, or it may be imposed by external forces.

3. The group members set *norms* that give direction and limits to their activity. Certain behaviors come to be rewarded; others are punished in some way.
4. The members develop a set of roles. Certain functions are performed by group members.
5. The group members develop a network of *interpersonal* attraction (likes and dislikes for each other).
6. The group works toward the satisfaction of the *individual needs* of the group members (p. 81).

Clearly, these characteristics will be present in varying degrees, depending on the type of group and the purpose of the group. The more in evidence they are, the more the likelihood that a group exists; the more these characteristics are lacking, the greater the chances that an aggregate or a simple collection of individuals exists. Large assembly programs in a school, for example, typically deal with aggregates. Usually, successful discussions, problem-solving, and counseling work through groups. A collection of individuals can still have utility for counselors. The point is simply that a distinction should be made between groups, which offer great potential inner resources for career guidance and counseling, and aggregates, which are a convenience. Pearson (1968) has termed work with aggregates as mass procedures. As opposed to group procedures, mass procedures are characterized by lack of interaction among individuals and do not typically satisfy individual needs. Other members of the mass in no way affect any given individual. Although mass procedures have some initial value in themselves for the acquisition of intellective and cognitive material and for establishing a psychological set (such as showing a film), there must be feedback and follow-up if an individual is to internalize the information in some meaningful fashion.

If the counselor works with true groups, then there must be some understanding of at least the basic elements of the way in which groups function. As a group interacts, it becomes dynamic; members are constantly adjusting and changing in relation to each other and to themselves. As a group restructures and adjusts, tensions are re-

duced, conflicts eliminated, and problems solved. The study of the variables underlying group movement is called group dynamics. Understanding group dynamics leads to evolving the techniques for effective group actions and decisions by using the forces that facilitate or inhibit group functioning. Such forces include the manner of interaction among the members, the amount of participation, the degree of group cohesiveness, the group values, the kind and quality of group leadership, and the internal structure of the group (degrees of permissiveness, competition, and communication).

The point is that the counselor skills necessary for effective functioning with groups are unique. Given sensitivity and communication ability as a base, however, the counselor can learn these skills and can apply them in the service of career guidance and counseling.

The Uses of Groups

The uses to which groups can be put in career guidance and counseling are limited only by the imagination and energy of the counselor. The following section presents some suggestions that provide an idea of the array of possibilities. Purposes for groups in career guidance are offered first; these are followed by a general discussion of the type of focus in career guidance groups.

Purposes. 1. *Information dissemination.* Information about the world of work is required in career decision-making. Certain elements of that information are pertinent only for given individuals; others are needed by all people. Information regarding the occupational structure, post–high school or postcollege educational and training opportunities, and courses of study at various educational levels, to cite but a few examples, are needed by every counselee and can be transmitted by means of group procedures, which will, of course, require follow-up.

2. *Motivation.* Motivation refers to the concept of convincing individuals of the value of some aspect of career guidance, whether this aspect involves the need for career planning in a broad sense or the need to take aptitude tests, for instance, in a much narrower sense. Readiness,

if lacking, and an orientation to planfulness must be established.

3. *Teaching*. The most obvious application of group techniques occurs in the teaching process. In fact, the primary strategy for career education, infusion (that is, teachers highlighting the career relevance of existing subject matter content in the classroom), relies on the teaching strategy. There is certainly a place for teaching in career guidance. Goldman (1962) has argued that group guidance often fails because counselors deal with guidance concerns by means of teacher behaviors. In other words, the *process* of teaching is seen as inappropriate for the *content* of guidance. This charge certainly is true in terms of the more affective elements of guidance content, but, as we have repeatedly stressed throughout this book, much of career guidance begins with a cognitive base. Goals ranging from the development of a vocabulary of work in youngsters to imparting decision-making skills in adults are effectively accomplished via a teaching strategy.

4. *Practice*. Role-playing, dramatization, gaming, and other simulation techniques allow individuals to rehearse or to practice career-related behaviors in groups. Whether the practice is as specific as role-playing a job interview or filling out an employment application, or is as broad as playing the Life Career Game, group situations permit the rehearsal of necessary career behaviors in a protected context.

5. *Attitude Development*. Attitudes are learned predispositions to respond in characteristic ways to certain stimuli. Since they are learned, they can be unlearned. Since they are learned within the family and other groups, they are logically unlearned and relearned within the group structure. Hence, the clarification of career attitudes and values and the crystallization and development of attitudes toward oneself can be fostered within groups.

6. *Exploration*. Since many individuals, whether school-aged or adult, are in the exploratory stage of career development, various group activities designed to enhance that exploration are beneficial. Ranging from field trips to career conferences to less structured activities, groups provide a vehicle for this exploration.

7. *Counseling*. Related somewhat to attitude developing but more specific is group counseling.

Some view group counseling as simply a remedial activity (for example, dealing with specific fears and anxieties, coping with intrapersonal difficulties, and so on). Others conceive of it as having a developmental focus (such as developing interpersonal and social skills, learning decision-making skills, and others). In either case, group counseling, as opposed to group guidance, is seen as a means of assisting individuals within a therapeutically created climate of respect and acceptance to recognize and to use their more affective aspects to their benefit.

Type of Focus. Fundamentally, group guidance and counseling should provide an opportunity to test or to discover one's own characteristics as related to particular environmental options. The following questions reflect such an intent: Knowing what I know about myself, how would I probably behave or perform in a situation with identified characteristics? Knowing what I know about a given occupation, what characteristics of mine can I compare and contrast with those required by the occupation? Through role-playing, case studies, selected audio-visual devices, discussion, speakers, structured exercises, and so on, an atmosphere can be created that will encourage individuals to project themselves vicariously into a given choice situation and to analyze how they, personally, would feel in that situation. Of course, it is not possible to create all the situations from which one might be able to choose or to have complete information. Also, it is possible to present irrelevant information to a group or to fail to encourage individuals to consider the characteristics of their behavior and performance that are related to choice-making.

Whether one deals with individual counseling or with group processes, the same questions are relevant. Both should support those experiences which reinforce for individuals the validity of the questions: Who am I? Am I able to be what I want to be? What is my life likely to be if I succeed in becoming what I choose to be?

Throughout the career guidance process, individually and in groups, the counselor not only must ensure that counselees have access to accurate, relevant information about their personal characteristics and create conditions which will help them understand the implications of this information, but the counselor also must ensure that counselees have accurate, relevant information about the options open to them. In the final analysis, people's self-perceptions or the self-labels that direct their behavior relate to persons, objects, and possibilities that lie outside the self. In other words, one's self-descriptions, whether they be such adjectives as bright-dull, capable-incapable, leader-follower, have meaning only in comparing oneself with others and with the requirements of specific situations. Appropriate information, much of which can be gleaned through groups, is vital to making good decisions about oneself as well as about what opportunities exist and what they require as one tests his or her personal fit with these opportunities.

A word of caution: too often a group strategy is employed simply because someone feels that it is time to launch a group guidance venture. Nothing comes before; very little comes after. The group guidance experience becomes a moment in time for its own sake. Group guidance is not "its own excuse for being." In a systematic approach to career guidance, one first determines goals and states them in behavioral terms; one then decides what activities are necessary and appropriate for achieving these goals; finally, one evaluates to discover if these goals have been achieved. One or more of the possible activities might involve the use of groups. This approach is quite a different matter from deciding to use a group strategy and then finding a focus for it. Intent determines strategy, not vice versa.

Much of career guidance and counseling can be accomplished via a group-helping strategy of one sort or another. Leading groups requires special skills of counselors, whether the purpose of the group is information dissemination, motivation, teaching, practice, attitude development, exploration, counseling, or some other aim. The use of group techniques is appropriate as a helping strategy in assisting individuals to answer a variety of career-related questions; it is not appropriate as an end in itself.

Summary

We have discussed two primary helping strategies in career guidance: individual and group processes. In one way or another, each of these strategies is designed to facilitate career decision-making. The internal personal attributes and values an individual brings to the career decision-making process must be balanced with the external realities of opportunities and cultural factors that constrain one's choices. Each helping strategy can be effected systematically in and of itself and within a systematic program of career guidance.

LEARNING ACTIVITIES

1. Describe the counseling theory to which you subscribe. Indicate orally or in writing how typical foci of career development and behavior can be addressed within the framework of this theory.

2. In a school or agency, observe a group intervention session relating to career development and behavior. Analyze the session in terms of content and process and in relation to the concepts and methods described in this chapter.

3. Select a population in need of a specific type of career intervention. Set up a course, workshop, or seminar designed to address the need. Include behavioral objectives, activities, materials, and evaluations.

4. Imagine that economic conditions, personal plans, or some other factor has caused you to seek a different career. You decide to seek help from a counselor. In terms of both content and process, what would you want that counselor to do for, with, or to you? Why?

5. Discuss with a classmate how such counseling process variables as diagnosis, exploration, clarification, integration, reflection, information-processing, implementation, and so on, relate to such variables as self-awareness, occupational awareness, and decision-making. How does the concept of "cognitive flexibility" fit into this relationship?

6. Reread Frank Parson's 1909 book, *Choosing a Vocation.* How have his notions of "study of

an individual, study of an occupation, and true reasoning" been broadened and redefined in current individual and group intervention strategies?

7. Make a videotape of a counseling interview in which is emphasized some specific aspect of career intervention (for example, developing self-awareness, increasing information-seeking behaviors, formulating an action plan, and so forth). Secure feedback from a supervisor or the class.

OBJECTIVES

After reading this chapter, engaging in the learning activities, and reading the suggested references, you should have met the objectives that follow. If you have not, it would probably be useful for you to review the material on helping strategies in career guidance before proceeding further.

1. Define individual counseling as a strategy for intervening in the career development and behavior of individuals.
2. Describe at least one example of a systematic individual counseling model.
3. List at least five examples of personal attribute factors, value structure factors, opportunity factors, and cultural forces factors influencing career choices.
4. Name at least five assumptions that undergird most decision-making intervention strategies.
5. Describe at least one decision-making program in some detail.
6. Present a rationale for the use of groups in career guidance and counseling.
7. List at least five uses of groups in career guidance and counseling.

15 | *Career Education: Concepts, Techniques, Status*

At various points in this book, the term career education has been used. Sometimes it has been used virtually interchangeably with the term career guidance; in other instances, it has been used primarily to describe a process of infusing into instructional content and method career development concepts by which the application of academic subject matter of any kind can be related to work or to self-exploration. In either case, the presence of career education as a federal priority has reestablished the fundamental importance of career guidance for youth and adults in the throes of planning and choosing among work opportunities. Indeed, it has affirmed that effective career education efforts are not likely without a strong career guidance program to complement and extend its activities. Some readers will believe that it is inappropriate to discuss career education in a separate chapter. However, we believe that the concepts involved are important enough to receive such treatment.

The concepts career education embodies strike to the heart of the relationship between education and work and, indeed, the needs of persons attempting to choose and adjust to a work environment that is in dramatic flux. Thus, the values and the substance that career education represents seem to be inherent in modernizing and industrializing societies throughout the world.

Career education, then, is not only a phenomenon of this nation. It took root in many parts of the world almost simultaneously as these nations entered social and occupational phases in their development in which the relationships between education and work were taking on new and independent forms, and as they became concerned about the creation of a labor force able to advance individual and national productivity.

Great Britain, France, West Germany, Canada, the Netherlands, the Scandinavian countries, East Germany, and the Soviet Union among other nations have each embarked on some form of career education since the late 1960s and early 1970s. Like American models, they have developed approaches to the infusion of subject matter with career development concepts, created decision-making courses and experiences, established career resource centers, expanded contacts between schools and the larger community and strengthened other career-related mechanisms in the schools, in ministries of labor, or in other community sectors. Each of these nations has strengthened its network of "employability" services in which the school may be the centerpiece but in which the employment service, vocational rehabilitation, and many other counseling agencies in the private and public sectors have clearly defined contributions. Many of these countries have developed work-study, career shadowing, apprenticeship schemes, or school-community linkages that are much more comprehensive than our own.

Obviously, the approaches to career education taken by other nations are shaped by their own political belief systems, economic conditions, cultural traditions, and conceptions of free and informed choice. Such models, then, are not necessarily interchangeable or transportable across national boundaries. That is not the point. The point is that nations experiencing particular levels of industrialization, occupational specialization and diversity, and magnitude of information about their work possibility structure apparently

417

must shift their educational content and career guidance processes in order to accommodate these conditions. Career education has tended to symbolize such efforts.

In this nation, career education was introduced as a federal priority by then U.S. Commissioner of Education Sidney Marland on January 23, 1971. In an unfortunately superficial way, many persons view that date as the spontaneous birth of career education. To do so, however, denies the evolutionary character of the concepts involved and their ongoing importance as a stimulus to strengthened programs of career development in schools and community agencies as well as to the fundamental necessity for comprehensive programs of career guidance in a time of social and occupational change. In this chapter we will examine the origins of career education, discuss what we have learned in the last ten to twelve years from the concepts and practices it represents, and make some projections about the likely future for such efforts.

THE EMERGENCE OF CAREER EDUCATION

The introduction of the term career education is widely attributed to an address entitled "Career Education Now," given by Sidney Marland on January 23, 1971 before the annual convention of the National Association of Secondary School Principals at Houston, Texas. Although this speech and the many that followed in rapid succession to various professional, civic, and industrial groups gave visibility and credibility to career education, neither the term nor the concepts it embraced were without precedent in American history. Indeed, it is fair to say that Marland's emphasis on career education extended an evolutionary process that had been building rapidly during the 1960s but had antecedents back into the early years of this nation.

Throughout 1960–1969 many significant pieces of legislation bearing on employment, educational innovation, and vocational education were passed by the Congress. Several prominent panels of advisors on national education and manpower issues were empowered to make recommendations on

needed policy. Both the policy and the legislation that emerged during the period became increasingly sensitive to the career development needs of persons, not just the needs of the occupational structure. Employability was seen as more than simply the acquisition by workers of occupation-task specific skills and needed to include attention to the types of educational, occupational, and personal information required by people choosing among diverse occupational and educational patterns, the effects of work values and attitudes, the ability to plan and choose, the ability to engage in industrial discipline and the affective components of work. Therefore, it became increasingly apparent that you could theoretically train the most competent machinist in the world but if this person did not value being a machinist, was unwilling to go to work at 8:00 A.M. each day, five days a week, did not have a commitment to personal productivity, you might just as well not train the person at all. There was a growing move to develop not just competent persons as defined by the needs of the occupational structure but personally competent people defined in broader terms. It was in this context that Commissioner Marland's predecessor James Allen actually used the term career education a year earlier than Marland when he addressed the National Association of Secondary School Principals' Convention in 1970. He said, "It is the renewed awareness of the universality of the basic human and social need for competence that is generating not only increased emphasis today on career education but a whole new concept of its character and its place in the total educational enterprise" (Allen, 1970).

Many persons then, as they do now, dismissed such observations as nothing more than the periodic rhetoric of the cyclical assaults on education that have occurred since the beginning of the Republic. Without overdrawing the matter, however, the issues were deeper and broader than that. The forces that gave rise to career education in the 1970s had been building intensely throughout the 1960s. The United States entered the 1960s in a climate of unemployment. Unemployment in the third recession since the Korean War exceeded 8.1 percent (unadjusted for seasonality in February 1961), causing it to become a key public issue for the first time since the 1930s. The focus of intensive debate was whether the cause of unemployment was slow economic growth and a deficient rate of job creation or inadequate skills among the work force in an economy of abundant but high-level employment opportunities. As the debate ensued through the decade, the U.S. Office of Education formulated a series of eleven conditions that allegedly justified educational reform through the medium of career education. They included (Hoyt, 1974):

1. Too many persons leaving our educational system are deficient in the basic academic skills required for adaptability in today's rapidly changing society.

2. Too many students fail to see meaningful relationships between what they are being asked to learn in school and what they will do when they leave the educational system. This is true of both those who remain to graduate and those who drop out of the educational system.

3. American education, as currently structured, best meets the educational needs of that minority of persons who will someday become college graduates. It fails to place equal emphasis on meeting the educational needs of that vast majority of students who will never be college graduates.

4. American education has not kept pace with the rapidity of change in the post industrial occupational society. As a result, when worker qualifications are compared with job requirements, we find overeducated and undereducated workers are present in large numbers. Both the boredom of the overeducated worker and the frustration of the undereducated worker have contributed to the growing presence of worker alienation in the total occupational society.

5. Too many persons leave our educational system at both the secondary and collegiate levels unequipped with the vocational skills, the self-understanding and career decision-making skills, or the work attitudes that are essential for making a successful transition from school to work.

6. The growing need for and presence of wom-

en in the work force has not been reflected adequately in either the educational or the career options typically pictured for girls enrolled in our educational system.

7. The growing needs for continuing and recurrent education on the part of adults are not being met adequately by our current systems of public education.

8. Insufficient attention has been given to learning opportunities which exist outside the structure of formal education and are increasingly needed by both youth and adults in our society.

9. The general public, including parents and the business-industry-labor community, has not been given an adequate role in formulation of educational policy.

10. American education, as currently structured, does not adequately meet the needs of minority, or economically disadvantaged persons in our society.

11. Post–high school education has given insufficient emphasis to educational programs at the sub-baccalaureate degree level (pp. 3–4).

Although each of these conditions was and is debated, collectively they call attention to conditions in society at large and in the educational structure per se that are seen as reducing the work ethic in America, inadequately providing the information and support to facilitate individual decision-making, and permitting a lack of meaningful linkage to occur between education and work. One solution to these problems that had been promoted during the 1960s was expanded vocational education. Indeed, the Vocational Education Act of 1963, its amendments in 1968, and various reports from the National Advisory Council on Vocational Education pointed out such a need. Both the legislation and the Advisory Council reports argued that vocational education programs needed reform and that they needed to be made more integral to the total educational process. The influential 1968 Report of the Advisory Council on Vocational Education entitled "Vocational Education: The Bridge Between Man and His Work," outlined a series of major characteristics viewed as essential to an adequate system of vocational education.

The scope of these recommendations was not limited to vocational education as traditionally defined. They struck at the very core of the educational process in the United States. The report alleged that as the educational outcomes of many young persons are appraised, the irrelevance and lack of specific skills found do not coincide with the philosophical and historical promise of American education.

Legislative authority under the 1968 amendments to the Vocational Education Act included direct support for many of the elements cited in the report by creating funding for exemplary programs and projects to test their validity in actual situations. Many of the projects that resulted became the early operational roots for career education after that term's introduction in 1971. In particular, such projects were to develop prevocational efforts in the elementary and junior high schools, create new curricular thrusts in vocational education and, in general, broaden the relationship of vocational education to the larger educational context of which it is a part. The explicit purposes of the legislation were (1) to identify effective ongoing programs that can serve as models for improving the vocational education of students at all levels, and (2) to stimulate interest in and provide the means for creating new, more efficient and effective methods for providing job preparation needs. Such perspectives emphasized a need in vocational education to become more person-oriented rather than focusing almost exclusively on skill acquisition.

The findings of career development research relating to how persons make occupational choices, the information they need, the effects of work values and attitudes on choice-making were seen in this legislation as important insights to be incorporated into vocational education. Indeed, the Exemplary Programs and Services Branch, Division of Vocational and Technical Education, USOE, stated in an internal memorandum that the Exemplary Programs and Projects funded by the 1968 Amendments to the Vocational Education Act were:

Early attempts to structure operating models of what is now coming to be referred to as a K through 12 career education system! The roots for such a system go back into many years of basic research on career development theory

(Exemplary Programs and Services Branch, USOE, 1971).

It is clear that although the climate in the U.S. Office of Education for career education was congenial for some years before 1971, the major implementation of the concept got underway after Commissioner Marland's speech in January 1971. However, since career education represented more than vocational education and more than a combination of other USOE-sponsored thrusts, there was, in early 1971, neither specific legislative support nor a single office in the USOE that was totally compatible with the emerging career education emphases. Such categorical support did not actually occur until career education was included in the Educational Amendments of 1974 (Section 406, PL 93-380), which created the Office of Career Education, the National Advisory Committee on Career Education, and authorized the expenditure of funds to demonstrate and to evaluate career education. In 1977, the Congress enacted PL 95-207, the Career Education Incentive Act, which provided incentive funds to states and local school districts for a five-year period to support the implementation of career education in those states voluntarily electing to participate under the provisions of law; it did not mandate such participation. In doing so, the federal government transferred, in effect, the power for leadership in career education to the State Department of Education (Hoyt, 1982).

National Models of Career Education

Immediately following the introduction of career education by Commissioner Marland in 1971, a major effort was begun to translate many of the notions he described into operational models. Such models occurred at both state and national levels. Although these models have now largely been integrated into the school systems or agencies where they were field-tested, and their original assumptions obscured by adaptations and refinements, it is useful to acknowledge their influence on the implementation of career education both conceptually and operationally.

Space does not permit examination of the state models or the models of private agencies that paralleled or evolved from the original national models. We will limit ourselves here to a consideration of the four national models that were federally funded and which were pioneering prototypes for much that has resulted in the past ten years. Each of these models was based on somewhat different assumptions, goals, and populations to be served. Each was also changed from its original form as demonstration projects played out and changed their form. Nevertheless, they remain important reference points from which to understand the current approaches to career education. The four national models were:

1. the school-based, or comprehensive career education model
2. the employer-based, or more recently, the experience-based career education model
3. the home/community-based career education model
4. the rural/residential-based career education model

A general overview of the goals and populations served by each of the models is provided in the subsequent sections.

The School-Based, Comprehensive Career Education Model. The school-based model originally began as an effort to revitalize education by infusing the curriculum from kindergarten to grade twelve with career education themes. Subsequently the model was extended from kindergarten to the graduate school. Extensive community, industrial, business involvement, widespread use of cooperative education, and the placement of every student departing the secondary school in either a job or a higher education program have each been stressed as essential to the success of the school-based model.

The original goals of the school-based model were to develop within each student:

- a concept of self that is in keeping with a work-oriented society
- positive attitudes about work, school, and society, and a sense of satisfaction resulting from successful experiences in these areas
- personal characteristics of self-respect, self-reliance, perseverance, initiative, and resourcefulness
- a realistic understanding of the relationships between the world of work and education

- a comprehensive awareness of career options in the world of work
- the ability to enter employment in an appropriate occupation at a productive level and/or to pursue further education.

In 1972, these goals were sharpened and re-ordered slightly, to ensure that students exit school with:

- a sense of purpose and direction
- self-identity and identification with society (and an idea of their relationship)
- basic skills and knowledge
- a comprehensive awareness of career options and the ability to enter employment and/or further education.

The school-based model was designed to re-orient the educational system from within, by infusing it with ideas, experiences, skills that have traditionally not been systematically provided to all students. Although the goals of the model have been frequently stated in educational philosophies, they have not been comprehensively carried forth in practice. Specifically, the purposes of the redirection of education as promoted by this model are: (1) to acquaint students more intimately with a variety of career opportunities through each of their school experiences, (2) to ensure that every student receives an education that integrates academic skills, social development, and career preparation; and (3) to provide students with a continuing awareness of educational choices for career planning. Weaving throughout the philosophy and practice of this model is an acknowledgement of the need for extensive guidance and counseling activities to help the student develop self-awareness, self-confidence, and mature attitudes, as well as to match his or her interests and abilities against potential careers.

In translating the philosophy and goals for the school-based model into instructional and guidance strategies and resources, the Ohio State Center for Vocational and Technical Education (the agency granted the U.S. Office of Education contract to develop the model) developed a matrix of over 1000 goals to guide the development of the model. These were subsequently field-tested in six school systems across the nation: Atlanta,

Georgia; Flint, Michigan; Hackensack, New Jersey; Jefferson County, Colorado; Los Angeles, California; and Mesa, Arizona. These goals were progressively sequenced, starting with career awareness in the elementary grades, career exploration in the junior high school grades, and career preparation in the senior high school grades. Figure 15.1 presents a graphic picture of the matrix of elements used as the intellectual framework for the school-based model. These elements were used to guide the development of curriculum and other educational activities based on the goals.

More complete definitions of the elements and their proposed outcomes as displayed in Figure 15.1 follow as a function of Miller's (1972) interpretations of these elements.

1. *Career awareness*. The individual entering school possesses some knowledge about, attitudes toward, and interest in careers. He or she knows something about career alternatives, associated life styles, rewards, leisure time, working conditions, and the education and training of some persons in some careers. Let us call that knowledge of careers career awareness. Through education, home, and community life we wish to assist the student in understanding the broad range of careers that are available, not only as they serve him or her, the community, or society at large, but also what is involved in the development, growth, behavior, training, and rewards of persons engaged in specific occupations. From this broad understanding of careers we want the student to

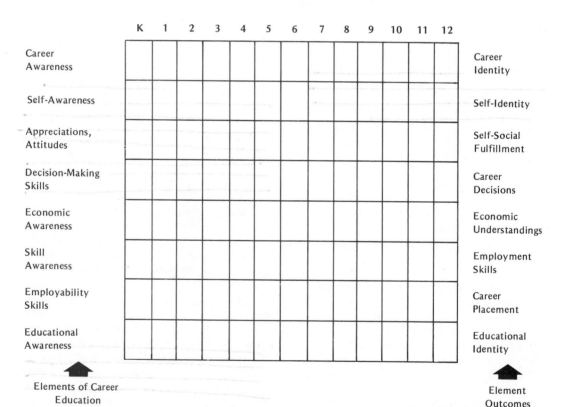

Figure 15.1
Comprehensive Career Education

experience active career exploration and preparation that lead to career identity. Career identity is defined as the individual selection of a role or roles within the world of work.

2. *Self-awareness.* The entering student has some knowledge and attitudes about him- or herself, what kind of person he or she is, and what he or she hopes to become. Let us call that self-awareness. Through career education and home and community experiences, we want the student to become involved in a planned, sequential process of self-assessment and self-evaluation that results in self-identity and a reasonably consistent internalized value system.

3. *Appreciations and attitudes.* The element, appreciations and attitudes, was included as a means of focusing attention on the affective component of career education. Through career education and supporting systems, the student should develop an internalized value system that includes the valuing of his or her own career role and the roles assumed by others. These positive attitudes toward a personal career role and the roles of others in society should lead to active and satisfying participation as a productive citizen and, thus, provide for both self-fulfillment and social-fulfillment. Self-social fulfillment is defined as the internalization of a value system that activates the individual as a self-actualized, self-fulfilling member of the world of work with appreciation for his or her own role and the roles of others.

4. *Decision-making.* The entering student has some understanding of the decision-making process and possesses some decision-making skills. If able to understand cause and effect relationships, the student is ready to examine the decision-making process. Through career education and supporting school and life experiences, the student will develop increasing skill and experience in the rational processes of decision-making, practice making decisions, and come to accept the responsibility for the outcomes of his or her decisions. The career decisions made during one's progress through the Comprehensive Career Education program will progress from very tentative and flexible career decisions to decisions that are increasingly irreversible or reversible only at some cost of time, effort, or money. A student should reach a decision that represents a careers direction setting by grade 10, or early enough to provide for the development of entry-level skills in a career direction setting, the product of a rational process, a plan for immediate, intermediate, and long-term career development.

5. *Economic awareness.* The child has observed and participated in the economic system to some extent before school entry. Building on this base of economic awareness, we wish to facilitate the student's systematic and thorough exploration of the economic system, both as it relates to career development and the community and society at large. Economic understanding is defined as those conceptual elements and networks which make it possible for the child or the adult to "read" the economic environment and resolve personal and social economic problems.

6. *Skill awareness and beginning competence.* The entering student has some awareness of the skills performed by workers in certain job roles and career fields. Building on this awareness, the career education program and its support systems will provide opportunities for the student to participate in both cognitive and psychomotor skill activities in order to develop employment skills. The development of these skills will both reinforce and be reinforced by learning experiences in other educational disciplines.

7. *Employability skills.* Employability skills are those elements of career education which have to do with searching for, locating, and obtaining career placement, both on an initial and advanced basis.

8. *Educational awareness.* The entering student has some awareness of the relationships between education and training, whether formal or experienced based, and the life roles assumed by self and others. From this basic educational awareness, the student will continue to develop and refine a thorough understanding of the part all education and training plays in relation to the "real world" and the changing world in which a more complete participation will occur. The student will also come to recognize the need for specific education and training for specific career roles.

9. *Educational identity.* One's educational identity combines an understanding of the relation between education and training and life roles, knowledge of oneself as a participant in education and training, one's learning style, pace,

capabilities and capacities, and the ability to select and evaluate educational avenues for the development of career plans.

In addition, it was intended that the output of the matrix development process would include eight basic career education elements leading to thirty-two pervasive career education themes. It was intended that within the themes would be 1500 specific goals and over 3000 performance objectives that could be appropriately placed at the various grade levels, K–12.

Although the goals and definitions cited were primarily oriented to the K–12 span, they were quickly recognized as the most elaborate and available definition of career education in terms of its expected effects on pupil learning. Thus, these goals were frequently modified for use in the other national career education models (discussed later) and condensed in ways that made them compatible with career education programs for college students and for other adult groups.

The approach taken by the school-based model in generating goals, objectives, strategies, and resources with which to infuse educational settings has had its critics. The goals were damned as anti-intellectual and antihumanistic, as ways of keeping minority students from going into higher education, and as too structured. Whether or not these criticisms are valid, however, the philosophical perspectives of the school-based model have done a great deal to create a climate conducive to the expansion of career guidance. In addition, the model's systematic approach to model-building and to goal-definition provided a significant format for facilitating systematic approaches to the purposes and delivery of career guidance elements.

The Employer-Based (Experience-Based) Model. Career Education Model II, the Employer-Based Model, was designed to meet the individual learning needs of a cross-section of young people, ages 13–18, who need or are seeking a significant alternative to their current educational environments. In contrast to the school-based model, which attempts to redirect the formal educational structure, this model assumed that some students are turned off by the formal educational structure and need a different way to acquire basic academic skills, self-understanding, and career awareness, as well as career preparation. The different way is to consider the community as a learning laboratory capable of providing many opportunities to individualize student experiences with the world of work. More specifically, the model was intended to demonstrate the relevance of the educational process to students through "intimate student involvement in professional and industrial operations." The program emphasizes educational experiences that are available in such settings as scientific and medical laboratories, warehouses, construction and housing projects, parks, museums, banks, insurance companies, hospitals, factories, and prisons. Specifically, employer-based career education begins with identification of learning elements that all students need to acquire, and then locates actual work or adult activity situations, managed by employers, in which students can learn these specific elements. Thus, students will experience adult-centered work while they acquire the same educational credentials as would be available through the formal educational structure. The original goals of the Employer-Based Model were to:

1. provide an alternative education program for students, ages 13–18, in an employer-based setting
2. unify the positive elements of academic, general, and vocational curricula into a comprehensive career education program
3. increase the relevance of the world of education to the world of work
4. broaden the base of community participation, particularly by involving public and private employers more directly and significantly in education

With respect to student learning, it was intended that the model would emphasize direct participation by students in learning experiences designed to:

1. review and reinforce students' educational competencies and interests
2. provide opportunities for a variety of activities with a variety of people other than the limited peer-group and teacher associations available in the public schools

3. develop a strong self-concept through participation in an individualized and self-directed learning program
4. provide multiple opportunities for obtaining directly relevant information concerning career opportunities and requirements, and advantages and disadvantages of a variety of career options

The essence of this program is its ability to individualize experience for each student through individual projects, individual contracts, work study, cooperative education, and other methods. Since the program's success involves a consortium of public and private employers, relatively few constraints were placed on the means by which knowledge, skills, attitudes, motivation, and experiences are imparted to students. In addition, it is intended that a student enter and reenter the program freely with options of returning to the traditional school program, getting a job, or moving on to further education.

The guidance system in this model has two functions: (1) to mediate actively between students and the interaction of their work-education community environments, and (2) to assist in the mapping of an individualized learning program for each student. This active involvement of guidance personnel is critical to the model's success, because student participation is voluntary. More importantly, it is expected that each student will participate in the selection of his or her own pattern of work or activity situations from a variety of opportunities, so that learning situations are most relevant to personal interests and needs.

When control of the funding of the four National Career Education Models was transferred from the U.S. Office of Education to the National Institute of Education in 1972, the employer-based model was renamed the experience-based model. This name change tended to shift the perspective of the model away from only those students turned off by the formal academic context and to employment/academic opportunities for such students to a greater emphasis on the instructional process being experiential in nature and that a range of community opportunities could be involved to accomplish career education goals.

Four regional educational laboratories held contracts to develop the experience-based models.

There were both similarities and differences among the models. Each of the four experience-based career education (EBCE) sites had the following objectives in common: (1) career development skills and knowledge; (2) self-knowledge of interests, abilities, and values; (3) reading skills; (4) problem-solving skills; (5) oral communications; (6) writing skills; (7) interpersonal skills; and (8) basic quantitative skills. In addition, two of the sites also had objectives in the following areas: (1) economic skills for daily living; (2) worker and employer rights and responsibilities; (3) political awareness; (4) inquiry skills; (5) physical fitness and health; (6) applied mathematics; (7) science; and (8) aesthetic expression.

Additional differences in the four experience-based models are the following:

1. In one program, students continue as essentially regular members of their original high schools, while students at the three other EBCE programs operate out of external learning centers. (These latter would be similar to what is called an alternative school in many communities.)
2. Instruction in basic skills ranges from the use of a programmed sequence of learning materials to informal on-the-job processes, sometimes supplemented by tutorial assistance.
3. Counseling in two cases has been provided as a separate service, while at the other two sites counseling has been made an integral element of the instructional program (National Association of Secondary School Principals, 1975).

Like the School-Based Model, the Employer/Experience-Based Model elevates the importance of career guidance to a central priority in the model's success. In the latter situation, it also demonstrates how guidance processes can be related to individualized instruction.

The Home/Community-Based Model. The third national career education model was the first to deal expressly with adult populations including those who are homebound. Of particular concern in this model are women who have been homebound while raising young children but now wish to reenter the labor market or to advance their education. In this model the home itself is used as a career education center in conjunction with three components: (1) a career-oriented educational television program, focused on building motivation in studying for a career, providing information about career opportunities, and some occupational competency instruction; (2) a home and community education system, using television, correspondence programs, and radio and instruction aids as well; and (3) career classes in the community to provide career guidance and counseling.

The purposes served by the home/community-based model included:

1. to develop educational delivery systems into the home and community
2. to provide new career education programs for adults
3. to establish a guidance and career placement system to assist individuals in occupational and related life roles
4. to develop more competent workers for the world of work
5. to enhance the quality of the home as a living center.

In essence, the home/community-based model was an effort to enhance the employability and career options of out-of-school adults through the systematic integration of mass media, referral centers, individual counseling, and community resources. Unlike the other models, this one did not attempt to teach skills and attitudes directly. Rather, it was seen as an information clearing-house and a vehicle by which interested persons can assess their career interests and identify ways by which these interests may be met in the local community.

Providence, Rhode Island, was the original national site for the Home/Community-Based Model. By 1975, the project had served more than 5000 adults from ages 16 to 70 who neither worked full-time nor were engaged in full-time education. The heart of this project is telephone interviews, career counseling, information, and referrals, conducted by paraprofessional counselors. In addition, a resource center provides information on employment and education opportunities as well as on such concerns as financial support, discrimination, child care, and testing.

The changes in this model since its inception are neither philosophical nor related to the clients served but rather focus on the delivery system. As the original objectives suggested, it was expected that cable and public television would be the major vehicles for information delivery. As it turns out, telephone interviews, referrals, and a resource center have emerged as highly important methods for this population. Further, it seems apparent that this project is quite literally an effort to provide career guidance and counseling on an outreach basis from a community level. As such, this model became an important spur to what have emerged as educational brokering centers for adults in many communities as well as to the educational information centers established by Title 1 of the Educational Amendments of 1976 (PL 94–482).

The Rural/Residential-Based Model. Career Education Model IV was basically an attempt to test the hypothesis that entire disadvantaged rural families can be helped to improve their economic and social conditions through an intensive program at a residential center. Therefore, rather than training only the head of a household in occupational skills, this project provided services for the entire family including: day care; elementary and secondary education; career and technical education; parent education; family-living assistance; medical and dental services; welfare services; counseling; and cultural and recreational opportunities for single and married students and their families.

In view of the scope of this model, its original objectives were few:

1. to provide families with employment capabilities suitable to the area
2. to provide leverage on the economic development of the area
3. to improve family living.

Only one site, the Mountain-Plains Education and Economic Development Program at Glasgow, Montana, implemented this model. The project focused on chronically underemployed, multi-problem rural families from six north central and northwestern states. Through a total intervention approach, it attempted to influence all significant activities of the family and to make it both economically and socially viable through career counseling, training, homemaking, family development skills, and occupational placement for the parents, as well as remedial education and guidance for the children. At any one time, approximately 210 families were in residence at the model site and remained there for an average of eight to nine months. Programs and services provided by this project included:

1. career guidance, required for both adults if it was an intact family
2. a career development program for the head-of-household and optionally for the spouse, including foundation education in math skills and communication skills, occupation preparation, and work experience
3. family and individual counseling for head-of-household and spouse and, based on need, for older children
4. a family core curriculum designed to provide both head-of-household and spouse with home management, health, consumer education, parenting, community organization, and recreation skills
5. limited basic medical, dental, and optical services through contracted services
6. financial support of the family while in the program
7. child development and care for preschool age youngsters
8. placement services
9. supportive follow-up after placement
10. research, documentation, and dissemination of the program.

The occupational preparation program stresses mastery of identified essential competencies for entry-level positions in the career areas of building trades and services, mobility and transportation; tourism and marketing; and office education. There are approximately fifty individual careers within the clusters we have identified for which occupational preparation is available.

In each of the required areas, the Mountain-Plains Program provided individualized diagnostic and prescriptive mechanisms for determining sequences of instruction for each student. Student plans were written to recognize existing skill levels as rated by pretests. Student progress was then monitored on a continuing basis with formal review every six weeks or at interim points, based on need. Completion of the Mountain-Plains Pro-

gram was defined as validation in all required program areas by both adults, including the requirement for validation in an occupational skill for the head of household. Validation is based on the achievement of competency or performance objectives as determined by posttests.

Although far more could be said about the beginnings of career education and about the early models designed to make operational the assumptions on which career education rests, it is useful to consider what has been learned from the attempts to implement career education since 1971. The categories of learning are diverse and represent the underlying structure from which projections about the future can be made.

The Changing Definition of Career Education

Among the trends and perspectives associated with the implementation of career education during the past decade has been a changing definition of career education itself.

Although there were many state definitions of career education by 1974 when the first federal definition was provided, that federal definition was a useful benchmark. It indicated that as a matter of federal policy, "Career Education is the totality of experiences through which one learns about and prepares to engage in work as part of her or his way of life" (Hoyt, 1974). This definition was buttressed by the description of career education found in the Education Amendments of 1974 (Section 406, PL 93–380), which created the Office of Career Education and officially made career education a federal priority. In this legislation, career education was considered to be a process designed to:

- increase the relationship between schools and society as a whole
- relate the curricula of schools to the needs of persons to function in society
- provide opportunities for counseling, guidance, and career development for all children
- extend the concept of the education process beyond the school into employment and the community
- foster flexibility in attitudes, skills and knowledge in order to enable persons to cope with accelerating change and obsolescence
- eliminate any distinction between education for

vocational purposes and general or academic education.

Since 1974 the federal definition of career education has gone through several iterations with the most recent one community-based rather than school-based. As such it introduces the concept of collaboration as a major emphasis. It is as follows:

Career Education is a community effort aimed at helping persons — youth and adults — better prepare themselves for work through acquiring adaptability skills that will enable them to change with change in society in such ways that work — paid and unpaid — will become a more meaningful and more rewarding part of their total lifestyle (Hoyt, 1979).

This definition goes on to identify the adaptability skills to be imparted through a career education effort. They are:

1. basic academic skills of reading, oral and written communication, and mathematics
2. work habits leading to productivity in the work place
3. a personally meaningful set of work values that lead the person to want to work
4. basic understandings of the American economic system that will enable the person to respect that system and function effectively within it
5. career decision-making skills
6. skills required for self-understanding and understanding of educational/occupational opportunities
7. job-seeking, job-getting, and job-holding skills
8. skills required to combat stereotyping as it impinges on full freedom of educational and occupational choice
9. skills required for the individual to humanize the workplace for himself/herself
10. skills required to find meaningful work in productive use of leisure time.

This definition of career education includes examples of career education activities, and resources for career education — the formal education system (all levels), the business/labor/industry/professional community, the home and family structure, and local government. Some examples

of the community organizations able to provide support to career education are the PTA, Chamber of Commerce, American Legion, Women's American ORT, Rotary, Kiwanis, National Urban Coalition, Central Labor Union Council, and many others. Possible local delivery systems able to collaboratively provide career education are junior achievement, 4-H clubs, National Alliance of Business, CETA, and so on. The definition concludes with a recommendation that the total effort be coordinated (but not managed) through some form of community career education council. It also suggests that the guidance and preparation of persons for work is a collaborative system to which many persons contribute, for example, teachers, school counselors, employment counselors, parents, community agencies, business and industry; it further suggests that employability services must acknowledge each other's contributions in a programmatic, coordinated fashion.

The implementation of such a perspective brings with it many issues: how it should be implemented, who has the power, how the school system and, indeed, the community must change to accommodate such shifts in the definition of career education. The conceptualization and evaluation of ways to respond to these matters will occupy career educators for some time.

Career Education and Education: Similarities and Differences

Flowing from the evolution of the federal definition of career education over the past decade has been greater clarity about whether career education and education are synonymous. They are not. They are, however, dynamic terms, not susceptible to a standardized definition so widely accepted as to eliminate any possible confusion of what each term represents. The early rhetoric of Marland and some others about all education being career education has confused many observers and caused misapprehension about the sweep of career education and what its meaning as an instrument of educational reform really is.

Nevertheless, the maturation of the federal and theoretical perspectives on career education suggests that although the terms education and career education are not synonymous, certain processes and content of education do have reciprocal effect. In its primary sense, career education is a systematic effort to right the balance between education and work by emphasizing among educational goals that of preparation for work — not just for some students but for all. It is assumed that other aspects of education can potentially contribute to the goals of career education and, indeed, that effective career education will likely enhance other basic goals of education. As Suhor (1979) has indicated, "Certain goals of career education and subject-area instruction will be seen as congruent; others as overlapping; still others as essentially distinctive" (p. 215). Perhaps the clearest statement on this matter appears in the second edition of the classic text, *Career Education: What It Is and How To Do It*, by Hoyt, Evans, Mackin, and Magnum (1972). Their perspectives about the matter are:

First, career education as the focus and substance of all education is untenable. Education as preparation for work was, after all, only one of the seven basic purposes of American education stated so eloquently in 1917. The other six purposes should not disappear with the advent of career education. . . .

Second, to acknowledge that one's work affects his or her entire lifestyle in no way justifies contending that all education is career education. There would be equal justification for saying that all education is citizenship education, all education is health education, or even all education is sex education. . . . To whatever extent one departs from the central and crucial importance of the four-letter word *work* in career education he misses the essential meaning of the concept itself.

In the third place, the general public would reject the contention that all education is career education. The business-labor-industry community, on the other hand, while willing to support and participate in that part of education concerned with preparation for work, sees no vital or urgent reason for participating in all of education.

In the fourth place, no new educational thrust claiming to constitute all of education has ever survived. . . . Career education advocates may be successful in promoting it as an additional reason for studying subject matter. They will

surely lose by pretending that the subject matter exists in order to impart career education concepts.

A final pragmatic reason for opposing the concept that all education is career education arises from the inevitability of some other slogan replacing career education as the number one priority of the U.S. Office of Education. If career education concentrates on picturing itself as only one of many worthy purposes of education, it is more likely to survive along with whatever new priority comes along (pp. 34–35).

Given that perspective, however, we also need to say that the 1970s have clarified what career education, or the concepts it embraces, can contribute to good education. Indeed, the evolving perspectives of career education have added considerable insight into the nature of basic education in a society as complex and diverse as the United States or other major industrial nations. Obviously, good education and basic education mean different things to different societies at different historical periods. Each of the educational movements — such as life adjustment, progressive, process, inquiry, affective, confluent, humanistic education — that have emerged in this century have represented a testimony to some alleged deficit in the education of the young or of the adult. Many of these movements have left a residue in legislation, regulations, and state or federal policies obligating school systems, industry, or other social institutions to respond in some way. Such a circumstance has caused school systems to have problems of priorities, increasing difficulties in monitoring how much of different types of content is being taught, and requirements for various evaluation processes to acknowledge compliance with one obligation or another.

Still the criticisms of education go on. In some cases criticism occurs because assessments of what students know suggest they do not know enough about certain bodies of organized knowledge. In other instances, criticism occurs because it is perceived that students have not acquired the generalized skills essential to becoming an effective person (however such a model is defined). In still other instances, criticism of education occurs because it has departed from the basics (usually defined as reading, writing, and computation) and gotten into areas better left to home, church, or community. Another category of criticism has dealt with the perceived meaninglessness or irrelevance of education to adult life. Implicit in each of these criticisms is a concern for the nature of basic education in today's society. Many prominent observers have argued for particular emphases that are, in fact, incorporated in career education content.

The Nature of Basic Education. Although there are many persons in every nation who wish to confine basic education to reading, writing, and computation skills, a growing number of people see basic education as a combination of both academic skills and other interpersonal and technical skills important to functioning effectively in today's knowledge society.

The importance of basic academic skills is reflected in Drucker's (1969) observations that: "The systematic acquisition of knowledge; that is organized formal education has replaced experience — acquired traditionally through apprenticeship — as the foundation for productive capacity and performance" (p. 40). Within this context, one might contend that reading, writing, and mathematics skills are the necessary but not sufficient skills in a highly bureaucratized, technologically oriented society.

Ginzberg (1971) has argued similarly that we tend to overlook "the fact that the preferred occupational preparation for a white collar society is the acquisition of skills in language, numbers, and analytical thinking. While a minority will earn their living in manual trades, the vast majority of the oncoming generation will work with paper and pencils, with typewriters, calculators, computers, and testing equipment" (p. 17).

Other observers would add to the perspectives of Drucker and Ginzberg. Darcy (1969), for example, has indicated that the basic skills related to work success include: communication skills, computational skills, manual dexterity or motor skills, and group organization and human relations skills. It is his position that employability, productivity, and earning power are enhanced by verbal skills (reading, writing, speaking); mathematics; manual skills; and the ability to work effectively with other people. He contends that

these skills are "basic, durable, versatile, transferable and open-ended; they represent human capital that is virtually immune to obsolescence." Marland (1972) has contended that interpersonal and organizational understanding are "survival skills" without which one simply cannot exist in a modern nation-state. Many of the perspectives on "affective work competencies," industrial discipline, and related phenomena reported in Chapters 2, 6, and 15 are also relevant here.

Coleman (1972), like some other observers, has argued that young people have been excluded from the "educational mainstream in their society." He cites several skills, basic from his perspective, that should be provided by the educational system before a student becomes 18. They include:

1. "intellectual skills," the kinds of things that schooling at its best teaches
2. skills of some occupation that may be filled by a secondary school graduate, so that every 18-year-old would be accredited in some occupation, whether he continued in school or not
3. decision-making skills: that is, those skills of making decisions in complex situations where consequences follow from decisions
4. general physical and mechanical skills: skills that allow the young person to deal with physical and mechanical problems he will confront outside work, in the home, or elsewhere
5. bureaucratic and organizational skills: how to cope with a bureaucratic organization, as an employee, a customer, a client, a manager, or an entrepreneur
6. skills and care of dependent persons: skills in caring for children, old persons, and sick persons
7. emergency skills: how to act in an emergency or unfamiliar situation, in sufficient time to deal with the emergency
8. verbal communication skills in argumentation and debate.

According to Coleman's (1974) report of the work of the Panel of Youth for the Science Advisory Committee of the President of the United States, environments for youth, including curricula and other schooling experiences, should be addressed to two broad classes of objectives.

"One is essentially self-centered. It concerns that acquisition of skills that expand the personal resources, and thus the opportunity of a young person. Schools have traditionally focused upon this class of objectives, and often narrowly so within this class" (p. 3). The report contends,

First among the self-centered class of objectives are those *cognitive and non-cognitive skills necessary for economic independence and for occupational opportunities.* Although survival in the modern world requires as a minimum a considerable capacity in the use of words and numbers, the range of necessary skills beyond that minimum varies widely as the distribution of occupations within the labor force.

. . . A second objective consists of developing the *capability of effective management of one's own affairs.* The emergent adult faces an increasingly complex world, in which self-direction and self-management are prerequisites to success. The current environments imposed on youth by society, in the form of schools, provide little experience with self-management, in large part because, where there is little freedom of choice, there is little self-responsibility. The need for experience is manifested in the frequency with which the freshman entering college, and seniors leaving high school, experience shock as a consequence of the enlargement of choice.

. . . A third objective within the self-centered class is to develop *capabilities as a consumer, not only of goods, but more significantly of the cultural riches of civilization.*

. . . As a final objective in this class, environments for youth should also develop in youth the *capabilities for engaging in intense concentrated involvement in an activity* (pp. 3–4).

Coleman argues further that the objectives of the second class, with activities directed toward other persons, are equally important. "Adulthood cannot be accomplished merely by the acquisition of self-serving capabilities. These must be augmented by capabilities for mutually rewarding involvement with others."

First, it is important for each person's horizons to be enlarged by *experience with persons differing in social class, subculture, and in age.*

A second facet of social maturation concerns *the experience of having others dependent on one's actions.* . . . Social maturity also develops in the context of involvement in *interdependent activities directed toward collaborative goals,* where the outcome for all depends on the coordinated efforts of each (p. 5).

According to Coleman and his colleagues on the panel, these kinds of social maturation are now accomplished haphazardly if at all. He adds,

It is important to develop in youth an additional set of attributes that arise from both classes of objectives, a sense of identity and self-esteem. These are attributes toward which environments for youth should be directed, for such identity and self-esteem form the foundations on which an adult life is built. Further, environments for youth can be assessed by these criteria just as well as by the objectives discussed earlier (p. 5).

The rise of curricular models in deliberate psychological education, values clarification, confluent education, affective education, moral-ethical reasoning, developmental education, and career education address alleged imbalances in the degree to which most subject matter or discipline-based curricula ignore what might be described as guidance learnings: learnings that broaden the content of basic skills and the experiential context in which they might occur, and that acknowledge the legitimacy and meaningfulness of content. Many of these skills were discussed in Chapter 1 in relation to work-context skills, guidance or career maturity skills, and decision-making skills.

However educational purposes and standards are defined, they immediately become part of some value domain. Every educational program proposes outcomes and rests on assumptions about intervention strategies. Also in each, organizational structures are suggested and alternative conceptual models are chosen. Each of these choices is value laden. Conflicts in educational philosophy essentially reflect differences in what people regard as most important. As Phenix (1973) has observed:

It follows that whenever people seek to frame new educational policy or to improve existing educational practices, they need to reflect on the values they wish to serve. Without such reflection it is easy to fall prey to the pressures of expediency, to sink into mindless routine, or to engage in capricious innovation. The clarity and consistency of a people's educational commitments evidently require conscious awareness of the values they seek to realize.

In a major sense the propositions that definitions of career education advance require individuals to confront their own values and, indeed, to change their own lives. Career education itself is an activist strategy. It expects persons to value work, to plan, to be purposeful, to be productive, to be serious about life's meaning, to be useful, and to be committed to growth and learning rather than to passively accept being unemployed or on welfare.

Career education, therefore, requires schools and other institutions, implicitly or explicitly, to accept or reject its values, in particular the direct connection between education and work. Whether a school district or board of education includes or excludes career education from its school program is a value issue frequently disguised as an economic issue or an intellectual one. Such realities are just becoming visible in the United States although much more research needs to be done in this matter.

Perspectives on the values that career education represents have not been well articulated in the literature, but some examples are worth consideration.

Values in Career Education. Swanson (1973) has suggested several value issues that relate to career education. Among them are:

The distribution of society's tasks and roles
Career education deals specifically with statuses, rewards, jobs, and the values that determine how these shall be rationed among the people of society. . . . If career education becomes available to all students, it will justify a view or a value that obligates the educational system to make the entire occupational hierarchy available to every student, not merely as an academic exercise, but as opportunities to be realized (pp. 43–45).

The work ethic
Career education has introduced much discussion about the validity of a work ethic and also with the possibility that career education is a kind of conspiracy to insure obedient and compliant workers for an industrial establishment. . . . Interpreted as useful activity, work may be gratifying and fulfilling whether regarded as an end or a means. In fact, career education offers unique opportunities to explore frontiers of self-discovery and fulfillment (p. 46).

Schools or non-schools
Community interaction is held to be an important element of career education. Much of this interaction involves work experience and other activities that are essentially nonformal (p. 47).

Equality of opportunity
The types of values represented by the demands of justice are of crucial importance to education and particularly to career education. They justify access to opportunity and self-development as a function of the institutional forms for providing career education. . . . (p. 48).

Phenix (1973) has pointed out the major significance and the complexity of eight basic value issues associated with career education. Three of these deal with meaning, one with the human condition, one with time, and three with society. He arrays these value issues using contrasting extremes in the following manner.

In the first three value issues, which are basically matters of semantics, he raises three questions: What is the meaning of career? What is the meaning of education? What is the meaning of gifted and talented? To consider each of these questions, he contrasts life and job, experience and schooling, person and function.

The fourth value issue has to do with the activities that best serve the realization of human ends. In this category, work and play are contrasted.

The fifth, pertaining to career education, is seen by Phenix as concerned with time, the context of relative transitoriness and mutability within a concern for order and stability. The contrast drawn here is between change and permanence.

The sixth, seventh, and eighth value issues relate to fundamental social values concerned with reconciling the competing claims of equality and difference and of unity and plurality. These issues are viewed in the contrasts of generalist and specialist, hierarchy and leveling, the person and the collective.

Phenix does not view these contrasts as dicotomous alternatives. Rather he sees them as axes of choice, with possibilities of any number of intermediate positions.

The significance of the value issues raised by both Swanson and Phenix deserve a great deal of discussion. Such is not the purpose of this chapter. The intent here is primarily to argue that neither the processes nor the content of career education is value free and to identify some of the values at least implicit in various definitions of career education. Although the value and conceptual issues discussed in this chapter are centered on career education, most of them have equal validity for career guidance in either an educational context or in other settings.

Evaluation in Career Education

A further trend during the past decade is an emphasis on evaluation in career education. A whole series of monographs and reports on the effects of career education has been published in the past ten years. Suffice it to say that in general career education comes out quite well on most of these findings. As Hoyt (1980) has suggested, collectively, the evaluation studies summarized in such monographs clearly demonstrate that a career education approach can — when correctly applied — provide students with the general employability/adaptability/promotability skills included in this first career education goal (p. 3). Some methodological matters and specific findings pertinent to career education are as follows:

1. By any measure, state and local efforts labeled as career education in content and goal are occurring throughout the United States. The largest amount of effort in career education has been at the elementary and the junior high levels, although there are less frequent examples at the senior high school and in higher education and the community.

2. Surveys of parents, teachers, and students about the goals or intent of career education

tend to be positive with almost no exceptions. When comparisons are possible, it is apparent that elementary school teachers are more enthusiastic about career education than are secondary school teachers. In specific settings and among some populations, ignorance of or confusion about career education continues to prevail.

3. Although career education efforts are taking place in one-third to one-half of the nation's school districts, relatively few instances of comprehensive K–12 programs are evident.

4. Little evidence is available of career education efforts being specifically tailored to the needs of special populations (e.g., the physically or mentally handicapped, ethnic groups, racial minorities).

5. In a number of projects, the term career seems to be misused. What is actually occurring is an occupational focus: an emphasis on immediate choices rather than intermediate and longer term planning. Similarly, in such approaches, very little emphasis seems to be given to volunteerism, leisure time activities, or implications of work conditions and characteristics for different life styles.

6. Successful career education programs tend to evidence considerable community involvement and the bringing of students and working adults together in some direct fashion.

7. In terms of specific results related to multicomponent career education efforts, the following could be estimated from the studies examined:

   a. On most career education outcomes, the results are mixed. While there are usually statistically significant changes reported on either pre-post or experimental/control bases, one can find non-significant results on the same controls at the same general grade level in some other evaluations and, in some few instances, situations where the controls exceed the experimentals. On balance, one finds career education evaluations reporting generally significant changes in knowledge of a wide range of occupations, in career/occupational awareness, in motivation, work habits and attitudes, and attitudes toward school. Self-concept changes, increases in academic achievement, changes on the *Career Development Inventory*, the *Career Education Questionnaire*, the *OVIS*, and *Coopersmith Self Esteem Scale* are more problematic. Some projects achieve significant differences, others do not. In the absence of standard assessments that a treatment, a process, a teacher behavior labelled the same really means the same from project to project, it is difficult to account for the variance in outcomes reported. Similarly, while career education goals may be titled in the same way from project to project, they are frequently assessed with quite different criterion measurements. Often these measures are uncorrelated with each other and thus the outcomes actually being measured are hard to interpret. If two projects seeking the same goal but measuring it with uncorrelated instruments each secure significant results, it is not clear what this means. If the contents of the measurement instruments are different, can the processes in the two projects be the same and do the significant outcomes mean the same? It is doubtful but difficult to know under the current conditions.

b. It is particularly interesting to note that in the studies reviewed here where academic achievement is a criterion variable, there are studies suggesting statistically significant increases in such achievement in favor of the career education groups and there are studies indicating no significant differences between experimental and control groups. There are no studies in which there are significant results in academic achievement favoring the control group. In essence, then, these studies suggest that on the one hand, career education is likely to increase the academic achievement of students; on the other, where there are not significant differences between experimentals and controls it suggests that career education does not harm academic achievement even though it adds other elements to the curriculum.

8. In the evaluations of experience-based career education efforts, results were not unlike those found in multi-component school-based career education programs. Academic achievement of students in these career education approaches either increased or remained the same as for the controls. Positive findings were also found in career maturity, attitudes toward school, personal responsibility, specific career planning, self-appraisal, and sense of achievement which exceeded those found with comparison groups. Students generally enjoyed the individualized, flexible, and community-based nature of these programs although they sometimes missed their friends and felt cut off from their regular schools. When queried about the experience-based programs, parents and employers were generally quite favorably disposed to them. They typically felt that such programs were good alternatives to traditional approaches. However, some concerns were expressed about the screening of students; some parents felt that students did not have control or discipline in the program and were not responsible enough themselves to be placed in such a situation.

9. In the several studies of specific decision-making courses, or short-term individual or group counseling directed to facilitating vocational development of students, generally positive results have been found. While there are several studies in which no significant results were found between experimental and control groups, the more specific the career planning experience to which students are exposed, the more positive the results tend to be. Students in experimental career planning courses or counseling groups tend to have higher academic achievement, more positive attitudes toward college (if they are college students), more certainty about completing their programs, higher measured career maturity, and they make more appropriate educational vocational choices than control students. There is some indication in these studies also that, in terms of sequence, if students can learn about themselves before they are exposed to occupational information, or if they can request such information as they are ready, then their learning will be significantly facilitated (Herr, 1978).

THE INGREDIENTS OF EFFECTIVE CAREER EDUCATION MODELS

The ingredients of *effective* career education efforts have become increasingly obvious. These have been dissected from major career education programs around the nation that have stood up to various types of evaluation by government agencies (Office of Career Education, 1979). Although no one model fits every circumstance, setting, or local emphasis, effective models of career education tend to share several ingredients:

1. They have administrative support that is visible and continuing.
2. The goals of career education are seen as major commitments of a school district, a higher education institution, or work setting. In this respect, they are seen as central to the institutional mission and to the facilitation of specific behaviors to be attained by graduates or by employees.
3. Career education is a planned, integrative dimension of an education or work setting, not a random add-on or by-product relegated to the responsibility of only one group of specialists. Representatives of all of the groups of educators, industrial personnel, and community persons affected by and making a contribution to career education are involved in the planning and selected advisory groups are used effectively.
4. Resources are provided for planning and for staff development and these emphases are matters of systematic effort. The planning and the staff development is based on theory and research in career behavior so that there is not only a concern about the how of career education but also the why.
5. Field experiences (whether internships, planned field trips, career shadowing, or something else) are planned to extend and to reinforce curriculum infusion and other career education instruction. They are not independent of the latter. The community is seen as a large learning laboratory and one that has responsibility to be in partnership with the schools in creating the most effective educational and occupational opportunities available.

6. Career education is not seen as something so different that the school system, teachers, counselors, and others must start from ground zero. Rather it acknowledges that experiences already in place have career education implications and further career education can be built on them. Organizational changes are planned and developed to facilitate the career education effort but they are not dramatized as so new as to be threatening to participants.
7. Career education and vocational education are not confused. Career education is seen as for all children, youth, or adults within the educational level or setting in which it is implemented; it is not confined in its scope to only the development of occupational task specific skills.
8. There is an evaluation process built into the planning and the implementation of career education so that its results can be examined and advocated as appropriate to policy-making bodies or other decision-makers.

RELATIONSHIP OF CAREER EDUCATION TO CAREER GUIDANCE

The models of career education described in this chapter clearly depend on the presence of career guidance. It is no overstatement to contend that career education has institutionalized, as major aspects of educational and manpower development missions, goals that have long been advanced by career guidance practitioners. Certainly, career education has made visible the complexity of many of these goals. It has reinforced the importance of cooperation between school and community, various networks of persons, and diverse processes and resources, if the goals of career education are to be met.

The Importance of Career Guidance Personnel

Career education has shown that no one group of persons can accomplish all its goals alone. But it has also made apparent that no other group of specialists is more important to its goals than career guidance personnel. Other elements of the school, community, or family may help to lay a broad base of career awareness or provide specific technical preparation for a chosen career. However, it remains the central task of career guidance to help individuals identify their career options, understand the personal implications of these options, plan the ways by which they can integrate the educational experiences necessary to achieve favored goals, and make decisions wisely when they must be made.

In Chapter 1 we discuss several competency statements that describe what the career guidance practitioner must be able to know and to do in order to be effective in career education, particularly in three major phases: planning and design, implementation, evaluation. You may want to review these.

With any concept, definitions are important to identifying the primary elements or boundaries to which that term relates. This is particularly true with such terms as career development, career education, and career guidance. In addition to the basic definitions given in Chapter 1, the three terms can be usefully differentiated in the following manner:

Career Development describes the lifelong behavioral processes and the influences upon them which lead to one's work values, choice of occupation(s), creation of a career pattern, decision-making style, role integration, self and career identity, educational literacy and related phenomena. As such, career development is not an intervention, but the object of intervention. Conceptual and research insights into career development comprise the theory of behavior which intervention strategies might modify in order to facilitate more positive and purposeful career development than would likely occur randomly.

If career development describes particular types of behavior, then career education and career guidance describe one intervention in such behavior. Although there is overlap in these processes, they can be usefully distinguished as follows:

Career Education has as its major goal improving the relationship between education and work. Career education tends to emphasize the teaching/learning process as the principal mode of intervention in career development and

teachers or instructors are seen as the principal actors in the intervention strategy.

Career Guidance is a set, preferably a systematic program, of processes, techniques, or services designed to assist an individual to understand and act on self-knowledge and knowledge of opportunities in work, education, and leisure, and to develop the decision-making skills by which one can create and manage one's career development. . . . Career guidance does not rely upon the teaching/learning process as its major intervention context or modality and counselors are typically seen as the primary actors (Herr, 1979).

Career Education in Settings Other Than Schools

Career education has had its major implementation in the elementary and secondary schools of the nation. But it would be wrong to conclude that its effects have been confined to those settings. College and universities and corporate settings have also instituted career education programs although not always under that title.

It appears that the significant increase in the number of colleges and universities expanding the functions of their placement centers to career development and placement centers is at least an indirect outcome of the influence of career education. Many of the characteristics and purposes of such centers have been described in Chapter 10. Particularly notable are their efforts in providing courses in decision-making and career-planning within majors, their use of computer-based career guidance systems, and the provision of workshops on job-search strategies, interviewing techniques, assertive training, and related topics. Most of these centers are developmental and proactive in their emphases. They use both instructional and counseling methodologies to make higher education settings more career relevant.

However, the effects of career education on higher education are not confined to what happens to college students through the auspices of career development and placement centers. There are also effects on the substance and process of preservice teacher or counselor preparation; expanded programs of in-service training in career education for practitioners of Career Education already in the field; increasing offerings of undergraduate credit courses in career exploration; greater attention to using work experience, internship, and work-study programs to assist students in the choice of and transition to work; greater communication and interaction between colleges and universities and business and industries; and closer working relationships between some four-year institutions and junior colleges on "two plus two" transfer programs designed around career ladder concepts (Jorgenson & Spooner, 1981).

It appears that career education has also influenced models of career development in business and industry, although this notion is somewhat more diffuse and harder to track than is the case of career development in higher education. Shifts in work values, the organization of work, employment and unemployment rates, concerns about work productivity have combined to stimulate new models of personnel *development*, not just personnel *management*. In Chapter 11 we described many of the models of career guidance in business and industry. As the concepts and practices embodied in these models are closely scrutinized, their resemblance to various career education models is clear, although the language of such implementations is that of business and industry rather than of education. In addition, in comparing career education for youth with that for adults, Rice (1981) has observed that the former has concentrated on the transition from school to work, whereas the latter has focused on the transition from work to school (retraining) or from work to work (midlife career change, moving from a part-time job to a long-term career, and so on). It seems quite likely that the implementation of career education concepts during the past decade has provided the stimulus and the conceptual mortar to bring together a life-span approach to career guidance.

THE FUTURE OF CAREER EDUCATION

Although much more could be said about the types of effects that have resulted from the implementation of career education during the past decade, it is useful to turn our attention briefly to the future as well as to some issues still to be played out.

First, with respect to the future of career education, there seems little doubt that its concepts and substance will continue to be important. Whether the term for these concepts, *career education*, will endure, is less certain, but that does not alter the fundamental need for and, indeed, the place already achieved by these notions. Let us look at some reasons for making such generalizations.

By 1976, over half of the nation's students were in school districts in which at least one major career education activity was implemented (McLaughlin, 1976). Under the influence of PL 95-207 and PL 94-482 the implementation of career education has expanded to additional districts or intensified where it was originally underway. In many, if not most, of these districts career education activities and concepts are now incorporated into the mainstream of the instructional or guidance processes and are likely to continue by inertia if for no other reason. A survey by the American Institute for Research in the Behavioral Sciences found that forty-seven states, Puerto Rico, and the District of Columbia participated in the Federal Career Education Act Incentive Program in fiscal years 1979 and 1980. New Mexico, South Dakota, and Nevada did not participate. Visits to nine participating states indicated strong support for career education, "with seven of the nine states using state funds as well as Incentives Act funds to support career education activities (American Institute for Research, 1981).

More important than the reasoning in the previous observations is the fact that many states have developed their own legislative and fiscal support for career education. These are not likely to be rescinded if the federal government pulls back its relatively small fiscal commitment to career education. Indeed, in some states (such as New Jersey), career education or career exploration instruction and outcomes as reflected in subject matter credits have become a part of graduation requirements. In others they have, more subtly, become part of the Educational Quality Assessment of schools (for example, Pennsylvania) or incorporated into competency-based examinations of students (for example, Florida). Responses to these statewide efforts obviously have their local corollaries embedded in the attitudes, knowledge base, and instructional activities to which students are exposed. Community expectations for such efforts are high and they are valued in such a way that retreat from them will not be easy.

These examples reflect the likely continuity of career education as a term and as a process for many years into the future. Misgivings about this matter lie with the lack of comprehensiveness of this continuity. In other words, many states and some school districts will not be affected by what will occur in other states and school districts. The young people in the areas without a career education opportunity will be disadvantaged in our judgment.

Also, whether or not career education is as firmly entrenched as has just been suggested that it is in some places, there is little doubt that the substance of the effort will continue for other reasons.

Tension between the academic and the vocational purposes of schooling has existed in this country for two hundred years. The forces that have kept that tension high have not abated and, indeed, will likely become more severe under the economic and energy problems of the foreseeable future. Career education represents a potential bridge between academic and vocational emphases in education without corrupting the essence of either. Beyond that, however, much of educational legislation as well as governmental or quasi-governmental statements have served to recommend institutionalization of the substance of career education without using the term. Certainly, prevocational aspects of the vocational education legislation since VEA of 1963 have permitted, encouraged, and supported efforts common to career education without using the term. Indeed, some aspects of the testimony of the American Vocational Association before the Congress over the last several years, including the recent language concerning the reauthorization of the Vocational Education Act, sound very much like career education although the term is not used. The aborted youth employability legislation of 1980 had many such emphases related to the substance of career education though rarely referring to the term itself. The provision of career exploration in many

CETA projects, and in many educational informational centers for adults has used career education models, materials, and processes. The rapidly growing introduction of career guidance in business and industry has, in fact, in several corporations institutionalized career education models defined within corporate parameters or those of specific governmental agencies such as NASA, Livermore Laboratory, GAO. The presence and growth of these models is a powerful counterforce to the rapid extinction of career education concepts and processes from American educational or social provisions.

Beyond these important factors there seem to be other even more subtle forces that make the continuation of career education concepts and processes likely. Some of these have been alluded to previously, but it is useful to reinforce them briefly here. One is that, in general, the factors giving rise to career education in the late 1960s and early 1970s have not really changed. They are problems basic to a society in major transition from an industrially oriented goods-producing economy to a postindustrial, service- and knowlege-oriented economy. They are major problems when there is less than full employment and when youth unemployment is a major social and economic matter. They become important where increasing evidence suggests that many adults are ill-equipped to deal with problems of living pertinent to work, to choice, to budgeting, to nutrition and to other matters of responsibility and commitment. They further occur where leisure time or increasing discretionary time is a very mixed blessing frequently inducing anxiety, conflict, substance abuse rather than renewal, refreshment, and other positive aspects. And they are of concern where shifts in occupational content will require different configurations of work, training, and discretionary time as well as different parameters of choice itself.

All of these changes and others too dim to perceive well at the moment speak directly to the need for the encouragement, the content, and the opportunities for experience that are represented by the term career education.

However positive such a view of the longevity of career education, or something like it, may be, several matters need to be anticipated, planned for, and dealt with. They include:

1. *Career education or occupational education.* In many instances, career education, when implemented, tends to deal with occupational or job choice, not the forging of a career that includes immediate, intermediate, and distant choices. Occupational education also involves forces that go beyond occupational models, in which the unit of concern has to do with self-understanding relating to self concept, personal values and preferences, risk-taking style, decision-making skills, industrial discipline and affective work competencies, role integration, reduction of sex-stereotyped choice-making, and similar matters.

2. *Career education's theoretical roots.* To date, the conceptualizations of career education have rested heavily on developmental and differential psychology that is embedded in career development theory and research. However important career development theory is as conceptual mortar for career education, it must to an increasing degree be embedded in economic perspectives, greater understanding of the differences among labor market characteristics, factors differentiating forms of employment and unemployment, and understandings of how employability and employment differ.

3. *Career education and special needs populations.* When we speak of career education, we sometimes overlook the fact that it requires attention to the specific needs and characteristics of subgroups within the general populations. Certainly, future models of career education will need to expand our ability to reduce the constraints on choice occasioned by both individual and institutional sex or racial bias. We will need to attend more fully to the needs of the physically disabled, not as a homogeneous group but as a group with great heterogeneity in functional limitations, aspirations, and abilities. Similarly, we need to be more conscious, before the fact, of the characteristics of the subpopulations who have considerable difficulty in mastering the school-to-work transition.

4. *Recurring concerns.* We must realize that in the future career education cannot confine itself to carving out new ground or refining old. It must also lay to rest some persistent myths, including: Career education and vocational education are synonyms. Career education is against higher education, or liberal arts. Career education is antiintellectual. Career education is antihumanistic. Career education is a conspiracy to limit the mobility of minority persons. These uninformed and simplistic observations create "noise" in the system and divert energies from the important issues of conceptualization and implementation that have been noted here and elsewhere. Part of the problem is that we have used terms related to career education too loosely and too imprecisely. Sometimes we have invested more energy in determining how to do career education than in why we are doing it or in discovering the conceptual background pertinent to it. Then we have not had answers to such concerns when we needed them. And, certainly, in other cases we have not invested our energies in the quality of staff development that career education has deserved.

5. *Converging concerns.* Finally, we must realize that many of the issues and goals of career education are beginning to converge with those of other educational emphases. Collaboration and linkages with the community are fundamental to career education, and they are matters in which research and conceptualization about different approaches are extremely important. But we must realize that they are similar to the emerging approaches to experiential education, to community education, to alternative high schools, and to similar phenomena. We cannot afford to overlook the successes and failures to be found in these areas and to learn from them. Similarly, we need to be alert to the points of congruence between career education, deliberate psychological education, values clarification and related movements. Career education and the approaches combined here under the term deliberate psychological education share many goals, although their descriptive language and emphases differ somewhat. For example, approaches to both career education and psychological education stress the importance to student development of self-understanding, planning and problem-solving, and decision-making skills. Both career education and psychological education express concern for modifying the school climate or its organizational structure including increasing the number of curricular options available to respond to a wider range of human talent than those primarily verbal and abstract. Many other parallels between these

movements could be drawn. That is not really necessary. What is important is that in the future career educators recognize the convergence of points of view with other educational movements, the conceptual content they might provide, and their possibilities for alliances in support of both the goals and processes of career education.

Summary

In this chapter we have discussed the past, present, and future of career education. Although it does represent continuity from the past, career education is more than vocational education and neither limited nor episodic as many earlier reform movements have been. Its roots and its substance speak to ideas deeply embedded in the American society as they reflect education for choice and the development of purposefulness in work. Such ideas and a press for educational accommodation of them are not likely to go away. Crucial to the implementation of career education is effective career guidance. Comprehensive career guidance programs are the catalysts by which the information and awareness stimulated by career education are personalized and translated into individual action.

LEARNING ACTIVITIES

1. Write a brief essay discussing the need for educational reforms in schools with which you are familiar. Are they similar to those cited by the USOE?
2. Compile a set of criteria by which school courses can be evaluated in order to determine whether they are preparing students for further education, for an entry-level job, or for both. Consider how schools of your acquaintance rate.
3. Construct a plan by which business, labor, and industrial organizations can be involved meaningfully with the educational system.
4. Prepare a presentation for a group of teachers describing how career education is humanistic or how it facilitates intellectual activities.
5. Inventory the contributions that general or academic education and vocational education can each make to career education.
6. Discuss with several employers their perceptions of and feelings about career education.

7. Visit a career education program in a school, a career development and placement center in a college and university, and a career guidance (personnel development or HRD) program in business and industry. Describe how the concepts and techniques are similar and how they are different.
8. Read the international economic news in a major newspaper for one week. Identify the themes that appear to support the implementation of career education in this country and in other nations.

OBJECTIVES

After reading this chapter, engaging in the learning activities, and reading the suggested references, you should have met the objectives that follow. If you have not, it would probably be useful for you to review the material in Chapter 15 before proceeding further. You should now be able to:

1. List at least five educational conditions that the USOE indicated required the initiation of career education.
2. State in your own words how vocational education and career education are different.
3. Describe five or more emphases that seem to be common to many career education projects.
4. Discuss the four original national career education models, state the assumptions of each, and identify the populations they were intended to serve.
5. Name the eight outcomes that the comprehensive career education model sought.
6. List ways that career guidance relates to each of the career education models.
7. Create a graph comparing the four national career education models in terms of the set-

ting, goals, organizing themes, population served, and other pertinent elements.

8. Construct an outline of differences between career education and career guidance and a list of ways in which they are related.

9. Compare and contrast the following: self-awareness, educational awareness, economic awareness, career identity, employability skills, and self-social fulfillment.

10. List a series of alternatives by which an experience-based career education model might be financed.

11. Discuss four value issues that are important to both career education and career guidance.

12. Define and contrast career development, career education, and career guidance.

16 / Information in Career Guidance and Counseling

Most people are conversant with very few occupations. They are aware, sometimes only vaguely, of the nature of the occupations of their immediate families and perhaps those of a small group of family-connected individuals. Because of the mass media, they may also be acquainted with an additional small number of occupations, frequently stereotyped. During the process of socialization, people have learned that some types of occupations are desirable and that others are taboo, at least within their cultural spheres. In attempting to relate self-characteristics to various occupations, then, they typically have few alternatives through which to sort unless some type of direct intervention occurs. This intervention usually takes the form of exposure to occupational information, mediated by a career guidance practitioner.

In addition to their need for occupational information, individuals require educational and personal information, if their career development is to be complete. Since educational decisions are intermediate choices within the total context of career decision-making, individuals must possess and be able to use information about various curricular opportunities, post-high school and post-college educational and training possibilities, and the relationship between education and work. If students make decisions to attend college, they need to understand such factors as how collegiate environments differ, how the overt characteristics of institutions of higher education (such as size, selectivity, geographical location, curriculum, and others) affect individuals, how to go about the application process, how to investigate financial aid opportunities, how to determine what

national tests are required, and how to cope with many other variables in the process of educational choice. If students or adults are specialty-oriented, they must have similarly important information about opportunities for training. Hence, whether counselees are adolescents in the process of exploration, college students in the process of delimiting choice, or adults involved in midcareer change, preretirement programs, CETA programs, or other career-related decision-making, information about educational or occupational opportunities can help individuals to accomplish the necessary tasks.

Both educational and occupational information have meaning only insofar as such data are evaluated within the framework of what individuals know about themselves. Self-information is crucial to individuals' seeing the relevance of the educational or occupational data which they receive. Counselees need an accurate picture and acceptance of their strengths and weaknesses in both the cognitive and the noncognitive domains in order to realize fully the value of the information regarding the worlds of work and education. They must be aware of their diverse aptitudes, interests, values, and attitudes toward learning and work. Only then can they truly evaluate the information they receive. In effect, one asks, "Knowing what I know about myself, how can I use this information?"

The process of career development requires that information continually reinforce planfulness; the interaction of educational or training alternatives, occupational alternatives, and self-characteristics is mandatory if good career decision-making is to occur. Suggestions for enhancing

442

the interaction of these topics have been offered in Chapter 14.

This chapter suggests processes to achieve the goals for career guidance offered earlier in this book. It offers a range of delivery systems by which the concepts, knowledge, and attitudes integral to career development can be attuned to the needs and characteristics of the various consumer publics. It seeks to identify the range of possibilities available within the many facets of the educational enterprise and within the community for reinforcing vocationalization – for helping the individual develop a vocabulary of work, acquire necessary career knowledge, develop healthy career attitudes, learn adequate decision-making skills, and so forth. Specifically, we will set forth in this chapter some principles for effectively using information and discuss the evaluation of information, types of delivery systems, and illustrations of some of the more promising systems. We include also a discussion of the work of the National Occupational Information Coordinating Committee (NOICC) and its state counterparts (SOICCs). A sampling of some of the specific materials available is also presented. Because of space limitations, we will concentrate primarily on occupational information.

PRINCIPLES FOR USING INFORMATION EFFECTIVELY

It is obvious that simple exposure to information is insufficient. The mere availability of information about occupations, educational and training opportunities, and the characteristics of an individual does not mean that the information will be used or, if used, that it will be employed effectively. In order to increase the probability that data will be efficiently utilized, one must consider aspects of motivation, the quality of the information, and how information is assimilated.

Motivation

O'Hara (1968) highlights the importance of the concepts of need and readiness. In emphasizing the more cognitive aspects of career learning, he suggests that all such learning is a function of motivation. Motivation, in turn, is based on a

person's attempt to satisfy a career-related need. In other words, no need, no action; no action, no career-related learning. To satisfy these conditions, O'Hara proposes, "Guidance personnel have an obligation to impose a formal learning situation, with formal academic sanctions, in order to create the goal-directedness necessary for increased understanding of the world of work and the numerous possible responses to it" (p. 638). The formal learning situation would emphasize the language of occupations to facilitate the vicarious exploration of the world of work. Without this experience, the individual is likely to be "vocationally deprived." O'Hara, then, points up the first principle in the use of information – motivation for use.

Cooley's (1969) view coincides with O'Hara's:

I believe a necessary ingredient would be an extensive guidance curriculum. Through a variety of approaches – such as independent study, small group discussions, career games, and computer-assisted instruction – principles involved in goal setting, planning toward goals, self-direction, and decision-making need to be taught. . . . Such a curriculum could provide the student with a body of relevant knowledge regarding those processes (goal setting and planning) so that the counselor and student can more easily work together in those tasks. The guidance curriculum must try to prepare the student to make effective use of the counseling interview (p. 65).

Although we are not necessarily advocating the development of a formal career curriculum, we agree with both O'Hara and Cooley that a great deal of career guidance is composed of cognitive learnings that need to be systematically planned and sequentially provided. Slater (1978), for example, defines career exploration as "good cognitive trips into a world of variously defined personal characteristics, job requirements, and so forth" (p. 133). Almost all learning theories place a premium on motivation, readiness, and the establishment of a set in the learner. Career guidance processes would do well to follow this example. To become motivated, individuals must be assisted to see how their needs are met by whatever information is delivered.

Motivation and the establishment of readiness pertain to all scholastic ability levels within an educational setting and to adults. Although there is some evidence that brighter students have more knowledge of high-level than low-level occupations (Banducci, 1970), more recent research suggests that academic achievers are no more knowledgeable about occupations than are lower achievers, and that the social status of the student is also not a factor in the accuracy of information (Nuckols & Banducci, 1974). Accuracy or inaccuracy of information also extends to sex-related stereotypes. Yanico (1980) found that college females demonstrated a lack of information about occupations nontraditional for their sex. Males do not. Birk, Tanney, and Cooper (1979) studied standard occupational information sources such as the *Occupational Outlook Handbook* and the *Encyclopedia of Careers* and concluded that members of minority groups and women are generally underrepresented and disproportionately pictured in traditional careers and roles and that this inaccurate image is therefore delimiting for women and minority users. These findings suggest that counselors should not make a priori assumptions regarding who needs occupational information and who does not.

Biggers (1971) has demonstrated that high school students do not know how to use information. In fact, he found high school students as limited as fourth graders in their ability to use information in career decision-making. These findings point to the necessity of helping individuals learn to use information. This end can be accomplished only after a learning set has been established.

Some people believe that the acquisition of information — not simply occupational, but all types of information — is a fundamental life skill. Hudson and Danish (1980) identify sixteen major categories of life information needs, two of which are related to employment and to education and schooling. These are skills related to defining and locating needed information to cope with a variety of crucial life events.

Readiness and motivation, then, are requisite to the effective use of occupational information at any intervention point in one's life span. Readiness assumes that we can accurately measure the level of an individual's occupational information.

Although some career maturity inventories use aspects of occupational information in their assessments (see Chapter 17), these efforts are thought to be less comprehensive than desirable. Consequently, Blank (1979) has developed Jobs-Career Key (JCK), a test of information in the domains of economic factors, education and training, job parts, and worker interactions. Although this instrument is not yet ready for general use, it is an example of promising developments in the assessment of occupational knowledge.

Evaluation of Information

A second factor in the effective use of information is the caliber of the data. Whatever the vehicle through which the information is transmitted — print, film, slide, record, computer, simulation, and such — there is a need to evaluate it in terms of some criteria of "good" information.

One important criterion is the source of the information. Some material is produced for recruitment, and although many such presentations are acceptable, some, because of their overzealousness, are misleading. Other materials are produced specifically for guidance purposes and thus can frequently be considered more accurate at face value.

Other important considerations are the currency, validity, and applicability of the data. Currency refers to the up-to-date nature of the information. Newness does not guarantee accuracy, but it is likely that information will be more accurate if it is recent. Validity refers to the accuracy of the information, insofar as the data may be affected by such factors as the zealous recruitment motive discussed earlier. Finally, applicability may be considered from two points of view: (1) Are the data presented in such a manner that they can be easily utilized? (2) Is the level at which the data are presented appropriate to the consumer?

Periodically, the National Vocational Guidance Association promulgates guidelines for the preparation and evaluation of career literature (NVGA, 1971, 1980). These guidelines form the bases for evaluating current career materials that appear in the *Vocational Guidance Quarterly*. There are both general guidelines and content guidelines that cover the following areas.

General Guidelines

Accuracy of Information-current and non-biased

Format-clear, concise, and interesting

Vocabulary-appropriate to target group

Bias and Stereotyping-gender-, race-, and religion-free information

Graphics-current and nonstereotyped

Dating and Revisions-frequent revisions required

Credits-who and where

Content Guidelines

Duties and Nature of the Work-purpose, activities, skills, specializations, and so on

Work Settings and Conditions-physical activities and work environment

Personal Qualifications-specific to a *particular* occupation

Social and Psychological Factors-satisfiers and limiters associated with an occupation; life style implications

Preparation Required-length and type, cost, difficulty of entry

Special Requirements-physical, personal, licensing, and so on

Methods of Entering-typical and alternate approaches

Earnings and Other Benefits-current ranges

Usual Advancement Possibilities-typical career ladders

Employment Outlook-short- and long-range

Opportunities for Experience and Exploration-part-time, summer, volunteer, and so on

Related Occupations-alternate possibilities

Sources of Education and Training-schools, agencies, and so on

Sources of Additional Information-where to go, whom to see

Use of Information

How individuals use information in career-related decision-making is, in many respects, a highly personalized matter. Several generalizations are possible, however, on the basis of research conducted by Halpern and Norris (1968). They investigated the role of information in the curriculum decisions of tenth-grade students.

1. The students tended to select information which counselors had judged to be most relevant.

2. Their information search sampled the available information areas with the exception of values, which tended to be neglected.

3. Their information-search pattern changed as they received information, i.e., information at first considered important was often reclassified as unimportant (and vice-versa) as new information was received.

4. The information area of abilities was considered the most important, plans and interests less important, and values least important (p. 240).

When these findings are coupled with the results of research reported in other chapters, namely, the concepts of cognitive dissonance (Festinger, 1957), primacy effect (Luchins, 1960), and bounded rationality (Simon, 1960), it is easy to understand that how information is assimilated, processed, and accepted or rejected is very complex and idiosyncratic. Just as the intake of information is individualized, so too is the output of information as it affects career-related decision-making.

One principle that seems to have been fairly well established through research is that behavioral reinforcement techniques are highly effective in promoting career information-seeking behaviors (Aiken & Johnston, 1973; Borman, 1972; Krumboltz & Schroeder, 1965; Krumboltz & Thoresen, 1964). Whether used with individuals or with groups, if motivation is present or lacking, verbal reinforcement of information-seeking statements of counselees apparently produces more information-seeking behaviors than not reinforcing. In a sense, counselors are establishing and stimulating a readiness of the type previously discussed.

The role of information in career decision making has not been clearly established. We have some preliminary research from Pitz and Harren (1980) which suggests that a person will seek information only if the perceived "payoff" is greater than the cost of the information. They cite the example of the impulsive decision maker who wants to terminate the decision process as quickly as possible and who thus makes a decision with minimum information. An agonizing decision maker, on the other hand, "may continually seek information to avoid the act of commitment to a particular choice and its attendant course of action" (p. 325). We do know that occupational information influences occupational perceptions and that the same information can produce varied perceptions on the basis of the perceiver's age and occupational status (Remeny & Fraser, 1977).

We know also that receiving occupational information tends to increase the simplicity with which one perceives occupations. Learning theorists call this phenomenon *cognitive complexity* (Bodden & James, 1976). What is more, the *type* of occupational information also affects cognitive complexity; that is, negative information is likely to produce a less simplified view of an occupation, whereas positive information decreases cognitive complexity (Haase et al., 1979). These studies suggest giving career decision makers both the positive and negative information about an occupation. Since most information now is either neutral or positive, these findings would argue for more description of negative features.

Finally, it would appear that level of occupational knowledge can affect even our most basic "tools of the trade." There are two ways to assess vocational preferences: by expressing preferences for job titles (such as mechanic) or by expressing preferences for behavioral activities (such as fixing a motor). Loesch and Sampson (1978) conducted research that suggests strongly that a client's job knowledge is related to the manner of assessing vocational preferences. Those with low-level knowledge should be assessed by behavioral activity preferences; those with high-level knowledge should be assessed on the basis of occupational titles.

Individualizing information appears to be a key requirement for its effective use. Hollis and Hollis (1969) argue, "The more information processes can be personalized, the better the individual can understand and integrate information through both his cognitive and affective processes" (p. vi). This means that there is a variety of approaches for gathering information and the effectiveness of these approaches will vary from individual to individual. As the counselor helps individuals to sort through, comprehend, assimilate, and find meaning in information, the effectiveness or lack of effectiveness of such data becomes apparent.

Drier (1980) has quite rightly indicated that career information is not simply career facts or job data. Career information results, he maintains, when a user attaches personal meaning to information. Borow (1980) also reminds us of two other essentials of occupational information, at least at the secondary school level. He argues that it should be presented to broaden the range of options and stimulate exploration rather than narrow choices and hurry decisions. And he urges that occupational information should evidence greater cognizance of the psychosocial characteristics of work, such as the interpersonal factors and peculiar values identified with various types of work.

Herr (1980) maintains that, again in terms of secondary schools, career information is deficient because: (1) it tends to be primarily national rather than substate or local and lacks local experience data; (2) it is more useful to adults who are making decisions than to students who are exploring; (3) there is little sharing between the Employment Service and schools; and (4) we have reached few clear conclusions about student uses of information. It is appropriate at this point to survey the types of delivery systems currently available in order to evaluate their potential effectiveness.

TYPES OF DELIVERY SYSTEMS

Until recently, virtually all occupational information was printed and was primarily descriptive (Flanders & Baxter, 1981). Beginning with the *Dictionary of Occupational Titles*, information became more complex and comprehensive and the possibilities for alternate ways of transmitting it became more numerous. The problem before us is a basic and complicated one — the acquisition, storage, retrieval, and dissemination of information. The information or knowledge explosion is a well-known reality. Knowledge in some fields doubles itself every few years. The generation of new knowledge, in fact, as achieved by various research and development programs, is mainly responsible for the changing occupational structure as described in Chapter 3. New jobs and occupations come about because new products, services, and industries evolve from new knowledge; these new jobs, in turn, generate more new jobs and occupations. The assault of information and new knowledge forces us to grope with new methods for storing the information so that it can be retrieved with maximum efficiency and disseminated in the most effective manner. McDaniel (1982) has urged that any future system of comprehensive career information must be built on four foundations:

1. wide-ranging multimedia approach
2. wide-ranging location of systems
3. wide-ranging appeal to users
4. wide range of sources of career information

The various delivery systems are outlined in the following pages along with representative listings of some of the more common modes.

Printed Matter

The most common and traditional form for career information is published material. These materials range from occupational briefs to the *Dictionary of Occupational Titles* and the *Occupational Outlook Handbook*, from biographies to popular magazines, from booklets, catalogues, and brochures to newspapers. There are diverse prepackaged or home-grown systems available. McDaniel (1980) points out that when counselors adopt a ready-made career information system, they are "buying a theory of career development; a type of access strategy; an evaluation of the appropriateness of the data base; a determination of the counselor component in the system; and a pre-selected point of counselor intervention" (p. 30). These are decisions that, in effect, are taken away from the counselor, with the quid pro quo being the convenience of the system.

There are all sorts of ways to file printed information. These are described in detail in several excellent texts (Hollis & Hollis, 1969; Isaacson, 1977; Norris et al., 1979; Hoppock, 1977). Also, an excellent article by Green (1979) discusses the various accessing systems, ranging from alphabetic to taxonomic.

Unfortunately, experience with occupational and educational literature indicates that all these systems present dissemination problems. The data are easily stored and readily retrieved, but they appear to be insufficiently utilized. Perhaps

the motivation of the individual is missing. Perhaps the effort of reading is too much. Perhaps the printed material is dry and uninspiring. Whatever the reason, it is clear that although students are aware of the types of printed information the school has stored and know that it can be retrieved, they do not in general make use of information. Likewise, adults surely know that they can get information at their public library, but they do not frequently exercise that option. It is apparent that methods other than or in addition to traditional printed materials are necessary or that counselors must deal more effectively with motivational concerns if individuals are to use printed data more extensively.

Acquisition of Information

The acquisition of educational and occupational information is a continual and formidable process. It requires a constant monitoring of commercial catalogues, professional publications, and other sources. Counselors must try to keep current with newer materials. The best way to do so is to consult the *Vocational Guidance Quarterly*, which offers periodic reviews of current career literature. There are several bibliographic sources which contain much useful information. Some of the more prominent compendia are:

- *Adult Career Education Counseling and Guidance Literature Resource*. Portland, Oregon: Commercial-Educational Distributing Services, 1974. Contains over 800 classified, annotated references relating to the career counseling, guidance, and education of adults. Research reports, professional literature, and instructional materials.
- *Career Index*. Moravia, New York: Chronicle Guidance Publications, 1983. An annual compilation of an annotated list of occupational and educational guidance materials available from about 700 public and private organizations.
- Horn, R. E. (Ed.). *The Guide to Simulations/ Games for Education and Training*. (3rd ed.). Cambridge, Mass.: Abt Publications, 1976. Over 1100 simulations and games listings with descriptive data and evaluations.
- *A Counselor's Guide to Occupational Informa-*

tion. Washington, D.C.: U.S. Department of Labor, Bureau of Labor Statistics, July 1980 (Bulletin 2042). An annotated listing of all government publications relating to careers and issued prior to the summer of 1979.

- M. H. Saterstrom (Ed.). *Educators Guide to Free Guidance Materials.* Randolph, Wisc.: Educators Progress Service, Inc., annual. Listing of almost 2500 free films, filmstrips and slides, tapes, scripts, and printed materials which are yours for the asking.
- B. Gale and L. Gale. *The National Career Directory for Free and Inexpensive Guidance Materials.* New York: Arco, 1978. More than 2000 sources of information.
- *Counselor's Information Service.* Washington, D.C.: B'nai B'rith Career and Counseling Services. Published four times per year, this newsletter presents an annotated bibliography of current literature on educational and vocational guidance. Special sections on adult education and the aging and on handicapped and rehabilitation counseling.
- Harry N. Drier, Jr. (Ed.). *Career Development Resources: A Guide to Audiovisual and Printed Materials for Grades K-12.* Worthington, Ohio: Charles A. Jones Publishing Company, 1973. Offers approximately 2200 titles of films, filmstrips, slides, tapes, scripts, games, kits, printed materials, songs, records, and other aids to help in integrating career development into a school curriculum. Classified by grade level and type of resource.
- *EPIE Career Education S*E*T.* New York: Educational Products Information Exchange Institute, 1975. Two volumes: Volume I deals with how to select and evaluate instructional career education materials; Volume II analyzes 750 films, printed materials, filmstrips, multimedia, and miscellanea, all by grade level.
- Gertrude Forrester. *Occupational Literature: An Annotated Bibliography.* New York: W. W. Wilson Co., 1980. A comprehensive, periodically updated listing and description of several thousand pieces of occupational data; has been a useful resource for many years.
- *NVGA Bibliography of Current Career Information* (7th edition). Washington, D.C.: National Vocational Guidance Association, 1980. Lists and evaluates, according to NVGA stan-

dards, over 2300 books, pamphlets, films, and so on.

Table 16.1 lists several references to occupational filing systems and to printed series that are useful for various career guidance purposes. This table is followed by a listing of magazines and journals devoted to career guidance, as well as a sampling of aids of particular interest to college students and adults.

The following magazines and journals are devoted wholly or in part to career guidance.

Career World. Curriculum Innovations, Highwood, Ill. Published monthly during the school year.

American Education. U.S. Department of Health, Education, and Welfare/Office of Education. Published ten times per year.

Career Education Digest. Education Properties. Published monthly during the school year.

Vocational Guidance Quarterly. National Vocational Guidance Association. Published four times per year.

Monthly Labor Review. U.S. Department of Labor. Published monthly.

Work and Occupations (formerly Sociology of Occupations). Sage Publications. Published four times per year.

Journal of Vocational Behavior. Academic Press, Inc. Published four times per year.

American Vocational Journal. American Vocational Association. Published ten times per year.

Journal of Employment Counseling. National Employment Counselors Association. Published four times per year.

Journal of College Placement. College Placement Council. Published four times per year.

Occupational Outlook Quarterly. U.S. Department of Labor. Published four times per year.

The following list is a sampling of aids for college students and adults:[1]

Abarbanel, K. and Siegel, G. *Women's Work Book.* New York: Praeger, 1975.

Angel, J. L. *The Complete Resume Book and Job Getter's Guide.* New York: Pocket Books, 1980.

[1] This list is presented solely as a random sampling of the scores of books in this genre. Inclusion is not necessarily an endorsement of any book.

Table 16.1
A Sampling of Printed Matter

Occupational Filing Systems

Name	Publisher	Description
Careerdex	Career Associates	1000+ card-file guide to sources of career information
Career Information Kit	Science Research Assoc.	600 pieces of current literature filed alphabetically by job families. Cross-referenced by Dewey Decimal System
Career Kits and Career Opportunity Boxes	Houghton Mifflin	5 boxes of job information (100–125 cards each) relating to English, social studies, math, foreign languages, and science
Career Skills Matrix	Westinghouse Learning Corporation	Entry-level jobs
The Job Box	Fearon Publishers	70 booklets relating to 7 job clusters for "special need" students
Mini-Briefs	Occupational Awareness	Data regarding 1800 occupations related to school subject matter areas
Occupational Library	Chronicle Guidance Publications, Inc.	Over 650 occupations by DOT classification. Supplemented by microfiche and viewdecks. An excellent resource
Occupational Profiles Kit	Johnson Publishing Co.	A system of retrieving DOT data on 20,000+ occupations via the use of slides
COPSystem Career Briefs Kit	EdITS	Over 400 cards describing occupations and organized by cluster sets. Tied to COPSystem interest inventory

Printed Volumes

Concise Handbook of Occupations	Doubleday & Company	300+ jobs described
Dictionary of Occupational Titles	U.S. Department of Labor	Described in detail elsewhere in this volume. A primary resource
Encyclopedia of Careers and Vocational Guidance (Hopke)	J.G. Ferguson Co.	650 occupations and 71 articles
Guide to Careers through College Majors and Guide to Careers through Vocational Training	Educational and Industrial Testing Service	As the titles suggest
Handbook of Job Facts	Science Research Assoc.	300 major occupations
Occupational Outlook Handbook and *Occupational Outlook Quarterly*	U.S. Department of Labor	Trends and outlook in over 800 occupations and industries with a quarterly supplement. Another primary resource
The College Handbook and the *College Handbook Index of Majors*	College Entrance Examination Board	Descriptions of over 2000 colleges and universities and indications of what majors are available where
Profiles of American Colleges, Vols. I and II	Barron's	Over 1400 colleges and universities described

Table 16.1 (continued)

Occupational Filing Systems

Name	Publisher	Description
Guide to Two-Year Colleges, Vols. I and II	Barron's	Information on over 1200 community colleges
College Learning Anytime, Anywhere	Harcourt, Brace, Jovanovich	Alternatives to a traditional college education
Comparative Guide to American Colleges and *Comparative Guide to Two-Year Colleges and Career Programs*	Harper & Row	Descriptions as indicated in titles with special emphasis on admissions criteria
Peterson's Annual Guides to Graduate Study	Peterson's Guides	Graduate and professional programs described in general or by specialty area
Printed Series		
Career Core Competencies	McGraw-Hill, Gregg Division	7 student text-workbooks, 7 filmstrips, 21 interview cassettes dealing with school and careers, decision-making, self-identity, communications at work, human relations at work, getting a job, keeping a job
Popeye Career Awareness Book and Poster Library (E)	King Comic Books	Popeye negotiates the USOE clusters
Career Education Books (E)	E. M. Hale and Co.	"Careers in" many occupations
Exploring Careers Series (E)	William Morrow and Co.	Many titles relating to careers
Highway to Work and Play (E)	McKnight	Activity oriented awareness readings
When You Grow Up (E)	Mini Productions	Cluster posters
Junior Guidance Booklets National Guidance Handbook Guidance Series Booklets New Rochester Occupational Reading Series	Science Research Assoc.	15 titles for Jr. High vocational and tech. ed 41 paperbacks re guidance work world exploration for non-academic students
Pete Saves the Day	Mafex	Text and workbook for practical employment skills
Learn to Earn A Good Worker		Stories about work-study Workbook for trainable young adults
Deciding Decisions and Outcomes	College Entrance Examination Board	Decision-making workbooks: Junior High School through adult
Decide for Yourself	Career Research and Advisory Centre	Decision-making workbook
Exploring Careers Series Vocations in Trades Series	William Morrow	A book for each cluster exploring trades occupations
World of Work: Readings in Interpersonal Relationships	McGraw-Hill	50 short stories about jobs
Career Exploration and Planning Finding Your First Job Career Education Program	Houghton Mifflin	Text and workbook stressing self-awareness and understanding Workbook for job-hunting skills K-12 career education lesson plans

Table 16.1 (continued)

Name	Publisher	Description
Catalyst: Career Opportunities Series, Educational Opportunities Series, Self-Guidance Series	Catalyst	Women and Careers
Messner Career Books	Julian Messner	"Your Career in" over 35 occupational areas
Finding a Job You Feel Good About	Argus Communications	Paperback and spirit master program 7-adult
Careers Wheels How To Select A Private Vocational School How to Complete Job Application Forms	American Personnel and Guidance Association	Career Information via disc-dial Caveats and how-to's
Vocational Biographies	Vocational Biographies, Inc.	475 career areas in biographical form
Careers in Depth	Richards Rosen Press	Series of books on various careers
How to Decide: A Guide for Women	Avon	Formulating goals and making decisions for women
Choices: Organizing and Teaching a Course in Personal Decision-Making	Pennant Educational Materials	Twenty-five learning activity packages
Resumes That Get Jobs	Arco	How to interview for a job and write a resume
Career Awareness: Discussion and Activities to Promote Self-Awareness	Creative Teaching Press	Workbook for grades 4–9 on self-awareness exercises
Career Capers	Teachers Press	Jr. High workbook based on the 15 USOE clusters
Me and Jobs	Educational Design	Workbook related to the job hunting process
Occupational Notebook Program	Research Press	Teaching unit on the transition from school to work
Yourself Ten Years from Now	Harcourt, Brace, Jovanovich	Future-oriented career-planning book for students
The INFO Job Resource Center	Perfection Form	11 categories describing hundreds of jobs
Job Power Now	Acropolis	How people with no work experience can get a job
I Can Be Anything: Careers and Colleges for Young Women	Bantam	Opportunities open especially to women
Vocational Guidance Paperback Series	Vocational Guidance Manuals	30 paperback books, each covering a broad area employment (with teacher's guide)

Applegath, J. *Working Free: Practical Alternatives to the 9 to 5 Job.* New York: Amacom, 1982.

Bolles, R. N. *What Color Is Your Parachute?* Berkeley: Ten Speed Press, 1983.

Borchard, D. C., Kelly, J. J., & Weaver, N. P. K. *Your Career: Choices, Chances, Changes* (2nd Ed.). Dubuque, Iowa: Kendall/Hunt, 1982.

Carkhuff, R. *The Art of Developing a Career.* Amherst, Mass.: Human Resources Development Press, 1974.

Crystal, J. C., & Bolles, R. N. *Where Do I Go from Here with My Life?* New York: Seabury Press, 1974.

Deutsch, A. R. *The Complete Job Book.* New York: Cornerstone Library, 1980.

Figler, H. E. *PATH: A Career Workbook for Liberal Arts Students.* Cranston, R.I.: Carroll Press, 1974.

Fox, M. R. *Put Your Degree to Work.* New York: W. W. Norton, 1979.

Hillstrom, J. K. *Steps to Professional Employment: With Special Advice to Liberal Arts Graduates.* New York: Barron, 1982.

Honigsberg, P. J. *The Unemployment Handbook.* New York: Ballantine, revised periodically.

Lathrop, R. *Who's Hiring Who.* Berkeley: Ten Speed Press, 1977.

Matteson, M. T., and Ivancevich, J. M. *Managing Job Stress and Health.* New York: Free Press, 1982.

Maurer, H. *Not Working.* New York: New American Library, 1979.

Pell, A. R. *The College Graduate Guide to Job Finding.* New York: Monarch Press, 1973.

Pogrebin, L. C. *Getting Yours: How to Make the System Work for the Working Woman.* New York: Avon, 1975.

Sweet, D. H. *The Job Hunter's Manual.* Reading, Mass.: Addison-Wesley, 1975.

Ulrich, H., and Connor, J. R. *The National Job-Finding Guide.* New York: Dolphin Books, 1982.

Woods, D. L. *My Job, My Boss, and Me.* Belmont, Calif.: Lifetime Learning Publications, 1980.

Wright, J. W. *The American Almanac of Jobs and Salaries.* New York: Avon, 1982.

Media Approaches

In addition to printed matter, various audio and visual means of disseminating information are used: bulletin boards and exhibits, commercial, educational, and closed-circuit television, slides, films, records, cassettes, filmstrips, microfilm, and microfiche. At the elementary school level, activities in this category might even include "show and tell" exercises.

A study by Norman (1969) suggests that the use of an audio aid often encourages students to seek additional career counseling. He transmitted career information to one group by means of a tape and presented the same information in mimeographed form to another group. More of the audio-group counselees returned for further counseling than did the printed material group. Other studies also demonstrate the effectiveness of an audio-visual presentation to disseminate occupational information. For example, Sankovsky (1973) showed that adult rehabilitation clients preferred a multimedia approach to acquire specific information. Johnson, Korn, and Dunn (1975) compared three methods of presenting occupational information to "reluctant learners" in high school. They found that students gained more information and were more receptive to a slide-tape presentation than they were to either of two other methods — written material or a tape cassette. These types of studies and others suggest that a multimedia approach is valuable, especially with low-motivation counselees and with adults.

Audio and visual approaches provide an interesting and sense-appealing method of transmitting information. The career education movement stimulated a remarkable number of multimedia approaches to occupational information. Table 16.2 represents a sampling of that prodigious output.

Interview Approaches

Educational or occupational information can be gathered by a variety of person-to-person and group interactions with individuals who represent various careers, occupations, jobs, and educational institutions or with individuals also learning about the world of work or educational opportunities. The career conference or career day is one such approach. Here adult individuals represent their vocations, and students are free to talk with or listen to as many as possible within a restricted amount of time. The dangers inherent in this

Table 16.2
Examples of Career Guidance Media

Films

Name	Publisher	Description
Library of Career Counseling Films	Counselor Films, Inc.	Over 30 films and sound filmstrips on the work world
Bread and Butterflies	Agency for Instructional Television	15 TV programs on careers for 9–12 year olds
The Working Worlds	Olympus Publishing	13 films on career clusters
Project WERC Film Series	American Personnel and Guidance Association	World of work exploration
Vocational Films	Houghton Mifflin	10 films on general and specific aspects of work
Career Decision Making	Counseling Films	Behavioral Emphasis

Other Media

Name	Publisher	Description
Career Kits for Kids (E)	Encyclopaedia Britannica Educational Corp.	Career awareness (6 occups.)
The Lollipop Dragon (E) Targo Explores the World of Work (E)	Singer Society for Visual Education, Inc.	World of work awareness 6 filmstrips introducing job clusters
Job Opportunities Now		
Exploring Careers Series	Singer Society for Visual Education, Inc.	9-part program for exploring 15 clusters
Getting Your Money's Worth		Consumer awareness
Career Development for Children Project (E)	McKnight	Career awareness, work activities, self awareness
Introduction to Careers Series		Exploration of various careers
DUSO: Developing Understanding of Self and Others (E)	American Guidance Service, Inc.	Understanding social and emotional behavior
TAD: Toward Affective Development (E)		Psychological or affective education
Compulearn Career Education Program	Random House	Elementary through adult individualized instruction in career education
Career Awareness Field Trips (E)	Guidance Associates	7 programs to simulate field trips to various industries
Career Values: What Really Matters to You?		Personal values and career decisions
Changing Work Ethic		Work attitudes and jobs
Jobs and Gender		Sex and career choice
Jobs for High School Students		Entry level jobs
The Paycheck Puzzle		Economic awareness
You and Your Job Interview		How-to-do-it

Table 16.2 (continued)

Name	Publisher	Description
What You Should Know Before You Go to Work		Employer expectations
Choosing Your Career		Holland's typology and choice
Job Hunting: Where to Begin		Sources of employment information
Career Discoveries Series		6 job groups explored
High School as a Tryout		Career exploration through high school
Focus on Self-Development (E)	Science Research Assoc.	Self-understanding and understanding of others and the environment
Job Family Series Booklets and Cassettes		Jobs and the clusters
Decision-Making for Career Development		Workbooks and Cassettes
WORK: Widening Occupational Roles Kit		Career Exploration
KEYS: Career Exploration Program		Career exploration related to interests
KNOW: Knowledge Needed to Obtain Work		64 transparencies related to selecting and applying for a job
Career Development: Education for Living	J.C. Penney	Exploration of work and work values
Preparing for an Interview	J.C. Penney	How-to-do-it
Career Decisions: Finding, Getting, and Keeping a Job		Influences on job choice
Career Clusters and the World of Work	AV Laboratory Educational Prop.	15 career clusters
Programmed Work Awareness Kit	Chronicle Guid.	33 weekly units
Fascinating World of Work	National Career Consultants	16 titles in various occupations
Careertapes	Macmillan	72 people in different occupations talk about exploration, entry, and training in their fields
Career Survival Skills	C.E. Merrill	Understanding the use of resources for career and life planning
Target Vocational Transparencies	Mafex	How to fill out forms
You're Hired	Classroom World Productions	Job-seeking behaviors
A Complete Learning System for Career Education	I(T) WORK(S), Inc.	12 monographs
The World of Work Series	Educational Resource Division of Educational Design, Inc.	3-part related to getting and keeping a job
Hard Choices: Strategies for Decision-Making		Decision-making skills

(E) = primarily for elementary school use

Table 16.2 (continued)

Name	Publisher	Description
Decision-Making: Dealing with Crises	Center for Humanities	Techniques for crisis management
Career Lab	Westinghouse Learning Corporation	9 units related to careers
Career Awareness Series	Aims Instructional Media Services	Scope of work in various career areas
Career Guidance and Counseling Filmstrip-Sound Materials	Charles W. Clark Co.	Many materials for career awareness and exploration
Me, Myself, and I (E)	EyeGate Instructional Materials	Elementary psychology course
Career Flashcards	CFI	Career awareness
Magic Circle Programs (E)	Human Development Training Institute	Interpersonal effectiveness exercises
Real People at Work (E)	Changing Times	Resource kits K–6
Career Directions: Planning for Career Decisions	Educational Service	4 units for career planning
Non-Traditional Careers for Women	Pathescope Educational Films	Filmstrips and cassettes regarding women's work roles past and present
Vocational Decisions	QED Productions	Filmstrips and cassettes for vocational awareness
Career Awareness Laboratory	Singer Career Systems	Electronic media and gaming for career awareness
Careers in Focus	McGraw-Hill	Career exploration and self-discovery
Career Information Center	Hoffman Educational Systems	Career exploration related to interests
Job Lab 1 and Job Lab 2	Houghton Mifflin	Career exploration via job description cards for elementary and secondary
Education/Career/Life Options	Educational Design	5 filmstrips, 5 cassettes, 24 spirit masters, and teacher's guide for career and life planning
Life Goals: Setting Personal Priorities	Human Relations Media Center	3 filmstrips and 3 cassettes for students
Vocational Skills for Tomorrow	Coronet	Bilingual career decision-making for non–college bound
First Jobs	Educational Design	9 filmstrips, 5 cassettes, 12 spirit masters
Increase Your Career Power	Universal Education and Visual Arts	Cassette and student workbook program
Occupation Photographs	Developmental Learning Materials	20 study prints of various non-sexist and nonracist occupational illustrations

Table 16.2 (continued)

Name	Publisher	Description
Job Skills for the Future	Newsweek	4 filmstrips, 4 cassettes, and 20 spirit masters
Selecting a Vocation	Coronet	8 filmstrips, 8 cassettes, and a teacher's guide
You're Hired	Multi-Media Productions	2 filmstrips and 1 cassette on job-hunting
Career Training	Westinghouse	6 filmstrips and cassettes and teacher's guide on the how, what, and where of career training
Career Education Clusters		16 filmstrips, cassettes, and teacher's guide related to USOE clusters
Entering the Working World	Butterick	4 filmstrips, cassettes, and text-workbook on the job hunt
Your Working Future	Encyclopedia Britannica	8 filmstrips and cassettes on various occupations
Careers — The Paraprofessional	Multi-Media Productions	6 filmstrips, 6 cassettes, and teacher's guide on a half-dozen paraprofessional occupations
Working Americans	Newsweek	filmstrip, cassette, 2 case studies units, and a career option packet regarding work in general
Black Americans at Work	Coronet	6 filmstrips and cassettes, and a teacher's guide. Interviews with blacks at work
Career Directions	Changing Times Educational Service	Six units ranging from deciding on a career to work behaviors; filmstrips, cassettes, spirit masters, and teacher's guide
Changing Times Mini-Units		6 reprints, transparencies, spirit masters, and teacher's guide on work behaviors
Job Interview Skills	Sunburst	3 filmstrips and cassettes and a teacher's guide
The Job of Job Hunting		2 filmstrips and cassettes and a teacher's guide
Self-Assessment: A Toll for Career Decision		3 filmstrips and cassettes and a teacher's guide
Careers and Values: Understanding the Choices		2 filmstrips and cassettes and a teacher's guide
On the Job Survival Skills		2 filmstrips and cassettes and a teacher's guide

Table 16.2 (continued)

Name	Publisher	Description
Livelyhoods	TSC	16 filmstrips and cassettes and a user's guide on workstyles and life styles for grades 7–12
COPSystem Occupational Cluster Charts	EdITS	Visual display of occupations related to COPS clusters

procedure are many: superficial or selective coverage of an occupational area, overemphasis on function to the exclusion of self-factors, proselytizing in the most negative sense, circus atmosphere, and such. Students sometimes go to hear people who represent jobs and occupations in which they are already interested and about which they already know something; thus, no new possibilities are explored. An educational analogue of this activity is the college night. In some cases, a professional organization (such as an AACD branch) organizes and conducts a regional job and educational opportunities "fair" (Pate, Tulloch, & Dassance, 1981).

This "trade fair" type of approach can be valuable to individuals if it is preceded by adequate preparation and followed by ample opportunity for feedback. A remarkably effective program of this type was conducted by Ms. Pam Wise, a counselor in the Clarence, New York, schools. After determining that the tentative career choices of girls in her high school were typically constricted, she planned and implemented, conjointly with teachers, one-week units in both English and social studies classes. During these sessions, topics ranged from factual material to attitudes relating to women and work. An all-day career conference was held on three successive days; forty carefully briefed women in atypical female careers were brought into the school and interacted with students. Students were excused from class to attend as many sessions as they wished over the three days. All sessions were videotaped to allow students to view any career presentation later which they could not personally attend. Evaluations showed that a large proportion of the girls indicated that they were exploring nontraditional careers as a result of the experience.

In a similar but more in-depth approach, students interview workers in various jobs or personnel directors who are familiar with the requirements of a relatively wide range of jobs. Students are not limited to those occupations represented at a career conference; they can explore any occupation available in the community. Students may be given an interview guide to ensure that important aspects of the occupation are covered in the conference. Again, however, this approach assumes that the student has some prior interest in an occupation and seeks to broaden knowledge of it.

A still more detailed and thorough approach is the job analysis. In this case, students supplement direct-interview data with information gathered from other sources, such as occupational literature. Although this technique offers a comprehensive and intensive view of a single occupation, it can be a tedious exercise that turns off students if their motivation, either intrinsic or extrinsic, is not relatively strong.

A final interview-type approach to occupational information is the job clinic. Whereas the career conference has long-range goals, the emphasis in the job clinic is on immediate goals, usually job placement. The job clinic brings together many individuals who have jobs to offer. Other individuals who need jobs come to the clinic and decide whether their attributes and interests match the available jobs. This type of activity is most common in employment agencies and college placement centers.

Simulation Approaches

There are many simulation or gaming techniques by which counselees can vicariously explore careers as well as educational opportunities. Simulation must be used properly – that is, not in isolation as an end in itself but along with meaningful discussion, follow-up, and explanatory materials. If used improperly, simulation can lead to distorted understandings (Kaplon & Gordon, 1967). When employed properly, however, simulation is valuable in that it brings down to manageable proportions a very complicated aspect of life. There is some disagreement about the relative merits of simulation. Cherryholmes (1966) has concluded that students who participate in simulation activities do not learn significantly more facts or principles than those engaged in other methods of learning. On the other hand, Boocock and Coleman (1966) have demonstrated that gaming has produced significant differences in learning, especially in the realm of attitudes. The worth of simulation is further demonstrated by the work of Fifield and Peterson (1978) who evaluated the use of thirty job simulation units in grades 4–6. Their results prove that career exploration through work simulation is effective and that it stimulates students to seek additional information.

The simplest form of simulation is role-playing. For example, individuals may role-play job interviews in order to become more relaxed and prepared when an actual employment interview comes. They may also dramatize potential conflicts in work situations (for example, supervisor-worker tensions) on the premise that such an exercise will serve as a preventive function when a similar situation is encountered in a real work situation.

Taking role-playing a step further, McCourt (1971) has conceived what he calls the vocational development lesson. In this type of simulation, groups of individuals are exposed to an occupation by means of a role model. Role models may be present in the form of a person, a film, or literature. Role models tell what they do, but, more important, they relate the personal meaning of their work – satisfactions, frustrations, and so on. In short, they give a picture of the kinds of people they are and help the group try to be for a short time a member of the occupation they represent. For example, a psychologist might present the group with a case study on a

client and invite the group to attempt a diagnosis and to prescribe treatment. After the role model has been presented, counselees are asked to engage in reflective thinking, to compare and contrast what they know about themselves with what they know about the role model and the role model's work. Thus, individuals vicariously explore the relevance to them of a particular occupation. This type of activity calls for the individual to use educational, occupational, and personal-social information in an integrated manner.

Using a similar premise, Krumboltz et al. (1967) have produced a series of vocational problem-solving kits that provide counselees with experiences in a variety of occupations. Students can, for example, reach some understanding of the work of an accountant by actually balancing a miniset of books. They can then read about the personal and educational requirements for the occupation of accounting. Hamilton and Krumboltz (1969) report that the initial effect of such simulated activities appears to be considerable. They used an Electronics Technician Kit with tenth-grade, non–college bound students and compared them with a group that used a less "real" type of experience. They found that the experimental group enjoyed the experience more, had a greater desire for further information, and wanted more experiences of the same sort. Their findings have been confirmed by Johnson (1971), who found that simulated experiences in particular occupations can generate interest in the occupation and in general career exploration.

Another type of simulation experience – job sampling – is simultaneously an assessment procedure. For example, the Singer Vocational Evaluation System provides actual work sample tasks for a variety of trade and skilled occupations. While the counselee is heuristically exploring some of the occupational functions, the counselor is able to assess aptitudes, attitudes, and interests. This system is but one example of numerous hands-on techniques for exploration. A related technique is that of "shadowing," whereby individuals are permitted to spend time on the job observing a worker who is engaged in an occupation in which they might have an interest.

Another potentially valuable simulation technique is gaming. Perhaps the best known occupational game is the Life Career Game, developed by Boocock (1968). The goals are to provide high school and college students with some ideas about the contours of the future, information about occupational and educational alternatives or opportunities, a feeling for the total life cycle of an individual, and practice in decision-making. The game is played by teams of from two to fifteen students, who compete against each other in making decisions about a fictitious individual for eight years into the future. Through this simulation, students presumably acquire an understanding of the labor market, educational opportunities, marriage, and leisure patterns.

Career clubs provide still another type of simulation activity. Future Teachers of America and Distributive Education Clubs are examples of this approach. In the former, youngsters with an interest in teaching as a career can hear speakers, go on field trips, and sometimes actually gain some experience in teaching. Prelaw, premedicine, and other professions-related clubs are also in operation. In Distributive Education Clubs, students gain real experience in setting up and running a business enterprise. Table 16.3 represents a sampling of the better known simulation and gaming materials that are available.

Field Trips

Field trips (to plants, offices, educational institutions, and so on) are a common method of gaining occupational and educational information. The opportunity to see work performed in an actual job setting and to interview those who perform the jobs, or the opportunity to get the feel of an educational institution can be a valuable experience. Too often, however, field trips are accomplished only en masse with little or no thought given to the interests of students. It is likely that a field trip program, individualized to the extent that arrangements can be made for a single student's visit, will be a better program, at least in relation to the exploratory phase of career development. Group trips can be useful, especially for career awareness and for expanding the educational and career worlds of the cul-

turally different, but they must be preceded by careful planning and followed up with feedback. Regarding preparation for field trips, Dale (1954) suggests the following points:

1. Arouse student interest in the trip (by class discussion, photographs, bulletin board, and other similar materials).
2. Discuss with students the problems that the trip can help solve.
3. Make clear to students the purpose or purposes of the trip.
4. Develop background by consulting reference materials.
5. Work out with students the specific points to observe during the trip.
6. Set up with the students the standards for safety and behavior.
7. Prepare and distribute to students any materials that can be used profitably in the course of the trip (p. 167).

Follow-up or debriefing activities include discussions individually and in groups, regarding the values gained from the trip. Such questions as, How does the information which I gained relate to me? and How does what I observed affect my decision-making? are appropriate.

Baca (1980) reports on an EXPO Program (Exploring Possible Occupations) for secondary school students. Monthly field trips to occupational sites were combined with speakers who gave presentations at the school. The student evaluations were most positive, although the participants were volunteers, and one might expect a more positive evaluation under these circumstances.

Working on the "If Mohammed can't come to the mountain" principle, Jepsen (1972) videotaped field trips into local industries. An experimental group viewed these videotapes and studied printed materials; a control group used only the printed materials. On a variety of outcome measures, the experimental group demonstrated more accurate images of the specific occupations studied. Videotaping is a relatively inexpensive technique in institutions that already have the necessary hardware. It may be an acceptable alternative or supplement to actual

Table 16.3
Examples of Career Guidance Simulations and Games

Name	Publisher	Description
Career Insights and Self-Awareness Games (E)	Houghton Mifflin	Insight and awareness
EXPO 10: Exploring Career Interests (E)	Science Research Assoc.	Occupational exploration
Job Experience Kits		20 occupations for work simulation
Grow Power: A Decision-Making and Personality Development Game (E)	Educational Activities	Physical, mental, social, and emotional growth awareness
Steady Job: A Vocational Orientation Game	Mafex	Attitudes and behavior related to employability
Generation Rap: The Parents and Kids Game	Spinnaker	Parent-child interaction
Scope Visuals 16: Career Crosswords	Scholastic Books	Careers through crossword puzzles
Life Career	Bobbs-Merrill	Career planning and decision-making
Game of Life	Milton Bradley Co.	Decision-making; 2–8 players
COMPULEARN	U.S. Office of Education	Computer simulation
Career Games	E.N. Chapman	Career search and decision-making for grades 8–13
Careers	Parker Brothers	8 occupations and success
Community Decisions Game	Education Ventures	Variety of decision-making situations
Edventure II: Career Guidance Game	Abt Associates	20 years in the future and choice in the educational marketplace
Edventure Lifelong Learning Simulation		Educational and work choices in the future
The Job Game	Employment Training Corp.	Finding jobs
Career Exploration Games	Educational Media Corp.	Four career exploration strategies
Career Decision Game	Instructo	Grades 4–10 board game relating to choosing a career
Pro's and Con's	Creative Learning Systems	Debating game on sex-role options

field trips, which frequently entail insurance, transportation, and supervision problems.

Formal Curriculum Approach

Earlier in this chapter, the views of O'Hara and Cooley were presented, regarding the need for a formal career guidance curriculum in educational institutions. We concur with that view to the extent that certain aspects of career development are perhaps best effected by means of structured and direct teaching-learning. The question is which of these experiences can be learned within an existing curriculum structure and which require a career guidance curriculum separate from subject matter classes? The career education strategy of infusion is consistent with developmental theory and, as research has demonstrated, it has proven effective when adequately planned and implemented. The great advantage of infusion is that in addition to career learnings, it seems to be a potent force in increasing student achievement. On the other hand, the effectiveness of "acceleration" in career guidance has been repeatedly demonstrated in cited studies. Especially at secondary education, higher education, and adult levels, the use of concentrated, intensive workshops, seminars, and courses has been shown to achieve desired goals of career guidance.

We do not want to imply that infusion and separate career guidance "courses" are an either-or proposition. Both can be useful. Our impressions of the career education infusion methodology is that through junior high school, teachers have generally embraced the concept. At the senior high school and higher educational levels, teacher resistance has appeared to be more marked; consequently, infusion has been less successful. Infusion may well be the primary method in elementary and middle schools, and discrete, structured career guidance group experiences the primary delivery mode beyond the middle school level. In either case, a systematic, planned program is required.

Direct Experience

The axiom that the best way to learn something is to do it probably holds true for the acquisition of information. Direct work experience clearly allows an individual to learn a great deal about a specific job. Work experience is, therefore, a valuable strategy in career guidance. Many schools offer work experience programs and many person power programs provide on-the-job training. In schools, distributive education students are freed from academic courses for a half-day to work in retail establishments. This cooperation provides on-the-job training and the benefit of experiential learning. Increasing numbers of collegiate institutions are offering work-study programs. Part-time and summer jobs also provide exploratory opportunities which make the individual more occupationally aware. Again,

however, these opportunities increase in value as participants have a chance for feedback to reinforce or stimulate career learnings.

Industrial "shadow" experiences are another form of acquiring experience of a sort. These visits to industry to observe and to experience work in situ are valuable for both counselors and students (Kelly, 1978; Kelly & Moore, 1979). For several years, the General Electric Company sponsored shadow experiences for counselors in order to give them a more realistic view of the work world. Counselees can also shadow workers for anywhere from a day to a week. Industry-education councils are also doing a great deal to provide valuable first-hand observation and experience for counselors and for students.

Computers

Throughout this chapter, a recurrent theme has been that "traditional" methods of occupational information acquisition, storage, retrieval, and dissemination have not proved so effective as desired. There are many possible reasons for this relative failure. In some cases, programs have been spontaneously mounted with no thought of what came before or of what would come after; they have lacked adequate preparation and feedback opportunities. Whatever the reasons, we are not suggesting that counselors give up traditional approaches. They require little expenditure of money, no fantastic hardware, no new educational system. It is equally clear, however, that a systematic approach to career guidance can utilize technology effectively.

Electronic data processing techniques were touted in the late 1960s and early 1970s as a potentially revolutionary mode for career guidance. Only now are they beginning to live up to that great promise. In the last ten years over three score projects have attempted to use computer technology in career guidance. Few survive today. Some were merely information vehicles; others were more ambitious, attempting something closer to an interactive counseling approach. Although the promise has not yet been completely fulfilled, the great potential is still there. So, too, are the potential pitfalls and disadvantages, ranging from the failure to accommodate human factors to the vulnerability of confidentiality

(Sampson, 1983). For these reasons and others, Sampson and Pyle (1983) urge that counselors mediate person-machine systems. Counselors can help to assuage problems of user anxiety that might impede effective use of a system, inadequately prepared users who are not at ease with the process of a system, inadequate follow-up after the counselee has accessed and experienced a system, out-of-date or inaccurate information in a system, and malfunctions or improper working of a system.

Unfortunately, the use of technology is not accomplished without concomitant problems. A financial outlay is necessary, of course, although microcomputers and time-sharing plans are beginning to bring costs down to manageable proportions. Beyond financial outlay, however, the use of technology opens other concerns. Walz (1970) points out that technology forces individuals to come to grips with their personal values and goals, which might otherwise remain unexamined. The result is frequently conflict. But this is true for much of career guidance. Invasion of privacy, or lack of safeguards for confidentiality, also can be troublesome. Faddism, intemperate usage, and "depersonalization" are further possible outcomes of technology. Super (1970) has suggested that counselors may be resistant to using computers because of a relatively unsophisticated mathematical orientation that makes counselors feel inadequate in relation to the computer's complexity, the computer's accuracy in contrast to the counselor's fallibility, the fear of a loss of autonomy, and the perceived deterministic character of the computer. Yet, with judicious planning and utilization, technology can provide a strong weapon among many in the counselor's arsenal.

Loughary (1970) delineates at least three ways computers can be used in career guidance. In the first application, computers serve as data processing tools for counselors by storing counselee data and subsequently retrieving them in various ways. Second, computers can be used as substitutes for some counselor functions that go beyond simple information processing. Here one may think in terms of reference systems that often permit the user and the computer to engage in a dialogue. Examples are the matching of stu-

dents and colleges or the matching of workers and jobs (such as Employment Service job data banks). In the third application, the machine is viewed as a substitute counselor, at least for some counseling functions which involve systematic, consistent, and selective use of a limited number of simple skills (such as Student Interactive Guidance and Information System).

In terms of the first two categories, Miller (1970) has divided information systems into four classes:

1. Educational development and planning systems are student information systems containing test scores, grades, personal characteristics, etc., and are usually state-based.
2. Locally oriented occupational information systems are designed to communicate general and local occupational information to students for use in vocational planning and placement.
3. Information systems to facilitate vocational decision-making emphasize providing the student with information about self, educational opportunities, and the world of work, and also helping him develop skills in effective vocational decision-making.
4. Information systems for staff training and program development contain information about current educational programs, practices, and research (pp. 215–216).

Computerized informational systems are typically based on one or another of the occupational classifications as described in Chapter 3 and one or another of the career development theories as described in Chapter 4. The DISCOVER II program, for example, incorporates Super's developmental stages and Tiedeman and O'Hara's decision making model along with the data-people-things orientation of the DOT and the Holland categories.

Studies which report on the effectiveness of the use of the computer in career guidance are generally positive. Pilato and Myers (1975) administered self-knowledge interest and aptitude instruments to eleventh grade boys and interpreted the data to groups of students by means of computer generated printouts, both in isolation and in relation to an occupational classification system. Their conclusion was that giving students information about their aptitudes and interests alone or giving students information about the occupational structure alone was an ineffective procedure; however, providing students with both types of information and using a computer-mediated approach produced effective results. A study by Price (1971) concluded that a computer-based system designed to assist high school students to explore and select courses was no more nor less effective than a counselor performing the same function. Melhaus, Hershenson, and Vermillion (1973) investigated the differential effects of computer-assisted counseling with high and low academic achievers in secondary school. They suggest that low readiness (achieving) students benefit less from computer-assisted counseling than do high readiness counselees. Cassie (1976) compared gains in career maturity between students who had and had not used the Ontario Ministry of Education Student Guidance Information Service (S.G.I.S.) and found that users increased their career maturity scores significantly more than did non-users.

In a comprehensive study of career planning among college students, Garis (1982) compared the effects of (1) the DISCOVER Career Guidance and Counselor Support system, (2) individual career counseling, and (3) combined DISCOVER/career counseling use. The sixty-seven college student subjects were randomly assigned to treatments or control conditions and given a variety of pretest and posttest measures of progress in career planning. Selected results were as follows:

1. All treatments produced positive effects on subjects' self-rated progress in educational/career planning as compared to the control group.
2. The DISCOVER use contributed to greater subject use of the career library than the counseling only condition.
3. The career counseling treatment was more effective than DISCOVER in stimulating subject contacts with career resource persons or services that could provide further assistance with educational/career planning.

4. Indications that the combined DISCOVER/counseling treatment produced stronger effects on career planning progress than either of its components used separately were inconclusive. Many criteria demonstrated no significant differences among treatment groups whereas one measure (Scale A Career Planning: Involvement in Thinking about the Future and Making Career Plans, College and University Form of the Career Development Inventory) indicated that the combined treatment produced the strongest effects on subject involvement in career planning.

These and other studies are instructive in that they point toward the effectiveness of computer-mediated techniques for the dissemination of occupational information. At the same time, they suggest that indiscriminate use of the computer may not be appropriate; some types of students benefit from computer generated information more than do others. Finally, research into the use of computers in career guidance confirms once again that information acquisition is merely a first, albeit important, step in career planning. Individuals must be assisted through a variety of techniques to utilize data in a personally meaningful manner.

Ryan, Drummond, and Shannon (1980) evaluated the effects of the Guidance Information System (GIS) as used in both schools and human service agencies in Maine. They concluded that the primary influence of the system is in increasing users' career awareness and information-gathering activities. Most users enjoyed the process, but a few became confused when what they thought were clearly formed career goals before using the system turned out to be less clear after the fact. The investigators suggest immediate counselor access for such users. At the college level, third- and fourth-generation computer career guidance systems are beginning to emerge. For example, the CECIL program (Computerized Educational and Career Information Link) was developed at Virginia Polytechnic Institute and State University by incorporating the best features of CVIS (Computerized Vocational Information System) and DISCOVER. The resulting hybrid, CECIL, was found effective as an outreach adjunct to the university's counseling and career services (Schenk, Murphy, & Shelton, 1980).

Information-handling technology is indeed increasing at a rapid rate. Individuals now possess and use everything from handheld calculators and instructional devices to personal computers with intelligent videodisc systems. Some of our graduate students have programmed their personal computers with common career guidance tools such as Holland's Self-Directed Search and similar instruments. This welding of common career guidance instruments to computer technology is also suggested by Price, Michal, and O'Neil (1978). Computers are now ubiquitous, and the variety of career-oriented commercial products is growing. Our software, however, is frequently crude and untested. Snipes and McDaniels (1981) offer some sensible questions for those who would assess or evaluate these systems.

1. On what theory of career development is the system designed?
2. Are the implications of the theory consistently manifested throughout the design of the system?
3. Are the assessment instruments valid and reliable?
4. What analytical skills are assumed to be entering behaviors of users?
5. What skills are taught in the system?
6. Is the system designed to provide opportunities for users to attain the outcomes listed as objectives for the system? (p. 313)

We here briefly describe only a few of the more commonly used computer-based systems.

DISCOVER II (Discover Foundation, Townson, Maryland; distributed by Chronicle Guidance Publications, Inc.; for a complete description see Rayman & Harris-Bowlsbey, 1977)

A carefully developed and field tested system for grades 7–12, colleges, and adults. Terminals are connected to a moderate or large computer. The system provides:

1. Assessment of interests (ACT instrument on-line, but can use extant results of SDS, OVIS, SCII, or Kuder E).
2. Assessment of aptitudes (self-rating of twelve

aptitudes or can use existing results of DAT, CPP, GATB, or ASVAB).
3. Assessment of values (fifteen values after Super's WVI).
4. Expected educational level.
5. User can enter occupational characteristics desired and program of study or college major.
6. DISCOVER II compares user input with job requirements, the ACT World of Work Map, and Holland codes and produces a list of jobs chosen from over 400 in storage.
7. Computer gives instructions on how to use the World of Work map.
8. Data in storage on
   a. 1800 four-year colleges
   b. statewide two-year colleges
   c. statewide trade and technical schools
   d. locally developed job information

GIS (THE GUIDANCE INFORMATION SYSTEM) TSC, Houghton Mifflin Co., Box 683, Hanover, N.H. 03755; for more complete information, see the *Guidance Information System Guide*, 1981)

A system organized by both U.S. Department of Labor interest areas and the Standard Occupational Classification groups described in Chapter 3. Although all data are national, some regions and states feed local information into the GIS system. There are five information files:

1. *Occupational Information File* (OCCU) contains 875 primary listings with reference to about 2500 related jobs. Typical information is stored for each occupation as well as sources for further information and the Quick Occupational Information File (Job Lab Series).
2. *Armed Services Occupational Information File* (ASOC) offers information relating to over 100 occupations in the military and gives comparable civilian occupations.
3. *Two-Year College Information File* (COL 2) and *Four-Year College Information File* (COL 4) contains typical information on more than 3400 institutions. This information is usually updated annually.
4. *Graduate and Professional School Information File* (GRAD) offers data of a traditional sort on over 1500 graduate and professional programs.

5. *Financial Aids Information File* (AIDS) gives information on national sources of financial assistance.

SIGI (SYSTEM OF INTERACTIVE GUIDANCE AND INFORMATION) Educational Testing Service (for a complete description see Katz, 1980).

A well-financed and technically well developed value-based system designed for college students. Students have a dialogue with a minicomputer that allows them to examine their values, identify and explore options, receive and interpret data, and practice decision-making. Six major subsystems are available.

Values – Users examine their own values and consider the place of values in decision-making. Ten values are explored in value-dilemma gaming exercises. The users examine their own values to pick up inconsistencies and indicate the weighting of their values.

Locate – Users put specifications on five values at a time and occupations are displayed that meet or exceed user specifications.

Compare – The users can ask specific questions about any three occupations at one time (such as work activities, entry requirements, outlook).

Prediction – Users get probability statements for various college programs based on the similarity of their data to those of previous students. Predictive data are unique to each college and are combined in regression formulae.

Planning – Users are assisted to determine how to enter an occupation and are permitted to see displays of rewards and risks associated with various occupations.

Strategy – For three occupations at a time, users review their values, occupational information, and predictions. Each occupation is assigned an index number to describe its overall desirability to the user. Desirability is then moderated by probability of success and choices are evaluated.

CAREER CENTERS

In the past decade, a career-center concept has surfaced (Jacobson, 1972; Circle et al., 1968; Laramore, 1969; Reardon, 1973; Simonis, 1973).

The term career resource center is most often used. The idea of a career resource center is to gather together in a single place all educational, occupational, and financial aid information; to provide individuals with professional assistance in using the information; and to allow for a physical space for counselees to meet with representatives of educational and training institutions and of occupations. The emphasis is on easy accessibility for users. Such a center may be a separate entity within an institution; such as the education information centers (EICs) established by PL 94-482 in the section devoted to the reauthorization of higher education (Title I); EICs have been established in the community for adults in shopping centers and other easily accessed public places; within guidance, counseling, or placement facilities; in a library; in a residence hall, and so on. It contains such components as microfilm viewers, view-decks, books, pamphlets, files, reference and resource volumes, catalogues, brochures – virtually every kind of information – and spaces in which counselees can utilize the information. It may also serve as a dissemination center for other units within an educational enterprise. At the elementary school level, it is sometimes called a guidance learning center. Initial evaluations suggest the popularity and effectiveness of such a center (Jacobson, 1975).

The original home/community-based career education model also provided some ingenious systems for the delivery of career information by means of modules, self-directed materials, and telephone "hotlines," as was discussed in Chapter 1.

Guidelines

As a result of their experience in the Newton, Massachusetts, schools, Circle et al. (1968) recommend eleven guidelines relating to the establishment and maintenance of a career center.

1. Responsibility for coordinating the career information service should be given to one person.
2. Funds must be budgeted for career materials on a regular basis.
3. Establish criteria for acquiring and evaluating materials.

4. Locate reliable sources of information (establish a listing of professional associations and organizations, commercial publishers, businesses and industries, and local, state, and national government sources).
5. Develop a workable classification and storage system.
6. Utilize good business management practices.
7. Establish open communication networks.
8. Location may determine effectiveness.
9. Work closely with existing school or community library services.
10. Keep career information up-to-date.
11. Establish sensible and practical administrative rules and regulations.

Other "how to" help with regard to the rudiments of setting up and evaluating a career center is also available (Martin, 1980; Reardon, Domkowski, & Jackson, 1980; Meerbach, 1978).

Career centers require planning and continual effort. They may require hiring a paraprofessional or training student or lay volunteer assistants. In any case, if career centers facilitate the acquisition, storage, retrieval, dissemination, and effective use of educational and occupational information, they are well worth the energy expenditure.

The National Occupational Information Coordinating Committee (NOICC)

The National Occupational Information Coordinating Committee was established in 1976 by act of Congress. Four federal agencies support the committee: the Bureau of Labor Statistics, the Employment and Training Administration, the Office of Vocational and Adult Education, and the National Center for Education Statistics. The same legislation provided for State Occupational Information Coordinating Committees (SOICCs) of which there are fifty-seven (Guam, American Samoa, Virgin Islands, Puerto Rico, Northern Marianas, and Trust Territory are included). The national group and the state groups are charged with the following responsibilities (Flanders, 1980):

• Develop an OIS (Occupational Information System) with standardized definitions, estimating procedures, and occupational classifications

that meets the common occupational information needs of vocational education programs and employment and training programs at the Federal, State, and local levels.
• Assist the State Committees.
• Improve coordination and communication among the developers and users of occupational information.
• Give special attention to the labor market information needs of youth (p. 22).

The various state groups engage in such worthwhile activities as identifying the types of occupational information required by users, inventorying sources of occupational data, collating extant resources, and preparing to implement on occupational information system. Career information delivery systems (CIDs) have been developed to improve the information and guidance received by clients. These CIDs include filmstrips and cassettes, various miniaturized information delivery vehicles (such as microfiche), and printed information. They may be used in schools, colleges, prisons, libraries, rehabilitation centers, and so forth. Included also in the system is a military/occupational information task group, which attempts to link military occupational information in NOICC and SOICC programs and CIDs (Flanders, 1981).

An *Occupational Information System (OIS) Handbook* is a three-volume work put out by NOICC and its subcontractors. Volumes I and II identify available sources of educational and occupational data and present specific methods for analyzing and assembling supply and demand information (NOICC, 1981). Volume III offers technical information in relation to the programs described in Volume I. As of this writing, although all three volumes have been completed, only Volume II has been published.

SOICCs in all states have been active in diverse programs. Delaware's Career Information Delivery System is an example of the type of CIDSs being developed by the SOICCs. It is called DELPHI and has five related but unique information systems.

1. an *occupational information system* to improve the planning and coordination of voca-

tional education and personpower training programs
2. a *career information system* to assist individuals and counselors with career exploration and decision-making
3. an *employment information system* to assist job seekers and job developers with job search and job development
4. an *educational information system* to assist students and teachers with educational program selection

5. an *economic information system* to assist the economic development process

What we have here in the NOICC/SOICC paradigm is basically an attempt at central planning and networking to reduce the potential chaos and overlap of existing government and private information systems and to extend in new directions occupational information gathering, storing, retrieving, and disseminating. Such objectives are appropriate to all systems of classifying information.

Summary

In this chapter we have discussed career guidance information in terms of criteria for "good" information and for effective use of information. Various possibilities for the storage, retrieval, and dissemination of information have been explored. Examples of the types of materials available have been offered. We have described the work of the NOICC as a useful model of a multisystem approach to the delivery of information at national, regional, state, and local levels. The underlying view in this chapter has been one of counselors helping individuals to integrate educational, occupational, and personal information in the decision-making process. The fostering of planfulness and career development involves not only helping counselees to acquire information but also assisting them to apply the knowledge to their personal characteristics.

LEARNING ACTIVITIES

1. Write to the sources listed in Appendices A and B of this volume and request catalogues and other materials that offer descriptions of educational and occupational materials, assessment instruments, and general career development aids. File such information in an accessible manner.
2. Select any occupation. For that occupation, locate three pieces of occupational information (such as Chronicle, *Occupational Outlook Handbook*, a professional association or

union). Compare the different pieces of data. Evaluate each according to NVGA guidelines.
3. Locate an edition of the *Occupational Outlook Handbook* that is at least five years old. Sample descriptions of several different occupations. paying special attention to the section relating to employment supply and demand projections. With the benefit of hindsight, make a judgment regarding the accuracy of such projections.
4. Obtain and "play" any of the games or simulations listed in this chapter. Discuss with your "playmates" pro and con reactions to the experience.
5. If your geographical area has an industry-education council, arrange to visit and discuss with the director, the services of the council.
6. Locate and visit a career center (or some similarly named organizational unit intended for the storage and use of occupational and educational resources). Form some judgments regarding completeness and ease of utilization.
7. Working with an elementary school librarian, make an inventory of the occupations represented by books in the elementary school collection. Form some judgments regarding the range of occupations which are represented and investigate whether sexism, racism or ageism are present.
8. Visit a state employment service office. Note especially the use of the job bank informa-

tion system. What other educational and occupation information is available? How is it used?

9. For a designated population, set up a structured group experience which has as its overall goal the acquisition of educational or occupational information of a specific nature. Include specific behavioral outcomes, activities, materials, and evaluations.

10. After suitable research, try writing an occupational brief that conforms to NVGA guidelines.

OBJECTIVES

After reading this chapter, engaging in the learning activities, and reading the suggested references, you should have met the objectives that follow. If you have not, it would probably be useful for you to review the material on information in career guidance before proceeding further.

1. Describe the importance of user motivation in relation to educational and occupational information.

2. List at least three criteria for the evaluation of information.

3. Define "individualizing information."

4. Identify at least three compendia of career or educational resources.

5. List at least three occupational filing systems.

6. Name at least three printed volumes of occupational information.

7. List at least four printed series of occupational information.

8. List at least three magazines or journals which address career development concerns.

9. Identify at least three sources of informational assistance in working with college students and adults.

10. List at least four media approaches for occupational information.

11. Describe various interview approaches to securing occupational information.

12. List at least two games or simulations.

13. Define the advantages of a field trip to obtain occupational information.

14. Describe the potential of electronic data processing techniques in relation to occupational information.

15. Define a "career center."

16. Describe the work of NOICC and SOICCs.

17 | *Assessment in Career Guidance and Counseling*

We have been told so often that we are living in an age of extraordinary complexity, specialization, and growth that we frequently fail to realize the implications. We take for granted the vast proliferation of knowledge, the social mobility and flux of social roles, and the substantial changes in occupational structure and opportunity that characterize our time. Yet, this "progress" presents us with problems unparalleled in world history.

Two problems directly relevant to career guidance are the training and allocation of personpower in order to ensure maximum utilization of this most valuable of all resources. We need talent of diverse specializations; we require a means of identifying that talent. The chief method that has evolved is the standardized test.

In addition, we have come to accept the premise that assessment procedures help individuals to understand themselves not only in terms of their talents but also in terms of their interests, values, and personality characteristics. The greater the self-understanding an individual has, it is assumed, the more likely that person is to make realistic, satisfying educational and career choices. Although self-understanding does not guarantee good decision-making, good decisions probably cannot be made without a realistic picture of one's abilities and interests. Again, assessment devices provide a vehicle that contributes to the self-understanding and accurate appraisal of counselees.

Testing by private employers is not typically extensive, although larger companies (more than 25,000 employees) tend to test more than smaller companies. In the public sector, merit systems cover the great majority of employees, and about

three-fourths of the systems use tests of some sort (Tenopyr, 1981). Tittle and Zytowski (1980) estimate that 3.5 million people take machine-scored interest inventories each year. Thus, the use of tests is substantial for both career exploration and employment purposes. Alternatives to testing, such as interviews, experience and educational factors, biodata instruments, and simulations, have been found to be less attractive than testing (Reilly & Chao, 1981). It behooves us, then, to use tests carefully in order to realize their full potential as an aid in career decision-making, exploration, and employment selection.

Over the past decade several significant changes have occurred in the type of test employed in the service of providing guidance and counseling and in the way such tests are used. Miller (1982), for example, points out that new types of instruments have been developed (such as career maturity inventories, large-scale assessment programs, such as the National Assessment of Educational Progress, and multimatrix instruments, such as the ACT and College Board career assessments to be described in this chapter). Further, we have witnessed the development of new techniques for administering, scoring, and reporting tests (such as DISCOVER II, discussed in Chapter 16), and we have responded more adequately to the needs of special populations.

In this chapter we will consider four major uses of tests or assessment procedures. We will deal first with the *predictive* uses of tests, with standardized appraisal data that forecast success in educational and career behaviors. Second, we will discuss the use of tests and inventories for *discrimination*, that is, for permitting individuals to

469

discover what occupational or educational groups they resemble. Together, predictive and discriminative use of tests deal with information pertinent to the content of choices. Third, the *monitoring* function of assessment will be discussed. In a systematic approach to career guidance, it is important that those responsible for intervention be able to identify the vocationalization stage of any individual or group; monitoring provides this information. In essence, monitoring deals with the process of choice or readiness for choice. Further, monitoring indicates whether career behaviors are serving an adaptive or a maladaptive function, as in the measurement of job satisfaction, for example. Finally, we will summarize the use of assessment in *evaluating* how well goals are being achieved with the interventions provided. Thus, the four purposes of assessment in career guidance are prediction, discrimination, monitoring, and evaluation. A sampling of appropriate instruments for each function will be offered and related issues discussed.

PREDICTION

When the effectiveness of a test is evaluated in career guidance, the concern is how well test performance predicts some future performance (such as success in training, success on the job, and so forth). The test is called a predictor; the variable being predicted, a criterion. The entire procedure is one of establishing the predictive validity of a test. The higher the predictive validity of a test (as summarized in a correlation coefficient), the more adequately we can forecast group achievement and, to a lesser extent, individual achievement.

Clinical Versus Statistical Prediction

The actual process of making a prediction on the basis of assessment data can take one of two forms or can combine elements of both. The first is the clinical or case study. Here the counselor operates as a clinician, and on the basis of an individual's test data and other observations, the counselor formulates some hypotheses about the counselee's behavior. This approach is largely intuitive and is probably the prevalent modus operandi for most counselors.

The second form of prediction is actuarial or statistical. Here the counselee's test data are classified into a category representing his or her performance. The counselor then uses an actuarial table that provides statistical frequencies of behavior of other persons classified in the same way. The data are thus mechanically combined (for example, by means of a regression equation or expectancy table), and a probability figure results.

A continuing argument in career guidance centers on the relative effectiveness of these two methods of making predictions from test data. Meehl's (1954) early work in this regard is instructive. He investigated nineteen studies with unambiguous results that predicted success in some kind of training or schooling, recidivism, or recovery from a major psychosis. Ten of these studies failed to find a difference between the two methods; nine found differences in favor of the statistical method of prediction; none produced a difference in favor of the clinical approach.

Meehl's pioneering work has been supported by later studies by Wiggins (1973) and Watley (1964). Watley used three groups of counselors (high school, university counseling center, and university advisor's office) and one group of freshmen college students as predictors to forecast grade point average, persistence in major, and extracurricular achievements for a group of college freshmen. In general, his results were as follows: Given basic data about individuals, increasing increments of information had no effect on predictive accuracy. There was very little difference between the predictive performance of groups of counselors from different settings, and their performance was not extraordinarily higher than that of the students who made predictions. The number of correct predictions made by statistical methods was higher than the same predictions made by different groups of clinical judges. There was great variability in the ability of individual counselors to make accurate predictions; generally, more accurate predictors were more capable in abstract verbal reasoning ability, more compulsive, least confident about their predictions, and they used no consistent model of prediction from case to case. There was some evidence to suggest that those counselors who predicted most accurately also did the best job of counseling.

The message that emerges from these studies is clear. In career guidance, the making of clinical predictions should be approached with extreme tentativeness. Further, whenever it is possible to collect the necessary data to make statistical predictions, this method is preferred. Therefore, it is mandatory that we know with what our tests correlate and precisely what we are predicting.

The Validity of Aptitude Tests for Career Guidance

It is safe to say that aptitude tests predict school performance and success in training better than they do performance in an occupation. This difference in favor of the training criterion is probably due to the narrower band of activity being predicted and to the fact that "success" in an occupation is very difficult to assess. The use of typical tests of scholastic aptitude produces correlation coefficients between test performance and grade point average at the graduate school level ranging from 0.20 to 0.60 with a mean of 0.40 and at the baccalaureate level from 0.30 to 0.70 with a mean of 0.50. At the high school level, ability and grades are correlated at about 0.60 (Lavin, 1965). Personality factors add very little to predictive accuracy when they are combined with intellective factors, because they are largely discriminant variables rather than predictive variables.

The prediction of success in an occupation shows more modest results. One of the monumental and highly publicized studies in this regard was carried out by Thorndike and Hagen (1959). Their results represent a devastating condemnation of the validity of tests in predicting job performance. Approximately 10,000 men who had taken a one and one-half day battery of tests during World War II as applicants for aircrew training were followed up twelve years later in civilian life. The tests yielded twenty separate scores in the areas of verbal, numerical, spatial, perceptual, and motor abilities. The sample was sorted into 120 occupational groups, with each subject rated in terms of "success in the occupation." Within each occupational grouping, success indicators were correlated with each of the twenty test scores.

There were group differences in mean scores in sensible directions (for example, accountants scored better on numbers tests than on any other tests and also scored better than writers, for in-

stance, on the measure of numerical ability). However, there was wide variability in the total group of 10,000 (such as some accountants had numerical scores as low as the lowest truck driver's score). In general, the 12,000 correlations clustered around zero with as many in the negative direction as in the positive direction. The conclusion reached was that tests given at about age 20 cannot predict occupational success twelve years later.

Thorndike and Hagen offer some possible explanations for their findings. The most valid of these is probably the proposition that beyond survival in an occupation, "success" is a meaningless concept. Because of the institutionalization of rewards in many occupations (civil service, unions, and so on), in which pay scales, hours, and outputs are set by schedules or agreements, it is virtually impossible to secure a differential measure of success in an occupation. Yet, even granting this fact, the results of the research are most discouraging and point, at best, to the need for short-range rather than long-range career counseling.

A brighter picture of the validity of occupational aptitude tests is offered by Ghiselli (1966, 1973). He reviewed all the studies made before 1965 on the accuracy of tests in predicting training success and proficiency in occupations. For all occupations, the average of the validity coefficients is 0.30 for training criteria and 0.19 for proficiency criteria. This difference on the order of 0.10 in favor of training criteria holds for just about all occupational groups. Thus, predicting success in training for a job is more accurate than predicting success in the job itself.

Table 17.1 also presents data on the comparison of validity coefficients by type of test. It is clear that although certain types of tests have significantly higher predictive power for training than for proficiency criteria, others do not. It seems that tests of intellectual, spatial, and mechanical abilities are more effective in predicting trainability than in predicting job proficiency. On the other hand, tests of perceptual accuracy and motor abilities predict trainability and job proficiency equally well.

Thus, the efficiency of aptitude tests in forecasting occupational success and trainability is moderate. For any given job, tests of one kind seem to give better predictions than others. The

Table 17.1
Comparison of Validity Coefficients for Training and Proficiency Criteria by Type of Test
and Proficiency Criteria by Type of Test

Type of Test	Mean Validity Coefficient		No. Pairs of Coefficients
	Train.	Prof.	
Intellectual abilities	.35	.19	38
Intelligence	.34	.21	16
Immediate memory	.23	.18	5
Substitution	.27	.23	4
Arithmetic	.42	.15	13
Spatial and mechanical abilities	.36	.20	28
Spatial relations	.38	.19	13
Location	.24	.17	6
Mechanical principles	.41	.24	9
Perceptual accuracy	.26	.23	15
Number comparison	.25	.24	4
Name comparison	.24	.29	3
Cancellation	.58	.19	1
Pursuit	.18	.17	4
Perceptual speed	.30	.27	3
Motor abilities	.18	.17	24
Tracing	.18	.15	4
Tapping	.15	.13	6
Dotting	.15	.14	4
Finger dexterity	.16	.20	7
Hand dexterity	.24	.22	2
Arm dexterity	.54	.24	1
Personality traits	.05	.08	2
Interest	.05	.08	2
All tests	.30	.19	107

predictive power of a test must be determined for a specific job. When this is done, the maximal power of tests to predict success in training jumps to 0.47 and success on the job itself to approximately 0.35.

Recent research, however, casts doubt on the situation-specific superiority of tests in prediction (Schmidt & Hunter, 1981; Schmidt, Hunter, & Urry, 1976). According to this research, standard aptitude tests (verbal, quantitative, mechanical, spatial, inductive and deductive reasoning, and so on) are valid predictors of performance on the job and in training *for all jobs and in all settings*. It is argued that differences such as those reported by Ghiselli are due to statistical artifacts and, therefore, that validities are generalizable. In

other words, it is claimed that all tests are valid at substantial levels for all jobs. Further, it is claimed that, based on recent large sample research, job performance is about as predictable as training (Pearlman, Schmidt, & Hunter, 1980). Further research is required to settle this dispute. In any case, researchers agree that tests can provide reasonably efficient prediction of training and job performance.

Finally, we have been speaking only of the predictive power of single tests. Combinations of tests yield greater validity. The evident conclusion is that tests can hold enough predictive power to be of practical value in the selection of personnel and of some value in counseling, depending on how they are used.

Appraisal and Career Guidance: Disillusionment

In recent years, several individuals have made derogatory and skeptical observations about the effectiveness of appraisal in career guidance. Career assessment procedures and their subsequent use have been variously termed "test 'em and tell 'em" activities and have been referred to as "three sessions and a cloud of dust." These are not the carpings of the ill-informed. In fact, some of the leading scholars in the field have expressed doubt about the usefulness of human assessment in enhancing career development and career choice (Goldman, 1972, 1982; Crites, 1974; Prediger, 1974a). These criticisms basically revolve around the fact that tests are still being used in the "square-peg, square-hole" trait-and-factor tradition and, usually, for purposes of informing immediate career choices rather than of enhancing general career development. Authorities generally agree, however, that if tests are not used in a mechanistic ritual, they can indeed be valuable for individuals. Crites (1974), for example, argues:

> Reconceptualizing vocational appraisal as an organic, ongoing part of career counseling casts it into the context of career development theory and research. It becomes a collaborative relationship engaged in by the counselor and client which (a) yields person and problem appraisals, (b) distinguishes between the content and process of career decision making, (c) recognizes the efficacy of communicating test results in response to client's thinking and talking about career choice, (d) furthers the client's present and future career development through active counselor intervention, and (e) applies principles of behavior modification as the modus operandi (p. 278).

Prediger (1974b) further suggests that assessment can be useful if employed in a proper manner. Among his recommendations are:

> It is essential to differentiate between assessments of human attributes and square-peg uses of the assessments. . . . The role of tests in career guidance is threefold: first, to stimulate, broaden, and provide focus to career exploration; second, to stimulate exploration of self in relation to career; and third, to provide "what

if" information with respect to various career choice options.

> Test data must go through a chain of transformations if it is to be useful in career guidance. First, test data must be transformed into information relevant to counseling and guidance. Next, this information must be transformed into exploratory activities and self-evaluated experiences. And, finally, these experiences must be transformed into career plans and decisions. Responsibilities for these transformations (in order of presentation) rest primarily with test publishers, counselors, and counselees.

> Because of the important and active roles of the counselor and counselee in these transformations, tests can best be used in the context of a developmental career guidance program (p. 21).

Prediger (1980) further stipulates that "the primary role of tests and other assessment procedures is to provide focus to career exploration" (p. 297).

With an increasing number of tests being interpreted by computer programs, the first of Prediger's suggestions regarding transformations is made much easier. Kleinmuntz (1975) has demonstrated that the computer can be programmed to provide excellent clinical interpretations of test data. It is then the responsibility of the counselor and the counselee to proceed from that point.

Finally, in terms of criticisms of testing and rejoinders, Leona Tyler (1978) has observed that the purposes that tests served in the past are no longer effective. She argues that tests used to be employed to sort individuals into suitable slots. They served to measure *vertical* differences among people — how high a level a person might attain or how much above or below average they might be. Tests, in that sense, encourage and perpetuate competition. As an alternative, Tyler suggests that tests should recognize *complementarity* as well as competition. She states:

> It is necessary that individuals play different roles, do different things, and these differences need not be scaled or graded. In schools, teachers are being challenged to find out how each individual learns most readily rather than

just how much he or she learns in a standard situation. In work places, new systems of organization are being explored, systems in which individual workers contribute in different ways to the functioning of work groups rather than acting as competitive units in an impersonal machine. Colleges that practice open enrollment must find for each individual who enters some fraction of the world's vast store of knowledge which will contribute to his or her intellectual development. Whatever one's occupation, one encounters opportunities for volunteer work and recreational activities from which choices can be made. Americans are coming to appreciate human diversity, to welcome the rich qualitative variety manifested in our population (p. 237).

In Tyler's view, then, "an individual is characterized by his or her total assortment of competencies, structures, styles, and strategies as well as by the amount of specified traits he or she possesses" (p. 238).

Test Interpretation

The effective use of tests in career guidance depends on the extent to which counselees understand and accept the results of test performance. Since we are considering the use of test results in a programmatic, systematic approach to career guidance, where everyone takes the same tests, our major concern is with group interpretation. Some research findings comparing various methods of group or individual interpretation are summarized below:

1. Whatever the method used, counselee attitudes toward the counselor or toward the value of the tests are much the same. However, recall of test results appears to be highest when the counselee has been dominant in an interpretation interview after a learning set for test interpretation has been established (Holmes, 1964).

2. Scholastic aptitude may be a significant variable in interpretation. Counselees with lower scholastic aptitude seem to recall scores more accurately with the use of audiovisual aids. There is also some evidence to suggest that acceptance of test results is facilitated in individual sessions more than in group sessions (Walker, 1965).

3. Those who have the most accurate pictures of themselves before testing tend to learn most about themselves as a result of test interpretation, regardless of the interpretive technique utilized (Gustad & Tuma, 1957).

4. There is a good deal of evidence that counselors should be extremely careful about the manner in which they interpret test results for women (Tittle, 1973), visible minorities (Samuda, 1975), the handicapped (Banas & Nash, 1966), and the older worker (Fozard & Nuttall, 1972; Rimmer & Myers, 1982).

5. Mode of interpretation effectiveness studies are conflicting. Oliver (1977), for example, found individual interpretation superior to multiple interpretation or programmed interpretation. Sharf (1978), on the other hand, found no differences in effectiveness of interpretation when comparing a computer-based narrative report with standard profiles.

What these and other illustrative studies suggest is that no one method of test interpretation can be considered superior for all counselees. Given this finding, the following recommendations for test interpretation offered by Lister and McKenzie (1966) are extremely helpful:

1. The counselee must experience a need for the test information. Therefore, the counselor's role in motivation is most important. Counselees must be assisted to see that a knowledge of test performance will be beneficial to them.

2. Counselees' questions must be translated into operational terms that are acceptable to them. This means that the interpretation must be made in terms of some criterion of importance to the counselee.

3. The information must be clearly communicated to the counselee. Lister and McKenzie argue that the evaluation of the effectiveness of test interpretation must be based on more than simple accurate recall of test information, that recall must be accompanied by significant behavior change. Some type of action must be taken. A counselee who understands and accepts test results given in the form of a probability statement would play the odds. The counselee's behavior would be consistent with the test results and with other data; that is, he or she would pursue alternatives with a reasonable prognosis of success

and would avoid alternatives for which chances of success are minimal (pp. 62–63).

These suggestions are similar to so-called person-referenced test interpretation (Bradley, 1978). In person-referenced interpretation a counselor assists a client to look at his or her performance in testing in order to consider possible ways of dealing with the data in a learning context. The goals for person-referenced counseling/learning test interpretation are such that the counselor: "(a) determines if the test was a valid experience for the client, (b) identifies the strengths and weaknesses of the client's test performances and the means of dealing with them, (c) considers how the information acquired can be used in decision-making, and (d) considers the norm or criterion-reference level of performance" (p. 132).

Kandor, Kendall, and Suggs (1977) suggest a small-group model for test interpretation that has four components. (1) Clients receive pretest information to increase their test-wiseness. (2) They are given pretest counseling to ensure positive motivation and attitudes toward the testing. (3) They acquire posttest information in which the results are presented and interpretated. (3) They are provided opportunity for posttest counseling in order to sort through the personal meaning of the results.

Another guideline for interpretation is provided by Garfield and Prediger (1982), who discuss the testing competencies and responsibilities of vocational counselors. They suggest that counselors rate their own interpretation skills by using the following key:

1 = I do this routinely – as a regular practice.
2 = I have done on occasion.
3 = I do not do – but ought to consider doing.
4 = Not applicable to the instrument(s) I am using.

Their list of interpretation responsibilities/competencies is as follows:

___ 1. Study suggestions for interpretation provided by the test manual (and/or score report form) and determine which of them are supported by the psychometric data provided for the test.

___ 2. Review, with the counselee, the purpose and nature of the test. Topics include:

___ a. Why the test was given; what the test can and *cannot* do.

___ b. Who will receive the test results.

___ c. What the test results cover and how they will be used.

___ 3. Interpret test results in the context of the testing experience, the counselee's background, and other assessments (if any) of the same characteristics by:

___ a. Encouraging a discussion of how the counselee felt about the testing experience, in general; his/her performance, in particular; and any difficulties or problems (e.g., nervousness, fatigue, distractions) encountered.

___ b. Examining the possibility that the counselee's background (race, sex, handicap, age, etc.) may have influenced the test results.

___ c. Seeking additional information to explain any inconsistencies that become evident.

___ 4. Apply good counseling techniques to test interpretation by:

___ a. Emphasizing "strengths" while objectively discussing "weaknesses."

___ b. Allowing sufficient time for the counselee to assimilate information and respond.

___ c. Listening attentively to the counselee's responses (i.e., attending to the counselee first and test results second).

___ d. Checking the counselee's understanding of the test results from time to time; correcting misconceptions.

___ 5. Help the counselee begin (or continue) the career (educational and vocational) planning process by:

___ a. Identifying, with the counselee, career options and steps for exploring each.

___ b. Providing assistance to the counselee through ongoing career guidance activities such as field trips, career conferences, filmstrips, library resources, etc.

___ c. Monitoring and encouraging career

planning efforts through progress reports, follow-through counseling sessions, etc.

Types of Aptitude Tests

Assessment in the cognitive domain is usually achieved by administering a standardized battery of tests or individual tests measuring common aptitudes for which adequate criterion data are available. An aptitude may be defined as "readiness for learning" (Thorndike & Hagen, 1969, p. 644). An aptitude test is, therefore, one that predicts success in some occupation or training course (Cronbach, 1970, p. 38). At present, the number of aptitudes for which psychologists have determined even minimally adequate validity data is limited. At best, it includes scholastic aptitude (verbal, numerical, and performance), perceptual speed and accuracy (clerical), manual dexterities, mechanical reasoning, spatial visualization, aesthetic judgment, artistic ability, and musical talent (Super & Crites, 1962). Of these, the last three are highly specialized and have limited application. Thus, we are left with five basic aptitudes.

Various individual tests are capable of assessing aptitudes in each of these areas. However, for purposes of career guidance testing, the selection of individual tests poses problems. The main obstacle is that they have been standardized on different populations, and therefore norms are not consistent from test to test. Also, some individual tests fail to provide specific educational or occupational norms that would be useful in career guidance. Finally, choosing individual tests to assess multiple potentialities can typically run to large costs and present clerical problems in scoring.

Because of these deficiencies, psychologists have developed the test battery. Here a number of tests are employed together to predict various criteria. Individuals have several aptitudes, or patterns of strengths and weaknesses, that contribute to their total potential. The battery yields a multi-score summary of these differential patterns. Since all the tests in a battery are standardized on the same group, norms take on added meaning. Several of the most widely used instruments of this sort are briefly described below.

THE DIFFERENTIAL APTITUDE TESTS (DAT). G. K. Bennett, H. G. Seashore, A. G. Westman. Psychological Corporation. Fifth Edition (1974). Grade 8–Adult.
Requires approximately four hours for a counselee to complete with Career Planning Program
Eight tests yielding nine scores
  Verbal Reasoning
  Numerical Reasoning
  Abstract Reasoning
  Space Relations
  Mechanical Reasoning
  Clerical Speed and Accuracy
  Spelling
  Language Usage
  Verbal + Numerical = general intelligence measure
Norms expressed in percentiles
Optional DAT/Career Planning Program developed by D. E. Super et al. gives computer print-out relating career and educational plans and preferences to scores on the test. Confirms plans or suggests alternative occupational areas.

THE GENERAL APTITUDE TEST BATTERY (GATB). United States Employment Service. Requires two and one-half hours for administration.
Twelve tests measuring nine factors
  Intelligence (G)
  Verbal Aptitude (V)
  Numerical Aptitude (N)
  Spatial Aptitude (S)
  Form Perception (P)
  Clerical Perception (Q)
  Motor Coordination (K)
  Finger Dexterity (F)
  Manual Dexterity (M)
Standard scores (Mean 100; standard deviation 20)
Cut-off scores for various occupational groups and job families according to DOT.
Can be administered by those in non–USOE agencies if counselors take a short training course.
Now related to USES interest inventory.

THE DAILEY VOCATIONAL TESTS. J. T. Dailey. Houghton Mifflin. Grade 8–Adult. Approximately two hours for administration.

Three tests
  Technical and Scholastic
  Business English
  Spatial Visualization
Assesses potential for training and success for occupations within the trade, technical, and business-secretarial fields.
Norms by grade and/or sex.
For use with noncollege bound.
Good "face" validity for specialty-oriented students.

APPRAISAL OF OCCUPATIONAL APTITUDES. A. Abbatiello. Houghton Mifflin. Grade 9–Adult. Approximately one and one-half hours for administration.
Eight tests
  Checking Letters
  Checking Numbers
  Filing Names
  Filing Numbers
  Posting Names
  Posting Numbers
  Arithmetical Computation and Reasoning
  Desk Calculator
Intended for selection and counseling regarding business and office careers.

FLANAGAN APTITUDE CLASSIFICATION TESTS (FACT). J. C. Flanagan. Science Research Associates. Approximately five and one-half hours to administer. Grade 12–Adult.
Fourteen tests
  Inspection
  Coding
  Memory
  Precision
  Assembly
  Scales
  Coordination
  Judgment and Comprehension
  Arithmetic
  Patterns
  Components
  Tables
  Mechanics
  Expression
Scores expressed in stanines and related to 30 oc-
cupations, mainly ranging from skilled to professional.
Self-scoring.
Various tests used in combination for various occupations in personnel selection, counseling, and screening.

ARMED SERVICES VOCATIONAL APTITUDE BATTERY (ASVAB). U.S. Department of Defense. High School level (mainly seniors).
Nine tests
  Coding Speed
  Word Knowledge
  Arithmetic Reasoning
  Tool Knowledge
  Space Perception
  Mechanical Comprehension
  Shop Information
  Automotive Information
  Electronics Information
Scores expressed in percentiles based on national norms.
Basically a recruitment device, but can yield valuable information at no cost.
Scores related to military and civilian occupations via the *U.S. Army Career and Education Guide*.
Cronbach (1979) maintains that the test requires interpretation by informed counselors and should not be given without such a safeguard.

GRAFLEX VOCATIONAL EVALUATION SYSTEM. Singer Education and Training Products. Seven days to administer all tests.
21 "work stations"
  Basic Tools
  Bench Assembly
  Drafting
  Electrical Wiring
  Plumbing and Pipe Fitting
  Wood Working and Carpentry
  Refrigeration, Air Conditioning, and Heating
  Welding and Soldering
  Clerk, Sales, and Office
  Needle Trades
  Masonry
  Sheet Metal Working
  Cooking and Baking
  Small Engine Service

Medical Service
Cosmetology
Data Calculation and Recording
Soil Testing
Photo Lab Technician
Production Machine Operating
Unlike other tests, this is a work sample, hands-on determination of career aptitudes, interests, and work tolerances, used primarily for screening purposes in rehabilitation centers, vocational-technical schools, job centers, business and industry, and so on.
Systems such as these are usually housed in a "Work Evaluation Center."
Orientation and instruction for each work station followed by goal-directed work.
Very expensive to purchase.

Other work sample batteries are available and are equally good. See, for example: VOCATIONAL INTEREST, TEMPERAMENT, AND APTITUDE SCALE (VITAS) (Abrams, 1979); TOWER: Testing, Orientation, and Work Evaluation in Rehabilitation (Institute for the Crippled and Disabled, 1967).

CAREER PLANNING PROGRAM (CPP). Grades 8–11 (Houghton Mifflin). Grades 12–13 (ACT).
Components of CPP 8–11
   1. Interest Scales
       Social Service
       Business Contact
       Business Detail
       Technical
       Science
       Creative Arts
   2. Experience Scales
       Career-related activities and experiences
   3. Ability Scales
       Mechanical Reasoning
       Space Relations
       Clerical Skills
       Numerical Skills
       Reading Skills
       Language Usage
Various other informal assessment components.
Related to *Exploring: You and Your Career* and *A Mini-Course in Career Planning.*
About two and one-half hours required for total program administration.

Abilities and interests reported in stanines.
Components of CPP 12–13
   1. Interest Scales
       Social Service
       Business Contact
       Business Detail
       Trades, technical
       Science
       Arts
       Health
   2. Ability Scales
       Space Relations
       Reading Skills
       Clerical Skills
       Numerical Computation, Math Usage
       Language Usage
       Mechanical Reasoning
       Nonverbal Reasoning
Related to ACT Occupational Classification System and World of Work Map for Job Families.
CPP 8–11 focus is primarily career exploration; CPP 12–13 emphasizes post-secondary planning.
Related to UNIACT Interest measure

VOCATIONAL PLANNING INVENTORY.
Science Research Associates. Two programs: High School Prediction Program that predicts grades in high school for eight major vocational curriculum areas and in vocational and academic courses as a whole (grades 8, 9, and 10); requires approximately three hours for administration. The Post-High School Prediction Program predicts grades for first years of post-high school training in seven major vocational curriculum areas and general areas (grades 11 and 12); approximately two and one-half hours.
Both combine various Flanagan Aptitude Tests, other SRA aptitude tests, and SRA value surveys to form a complete battery.
Curriculum areas predicted are:
   General Academic
   General Vocational
   Business
   Mechanical and Mechanical Maintenance
   Drafting and Design
   Metal Trades
   Home Economics and Health
   Construction Trades
   Electronics and Electrical Trades
   Agriculture

Scores reported in terms of predicted grade range.

CAREER ABILITY PLACEMENT SURVEY (CAPS). Edits. The battery consists of eight five-minute ability tests. Results are reported in terms of stanines.

Mechanical Reasoning
Spatial Relations
Verbal Reasoning
Numerical Ability
Language Usage
Word Knowledge
Perceptual Speed and Accuracy
Manual Speed and Dexterity

May be used separately, but intended to accompany COPSystem interest and value measurement instruments and related to COPSystem career clusters (Service, Science, Technology, Outdoor, Business, Clerical, Communication, and Arts).

Norms for grades 8–12, community college, and selected occupational groups. Very short tests correlate moderately with longer tests (such as DAT, GATB). Contention is that when consideration of testing time is important, one can get as good prediction of high school grades with CAPS as with the GATB (Knapp et al., 1978).

APTITUDE TESTS FOR OCCUPATIONS. W. S. Roeder. Bobbs-Merrill. High school through adult. Purpose to acquire "a quick but valid" general vocational profile of an individual. Hand- or machine-scored. Six tests (107 minutes):

Personal-Social Aptitude (20 minutes)
Mechanical Aptitude (20 minutes)
General Sales Aptitude (20 minutes)
Clerical Routine Aptitude (12 minutes)
Computational Aptitude (15 minutes)
Scientific Aptitude (20 minutes)

Occupations related to each aptitude are offered in interpretation, but there are no occupational norms. Norms in percentiles by grade level (9–13).

DISCRIMINATION

It is generally conceded that at least two types of measurement are required for career guidance, where choice content is the purpose: assessment of various capacities or aptitudes and assessment of interests. Each of these two should be surveyed at various stages of an individual's development. The results should be communicated to the counselee in two ways: first, in terms of the groups in which the counselee may succeed, and second, in terms of the groups that the counselee most resembles with regard to interests, values, personality, and such. The "most like" description is achieved by means of a statistical technique called discriminant analysis. The former "goodness" probability statement emerges as a result of the regression analysis procedure discussed earlier. Hence, it is desirable to assess personal traits from both the cognitive (aptitudes) and noncognitive domains (interests) and to report results both in terms of the groups an individual is most like (discriminant analysis) and in terms of that individual's probability of success in given groups (regression analysis) (Sprinthall, 1967; Prediger, 1974). In terms of the group an individual most resembles, for example, Laing, Lamb, and Prediger (1982) in a large-scale study have affirmed the use of basic interest scales in suggesting college majors to explore. Interest measurement is the most common application of discriminant analysis in career guidance. Although it is possible to use interest inventories for prediction, we do not view prediction as their primary value.

Interests

Super and Crites (1962) have observed that we may assess an individual's interests in four ways. We may look to *expressed* interests — what an individual expresses an interest in. Second, we may observe *manifest* interests — what an individual actually does as an indiction of what one's interests are. Third, we may assess interests by *testing* — using an instrument like the Michigan Vocabulary Test, on the grounds that if an individual is really interested in something, that person will know the vocabulary involved in that area. Finally, we may examine *inventoried* interests — determining the pattern of an individual's interests from his or her responses to lists of occupations or activities.

This last technique is by far the most common means of assessing interests. Basically, two types of inventories have emerged. One is the so-called empirically keyed or criterion-keyed inventory, which results in interest scores related to specific occupations. The other is the ipsatively determined, or nonempirically keyed inventory, which yields score profiles in areas rather than in specific occupations and in relation to each other area rather than absolutely.

Research conducted by Reilly and Echternacht (1979) casts some doubts on the manner in which criterion-keying has been effected. Criterion-keying has been done without regard to the dimension of job satisfaction. There is now some evidence to suggest that job satisfaction within occupations should be considered in criterion-keyed interest scales. Elements of both types of scoring may be combined in a given inventory.

The interpretation of interest inventories is no more informed by definitive research than is the interpretation of other tests as discussed earlier in this chapter. Sharf (1974) offers a thoughtful paradigm to serve as a structure for research into the question of differential effectiveness in test interpretation. His model would investigate the interaction of client variables, such as sex or age, with type of interpretation, such as programmed or computerized. Table 17.2 is a schematic of Sharf's model.

Of course, some suggestions for interpretation are available in the manuals for the various inventories. Other suggestions are contained in the professional literature. Weinrach (1980) has resurrected an old technique that he calls "discrepancy

identification." By this he means that clients simply predict their Kuder DD results and then compare them to actual outcomes. One often-used variation on this theme is to have parents predict the interest inventory results of their children. Their predictions rarely conform to actual profile results. The discrepancy serves as a stimulus for parent training. Such activities stem, in general, from expectancy theory (Synder, 1979), which was discussed in Chapter 4.

Other researchers advocate a so-called integrative approach to test interpretation (Rubinstein, 1978; Lange & Coffman, 1981). In this method, the counselor begins with the unique needs of the individual, compares these needs to those expressed by people in various occupations, and helps the individual to integrate this knowledge with an overview of the world of work. Several researchers urge the adoption of a systematic approach to the use and interpretation of tests; that is, specification of objectives, activities to achieve them, careful evaluation of results (Brown & Koltveit, 1977). Obviously, we are in favor of such an approach.

Interest Inventories

Several of the most commonly used interest inventories are briefly described here:

OHIO VOCATIONAL INTEREST INVENTORY (OVIS). A. G. D'Costa, D. W. Winefordner, J. G. Odgers, and P. B. Koons, Jr. Harcourt Brace

Table 17.2
A Design Suggesting Future Directions in Research in Interest Inventory Interpretation

| Client Variables | Type of Interest Inventory Interpretation | | | |
	Standard Profile Interpretation	Programmed Interpretation	Audio-video Interpretation	Computerized Interpretation
Sex				
Age				
Education level				
Cultural group				
Personality type				
Type of vocational problem				

Jovanovich, and others. Approximately one and one-half hours. Grades 8–13.

Twenty-four interests scales and a scale clarity score

  Manual Work
  Machine Work
  Personal Services
  Caring for People or Animals
  Clerical Work
  Inspecting and Testing
  Crafts and Precise Operations
  Customer Services
  Nursing and Related Technical Services
  Skilled Personal Services
  Training
  Literary
  Numerical
  Appraisal
  Agriculture
  Applied Technology
  Promotion and Communication
  Management and Supervision
  Artistic
  Sales Representative
  Music
  Entertainment and Performing Arts
  Teaching, Counseling, and Social Work
  Medical

Scores expressed in stanines and percentiles.

Based on cubistic model (people, data, things) of DOT.

Includes a *Student Information Questionnaire* (six questions and one open-ended for a school to ask eight more questions of a locally pertinent nature).

Provides a *Student Report Folder* and a *Guide to Career Exploration* to link interests to the world of work.

VOCATIONAL INTERESTS, EXPERIENCE, AND SKILL ASSESSMENT (VIESA). Houghton Mifflin. Grades 8–12. Approximately 45 minutes.

Yields six job clusters (comparable to Holland's typology) and 25 job families that include 650 occupations. Self-scored.

Related to *Career Planning Program* described elsewhere in this chapter.

Not a great deal of data yet accumulated regarding this instrument.

STRONG-CAMPBELL INTEREST INVENTORY (SCII).[1] E. K. Strong and D. P. Campbell. Stanford University Press (various distributors). Grade 11–Adult. Approximately 30–45 minutes. Revised and extended form combining separate SVIBs for men and women.

1981 Revised Norms. Yields 6 General Occupational Theme Scales (à la Holland) with 20 items in each scale. These are related to 23 Basic Interest Scales.

  Realistic Theme
    Agriculture
    Nature
    Adventure
    Military Activities
    Mechanical Activities
  Investigative Theme
    Science
    Mathematics
    Medical Science
    Medical Service
  Artistic Theme
    Music/Dramatics
    Art
    Writing
  Social Theme
    Teaching
    Social Service
    Athletics
    Domestic Arts
    Religious Activities
  Enterprising Theme
    Public Speaking
    Law/Politics
    Merchandising
    Sales
    Business Management
  Conventional Theme
    Office Practices

Also yields scores on 124 Occupational Scales, primarily professional level.

Individuals may still compare scores to both men and women, although much sexism has been eliminated.

[1]Because of the sexism charges that have surrounded the SVIB-M and SVIB-W forms, they are not discussed here. Rather, we present the combined, newer form. See, for example, Birk (1974); Campbell et al. (1974), Harmon (1973), Diamond (1975), Lamb and Prediger (1979), Lunneborg (1980), and Betz and Wolfe (1981).

Still has an Academic Orientation Scale (AOR) and an Introversion-Extroversion Scale (I-E). Older Masculinity-Femininity Scale (M-F) has been eliminated.

Usually scored and interpreted by computer.

BRAINARD OCCUPATIONAL PREFERENCE INVENTORY. P.O. and R. F. Brainard. Psychological Corporation. Grades 8-12. Approximately 30 minutes.

Yields scores in 6 broad fields
Commercial
Mechanical
Professional
Aesthetic
Scientific
Agriculture (males)
Personal Service (females)

Scores expressed in percentiles for males and females.

CALIFORNIA OCCUPATIONAL PREFERENCE SURVEY (COPS). R. R. Knapp and others. Educational and Industrial Testing Service. Grades 9-12. Approximately 40 minutes. Yields scores in 8 major groups according to 2 levels each (professional and skilled) à la Roe.
Science
Technology
Business
Linguistic
Aesthetic
Service
Outdoor
Clerical

Scores expressed in percentiles for males and females.

OCCUPATIONAL INTERESTS INVENTORY (OII). E. A. Lee and L. P. Thorpe. California Test Bureau. Grade 7-Adult. Approximately 40 minutes.

Yields scores in 6 fields of interests and three types of interests (verbal, manipulative, and computational)
Personal-Social
Natural
Mechanical
Business
Arts
Sciences

A similar instrument in pictorial form, the Picture Interest Inventory (PII) by K. P. Weingarten, is also published by the California Test Bureau.

MINNESOTA VOCATIONAL INTERESTS INVENTORY (MVII). K. E. Clark. Psychological Corporation. Males, ages 15+. Approximately 45 minutes.

Yields nine general interest scales
Mechanical
Health Service
Office Work
Electronics
Food Service
Carpentry
Sales Office
Clean Hands
Outdoor

Also yields 21 Occupational Scales for skilled occupations (baker, carpenter, plumber, and so on).

Results expressed in T scores.

Intended for noncollege bound.

CAREER ASSESSMENT INVENTORY (CAI). C. B. Johannson. National Computer Systems. Grade 8-Adult. Approximately 45 minutes.

Yields scores according to Holland's six types and 22 basic interests.
Realistic
Mechanical/Fixing
Electronics
Carpentry
Manual/Skilled Trades
Agriculture
Nature/Outdoors
Animal Service
Investigative
Science
Numbers
Artistic
Writing
Performing/Entertaining
Arts/Crafts
Social
Social Service
Teaching
Child Care
Medical Service
Religious Activities

Enterprising
  Business
  Sales
Conventional
  Office Practices
  Clerical/Clerking
  Food Service
Also yields 42 specific occupational scores.
Intended for undecided, noncollege bound individuals.
Concentrates on subprofessional levels, whereas SCII emphasizes professional level occupations.
Results presented in standard score form.

KUDER PREFERENCE RECORDS AND INTEREST SURVEYS. G. F. Kuder. Science Research Associates. There are 3 Preference Records (Forms C, A, and D) and 2 Surveys (Forms E and DD). Only the latter two instruments are described below.

KUDER GENERAL INTEREST SURVEY (FORM E). Grades 7-12. Approximately 50 minutes.
Yields 10 interest scales plus verification (V) score
  Outdoor
  Mechanical
  Computational
  Scientific
  Persuasive
  Artistic
  Literary
  Musical
  Social Service
  Clerical
Scores expressed in national percentiles.
Can be hand scored.

KUDER OCCUPATIONAL INTEREST SURVEY (OIS) (FORM DD). Grades 9-12 and adults. Approximately 30 minutes.
Yields 77 occupational scales and 29 college major scales for men; 57 occupational scales and 27 college major scales for women. Many of the male scales can be applied to women. Verification (V) scale and eight experimental scales.
Scores reported in terms of modified biserial correlations. Must be machine scored.
All Kuder Preference Records and Surveys may be related to careers through Lombard (1973).

VOCATIONAL PREFERENCE INVENTORY (VPI). J. L. Holland. Consulting Psychologists Press. Grade 9-Adult. Approximately 30 minutes.
Yields 6 personality scales and 5 experimental scales
  Realistic
  Intellectual
  Social
  Conventional
  Enterprising
  Artistic
  Self-Control
  Masculinity
  Status
  Infrequency
  Acquiescence
Self-scored.
Whether this instrument is a personality measure, and interest measure, or both, is still moot.

VOCATIONAL INTEREST INVENTORY (VII). P. W. Lunneborg. Western Psychological Services. High school population at grade 12 reading level. Intended for undecided students whose interests are not well differentiated. Approximately 20 minutes.
Forced choice format yields relative strength of interests in Roe's 8 areas:
  Service
  Business Contact
  Organization
  Technical
  Outdoor
  Science
  General Cultural
  Arts and Entertainment
Machine scored. Scores reported in terms of percentiles and T scores for each scale.
Controls for sex bias at item level and encourages exploration of nontraditional careers.

JACKSON VOCATIONAL INTEREST SURVEY. D. N. Jackson. Research Psychologists Press. Grade 7-Adult. Approximately 40 minutes.
A Canadian-developed instrument that measures preferences in terms of vocational roles and vocational styles (activities and work environments).
34 basic interest scales arranged in 11 categories:
  The Arts
  Science and Mathematics
  Practical, Outdoor Activities

Service Activities
Medicine and Health
Interpersonal and Job-Related Work Styles
Teaching and Social Welfare Activities
Business, Administrative, and Related Activities
Legal, Professional, Persuasive Work Roles
Literary, Academic
Work Styles Related to Job Activities
Hand or machine scored.
Males and females measured equally.
10 general occupational themes (expressive, logical, inquiring, practical, assertive, socialized, helping, conventional, enterprising, and communicative).
Academic orientation scale.
This inventory was carefully developed in terms of its psychometric qualities.

GEIST PICTURE INTEREST INVENTORY. H. Geist. Western Psychological Services. Grade 8–Adult. Some occupational norms. Intended for culture-limited and educationally deprived populations.

UNIACT (Unisex edition of the ACT Interest Inventory (ACT-IV). American College Testing Program. 90-item inventory yielding scores on the 6 Holland scales (15 items per scale).
Attempt to reduce and virtually eliminate sex differences in vocational interest scores.
Activity- rather than occupation-based instrument.

INTEREST DETERMINATION, EXPLORATION, AND ASSESSMENT SYSTEM (IDEAS). C. B. Johannson. NCS Interpretive Scoring Systems. Approximately 30–40 minutes. Grades 6–12.
14 basic interest scales
Mechanical/Fixing
Electronics
Nature/Outdoor
Science
Numbers
Writing
Arts/Crafts
Social Service
Child Care
Medical Service
Business

Sales
Office Practices
Food Service
Scores reported in raw scores and standard score form.
Related to *Occupational Outlook Handbook* and DOT.
Self-scoring
Emphasis generally on occupations not requiring college education.

MONITORING

It is useful to have some assessment of the stage of career development or career maturity of an individual or groups. In one sense, monitoring can be thought of as an evaluation of an individual's career progress. Depending on the instrument used, it can tell us about individual readiness for choice rather than the content of choice. It tells us where individuals are vocationally and where they have to go. In another sense, monitoring informs us of such work-related factors as work values, job satisfaction, and a wide variety of other measurable variables pertinent to work life.

The career-related needs of individuals determine the goals to be achieved in a systematic approach; monitoring permits a continued check on these needs. There are diverse types of measures, both extant and in-process, that relate to this function. In development, for example, there are scales to determine degree of career "undecidedness" (see Chapter 14). Instruments exist to assess everything from work environment preference to career education needs assessment to job satisfaction and satisfactoriness. In the following section, we will consider some of the more prominent monitoring instruments in four distinct areas: career maturity, work values, career planning, and job satisfaction.

Career Maturity

As discussed at length in Chapter 4, career maturity is a construct that naturally emerges from developmentally oriented career theories. If people do indeed go through a systematic series of stages in career development, then it ought to be possible to measure the rate and progress of that sequence and to compare where an individual is along that developmental line, both in terms of where one might reasonably be expected to be and in terms of where one's age peers are (Jordaan, 1974; Super, 1974; Crites, 1974). Depending on how far they depart from an expected norm, we may then classify them according to career maturity. Crites (1974a) has suggested that the measurement of career maturity has at least two types of utility: (1) a *research function* in that it enables us to "test" theoretical aspects of career development; and (2) a *practical function* in that it diagnoses the rate and progress of the career development of an individual and consequently suggests intervention strategies to enhance that development. In the latter sense, career maturity measurement can be used as both a type of needs analysis and as a criterion variable in the evaluation of the effectiveness of certain types of intervention strategies.

Generally, career maturity may be defined as the place reached on a continuum of career development from exploration to decline. Note that no current career maturity measure assesses any career-related maturational variables in the growth stage — that stage hypothesized to precede the exploratory stage. In broader terms, career maturity measures are an attempt to assess "the readiness of the individual to make decisions that are called for at a given decision point" (Super, 1974, p. 10).

A number of instruments designed to appraise career maturity from adolescence through adulthood have been devised.

Career Maturity Measures

CAREER DEVELOPMENT INVENTORY (CDI). D. E. Super, A. S. Thompson, R. H. Lindeman, J. P. Jordaan, and R. A. Myers. Consulting Psychologists Press. About one hour to complete. School form and college and university form. 8 scales:

Career Planning (CP) — 20 items
Career Exploration (CE) — 20 items
Decision-Making (DM) — 20 items
World-of-Work Information (WW) — 20 items
Knowledge of Preferred Occupational Group (PO) — 40 items

Career Development Attitudes (CDA) — (CP & CE Combined)
Career Development, Knowledge and Skills (CDK) — (DM & WW Combined)
Career Orientation Total (COT) — CP, CE, DM, & WW Combined

Generally acceptable discriminant validity (Kuhlman-Harrison & Neely, 1980).

ADULT CAREER CONCERNS INVENTORY. D. E. Super and others (in process). 120 items. Adult populations (few normative data as yet). Being used in Career Pattern Study. 15–30 minutes. 12 substages (10 items each):

Exploration
1. crystallization
2. specification
3. implementation

Establishment
4. stabilization
5. consolidation
6. advancement

Maintenance
7. holding
8. updating
9. innovating

Disengagement
10. deceleration
11. retirement planning
12. retirement living

Subject rates self in relation to statements (e.g., "using new methods and ideas on the job") on a 1–5 scale (1 = I have not yet thought much about it; 5 = I have already done this). Two separate scoring methods.

CAREER MATURITY INVENTORY (Formerly called the Vocational Development Inventory). John O. Crites. 50 attitude items. 100 competence items. Normative data for grades 6–13. 20–30 minutes for attitude test. Two to two and one-half hours for competency test.

Attitude Test
True-false format measuring 5 presumed attitude clusters with a total score.
1. Involvement in the choice process
2. Orientation toward work
3. Independence in decision-making
4. Preference for choice factors
5. Conceptions of the choice process

Competency Test

5 multiple-choice tests: separate and total scores
1. Problems: problem-solving in career decision-making
2. Planning: logical steps to career goals
3. Occupational Information: job duties and tasks, employment trends, and so on
4. Self-Appraisal: assessment of hypothetical person's assets and liabilities in relation to career success and satisfaction
5. Goal Selection: choosing the most realistic occupation for a fictitious individual

Attitude Test has been much more widely used than Competency Test up to this point.

COGNITIVE VOCATIONAL MATURITY TEST (CVMT). B. W. Westbrook. 120 multiple choice items. 80–90 minutes. Normative data for grades 6–9.
6 subtests
1. Fields of Work (20 items)
2. Job Selection (15 items)
3. Work Conditions (20 items)
4. Education Required (20 items)
5. Attributes Required (20 items)
6. Duties (25 items)

Reading level below grade 3
Includes occupations in all Roe interests fields
Subtests and total scores

READINESS FOR CAREER PLANNING (RCP). (Formerly Readiness for Vocational Planning RVP). W. D. Gribbons and P. R. Lohnes. Originally 45 items; now 22 items. Semi-structured interview. Grades 8–10.
8 original scales
1. Factors in Curriculum Choice
2. Factors in Occupational Choice
3. Verbalized Strengths and Weaknesses
4. Accuracy in Self-Appraisal
5. Evidence of Self-Rating
6. Interests
7. Values
8. Independence of Choice

Eight original scales reduced to univariate treatment of career maturity mainly to allow for statistical treatments.

ADULT VOCATIONAL MATURITY INVENTORY (AVMI). D. I. Sheppard. Male adults. Two forms: Form I, true-false; Form II, 5-point Likert scale. 40 items.
5 dimensions
1. Involvement in the vocational choice process
2. Orientation toward work
3. Independence in decision-making
4. Preference for vocational choice factors
5. Conceptions of the choice process

Small normative sample

Westbrook (1974) has reviewed four of the inventories cited herein and two others that are less rigidly devised attempts to measure the construct. He has evolved a composite outline of the career behaviors which the tests are attempting to assess. In abbreviated form, the outline is:

I. Cognitive Domain (What the learner knows)
   A. Individual attributes
   B. Occupational information
   C. Job selection
   D. Course and curriculum selection
   E. School and career planning
   F. School and career problem solving
II. Psychomotor Domain (What the learner says he has done)
   A. Involvement in career planning activities
   B. Involvement in wide range of worker activities
   C. Involvement in activities related to preferred occupation(s)
III. Affective Domain (Attitudes, preferences, and perceptions of learner)
   A. Attitudes
   B. Preferences
   C. Perceptions

The six measures described above are clearly attempts to appraise the construct of career maturity. All are in the process of development, that is, they are being researched to determine their criterion-related validity and their construct validity and to discover what variables affect performance. Hundreds of studies have already been accomplished, and some useful data have emerged. For example, several studies have clearly demonstrated that race per se is not a significant variable in career maturity (Ansell & Hansen, 1971; Maynard & Hansen, 1970; Dillard, 1976). On the other hand, still moot are the relationships between such variables as sex, socioeconomic class, and intelligence and career maturity. Some studies have found high loadings of these factors in career maturity; other studies have found them to be independent of career maturity. In short, studies have thus far produced conflicting findings, although the weight of evidence is beginning to accumulate to provide answers. One disturbing finding, however, is the fact that the correlations between aspects of certain instruments which purport to measure the same variables in the construct are low (Westbrook & Mastie, 1973). In any case, attempts to operationalize and measure the construct of career maturity represent a most exciting and potentially valuable development in career guidance and counseling.

Work Values

A second type of monitoring instrument that is useful in both research and in career guidance is the work values measure. The values that one holds are clearly a determinant of career choice (Katz, 1973); therefore, an objective measure of the hierarchical structure of those values provides an individual with important input data for career decision-making. Often these measures simply clarify what an individual already knows. Frequently, however, they open up hidden areas for exploration and consideration; they bring to the surface that which had remained dormant. Work values are sometimes confused with work interests. In fact, the two are distinctive domains, each measuring different variables (Breme & Cockriel, 1975). Work values measures are briefly described here.

WORK VALUES INVENTORY (WVI). D. E. Super. Houghton Mifflin. Grade 7–Adult. 15 minutes.
15 values relating to job success and satisfaction, combined into four factors: material, goodness of life, self-expression, and behavior control.
1. intellectual stimulation
2. job achievement
3. way of life
4. economic returns
5. altruism
6. creativity
7. relationship with associates
8. job security

9. prestige
10. management of others
11. variety
12. aesthetics
13. independence
14. supervisory relations
15. physical surroundings

Factor analysis of the WVI suggests 6 second-order dimensions (rather than the structural 4 into which the 15 values were organized): stimulating work, interpersonal satisfaction, economic security, responsible autonomy, comfortable existence, and esthetic concerns (Bolton, 1980).

SURVEY OF WORK VALUES (SWV). S. Wollack, J. G. Goodale, J. P. Wijting, and P. C. Smith. Late adolescent–Adult. Measures intrinsic (work-related values) and extrinsic (reward-related values) aspects of the Protestant work ethic.
54 items and 6 scales (9 items per scale)
1. Social status of job
2. Activity preference
3. Upward striving
4. Attitude toward earnings
5. Pride in work
6. Job involvement

HALL OCCUPATIONAL ORIENTATION INVENTORY. Scholastic Testing Service.
Three levels: Grades 3–7; high school and college; handicapped adults. Based on Maslow's personality need theory and DOT.
Yields scale scores
Creativity, Independence
Risk
Information, Knowledge
Belongingness
Security
Aspiration
Esteem
Self-Actualization
Personal Satisfaction
Routine-Dependence
Data Orientation
Things Orientation
People Orientation
Location Concern
Aptitude Concern
Monetary Concern

Physical Abilities Concern
Environment Concern
Coworker Concern
Qualifications Concern
Time Concern
Defensiveness

OHIO WORK VALUES INVENTORY (OWVI).
L. W. Hales and B. J. Fenner. Publishers Test Service. Grades 4–12; 30 minutes to complete. 77 items yielding scores on 11 work values:

Altruism
Object orientation
Security
Control
Self-realization
Independence
Money
Task satisfaction
Solitude
Ideas/data orientation
Prestige

MINNESOTA IMPORTANCE QUESTIONNAIRE (MIQ). Vocational Psychology Research, University of Minnesota. Based on Theory of Work Adjustment (R. V. Dawis, L. H. Lofquist, and D. J. Weiss). Actually a measure of vocational needs rather than values. Most common form 1975 paired format with machine scoring. Fifth-grade reading level. 30–40 minutes. 20 statements representing 20 needs (e.g., authority: I could tell people what to do) are paired with each other for a forced choice, then each of the 20 is rated absolutely.
Yield is scores on the 20 needs:

Ability utilization
Achievement
Activity
Advancement
Authority
Company Policies and Practices
Compensation
Coworkers
Creativity
Independence
Moral Values
Recognition
Responsibility
Security

Social Service
Social status
Supervision – Human Relations
Supervision – Technical
Variety
Working Conditions

Occupational Reinforcer Patterns (ORPs) are descriptions of reinforcer systems of selected occupations. Scores also on 9 clusters of ORPs).

There are many other general values measures and many other work values instruments, but none of the latter has been so carefully devised and tested as the four we have listed. Measures devised by Centers (1949), Fretz (1972), and Stefflre (1959) are examples of other work values instruments that have been utilized in research but for which construct validity has been less clearly established.

Other Career Assessment Devices

Several other instruments have been devised to assess the knowledge or attitudes of individuals with regard to selected aspects of career development. These devices are intended to give both individuals and those responsible for career interventions a gauge of career-related awareness, knowledge, and attitudes. Some are criterion-referenced, and others are norm-referenced. Some are based on psychological constructs; some are not. They are, by and large, content measures. A sampling of some of these instruments follows.

BOXSCORE. S. N. Feingold, S. Swerdloff, and J. E. Barber. Chronicle Guidance Publications. Grades 7–11. One class period. Measures basic knowledge of occupational information.
5 groups of questions (100 items)
1. Occupational outlook or world of work in general (40 items)
2. Occupational earnings (10 items)
3. Relationship between education and occupations (20 items)
4. Licensing requirements for occupations (20 items)
5. Descriptions of occupations (10 items)

CAREER SKILLS ASSESSMENT PROGRAM. College Entrance Examination Board. A still ex-

perimental program offering exercise booklets dealing with five areas of career assessment:
1. Self-evaluation and development skills (e.g., understanding individual differences, locating and interpreting information about self)
2. Career awareness skills (e.g., relating abilities, values, needs, and experience to career choice; knowing facts about career opportunities)
3. Employment-seeking skills (e.g., anticipating job prospects, evaluating when a specific job fits a person's needs and interests)
4. Career decision-making skills (e.g., skills and knowledge in various aspects of career decision-making)
5. Work effectiveness skills (e.g., developing effective work habits, planning job changes)

Machine scored.

WORLD OF WORK INVENTORY. J. W. Hudson and K. S. Hudson. World of Work, Inc. Grade 8–Adult.
3 sections:
1. Career Interest Activities
2. Job Satisfaction Indicators
3. Vocational Training Potentials

Excellent interpretive manual.

COMPREHENSIVE CAREER ASSESSMENT SCALES (CCAS). S. L. Jackson and P. M. Goulding. Learning Concepts. Three scales: grade 3–7; grade 8–12+; teachers
Assesses familiarity with 75 occupations in the USOE clusters. Yields interest and familiarity profiles. Can be used for needs assessment, curriculum planning, and/or evaluation.

OLYMPUS CAREER EDUCATION NEEDS ASSESSMENT INSTRUMENTS. A. C. Blome and G. D. Rask. Olympus Publishing. Four levels: K–3; 4–6; 7–12; teachers and administrators. Provides information about state of occupational understanding, self-awareness, attitudes, and career concepts.

SELF-DIRECTED SEARCH (SDS) FORM E. J. L. Holland. Consulting Psychologists Press. Self-administered and scored. Grade 4–Adult. 40 minutes.
Self-reports and estimates regarding:

1. Occupational daydreams
2. Preference for activities
3. Competencies
4. Preferences for kinds of occupations
5. Abilities in various occupational areas

Yields summary codes according to Holland's scales and refers taker to *Jobs Finder*.

The Self-Directed Search has been combined with a Vocational Card Sort (VCS), an instructional booklet, and an action plan into the Vocational Exploration and Insight Kit (VEIK). In research on the VEIK, it is interesting to note that the VEIK failed to exceed the effect of its components (VCS and SDS) (Takai & Holland, 1979).

The Self-Directed Search is illustrative of self-administered, self-scored, and essentially self-interpreted instruments. Although the approach is promising and certainly has been and is being subjected to research to establish its validity and effectiveness, there are several caveats to be noted. First, the SDS (and, we may infer, similar instruments) may yield inaccurate results in a substantial number of cases, simply because of self-scoring errors and despite efforts to simplify the instrument (Christensen, Gelso, Williams, & Sedlacek, 1975; Gelso, Collins, Williams, & Sedlacek, 1973; O'Neil, Price, & Tracey, 1979; and Tracey & Sedlacek, 1980). Holland has responded by producing Form E (for easy), which yields only a two-letter code, but there is no evidence to suggest that this instrument, as well as other self-administered, self-scored, and self-interpreted devices, is any less susceptible to error. Second, the ability of individuals to estimate their own aptitudes is still a moot issue. Although some studies have suggested that counselees can accurately self-estimate aptitudes with which they have most familiarity (such as verbal and numerical), other studies have suggested that a significant proportion of individuals cannot accurately self-estimate either familiar or unfamiliar (for example, mechanical reasoning, clerical speed and accuracy, and such) aptitudes (Hodgson & Cramer, 1977; Bailey & Bailey, 1971; Pohlmann & Beggs, 1974; Tierney & Herman, 1973; Tuck, 1972; Kelso, Holland, & Gottfredson, 1977; DeNisi & Shaw, 1977). Third, there appears to be some disagreement regarding how much, if any, counselor assistance is or should be required in relation to interpreting the SDS (Brown, 1975; Holland, 1975). In view of these three factors and others, perhaps the best advice that can be offered to counselors is that they proceed cautiously and accumulate their own data for evaluation.

PERSONAL CAREER DEVELOPMENT PRO-FILES. V. Walter. Institute for Personality and Ability Testing. Computer scored. Adolescent–Adult.
Yields computerized narrative report regarding overview, problem-solving patterns, patterns for coping with stressful conditions, patterns of interpersonal interaction, and career development considerations, all based on Cattell's *16 Personality Factor Questionnaire.*

CAREER DECISION-MAKING SYSTEM. T. J. Harrington and A. J. O'Shea. American Guidance Service. Junior high–Adult. Either self-scored or computerized. Based on Holland's hexagonal theory of career development. Presumably systematic use of basic Holland-type data in decision-making.

PLANNING CAREER GOALS (PCG). American Institutes for Research. Measures of interests, ability, career information, and a life and career plan inventory all in one package. This system is an outgrowth of Project Talent data.

THE VOCATIONAL ACTION PLAN. William Bloomfield and Associates, Inc. Independently functioning adults (special adolescent materials available).
A combination assessment, counseling, and placement system, consisting of 5 stages:
  1. Preassessment Interview
  2. In-Depth Assessment Interview
  3. Development of Individual Action Plan
     a. Discovering Myself: Attitudes, Beliefs, and Ideas
     b. Options in Work, Jobs, and Careers
     c. The Job Search
  4. Implementation of Patient Plan
  5. Closure and Recommendations

JOB-O. A. Cutler, F. Ferry, R. Kauk, and R. Robinett. Publishers Test Service. Grade 7–Adult.

Career exploration instrument that measures educational aspirations, occupational interests, and interpersonal and physical characteristics of occupations. Available with a JOB-O Dictionary containing definitions related to about 120 job titles.

SELF-EXPLORATION INVENTORIES. J. L. Lee and C. J. Pulvino. Careers, Inc. High school and college. 16 self-administered and self-scored inventories, ranging from a career planning questionnaire to occupational values, to problem-solving style. No indication that validity and reliability have been carefully researched.

OCCU-SORT. L. K. Jones. North Carolina State University Office of Publications. An occupational card sort that consists of sets of cards (60 cards in all) categorized by educational level and by Holland's categories. Self-guided and yielding a 3-letter Holland code. Reportedly compares favorably with the SDS (Jones & DeVault, 1979) and can be used in University Placement Centers (Harris & Jones, 1981).

Job Satisfaction Measures

There are hundreds of measures of job satisfaction, worker attitudes, preference for work environments, and so on. A comprehensive annotation of these measures may be found in Cook, Hepworth, Wall, and Warr (1981). Discussions of job satisfaction are contained in Chapters 2 and 13. We here present a sampling of some widely used instruments.

JOB SATISFACTION BLANK. R. Hoppock. Venerable overall measure of job satisfaction, containing only 4 basic questions. Respondents check alternatives that best tell how they feel about their jobs.

JOB DESCRIPTIVE INDEX. P. C. Smith, L. M. Kendall, and C. L. Hulin. A heavily used instrument. 5 subscales (Type of Work – 18 items; Promotion Opportunities – 9 items; Supervision – 18 items; Pay – 9 items; and Co-workers – 18 items). Each of the 72 items is an adjective or phrase and respondents indicate yes, uncertain, or no whether it describes the job aspect. Can also combine subscales for an overall score.

MICHIGAN ORGANIZATIONAL ASSESSMENT QUESTIONNAIRE. C. Cammann, M. Fichman, D. Jenkins, and J. Klesh. Contains measures of overall job satisfaction (3-item scale), intrinsic and extrinsic rewards, social rewards satisfaction, work attitudes and perceptions, job involvement, internal work motivation, task, job, and role characteristics, supervision, and work group functioning.

ORGANIZATIONAL COMMITMENT QUESTIONNAIRE. L. W. Porter and F. J. Smith. 15 items responded to on a 7-point scale. Organizational commitment is assumed to be more global and less transitory than job satisfaction. Measures how strongly an individual identifies with and is involved in a particular organization.

JOB-RELATED TENSION SCALE. R. L. Kahn, D. M. Wolfe, R. P. Quinn, J. D. Snoek, and R. Rosenthal. 15 items responded to on a 5-point scale. Respondents indicate how frequently they are bothered at work by each item (e.g., "Feeling that you may not be liked and accepted by the people you work with").

WORK PREFERENCE QUESTIONNAIRE (WPQ). S. Fineman. Measures need for achievement in occupational settings. 24 forced-choice items yield scores on 9 aspects of an achievement (e.g., responsibility, risk-taking, competitiveness).

ROLE AMBIGUITY AND ROLE CONFLICT SCALES. J. Rizzo, R. J. House, and S. I. Lirtzman. 6-item scale measuring role ambiguity ("predictability of outcomes of one's behavior and the existence of environmental guidelines to provide knowledge that one is behaving appropriately") and 8-item scale measuring role conflict (incompatibility of demands).

EVALUATION

Because a comprehensive discussion of evaluation in a systematic approach to career guidance was presented in Chapter 6, the following remarks are intended primarily as a summary. Built into any systematic approach is the process of evaluation. Evaluation is simply a series of activities designed to determine how well goals have been achieved. As such, evaluation implies valuing – saying what is desirable or good. Wellman (1970) proposes, "The ultimate goal of evaluation is to provide the kinds of information needed to predict the probability that a specified outcome will result when a defined guidance process is used in a particular situation with a given type of student."

In a systematic approach, one looks for a relationship between career guidance processes (input) and counselee behavioral outcomes (output). In order to determine the strength of such a relationship, one must consider certain elements in the systematic model. These have been dealt with in earlier chapters; by way of review, selected aspects of the components of a systematic approach are presented as they have been classified by Wellman (1970).

1. *Needs.* The various developmental stages through which individuals pass determine their needs at various developmental levels and, in turn, determine the goals of career guidance.

2. *Objectives.* Objectives or goals, which arise from counselee needs, are stated in both global and behaviorally specific terms. (More about this crucial variable in evaluation will be given after this list.)

3. *Process.* Process or treatment refers to specific activities carried out to achieve objectives. Treatments are dependent on and arise from the base built prior to their implementation and subsequently determine future process.

4. *Counselee variables.* Since certain career guidance processes are dependent on selected characteristics of the counselees who are exposed to those processes, it is frequently necessary in evaluation to conduct cross-breaks – that is, to determine differential effects of process on counselees because of differences in sex, socioeconomic level, culture, ability, and so on.

5. *Situational variables.* It is equally likely that career guidance processes may have differential effects in different situations. What works in a vocational school may not work in a comprehensive high school; what works in a liberal arts college may not work in a more technically oriented

institution; what is effective in a rural area may not be effective in an urban area, and so on.

6. *Outcome variables.* Outcome variables are defined by objectives that are behaviorally specific and must, in some cases, present immediate, intermediate, and long-range goals.

7. *Feedback.* This concept refers to the need for continuous evaluation. Just as one continually uses monitoring procedures to keep aware of counselees' career needs, the counselor employs continual evaluation to determine how closely goals are being achieved. If goals are not being achieved, then processes must be changed for future groups.

For a detailed description of evaluation techniques that even the counselor who is unsophisticated in research procedures can accomplish, see Cramer, Herr, Morris, and Frantz (1970).

In summary, the procedures for evaluation within a systematic approach to career guidance are as follows:

1. Formulate the broad goals of the career guidance program.

2. Classify these goals so that an economy of thought and action can be achieved. Decide what developmental stages require which guidance processes for implementation.
3. Define objectives in behavioral terms.
4. Suggest situations in which the desired objectives and behaviors might be observed.
5. Develop or select appraisal techniques such as standardized tests, monitoring instruments, questionnaires, and so on.
6. Gather and interpret performance data and compare these data with the stated behavioral objectives.

This system of evaluation is, in a sense, an absolute system, since no comparisons are made between the career guidance program in a given institutional setting and the program in any other comparable setting. Those responsible for planning, implementing, and evaluating a systematic approach to career guidance may wish to make such comparisons to determine relative effectiveness.

Summary

In this chapter we have discussed the use of measurement and assessment procedures in four areas relating to career guidance: prediction, discrimination, monitoring, and evaluation. Selected aspects of each of these areas, with descriptions of a sampling of illustrative instruments, were presented. Prediction and discrimination techniques provide data for individual decision-making; monitoring and evaluation procedures enable counselors to plan more effectively in providing career guidance within a systematic framework. The use of any specific appraisal instrument, whether commerically standardized or locally developed, depends on the unique characteristics of a given population. Therefore, there is no such thing as *the* testing program in career guidance or *the* evaluation instruments. Institutions should be flexible and imaginative, as they build their own appraisal programs.

LEARNING ACTIVITIES

1. Self-administer two instruments that purport to measure the same variables (such as interests, career maturity, aptitudes, work values, job satisfaction). Compare the results. What conclusions can you draw?
2. Two very different views of the validity of occupational aptitude tests are presented in Thorndike and Hagen (1959) and Ghiselli (1966). Read each of these books. What factors might account for the differing conclusions?
3. Select any aptitude battery and evaluate it according to the criteria outlined in the APA's *Standards for Educational and Psychological Tests.*
4. Assume a need for some sort of assessment in a given situation. Using a systematic model,

describe a delimited program of assessment and interpretation to assist in career development. Include behavioral objectives, activities, materials, and evaluation.

5. In *Testing and Fair Employment* (New York University Press, 1968), Kirkpatrick, Ewen, Barrett, and Katzell recommend separate test validation and standardization for the different ethnic and racial groups. Discuss with a classmate the possible arguments for and against such a proposal.
6. Microcomputers are now available at a relatively small purchase cost (for example, Apple, IBM PC, Commodore, Texas Instruments). It is likely that your institution will have one. Using an existing program, run a simple linear regression with real or imagined ined data.
7. Pair off with someone. Reciprocally administer and interpret one or two tests or inventories. Provide feedback to your partner regarding your reactions to the interpretation.
8. Write to test publishers listed in Appendix A of this volume, requesting catalogues and asking that you be placed on their mailing lists. Begin building an up-to-date test source library.
9. Read the following article: D. J. Willis and J. H. Becker, "The Assessment Center in the Post-Griggs Era," *Personnel and Guidance Journal*, 55 (December 1976): 201-205. Do you agree or disagree with the authors' proposed solutions for equitable personnel decisions? Why?
10. Write an essay in which you justify and describe the role of assessment in career guidance.

OBJECTIVES

After reading this chapter, engaging in the learning activities, and reading the suggested references, you should have met the objectives that follow. If you have not, it would probably be useful for you to review the material on assessment in career guidance before proceeding.

1. List the four major uses of assessment procedures in career guidance.
2. Distinguish between clinical and actuarial prediction.
3. Describe in general terms the validity of aptitude tests in predicting success in training and job success.
4. Distinguish between tests used in a narrow trait-and-factor sense and tests used in enhancing general career development.
5. List at least three general principles of test interpretation.
6. Name at least three aptitude test batteries.
7. Define the discriminant function of tests and inventories.
8. Name at least five interest inventories.
9. Define the monitoring function of assessment in career guidance.
10. Define the construct of career maturity.
11. Name at least three career maturity measures.
12. Name at least one work values measure.
13. Name at least two other monitoring instruments for career guidance.
14. Name at least two job satisfaction measures.
15. Write a three-level behavioral objective (goal statement, minimum level, desired level).
16. List the six-steps for evaluation within a systematic approach to career guidance.

18 / Research and Social Issues in Career Guidance and Counseling

It is apparent from the many studies and forms of speculation that have been cited in this book that research and theory pertinent to career guidance are abundant, even if the quality and comprehensiveness are uneven. Since the term career guidance is essentially representative of a large inventory of processes and techniques applied to career behavior, it is logical to suggest that relevant research and theory can be found in many academic disciplines and at many levels of quality and sophistication. This same observation can be made about virtually any realm of human behavior, but it nevertheless suggests the difficulty of being encyclopedic in a book such as this or in analyzing the research base as fully as some readers might desire.

Although it is probably fair to suggest that, in general, the theoretical speculation about career-related behavior across the life span has stimulated research, it is also equally fair to assert that there are many questions and hypotheses yet to be considered and the effects of many career guidance interventions yet to be assessed. Since the content of career guidance (for example, type of work options, freedom of opportunity, achievement images, systems of job information) is so dynamic and so intimately tied to changes in the occupational, political, social, and economic contexts of the nation, one could hardly expect that research on these matters would be static and totally encompassing. Individual behavior is a function of transactions with environmental expectations and opportunities intertwined with personal values, abilities, and skills. As any of these ingredients changes, so does the system within which individual behavior is triggered. In a sense, theory and research are virtually always running to catch up with such circumstances.

Much of the theory and research on career development to the present has assumed that individual action has been the predominant effect on how careers are forged and where intervention in such career behavior should be aimed. This is, of course, a view in which the lens is primarily psychological. However, as we discussed in Chapter 4, this view tends to underestimate the degree to which environments create and reinforce work roles and career opportunities; the degree to which persons are chosen rather than do the choosing. The latter views are predominantly sociological, anthropological, and economic. The influence of such perspectives on how individual career behavior is influenced and shaped have not yet been as fully integrated into the conceptual and empirical bases of career guidance as is likely to emerge during the next decade.

The state of the conceptual and empirical bases of career guidance is fundamental to the quality of services that practitioners offer in any setting. But these are not the only important questions to be raised. Also of concern are questions of social effects. As we have suggested, career guidance does not occur in a political or social vacuum. Its content is derived from the larger society. Indeed, the types of questions that youth and adults bring to counselors are related to how they view current societal belief systems about personal choice, achievement, social interaction, self initiative, marriage, prestige, occupational or educational status, role integration, and many

494

other aspects of life. The resulting anxieties, deficits, or indecisiveness that persons experience as they compare themselves with what society's representatives (such as parents, employers, teachers, peers, spouses, the mass media) say they should believe or do is the content with which counselors deal. Societal filters also permit or discourage persons asking certain questions about themselves or their opportunities. And different societies, deliberately or inadvertently, support the use of some guidance and counseling techniques as ethical or appropriate and restrict or prohibit the use of other forms of intervention. From such a perspective, the question of social effects can be succinctly stated as: Because one can change behavior in certain ways, should one do so? The answers to such questions are not necessarily empirical; they are more likely to be philosophical and value oriented.

The term career guidance represents deliberate instructional, counseling, and direct experiential interventions in the career development of youth and adults. Such different approaches to career guidance stimulate hypotheses that ask if certain types of career guidance or related processes (such as career education) are implemented, what specific student or client behaviors will result to benefit the individual or society? Many of the assumptions and much of the research on which current models of career guidance rest have already been referred to in this book. But not every observer accepts the assumptions stated, asks the same questions as those who advocate career guidance or career education, or believes that the existing research base is adequate to endorse expanding or even retaining career guidance in its present forms. Questions continue to be raised and criticisms leveled at the effectiveness or the appropriateness of these processes in relation to the characteristics of the nation's economy, shifting values of the population, legitimate expectations of schooling, the potential social effects of the techniques used, and the status of research underlying these processes.

Although we hope that we have made a case for career guidance in the preceding chapters, we continue to realize that many relevant research questions and social issues still need to be explored. Some are matters of substance; others, of methodology; still others, of philosophy. In this chapter we will briefly discuss some of the current views on these matters, identify some methodological issues, and inventory some research needs.

PERSPECTIVES ON RESEARCH AND THEORY

Depending on the training and interests of given observers, current perspectives on the state of the art of research in career guidance differ somewhat, although there are certain overarching views. For example, Healy (1982, pp. 586–588) has identified five research priorities pertinent to career development. In abridged form they include:

1. Counseling treatments must be specified in greater detail, ideally delineating factors such as key concepts and principles; the kinds of materials and exercises used in counseling and as homework; the quality of learning interaction; the total time for counseling and homework; the client's starting and closing mastery of concepts, principles, and skills; and the degree to which the client voluntarily selected and created the counseling program....

2. Reports need to describe clients more comprehensively at the start and conclusion of counseling, using psychodiagnostic systems. . . . Demographics such as age, sex, grade and previous counseling are useful but insufficient. Replication and transportability require information about strengths and weaknesses of the clients and their environments and data about client's aspirations and the urgency of their quest.

3. Counselors need to examine the modifications of traditional treatments, which may be necessary to serve atypical populations. . . . Relationships between client type and counseling method promise to be an important research concern.

4. Counselors need to test whether and how expansion of counseling to include strategies such as assigned reading, extracounseling practice, mastery tests, and securing privileged

access to resources for a client contribute to career advancement. . . .

5. Counselors need to improve their research designs. . . .

Healy's observations are helpful in defining some of the major problems associated with improving research in career guidance. A primary problem is methodological.

The Search for Acceptable Methodology

Gelso (1979) has suggested that in recent years counseling has experienced a polarization of views on what constitutes an acceptable methodology. He further suggests that it may well be the most prominent trend in the field and a healthy state of affairs "if it represents an expansion of what the field views as permissible bases for evidence, and if the strengths and limitations of each investigative style are recognized" (p. 9).

This chapter is not supposed to be a research primer, but it is useful to note that the maturing of theory development pertinent to career behavior and the understanding of the effects of career guidance "treatments" are likely to require all the research tools now available: for example, descriptive, correlational, case study, naturalistic, single subject, factorial, subjective and qualitative, experimental, cross-sectional, longitudinal, and a combination of these. It is unlikely that single studies, however large in scale, can answer all of the important research questions that lie before us. Rather, we are likely to continue to rely on the aggregate effects of several studies, each true to the assumptions and design precautions appropriate to the specific questions being studied.

It is often true that the research techniques available are significantly ahead of practice in the field or that there are more powerful ways to study certain questions than are used. The study of "treatment effects" is one example. Gelso (1979) appropriately notes the effects of Kiesler's work (1971) in using factorial designs to study both main effects of treatment and organismic or individual differences variables. Thus, in such designs one can study two or more treatments in comparison to the outcomes associated with control groups as well as the effects of such treat-

ments on different client populations defined by age, gender, experience, and so on, across time and as provided by counselors of different types. The study of interaction inherent in such factorial designs permits one to test several hypotheses simultaneously as one studies treatment effects against differences in client populations, counselor style, outcome measures, repeated observations, or other pertinent criteria. Factorial approaches typically involve analysis of variance or covariance or multivariate analysis of variance as the statistic of choice in addition to a post hoc significance test, although correlation or regression analysis is frequently the appropriate statistical approach.

As important as factorial designs are for comparative and for experimental studies of "treatment effects" on different types of presenting problems, they are less useful for predicting patterns of longitudinal career development. For such purposes it is more likely that some type of regression analysis or discriminant function procedure will be used.

The Issue of "Careers." In 1969 (Super 1969a; 1969b) Super discussed the state of methodology bearing on such issues. He began with the premise that vocational psychology from the beginning of this century until shortly after 1950 was a "psychology of occupations." Since that period we have also had emerging a "psychology of careers." Methodological models in a psychology of occupations typically focus on the occupations as the subject and the persons in the occupations as the source of data about the occupation. According to Super (1969a) this model takes predictor data at an early stage of a career and uses regression methods to predict later success in one occupation or it uses discriminant analysis as a means of assessing the likelihood of being found – later – in each of several possible occupations. But such approaches tend to represent differential psychology, the study of individual differences, in a somewhat static sense. The psychology of careers requires more than differential diagnosis.

Careers are by definition developmental. Indeed, career development is itself a rubric for the complex interactions between the affective, cognitive, and psychomotor characteristics of persons potentially mediated by their values, family history, school climate, community reward system and many other possible variables that may or may not be affected by time. In a career model we are interested in predicting the sequence of positions that a person will occupy in pursuing a career (Super, 1969a). To achieve this understanding of careers, however, we need to understand not only the positions people occupy during their working life but also the interrelationship of factors that caused them to anticipate, plan, and implement one position rather than another at any given point in their life as well as the threads that link one choice to another or one position to the subsequent one. Our progress toward such goals has depended on the availability of statistical methods capable of handling the myriad of factors feeding into career development and on hardware (computers primarily) that allow a researcher to cope with sophisticated analyses of an enormous number of data points. Hardware problems are rapidly disappearing, but questions of statistical methodology continue to be formidable obstacles as we move forward with time series data.

Obviously, not all elements of career development require the same levels of sophistication or the same purpose as do time series questions. It is necessary to conduct survey research by which the variables deserving systematic study in career development can be identified. Some questions that fall within this category are: What career behaviors develop as the individual matures? Are there group differences in the development of career behavior? What are the career behaviors essential to success in different work settings?

Technique research is also necessary to career development – for example, the work of Crites on the Career Maturity Inventory, Holland on the Self-Directed Search and the Vocational Preference Inventory, Westbrook on the Cognitive Vocational Development Inventory, Super on the Work Values Inventory, the Career Development Inventory, or Adult Career Concerns Survey – are examples of efforts to create ways of collecting information that is pertinent to career development and quantifiable. Such research concerns the internal structure of available instruments as well as their relationship to external criteria de-

termined largely by survey research to be important to career development.

Theoretical Research. Theoretical research has represented a stimulus to or an outcome of the survey and technique research cited. In the theoretical arena, hypothesis testing has attempted to evaluate the gross assumptions that career development is continuous and longitudinal, that it can be described as composed of different developmental tasks at different life periods, that career development and personal development more broadly conceived are related, that career development can be modified by certain forms of intervention or that specific variables are associated with the character of career development at some point in time. Much of this research is concerned with understanding the structure of career behavior as well as how it changes over time. Applied research, too, has been moving forward in testing various attempts to facilitate career development through the formal processes of schooling or other educative methods.

Statistical Methods. To reiterate to some degree what has already been said about methodology, the statistical methods used in these four research areas have included the following:

1. *Discriminant analysis* is a way of examining predictive validity in regard to group membership particularly where the criterion variables are nominal or ordinal, rather than continuously measured traits, or where the predictor variables are multidimensional as found in personality profiles. This approach has been important to our understanding of the personality variables by which career or curriculum groups are separated in measurement space – how persons resemble groups of persons engaging in an occupation or curriculum, for example.

2. *Analysis of variance* (factorial approaches), although important as a part of discriminant analysis strategy and frequently the statistic of choice for testing the null hypothesis, has often been used as a descriptive or classification method rather than in an experimental form. As such it has helped in the identification of shifts in means or variance on some

dependent variable over time but has not advanced our understanding of the dynamics underlying such shifts as much as we would hope.

3. *Correlational analysis* has also been widely used to determine the predictive power of certain individual traits or trait sets to different classes of career-related criterion variables — academic decisions, vocational aspirations, and vocational adjustment. Indeed, the various correlational modes, parametric and nonparametric, have been highly valuable, particularly in identifying associations between variables requiring further study. Certainly, multiple regression and partial correlation have been exceedingly valuable in our understanding of the ranking or weights of predictive variables in relation to each other. In some instances, canonical correlations have been helpful in analyzing the stability of the dispersion of scores over time (Gribbons & Lohnes, 1969, p. 32), determining the full extent of the interrelatedness of two sets of scores, and indexing the amount of common variance shared by the functions of two sets of measurement.

Essentially, the approaches that have just been identified are linear and represent an independent-variable-predicting-dependent-variables paradigm in which "the criterion variable is 'explained' by the pattern of its statistical dependency on a set of predictors. . . . Generally, the effort is to account for as much of the variance in the criterion as possible from the predictors' variance-covariance" (Gribbons & Lohnes, 1969, p. 185). Gribbons and Lohnes have attempted to move outside this perspective by using a stochastic model, in particular Markov chain analysis, to examine the outcomes of a discrete measurement variable. Markov chains are probability models that can tell us how much of the variance in developmental outcomes can be explained by a theoretical model of the process itself without recourse to functional or statistical relations with outside variables (p. 186). Essentially, the model observes the paths taken by the subjects through the states of the variable over temporally separated stages to see if there is a probability law inherent in the "process" (the tree structure) of possible paths through the states over the stages.

Treating Career Data. Super (1969b) suggested in 1969 that four approaches might be useful to treating career data: lattice theory, Markov chains theory, path analysis, and the career tree. Although each of these approaches has been used in other disciplines, particularly sociology, over the fifteen years since Super's observations were made, these approaches have rarely been used in career development research.

Significant exceptions to the above generalization are the twenty-year longitudinal study of Gribbons and Lohnes (1968; 1982) in which the use of Markov chains is a prominent feature, and the work of Cooley and others (for example, Flanagan & Cooley, 1966), which have applied the career tree approach to Project Talent data. Although there are some examples of the use of path analysis (O'Reilly, 1973; Enderlein, 1974; Watanabe, 1980) with career data, this methodology may soon be superceded by new approaches to causal modeling (Jackson, 1983).

Path analysis and causal modeling are among the best methods we now know to handle longitudinal data, not simply cross-sectional data at different points in time. More important, perhaps, is the fact that most of the statistical techniques we have used deal with direct effects, X on Y, rather than indirect effects among variables. However, path analysis facilitates the examination of the cumulative indirect effects of a variable on some other variable.

Causal modeling techniques incorporate the functions of path analysis and increase the power to study alternative models of structural equations hypothesized to represent certain relationships occurring over a period of time (Bentler, 1980). It is also possible to examine the effect of several measured variables on one latent variable (unobserved) and therefore to increase the number of hypotheses that can be considered in relationship to how underlying structures affect career outcomes across time, whether the question is the direct and indirect effects of latent variables on each other or the composition of latent variables themselves. Although it is tempting to analyze each of these methods and the studies that have used them in some depth, that would be beyond the purpose of this chapter. Interested researchers are encouraged to read the references cited for elaboration of each of the techniques identified.

Suffice it to say here that methodologies useful to increasingly sophisticated study of career-related human behavior and the effects of interventions on this process are rapidly emerging. Even so, however, the complexity of the phenomena about which career guidance practitioners are concerned is vast enough to accommodate a wide range of research designs and statistical tools. In any case, there will continue to be an overarching need for what Goldman (1979) has called "disciplined creative search": "ideas and theories which come from the imagination and vision of people who look at and listen to career development issues and behaviors, counseling, career guidance, social trends with openness and an urge to understand and conceptualize" (p. 44). Such creativity and vision yield the theory, ideas, and hypotheses that then lead to the methodological issues cited here as they relate to the testing of such ideas.

The Character of Career Development Theory

However important methodological issues are to understanding the "state of the art" of research in career guidance, they are not the only matters of concern. The character of career development theory itself is important.

Theoretical Base. Chapter 4, and indeed other chapters, has described the conceptual streams of thought that make up the current theoretical base in career development. Much of this material is still speculative, however perceptive and logical, and untested. There are also other characteristics worthy of note.

Many of the hypotheses and, indeed, existing principles of career development have come from small samples of middle-class white males. There are as yet few comprehensive perspectives on the career development of women (indeed, Fitzgerald and Crites (1980) in a major review article have discussed the limited knowledge available about the career psychology of women); nor is there much systematic information pertinent to the career development of minority group members whether classified racially, ethnically, or religiously. Much less attention has been given to the career development of the rural poor than to that of the urban poor. Likewise, systematic study of the effects of congenital versus adventitious

physical handicaps on career development is yet to be undertaken. Virtually no attention has been given to the career development of gay persons, the employment limitations they face, or appropriate career guidance strategies.

Much career development theory has evolved from descriptive research with samples restricted in size and in composition. As a result, many relationships and hypotheses about career behavior, the influences on them, or the effect of attempts to intervene in them remain to be tested. Indeed, interpretations of existing findings are often made without the benefit of validation or replication across samples that diverge in characteristics from those on whom the original findings were obtained.

In addition to any other criticisms of samples from which career development theory or research has come, many sample subjects have been students. In longitudinal samples, it makes sense to begin studying career development when individuals are in the early years of schooling and then watch their progression into and through adulthood. However, secondary school and university student samples have been the rule not only for longitudinal studies but for cross-sectional studies as well. Since most investigations of career development are conducted by persons in colleges and other educational settings, student samples are convenient, but they do not offer insight into the whole of career development, particularly its characteristics in adulthood and in persons with minimal educational experience.

In the few longitudinal studies now being conducted, the original student samples are maturing and proceeding through adulthood, but little has been published about them other than in terms of adolescent exploration and the early stages of young adulthood. As a result, we know less about the predictive validity of various patterns of early career development in relationship to the linearity of later career development, midcareer change, or occupational dislocation than we need if we are to make career guidance procedures more effective for persons beyond adolescence. For example, we know comparatively little about the developmental progression of persons into retirement, although there is a growing demand for career guidance at this life stage. Thus, questions of when such career guidance should begin, what its emphases should be — use of leisure, volunteer possibilities, part-time work, economic planning — remain vague. Much the same could be said about the comprehensiveness of knowledge available about second careerists, midcareer dislocated, and other segments of the adult population.

Each of these observations is well known to researchers and theorists, and attempts to modify these voids, move away from restrictive samples, and improve the quality of theory and research in career development are proceeding apace. However, there is a new challenge that will likely affect the conceptualization of emerging programs of career development speculation and research. This challenge is founded principally in life-span psychology.

Influence of Life-Span Psychology. Among other life-span psychologists, Vondracek and Lerner (1982) and Vondracek, Lerner, and Schulenberg, (in press) have been most analytic in their view of the weaknesses of current views of career development as seen from the perspective of life-span psychology. They strongly suggest that many of the existing models of career development are personological and unidimensional rather than dynamic and interactional as would be useful. Citing the study of adolescents, in particular, they advocate the need for three key perspectives in the study of adolescent vocational role development: developmental, contextual, and relational. In a *developmental perspective*, "events prior to adolescence need to be considered as possible antecedents of vocational development; in turn, adolescent developments provide key antecedents of development in later life" (Vondracek & Lerner, 1982, p. 604). Longitudinal studies using Markov chains, path analysis, and causal modeling (mentioned in the previous section) would likely be of significant use in this area. A *contextual perspective* would emphasize the nature of the social (including political and economic), physical, and cultural milieu of adolescent vocational role development. "Thus the individual characteristics of the developing adolescent must be considered in relation to the particular features of the context within which the person is developing" (p. 604). A *relational perspective* would consider the goodness of fit between adolescent and contextual developments. It is further argued that although several impor-

tant longitudinal studies of career development have been carried out (*The Career Pattern Study*, Super et al., 1957; *Project TALENT*, Flanagan, Shaycroft, Richards, & Claudy, 1971; *The Career Development Study*, Gribbons & Lohnes, 1969, 1982, and the *Youth in Transition Study*, Bachman et al., 1970) none of these has employed a historical (for example, sequential) design suitable for appraising age-, cohort-, and time-related variance.

Vondracek and Lerner (1982) further assert:

Although the current research literature on vocational development reflects a growing emphasis on a developmental perspective, there are still major shortcomings in the implementation of these orientations. These shortcomings involve problems of research design as well as problems of conceptualization – that is, a commitment to a life span developmental perspective cannot be best actualized in our view, through reliance on personalogical, organismic conceptions of vocational-role development. Instead, an appreciation of mutually adaptive interchanges between adolescents and their contexts must be attained (p. 609).

From such a perspective, Vondracek and Lerner (1982) then contend, "Traditional interventions in vocational development need to be broadened to incorporate interventions targeted to the individual, the family, the community, and its institutions, and finally, social policy" (p. 612).

The challenge and observations posed by Vondracek and his colleagues are certainly not confined to thinking about the career development of adolescents. Rather, such views are equally pertinent to understanding the career development of adults and particularly the effects of context and fit with context. To some degree this matter was discussed in Chapter 2 with regard to the meaning of work and person-job relationships. It was also dealt with in Chapter 4 as situational approaches to career development were described.

The Effects of Cultural and Economic Factors

As one might expect if the observations about a need for more attention to context are valid, little is known about the effects of economic or cultural change on career behavior. Although most career development theorists have addressed the importance of situational variables to career development, they frequently have done so in abstract terms rather than researched the effects of such conditions on personal choicemaking and commitments. It is clear that the family history, community in which reared, and socioeconomic status of the person all affect career development. The questions are, How much, when, under what conditions, and for whom? We often continue to treat persons described by a group characteristic — racial, ethnic, religious, age, sex — as though they are part of a homogeneous group. We tend not to take into account the extent of variance that operates in any group and examine its implications for given individuals.

Cross-Cultural Information. The same point can be made about cultures other than American. We know little about the socialization of career behavior in developing nations, or indeed, in many of the contemporary developed or postindustrial societies. In some instances this situation occurs because pertinent research has not been done in other societies in which we might be interested; in other cases the research is not developmentally focused; in still others, useful research findings exist but have not been assimilated into the American view of career development. For example, many excellent publications on career development, occupational classification systems, and career interventions have been developed by the Occupational and Career Analysis and Development Branch of the Canadian Employment and Immigration Commission in Ottawa under the leadership of D. Stuart Conger. Similarly, excellent material is available from the Federal Employment Institute of West Germany under the leadership of Reinhard Wolleben. Other examples of guidance interventions or career development theory could be identified in other nations. The point is, however, that even when such material is available it is not typically known and used in the United States.

Obviously, one way of testing the effects of cultural and economic factors in career development is to study the fit of current American views of career development in societies with different economic characteristics, belief systems regarding

work values, or political assumptions about individual choice and development. One major example of such an effort began in September 1976 to test the validity of Super's theoretical concepts with a British population. Based at the National Institute for Careers Education and Counseling in Cambridge, this research will be a longitudinal effort to replicate many of the American findings from Super's research with samples of British youth and adults. One of the early outcomes of this project is *Career Development in Britain* (Watts, Super, & Kidd, 1981). Among its many useful aspects, the book addresses the current state of the art in careers theory in Britain and introduces to the American reader the powerful influence that sociological perspectives play in such careers theory. From such a frame of reference, American theories of career development are contrasted with those of the British, and several concepts new to most American readers (such as low autonomy-high autonomy) are provided as ways of analyzing career history. In addition to *Career Development in Britain*, the work at the National Institute of Careers Education and Counselling has become part of a fourteen-nation Work Importance Study directed by Donald Super. More cross-cultural efforts to examine the effects of political, economic, and other social factors on career development should become increasingly evident in the American literature and as a fertile arena for international cooperation.

Cross-cultural studies of career development are principally seen as useful in macro terms. The emphasis tends to be on the comparisons of nations. At this level, frequent comparisons are made between the underdeveloped, developing, or developed nations, or between the nations of the Northern and the Southern Hemisphere or some other similar classification scheme. However useful such comparisons are across nations to study major cultural dimensions, it is also worth acknowledging the importance of such inquiry at a micro- or subnational level. Many nations, particularly the United States and increasingly the countries of Western Europe, are becoming pluralistic in the population groupings they contain. Therefore, within nations there are groups of persons who could be considered underdeveloped, developing, and developed. Undoubtedly, the career development of each of the groups differs in ways that could be illuminated by applying paradigms similar to those useful in studies at national levels, and many of the cross-cultural constructs thought to be useful only to make national comparisons would also be helpful within multiethnic, multicultural populations.

Ultimately, as part of the analyses of the career development of different cultural groups, it will be necessary to identify those factors related to restricted socioeconomic status or other variables which limit people's ability to cope with skill mastery, attitude development, or achievement motivation, and design experiences which can systematically overcome such deficits. In essence, it would be helpful to know not only whether our theories of career development are culture-bound or generally applicable but also whether our methods of intervening in career development are culture-bound.

Changing Sex Roles. A related issue is that of changing sex roles. As a cultural phenomenon, the elimination of sex-role stereotyping — "masculine" versus "feminine" occupations — tends to be proceeding rapidly. However, very little research has yet been directed to the career guidance processes most effective in facilitating this movement, when such interventions should occur, or how to most effectively help women or men reconsider their values in this area and consider nontraditional educational or occupational opportunities. Here again, it would be helpful to consider the experiences of other nations in dealing with such problems and how their career guidance responses might be adapted in this country.

Importance of Economic Factors. Not only does career development research need to include greater attention to cultural factors and to sociological insights, it also needs greater attention to economic factors. Free and Tiedeman (1980) have recently contended that both econometric and psychometric models need to be included in the foundational study of individual behavior and counseling. In their view, "Economics . . . focuses on interdependent choice and decision making in production, distribution and consumption as a control consideration just as counselors focus on these processes in the time choices and

decision making that define personality" (p. 361). The study of economics extends the counselor's view of the individual in the environment and, indeed, of the ways the individual can construct desirable futures, both personal and societal. Free and Tiedeman contend, in fact, that the individual (client, counselee) "requires comprehension of the economic system itself to be an active participant in determining his or her economic future" (p. 362).

A greater attention to economic factors in career development should also include increased research concern for the implications for career guidance of different forms of employment or unemployment. These terms are frequently treated as though, for example, all unemployment were caused by the same factors and affected every person in the society equally. Recall from previous discussion that depending on the definitions used, unemployment can be divided into at least four types: seasonal, frictional, cyclical, and structural. Each of these types of unemployment differs in its severity, its causes and the groups most affected (Pierson, 1980). Determining which career guidance approaches are useful in reducing the severity or duration of these different forms of unemployment is an important research question that has rarely been asked. The question is likely to gain prominence in the next decade as the nation wrestles intensely with the wide-ranging effect of structural unemployment.

A few of the research concerns related to structural unemployment might be:

1. developing career information that identifies which occupations are likely to be most vulnerable to shifts in technology
2. assessing during major shifts in industrial processes, what worker skills are most elastic — able to be transferred across boundaries with the least amount of retraining
3. creating models of choice that help persons understand the knowledge bases and skills inherent in new occupational configurations
4. examining changes in work organization and their effects on dual-career families, length of work life, retirement, the availability of overtime or leisure time
5. understanding more fully which persons

function best under conditions of low- or high-autonomy in the work place; identifying how differences in supervisory style or the psychological conditions of the work place affect individual productivity

6. examining the direct relationships between education and work, training and retraining as work technologies rapidly change

7. studying how affective work competencies or industrial discipline change as a result of changes in the work place occasioned by automation, computerization, robotics

8. studying what happens to those persons in the work force who are functionally illiterate, whose basic academic skills are inadequate to learning the skills necessary to new occupational technologies. Do we simply assume that under major occupational transitions that some persons are destined to be unemployed and that one of the roles of career guidance is to assist such persons to prepare for unemployment just as one prepares for work?

9. considering what advocacy roles career guidance has in assisting employers recognize their employees as human capital, resources to be developed and nurtured, just as they have historically emphasized the preventive maintenance of equipment; identifying what are the most effective models of career guidance in business and industry as shifts are made from personnel management to personnel development

Such research areas are only the most superficial of possibilities as the implications of structural unemployment for career guidance are studied in the years ahead. Suffice it to say that ways will need to be found to increase the understanding of career guidance practitioners of the dynamics of employment and unemployment. Although career guidance is likely to facilitate "employability" in persons, help them to plan for work more knowledgeably and purposefully, and assist them in their adjustment to work, it cannot create jobs or employment for them; the latter is a function of many complex factors such as population demographics, international competition, fiscal policies, which cannot be decisively influenced by career guidance. Therefore, to argue that career guidance will "reduce unem-

ployment" is to misunderstand the dynamics of unemployment and to naively overpromise what career guidance cannot deliver.

From the standpoint of social effects as well as research concerns, it is useful to note that uninformed understandings of the factors initiating and maintaining unemployment cause some counselors, like lay citizens, to assume that after receiving career guidance or training, if one is still unemployed, one must want to be. That might be a reasonable assumption if the nation were providing full employment or if it were not in the middle of a major structural transition in work technology, but it is not providing full employment and it is engaged in a major structural transition. Therefore, we sometimes inadvertently blame the victims of unemployment for being victims and unintentionally intensify the feelings of frustration or helplessness they experience (Herr & Watts, 1981).

Another area of research concern still within the broad rubric of economic and cultural factors has to do with the characteristics of labor markets. Doeringer and Piore (1971) have described a dual labor market in the United States that has different "ports of entry" for workers depending on the industry involved; different levels of security, benefits, and training; and, different possibilities for internal mobility. The primary and secondary labor markets, as they are known, require different job search strategies, skills, and personal characteristics. The career ladders available, the commitments to and processes of on-the-job training and retraining, the sources of workers, and the hiring processes in the primary and secondary labor markets are each worthy of far more research attention than has been given to such matters to date. Without being aware of such distinctions in the labor force, career guidance practitioners and job seekers are likely to expend energies in efforts which are insufficiently tailored to the actual dynamics which occur in the various components of the structure. It is also likely that a person concentrating on seeking work in either the primary or secondary labor market underestimates the possibilities of self-employment (Gershuny & Pahl, 1979-1980). It seems likely that more work in the future than in the past will be subcontracted from large corporations to small entrepreneurs. In addition, consumers seem to be evidencing increased interest in handmade, quality goods available from individual or small groups of craftsmen as discretionary income continues to rise. However, again, self-employment, its availability, and the specific skills required in such informal labor markets has not typically been the subject of research in career guidance. Until it is, the employment potential in such areas will be less systematically sought and prepared for than would otherwise be appropriate.

Awareness of Cost-Benefit Effects

One of the major research arenas of the future must be the cost-benefit effects of career guidance. Each of the research or evaluation studies that show either positive or negative outcomes for career guidance is important in an empirical sense, for its value in testing some theoretical proposition or in evaluating the efficacy of a particular treatment in relation to some factor of age, gender, or population type. As suggested throughout this chapter and the rest of the book, we need more and better research about all sorts of questions.

The point of this section is, however, that research findings, particularly in career guidance, have meaning beyond the empirical. They are also important in cost-benefit terms: for example private benefits that accrue directly to the individual as in greater job satisfaction and work productivity; external benefits that accrue to a third party, perhaps an employer, as in increased worker satisfactoriness or less absenteeism from work; social benefits that accrue to society as a whole as in reduced welfare payments or in increased contributions to taxes and charitable agencies. On the cost side are the expenditures for facilities, staff training, materials purchased, employee released time from work and the money, energy, or time required to produce some form(s) of benefit. The central questions of cost-benefit analyses are: How much does it cost to have a career guidance program? How much will it cost not to have a career guidance program? What are the cost-benefit ratios and the economic tradeoffs or payoffs of having or not having career guidance programs? Under the pressures for accountability and the wise management of scarce resources, such questions will be essential

to the future availability of career guidance programs in many settings.

Cost-benefit analyses of career guidance are not easy, and they typically require a somewhat different mentality than ordinarily characterizes the practitioners of the field. For example, cost-benefit analyses really require theorists, researchers, and practitioners to be willing to risk evaluating what they do, using as a criterion economic benefits that exceed economic costs. Within such a construct, if the economic benefits to individuals or to society exceed the cost of career guidance, one can argue that counselors are generators of resources not simply consumers of them.

One might further argue that each of the positive effects of career guidance cited throughout this book makes a direct or indirect contribution to the gross national product by increasing educational and occupational attainment or productivity, by decreasing losses associated with absence or vandalism, or by precluding the need for more expensive treatment in the future (Herr, 1982a, 1982b). The logic of such a perspective seems unassailable, but the connections between the empirically derived findings about career guidance effects and the economic health of individuals or the society at large have not typically been made. Although there are useful examples of such efforts within industry (Olbrisch, 1977; Alander & Campbell, 1975; Warren, 1978; Reardon, 1976), vocational rehabilitation (Worrall, 1978), and in health insurance plans (Cummings, 1977), the systematic comparison of the economic benefit/cost ratios of career guidance to other systems of intervention is still in a primitive state. However, it has extraordinary promise.

Developing Measures of Career Development

Since much of our understanding of career development comes from observations of restricted samples, often not adequately representing women or minority persons, existing measures of career development can be considered susceptible to limited sensitivity in their observations of career behavior. When such instruments are applied to persons who might be different in their characteristics, they may miss, exclude, or overemphasize material relevant to the latter.

Obviously, this criticism differs in its importance depending on whether the instrument is assessing values or unequivocal factual information, or making judgments about the level of career maturity. The last is most problematic, although each must be viewed with caution depending on the procedures followed in developing and validating the instrument.

No specific instruments are mentioned here because the concerns expressed are well known to test developers and they are working diligently to correct imbalances in samples represented in the validation procedures. Nevertheless, because of the unevenness of coverage in current theories of career development of women and minority groups, the construction of instruments to assess career behavior across all population types will be difficult.

What also needs to be noted in the measurement of career development is that only some of the dimensions of current models of vocational or career maturity are well established or measured. Super and Hall (1978) observe that the most highly developed instruments assess only one to six factors out of a total list of eighteen in the Crites' model or nineteen in the Super model. Some of the other factors (such as realism) have been measured, but in unstandardized ways that make the comparison of results difficult. Furthermore, some factors (such as realism and consistency of preferences), appear to be meaningful theoretically and significant practically at some ages but not at others. Although Super has proposed a developmental model of vocational maturity that is based on both theory and research, there is a great deal to be done in establishing the ages at which each factor begins to assume, and perhaps ceases to have, significance.

Finally, the predictive validity of our measures of vocational maturity remains to be established. The pioneer measures devised by the Career Pattern Study have been proved to have some predictive validity over a span of about seven years, but not over eighteen years. But these measures were not designed for practical use, and those which have been designed from them and made available for use in research and evaluation have not yet produced adolescent scores validated against adult criteria (p. 348).

Another area related to the measurement of career development that has received almost no research attention is records management. Career development implies assessment different from standard aptitude and interest measurement. For example, aptitude measurement is basically used to predict the probable *performance* of an individual in various learning or occupational settings. Such aptitude scores are usually acquired infrequently, because it is assumed that these are reasonably stable characteristics of an individual particularly after mid- to late adolescence. Thus, the individual's aptitudes are usually expressed in his or her records as a series of scores in those aptitudes considered most pertinent to predictions of major concern or those which have the most generalized character.

Interest assessment has as its major emphasis predicting a person's *compatibility* with or *similarity* to distinctive groups of students or workers. Again, the interest scores are typically taken only twice or three times during the course of one's schooling or once in most agencies. Even though more dynamic than aptitude scores, interest scores obtained after midadolescence are assumed to be reasonably stable. These scores, too, are usually expressed as a series in the person's clinical or interview record that reflect the major weightings of interests at particular points in time.

Career development measurement, however, has a somewhat different purpose than either aptitude or interest assessment. It is intended to identify the person's status in terms of the various dimensions considered to be part of career maturity (for example, orientation to planning, information about alternative actions, possession of occupational information, accurate self-appraisal, independent judgment) and to reveal any deficits the person might have. Since the elements of career maturity change (they are related to age and education level), the assessment of career development requires a *monitoring* function. Thus, in the case of schools, for example, a career development data system would specify and report on the kinds of behaviors students would be expected to demonstrate at each educational level in each of the domains pertinent to career development and whether or not these have been achieved. Basically, the types of behavioral expectations established in the stages identified in Chapter 4 and 6 would appear in this data system, and the student's relevant knowledge and skills would be assessed so that appropriate individual experiences can be planned to correct any deficits identified. Such a goal would require far more comprehensive records and more frequent monitoring than that traditionally associated with either aptitude or interest assessment. It could be conceived in the same format and magnitude as instructional report cards now take. If one were also to apply such career development goal-setting to the work place using Schein's (1968) notion of organizational socialization and transitions as deliberate management strategy, the implications for records management would again be worthy of serious investigation.

At any rate, the design and monitoring of career development data systems, whether in educational or industrial settings, need more analysis than has so far appeared in the professional literature. Perhaps even more significant than the planning and effort involved in such data systems are the possible legal implications. Since the passage of the so-called Buckley Amendment in 1974 and the earlier recommendations on pupil data systems formulated by the Russell Sage Foundation, both the appropriate content of and access to client or student data systems have come under considerable scrutiny and control. In some instances, no data other than objective fact (such as achievement record, aptitude tests) can be maintained by a school or a college about a student for other than very short periods of time. If brought to a court test, would career development information be considered objective fact or subjective and impressionistic speculation? Would such assessment and monitoring be considered a reasonable educational procedure? How would such personnel data systems be construed within a business or industrial setting? This issue has yet to be resolved.

Research and Career Guidance Interventions

As suggested in the observations of Healy (1982) cited earlier, research efforts too often have neglected to describe specifically enough for replication the type of career counseling or career guidance approach undertaken in regard to some criterion — occupational or self-exploration, development of planning skills, choice of vocational education, work adjustment. These limitations significantly reduce our knowledge of the specificity of effects among treatments or consumers' expectancies of action. As Holland, Magoon, and Spokane (1981) have observed, the forms of career assistance have grown rapidly if not explosively but the proliferation of materials and techniques has not been accompanied by a similar interest in evaluation. Therefore, the distribution of research about the many forms of career assistance is uneven.

Aside from the extensive work accumulating about the efficacy of behavioral approaches to information-seeking and other exploratory behavior pertinent to decision-making, little can be said about the likely effects of different types of career guidance or counseling techniques in relation to specific categories of individual problems or needs. More research is needed that links client goals to treatment using goal-attainment scaling (Cytrynbaum, Ginath, Birdwell, & Brandt, 1979) or diagnostic procedures (Jepsen & Prediger, 1981; Campbell & Cellini, 1981) to extend existing knowledge of client treatment interactions (Holland, Magoon, & Spokane, 1981). Equally important is a lack of information about the long-term effects of different career guidance interventions. Most of the data available about the comparative advantages of career guidance modes are based on the outcomes that can be assessed at the termination of contact with a student or client rather than over time.

At a somewhat different level there remains a major question about the focus of career guidance. Are our interventions really directed to careers — intermediate and long-range planning, life style options, self-definition — as an evaluative base for educational and occupational choice? Or, are we really talking about the choice of jobs or occupations — immediate choices couched in economic rather than affective terms? Are we really trying to help build strengths to generalize to various decision points in the future or resolve immediate and limited dilemmas? The answers with regard to what actually occurs in career guidance interventions are not clear.

Advances in Occupational Information

Considerable progress has been made during the last decade in developing both affective and cognitive information about various forms of work that is sensitive to sexual stereotyping and responsive to the types of questions and conceptual ability pertinent to persons at various developmental levels. However, more can be done.

Specifically, research needs to address such questions as, Do students or adults think in terms of careers or entry jobs, school subjects, and college majors or clusters of interests? How do such perspectives bear on achievement motivation, career motives, and occupational valuing as these bear upon planning or adjustment to work? How much information do persons need before they can make a commitment at a given choice point? What are the effects of the tentative goal-setting of preadolescent youth on later choice and how is available information related to such choice-making? Are there differences among various population groups (defined by sex, race, ethnicity) in the types of occupational and career information preferred?

Another research issue concerning occupational or career information has to do with how to make it more localized. Most available information is national and, therefore, quite broad in its description of occupations and careers. Some research, however, has shown that local information, when it is available, is more important in decision-making than is national information. But aside from Department of Labor regional labor surveys, the prototype computerized occupational information systems, job data bank information that is regionalized or localized in some areas in the country, or occasional community surveys taken by counselors, there is very little local occupational or career information useful for decision-making. How such information can be effectively secured, what its characteristics are, and how valuable it is for different kinds of decisions are other important areas for research.

The Question of Work Values

A body of literature on worker alienation has emerged over the past several decades. Some

speculate that its revelations about the tedium and limitations for personal fulfillment in work have turned many young people against a work ethic. Other speculation interspersed with some research suggests that young people want to work but primarily in occupations that are challenging, of service to mankind, and personally gratifying.

It is not now clear how or if such concepts have affected the thinking of most youth. For example, do vocational education and college preparatory students share similar perspectives on the meaning of work? Nor is it clear how youth view decision stress or the increasing burdens of psychological responsibility being portrayed by many writers as emerging social problems. Many research questions are pertinent to such emphases. Some examples follow.

Are youth experiencing indecisiveness as a general behavior pattern? Is it restricted to career choice? How widespread is indecisiveness among student populations of different socioeconomic or racial characteristics and at different educational levels? What characteristics and conditions differentiate those who are guided by security from those who are risk-takers in decision-making? Are student values about work shifting dramatically? How? Are student values about education shifting? How? What forms of or emphases in career guidance do youth most value or desire? What career incentives do youth currently find most attractive (for example, contributions to others, service to society, high income, prestige) and what differences do these desires actually make at the point of choice? In a shifting employment picture, do youth find unemployment compensation, welfare, or other governmental subsidies attractive alternatives to work? Can youth or adults find personal significance outside of paid work if their physiological and security needs are met? Do the work values of youth and adults really differ or is this an intergenerational straw man?

Many of these questions might also be asked of various adult populations and the answers related to choices made. A fundamental question in either youth or adult populations is whether economic or psychological contingencies are really the more important at the point of choice for most persons in a highly industrialized society. A nagging concern among such questions is what is the influence of the mass media in shaping personal aspirations and questions of psychological identity as compared with other mechanisms in the environment or the individual's intrinsic need structure?

The Question of Counselor Characteristics

Counselor role and function studies have a long and sometimes questionable history. Examples of recent position statements on counselor role in career guidance and in career education were cited in Chapter 1. For the most part, these position statements are based on speculation, not research about the most important functions of counselors in discharging their responsibilities in career guidance. Other research questions also remain.

What is the relationship of the counselor's socioeconomic background and work history to knowledge of careers or occupations, to attitudes toward decision-making and exploratory behavior, to the place of career guidance within a repertoire of counselor priorities? What are the effects of counselor preparation in nonschool settings (for example, industrial internships, different amounts or types of paid employment, intern experiences in community and government agencies) on subsequent counselor effectiveness in career guidance? What are the relationships between the counselor's effectiveness in career guidance and previous occupational experience? How do the career guidance skills and emphases differ among counselors working in a vocational education setting, a comprehensive educational setting, and a community agency? What do counselors in different settings actually know about vocational education? How do counselors rate their competencies on the various career guidance skills recommended in the position statements cited in Chapter 1? What do counselors know about employment and unemployment? About skill elasticities across occupations and settings? About the primary and secondary labor markets? What types of retraining or preservice models are most effective in preparing career counselors for the needs of the future?

RESEARCH FOR THE FUTURE: SOME MAJOR QUESTIONS

Throughout the previous sections, some of the major areas of necessary research have been suggested. In this section we will summarize some additional questions that warrant future attention and identify studies pertinent to them.

The Career Development of Females

- Are there differences in career salience between men and women? If so, what are the factors related to such differences? (Hardesty & Betz, 1980; Sekaran, 1982)
- What are the reciprocal effects of women's career and family attitudes and career behavior across the life span? (Faver, 1982).
- What are the predictors of preferences for traditional or egalitarian marriages on women? What are their implications for career choice and for dual-career families? (Kassner, 1981).
- How do women who choose nontraditional careers differ from women who choose traditional careers? (Wolfe & Betz, 1981).
- What social-psychological determinants relate to achievement (individualism) in high school girls and women? (Smith, 1980).
- How does the pressure of multiple role expectations, opportunities, and choices differentiate women who pursue homemaker, career, or homemaker-career orientations? (Tinsley & Faunce, 1980; Betz, 1982).
- Are background factors or characteristics of the present context and role expectation of others more effective in accounting for achievement motivation in high school girls? What are the resulting implications for career guidance interventions? (Farmer, 1980).

Career Decision-Making and Career Guidance Interventions

- What happens at the actual interface of school and work? How can this process best be conceptualized? (Lokan & Biggs, 1982).
- How can client personality types be most effectively matched to different career guidance

approaches? (Kivligham, Hageseth, Tipton, & McGovern, 1981).

- How are career decision-making styles related to locus of control, social desirability, and passivity/activism? (Hesbeth, 1982).
- What are the factors related to commitment to change? How can such information be used in the career exploration process? (Dixon & Claiborn, 1981).
- What types of career intervention are most effective with persons experiencing high levels of indecisiveness and poor vocational identity? (Fretz & Leong, 1982).
- In what ways are conceptual level of cognitive style related to career decision-making behavior? What are the implications for career guidance interventions? (Warner & Jepsen, 1979; Lokan & Biggs, 1982).
- How are differential counseling interventions most effectively related to stage and style of decision-making? (Harren, Kass, Tinsley & Morehead, 1978).
- What elements should be included in ideal career guidance programs for different settings? (Goodson, 1982).
- What are the effects of different counseling environments on client perceptions of those environments and on client behavior? (Kerr, 1982).
- How do career indecision subtypes differ? Should career counseling be conducted with different content or different processes to maximize the benefits to different subtypes? (Barak & Friedkes, 1982).
- What are the effects of peers, faculty, and other models in developing career decision-making skills? Are these the prime sources of social reinforcement in career choice? (Ware, 1980).
- Are models of career decision-making most effectively conceptualized as idealized views of rationality toward which persons might strive? (Pitz & Harren, 1980).
- What factors (such as anxiety, organizational variables, work role salience) lead to employees' exploration as they proceed through various stages of career development?
- What are the major factors in occupational preference in relation to valence, instrumen-

tality, cost-benefit perceptions? (Wheeler & Mahoney, 1981).

- How can career interventions be evaluated on cost-benefit terms as well as preferences of users? (Reardon, Bonnell, & Huddleston, 1982).

Job Search Process and Work Adjustment

- How do labor market factors and individual characteristics interact to affect the job search process? What are the relationships between types of formal and informal job sources and subsequent work adjustment? (Allen & Kaveny, 1980).
- How do value differences between workers and supervisors affect the work adjustment process? Do such factors and other demographic variables significantly moderate both communication behavior and employee performance? (Vecchiotti & Korn, 1980; Penley & Hawkins, 1980).
- What sources of hiring bias exist in relation to disabled interviewees? How can job search techniques be devised to reduce prejudicial employment practices and attitudes toward the disabled?
- Can differences in intraoccupational characteristics of specific job activities and organizational settings be identified in order to maximize the best match between an individual and job? (Erez & Shneorson, 1980).

Implications of Mid-life Career Changes

- Do different kinds of career transitions require different kinds of support systems to be provided by work organizations? (Schlossberg & Leibowitz, 1980).
- What factors differentiate voluntary from involuntary career changers? How do their needs for career counseling differ? (Isaacson, 1981).
- Are decision-making styles interdependent throughout life or do they differ at various stages of life? (Phillips, 1982).
- Can a typology of midlife career changes be established that includes blue-collar, professional, or management changes, personal desire for change versus external pressures to leave, radicalness of change, obstacles to change, and

levels of satisfaction? (Thomas, 1980; Neopolitan, 1980).
- Are there motivators of retraining that can be identified and related to potential programs? (Schwarzwald & Shoham, 1981).

Work and Leisure

- Do population groups differing in age, gender, and ethnicity differ in their understanding of the concepts of work, leisure, education, future and self? What do these findings imply for the work-leisure relationship or for comprehensive career guidance approaches? (Rimmer & Kahnweiler, 1981).
- To what degree can occupation alone meet the psychological needs of the work force? How do occupations differ on this matter? What are the implications for a theory of leisure and of career guidance? (Bloland & Edwards, 1981).
- Are there relationships between personality and the selection of leisure activities? Does leisure have a compensatory effect for the vocationally dissatisfied? (Melamed & Meir, 1981).

Occupational/Career Information

- How can occupational information be most effectively clustered around transferability of skills? (Gottfredson, 1982).
- What are the effects of different types of occupational information on cognitive complexity/simplicity of different types of vocational undecidedness? (Cesari, Winer, Zychlinski, & Laird, 1982).

Summary Reviews of Research Needs

In the *Annual Review of Psychology* and the *Journal of Vocational Behavior*, as well as other pertinent journals, major summaries of the research literature and analyses of research needs in that literature are published. To conclude this chapter, selected highlights of recent reviews that go beyond what has been discussed earlier in this chapter will be summarized here.

For example, Bartol (1981) suggested,

As greater emphasis is placed on the working

life of individuals after initial occupational choices are made, researchers on vocational behavior and career development will increasingly find it necessary to synthesize research findings from the areas of industrial/organizational psychology, organizational sociology, and organizational behavior and theory. This factor may suggest greater collaboration among researchers across these fields in the future. In any event, the broadening base of relevant research, while challenging, also is an exciting development with rich potential for increased knowledge of vocational behavior (p. 151).

Fretz and Leong (1982) add to this perspective with their observations that more researchers are attending to environmental and organizational variables as major factors in career development:

The affirmative results from this emphasis will have to be asserted repeatedly to counter the impact of several generations of intrapsychically oriented career counselors and researchers. Understanding both the unique and interactive contributions of environmental and organizational, as well as organismic, variables to the development and implementation of careers may well be a challenge we can meet in the 1980's (p. 152).

That research on programs planned for career development in work settings is still limited is evident in the 1978 review of Super and Hall. In their view most of the research has involved field studies of such matters as assignments to challenging jobs or various types of job enrichment. They contend that there is "a need for more research on how career identities develop and are shaped by work experiences, as well as studies of how people maintain or increase adaptability in the face of advancing age or technology" (p. 366). Just as is true in other settings, Super and Hall contend that there are needs for more experimental studies to evaluate career development interventions and comparative studies of the relative effectiveness of different interventions.

Super and Hall also express surprise that career theory has been used so little in trying to deal with career problems in the organizational context. In particular, they cite how the work of Schein (1968, 1971), Super (1974), and Holland (1973) might be used to explore various career problems and to refine present theoretical conceptions in order to build stronger analytic tools. Finally, they suggest that perhaps the most troubling questions both in theoretical and practical terms are, What is development in the work career? in occupational success? in satisfaction? in growth and development of skills? in successful movement through life stages? (p. 367). Such questions, of course, return us to our earlier observation that many of our research concerns are not empirical, but rather philosophical or value-oriented.

A final representative set of research needs are those suggested by Holland, Magoon, and Spokane (1981) in their comprehensive review of research and theory on career interventions. Among their suggestions are the following:

- More rigorous evaluations of all forms of vocational interventions are still required. The analysis of how interventions work needs to be continued and reexamined in the context of instructional technology, decision-making, and information processing.
- More analytical evaluations in which client goals are linked to treatments are needed to acquire a comprehensive knowledge of client treatment interactions and related outcomes.
- More potent treatments should be developed by incorporating the influential characteristics of past treatments.
- The ordering effects of treatment chains should be investigated.
- The neglected but painfully relevant topics of job finding, placement strategies, and vocational adaptation require more attention.
- The classification research should be more completely exploited (pp. 298–300).

Summary

In this chapter we have examined a broad spectrum of research issues and needs of relevance to fuller understanding of both career behavior and potential interventions in such behavior. Research and statistical methods were discussed in relation to how different statistical techniques are used to analyze particular types of questions. Also discussed was the importance to longitudinal career development studies of path analysis and causal modeling. We also identified the areas in which research questions in career guidance or career development are present and inventories of such questions are provided. The range of such questions illustrates the complexity of career development processes and their dynamic quality. They also affirm that many of the major questions of concern to career guidance are not empirical, but rather matters of philosophy or values.

LEARNING ACTIVITIES

1. Discuss with career counselors in a school, college, or community agency areas in which they feel more research or development would

improve career guidance practice. Compare their responses to the needs identified in this chapter.

2. Review the chapters in this book dealing with career development theory (Chapters 2, 4, and 6 particularly) and find evidence that the observations in this chapter about the limitations of sample size and composition and cross-cultural factors is accurate.

3. Review the chapters dealing with the application of career guidance in different settings and with different populations. Construct a matrix with career guidance approaches (treatments, interventions) down the left column and age or population groups across the top, and identify the types of problems each approach addresses.

4. Refer to textbooks on research design or statistics and identify the meanings of the different research approaches listed in this chapter (such as single subject, naturalistic, factorial, correlational) and consider how each might be matched to some of the specific research questions suggested later in the chapter.

5. Brainstorm with your colleagues what sorts of

research questions are most important in your setting or in relation to the population with whom you hope to work. Construct a plan by which you might obtain information of concern to you, identify data sources, possible ways of analyzing the information, and potential uses of the information.

OBJECTIVES

After reading this chapter, participating in the learning activities, and reading additional suggested resources, you should have achieved the following objectives. If you have not, please review the chapter.

1. Identify at least five categories of needs for research and development in career guidance.
2. Discuss three or more factors that limit the applicability of career development theory to all segments of the population.
3. Describe the relationship of career guidance content to social, economic, political, and occupational trends in the society.
4. Summarize three or more characteristics of the state of the art of research in career guidance.
5. Differentiate methodological issues pertinent to psychology of occupations from those pertinent to a psychology of careers.
6. Identify the emphases that life span psychology would add to career models of career development.
7. Discuss why economic understandings are important to a career guidance practitioner and give examples of types of knowledge of particular interest.
8. Describe why cost-benefit effects of career guidance are an important, emerging research area.
9. Discuss two issues relating to the assessment of career development.

Appendix A

Directory of Publishers of Commercial Educational,
Occupational, and Career Development Materials and Tests

Aaron Press	14 E. 2700 South	Salt Lake City, UT 84115
Abelard Schuman Ltd.	6 N. 57th Street	New York, NY 10019
Abingdon Press	201 Eighth Ave., S.	Nashville, TN 37202
Abt Publications	55 Wheeler Street	Cambridge, MA 02138
Academic Press, Inc.	11 Fifth Avenue	New York, NY 10003
Addison-Wesley	South Street	Reading, MA 01867
Aims Instructional Media Services, Inc.	P.O. Box 1010	Hollywood, CA 90028
Allyn and Bacon, Inc.	470 Atlantic Avenue	Boston, MA 02110
Alp Publications	3048 North 34th St.	Milwaukee, WI 53210
American Book Company	55 Fifth Avenue	New York, NY 10003
American College Testing Prog.	P.O. Box 168	Iowa City, IA 52240
American Guidance Service	Publishers' Building	Circle Pines, MN 55014
American Personnel and Guidance Association	1607 New Hampshire Ave., N.W.	Washington, DC 20009
American Psychological Assn.	1200 17th St., N.W.	Washington, DC 20036
American Vocational Assn.	1025 15th St., N.W.	Washington, DC 20005
Arco Publishing Co., Inc.	219 Park Avenue South	New York, NY 10003
Argus Communications	7440 Natchez	Niles, IL 60648
Association Films, Inc.	347 Madison Avenue	New York, NY 10017
Association Press	291 Broadway	New York, NY 10007
Avid Corporation	Ten Tripps Lane	East Providence, RI 02914
Bailey Film, Inc.	6509 De Longpre Avenue	Hollywood, CA 90028
Barron's Educational Series, Inc.	113 Crossways Park Dr.	Woodbury, NY 11797
Benefic Press	10300 W. Roosevelt Rd.	Westchester, IL 60153
BFA Educational Media	2211 Michigan Avenue	Santa Monica, CA 90404
B'nai B'rith Career and Counseling Services	1640 Rhode Island Av., N.W.	Washington, DC 20036
Bobbs-Merrill Co., Inc.	4300 W. 62nd Street	Indianapolis, IN 46206
Bowmar Publishing Corp.	622 Rodier Drive	Glendale, CA 91201
Bunting & Lyon, Inc.	238 North Main Street	Wallingford, CT 06490
Bureau of Publications	Teachers College, Columbia Univ. 525 West 120th St.	New York, NY 10027
Burgess Publishing Company	426 South Sixth St.	Minneapolis, MN 55415
California Test Bureau	Del Monte Research Park	Monterey, CA 93940
Career Associates	P.O. Box 2316	Newport Beach, CA 92663
Career Associates	P.O. Box 505	Lansdale, PA 19446
Career Films, Inc.	2100 Locust Street	Philadelphia, PA 19103
Careers, Inc.	P.O. Box 135	Largo, FL 33540
Carlton Films	2870 Bartells Drive	Beloit, WI 53511
Catalyst	14 E. 60th Street	New York, NY 10022

Center for Humanities	2 Holland Avenue	White Plans, NY 10603
Centron Corp.	18 East 41st Street	New York, NY 10000
Changing Times Education		
Service	1729 H Street, N.W.	Washington, DC 20006
Channing L. Bete Co., Inc.	45 Federal Street	Greenfeld, MA 01301
Charles W. Clark Co., Inc.	564 Smith Street	Farmingdale, NY 11735
Children's Press	1224 W. Van Buren St.	Chicago, IL 60607
Chronicle Guidance		
Publications, Inc.		Moravia, NY 13118
Classroom World Productions	22 Glenwood Avenue, Box 2090	Raleigh, NC 27602
John Colburn Associates, Inc.	265 Alice Street	Wheeling, IL 60090
College Entrance		
Examination Board	888 Seventh Avenue	New York, NY 10019
Commercial Educational		
Distributing Services	P.O. Box 3711	Portland, OR 97208
Consulting Psychologists Press	577 College Avenue	Palo Alto, CA 94306
Continental Publishing Co.	1261 Broadway	New York, NY 10001
David C. Cook Publishing Co.	850 North Grove Avenue	Elgin, IL 60120
Coronet Films	65 E. South Water St.	Chicago, IL 60600
Counseling Films, Inc.	P.O. Box 1047	Madison, WI 53701
Counselor Films, Inc.	1728 Cherry Street	Philadelphia, PA 19103
Coward McCann, Inc.	200 Madison Avenue	New York, NY 10016
Croner Publications	211 Jamaica Avenue	Queens Village, NY 11428
Thomas Y. Crowell Company	201 Park Ave., South	New York, NY 10003
Curriculum Innovations, Inc.	501 Lake Forest Avenue	Highwood, IL 60040
John Day Co., Inc.	200 Madison Avenue	New York, NY 10016
Denoyer-Geppert	5235 Ravenswood Avenue	Chicago, IL 60640
Louis De Rochemont		
Associates, Inc.	18 F. 48th Street	New York, NY 10017
Dodd, Mead & Company	79 Madison Avenue	New York, NY 10016
Dorsey Press	1818 Ridge Road	Homewood, IL 60430
Doubleday & Company, Inc.		
School and Library Division		Garden City, NY 11530
Dowling Pictures	1056 South Robertson Blvd.	Los Angeles, CA 90000
E. P. Dutton & Company	201 Park Avenue South	New York, NY 10003
Education Achievement Corp.	P.O. Box 7310	Waco, TX 76710
Educational Activities, Inc.		Freeport, NY 11520
Educational Design, Inc.		
Educational Resources Div.	47 West 13th Street	New York, NY 10011
Educational Dimensions	Box 146	Great Neck, NY 11023
Educational Enrichment		
Materials, Inc.	83 East Avenue	Norwall, CT 06851
Educational Horizons Press	Box 751	Melville, NY 11746
Educational and Industrial		
Testing Service	P.O. Box 7234	San Diego, CA 92107
Educational Media Corp.	Box 847	Madison, WI 53701
Educational Progress Corp.	8538 East 41st St.	Tulsa, OK 74415
Educational Resources, Inc.	P.O. Box 353	
	Old Chelsea Station	New York, NY 10011
Educational Testing Service	20 Nassau Street	Princeton, NJ 08540
Education Ventures, Inc.	209 Court Street	Middletown, CT 06457
Edu-Craft, Inc.	6475 DuBois	Detroit, MI 48200
Elkins Company	10031 Commerce Street	Tujunga, CA 91042
Employment Training Corp.	300 Central Park West	New York, NY 10024
Encyclopedia Britannica Films,		
Inc.	425 N. Michigan Avenue	Chicago, IL 60611
EPIE Institute	463 West Street	New York, NY 10014
Eye Gate Instructional Materials	146-01 Archer Avenue	Jamaica, NY 11435
Farrar, Straus & Giroux, Inc.	19 Union Square W.	New York, NY 10003
Fearon Publishers, Inc.		
Div. of Pittman Publ. Inc.	6 Davis Drive	Belmont, CA 94002

J.G. Ferguson	Six N. Michigan Avenue	Chicago, IL 60602
Fieldler Company	31 Ottawa, N. W.	Grand Rapids, MI 49500
Finney Company	3350 Gorham Avenue	Minneapolis, MN 55426
Gordon Flesch Company	225 Beltline Hy., N.	Madison, WI 53713
Follett Publishing Company	1000 N. Washington Blvd.	Chicago, IL 60607
Friendship Press	475 Riverside Drive	New York, NY 10027
Frith Films	1816 North Highland Dr.	Hollywood, CA 90028
Garrard Press	510–522 N. Hickory St.	Champaign, IL 61820
Ginn & Company	P.O. Box 191	Boston, MA 02100
Golden Press, Inc.	850 Third Avenue	New York, NY 10022
Grosset & Dunlop Publishing Company	51 Madison Avenue	New York, NY 10010
Guidance Associates	757 Third Avenue	New York, NY 10017
Guidance Exchange	3310 Rochambeau Avenue	Bronx, NY 10467
E. M. Hale and Company		Eau Claire, WI 54701
Halewyn Films	106 John Street	Toronto, Canada
Harcourt Brace Jovanovich	757 Third Avenue	New York, NY 10017
Harper & Row, Publishers	Keystone Industrial Pk.	Scranton, PA 18512
Hastings House Publishers, Inc.	151 E. 50th Street	New York, NY 10022
Hawthorne Books, Inc.	70 Fifth Avenue	New York, NY 10011
D. C. Heath & Company	285 Columbus Avenue	Boston, MA 02116
Henk Newenhouse, Inc.	1825 Willow Road	Northbrook, IL 60093
Hoffman Educational Systems	4423 Arden Drive	El Monte, CA 91734
Holt, Rinehart, & Winston	383 Madison Avenue	New York, NY 10017
Houghton Mifflin	1 Beacon Street	Boston, MA 02107
Human Resources Consultants	1950 Allison Park Dr.	Richland Center, WI 53581
Institute for Personality and Ability Testing	1602 Coronado Drive	Champaign, IL 61822
Instruction Media Company	P.O. Box 185	Green Lake, WI 54941
I(T) WORK(S), Inc.	1204 Rio Grande	Denton, TX 76201
Thomas Jacobson	5945 Highgate Court	La Mesa, CA 92041
Jam Handy, Inc.	2861 East Grand Blvd.	Detroit, MI 48211
Johnson Press, Inc.	P.O. Box 4156	Rockford, IL 61100
Johnson Publishing Company	428 South Wilbur	Mesa, AZ 85202
King Comic Books	235 E. 45th Street	New York, NY 10017
Alfred A. Knopf, Inc.	201 E. 50th St.	New York, NY 10022
Knowledge Aid	6633 West Howard St.	Niles, IL 60648
Lantern Press	257 Park Avenue, South	New York, NY 10003
Lawren Productions, Inc.	P.O. Box 1542	Burlingame, LA 94010
Learning Corporation of America	711 Fifth Avenue	New York, NY 10022
J. P. Lippincott Company	E. Washington Square	Philadelphia, PA 19105
Lithrop Publishing Company	105 Madison Avenue	New York, NY 10006
Little, Brown and Company	34 Beacon Street	Boston, MA 02106
Lyons and Carnahan	407 East 25th Street	Chicago, IL 60610
Macmillan Library Services	255 B. Brown Street	Riverside, NY 08075
Maco Publishing Co., Inc.	757 Third Avenue	New York, NY 10017
Mafex Associates	111 Baron Avenue, Box 519	Johnstown, PA 15907
Magic Circle People	7574 University Avenue	La Mesa, CA 92041
Manpower Administration U.S. Department of Labor		Washington, DC 20210
McCormick Mathers	300 Pike Street	Cincinnati, OH 45202
McGraw-Hill Book Company	1221 Avenue of the Americas	New York, NY 10036
David C. McKay Co., Inc.	750 Third Avenue	New York, NY 10017
McKnight Publishing Company	Box 854	Bloomington, IL 61701
Melmount Publishers, Inc.	1224 North Van Buren St.	Chicago, IL 60607
Mercer Enterprises	4241 Norman Avenue	Hollywood, CA 90029
Merchandiser Film Prod.	419 Park Avenue, South	New York, NY 10016
Meredith Press	1716 Locust Street	Des Moines, IA 50303
Charles E. Merrill Publishing Company	1300 Alum Creek Drive	Columbus, OH 43216
Julian Messner	One West 39th Street	New York, NY 10018

MINCOMP	1780 S. Bellaire St.	Denver, CO 80222
Mini Productions	192 Hyeholde Drive	Coraopolis, PA 15108
William Morrow & Company	105 Madison Avenue	New York, NY 10016
National Association of Trade and Technical Schools	2021 L Street, N.W.	Washington, DC 20036
National Career Consultants, Inc.	9978 Monroe Drive	Dallas, TX 75220
National Computer Systems	4401 W. 76th Street	Minneapolis, MN 55435
Thomas Nelson & Sons	Copewood & Davis Sts.	Camden, NJ 08103
Neubacker Productions	10609 Bradbury Road	Los Angeles, CA 90064
NEWIST	P.O. Box 7711	Green Bay, WI 54303
Occupational Awareness	P.O. Box 5098	Los Angeles, CA 90055
Occupational Outlook Service Bureau of Labor Statistics U.S. Department of Labor		Washington, DC 20212
Occu-Press	P.O. Box 1464 Grand Central P.O.	New York, NY 10003
Oceans Publications, Inc.	40 Cedar Street	Dobbs Ferry, NY 10522
Odyssey Press, Inc.	55 Fifth Avenue	New York, NY 10003
Olympus Publishing Company	1670 E. Thirteenth, S.	Salt Lake City, UT 84115
Oxford University Press	200 Madison Avenue	New York, NY 10016
Palmer Publications	25 West 45th Street	New York, NY 10036
Parker Brothers, Inc.		Salem, MA 01970
Park Publishing House	414 West Vleet Street	Milwaukee, WI 53208
Pathescope Educ. Films	71 Weyman Avenue	New Rochelle, NY 10802
Pennant Educational Materials	P.O. Box 236	Northfield, IL 60093
J. C. Penney, Inc.	1301 Avenue of the Americas	New York, NY 10019
Personnel Press, Inc.	200 Nassau Street	Princeton, NJ 08540
Personnel Services	P.O. Box 306	Jaffrey, NH 03452
George A. Pflaum, Publishers	38 West Fifth Street	Dayton, OH 45402
Pitman Publishing Company	20 East 46th Street	New York, NY 10017
R. L. Polk & Company	130 4th Avenue, North	Nashville, TN 37219
Prentice-Hall, Inc.		Englewood Cliffs, NJ 17632
The Psychological Corporation	757 Third Avenue	New York, NY 10017
Psychological Test Specialists	Box 1441	Missoula, MT 59804
Psychometric Affiliates	Box 3167	Munster, IN 46321
G. P. Putnam's	200 Madison Avenue	New York, NY 10016
Q E D Productions	Box 1608	Burbank, CA 91507
Rand McNally & Company	P.O. Box 7600	Chicago, IL 60680
Random House	201 E. 50th St.	New York, NY 10022
Research Publishing Company	Box 1474	Madison, WI 53701
Research Psychologists Press		Goshen, NY 10924
Richtext Press	1224 West Van Buren St.	Chicago, IL 60607
R.O.A.'s Films	1696 North Astor St.	Milwaukee, WI 53202
Roche Testing Service Hoffman-La Roche, Inc.		Nutley, NJ 07110
Ronald Press	15 East 26th Street	New York, NY 10010
Richards Rosen Press	29 East 21st Street	New York, NY 10010
Scholastic Book Services Div. Scholastic Magazines	906 Sylvan Avenue	Englewood Cliffs, NJ 07632
Scholastic Magazines, Inc.	902 Sylvan Avenue	Englewood Cliffs, NJ 07632
Scholastic Testing Service	480 Meyer Road	Bensenville, IL 60106
Science Research Associates	259 E. Erie Street	Chicago, IL 60611
Scott Foresman & Company	1900 E. Lake Avenue	Glenview, IL 60025
Charles Scribners	597 Fifth Avenue	New York, NY 10017
The Seabury Press	815 Second Avenue	New York, NY 10017
Sextant Systems, Inc.	3048 N. 34th Street	Milwaukee, WI 53210
Sheridan Psychological Services	P.O. Box 837	Beverly Hills, CA 90213
Silver Burdett Company	Park Avenue	Morristown, NJ 07960
Simon & Schuster	630 Fifth Avenue	New York, NY 10020
Singer Career Systems	80 Commerce Drive	Rochester, NY 14623

Singer Society for Visual Education, Inc.	1345 Diversey Parkway	Chicago, IL 60614
S. L. Flim Productions	5126 Hartwick Street	Los Angeles, CA 90041
Southwestern Publishing Co.	5101 Madison Road	Cincinnati, OH 45227
Springer Publishing Co., Inc.	200 Park Avenue South	New York, NY 10003
Stanford University Press		Palo Alto, CA 94305
Sterling Educational Films, Inc.	6 East 39th Street	New York, NY 10023
Sterling Publishing Company	419 Fourth Avenue	New York, NY
C. H. Stoetling Company	424 North Homan Ave.	Chicago, IL 60624
R. A. Stone Products	18279 Livernois	Detroit, MI 48221
Studies for Urban Man, Inc.		Tempe, AZ 85281
Success Motivation Institute	P.O. Box 7614	Waco, TX 76700
Success Research Consultants, Inc.	17055 S. Oak Park Ave.	Tinley Park, IL 60477
Teaching Films Custodians	25 West 43rd Street	New York, NY
Troll Associates	E. 64 Midland Avenue	Paramus, NJ 07652
United World Films, Inc.	221 Park Avenue South	New York, NY 10003
U. S. Department of Labor Bureau of Labor Statistics	GAO Building	Washington, DC 20212
United States Employment Service		Washington, DC 20210
U. S. Government Film Service	245 West 55th Street	New York, NY 10019
U. S. Government Printing Office Superintendent of Documents		Washington, DC 20402
Valient, Inc.	237 Washington Ave.	Hackensack, NJ 07602
Vantage Press, Inc.	120 West 31st Street	New York, NY 10001
Viking Press	625 Madison Avenue	New York, NY 10022
Visual Education Consultants	2066 Helena Street	Madison, WI 53701
Vocational Biographics, Inc.	Box 146	Sank Centre, MN 56378
Vocational Films	111 Euclid Avenue	Park Ridge, IL 60068
Vocational Guidance Manuals	235 East 45th Street	New York, NY 10017
Wadsworth Publishing, Inc.	10 Davis Drive	Belmont, CA 94002
Henry Z. Walck, Inc.	19 Union Square, West	New York, NY 10003
Franklin Watts	575 Lexington Avenue	New York, NY 10022
Western Psychological Services	12035 Wilshire Blvd.	Los Angeles, CA 90025
Western Publishing Company	850 Third Avenue	New York, NY 10022
Westinghouse Learning Corp.	100 Park Avenue	New York, NY 10017
Westminster Press	Witherspoon Building	Philadelphia, PA 19107
Albert Whitman & Company	560 West Lake Street	Chicago, IL 60606
John Wiley & Sons, Inc.	605 Third Avenue	New York, NY 10016
H. H. Wilson Company	950 University Avenue	Bronx, NY 10452
E. F. Wonderlic & Associates, Inc.	P.O. Box 7	Northfield, IL 60093
World Publishing Company	2231 West 110th St.	Cleveland, OH 44102

Appendix B

Sources of Occupational Information—Upon written request, these agencies are willing to provide up-to-date career information to individuals or to a school representative that can be utilized in developing a career information file.

Academy of Aeronautics
LaGuardia Airport
Flushing, NY 11371

Accounting Careers Council
National Distribution Center
P.O. Box 650
Radio City Station
New York, NY 10019

Accredited Council School of
Journalism
University of Missouri
Box 838
Columbia, MO 65205

Accredited Journalism and
Mass Communication Education
The Newspaper Fund, Inc.
P.O. Box 300
Princeton, NJ 08540

Advertising Education
Publications
3429 556th Street
Lubbock, TX 79412

Aerospace Industries
Association of American
Industries
1725 DeSales Street NW
Washington, DC 20036

Aerospace Medical Association
Washington National Airport
Washington, DC 20036

Agency for International
Development
Washington, DC 20523

Agricultural Research Service
U.S. Department of Agriculture
Hyattsville, MD 20782

Air-Conditioning and
Refrigeration Institute
1815 North Fort Myer Drive
Arlington, VA 22091

Air Force Recruiting Service
6209 18th Avenue
Brooklyn, NY 11204

Air Transport Association
of America
1709 New York Avenue NW
Washington, DC 20006

Air Transportation
TSA Atterboard Airport
80 Moonachie Avenue
Teterboard, NJ 07608

Allis Chalmers
Milwaukee, WI 53200

Alumnae Advisory Center, Inc.
541 Madison Avenue
New York, NY 10022

Amalgamated Clothing and
Textile Workers, Inc.
15 Union Square
New York, NY 10003

Amalgamated Meat Cutters and
Butcher Workmen of North
America
2800 North Sheridan Road
Chicago, IL 60657

American Accounting Association
School of Commerce

University of Wisconsin
Madison, WI 53715

American Arbitration Association
140 West 51st Street
New York, NY 10020

American Association of
Advertising Agencies
666 Third Avenue
New York, NY 10017

American Association for Health,
Physical Education and
Recreation
1201 16th Street NW
Washington, DC 20036

American Association of
Nurserymen, Inc.
230 Southern Building
Washington, DC 20005

American Association of
Petroleum Landmen
2408 Continental Life Building
P.O. Box 1884
Fort Worth, TX 76101

American Astronomical Society
Mr. H. M. Gurhu, Executive
Director
211 Fitz Randolph Road
Princeton, NJ 08405

American Bakers Association
Suite 650
1700 Pennsylvania Avenue NW
Washington, DC 20036

American Bar Association
Information Service

Appendix B was developed and revised by Dr. Nancy Ryan Prince, Career Management Consultant, Chattanooga, Tennessee. The authors are most grateful for her contribution.

1155 East 60th Street
Chicago, IL 60637

American Board of Funeral
  Services Education
201 Columbia Street
P. O. Box 2090
Fairmont, WV 26554

American Camping Association
Bradford Woods
Martinsville, IN 46151

American Chemical Society
1155 Sixteenth Street NW
Washington, DC 20036

American College of Hospital
  Administration
840 North Lake Shore Drive
Chicago, IL 60611

American College of Physicians
4200 Pine Street
Philadelphia, PA 19104

American College of Surgeons
55 East Eric Street
Chicago, IL 43214

American Council of Education
  for Journalism
School of Journalism
University of Missouri
Columbia, MO 65201

American Dental Assistants
  Association
American Dental Association
211 East College Avenue
Chicago, IL 60611

American Dental Hygienists
  Association
American Dental Association
  Council on Dental Education
211 East Chicago Avenue
Chicago, IL 60611

American Dietetic Association
620 North Michigan Avenue
Chicago, IL 60611

American Federation of Labor
  and Congress of Industrial
  Organization Building and
  Construction Trade Department
815 16th Street NW
Washington, DC 20006

American Federation of
  Technical Engineers
1126 16th Street NW
Washington, DC 20009

American Forest Association
1319 18th Street NW
Washington, DC 20036

American Guild of Musical Artists
1841 Broadway
New York, NY 10020

American Guild of Organists
630 Fifth Avenue
New York, NY 10021

American Historical Association
400 A Street SE
Washington, DC 20003

American Hospital Association
840 North Lake Shore Drive
Chicago, IL 60611

American Hotel and Motel
  Association
Kellogg Center
Michigan State University
East Lansing, MI 48823

American Industrial Arts
  Association
1210 16th Street NW
Washington, DC 20005

American Institute of Aeronautics
  and Astronautics, Inc.
1290 Avenue of Americas
New York, NY 10019

American Institute of Architects
1735 New York Avenue NW
Washington, DC 20006

American Institute of Certified
  Public Accounting
1211 Avenue of the Americas
New York, NY 10036

American Institute of
  Chemical Engineering
345 East 47th Street
New York, NY 10017

American Legion Education and
  Scholarship Program
Americanism Division
P.O. Box 1055
Indianapolis, IN 46206

American Library Association
  Office for Recruitment
50 East Huron Street
Chicago, IL 60611

The American Management
  Association
135 West 50th Street
New York, NY 10020

The American Medical
  Association
535 North Dearborn Street
Chicago, IL 60061

American Meteorological Society
45 Beacon Street
Boston, MA 02103

American Model Festival
P. O. Box 100
Croton-on-Hudson, NY 10502

American Osteopathic
  Association
312 East Ohio Street
Chicago, IL 60611

American Paper Institute, Inc.
260 Madison Avenue
New York, NY 10016

American Petroleum Institute
1801 K Street NW
Washington, DC 20036

American Physiological Society
Education Office
9650 Rockville Pike
Bethesda, MD 20014

American Podiatry Association
20 Chevy Chase Circle NW
Washington, DC 20036

The American Red Cross
National Headquarters
Washington, DC 20015
American Rehabilitation
  Counseling Association
1607 New Hampshire Avenue NW
Washington, DC 20009

American School Counselor
  Association
1605 New Hampshire Avenue NW
Washington, DC 20009

American Society of Astronomy
677 Sego Road
Madison, WI 52700

American Society for Engineering
  Education, Publication Sales
Suite 400
One Dupont Circle
Washington, DC 20036

American Society of Heating,
  Refrigeration, and Air-
  Conditioning Engineers, Inc.
1791 Tulie Circle NE
Atlanta, GA 30329

American Society of Limnology
  and Oceanography
W. W. Kellogg Biological Station
Michigan State University
Hickory Corners, MI 49060

American Society for Metals
Metals Park, OH 44073

American Society of Personnel
  Administration
19 Church Street
Berea, OH 44017

American Society of
  Pharmacology and
  Experimental Therapeutics
9650 Rockville Pike
Bethesda, MD 20014

American Society of
  Photogrammetry
105 North Virginia Avenue
Falls Church, VA 22046

American Society of Radiologic
  Technologists
Suite 836
500 North Michigan Avenue
Chicago, IL 60611

American Speech-Language and
  Hearing Association
10801 Rockville Pike
Rockville, MD 20850

American Statistics Association
Biometric Society, Eastern and
Western, North American Regions
Institute of Mathematical
  Statistics
806 15th Street NW
Washington, DC 20036

The American Trucking
  Association, Inc.
1616 P Street NW
Washington, DC 20036

American Veterinary Medical
  Association
930 North Meacham Road
Schaumburg, IL 60198

American Watchmakers Institute
P. O. Box 11011
Cincinnati, OH 45211

Apprenticeship Committee
National Association of
  Plumbing, Heating, and Coiling
  Contractors
1016 20th Street NW
Washington, DC 20036

ARCO
515 South Flower Street
Box 2679-TA
Los Angeles, CA 90051

Associated Fur Manufacturers
101 West 30th Street
New York, NY 10001

Association of American Railroads
Office of Information and
  Public Affairs
1920 L Street NW
Washington, DC 20036

Association for Computing
  Machinery
1133 Avenue of the Americas
New York, NY 10036

Association for Education in
  Journalism
425 Henry Hall
University of Wisconsin
Madison, WI 53715

The Association of General
  Contractors of America
1957 E Street NW
Washington, DC 20036

Association of Home Appliance
  Manufacturers
20 North Wacker Drive
Chicago, IL 60606

Association of Independent
  Colleges and Schools
1730 M Street NW
Washington, DC 20036

Association of Master Barbers
  and Beauticians of America
P. O. Box 22078
Charlotte, NC 28222

Association of Operating Room
  Technicians
Denver Technological Center
8085 East Prentice Avenue
Englewood, CA 80110

Atlas Chemical Industries
Wilmington, DE 19899

Automobile Manufacturers
  Association, Inc.
320 New Center Building
Detroit, MI 48202

Blue Cross Association
840 North Lake Shore Dr.
Chicago, IL 60611

Botanical Society of America
School of Biological Sciences
University of Kentucky
Lexington, KY 40506

Building and Construction
  Trades Department
American Federation of Labor
  and Congress of Industrial
  Organization
Suite 603
815-16th Street NW
Washington, DC 20006

Bureau of Apprenticeship and
  Training
U.S. Department of Labor
Washington, DC 20212

Bureau of Land Management
Denver Service Center
Federal Center Building 50
Denver, CO 80225

Canadian Occupations Monograph
  Queens
Printer and Controllers of
  Stationery
Ottawa, Canada

Careers
Washington, DC 20202

Clothing Manufacturers
  Association of America
135 West 50th Street
New York, NY 10020

The College Placement Council
42 Highland Avenue
Bethlehem, PA 18017

Communications Workers of
  America
1925 K Street NW
Washington, DC 20006

Consumer Protection and
  Environmental Health Services
Department of Health, Education
  and Welfare
200 C Street NW
Washington, DC 20204

Coordinator, Independent Study
  Program
FBI Department of Justice
Washington, DC 20535

Department of the Navy
U.S. Navy Oceanographic Office
NSTL Station
Bay St. Louis, MS 39521

Department of Paper Science and
  Engineering
Western University of Michigan
Kalamazoo, MI 49008

Education Program
P. O. Box 1055
Indianapolis, IN 46206

Educational Council on Graphic
  Arts
4615 Forbes Avenue
Pittsburgh, PA 15213

Educational Testing Service
Suite 2020
250 Piedmont Avenue NE
Atlanta, GA 30308

ERIC/Clearinghouse
1960 Kenny Road
Columbus, OH 43210

Fashion Design
Chamberlayne Junior College
128 Commonwealth Avenue
Boston, MA 02116

Fashion Institute of Technology
227 West 27th Street
New York, NY 10001

Forging Industry Association
55 Public Square
Cleveland, OH 44113

General Electric Educational
Relations
New York, NY 10022

General Motors Corporation
Public Relations Staff
General Motors Boulevard
Detroit, MI 48202

Graphic Communications
Education Council of the Graphic
Arts Industry
4615 Forbes Avenue
Pittsburgh, PA 15213

Gypsum Drywall Contractors
International
234 South Wabash Avenue
Chicago, IL 60604

Health Manpower Division
United Hospital Fund
3 East 54th Street
New York, NY 10022

The Institute of Electrical and
Electronics Engineering
245 East 47th Street
New York, NY 10017

Institute of Mathematical
Statistics
Department of Statistics
California State College at
Hayward
Hayward, CA 94542

Insurance Information Institute
110 William Street
New York, NY 10038

Internal Revenue Service
U.S. Treasury Department
Washington, DC 20036

Interagency Board of Civil Service
Examiners for Washington, D.C.
19000 E Street NW
Washington, DC 20036

International Association of
Firefighters

905 16th Street NW
Washington, DC 20006

International Association of
Machinists and Aerospace
Workers
1300 Connecticut Avenue
Washington, DC 20036

International Brotherhood of
Electric Workers
1125 15th Street NW
Washington, DC 20005

International Brotherhood of
Painters and Allied Trades
United Unions Building
1750 New York Avenue NW
Washington, DC 20006

International Chiropractors
Association
741 Brady Street
Davenport, IA 52805

International Ladies Garment
Union
1710 Broadway
New York, NY 10019

International Oceanographic
Foundation
1 Rickenbacker Causeway
Virginia Key
Miami, FL 33141

International Union of Machinists
and Aerospace Workers
1300 Connecticut Avenue NW
Washington, DC 20036

Laborer's International Union of
North America
905 16th Street NW
Washington, DC 20006

Management
Northwest University Department
of Admissions
360 Huntington Avenue
Boston, MA 02115

Manufacturing Chemists
Association
1825 Connecticut Avenue NW
Washington, DC 20009

Master Photo Dealers and Finishers
Association
603 Lansing Avenue
Jackson, MI 49202

Mathematics Association of
America
1529 18th Street NW
Washington, DC 20036

McKnight Publishing Company
Career Materials
Bloomington, IL 61701

Medical Technology
Veterans Administration
Washington, DC 20420

Milk Industry Foundation
910 17th Street NW
Washington, DC 20006

Motor Vehicle Manufacturers
Association of the United
States, Inc.
300 New Center Building
Detroit, MI 48202

Music Editors National Conference
National Educational Association
of United States
1201 16th Street NW
Washington, DC 20009

National Air Transportation
Association
Aerospace (NATA)
1010 Wisconsin Avenue NW
Suite 405
Washington, DC 20007

National Art Education
Association
c/o Mrs. J. Theodore Anderson
1916 Association Drive
Reston, VA 22091

National Association of
Broadcasters
1771 N Street NW
Washington, DC 20036

National Association of
Emergency Medical Technicians
P. O. Box 334
Newton Highlands, MA 02161

National Association of Legal
Secretaries (International)
3005 East Shelly Drive
Tulsa, OK 74105

National Association of
Plumbing-Heating-Cooling
Contractors
1016 20th Street NW
Washington, DC 20036

National Association of Trade
and Technical Schools
2021 L Street NW
Washington, DC 20036

National Board of Coat and Shirt
Industries
450 Seventh Avenue
New York, NY 10001

National Consumer Finance
  Association
1000 16th Street NW
Washington, DC 20036

National Electrical Contractors
  Association
1730 Rhode Island Avenue
Washington, DC 20036

National Fire Protection
  Association
Batterymarch Park
Quincy, MA 02269

National Forest Products
  Association
Wood Industry Careers
1619 Massachusetts Ave.
Washington, DC 20036

National Home Study Council
1601 18th Street NW
Washington, DC 20009

National Secretaries Association
  (International)
224 Pershing Road
Suite G 10
Kansas City, MO 64108

National Science Teachers
  Association
1742 Connecticut Ave.
Washington, DC 20009

The National Society of Public
  Accountants
Executive Offices
1010 North Fairfax St.
Alexandria, VA 22314

National Tool, Die and Precision
  Machining Association
9300 Livingston Road
Washington, DC 20022

Newspaper Fund, Inc.
Box 300
Princeton, NJ 08540

Bibliography

Abbott, J., McClean, K., & Davidshofer, C. O. (1978). *Career development group: Leader's manual.* Fort Collins, CO: Colorado State University Counseling Center.

Abdel-Halim, A. A. (1981). Effects of role stress-job design — technology interact in employee work satisfaction. *Academy of Management Journal, 24*(2), 260–273.

Abdelnour, B. T., & Hall, D. T. (1980). Career development of established employees. *Career Development Bulletin, 2*(1), 5–8.

Abeles, R. P., Steel, L., & Wise, L. L. (1980). Patterns and implications of life-course organization: Studies from Project TALENT. In P. B. Baltes & O. G. Brim, Jr. (Eds.), *Life-span development and behavior* (pp. 308–339). New York: Academic Press.

Abrams, M. (1979). A new work sample battery for vocational assessment of the disadvantaged: VITAS. *Vocational Guidance Quarterly, 28*(1), 35–43.

ACES Position Paper. (1976). *Commission on counselor preparation for career development/career education.* Washington, DC: Association for Counselor Education and Supervision.

Adams, A. V., & Mangum, G. (1978). *The lingering crisis of youth unemployment.* Kalamazoo, MI: Upjohn Institute for Employment Research.

Adams, A. V., Mangum, G. & Lenninger, S. F. (1978). The nature of youth unemployment. In A. Adams and G. L. Mangum (Eds.), *The lingering crisis of youth unemployment* (pp. 1–13). Kalamazoo, MI: Upjohn Institute for Employment Research.

Adams, G. A. (1974). Preventative career counseling proving that it works. *Journal of College Placement, 34*(3), 26–33.

Adler, A. (1927). *The practice and theory of individual psychology.* New York: Harcourt.

Adler, A. (1935). The fundamental views of individual psychology. *International Journal of Individual Psychology, 1*, 5–8.

Advisory Council on Vocational Education. (1968). Vocational education: The bridge between man and his work. *Highlights and recommendations from the General Report.* Washington, DC: U.S. Office of Education.

Aging in America: Trials and triumphs. (1980). New York: Research and Forecast, Inc. (for Americana Health Care Corporation).

Aiken, J., & Johnston, J. (1973). Promoting career information-seeking behaviors in college students. *Journal of Vocational Behavior, 3*, 81–87.

Ainsworth, J., & Fifield, M. G. (1973, May). *Work simulation: An approach to vocational exploration.* Training paper, Logan, UT: Utah State University, Exceptional Child Center.

Alander, R., & Campbell, T. (1975). An evaluative study of an alcohol and drug recovery program: A case study of the Oldsmobile experience. *Human Resource Management, 14*, 14–18.

Allen, J. E., Jr. (1970, February). *Competence for all as the goal for secondary education.* Paper presented to the National Association of Secondary School Principals, Washington, DC.

Allen, L. R. (1980). Leisure and its relationship to work and career guidance. *Vocational Guidance Quarterly, 28*(3), 257–262.

Allen, R. E., & Keareny, T. J. (1980). The relative effectiveness of alternative job sources. *Journal of Vocational Behavior, 16*, 18–42.

Almquist, E. M. (1974). Sex stereotypes in occupational choice: The case for college women. *Journal of Vocational Behavior, 5*, 13–21.

Amara, R. (1978, December). *The U.S. in the decade ahead: An inventory of resources.* Speech presented to the American Vocational Association.

Amatea, E. S., & Cross, E. G. (1980). Going places: A career guidance program for high school students and their parents. *Vocational Guidance Quarterly, 28*(3), 274–282.

American Institute for Research. (1975). *Developing comprehensive career guidance programs.* Palo Alto, CA: AIR.

American Institute for Research in the Behavioral Sciences. (1981, August). Rapid feedback evaluation of the career education incentive act program (Phase II — Technical Report). Quoted in *Education and Work,* p. 3.

American Personnel and Guidance Association. (1975, March). *Career guidance: Role and functions of counseling and guidance practitioners in career education* (Position paper). Washington, DC: The Association.

American Psychological Association. (1974). *Standards for educational and psychological tests.* Washington, DC: APA.

American Psychological Association. (1979). Principles concerning the counseling and therapy of women. *The Counseling Psychologist, 8*(1), 21.

American School Counselors Association. (1977, August). *The unique role of the elementary school counselor* (Position paper adopted by ASCA Governing Board).

American School Counselors Association. (1977, August). *The unique role of the middle/junior high school counselor* (Position paper adopted by ASCA Governing Board).

American School Counselors Association. (1981). The practice of guidance and counseling by school counselors. *The School Counselor, 29*(1), 7-12.

Anderson, K. L. (1980). Educational goals of male and female adolescents: The effects of parental characteristics and attitudes. *Youth and Society, 12,* 173-188.

Aneshensel, C. W., & Rosen, B. C. (1980). Domestic roles and sex differences in occupational expectations. *Journal of Marriage and the Family, 42,* 121-131.

Angresano, J. (1980). Results of a survey of employer hiring practices. *Vocational Guidance Quarterly, 28*(4), 335-342.

Anguist, S. (1972). Changes in women's work aspirations during college. *International Journal of Sociology of the Family, 2,* 87-97.

Ansell, E. M., & Hansen, J. C. (1971). Patterns of vocational development in urban youth. *Journal of Counseling Psychology, 18,* 505-508.

Anthony, W. A. (1980). *The principles of psychiatric rehabilitation.* Baltimore: University Park Press.

Anthony, W. A., & Buell, G. (1974). Predicting psychiatric rehabilitation outcomes using demographic characteristics: A replication. *Journal of Counseling Psychology, 21*(5), 421-422.

Appel, V., Haak, R., & Witzke, D. (1970). Factors associated in the indecision about collegiate major and career choices. *Proceedings of the 78th Annual Convention of the American Psychological Association,* (5), 667-668.

Arbeiter, S., Aslanian, C. B., Schmerbeck, F. A., & Brickell, H. M. (1978). *40 million Americans in career transition: The need for information.* New York: College Entrance Examination Board.

Arbuckle, D. S. (1963). Occupational information in the elementary school. *Vocational Guidance Quarterly, 12,* 77-84.

Argeropoulos, J. (1981). *Burnout, stress management, and wellness.* Moravia, NY: Chronicle Guidance.

Armstrong, J. C. (1981). Decision behavior and outcomes of midlife career changes. *Vocational Guidance Quarterly, 29*(3), 205-211.

Arroba, T. (1977). Styles of decision-making and their use: An empirical study. *British Journal of Guidance and Counseling, 5*(2), 149-158.

Asbury, F. A. (1968). Vocational development of rural disadvantaged eighth grade boys. *Vocational Guidance Quarterly, 17,* 109-113.

Ash, K. S., & Mandelbaum, D. (1982). Using peer counselors in career development. *Journal of College Placement, 42*(3), 47-51.

Ashby, J. D., Wall, H. W., & Osipow, S. H. (1966). Vocational certainty and indecision in college freshmen. *Personnel and Guidance Journal, 44,* 1037-1041.

Ashley, W. L., Cellini, J., Faddis, C., Pearsol, J., Wiant, A., & Wright, B. (1980). *Adaptation to work: An exploration of processes and outcomes.* Columbus, OH: National Center for Research in Vocational Education, Ohio State University.

Aslanian, C. B., & Brickell, H. M. (1980). *Americans in transition: Life changes as reasons for adult learning.* New York: College Entrance Examination Board.

Association for Counselor Education and Supervision. (1976, April). *Position paper on counselor preparation for career development/career education.* Washington, DC: The Association.

Astin, H. S. (1967). Career development during the high school years. *Journal of Counseling Psychology, 14,* 94-98.

Astin, H. S., & Myint, T. (1971). Career development of young women during the post-high school years (Monograph). *Journal of Counseling Psychology, 18*(4), 369-393.

Atchley, R. C. (1976). *The sociology of retirement.* New York: Wiley.

Atchley, R. C. (1979). Issues in retirement research. *The Gerontologist, 19*(1), 44-54.

Atkinson, D. R., Morten, G., & Sue, D. W. (1983). *Counseling American minorities,* Dubuque, IA: William C. Brown.

Atlas, J. W. (1978). Career planning needs of unemployed minority persons. *Journal of Employment Counseling, 15*(4), 171-179.

Aubrey, R. G. (1977). *Career development needs of thirteen-year-olds: How to improve career development programs.* Washington, DC: National Advisory Council for Career Education.

Auster, C. J., & Auster, D. (1981). Factors influencing women's choice of nontraditional careers: The role of family, peers, and counselors. *Vocational Guidance Quarterly, 29,* 253-263.

Axelrod, W. L., & Gavin, J. F. (1980). Stress and strain in blue-collar and white-collar management staff. *Journal of Vocational Behavior, 17,* 41-49.

Ayres, M. E. (1979). Counseling Hispanic Americans. *Occupational Outlook Quarterly, 23,* 3-8.

Babcock, R. J., & Kaufman, M. A. (1976). Effectiveness of a career course. *Vocational Guidance Quarterly, 24*(3), 261-266.

Baca, P. M. (1980). Ex-P.O.: Exploring possible occupations. *The School Counselor, 28*(1), 54-58.

Bach, R. L. (1980). The new Cuban immigrants: Their background and prospects. *Monthly Labor Review, 103*(10), 39-46.

Bach, R. L., & Bach, J. B. (1980). Employment patterns of southeast Asian refugees. *Monthly Labor Review, 103*(10), 31-38.

Bachman, J. G., Kahn, R. L., Mednick, M., Davidson, T. N., & Johnston, L. D. (1970). *Youth in transition* (Vol. 2). Ann Arbor: University of Michigan, Institute for Social Research.

Backman, M. E., Lynch, J. J., & Loeding, D. J. (1979). Sex and ethnic differences in vocational aptitude patterns. *Measurement and Evaluation in Guidance, 12*(1), 35–43.

Bailey, L. J., & Stadt, R. (1973). *Career education: New approaches to human development.* Bloomington, IL: McKnight.

Bailey, R. C., & Bailey, K. G. (1971). Perceived ability in relation to actual ability and academic achievement. *Journal of Clinical Psychology, 27,* 461–463.

Baker, H. (1944). *Employee counseling.* Princeton, NJ: Princeton University Press.

Bamundo, P. J., & Kopelman, R. E. (1980). The moderating effects of occupation, age, and urbanization on the relationship between job satisfaction and life satisfaction. *Journal of Vocational Behavior, 17,* 106–123.

Banas, P., & Nash, A. (1966). Differential predictability: Selection of handicapped and nonhandicapped. *Personnel and Guidance Journal, 45,* 277–230.

Banducci, R. (1970). Accuracy of occupational stereotypes of grade twelve boys. *Journal of Counseling Psychology, 17,* 534–539.

Bandura, A. (1977). Self-efficacy: Toward a unifying theory of behavioral change. *Psychological Review, 84,* 191–215.

Bandura, A. (1982). The psychology of chance encounters and life paths. *The American Psychologist, 37*(7), 747–755.

Bandura, A., Adams, N. E., & Meyer, J. (1977). Cognitive processes mediating behavior change. *Journal of Personality and Social Psychology, 35,* 125–139.

Bank, I. M. (1969). Children explore careerland through vocational role models. *Vocational Guidance Quarterly, 17,* 284–289.

Barad, C. B. (1977). Developing and using an in-house interest inventory. *Personnel, 54,* 57–61.

Barak, A., & Friedkes, R. (1982). The mediating effects of career indecision subtypes on career counseling effectiveness. *Journal of Vocational Behavior, 20,* 120–128.

Barak, A., & Rabbi Ben-Zion. (1982). Predicting persistence, stability, and achievement in college by major choice consistency: A test of Holland's consistency hypothesis. *Journal of Vocational Behavior, 20,* 235–243.

Barbee, J. R., & Keil, E. C. (1973). Experimental techniques of job interview training for the disadvantaged: Videotape feedback behavior modification, and microcounseling. *Journal of Applied Psychology, 58,* 209–213.

Barnett, R. (1971). Personality correlates of vocational planning. *Genetic Psychology Monographs, 83,* 309–356.

Baron, A. S. (1977). Selection, development, and socialization of women into management. *Business Quarterly, 42*(4), 61–67.

Barrett, T., & Tinsley, H. (1977). Vocational self-concept crystallization and vocational indecision. *Journal of Counseling Psychology, 24,* 301–307.

Bartlett, W. E., & Oldham, D. (1978). Career adjustment counseling of "young-old" women. *Vocational Guidance Quarterly, 27*(2), 156–164.

Bartol, K. M. (1981). Vocational behavior and career development, 1980: A review. *Journal of Vocational Behavior, 18,* 123–162.

Bartsch, K., & Hackett, G. (1979). Effect of a decision-making course on locus of control, conceptualization, and career planning. *Journal of College Student Personnel, 20*(3), 230–235.

Baruch, G. K. (1972). Maternal influences upon college women's attitudes toward women and work. *Developmental Psychology, 6,* 32–37.

Basow, S. A., & Howe, K. G. (1979). Model influences on career choices of college students. *Vocational Guidance Quarterly, 27*(3), 239–243.

Baumgardner, S. R. (1977). Vocational planning: The great swindle. *Personnel and Guidance Journal, 56,* 17–22.

Bayer, A. E. (1972). *The Black college freshman: Characteristics and recent trends.* Washington, DC: American Council on Education.

Beane, A. L., & Zachmanoglou, M. A. (1979). Career education for the handicapped: A psychosocial impact. *Vocational Guidance Quarterly, 28*(1), 44–47.

Beard, J. H., Malamud, T. J., & Rossman, E. (1978). Psychiatric rehabilitation and long-term hospitalization rates: The findings of two research studies. *Schizophrenia Bulletin, 4,* 622–635.

Beck, C. E. (1963). *Philosophical foundations of guidance.* Englewood Cliffs, NJ: Prentice-Hall.

Becker, B. E., & Krzystojiak, F. J. (1982). The influence of labor market discrimination on locus on control. *Journal of Vocational Behavior, 21,* 60–70.

Beckman, L. J. (1978). The relative rewards and costs of parenthood and employment for employed women. *Psychology of Women Quarterly, 2*(3), 215–234.

Beley, W., & Felker, S. (1981). Comprehensive training evaluation for clients with psychiatric impairments. *Rehabilitation Literature, 42,* 194–201.

Bell, B. D. (1978). Life satisfaction and occupational retirement: Beyond the impact year. *International Journal of Aging and Human Development, 9*(1), 31–50.

Bem, S. L., & Bem, D. J. (1973). *Training the woman to know her place: The social antecedents of women in the world of work.* Harrisburg, PA: Pennsylvania Department of Education.

Bender, J. (1973). What is typical of assessment centers? *Personnel Journal, 50*(4), 50–57.

Bentler, P. M. (1980). Multivariate analysis with latent variables: Causal modeling. In M. R. Rosenzweig & L. W. Porter (Eds.), *The Annual View of Psychology* (Vol. 31). Palo Alto, CA: Annual Reviews.

Berdie, R. (1968). Personality changes from high school entrance to college matriculation. *Journal of Counseling Psychology, 15,* 376–380.

Berg, I. (1975). *Education and jobs: The great training robbery.* Boston: Beacon Press.

Bergland, B. W. (1974). Career planning: The use of sequential evaluated experience. In. E. L. Herr (Ed.), *Vocational guidance and human development* (pp. 350–380). Boston: Houghton Mifflin.

Bergland, B. W., & Krumboltz, J. D. (1969). An optimal grade level for career exploration. *Vocational Guidance Quarterly, 18,* 29-33.

Berman, E. (1980). *Re-entering.* New York: Crown.

Bernard, J. (1970). Women, marriage, and the future. *The Futurist, 4*(2), 41-43.

Bernard, J. (1981). The good provider role: Its rise and fall. *American Psychologist, 6*(1), 1-12.

Berry, E. (1979). Guidance and counseling in the elementary school. Its theoretical base. *The Personnel and Guidance, 57*(10), 513-520.

Betz, E. L. (1982). Need fulfillment in the career development of women. *Journal of Vocational Behavior, 20,* 53-66.

Betz, N. E., & Wolfe, L. K. (1981). Comparison of the utility of two approaches to sex-balanced interest scales for college women. *Journal of Vocational Behavior, 19,* 61-77.

Betz, R. L., Engle, K. B., & Mallinson, G. G. (1969). Perceptions of non-college-bound, vocationally oriented high school graduates. *Personnel and Guidance Journal, 47,* 988-994.

Beutell, N. J., & Greenhaus, J. H. (1982). Interrole conflict among married women: The influence of husband and wife characteristics on conflict and coping behavior. *Journal of Vocational Behavior, 21,* 99-110.

Bielby, D. D. V. (1978). Maternal employment and socioeconomic status as factors in daughters' career salience: Some substantive refinements. *Sex Roles, 4*(2), 249-265.

Bienstock, J. K. (1981). Reading and writing and the study of careers. *The College Board Review, 110,* 14-16.

Biggers, J. L. (1971). The use of information in vocational decision making. *Vocational Guidance Quarterly, 19*(3), 171-176.

Bigoness, W. J. (1978). Correlates of faculty attitudes toward collective bargaining. *Journal of Applied Psychology, 63*(2), 228-233.

Bird, C. (1975). *The case against college.* New York: David McKay.

Birk, J. M. (1974). Interest inventories: A mixed blessing. *Vocational Guidance Quarterly, 22*(4), 280-286.

Birk, J. M., Tanney, M. F., & Cooper, J. F. (1979). A case of blurred vision: Stereotyping in career information illustrations. *Journal of Vocational Behavior, 15,* 247-257.

Bjorkquist, D. C. (1970). Technical education for the underemployed and unemployed. *Vocational Guidance Quarterly,* 264-272.

Blai, B. (1982). Programs for older persons: A compendium. *Journal of Employment Counseling 19*(3), 98-105.

Blaikie, N. W. H. (1971). Towards a theoretical model for the study of occupational choice. *Sociology, 5,* 313-333.

Blank, J. R. (1979). Jobs-career key: A test of occupational information. *Vocational Guidance Quarterly, 28*(1), 6-17.

Blau, P. M., & Duncan, O. D. (1967). *The American occupational structure.* New York: Wiley.

Blau, P. M., Gustad, J. W., Jessor, R., Parnes, H. S., & Wilcock, R. C. (1956). Occupational choice: A conceptual framework. *Industrial Labor Relations* (rev. ed.), *9,* 531-543.

Blocher, D. (1966). Wanted: A science of human effectiveness. *Personnel and Guidance Journal, 44,* 729-733.

Blocher, K., & Rogers, J. (1977). Career development for the majority. *Journal of College Placement, 37*(1), 69-72.

Bloland, P. A., & Edwards, P. B. (1981). Work and leisure: A counseling synthesis. *Vocational Guidance Quarterly, 30*(2), 101-108.

Bloom, B. S., Engelhart, M. D., Furst, E. J., Hill, W. H., & Krathwohl, D. R. (1956). *Taxonomy of educational goals, handbook I: Cognitive domain.* New York: Longmans, Green.

Bocknek, G. (1976). A developmental approach to counseling adults. *The Counseling Psychologist, 6*(1), 37-40.

Bodden, J., & James, L. (1976). Influence of occupational information giving on cognitive complexity. *Journal of Counseling Psychology, 23,* 280-282.

Boese, R. R., & Cunningham, J. W. (1976). Systematically derived dimensions of human work. *JSAS Catalog of Selected Documents in Psychology, 6,* 57 (Ms. No. 1270).

Bohn, M. J., Jr. (1966). Vocational maturity and personality. *Vocational Guidance Quarterly, 15,* 123-126.

Boll, A. S., & Briggs, J. I. (1979). Informational interviewing: Easing the student's entry into the working world. *Journal of College Placement, 39*(2), 53-55.

Boocock, S. S. (1967). The life career game. *Personnel and Guidance Journal, 45* 328-334.

Boocock, S. S. (1968). *Instructor's manual for life career.* New York: Bobbs-Merrill.

Boocock, S. S., & Coleman, J. S. (1966). Games with simulated environments in learning. *Sociology of Education, 33,* 215-236.

Booth, A. (1977). Wife's employment and husband's stress: A replication and a reputation. *Journal of Marriage and the Family, 39,* 645-650.

Bordin, E. S. (1946). Diagnosis in counseling and psychotherapy. *Education and Psychological Measurement, 6,* 169-184.

Bordin, E. S. (1955). *Psychological counseling.* New York: Appleton-Century-Crofts.

Bordin, E. S., & Kopplin, D. A. (1973). Motivational conflict and vocational development. *Journal of counseling psychology, 20*(2), 154-161.

Bordin, E. S., Nachmann, B., & Segal, S. J. (1963). An articulated framework for vocational development. *Journal of Counseling Psychology, 10,* 107-116.

Borgen, F. H., Weiss, D. J., Tinsley, H. E. A., Dawis, R. V., & Lofquist, L. H. (1972). *Occupational reinforcer patterns: I.* Minneapolis, MI: Vocational Psychology Research, Department of Psychology.

Borman, C. (1972). Effects of reinforcement style of counseling on information-seeking behavior. *Journal of Vocational Behavior, 2,* 255–259.

Borow, H. (1961). Vocational development research: Some problems of logical and experimental form. *Personnel and Guidance Journal, 40,* 21–25.

Borow, H. (1970). Career development: A future for counseling. In W. Van Hoose & J. Pietrofesa (Eds.), *Counseling and guidance in the twentieth century* (pp. 30–46). Boston: Houghton Mifflin.

Borow, H. (1980). Career guidance uses of labor market information: Limitations and potentialities. In H. N. Drier and L. A. Pfister (Eds.), *Career and labor market information: Key to improved individual decision-making* (pp. 7–19). Columbus, OH: National Center for Research in Vocational Education.

Boston, B. (1980). Second-order dimensions of the Work Values Inventory (WVI). *Journal of Vocational Behavior, 17,* 33–40.

Boswell, J. (1981). The dual-career family: A model for egalitarian family politics. *Elementary School Guidance and Counseling, 15*(3), 262–269.

Bottoms, J. R., & Matheney, K. (1969, March). *Occupational guidance, counseling, and job placement for junior high and secondary school youth.* Paper presented at the National Conference of Exemplary Programs and Projects Section of the Vocational Education Act, Amendment of 1968, Atlanta, Georgia.

Bowlby, J. A. (1958). The nature of the child's tie to his mother. *International Journal of Psychoanalysis, 39,* 350–373.

Boy, A. V., & Pine, G. J. (1963). *Client-centered counseling in the secondary school.* Boston: Houghton Mifflin.

Bradburn, N. M. (1963). The cultural context of personality theory. In J. M. Nepman and R. W. Heine (Eds.), *Concepts of personality.* Chicago: Aldine.

Bradley, R. W. (1978). Person-referenced test interpretation: A learning process. *Measurement and Evaluation in Guidance, 10*(4), 201–210.

Bramel, D., & Friend, R. (1981). Hawthorne, the myth of the docile worker, and class bias in psychology. *The American Psychologist, 36*(8), 867–878.

Brammer, L. M., & Shostrom, E. L. (1960). *Therapeutic Psychology.* Englewood Cliffs, NJ: Prentice-Hall.

Brass, D. J. (1981). Structural relationships, job characteristics, and worker satisfaction and performance. *Administrative Science Quarterly, 26*(3), 331–348.

Braude, L. (1975). *Work and workers: A sociological perspective.* New York: Praeger.

Braun, J. S., & Bayer, F. (1973). Social desirability of occupations revisited. *Vocational Guidance Quarterly, 21,* 202–205.

Brayfield, A. H., & Crites, J. O. (1964). Research on vocational guidance: Status and prospect. In H. Borow (Ed.), *Man in a world of work* (pp. 310–340). Boston: Houghton Mifflin.

Breed, W. (1963). Occupational mobility and suicide among white males. *American Journal of Sociology, 28*(2), 179–188.

Breme, F. J., & Cockriel, I. W. (1975). Work values and work interests: Are they the same? *Journal of Vocational Behavior, 6,* 331–336.

Brenner, D., & Gazda-Grace, P. A. (1979). Career decision-making in women as a function of sex composition of career-planning groups. *Measurement and Evaluation in Guidance, 12*(1), 8–13.

Brenner, M. H. (1973). *Mental illness and the economy.* Cambridge: Harvard University Press.

Brill, A. A. (1948). *Psychoanalytic psychiatry.* London: John Lehman.

Brim, O. G., Jr. (1976). Theories of male mid-life crisis. *The Counseling Psychologist, 6*(1), 2–9.

Brito, P. K., & Jusenius, C. L. (1978). A note on young women's occupational expectations for age 35. *Vocational Guidance Quarterly, 27*(2), 165–175.

Brolin, D. E. (1975). Agency settings for career guidance. *Personnel and Guidance Journal, 53*(9), 686–690.

Brolin, D. E., & Gysbers, N. C. (1979). Career education for persons with handicaps. *Personnel and Guidance Journal, 58*(4), 258–262.

Bross, I. D. (1953). *Design for decision.* New York: MacMillan.

Brough, J. R. (1969). A profile of junior high school counseling. *The School Counselor, 17,* 67–72.

Brown, C. W., & Ghiselli, E. E. (1952). The relationship between the predictive power of aptitude tests for trainability and for job proficiency. *Journal of Applied Psychology, 37,* 370–372.

Brown, D. (1981). Emerging models of career development groups for persons at midlife. *Vocational Guidance Quarterly, 29*(4), 332–340.

Brown, D., & Feit, S. S. (1978). Making job placement work. *Vocational Guidance Quarterly, 27*(2), 176–183.

Brown, D. A. (1980). Life-planning workshop for high school students. *The School Counselor, 29*(1), 77–83.

Brown, G. S., & Strange, C. (1981). The relationship of academic major and career choice status to anxiety among college freshmen. *Journal of Vocational Behavior, 19,* 328–334.

Brown, J., & Koltveit, T. (1977). Individual assessment: A systematic approach. *Personnel and Guidance Journal, 55*(5), 271–276.

Brown, J. H., & Brown, C. S. (1977). *Systematic counseling: A guide for the practitioner.* Champaign, IL: Research Press.

Brown, S. J. (1975). Career planning inventories: "Do-it-yourself" won't do. *Personnel and Guidance Journal, 53,* 512–517.

Bruch, M. A., & Krieshok, T. S. (1981). Investigative versus realistic Holland types and adjustment in theoretical engineering majors. *Journal of Vocational Behavior, 18,* 162–173.

Brugnoli, G. A., Campion, J. E., & Basen, J. A. (1979). Racial bias in the use of work samples for personnel selection. *Journal of Applied Psychology, 64*(2), 119–123.

Bruner, J. (1973). Continuity of learning. *Saturday Review of Education, 1* (2), 21-24.

Brunkan, R. (1965). Perceived parental attitudes and parental identification in relation to field of vocational choice. *Journal of Counseling Psychology, 12,* 39-47.

Brunkan, R., & Crites, J. O. (1964). An inventory to measure the parental attitude variable in Roe's theory of vocational choice. *Journal of Counseling Psychology, 11,* 3-11.

Bryson, R. B., Bryson, J. B., Licht, M. H., Licht, B. G. (1976). The professional pair: Husband and wife psychologists. *The American Psychologist, 31*(1), 10-16.

Buckingham, L. & Lee, A. M. (1973). *Placement and follow-up in career education.* Raleigh, NC: Center for Occupational Education, North Carolina State University.

Buehler, C. (1933). *Der menschliche lebenslauf als psychologisches problem.* Leipzig: Hirzel.

Bunda, R., & Mezzano, J. (1968). A study of the effects of a work-experience program on performance of potential dropouts. *The School Counselor, 15,* 272-274.

Burack, E. H. (1977). Why all of the confusion about career planning? *Human Resources Management,* 21-23.

Burack, E. H., & Mathys, N. J. (1980). *Career management in organizations: A practical human resources planning approach.* Lake Forest, IL: Brace-Park Press.

Burdetsky, B. (1976). Troubled transition: From school to work. *Worklife, 1*(11), 2-6.

Burke, R. J., & Weir, T. (1976). Some personality differences between members of one-career and two-career families. *Journal of Marriage and the Family, 38*(3), 453-459.

Burke, R. J., & Weir, T. (1978). Maternal employment status, social support, and adolescents' well-being. *Psychological Reports, 42,* 1159-1170.

Burkhauser, R. V., & Tolley, G. S. (1978). Older Americans and market work. *The Gerontologist, 8*(5), 449-453.

Burnstein, E. (1963). Fear of failure, achievement motivation, and aspiriing to prestigeful occupations. *Journal of Abnormal and Social Psychology, 67,* 189-193.

Burr, P. L. (1980). Women: The emerging labor force. In C. S. Sheppard & D. C. Carroll (Eds.), *Working in the twenty-first century* (pp. 98-105). New York: Wiley.

Burtnett, F. E. (Ed.). (1980). *The school counselor's involvement in career education.* Falls Church, VA: APGA press.

Butler, M., & Paisley, W. (1977). Status of professional couples in psychology. *Psychology of Women Quarterly, 1*(4), 307-318.

Butler, R. N. (1975). *Why survive? Being old in America.* New York: Harper and Row.

Byham, W. C. (1982). Applying a systems approach to personnel activities. *Training and Development Journal, 36,* 70-75.

Byrne, R. H. (1975). Proposed revisions of the Borden-Pepinsky Diagnostic Constructs. *Journal of Counseling Psychology, 5,* 184-187.

Calhoun, R. E. (1980). The new work ethic. *Training and Development Journal, 34,* 127-130.

California State Department of Education. (1972). *Identification of major occupational groups and entry level jobs in civilian public service.* Sacramento, CA: The Department.

Campbell, D. P., Crichton, L., Hansen, J. L., & Webber, P. (1974). A new edition of the SVIB: The Strong-Campbell interest inventory. *Measurement and Evaluation in Guidance, 7,* 92-95.

Campbell, D. P., & Holland, J. L. (1972). A merger in vocational interest research: Applying Holland's theory to Strong's data. *Journal of Vocational Behavior, 2,* 353-376.

Campbell, R. E. (1968). *Vocational guidance in secondary education: A national survey.* Columbus, OH: The Center for Vocational Education.

Campbell, R. E., & Cellini, J. V. (1981). A diagnostic taxonomy of adult career problems. *Journal of Vocational Behavior, 19*(2), 175-190.

Campbell, R. E., & Parsons, J. L. (1972). Readiness for vocational planning in junior high school: A socioeconomic and geographic comparison. *Journal of Vocational Behavior, 2,* 401-417.

Campbell, R. E., Suzuki, W. N., & Gabria, M. J., Jr. (1972). A procedural model for upgrading career guidance programs. *American Vocational Journal, 47*(1), 101-103.

Caplow, T. (1954). *The sociology of work.* Minneapolis: University of Minnesota Press.

Caplow, T. (1976). *Principles of organization.* New York: Harcourt, Brace Jovanovich.

Cappeto, M. A. (1977). Liberal arts versus business administration. *Journal of College Placement, 37*(1), 37-39.

Card, J. J., Steel, L., & Abeles, R. P. (1980). Sex differences in realization of individual potential for achievement. *Journal of Vocational Behavior, 17,* 1-21.

Career development activities: (1979). Practices, focuses, concerns. *Career Development Bulletin, 1*(1), 5-14.

Career Guidance, Counseling, and Placement Project. (1973). *Elements of an illustrative guide, career guidance, counseling and placement for state department of education.* Columbia, MO: University of Missouri-Columbia.

Carey, M. L. (1980). Evaluating the 1975 projections of occupational employment. *Monthly Labor Review, 103,* 10-12.

Carey, M. L. (1981a). Three paths to the future: Occupational projections, 1980-90. *Occupational Outlook Quarterly, 25*(4), 3-11.

Carey, M. L. (1981b). Occupational employment growth through 1990. *Monthly Labor Review, 104,* 42-55.

Carkhuff, R. R. (1983). *The art of helping* (5th ed.). Amherst, MA: Human Resources Development Press.

Carney, C. G., & Barak, A. (1976). A survey of student needs and student personnel services. *Journal of College Student Personnel, 17,* 280-284.

Carter, H. D. (1940). The development of vocational attitudes. *Journal of Consulting Psychology, 4,* 185–191.

Cass, J. C., & Tiedeman, D. V. (1960). Vocational development and the election of a high school curriculum. *Personnel and Guidance Journal, 38,* 538–545.

Cassel, R. N., & Mehail, T. (1973). The Milwaukee computerized vocational guidance system (VOCGUID). *Vocational Guidance Quarterly, 21,* 206–213.

Cassie, J. R. B. (1976). *An assessment of the effects of a computer-assisted career maturity of Ontario students in grades nine, ten, and eleven.* Ph.D. dissertation, State University of New York at Buffalo.

Cedoline, A. J. (1982). *Job burnout in public education: Symptoms, causes, and survival skills.* New York: Teachers College Press.

Cellarius, R., & Platt, J. (1972). Classification of crisis research studies by project areas. In R. Theobald (Ed.), *Futures conditional* (pp. 336–346). Indianapolis: Bobbs-Merrill.

Centers, R. (1949). *Psychology of social class.* Princeton, NJ: Princeton University Press.

Cesari, J. P., Winer, J. L., Zychlinski, F., & Laird, I. O. (1982). Influence of occupational information giving on cognitive complexity in decided versus undecided students. *Journal of Vocational Behavior, 21,* 224–230.

Chansky, N. M. (1965). Race, aptitude and vocational interests. *Personnel and Guidance Journal, 43,* 783–784.

Chapman, W., & Katz, M. R. (1981). *Survey of career information systems in secondary schools: Final report of study.* Princeton, NJ: Educational Testing Service.

Cheloha, R. S., & Farr, J. L. (1980). Absenteeism, job involvement, and job satisfaction in an organizational setting. *Journal of Applied Psychology, 65,* 467–473.

Cherichello, F. J., & Gillian, C. (1980). An alumni panel: A component for National Career Guidance Week at Essex. *Journal of College Student Personnel, 21,* 170.

Cherniss, C. (1980a). *Staff burnout: Job stress in the human services.* Beverly Hills, CA: Sage Publications.

Cherniss, C. (1980b). *Professional burnout in human service organizations.* New York: Praeger.

Cherryholmes, C. (1966). Some current research on effectiveness of educational simulations: Some implications for alternative strategies. *American Behavioral Scientist, 10,* 4–7.

Chervenik, E., Nord, D., & Aldridge, M. (1982). Putting career planning and placement together. *Journal of College Placement, 42*(2), 48–51.

Chiko, C. H., Tolsma, R. J., Kahn, S. E., & Marks, S. E. (1980). A model to systematize compentencies in counselor education. *Counselor Education and Supervision, 19*(4), 283–292.

Christensen, K. C., Gelso, C. J., Williams, R. O., & Sedlacek, W. E. (1975). Variations in the administration of the self-directed search, scoring accuracy, and satisfaction with results. *Journal of Counseling Psychology, 22,* 12–16.

Christy, P. T., & Horowitz, K. J. (1979). An evaluation of BLS projections of 1975 production and employment. *Monthly Labor Review, 102,* 8–19.

Ciardello, J. A., & Bingham, W. C. (1982). The career maturity of schizophrenic clients. *Rehabilitation Counseling Bulletin, 26*(2), 3–9.

Circle, D. F., Clemens, D. B., Kroll, A. M., & Overholt, D. C. (1968). *Career information service.* Boston: Department of Education, Commonwealth of Massachusetts.

Clack, R. J. (1968). Occupational prestige and vocational choice. *Vocational Guidance Quarterly, 16,* 282–286.

Clark, A. K. (1975). Career entry skills gap in the guidance chain. *Canadian Counselor, 9*(2), 126–131.

Clark, A. M., & Seals, J. M. (1975). Student perceptions of the social status of careers for college graduates. *Journal of College Student Personnel, 16*(4), 293–298.

Clark, B. R., & Trow, M. (1966). The organizational context. In T. M. Newcomb & E. K. Wilson (Eds.), *College peer groups.* Chicago: Aldine.

Clark, E. T. (1967). Influence of sex and social class on occupational preference and perception. *Personnel and Guidance Journal, 45,* 440–444.

Clarke, R., Gelatt, H. B., & Levine, L. (1965). A decision-making paradigm for local guidance research. *Personnel and Guidance Journal, 44,* 40–51.

Cleveland, H., Orr, W., et al. (1975). The young manager: Is career planning a useless exercise? *Advanced Management Journal, 40,* 52–62.

Clopton, W. (1973). Personality and career change. *Industrial Gerontology, 17*(2), 9–17.

Cochran, D. J., Hetherington, C., & Strand, K. H. (1980). Career choice class: Caviar or caveat? *Journal of College Student Personnel, 21,* 402–406.

Cochran, D., Hoffman, S., Strand, K., & Warren, P. (1977). Effects of client/computer interaction in career decision-making processes. *Journal of Counseling Psychology, 24,* 308–312.

Cohen, B. S. (1977). *Career development in industry: A study of selected programs and recommendations for program planning.* Princeton, NJ: Educational Testing Service.

Cohn, A. E. (1972). *Achievement motivation.* Corning, NY: Corning Community College.

Cohn, R. M. (1979). Age and the satisfaction from work. *Journal of Gerontology, 34*(2), 264–272.

Coleman, J. S. (1972). How do the young become adults? *Review of Educational Research, 42.*

Coleman, J. S. (1974). *Youth: Transition to adulthood.* Chicago: University of Chicago Press.

Collin, A. (1979). Mid-life crisis and its implications in counseling. *British Journal of Guidance and Counseling, 7*(2), 144–152.

Collins, J., Reardon, M., & Waters, L. K. (1980). Occupational interest and perceived personal success: Effects of gender, sex-role orientation, and the sexual composition of the occupation. *Psychological Reports, 47,* 1155–1159.

Comas, R. E., & Day, R. W. (1976). College students explore careers. *Vocational Guidance Quarterly, 25*(1), 76–79.

Connelly, S. L. (1979). Career development: Are we asking the right questions? *Training and Development Journal, 33*(3), 8–12.

Conyne, R. K., & Cochran, D. J. (1973). Academia and career development: Toward integration. *Personnel and Guidance Journal, 52,* 217–223.

Cook, J. D., Hepworth, S. J., Wall, T., & Warr, P. B. (Eds.). (1981). *The experience of work.* New York: Academic Press.

Cook, H. E. (1968). Vocational guidance materials: A survey for teachers. *American Vocational Journal, 13,* 25–28.

Cooker, P. G. (1973). Vocational values of children in grades four, five, and six. *Elementary School Guidance and Counseling, 8*(12), 112–118.

Cooley, W. W. (1964). Research frontier: Current research on the career development of scientists. *Journal of Counseling Psychology, 11,* 88–93.

Cooley, W. W. (1969). Computer systems for guidance. In *Computer-based vocational guidance systems* (pp. 61–71). Washington, DC: U.S. Government Printing Office.

Cooper C. L., & Marshall, J. (1976). Occupational sources of stress: A review of the literature relative to coronary heart disease and mental ill health. *Journal of Occupational Psychology, 49,* 11–28.

Cooper, C. L., & Marshall, J. (1980). *White collar and professional stress.* New York: Wiley.

Costello, T. W., & Zalkind, S. S. (Eds.), (1963). *Psychology in administration: A research orientation.* Englewood Cliffs, NJ: Prentice-Hall.

Counts, G. S. (1925). Social status of occupations. *School Review, 33,* 16–27.

Craft, J. A., Doctors, S. I., Shkop, Y. M., & Benecki, T. J. (1979). Simulated management perceptions, hiring decisions, and age. *Aging and Work, 2*(2), 95–102.

Cramer, J. C. (1980). Fertility and female employment: Problems of causal direction. *American Sociological Review, 45,* 167–190.

Cramer, S. H., Herr, E. L., Morris, C. N., & Frantz, T. T. (1970). *Research and the school counselor.* Boston: Houghton Mifflin.

Cramer, S. H., Wise, P. S., & Colburn, E. D. (1977). An evaluation of treatment to expand the career perceptions of high school girls. *The School Counselor, 25,* 125–129.

Crawford, L. (1976). Imperatives regarding placement services in secondary schools. In T. H. Hohenshil (Ed.), *New dimensions in placement services.* Blacksburg, VA: VPI and State University, 16–28.

Creason, F., & Schilson, D. L. (1970). Occupational concerns of sixth-grade-children. *Vocational Guidance Quarterly, 18,* 219–224.

Cremin, L. A. (1961). *The transformation of the school.* New York: Alfred Knopf.

Crites, J. O. (1961). A model for the measurement of vocational maturity. *Journal of Counseling Psychology, 8,* 255–259.

Crites, J. O. (1962). An interpersonal relations scale for occupational groups. *Journal of Applied Psychology, 46,* 87–90.

Crites, J. O. (1965). Measurement of vocational maturity in adolescence: Attitude test of the vocational development inventory. *Psychological Monographs, 79, (1, Whole No. 595).*

Crites, J. O. (1969). *Vocational psychology.* New York: McGraw-Hill.

Crites, J. O. (1973). *Career maturity inventory.* Monterey, CA: California Test Bureau/McGraw-Hill.

Crites, J. O. (1974a). Career development processes: A model for vocational maturity. In E. L. Herr (Ed.), *Vocational guidance and human development* (pp. 296–320). Boston: Houghton Mifflin.

Crites, J. O. (1974b). Methodological issues in the measurement of career maturity. *Measurement and Evaluation in Guidance, 6,* 200–209.

Crites, J. O. (1974c). Problems in the measurement of vocational maturity. *Journal of Vocational Behavior, 4,* 25–31.

Crites, J. O. (1974d). A reappraisal of vocational appraisal. *Vocational Guidance Quarterly, 22*(4), 272–279.

Crites, J. O. (1976). A comprehensive model of career development in early adulthood. *Journal of Vocational Behavior, 9,* 105–118.

Crites, J. O. (1978). *Theory and research handbook for the career maturity inventory.* Monterey, CA: CTB/McGraw-Hill.

Crites, J. O. (1981). *Career counseling: Models, methods, and materials.* New York: McGraw-Hill.

Crites, J. O., & Semler, I. J. (1967). Adjustment, educational achievement, and vocational maturity as dimensions of development in adolescence. *Journal of Counseling Psychology, 14,* 489–496.

Cronbach, L. J. (1970). *Essentials of psychological testing* (3rd ed.). New York: Harper & Row.

Cronbach, L. J. (1979). The Armed Services Vocational Aptitude Battery – A test battery in transition. *Personnel and Guidance Journal, 57*(5), 232–237.

Cronbach, L. J., & Glaser, G. C. (1957). *Psychological tests and personnel decision* (2nd ed.). Urbana, IL: University of Illinois Press.

Csikszentmihalyi, M. (1975). *Beyond boredom and anxiety.* San Francisco: Jossey-Baas.

Cummings, N. A. (1977). The anatomy of psychotherapy under national health insurance. *American Psychologist, 32*(9), 711–718.

Cummings, S. (1980). White ethnics, racial prejudice, and labor market segmentation. *American Journal of Sociology, 86,* 938–950.

Cunningham, J. W. (1969). *The cluster concept and its curricular implications.* Center Monograph No. 4. Raleigh, NC: Center for Occupational Education.

Cytrynbaum, S., Ginath, Y., Birdwell, J., & Brandt, C. (1979). Goal attainment scaling. *Evaluation Quarterly, 3,* 5–40.

Daane, C. J. (1971). *Vocational exploration group* (3rd ed.). Leader manual. Tempe, AZ: Studies for Urban Man.

Dale, E. (1954). *Audio-visual methods in teaching.* New York: Dryden Press.

Daley, M. R. (1979). Burnout: Smoldering problem in protective services. *Social Work, 24,* 375–379.

D'Alonzo, C. A., & Fleming, A. J. (1973). Occupational

psychiatry through the medical periscope. In R. L. Noland (Ed.), *Industrial mental health and employee counseling.* New York: Behavioral Publications, 160–167.

Dalton, G., Thompston, P., & Price, R. (1977). Career stages: A model of professional careers in organizations. *Organizational Dynamics, 6,* 19–42.

Daniels, M. H. (1982). The heuristic value of Harren's career decision-making model for practitioners. *Journal of College Student Personnel, 23*(1), 18–24.

Danish, S. J. (1981). Life-span human development and intervention: A necessary link. *The Counseling Psychologist, 9*(2), 40–43.

Darcy, R. L. (1969). Manpower in a changing curriculum. *American Vocational Journal, 44*(3), 57–60.

Davidshofer, C. O. (1976). Risk-taking and vocational choice: A re-evaluation. *Journal of Counseling Psychology, 23*(2), 151–154.

Davidson, D., Suppes, P., & Siegel, S. (1957). *Decision-making: An experimental approach.* Stanford, CA: Stanford University Press.

Davis, E. (1979). Changing priorities for mental health. In I. Robinault & M. Weisinger (Eds.), *Mobilization of community resources* (3rd ed.). New York: ICD Rehabilitation and Research Center.

Davis, P. A., Hagen, N., & Strouf, J. (1962). Occupational choice of twelve-year-olds. *Personnel and Guidance Journal, 40,* 628–629.

Dawis, R. V., & Lofquist, L. H. (1978). A note on the dynamics of work adjustment. *Journal of Vocational Behavior, 12,* 76–79.

Dawis, R. V., Lofquist, L. H., Henly, G. A., & Rounds, J. B., Jr. (1979). *Minnesota Occupational Classification System II (MOCS II).* Minneapolis: Vocational Psychology Research Work Adjustment Project.

Day, S. R. (1966). Teacher influence on the occupational preferences of high school students. *Vocational Guidance Quarterly, 14,* 215–219.

Dearman, N. B., & Plisko, V. W. (1981). *The condition of education* (1980 edition). Washington, DC: National Center for Educational Statistics.

Deeg, M. E., & Paterson, D. G. (1947). Changes in social status of occupations. *Occupations, 25,* 205–208.

DeFreitas, G. E. (1981). What is the occupational mobility of black immigrants? *Monthly Labor Review, 104,* 44–45.

Dellas, M., Gaier, E. L., & Emihovich, C. A. (1979). Maternal employment and selected behaviors and attitudes of preadolescents and adolescents. *Adolescence, 14,* 579–589.

DeNisi, A. S., & Shaw, J. B. (1977). Investigation of the uses of self-reports of abilities. *Journal of Applied Psychology, 62,* 641–644.

Derr, C. B. (1980). More about career anchors. In C. B. Derr (Ed.), *Work, family, and the career.* New York: Praeger, 166–187.

Dewey, J. (1931). *Democracy and education.* New York: Macmillan.

Dewey, J. (1956). *School and society.* Chicago, IL: University of Chicago Press. (Originally published, 1900).

Diamond, E. (Ed.). (1975). *Issues of sex bias and sex fairness in career interest measurement.* Washington, DC: National Institute of Education.

Dickson, P. (1977). *The future file.* New York: Rawson Associates.

Dillard, J. M. (1976). Socioeconomic background and the career maturity of black youths. *Vocational Guidance Quarterly, 25*(1), 65–70.

Dillard, J. M. (1980). Some unique career behavior characteristics of blacks: Career theories, counseling practice, and research. *Journal of Employment Counseling, 17*(2), 288–298.

Dillard, J. M. (1982). Life satisfaction of nearly retired workers. *Journal of Employment Counseling, 19*(3), 131–134.

Dillard, J. M., & Campbell, N. J. (1981). Influences of Puerto Rican, black, and Anglo parents' career behavior in their adolescent children's career development. *Vocational Guidance Quarterly, 30*(2), 129–148.

Dilley, J. S. (1967). Decision-making: A dilemma and a purpose for counseling. *Personnel and Guidance Journal, 45,* 547–551.

DiPrete, T. A. (1981). Unemployment over the life cycle: Racial differences and the effect of changing economic conditions. *American Journal of Sociology, 87*(2), 286–307.

District of Columbia Schools. (1976). *Career education in the inner city.* Interdisciplinary curriculum, grades 1–6. Washington, DC: The Schools.

Division 17, Education and Training Committee. (1982). A position paper: Cross-cultural counseling competencies. *The Counseling Psychologist, 10*(2), 45–52.

Dixon, D. N., & Claiborn, C. D. (1981). Effects of need and commitment on career exploration behaviors. *Journal of Counseling Psychology, 28*(5), 411–415.

Doane, C. J. (1971). *Vocational exploration group* (3rd ed.). *Leader Manual.* Tempe, AZ: Studies for Urban Man.

Doeringer, P. B., & Piore, M. J. (1971). *Internal labor markets and manpower analysis.* Lexington, MA: Lexington Books.

Doty, M., & Betz, N. E. (1979). Comparison of the concurrent validity of Holland's theory for men and women in an enterprising occupation. *Journal of Vocational Behavior, 15,* 207–216.

Drasgow, J., & Carkhuff, R. R. (1964). Kuder neuropsychiatric keys before and after psychotherapy. *Journal of Counseling Psychology, 11,* 67–69.

Dreher, G. F. (1980). Individual needs as correlates of satisfaction and involvement with a modified Scanlon Plan company. *Journal of Vocational Behavior, 17,* 89–94.

Drier, H. N. (1971, June). Implementing career development programs in high schools. Paper presented at the Workshop on the Development of Guidelines for Planning Career Development Programs, K–12. Columbus, Ohio.

Drier, H. N. (1980). Career information for youth in transition: The need, system, and models. *Vocational Guidance Quarterly, 29*(2), 135–143.

Droege, R. C., & Padgett, A. (1979). Development of an interest-oriented occupational classification system. *Vocational Guidance Quarterly, 27*(4), 302–310.

Drucker, P. F. (1969). *The age of discontinuity: Guidelines to our changing society.* New York: Harper & Row.

Drucker, P. F. (1982). *The changing world of the executive.* New York: Truman Talley.

Drummond, R. J., McIntire, W. G., & Skaggs, C. T. (1978). The relationship of work values to occupational level in young adult workers. *Journal of Employment Counseling, 15*(3), 117–121.

Ducat, D. E. (1980). Cooperative education, career exploration, and occupational concepts for community college students. *Journal of Vocational Behavior, 17,* 195–203.

Dudley, G. A., & Tiedeman, D. V. (1977). *Career development, exploration and commitment.* Muncie, IN: Accelerated Development.

Dunham, J. R., & Dunham, C. S. (1978). Psychosocial aspects of disability, in R. M. Goldenson (Ed.), *Disability and rehabilitation handbook.* New York: McGraw-Hill.

Dunlop, K. H. (1981). Maternal employment and child care. *Professional Psychology, 12*(1), 67–75.

Dunne, F., Elliott, R., & Carlsen, W. S. (1981). Sex differences in the educational and occupational aspirations of rural youth. *Journal of Vocational Behavior, 18,* 56–66.

Dwight, A. H. (1979). Public relations design for college career counseling services. *Personnel and Guidance Journal, 58,* 205–207.

Echols, F. H. (1971). Rehabilitation counselor's responsibility for placement. *Journal of Applied Rehabilitation Counseling, 3*(2), 72–75.

Eckerdt, D. J., Bosse, R., & Mogery, J. M. (1980). Concurrent change in planned and preferred age for retirement. *Journal of Gerontology, 35*(2), 232–240.

Edelwich, J., & Brodsky, A. (1980). *Burnout: Stages of disillusionment in the helping professionals.* New York: Human Sciences Press.

Edward, P. B. (1980). *Leisure counseling techniques, individual and group counseling step by step.* Los Angeles, CA: Constructive Leisure.

Eggeman, D. F., Campbell, R. E., & Garbin, A. P. (1969, December). *Problems in the transition from school to work as perceived by youth opportunity center counselors.* Columbus, OH: Center for Vocational and Technical Education, Ohio State University.

Elleson, V. J., & Onnink, A. G. (1976). Jobs Inc., In-school career education/experience. *Elementary School Guidance and Counseling, 10*(4), 290–292.

Elliott, E. D. (1973). Effects of female role models on occupational aspiration levels of college freshman women. *Dissertation Abstracts International, 34,* 1075a.

Ellis, A. (1962). *Reason and emotion in psychotherapy.* Secaucus, NJ: Lyle Stuart.

Ellis, L. (1976). America's convicts: How to let them go. *Offender Rehabilitation, 1*(1), 5–15.

Elton, C. F. (1967). Male career role and vocational choice: Their prediction with personality and aptitude variables. *Journal of Counseling Psychology, 14,* 99–105.

Emener, W. G., & Rubin, S. E. (1980). Rehabilitation counselor roles and functions and sources of role strain. *Journal of Applied Rehabilitation Counseling, 11*(2), 57–69.

Employment and Training Administration, U. S. Department of Labor. (1980). *Self-directed job search: An introduction.* Washington, DC: The Department.

Enderlein, T. E. (1974). *Causal relationships of student characteristics related to satisfaction in post high school employment.* Unpublished doctoral dissertation, Pennsylvania State University.

Enderlein, T. E. (1975). Causal patterns related to post high school employment satisfaction. *Journal of Vocational Behavior, 7,* 67–80.

Endicott, F. S. (1965; 1975). *The Endicott Report.* Evanston, IL: Northwestern University.

Eng, J. E., & Gottsdanker, J. S. (1979). Positive changes from a career development program. *Training and Development Journal, 33*(1), 3–7.

Entine, A. (1977). Counseling for mid-life and beyond. *Vocational Guidance Quarterly, 24*(4), 332–336.

Entrekin, L. V., & Everett, J. E. (1981). Age and mid-career crisis: An empirical study of academics. *Journal of Vocational Behavior, 19*(1), 84–97.

Entwisle, D. R., & Greenberger, E. (1972). Adolescents' views of women's work role. *American Journal of Orthopsychiatry, 42*(4), 648–656.

Epstein, C. F. (1971). Law partners and marital partners. *Human Relations, 24*(6), 549–564.

Erez, M., & Shneorson, Z. (1980). Personality types and motivational characteristics of academics versus professionals in industry in the same occupational disciplines. *Journal of Vocational Behavior, 17,* 95–105.

Erickson, R. J. (1980). The changing workplace and workforce. *Training and Development Journal, 34,* 62–65.

Erikson, E. H. (1950). *Childhood and society.* New York: Norton.

Erikson, E. H. (1963). *Childhood and society* (2nd ed.). New York: Norton.

Ermalinski, R., & Ruscelli, V. (1971). Incorporation of values by lower and middle socioeconomic class preschool boys. *Child Development, 42,* 629–632.

Erwin, T. D. (1982). The predictive validity of Holland's construct of consistency. *Journal of Vocational Behavior, 20,* 180–182.

Etaugh, C. (1974). Effects of maternal employment on children: A review of recent research *Merrill-Palmer Quarterly of Behavior and Development, 29*(2), 71–98.

Etaugh, C. (1980). Effects of nonmaternal care on children: Research evidence and popular views. *American Psychologist, 35*(4), 309–319.

Evans, J., & Rector, A. (1978). Evaluation of a college course in career decision-making. *Journal of College Student Personnel, 19,* 163–169.

Evans, J. R., & Cody, J. J. (1969). Transfer of decision-making skills learned in a counseling-like setting to similar and dissimilar situations. *Journal of Counseling Psychology, 16,* 427–432.

Evans, R. N., & Herr, E. L. (1978). *Foundations of voca-

tional education (2nd ed.). Columbus, OH: Charles E. Merrill.

Fain, T. S. (1980). Self-employed Americans: Their number has increased. *Monthly Labor Review, 103,* 3–8.

Farber, B. A., & Heifetz, L. J. (1981). The satisfaction and stresses of psychotherapeutic work: A factor analytic study. *Professional Psychology, 12*(5), 621–630.

Farmer, H. S. (1976). What inhibits achievement and career motivation in women. *The Counseling Psychologist, 6,* 12–14.

Farmer, H. S. (1980). Environmental, background, and psychological variables related to optimizing achievement and career motivation for high school girls. *Journal of Vocational Behavior, 17,* 58–70.

Farrell, M. P., & Rosenberg, S. D. (1981). *Men at midlife.* Boston: Auburn House.

Faunce, P. (1971). Vocational interests of high ability college women. *Journal of College Student Personnel, 12,* 430–431.

Faver, C. A. (1982). Achievement orientation, attainment values, and women's employment. *Journal of Vocational Behavior, 20,* 67–80.

Fay, D. W., Massey, F. H., Duer, J. D., Ross, J. M., & Wooten, K. S. (1979). Social skills training to improve alcoholics' vocational interpersonal competency. *Journal of Counseling Psychology, 26*(2), 128–132.

Feather, N. T., & Davenport, P. R. (1981). Unemployment and depressive affect: A motivational and attributional analysis. *Journal of Personality and Social Psychology, 41*(3), 422–436.

Feld, S. (1963). Feelings of adjustment. In F. I. Nye & L. W. Hoffman (Eds.), *The employed mother in America.* Chicago: Rand McNally, 331–352.

Feree, M. (1976). Working class jobs: Housework and paid work as sources of satisfaction. *Social Problems, 23,* 431–441.

Feree, M. (1980). Working class feminism: A consideration of the consequences of employment. *The Sociological Quarterly, 21,* 173–184.

Ference, T. P., Stoner, J. A. F., & Warren, E. K. (1977). Managing the career plateau. *Academy of Management Review, 2,* 606–612.

Ferrini, P., & Parker, L. S. (1978). *Career change, a handbook of exemplary programs in business and industrial firms, education institutions, government agencies, professional associations* (p. 64). Cambridge, MA: Technical Education Research Centers.

Festinger, L. A. (1957). *A theory of cognitive dissonance.* Stanford, CA: Stanford University Press.

Field, H. S., & Holley, W. H. (1976). Resume preparation: An empirical study of personnel managers' perceptions. *Vocational Guidance Quarterly, 24,* 229–237.

Fifield, M., & Petersen, L. (1978). Job simulation: A model of vocational exploration. *Vocational Guidance Quarterly, 26*(4), 326–333.

Figler, H. E. (1973). PATH: Vocational exploration for liberal arts students. *Journal of College Placement,*

34(1), 40–50.

Figler, H. E. (1978). Career counseling for the obscure, the meek, and the ugly. *Journal of College Placement, 39*(1), 31–39.

Finegan, T. A. (1978). Improving our information on discouraged workers. *Monthly Labor Review, 101*(9), 15–25.

Finnegan, R., Westefeld, J., & Elmore, R. (1981). A model for a midlife career decision-making workshop. *Vocational Guidance Quarterly, 18*(3), 69–72.

Fitzgerald, L. F., & Crites, J. O. (1980). Toward a career psychology of women: What do we know? What do we need to know? *Journal of Counseling Psychology, 27,* 44–62.

Fitzpatrick, E. W. (1979). Evaluating a new retirement planning program: Results with hourly workers. *Aging and Work, 2*(2), 87–94.

Fitzpatrick, E. W. (1980). An introduction to NCOA's Retirement Planning Program. *Aging and Work, 3*(1), 20–26.

Flake, M. H., Roach, A. J., Jr., & Stenning, W. F. (1975). Effects of short-term counseling on career maturity of tenth-grade students. *Journal of Vocational Behavior, 6,* 73–80.

Flanagan, J. C. (1978). *Perspectives on improving education: Project Talent's young adults look back.* New York: Praeger.

Flanagan, J. C., & Cooley, W. W. (1966). *Project Talent: One-year follow-up studies.* Pittsburgh, PA: University of Pittsburgh Press.

Flanagan, J. C., Shaycroft, J. F., Richards, J., Jr., & Claudy, J. G. (1971). *Project Talent: Five years after high school.* Pittsburgh, PA: American Institute for Research.

Flanders, R. B. (1980). NOICC: A coordinator for occupational information. *Occupational Outlook Quarterly, 24*(4), 22–28.

Flanders, R. B. (1981, December). *Military/vocational linkages.* Speech to the American Vocational Association Convention, Atlanta, GA, 4–8, December 1981.

Flanders, R. B., & Baxter, N. (1981). The seat of their brows: A look back over occupational information and career counseling. *Occupational Outlook Quarterly, 25*(3), 9–11.

Flannagan, T. (1974). Whatever happened to job placement? *Vocational Guidance Quarterly, 22*(3), 209–213.

Fleishman, E. A. (1968). Attitudes versus skill factors in work group productivity. *Personnel Psychology, 18,* 253–266.

Fleming, K. (1974). Reflections on manpower. *Vocational Guidance Quarterly, 22*(3), 224–229.

Fletcher, B. J. (1976). Thoughts on parental involvement in the guidance program. Middle/junior high school counselor's corner. *Elementary School Guidance and Counseling, 10*(3), 210–213.

Flores, T. R., & Olsen, L. C. (1967). Stability and realism of occupational aspiration in eighth and twelfth-grade males. *Vocational Guidance Quarterly, 16,* 104–112.

Florian, V. (1978). Employers' opinions of the disabled

person as worker. *Rehabilitation Counseling Bulletin, 22,* 38–43.

Foote, B. (1980). Determined and undetermined students: How different are they? *Journal of College Student Personnel, 21*(1), 29–34.

Forney, D. S., Wallace-Schutzman, F., & Wiggens, T. T. (1982). Burnout among career development professionals: Preliminary findings and implications. *Personnel and Guidance Journal, 60,* 435–439.

Fort, M. K., & Cordisco, J. H. (1981). Career development for women in industry. *Training and Development Journal, 35,* 62–64.

Fortner, M. L. (1970). Vocational choices of high school girls: Can they be predicted? *Vocational Guidance Quarterly, 18,* 203–206.

Fottler, M. D. (1978). Retention of the hard-core unemployed. *Academy of Management Journal, 21*(3), 366–379.

Fottler, M. D., & Bain, T. (1980a). Managerial aspirations of high school seniors: A comparison of males and females. *Journal of Vocational Behavior, 16,* 83–95.

Fottler, M. D., & Bain, T. (1980b). Sex differences in occupational aspirations. *Academy of Management Journal, 23*(1), 144–149.

Fox, G. L. (1973–1974). Some observations and data on the availability of same sex role models as a factor in undergraduate career choice. *Sociological Focus, 7,* 15–30.

Fozard, J. L., & Nuttall, R. L. (1972). General aptitude test battery scores for men in different age and socioeconomic groups. In G. M. Shatto (Ed.), *Employment of the middle aged.* Springfield, IL: Charles C. Thomas.

Frederickson, R. H., Rowlery, D. J., & McKay, F. E. (1975). Multipotential – A concept for career decision-making. *Impact, 3*(6), 36–39.

Free, C. G., & Tiedeman, D. V. (1980). Counseling and comprehension of the economics of change. *Personnel and Guidance Journal, 58*(5), 358–367.

Fretz, B. R. (1972). Occupational values as discriminants of preprofessional student groups. *Journal of Vocational Behavior, 2,* 233–237.

Fretz, B. R., & Leong, F. T. L. (1982a). Career development status as a predictor of career intervention outcomes. *Journal of Counseling Psychology, 29*(4), 388–393.

Fretz, B. R., & Leong, F. T. L. (1982b). Vocational behavior and career development, 1981: A review. *Journal of Vocational Behavior, 21*(2), 123–163.

Freud, S. (1955). Civilization and its discontents (1930). In J. Strachey (Ed.), *Complete psychological works.* London: Hogarth Press.

Freudenberger, H. J. (1974). Staff burnout. *Journal of Social Issues, 30*(1), 159–165.

Freudenbeger, H. J., & Richelson, G. (1980). *Burnout: The high cost of high achievement.* Garden City: NY: Anchor Press.

Friedman, M. (1974). *Type A behavior and your heart.* New York: Knopf.

Froelich, C. P. (1949). *Evaluating guidance procedures.*

Washington, DC: U.S. Office of Education.

Frost, F., & Diamond, E. E. (1979). Ethnic and sex differences in occupational stereotyping for elementary school children. *Journal of Vocational Behavior, 15,* 43–54.

Fryer, D. (1922). Occupational-intelligence standards. *School and Society, 16,* 273–277.

Fuchs, K. D. (1978). Intervention and life-span developmental psychology. *Human Development, 21,* 370–373.

Fullerton, H. N., Jr. (1980). The 1995 labor force: A first look. *Monthly Labor Review, 103,* 11–21.

Galassi, J. P., & Galassi, M. D. (1978). Preparing individuals for job interviews. Suggestions from more than 60 years of research. *Personnel and Guidance Journal, 57*(4), 188–192.

Gallagher, R. P., & Scheuring, S. B. (1979). A more efficient way of planning outreach programming at a university counseling and placement service. *Journal of College Student Personnel, 20,* 360–361.

Gambrill, T. R. (1979). Career counseling: Too little, too late. *Training and Development Journal, 33,* 24–27.

Gammuto, J. J. (1980). Technical training: A systematic approach. *Training and Development Journal, 34,* 82–90.

Gannaway, T. W., Sink, J. M., & Becket, W. C. (1980). A predictive validity study of a job sample program with handicapped and disadvantaged individuals. *Vocational Guidance Quarterly, 29*(1), 4–11.

Garbin, A. P. (1967). Occupational choice and the multidimensional rankings of occupations. *Vocational Guidance Quarterly, 16,* 17–25.

Garbin, A. P., Campbell, R. E., Jackson, D. P., & Feldman, R. (1967). *Problems in the transition from high school to work as perceived by vocational educators.* Columbus, OH: Center for Vocational and Technical Education, Ohio State University.

Garbin, A. P., Salomone, J. J., Jackson, D. P., & Ballweg, J. A. (1970). *Worker adjustment problems of youth in transition from high school to work.* Columbus, OH: Center for Vocational and Technical Education, Ohio State University.

Gardner, E. R., & Hall, R. C. W. (1981). The professional stress syndrome. *Psychosomatics, 22,* 672–680.

Garfield, N. J., & Prediger, D. J. (1982). Testing competencies and responsibilities: A checklist for vocational counselors. In J. T. Kapes and M. M. Mastie (Eds.), *A counselor's guide to vocational guidance instruments.* Washington, DC: National Vocational Guidance Association.

Garis, J. W. (1982, August). *The integration of a computer-based system in a college counseling center: A comparison of the effects of DISCOVER and individual counseling upon career planning.* Unpublished doctoral dissertation, Pennsylvania State University.

Garland, H., & Smith, G. B. (1981). Occupational achievement motivation as a function of biological sex, sex-linked personality, and occupational stereotypes. *Psychology of Women Quarterly, 5*(4), 568–585.

Garraty, S. A. (1978). *Unemployment in history, economic thought and public policy.* New York: Harper & Row.

Garrison, H. H. (1979). Gender differences in the career aspirations of recent cohorts of high school seniors. *Social Problems, 27*(2), 170-185.

Garte, S. H., & Rosenblum, M. L. (1978). Lighting fires in burned-out counselors. *Personnel and Guidance Journal, 57*(3), 158-160.

Geis, H. J. (1970). Toward a comprehensive framework unifying all systems of counseling. *Educational Technology, 9*, 19-28.

Gelatt, H. B. (1962). Decision-making: A conceptual frame of reference for counseling. *Journal of Counseling Psychology, 9*, 240-245.

Gelatt, H. B., Varenhorst, B., & Carey, R. (1972). *Deciding.* New York: College Entrance Examination Board.

Gelatt, H. B., Varenhorst, B., Carey, R., & Miller, G. P. (1973). *Decisions and outcomes.* New York: College Entrance Examination Board.

Gelso, C. J. (1979). Research in counseling: Methodological and professional issues. *The Counseling Psychologist, 8*(3), 7-36.

Gelso, C. J., Collins, A. M., Williams, R. O., & Sedlacek, W. E. (1973). The accuracy of self-administration and scoring on Holland's self-directed search. *Journal of Vocational Behavior, 3*, 375-382.

Gerler, E. R., Jr. (1980). Mental imagery in multimodal career education. *Vocational Guidance Quarterly, 28*(4), 312.

Gershuny, J. I., & Pahl, R. E. (1979-80). Work outside employment: Some preliminary speculations. *New Universities Quarterly, 34*(1), 120-135.

Gerstein, M. (1982). Vocational counseling for adults in varied settings: A comprehensive view. *Vocational Guidance Quarterly, 30*(4), 315-321.

Gesell, A., Ilgi, F. L., & Ames, L. (1956). *Youth: The years from ten to sixteen.* New York: Harper.

Ghiselli, E. E. (1966). *The validity of occupational aptitude tests.* New York: Wiley.

Ghiselli, E. E. (1973). The validity of aptitude tests in personnel selection. *Personnel Psychology, 26*, 461-477.

Gibson, R. L. (1962). Pupil opinions of high school guidance programs. *Personnel and Guidance Journal, 40*, 453-457.

Gibson, R. L. (1972). *Career development in the elementary school.* Columbus, OH: Charles Merrill.

Gilbert, H. G. (1966). *Children study American industry.* Dubuque, IA: William C. Brown.

Gilbert, L. A., Holahan, C. K., & Manning, L. (1981). Coping with conflict between professional and maternal roles. *Family Relations, 30*(3), 419-426.

Giles, W. F., & Feild, H. S. (1982). Accuracy of interviewers' perceptions of the importance of intrinsic and extrinsic job characteristics to male and female applicants. *Academy of Management Journal, 25*(1), 148-157.

Gill, S. J., & Fruehling, J. A. (1979). Needs assessment and the design of service delivery systems. *Journal of College Student Personnel, 20*, 322-328.

Gillingham, W. H., & Lounsbury, J. E. (1979). A description and evaluation of career exploration course. *Journal of College Student Personnel, 20*, 525-529.

Gilmore, D. C., Beehr, T. A., & Richter, D. J. (1979). Effects of leader behaviors in subordinate performance and satisfaction: A laboratory experiment with student employees. *Journal of Applied Psychology, 64*(2), 166-172.

Gingrich, D. E. (1982). The dual career couple dilemma. *Journal of College Placement, 42*(2), 26-30.

Ginn, R. (1973-1974). Counseling the undecided student. *Journal of College Placement, 35*(2), 42-45.

Ginzberg, E. (1971). *Career guidance: Who needs it, who provides it, who can improve it.* New York: McGraw-Hill.

Ginzberg, E. (1972). Restatement of the theory of occupational choice. *Vocational Guidance Quarterly, 20*(3), 169-176.

Ginzberg, E. (1975). *The manpower connection, education, and work.* Cambridge, MA: Harvard University Press.

Ginzberg, E. (1982, September). The mechanization of work. *Scientific American, 247*(3), 66-75.

Ginzberg, E., Ginsburg, S. W., Axelrad, S., & Herma, J. (1951). *Occupational choice: An approach to a general theory.* New York: Columbia University Press.

Glamser, F. D. (1980). The impact of preretirement programs in the retirement experience. *Journal of Gerontology, 36*(2), 244-250.

Glenn, N. D., Taylor, P. A., & Weaver, C. N. (1977). Age and job satisfaction among males and females: A multivariate multisurvey. *Journal of Applied Psychology, 62*, 189-193.

Goeke, J. D., & Salomone, P. R. (1979). Job placement and the school counselor. *Vocational Guidance Quarterly, 27*(3), 209-215.

Goff, W. H. (1967, December). *Vocational guidance in elementary schools: A report of Project P.A.C.E.* Paper presented at the American Vocational Association Convention, Cleveland, OH.

Gold, D., & Andres, D. (1978). Developmental comparisons between adolescent children with employed and nonemployed mothers. *Merrill-Palmer Quarterly, 24*, 243-254.

Goldman, L. (1961). *Using tests in counseling.* New York: Appleton-Century-Crofts.

Goldman, L. (1962). Group guidance: Content and process. *Personnel and Guidance Journal, 40*, 518-522.

Goldman, L. (1971). *Using tests in counseling* (2nd ed.). New York: Appleton-Century-Crofts.

Goldman, L. (1972). Tests and counseling: The marriage that failed. *Measurement and Evaluation in Guidance, 4*(4), 213-220.

Goldman, L. (1979). Research is more than technology. *The Counseling Psychologist, 8*(3), 41-44.

Goldman, L. (1982). Assessment in counseling: A better way. *Measurement and Evaluation in Guidance, 15*(1), 70-73.

Golembiewski, R. T. (1978). Mid-life transition and midcareer crisis: A special case for individual development. *Public Administration Review, 38*(3), 215–222.

Goodman, H. H. (1981). Adult education and counseling: An emerging synthesis. *Personnel and Guidance Journal, 59*(7), 465-469.

Goodman, P. S., & Friedman, A. (1971). An examination of Adams; theory of inequity. *Administrative Science Quarterly, 16,* 271-288.

Goodson, W. D. (1978). Which do college students choose first – Their major or their occupation? *Vocational Guidance Quarterly, 27*(2), 150–155.

Goodson, W. D. (1982). Status of career programs on colleges and university campuses. *Vocational Guidance Quarterly, 30*(3), 230-235.

Goodstein, L. D. (1972). Behavioral views of counseling. In B. Stefflre & W. H. Grant (Eds.), *Theories of counseling* (pp. 243-286). New York: McGraw-Hill.

Gordon, M. (1974). *Higher education and the labor market.* New York: McGraw-Hill.

Gordon, M. (1979). Women and work: Priorities for the future. In C. Kerr, & J. M. Rosow (Eds.), *Work in America: The decade ahead* (pp. 111–137). New York: Van Nostrand.

Gordon, V. (1981). The undecided student: A developmental perspective. *Personnel and Guidance Journal, 49*(7), 433-439.

Gottfredson, G. D. (1977). Career stability and redirection in adulthood. *Journal of Applied Psychology, 62*(4), 436-445.

Gottfredson, G. D. (1982). An assessment of a mobility-based occupational classification for placement and counseling. *Journal of Vocational Behavior, 21,* 71-98.

Gottfredson, L. S. (1980). Construct validity of Holland's occupational typology in terms of prestige, census, Department of Labor, and other classification systems. *Journal of Applied Psychology, 65*(6), 697-714.

Gottfredson, L. S. (1978). Providing black youth more access to enterprising work. *Vocational Guidance Quarterly, 27*(2), 114-123.

Gottfredson, L. S., & Becker, H. J. (1981). A challenge to vocational psychology: How important are aspirations in determining male career development? *Journal of Vocational Behavior, 18,* 121-137.

Gottlieb, D. (1967). Poor youth do want to be middle-class but it's not easy. *Personnel and Guidance Journal, 46,* 116-122.

Goudy, W. J. (1981). Changing work expectations: Findings from the retirement history study. *The Gerontologist, 21*(6), 644-649.

Gould, R. (1978). *Transformations: Growth and change in adult life.* New York: Simon and Schuster.

Gould, R. (1972). The phases of adult life: A study of developmental psychology. *American Journal of Psychiatry, 1929*(11), 33-43.

Gould, S. (1979). Age, job complexity, satisfaction, and performance. *Journal of Vocational Behavior, 14,* 209-223.

Gould, S. (1982). Correlates of career progression among Mexican-American college graduates. *Journal of Vocational Behavior, 20,* 93-110.

Gould, S., & Hawkins, B. L. (1978). Organizational career stage as a moderator of the satisfaction-performance relationship. *Academy of Management Journal, 21*(3), 434-450.

Goulet, L. R., & Bates, P. B. (Eds.). (1970). *Life-span developmental psychology: Research and theory.* New York: Academic Press.

Graney, J. J., & Cottam, D. M. (1981). Labor force non-participation of older people: United States, 1890-1970. *The Gerontologist, 21*(2), 138-141.

Graney, J. J., & Zimmerman, R. M. (1981). Causes and consequences of health self-report variations among older people. *International Journal of Aging and Human Development, 12*(4), 291-300.

Granovetter, M. S. (1974). *Getting a job: A study of contacts and careers.* Cambridge, MA: Harvard University Press.

Graves, J. P., Dalton, G. W., & Thompson, P. H. (1980). Career stages in organizations. In C. B. Derr (Ed.), *Work, family, and the career.* New York: Praeger, 18-37.

Gray, J. D. (1980). Counseling women who want both a profession and a family. *Personnel and Guidance Journal, 59*(1), 43-46.

Gray, S., & Morse, D. (1980). Retirement and re-engagement: Changing work options for older workers. *Aging and Work, 3*(2), 103-111.

Green, C. H. (1979). Managing career information: A librarian's perspective. *Vocational Guidance Quarterly, 28*(1), 83-91.

Green, L. B., & Parker, H. J. (1965). Parental influences upon adolescent's occupational choice: A test of an aspect of Roe's theory. *Journal of Counseling Psychology, 12,* 379-383.

Greenfeld, S., Greiner, L., & Wood, M. M. (1980). The "feminine mystique" in male-dominated jobs: A comparison of attitudes and background factors of women in male-dominated versus female-dominated jobs. *Journal of Vocational Behavior, 17,* 291-309.

Greenhaus, J. H. (1971). Self-esteem as an influence on occupational choice and occupational satisfaction. *Journal of Vocational Behavior, 1,* 75-83.

Greenhaus, J. H., & Sklarew, N. D. (1981). Some sources and consequences of career exploration. *Journal of Vocational Behavior, 18,* 1-12.

Gregg, C. H., & Dobson, K. (1980). Occupational sex role stereotyping and occupational interests in children. *Elementary School Guidance and Counseling, 15*(1), 66-75.

Gribbons, W. D., & Lohnes, P. R. (1966). A five-year study of students' educational aspirations. *Vocational Guidance Quarterly, 14,* 66-69.

Gribbons, W. D., & Lohnes, P. R. (1968). *Emerging careers.* New York: Teachers College Press, Columbia University.

Gribbons, W. D., & Lohnes, P. R. (1969). *Career development from age 13 to 25.* (Final Report, Project No. 6-2151.) Washington, DC: U. S. Department of Health, Education, and Welfare.

Gribbons, W. D., & Lohnes, P. R. (1975). *Readiness for career planning* (revised). Buffalo, NY: State University of New York at Buffalo, Department of Educational Psychology.

Gribbons, W. D., & Lohnes, P. R. (1982). *Careers in theory and experience: A twenty-year longitudinal study.* Albany, NY: State University of New York Press.

Griffith, A. R. (1980). A survey of career development in corporations. *Personnel and Guidance Journal, 58*(8), 537-543.

Griffith, A. R. (1981). A survey of career development in state and local government. *Journal of Employment Counseling, 18*(1), 12-23.

Grite, T. J. (1981). Being "undecided" might be the best decision they could make. *The School Counselor, 29*(1), 41-46.

Gronlund, N. E. (1970). *Stating behavioral objectives for classroom instruction.* New York: Macmillan.

Gross, E. (1967). A sociological approach to the analysis of preparation for work life. *Personnel and Guidance Journal, 45,* 416-423.

Gross, E. (1975). Patterns of organizational and occupational socialization. *Vocational Guidance Quarterly, 24*(2), 140-149.

Gross, H. E. (1980). Dual-career couples who live apart: Two types. *Journal of Marriage and the Family, 42*(3), 567-576.

Guidance information system guide: Edition 12. (1981). Hanover, NH: TSC, Houghton Mifflin.

Gunnings, T. S. (1976). *A systemic approach to counseling.* East Lansing, MI: Michigan State University, Department of Psychiatry.

Gunter, B. G., & Gunter, N. (1980). Leisure styles: A conceptual framework for modern leisure. *The Sociological Quarterly, 21,* 361-374.

Gurin, P., & Gaylord, C. (1976). Educational and occupational goals of men and women at black colleges. *Monthly Labor Review, 99,* 10-16.

Gurin, P., & Pruitt, A. (1978). *Counseling implications of black women's market position, aspirations, and expectancies* (pp. 87-154). Research papers presented at the conference on the educational and occupational needs of Black women. Washington, DC: The National Institute of Education.

Gustad, J. W., & Tuma, A. (1957). The effects of different methods of test introduction and interpretation on client learning in counseling. *Journal of Counseling Psychology, 4,* 313-317.

Guthrie, W. R., & Herman, A. (1982). Vocational maturity and its relationship to Holland's theory of vocational choice. *Journal of Vocational Behavior, 21*(2), 196-205.

Gutmann, D. (1967). Aging among the Highland Maya: A comparative study. *Journal of Personality and Social Psychology, 7*(1), 28-35.

Gutteridge, T. G., & Otte, F. (1983). Organizational career development: What's going on out there? *Training and Development Journal, 37,* 22-26.

Guttmann, D. (1978). Life events and decision making by older adults. *The Gerontologist, 18*(5), 462-467.

Gysbers, N. C. (1969, March). *Elements of a model for promoting career development in elementary and junior high school.* Paper presented at National Conference on Exemplary Programs and Projects Section of the Vocational Education Act, Amendments of 1968, Atlanta, GA.

Gysbers, N. C., & Moore, E. J. (1981). *Improving guidance programs.* Englewood Cliffs, NJ: Prentice-Hall.

Gysbers, N. C., & Pritchard, D. H., II. (1970, October). *Proceedings, National Conference on Guidance, Counseling, and Placement in Career Development and Educational-Occupational Decision-Making.* University of Missouri, Columbia, MO.

Gysbers, N., Moore, E. J., Magnuson, C., Peters, C., & Sturgis, B. (1973). *Elements of an illustrative guide, career guidance and counseling and placement for state departments of education.* University of Missouri, Columbia, MO.

Haase, R. F., Reed, C. F., Winer, J. L., & Bodden, J. L. (1979). Effect of positive, negative, and mixed occupational information on cognitive and affective complexity. *Journal of Vocational Behavior, 15,* 294-302.

Haber, S. (1980). Cognitive support for the career choices of college women. *Sex Roles, 6*(1), 129-138.

Haccoun, R. R., & Campbell, R. E. (1972). *Work entry problems of youth: A literature review.* Center for Vocational Technical Education, Ohio State University, Columbus, OH.

Hackett, D. F. (1966). Industrial element for the elementary school. *School Shop, 25,* 58-62.

Hackett, G., & Betz, N. E. (1981). A self-efficacy approach to the career development of women. *Journal of Vocational Behavior, 18,* 326-339.

Hackman, J. R., & Oldham, G. R. (1981). Work redesign: People and their work. In J. O'Toole, J. L. Scheiber, & L. C. Wood (Eds.), *Working, changes and choices* (pp. 173-182). New York: Human Sciences Press.

Hager, P. C., & Elton, C. F. (1971). The vocational interests of Black males. *Journal of Vocational Behavior, 1,* 153-158.

Hageseth, J. A. (1982). A modular approach to career programming at a university counseling center. *Journal of College Student Personnel, 23,* 154-157.

Hahn, W. A. (1980). The post-industrial boom in communications. In C. S. Sheappard, & D. C. Carroll (Eds.), *Working in the twenty-first century.* New York: Wiley, 30-38.

Hakel, M. D., Hollman, T. D., & Dunette, M. D. (1968). Stability and change in the social status of occupations over 21 and 42 year periods. *Personnel and Guidance Journal, 46,* 762-764.

Hale, L. L. (1974). A bold new blueprint for career planning and placement: Part L. *Journal of College Placement, 35*(2), 34-40.

Hales, L. W., & Fenner, B. (1972). Work values of 5th, 8th, and 11th grade students. *Vocational Guidance Quarterly, 20*(3), 199-203.

Hales, L. W., & Fenner, B. (1973). Sex and social class differences in work values. *Elementary School Guidance and Counseling, 8*(1), 26-32.

Hall, C. S., & Lindzey, G. (1957). *Theories of personality*. New York: Wiley.

Hall, D. T. (1976). *Careers in organizations*. Pacific Palisades, CA: Goodyear.

Hall, D. T., & Lawler, E. E. (1971). Job pressures and research performance. *American Scientist, 59*, 64–73.

Hall, D. T., & Schneider, B. (1973). *Organizational climates and careers: The work lives of priests*. New York: Seminar Press.

Hall, F. S., & Hall, D. T. (1978). Dual careers: How do couples and companies cope with the problem? *Organizational Dynamics, 6*, 57–77.

Halpern, G., & Norris, L. (1968). Student curriculum decisions. *Personnel and Guidance Journal, 47*, 240–243.

Halverson, P. M. (1970, January). A rationale for a career development program in the elementary school. Paper presented to the Program Development Committee of the Cobb County, Georgia, Schools.

Hamilton, J. A., & Jones, G. B. (1971). Individualizing educational and vocational guidance: Developing a prototype program. *Vocational Guidance Quarterly, 19*(4), 293–299.

Hamilton, J. S., & Krumboltz, J. D. (1969). Simulated work experience: How realistic should it be? *Personnel and Guidance Journal, 48*, 39–44.

Hamilton, R. F., & Wright, J. D. (1976). *College-educated blue collar workers*. Paper presented at the meeting of the American Sociological Association, New York.

Hamrin, R. D. (1981). The information economy. *The Futurist, 15*(4), 25–30.

Handel, L. (1973). Three tips on career guidance activities. *Elementary School Guidance and Counseling, 7*(4), 290–291.

Hannson, R. O., O'Connor, M. E., Jones, W. H., & Blocker, T. J. (1981). Maternal employment and adolescent sexual behavior. *Journal of Youth and Adolescence, 10*(1), 55–60.

Hansen, J. C., & Cramer, S. H. (Eds.). (1971). *Group guidance and counseling in the schools*. New York: Appleton-Century-Crofts.

Hansen, L. S. (1964–1965). The art of planmanship. *Chronicle guidance professional services*. Moravia, NY: Chronicle Guidance Publications.

Hansen, L. S., & Keierleber, D. L. (1978). Born free: A collaborative consultation model for career development and sex-role stereotyping. *Personnel and Guidance Journal, 56*(7), 395–399.

Hansen, L. S., & Tenneyson, W. W. (1975, May). A career management model for counselor involvement. *Personnel and Guidance Journal, 53*(9), 638–646.

Happ, D. A., & Altmair, E. M. (1982). Counseling the hearing-impaired: Issues and recommendations. *Personnel and Guidance Journal, 60*(9), 556–559.

Hardesty, S. A., & Betz, N. E. (1980). The relationships of career salience, attitudes toward women, and demographic and family characteristics to marital adjustment in dual-career couples. *Journal of Vocational Behavior, 17*(2), 242–250.

Harlow, H. F. (1953). Mice, monkeys, men, and motives. *Psychological Review, 60*, 23–32.

Harmon, L. W. (1973). Sexual bias in interest measurement. *Measurement and Evaluation in Guidance, 5*, 496–501.

Harren, V. (1966). The vocational decision-making process among college males. *Journal of Counseling Psychology, 13*, 271–277.

Harren, V. (1979). A model of career decision-making for college students. *Journal of Vocational Behavior, 14*, 119–133.

Harren, V. A., Kass, R. A., Tinsley, H., & Morehead, J. R. (1978). Influence of sex role attitudes and cognitive styles on career decision-making. *Journal of Counseling Psychology, 25*(5), 390–398.

Harrington, C. C. (1975). A psychological anthropologist's view of ethnicity and schooling. *IRCD Bulletin, 10*(4).

Harris, J. S. (1968). The computerization of vocational information. *Vocational Guidance Quarterly, 17*, 21–20.

Harris, M. (1981). *America now: The anthropology of a changing culture*. New York: Simon & Schuster.

Harris, M. B., & Jones, L. (1981). Occu-Sort: A new career planning tool. *Journal of College Placement, 42*(1), 47–50.

Harris, T. L., & Wallin, J. S. (1978). Influencing career choices of seventh grade students. *Vocational Guidance Quarterly, 28*(1), 50–54.

Harrison, B. (1973). *Education, training, and the urban ghetto*. Baltimore: Johns Hopkins University Press.

Harrison, L., & Entine, A. D. (1977). Existing programs and emerging strategies. In N. K. Schossberg & A. D. Entine (Eds.), *Counseling adults* (pp. 108–121). Monterey, CA: Brooks/Cole.

Harrison, R. (1976). The demoralizing experience of prolonged unemployment. *Department of Employment Gazaette, 84*(4), 339–348.

Hart, D. H., Rayner, K., & Christensen, E. R. (1971). Planning, preparation and chance in occupational entry. *Journal of Vocational Behavior, 1*, 279–285.

Hartman, B., & Hartman, P. (1982). The concurrent and predictive validity of the career decision scale adapted for high school students. *Journal of Vocational Behavior, 20*, 244–252.

Hartman, B., Utz, P., & Farnum, S. (1979). Examining the reliability and validity of an adapted scale of educational-vocational undecidedness in a sample of graduate students. *Journal of Vocational Behavior, 15*, 224–230.

Hatt, P. K. (1962). Occupation and social stratification. In S. Nosow, & W. H. Form (Eds.), *Man, work, and society* (pp. 238–249). New York: Basic Books.

Havighurst, R. J. (1953). *Human development and education*. New York: Longmans, Green.

Havighurst, R. J. (1965). Counseling adolescent girls in the 1960's. *Vocational Guidance Quarterly, 13*, 153–160.

Hawkins, J., Bradley, R., & White, G. (1977). Anxiety and the process of deciding about a major and a vocation. *Journal of Counseling Psychology, 24*(5), 398–403.

Hawley, P. (1980). *Sex-fair career counseling*. Washington, DC: National Vocational Guidance Association.

Hayes, D. G. (1982). Future shock and the counselor.

In E. L. Herr, & N. M. Pinson (Eds.), *Foundations for policy in guidance and counseling* (pp. 20-33). Washington, DC: American Personnel and Guidance Association.

Hayes, J., & Nutman, P. (1981). *Understanding the unemployed: The psychological effects of unemployment.* London: Tavistock.

Hayes, R. L. (1979). High school students' occupational interest as a function of projected sex ratios in male-dominated occupations. *Journal of Applied Psychology, 84*(3), 275-279.

Hayghe, H. (1981). Husbands and wives as earners: An analysis of family data. *Monthly Labor Review,* U. S. Department of Labor, Bureau of Labor Statistics, *104*(2), 47.

Hazel, E. R. (1976). Group counseling for occupational choice. *Personnel and Guidance Journal, 54,* 436-438.

Healy, C. C. (1968). Relation of occupational choice to the similarity between self-ratings and occupational ratings. *Journal of Counseling Psychology, 15,* 317-323.

Healy, C. C. (1973). Toward a replicable method of group career counseling. *Vocational Guidance Quarterly, 21,* 214-221.

Healy, C. C. (1974). Evaluation of a replicable group career counseling procedure. *Vocational Guidance Quarterly, 22,* 34-40.

Healy, C. C. (1982). *Career development, counseling through the life stages.* Boston: Allyn & Bacon.

Heath, D. (1976). Adolescent and adult predictors of vocational adaptation. *Journal of Vocational Behavior, 9,* 1-19.

Hedges, J. N., & Sekscenski, E. S. (1979). Workers on late shifts in a changing economy. *Monthly Labor Review, 102,* 14-22.

Hedstrom, J. E. (1978). Jobs for kids. *Elementary School Guidance and Counseling, 13*(2), 132-134.

Heilman, M. E. (1979). High school students' occupational interest as a function of projected sex ratios in male-dominated occupations. *Journal of Applied Psychology, 84*(3), 275-279.

Helliwell, T. (1981). Are you a potential burnout? *Training and Development Journal, 35,* 25-29.

Helmstadter, G. C. (1964). *Principles of psychological measurement.* New York: Appleton-Century-Crofts.

Helpingstine, S. R., Head, T. C., & Sorensen, P. F. (1981). Job characteristics, job satisfaction, motivation and satisfaction with growth: A study of industrial engineers. *Psychological Reports, 49,* 381-382.

Helwig, A. A. (1979). Role conflict and ambiguity of employment counselors. *Journal of Employment Counseling, 16*(2), 72-81.

Heppner, M. J., & Olson, S. K. (1982). Expanding college career centers to meet the needs of adults. *Journal of College Student Personnel, 23,* 123-127.

Heppner, P. P., & Krause, J. B. (1979). A career seminar course. *Journal of College Student Personnel, 20,* 300-305.

Herr, E. L. (1969, March). *Unifying an entire system of education around a career development theme.* Paper presented at the National Conference of Exemplary Programs and Projects Section of the 1968 Amendments to the Vocational Education Act, Atlanta, GA.

Herr, E. L. (1970). *Decision-making and vocational development.* Boston: Houghton Mifflin.

Herr, E. L. (1972). *Review and synthesis of foundations for career education.* Columbus, OH: Center for Vocational and Technical Education, Ohio State University.

Herr, E. L. (1974). The decade in prospect: Some implications for vocational guidance. E. L. Herr (Ed.), *Vocational guidance and human development* (Chapter 22). Boston: Houghton Mifflin.

Herr, E. L. (1976a). Counseling accountability, reality, credibility. *Journal of Counseling Services, 1*(1), 14-23.

Herr, E. L. (1976b). *Introduction. Career education in the elementary school.* Lewisburg, PA: Central Susquehanna Intermediate Unit, Career Development Field Guide Project.

Herr, E. L. (1976c). *Introduction to career education in the senior high school.* Harrisburg, PA: Central Susquehanna Intermediate Joint Career Development Field Guide Project.

Herr, E. L. (1976, April). *Does counseling work?* Speech presented to the Seventh International Roundtable for the Advancement of Counseling, University of Würzburg, Germany.

Herr, E. L. (1977a). The roots of career education. *College Board Review, 105,* 6-17, 32-33.

Herr, E. L. (1977b). *Career education: The state of research.* Columbus, OH: ERIC Clearinghouse for Career Education.

Herr, E. L. (1977c). Vocational planning: An alternate view. *Personnel and Guidance Journal, 56,* 25-27.

Herr, E. L. (1978a). Career development concepts and practices: Some international perspectives. *Counseling and Human Development, 11*(1), 1-11.

Herr, E. L. (1978b). *Research in career education: The state of the art.* Columbus, OH: ERIC Clearinghouse for Career Education.

Herr, E. L. (1979). The outcomes of career guidance. *Journal of Counseling Services, 3*(2), 6-15.

Herr, E. L. (1980). Recommendations for the improved use of labor market information in secondary schools. In H. N. Drier and L. A. Pfister (Eds.), *Career and labor market information: Key to improved individual decision-making.* Columbus: The National Center for Research in Vocational Education, 43-60.

Herr, E. L. (1981). Policy in guidance and counseling: The U. S. Experience. *Bulletin of the International Association of Education and Vocational Guidance* (Special Issue).

Herr, E. L. (1982a). Career development and vocational guidance. H. F. Silberman (Ed.), *Education and work* (Chapter 6). Chicago: University of Chicago Press.

Herr, E. L. (1982b). Perspectives on the philosophical, empirical, and cost-benefit effects of guidance and counseling: Implications for political action. *The Personnel and Guidance Journal, 60*(10), 594-597.

Herr, E. L (1982c). Comprehensive career guidance: Future impact. *Vocational Guidance Quarterly, 30*(4), 367-376.

Herr, E. L. (1982d). The effects of guidance and counseling: Three domains. In E. L. Herr & N. M. Pinson (Eds.), *Foundations for policy in guidance and counseling.* Washington, DC: APGA Press.

Herr, E. L. (1982, May). Counselor education programs: Training for career development for exceptional people. Paper presented at Johns Hopkins University, Baltimore.

Herr, E. L., & Cramer, S. H. (1968). *Guidance of the college-bound: Problems, practices, and perspectives.* New York: Appleton-Century-Crofts.

Herr, E. L., & Cramer, S. H. (1972). *Vocational guidance and career development in the schools: Toward a systems approach.* Boston: Houghton Mifflin.

Herr, E. L., & Enderlein, T. (1976). Vocational maturity: The effects of school, grade, curriculum, and sex. *The Journal of Vocational Behavior, 8,* 227–238.

Herr, E. L., Horan, J. J., & Baker, S. G. (1973). Clarifying the counseling mystique. *American Vocational Journal, 48*(4), 66–68.

Herr, E. L., & Watts, A. G. (1981). The implications of youth unemployment for career education and for counseling. *Journal of Career Education, 7*(3), 184–202.

Herr, E. L., Weitz, A., Good, R., & McCloskey, G. (1981). *Research on the effects of secondary school curricular and personal characteristics upon post-secondary educational and occupational patterns* (NIE-G-80-0027). University Park, PA: The Pennsylvania State University.

Herrera, J. A. (1978). The occupational status of the Latino in the United States. *Journal of Employment Counseling, 15*(4), 157–163.

Hershenson, D. B. (1967). Sense of identity, occupational fit, and exculturation in adolescence. *Journal of Counseling Psychology, 14,* 319–324.

Hershenson, D. B. (1968). Life-state vocational development system. *Journal of Counseling Psychology, 15,* 23–30.

Hershenson, D. B. (1974). Vocational guidance and the handicapped. In E. L. Herr (Ed.), *Vocational guidance and human development* (pp. 478–501). Boston: Houghton Mifflin.

Hershenson, D. B., & Roth, R. M. (1966). A decisional process model of vocational development. *Journal of Counseling Psychology, 13,* 368–370.

Herzberg, F. (1968). One more time: How do you motivate employees? *Harvard Business Review, 46*(1), 53–62.

Herzberg, F., Mausner, B., & Snyderman, B. (1959). *The motivation to work.* New York: Wiley.

Hesketh, B. (1982). Decision-making style and career decision-making behaviors among school learners. *Journal of Vocational Behavior, 20,* 223–234.

Hiestand, D. C. (1971). *Changing careers after 35.* New York: Columbia University Press.

Hill, R. E., & Miller, E. L. (1981). Job change and the middle seasons of a man's life. *Academy of Management Journal, 24*(1), 114–127.

Hiller, D. V., & Philliber, W. W. (1982). Predicting marital and career success among dual-worker couples. *Journal of Marriage and the Family, 44*(1), 53–62.

Hills, J. R. (1964). Decision theory and college choice. *Personnel and Guidance Journal, 43,* 17–22.

Hilton, T. J. (1962). Career decision-making. *Journal of Counseling Psychology, 9,* 291–298.

Hitchcock, A. A. (1980). Public policy and adult career/occupational services. In R. E. Campbell, & P. Shaltry (Eds.), *Perspectives on adult career development and guidance.* Columbus, OH: The National Center for Research in Vocational Education N. 181.

Hochschild, A. R. (1973). *The unexpected community.* Englewood Cliffs, NJ: Prentice-Hall.

Hodanish, M. J. (1976–1977). Rehabilitation through employment. *Offender Rehabilitation, 1*(2), 147–161.

Hodge, R. W., Siegel, P. M., & Rossi, P. H. (1964). Occupational prestige in the United States: 1925–1963. *American Journal of Sociology, 70,* 286–302.

Hodgson, M., & Cramer, S. H. (1977). The relationship between selected self-estimated and measured abilities in adolescents. *Measurement and Evaluation in Guidance, 10*(2), 98–105.

Hoffman, D. (1973). Teaching self-understanding for productive living. *N.A.S.S.P. Bulletin, 57,* 74–79.

Hoffman, L. W. (1979). Maternal employment: 1979. *American Psychologist, 34*(10), 859–865.

Hogan, D. P., & Pazul, M. (1981). The career strategies of Black men. *Social Forces, 59*(4), 1217–1228.

Hogan, D. P., Pazul, M. (1982). The occupational and earnings returns to education among Black men in the North. *American Journal of Sociology, 87*(4), 905–920.

Hoggart, R. (1957). *The uses of literacy.* London, England: Chatto and Windus.

Hohenshil, T. H. (1980). The vocational education view of guidance and counseling. *Personnel and Guidance Journal, 58*(10), 668–669.

Holahan, C. K. (1981). Lifetime acheivement patterns, retirement and life satisfaction of gifted aged women. *Journal of Gerontology, 36*(6), 741–749.

Holahan, C. K., & Gilbert, L. A. (1979). Interrole conflict for working women: Careers versus jobs. *Journal of Applied Psychology, 64*(1), 86–90.

Holland, J. L. (1963). Explanation of a theory of vocational choice: Vocational images and choices. *Vocational Guidance Quarterly, 11,* 232–239.

Holland, J. L. (1966). *The psychology of vocational choice.* Waltham, MA: Blaisdell.

Holland, J. L. (1970). *Self-directed search.* Palo Alto: CA: Consulting Psychologists Press.

Holland, J. L. (1972). The present status of a theory of vocational choice. In J. M. Whitely, & A. Resnikoff (Eds.), *Perspectives on vocational development* (Chapter 3). Washington, DC: APGA Press.

Holland, J. L. (1973). *Making vocational choices: A theory of careers.* Englewood Cliffs, NJ: Prentice-Hall.

Holland, J. L. (1975). Dilemmas and remedies. *Personnel and Guidance Journal, 53,* 517–519.

Holland, J. L., & Gottfredson, G. (1976). Using a typology of persons and environments to explain career: Some extensions and clarifications. *The Counseling Psychologist, 6*(3), 20–29.

Holland, J. L., Gottfredson, G., & Nafzinger, D. (1975). Testing the validity of some theoretical signs of vocational decision-making ability. *Journal of Counseling Psychology, 22,* 411–422.

Holland, J. L., Gottfredson, G., & Power, P. (1980). Some diagnostic scales for research in decision-making and personality: Identity, information, and barriers. *Journal of Personality and Social Psychology, 39*(6), 1191–1200.

Holland, J. L., & Holland, J. E. (1977a). Distributions of personalities within occupations and fields of study. *Vocational Guidance Quarterly, 25*(3), 226–231.

Holland, J. L. & Holland, J. E. (1977b). Vocational indecision: More evidence and speculation. *Journal of Counseling Psychology, 24,* 404–414.

Holland, J. L., Magoon, T. M., & Spokane, A. R. (1981). Counseling psychology: Career interventions, research, and theory. *Annual Review of Psychology, 32,* 279–300.

Holland, J. L., & Nichols, R. C. (1964). Explorations of a theory of vocational choice: III. A longitudinal study in charge of major field of study. *Personnel and Guidance Journal, 43,* 235–242.

Holland, J. L., Viernstein, M. C., Kuo, H. M., Karweit, N. L., & Blum, S. D. (1970, November). A psychological classification of occupations. Report No. 90, Center for the Study of Social Organization of Schools. Baltimore, MD: Johns Hopkins University.

Holland, M. (1981). Relationships between vocational development and self-concept in sixth grade students. *Journal of Vocational Behavior, 18,* 228–236.

Hollander, M. A., & Parker, H. J. (1969). Occupational stereotypes and needs: Their relationship to vocational choice. *Vocational Guidance Quarterly, 18,* 91–98.

Hollander, M. A., & Parker, H. J. (1972). Occupational stereotypes and self-descriptions: Their relationship to vocational choice. *Journal of Vocational Behavior, 2,* 57–65.

Hollender, J. W. (1967). Development of a realistic vocational choice. *Journal of Counseling Psychology, 14,* 314–318.

Hollender, J. W. (1972). Differential parental influence on vocational interest development in adolescent males. *Journal of Vocational Behavior, 2,* 67–76.

Hollender, J. W. (1974). Development of vocational decisions during adolescence. *Journal of Counseling Psychology, 18*(3), 244–248.

Hollingshead, A. B. (1949). *Elmtown's youth.* New York: Wiley.

Hollis, J. W., & Hollis, L. U. (1969). *Personalizing information processes.* New York: Macmillan.

Hollis, J. W., & Hollis, L. U. (1976). *Career and life planning.* Muncie, IN: Accelerated Development.

Holmes, J. (1964). The presentation of test information to college freshmen. *Journal of Counseling Psychology, 11,* 54–58.

Holmes, T. H., & Rahe, R. H. (1967). The social readjustment rating scale. *Journal of psychosomatic research, 11*(2), 213–218.

Holmstrom, L. L. (1972). *The two-career family.* Cambridge, MA: Schenkman.

Hood, B. I., & Brown, B. F. Students with epilepsy: Guidelines for vocational counseling. *School Counselor, 26*(5), 342–345.

Hopke, W. (1979). Work classification in ancient times. *Journal of Employment Counseling, 16*(1), 26–31.

Hoppock, R. (1935). *Job satisfaction.* New York: Harper.

Hoppock, R. (1970). Presidential address 1950. *Occupations, 28,* 497–499.

Hoppock, R. (1976). *Occupational information: Where to get it and how to use it in career education, career counseling, and career development* (4th ed.). New York: McGraw-Hill.

Hopson, B., & Scully, M. (1981). *Lifeskills teaching.* London: McGraw-Hill.

Hosford, R. E. (1970). Behavioral counseling: A contemporary overview. *The Counseling Psychologist, 1,* 1–32.

Hosie, T. W. (1979). Preparing counselors to meet the needs of the handicapped. *Personnel and Guidance Journal, 58*(4), 271–275.

House, J. S. (1974). Effects of occupational stress on physical health. In J. O'Toole (Ed.), *Work and the quality of life.* Cambridge, MA: MIT Press.

Houseknecht, S. K., & Macke, A. S. (1981). Combining marriage and career: The marital adjustment of professional women. *Journal of Marriage and the Family, 43*(3), 651–661.

Howard, J. H. (1975). Management productivity, rushing out of burning out. *The Business Quarterly, 40,* 44–49.

Hoyt, K. B. (1965). High school guidance and the specialty oriented student research program. *Vocational Guidance Quarterly, 13,* 229–236.

Hoyt, K. B. (1974). *An introduction to career education.* U.S. Office of Education Policy Paper. Washington, DC: The Office.

Hoyt, K. B. (1975). *Career education: Contributions to an evolving concept.* Salt Lake City: UT: Olympus.

Hoyt, K. B. (1978). Refining the concept of collaboration in career education. *Monographs on Career Education.* Washington, DC: U.S. Office of Education.

Hoyt, K. B. (1979). *A primer for career education.* Washington, DC: Office of Career Education.

Hoyt, K. B. (1980). Contracts between the guidance and the career education movements. In F. E. Burtnett (Ed.), *The school counselor's involvement in career education.* Falls Church, VA: American Personnel and Guidance Association.

Hoyt, K. B. (1982). Federal and state participation in career education: Past, present, and future. *Journal of Career Education, 9*(1), 5–15.

Hoyt, K. B., Evans, R., Mackin, E. F., & Mangum, G. L. (1972). *Career education: What it is and how to do it* (2nd ed.). Salt Lake City, UT: Olympus.

Hudson, J., & Danish, S. J. (1980). The acquisition of information: An important life skill. *Personnel and Guidance Journal, 59*(3), 164–167.

Huffine, C. L., & Clausen, J. A. (1979). Madness and work: Short and long-term effects of mental illness on occupational careers. *Social forces, 57*(4), 1049–1062.

Hughes, H. M. (1972). Vocational choice, level, and consistency: An investigation of Holland's theory on an employed sample. *Journal of Vocational Behavior, 2,* 377–388.

Hultman, E. E., & Cunningham, G. (1978). Preparing employees for upward mobility. *Training and Development Journal, 32*(2), 10–14.

Hummel, R., & Sprinthall, N. (1965). Underachievement related to interests, attitudes, and values. *Personnel and Guidance Journal, 44,* 388–395.

Hunt, E. E. (1970). Career development K-6; A background paper of initial suggestions. Paper presented to the Program Development Committee of the Cobb County Schools, GA.

Hunt, J. M. (1961). *Intelligence and experience.* New York: Ronald Press.

Huser, W. R., & Grant, C. W. (1978). A study of husbands and wives from dual career and traditional career families. *Psychology of Women Quarterly, 3*(1), 78–89.

Hutchinson, T., & Roe, A. (1968). Studies of occupational history: Part II. Attractiveness of occupational groups of the Roe system. *Journal of Counseling Psychology, 15,* 107–110.

Ibrahim, F., & Herr, E. L. (1982). Attitude modification toward disability: Differential effect of two educational modes. *Rehabilitation Counseling Bulletin, 26*(8), 29–36.

Iglitzin, A. B. (1972). A child's-eye view of sex roles. *Today's Education, 61,* 23–25.

Ilfield, F. W. (1976). Characteristics of current social stressors. *Psychological Reports, 39*(3), 1231–1247.

Illfelder, J. K. (1980). Fear of success, sex role attitudes, and career salience and anxiety level of college women. *Journal of Vocational Behavior, 16,* 7–17.

Institute for the Crippled and Disabled. (1967). *TOWER: Testing, orientation, and work evaluation in rehabilitation.* New York: Institute for the Crippled and Disabled.

Instructor Special Report. (1979). Teacher burnout: How to cope when your world goes black. *Instructor, 88,* 56–62.

International Labor Office. (1977a). *The ILO and the world of work.* Geneva, Switzerland: The Office.

International Labor Office. (1977b). Why it's hard to cut youth unemployment. *ILO Information, 5*(1).

Iorachine, E. V., & Abond, R. R. (1981). A look at counselor education programs in light of Section 504 of the Rehabilitation Act of 1973. *Counselor Education and Supervision, 21*(2), 109–118.

Irvin, F. S. (1968). Personality characteristics and vocational identification. *Journal of Counseling Psychology, 15,* 329–333.

Isaacson, L. E. (1977). *Career information counseling and teaching* (2nd ed.). Boston: Allyn and Bacon.

Isaacson, L. E. (1981). Counseling male midlife career changes. *Vocational Guidance Quarterly, 29*(4), 324–331.

Ivey, A. E. (1976). Counseling psychology, the psychoeducator model and the future. *The Counseling Psychologist, 6*(3), 72–75.

Jackson, D. N., & Williams, D. R. (1975). Occupational classification in terms of interest patterns. *Journal of Vocational Behavior, 6,* 269–280.

Jackson, G., Masnick, G., Bolton, R., Bartlett, S., & Pitkin, J. (1981). *Regional diversity: Growth in the United States, 1960-1990.* Boston: Auburn House Publishing Company.

Jackson, L. M. (1983). *Linear structural equation: Analysis of technical versus nontechnical career paths of engineers.* Unpublished doctoral dissertation, Pennsylvania State University.

Jacobs, R., & Solomon, T. (1977). Strategies for enhancing the prediction of job performance from job satisfaction. *Journal of Applied Psychology, 62,* 417–421.

Jacobson, T. J. (1972). Career guidance centers. *Personnel and Guidance Journal, 50,* 599–604.

Jacobson, T. J. (1975). Career center implementation and evaluation. *Impact, 3,* 32–39.

Jaffe, A. J. (1978). Notes on the recent labor force experience of older workers. *Aging and Work, 1*(2), 135–138.

Jahoda, M. (1979). The impact of unemployment in the thirties and seventies. *British Psychological Society Bulletin, 32,* 309–314.

Jahoda, M. (1981). Work, employment and unemployment. *American Psychologist, 36*(2), 184–191.

James, F., III. (1963). Comment on Hilton's model of career decision making. *Journal of Counseling Psychology, 10,* 303–304.

Janis, I., & Mann, L. (1977). *Decision-making: A psychological analysis of conflict, choice, and commitment.* New York: The Free Press.

Jencks, C. (1972). *Inequality.* New York: Harper & Row.

Jepsen, D. A. (1972). The impact of videotaped occupational field trips on occupational knowledge. *Vocational Guidance Quarterly, 21,* 54–62.

Jepsen, D. A. (1974). Vocational decision-making strategy-types: An exploratory study. *Vocational Guidance Quarterly, 23*(2), 17–23.

Jepsen, D. A., & Dilley, J. S. (1974). Vocational decision-making models: A review and comparative analysis. *Review of Education Research, 44*(3), 331–349.

Jepsen, D. A., & Prediger, D. (1981). Dimensions of adolescent career development: A multi-instrument analysis. *Journal of Vocational Behavior, 18,* 350–368.

Johnson, C. L., & Johnson, F. A. (1977). Attitudes toward parenting in dual career families. *American Journal of Psychiatry, 134*(4), 391–395.

Johnson, M., Jr., Busacker, W. E., & Bowman, F. Q., Jr. (1961). *Junior high school guidance.* New York: Harper & Brothers.

Johnson, R. G. (1970). Simulation techniques in career development. *American Vocational Journal, 45,* 30–32.

Johnson, R. G. (1971). Job simulations to promote vocational interests. *Vocational Guidance Quarterly, 20,* 25–30.

Johnson, R. H., & Myrick, R. D. (1971). MOLD: A new approach to career decision making. *Vocational Guidance Quarterly, 21*(1), 48–53.

Johnson, R. P., & Riker, H. C. (1981). Retirement maturity: A valuable concept for preretirement counselors. *Personnel and Guidance Journal, 59*(5), 291-295.

Johnson, W. F., Korn, T. A., & Dunn, D. J. (1975). Comparing three methods of presenting occupational information. *Vocational Guidance Quarterly, 24,* 62-66.

Joint Economic Committee, U. S. Congress. (1980, November). *Human resources and demographics: Characteristics of people and policy.* Washington, DC: The Committee.

Jones, B., & Krumboltz, J. D. (1970). Stimulating vocational exploration through film-mediated problems. *Journal of Counseling Psychology, 17,* 107-114.

Jones, G., & Chenery, M. (1980). Multiple subtypes among vocationally undecided college students: A model and assessment instrument. *Journal of Counseling Psychology, 27,* 469-477.

Jones, G. B., Helliwell, C. B., & Ganschow, L. H. (1975). A planning model for career guidance: *Vocational Guidance Quarterly, 23*(3), 220-226.

Jones, L. K. (1979). Occu-Sort: Development and evaluation of an occupational card sort system. *Vocational Guidance Quarterly, 28*(1), 56-62.

Jones, L. K. (1980). Holland's typology and the new guide for occupational exploration: Bridging the gap. *Vocational Guidance Quarterly, 29*(1), 70-75.

Jones, L. K., & DeVault, R. M. (1979). Evaluation of a self-guided career exploration system: The Occu-Sort. *The School Counselor, 26*(5), 334-341.

Jones, L. M., & McBridge, J. L. (1980). Sex role stereotyping in children as a function of maternal employment. *Journal of Social Psychology, 3*(2), 219-223.

Jordaan, J. P. (1963). Exploratory behavior: The formation of self and occupational concepts. In D. Super, R. Starishevsky, R. Matlin, & J. P. Jordaan (Eds.), *Career development: Self-concept theory* (pp. 42-78). New York: College Entrance Examination Board.

Jordaan, J. P. (1974). Life stages as organizing modes of career development. In E. L. Herr (Ed.), *Vocational guidance and human development.* Boston: Houghton Mifflin, 263-295.

Jordaan, J. P., & Heyde, M. (1979). *Vocational maturity during the high school years.* New York: Teachers College Press.

Jorgenson, D. D., & Spooner, S. E. (1981). Career education in colleges and universities. *Journal of Career Education, 7*(3), 253-259.

Jourard, S. M., & Jaffe, P. L. (1970). Influence of an interviewer's disclosure on the self-disclosing behavior of interviewers. *Journal of Counseling Psychology, 17,* 252-257.

Jurgensen, C. E. (1978). Job preferences (What makes a job good or bad?) *Journal of Applied Psychology, 63,* 267-276.

Justice, B., Gold, R. S., & Klein, J. P. (1981). Life events and burnout. *Journal of Psychology, 108,* 219-226.

Kaback, G. R. (1960). Occupational information in elementary education. *Vocational Guidance Quarterly, 9,* 55-59.

Kaback, G. R. (1966). Occupational information for groups of elementary school children. *Vocational Guidance Quarterly, 14,* 163-168.

Kahnweiler, J. B., & Kahnweiler, W. M. (1980). A dual-career family workshop for college undergraduates. *Vocational Guidance Quarterly, 28*(3), 225-230.

Kaiser, M. A., Peters, G. R., & Babchuk, N. (1982). When priests retire. *The Gerontologist, 22*(1), 89-94.

Kalder, D. R., & Zytowski, D. G. (1969). A maximizing model of occupational decision-making. *Personnel and Guidance Journal, 47,* 781-788.

Kalleberg, A. L., & Griffin, L. J. (1978). Positional sources of inequality in job satisfaction. *Sociology of Work and Occupations, 5*(4), 371-401.

Kando, T. M., & Summers, W. C. (1971). The impact of work on leisure: Towards a paradigm and research strategy. *Pacific Sociological Review, 14,* 310-327.

Kandor, J. R., Kendall, D., & Suggs, R. C. (1977). A model for improving test experience through small groups. *Measurement and Evaluation in Guidance, 9*(4), 178-183.

Kantor, L. M., & Bartlett, L. R. (1974). Span of life discussions for college students: Their impact and implications. *Journal of College Student Personnel, 15,* 145-148.

Kantor, R. M. (1977). *Work and family in the United States: A critical review and agenda for research and policy.* New York: Russell Sage.

Kanzaki, G. A. (1976). Fifty years of stability in the social status of occupations. *Vocational Guidance Quarterly, 25,* 101-105.

Kapes, J. T., & Mastie, M. M. (1982). *A counselor's guide to vocational guidance instruments.* Falls Church, VA: National Vocational Guidance Association.

Kapes, J. T., & Strickler, R. T. (1975). A longitudinal study of change in work values between ninth and twelfth grade as related to high school curriculums. *Journal of Vocational Behavior, 6*(1), 81-93.

Kaplon, A. J., & Gordon, M. S. (1967). A critique of war and peace: A simulation game. *Social Education, 31,* 383-387.

Karayani, M. (1981). Career maturity of emotionally maladjusted high school students. *Vocational Guidance Quarterly, 29*(3), 213-220.

Karpicke, S. (1980). Perceived and real sex differences in college students' career planning. *Journal of Counseling Psychology, 27*(3), 240-245.

Karre, I. (1976). Self-concept and sex role stereotype: An empirical study with children. *Dissertation Abstracts International, 36,* 4850-4851.

Kasl, S. V. (1977). Work and mental health: Contemporary research evidence. In W. J. Heisler, & J. W. Houck (Eds.), *A matter of dignity.* South Bend, IN: University of Notre Dame Press.

Kasl, S. V., Gore, S., & Cobb, S. (1975, March-April). The experience of losing a job: Reported changes in health, symptoms, and illness behavior. *Psychosomatic Medicine, 371*(2), 106-122.

Kassarjian, W. M., & Kassarjian, H. H. (1965). Occupational interests, social values, and social character. *Journal of Counseling Psychology, 12,* 48-54.

Kasschau, P. L. (1974). Reevaluating the need for retirement preparation programs. *Industrial Gerontology, 19*(1), 42-59.

Kassner, M. (1981). Will both spouses have careers? Predictions of preferred traditional or egalitarian marriage among university students. *Journal of Vocational Behavior, 18,* 340-355.

Katz, M. (1958). *You: Today and tomorrow.* Princeton, NJ: Educational Testing Service.

Katz, M. (1963). *Decisions and values: A rationale for secondary school guidance.* New York: College Entrance Examination Board.

Katz, M. (1966). A model of guidance for career decision-making. *Vocational Guidance Quarterly, 15,* 2-10.

Katz, M. (1969). Can computers make guidance decisions for students? *College Board Review. 13.* 13-17.

Katz, M., Norris, L., & Pears, L. (1978). Simulated occupational choice: A diagnostic measure of competencies in career decision-making. *Measurement and Evaluation in Guidance, 10,* 222-232.

Katz, M. (1973). The name and nature of vocational guidance. In H. Borow (Ed.), *Career guidance for a new age* (pp. 83-134). Boston: Houghton Mifflin.

Katz, M. (1980). SIGI: An interactive aid to career decision-making. *Journal of College Student Personnel, 21*(1), 34-40.

Katz, R. L. (1974). Skills of an effective administrator. *Harvard Business Review, 52,* 90-102.

Katzell, R. A. (1964). Personal values, job satisfaction, and job behavior. In H. Borow (Ed.), *Man in a world at work.* Boston, MA: Houghton Mifflin.

Katzell, R. A. (1979). Changing attitudes toward work. In C. Ken, & J. M. Rosow (Eds.), *Work in America: The decade ahead.* New York: Van Nostrand.

Kauffman, J., Schaefer, C., Lewis, M. V., Steven, D. W., & House, E. W. (1967). *The role of the secondary school in the preparation of youth for employment.* University Park, PA: Institute for Human Resources.

Kaufman, R. L., & Spilerman, S. (1982). The age structure of occupations and jobs. *American Journal of Sociology, 87,* 827-851.

Kazanas, H. C. (1978). *Affective work competencies for vocational education.* Columbus, OH: National Center for Research in Vocational Education, Ohio State University.

Keith, P. M. (1981). Sex-role attitudes, family plans, and career orientations: Implications for counseling. *Vocational Guidance Quarterly, 29*(3), 244-252.

Keith, P. M., Goudy, W. J., & Powers, E. A. (1981). Employment characteristics and psychological well-being of men in two-job families. *Psychological Reports, 49,* 975-978.

Keith, P. M., & Schafer, R. B. (1980). Depression in one and two job families. *Psychological Reports, 47*(2), 669-670.

Kelleher, C. H. (1973). Second careers: A growing trend. *Industrial Gerontology, 17*(2), 1-8.

Kelly, E. W., Jr. (1978). Industrial shadow experiences: Career counseling from an experiential base. *Vocational Guidance Quarterly, 26*(4), 342-348.

Kelly, E. W., Jr., & Moore, P. R. (1979). Process analysis

of industrial shadow experiences. *Vocational Guidance Quarterly, 27*(3), 244-249.

Kelly, J. R. (1981). Leisure interaction and the social dialectic. *Social Forces, 60*(2), 304-322.

Kelso, G. I., Holland, J. L., & Gottfredson, G. D. (1977). The relation of self-reported competencies to aptitude test scores. *Journal of Vocational Behavior, 10,* 99-103.

Kerr, B. A. (1982). The setting of career counseling. *Vocational Guidance Quarterly, 30*(3), 210-218.

Kessler, R. C., & McRae, J. A. (1982). The effects of wives' employment on the mental health of married men and women. *American Sociological Review, 47,* 216-227.

Kieffer, J. A. (1980). Counselors and the older worker: An overview. *Journal of Employment Counseling, 17*(1), 8-16.

Kiesler, D. J. (1971). Experimental designs in psychotherapy research. In A. E. Bergin, & S. J. Garfield (Eds.), *Handbook of psychotherapy and behavior change.* New York: Wiley.

Kimball, R. L., Sedlacek, W. E., & Brooks, G. C. (1973). Black and white vocational interests in Holland's Self-Directed Search (SDS). *Journal of Negro Education, 42,* 1-4.

Kingson, E. R. (1981). Retirement circumstances of very early retirees: A life cycle perspective. *Aging and Work, 4*(3), 161-174.

Kinnick, B. C. (1968). Group discussion and group counseling applied to student problem solving. *The School Counselor, 15,* 350-356.

Kirligham, D., Hagesth, J., Tipton, R., & McGovern, T. (1981). Effects of matching treatment approaches and personality types in group vocational counseling. *Journal of Counseling Psychology, 28,* 315-320.

Kirts, D. K., & Fisher, R. B. (1973). TRIPOD — A systems approach to career planning. *Journal of College Placement, 34*(4), 42-49.

Kitabachi, G., Murrell, P. H., & Crawford, R. L. (1979, December). Career/life planning for divorced women: An overview. *Vocational Guidance Quarterly,* 137-145.

Kitson, H. D. (1934). Getting rid of a piece of educational rubbish. *Teachers College Record, 36,* 30-34.

Kivligham, D. M., Jr., Hageseth, J. A., Tipton, R. M., & McGovern, T. V. (1981). Effects of matching treatment approaches and personality types in group vocational counseling. *Journal of Counseling Psychology, 28*(4), 315-320.

Kleinmuntz, B. (1975). The computer as clinician. *American Psychologist, 30*(3), 379-387.

Knapp, D. L., & Bedord, J. H. (1967). *The parent's role in career development.* Washington, DC: National Guidance Association.

Knapp, L., Knapp, R. R., Strand, L., & Michael, W. B. (1978). Comparative validity of the Career Ability Placement Survey (CAPS) and the General Aptitude Test Battery (GATB) for predicting high school course marks. *Educational and Psychological Measurement, 38,* 1053-1056.

Knapp, L., & Michael, W. B. (1980). Relationship of work values to corresponding academic success.

Educational and Psychological Measurement, 40, 487-494.

Knefelkamp, L. L., & Slepitza, R. (1976). A cognitive developmental model of career development – an adaptation of the Perry scheme. *The Counseling Psychologist, 6*(3), 53-58.

Knell, S., & Winer, G. A. (1979). Effects of reading content on occupational sex role stereotypes. *Journal of Vocational Behavior, 14,* 78-87.

Knierim, K., & Stiffler, T. (1979). Peer outreach: Two viewpoints. *Journal of College Placement, 39*(2), 56-61.

Knowdell, R. L. (1982). Comprehensive career programs in the workplace. *Vocational Guidance Quarterly, 30*(4), 323-326.

Knowles, M. (1977). The adult learner becomes less neglected. *Training, 14*(9), 16-18.

Koehn, S. (1978). Who's doing what? An update survey of career planning programs. *Journal of College Student Personnel, 18,* 523-526.

Kohlan, R. G. (1968). Relationship between inventoried interests and inventoried needs. *Personnel and Guidance Journal, 46,* 592-598.

Kohlberg, L. (1968). The child as a moral philosopher. *Psychology Today, 2*(4), 24-30.

Kolb, D. A., & Plovnik, M. S. (1977). The experiential learning theory of career development. In J. V. Maanen (Ed.), *Organizational career: Some new perspectives* (pp. 65-87). New York: Wiley.

Koyl, L. F. (1974). *Employing the older worker: Matching the employee to the job.* Washington, DC: National Council on Aging.

Kramer, H. C., Berger, F., & Miller, G. (1974). Student concerns and sources of assistance. *Journal of College Student Personnel, 15*(5), 389-393.

Krasnow, B. S. (1968). Occupational information as a factor in the high school curriculum chosen by ninth-grade boys. *The School Counselor, 15,* 275-280.

Krathwohl, D. R., Bloom, B. S., & Masia, B. B. (1964). *Taxonomy of educational objectives, handbook II: The affective domain.* New York: David McKay.

Krau, E. (1981). Immigrants preparing for their second career: The behavioral strategies adopted. *Journal of Vocational Behavior, 18,* 289-303.

Krau, E. (1982). The vocational side of a new start in life: A career model of immigrants. *Journal of Vocational Behavior, 20,* 313-330.

Krefting, L. A., & Berger, P. K. (1979). Masculinity-feminity perceptions of job requirements and their relationship to job-sex stereotypes. *Journal of Vocational Behavior, 15,* 164-174.

Kriedberg, B., Butcher, A. L., & White, K. M. (1978). Vocational role choice in second- and sixth-grade children. *Sex Roles, 4,* 145-181.

Krippner, S. (1965). The educational plans and preferences of upper-middle class junior high school pupils. *Vocational Guidance Quarterly, 13,* 257-260.

Krivasky, S., & Magoon, T. (1976). Differential effects of three vocational counseling treatments. *Journal of Counseling Psychology, 43,* 112-118.

Krolik, J. J., & Nelson, J. L. (1980). A conference approach: Expanding career alternatives. *Journal of*

College Student Personnel, 21, 90-91.

Kroll, A. M. (1976). Career education's impact on employability and unemployment: Expectations and realities. *Vocational Guidance Quarterly, 24*(3), 209-218.

Krumboltz, J. D. (1966). *Stating the goals of counseling.* Fullerton, CA: California Personnel and Guidance Association.

Krumboltz, J. D. (1979). A social learning theory of career decision making. In A. M. Mitchell, G. G. Jame, & J. D. Krumboltz (Eds.), *Social learning and career decision making.* Cranston, RI: Carrole Press, 19-49.

Krumboltz, J. D., Mitchell, A., & Gellat, H. G. (1975). Applications of social learning theory of career selection. *Focus on Guidance, 8*(3), 1-16.

Krumboltz, J. D., & Schroeder, W. W. (1965). Promoting career planning through reinforcement and models. *Personnel and Guidance Journal, 44,* 19-26.

Krumboltz, J. D., Sheppard, L. E., Jones, G. B., Johnson, R. G., & Baker, R. D. (1967). *Vocational problem-solving experiences for simulating career exploration and interest.* Final report of Project OE 5-85-059, U.S. Office of Education.

Krumboltz, J. D., & Thoresen, C. E. (1964). The effect of behavioral counseling in groups and individual settings on information seeking behavior. *Journal of Counseling Psychology, 11,* 324-333.

Krumboltz, J. D., Varenhorst, B., & Toresen, C. E. (1967). Non-verbal factors in effectiveness of models in counseling. *Journal of Counseling Psychology, 14,* 412-418.

Kryger, G. R., & Shikiar, R. (1978). Sexual discrimination in the use of letters of recommendations: A case of reverse discrimination. *Journal of Applied Psychology, 63*(3), 309-314.

Kuehn, J. (1974). Group counseling with undecided college students. *Vocational Guidance Quarterly, 22,* 232-234.

Kuhlman-Harrison, J., & Neely, M. A. (1980). Discriminant validity of career development inventory scales in grade 10 students. *Educational and Psychological Measurement, 40,* 475-478.

Kurolesky, W. P., Wright, D. E., & Juarez, R. Z. (1971). Status projections and ethnicity: A comparison of Mexican American, Negro, and Anglo youth. *Journal of Vocational Behavior, 1,* 137-151.

Kurtz, R. R. (1974). Using a transactional analysis format in vocational group counseling. *Journal of College Student Personnel, 15,* 447-451.

LaFitte, P. C., & Phillips, B. (1980). Assertive job hunting: A lesson in integration. *Journal of College Student Personnel, 21,* 92-93.

LaGory, M., & Magnani, R. J. (1979). Structural correlates of black-white occupational differentiation: Will U.S. regional differences in status remain? *Social Problems, 27*(2), 157-168.

Laing, J., Lamb, R. R., & Prediger, D. J. (1982). An application of Strong's validity criteria to basic interest scales. *Journal of Vocational Behavior, 20,* 203-214.

Lamb, R. R., & Prediger, D. J. (1979). Criterion-related validity of sex-restrictive and unisex interest scales:

A comparison. *Journal of Vocational Behavior, 15,* 231-246.

Lamb, S. H. (1980). Student interchange with business and industry. *Journal of College Student Personnel, 21,* 176-177.

Lance, L. M., Lourie, J., & Mayo, C. (1979). Needs of reentry university students. *Journal of College Student Personnel, 20,* 479-485.

Lang, K. A. (1978). Suggestions for counseling women who want to enter a nontraditional occupation. *Journal of Employment Counseling, 15*(4), 180-187.

Lange, S., & Coffman, J. S. (1981). Integrative test interpretation: A career counselor tool. *Vocational Guidance Quarterly, 30*(1), 73-77.

Laramore, D. (1969). Career information center: An approach to occupational information. *Personnel and Guidance Journal, 48,* 55-56.

Laramore, D. (1979). Career counseling for families (and other multi-age groups). *The Personnel and Guidance Journal, 57*(10), 555-556.

Laramore, D., & Thompson, J. (1970). Career experiences appropriate to elementary school grades. *The School Counselor, 17,* 262-263.

Larkin, J. C., & Pines, H. A. (1979). No fat persons need apply: Experimental studies of the overweight stereotype and hiring preference. *Sociology of Work and Occupations, 6*(1), 312-327.

Larkin, T. (1975). Removing the ex-offender's catch 22. *Journal of Employment Counseling, 12*(3), 126-131.

Lasker, H., Moore, J., & Simpson, E. L. (1980). *Adult development and approaches to learning.* Washington, DC: National Institute of Education.

Lassiter, R. A. (1981, December). *Work evaluation and work adjustment for severely handicapped people. A counseling approach* (pp. 13-18). Paper presented at the International Roundtable for the Advancement of Counseling Consultation on Career Guidance and Higher Education, Cambridge, England.

Lattanzi, M. E. (1981). Coping with work-related losses. *Personnel and Guidance Journal, 59*(6), 350-351.

Laudeman, K. A., & Griffith, P. (1978). Holland's theory of vocational choice and postulated value dimensions. *Educational and Psychological Measurement, 38,* 1165-1175.

Lavin, D. E. (1965). *The prediction of academic performance.* New York: Russell Sage Foundation.

Law, B. (1973). *Decide for yourself.* Cambridge, England: Careers Research and Advisory Center.

Lawler, E. E. (1973). *Motivation in work organizations.* Monterey, CA: Brooks/Cole.

Lawler, E. E. III. (1982). Strategies for improving the quality of work life. *American Psychologist, 37*(5), 486-493.

Lazarus, A. A. (1976). *Multimodal behavior therapy.* New York: Springer.

Leacock, E. (1968). The concept of culture and its significance for school counselors. *Personnel and Guidance Journal, 46*(9), 844-851.

Leclair, S. W. (1982). The dignity of leisure. *The School Counselor, 29*(4), 289-296.

Lee, R. (1982). The moderating effect of sex on the prediction of job satisfaction in the public sector. *Journal of Employment Counseling, 19*(1), 34-44.

Lee, R., Mueller, L., & Miller, K. J. (1981). Sex, wage-earner status, occupational level, and job satisfaction. *Journal of Vocational Behavior, 18,* 362-373.

Lefkowitz, J., & Brigando, L. (1980). The redundancy of work alienation and job satisfaction: Some evidence of convergent and discriminant validity. *Journal of Vocational Behavior, 16,* 115-131.

Legislative Provisions for the Improvement of Guidance Programs and Personnel Development. (1979). *Various Modules.* Columbus, OH: National Center for Research in Vocational Education.

Leibowitz, Z. B., & Schlossberg, N. K. (1981). Training managers for their role in a career development system. *Training and Development Journal, 35,* 72-79.

Lemkau, J. P. (1979). Personality and background characteristics of women in male-dominated occupations: A review. *Psychology of Women Quarterly, 4*(2), 221-240.

Lenz, E., & Shavitz, M. H. (1977). *So you want to go back to school.* San Francisco: McGraw-Hill.

Leonard, G. E. (1972). Career guidance in the elementary school. *Elementary School Guidance and Counseling, 6,* 283-286.

Leonard, G. E., & Brooks, L. P. (1980). Developmental career guidance for girls and young women. In E. Waters, & J. Goodman (Eds.), *Resocializing sex roles: A guide for education.* Washington, DC: The National Vocational Guidance Association.

Leonards, J. T. (1981). Corporate psychology: An answer to occupational mental health. *Personnel and Guidance Journal, 30*(1), 47-51.

Leveson, I. (1980). Technology and society in the next thirty years: We have manageable choices. In C. S. Sheppart, & D. C. Carroll (Eds.), *Working in the twenty-first century.* New York: Wiley, 39-48.

Levine, A. (1976). Educational and occupational choice: A synthesis of literature from sociology and psychology. *Journal of Consumer Research, 2,* 276-289.

Levine, S. V. (1979). The psychological and social effects of youth unemployment. *Children Today, 8*(6), 6-9, 40.

Levinson, D. J. (1977). The mid-life transition: A period in adult psychosocial development. *Psychiatry, 40,* 99-112.

Levinson, D. J., Darrow, C. N., Klein, E. B., Levinson, M. H., & McKee, B. (1978). *The seasons of a man's life.* New York: Knopf.

Levitan, S., Johnson, W., & Taggart, R. (1974). Manpower programs and black progress. *Manpower, 6*(6), 2-10.

Leviton, L. C., & Whitely, S. E. (1981). Job seeking patterns of female and male Ph.D. recipients. *Psychology of Women Quarterly, 5*(5), 690-701.

Lewis, J. A., & Lewis, M. D. (1977). *Community counseling: A human services approach.* New York: Wiley.

Ley, R. (1966). Labor turnover as a function of worker difference. *Journal of Applied Psychology, 50*(6), 497-500.

Liem, R., & Rayman, P. (1980). Health and social costs

of unemployment. *American Psychologist, 37*(10), 1116-1123.

Lilley, W. (1978). Job hunters, beware. *Canadian Business, 51,* 36-37; 99-100.

Lipman-Blumen, J., & Leavitt, H. S. (1977). Vicarious and direct achievement patterns in adulthood. In N. K. Schlossberg and A. D. Entine (Eds.), *Counseling adults.* Monterey, CA: Brooks/Cole.

Lipsett, L. (1962). Social factors in vocational development. *Personnel and Guidance Journal, 40,* 432-437.

Lipsett, L. (1980a). A career counselor in industry. *Vocational Guidance Quarterly, 28*(4), 269-273.

Lipsett, L. (1980b). Career path charts as counseling aids. *Vocational Guidance Quarterly, 30*(4), 360-368.

Lister, J. L., & McKenzie, D. H. (1966). A framework for the improvement of test interpretation in counseling. *Personnel and Guidance Journal, 45,* 61-66.

Little, C. (1976). Technical-professional unemployment: Middle class adaptability to personal crisis. *The Sociological Quarterly,* 17i, 262-274.

Livingston, J. S. (1970). The troubled transition: Why college and university graduates have difficulty developing careers in business. *Journal of College Placement, 30,* 34-41.

LoCascio, R. (1967). Continuity and discontinuity in vocational development theory. *Personnel and Guidance Journal, 46,* 32-36.

Locksley, A. (1980). On the effects of wives' employment on marital adjustment and companionship. *Journal of Marriage and the Family, 42,* 337-346.

Lockwood, O., Smith, D. B., & Trezise, R. (1966). Four worlds: An approach to vocational guidance. *Personnel and Guidance Journal, 45,* 641-643.

Loesch, L. C. (1980). Life-flow leisure counseling for older persons. *Journal of Employment Counseling, 17*(1), 49-56.

Loesch, L. C., & Sampson, J. P., Jr. (1978). Job knowledge and vocational preferences. *Vocational Guidance Quarterly, 27*(1), 55-60.

Loevinger, J. (1976). *Ego development: Conceptions and theories.* San Francisco: Jossey-Bass.

Lofquist, L. H., & Dawis, R. (1969). *Adjustment to work, a psychological view of man's problems in a work-oriented society.* New York: Appleton-Century-Crofts.

Lofquist, L. H., & Dawis, R. V. (1975). *Counseling and use of the Minnesota Importance Questionnaire.* Minneapolis: University of Minnesota Vocational Psychology Work Adjustment Project.

Lokan, J., & Biggs, J. (1982). Student characteristics and motivational and process factors in relation to styles of career development. *Journal of Vocational Behavior, 21,* 1-16.

Lombana, J. H. (1979). Facilitating career guidance of deaf students: Challenges and opportunities for counselors. *Vocational Guidance Quarterly, 27*(4), 350-358.

Lombard, J. W. (1973). *Career guidance and the Kuder interest inventories.* Chicago: Science Research Associates.

London, M., & Stumpf, S. A. (1982). *Managing careers.* Reading, MA: Addison-Wesley.

Loughary, J. W. (1970). The computer is in! *Personnel and Guidance Journal, 49,* 185-191.

Lowe, B. (1981). The relationship between vocational interest differentiation and career undecidedness. *Journal of Vocational Behavior, 19,* 346-349.

Lowenthal, M. F. (1977). Toward a sociopsychological theory of change in adulthood and old age. In J. E. Birren & K. W. Schaie (Eds.), *Handbook of the psychology of aging.* New York: Van Nostrand-Rienhold.

Lowenthal, M. F., Thurnher, M., Chiroboga, D., and Associates. (1976). *Four stages of life.* San Francisco: Jossey-Bass.

Lowenthal, M. F., & Weiss, L. (1976). Intimacy and crisis in adulthoood. *The Counseling Psychologist, 6*(1), 10-15.

Luchins, A. S. (1960). Influences of experiences with conflicting information and reactions to subsequent conflicting information. *Journal of Social Psychology, 5,* 367-385.

Lundborg, U., & Theorell, T. (1976). Scaling off life changes: Differences between three diagnostic groups and between recently experienced and nonexperienced events. *Journal of Human Stress, 2,* 8-16.

Lunneborg, C. E. (1982a). Role model influences of nontraditional professional women. *Journal of Vocational Behavior, 20,* 276-281.

Lunneborg, C. E. (1982b). Systematic biases in brief self-ratings of vocational qualifications. *Journal of Vocational Behavior, 20,* 255-275.

Lunneborg, P. (1975). Interest differentiation in high school and vocational indecision in college. *Journal of Vocational Behavior, 7,* 297-303.

Lunneborg, P. (1976). Vocational indecision in college graduates. *Journal of Counseling Psychology, 23*(4), 402-404.

Lunneborg, P. (1978). Sex and career decision-making styles. *Journal of Counseling Psychology, 25,* 299-305.

Lunneborg, P. (1980). Reducing sex bias in interest measurement at the item level. *Journal of Vocational Behavior, 16,* 226-234.

Luther, R. K., & Smith, V. M. (1974). A functional model for career development. *NASPA Journal, 12,* 60-66.

Lynch, R. K., & Maki, D. R. (1981). Searching for structure: A trait-factor approach to vocational rehabilitation. *Vocational Guidance Quarterly, 30*(1), 61-68.

Lyson, T. A., & Brown, S. S. (1982). Sex-role attitudes, curriculum choice, and career ambition: A comparison between women in typical and atypical college majors. *Journal of Vocational Behavior, 20,* 366-375.

Lytel, R. (1978). Aptitutdes and self-perceptions related to the employability of the emotionally disabled. *Journal of Employment Counseling, 15,* 134-143.

MacArthur, J. D. (1980). Career services for university international students. *Vocational Guidance Quarterly, 29,* 178-181.

Maccoby, M. (1976). *The gamesman.* New York: Simon and Schuster.

Maccoby, M. (1980). Work and human development. *Professional Psychology, 11*, 509–519.

Maccoby, M., & Terzi, K. (1981). What happened to the work ethic? In J. O'Toole, J. L. Scheiber, & L. C. Wood, (Eds.), *Working, changes and choices.* New York: Human Sciences Press, pp. 162–171.

Mackay, W. R., & Miller, C. A. (1982). Relations of socioeconomic status and sex variables to the complexity of worker functions in the occupational choice of elementary school children. *Journal of Vocational Behavior, 20*, 31–39.

Macke, A. S., Bohrstedt, G. W., & Bernstein, I. N. (1979). Housewives' self-esteem and their husbands' success: The myth of vicarious involvement. *Journal of Marriage and the Family, 40*, 51–57.

Macke, A. S., & Morgan, W. R. (1978). Maternal employment, race, and work orientation of high school girls. *Social Forces, 57*(1), 187–203.

Mackin, R. K., & Hansen, L. S. (1981). A theory-based career development course: A plant in the garden. *The School Counselor, 28*(5), 325–334.

MacKota, C. (1976). Using work therapeutically. In H. Lamb (Ed.), *Community surivial in long term patients.* San Francisco: Jossey-Bass.

MacMichael, D. C. (1974). Work ethics: Collision in the classroom. *Manpower, 6*, 15–20.

Maddox, G. L. (1972). Retirement as a social event in the United States. In B. L. Neugarten (Ed.), *Middle age and aging.* Chicago: University of Chicago Press.

Mager, R. F. (1962). *Preparing instructional objectives.* Palo Alto, CA: Fearon.

Magoon, T. M. (1969). Developing skills for solving educational and vocational problems. In J. D. Krumboltz, & C. E. Thoresen (Eds.), *Behavioral counseling: Cases and techniques.* New York: Holt, Rinehart and Winston.

Mahone, C. H. (1960). Fear of failure and unrealistic vocational aspiration. *Journal of Abnormal and Social Psychology, 60*, 253–261.

Malnig, L. R. (1967). Fear of paternal competition: A factor in vocational choice. *Personnel and Guidance Quarterly, 46*, 235–239.

Manneback, A. J., & Stillwell, W. E., (1974). Installing career education: A systems approach. *Vocational Guidance Quarterly, 22*, 180–188.

Mansfield, C. (1976). We hear you Mr./Ms. Business: The resume and career letter. *ABCA Bulletin, 39*, 20–23.

Maples, M. F. (1981). Dual career marriages: Elements for potential success. *Personnel and Guidance Journal, 60*(1), 19–23.

Marbach, G. (1968). *Job re-design for older workers.* Paris: Organization for Economic Cooperation and Development.

Marinoble, R. M. (1980). Community jobs for handicapped students: A career education technique. *Vocational Guidance Quarterly, 29*(2), 172–177.

Marland, S. P. (1972). Career education 300 days later. *American Vocational Journal, 47*(2), 14–17.

Marland, S. P. (1974). *Career education: A proposal for reform.* New York: McGraw-Hill.

Marlowe, A. F. (1981). Passages: A program for career and life planning. *Vocational Guidance Quarterly, 29*(4), 355–361.

Marr, E. (1965). Some behaviors and attitudes relating to vocational choice. *Journal of Counseling Psychology, 12*, 404–408.

Marsden, D. (1975). *Workless.* Harmondsworth, England: Penguin.

Marshall, A. E. (1979). Assisting college students to apply to graduate school: A career planning service. *Journal of College Student Personnel, 20*, 556–557.

Marshall, S. J., & Wijting, J. P. (1980). Relationships of achievement motivation and sex-role identity to college women's career orientation. *Journal of Vocational Behavior, 16*, 299–311.

Martin, G. M. (1979). Getting chosen: The job interview and before. *Occupational Outlook Quarterly, 23*(1), 2–9.

Martin, G. M. (1980). A guide to setting up a career resource information center. *Occupational Outlook Quarterly, 24*(3), 12–17.

Maslach, C. (1976). Burned out. *Human Behavior, 5*(9), 16–22.

Maslach, C. (1978). The client role in staff burnout. *Journal of Social Issues, 34*(4), 111–124.

Maslach, C. (1981). Burnout: A social psychological analysis. In J. W. Jones (Ed.), *The burnout syndrome: Current research, theory, interventions.* Park Ridge, IL: London House Press.

Maslach, C., & Jackson, J. E. (1981). The measurement of experienced burnout. *Journal of Occupational Behavior, 2*, 99–113.

Maslow, A. H. (1954). *Motivation and personality.* New York: Harper & Row.

Matthay, E. R., & Linder, R. (1982). A team effort in planning for the academically disadvantaged. *The School Counselor, 29*(3), 226–231.

Maurer, J. G., Vrendenburgh, D. J., & Smith, R. L. (1981). An examination of the central life interest scale. *Academy of Management Journal, 24*(1), 174–182.

Maynard, M. (1979). The occupational, learning, and social support orientations of employees. *Journal of Employment Counseling, 16*(2), 94–109.

Maynard, P. E., & Hansen, J. C. (1970). Vocational maturity among inner city youths. *Journal of Counseling Psychology, 17*, 400–404.

McAshan, H. H. (1969). *Writing behavioral objectives.* Gainesville, FL: Florida Educational Research and Development Council.

McAshan, H. H. (1970). *Writing behavioral objectives: A new approach.* New York: Harper & Row.

McClellan, D. C. (1965). Toward a theory of motive acquisition. *American Psychologist, 20*, 321–333.

McCourt, H. (1971). The vocational development lesson. In J. C. Hansen and S. H. Cramer (Eds.), *Group guidance and counseling in the schools* (pp. 172–183). New York: Appleton-Century-Crofts.

McDaniel, C. (1978). The practice of career guidance and counseling. *INFORM, 7*(1), 1–2, 7–8.

McDaniel, C. (1982). Comprehensive career information systems for the 1980s. *Vocational Guidance Quarterly, 30*(4), 344-350.

McDaniel, J. W. (1963). Disability and vocational development. *Journal of Rehabilitation, 29*(4), 16-18.

McDaniels, C. (1968). Youth: Too young to choose. *Vocational Guidance Quarterly, 16,* 242-249.

McDaniels, C. (1980). Labor market information: How well equipped are counselors to assist students? In H. N. Drier, & L. A. Pfister (Eds.), *Career and labor market information: Key to improved individual decision making* (pp. 27-39). Columbus, OH: The National Center for Research in Vocational Education.

McDowell, C. F. (1976). *Leisure counseling: Related lifestyle processed.* Eugene, OR: University of Oregon.

McFarland, R. A. (1973). The need for functional age measures in industrial gerontology. *Industrial Gerontology, 19*(3), 1-19.

McGee, L., & Stillman, B. (1982). Interest measurement as a basis for elementary career awareness activities. *Elementary School Guidance and Counseling, 16*(3), 172-179.

McGehee, W., & Tullar, W. L. (1979). Single question measures of overall job satisfaction: A comment on Quinn, Staines, and McCullough. *Journal of Vocational Behavior, 14,* 112-117.

McGinnis, R. D., et al. (1977). Probation and employment. *Offender Rehabilitation, 1*(4), 323-333.

McGovern, T. V., & Jones, B. W., & Morris, S. E. (1979). Comparison of professional versus student ratings of job interviewee behavior. *Journal of Counseling Psychology, 26*(2), 176-179.

McGovern, T. V., & Tinsley, H. (1978). Interviewer evaluations of interviewee nonverbal behavior. *Journal of Vocational Behavior, 13,* 163-171.

McKay, W. R., & Miller, C. A. (1982). Relations of socioeconomic status and sex variables to the complexity of worker functions in the occupational choices of elementary school children. *Journal of Vocational Behavior, 20,* 31-39.

McLaughlin, R. (1976). *Career education in the public schools 1974-75: A national study.* Washington, DC; The Office of Career Education.

McLaughlin, S. D. (1978). Occupational sex identification and the assessment of male and female earnings inequality. *American Sociological Review, 43,* 909-921.

McLean, A. A. (1973). Occupational mental health: Review of and emerging art. In R. L. Noland (Ed.), *Industrial mental health and counseling* (Chap. 7). New York: Behavioral Publications.

McMahon, G. G. (1970). Technical education: A problem of definition. *American Vocational Journal, 44,* 22-23.

McMorrow, F. (1974). *Midolescence: The dangerous years.* New York: Quadrangle/New York Times Co.

McPherson, B., & Guppy, N. (1975). Pre-retirement life style and planning for retirement. *Industrial Gerontology, 2,* 95-109.

Meckel, N. T. (1981). The manager as career counselor. *Training and Development Journal, 35,* 65-69.

Medvene, A. M. (1973). Early parent child interactions of educational, vocational, and emotional-social clients. *Journal of Counseling Psychology, 20,* 94-95.

Medvene, A. M., & Collings, A. (1974). Occupational prestige and its relationship to traditional and nontraditional views of women's roles. *Journal of Counseling Psychology, 21,* 139-143.

Meehl, P. E. (1954). *Clinical versus statistical prediction.* Minneapolis, MN: University of Minnesota Press.

Meerback, J. (1978). *Career resource centers.* New York: Haman Services Press.

Meichenbaum, D. (1977). *Cognitive-behavior modification.* New York: Plenum.

Meier, E. L. (1975). Over 65: Expectations and realities of work and retirement. *Industrial Gerontology, 2,* 95-109.

Meir, E. I. (1978). A test of the independence of fields and levels in Roe's occupational classification. *Vocational Guidance Quarterly, 27*(2), 124-129.

Melamed, S., & Meir, E. (1981). The relationship between interests – job incongruity and selection of avocational activity. *Journal of Vocational Behavior, 18,* 310-325.

Melhaus, G. E., Hershenson, D. B., & Vermillion, M. E. (1973). Computer assisted versus traditional vocational counseling with high school and low readiness clients. *Journal of Vocational Behavior 3,* 137-144.

Mencke, R. A., & Cochran, D. J. (1974). Impact of a counseling outreach workshop on vocational development. *Journal of Counseling Psychology, 21,* 185-190.

Menning, A. (1981). How career services can assist undeclared majors. *Journal of College Placement, 41*(3), 44-47.

Menning, A., & Whittmayer, C. (1979). Administrative and program provisions for undecided students. *Vocational Guidance Quarterly, 28*(2), 175-181.

Mercado, P., & Atkinson, D. R. (1982). Effects of counselor sex, student sex, and student attractiveness in counselors' judgments. *Journal of Vocational Behavior, 20,* 304-312.

Merman, S. K., & McLaughlin, J. E. (1982, August). *Unleashing human potential: The role of the career counselor in industry.* Paper presented to the International Federation of Training and Development Organizations, Calgary, Alberta, Canada.

Mesa Public Schools. (1974). *Toward accountability.* A report on the Mesa approach to career guidance, counseling, and placement. Mesa, AZ: The Public Schools.

Meyer, J. B., Strowig, W, & Hosford, R. E. (1970). Behavioral-reinforcement counseling with rural high school youth. *Journal of Counseling Psychology, 17,* 127-132.

Meyers, C. E., Drinkard, K., & Zinner, E. G. (1975). *What I like to do.* Chicago: Science Research Associates.

Miles, L. (1981). Midlife career change for Blacks: Problems and issues. *Vocational Guidance Quarterly, 30*(1), 5-13.

Millan, B. H. (1979). Providing assistance to displaced workers. *Monthly Labor Review, 102*(5), 17–32.

Miller, A. J. (1972, April) *The emerging school based comprehensive education model*. Paper presented to the National Conference on Career Education for Deans of Colleges of Education, Columbus, OH.

Miller, A. L., & Tiedeman, D. V. (1972). Decision making for the 70's: The cubing of the Tiedeman paradigm and its application in career education. *Focus on Guidance, 5*(1), 1–15.

Miller, A. L., & Tiedeman, D. V. (1977). Structuring responsibility in adolescents actualizing "I" power through curriculum. In G. D. Miller (Ed.), *Developmental theory and its application in guidance programs: Systematic efforts to promote personal growth* (pp. 123–166). Minneapolis, MN: Minnesota Department of Education.

Miller, A. W. (1968). Learning theory and vocational decisions. *Personnel and Guidance Journal, 47,* 18–23.

Miller, C. (1973). Historical and recent perspectives on work and vocational guidance. In H. Borow (Ed.), *Career guidance for a new age*. Boston: Houghton Mifflin.

Miller, C. D., & Oetting, G. (1977). Barriers to employment and the disadvantaged. *Personnel and Guidance Journal, 56*(2), 89–93.

Miller, C. H. (1974). Career development theory in perspective. Chapter 10. In E. L. Herr (Ed.), *Vocational guidance and human development*. Boston, MA: Houghton Mifflin.

Miller, D. C., & Form, W. H. (1951). *Industrial sociology*. New York: Harper.

Miller, D. C., & Thomas, D. L. (1966). Relationships between education and vocational interests. *Vocational Guidance Quarterly, 15,* 113–118.

Miller, D. W., & Starr, M. K. (1967). *The structure of human decisions*. Englewood Cliffs, N.J.: Prentice-Hall.

Miller, G. (1980). The interpretation of nonoccupational work in modern society: A preliminary discussion and typology. *Social Problems, 27*(4), 381–391.

Miller, J. (1970). Information retrieval systems in guidance. *Personnel and Guidance Journal, 49,* 212–218.

Miller, J. (1977). *Career development needs of nine-year-olds: How to improve career development programs*. Washington, DC: National Advisory Council for Career Education.

Miller, J. (1980). Individual and occupational determinants of job satisfaction. *Sociology of Work and Occupations, 7*(3), 337–366.

Miller, J. V. (1982). Lifelong career development for disadvantaged youth and adults. *Vocational Guidance Quarterly, 30*(4), 359–366.

Miller, J. V. (1982). 1970's trends in assessing career counseling, guidance, and education. *Measurement and Evaluation in Guidance, 15*(2), 142–146.

Miller, M. F. (1974). Relationship of vocational maturity to work values. *Journal of Vocational Behavior, 5,* 367–371.

Miller, M. F. (1978). Childhood experience antecedents

of career maturity attitudes. *Vocational Guidance Quarterly, 27*(2), 137–143.

Milley, D. J., & Bee, R. H. (1982). A conditional logic model of collegiate major selection. *Journal of Vocational Behavior, 20,* 81–92.

Milliken, R. L. (1962). Realistic occupational appraisal by high school seniors. *Personnel and Guidance Journal, 40,* 541–544.

Minton, E. B. (1977). Job placement: Strategies and techniques. *Rehabilitation Counseling Bulletin, 21*(2), 141–149.

Mitchel, J. O. (1982). Careers at the agency level. *Managers Magazine, 53*(3), 28–35.

Mitchell, A. M. (1975). Emerging career guidance competencies. *Personnel and Guidance Journal, 53*(9), 700–705.

Mitchell, A. M. (1977). *Career development needs of seventeen year olds: How to improve career development programs*. Washington, DC: National Advisory Committee for Career Education.

Mitchell, J. S. (1973). Decisions by catalytic counseling. *The School Counselor, 20*(3), 197–201.

Moch, M. K. (1980). Racial differences in job satisfaction: Testing four common explanations. *Journal of Applied Psychology, 65,* 299–306.

Mogul, K. M. (1979). Women in midlife: Decisions, rewards, and conflicts related to work and careers. *American Journal of Psychiatry, 136*(9), 1139–1143.

Moir, E. (1981). Career resource centers in business and industry. *Training and Development Journal, 35*(2), 54–57.

Moore, G. D. (1961). A negative view toward therapeutic counseling in the schools. *Counselor Education and Supervision, 1,* 60–65.

Moore, K. (1976). Faculty advising: Panacea or placebo? *Journal of College Student Personnel, 17,* 371–375.

Moore, K., & Veres, H. (1976). Traditional and innovative career plans of two-year college women. *Journal of College Student Personnel, 17*(1), 34–38.

Moreland, J., Harren, V., Krimski-Montague, E., & Tinsley, H. (1979). Sex role concept and career decision-making. *Journal of Counseling Psychology, 26,* 329–336.

Morgan, M., Hall, D., & Martier, A. (1979). Career development strategies in industry: Where are we and where should we be? *Personnel, 56,* 13–30.

Morrill, W. H., & Forrest, D. J. (1970). Dimensions of counseling for career development. *Personnel and Guidance Journal, 49,* 299–306.

Morris, J. L. (1966). Propensity for risk taking as determinant of vocational choice. *Journal of Personality and Social Psychology, 3,* 328–335.

Morrison, M. (1975). The myth of employee planning for retirement. *Industrial Gerontology, 2*(2), 135–143.

Morrow, P. C. (1981). Retirement planning programs: Assessing their attendance and efficacy. *Aging and Work, 4*(4), 244–252.

Morse, N., & Weiss, R. S. (1962). The function and meaning of work and the job. In S. Nosow & W. Form (Eds.), *Man, work, and society*. New York: Basic Books.

Morse, W. (1963). *Foreword to the vocational education act of 1963*. PL88210. Washington, DC.

Moser, H. P., Dubin, W., & Shelsky, I. (1956). A proposed modification of the Roe occupational classification. *Journal of Counseling Psychology, 3,* 27–31.

Moses, J. L., & Byham, W. C. (Eds.). (1977). *Applying the Assessment center method*. New York: Pergamon Press.

Mossholder, K. W., Dewhirst, H. D., & Arvey, R. P. (1981). Vocational interest and personality differences between development and research personnel: A field study. *Journal of Vocational Behavior, 19,* 233–243.

Motsch, P. (1980). Peer social modeling: A tool for assisting girls with career exploration. *Vocational Guidance Quarterly, 28*(3), 231–240.

Moynihan, D. P. (1964). Morality of work and immorality of opportunity. *Vocational Guidance Quarterly, 12,* 229–236.

Muchinsky, P. M. (1978). Age and job facet satisfaction: A conceptual reconsideration. *Aging and Work, 1*(3), 175–179.

Muchinsky, P. M., & Tuttle, M. L. (1979). Employee turnover: An empirical and methodological assessment. *Journal of Vocational Behavior, 14,* 43–77.

Mueller, C. F. (1981). Migration of the unemployed: A relocation assistance program. *Monthly Labor Review, 104*(4), 62–64.

Mund, S. (1978). Vocational rehabilitation, employment, self-employment: Vocational rehabilitation process. In R. M. Goldenson (Ed.), *Disability and Rehabilitation Handbook*. New York: McGraw-Hill, 67–71.

Murphy, G. (1947). *Personality: A biosocial approach to origins and structure*. New York: Harper & Row.

Murphy, S. T. (1977). A critical view of job placement inquiry. *Rehabilitation Counseling Bulletin, 21*(2), 166–175.

Murray, H. (1938). *Explorations in personality*. New York: Oxford University Press.

Myers, R. A., Linderman, R. H., Thompson, A. S., & Patrick, T. A. (1975). Effects of educational and career exploration systems on vocational maturity. *Journal of Vocational Behavior, 6,* 245–254.

Nafziger, D. H., Holland, J. L., Helms, S. T., & McPartland, J. M. (1974). Applying an occupational classification to the work histories of young men and women. *Journal of Vocational Behavior, 5,* 331–345.

Naisbitt, J. (1982). *Megatrends: Ten new directions transforming our lives*. New York: Warner Books.

National Association of Secondary School Principals. (1975). EBCE: A design for career education. *Curriculum Report 4*(3), 1–11.

National Center for Educational Statistics. (1980). *Condition of education, 1980*. Washington, DC: The Center.

National Center for Educational Statistics. (1981). *Digest of educational statistics, 1981*. Washington, DC: The Center.

National Center for Research in Vocational Education. (1982). Factors relating to the job placement of former secondary vocational education students. *CENTERGRAM, 17*(3), 1–2.

National Opinion Research Center. (1947). Jobs and occupations: A popular evaluation. *Opinion News, 9,* 3–13.

National Vocational Guidance Association. (1981, September). *Vocational/Career Counseling Competencies Approved by the board of Directors*. Falls Church, VA.

National Vocational Guidance Association/American Vocational Association. (1973). *The position paper on career development*. Washington, DC: The Association.

Navin, S. (1972). Future planning of college women: Counseling implication. *Vocational Guidance Quarterly, 21*(4), 12–17.

Nealer, J. K., & Papalia, A. S. (1982). *So you want to get a job: A manual for the job seeker and vocational counselor*. Moravia, NY: Chronicle Guidance.

Neapoliton, J. (1980). Occupational change in midcareer: An exploratory investigation. *Journal of Vocational Behavior, 16,* 212–225.

Near, J. P., Rice, R. W., & Hunt, R. G. (1980). The relationship between work and nonwork domains: A review of empirical research. *Academy of Management Review, 5,* 415–429.

Neely, M. A. (1980). Career maturity inventory interpretations for grade 9 boys and girls. *Vocational Guidance Quarterly, 29*(2), 113–124.

Neely, M. A., & Kosier, M. W. (1977). Physically impaired students and the vocational exploration group. *Vocational Guidance Quarterly, 26*(1), 37–44.

Neff, W. S. (1977). *Work and human behavior* (2nd ed.). Chicago: Aldine.

Neice, D., & Bradley, R. (1976). Relationship of age, sex, and educational groups to career decisiveness. *Journal of Vocational Behavior, 14,* 271–278.

Nelson, A. G. (1956). Vocational maturity and client satisfaction. *Journal of Counseling Psychology, 3,* 254–256.

Nelson, R. C. (1963). Knowledge and interest concerning sixteen occupations among elementary and secondary students. *Educational and Psychological Measurement, 27,* 741–754.

Nelson, R. C. (1979). The CREST program: Helping children with their choices. *Elementary School Guidance and Counseling, 14*(4), 286–298.

Nelson, R. E. (1979). *Perceptions concerning occupational survival skills*. Springfield, IL: Department of Adult, Vocational and Technical Education, Illinois Office of Education.

Neopolitan, J. (1980). Occupational change in midcareer: An exploratory investigation. *Journal of Vocational Behavior, 16*(2), 212–225.

New Jersey State Department of Education. (1973). Technology for children (T4C). *Elementary School Guidance and Counseling, 7*(3), 235.

Newberry, P., Weissman, M. M., & Myers, J. K. (1979). Working wives and housewives: Do they differ in mental status and social adjustment? *American Journal of Orthopsychiatry, 49*(2), 282–291.

Newman, M. J. (1978). A profile of Hispanics in the

U. S. work force. *Monthly Labor Review, 101,* 3-14.

Nieva, V. G., & Gutek, B. A. (1981). *Women and work.* New York: Praeger.

NOICC. (1981). *Occupational information system handbook: Volume II, occupational information analysis, presentation, and delivery.* Washington, DC: U. S. Government Printing Office.

Nolan, R. L. (Ed.). (1973). *Industrial mental health and employment counseling.* New York: Behavioral Objectives.

Norman, R. P. (1969). The use of preliminary information in vocational counseling. *Personnel and Guidance Journal, 47,* 693-697.

Norris, W. (1963). *Occupational information in the elementary school.* Chicago: Science Research Associates.

Norris, W., Zeran, F. R., Hatch, R. N., & Engelkes, J. R. (1979). *The information service in guidance* (4th ed.). Chicago: Rand McNally.

Norton, J. L. (1970). Current status of the measurement of vocational maturity. *Vocational Guidance Quarterly, 18,* 165-170.

Novaco, R. (1976). Treatment of chronic anger through cognitive and relaxation controls. *Journal of Consulting and Clinical Psychology, 44,* 681.

Nuckols, T. E., & Banducci, R. (1974). Knowledge of occupations – Is it important in occupational choice? *Journal of Counseling Psychology, 21,* 191-195.

NVGA. (1971). *Guidelines for the preparation and evaluation of career information media: Films, filmstrips, and printed materials.* Washington, DC: American Personnel and Guidance Association.

NVGA. (1980). Guidelines for the preparation and evaluation of career information literature. *Vocational Guidance Quarterly, 28*(4), 291-296.

Nye, F. I. (1963). Marital interaction. In F. I. Nye, & L. W. Hoffman (Eds.), *The employed mother in America.* Chicago: Rand McNally, 263-281.

Oakland, J. A. (1969). Measurement of personality correlates of academic achievement in high school students. *Journal of Counseling Psychology, 16,* 452-457.

Obgu, J. (1974). *The next generation.* New York: Academic Press.

O'Bryant, S. L., Durrett, M. E., & Pennebaker, J. W. (1978). Students' ratings of occupational dimensions of traditionally male and traditionally female occupations. *Journal of Vocational Behavior, 12,* 297-304.

O'Hara, R. P. (1966). Vocational self-concepts and high school achievement. *Vocational Guidance Quarterly, 15.* 106-112.

O'Hara, R. P. (1968). A theoretical foundation for the use of occupational information in guidance. *Personnel and Guidance Journal, 46,* 636-640.

O'Hara, R. P. (1969). Comment on Super's papers. *The Counseling Psychology, 1,* 29-31.

Okun, M. A. (1976). Adult age and cautiousness in decision-making. *Human Development, 19,* 220-233.

Olbrisch, M. E. (1977). Psychotherapeutic intervention in physical health: Effectiveness and economic efficiency. *American Psychologist, 32*(9), 761-777.

Olive, H. (1973). Sex differences in adolescent vocational preferences. *Vocational Guidance Quarterly, 21*(3), 199-201.

Oliver, L. (1975). The relationship of parental attitudes and parent identification to career and homemaking orientation in college women. *Journal of Vocational Behavior, 7,* 1-12.

Oliver, L. W. (1977). Evaluating career counseling outcome for three modes of test interpretation. *Measurement and Evaluation in Guidance, 10*(3), 153-161.

Olney, R. J. (1982). How employees view resumes: 1974-1981. *Journal of College Placement, 42*(3), 64-67.

Olson, S. K. (1981). Current status of corporate retirement preparation programs. *Aging and Work, 4*(3), 175-187.

Omvig, C. P., & Thomas, E. G. (1974). A socioeconomic comparison of vocational interests: Implications for counseling. *Journal of Vocational Behavior, 5,* 147-155.

O'Neil, J. M., & Heck, E. J. (1980). A sequential, self-help, job seeking training manual to help college students in the job-search process. *Journal of College Student Personnel, 21,* 170-171.

O'Neil, J. O., Price, G. E., & Tracy, T. J. (1979). The stimulus value, treatment effects, and sex differences when completing the Self-Directed Search and Strong-Campbell Interest Inventory. *Journal of Counseling Psychology, 26,* 45-50.

O'Neill, J., Ohlde, C., Tolefson, N., Barke, C., Piggott, T., & Watts, D. (1980). Factors, correlates, and problem areas affecting career decision-making of a cross-sectional sample of students. *Journal of Counseling Psychology, 27,* 571-580.

O'Reilly, P. A. (1973). *Predicting the stability of expressed occupational choices of secondary students.* Unpublished doctoral dissertation, Pennsylvania State University.

Orpen, C. (1978). Work and nonwork satisfaction: A casual-correlation analysis. *Journal of Applied Psychology, 63,* 530-532.

Osipow, S. (1977). The great expose swindle: A reader's reaction. *Personnel and Guidance Journal, 56,* 23-24.

Osipow, S. (1980). *Mannual for the career decision scale.* Columbus, OH: Marathon Consulting and Press.

Osipow, S., Carney, C., & Barak, A. (1976). A scale of educational-vocational undecidedness: A typological approach. *Journal of Vocational Behavior, 9,* 233-243.

Osipow, S. H. (1968). *Theories of career development.* New York: Appleton-Century-Crofts.

Osipow, S. H. (1977). Will the real counseling psychologist please stand up? *The Counseling Psychologist, 7*(2), 93-94.

Osipow, S. H. (1982). Counseling psychology: Applications in the world of work. *The Counseling Psychologist, 10*(3), 19-25.

Osipow, S. H. (1983). *Theories of career development* (3rd Ed.). Englewood Cliffs, NJ: Prentice-Hall.

Osipow, S. H., Ashby, J. D., & Wall, H. W. (1966). Personality types and vocational choice: A test of Holland's theory. *Personnel and Guidance Journal, 45,* 37-42.

Osipow, S. H., Carney, C. G., Winer, J. L., Yanico, B. J. & Koschir, M. (1976). *Career decision scale.* Columbus, OH: Marathon Consulting and Press.

Osipow, S. H., & Gold, J. A. (1967). Factors related to inconsistent career preference. *Personnel and Guidance Journal, 46,* 342-349.

Osterman, P. (1980). *Getting started: The youth labor market.* Cambridge, MA: MIT Press.

O'Toole, J. (Ed.) (1973). *Work in America.* Cambridge, MA: MIT Press.

O'Toole, J. (1975). *The reserve army of the underemployed.* Monographs on Career Education. Washington, DC: U.S. Department of Health, Education, and Welfare.

O'Toole, J. (1981). Work in America in J. O'Toole, J. L. Schiber, & L. C. Wood (Eds.) Working: *Changes and choices.* New York: Human Sciences Press. 12-17.

O'Toole, J. (1982). How to forecast your own working future. *The Futurist, 16*(1), 5-11.

Ott, M. D. (1978). Differences between male and female freshmen engineers. *Journal of College Student Personnel, 19*(6), 552-557.

Otte, F. L., & Sharpe, D. L. The effects of career exploration on self-esteem, achievement motivation, and occupational knowledge. *Vocational Guidance Quarterly, 28*(1), 63-70.

Ouchi, W. G. (1981). *Theory Z: How American business can meet the Japanese challenge.* Reading, MA: Addison-Wesley.

Ouchi, W. G., & Jaeger, A. M. (1978). Type Z organization: Stability in the midst of mobility. *Academy of Management Reveiw, 3,* 305-314.

Palmo, A. J., & DeVantier, J. (1976). An examination of the counseling needs of Voc-Tech students. *Vocational Guidance Quarterly, 25,* 170-176.

Paloma, M. M., & Garland, T. N. (1971). The married professional woman: A study in the tolerance of domestication. *Journal of Marriage and the Family, 33*(3), 531-540.

Paolitto, D. P. (1977). Group counseling in the junior high: Counselors and teachers as coleaders. *Focus on Guidance, 9*(2), 1-16.

Papalia, A. S., & Kaminski, W. (1981). Counseling and counseling skills in the industrial environment. *Vocational Guidance Quarterly, 30*(1), 37-42.

Papalia, A. S., & Moore, S. J. (1979). Applying educational counseling skills in industry: A role expansion model for counselors. *Journal of College Student Personnel, 20*(1), 23-27.

Parasuraman, S., & Alutto, J. A. (1981). An examination of the organizational antecedents of stress at work. *Academy of Management Journal, 24*(1), 48-67.

Pardine, P., Higgins, R., Szeglin, A., Beres, J., Kravitz, R., & Fotis, J. (1981). Job-stress worker-strain relationship moderated off-the-job experience. *Psychological Reports, 48,* 963-970.

Parelius, A. P. (1975). Change and stability in college women's orientations toward education, family, and work. *Social Problems, 22,* 420-432.

Parker, C. (1974). Student development: What does it mean? *Journal of College Student Personnel, 15,* 248-256.

Parker, C., Bunch, S., & Hagberg, R. (1974). Group vocational guidance with college students. *Vocational Guidance Quarterly, 23,* 168-172.

Parker, D. A., Parker, E. S., Wolz, M. W., & Harford, T. C. (1980). Sex roles and alcohol consumption: A research note. *Journal of Health and Social Behavior, 21,* 43-48.

Parker, H. J. (1970). 29,000 seventh-graders have made occupational choices. *Vocational Guidance Quarterly, 18,* 219-224.

Parker, M., Peltier, S., & Wolleat, P. (1981). Understanding dual career couples. *Personnel and Guidance Journal, 60*(1), 14-18.

Parker, V. (1975). Placement programs: A new philosophy. *Community and Junior College Journal, 45,* 30-31, 34.

Parkes, C. M. (1971). Psycho-social transitions: A field for study. *Social Science and Medicine, 5*(2), 101-115.

Parkinson, T., Bradley, R., & Lawson, G. (1979). Career counseling revisited. *Vocational Guidance Quarterly, 28*(2), 121-129.

Parsons, F. (1909). *Choosing a vocation.* Boston: Houghton Mifflin.

Parsons, T. (1951). *The social system.* Glencoe, IL: The Free Press.

Partin, R. L., & Gargiolo, R. N. (1980). Burned out teachers have no class! Prescriptions for teacher burnout. *College Student Journal, 14*(4), 365-380.

Pascal, A. H., et al. (1975a). *An evaluation of policy-related research on programs for mid-life career redirection: Volume I – major findings* (R-1582/2-NSF). Washington, DC: National Science Foundation.

Pascal, A. H., et al. (1975b). *An evaluation of policy-related research on programs for mid-life career redirection: Volume II – Major findings.* Santa Monica, CA: Rand.

Pate, R. H., Jr., Simpson, L. A., & Burks, H. M. (1969-1970). A pilot program for group counseling. *Journal of College Placement, 30*(2), 79-82.

Pate, R. H., Jr., Tulloch, J. B., & Dassance, C. R. (1981). A regional job and educational opportunities fair. *Personnel and Guidance Journal, 60*(3), 187-189.

Paterson, D. G. (1938, January). The genesis of modern guidance. *Educational Record, 19,* 36-46.

Paykell, E. S., Prusoff, B. A., & Vienhuth, E. H. (1971). Scaling life events. *Archive of General Psychiatry, 25* (4), 340-347.

Peace, C. H. (1973). Pastoral counseling with the problem employee. In R. L. Noland (Ed.), *Industrial mental health and employee counseling* (Chap. 22). New York: Behavioral Publications.

Pearlin, L. J. (1975). Status inequality and stress in

marriage. *American Sociological Review, 40*, 344–357.

Pearlman, K., Schmidt, F. L., & Hunter, J. E. (1980). Validity generalization results for tests used to predict job proficiency and training success in clerical occupations. *Journal of Applied Psychology, 65*, 373–406.

Pearson, R. (1968). Working with the disadvantaged through groups. In W. E. Amos & J. D. Grambo (Eds.), *Counseling the Disadvantaged youth.* Englewood Cliffs, NJ: Prentice-Hall.

Peatling, J. H., & Tiedeman, D. V. (1977). *Career development, designing self.* Muncie, IN: Accelerated Development.

Peck, R. C. (1975, April). Psychological developments in the second half of life. In J. E. Anderson (Ed.), *Psychological aspects of aging* (pp. 44–49). Proceedings of a Conference on Planning Research, Bethesda, Maryland.

Pederson, P., Holwill, C. F., & Shapiro, J. (1978). A cross-cultural training procedure for classes in counselor education. *Counselor Education and Supervision, 17*(3), 233–237.

Pedro, J. D. (1982). Career maturity in high school females. *Vocational Guidance Quarterly, 30*(3), 243–251.

Pedro, J. D., Wolleat, P., & Fennema, E. (1980). Sex differences in the relationship of career interests and mathematics plans. *Vocational Guidance Quarterly, 29*(1), 25–34.

Pelletier, D. M. (1981). The sales approach to the job hunt. *Journal of College Placement, 41*(4), 48–50.

Penley, L. P., & Hawkins, B. L. (1980). Organizational communication, performance, and job satisfaction as a function of ethnicity and sex. *Journal of Vocational Behavior, 16*, 368–384.

Perovich, G. M., & Mierzwa, J. A. (1980). Group facilitation of vocational maturity and self-esteem in college students. *Journal of College Student Personnel, 21*, 206–211.

Perrone, P. A. (1964). Factors influencing high school seniors' occupational preference. *Personnel and Guidance Journal, 42*, 976–979.

Perrone, P. A. (1973). A longitudinal study of occupational values in adolescents. *Vocational Guidance Quarterly, 22*(2), 116–123.

Perrone, P. A., Male, R. A., & Karshner, W. W. (1979). Career development needs of talented students: A perspective for counselors. *The School Counselor, 27*(1), 16–23.

Perrone, P. A., Wolleat, P. L., Lee, J. L., & Davis, S. A. (1977). Counseling needs of adult students. *Vocational Guidance Quarterly, 28*(1), 27–36.

Perry, L. (1982). Special populations: The demands of diversity. In E. L. Herr, & N. M. Pinson (Eds.), *Foundations for policy in guidance and counseling.* Washington, DC: American Personnel and Guidance Association.

Perry, W. G. (1968). *Forms of intellectual and ethical development in the college years: A scheme.* New York: Holt, Rinehart & Winston.

Petersen, M. L. (1974, July). *Simulated instructional systems "SIS" utilizing simulated occupational units in a career education program.* Paper presented at the meeting of the Utah Vocational Association, Salt Lake City.

Phelps, L. A., & Lutz, R. J. (1977). *Career exploration and preparation for the special needs learner.* Boston: Allyn and Bacon.

Phenix, P. H. (1973, March). *Basic values issues in career education for the gifted and talented.* Paper presented at the First National Invitational Seminar on Career Education for the Gifted and Talented Students, University of Maryland.

Phillips, M. G. (1966). Learning materials and their implementation. *Review of Educational Research, 36*(3), 373–379.

Phillips, S. D. (1982a). Career exploration in adulthood. *Journal of Vocational Behavior, 20*, 129–140.

Phillips, S. D. (1982b). The development of career choices: The relationship between patterns of commitment and career outcomes in adulthood. *Journal of Vocational Behavior, 29*, 141–152.

Phillips, J. S., Barrett, G. V., & Rush, M. C. (1978). Job structure and age satisfaction. *Aging and work, 1*(2), 109–119.

Phillips, L., & Weiss, B. (1972). Career development for handicapped youth. *Elementary School Guidance and Counseling, 7*(2), 154–155.

Phillips, S., & Strohmer, D. (1982). Decision-making style and vocational maturity. *Journal of Vocational Behavior, 20*(2), 215–222.

Phillips-Jones, L., Jones, G. B., & Drier, H. N. (1981). *Developing training competencies for career guidance personnel.* Falls Church, VA: National Vocational Guidance Association.

Piaget, J. (1929). *The child's conception of the world.* New York: Harcourt, Brace.

Pierson, F. C. (1980). *The minimal level of unemployment and public policy.* Kalamazoo, MI: The W. E. Upjohn Institute for Employment and Research.

Pietrofesa, J. J., & Splete, H. (1975). *Career development: Theory and research.* New York: Grune and Stratton.

Pilato, G. T., & Myers, R. A. (1975). The effects of computer-mediated vocational guidance procedures on the appropriateness of vocational preference. *Journal of Vocational Behavior, 6*, 61–72.

Pilot, M. (1980). Job outlook projections: Why do them? How are they made? How accurate are they? *Occupational Outlook Quarterly, 24*, 3–8.

Pine, G. J. (1964-1965). Occupational and educational aspirations and delinquent behavior. *Vocational Guidance Quarterly, 13*, 107–111.

Pines, A., Aronson, E., & Kafry, D. (1981). *Burnout: From tedium to personal growth.* New York: The Free Press.

Pines, A., & Maslach, C. (1978). Characteristics of staff burnout in mental health settings. *Hospital and Community Psychiatry, 29*, 233–237.

Pines, A., & Maslach, C. (1979). Burnout: The loss of human caring. In *Experiencing social psychology.* New York: Random House.

Pines, A., & Maslach, C. (1980). Combatting staff

burnout in a day care center: A case study. *Child Care Quarterly, 9,* 5–16.

Pingree, S., Butler, M., Paisley, W., & Hawkins, R. (1978). Anti-nepotism's ghost: Attitudes of administrators toward hiring professional couples. *Phychology of Women Quarterly, 3*(1), 22–29.

Pinson, N. M. (1980). School counselors as interpreters for and of the community: New roles in career education. In Chapter 3, F. E. Burtnett (Ed.), *The school counselor's role in career education.* Falls Church, VA: APGA Press.

Piost, M. (1974). Effect of sex and career models on occupational preferences of adolescents. *Audiovisual Communication Review, 22,* 41–50.

Pitz, G. F., & Harren, V. A. (1980). An analysis of career decision-making from the point of view of information-processing and decision theory. *Journal of Vocational Behavior, 16,* 320–346.

Plata, M. (1975). Stability and change in the prestige rankings of occupations over 49 years. *Journal of Vocational Behavior, 6,* 95–99.

Plata, M. (1981). Occupational aspirations of normal and emotionally disturbed adolescents: A comparative study. *Vocational Guidance Quarterly, 30*(2), 130–138.

Pleck, J. H., Staines, G. L., & Lang, L. (1980). Conflicts between work and family life. *Monthly Labor Review, 103*(3), 29–31.

Pohlman, J. T., & Beggs, D. L. (1974). A study of the validity of self-reported measures of academic growth. *Journal of Educational Measurement, 11,* 115–119.

Poloma, M. M., & Garland, T. N. (1971). The married professional woman: A study in the tolerance of domestication. *Journal of Marriage and the Family, 33*(3), 531–540.

Pope John Paul II. (1981, September #21). Laboreum exercens (on human work): Papal Encyclical. *The Catholic Register,* p. 7.

Porter, L. (1970). Adults have special counseling needs. *Adult leadership, 19*(9), 275–277.

Porter, L. W., & Lawler, E. E. (1968). *Managerial attitudes and performance.* Homewood, IL: Richard P. Irwin.

Portigal, A. H. (1976). *Towards the measurement of work satisfaction.* Paris: Organization for Economic Cooperation and Development.

Potter, B. A. (1980). *Beating job burnout.* San Francisco: Harbor Publishing.

Pound, R. E. (1978). Using self-concept subscales in predicting career maturity for race and sex subgroups. *Vocational Guidance Quarterly, 27*(1), 61–70.

Powell, M., & Bloom, V. (1963). Development of and reasons for vocational choices of adolescents through the high school years. *Journal of Educational Research, 50*(3), 126–133.

Prager, K. J., & Freeman, A. (1979). Self-esteem, academic competence, educational aspiration and curriculum choice of urban community college students. *Journal of College Student Personnel, 20*(5), 392–397.

Prediger, D. J. (1974a). The role of assessment in career guidance: A reappraisal. *Impact, 3,* 3–4, 15–21.

Prediger, D. J. (1974b). The role of assessment in career guidance. In E. L. Herr (Ed.), *Vocational guidance and human development* (pp. 325–349). Boston: Houghton Mifflin.

Prediger, D. J. (1980). The marriage between tests and career counseling: An intimate report. *Vocational Guidance Quarterly, 28*(4), 297–305.

Prediger, D. J., & Noeth, R. J. (1979). Effectiveness of a brief counseling intervention in stimulating vocational explanation. *Journal of Vocational Behavior, 14,* 352–368.

Prediger, D. J., Roth, J. D., & Noeth, R. J. (1973). *Nationwide study of student career development: Summary of results.* Iowa City, IA: The American College Testing Program.

Price, G. E. (1971, March). *Computerized course exploration and selection – A comparison of the effectiveness of a computer-based system with a counselor-based system.* Paper presented at the American Personnel and Guidance Association, Atlantic City, NJ.

Price, G. E., Michal, R. D., & O'Neil, J. M. (1978). Using the computer to minimize ADS user error rate and facilitate SDS interpretation and research. *Measurement and Evaluation in Guidance, 11*(3), 150–154.

Pursell, D. E., & Torrence, W. D. (1980). The older woman and her search for employment. *Aging and Work, 3*(2), 121–128.

Quinn, J. F. (1981). The extent and correlates of partial retirement. *The Gerontologist, 21*(6), 634–643.

Quinn, R. P., et al. (1971). *Survey of working conditions* (Document 2916-0001). Washington, DC: U.S. Government Printing Office.

Quinn, R. P., & Mandilovitch, M. S. B. (1980). Education and job satisfaction: 1962–1977. *Vocational Guidance Quarterly, 29*(2), 100–111.

Quinn, R. P., Staines, G. L., & McCullough, M. R. (1974). Job satisfaction: Is there a trend? *Manpower Research Monograph, 30.* Washington, DC: U. S. Department of Labor.

Rabinowitz, W., Falkenbach, K., Travers, J. R., Valentine, C. G., & Weener, P. (1983). Worker motivation: Unsolved problems or untapped resources? *California Management Review, 25*(2), 45–56.

Radloff, L. (1975). Sex differences in depression: The effects of occupation and marital status. *Sex Roles, 1*(3), 249–265.

Raines, M. R. (1972). Community Services. In T. O'Banion, & A. Thurston (Eds.), *Student development programs in the community junior college* (pp. 147–155). Englewood Cliffs, NJ: Prentice-Hall.

Rapoport, R., & Rapoport, R. N. (1971). *Dual-career families.* Middlesex, England: Penguin Books.

Rapoport, R., & Rapoport, R. N. (1976). *Dual-career families re-examined.* London: Martin Robertson & Co.

Raskin, A. H. (1980). Toward a more participative work force. In C. S. Sheppard & D. C. Carroll (Eds.), *Working in the twenty-first century* (pp. 90–97). New York: Wiley.

Raths, L., Harmin, M., & Simon, S. (1966). *Values and teaching*. Columbus, OH: Charles E. Merril.

Rayman, J. R., & Harris-Bowlsbey, J. A. (1977). DISCOVER: A model for a systematic career guidance program. *Vocational Guidance Quarterly, 26*(1), 4–12.

Raynor, J. O., & Entin, E. E. (1982). *Motivation, career striving, and aging*. New York: Hemisphere.

Reardon, R. C. (1973). The counselor and career information services. *Journal of College Student Personnel, 14*(6), 495–500.

Reardon, R. C., Bonnell, R. O., & Huddleston, M. R. (1982). Self-directed career exploration: A comparison of choices and the self-directed search. *Journal of Vocational Behavior, 20*, 22–30.

Reardon, R. C., Domkowski, D., & Jackson, E. (1980). Career center evaluation methods: A case study. *Vocational Guidance Quarterly, 29*(2), 150–158.

Reardon, R. C., Zunker, V., & Dyal, M. A. (1979). The status of career planning programs and career centers in colleges and universities. *Vocational Guidance Quarterly, 28*, 154–159.

Reardon, R. W. (1976). Help for the troubled worker in a small company. *Personnel, 53*(1), 50–54.

Redfering, D. L., & Cook, D. (1980). Relationships among vocational training, income, and job complexity of high school dropouts and high school graduates. *Journal of Vocational Behavior, 16*, 158–162.

Reeves, D. J., & Booth, R. F. (1979). Expressed vs. inventoried interests as predictors of paramedical effectiveness. *Journal of Vocational Behavior, 15*, 155–163.

Regehr, C. N., & Herman, A. (1981). Developing the skills of career decision making and self assessment in ninth grade students. *Vocational Guidance Quarterly, 28*(5), 335–342.

Reid, G. L. (1972). Job search and the effectiveness of job-finding methods. *Industrial and Labor Relations Review, 25*, 479–495.

Reilly, R. R., & Chao, G. T. (1981). *Validity and fairness of alternative employee selection procedures*. Unpublished manuscript, American Telephone and Telegraph Company, Morristown, NJ.

Reilly, R. R., & Echternacht, G. (1979). Some problems with the criterion-keying approach to occupational interest scale development. *Educational and Psychological Measurement, 39*, 85–94.

Remeny, A. C., & Fraser, B. J. (1977). Effects of occupational information on occupational perceptions. *Journal of Vocational Behavior, 10*, 53–68.

Renwick, P. A., & Tosi, H. (1978). The effects of sex, marital status, and educational background on selection decisions. *Academy of Management Journal, 21*, 93–103.

Research and Forecasts, Inc. (1980). Retirement preparation: Growing corporate involvement. *Aging and Work, 3*(1), 1–13.

Research Utilization Branch. (1968, September). *Youth in trouble: A vocational approach*. Research brief. Washington, DC: Division of Research Demonstration Grants, Social and Rehabilitation Service,

Department of Health, Education, and Welfare.

Reubens, B. G. (1974). Vocational education. Performance and potential. *Manpower, 6*(7), 23–30.

Rhodes, S. R. (1983). Age-related differences in work attitudes and behavior: A review and conceptual analysis. *Psychological Bulletin, 93*(2), 328–367.

Rice, D. G. (1979). *Dual-career marriage: Conflict and treatment*. New York: The Free Press.

Rice, J. K. (1981). Career education comes of age. *Journal of Career Education, 7*(3), 212–219.

Rice, R. W., Near, J. P., & Hunt, R. G. (1980). The job satisfaction/life satisfaction relationship: A review of empirical research. *Basic and applied social psychology, 1*, 37–64.

Rich, N. S. (1979). Occupational knowledge: To what extent is rural youth handicapped? *Vocational Guidance Quarterly, 27*(4), 320–325.

Richardson, J. G. (1979). Wife occupational superiority and marital troubles: An examination of the hypothesis. *Journal of Marriage and the Family, 41*, 63–72.

Richardson, M. S. (1974). The dimensions of career and work orientation in college women. *Journal of Vocational Behavior, 5*, 161–172.

Ridener, J. (1973). Careers of the month program. *Elementary School Guidance and Counseling, 7*(3), 235–236.

Riegle, D. W., Jr. (1982). Psychological and social effects of unemployment. *American Psychologist, 37*(10), 113–115.

Riley, M. W. (1982, April). Implications for the middle and later years. In P. W. Berman and E. R. Ramey (Eds.), *Women: A developmental perspective*. (NIH Publication No. 82–2298, 399–405.) Washington, DC.

Riley, P. J. (1981). The influence of gender on occupational aspirations of kindergarden children. *Journal of Vocational Behavior, 19*, 244–250.

Rimmer, S. M. (1981). A systems approach model for counselor education program development and redefinition. *Counselor Education and Supervision, 21*, 7–15.

Rimmer, S. M., & Kahnweiler, W. M. (1981). The relationship among work, leisure, education, future, and self: An empirical investigation. *Vocational Guidance Quarterly, 30*(2), 109–116.

Rimmer, S. M., & Myers, J. W. (1982). Testing and older persons: A new challenge for counselors. *Measurement and Evaluation in Guidance, 15*(3), 182–193.

Ritzer, G. (1977). *Working: Conflict and change* (2nd ed.) Englewood Cliffs, NJ: Prentice-Hall.

Robb, W. D. (1979). Counseling and placement: Must they be separate entities? *Journal of College Placement, 34*(4), 67–71.

Robbins, P. I., Thomas L. E., Harvey, D. W., & Kandefer, C. (1978). Career change and congruence of personality type: An examination of DOT-derived work environment designations. *Journal of Vocational Behavior, 13*, 15–25.

Roberts, B. (1978). A look at psychiatric decision making. *American Journal of Psychiatry, 135*(11), 1384–1387.

Roberts, K. (1968). The entry into employment: An approach toward a general theory. *Sociological Review, 16*, 165-184.

Roberts, K. (1977). *From school to work, a study of the youth employment service*. Newton Abbott, England: David and Charles.

Robinson, F. P. (1963). Modern approaches to counseling diagnosis. *Journal of Counseling Psychology, 10*, 325-333.

Roche, G. R. (1979). Much ado about mentors. *Harvard Business Review, 57*(1), 14-28.

Rockwell, L. K., Hood, A. A., & Lee, V. F. (1980). APGA members in retirement and their advice to the rest of us. *Personal and Guidance Journal, 59*(3), 135-139.

Roe, A. (1953). A psychological study of eminent psychologists and anthropologists and a comparison with biological and physical scientists. *Psychological Monographs, 67*(2), 1-55.

Roe, A. (1954). A new classification of occupations. *Journal of Counseling Psychology, 1*, 215-220.

Roe, A. (1956). *The psychology of occupations*. New York: Wiley.

Roe, A., & Siegelmen, M. (1964). *The origin of interests*. Washington, DC: American Personnel and Guidance Association.

Roland, R. L. (1973). *Introduction to industrial mental health and employee counseling*. New York: Behavioral Publications.

Rones, P. L. (1980a). Moving to the sun: Regional job growth, 1968 to 1978. *Monthly Labor Review, 103*, 12-19.

Rones, P. L. (1980b). The retirement decision: A question of opportunity. *Monthly Labor Review, 103*(11), 14-17.

Root, N. (1981). Injuries at work are fewer among older employees. *Monthly Labor Review, 104*(3), 30-34.

Roscow, I. (1974). *Socialization to old age*. Berkely: University of California Press.

Roscow, J. M. (1983). Personnel policies for the 1980s. In J. S. Manuso (Ed.), *Occupational clinical psychology*. New York: Praeger.

Rose, H. A., & Elton, C. F. (1973). Sex and occupational choice. *Journal of Counseling Psychology, 18*(5), 456-461.

Rose, H. A., & Elton, C. F. (1982). The relation of congruence, differentiation and consistency to interest and aptitude scores in women with stable and unstable vocational choices. *Journal of Vocational Behavior, 20*(2), 162-174.

Rosen, B. C., & Aneshensel, C. S. (1978). Sex differences in the educational-occupational expectation process. *Social Forces, 57*(1), 164-185.

Rosen, G., Jerdee, T. H., & Presturch, T. L. (1975). Dual career marital adjustment: Potential effects of discriminatory managerial attitudes. *Journal of Marriage and the Family, 37*(3), 565-572.

Rosenfeld, C., & Brown, S. C. (1979). The labor force status of older workers. *Monthly Labor Review, 102*(11), 12-18.

Rosenfeld, R. A. (1979). Women's occupational careers: Individual and structural explanations. *Sociology of Work and Occupations, 6*(3), 283-311.

Rosengarten, W. (1936). *Choosing your life work* (3rd ed.). New York: McGraw-Hill.

Rosenthal, D. A., & Chapman, D. C. (1980). Sex-role stereotypes: Children's perceptions of occupational competence. *Psychological Reports, 44*, 135-139.

Rosove, B. (1982). Employability assessment: Its importance and one method of doing it. *Journal of Employment Counseling, 19*(3), 113-123.

Rothstein, M., & Jackson, D. N. (1980). Decision making in the employment interview. *Journal of Applied Psychology, 65*(3), 271-283.

Rounds, J. B., Jr., Davison, M. L., & Davis, R. V. (1979). The fit between Strong-Campbell Interest Inventory general occupational themes and Holland's hexagonal model. *Journal of Vocational Behavior, 15*, 303-315.

Rounds, J. B., Jr., Henly, G. A., Dawis, R. V., & Lofquist, L. H. (1981). *Manual for the Minnesota Importance Questionnaire: A measure of needs and values*. Minneapolis, MN: Vocational Psychology Research, University of Minnesota.

Rounds, J. B., Jr., Shubsachs, A. P. W., Dawis, R. V., & Lofquist, L. H. (1978). A test of Holland's formulations. *Journal of Applied Psychology, 63*(5), 609-616.

Royston, W., Jr. (1970). Forsyth County Vocational High: An investment in youth. *American Vocational Journal, 45*, 58-61.

Rubinstein, M. R. (1978). Integrative interpretation of vocational interest inventory results. *Journal of Counseling Psychology, 25*, 306-309.

Rubinton, N. (1980). Instruction in career decision-making and decision-making styles. *Journal of Counseling Psychology, 27*, 581-588.

Ruch, R. S. (1979). A path analytic study of the structure of employee job satisfaction: The critical role of top management. *Journal of Vocational Behavior, 15*, 277-293.

Rudd, N. M., & Coveny, A. R. (1979). Employment experience, attitudes, and aspirations of low-income men in a developing rural area. *Journal of Employment Counseling, 16*(3), 159-163.

Rudnick, D. T., & Wallach, E. J. (1980). Women in technology: A program to increase career awareness. *Personnel and Guidance Journal, 58*(6), 445-448.

Ruiz, R. A., & Padilla, A. M. (1977). Counseling Latinos. *The Personnel and Guidance Journal, 55*, 401-408.

Russel, J. H., & Sullivan, T. (1979). Student acquisition of career decision-making skills as a result of faculty advisor intervention. *Journal of College Student Personnel, 20*, 291-296.

Russella, J. J., & Brophy, A. L. (1982). Counseling psychologists in Veterans Administration regional offices. *Professional Psychology, 13*(5), 647-653.

Ryan, C. W., & Drummond, R. J. (1981). University based career education: A model for infusion. *Personnel and Guidance Journal, 60*, 89-92.

Ryan, C. W., Drummond, R. J., & Shannon, M. D. (1980). Guidance information systems: An analysis of impact on school counseling. *The School Counselor, 28*(2), 93-97.

Ryan, M. K. (1972). Middle school community program. *Elementary School Guidance and Counseling, 6*(4), 279–280.

Ryan, T. (1974). A systems approach to career education. *Vocational Guidance Quarterly, 22*, 172–179.

Ryan, T., & Krumboltz, J. D. (1964). Effect of planned reinforcement counseling on client decision-making behavior. *Journal of Counseling Psychology, 11*, 315–323.

Ryscavage, P. M. (1979). BLS labor force projections: A review of methods and results. *Monthly Labor Review, 103*, 12–19.

Rytina, N. F. (1981). Occupational segregation and earnings differences by sex. *Monthly Labor Review, 104*, 49–53.

Sacks, S., & Eisenstein, H. (1979). Feminism and psychological autonomy. *Personnel and Guidance Journal, 57*(8), 419–423.

Sagal, K., & DeBlassie, R. (1981). The male midlife crisis and career change. *Journal of Employment Counseling, 18*(1), 34–42.

Salimi, L., & Hsi, M. L. (1977). Career counseling and the foreign student. *Journal of College Placement, 37*(1), 30–31.

Salipante, P., & Goodman, P. (1976). Training, counseling, and retention of the hard-core unemployed. *Journal of Applied Psychology, 61*(1), 1–11.

Salomone, P. R., & Slaney, R. B. (1981). The influence of chance and contingency factors on the vocational choice process of nonprofessional workers. *Journal of Vocational Behavior, 19*, 25–35.

Samaan, M. K., & Parker, C. A. (1973). Effects of behavioral (reinforcement) and advice-giving counseling on the information-seeking behavior. *Journal of Counseling Psychology, 20*, 193–201.

Samby, G., & Healy, C. (1979). Developing a replicable career decision-making counseling procedure. *Journal of Counseling Psychology, 26*, 210–216.

Samler, J. (1968). Vocational counseling: A pattern and a projection. *Vocational Guidance Quarterly, 17*, 2–11.

Sampson, J. P. (1980). Using college alumni as resource persons for providing occupational information. *Journal of College Student Personnel, 21*, 172.

Sampson, J. P., Jr. (1983). Computer-assisted testing and assessment: Current status and implications for the future. *Measurement and Evaluation in Guidance, 15*(3), 293–299.

Sampson, J. P., & Loesch, L. C. (1981). Relationship among work values and job knowledge. *Vocational Guidance Quarterly, 29*(3), 229–235.

Sampson, J. P., Jr., & Pyle, K. R. (1983). Ethical issues involved with the use of computer-assisted counseling, testing, and guidance systems. *Personnel and Guidance Journal, 61*(3), 283–287.

Samuda, R. J. (1975). *Psychological testing of American minorities: Issues and consequesces*. New York: Dodd, Mead.

Sander, D., Westerberg, V., & Hedstrom J. E. (1978). Career education through children's literature. *Elementary School Guidance and Counseling, 13*(2), 129–132.

Sandmeyer, L. E. (1980). Choices and changes: A workshop for women. *Vocational Guidance Quarterly, 28*(4), 352–359.

Sankovsky, R. (1973). Audiovisuals: A valuable tool. *Journal of Rehabilitation, 39*, 14–15.

Sarason, I. G., & Johnson, J. H. (1979). Life stress, organizational stress, and job satisfaction. *Psychological Reports, 44*, 75–79.

Sarason, S. B. (1977). *Work, aging, and social change*. New York: The Free Press.

Sarason, S. B., Sarason, E., & Cowden, P. (1975). Aging and the nature of work. *American Psychologist, 30* 584–592.

Sarata, B. P. Y., & Jeppesen, J. C. (1977). Job design and staff satisfaction in human service settings. *American Journal of Community Psychology, 5*, 229–236.

Sauter, D., Seidl, A., & Karbon, J. (1980). The effects of high school counseling experience and attitudes toward women's roles on traditional or nontraditional career choice. *Vocational Guidance Quarterly, 28*(3), 242–249.

Savicki, V., & Cooley, E. J. (1982). Implications of burnout research and theory for counselor educators. *Personnel and Guidance Journal, 60*, 415–419.

Scanlan, T. J. (1980). Toward an occupational classification for self-employed men; An investigation of entrepreneurship from the perspective of Holland's theory of career development. *Journal of Vocational Behavior, 16*, 163–172.

Scanzoni, J. (1979, November). Work and fertility control sequences among younger married women. *Journal of marriage and the family*, 739–748.

Schaffer, K. (1976). Evaluating job satisfaction and success for emotionally maladjusted men. *Journal of Vocational Behavior, 9*, 329–335.

Schein, E. H. (1968). Organizational socialization and the process of management. *Industrial Management Review, 9*, 1–16.

Schein, E. H. (1971). The individual, the organization, and the career: A conceptual scheme. *Journal of Applied Behavioral Science, 7*(4), 415–416, 421–424.

Schein, E. H. (1978). *Career dynamics: Matching individual and organizational needs*. Reading, MA: Addison-Wesley.

Schenk, G. E., Murphy, P. P., & Shelton, R. L. (1980). Computerized career information systems of the college campus: A low-cost, do-it-yourself-approach. *Personnel and Guidance Journal, 58*(8), 516–520.

Schlichter, K. J., & Horan, J. J. (1981). Effects of stress inoculation on the anger and aggression management skills of institutionalized juvenile delinquents. *Cognitive Therapy and Research, 5*(4), 359–365.

Schlossberg, N. K. (1976). The case for counseling adults. *The Counseling Psychologist, 6*(1), 33–36.

Schlossberg, N. K. (1978). Five propositions about adult development. *Journal of College Student Personnel, 19*(5), 418–423.

Schlossberg, N. K. (1981). A model for analyzing

human adaptation to transition. *The Counseling Psychologist, 9*(2), 2–18.

Schlossberg, N. K., & Leibowitz, Z. (1980). Organizational support systems as buffers to job loss. *Journal of Vocational Behavior, 17*, 204–217.

Schmeiding, O. A., & Jensen, S. (1968). American Indian students: Vocational development and vocational tenacity. *Vocational Guidance Quarterly, 17*, 120–123.

Schmidt, F. L., & Hunter, J. E. (1981). Employment testing: Old theories and new research findings. *American Psychologist, 36*, 1128–1137.

Schmidt, F. L., Hunter, J. E., & Urry, V. (1976). Statistical power in the criterion-related validity studies. *Journal of Applied Psychology, 61*, 473–485.

Schmidt, J. A. (1976). Self-concepts and career exploration. *Elementary School Guidance and Counseling, 11*(2), 145–153.

Schmitt, N., & McCune, J. T. (1981). The relationship between job attitudes and the decision to retire. *Academy of Management Journal, 24*(4), 795–802.

Schmitt, N., & Mellon, P. M. (1980). Life and job satisfaction: Is the job central? *Journal of Vocational Behavior, 16*, 51–58.

Schoen, R., & Cohen, L. E. (1980). Ethnic endogamy among Mexican-American grooms: A reanalysis of generational and occupational effects. *American Journal of Sociology, 86*(2), 359–366.

Scholz, N. T., Prince, J. S., & Miller, G. P. (1975). *How to decide: A guide for women*. New York: College Entrance Examination Board.

Schontz, F. C. (1975). *The psychological aspects of physical illness and disability*. New York: Macmillan.

Schrank, F. A. (1982). A faculty/counselor implemented career planning course. *Journal of College Student Personnel, 23*, 83–84.

Schriesheim, C. A. (1978). Job satisfaction, attitudes toward unions, and voting in a union representation election. *Journal of Applied Psychology, 63*(5), 548–552.

Schumacher, E. F. (1981). Good work. In J. O'Toole, J. L. Scheiber, and L. C. Wood (Eds.), *Working, changes, and choices*. New York: Human Sciences Press, pp. 25–32.

Schwab, R. L. (1981). The relationship of role conflict, role ambiguity, teacher background variables and perceived burnout among teachers. (Doctoral dissertation, University of Connecticut, 1980). *Dissertation Abstracts International, 41*(9), 3823–A.

Schwarzwald, J., & Shoham, M. (1981). A trilevel approach to motivation for retraining. *Journal of Vocational Behavior, 18*, 265–276.

Scott, T. B., & Anadon, M. (1980). A comparison of the vocational interest profiles of Native Americans and Caucasian college-bound students. *Measurement and Evaluation in Guidance, 13*(1), 35–42.

Sehgal, E., & Vialet, J. (1980). Documenting the undocumented: Data, like aliens, are elusive. *Monthly Labor Review, 103*, 18–21.

Sekaran, U. (1982). An investigation of career salience for men and women in dual-career families. *Journal of Vocational Behavior, 20*, 111–119.

Sell, M. V., Brief, A. P., & Aldag, R. J. (1979). Job satisfaction among married working women. *Journal of Employment Counseling, 16*(1), 38–42.

Seltz-Petrash, A. (1980). The great woman hunt. *Occupational Outlook Quarterly, 24*, 14–16.

Selye, H. (1975). *Stress without distress*. New York: Signet.

Selz, N., Jones, J. S., & Ashley, W. L. (1980). *Functional competencies for adapting to the world of work*. Columbus, OH: National Center for Research in Vocational Education, Ohio State University.

Sewell, W. H., & Orenstein, A. M. (1965). Community of residence and occupational choice. *American Journal of Sociology, 70*, 551–563.

Shane, H. G. (1970). A curriculum continuum: Possible trends in the 70's. *Phi Delta Kappan, 51*, 389–392.

Shapiro, D., & Mott, F. L. (1979). Labor supply behavior of prospective and new mothers. *Demography, 16*(2), 199–208.

Shapiro, E. C., Haseltine, F. P., & Rowe, M. P. (1978). Moving up: Role models, mentors, and the patron system. *Sloan Management Review, 19*(3), 51–55.

Sharf, R. S. (1970). Relative importance of interest and ability in vocational decision making. *Journal of Counseling Psychology, 17*, 258–262.

Sharf, R. S. (1974). Interest inventory interpretation: Implications for research and practice. *Measurement and Evaluation in Guidance, 7*(1), 16–23.

Sharf, R. S. (1978). Evaluation of a computer-based narrative interpretation of a test battery. *Measurement and Evaluation in Guidance, 11*(1), 50–53.

Shaw, M. C. (1968). *The function of theory in guidance programs*. Guidance Monograph Series I: Organizations and Administration. Boston: Houghton Mifflin.

Sheehy, G. (1976). *Passages: Predictable crises of adult life*. New York: Dutton.

Sheehy, G. (1981). *Pathfinders*. New York: Bantam Books.

Shepard, J. M., Kim, D. I., & Houghland, J. G. (1979). Effects of technology in industrialized and industrializing societies. *Sociology of Work and Occupations, 6*(4), 457–481.

Sheppard, D. I. (1971). The measurement of vocational maturity in adults. *Journal of Vocational Behavior, 1*, 399–406.

Sherman, V. S. (1967). *Guidance curriculum for increased self-understanding and motivation for career planning*. American Institute for Research in Behavioral Science. (ERIC Document ED 010626).

Shontz, F. C. (1975). *The psychological aspects of physical illness and disability*. New York: Macmillan.

Shultz, J. T. (1979). The private sector: A new frontier? *Vocational Guidance Quarterly, 27*(3), 276–280.

Siegel, C. L. F. (1973). Sex differences in the occupational choices of second graders. *Journal of Vocational Behavior, 3*, 15–19.

Siegried, W. D., MacFarlane, I., Graham, D. G., Moore, N. A., & Young, P. L. (1981). A reexamination of sex differences in job preferences. *Journal of Vocational Behavior, 18*, 30–42.

Sievert, N. W. (1972). The role of the self-concept in determining an adolescent's occupational choice. *Journal of Industrial Teacher Education, 9*(3), 47-53.

Simmons, D. (1962). Children's ranking of occupational prestige. *Personnel and Guidance Journal,* 1962, *41,* 332-336.

Simon, H. A. (1960). *The new science of management decisions.* New York: Harper & Row.

Simon, J. B. (1966). An existential view of vocational development. *Personnel and Guidance Journal, 44,* 604-610.

Simonis, S. (1973). The counselor's workshop: An approach to developmental guidance. *Elementary School Guidance and Counseling 8,* 58-63.

Simpson, E. J. (1972). The classification of educational objectives in the psychomotor domain. *The psychomotor domain: A resource book for media specialists* (pp. 43-56). The National Special Media Institutes. Washington, DC: Gryphon House.

Sinick, D. (1975). Counseling older persons: Careers, retirement, dying. Ann Arbor, MI: ERIC Clearing House on Counseling and Personnel Services (CG400 129), 97.

Sinick, D. (1979). Career counseling with handicapped persons. *Personnel and Guidance Journal, 58*(4), 252-257.

Skinner, D. A. (1980). Dual-career family stress and coping: A literature review. *Family Relations, 29*(4), 473-481.

Slakter, M. J., & Cramer, S. H. (1969). Risk-taking and vocational or curriculum choice. *Vocational Guidance Quarterly, 17*(2), 127-132.

Slaney, R. (1980). Expressed vocational choice and vocational indecision. *Journal of Counseling Psychology, 27,* 122-129.

Slaney, R., Palko-Nonemaker, D., & Alexander, R. (1981). An investigation of two measures of indecision. *Journal of Vocational Behavior, 18,* 92-103.

Slaney, R. B. (1980). An investigation of racial differences on vocational values among college women. *Journal of Vocational Behavior, 16,* 197-207.

Slaney, R. B., Stafford, J. J., & Russell, J. E. A. (1981). Career indecision in adult women: A comparative and descriptive study. *Journal of Vocational Behavior, 19*(3), 335-345.

Slater, J. M. (1978). Career exploration: Theory, practice, and assessment. *Vocational Guidance Quarterly, 27*(2), 130-136.

Slocum, W. L. (1966). *Occupational careers.* Chicago: Aldine.

Slocum, W. L., & Bowles, R. T. (1968). Attractiveness of occupations to high school students. *Personnel and Guidance Journal, 46,* 754-761.

Smallwood, K. B. (1980). What do adult women college students really need? *Journal of College Student Personnel, 21,* 65-73.

Smith, A., & Chemers, M. M. (1981). Misperceptions of motivation of economically disadvantaged employees in work settings. *Journal of Employment Counseling, 18*(1), 24-33.

Smith, E. D. (1968). Innovative ideas in vocational guidance. *American Vocational Journal, 43,* 19-21.

Smith, E. D. (1977, September). Personal communication.

Smith, E. J. (1975). Profile of the Black individual in vocational literature. *Journal of Vocational Behavior, 6,* 41-59.

Smith, E. J. (1980). Career development of minorities in nontraditional fields. *Journal of Non-White Concerns, 8,* 141-156.

Smith, E. J. (1981). The working mother: A critique of the research. *Journal of Vocational Behavior, 18,* 191-211.

Smith, E. R. (Ed.) (1979a). *The subtle revolution.* Washington, DC: The Urban Institute.

Smith, E. R. (1979b). *Women in the labor force in 1990.* Washington, DC: The Urban Institute.

Smith, E. R. (1980). Desiring and expecting to work among high school girls: Some determinants and consequences. *Journal of Vocational Behavior, 17*(2), 218-230.

Smith, M. (1943). An empirical scale of prestige status occupations. *American Sociological Review, 8,* 185-192.

Smith, R. D., & Evans, J. R. (1973). Comparison of experimental group guidance and individual counseling as facilitators of vocational development. *Journal of Counseling Psychology, 20*(3), 202-208.

Smith, R. I. & Southern, C. (1980). Multimodal career counseling: An application of the "BASIC ID." *Vocational Guidance Quarterly, 29*(1), 56-64.

Smith, R. R., & Warner, R. W. (1977). Healthy employment and career development for adult offenders. *Offender Rehabilitation, 1*(4), 335-341.

Smith, S. M., & Golden, B. J. (1982). Vocational services for older adults or "I want to work, but." *Journal of Employment Counseling, 19*(1), 29-33.

Snipes, J. K., & McDaniels, C. (1981). Theoretical foundations for career information delivery systems. *Vocational Guidance Quarterly, 29*(4), 307-314.

Snodgrass, G., & Healy, C. C. (1979). Developing a replicable career decision-making counseling procedure. *Journal of Counseling Psychology, 26,* 210-216.

Snyder, J. F., Hill, C. E., & Derksen, T. P. (1974). Why some students do not use university counseling services. *Journal of Counseling Psychology, 19*(4), 263-268.

Snyder, R. A.. (1979). Improving interest measurement through the use of expectancy theory. *Vocational Guidance Quarterly, 28*(2), 160-165.

Snyder, R. A., Howard, A., & Hammer, T. H. (1978). Mid-career change in academia: The decision to become an administrator. *Journal of Vocational Behavior, 13*(2), 229-241.

Sobol, M. G. (1978). Use of labor market forecasts by high school counselors. *The School Counselor, 26*(1), 57-61.

Sorokin, P. (1927). *Social mobility* (pp. 225 & 238). New York: Harper.

Sovilla, E. S. (1970). A plan for career planning. *Journal of College Placement, 21*(1), 50-58.

Spaeth, J. L. (1968). Occupation prestige expectations among male college graduates. *American Journal of Sociology, 73*, 548–558.

Special Task Force to the Secretary of Health, Education and Welfare. (1973). *Work in America*. Cambridge, MA: The MIT Press.

Spicuzza, F. J., & DeVoe, M. W. (1982). Burnout in the helping professions: Mutual aid as self-help. *Personnel and Guidance Journal, 61*(2), 95–99.

Spitze, G. D., & Huker, J. (1980). Changing attitudes toward women's nonfamily roles: 1938–1978. *Sociology of Work and Occupations, 7*(3), 317–335.

Spitze, G. D., & Waite, L. J. (1980). Labor force and work attitudes: Young women's early experiences. *Sociology of Work and Occupations, 7*(1), 3–32.

Spokane, A. R. (1979). Validity of the Holland categories for college women and men. *Journal of College Student Personnel, 20*(4), 335–340.

Spokane, A. R., & Oliver, L. W. (1983). The outcomes of vocational intervention. In S. H. Osipow, & W. B. Walsh (Eds.), *Handbook of Vocational Psychology* (Vol. 2), Hillsdale, N.J.: Erlbaum. 99–136.

Sprague, D. G., & Strong, D. J. (1970). Vocational choice group counseling. *Journal of College Student Personnel, 45*, 35–36.

Spranger, E. (1928). *Types of men: The psychology and ethics of personality* (Paul J. W. Pigors, Trans.). Halle, Germany: Max Niemeyer Verlag.

Spreitzer, E., Snyder, E., & Larson, D. (1980). The relative effects of health and income in life satisfaction. *International Journal of Aging and Development, 10*(3), 283–288.

Sprinthall, N. A. (1967). Test interpretation: Some problems and a proposal. *Vocational Guidance Quarterly, 17*(4), 248–256.

Sprinthall, N. A., Whiteley, J. M., & Mosher, R. L. (1966). Cognitive flexibility: A focus for research on counselor effectiveness. *Counselor Education and Supervision, 5*, 188–197.

Srivastva, S., Salipante, P., Cummings, T., Notz, W., Bigelow, J., & Waters, J. (1975). *Job satisfaction and productivity*. Cleveland: Case Western Reserve.

St. John Parsons, D. (1978). Continuous dual-career families: A case study. *Psychology of Women Quarterly, 3*(1), 30–42.

Stagner, R. (1979). Propensity to work: An important variable in retiree behavior. *Aging and Work, 2*(3), 161–181.

Staines, G. L., Preck, J. H., Shepard, L. J., & O'Connor, P. (1978). Wives' employment status and mental adjustment: Yet another look. *Psychology of Women Quarterly, 3*(1), 90–120.

Stake, J. E. (1979). Women's self-estimates of competence and the resolution of the career/hope conflict. *Journal of Vocational Behavior, 14*, 33–42.

Stake, J. E., & Levitz, E. (1979). Career goals of college women and men and perceived achievement-related encouragement. *Psychology of Women Quarterly, 4*(2), 151–159.

Stamm, M. L., & Nissman, B. S. (1973). The counselor's view of the middle school student. *The School Counselor, 21*(1), 34–38.

Standley, K., & Soule, B. (1974). Women in male-dominated professions: Contrasts in their personal and vocational histories. *Journal of Vocational Behavior, 4*, 245–258.

Steers, R. M., & Porter, L. W. (1975). *Motivation and work behavior*. New York: McGraw-Hill.

Stefflre, B. (1959). Concurrent validity of the vocational values inventory. *Journal of Educational Research, 52*, 339–352.

Stefflre, B. (1966). Vocational development: Ten propositions in search of a theory. *Personnel and Guidance Journal, 44*, 611–616.

Stein, L. I., & Test, M. A. (1980). Alternative to mental hospital treatment: Conceptual model, treatment program, clinical evaluation. *Archives of General Psychiatry, 27*(4), 392–397.

Stephens, D. B., Watt, J. T., & Hobbs, W. S. (1979a). Employer preferences for the form and substance of employment application cover letters. *Journal of Employment Counseling, 16*(4), 238–243.

Stephens, D. B., Watt, J. T., & Hobbs, W. S. (1979b). Getting through the resume preparation maze: Some empirically based guidelines for resume format. *Vocational Guidance Quarterly, 28*(1), 25–34.

Stephens, W. R. (1970). *Social reform and the origins of vocational guidance*. Washington, DC: National Vocational Guidance Association.

Stern, B. E. (1977). *Toward a federal policy on education and work*. Washington, DC: U.S. Department of Health, Education and Welfare.

Sternberg, C. (1956). Interests and tendencies toward maladjustment in a normal population. *Personnel and Guidance Journal, 35*, 94–99.

Stevens, G., & Marquette, R. P. (1979). Women on the move. *Journal of College Placement, 39*(4), 43–45.

Stevens, N. D. (1973). Job seeking behavior: A segment of vocational development. *Journal of Vocational Behavior, 3*, 209–219.

Stevenson, W. (1978). The transition from school to work. In A. Adams and G. L. Mangum (Eds.), *The lingering crisis of youth unemployment*. Kalamazoo, MI: Upjohn Institute for Employment Research, pp. 65–90.

Stevic, R., & Uhlig, G. (1976). Occupational aspirations of selected Appalachian youth. *Personnel and Guidance Journal, 45*, 435–439.

Stewart, N. (1947). AGCT scores of army personnel grouped by occupations. *Occupations, 26*, 5–41.

Stewart, N. R., Winborn, B. B., Johnson, R. G., Burks, H. M., & Engelkes, J. R. (1978). *Systematic counseling*, Englewood Cliffs, NJ: Prentice-Hall.

Stockton, N., Berry, J., Shepson, J., & Utz, P. (1980). Sex role and innovative major choice among college students. *Journal of Vocational Behavior, 16*, 360–367.

Stodden, R. A., Casale, J., & Schwartz, S. E. (1977). Work evaluation and the mentally retarded: Review and recommendations. *Mental Retardation, 15*(4), 25–27.

Stone, C. I., & Sawatzki, B. (1980). Hiring bias and the disabled interviewee: Effects of manipulating work history and disability information of the disabled job applicant. *Journal of Vocational Behavior, 16*, 96–104.

Storey, W. D. (Ed.). (1978). *A guide for career development inquiry*. Madison, WI: American Society for Training and Development.

Stratemeyer, F. B., Forkner, H. L., McKim, M., & Passow, A. W. (1957). *Developing a curriculum for modern living*. New York: Teachers College, Columbia University.

Strong, E. K., Jr. (1943). *Vocational interests of men and women*. Palo Alto, CA: Stanford University Press.

Stryker, L. E., & Scorzelli, J. F. (1977). Work, counseling, and ex-offenders. *Offender Rehabilitation, 1*(3).

Stumpf, S. A., & Rabinowitz, S. (1981). Career stage as a moderator of performance relationships with facets of job satisfaction and role perceptions. *Journal of Vocational Behavior, 18*, 202–218.

Suhor, C. (1979). Goals of career education and goals of subject-area instruction: A model. *Journal of Career Education, 5*(3), 215–219.

Sundby, D. Y. (1980). The career quad: A psychological look at some divergent dual-career families. In C. B. Derr (Ed.), *Work, family, and the career. New frontiers in theory and research*. New York: Praeger, 329–353.

Sundstrom, E., Burt, R. E., & Kamp, D. (1980). Privacy at work: Architectural correlates of job satisfaction and job performance. *Academy of Management Journal, 23*(1), 101–117.

Super, D. E. (1951). Vocational adjustment: Implementing a self-concept. *Occupations, 30,* 88–92.

Super, D. E. (1953). A theory of vocational development. *American Psychologist, 8,* 185–190.

Super, D. E. (1954). Career patterns as a basis for vocational counseling. *Journal of Counseling Psychology, 1,* 12–20.

Super, D. E. (1957). *The psychology of careers*. New York: Harper & Row.

Super, D. E. (1962). The structure of work values in relation to status, achievement, interest, and adjustment. *Journal of Applied Psychology, 46,* 227–239.

Super, D. E. (1969a). Vocational development theory: Persons, positions, and processes. *The Counseling Psychologist, 1,* 2–9.

Super, D. E. (1969b). The natural history of a study of lives and of vocations. *Perspectives on Education, 2,* 13–22.

Super, D. E. (1970). *Computer-assisted counseling*. New York: Teachers College Press.

Super, D. E. (1974). The broader context of career development and vocational guidance: American trends in world perspective. In E. L. Herr (Ed.), *Vocational guidance and human development* (Chap. 3). Boston, Houghton Mifflin.

Super, D. E. (1974). Vocational maturity theory: Toward implementing a psychology of careers in career education and guidance. In D. E. Super (Ed.), *Measuring vocational maturity for counseling and evaluation* (Chap. 1). Washington, DC: American Personnel and Guidance Association, 9–21.

Super, D. E. (1976). *Career education and the meaning of work*. Monographs on career education. Washington, DC: The Office of Career Education, U. S. Office of Education.

Super, D. E. (1977, June). Vocational maturity in mid-career. *Vocational Guidance Quarterly, 25*(4), 294–302.

Super, D. E. (1980). A life-span, life space approach to career development. *Journal of Vocational Behavior, 16*(3), 282–298.

Super, D. E. (1981). Approaches to occupational choice and career development. In A. G. Watts, D. E. Super, & J. M. Kidd (Eds.), *Career development in Britain*. Cambridge, England: Hobsons Press.

Super, D. E. (1982). The relative importance of work: Models and measures for meaningful data. *The Counseling Psychologist, 10*(4), 95–104.

Super, D. E., & Bohn, M. J., (1970). *Occupational psychology*. Belmont, CA: Wadsworth.

Super, D. E., Bohn, M. J., Forrest, D. J., Jordaan, J. P., Lindeman, R. H., & Thompston, A. A. (1971). *Career development inventory*. New York: Teachers College, Columbia University.

Super, D. E., & Crites, J. O. (1962). *Appraising vocational fitness*. New York: Harper & Row.

Super, D. E., Crites, J. O., Hummel, R. C., Moser, H. P., Overstreet, P. L., & Warnath, C. F. (1957). *Vocational development: A framework for research*. New York: Teachers College, Columbia University.

Super, D. E., et al. (1974). *Measuring vocational maturity for counseling and evaluation*. Washington, DC: National Vocational Guidance Association.

Super, D. E., Starishevsky, R., Matlin, N., & Jordaan, J. P. (1963). *Career development: Self-concept theory*. New York: College Entrance Examination Board.

Super, D. E., & Forrest, D. J. (1972). *Preliminary manual: Career development inventory*. New York: Columbia University Teachers College.

Super, D. E., & Hall, D. T. (1978). Career development: Exploration and planning. *Annual Review of Psychology, 29*, 333–372.

Super, D. E., & Kidd, J. M. (1979). Vocational maturity in adulthood: Toward turning a model into a measure. *Journal of Vocational Behavior, 14*(3), 255–270.

Super, D. E., & Overstreet, P. L. (1960) *The vocational maturity of ninth-grade boys*. New York: Teachers College, Columbia University.

Suziedelis, A., & Steimel, R. J. (1963). The relationship of need hierarchies to inventoried interest. *Personnel and Guidance Journal, 42*, 393–396.

Swanson, G. (1973). Philosophical bases for career education. In J. Magisos (Ed.), *Career education*. Third Yearbook of the American Vocational Association. Washington, DC: The Association, 40–49.

Swatko, M. K. (1981). What's in a title? Personality, job aspirations, and the nontraditional women. *Journal of Vocational Behavior, 18*, 174–183.

Szilagyi, A. D., & Holland, W. E. (1980). Changes in social density: Relationships with functional interaction and perceptions of job characteristics, role stress, and work satisfaction. *Journal of Applied Psychology, 65*(1), 28–33.

Taber, T. D., Walsh, J. T., & Cooke, R. A. (1979). Developing a community-based program for reducing the social impact of a plant closing. *Journal of Applied Behavioral Sciences, 15*(2), 133–155.

Takai, R., & Holland, J. L. (1979). Comparison of the Vocational Card Sort, the SDS, and the Vocational Exploration and Insight Kit. *Vocational Guidance Quarterly, 27*(4), 312–318.

Taylor, D. E. (1981). Education, on-the-job training, and the Black-White earnings gap. *Monthly Labor Review, 104*, 28–34.

Taylor, K. E., & Weiss, D. J. (1972). Prediction of individual job termination from measured job satisfaction and biographical data. *Journal of Vocational Behavior, 2*, 123–132.

Teglasi, H. (1981). Children's choices of and value judgments about sex-typed toys and occupations. *Journal of Vocational Behavior, 18*, 184–195.

Tennyson, W. W. (1967). The psychology of developing competent personnel. *American Vocational Journal, 42*, 27–29.

Tennyson, W. W., Hansen, L. S., Klaurens, M. K., & Antholz, M. B. (1975). *Educating for career development*. St. Paul, MN: Minnesota Department of Education (Revised 1980, National Vocational Guidance Association).

Tenopyr, M. L. (1981). The realities of employment testing. *American Psychologist, 36*, 1120–1127.

Tesolowski, D. G., & Halpin, G. (1979). Modifying work personalities of the handicapped. *Vocational Guidance Quarterly, 27*(4), 334–340.

This, L. E. (1970). What is simulation? *American Vocational Journal, 45*, 20–22.

Thomas, G. P. (1972). Feasible alternatives counseling. *The School Counselor, 19*, 237–242.

Thomas, H. B. (1974). The effects of social position, race, and sex on work values of ninth-grade students. *Journal of Vocational Behavior, 4*, 357–364.

Thomas, L. E. (1979). Causes of mid-life change from high-status careers. *Vocational Guidance Quarterly, 27*(3), 202–208.

Thomas, L. E. (1980). A typology of mid-life career changes. *Journal of Vocational Behavior, 16*(2), 173–182.

Thomas, W. G. (1966). Placement's role in the university. *Journal of College Placement, 26*(4), 87–92.

Thompson, J. (1976). Patrons, rabbis, mentors – whatever you call them, women need them too. MBA, *10*(2), 26.

Thompson, J. W. (1980). Burnout in group home houseparents. *American Journal of Psychiatry, 137*(6), 710–714.

Thompson, O. E. (1966). Occupational values of high school students. *Personnel and Guidance Journal, 44*, 850–853.

Thoni, R. J., & Olsson, P. M. (1975). A systematic career development program in a liberal arts college. *Personnel and Guidance Journal, 53*, 672–675.

Thoresen, C. E., & Krumboltz, J. D. (1968). Similarity of social models and clients in behavioral counseling: Two experimental studies. *Journal of Counseling Psychology, 15*, 393–401.

Thoresen, C. E., Krumboltz, J. D., & Varenhorst, B. (1967). Sex of counselors and models: Effect on client career exploration. *Journal of Counseling Psychology, 14*, 503–508.

Thoresen, C. E., & Mehrens, W. A. (1967). Decision theory and vocational counseling: Important concepts and questions. *Personnel and Guidance Journal, 46*, 165–172.

Thorndike, R. L. (1963). The prediction of vocational success. *Vocational Guidance Quarterly, 11*, 179–187.

Thorndike, R. L., & Hagen, E. (1959). *10,000 careers*. New York: Wiley.

Thorndike, R. L., & Hagen, E. (1969). *Measurement and evaluation in psychology and education*. New York: Wiley.

Thorndike, R. L., Weiss, D. J., & Dawis, R. V. (1968). Canonical correlation of vocational interests and vocational needs. *Journal of Counseling Psychology, 15*, 101–106.

Thurnher, M. (1974). Goals, values, and life evaluations at the preretirement stage. *Journal of Gerontology, 29*(1), 85–96.

Tiedeman, D. V. (1958, December). The Harvard studies in career development in current perspective.

Tiedeman, D. V. (1961). Decision and vocational development: A paradigm and its implications. *Personnel and Guidance Journal, 40*, 15–20.

Tiedeman, D. V. (1979). Burning and copping out of counseling. *Personnel and Guidance Journal, 57*, 328–330.

Tiedeman, D. V., & Miller-Tiedeman, A. (1977). An "I" power primer: Part one: Structure and its involvements of intuition. *Focus on Guidance, 9*(7), 1–16.

Tiedeman, D. V., & O'Hara, R. P. (1963). *Career development: Choice and adjustment*. New York: College Entrance Examination Board.

Tierney, R. J., & Herman, A. (1973). Self-estimate ability in adolescence. *Journal of Counseling Psychology, 20*, 298–302.

Tillar, T. C., & Hutchins, D. E. (1979). The effectiveness of the components of a model program of career exploration for college freshmen. *Journal of College Student Personnel, 20*, 538–545.

Tillinghast, B. S., Jr. (1964). Choice orientations of guidance. *Vocational Guidance Quarterly, 13*, 18–20.

Tinsley, D. J., & Faunce, P. S. (1980). Enabling, facilitating, and precipitating factors associated with women's career orientation. *Journal of Vocational Behavior, 17*, 183–194.

Titley, R. W., & Titley, B. S. (1980). Initial choice of college major: Are only the "undecided" undecided? *Journal of College Student Personnel, 21*, 293–298.

Tittle, C. K. (1973). Sex bias in educational measurement: Fact or fiction? *Measurement and Evaluation in Guidance, 6*, 219–226.

Tittle, C. K., & Zytowski, D. G. (Eds.). (1980). *Sex-*

fair interest measurement: Research and implications. Washington, DC: National Institute of Education, U.S. Government Printing Office.

Toffler, A. (1980). *The third wave*. New York: Morrow.

Toomer, J. E. (1982). Counseling psychologists in business and industry. *The Counseling Psychologist, 10*(3), 9–18.

Townshend, A., & Gurin, P. (1981). Re-examining the frustrated homemaker hypothesis: Role fit, personal satisfaction, and collective discontent. *Sociology of Work and Occupations, 8*(4), 464–488.

Tracey, T. J., & Dedlacek, W. E. (1980). Comparison of error rates on the original Self-Directed Search and the 1977 version. *Journal of Counseling Psychology, 27*, 299–301.

Trantow, D. J. (1970). An introduction to evaluation: Program effectiveness and community needs. *Rehabilitation Literature, 31*, 2–10.

Treiman, D. J. (1977). *Occupational prestige in comparative perspective*. New York: Academic Press.

Tremaine, L. S., & Schau, C. G. (1979). Sex role aspects in the development of children's vocational knowledge. *Journal of Vocational Behavior, 14*, 317–328.

Triandis, H. C., Feldman, J. M., Weldin, D. E., & Harvey, W. M. (1975). Ecosystem distrust in the hard-to-employ. *Journal of Applied Psychology, 60*, 44–56.

Troll, L. E., & Nowak, C. (1976). How old are you? The question of age bias in the counseling of adults. *The Counseling Psychologist, 6*(1), 41–44.

Tschirgi, H. D., & Huegli, J. M. (1979). Monitoring the employment interview. *Journal of College Placement, 39*(2), 37–39.

Tseng, M. S. & Carter, A. R. (1970). Achievement motivation and fear of failure as determinants of vocational choice, vocational aspiration, and perception of vocational prestige. *Journal of Counseling Psychology, 17*, 150–156.

Tuck, B. J. (1972). Self-evaluation and realism of vocational aspiration. *New Zealand Journal of Educational Studies, 7*, 30–37.

Tucker, D. H., & Rowe, P. M. (1979). Relationship between expectancy, causal attributions, and final hiring decisions in the employment interview. *Journal of Applied Psychology, 64*(4), 27–34.

Tung, R. L. (1980). Comparative analysis of the occupational stress profiles of male versus female administrators. *Journal of Vocational Behavior, 17*, 344–355.

Turner, C. (1979). Systematic decision-making by career counselors. *Vocational Guidance Quarterly, 27*(4), 341–349.

Turner, R. G., & Whitaker, W. M. (1973). The impact of mass layoffs on older workers. *Industrial Gerontology, 16*(1), 14–21.

Turner, S. A., Johnson, J. K., & Patterson, C. (1981). Career development of minorities. *Journal of College Placement, 41*(3), 38–42.

Tyler, L. E. (1961). *The work of the counselor* (3rd ed.). New York: Appleton-Century-Crofts.

Tyler, L. E. (1978). *Individuality*. San Francisco: Jossey-Bass.

Tyler, L. E., Sundberg, N. D., Rohila, P. K. & Greene, M. M. (1968). Patterns of choice in Dutch, American, and Indian adolescents. *Journal of Counseling Psychology, 15*, 522–529.

Tyler, R. W. (1950). *Basic principles of curriculum and instruction*. Chicago: University of Chicago Press.

U.S. Bureau of the Census. (1982, March). *Provisional estimates of social, economic, and housing characteristics*. 1980 Census of population and Housing. Supplementary Report. Washington, DC: U.S. Department of Commerce, 25–35.

U.S. Civil Service Commission. (1968). *Position-classification standards*. (Psychology Series), 29 pages.

U.S. Department of Health, Education, and Welfare. (1973). Special Task Force. *Work in America*. Cambridge, MA: MIT Press.

U.S. Department of Labor. (1974). *Job satisfaction: Is there a trend?* (Manpower Research Monograph No. 30). Washington, DC: U.S. Government Printing Office.

U.S. Department of Labor. (1974a). *Manpower report of the president, 1974*. Washington, DC: U.S. Government Printing Office.

U.S. Department of Labor. (1974b). *The United States economy in 1985*. Washington, DC: U.S. Government Printing Office.

U.S. Department of Labor. (1979). *International comparisons of unemployment*. Washington, DC: U.S. Government Printing Office.

U.S. Department of Labor. (1980). *Occupational outlook handbook, 1980-1981 edition*. Washington, DC: U.S. Government Printing Office.

U.S. Department of Labor (1980). Self-directed job search: An introduction. Washington, DC: Employment and Training Administration.

U.S. Department of Labor. (1981). *Monthly Labor Review, 104*(2). Washington, DC: Bureau of Labor Statistics.

U.S. Office of Management and Budget. (1972). *Standard industrial classification manual*. Washington, DC: U.S. Government Printing Office.

Ullrich, M. F. (1973). Several measures of expectancy of vocational counseling. *Psychological Reports, 33*, 299–304.

Underhill, R. (1966). Values and postcollege career change. *American Journal of Sociology, 72*, 163–172.

Vaillant, G. E. (1977). *Adaptation to life*. Boston: Little, Brown.

Vaitenas, R., & Wiener, Y. (1977). Developmental, emotional, and interest factors in voluntary midcareer change. *Journal of Vocational Behavior, 11*(3), 291–304.

Valenzi, E., & Dessler, G. (1978). Relationships of leader behavior, subordinate role ambiguity, and subordinate job satisfaction. *Academy of Management Journal, 21*(4), 671–678.

Vandergoot, D., & Engelkes, J. R. (1977). An application of the theory of work adjustment to vocational counseling. *Vocational Guidance Quarterly, 26*(1),

45-53.

Varenhorst, B. B. (1969). Learning the consequences of life's decisions. In J. D. Krumboltz, & C. E. Thoresen (Eds.), *Behavioral counseling: Cases and techniques* (pp. 306-319). New York: Holt, Rinehart and Winston.

Vecchio, R. P. (1980). The function and meaning of work and the job: Morse and Weiss (1955) revisited. *Academy of Management Journal, 23*(2), 361-367.

Vecchio, R. P. (1980a). The test of moderator of the job satisfaction – job quality relationship: The case of religious affiliation. *Journal of Applied Psychology, 65*(2), 195-201.

Vecchio, R. P. (1980b). Worker alienation as a moderator of the job quality – job satisfaction relationship: The case of racial differences. *Academy of Management Journal, 23*(3), 479-486.

Vecchiotti, D. I., & Korn, J. H. (1980). Comparison of student and recruiter values. *Journal of Vocational Behavior, 16*, 43-50.

Veninga, R. L., & Spradley, J. P. (1981). *The work/stress connection: How to cope with job burnout.* Boston: Little, Brown.

Veroff, J., Kulka, R. A., & Douvan, E. (1981). *Mental health in America: Patterns of help-seeking from 1957 to 1976.* New York: Basic Books.

Vincenzi, H. (1977). Minimizing occupational stereotypes. *Vocational Guidance Quarterly, 25*(3), 265.

Voight, N. L., Lawler, A., & Fulkerson, K. F. (1980). Community-based guidance: A "Tupperware Party" approach to mid-life decision-making. *Personnel and Guidance Journal, 59*(2), 106-107.

Von der Embse, T. J., & Childs, J. M. (1979). Adults in transition: A profile of the older college student, *Journal of College Student Personnel, 20*, 475-479.

Vondracek, F. W., & Learner, R. M. (1982). Vocational role development in adolescence. In B. Wolman (Ed.), *Handbook of developmental psychology* (Chap. 33). Englewood Cliffs, NJ: Prentice-Hall.

Vondracek, F. W., Lerner, R. W., & Schulenberg, J. E. The concept of development in vocational theory and intervention. *The Journal of Vocational Behavior* (in press).

Vondracek, S. I., & Kirchner, E. P. (1974). Vocational development in early childhood: An examination of young children's expressions of vocational aspirations. *Journal of Vocational Behavior, 5*, 251-260.

Voss, J. (1980). Concepts of self, ideal self, and ideal woman held by college men and women: A comparison study. *Journal of College Student Personnel, 21*(1), 50-57.

Voss, J. H., & Skinner, D. A. (1975, May). Concepts of self and ideal woman held by college women: A replication. *Journal of College Student Personnel*, 210-213.

Voydanoff, P. (1980). Perceived job characteristics and job satisfaction among men and women. *Psychology of Women Quarterly, 5*(2), 177-185.

Vriend, J. (1968). *The vocational maturity of inner city boys.* Paper presented at the American Psychological Association Convention, San Francisco.

Vroom, V. H. (1964). *Work and motivation.* New York: Wiley.

Wade, A., & Shertzer, B. (1970). Anxiety reduction through vocational counseling. *Vocational Guidance Quarterly, 19*(1), 46-49.

Wagman, M. (1968). Perceived similarities in occupational value structure. *Vocational Guidance Quarterly, 16*, 275-281.

Waldman, E., Grossman, A. S., Hayghe, H., & Johnson, B. L. (1979). Working mothers in the 1970's: A look at the statistics. *Monthly Labor Review, 102*, 39-49.

Walker, J. E., Tansky, C., & Oliver, D. (1982). Men and women at work: Similarities and differences in work values within occupational groupings. *Journal of Vocational Behavior, 21*, 17-36.

Walker, J. L. (1965). Four methods of interpreting test scores compared. *Personnel and Guidance Journal, 44*, 402-404.

Walker, J. W., Kimmel, D. C., & Price, K. F. (1981). Retirement style and retirement satisfaction: Retirees aren't all alike. *International Journal of Aging and Human Development, 72*, 267-281.

Walker, J. W., & Gutteridge, T. G. (1979). *Career planning practices: An AMA survey report.* American Management Association.

Walker, J. W., & Lazar, H. L. (1978). *The end of mandatory retirement: Implications for management.* New York: Wiley.

Walker, L. S., & Walker, J. I. (1980). Trait anxiety in mothers: Differences associated with employment status, family size, and age of children. *Psychological Reports, 47*(1), 295-299.

Walls, R. T., & Gulkus, S. P. (1974). Reinforcers and vocational maturity in occupational aspiration, expectation, and goal deflection. *Journal of Vocational Behavior, 5*, 381-390.

Wallston, B. S., Foster, M. A., & Berger, M. (1978). I will follow him: Myth, reality or forced choice – job seeking experiences of dual-career couples. *Psychology of Women Quarterly, 3*(1), 9-21.

Walsh, W. B., Bingham, R., Horton, J. A., & Spokane, A. (1979). Holland's theory and college degreed working Black and white women. *Journal of Vocational Behavior, 15*, 217-223.

Walters, L., & Saddlemire, G. (1979). Career planning needs of college freshmen and their perceptions of career planning. *Journal of College Student Personnel, 20*, 224-229.

Walter-Samli, J. H., & Samli, A. C. (1979). A model of career counseling for international students. *Vocational Guidance Quarterly, 28*(1), 48-55.

Walz, G. (1970). Technology in guidance: A conceptual overview. *Personnel and Guidance Journal, 49*, 175-182.

Ward, C. M., & Walsh, W. B. (1981). Concurrent validity of Holland's theory for non-college degreed Black women. *Journal of Vocational Behavior, 18*, 356-361.

Ward, R. A. (1979). *The aging experience.* New York: J. B. Lippincott.

Ware, M. E. (1980). Antecedents of educational/career

preferences and choices. *Journal of Vocational Behavior, 16*, 312–319.

Warnath, C. F. (1975). Vocational theories: Directions to nowhere. *Personnel and Guidance Journal, 53*, 422–428.

Warnath, C. F. (1979). Counselor burnout: Existential crisis or a problem for the profession? *Personnel and Guidance Journal, 57*, 325–328.

Warnath, C. F. & Shelton, J. L. (1976). The ultimate disappointment: The burned-out counselor. *Personnel and Guidance Journal, 55*, 172–175.

Warner, S. G., & Jepsen, D. L. (1979). Differential effects of conceptual level and group counseling format on adolescent career decision-making processes. *Journal of Counseling Psychology, 26*(6), 497–503.

Warner, W. L., Melker, M., & Eells, K. (1949). *Social class in America.* Chicago: Science Research Associates.

Warren, J. M. (1978). Changing attitudes of supervisors. *Labor-Management Alcoholism Newsletter, 1*, 9.

Wasil, R. (1974). Job placement: Keynote of career development. *American Vocational Journal, 49*, 32.

Watanabe, A. (1980). *Developing a causal model for predicting college adjustment from pre-college characteristics.* Unpublished doctoral dissertations. Pennsylvania State University.

Waters, E., & Goodman, J. (1977). Career counseling for adults: Why, when, where, how. *Vocational Guidance Quarterly, 25*(4), 337–343.

Watley, D., & Vance, F. L. (1964). *Clinical versus actuarial prediction of college achievement and leadership activity.* (Final Report, Project No. 22-2, Cooperative Research Program.) Washington, DC: Office of Education, U.S. Department of Health, Education, and Welfare.

Watley, D. J. (1966). Student decisions influenced by counselors and teachers. *Vocational Guidance Quarterly, 15*, 36–40.

Watson, G. (1966). Resistance to change. In G. Watson (Ed.), *Concepts for social change.* Washington, DC: National Training Laboratories.

Watts, A. G., & Herr, E. L. (1976). Career(s) education in Britain and the U.S.A.: Contrasts and common problems. *British Journal of Guidance and Counseling, 4*(2), 129–142.

Watts, A. G., Super, D. E., & Kidd, J. M. (1981). *Career development in Britain.* Cambridge, England: Hobson's Press.

Weagraff, P. J. (1974). The cluster concept: Development of curricular materials for the public service occupations cluster. *Journal of Research and Development in Education, 7*(3), 45–54.

Weaver, C. N. (1978). Black-white correlates for job satisfaction. *Journal of Applied Psychology, 63*, 255–258.

Weaver, C. N. (1980). Job satisfaction in the United States in the 1970's. *Journal of Applied Psychology, 65*, 364–367.

Weeks, M., Thornburg, K. R., & Little, L. F. (1977). The impact of exposure to nontraditional vocational role models on the vocational role preferences of five-year-old children. *Journal of Vocational Behavior, 10*, 139–145.

Weinrach, S. G. (1980). Discrepancy identification: A model for the interpretation of the Kuder DD and other interest inventories. *Vocational Guidance Quarterly, 29*(1), 42–55.

Weinstein, M. (1979). A primer on unemployment. *Occupational Outlook Quarterly, 23*(1), 24–27.

Weishaar, M. E., Green, B. J., & Craighead, L. W. (1981). Primary influences of initial vocational choices of college women. *Journal of Vocational Behavior, 18*, 67–78.

Weiss, H. M. (1978). Social learning of work values in organizations. *Journal of Applied Psychology, 63*(6), 711–718.

Weissberg, M., Berentsen, M., Cote, A., Cravey, B., & Heath, K. (1982). As assessment of the personal, career, and academic needs of undergraduate students. *Journal of College Student Personnel, 23*, 115–122.

Weissman, S., & Krebs, D. O. (1976). A decision-making model for career exploration. *Personnel and Guidance Journal, 54*(10), 517–518.

Wellington, J. A., & Olechowski, N. (1966). Attitudes toward the world of work in elementary school. *Vocational Guidance Quarterly, 14*, 160–162.

Wellman, F. E. (1970, December). *Evaluation of vocational guidance: Local level.* Paper presented at the 64th annual Vocational Convention, New Orleans, LA.

Werts, C. E. (1968). Paternal influence on career choice. *Journal of Counseling Psychology, 15*, 48–52.

Westbrook, B. W. (1974). Content analysis of six career development tests. *Measurement and Evaluation in Guidance, 7*(3), 172–180.

Westbrook, B. W. (1978). *Career development needs of adults. How to improve career development programs.* Washington, DC: National Vocational Guidance Association and the Association for Measurement and Evaluation in Guidance.

Westbrook, B. W., & Cunningham, J.W. (1970). The development and application of vocational maturity measures. *Vocational Guidance Quarterly, 18*, 171–175.

Westbrook, B. W., & Mastie, M. M. (1973). Three measures of vocational maturity: A beginning to know about. *Measurement and Evaluation in Guidance, 6*(1), 8–16.

Westbrook, B. W., & Parry-Hill, J. W., Jr. (1973a). *The construction and validation of a measure of vocational maturity* (ERIC document #ED 101 145). Raleigh, NC: Center for Occupational Education, North Carolina State University.

Westbrook, B. W., & Parry-Hill, J. W., Jr. (1973b). The measurement of cognitive vocational maturity. *Journal of Vocational Behavior, 3*, 239–252.

Wheeler, C. L., & Carnes, E. F. (1968). Relationships among self-concepts, ideal self-concepts, and stereotypes of probable and ideal vocational choices. *Journal of Counseling Psychology, 15*, 530–535.

Wheeler, K. G., & Mahoney, T. A. (1981). The expectancy model in the analysis of occupational preference and occupational choice. *Journal of Vocational Behavior, 19*, 113-122.

White, L., & Brinkerhoff, D. B. (1981). The sexual division of labor: Evidence from childhood. *Social Forces, 60*(1), 170-181.

White, P., Reardon, R., Barker, S., & Carlson, A. (1979). Increasing career center accessibility for the blind. *Personnel and Guidance Journal, 58*(4), 292-295.

Whitson, K. S., Drier, H. N., Frank, R. L., Herr, E. L., Jacobson, M. B., & Stein, W. L. (1979). *Urban guidance services for CETA participants*. Columbus, OH: The National Center for Research in Vocational Education.

Wiener, Y., Vardi, Y., Muczyk, J. (1981). Antecedents of employees' mental health − The role of career and work satisfaction. *Journal of Vocational Behavior, 19*, 50-60.

Wiener, Y., & Vaitenas, R. (1977). Personality correlates of voluntary midcareer change enterprising occupations. *Journal of Applied Psychology, 62*(6), 706-712.

Wiggins, J. S. (1973). *Personality and prediction: Principles of personality assessment*. Reading, MA: Addison-Wesley.

Wigington, J. H. (1982). Career maturity aspects of the Kuder Occupational Interest Survey. *Journal of Vocational Behavior, 20*, 175-179.

Wijting, J. P., Arnold, C. R., & Conrad, K. A. (1977). Relationships between work values, socio-educational and work experiences, and vocational aspirations of 6th, 9th, 10th, and 12 graders. *Journal of Vocational Behavior, 11*(1). 51-65.

Wiley, M. O., & Magoon, T. M. (1982). Holland high point social types: Is consistency related to persistence and achievement? *Journal of Vocational Behavior, 20*, 14-21.

Wilkie, J. R. (1981). The trend toward delayed parenthood. *Journal of Marriage and the Family, 43*(3), 583-591.

Wilkinson, L., & Rosenberg, H. (1979). Resume preparation workshop for university students. *Journal of Employment Counseling, 16*(3), 153-163.

Williams, G. D., Lindsay, C. A., Burns, M. A., Wyckoff, J. H., & Wall, H. W. (1973). Urgency and types of adult counseling needs among continuing education students. *Journal of College Student Personnel, 14*(6), 501-506.

Williams, W. G. (1980). Civic education in a stressful society: A program of value clarity and tension reduction. In F. J. McGuigan, W. E. Sime, & J. M. Wallace (Eds.), *Stress and tension control* (pp. 17-35). New York: Plenum Press.

Williamson, E. G. (1939). *How to counsel students*. New York: McGraw-Hill.

Williamson, E. G. (1965). *Vocational counseling: Some historical, philosophical, and theoretical perspectives*. New York: McGraw-Hill.

Willis, M. L. (1979). *The organization of household work and role problems for employed men and women*, ED176002, Ann Arber: ERIC, 36 pp.

Wilson, J., & Daniel, R. (1981). The effects of a career-options workshop on social and vocational stereotypes. *Vocational Guidance Quarterly, 30*(4), 341-349.

Wilson, K. L., & Butler, J. S. (1978). Race and job satisfaction in the military. *The Sociological Quarterly, 19*, 626-638.

Wilson, R. N. (1981). The courage to be leisured. *Social Forces, 60*(2), 282-302.

Winer, J. L., Cerari, J., Haase, R. F., & Bodden, J. L. (1979). Cognitive complexity and career maturity among college students. *Journal of Vocational Behavior, 15*, 186-192.

Winkles, E. J., & Johnson, R. H. (1973). A model for developing a career decision-making program. *Canadian Counselor, 7*(2), 139-143.

Winter, J., & Schmidt, J. S. (1974). A replicable career program for junior high. *Vocational Guidance Quarterly, 23*(2), 177-180.

Wircenski, J. L., Fales, J. G., & Wircenski, S. L. (1978). Career guidance in the elementary school. *Elementary School Guidance and Counseling, 12*(3), 212-215.

Wise, R., Charner, I., & Randour, M. A. (1978). A conceptual framework for career awareness in career decision-making. In J. Whitely and A. Resnikoff (Eds.), *Career counseling* (pp. 216-231). Monterey, CA: Brooks/Cole.

Wish, P. A., & Hasazi, J. W. (1973). Motivational determinants of curricular choice in college males. *Journal of Counseling Psychology, 20*, 127-131.

Withers, W. (1974). Some irrational beliefs about retirement in the U. S. *Industrial Gerontology, 1*(1), 23-32.

Wittmer, J., Bostic, D., Phillips, T. D., & Waters, W. (1981). The personal, academic, and career problems of college student athletes: Some possible answers. *Personnel and Guidance Journal, 60*(1), 52-55.

Witwer, G., & Stewart, L. H. (1972). Personality correlates of preference for risk among occupation oriented junior college students. *Vocational Guidance Quarterly, 20*(4), 259-265.

Wolfe, L. K., & Betz, N. E. (1981). Traditionality of choice and sex-role identification as moderators of the congruence of occupational choice in college women. *Journal of Vocational Behavior, 18*, 43-55.

Wollack, S., Goodale, J. G., Wijting, J. P., & Smith, P. C. (1971). Development of the survey of work values. *Journal of Applied Psychology, 55*, 331-338.

Wollman, M., Johnson, D. A., & Bottoms, J. E. (1975). Meeting career needs in two-year institutions, *Personnel and Guidance Journal, 53*, 676-679.

Women's Bureau. (1982). *20 facts on women workers*. Washington, DC: U.S. Department of Labor.

Woody, R. H. (1968). Vocational counseling with behavioral techniques. *Vocational Guidance Quarterly, 17*, 97-103.

Wool, S. T. (1974, Fall). Queries, influences, and vocational interests of junior high school students. *Journal of Career Education, 2*, 55-62.

Work in America Institute. (1980). *The future of older*

workers in America. Scarsdale, NY: The Institute.

Worrall, J. (1978). A benefit-cost analysis of the vocational rehabilitation program. *The Journal of Human Resources, 13*(2), 285–298.

Worrell, J. (1980). New directions in counseling women. *Personnel and Guidance Journal, 58*(7), 477–484.

Wortley, D. B., & Amatea, E. S. (1982). Mapping adult life changes: A conceptual framework for organizing adult development theory. *Personnel and Guidance Journal, 60*(8), 477–482.

Wrenn, C. G. (1964). Human values and work in American life. In H. Borow (Ed.), *Man in a world of work*. Boston: Houghton Mifflin.

Wright, B. A. (1960). *Physical disability: A psychological approach*. New York: Harper Bros.

Wright, D., & Gutkin, T. B. (1981). School psychologists' job satisfaction and discrepancies between actual and desired work functions. *Psychological Reports, 49*, 735–738.

Wright, E. W. (1959). Multiple counseling: Why? When? How? *Personnel and Guidance Journal, 37*, 551–557.

Wright, G. N. (1980). *Total rehabilitation*. Boston: Little, Brown.

Wright, J. D. (1978). Are working women really more satisfied? Evidence from several national surveys. *Journal of Marriage and the Family, 40*, 301–313.

Wright, J. D., & Hamilton, R. F. (1979). Education and job attitudes among blue-collar workers. *Sociology of Work and Occupations, 6*(1), 59–83.

Yabroff, W. (1969). Learning decision-making. In J. D. Krumboltz & C. E. Thoresen (Eds.), *Behavioral counseling; Cases and techniques* (pp. 329–343). New York: Holt, Rinehart and Winston.

Yanico, B. J. (1980). Students' self-reported amount of information about masculine and femine occupations. *Vocational Guidance Quarterly, 28*(4), 244–350.

Yanico, B. J. (1981). Sex-role self concept and attitudes related to occupational daydreams and future fantasies of college women. *Journal of Vocational Behavior, 19*, 290–301.

Yanico, B. J., & Hardin, S. I. (1981). Sex-role self-concept and persistence in a traditional versus non-traditional college major for women. *Journal of Vocational Behavior, 18*, 219–227.

Yankelovich, D. (1981). The meaning of work. In J. O'Toole, J. L. Scheiber, & L. C. Wood (Eds.), *Working, changes and choices* (pp. 33–34). New York: Human Sciences Press.

Yankelovich, D., & Lefkowitz, B. (1982). Work and American expectations. *National Forum, 62*(2), 3–5.

Yates, J. E. (1979). *Managing stress*. New York: AMALOM.

Yogev, S. (1981). Do professional women have egalitarian marital relationships? *Journal of Marriage and the Family, 43*(4), 865–871.

Young, A. M. (1980). Trends in educational attainment among workers in the 1970's. *Monthly Labor Review, 103*, 44–47.

Young, D. M., & Beier, E. G. (1977). The role of applicant nonverbal communication in the employment interview. *Journal of Employment Counseling, 14*, 154–165.

Young, D. M., Beier, E. G., & Beier, S. (1979). Beyond words: Influence of nonverbal behavior of female job applicants in the employment interview. *Personnel and Guidance Journal, 57*(7), 346–350.

Young, J. M. (1974). Community-oriented exploration program. *Elementary School Guidance and Counseling, 8*(3), 209–212.

Young, R. A., (1979). The effects of value confrontation and reinforcement counseling on the career planning attitudes and behavior of adolescent males. *Journal of Vocational Behavior, 15*, 1–11.

Zaccaria, J. S. (1965). Developmental tasks: Implications for the goals of guidance. *Personnel and Guidance Journal, 44*, 372–375.

Zaccaria, J. S. (1969). *Approaches to guidance in contemporary education*. Scranton, PA: International Textbook.

Zadney, J. J., & James, L. F. (1977). Time spent in placement. *Rehabilitation Counseling Bulletin, 21*(1), 31–35.

Zaslow, M. J., & Pederson, F. A. (1981). Sex role conflicts and the experience of childbearing. *Professional Psychology, 12*(1), 47–55.

Zehring, J. W. (1975). Rejection shock. *Journal of College Placement, 35*(4), 34–35.

Zehring, J. W. (1976) Employing students as paraprofessional counselors. *Journal of College Placement, 36*(1), 43–47.

Zehring, J. W. (1979). Job sources for liberal arts graduates. *Journal of College Placement, 39*(2), 28–31.

Zelenak, B. M. (1978). Using assertive training to develop positive job interviewing skills. *Journal of College Student Personnel, 19*(5), 410–414.

Zenger, J. H. (1981). Career planning: Coming in from the cold. *Training and Development Journal, 35*, 47–52.

Ziller, R. C. (1957). Vocational choice and utility for risk. *Journal of Counseling Psychology, 4*, 61–64.

Zito, R. J., & Bardon, J. I. (1968). Negro adolescents' success and failure imagery concerning work and school. *Vocational Guidance Quarterly, 16*, 181–184.

Zuckerman, D. M. (1979). The impact of education and selected traits on sex-role related goals and attitudes. *Journal of Vocational Behavior, 14*, 248–254.

Zytowski, D. G. (1965). Avoidance behavior in vocational motivation. *Personnel and Guidance Journal, 43*, 746–750.

Zytowski, D. G. (1969). Toward a theory of career development for women. *Personnel and Guidance Journal, 47*, 660–664.

(continued from page iv)

Counselor Education and Supervision, April 1976), pp. 10–11. Copyright 1976, American Association for Counseling and Development. Reprinted with permission. *Page 18:* From Anita M. Mitchell, "Emerging career guidance competencies," *Personnel and Guidance Journal,* May 1975, *53*(9), pp. 701–702. Copyright 1975, American Association for Counseling and Development. Reprinted with permission. *Page 35:* Reprinted by permission of the publishers from THE MANPOWER CONNECTION by Eli Ginzberg, Cambridge, MA: Harvard University Press, copyright © 1975 by the President and Fellows of Harvard College. *Page 42:* From Lloyd H. Lofquist and Rene V. Dawis, *Adjustment to work, a psychological view of man's problems in a work-oriented society* (New York: Appleton-Century-Crofts, 1969), pp. 45–50. Reprinted by permission. *Page 118:* From J. L. Holland and G. D. Gottfredson, "Using a typology of persons and environments to explain careers: Some extensions and clarification," *The Counseling Psychologist,* 1976, *6*(3), pp. 21–22. Reprinted by permission. *Page 121:* From R. Hoppock, *Occupational Information: Where to Get It and How to Use it in Career Education, Career Counseling and Career Development* (4th ed.) (New York: McGraw-Hill Book Company, 1976), pp. 111–112. Reprinted by permission. *Page 133:* Reprinted by permission of the publisher from Warren D. Gribbons and Paul R. Lohnes, EMERGING CAREERS (New York: Teachers College Press, © 1968 by Teachers College, Columbia University. All rights reserved.), pp. 15 and 16. *Page 175:* From J. S. Zaccaria, "Developmental tasks: Implications for the goals of guidance," *Personnel and Guidance Journal,* 1965, *44*, p. 373. Copyright 1965, American Association for Counseling and Development. Reprinted with permission. *Page 223:* From OCCUPATIONAL INFORMATION IN THE ELEMENTARY SCHOOL by Willa Norris. © 1963, Science Research Associates, Inc. Reprinted by permission of the publisher. *Page 223:* From I. M. Bank, "Children explore careerland through vocational role models," *Vocational Guidance Quarterly,* 1969, *17*, p. 285. Copyright 1969, American Association for Counseling and Development. Reprinted with permission. *Page 308-309:* From *The Complete Job Search Handbook* by Howard Figler. Copyright © 1979 by Howard Figler. Reprinted by permission of Holt, Rinehart & Winston, Publishers. *Pages 357-358:* From R. C. Atchley, "Issues in retirement research." Reprinted by permission of *The Gerontologist/ The Journal of Gerontology,* 1979, *19*(1), pp. 47–48. *Page 429:* From Hoyt, Evans, Mackin and Mangum, *Career Education: What It Is and How to Use It* (2nd ed.) (Salt Lake City, Utah: Olympus Publishing, 1974), pp. 34–35. Reprinted by permission. *Page 431:* From James S. Coleman et al., *Youth: Transition to Adulthood* (Chicago, IL: University of Chicago Press, 1974), pp. 3–5.

FIGURES
Figure 1.1: From Frank E. Burtnett (Ed.), *The School Counselor's Involvement in Career Education* (Falls Church, VA: APGA Press, 1980), p. 18. Copyright 1980, American Association for Counseling and Development. Reprinted by permission. *Figure 1.2:* From A. G. Watts and E. L. Herr, "Career(s) education in Britain and the U.S.A.: Contrasts and common problems," *British Journal of Guidance and Counseling,* July 1976, *4*(2), pp. 129–142. Reprinted by permission. *Figure 3.2:* From Figure 1 "A Scheme for Classifying Occupations by Level, Field and Enterprise" (p. 48) in THE PSYCHOLOGY OF CAREERS by Donald Super. Copyright © 1957 by Donald E. Super. By permission of Harper & Row, Publishers, Inc. *Figure 4.1:* Reprinted with permission from *Deciding* by H. B. Gelatt, Barbara Varenhorst, and Richard Carey, copyright © 1972 by the College Entrance Examination Board, New York. *Figure 4.2:* From Peter M. Blau, John W. Gustad, Richard Jesser, Herbert S. Parnes, and Richard C. Wilcock, "Occupational Choice: A Conceptual Framework." Reprinted with permission from the *Industrial and Labor Relations Review,* Vol. 9, No. 4 (July 1956), pp. 531–543. Copyright © 1956 by Cornell University. All rights reserved. *Figure 4.3:* From John L. Holland, "The present status of a theory of vocational choice," in J. M. Whitely and A. Resnikoff (Eds.), *Perspectives on Vocational Development,* p. 54. (Washington, DC: APGA, 1972). Copyright 1972 American Association for Counseling and Development. Reprinted with permission. *Figure 4.4:* From D. E. Super, "Approaches to occupational choice and career development," in A. G. Watts, D. E. Super, and Jennifer Kidd (Eds.), *Career Development in Britain,* p. 35. (Cambridge, England: Hobson Press, 1981). Reprinted by permission. *Figure 4.5:* From Donald E. Super, "A Life-span, Life-space approach to career development," *Journal of Vocational Behavior,* 1980, *16,* p. 295. Reprinted by permission. *Figure 4.6:* From L. Lee Knefelkamp and Ron Slepitza, "A cognitive-developmental model of career development—An adaptation of the Perry Scheme," *The Counseling Psychologist,* 1976, *6*(3), p. 55. Reprinted by permission. *Figure 6.1:* From Paul Ferrini and L. Allen Parker, *Career Change, A Handbook of Exemplary Programs in Business and Industrial Firms, Educational Institutions, Government Agencies, Professional Associations,* p. 64 (Cambridge, MA: Technical Education Research Center, 1978). Reprinted by permission. *Figure 9.1:* From Laurence Lipsett, "Career path charts as counseling aids," *Vocational Guidance Quarterly,* 1980, *30*(4), p. 364. Copyright 1980, American Association for Counseling and Development. Reprinted by permission. *Figure 9.2:* From Laurence Lipsett, "Career path charts as counseling aids," *Vocational Guidance Quarterly,* 1980, *30*(4), p. 366. Copyright 1980, American Association for Counseling and Development. Reprinted with permission. *Figure 9.3:* From Laurence Lipsett, "Career path charts as counseling aids," *Vocational Guidance Quarterly,* 1980, *30*(4), p. 366. Copyright 1980, American Association for Counseling and Development. Reprinted with permission. *Figure 10.1:* From R. K. Luther and V. M. Smith, "A functional

572

Index

Bailey, R. C., 489
Bain, T., 256, 258
Baker, H., 320
Baker, S. G., 392
Ballweg, J. A., 53
Baltes, P. B., 86, 336
Bamundo, P. J., 384
Banas, P., 474
Banducci, R., 444
Bandura, A., 41, 99-100, 105-106
Bank, I. M., 223
Barad, C. B., 324
Barak, A., 120, 292, 411, 509
Barbee, J. R., 380
Bardon, J. I., 108
Barker, S., 165
Barnett, R., 148
Baron, A. S., 147
Barrett, G. V., 352
Barrett, T., 403, 404
Bartlett, L. R., 303
Bartlett, W. E., 150
Bartol, K. M., 510
Bartsch, K., 303, 412
Baruch, G. K., 145
Basen, J. A., 153
Basow, S. A., 95
Baumgardner, S. R., 395, 397
Baxter, N., 446
Bayer, A. E., 154
Bayer, F., 76
Beard, J. H., 329
Becker, B. E., 153
Becker, H. J., 97
Becket, W. C., 164-165
Beckman, L. J., 372
Bedford, J. H., 221
Bee, R. H., 403
Beggs, D. L., 489
Beier, E. G., 380
Beier, S., 380
Beley, W., 329
Bell, B. D., 354, 384
Bem, D. J., 143
Bem, S. L., 143
Bender, J., 323
Benecki, T. J., 352
Bentler, P. M., 498
Berdie, R., 96-97
Berg, I., 65
Berger, F., 13, 292
Berger, M., 375
Berger, P. K., 144
Bergland, B. W., 409
Berman, E., 348
Bernard, J., 348-349, 374
Bernstein, I. N., 372
Berry, E., 215
Betz, E. L., 145, 146
Betz, N., 120, 144, 146, 375, 508

Betz, R. L., 250
Beutell, N. J., 371, 374
Bielby, D. D., 147-148, 371
Bienstock, J. K., 272
Biggers, J. L., 220, 444
Biggs, J., 508, 509
Bigoness, W. J., 384
Binet, A., 2
Bingham, R., 120
Bingham, W. C., 329
Biosciences, 64
Bird, C., 65
Birdwell, J., 506
Birk, J. M., 444
Bjorkquist, D. C., 41, 65
Blacks, career development of, 152-154
Blai, B., 356
Blaikie, N. W. H., 403, 405-406
Blank, J. R., 444
Blau, P. M., 66, 103, 110
Blocher, D. R., 188
Blocher, K., 296
Bloland, P. A., 23, 510
Bloom, B. S., 195
Bloom, V., 238
Blum, S. D., 117
Bocknek, G., 341
Bodden, J. L., 92, 446
Boese, R. R., 74
Bohn, M. J., Jr., 93, 330
Bohrnstadt, G. W., 372
Boll, A. S., 307
Bonnell, R. O., 509
Boocock, S. S., 458, 459
Booth, A., 372
Booth, R. P., 94
Bordin, E. S., 7, 8, 93, 112, 116, 306
Borman, C., 445
Borow, H., 87, 216, 446
Bosse, R., 354
Boswell, J., 377
Bottoms, J. R., 251, 302
Bowlby, J. A., 371
Bowles, R. T., 76
BOXSCORE, 488
Boy, A. V., 10
Bradburn, N. M., 88
Bradley, R. W., 397, 403, 404, 475
Brainard Occupational Preference Inventory, 482
Bramel, D., 40
Brammer, L. M., 9, 392
Brandt, C., 506
Brass, D. J., 384
Braude, L., 32
Braun, J. S., 76
Brayfield, A. H., 102
Breed, W., 362
Breme, F. J., 487

Brenner, D., 151, 403
Brenner, M. H., 45, 362
Brickell, H. M., 56
Brief, A. P., 384
Brigando, L., 384
Briggs, J. I., 307
Brill, A. A., 112
Brim, O. G., Jr., 343
Brinkerhoff, D. B., 94
Brito, P. K., 144
Brodsky, A., 365
Brolin, D. E., 165-166, 330, 332
Brooks, G. C., 154
Brophy, A. L., 330
Bross, I. D., 100
Brough, J. R., 236
Brown, B. F., 165
Brown, C. S., 392
Brown, C. W., 91
Brown, D. A., 267, 287, 346
Brown, G. S., 404
Brown, J. H., 392, 480
Brown, S. C., 354
Brown, S. S., 147
Bruch, M. A., 120
Brugnoli, G. A., 153
Bruner, J., 265
Brunkan, R. M., 115
Bryson, R. B., 375
Buckingham, L., 286
Buehler, C., 87, 124, 319, 336-337
Bunch, S., 305
Burack, E. H., 315
Burdetsky, B., 52
Bureau of the Census, U.S., 66, 75
Bureau of Labor Statistics (BLS), 39, 62, 63, 67, 69, 73
Burke, R. J., 371, 376
Burkhauser, R. V., 354
Burks, H. M., 305
Burnout, 364
  defined, 364-368
  prevention and treatment of, 368-369
Burnstein, E., 97
Burr, P. L., 64
Butler, J. S., 384
Butler, M., 375
Butler, R. N., 354
Byham, W. C., 169, 323
Byrne, R. H., 7, 8

Calhoun, R. E., 34
California Occupational Preference Survey (COPS), 482
Campbell, D. P., 93
Campbell, N. J., 152, 257
Campbell, R. E., 53, 57, 236, 272, 282, 338, 506

Garrison, H. H., 258
Garte, S. H., 369
Gavin, J. F., 366
Gaylord, C., 152
Gazda-Grace, P., 151, 403
Geis, H. J., 390
Geist Picture Interest Inventory, 484
Gelatt, H. B., 100-101, 102, 103-104, 188, 269, 406
Gelso, C. J., 489, 496
General Aptitude Test Battery (GATB), 43, 73, 328, 476
George-Dean Act (1938), 5
Gerler, E. R., Jr., 392
Gershuny, J. I., 23, 503
Gerstein, M., 346
Ghiselli, E., 72, 91, 471, 472
Gibson, R. L., 232
Gilbert, L. A., 372, 376
Giles, W. F., 381
Gillian, C., 307
Gillingham, W. H., 303
Gilmore, D. C., 383
Ginath, Y., 506
Gingrich, D. E., 376-377
Ginn, R., 305
Ginsburg, S. W., 122, 124, 174
Ginzberg, E., 22, 35-37, 64, 122, 123, 124, 135, 136, 174, 219, 294-295, 430
Glamser, F. D., 354, 356
Glaser, G. C., 100
Glenn, N. D., 383
Goeke, J. D., 286
Goff, W. H., 227
Gold, D., 371
Gold, J. A., 96, 109
Gold, R. S., 365
Golden, B. J., 353
Goldman, L., 397, 414, 473, 499
Golembiewski, R. T., 346
Good, R., 261
Goodman, H. H., 338-339
Goodman, J., 346
Goodman, P. S., 22, 363-364
Goodson, W. D., 297, 509
Goodstein, L. D., 191
Gordon, M., 64, 65
Gordon, M. S., 458
Gordon, V., 404
Gore, S. N., 362
Gottdanker, J. S., 323
Gottfredson, G. D., 89, 118, 344, 411, 489, 510
Gottfredson, L. S., 97, 120-121, 154
Gottlieb, D., 108
Goudy, W. J., 354, 372
Gould, P., 88, 136
Gould, R., 336
Gould, S., 156, 384

Goulet, L. R., 86, 336
Graflex Vocational Evaluation System, 477-478
Graney, J. J., 351, 354
Granovetter, M. S., 378
Grant, C. W., 375, 376
Graves, J. P., 319
Gray, J. D., 377
Gray, S., 354
Green, B. J., 147
Green, C. H., 447
Green, L. B., 115
Greenberger, E., 236
Greene, M. M., 57
Greenfeld, S., 145
Greenhaus, J. H., 371, 374, 384
Greiner, L., 145
Gribbons, W. D., 109, 132-134, 138, 174, 184, 188, 337, 498, 500
Griffin, L. J., 383
Griffith, A. R., 313
Griffith, P., 119
Grite, T. J., 411
Gronlund, N. E., 195, 199
Gross, E., 38, 88, 137, 188
Gross, H. E., 375
Group
  activities, 229-231
  counseling, 303-305, 412-415
  guidance processes, 288-289
Guidance learnings, 25
Guide for Occupational Literature, 120
GULHEMP, 352
Gulkus, S. P., 97
Gunnings, T. S., 392
Gunter, B. G., 49
Gunter, N., 49
Guppy, N., 48, 354
Gurin, P., 152, 158, 372
Gustad, J. W., 103, 110, 474
Gutek, B. A., 238
Guthrie, W. R., 344
Gutkin, T. B., 383
Gutteridge, T. G., 313
Guttmann, D., 344, 403
Gysbers, N. C., 14, 165-166, 219, 222-223, 242, 263, 287

Haak, R., 412
Haase, R. F., 92, 446
Haber, S., 371
Haccoun, R. R., 53
Hackett, G., 144, 303, 412
Hackman, J. R., 40
Hagan, N., 216
Hagberg, R., 305
Hagen, E., 73, 91, 471, 476
Hager, P. C., 154
Hageseth, J. A., 300, 412, 509
Hahn, W. A., 64

Hakel, M. D., 76
Hale, L. L., 296
Hales, L. W., 94, 216, 236, 260
Hall, C. S., 113
Hall, D. T., 41-42, 313, 314, 318, 319, 373, 376, 404, 505, 510-511
Hall, F. S., 376
Hall, G. S., 2
Hall, R. C. W., 366, 369
Hall Occupational Orientation Inventory, 487-488
Halpern, G., 445
Halpin, G., 165
Halverson, P. M., 219, 223
Hamilton, J. A., 406
Hamilton, J. S., 458
Hamilton, R. F., 37, 39
Hammer, T. H., 344
Hamrin, R. D., 63
Handel, L., 227
Hannson, R. O., 371
Hansen, J. C., 108, 412-413, 486
Hansen, L. S., 14, 15, 23, 24, 103, 199, 269
Happ, D. A., 165
Hardesty, S., 375, 508
Hardin, S. I., 147
Harford, T. C., 372
Harlow, H. F., 371
Harper, W. R., 2
Harren, V. A., 89, 100, 403, 404, 408, 412, 445, 509
Harrington, C. C., 110
Harris, T. L., 250
Harris-Bowlsby, J. A., 464
Harrison, B., 65
Harrison, L., 327, 333
Harrison, R., 51, 362
Hart, D. H., 106
Hartman, B., 411
Hartman, P., 411
Harvey, D. W., 344
Hasazi, J. W., 403
Hatt, P. K., 72
Havighurst, R. J., 124, 135, 174, 175, 182, 238
Hawkins, B. L., 384, 509
Hawkins, J., 404
Hawley, P., 238
Hayes, D. G., 64
Hayes, J., 362, 363
Hayes, R. L., 256
Hazel, E. R., 305
Head, T. C., 384
Health, Education, and Welfare, U. S. Department of, 65
Healy, C. C., 97, 412, 495-496, 506
Healy, G. A., 385
Heath, D., 96
Heck, E. J., 307